The Routledge Handbook of Chinese Studies

This *Handbook* approaches Chinese Studies from an interdisciplinary perspective while attempting to establish a fundamental set of core values and tenets for the subject, in relation to the further development of Chinese Studies as an academic discipline. It aims to consolidate the current findings in Chinese Studies, extract the essence from each affiliated discipline, formulate a concrete set of ideas to represent the 'Chineseness' of the subject, establish a clear identity for the discipline and provide clear guidelines for further research and practice.

Topics included in this *Handbook* cover a wide spectrum of traditional and newly added concerns in Chinese Studies, ranging from the Chinese political system and domestic governance to international relations, Chinese culture, literature and history, Chinese sociology (gender, middle class, nationalism, home ownership, dating) and Chinese opposition and activism. The *Handbook* also looks at widening the scope of Chinese Studies (Chinese psychology, postcolonialism and China, Chinese science and climate change), and some illustrations of innovative Chinese Studies research methods.

The Routledge Handbook of Chinese Studies is an essential reference for researchers and scholars in Chinese Studies, as well as students in the discipline.

Chris Shei was educated in Taiwan and studied at the Universities of Cambridge and Edinburgh, UK. He has worked at Swansea University, UK, since 2003. He teaches and researches in linguistics and translation and also edits books and online publications across the broad spectrum of Chinese studies, including Chinese politics and governance, Chinese sociology, Chinese history and cultural studies and so on. He is the General Editor for three Routledge book series: *Routledge Studies in Chinese Discourse Analysis*, *Routledge Studies in Chinese Translation*, and *Routledge Studies in Chinese Language Teaching* (with Der-lin Chao).

Weixiao Wei has been working with Taiyuan University of Technology as a lecturer at the College of Foreign Languages and Literatures since she obtained her MA degree in 2010. In July 2017, she obtained a visiting scholarship from the China Scholarship Council (CSC) to visit Swansea University, UK, for a year. Since then, she has published a monograph and three book chapters with Routledge. In addition to preparing research papers, monographs, and edited volumes for further publication, she started pursuing her PhD study in rhetoric and composition at the University of Houston in August 2020.

The Routledge Handbook of Chinese Studies

Edited by Chris Shei and Weixiao Wei

First published 2021
by Routledge
2 Park Square, Milton Park, Abingdon, Oxon OX14 4RN

and by Routledge
605 Third Avenue, New York, NY 10158

Routledge is an imprint of the Taylor & Francis Group, an informa business

British Library Cataloguing-in-Publication Data
A catalogue record for this book is available from the British Library

Library of Congress Cataloging-in-Publication Data
A catalog record has been requested for this book

ISBN: 978-0-367-18139-0 (hbk)
ISBN: 978-0-367-76090-8 (pbk)
ISBN: 978-0-429-05970-4 (ebk)

DOI: 10.4324/9780429059704

Typeset in Times New Roman
by Deanta Global Publishing Services, Chennai, India

Contents

Figures

Tables

Contributors

Sampson Lee Blair focuses his research on parent-child relationships, with particular emphasis on child and adolescent development. He has served as chair of the Children and Youth research section of the American Sociological Association, as senior editor of *Sociological Inquiry*, and on the editorial boards of journals. In 2018, he was elected as Vice President (North America) of the Research Committee on Youth (RC34), in the International Sociological Association. Since 2011, he has served as the editor of *Contemporary Perspectives in Family Research.*

André Bueno is Adjunct Professor of Oriental History in State University of Rio de Janeiro [Universidade do Estado do Rio de Janeiro–UERJ], Brazil. He has experience in the area of History and Philosophy, with emphasis on Sinology, acting mainly on the following themes: Chinese thought, Confucianism, ancient history and philosophy, East–West cultural dialogues, and history teaching.

Maria Adele Carrai is Assistant Professor of Global China Studies at NYU Shanghai. Her research explores the history of international law in East Asia and investigates how China's rise as a global power is shaping norms and redefining the international distribution of power. Prior to joining NYU Shanghai, she was a recipient of a three-year Marie Curie Fellowship at KU Leuven. She was also a Fellow at the Italian Academy of Columbia University, Princeton-Harvard China and the World Program, Max Weber Program of the European University Institute of Florence, and New York University Law School.

Yu-Wen Chen is Professor of Chinese Studies at the University of Helsinki in Finland and Hosting Professor of Asian Studies at Palacký University in Czech Republic. Chen's research concerns China's international relations and ethnic politics in China.

John J. Chin manages the research lab at the Center for International Relations and Politics at Carnegie Mellon University (CMU) and is a 2020–2021 nonresident research fellow with the International Center for Nonviolence Conflict. He previously was a post-doctoral fellow in CMU's Institute for Politics and Strategy, where he taught diplomacy and statecraft, nonviolent conflict and revolution, the future of democracy, and writing for political science and policy. He earned a BA from the University of Notre Dame, MPP from the University of Michigan, and PhD from Princeton University. His has written for the *Journal of Chinese Political Science*, *Georgetown Journal of International Affairs*, the *CIRP Journal*, *Political Violence at a Glance*, *The Monkey Cage*, and the *Washington Post*. Prior to academia, he was an international affairs analyst at the US Congressional Budget Office and worked on China policy at the Rand Corporation, the US Treasury Department, and the US State Department.

Pavel Deriugin is a professor in the Department of Applied and Sectoral Sociology at the Faculty of Sociology, St. Petersburg State University. His research interests are related to network research of values in Russia and China, the use of big data analysis in the study of sociopsychological characteristics and comparative studies of Russian and Chinese society, the development of methods for applied research and diagnostics of interpersonal relations, in particular, in business and educational organizations, corporate culture in Russian and joint ventures, features of human capital in the post-Soviet space.

Andrew Flynn is a reader in environmental policy in the School of Geography and Planning at Cardiff University. His research focuses on three themes: the changing nature of the local state and how it is increasingly performing multiple environmental functions; the ways in which sustainability is constructed through the activities of local and state actors; and private interests and standard setting which involves analysing the ways in which private interests interact with public bodies to produce standards that are, in turn, shaping ideas of the environment and the role of government.

David S.G. Goodman is Professor of China Studies at Xi'an Jiaotong-Liverpool University, Suzhou, where he is also Vice President for Academic Affairs. A graduate of the University of Manchester, Peking University, and the London School of Oriental and African Studies, his research concentrates on social and political change in China, especially at the local level. Current projects include preparation of a two-volume work on *Class and the CCP: A Hundred Years of Social Change* (Routledge, 2021); research into the social background of China's current new economic elites; and the preparation of ethnographies of inequality in China.

Patrick Gorman received his PhD in political science from the Department of Politics and Public Administration at The University of Hong Kong in 2018. Gorman's research areas include internet governance, online politics, Chinese politics, nationalism and ideology, and political economy of the media.

Gerry Groot is Senior Lecturer in Chinese Studies in the Department of Asian Studies, School of Social Sciences at the University of Adelaide. He teaches, researches, and writes on Chinese politics and Asian studies. His research interests include the Chinese Communist Party's united front work, social change in China, the idea and forms of soft power, and Asian influences on the world both past and present. He would like to one day also finish his papers on cookbooks.

Nick Hacking is a lecturer in geography and planning at Cardiff University's School of Geography and Planning. His research on the circular economy and the hydrogen economy involves case study comparisons of the governance of sustainability transitions in Europe and China. He has several strands of interest: (1) community-led contestations over social constructions of sustainability; (2) the failures of neoliberal environmental governance including public participation in national planning systems; and (3) improving the links between environmental governance theory and policy.

Kamila Hladíková is an assistant professor of Chinese literature at Palacký University in Olomouc, Czech Republic. She graduated from sinology at Charles University in Prague and completed her PhD in 2011. In her research she has been focusing on questions of identity, ideology, and censorship in literature, film, and popular media, with specific interest in modern Chinese society and contemporary Tibetan issues. She is a translator of works of Chinese and Sinophone Tibetan literature into Czech.

Obert Hodzi is a lecturer in politics at the University of Liverpool, UK. Hodzi is an international relations scholar focusing on international politics, conflict and security, and non-western emerging powers in global governance with empirical expertise in China and Africa. This chapter was written when Hodzi was a postdoctoral researcher at the Department of Cultures at the University of Helsinki.

Chen Jie is an associate professor working on transnational politics of China. He received PhD from the Australian National University in 1995, and currently teaches at the Political Science and International Relations, the University of Western Australia. He has published in various refereed journals.

Iris Levin is an architect, urban planner, and researcher. She has a passion for working with diverse communities and understanding the effects of migration on the built environment. She is interested in housing, social planning, migration, and social diversity in cities. Iris is currently Senior Research Fellow at the Centre for Urban Transitions, Swinburne University, Melbourne.

Eric Li received his PhD in marketing from the Schulich School of Business at York University, and he received his MA in anthropology from the Chinese University of Hong Kong. Li's research interests include global consumer culture, consumer health and well-being, online consumer privacy, food consumption, fashion and culture, and digital marketing and consumption. His work has been published and presented in several academic journals and conferences.

He Li is a professor of political science at Merrimack College, United States. Li is the author of three books and has written widely in the field of Chinese Studies. His most recent book is *Political Thought and China's Transformation: Ideas Shaping the Reform in Post-Mao China* (2015). Li has been a Senior Fulbright Research Scholar in China (2015) and Taiwan (2004) and a recipient of several major research grants and fellowships such as Ford Foundation, Henry Luce Foundation, Tinker Foundation, and Chiang Ching-Kuo Foundation for International Scholarly Exchange.

Wenjing Li is specialized in medical intelligence. She received her PhD in human biology from Universitätsklinikum Hamburg-Eppendorf (UKE). She has international experience working in both medical academia and the pharmaceutical industry in China, Germany, and Switzerland. She has studied and written on a broad range of medical topics, particularly medical information, health policy, psychiatry, emerging infectious disease, and chronic noncommunicable disease.

Lebedintseva Liubov is a sociologist-economist who graduated from the Faculty of Sociology, St. Petersburg State University in 1996. From 2002 to the present, she has been working as Associate Professor at the Faculty of Sociology of St. Petersburg State University. Her research interests concern, first of all, theoretical issues of the development of sociology in China and the Chinese world, as well as modern processes taking place in Chinese society; in particular, changes in social structure, the evolution of modern universities, and social security.

Veselova Liudmila obtained her BA and MA from St. Petersburg State University's Faculty of Oriental Studies. She is Associate Professor at the National Research University 'Higher School of Economics' (St. Petersburg). She currently acts as Academic Director of the MA Program 'Business and Politics in Modern Asia' at the NRU Higher School of Economics (St. Petersburg). Her research interests concern the modern history of China, informal relations (guanxi), the Chinese middle class, social changes in China, talent management, the development of sociology in China, and Chinese ethnopsychology.

Yuanyi Ma received her PhD from the Hong Kong Polytechnic University. Her research interests include systemic functional linguistics, translation studies, discourse analysis, and language description. She is a lecturer at Guangdong Polytechnic of Science and Technology.

Christina Maags is Lecturer in Chinese Studies at the School of East Asian Studies, University of Sheffield. She has studied in Bonn, Frankfurt, and Oxford, specializing in Chinese politics. Her research interests focus on Chinese cultural heritage politics particularly surrounding 'intangible cultural heritage'. In a new research project, she examines the politics of demographic change in China focusing on elderly care.

Joshua Mason is Assistant Professor of Philosophy at Loyola Marymount University. His research focuses on Chinese philosophy, cross-cultural comparison, and ethics.

William Matthews is Fellow in the Anthropology of China at the London School of Economics, where he teaches on the course 'China in Comparative Perspective'. His research concerns the relationship between cosmology, cognition, and the politics of knowledge in contemporary and early China. He has carried out ethnographic research on *Yijing* divination in Hangzhou.

Mikael Mattlin is Professor of Political Science (act.) at the University of Turku. He was recently also Professor of Chinese Studies (act.) at the University of Helsinki. Mattlin's most recent book, *Politicized Society: Taiwan's Struggle with its One-Party Past*, was published in 2018 by NIAS Press (Copenhagen University). The book is a revised and expanded second edition of his acclaimed 2011 book. His peer-reviewed journal articles have appeared in *The China Quarterly, Information, Communication & Society, Cooperation and Conflict, Journal of Contemporary China, Simulation & Gaming, Journal of Political Science Education, Asia-Europe Journal, European Political Science, Issues & Studies, Internasjonal Politikk, China Perspectives* and *East Asia*, among others.

William McBride pursued graduate work in philosophy at Yale University, where he received his MA and PhD and then taught for nine years. He has been a member and chair of the Committee on International Cooperation of the American Philosophical Association and, in the latter capacity, a member of its Board of Directors; was cofounder and first Director of the Sartre Society of North America; and was President of the North American

Society for Social Philosophy from 2000 to 2005. He was one of the two American members of the International Federation of Philosophical Societies (FISP) from 1998 to 2003.

Marius Meinhof received his PhD degree in 2017 from Bielefeld University. In 2016, he joined the faculty of sociology at Bielefeld University as a "wissenschaftlicher Mitarbeiter" (research associate). His fields of research are postcolonialism in China, discourses on modernity/backwardness in China, and consumption in China, placing an emphasis on governmentality in consumption. His works so far have mainly treated the pervasiveness of notions of "Chinese backwardness" and the urge to 'catch up to modernity', which are used to legitimize and propel the engineering of 'modern' subjects, for example through reeducation, spatial restructuring, or population politics. He recently started a project on how recent claims about Chinese traditional culture are related to this older discourse on modernity and backwardness.

Sabine Mokry is a PhD candidate at Leiden University's Political Science Department, a visiting researcher at the German Institute for Global and Area Studies (GIGA) in Hamburg and teaches at the University of Hamburg.

Florin-Stefan Morar is Assistant Professor in the Linguistics and Translation Department at the City University of Hong Kong. He received his PhD from the History of Science Department at Harvard University in 2019. His work focuses on scientific knowledge in the cross-cultural exchanges between China and the West and on the translation of scientific knowledge.

Liselotte Odgaard is a senior fellow at Hudson Institute in Washington D.C. Odgaard has been a visiting scholar at institutions such as Harvard University, the Woodrow Wilson International Center for Scholars, and the Norwegian Nobel Institute.

Elena Perez-Alvaro is Adjunct Professor of Oriental History in State University of Rio de Janeiro [Universidade do Estado do Rio de Janeiro–UERJ], Brazil. She has experience in the area of history and philosophy, with emphasis on Sinology, acting mainly on the following themes: Chinese thought, Confucianism, ancient history and philosophy, East–West cultural dialogues and history teaching.

Elise Pizzi is an assistant professor of political science at the University of Iowa. Her primary research focus is rural development in China, but she also studies natural resource management, migration, and ethnic politics. Most of her time in China is spent in rural villages in Guizhou province, where all of these issues and challenges converge.

Jesper Schlæger is a specially appointed researcher at Sichuan University. He received his PhD in political science from the University of Copenhagen in 2012 and has postdoctoral experience from Lund University. His main field of research is Chinese public administration with a focus on e-government. He is a section editor on the open-access journal *Chinese Public Administration Review* (cpar.net).

Jim Schnell is an analyst with the Indo-Pacific Culture and Regional Studies Program in the Special Operations Command at Fort Bragg, North Carolina. He is a two-time Fulbright Scholar (Cambodia 2005–2006, Myanmar 2018–2019) and has held faculty positions at Cleveland State University, Ohio State University, University of Cincinnati, Miami University, Ohio University, Beijing Jiaotong University, Fudan University, Duy Tan University, and the Royal University of Phnom Penh. He retired from the US Air Force, at the rank of Colonel, where his final 14 years were in assignment as an Air Force Attache at the US Embassy in Beijing, China.

Eric Setzekorn is an adjunct faculty member at George Mason University and a historian with the US Army Center of Military History. He specializes in the military history of China and Taiwan. His book, *The Rise and Fall of an Officer Corps: The Republic of China Military, 1942–1955*, was published in 2018. The views presented in this article represent his personal opinions and are not those of his employer.

Hui Shi completed her MA at Taiyuan University of Technology. She works at the Armed Police Corps in Taiyuan as a senior computer engineer.

Elina Sinkkonen is a senior research fellow at the Finnish Institute of International Affairs. She received her PhD from the Department of Politics and International Relations, University of Oxford, UK. Her research interests include Chinese nationalism, public opinion issues in China, authoritarian regimes, regional security in East Asia, and domestic-foreign policy nexus in IR theory. Sinkkonen is currently conducting a multiyear project on authoritarian resilience, funded by the Kone Foundation. A list of her publications with links can be accessed at www.elinasinkkonen.com.

Jacquelien van Stekelenburg focuses her research on moderate and radical protest. With a background in social psychology, she combines a social psychological approach with sociological insights. She conducted an international comparative study on street demonstrations with Klandermans and Walgrave funded by the European-Science-Foundation entitled *Caught in the act of protest: Contextualized Contestation*, and a study on emerging networks and feelings of belonging funded by the Dutch Royal Academy of Science entitled 'The Evolution of Collective Action in Emerging Neighbourhoods'. Currently she is involved in the major project Determinants of 'Mobilisation' at Home and Abroad: Analysing the Micro-Foundations of Out-Migration and Mass Protest.

Wendy M. Stone leads the Housing Research Program within the Centre for Urban Transitions at Swinburne University of Technology and is Director of the Australian Housing and Urban Research Institute-Swinburne Research Centre. Her research examines the intersection of social change with housing and urban transitions. Her recent research analyses changing housing aspirations and generational opportunities, emerging housing inequalities such as those affecting children, as well as housing solutions.

Christina Ting is an early career social science researcher. Her research interests are sustainable living among ethnic groups, circular economy and zero waste in urban and rural contexts. She also contributes to the Eastern Regional Organisation for Planning and Human Settlements (EAROPH) Australia and the World Resource Institute's Ross Center Prize for Cities.

Mariano Treacy is a PhD in Social Sciences (UBA) and research professor at the General Sarmiento University (UNGS), where he heads an investigation project on Latin American regional integration processes in a context of strong international volatility. He has specialized in research lines linked to international relations and the links between North–South relations, inequality and dependency, and in Latin American economic and social thought. He holds an MSc in political economy (FLACSO) and a degree in economics (UBA). He is a member of the Critical Economy Society of Argentina and Uruguay (SEC).

Wen-Hsuan Tsai is an associate research fellow at the Institute of Political Science, Academia Sinica, Taiwan. His main research interests are Chinese political development, Chinese governance and innovation, comparative politics, and comparative authoritarian regimes. He has recently published in *The China Journal*, *The China Quarterly*, the *Journal of Contemporary China*, *Modern China*, *Asian Survey*, the *China Review*, *China Information*, *China: An International Journal*, *Problems of Post-Communism*, the *Journal of East Asian Studies*, and *Issues & Studies*.

Eduardo Tzili-Apango is a professor and researcher at the Autonomous Metropolitan University-Xochimilco, Mexico. He is a founding member of the Eurasia Studies Group in Mexico (GESE).

Alan Walker has been researching and writing on aspects of ageing and social policy for more than 40 years and has published more than 30 books and over 300 scientific papers. He has also directed several major national and European research programmes and projects. He was the Economic and Social Research Councils' first Impact Champion in 2013,appointed CBE for Services to Social Science in 2014 and made a Fellow of the Gerontology Society of American in 2016. He is cofounder and codirector of the University of Sheffield's Healthy Lifespan Institute.

Bo Wang received his PhD from the Hong Kong Polytechnic University. His research interests include systemic functional linguistics, translation studies, discourse analysis and language description. He is coauthor of *Lao She's Teahouse and Its Two English Translations*, *Systemic Functional Translation Studies*, and *Translating Tagore's Stray Birds into Chinese*. He is currently an associate research fellow at the School of International Studies, Sun Yat-sen University, China.

Ching-Hsing Wang is an assistant professor in the Department of Political Science at National Cheng Kung University. His research interests are political behavior, public opinion, political psychology, Asian politics, and research methods. He has published articles in *Electoral Studies*, *International Political Science Review*, *Party Politics*, *Sexuality Research and Social Policy*, *Social Science Quarterly*, and other scholarly journals.

Chen Xia has been engaged in interdisciplinary research for years, and recently focused on classic Chinese poetry and its English translation based on cross-cultural communication and cultural social psychology. Her broad research interests relate to the cultural and social psychological processes involved in the cross-cultural communication of Chinese literature and cultures. She received her PhD in Personality and Social Psychology from Peking University, and she is currently an associate professor at the College of Literature and Journalism at Sichuan University, Chengdu, China.

Ting Xue is an associated professor of Tianjin University of Traditional Chinese Medicine in China, in the department of Applied Psychology. During 2014–2015, she visited VU

University Amsterdam, working with Jacquelien van Stekelenburg and Bert Klandermans. Her research interests focus on the social psychological mechanisms of collective action in China and the correlation between online hot events and public emotion.

Fan Yang is a PhD candidate at the School of Communication and Creative Arts, Deakin University. She researches the effects of large-scale international social media platforms in terms of cross-jurisdictional tensions and expectations, and their cross-border effects on political activity and identity. Her research also includes the globalisation of non-Western technologies and social media platforms, smart cities and surveillance and information privacy.

Andy Xiao-Ping Yue graduated from the Master of Arts in Interdisciplinary Graduate Studies at the University of British Columbia–Okanagan campus. His research interests include online game consumption and marketing, Chinese consumer culture, youth consumption. He worked for Disney Interactive in Canada and is currently working as an entrepreneur with Magic Fruit English in Nanjing, China.

Luyang Zhou holds a PhD in sociology at McGill University (2018) and is starting his appointment as associate professor at Zhejiang University (2020), after finishing his postdoctoral research fellowship at Watson Institute for International and Public Affairs at Brown University (2018–2020). His research interests cover comparative historical sociology, revolution, empire, nationalism, war, with a special focus on Russia and China. He is currently writing a book comparing the Bolshevik and the Chinese Communist Revolutions on their relationships with nationalism. His research has appeared in *European Journal of Sociology*, *Nations and Nationalism*, *Communist and Post-Communist Studies*, and *Journal of Historical Sociology*.

Lu Zhouxiang is Lecturer in Chinese Studies within the School of Modern Languages, Literatures and Cultures at Maynooth University, Ireland. His research interests are nationalism, national identity, modern Chinese history, Chinese martial arts, and China's sport policy and practice, and he has published extensively in these areas.

Huoyun Zhu is an associate professor of social security in the School of Public Administration and Public Emergency, Jinan University, Guangzhou, China. His research interests mainly focus on population ageing and relevant social policy. He hosts a national academic project on social service provision for older people in Chinese rural areas and has published many papers in international journals discussing the Chinese pension system reform.

Foreword

In the beginning there was sinology, which signified a 'harmless' interest in Chinese people and their culture (according to Webster's Dictionary, sinology is 'the study of the Chinese and especially their language, literature, history, and culture'). Then there is 'Chinese Studies', which ventures further into the realm of politics and other humanities ushering in the next stage where there are billions of possibilities of studying the subject, from I-Ching to Li Bai, from Chinese feudalism to the opium wars, and from the Cultural Revolution to the June Fourth military operation. In the 1990s, China starts to shake the world with an economic juggernaut and a political agenda under the slogan of 'peaceful rise', with a sting in the tail for those wanting to share the economic boom but unable to remain 'peaceful' in China's terms. This is when the discipline goes into the third phase, rebranded as 'China Studies' by some forerunners of the academic marathon who probably saw the dragon looming as large as the Earth in the sky and forecast an unpredictable future for the globe. In this context, 'China Studies' signifies a change of focus from people and artifacts to nation and governance. This time, the world has to quickly figure out what China really is and is capable of before they all become 'part of China': The second largest economy in the world is reclaiming its past glory with a vengeance, leaving no stone unturned. The investigation has to be critical, comprehensive, and persevering in order to reveal the truths amid persistent political turmoil and chaos. One example of a hastily-drawn conclusion is to say that China has dealt with the coronavirus outbreak more efficiently than a democratic country due to the 'merit' of the authoritarian approach. A clear counterexample to this is Taiwan, a democratic homeland to a population of 24 million made up of indigenous peoples, Han Chinese immigrants, and new residents from Indonesia, Vietnam, the Philippines, and so on. Taiwan has managed COVID-19 very well, with total cases of 22 per million population up to October 5, 2020; considerably better than China's 59 per million. Other authoritarian states have done as badly as or even worse than some democratic countries; for example, Belarus had 8,582 cases per million population as of October 5, Kazakhstan had 5,750, and China's close ally, Russia, had 8,479.

China's domestic governance and foreign policies are often innovative and effective (and decidedly cunning, as described in Gerry Groot's chapter on united front work in this volume), and some of them are only systematically analyzed for the first time in this volume, a major academic work. Who would imagine that LOVE as a sublime feeling of affection is used as a tool to replace the censored criticism and protests on social media in a national crisis to disperse antigovernment sentiments (as revealed in Patrick Gorman's chapter on management of public opinion)? Meanwhile, all the steam that has to be let off is directed toward the foreign imperialists (especially America and Japan) and the 'separatists' (the Taiwan government and Hong Kong democratic fighters) to merge patriotism with ruling legitimacy. There is very little room left for critical and independent thinking when all the dissenting voices have been stifled and the attention of the rest guided toward love for the motherland, gratitude to the party for a good living, and the indisputable 'Chinese Dream'. To carry out a proper assessment of contemporary China then, a forest view from above and outside is mandatory. In addition, a holistic approach must be taken to encourage interdisciplinary debates and transdisciplinary integration. To that end, this handbook has collected a useful number of essays on interrelated themes across miscellaneous disciplines. All basic enquiries in the three stages of Chinese Studies are represented, including the literary pursuit of sinology, the sociopolitical concerns of Chinese Studies, and the current focus of China Studies on the interplay between economy, technology, geopolitics, military aggression, and so on. The handbook adopts the more traditional title of 'Chinese Studies' to reflect its mission to connect the past and the present, and to plan for the future. As a sequel, the online *Routledge Research Encyclopaedia of Chinese Studies* will soon follow under my general editorship, which will probe deeper into the topics considered in this volume and more. As initiator of the project and the content editor of this handbook, I am solely responsible for the selection of authors and the review and acceptance (or rejection) of papers. I thank my coeditor for their postcontent selection editorial job and for helping to write the introduction. I also thank the Routledge assistant editors and senior publisher for their generous support in the process of preparing the book.

Chris Shei

Introduction

Weixiao Wei

To understand what the academic circles are writing about China, a bibliography of journal papers in the Web of Science (WoS) core collection was assembled in September 2020 consisting of 20,000 titles and abstracts. All of these journal papers include 'China' as a topic and were due to be published between May and December 2020. To understand the key concepts surrounding the topic of 'China' in today's academic publications, we used the scientometric analysis tool *CiteSpace*, developed by Dr. Chaomei Chen, to process the bibliographic records exported from WoS.

We further classified the first 100 keywords found by *CiteSpace* into five concept groups as shown below (each category illustrated by some of its higher frequency keywords):

- Generic terms: Impact (1489), model (1128), system (572), prevalence (524)
- Environment and health: Climate change (607), health (455), water, (402), pollution (376)
- Biology and medicine: COVID-19 (971), evolution (476), behavior (429), mortality (355)
- Business and economy: Performance (746), management (690), risk (547), policy (321)
- Other science: Heavy metal (241), simulation (237), energy (223), nitrogen (212)

We then count the frequency of all keywords allocated to each concept group among the top 100 in the list. The result is shown in Table 0.1.

It is obvious that generic terms such as *model* and *system* are predominantly used in the corpus to describe the other categories such as business and sciences. We were surprised to find no top keywords that seem to relate exclusively to traditional Chinese Studies categories such as China's history, languages and cultures, or even terms from political and social sciences. Within the 20,000 bibliographic records, *politics* as a keyword appears only 101 times, *culture* 98, and *history* 88 times. We can surmise two reasons for this. First, the study of Chinese language and literature may have gone out of fashion. Second, as the majority of authors writing about China also write these articles from China, it is understandable that scientific publications are encouraged a lot more than politics and sociology. Figure 0.1 shows the composite of the top ten countries where the authors (including coauthors) of these 20,000 papers reside in (Likewise, the information was extracted by *CiteSpace*).

As can be seen from Figure 0.1, more than two-thirds (71%) of the authors writing papers about 'China' work from an institution based in China, where politics is rarely a topic open for discussion. Most of the papers dwell on safe and meaningful topics to the context such as

DOI: 10.4324/9780429059704-1

Table 0.1 Categories of concepts represented by the first 100 keywords and their frequencies

Concept	*Count*	*Percentage*
Generic terms	36	36%
Environment and health	24	24%
Biology and medicine	18	18%
Business and economy	13	13%
Other science	9	9%

science and health. To fill in the gaps, this handbook collects much needed research findings from literary studies and social sciences with a view to providing a more balanced reference framework for current and future Chinese Studies in both domestic and international settings.

This handbook is an in-depth journey within and around China, providing a window into a better understanding of the country after making six stops along the journey. Part I, *China's global interests and foreign policy*, is our first stop, which offers a mountain-peak view to guide the reader on the direction of travel. Mariano Treacy first pulls back the curtains drawn by China's *Tao Guang Yang Hui* policy in Chapter 1. This foreign policy gives China an unprecedented opportunity to start an interrelationship of game playing with

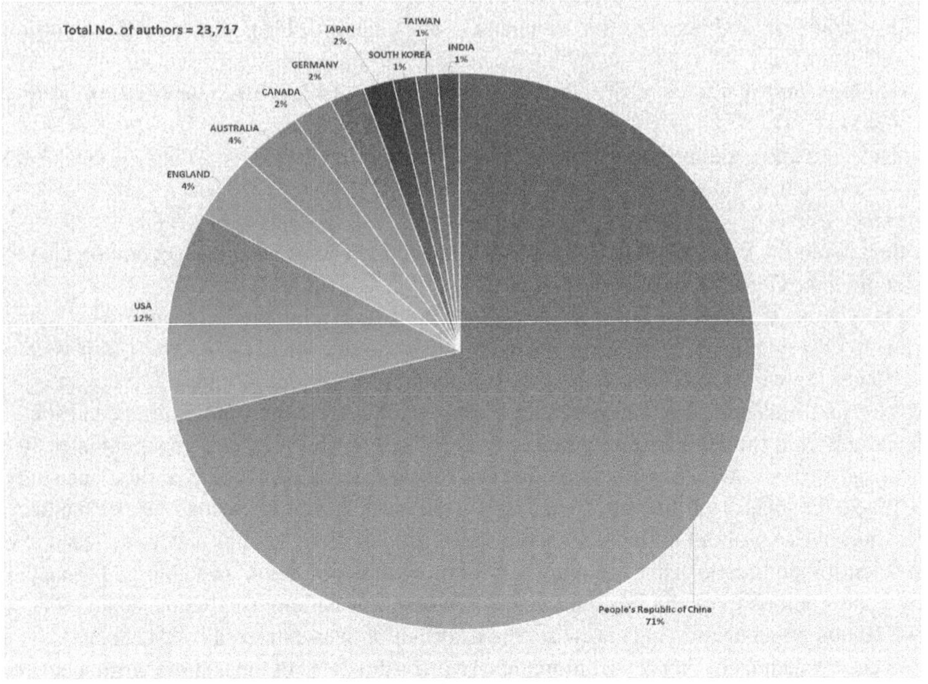

Figure 0.1 Percentages of top 10 countries of origin among authors of the 20,000 papers sampled.

America. Policies and economics are inextricably linked. Thereafter, Chapter 2 offers a well-deserved account on politics and economy, where Mikael Mattlin delves into normative economic statecraft policy to show how China uses economic and financial means to support its foreign policy. In Chapter 3, Gerry Groot explains how the 'united front work' serves the Chinese Communist Party as a crucial mobilization tool in both historical and contemporary settings. Different contexts, missions, and strategies of the united front work department are critically analyzed in different historical periods. Chapter 4 is another contribution on China's economic policy in which Eduardo Tzili-Apango goes a great way into explaining why the Belt and Road Initiative (BRI) is the sure choice for global public good provision and how it serves its purpose. Chapter 5 analyzes the 'China model' in four dimensions and explores the three waves of related debates surrounding the topic. By so doing, the two authors draw a relatively clear picture of the rise and fall of this model and predict where it is heading. In Chapter 6, Liselotte Odgaard offers a detailed account of China's active defense strategy and discusses how the BRI and peaceful coexistence concept are used to solicit cooperation in Central Asia. Chapter 7 details the role of context in human source collection and concludes that China and the United States differ in regard to context culture, which mirrors the complex nature of China–US relations.

Next, we arrive at our second stop, *China's political system and governance*. Politics is the backbone of a country. It determines nation-related economic systems, cultural orientation, and the living conditions of the people. In Chapter 8, Elina Sinkkonen describes the elite level dynamics in China, including power concentration and state control over economic assets, and explores how the trend of deepening autocratization is related to authoritarian resilience. Chapter 9 raises awareness about the unique and irreproducible meritocracy in China which facilitates China's economic success and global rise. The inspiration derived from this political model and its influence may be enormous and ever-widening. Chapter 10 highlights a case study to signal how the major social media platform Sina Weibo works within the bounds and demands of the government. The importance of network front to the management of China's domestic politics comes to the fore. Chapter 11 takes readers through the more interesting byways of the research and practice of e-government in China, which appears to be revolutionary not only in improving people's life by streamlining the administrative procedures but also in terms of government efficiency. Chapter 12 provides insights on intangible cultural heritage which add food for thought to this debate on cultural heritage politics. The reasons, processes, and effects of the revitalization of cultural heritage are illustrated by a case study. Next, Chapter 13 touches upon the all-important issue of population ageing in China. The authors take us through the review of some of the serious problems and challenges the government faces in respect of an ageing population. They also propose the concept of active ageing to meet future challenges in population ageing. Finally in this section, we offer a glimpse of China's waste policy to end this leg of the journey. The authors of Chapter 14 veer away from the traditional Ecological Modernisation (EM) and Chinese governmentality approaches to waste disposal and propose the Protean Environmental State model, which will certainly expand the horizon of environmental governance in China.

Our third stop, *Chinese culture and history*, is a treasure trove waiting to be discovered on this journey. Many aspects of Chinese culture and history are discussed in great detail or a new light. In Chapter 15, for example, Eric Setzekorn paints a dramatically different picture of Qing military history from the stereotypical impression of Chinese military capacity. Chapter 16 offers a broader perspective on the history of international law in China: Maria Adele Carrai points out that in previous studies, a heavy emphasis on Eurocentrism resulted in significant losses of Sinocentrism. Next, William McBride in Chapter 17 explains how Marxism's cult status came about as a result of the guidance it provided for Chinese revolution and construction. He reviews how the Chinese revolutionaries lived at the dawn of this philosophy and explores its relevance to the current situation in China. In Chapter 18, William Matthews provides insights into correlative cosmology and its relationship with the Chinese view of the world. Having worked up an appetite for this little-researched area of knowledge, Joshua Mason in Chapter 19 further explores the topic of Chinese correlative cosmology in the richness of hermeneutics in order to assess the significance of metaphor in Chinese philosophy. Next, Chapter 20 dwells on classical Chinese poetry and shows how it is deeply entrenched in Chinese cultural tradition. The author of the chapter, Chen Xia, takes the reader for a pleasant swim in classic poems and reveals the close relationship between Chinese poetry and emotion. Monumentally important sutra translation holds a vital position in the history of Chinese culture and ideology. Chapter 21 sees the translation of Chinese sutra through a new lens and demystifies the skills sutra translators used in this heroic feat. The article also reveals how Chinese culture is enriched through the avenue of translation and the zealous effort of monk translators. Chapter 22 takes over the story and introduces Shaolin as a prestigious symbol of Chinese culture in the historical turning points of Chan Buddhism. The ups and downs of Shaolin in Chinese history and the significance and influence attached to it are described in detail.

After absorbing China's political landscape and cultural phenomena, we step into the fourth stop to learn about *Chinese people and society*. Chapter 23, written by David Goodman, sets out to introduce the middle class from an all-embracing perspective and highlights the fact that this significant force has an inextricable link to Chinese society, especially in maintaining its political stability. Elise Pizzi in Chapter 24 keeps her focus on the domestic labor migration trend in China, its positive consequences, and the benefits it brings to rural areas. Chinese nationalism is a theory, movement, and belief that involves culture, history, geography, and politics. Chapter 25 reviews three major debates in comparative studies of Chinese nationalism and looks forward to further possible topics in this field in the future. Chapter 26 describes a groundswell of concerns about populism and its research considerations. Currently, Chinese populism is still an online movement targeting the elite and the capitalists, but its further development is unpredictable and its political implications are enormous. Chapter 27 offers a window into a further understanding of sociology in China by depicting the social conditions for its emergence, formation, and development. Compared to Western sociocultural tradition, Chinese sociology has its own historical background and unique features. Chapter 28 discusses the concept of 'Chineseness' within Chinese ethnic media developed in Australia. This study covers a wide range of historical materials with a time span from the 1850s to the present. Chapter 29 investigates a rarely explored area in the cultural meanings of home ownership for China-born migrants in Australia. Their findings reveal that the meaning of home ownership originating in the home country persists after migration. On a different note, but still related to the family domain, one reason for the surging interest in dating and mate selection no doubt lies in the persistence of traditional requirements and the complexity of modern life. In this regard, Chapter 30 analyzes the ever-changing dating behavior and mate selection criteria in China. Although a multitude of factors may influence their decisions, starting a family is still the ultimate goal for most young people. Finally, in this section, Chapter 31 investigates digital youth in Shanghai and concludes that online gaming is a way of shaping and reconstructing gender identity and relationships in contemporary Chinese society.

As China progresses, curiosities of its success steadily increase. The following leg of the journey is a sobering reaction to this thought. The section on *oppression and opposition* starts from Chapter 32, which puzzles out the outlook of nonviolent pro-democracy revolutions in China by reviewing several outbreaks since 1949. Next, the topic of the overseas Chinese democracy movement is considered in Chapter 33. Compared to the relatively sketchy and fragmentary previous research, this chapter lays the foundation stone of a research strand that may loom large in the future. Network technology serves a strut of governance in the current world. How does it work in China? Chapter 34 discusses how China's media management skills improve as network technology advances. In particular, a cutting-edge analysis of media administration during the COVID-19 pandemic is offered as an example. In Chapter 35, the history of Chinese literary censorship is introduced. The author shows how (self-)censorship shapes every niche of production and reception of Chinese literature and reflects core socialist values. Chapter 36 contributes a new framework of on- and off-line collective actions in contemporary China by integrating pertinent theory and research findings from home and abroad. Speaking of public protest, researchers seldom pay attention to how personality affects people's willingness to participate. Chapter 37 explores how personality traits play a pivotal role in contentious participation among Chinese people using a reproducible research method.

Chinese studies: Scope and methodology is the coda to this long-distance travel, and showcases some of the remaining concerns of the discipline and examples of research methodology. As a kickoff, Chapter 38 describes the rich and intricate history of Chinese Studies in Brazil, which is well above expectations. The author details the trajectory of its development from the word go and highlights some of the recent advances of the field in Brazil. In Chapter 39, the author laments that there is so far no consistent body of literature on postcolonial research in China and undertakes to provide an overview, focusing on three key topics: modernity, orientalism, and occidentalism. The author of Chapter 40 starts by asking why modern science did not happen in China, and then goes on to discuss the formation of science in China up to the present. Chapter 41 presents the historical origins of modern psychiatry in China via a process of transnational knowledge transfer and cultural adaptation. Chapter 42 examines the interplay between climate change and cultural heritage and how this may cause ethical issues affecting China and its citizens. The preservation of culture and the safeguarding of citizens identity become important tasks for the future. Next, Chapter 43 introduces frame analysis techniques that work on Chinese official documents to uncover the government's policy priorities. Finally, Chapter 44 constructs an analytical framework combining lexicogrammatical and contextual analyses based on Systemic Functional Linguistics (SFL) hoping to show that Chinese media language is heavily influenced by socialist ideology.

Our journey involves learning to see a multifaceted China. As editors, we sincerely hope that readers have a good opportunity to hear the full range of different voices from a multitude of scholars in multiple disciplines. With the continued upward trend of China in economy and technology, increasing numbers of people across the world will be attracted to this once-mysterious land of the East, embrace China's rapid growth, and continue to receive the dividends it pays.

Part I

China's global interests and foreign policy

1

Great chaos under heaven

Strategies and challenges for consolidating China's global hegemony in the 21st century

Mariano Treacy

Introduction

The 21st century will be marked by the struggle for global hegemony between the United States of America and the People's Republic of China. China's rise has led to a heated debate in the world of international politics about how this struggle will unfold. Will the rise of China be peaceful, or will it imply an increase in conflict, leading to a new 'Cold War' characterized by a race for technological supremacy? Will this technological race lead to separate and politically divided technological spheres of influence? Will Beijing seek to export its development model?

After the 2008 economic crisis, trends of globalization came to a halt. This led to numerous attempts to understand how China's rise was affecting globalization. Some authors argue that globalization is unstoppable and that the integration of national economies makes it harder to escalate bilateral or multilateral conflicts. Meanwhile, other authors talk about 'decoupling trends' in national economies, pointing to the decline of international trade of goods, the slowdown in international capital flows, and the reappearance of protectionist measures.

The trade war that started in March 2018 is only a superficial aspect of the deep geopolitical tensions that exist between the United States and China. The United States argued that China had a history of unfair trade practices and intellectual property theft to justify imposing tariffs on imports of Chinese products, but the underlying conflict is the dispute over global hegemony in the 21st century. China's ability to weather a long-term trade conflict with the United States is a key factor shaping this dispute.

I have previously explored how China went from a closed and centralized economy to a more open, decentralized, and diversified economy, without the Chinese Communist Party (CCP) losing political power or control of strategic state-owned enterprises (Treacy 2020). The policies of structural reform carried out since 1978 allowed the CCP to regain its legitimacy after significant catastrophes, such as the Great Leap Forward, the Hundred Flowers Campaign, and the Cultural Revolution. The modernization program and the CCP's central role in this process led to the so-called 'Chinese miracle'.

In this chapter, I explore the strategic actions that the Chinese government is taking to consolidate itself as a global leader in the 21st century. I analyze the economic, financial,

DOI: 10.4324/9780429059704-3

technological, productive, and geopolitical aspects of these actions and the challenges that China will face in the pursuit of its objective. First, I describe why the United States is concerned about the rise of China. Next, I discuss the idea of the great decoupling and the Thucydides trap in the framework of hegemonic transitions and systemic cycles of accumulation. Then I explain the Chinese development model and the foreign policy strategy known as Tao Guang Yang Hui. After that, I characterize the launch of the new Silk Road as part of China's strategy of a peaceful rise and the United States' geostrategic responses in its 'America First' policy. Finally, I describe the economic and technological race between the two global superpowers and some challenges and tensions regarding the rise of China.

America's concerns over China's growth

After World War II, the United States became a superpower, consolidating its global hegemony. To this day, the United States has maintained military, economic, financial, technological, cultural, and ideological supremacy. This power is extended by US control of the North Atlantic Treaty Organization (NATO) and major multilateral organizations, including the World Bank (WB), the International Monetary Fund (IMF), and the World Trade Organization (WTO). Since Bretton Woods, but especially after the crisis of the 1970s, American supremacy has been threatened by emerging powers such as the Soviet Union, Germany and Japan. However, in recent years there have been signs that this power is waning because of the rise of China.

In this new era of power competition between states, China and Russia have been designated as the main 'strategic competitors' and the objective of US foreign policy is to ensure its hegemony by containing their economic, military, and ideological rise (Woodward 2017).

In 2017–2018, the United States issued official documents assessing the international situation and challenges to national security posed by the relocation of global hegemony to the East. In the 2018 National Defense Strategy, former US Secretary of Defense Jim Mattis stated that the United States was entering a new era where 'inter-state strategic competition, not terrorism, is the primary concern in US national security'. The document also described 'the central challenge to US prosperity and security [as] the reemergence of long-term, strategic competition by what the National Security Strategy classifies as revisionist powers'. According to the Secretary of Defense, China and Russia are willing to 'shape a world consistent with their authoritarian model – gaining veto authority over other nations' economic, diplomatic and security decisions' (NDS 2018).

According to one of the Pentagon's top military officers, Gen. Joseph Dunford, China will likely pose the greatest threat to the United States by 2025 (Mahbubani 2019). Donald Trump's vice president Mike Pence characterized China as a major competitor and imminent threat to American democracy, its geopolitical power, and global economic supremacy. With the same sentiment, US Deputy National Security Advisor Matt Pottinger stated, 'We at the administration have updated our China policy to bring the concept of competition to the forefront' (Zhao 2019).

Concern among US officials is largely driven by Chinese economic growth, the amount of US debt that China holds in its banks, and the invasion of cheap goods into the North American market. The threat to American national security is twofold. First, China and the United States are competing over natural and mineral resources, as well as to control trade flows through the management of and access to trade routes and ports. Second, they are competing over the development of crucial assets such as knowledge and innovation, and associated infrastructure such as communication networks and computing capacities.

Although the United States still maintains its supremacy, China's rise considerably reduced the gap between the two countries (Zhao 2019). China is already the world's top economy if measured according to GDP with Purchasing Power Parity (PPP). Its share of global GDP increased from 2.3% in 1980 to 18.7% in 2018. The average yearly growth of the Chinese economy between 1980 and 2018 was 12.36% and its GDP per capita increased at an average annual rate of 11% for almost 40 years (IMF Database, 2019). With this performance, China has been doubling real living standards at a rate of every 13 years. Because of this, it has raised 620 million people out of poverty and increased life expectancy from 32 to 65 years between 1949 and 1976, with life expectancy currently standing at 76 years (WB World Development Indicators, 2019). China is also the world's principle export economy (12.8% of world exports) and second largest importer (with 10.8% of world imports) (WTO World Trade Statistical Review 2019). Additionally, it is one of the main emitters and receivers of Foreign Direct Investment (FDI) and the United States' main creditor.

Fortune's 2019 Global list of top 500 companies by revenue included 119 Chinese firms. These firms are global leaders in finance, energy and materials, of which 15 of the top 24 firms are Chinese, including massive entities such as China Minmetels, Amer International Group, and China Baowu Steel Group (China Power Team). The high profitability of Chinese companies is linked to their investment in research and development and their leap forward in the most dynamic emerging sectors.

China is already a global leader in consumer-oriented digital technologies and electronic payments. It has the largest e-commerce market in the world and invests venture capital in autonomous vehicles, 3D printing, robotics, and drones. It also has the largest data market in the world, which gives it an unmatched comparative advantage in the development of artificial intelligence. Currently, more than 20% of the world's R&D investment is made in China. Between 1996 and 2017, China steadily increased its share of R&D expenditure

Table 1.1 Main Economic Indicators, United States and China 1980 and 2018

	1980[1]			*2018*		
	United States	*China*	*China % US*	*United States*	*China*	*China % US*
GDP (billion US$)	2,857	305.3	11%	20,580 (1st)	13,368 (2nd)	65%
GDP (PPP) (billion US$)	2,857	305.6	11%	20,580 (2nd)	25,279 (1st)	123%
Per Capita GDP (PPP)	12,553	310	2%	62,869 (12th)	18,116 (88th)	29%
% World Exports	11.2	1.2	11%	8.8 (2nd)	13.1 (1st)	149%
% World Imports	14.3	1.1	8%	13.5 (1st)	10.8 (2nd)	80%
Int. Reserves (mill. US$)	171,413	10,091	6%	449,907 (7th)	3,168,216 (1st)	704%
Military Exp. (mill. US$)	304,085	11,403	4%	648,798 (1st)	249,997 (2nd)	39%
R&D Exp. (2010 mill. US$)	235,642	13,414	6%	483,676 (1st)	444,755 (2nd)	92%
Patent applications (residents and nonresidents)	115,235	8,558	7%	597,141 (2nd)	1,542,002 (1st)	258%

Source: Own elaboration with data from IMF World Economic Outlook Database, WB World Development Indicators Database, National Bureau of Statistics of China (NBS), WTO World Trade Statistical Review 2019, SIPRI Database & OECD Main Science and Technology Indicators

[1] For the military expenditure set, we use the year 1989; for the R&D expenditure set, we use 1991, and for the patent application set, we use the year 1985 because they are the first available data in the respective databases,

on GDP from 0.56% to 2.13% and plans to continue doing so within the framework of its plan 'Made in China 2025'. Additionally, China incorporates 30% of total robots produced worldwide, filed more than 1.5 million patent applications in 2018, and recently surpassed the United States in the number of nationally manufactured machines to appear on the list of the 500 fastest computers in the world (Hernández 2018).

In terms of military competition, the United States continues to be dominant but China has become the second world power. The United States had the highest military spending in 2018 with $649 billion. This figure represents 36.4% of total global spending. The United States maintains more than 800 military bases outside its territory, has ongoing military conflicts in at least eight countries, and deploys over 240,000 military personnel in 172 countries (Arceo 2018). China followed the United States as the country with the second highest military expenditure in 2018 with $250 billion, 14% of global spending and 38.5% of US military spending (SIPRI 2019). Leaving aside conflicts in some Chinese regions such as Hong Kong, Tibet, and Xinjiang and in a disputed region like Taiwan, China has not been at war and has not made military interventions in other countries for decades.[1]

China took advantage of the protection cost the United States had to pay in order to maintain its global hegemony and invested its surplus in gross formation of fixed capital and R&D. Between 2000 and 2007, gross fixed capital formation in China averaged 39.4% and, between 2008 and 2018, more than 45% of GDP, doubling the figures of the United States, which invested around 22% (WEO).[2] Similarly, Chinese economic productivity has increased by 9.9% annually between 2008 and 2018, while US productivity grew 1.2% in the same period (Arceo 2018). China currently only has one overseas military base, in Djibouti, although it is believed to be planning others.

The World Power Index (WPI) calculates the accumulation of a state's national capacities to exercise its power in the international system. It is the sum of the other three subindices of National Power reflecting states' economic-military and socio-institutional power and broader cultural hegemony. These indices account for material capacities (national production, total surface area, defense, international commerce, finances, and research and development), semimaterial capacities (production per capita, population, consumption, energy, education, and health) and immaterial capacities (government expenditure, tourist appeal, expenditure on international aid, number of telephone lines, and academic influence and cosmopolitanism) (Morales Ruvalcaba 2019).

As Table 1.2 shows, the United States has led the WPI since that index began to be recorded. Geopolitical changes and hegemonic disputes can be observed through the ups and downs of the different countries in the remaining positions. In the 1970s, in the midst of the Cold War, Germany and the Soviet Union fought for second place. Following the collapse of the Soviet Union, Japan rose, while Germany and France maintained their central place. After the 2008 economic crisis, China begins to rise, entering to the WPI Top 5 in 2011 and in the Top 2 in 2015.

These indicators are useful, but they do not account for the whole meaning of global hegemony. Economic, technological, financial, and military supremacy are not the only factors that make a state power hegemonic. Other factors such as internal cohesion, the state's ability to discipline the ruling class and workers, foreign policy strategies, and the use of soft and silent diplomacy must also be considered.

The great decoupling, the Thucydides trap, and a new world order

In International Relations, hegemony refers to the way in which a state power exercises leadership and government functions over a system of foreign sovereign states.

Table 1.2 World Power Index (WPI)

	1975	*1985*	*1995*	*2005*	*2015*
1st	United States	United States	United States	United States	United States
2nd	Germany	Japan	Japan	Japan	China
3rd	USSR	Germany	Germany	Germany	Japan
4th	France	France	France	France	Germany
5th	Japan	USSR	United Kingdom	United Kingdom	France

Source: Own elaboration from Morales Ruvalcaba (2019)

This geopolitical, economic, military, scientific-technological, cultural, moral, and intellectual leadership is exercised through mixed forms of coercion and consensus and is perceived by other nations as a way of achieving the general interest. World hegemony is a historical construction that results from disputes between major powers. In Arrighi's words, 'the modern system itself has been formed by, and has expanded on the basis of, recurrent fundamental restructuring led and governed by successive hegemonic states' (Arrighi 1994: 30).

Interstate conflicts over world hegemony have marked the transitions between Systemic Cycles of Accumulation (SCA) composed of stages of emergence, consolidation, and decline of hegemonic states in the world system (Arrighi 1994). In the first stage, productive and material expansion is combined with growing political and technological leadership that results in greater control of innovations and geopolitical changes. In the stage of decline and crisis, the Hegemon loses competitive leadership due to the financialization of its economic surplus and appearance of other competitors.

Capitalism's logic of competition leads large corporations to transcend national spaces to find resources, markets, and an abundant and cheap labor force. States support their corporations' interests by building military arsenals and negotiating with and putting pressure on other countries. Competition between capitals can lead to competition between rival states to delimit the rules of the international system and the place occupied by each country in the international division of labor. This competition sometimes leads to war and produces changes in the command of world hegemony, leading to new SCA.

The reorganization of the world that took place between 1980 and the 2008 crisis under US hegemony turned East Asia into a center of global capital accumulation with China at its center. In the 1980s and 1990s, US corporations restructured the economy to reestablish their domination over Japan and Germany, the two rival states of the time. The United States played a major role in assimilating many of the former Soviet Socialist Republics into the world order. The United States' core strategy for hegemony was based on integrating its former and potential competitors into a global order under its domain (Smith 2016). This strategy was successful until the rise of China, which represents a systemic threat to the American model of civilization and refuses to be integrated as a minor partner in the current world order.

Many analysts argue that the 2008 crisis and the stagnation and partial reversal of the globalization process is an outcome of how the accumulation crisis of the 1970s was resolved, expressing the limits of US hegemony. Many analysts even argue that in recent years the world has gone from a unipolar order with the United States in the center to a bipolar order with China sharing the status of supreme power (Xuetong 2011).

The United States has been maintaining a structural trade and current account deficit since 1974, with China making up the largest part of that deficit. In 2018, 82% of US total current account deficit came from a bilateral deficit with China, which has been reducing its holdings of US debt but is still the largest American debt holder with $1.12 trillion (BEA). Therefore, many authors speak of a strategic partnership between the two countries, which allows the former to sell their goods and the latter to artificially sustain its level of consumption through access to cheaper goods and public and private indebtedness (Arceo 2018).

The main hypothesis according to which an armed conflict would not erupt is that, unlike many other hegemonic disputes, the Chinese and American economies are highly integrated. Since the end of World War II, economic integration has served as a mechanism to reduce the likelihood of conflict between countries. When competition prevails between economic actors of two opposing powers, the objective conditions bring them to try to annihilate each other. When there are commercial and financial partnerships between actors from different countries, economic powers try to seek peaceful solutions to the conflict. The coalition of interests between corporations and states would prevent the destruction of capital that would result in the case of an armed conflict.

Productive and financial integration between the United States and China has shaped the form of capital accumulation since the 1980s. Foreign capital has been invited to enter the Chinese economy as a subordinate actor and virtually all large multinational companies have developed global value chains and become tied to Chinese interests. The fragmentation and relocation of production, the configuration of global value chains, and the consolidation of the dollar as a reserve of global value and China as the world's leading creditor configured a win-win relationship. Thanks to those relationships and certain strategic policies, China has made progress in high-tech industries and begun to catch-up with US technological prowess. This articulation allowed China to maintain some geopolitical autonomy from American interests and rise as a 'Contender State' (Fusaro 2017).

However, the limits to this strategic partnership have been showing for years and economic interdependence between China and the United States is being reversed in a movement that some analysts characterize as 'the great decoupling' (Actis & Creus 2019; Bremmer & Kupchan 2020). As a sign of this decoupling process, we see the interruption of the development of production chains and the dismantling of global value chains, a decrease in R&D cooperation and the flow of academic and technological exchanges, and a decrease in the level of bilateral investments. The United States fears losing its economic and military hegemony and China is preparing to autonomize its development process. The 'great decoupling' process could slowly reverse the integration between the two countries and increase the likelihood of conflict.[3] However, the size of the Chinese domestic market and the advantages of efficiency in supply chains limit the shift of some manufacturing activities out of the country (Orr 2018).

China's rise increased competition and tension with the United States because China is not content to participate in the world order as a minor partner. The Thucydides trap refers to the pattern of structural stress that results when a rising power challenges a ruling one. In the past 500 years, there have been 16 occasions in which a rising power threatened to displace the consolidated power and 12 of those ended with war. There were only four occasions that did not end in war: Spain against Portugal in the 15th century, the United States against the United Kingdom at the beginning of the 20th century, the USSR against the United States throughout the 20th century, and Germany and Japan against the United States in the late 20th century (Allison 2017). Of these experiences, the dispute between the United States and the USSR was probably the one that compares the most to the current hegemonic dispute. Many analysts are already calling the great decoupling a 'new cold war' (Roubini 2020; Smith 2018).

For Beijing, the time during which Western powers dominated the world has been nothing more than a parenthesis before history recovers its 'Sinocentric course' (Rousset 2018). Currently, we could be witnessing the beginning of a transition toward a new systemic cycle of accumulation focused on Asia and particularly China. The 'Chinese cycle', if it exists, will be the result of a historical construction and dialectical contradiction that has been taking place for several decades. China will not replace the United States but rather put it in its place as a first among equals. It is difficult to envision a warlike future between these competing powers because China does not have the military force to threaten the United States nor is that included in China's foreign policy guidelines, based on the Tao Guang Yang Hui strategy of a peaceful rise to power. However, as Allison (2017) argues, 'When one great power threatens to displace another, war is almost always the result – but it doesn't have to be'.

Chinese development model and Tao Guang Yang Hui (TGYH) strategy of a peaceful rise

For some Western analysts, the takeoff of the Chinese economy is associated with the modernization and liberalization and market-oriented reforms initiated by Deng Xiaoping in 1978. This rise is often presented as a victory of the market economy over the state-oriented economy. However, many of the aspects that made China's exceptional growth possible are linked to the specific characteristics of its model.

Trying to characterize the Chinese model as 'capitalist' or 'socialist' is not helpful for understanding it. As Roberts (2017) points out, 'China will remain an economy that is fundamentally state-controlled and directed, with the "commanding heights" of the economy under public ownership and controlled by the party elite'. Undoubtedly, China has learned and internalized the rules of capitalist competition, but has also taken advantage of the strength of a single-party political system and a regime with a strong capacity for discipline and planning and high approval rates.

China has proven to be a rising power with a stable political system, in which the Communist Party plans the long-term strategic guidelines involving the government, the banks, and companies. The Chinese threat to the current world order lies in the systemic risk involved in the dispute between a model of market capitalism versus a model of state capitalism or socialism with Chinese characteristics. Unlike the USSR, however, the internationalization of communism or the export of its political and ideological system does not appear (at least until now) among the Chinese government's objectives.

The Chinese national state remains a dominant agent in decision making, especially when it comes to industrial and technological upgrading. The Chinese state exercises greater control over its economy than any other country in the world. The public sector controls investment, employment, and production decisions in strategic sectors such as banking, telecommunications, petrochemicals, power generators, civil aviation, and armament factories and exerts significant influence over others such as machinery and equipment, steel, and chemicals (China Power Team; Fan, Morck, & Yeung 2011).

The state-owned Assets Supervision and Administration Commission (SASAC) controls about 120 companies, defines the prices of goods, limits exports, and appoints executives of the main firms. Additionally, the Chinese state excludes foreign companies from certain activities, subsidizes strategic sectors and controls access to inputs such as bauxite, coke, silicon, and magnesium (Dorn & Cloutier 2013). There are 102 key state-owned enterprises (SOEs), whose total assets are worth 50 trillion yuan, such as oil companies, telecommunications operators, power generators, and weapons manufacturers.[4] These companies, which have assimilated Western technologies, contributed 60% of the Chinese FDI in 2016 (Roberts 2017). The share of GDP owned and controlled by the state is approximately 50%. China has a stock of public sector assets worth 150% of the annual GDP and China's public investment to GDP ratio is around 16% (Szamosszegi & Kyle 2011).

Far from the false statist or free-market dichotomies that predominate in international political economy debates, Chinese politics since 1978 has been characterized by pragmatism. Recently, Chinese leaders have worked in a consistent development program called the 'Chinese Dream' to convey the impression that China's rise is inevitable. The government has launched the Made in China 2025 project and the Belt and Road Initiative (BRI) to develop independent technological capabilities, move up the global value chain, and consolidate its scientific-technological, geopolitical, and cultural leadership.

Chinese leadership strategy is based on the Tao Guang Yang Hui (韬光养晦) doctrine elaborated by Deng Xiaoping. Also known as the '24-Character Strategy' or 'Pacific rise', this doctrine is now Chinese official foreign policy. Briefly, TGYH means to 'observe calmly, secure the position and slowly cope with affairs, keeping a low profile and working hard for some years until slowly getting more weight in international affairs' (Chen & Wang 2011).

TGYH foreign policy is based on strategic moderation. Under the rule of Xi Jinping, China launched the 'Peaceful Rise 2.0' foreign policy strategy (Zhang 2015). The goal of this strategy is to transform China into a builder of global peace, contributor to development of global governance, and protector of international order, without sacrificing its national core interests. Unlike the TGYH strategy, however, China has abandoned its low profile and tries to move toward building a multipolar world order without challenging US hegemony. China has openly stated that it will not accept an international system that reflects the interests of the winners of World War II.

The international order ruled by the United States and crystallized in the Bretton Woods accords after the end of World War II is clearly coming to an end. It is possible that there will be a transition in which the Chinese government will integrate the main institutions as it has been doing so far. But sooner or later, China will try to reform the global governance system to adapt it to the situation of multipolar hegemony of today's world. The outcome of this process will depend, among other elements, on the result of the most ambitious economic integration strategy in history, the BRI.

The BRI as the Chinese strategy for regional leadership and the US geostrategic response

The main leaders of the CCP have long argued that China's stability and prosperity depends on the stability and prosperity of its neighbors. With this idea, Beijing has planned on building its regional leadership using soft power by increasing its positions in international organizations and through economic, financial and political integration agreements. The main goal is to diversify commercial partners and commodity suppliers and to gradually consolidate an area of influence of its currency, the yuan.

In 2013 China launched the BRI, also known as the new Silk Road. The BRI is one of the most ambitious regional integration projects since the Marshall Plan as it includes almost 70 countries, 75% of the world's known energy reserves, 65% of the world's population, and 40% of the world's GDP. This project is intended to develop six land and sea corridors to expand Asia's economic and political integration with the Middle East, Europe, Africa, and Latin America. In the preliminary draft, the BRI includes investment in all sectors (from tourism to mining, electronics, and solar energy), the creation of industrial parks and port areas, large public works (railroads, bridges, tunnels, dams), and energy equipment (oil and gas pipelines, power plants, wind fields) (Rousset 2018). Through the construction of infrastructure, the opening of markets, and the realization of investments, the BRI is expected to project Chinese industrial interests and strengthen Chinese political and cultural influence all over the world. This initiative would also allow the Chinese government to safeguard its border areas and begin a pacific expansion to the west, ensuring a geostrategic access to mineral deposits, oil, land, markets, and influences.

In addition to promoting the new Silk Road, the Chinese government has also promoted large integration and investment projects such as the Regional Comprehensive Economic Partnership (RCEP) and Asia-Pacific Free Trade Area (FTAAP). Chinese geostrategic projects are leading to new tensions with the United States, Russia, and India as they cross their main areas of influence in the Eurasian land mass and the South China Sea.[5] The Shanghai Cooperation Organization (SCO) (seen by the United States as a parallel NATO) raises another point of tension with the United States. Very intelligently, China has already begun to negotiate partnerships with countries such as Germany, the United Kingdom, France, and South Korea (among others) that are already part of the Asian Infrastructure Investment Bank. Beijing is also trying to include India and the United States in the BRI, something that is unlikely to happen (Rousset 2018).

United States foreign policy strategy during the Trump administration (2017–2020) has been realigned with national security objectives and the 'America First' policy to restore its political, economic, and military leadership (Smith 2018). In this period, the United States implemented protectionist measures,[6] withdrew from the Trans Pacific Partnership (TPP), froze the Transatlantic Trade and Investment Treaty (TTIP), renegotiated existing free trade agreements, and launched the 'Free and Open Indo-Pacific Strategy', which aims to counterbalance the Chinese BRI. Along those lines, the US government increased the defense budget, launched the Quadrilateral Dialogue (QUAD) with Australia, Japan, and India,[7] increased its naval patrols in the South China Sea, restricted Chinese FDI in sensitive sectors, and pressured its allies not to participate in the BRI and not allow China to enter in key sectors such as artificial intelligence and 5G networks.

The trade war has been part of the United States' 'America First' geostrategic response to the rise of China (Smith 2018). In 2018, Trump accused Beijing of carrying out unfair trade attacks that caused unemployment and the closure of American factories. For the United States, the Asian power based its economic rise on unfair practices such as violations of intellectual property rights, nontariff trade barriers, subsidies to domestic firms, and forced demands for technology transfers to foreign direct investments (The White House 2017). In response, the US government has begun to impose tariff barriers and fines, restricted investments, and filed lawsuits against China in the WTO. In reaction to the United States' protectionist measures, the Chinese government raised tariffs on Made in USA products and threatened to stop buying sorghum and soybeans, to change the supplier of Boeing airplanes and General Motors automobiles, and to boycott the consumption of American products and Chinese tourism to the United States. Beijing also threatened to stop buying American public debt and to get rid of the bonds it already has.

In January 2020, top representatives of the US and Chinese governments signed the first phase of an agreement to mitigate the effects of the trade war and tensions between the two countries. China has pledged to buy more agricultural products, such as soybeans and pork, in exchange for a reduction in import tariffs. In addition, China suspended tariffs on US products such as corn, cars and auto parts, and suspended taxes on imports of electronic goods and toys. The agreement includes some points related to technology transfers, intellectual property rights, and the foreign exchange market. China would stop demanding technology transfers to foreign companies and the United States would stop accusing Beijing of currency manipulation (Kirbi 2020).

Despite having advanced in a partial agreement to end the trade war, the global situation stemming from the spread of the COVID-19 virus rekindled geopolitical tensions between the United States and China. The United States underestimated the risks of the outbreak and inequities in its health system have been revealed to the world. China demonstrated an ability to contain the disease through mass surveillance of its citizens and used the critical situation to expand its soft power by assisting the countries most affected by the pandemic. Many analysts argue that the current crisis demonstrates the absence of multilateral coordination, the limits of the Western model, and the emergence of a more authoritarian, but more effective, Eastern model for crisis management and social control. COVID-19 could be accelerating the trends of the reversal of globalization, the great decoupling, and the generation of a new world economic and political architecture.

In this dynamic scene, however, it is difficult to predict how things will turn out. There is still a long-term risk that trade, currency, technological and geopolitical disputes intensify and that a new cold war breaks out between Washington and Beijing. However, unlike the 20th-century Cold War, in the current context, no country would be willing to choose only one side and it is highly unlikely that there would be a clear winner.

Economic and technological aspects of China's rise and its main challenges

Over the course of a few decades, China went from being the industrial Mecca of foreign investments in low value-added manufactured goods with low wage costs to being a global center of research and technological development, exporting complex products and services, and one of the main issuers of foreign investment.

After the Third Plenary Session of the 18th National Congress of the Communist Party of China in 2013, new strategic objectives were launched for the centenary of the Republic in 2049. The main objective, according to Xi Jinping, is to 'rejuvenate the Chinese nation' by deepening economic reforms and resolving tensions between unbalanced development and the living conditions of Chinese citizens. While economic growth benefited the vast majority of the Chinese population, it widened the gaps between the countryside and the city and also within large cities, where large inequalities have developed between the middle classes with increasing purchasing power and migrant workers.[8]

The 'Chinese Dream' anticipates an economic advance in terms of GDP and per capita income growth[9] associated with a reduction of internal inequality and external vulnerability. China's current main challenge lies in transitioning from the export-oriented growth model to a model based on strengthening the domestic market. To achieve this, the government developed an economic plan to shift an economy based on heavy industry into one based on high-tech service (Woetzel 2015). Both the new Silk Road and the Made in China 2025 (MIC2025) plan are the main projects that would enable the country to promote higher value-added exports and open new markets.

MIC2025 was launched in 2015 to develop more innovative industry and increase autonomy in strategic sectors through more local production of essential parts and materials. To do so, it calls for an increase in R&D investment from 0.95% to 2% of GDP and establishes priority development areas in integrated circuits, communication equipment, information technology and 5G networks, cybersecurity, operating systems, big data,[10] the Internet of Things (IoT), machine tool control, robots, aerospace and aeronautical equipment, oceanographic equipment, rail equipment, low consumption vehicles, medical devices, and aerospace technology. The goal is to turn China into a center of global innovation in artificial intelligence (AI) by 2030 (Girado 2017).

Since 2015, the US government has been suspicious of China's technological rise. It banned Intel from selling chips to China to prevent the Tianhe 2 supercomputer from displacing an American one on the list of the 500 fastest supercomputers. In recent years, American industry has become increasingly dependent on Chinese chips, increasing its vulnerability to hacking. Following Trump's victory in 2016, major changes took place in US foreign policy. The Trump administration's military, industrial, and national defense policy is oriented toward reversing the influence of Beijing and restoring national security.

In September 2018, the US Defense Department published a study on 'Assessing and Strengthening the Manufacturing and Defense Industrial Base and Supply Chain Resiliency of the United States' that identifies supply chains' dependence on China as a national security threat (ITF 2018). Following that report, the White House included Huawei Technologies Co. Ltd. on the US Commerce Department blacklist and banned US companies such as Qualcomm, Intel, and Google from selling them certain key components or doing business with the Chinese firm. The White House also banned American high-tech companies from supplying the Chinese telecommunications corporation ZTE. Additionally, it restricted its own purchases of goods and services from Chinese companies and persuaded European Union partners to do the same.

These 'decoupling' measures were taken to preserve the US core interest in maintaining supremacy over AI, quantum computing, 5G, supercomputing and semiconductors technologies (Bremmer & Kupchan 2020). The key to this conflict is the dispute over the 5G network, which is 40 times faster than 4G. Huawei has already invested in infrastructure and developed technological processes for the 5G network. Google is lagging behind in this race since its core business is in data processing (Zuazo 2019). The Trump administration pressured Australia, New Zealand, Canada, and the United Kingdom to ban Huawei from building 5G communication infrastructure in their countries, claiming that China would use it to carry out illegal espionage (Smith 2018). Despite US warnings, the United Kingdom authorized the Chinese company to develop 5G networks but imposed some restrictions such as a 35% market share and exclusion from strategic sectors such as nuclear and military installations (Drezner 2020).

China is rapidly becoming an economic and technological superpower. In this economic cold war, most countries will probably have to choose between US and Chinese contractors. The Thucydides trap is about to arrive and the conflict between China and the United States over commercial and technological leadership could lead to a decoupling of the global economy and a new cold war with Chinese characteristics.

Conclusion

This chapter identified the main factors that make the People's Republic of China a strategic competitor of the United States for world hegemony. In the past 40 years, China has narrowed the gap in production, per capita income, foreign trade, international reserves, military spending, R&D spending, and patent applications. Fixed capital formation and increased productivity allowed China to double living standards every 13 years and its companies have established themselves as leaders in the most dynamic technology sectors.

For many years, China and the United States acted as strategic partners because economic integration produced reciprocal benefits. However, recently China's leadership in key technology areas has been characterized as a threat to American national security. This led to a slow process of decoupling. The main challenge of the Xi Jinping administration is to build a multipolar world order, for which it has sustained the foreign policy strategy of peaceful rise and strategic moderation (Zhao 2015). Beijing has promoted the BRI and the MIC2025 program. Together, they form a coherent strategy of economic development that aims to transition from the export-oriented model to a model based on strengthening the domestic market and the production and export of high value-added services, with diversified business partners and expanding the yuan's area of influence. The United States has modified its foreign policy and launched the America First program. Under this framework, it has implemented protectionist measures to regain its political, economic, and military leadership and also made geostrategic agreements with Australia, Japan, and India to contain China's advance.

The 21st century will definitely be marked by struggle between the United States and China in the construction of a new world order. The success or failure of the Chinese strategy of a peaceful rise will depend, among other factors, on the outcome of the New Silk Road project and the MIC2025 plan. China's rise represents a challenge to the United States' national security but, above all, a systemic risk to its world hegemony as it seeks to forge an order that reflects its supremacy. For Beijing's interests, the convulsion that the world is currently going through is an unprecedented opportunity to assert itself on the international political stage and lead the building of a new order. As the Mao Zedong quote goes, 'There is great chaos under heaven, the situation is excellent'.

Notes

1 Numerous illegal detentions of members of minorities belonging to Muslim ethnic groups such as the Uyghurs, Kazakhs, and other Turkik minorities have been reported in Xinjiang Province (Human Rights Watch).
2 In the United States, the investment rate falls and labor productivity grows well below than in China. Industry participation in the GDP decreased from 21% in 1974 to 11.7% in 2016. The share of finance, insurance, and real estate increased from 13.6% to 19.7% of GDP (Arceo 2018).
3 The conservative wing of the Republican Party (led by Steve Bannon and Robert Lighthizer) characterized the coming world as one in which the win-win relationship would no longer be possible. The conservative wing of the Chinese Communist Party also welcomes economic self-sufficiency in a context of greater geopolitical tensions. President Xi Jinping has called for a new 'Long March' to break China's technological dependence on the United States (Bremmer & Kupchan 2020).
4 The link between the leaders of the largest SOEs (like Sinopec or ICBC) and the CCP is clear: the CCP places top executives in important party roles, with SOEs leaders accounting for 18 of the 172 alternate members of the Central Committee (Macro Polo).
5 One of the most sensitive points of the geopolitical dispute between China and the United States is the South China Sea, an area of great oil projection and the densest sea route in the world. Currently there are disputes with Vietnam and Taiwan for the Paracel Islands and with those two countries and the Philippines, Brunei, Indonesia, and Malaysia for the Spratly Islands (Rousset 2018).
6 In addition to implementing protectionist measures, the United States refused to replace two of the judges of the WTO Appellate Body, leaving the organization unable to operate (Duesterberg 2019).
7 In the framework of the Indo-Pacific Strategy to contain China's expansion in the Asia Pacific, the United States, and India signed in a $3 billion military agreement in February 2020 to modernize the Indian armed forces with US equipment (India Today).

8 Expelled from their lands due to government intervention in the grain market that limited increases in agricultural prices and stripped them of public services as a result of the dismantling of rural communes, migrant workers (Mingong) moved away from the countryside to large factories on the east coast of the country, accepting low wages and poor working conditions.
9 The Chinese five-year plan has goals of increasing per capita income from the current $18,000 to $20,000 in 2022 and $40,000 in 2049 (Woetzel 2015).
10 Reporters Without Borders has characterized President Xi Jinping as the 'world's leading censor'. The Chinese Government controls the world's largest mass of internet users (802 million) through its social networks such as Tencent, Weibo, WeChat, and commercial platforms such as Alibaba and has installed a large firewall to control what information circulates. The metadata of this population is a highly desired asset for the world's leading companies, such as Google, Amazon, Facebook, Apple, and Microsoft (GAFAM) (Lee & Woetzel 2017).

References

Actis, E. & Creus, N. (2019). Estados Unidos, China y el 'desacople'. *El Economista*, May 28. Available at https://www.eleconomista.com.ar/2019-05-estados-unidos-china-y-el-desacople/ (accessed January 8, 2020).

Allison, G. (2017). *Destined for War. Can America and China Escape Thucydides's Trap?* New York: Houghton Mifflin Harcourt.

Arceo, E. (2018). China: ¿El Nuevo Poder hegemónico? *Realidad Económica*, *47*(319), 9–40.

Arrighi, G. (1994). *The Long 20th Century: Money, Power and the Origins of Our Times*. London: Verso.

Bremmer, I. & Kupchan, C. (2020). Risk 2: The Great Decoupling. Top Risks 2020. *Eurasia Group Report*. Available at https://www.eurasiagroup.net/live-post/risk-2-great-decoupling (accessed January 8, 2020).

Chen, D. & Wang, J. (2011). Lying Low No More? China's New Thinking on the Tao Guang Yang Hui Strategy. *China: An International Journal*, *9*(02), 195–216.

China Power Team. How Dominant Are Chinese Companies Globally? *China Power*. Available at https://chinapower.csis.org/chinese-companies-global-500/.

Dorn, J.W. & Cloutier, C. (2013). *Report on Chinese Industrial Policies*. London: King & Spalding.

Drezner, D. (2020). What I Learned at the 2020 Munich Security Conference (February 17th, 2020). *The Washington Post*. Available at https://www.washingtonpost.com/outlook/2020/02/17/what-i-learned-2020-munich-security-conference/ (accessed on March 4, 2020).

Duesterberg, T. (2019). Now Is a Good Time to Modernize the WTO (December 1, 2019). *The Wall Street Journal*. Available at https://www.wsj.com/articles/now-is-a-good-time-to-modernize-the-wto-11575229069 (accessed December 5, 2019).

Fan, J., Morck, R., & Yeung, B. (2011). *Capitalizing China (No. w17687)*. Cambridge: National Bureau of Economic Research.

Fusaro, L. (2017). Why China Is Different: Hegemony, Revolutions and the Rise of Contender States. In *Return of Marxian Macro-Dynamics in East Asia* (pp. 185–223). London: Emerald Publishing Limited.

Girado, G. (2017). *¿Cómo lo hicieron los chinos: Algunas de las causas del gran desarrollo del gigante asiático*. Buenos Aires: Editorial Astrea.

Hernández, M. (Ed.) (2018). *La situación de la clase obrera en China*. Buenos Aires: Editorial Metrópolis.

Interagency Task Force (ITF) (2018). Assessing and Strengthening the Manufacturing and Defense Industrial Base and Supply Chain Resiliency of the United States. September. Available at https://media.defense.gov/2018/Oct/05/2002048904/-1/-1/1/assessing-and-strengthening-the-manufacturing-and%20defense-industrial-base-and-supply-chain-resiliency.pdf (accessed January 6, 2020).

International Monetary Fund, World Economic Outlook Database. October 2019. Available at https://www.imf.org/external/pubs/ft/weo/2019/02/weodata/index.aspx.

Kirbi, J. (2020). Trump Signed a 'Phase One' Trade Deal with China. Here's What's in it — And What's Not. Available at ‹https://www.vox.com/world/2020/1/15/21064070/trump-china-phase-one-trade-deal-signing› (consulted February 7, 2020).

Lee, K.F. & Woetzel, J. (2017). China, the Digital Giant. *Project-Syndicate*, December 4. Available at https://www.project-syndicate.org/commentary/china-digital-age-innovation-by-kai-fu-lee-and-jonathan-woetzel-2017-12 (accessed January 7, 2020).

Macro Polo: Decoding China's Economic Arrival. Available at https://macropolo.org/digital-projects/the-committee/.

Mahbubani, K. (2019). El destino manifiesto de China. *Le Monde Diplomatique, Edición No 238*, April. Available at https://www.eldiplo.org/238-como-salir-de-la-grieta/el-destino-manifiesto-de-china/ (accessed November 27, 2019).

Morales Ruvalcaba, D. (2019). *World Power Index Database*. Available at https://www.worldpowerindex.com/data-wpi/.

National Defense Strategy (2018). Summary of the 2018 National Defense Strategy of the United States of America: Sharpening the American Military's Competitive Edge. Available at https://dod.defense.gov/Portals/1/Documents/pubs/2018-National-Defense-Strategy-Summary.pdf (accessed December 6, 2019).

Organization for Economic Co-operation and Development Database (OECD) Economic Outlook. November 2019. Available at https://stats.oecd.org/.

Orr, G. (2018). What Can We Expect in China in 2019? *McKinsey Quarterly*, November. Available at https://www.mckinsey.com/featured-insights/china/what-can-we-expect-in-china-in-2019 (accessed December 7, 2019).

Roberts, M. (2017). Xi Takes Full Control of China's Future. *The Next Recession*, October 25. Available at https://thenextrecession.wordpress.com/2018/06/07/china-workshop-challenging-the-misconceptions/ (accessed December 1, 2019).

Roubini, N. (2020). *The Specter of Deglobalization and the Thucydides Trap. Horizons No. 15*. Center for International Relations and Sustainable Development, Winter. Available at https://www.cirsd.org/en/horizons/horizons-winter-2020-issue-no-15/the-specter-of-deglobalization-and-the-thucydides-trap (accessed January 3, 2020).

Rousset, P. (2018). Géopolitique chinoise: Continuités, inflexions, incertitudes. *Europe Solidaire Sans Frontieres*, July 1. Available at http://www.europe-solidaire.org/spip.php?article45040 (accessed December 1, 2019).

SIPRI Military Expenditure Database. 2019. Available at https://www.sipri.org/databases/milex.

Smith, A. (2016). The Asymmetric World Order: Interimperial Rivalry in the Twenty-First Century. *International Socialist Review*, *100*, Spring. Available at https://isreview.org/issue/100/asymmetric-world-order (accessed January 6, 2020).

Smith, A. (2018) The Road to a New Cold War with China. *Socialist Worker*, October 22. Available at https://socialistworker.org/2018/10/22/the-road-to-a-new-cold-war-with-china (accessed December 4, 2019).

Szamosszegi, A. & Kyle, C. (2011). *An Analysis of State-Owned Enterprises and State Capitalism in China* (Vol. 52). Capital Trade, Incorporated for US–China Economic and Security Review Commission. Available at https://www.uscc.gov/research/analysis-state-owned-enterprises-and-state-capitalism-china (accessed December 14, 2019).

The White House (2017). National Security Strategy of the United States of America. December. Available at https://www.whitehouse.gov/wp-content/uploads/2017/12/NSS-Final-12-18-2017-0905.pdf (accessed December 6, 2019).

Treacy, M. (2020). The Past Can Be Discussed in the Future: From the Modernization of Deng Xiaoping to the Tensions of China Becoming a World Power. *Izquierdas*, *49*, 159–177.

US Bureau of Economic Analysis (BEA) Database. 2019. Available at https://www.bea.gov/data/intl-trade-investment/international-transactions.

Woetzel, J. (2015). Five Myths about the Chinese Economy. *McKinsey Quarterly*, November. Available at https://www.mckinsey.com/featured-insights/china/five-myths-about-the-chinese-economy (accessed December 5, 2019).

Woodward, J. (2017). *The US Vs China: Asia's New Cold War?* Manchester: Manchester University Press.

World Development Indicators (WDI). Available at https://databank.worldbank.org/source/world-development-indicators#.

World Trade Organization (WTO). *World Trade Statistical Review 2019*. Available at https://www.wto.org/english/res_e/statis_e/wts2019_e/wts2019_e.pdf.

Xuetong, Y. (2011). From a Uni-Polar to a Bi-Polar Superpower System: The Future of the Global Power Dynamic. *Carnegie Tsinghua Center For Global Policy*. Available at https://carnegietsinghua.org/2011/12/30/from-unipolar-to-bipolar-superpower-system-future-of-global-power-dynamic-pub-47688 (accessed January 6, 2020).

Zhang, J. (2015). China's New Foreign Policy Under Xi Jinping: Towards 'Peaceful Rise 2.0'? *Global Change, Peace & Security*, *27*(1), 5–19.

Zhao, M. (2019). Is a New Cold War Inevitable? Chinese Perspectives on US–China Strategic Competition. *The Chinese Journal of International Politics*, 12(3), 371–394.

Zhao, S. (2015). Rethinking the Chinese World Order: The Imperial Cycle and the Rise of China. *Journal of Contemporary China*, *24*(96), 961–982.

Zuazo, N. (2019). La tecnología, arma de negociación. *Le Monde Diplomatique EDICIÓN N°240*, June. Available at https://www.eldiplo.org/240-el-ultimo-sosten-de-macri/la-tecnologia-arma-de-negociacion/ (accessed November 27, 2019).

2

Normative economic statecraft

China's quest to shape the world in its image

Mikael Mattlin

Introduction

As China's economy has grown, scholars and pundits have pondered whether China will be satisfied with the *status quo* world order or wishes to transform it (Johnston 2003). Until the 2012 arrival of Xi Jinping as China's leader, the general view on China's relationship with the existing global order was one of peaceful coexistence and integration into a Western-led world order. China was seen as having integrated reasonably well into this order and become adept at defending its own national interests within its confines, but not interested in overturning it. Some influential scholars mused that China might even come to strengthen the 'liberal international order' (Chan 2006; Ikenberry 2012; Foot & Walter 2012; McNally 2012).

Beijing was seen as being reluctant to proactively promote international norms, believing it to be a dangerous game to engage in. Despite its systemic importance, China was a relatively passive participant in the system, a 'rule-taker' that tended to be active mainly when its own domestic development priorities were jeopardized by global governance actions (Foot & Walter 2012: 15; Bo 2010: 20–23). China thus shunned the role of 'norm entrepreneur' (Finnemore & Sikkink 1998). The most prominent norm-making efforts originated, not from the Chinese government, but from Chinese International Relations (IR) scholars like Yan Xuetong, who advocates that China ought to promote international norms based on traditional Chinese moral norms, e.g., 'humane authority' (Yan 2011).

The Xi Jinping era has shown a different China. Representatives of the Chinese state now act more self-assuredly and assertively on the world stage, at times even aggressively, e.g., in the context of some Chinese diplomats' public verbal attacks in 2019–2020 (the 'wolf-warrior' phenomenon). China's current approach to global governance is nuanced and multifaceted, with varying levels of support and contestation, depending on the governance area (Johnston 2019). Increasingly, China is attempting to become also a *norm-maker*. One leading scholar has used the expression 'revisionist stakeholder' (Zhao 2018).

This chapter provides an overview of state-of-the-art research revolving around China's use of economic/financial statecraft, i.e., using various economic or financial means to serve foreign policy objectives, particularly objectives with normative implications. The chapter

DOI: 10.4324/9780429059704-4

discusses how Beijing uses economic statecraft in effecting preferred changes to existing international norms in different contexts. The discussed cases have been chosen to cover the diversity of China's economic statecraft. The article also highlights how China impacts global economic governance through its alternative *modus operandi.*

International norms and economic statecraft

Norms have been an important topic in IR since the 1980s. The late 1990s and early 2000s saw influential scholarship on norms within constructivist IR theory. Constructivists usually define norms as (expectations about) appropriate behavior held by a collectivity, or for a given identity (Finnemore & Sikkink 1998: 891; Checkel 1998: 83). Much of that scholarship was globalist and 'progressive' in its orientation, with case studies on active normative change to 'make the world a better place', e.g., by abolishing the death sentence, or raising awareness of environmental hazards or the climate crisis, to prompt politicians into action (see, e.g., Manners 2002; Björkdahl 2002).

In world politics, norms tend to be contested and less-than-universally accepted, or not strongly internalized (Goertz 2003; cf. Wendt 2010). Governments do not share a universally accepted normative view on global governance. World politics also lacks a world government, a shared legal system and enforcement mechanisms. International norms do not get established in a vacuum, they tend to reflect the outcomes of power-constellations and long-term struggles to establish certain norms, e.g., on protection of civilians during war, or the concept of freedom of the seas. While norm entrepreneurs (Finnemore & Sikkink 1998) or epistemic communities (Haas 1992) may be a transnational group of individuals, e.g., scientists and activists, the influence of powerful states (Great Powers) on the normative order is important (Bull 1977 [2002]). Powerful states have throughout history sought to use their dominant position to 'lay down the rules of the land'. Think e.g., of the Roman empire's Pax Romana or the Qin-dynasty unification of China and setting of common standards across the newly erected empire. Based on a conceptual analysis of the EU, Forsberg argues that normative power can be exercised by persuasion, invoking norms, shaping the discourse or leading through example (Forsberg 2009).

The contemporary global economic system, born on the ruins of World War II, was largely an American design. Although many other nations participated in the famous Bretton Woods discussions in 1944, the most important talks were held between American and British negotiators, i.e., the emerging and receding leading powers (Kindleberger 1986). Ultimately, the American view often prevailed, reflecting the already vast power-differential between the two countries at the time (Subramanian 2011: 16–19). Later, this normative order was cemented in Western Europe and Japan, e.g., through the Marshall Plan and institutions such as the Organisation for Economic Co-operation and Development (OECD) and NATO, although the Western bloc was seldom as unified on economic governance as is later remembered (Ibid). Nevertheless, differences were held in check by the larger strategic backdrop and security dependence on the United States. China is perceived as challenging established governance norms because it represents values different from those of the (mainly Western) countries that for decades dominated the normative game (Yan 2018), and it is not part of Western security arrangements.

Ironically, right at the time when the United States and the US dollar seem in danger of losing their preponderant position in the global economic system – as the United Kingdom and Pound sterling did after the First World War (Kindleberger 1986) – the raw nature of this underlying reality comes to the fore. Susan Strange, the grandmother of British

International Political Economy (IPE), drew early attention to finance as a channel of power through which the United States is able to wield important, albeit largely hidden, power, through the dominance of the US dollar and Wall Street in financial markets (Strange 1997: 179–186). This latent financial power gradually became more visible in the war on terror (Zarate 2013) and later related to Russian annexation of Crimea and Iran's nuclear program, as well as Washington's allegations of China using American technology to strengthen its military or surveillance capabilities. Washington imposes economic sanctions on states whose actions it disagrees with. During the Trump administration, the blunt nature of US financial power to shape the global order became evident. Today, Washington shows little inhibition in turning the architecture and channels of global interdependence into the service of its foreign policy – a phenomenon that Farrell and Newman (2019) aptly call 'weaponized interdependence'.

Other major powers, such as Russia and China, even the EU, now also seem to be experimenting with how to turn their economic strengths into foreign policy tools. For Russia, this naturally revolves around energy, in particular oil and gas (see, e.g., Wigell & Vihma 2016). For the EU, the natural strength is the vast single market. China, in particular, seems to have borrowed a leaf or two from the US playbook. China has a broad array of economic and financial tools at its disposal, as well as the global ambition to match the United States.

The discussion on states' use of economic tools of foreign policy (to effect policy changes in other states) has traditionally been conducted within the IPE subbranch of IR under the broad concept of *economic statecraft*. This encompasses different scholarly approaches, albeit predominantly Realist-tinged, beginning with Friedrich List's and Albert Hirschman's early writings on economic nationalism (see, e.g., Baldwin 2020; Gilpin 2001; Hirschman 1980; Drezner 1999; Breslin 2011). There is no widely accepted clear definition of economic statecraft, although Baldwin (2020: 28–39) has recently engaged in conceptual clarification. While the term covers also economic inducements, it has tended to be associated more with sanctions and coercion (Drezner 1999). Some scholars have also tried to delineate a more specific subset of *financial statecraft* that refers to 'those aspects of economic statecraft that are directed at influencing international capital flows' (Steil & Litan 2008; cf. Wu & De Wei 2014: 783), but this discussion has been mainly centered around a few scholars (e.g., Armijo & Katada 2014, 2015). Another term, *geoeconomics* – that harks back to Edward Luttwak's writings on geoeconomic power (Luttwak 1990, 1993; Mattlin & Wigell 2016) – has also seen a resurrection. The geoeconomics concept has caught on and gained ground at the expense of economic statecraft. However, it suffers from even less definitional clarity (cf. Wigell 2016: 137; Youngs 2011: 14; Blackwill & Harris 2016), and has conceptually drifted away from Luttwak's original understanding.

With regard to economic statecraft, there is a common thread that revolves around a nation-state using various forms of economic/financial means to achieve foreign policy ends. In this chapter we focus especially on *normative economic statecraft*, by which I refer to economic or financial means used by a state in pursuit of foreign policy goals with normative implications.

Dollar diplomacy and the One-China principle

One of the earliest examples of China attempting to mold other states' behavior to its liking is the so-called dollar diplomacy contest between the People's Republic of China (PRC) and Republic of China (ROC, Taiwan) over diplomatic recognition. Until the economic boom gave China rich financial resources, the ROC government was apt at using various economic incentives to induce small and poor developing countries to support it, notwithstanding the goodwill that the PRC had garnered particularly in Africa through early aid programs, such as the Tanzara railway line – still one of the largest development projects completed by China outside its borders. Especially the contest for recognition of Central American states and micro-states in the Pacific Ocean has been intense, with countries often switching allegiance based on the highest bid, in one case up to six times (Wu & De Wei 2014: 795–801; Shattuck 2020). This phenomenon has been described as 'recognition auctions' (Fossen 2007). With micro-states, relatively small sums of money can induce diplomatic switches, or even flip-flopping, as in the cases of Nauru (ROC-Nauru diplomatic relations ended in 2002 but were reestablished in 2005) and Vanuatu, which maintained diplomatic relations with the ROC for a week in 2004.

What form does China's dollar diplomacy then take? Much of it is promises of loans, assistance and contracts for development projects and infrastructure construction that are large relative to the size of the economies, and transactional in nature (Wu & De Wei 2014: 795–801; Shattuck 2020: 345–346). However, there are also harder-to-prove allegations of elite corruption and influence-buying among local political leaders, often made by the opposition in the target country, or the other side of the diplomatic conflict. China's infamous lack of transparency regarding its bilateral loans does not lessen such suspicions. Similar claims have earlier also been made about Taiwan's dollar diplomacy (Fossen 2007: 135–139, Shattuck 2020: 347; Wu & De Wei 2014: 798). After Tsai Ing-wen was elected ROC president in 2016, the ROC government signaled that it would no longer use monetary incentives to retain its allies (Shattuck 2020). Beijing, in turn, ended the diplomatic truce with Taipei, which had been in effect during Tsai's predecessor Ma Ying-jeou's term in office (2008–2016). Consequently, the ROC has lost six diplomatic allies since 2016.

The history of Cross-Taiwan Strait relations is full of cumbersome diplomatic semantics and subtle connotations that often are lost on an international audience. One key difference concern having a One-China *policy* versus adhering to the One-China *principle*. Since switching diplomatic recognition in 1979, the United States has consistently maintained its One-China policy interpretation, that there is only one sovereign state under the name 'China'. To balance the diplomatic switch, the US Congress passed the Taiwan Relations Act (TRA), which enables the United States to continue cooperation with Taiwan on a subdiplomatic level (Vogel 2011: 323, 479–480). The EU similarly follows a One-China policy.

Beijing, however, consistently talks of the One-China *principle*, which means that Taiwan and the mainland are inalienable parts of a single China (which the world in practice understands as the PRC). The small but crucially important semantic difference is that a consistent One-China *policy* does not recognize Taiwan as belonging to the PRC, either as a matter of principle or practice. Since 2016, Beijing has doubled down on its insistence on the One-China principle. Earlier, many smaller countries did not mind signing up to joint statements that lent support to the One-China principle, and Beijing opportunistically sought to include such statements wherever it could. Recent years, however, have witnessed a more concerted effort to conflate this distinction, and require that not just other governments, but also international organizations and corporations toe Beijing's line. This has been visible in an active campaign to compel changes to the indicated status of Taiwan, e.g., in various online listings and booking systems – from a separate listing for Taiwan to an entry under the PRC, often with the addition of 'Province of China'. In 2018, Beijing, e.g., demanded that international airlines and other companies change how they refer to Taiwan by a specific deadline (BBC 25.6.2018).

It is often difficult to gauge what exact economic measures Beijing has used (or threatened to use) against individual companies [fines, website blockings and regulator's reprimands have been reported (Sui 2018)]. Nonetheless, for corporations with extensive business in China, the potential economic repercussions of official displeasure, in terms of lost contracts or market access, are clear enough in an economic system, where the state is dominant. International companies therefore often quickly accommodate Beijing's sensitivities, or publicly apologize for alleged transgressions against such sensitivities.[1] Some major international companies with extensive business in China have even proactively come out in favor of Chinese political initiatives, such as the Hong Kong national security law enacted in 2020 (Groffman 2020).

The Taiwan issue came to the fore also with COVID-19. Due to Beijing's strong resistance, Taiwan is not a World Health Organisation (WHO) member, and even lost the World Health Assembly (WHA) observer status it had in 2009–2016. Taiwan successfully handled the first wave of COVID-19 with few cases and very low fatalities, despite its proximity to Wuhan. Against this backdrop, Taiwan lobbied hard to attend the 2020 WHA, with flank support from the USA, but was voted down, as Beijing commanded stronger support among WHO members. The Trump administration claimed that the organization was colluding with China. Subsequently, the United States formally announced its withdrawal from the organization (Garrett 2020).

Bilateral lending, conditionality, and debt traps

One intriguing form of potential influence that China wields is through its vast bilateral lending commitments that encompass most of the Global South, but also advanced economies (PRC State Council 2021). This is a potent tool in advancing China's foreign policy goals, as it is a central element of China's bilateral relations that other governments come into direct contact with.

China's lending patterns take different forms from development lending by Western governments. Since China is not a member of the OECD Development Assistance Committee (DAC), it does not need to report its lending terms (Brautigam 2011). Typically, China's bilateral lending takes places through Chinese policy banks (China Exim Bank and China Development Bank), with China Exim Bank responsible for disbursing concessional loans that are tied to procurement from China (Corkin 2013: 63–68). Exim Bank is also actively involved in a broad range of export-financing activities, which makes it difficult to distinguish concessional loans from other forms of lending (European Parliament 2011). A bilateral framework agreement is usually drawn up between governments, followed by more specific project loan and contractual agreements (Mattlin & Nojonen 2015; Corkin 2013: 68). Framework agreements offer the Chinese government an opportunity to get recipient country commitments to broad political objectives, e.g., adherence to the One-China principle, while the contractual agreements introduce more specific project-related requirements. Chinese lending terms are often secretive to the extent that even incoming governments in recipient countries often struggle to gauge what debt commitments have been incurred, as happened in the Maldives and some African countries.

Much has been written about the supposed no-strings-attached nature of China's bilateral loans. China's traditional insistence on noninterference and sovereignty (Brautigam 2007) has ushered in an impression that, unlike Western governments or Western-controlled institutions, Chinese financing institutions grant loans and other forms of financing without attaching conditionality, i.e., without requiring that the recipient government adheres to certain political standards or adjusts its economic policies (e.g., Diao & Fan 2008; Zhou 2008; Foster et al. 2008; Chin & Helleiner 2008; Woods 2008). Later, scholars have realized that the no-strings-attached picture is too simplistic, even naïve. Mattlin and Nojonen (2015), e.g., argued that one can identify four different types of conditionality associated with Chinese bilateral lending: political conditions, embedded conditions, cross-conditionality and emergent conditionality. Of these, *emergent conditionality* is the most intriguing, as it refers to the potential for recipient countries' policy choices to gradually become restricted or redirected through path-dependent processes, even as the Chinese government officially shuns such policy conditionality (Ibid, 715–716). Countries that become overly reliant on Chinese lending for their development give leverage to Beijing and may even become beholden to it. The possibility is clearest in smaller countries, e.g., Cambodia, where China has a large economic and political footprint.

A somewhat similar argument has later been made by other scholars regarding so-called *debt-trap diplomacy* (Chellaney 2017; Parker & Chefitz 2018) associated with Chinese lending terms. The issue came to the fore when the Sri Lankan government was forced to hand over control of the Hambantota harbor to Chinese lenders. The harbor had been pledged as collateral for loans that Sri Lanka was unable to repay. Similar collateral fears have surfaced, e.g., in Kenya. The discussion has become highly politicized, as the Trump administration adopted the 'debt-trap' term to condemn China and warn other governments, leading some scholars to call the term a 'meme' (Brautigam 2020). An important difference between emergent conditionality and debt-trap diplomacy, is that the former regards such adverse outcomes as an emergent path-dependent consequence of the complex ways that projects with Chinese lending are set up and implemented by a multitude of Chinese organizations pursuing different goals, rather than an outcome intended by (devious) design. Interestingly, China's 2021 development policy White paper explicitly discusses planning assistance to other governments, and better coordination of Chinese development policy and BRI projects. Recurrence of the phrase 正确义利观 could be interpreted as an indirect admission that there were tensions between Chinese interests and local development needs with adverse consequences in the previous, less coordinated, approach (PRC State Council 2021).

The BRI as a geostrategic tool to push favored political objectives

China's most ambitious international initiative is the Belt and Road Initiative (BRI) that was launched by China's leader Xi Jinping in two international speeches given in 2013, and coupled with several large funding schemes, such as the Silk Road Fund and the Asian Infrastructure Investment Bank (AIIB), as well as several other regional funds (Zhao 2019). Comparisons have been made between the BRI and the American Marshall Plan for the postwar reconstruction of Western Europe and Japan–in the process turning them into American spheres of influence, as well as expanding and opening up their markets for US products (Mattlin and Gaens 2018). The BRI Initiative aims to connect the Eurasian continent's infrastructure and trade networks and shape the entire megaregion in the vision of China's leaders. The BRI covers more than 60 countries, with special emphasis on developing countries in Central and Southern Asia (Fu 2017).

As the BRI has a prominent geographical element to it, and echoes century-old works on geopolitics (MacKinder 1904; Mattlin and Wigell 2016), scholars have, unsurprisingly, approached it through the lenses of geoeconomics and geostrategy (Zhao 2019). Chan (2020), e.g., argues that the BRI 'can be understood via the lens of regional ordering, whereby China attempts to redefine the shared goals and values for the region of Eurasia and to socialize regional states into the new values in order to have their consent to its leadership'. Another prominent strand of BRI research revolves around (critical) political economy that dissects the underlying power structures in state-business relationships. One of its observations is that underlying BRI is a concern with cutting industrial overcapacity in China that has been a by-product of China's growth model (Shen 2018: 2688).

The BRI offers China a convenient channel for pushing other political objectives, such as internationalization of the Chinese currency, the renminbi – an explicitly stated goal of BRI that has seen some success (Zhao 2019; Cai & Li 2017; Shen 2018). Chinese leaders have not favored free convertibility of the renminbi and full opening of their capital account. Instead, they have opted for maintaining political control of the currency and managed opening, setting up channels ('pipelines') for its wider use, e.g., through bilateral swap agreements with other central banks, and increased use of the currency by Chinese state-owned enterprises (SOEs) and in cross-border trade (McNally 2012; Song & Xia 2019).

Another project that China has promoted through the BRI Initiative is the Digital Silk Road. The charitable view is that the project promotes digital connectivity and enables the Chinese state to capitalize on vibrant Chinese digital economy companies (Shen 2018). However, there are suspicions that allowing Chinese companies to build overseas digital infrastructure also enables them to export Chinese surveillance technology and related practices to BRI countries, especially in Central Asia, where authoritarian governments dominate. The BRI has been controversial from its inception, as it has been designed to win diplomatic allies, markets, and natural resources for China, albeit amid win-win cooperation rhetoric. Framed by Chinese leaders as Chinese benevolence to other countries and magnanimous provision of public goods, realist critics tend to portray it as a power-grab (Zhao 2019). The governments of some BRI countries have also later woken up to overpricing in BRI projects, and demanded renegotiation of terms, e.g., in a massive Malaysian railway project (Lim et al. 2021). Overpricing projects provides opportunities for different contracting parties to 'take cuts' and can thus be used to buy loyalty among local elites.

An important distinction in the academic debate on China runs between *intentions* and *outcomes*. As with debt trap diplomacy, discussions on BRI have tended to focus on China's ambitions to use economic tools for geostrategic gain. Yet closer case analysis has often highlighted a more complex reality. Much current analysis, e.g., assumes that China has an almost limitless capacity to complete BRI projects, or to turn economic dependence into political influence. China's troubled efforts to complete the China–Myanmar Economic Corridor, because of major security challenges and instability, is a case-in-point. In the Belgrade–Budapest railway case, China miscalculated Hungary's ability to get project approval from the EU, and a local backlash against mounting debt. In Venezuela, China is in danger of not having its loans repaid and is in the crosshairs of US sanctions against Venezuela, while failing to secure a stable oil supply. The list goes on.

Coercive economic diplomacy and undeclared sanctioning actions

Coercive diplomacy is an integral part of economic statecraft, especially for major powers. However, unlike the United States (see, e.g., Zarate 2013), and to a lesser extent the EU, formal economic sanctions have not played a prominent role in PRC foreign policy. Earlier, China has itself been on the receiving end of economic sanctions, e.g., an embargo during the Korean war and sanctions after the Tiananmen crackdown in 1989. However, China is no stranger to sanctioning. One of the prominent themes of China's foreign policy in recent years has been the ever-more-frequent and broader range of *sanctioning actions* used by the

Chinese state to indicate displeasure with the foreign policy of other countries. China's traditional dollar diplomacy, based on public or private economic incentives (carrots), has also in recent years been complemented with other harder economic and political means (sticks).

China has used various forms of coercive economic diplomacy on a number of countries and foreign companies. Intriguingly, however, China typically does not declare formal sanctions. Instead, it is often mum about having imposed such sanctions, or even denies it, which may be linked to China's self-avowed policies of peaceful rise and never seeking concessions from other countries (Lai 2018) that harks all the way back to the 1964 visit of then-Premier Zhou Enlai to Africa. This pattern of behavior was observable already in the late 1990s and early 2000s when the PRC government showed displeasure with various European governments, e.g., for receiving the Dalai Lama, by temporarily freezing or cancelling economic exchanges and imposing temporary trade restrictions (Mattlin 2012; Lai 2018). The pattern was taken further with Norway, where some parts of economic cooperation remained frozen for six years after the Nobel Peace Prize was awarded to Liu Xiaobo in 2010.

Other governments that have encountered economic repercussions include South and North Korea, the Philippines, Japan, and recently Australia. In 2020, Sino-Australian relations significantly deteriorated, with Beijing accusing Australia of undermining bilateral relations through a range of policy measures, including blocking Huawei from its telecommunications networks, new legislation on foreign influence, and calling for an international inquiry into the origins of the COVID-19 virus. To show its displeasure, China took various actions to block or restrict a broad range of imports from Australia, from wine to coal. Sweden has also been the object of sustained public criticism by Chinese diplomats. In some cases, even individual companies have been caught up in foreign policy tussles and become a target of Chinese economic measures, as happened with South Korean Lotte Group. The United States intended to place an anti-missile system on land sold to it by Lotte (Shattuck 2020: 347–348). Recently, China has also used formal sanctions in a tit-for-tat with the United States. In the summer of 2020, Beijing announced sanctions on American politicians, NGOs, and military manufacturers, for allegedly interfering with Chinese 'internal matters' (Xinjiang or Taiwan).

It is notable that China's use of coercive economic diplomacy has tended to focus mostly on developed countries in Asia, Europe, and North America. The one exception is the Philippines, which in 2012 found its bananas held up in ports due to its dispute with China in the South China Sea (Lai 2018). This sets China apart from the United States and the EU, whose sanctions tend to target non-Western developing countries. China, it seems, has been keen to maintain good public relations with developing countries – in keeping with its South–South cooperation rhetoric – although it is harder to gauge what might be going on behind closed doors.

China's coercive economic diplomacy tends towards retaliatory actions against developed countries and is partly pushed by China's reactivity to similar American actions towards itself. A case in point is the order issued by the Ministry of Commerce in early 2021 that may prohibit the application of foreign laws against Chinese entities, where these are deemed 'unjustified', and allows for compensation claims and countermeasures by the Chinese government (PRC Ministry of Commerce 2021).

More frequent use of coercive measures is a double-edged sword for China. Smaller countries often bend to China eventually. For example, Norway's government was forced to give in to China in order to normalize bilateral relations in late 2016. The Norwegian government signed a joint statement, where it pledged its commitment to the One-China policy, China's sovereignty, territorial integrity, core interests and major concerns, and further promised not to support actions that undermine them or damage bilateral relations (Statement 2016). However, in countries that have been recent targets of China's coercive diplomacy, views on China have tended to take a negative turn. While cause and effect are hard to attribute, the negative media coverage associated with sanctions seems to play a part. Japan, South Korea, the Philippines, Australia, and Sweden are all among countries that have the most unfavorable views of China, according to Pew opinion surveys (Silver et al. 2019).

China's alternative set of economic governance norms gaining ground

Until recently, China's government disavowed exporting any model or ideology – conscious of the apprehension that China's past export of revolutionary communism to South-East Asia and Africa still evokes (Jones & Johnson 2013). The alternative norms and values that China espoused were more in the eye of external beholders. For example, the discussion around the so-called Beijing Consensus as an alternative to the discredited Washington Consensus (Williamson 2004; Patomäki & Teivainen 2004; Woods 2008), was born and waged among scholars and external observers, many of them Western (Ramo 2004; Li, Brodsgaard, & Jakobsen 2010; Breslin 2011). The example that China sets by being a successful economy and major geoeconomic player, pursuing a development path that does not neatly dovetail with received Western policy prescriptions, has only grown in importance. China increasingly is setting new standards for many global governance practices, and has forced, or speeded up, reconsideration of many aspects of global economic governance. China has thus used the 'power of example' (Manners 2002; Forsberg 2009). As such, China's importance lies also in what it is *not*, and what it does *not* stand for (Breslin 2011). Table 2.1 lists some norms that China indirectly or passively challenges by its different *modus operandi*.

One such area concerns development aid, where 'emerging donors' (foremost China), by offering an attractive alternative, pose a challenge for traditional donors (OECD-DAC), who increasingly feel compelled to rethink their own aid practices (Woods 2008). While the no-strings-attached view is too simplistic, compared to many traditional donors China requires

Table 2.1 Global economic governance norms that China's alternative indirectly challenges

Norm	*China's Alternative*
Development aid conditional on sound economic policies and good governance	Few upfront aid conditionalities; aid as integral part of broader investment and trade relations
Free capital account (convertibility) as a precondition for inclusion in IMF's SDR	Partial capital account convertibility sufficient; certain capital controls appropriate
Open-trade regime	Protectionism of strategic industries and key domestic markets
Upholding market competition (antitrust regime)	Active industrial policies favoring national state-owned champions
Relatively clear distinction between state and private sector (WTO context)	State-led capitalism with unclear state/private distinctions, and a role for the state also in private enterprises

less *upfront* aid conditionalities. The attractiveness is further increased as Chinese aid tends to be complementary to regular investment and trade (Davies et al. 2008). Developing countries have long wished to relinquish aid dependence for normal economic relations based on investment and trade on fair terms. China offers a large market for their goods and long-term investment – two functions that Kindleberger identified as important for a leading economy (Kindlberger 1986; Mattlin 2017).

After the global financial crisis (2007–2009), the Chinese government, along with other emerging powers, talked of 'democratizing world politics.' China and Brazil also vociferously called for fundamental reform of the international monetary system, with the current system considered profoundly unfair and unrepresentative by many Chinese policy commentators (Zhou 2009; Madhur 2012). They were lent flank support by some Western scholars and policymakers (Barnett & Finnemore 2004; Tooze 2018: 266–8). In an increasingly polyphonic domestic policy debate (Ferchen 2012), there was an emerging acceptance that China must play a larger role in shaping the 'rules of the game' of post-financial crisis global economic and financial governance (Ching 2012). An early sign of China's views gaining ground globally, was in the symbolic victory achieved when the IMF's Executive Board in November 2015 concluded that the renminbi was 'freely usable' and could be included in the IMF's Special Drawing Rights (SDR) basket of currencies (IMF 2015) – sometimes called the world's most exclusive club, as it only has five members. This was a remarkable achievement, given that China formally still maintains relatively strict controls on its capital account (Prasad & Ye 2012), and free convertibility has been an IMF requirement. Furthermore, in 2015–2016 China actually tightened capital controls. Chinese leaders had argued that China's currency, while not freely convertible, is 'free enough' and should be included in the basket. Earlier the IMF had maintained that China's capital account was not sufficiently open and China's currency therefore not yet freely convertible. Underlying the decision was a reevaluation within the IMF on capital controls. Having earlier been a strong advocate of free capital flows, the IMF now considers some capital controls as reasonable, albeit temporary, measures (IMF 2011; Chin 2010: 702, 711; Keukeleire et al. 2011: 17–18; Tooze 2018: 475). The IMF has thus come around to China's position, as China's central bank has also advocated maintaining capital controls in critical areas (*Sina* 2012).

Following the United States' embrace of protectionism and trade wars during the Trump administration, China initially attempted to portray itself as a champion of free trade and an open international economy, most notably in the speech given by China's leader in Davos in early 2017 (Kellogg 2017). To many observers, this claim rang hollow. While China has been the biggest beneficiary of global trade in recent decades, and broadly has been a constructive participant in the WTO, China itself has not opened up its domestic markets to the extent expected in Europe and the United States (European Commission 2019; Campbell & Ratner 2018; Lau 2020), leading scholars to talk of a mercantilistic approach to trade (Holslag 2006). In practice, China maintains a long list of support measures (e.g., favorable finance terms, local government support) for state-owned enterprises operating in strategic industries and has been slow to liberalize some of these markets for foreign enterprises, e.g., by maintaining investment lists (later negative lists) and bureaucratic red tape. Neither can China's BRI be regarded as a vehicle for an open-trade regime, as it is 'embedded in a China-dominated tied aid architecture' (Chan 2020).

Relatedly, while China adopted competition (i.e., antitrust) laws already in 2008, there were from the start doubts as to whether these would be applied also to strategic SOEs or used more to block foreign competitors from gaining significant market share. The most notable antitrust action has been against the publicly listed, but private-origin, Alibaba Group and its affiliated company Ant Group. Alibaba Group's prominent co-founder and former executive chair had been publicly critical against authorities and regulators shortly before the antitrust case was launched in late 2020. However, China has been actively pursuing a strategy of building state-controlled national champions in strategic industries, *inter alia* by way of state-directed mergers of SOEs to create global industrial behemoths (Mattlin 2007). The Fortune Global 500 lists 24 Chinese companies among the top one-hundred (Fortune 2020), almost all of which are ultimately state-controlled – mostly strategic SOEs under the State-Owned Assets Supervision and Administration Commission (SASAC) or state-controlled financial institutions. In contrast, one of the strongest features of the EU has been its single market and strict upholding of market competition by a succession of active EU competition commissioners, including by blocking intra-EU mergers, if necessary. Until recently, championing activist industrial policy and national/EU industrial champions was not considered the EU way. But the norm of upholding market competition under all circumstances has rapidly become more nuanced due to China, with even the competition commissioner now urging EU member states to take stakes in European industrial companies to prevent Chinese takeovers (European Commission 2020, *Financial Times* 12.4.2020). China is thus indirectly prompting reconsideration of this sacrosanct EU norm.

Finally, the Chinese mode of state-led capitalism is also challenging conceptions of the distinction between the public and private sector. Corporate structures in China are famously opaque and complicated.[2] While the Chinese 'private sector' has been growing rapidly, there are perennial doubts as to how independent enterprises in China really can be of the state, given that, e.g., bank loans are highly reliant on good political connections (Cheng & Wu 2019); the party maintains party committees in the vast majority of private companies, as well as some foreign-invested companies (Russo 2019); and state-controlled banks have a legally-designated role in implementing public policy. The trend within China over the past decade has been described as one of *guo jin, min tui* (国进民退), indicating that the state-owned sector advances, while the private sector recedes.

Concretely, the blurred distinctions between the party-state and private sector have led to legal discussions within the WTO framework on how to determine what is a 'public body', i.e., which Chinese enterprises, banks and entities are to be considered extensions of the Chinese state. The debate is not purely academic, as several recent WTO disputes related to China have revolved around this issue. The WTO prohibits certain forms of subsidies, if they are provided by governments and their associated entities, including public bodies – a legal concept created by the WTO drafters. Cross-subsidies provided by private firms are, however, not prohibited. Prior to China's WTO accession, there was no major issue as to what constituted a public body. One blank spot for drafters was when an entity provides, rather than receives, a subsidy. Such situations may occur, e.g., if a state-controlled bank, legally tasked with quasi-governmental economic policy duties, provides a preferential loan to a company, or an SOE sells its products at discounted prices to another SOE (Wu 2016: 301–305; Chiang 2018; see also Benitah 2019). Given the opaqueness of ownership structures in China, ownership alone may not be a sufficient criterion to determine demarcations between public and private, which challenges conventional understandings.

Economic statecraft: Stated and concealed normative objectives

Research on China's economic statecraft, as it relates to international norms, has become a hot topic within Chinese studies and IPE. Researchers have dissected and methodically analyzed China's evolving use of economic statecraft in different areas of global economic governance, typically by scrutinizing policy documents and through case studies. Until recently, China's tentative exercise of normative power revolved mainly around the 'power of example'. However, since the work report by Xi Jinping during the 18th Party Congress in October 2017, China has taken a more active approach to promoting its preferred norms and standards in various areas of global governance, trying to seize 'discourse power' (话语权) and offering 'China solutions' (Zhao 2018). China has been moving towards actively challenging selective aspects of the 'liberal international order', yet without always openly proclaiming so. I therefore postulate a key analytical distinction: between *stated* and *concealed* normative objectives. Stated normative objectives are present when state leaders signal what normative change they desire in other actors. When there is an unrevealed intention to subtly undermine a prevalent international norm and support an alternative norm, the normative objective is concealed. Much of China's challenge to global economic governance norms is indirect and concealed.

China now increasingly also uses economic statecraft to actively push for normative change, but it does so in ways that differ from, e.g., the United States or Russia. While there is traditionally a tendency within economic statecraft studies to focus on economic coercion (e.g. economic sanctions), China has brought a new twist to these studies, as its use of economic statecraft has tended to focus more on economic inducements (e.g., dollar diplomacy and BRI), as well as offering alternative economic institutions and interpretations of economic norms. Ironically, China's economic statecraft has, however, itself shifted from being predominantly 'carrots' (aid, loans, investments, and private economic inducements) towards experimentation with 'sticks' (coercive diplomacy, sanctioning acts, recently also formal sanctions). Notably, China's more coercive economic statecraft is creating an international backlash that undermines its efficacy.

The importance of China for academic discussions on economic statecraft and geoeconomics should not be underestimated. China has revitalized old debates that had become rather stale, as they tended to revolve mainly around the United States. This is one of the subfields of China studies that has a clear scholarly impact beyond the narrow confines of the area studies specialization.

Acknowledgments

The author acknowledges financial support from the Academy of Finland (grant 338145) and the Turku Institute for Advanced Studies. The author would also like to thank Matt Ferchen, Tuomas Forsberg, Iikka Korhonen, Chris Shei, Elina Sinkkonen, Teivo Teivainen, and Henri Vogt for excellent comments on the article draft.

Notes

1 For a website listing international companies that have publicly apologized to China since 2017, see https://signal.supchina.com/all-the-international-brands-that-have-apologized-to-china/.

2 For a nice illustration of this, consider the following depiction contained in a stock market notification on a large shareholding: *'BOC Aviation is a company controlled by Sky Splendor Limited, which in turn is controlled by Bank of China Group Investment Limited, which in turn is controlled by Bank of China Limited, which in turn is controlled by Central Huijin Investment Ltd, which in turn is controlled by China Investment Corporation which is owned by the government of The People's Republic of China'* (Oslo Børs 2020).

References

Armijo, L.E. and S.N. Katada, eds. (2014) *The Financial Statecraft of Emerging Powers. Shield and Sword in Asian and Latin America*. Houndmills: Palgrave MacMillan.

Armijo, L.E. and S.N. Katada (2015) 'Theorizing the financial statecraft of emerging powers', *New Political Economy* 20(1): 42–62.

Baldwin, D.A. (2020) *Economic Statecraft: New Edition*. Princeton: Princeton University Press.

Barnett, M. and M. Finnemore (2004) *Rules for the World: International Organizations in Global Politics*. Ithaca: Cornell University Press.

BBC (2018) 'Three biggest US airlines bow to China Taiwan demand as deadline passes', 25 July. https://www.bbc.com/news/world-asia-china-44948599 [accessed 4.7.2020].

Benitah, M. (2019) '"China's industrial subsidies": Is the WTO's AB jurisprudence about the definition of a "public body" an instance of the worst form of judicial activism?' https://worldtradelaw.typepad.com/ielpblog/2019/05/chinas-industrial-subsidies-is-the-wtos-ab-jurisprudence-about-definition-of-a-public-body-an-instan.html [accessed 5.7.2020].

Björkdahl, A. (2002) *From Idea to Norm: Promoting Conflict Prevention*. Lund Political Studies 125, Lund University.

Blackwill, R.D. and J. Harris (2016) *War By Other Means: Geoeconomics and Statecraft*. Cambridge, MA: Belknap Press.

Bo, Q. (2010) 'Dynamic engagement: China's preference to the international monetary system', Paper presented at the 2nd GLF Colloquium, 3 May, Princeton University.

Brautigam, D. (2007) 'China, Africa and the international aid architecture', *African Development Bank Group Working Paper Series* 107: 37–40.

Brautigam, D. (2011) 'Aid with "Chinese characteristics": Chinese foreign aid and development finance meet the OECD-DAC aid regime', *Journal of International Development* 23(5): 752–764.

Brautigam, D. (2020) 'A critical look at Chinese "debt-trap diplomacy": The rise of a meme', *Area Development and Policy* 5(1): 1–14.

Breslin, S. (2011) 'The "China model" and the global financial crisis: From Friedrich List to a Chinese mode of governance?' *International Affairs* 87(6): 1323–1343.

Bull, H. (1977 [2002]) *The Anarchical Society. A Study of Order in World Politics*, 4th ed. New York: Columbia University Press.

Cai, X. and X. Li (2017) 'RMB use to grow in belt, road economies', *China Daily*, June 7. http://www.chinadaily.com.cn/business/2017-06/07/content_29645681.htm [accessed 14.7.2020].

Campbell, K.M. and E. Ratner (2018) 'The China reckoning', *Foreign Affairs* 97: 60–70.

Chan, G. (2006) *China's Compliance in Global Affairs: Trade, Arms Control, Environmental Protection, Human Rights*. Singapore: World Scientific.

Chan, L.-H. (2020) 'Can China remake regional order? Contestation with India over the belt and road initiative', *Global Change, Peace and Security* 32(2): 199–217.

Checkel, J. (1998) *The Constructivist Turn in International Relations Theory*. Cambridge: Cambridge University Press.

Chellaney, B. (2017) 'China's debt-trap diplomacy', *Project Syndicate*, 23 January. https://www.project-syndicate.org/commentary/china-one-belt-one-road-loans-debt-by-brahma-chellaney-2017-01?barrier=accesspaylog [accessed 5.7.2020].

Cheng, W. and Y. Wu (2019) 'Bank finance for private firms in China: Does political capital still pay off?', *The World Economy* 42: 242–67.

Chiang, T.-W. (2018) 'Chinese state-owned enterprises and WTO's anti-subsidy regime', *Georgetown Journal of International Law* 49: 845–86.

Chin, G.T. (2010) 'Remaking the architecture: The emerging powers, self-insuring and regional insulation', *International Affairs* 86(3): 693–715.

Chin, G.T. and E. Helleiner (2008) 'China as a creditor: A rising financial power?', *Journal of International Affairs* 62(1): 87–102.

Ching, F. (2012) 'Who defines the "international community"?', *The Diplomat*, 12 September.

Corkin, L. (2013) *Uncovering African Agency. Angola's Management of China's Credit Lines*. Farnham: Ashgate.

Davies, M., H. Edinger, N. Tay, and S. Naidu (2008) *How China Delivers Development Assistance to Africa*. Stellenbosch: Centre for Chinese Studies, University of Stellenbosch.

Diao, L. and H. Fan 刁莉, 何帆 (2008) '中国的对外发展援助战略反思' [Strategic reflections on China's bilateral development aid], 当代亚太 *(Journal of Contemporary Asia-Pacific Studies)* 6: 120–33.

Drezner, D.W. (1999) *The Sanctions Paradox: Economic Statecraft and International Relations*. Cambridge: Cambridge University Press.

European Commission (2019) 'EU–China – A strategic outlook', *European Commission and HR/VP Contribution to the European Council*, 12 March.

European Commission (2020) 'Guidance to the member states concerning foreign direct investment and free movement of capital from third countries, and the protection of Europe's strategic assets, ahead of the application of regulation', (EU) 2019/452 (FDI Screening Regulation).

European Parliament (2011) 'Export finance activities by the Chinese government', Directorate-General for External Policies of the Union, Policy Department Briefing Paper, EXPO/B/INTA/FWC/2009-01/Lot7/15.

Farrell, H. and A.L. Newman (2019) 'Weaponized interdependence: How global economic networks shape state coercion', *International Security* 44(1): 42–79.

Ferchen, M. (2012) 'Whose China model is it anyway? The contentious search for consensus', *Review of International Political Economy* 20(2): 1–31.

Financial Times (2020) 'Vestager urges stakebuilding to block Chinese takeovers', 12 March.

Finnemore, M. and K. Sikkink (1998) 'International norm dynamics and political change', *International Organization* 52(4): 887–917.

Foot, R. and A. Walter (2012) 'Global norms and major state behaviour: The cases of China and the United States', *European Journal of International Relations* 19(2): 1–24.

Forsberg, T, (2009) 'Normative power Europe, once again: A conceptual analysis of an ideal type', *Journal of Common Market Studies* 49(6): 1184–1204.

Fortune Global 500 (2020). Available at: https://fortune.com/global500/ [accessed 29.12.2020].

Foster, V., W. Butterfield, C. Chen and N. Pushak (2008) *Building Bridges: China's Growing Role as Infrastructure Financier for Sub-Saharan Africa*. Washington, DC: World Bank.

Fu, Y. (2017) 'China's vision for the world: A community of shared future', *The Diplomat*, 22 June. https://thediplomat.com/2017/06/chinas-vision-for-the-world-a-community-of-shared-future/ [accessed 12.7.2020].

Garrett, L. (2020) 'Trump scapegoats China and WHO – And Americans will suffer', *Foreign Policy*, 30 May. https://foreignpolicy.com/2020/05/30/trump-scapegoats-china-and-who-and-americans-will-suffer/ [accessed 14.7.2020].

Gilpin, R. (2001) *Global Political Economy. Understanding the International Economic Order*. Princeton: Princeton University Press.

Goertz, G. (2003) *International Norms and Decision-making. A Punctuated Equilibrium Model*. Lanham, MD: Rowman & Littlefield Publishing Group.

Groffman, N. (2020) 'National security law: UK needs a new law too, or more firms like HSBC will side with China on Hong Kong', *South China Morning Post*, 7 July. https://www.scmp.com/week-asia/opinion/article/3092062/national-security-law-uk-needs-new-law-too-or-more-firms-hsbc [accessed 12.7.2020].

Haas, P.M. (1992) 'Introduction: Epistemic communities and international policy coordination', *International Organization* 46(1): 1–35.

Hirschman, A.O. (1980) *National Power and the Structure of Foreign Trade*. Berkeley: University of California Press.

Holslag, J. (2006) 'China's new mercantilism in Central Africa', *African and Asian Studies* 5(2): 133–69.

Ikenberry, G.J. (2012) *Liberal Leviathan: The Origins, Crisis and Transformation of the American World Order*. Princeton: Princeton University Press.

IMF (2011) *Recent Experiences in Managing Capital Inflows: Cross-Cutting Themes and Possible Policy Framework*. Washington, DC: International Monetary Fund.

IMF (2015) 'Chinese renminbi to be included in IMF's special drawing right basket', 1 December. http://www.imf.org/external/pubs/ft/survey/so/2015/new120115a.htm [accessed 14.7.2020].

Johnston, A.I. (2003) 'Is China a status quo power?', *International Security* 24(4): 5–56.

Johnston, A.I. (2019) 'China in a world of orders: Rethinking compliance and challenge in Beijing's international relations', *International Security* 44(2): 9–60.

Jones, S.G. and P.B. Johnson (2013) 'The future of insurgency', *Studies in Conflict & Terrorism* 36(1): 1–25.

Kellogg, T. (2017) 'Xi's Davos speech: Is China the new champion for the liberal international order?', *The Diplomat*. http://thediplomat.com/2017/01/xis-davos-speech-is-china-the-new-champion-for-the-liberal-international-order/ [accessed 27.6.2020].

Keukeleire, S., M. Mattlin, B. Hooijmaaijers, T. Behr, J. Jokela, M. Wigell and V. Kononenko (2011) *The EU Foreign Policy Towards the BRICS and Other Emerging Powers: Objectives and Strategies*. Brussels: European Parliament.

Kindleberger, C. (1986) *The World in Depression: 1929–1939*. Berkeley: University of California Press.

Lai, C. (2018) 'Acting one way and talking another: China's coercive economic diplomacy in East Asia and beyond', *The Pacific Review* 31(2): 169–87.

Lau, S. (2020) 'EU leaders talk tough to Beijing over long list of unmet promises', *SCMP*, 23 June. https://www.scmp.com/news/china/diplomacy/article/3090198/eu-leaders-talk-tough-beijing-over-long-list-unmet-promises [accessed 4.7.2020].

Li, X., K.E. Brodsgaard and M. Jacobsen (2010) 'Redefining Beijing consensus: Ten economic principles', *China Economic Journal* 2(3): 297–311.

Lim, G., C. Li and X. Ji (2021) 'Chinese financial statecraft in Southeast Asia: An analysis of China's infrastructure provision in Malaysia', *The Pacific Review*, DOI: 10.1080/09512748.2020.1868556.

Luttwak, E.N. (1990) 'From geopolitics to geo-economics: Logic of conflict, grammar of commerce', *National Interest* 20: 17–24.

Luttwak, E.N. (1993) 'The coming global war for economic power: There are no nice guys on the battlefield of geo-economics', *International Economy* 7(5): 18–67.

MacKinder, H. (1904) 'The geographical pivot of history', *Geographical Journal* 23(4): 421–37.

Madhur, S. (2012) 'Asia's role in the twenty-first century global economic governance', *International Affairs* 88(4): 817–33.

Manners, I. (2002) 'Normative power Europe: A contradiction in terms?', *Journal of Common Market Studies* 40(2): 235–58.

Mattlin, M. (2007) 'The Chinese government's new approach to ownership and financial control of strategic state-owned enterprises', *BOFIT Discussion Papers 10*. Helsinki: Bank of Finland.

Mattlin, M. (2012) 'Dead on arrival: Normative EU policy towards China', *Asia Europe Journal* 10 (2–3): 181–98.

Mattlin, M. (2017) 'China as a leading economic power: Could China stabilise the global economic system in times of crisis?', *FIIA Working Paper* 97: 1–26.

Mattlin, M. and B. Gaens (2018) 'Development lending as financial statecraft? A comparative exploration of the practices of China and Japan', in M. Wigell, S. Scholvin and M. Aaltola (eds), *Geo-Economics and Power Politics in the 21st Century: The Revival of Economic Statecraft*. London: Routledge, pp. 145–63.

Mattlin, M. and M. Nojonen (2015) 'Conditionality and path dependence in Chinese lending', *Journal of Contemporary China* 24(94): 701–20.

Mattlin, M. and M. Wigell (2016) 'Geo-economics in the context of restive regional powers', *Asia Europe Journal* 14(2): 125–34.

McNally, C.A. (2012) 'Sino-capitalism: China's re-emergence and the international political economy', *World Politics* 64(4): 741–76.

Oslo Børs (2020) 'Norwegian air shuttle ASA–disclosure of large shareholding', https://newsweb.oslobors.no/message/506074 [accessed 28.6.2020].
Parker, S. and G. Chefitz (2018) 'Debtbook diplomacy', *Belfer Center for Science and International Affairs, Harvard Kennedy School*, 24 May. https://www.belfercenter.org/publication/debtbook-diplomacy [accessed 5.7.2020].
Patomäki, H. and T. Teivainen (2004) *A Possible World. Democratic Transformations of Global Institutions*. London: Zed Books.
Prasad, E. and L. Ye (2012) 'The renminbi's role in the global monetary system', *IZA Discussion Papers, No. 6335*, February.
PRC Ministry of Commerce 中华人民共和国商务部 (2021) 阻断外国法律与措施不当域外适用办法, 商务部令, No. 1. Beijing.
PRC State Council (2021) *China's International Development Cooperation in the New Era*. Beijing: Information Office of the State Council.
Ramo, J. (2004) *The Beijing Consensus*. London: Foreign Policy Centre.
Russo, F. (2019) 'Politics in the boardroom: The role of Chinese Communist party committees', *The Diplomat*, 24 December. https://thediplomat.com/2019/12/politics-in-the-boardroom-the-role-of-chinese-communist-party-committees/ [accessed 5.7.2020].
Shattuck, T.J. (2020) 'The race to zero? China's poaching of Taiwan's diplomatic allies', *Orbis* 64(2): 334–52.
Shen, H. (2018) 'Building a digital silk road? Situating the internet in China's belt and road initiative', *International Journal of Communications* 12: 2683–701.
Silver, L., K. Devlin and C. Huang (2019) *People Around the World Are Divided in Their Opinions on China*. Pew Research Center. https://www.pewresearch.org/fact-tank/2019/12/05/people-around-the-globe-are-divided-in-their-opinions-of-china/ [accessed 13.7.2020].
Sina. (2012) '央行课题组：加快资本账户开放条件基本成熟' [Central bank research department: The conditions for speeding-up capital account opening are basically mature], 27 February.
Song, K. and L. Xia (2019) 'Bilateral swap agreement and Renminbi settlement in cross-border trade', *BOFIT Discussion Papers 19/2019*.
Statement of the Government of the People's Republic of China and the Government of the Kingdom of Norway on Normalization of Bilateral Relations. https://www.regjeringen.no/en/aktuelt/normalization_china/id2524797/ [accessed 13.7.2020].
Steil, B. and R.E. Litan (2008) *Financial Statecraft: The Role of Financial Markets in American Foreign Policy*. New Haven: Yale University Press.
Strange, S. (1997) *Casino Capitalism*, 2nd edition. Manchester: Manchester University Press.
Subramanian, A. (2011) *Eclipse. Living in the Shadow of China's Economic Dominance*. Washington: Peterson Institute for International Economics.
Sui, C. (2018) 'China warns Western firms over Taiwan', *BBC*, 29 June. https://www.bbc.com/news/business-44614106 [accessed 29.12.2020].
Tooze, A. (2018) *Crashed: How a Decade of Financial Crises Changed the World*. London: Penguin Books.
Van Fossen, A. (2007) 'The struggle for recognition: Diplomatic competition between China and Taiwan in Oceania', *Journal of Chinese Political Science* 12(2): 126–46.
Vogel, E.F. (2011) *Deng Xiaoping and the Transformation of China*. Cambridge, MA & London: Belknap Press of Harvard University Press.
Wendt, A. (2010 [1999]) *Social Theory of International Politics*. Cambridge: Cambridge University Press.
Wigell, M. (2016) 'Conceptualizing regional powers' geoeconomic strategies: Neo-imperialism, neo-mercantilism, hegemony, and liberal institutionalism', *Asia Europe Journal* 14(2): 135–51.
Wigell, M. and A. Vihma (2016) 'Geopolitics versus geo-economics: The case of Russia's geostrategy and its effects on the EU', *International Affairs* 92(3): 605–27.

Williamson, J. (2004) 'A short history of the Washington consensus', Paper presented in the conference From the Washington Consensus to a new Global Governance. Barcelona, 24 September.

Woods, N. (2008) 'Whose aid? Whose influence? China, emerging donors and the silent revolution in development assistance', *International Affairs* 84(6): 1205–21.

Wu, F. and K. De Wei (2014) 'From financial assets to financial statecraft: The case of China and emerging economies of Africa and Latin America', *Journal of Contemporary China* 23(89): 781–803.

Wu, M. (2016) 'The "China, Inc." challenge to global trade governance', *Harvard International Law Journal* 57(2): 261–324.

Yan, X. (2011) 'International leadership and norm evolution', *The Chinese Journal of International Politics* 4: 233–64.

Yan, X. (2018) 'Chinese values vs. liberalism: What ideology will shape the international normative order?', *The Chinese Journal of International Politics* 11(1): 1–22.

Youngs, R. (2011) 'Geo-economic futures', in A. Martiningui and R. Youngs (eds), *Challenges for European Foreign Policy in 2012: What Kind of Geo-Economic Europe?* Madrid: FRIDE, 13–17.

Zarate, J.C. (2013) *Treasury's War. The Unleashing of a New Era of Financial Warfare*. New York: Public Affairs.

Zhao, S. (2018) 'A revisionist stakeholder: China and the post-world war II world order', *Journal of Contemporary China* 27(113): 643–58.

Zhao, S. (2019) 'China's belt-road initiative as the signature of president Xi Jinping diplomacy: Easier said than done', *Journal of Contemporary China* 29(123): 319–35.

Zhou, H. 周弘 (2008) 中国对外援助与改革开放30年 [China's foreign aid and 30 years of reform and opening-up], 世界经济与政治 11: 33–43.

Zhou X. 周小川 (2009) '关于改革国际货币体系的思考' [Reflections on reforming the international monetary system]. People's Bank of China, 24 March.

3

The CCP's united front work department

Roles and influence at home and abroad

Gerry Groot

Introduction

The Chinese Communist Party's (CCP) extensive history and practice of united front work is an area few outside the Party itself were interested in after the Cold War (1946–1991). The last comprehensive overview in English, van Slyke's *Enemies and Friends*, was in 1967. Yet invoking of ties of 'friendship' and demarking of enemies remains a basic element of every day CCP practice, let alone united front work. Likewise, the contribution of this work to China's growing importance has remained obscure. Until around 2017 it still rarely attracted attention. That united front work is again attracting outside scrutiny has much to do with the elevation of Xi Jinping to CCP General Secretary in 2012 and Xi's subsequent active endorsement of it. Domestically, this work is again a powerful tool of assimilation while abroad it is one of mobilization of support and neutralization of critics. The most recent turning point has been the emergence of the COVID-19 pandemic, which emanated from Wuhan in late 2019.

Even this pandemic, a major historical event, is entangled in various arms of the CCP's United Front Work Department (UFWD), under direct control of the Party Central Committee and the Small Leading Group on United Front Work appointed by Xi himself. These manifestations have included a scandal involving a 'democratic party' member at a Wuhan virology lab and the use of such parties to rally expertise to fight the virus.

The most salient manifestations outside of China were the mobilization of united front groups throughout Europe, Australia, and North America, to buy up and send 'home' bulk supplies of personal protection equipment (PPE) and medical equipment in the first few months of 2020. This activity occurred only weeks before countries belatedly recognized the dangers of the virus to their own populations but then at its peak within China. Together with the accelerating spread of the pandemic, these factors helped precipitate crises over inadequate medical supplies. These in turn generated waves of anti-China sentiment, which sometimes included racist attacks on individuals assumed to be Chinese. Then, as China's domestic conditions eased, the Party-state again began exporting PPE, sometimes with united front-linked groups distributing it to generate positive publicity for China.

DOI: 10.4324/9780429059704-5

The virus also had other unanticipated consequences for united front work. In Hong Kong, protestors who in 2019 had been out in vast numbers demonstrating against increasing direct interference from the People's Republic of China (PRC) in the former colony, disappeared off the streets. Despite decades of united front work and consequent strong ties with the city's elites (Loh 2010), the CCP had been unprepared for the resistance it was increasingly facing. Then, in April 2020 the CCP's representative office declared it was not bound by key parts of the agreement signed between the Party and Britain to facilitate the city's return to Chinese sovereignty in 1997. For good measure, the protestors were labelled a 'political virus' requiring elimination. This turn was compounded with Beijing promulgating a *National Security Law* for Hong Kong on July 1. This law immediately criminalized most actions of its critics as 'terrorism' or secession and allowed for trials in China proper. Hong Kong's legal independence was neutered. These acts also effectively killed off the CCP's key united front promise of 'One-Country–Two-Systems' (OCTS).

This effective end of OCTS also meant that the central promise being held out to solve the CCP's largest bit of unfinished business, gaining effective sovereignty over the remnant Republic of China on Taiwan, also evaporated. As part of united front work aimed at national unification, Taiwan, like Hong Kong, has been promised it would be able to maintain its own civil service, police, judiciary, etc. – the Two Systems – *if* it accepts PRC sovereignty – the One Country. Meanwhile, Taiwan, democratic since the 1990s, had already emerged from the pandemic both unscathed and with its international status enhanced: the exact opposite of united front work's intended purpose.

The year 2020 may well have seen the end of the rise of China's soft power in the world. This is not only because the pandemic forced foreign reappraisals of CCP's promises and intentions; it also resulted in a greater willingness to examine other elements of the Party's actions which conflict with Western values and interests. Moreover, many of these actions have united front work connections to the UFWD or its partner body, the CCP's International Liaison Department (ILD), in ways that earlier generations of scholars often found hard to see or easy to ignore. These actions include a renewed emphasis on the 'Sinification' of religious beliefs like Christianity, forced assimilation of ethnic minorities (notably Muslim Uyghurs) in the name of eliminating the 'virus of religion,' and the elimination of civil society–like spaces for emerging professional classes.

Meanwhile, the actions of united front groups abroad are now also of growing concern to increasing numbers of foreign governments as potentially compromising their political systems, universities and Diaspora populations. At the same time, the importance of the CCP's domestic cooptation of groups to maintain power and respond to social and economic change, key elements of its 'consultative democracy', is under appreciated. To understand these issues though, some history is crucial.

A brief history of united front work

Seizing power

In 1939 Mao Zedong famously declared that the CCP's survival to-date, against all odds, was based its three 'magic' (or 'secret') weapons; united front work, armed struggle and Party-building (Mao 1939). In October 1949 when the Party finalized its rise to power by force by militarily defeating the Nationalists, the truth of Mao's claim was established. The CCP had taken cooperation with parties, groups, and individuals who might otherwise oppose them and used them to help win power. Significantly, the Party had eventually taken united front policies forced on it and adapted these to become intrinsic to its work and structures. These policies recognized inherent weaknesses vis-à-vis enemies and justified strategic and tactical cross-class and interest group collaboration to secure Party goals. When the Party was strong enough, it could abandon, 'reeducate', or eliminate former 'friends' as it saw fit.

The CCP's first experience of united front work was that determined by the Comintern in 1924 and implemented by its agents including Henk Sneevliet (1883–1942) and Mikhail Borodin (1884–1951). In 1924, using his East Indies experience, Sneevliet organized a bloc-within-united-front between CCP and the Chinese Nationalist Party or Kuomintang (KMT) led by a sympathetic Sun Yatsen (1866–1925). Importantly, the theoretical basis for such alliances is Lenin's 1920 pamphlet, '"Left-Wing" Communism: An Infantile Disorder', in which Lenin justified communists compromising with other groups and classes to promote eventual revolutionary success (Armstrong 1977: 13–20).

In 1924, the KMT (1912–) was China's only advanced and successful anti-imperialist revolutionary party. The CCP, only formed in 1921, was tiny, fragmented, and inexperienced. The bloc-within was a strategy to learn from the KMT, radicalize it, and eventually take it over. Sun's successor Chiang Kaishek (1887–1975), however, turned on the CCP and leftists in April 1927, killing thousands.

While the CCP lost many members and survivors had to flee to remote rural areas or go underground, it was nevertheless much larger, tempered and far more experienced than in 1924. It also learnt the necessity of maintaining independence and leadership in any united front form. But for much of the next decade, isolated in faraway revolutionary soviets, the CCP asserted revolutionary purity. Its 'red terror' violence, murder of landlords, and radical land redistribution, failed to bring lasting economic benefits and turned otherwise neutral or supportive wealthier groups into fearful active enemies. To secure the revolution, it became clear that the Party needed wider support. When the failures of its ultra-left policies and increasing attacks by the KMT forced the Party on the Long March (late 1934–1935), the value of support from ethnic minorities in borderlands also became clear.

The increasing influence of Japanese expansion in China from the 1930s and its eventual full-scale invasion in 1937 allowed the CCP to call on China's urban patriots to pressure the KMT to cease attacking it and face the common enemy. Yet it was another intervention by the Communist International under Stalin, which resulted in the second period of cooperation with the Chiang and the Nationalists from 1937 onward.

This cooperation, in turn, formed but one part of much wider CCP united front efforts in which the Party played down its ultimate revolutionary goals and made material concessions to groups such as landlords, gentry, capitalists, and urban intellectuals – as long as these resisted Japan and pressured the KMT to stop attacking communists and their progressive allies. Publicly, the CCP promoted a platform that seemingly moved it close to Sun Yatsen's 'Three Principles of the People' (Nationalism, Democracy, and People's Livelihood) program. It now also incorporated local notables in assemblies based on a 'three-thirds' principle: one-third CCP, one-third 'progressives,' and one-third others who were not explicitly hostile and vetted by the Party. It is a principle reflected today in every level of the Chinese People's Political Consultative Conference (CPPCC), the political representative system and apex of the united front system and which grew out of this experience.

Just as importantly, the second bout of nominal CCP–KMT cooperation also resulted in the legalization of the CCP in KMT-controlled urban areas where it again was able to work with as many political groups, factions, and influential individuals it could find. China's so-called minor 'democratic' parties and groups (MPGs) were wooed, assisted, infiltrated, and later sometimes even established by underground communists. They were used to access and to influence urban intellectuals and even international, especially American audiences, as well as access the KMT and glean intelligence.

The immediate goal was to pressure the KMT to only fight the Japanese and hence become weaker while the CCP built up its strength in the hinterlands. At the end of the war with Japan, the goodwill generated and influence exercised through united front work, meant that if the KMT ever allowed its long-promised national elections, the CCP would have numerous urban allies and proxies. In the meantime, compromised allies like the China Democratic League helped convince some key foreign observers that China had 'liberal' elements between the KMT and CCP extremes, which might balance the two big armed parties and even be a force for democratization.

From 1936 onwards, the survival of the Party itself was its central concern. Hence much united front work was devoted to this end and included mobilizing urban and other groups to pressure the KMT to desist from anti-CCP actions, to weaken KMT legitimacy and isolate it politically as much as possible, and to access the many disparate groups that made up the Nationalist forces. These elements of anti-KMT united front work overlapped with and often fused with intelligence work. Using altruistic appeals such as 'Resist Japan!' patriotism, 'peace', and 'democracy', combined with personal appeals, compromises, inducements, and other promises, led to major successes, such as surrenders of leaders and soldiers to CCP forces. Before the outbreak of open civil war between the two, the kidnapping of Chiang Kai-shek by the warlords Zhang Xueliang (1901–2001) and Yang Hucheng (1893–1949) in 1936 was but one important factor in bringing about the Second Period of CCP-KMT Cooperation. This had been preceded by talks with Zhou Enlai and the use of MPG supporters in their offices. Among the MPGs aided by the CCP to draw support from the KMT's more left-wing elements was the Third Party originally established by Deng Yanda (1895–1931). This lives on as today's China Peasants and Workers Democratic Party.

With the subsequent outbreak of full-scale civil war between the CCP and KMT (1946–1949), the MPGs still provided the CCP invaluable access to urban populations and resources while using their access to the KMT, business, bureaucracies, schools, and universities to recruit, propagandize, and organize. To convince urban and educated Chinese that the CCP had the broadest support, it also became imperative to prevent the possibility of the MPGs trying to establish some middle way or third road between it and the KMT. Only the CCP should be seen as 'democratic,' inclusive, and able to bring about peace (Groot 2004).

When on May 1, 1948, the CCP made a call for allies, most MPGs rallied to it and allowed the CCP to symbolically demonstrate its claim to represent the majority of China's people and classes as it already claimed peasants, workers, and soldiers as its natural constituencies. United front successes allowed the Party to claim popular legitimacy at the KMT's expense. The military victory needed to allow unfettered revolutionary change without compromise was now inevitable. In the interim, united front work to disintegrate and drain support from the Nationalists and their armies continued unabated.

In this revolutionary stage of seizing power, united front work was part of the CCP's general strategy and tactics of seeking to undermine and delegitimize the KMT as its principal enemy. Friends or potential friends were any whose interests were inimical to the Nationalists. Friends (groups or influential individuals) could be won over by any combination of personal persuasion, material concessions, altruistic appeals (patriotism, peace, democracy, etc.), or coercion.

In this zero-sum context, even convincing symbolically and/or instrumentally important groups and key individuals to move from active support of the enemy to neutrality constituted a win for the CCP as its effective strength and legitimacy increased at the KMT's expense. In many cases, apparent neutrality of allies was also better than active endorsement of the CCP. As Sun Yatsen's widow and from a key family, Song Qingling (1893–1981) remained influential among urban elites and Overseas Chinese and it was more useful to have her as nominally independent. Others, towering intellectuals like Huang Yanpei (1878–1965), had extensive social networks and academic connections while serving as models for those who aspired to be like them. Still others, like He Xiangning (18781972), widow of left-wing KMT leader Liao Zhongkai (1877–1925) who was assassinated by the KMT in 1925, could be relied on to attack CCP critics as a leader of the National Salvation Leagues encouraged by the CCP, or later as a leader of an MPG. Much of this took place in the comparatively open civil society–type spaces allowed by the Nationalists, especially in big cities like Shanghai where the CCP could take advantages of the relative freedom to launch protests and demonstrate against the KMT's failings in controlling inflation, providing jobs, and allying with the United States. This activity became the CCP's second front against the KMT.

Public attacks on CCP enemies or wavering 'friends' by the likes of He to support CCP goals remains a key use of united front bodies and figures and represents the principle of 'unity with struggle'. It is the effective equivalent of the CCP's Party-building ideological indoctrination. In groups such as MPGs, underground CCP members or trusted leftists engaged in sometimes fierce political browbeating and emotional blackmail based on the bonds of friendship, so that allies would learn their 'correct' political positions. The invoking of the affective ties of friendship, particularly important in Chinese culture, and the demarking of enemies remains a basic element of every day united front work at its most basic.

Another persistent united front work characteristic is the use of individuals with family links to it, not just Xi Jinping. He and Liao's son Liao Chengzhi, for example, became important for his involvement with Overseas Chinese work and Japan (Radtke 1990) while his son, Liao Hui, became a director of the Hong Kong and Macau Affairs Office of the State Council and a vice chairman of the CPPCC, also involved in Hong Kong and Macau issues. In many Chinese circles, such individuals carry the authority and credibility of their family connections.

During this revolutionary period, the key goals of united front work were supporting the survival and eventual success of the CCP by undermining the legitimacy and capacities of KMT. This was a period of expansion of the net of friends and allies, when the CCP's enemies could be 'friends' if critical of the KMT. It was a period of looseness-*fang* (放) and inclusion rather than tightening or control-*shou* (收), an approach determined by the CCP's relative weakness. Once it was in power, the balance of power shifted dramatically and the nature of united front work changed accordingly.

Consolidating power, constructing socialism, destroying enemies, and assimilating allies

Having secured final victory by force in October 1949, and thus eliminating the need for any constraining concessions, the CCP rapidly adapted united front work to help manage its transformation into the state power and prepare for the eventual transition to socialism. In doing so the Party expanded understandings and practice of such work well beyond that envisaged by Lenin. This transformation was presented as delivering Mao Zedong's 1940 promise of 'New Democracy' with its 'long-term' coexistence of different classes and forms of ownership. Yet these economic and social revolutions went together with intense ideological indoctrination. The UFWD rationalized and reorganized the MPGs along clear corporatist lines and established the All-China Federation of Industry and Commerce (ACFIC, 1953-) to help organize ideological and ownership transformations.

So-called red capitalists like Rong Yiren (1916–2005) became famous for publicly signing over their wealth and 'transforming their thinking' thereby encouraging others to emulate them. Many of the more important capitalists became members of the China National Democratic Construction Association MPG established in 1945 for just this purpose. Together with the ACFIC they played important roles in organizing the socialization of industry and commerce as well as the surveilling, coopting, and ideological indoctrination of the capitalists and bourgeoisie using unity-and-struggle, cooption, and coercion (Cheng 2019).

The social change necessary to accompany the economic transformation towards socialism also included united front work. All protestant churches were merged into one new entity using sympathetic left-wing clergy and creating a single Three-Selfs Patriotic Movement: self-governance, self-supporting, and self-propagation (i.e., independent of any foreign connections). Catholics were called on to submit to a reorganized 'Patriotic' Catholic Church fully independent of the Pope in Rome. All churches and any links abroad came under the authority of the State Administration of Religious Affairs (1951–2018) and the UFWD. Buddhism, Daoism, and Islam were also placed under state control via united front work.

Ethnicity also became an issue of deep concern and China's myriad ethnic, language, and cultural groups were investigated and categorized to develop the CCP's 'fifty-five minorities + the Han majority' and the 92% Han + 8% minorities formulations. Some, like the Uyghurs in Xinjiang and Mongolians, were subsequently awarded nominal homelands that they could administer, the so-called autonomous regions. After the CCP forcibly annexed Tibet in 1950–1951, united front work became a key means of asserting Party-state control over the area and its peoples, although it had to be adapted to suit very different conditions (Weiner 2020). The state body that oversaw this work was the National Ethnic Affairs Commission established in 1949 but, again, the UFWD was heavily influential even if often in the background, at least to foreigners. Li Weihan (1896–1984) was a key figure in united front work with ethnic minorities and theorizing on 'nationalities issues' and his influence outlasted him (Li, 1980).

Another key constituency was that of Overseas Chinese and returnees whose importance was recognized with the 1949 establishment of what became the Overseas Chinese Affairs Office of the State Council. Invaluable sources of funds, expertise, and political influence at home and abroad, post-1949 the CCP continued to compete with the KMT for their support. Key representatives were accorded seats in CPPCCs while the Zhigong Dang or Public Interest Party became the MPG to liaise with groups abroad such as Hongmen (洪门) societies and triads (Jourda 2019).

Although defeated and now isolated on Taiwan, Chiang and the Nationalist rump remained a focus of CCP efforts to assert sovereignty over them, a goal that would include military threats, diplomatic efforts, economic integration and united front work, though the latter only began returning to prominence after the CCP's post-1978 opening up and reform period. Finally gaining control of Taiwan remained the Party's great unfinished business. As a result, after 1949, the CCP constantly sought ways to appeal to KMT figures abroad, family members left behind or those who returned from Taiwan. The former were officially represented by the Revolutionary Committee of the KMT while those communists who fled Taiwan to escape the KMT were recruited into the Taiwan Democratic Self Government League. As implied, this MPG nominally stands for a degree of autonomy for Taiwan and is used to reach out to groups on the island and collect intelligence. From early on then, the CCP recognized the benefits of offering Taiwanese more space than allowed on the Mainland.

The other major group of concern consisted of the rare and valuable intellectuals outside of the Party itself. These were represented by the MPGs or by so-called non-partypersonages. Many of the latter did not fit the corporatist categories of the MPGs, didn't want to join one, or the UFWD believed their independent status was more useful. It would be some time before enough proletarian intellectuals were nurtured through the education system to replace those who had grown up in the old so-called semicolonialism, semifeudal society.

One of the reasons for the success of united front work before and after 1949 was undoubtedly because so many of the CCP's most able people directed it. Zhou Enlai, Deng Xiaoping, Liu Shaoqi, Liao Chengzhi, Li Weihan, Dong Biwu, and Xi Jinping's father, Xi Zhongxun were all influential at different times. The problem was with Mao's impatience. New Democracy, which had promised long-term coexistence, ended abruptly in 1956 when Mao arbitrarily declared the basic transition to socialism achieved. Henceforth, united front became increasingly about rapid assimilation.

Mao had begun to lose interest in united front work when during his attempt to reinvigorate the CCP using external criticism, the Hundred Flowers Campaign of 1957, some MPG leaders and ostensible members, dared criticize their treatment and even Mao himself. Mao's response, the Anti-Rightist Campaign (1957–1959), not only resulted in the mistreatment, torture, imprisonment and deaths of many allies, it also significantly delegitimized united front work and the UFWD itself. When in 1966, Mao launched what would become his Great Proletarian Cultural Revolution and its attacks on the 'Four Olds', united front work and the UFWD largely ceased, criticized heavily for its past associations with capitalists, foreigners, and others now deemed enemies. Even after Mao's death in 1976, the UFWD's connections with groups in disgrace for two decades; former capitalists, intellectuals, those with Overseas educations or connections, KMT links, religious believers, etc., were nearly all still labelled as 'bad class elements,' treated with suspicion and as targets for persecution whenever political necessity required.

The period from 1957 to 1976 and particularly during the Cultural Revolution can be seen as a particularly acute time of *fang*, of tightening and assimilation if not elimination, one when Mao believed that most allies were now dispensable. Yet the cost of Mao's attitudes to this work and other areas meant that living standards soon fell below those reached in 1956. Treating the potential contributions of millions of Chinese foregone in favor of treating them as enemies constituted an opportunity cost of enormous proportions. Little wonder then that among the many pre-1956/1957 policies to be rapidly reinstated after his death were those of united front work.

As the ideas of opening up and reform took hold, leaders such as Deng Xiaoping quickly recognized that some of the knowledge and connections now needed could be found within the ranks of surviving UF target groups like non-Party intellectuals, the MPGs, ACFIC, and among the Chinese in Hong Kong, Macau, Taiwan, and elsewhere. The pendulum swung back towards relaxation, rehabilitation, and inclusion.

The one area in which united front ideas did briefly flourish under high Maoism was its extrapolation to international diplomacy. Again, this extension owed much to Lenin but Mao's emphasis on contradictions became increasingly important (Armstrong 1977: 24–38). This international application became part of Mao's pitch for support from and leadership of third world countries in the 1960s but outlasted him as leaders such as Deng Xiaoping became worried about threats from the Soviet Union Mao's Three World Theory

(Yee 1983). The other important crossover was Liao Chengzhi's work, which included not only directing united front work among Overseas Chinese but also building up relations with Japan (Radtke 1990).

United front work 1976–1989

United front work after Mao and before Xi can be usefully divided into two periods. The first, 1978–1989, consisted of harnessing it to mostly economic and technological development. In hindsight, this era might even be seen as a golden one of expansion, inclusion, and contribution.

Mao's policies of violent class struggle and his economic model of socialist ownership and autarkic development meant there was no place for markets, capitalists, entrepreneurs, or profit. As the reformers cautiously allowed the reemergence of agricultural markets, limited private enterprise, and foreign investment, 'bourgeois' knowledge of economics, law, Western technology, and connections was again needed. Indeed, these were key to achieving the 'Four Modernizations' of agriculture, industry, defense, science and technology necessary for national development and turning China into a rich and prosperous nation, preconditions for achieving other key goals such as the return of Hong Kong and Macau and winning control of Taiwan. The knowledge and foreign connections of intellectuals and business persecuted under Mao were again validated and called on. The UFWD was now tasked with helping rehabilitate and mobilizing such knowledge and connections, though a considerable number of old allies had died from mistreatment or suicide.

Surviving experts within the MPGs now became involved in setting up schools, mainly vocationally oriented, and helping to overcome failings and shortfalls in the education systems, particularly at provincial and municipal levels and related to the needs of reform. The China Democratic Construction Association and ACFIC sought out old capitalists and entrepreneurs to help modernize business and the economy. They were now encouraged to start new businesses, some with belated payouts from the confiscation of their businesses in the 1950s. Other talents were pressed into service to restart stock exchanges and investment organizations. China International Trust Investment Corporation (CITIC) with Rong Yiren as at its head was one example. The proposal for Special Economic Zones (SEZ) in which foreign investors gained special concessions in exchange for setting up export-oriented businesses, was first floated in the Guangdong Provincial CPPCC.

The SEZs were very attractive to Overseas Chinese investors and manufacturers. Capitalists from Hong Kong, Macau, and Taiwan could utilize their special compatriot status to work with local UFWDs to deliver investment in return for concessions. Overtime, increasing numbers became local CPPCC delegates. The success of this work helps explain why economic development took off in China's south first.

In the areas of religion and ethnic policy, there was also increasing relaxation though the Party was always aware of the potential for social unrest. The guiding slogan was, 'there are no "small issues" in religious work'. Foreign connections were again allowed and even encouraged if these helped with improving technical and other capacities, such as by importing advanced printing machines for diocesan purposes. Local authorities often ignored foreigners who preached Christianity under the cover of teaching in local institutions because they were developing foreign language capacities. With new relative freedoms, many Chinese again openly sought out the solace of religious belief. Muslims were also once again much freer to attend mosques and increasingly, to undertake the Hajj to Mecca with local approval.

When the CCP adopted its One Child Policy in the early 1980s, minorities were excluded while preferential policies allowed some of their brightest students to enter higher education. At home, local languages were taught in schools and some amends were made for humiliations of the Cultural Revolution. Over time, significant minorities among many of the ethnic groups, such as Tibetans and Uyghurs, also became successful in business.

By the late 1980s, the general success of economic reform and united front work and the increasing complexity of trying to manage a diversifying economy but one still dominated by state-owned enterprises and work units as well a much greater degree of openness began to give rise to problems including, corruption, inflation, and a breakdown of the work allocation system. The MPGs and others were called on to help research problems in their areas of expertise and provide policy suggestions to the CCP. The most notable example was the MPGs criticism of the proposed Three Gorges Dam Project, which they suggested was too expensive and risky. Premier Zhao Ziyang, sympathetic to reform, mooted a greater role for united front allies and the CPPCC system as a way of increasing the effectiveness and representativeness of the political system. When in 1989 university students in Beijing and elsewhere started worrying about their conditions and futures, and then began calling for dramatic reforms including more democracy, many of the MPGs even marched in support.

The bloody suppression of the student movement by the People's Liberation Army in Beijing on June 4, 1989 (六四) and the wave of arrests elsewhere, had consequences for united front work. It abruptly terminated Zhao's ideas about expanding representation and freedoms within the united front system in favor of renewed ideological education. Moreover, the escape of student activists abroad made the CCP concerned about the role of smugglers and triads from Hong Kong in whisking its enemies away. In the future, such groups had to be neutralized or come to work more closely with the Party. Criminal intelligence work and united front work came to overlap (Jourda 2019). The results of this underground united front cooperation would be seen on the streets of Hong Kong decades later.

United front work 1990–2012

Counter intuitively, the MPGs were only subject to a brief period of suppression despite their support of the students but their promised increased freedoms and independence within an expanded CPPCC system, this time implied if not promised by Zhao, failed to eventuate. They did soon resume growing, but very slowly (Groot 2004).

This period 1990–2012, which ends with the rise of Xi Jinping, largely consisted of expanding the UF system to cope with changes brought about by the successes of economic reform, successes in part the result of united front work. The rapid growth of the economy due to large levels of foreign investment, which increasingly came from multinationals, was giving rise to new interest groups of returned Overseas Chinese, foreign trained PRC nationals and local managers and other professionals. These new interest groups did not readily fit existing united front categories but were to be allowed to develop outside of Party scrutiny and influence. They could not be categorized as new classes; that was too reminiscent of Maoism. They are now called new social strata (Guo 2016).

How this profusion could be accommodated politically had been a sensitive issue since June 4, when support of the student movement by businesspeople, among others, alarmed the Party. There was also the problem posed by Western political theory that capitalists seeking to protect their property rights would demand democratic reforms. The MPGs argued with the UFWD and among themselves to expand to include new groups such as lawyers and managers, with limited success. Among the measures adopted by the UFWD was the creation of new associations to represent the new strata and extension of united front work into places like law firms (Groot & O'Brien 2012).

The biggest beneficiary of these changes was the ACFIC, which was greatly revitalized and flourished with the influx of millions of increasingly rich members. To make management easier, affiliated associations for specific types of businesses were created and the associations themselves divided into two. Chambers of commerce were established to help deal with business-related elements and as the public face for foreigners, while the association handled the political education and selection of representatives

This period was also marked by a new wave of Chinese emigration. However, instead of the almost moral panic about a brain drain in the 1980s and even after June 4, these migrants and those students and researchers who stayed abroad came to be seen by the Party as potential sources of support and this latest group became a new united front target group. They joined émigré Tibetans and Uyghurs, some of whom wanted independence for their homeland, June 4 democracy activists, supporters of Taiwanese independence and, after 1999, refugee Falungong members and their followers abroad: the CCP's 'Five Evils'. These suspect groups became a target of both CCP surveillance and united front work even when living in Western democracies including Sweden, Australia, and Britain. More recently, the many new migrants leaving China to establish businesses or for their children's education have often benefitted from the Party's policies and can generally be relied on for support abroad while also acting to dilute the influence of the Party's enemies including that of the five evils.

The return of Hong Kong and Macau also became key issues in this time. Appointments to CPPCCs of prominent business identities expanded during and after the Sino-British negotiations as the CCP sort to inform itself of local conditions and prepare the way for its assumption of sovereignty of Hong Kong on July 1, 1997, and Macau in 1999. The promise of One-Country–Two-Systems was to be the principle to assuage both the fears of the colonies' citizens and the consciences of the colonial powers.

At the same, the anticipated success of this promise was intended to also signal to those in Taiwan that success in the colonies would also mean they too should welcome coming under the umbrella of the 'Motherland'. In the case of Taiwan, however, the rise of a new form of Taiwan identity through the 1990s and into the 2000s, particularly among youth, was to prove a growing obstacle.

Growth in religious belief was also a notable phenomenon of this period. The exposure to Christians and proselytizing while living abroad, as well as the activities of missionaries within China, helped not only to increase the numbers of believers but also to fracture them into numerous denominations. House churches began appearing, often operating in the cracks between local governments and UFWDs. In places such as Wenzhou in Zhejiang Province, 'boss Christians' began building new churches and spreading the word among their employees. At the same time, success in business by some Tibetans and Muslims resulted in them using their new wealth to reassert their ethnic and/or religious identities, not necessarily make them more 'Chinese' as Party theory had assumed.

Even worse, in regions like Xinjiang, discontent and increasing exposure to what was happening abroad also resulted in some Uyghurs becoming attracted to Islamic extremism and violent jihad. All these issues were extremely confronting for a CCP always obsessed by maintaining social stability and they threw into doubt some of the Party's assumptions about the consequences of economic development for national unity. Rising ethnic consciousness among some groups and more religious believers had not been anticipated while the contributions of these factors to the collapse of the USSR weighed heavily on some minds.

The structure and nature of united front work under Xi Jinping since 2012

Although some of the changes to united front work that have become well known since Xi became Party leader in 2012 were already underway, notably the crackdown on Uyghurs, Xi is notable for his active championing of united front work and more so than any leader since Deng. Heir to his father's legacy and his own experience in Fujian and Zhejiang including working with Overseas Chinese, which he wrote about in 1995, Xi was almost certainly also involved with work directed at Taiwan which has also involved his siblings (Joske 2020: 8). Xi's revitalization of this work is accompanied by greatly increased emphasis on ideology and Party-building and improving the military – all three of Mao's 'magic weapons'.

With Xi's authority firmly behind the UFWD, the department held a major national conference in 2015 which Xi attended, and he established a Small Leading Group for its work, increasing his direct influence (Joske 2019b). One of the conference announcements was a formalization of Chinese students abroad, internet celebrities, and young entrepreneurs as new united front targets (*Chinadaily* 2015).

In 2018 the department itself was reorganized in two important ways. Three state organizations hitherto separate (The State Administration for Religious Affairs, the Overseas Chinese Affairs Office, and the National Ethnic Affairs Commission) were subsumed into the CCP's own UFWD, presumably to increase control and consistency of policy implementation across China. The second change was to increase the UFWD's work bureaus from nine to twelve: A Democratic Parties Bureau; Ethnic Affairs Bureau; the Hong Kong, Macau, and Taiwan Bureau; Nonpublic Economy Work Bureau; Nonaffiliated Intellectuals Bureau; New Social Strata Bureau; Tibet Work Bureau; Xinjiang Work Bureau; Overseas Chinese Affairs General Bureau; Overseas Chinese Affairs Bureau; Religious Work Bureau 1; and Religious Work Bureau 2 (Joske 2019a).

Not only does Xi have a personal interest in united front work, but it also needs to support the Party's greater goals summed up in Xi's 'China Dream' of national rejuvenation. While the details are vague, the dream's foundations include social stability, unity and prosperity, technological and cultural advancement, full sovereignty and control over Hong Kong, Macau, and Taiwan and to speak for all Chinese, everywhere. These foundations help explain the UFWD's dramatic shift in focus towards the assimilation of ethnic minorities, promotion of sinicization among religious believers at home and the stepping up of work in Hong Kong, toward Taiwan and among Overseas Chinese.

The growing social unrest in Hong Kong, itself in part a response to an overreliance on united front work focused on business and social elites to the exclusion of increasingly alienated youth which developed from attempts to impose patriotic education in 2012, alarmed the CCP and its local supporters (Chan 2013). The subsequent rise of the 2014 Umbrella Movement calling for more democracy intensified CCP fears and highlighted the shallowness of much of its appeal. However, united front work did allow the mobilization of allied groups in the city, including hometown associations, clan, and lineage groups from the New Territories, unions, and triads, to come out in support of Beijing and the city's government. This was repeated for more unrest in 2019 and it was the COVID-19 pandemic which finally cleared the streets. This was united front work for coercive, not inclusive, purposes and marked the fruition of the work with Triads initiated after 1989.

The CCP's political warfare work trying to win over Taiwanese has a similar narrower focus, concentrating mainly on the KMT, its leaders and members and using its plethora of organizations, like the Alumni Association of the Huangpu (Whampoa) Military Academy

(*Chinadaily* 2020), to reach out to those disaffected by changes in Taiwan or attracted to China's success and Xi's appeals. Its allies in Taiwan include business owners, gangsters, and 'Red' media owners (Cole 2019). In the lead-up to the early 2020 general election, and following a UFWD meeting in late 2019, this work, including united front work, was intensified to include internet and other celebrities urged to play their part by UFWD head, You Quan, and 'play an active role in guiding public opinion' (Zhong 2020). Like Hong Kong though, the return of Tsai Ing-wen and her Democratic Progressive Party and the defeat of the Beijing-supported Han Kuo-yu indicates that much of this work may be counterproductive. It is not even clear that the promises of One-Country–Two-Systems still have any appeal even to KMT diehards.

For the more than 50 million Overseas Chinese, their numbers continuously boosted by new emigrants who generally continue to support the Party-state, there is Xi's Grand Overseas Chinese Work (Aisixiang 2015). Based on Xi's 1995 essay, this work sees the Party speaking for all of them, supporting them, and in turn, wanting their support whether that be investing back home, helping the nation's technological, scientific, and military development or helping defeat the Party's enemies, such as the five evils, as well as becoming politically active in their adopted lands. It is the influence of this work that has largely generated the unprecedented outside attention to the activities of the UFWD. This was particularly the case in places, such as Australia, New Zealand, and Canada (Brady 2017, Manthorpe 2019, Hamilton & Ohlberg 2020), but increasingly also in Europe, in the Arabian Gulf (Al-Sudairi 2018) and wherever there are enough Chinese.

In places such as Australia, this work has taken the form of encouraging the proliferation of civil society groups of all sorts, catering for businesses, for cultural activities, hometown associations, etc. The main umbrella groups are often Associations for the Peaceful Unification of China (Dotson 2018). In 2020 such groups were obvious for their public declarations of support for the new National Security Law to quell unrest in Hong Kong. It was the ability of 'the Motherland' to call on all of these groups to do their bit, which also helps explain how they could be mobilized in early 2020 to buy up medical supplies and PPE around the world to cope with COVID-19. There was little nefarious in such actions, merely many Chinese doing what they could to help tackle a terrible situation at home. In doing so they were also reasserting and cementing their Chineseness and (CCP fashioned) patriotism. At the same time, however, they were also helping the CCP prove to its domestic audience that it had overseas support and influence.

Within China, the most striking and worrying manifestations of the historical shifts in united front work include the dramatic switch to assimilation. Western attention was on the internment of possibly upwards of a million Muslim Uyghurs in prisons labelled as reeducation centres with many subsequently sent out as labour for private firms (Xu et al. 2020) in the name of preventing terrorism. At the same time, religious observance came under increasing surveillance while thousands of mosques have been destroyed or abandoned. In September 2020 some of China's Mongolians protested the apparent dropping of school instruction in Mongolian in favor of Mandarin Chinese. Around the same time, there were also indications that some of the policies being applied to Uyghurs, might also be extended to Tibetans. In the case of all three groups, ethnic identity is closely associated with religious identity, and policies toward that have also shifted.

China's Christians are another united front target group under apparent increased pressure since Xi's ascent. In provinces such as Zhejiang, cross removals and demolitions of churches deemed illegal structures may have peaked around 2015–2016 but did not cease entirely.

Increasingly, the emphasis in religious united front work has been on promoting sinicization of both Protestant and Catholic Christianity. Moreover, now the UFWD dominates religious work policy implementation, it is probably far harder for any groups to play in the spaces between Party and local government (Wang & Groot 2018). At the same time it seems that Beijing has come to an accommodation with the Vatican it can live with and the Church has seemingly accepted despite the ongoing general suppression of religion (Rocca & Chin 2020).

In September 2020 there was another major united front work announcement, this time reemphasising the UFWD's work with China's private (or nonpublic) enterprises. State-owned enterprises with enough Party members also have their own united front departments while private firms are also required to have Party cells that have united front functions. This 2020 policy, though, was yet another attempt to ensure that the increasingly wealthy and powerful capitalists and their key employees recognize their debts to the CCP, accept its leadership and work in support of its goals (Chen 2020).

Conclusion

This overview of CCP united front work reflects the dramatic changes in the Party's relative strength over almost a century. While there have been some failures in recent times, notably in Hong Kong (although, conspicuously, not in Macau where integration has been remarkably smooth). The Party's alliances and concessions have generally only lasted as long as necessary. It seems that with Party and Xi apparently judging that the time suits them, it is also time to wind back concessions in favor of greater control and assimilation. This approach makes even more sense in light of Xi's reemphasising of ideology and stressing the necessity of Marxism.

While united front work has brought many successes over many decades in wildly different circumstances, it was Mao's all too hasty abandonment of it which led in part, to the need to reinstate it. The post-handover failures in Hong Kong and lack of dramatic success in Taiwan also point to other problems in addition to those that result from the inherent limits of its corporatist forms within China (Groot 2012). These point to wider problems of democratic deficit and exclusion which are only likely to intensify under the top-down style of leadership developing under Xi. The CCP's increasing reliance on coercion and violence in Hong Kong at the expense of concessions and inclusion does not bode well for China more generally.

References

Aisixiang (2015) '习近平 "大侨务" 观念的确立 The Establishment of Xi Jinping's Grand Overseas Chinese Work(originally in 《战略与管理》)', http://www.aisixiang.com/data/93625.html.

Al-Sudairi, M. (2018) 'The Communist Party of China's United Front Work in the Gulf: The "Ethnic Minority Overseas Chinese" of Saudi Arabia as a Case Study', *Dirasat*, vol. 34 https://kfcris.com/pdf/364dd98d47dae1c81e9eb8362a086bf85af3e7e7f302e.pdf.

Armstrong, J.D. (1977) *Revolutionary Diplomacy: Chinese Foreign Policy and the United Front Doctrine*, Irvine, University of California Press.

Brady, A. (2017) *Magic Weapons: China's Political Influence Activities under Xi Jinping*, Wilson Centre, https://www.wilsoncenter.org/article/magic-weapons-chinas-political-influence-activities-under-xi-jinping.

Chan, C. (2013) 'Young Activists and the Anti-Patriotic Education Movement in Post-Colonial Hong Kong: Some Insights from Twitter', *Citizenship, Social and Economics Education*, vol. 12, no. 3, pp. 148–162.

Chen, F. (2020) 'Follow Party's Lead, Beijing Tells Private Firms', *Asiatimes*, 17 September. https://asiatimes.com/2020/09/follow-partys-lead-beijing-tells-private-firms/.

Cheng, G. (2019) *Secrets of the CCP's United Front Work Department: Memoir of a United Front Cadre*, Washington, Citizen Press.

ChinaDaily.com (2015) 'Xi Urges Strengthening of United Front', http://www.chinadaily.com.cn/china/2015–05/21/content_20785494.htm.

ChinaDaily.com (2020) 'Alumni Association of Huangpu Military Academy Holds Spring Festival Tea Party in Beijing', https://www.chinadaily.com.cn/a/202001/20/WS5e25728da310128217272 4e6.html.

Cole, M.J. (2019) 'Taiwan and CCP Political Warfare: A Blueprint', *Sinopsis*, December 27. https://si nopsis.cz/en/taiwan-and-ccp-political-warfare-a-blueprint/.

Dotson, J. (2018) 'The United Front Work Department in Action Abroad: A Profile of the Council for the Promotion of the Peaceful Reunification of China', *China Brief*, vol. 18, no. 2. https://jamesto wn.org/program/united-front-work-department-action-abroad-profile-council-promotion-peaceful -reunification-china/.

Groot, G. (2004) *Managing Transitions: The Chinese Communist Party, United Front Work, Corporatism and Hegemony*, New York, Routledge.

Groot, G. (2012) 'A Self-Defeating Secret Weapon? The Institutional Limitations of Corporatism on United Front Work Effectiveness in 21st Century China', in J. Hsu and R. Hasmath (Eds.), *The Chinese Corporatist State: Adaptation, Survival and Resistance*, New York, Routledge, pp. 41–73.

Groot, G. and O'Brien, R. (2012) 'The Chinese Communist Party's United Front Work with the Legal Profession', *Hong Kong Law Journal*, vol. 42, no. 3, pp. 939–970.

Guo, Y. (Ed.) (2016) *Handbook on Class and Social Stratification in China*, Cheltenham, Edward Elgar Publishing.

Hamilton, C. (2018) *Silent Invasion: China's Influence in Australia*, Richmond, Hardie Grant.

Hamilton, C. and Ohlberg, M. (2020) *Hidden Hand: Exposing how the Chinese Communist Party is Reshaping the World*, Richmond, Hardie Grant.

Joske, A. (2019a) 'Reorganizing the United Front Work Department: New Structures for a New Era of Diaspora and Religious Affairs Work', *China Brief*, vol. 19, no. 9, pp. 6–14. https://jamestown.org/program/reorganizing-the-united-front-work-department-new-structures-for-a-new-era-of-diaspora-and-religious-affairs-work/.

Joske, A. (2019b) 'The Central United Front Work Leading Small Group: Institutionalising United Front Work', *Sinopsis*, 23 July, pp. 1–14. https://sinopsis.cz/en/joske-united-front-work-lsg/.

Joske, A. (2020) *The Party Speaks for You: Foreign Interference and the Chinese Communist Party's United Front System*, Australian Strategic Policy Institute, Policy Brief, June.

Jourda, E. (2019) 'Le Parti Communiste Chinois, le Front Uni et les Triades: Patriotisme, Business et Crime Organisé', *Sociétés Politiques Comparées*, vol. 47, January–April pp. 1–27. http://www .fasopo.org/sites/default/files/varia3_n47.pdf.

Li, W. 李维汉 (1980) 关于民族理论和民族政策的若干问题(*Certain Questions on Nationalities Theory and Nationalities Policies*)人民出版社 (People's Publishing House)北京 (Beijing).

Loh, C. (2010) *Underground Front: The Chinese Communist Party in Hong Kong*, Hong Kong, Hongkong University Press.

Manthorpe, J. (2019) *Claws of the Panda: Beijing's Campaign of Influence and Intimidation in Canada*, Toronto, Cormorant Books.

Mao, T.-t. (1939) 'Introducing the Communist', *Selected Works of Mao Tse-Tung II*, Peking, https://www.marxists.org/reference/archive/mao/selected-works/volume-2/index.htm.

Radtke, K.W. (1990) *China's Relations with Japan, 1945–83: The Role of Liao Chengzhi*, Manchester, Manchester University Press.

Rocca, F.X. and Chin, J. (2020) 'Vatican Looks to Extend Church Leadership Agreement With China Despite Criticism', *The Wall Street Journal*, 15 September. https://www.wsj.com/articles/vatican -looks-to-extend-church-leadership-agreement-with-china-despite-criticism-11600179880.

Van Slyke, L. (1967) *Enemies and Friends: The United Front in Chinese Communist History*, Stanford, Stanford University Press.
Wang, R. and Groot, G. (2018) 'Who Represents? Xi Jinping's Grand United Front Work, Legitimation, Participation and Consultative Democracy', *Journal of Contemporary China*, vol. 27, no. 112, pp. 569–583.
Wiener, B. (2020) *The Chinese Revolution on the Tibetan Frontier*, Ithaca, Cornell University Press.
Xu, V.X., Cave, D., Leibold, J., Munro, K. and Ruser, N. (2020) *Uyghurs for Sale*, Australian Strategic Policy Institute, https://www.aspi.org.au/report/uyghurs-sale.
Yee, H.S. (1983) 'The Three World Theory and Post-Mao China's Global Strategy', *Royal Institute of International Affairs*, vol. 59, no. 2, pp. 239–249.
Zhong, R. (2020) 'Awash in Disinformation Before Vote, Taiwan Points Finger at China', *New York Times*, 6 January. https://www.nytimes.com/2020/01/06/technology/taiwan-election-china-disinformation.html.

4

The discursive construction of the Belt and Road Initiative as a global public good

Eduardo Tzili-Apango

Introduction

After Xi Jinping's speech proposing to restore the ancient silk road in 2013, the Chinese government started huge efforts to consolidate what is now called the 'Belt and Road Initiative' (BRI), which intends to connect the Eurasian continent through infrastructure projects. Among these efforts is the elaboration of a discourse that characterizes the BRI as a global public good, especially after the Chinese foreign minister Wang Yi declared in 2015 that 'the Belt and Road Initiative is the public good that China provides to the world' (China News Service 2015). From this point, several Chinese government officials and scholars, as well as Chinese official media, have agreed with the Chinese government position, and have helped construct a perception of the BRI as a global public good.

Among the initial elements of the BRI as a public good is that the initiative offers a framework for international cooperation and regional connectivity, echoing some policy papers' proposals of the Asian Development Bank (ADB 2014). Then, as the 'BRI discourse' evolved, it also included ideas such as the BRI being a manifestation of China's great power status, an evolution of China's foreign policy, and China's commitment to the world's development, all these profoundly related with Xi Jinping's project to convert China into a world power (Xinhuanet 2018). Linked to this end, most importantly, is the notion of China as a responsible world power by supplying global public goods precisely through the BRI, an intention that even came to be reflected in documents and resolutions of traditional international organizations like the United Nations General Assembly and the Security Council (UNSC 2017).

The main argument of this chapter is that the choice of characterizing the BRI as a global public good is not accidental since it implies the major political purpose of consolidating economic and political resources to make China a new world power. Beyond debating if this is right or wrong, the construction of the BRI as a global public good is eminently a realist process seen through the International Relations' (IR) theoretical perspective. This is because the analytical category 'public good provision' and the category 'public good provider' are connected, and in IR theories, in the absence of world government the provision of global public goods is possible through cooperation or through hegemony. This chapter

 DOI: 10.4324/9780429059704-6

emphasizes the construction of public opinion and perceptions as an important element of world power, side-by-side with other elements like economic and military power. Therefore, the main research question is: Why has China constructed the BRI as a global public good? As the hypothesis, this chapter affirms that China has constructed the idea of the BRI as a global public good in order to construct a power of shaping opinions and perceptions, which ultimately aims to consolidate China's world power and which will enable China to provide global public goods.

This intention is dialectical, so it is useless to see it through the lens of the chicken-or-the-egg causality dilemma. In order to maintain its economic development, China has to assure the global market functional operation, and in order to assure this situation, China has to solve market failures that could harm its economic development. Some under-supplied public goods, such as the lack of infrastructure, are market failures that China has to provide if it wants to overcome an obstacle for its development. To provide public goods adequately in the absence of a world government, China first needs to promote cooperation or to reach a hegemonic status that makes available the necessary material resources for public goods' provision. Since international cooperation and/or world hegemony are mainly political processes, and again in the absence of a world government as an 'enforcer' of political processes, to build world power is to build the capacity to promote these processes (Brucan 1971). Then, to build world power is to build the capacity to effectively provide global public goods, and in the case of this chapter's study object, to construct the BRI as a global public good is to build an important element of world power. To sum up, to construct the BRI as a global public good contributes to consolidate the BRI as a prerequisite for achieving China's aim to become a world power.

The chapter is divided into four sections. The first section has the objective of understanding the notion of the 'public' in a Chinese context, since public goods is the topic under discussion. The reader may take notice of the formation of a Chinese public sphere, in which the provision of public goods serve for political and social purposes. The second section aims to understand the connection between 'world power' and 'global public good provision'. In this sense, it is important to highlight that the capacity of providing a global public good is a sign of a world power status. The third section analyses the discourse of Chinese government officials, news media and scholars around the BRI. The results of this analysis suggest that an important concern is solving the classical public good problem of the 'free-rider' by securing the participation of a wide range of countries, and reproducing the principles of the Chinese public sphere in the international arena. The fourth and last section offers some concluding remarks.

The formation of the Chinese public sphere

In this section, I argue that the provision of public goods in the global arena is intrinsically related to the process of obtaining international political power as it implies building world authority and legitimacy. For this, I first define 'public authority' and then share some thoughts about the public arena in the Chinese cultural and political contexts. Then, I define 'public goods' in the context of a hypothetical 'public authority with Chinese characteristics'. Lastly, I offer an argument of how the provision of global public good constructs world power.

In contradistinction to Western history, in Asian history the public realm has subordinated the private. In some historical events the private has even been subjected to attacks and condemnation for the sake of the public (Tan 2009), such as in China's Cultural Revolution, or during the Khmer Rouge rule of Cambodia. Perhaps there is no better explanation of this than a phrase contained in the Book of Rites attributed to Confucius when he explained the ideal society and government: 大道之行也, 天下為公, 'When the great *dao* is pursued, all-under-heaven becomes public'. Among other things, with this sentence Confucius elucidates the need for merit, instead of family lineage, in order to become a public servant; in other words, he prioritized a public value to govern in lieu of a private value. In addition, it is possible to find another meaningful explanation of the importance of the public in the Book of Poetry which is then used in Mencius in a discussion about the proper way of governing: 雨我公田, 遂及我私, 'May the rain fall upon our public fields, and then into our private fields'. Unlike in Western tradition, the consolidation of the 'public authority' in China is not just a means to dominate the public political realm, but it is a manifestation of a 'healthy' or a 'good' public realm.

In Chinese history strong public authority was maintained paradoxically because of highly autonomous local political forces. This has caused some scholars to affirm that, from the 18th century to the first half of the 20th century, a particular Habermasian 'public sphere'[1] developed in China, as well as an assurance of the provision of public goods (Rankin 1993; Wong 2019). The Chinese public sphere did not develop in the same way as in Western countries, although there are some parallels, such as the intensification of long-distance trade and the formation of financial institutions (although it did not promote the emergence of a capitalist structure), as well as the establishment of complex urban structures like the printing press, public spaces in the form of the Chinese teahouse, and public associations such as 'secret societies' and freemasonry (MacKinnon 1997; Qin 1998). Nevertheless, unlike Western countries, in China the public sphere was characterized by the absence of a strong bourgeois social class that could direct political revolution, and instead of public discussions it is possible to see management and locally deposited public responsibilities as main features (Rankin 1993: 162; Scalapino & Schiffrin 1959: 331). This is reflected in the fact that Sun Yat-Sen, as one of the main leaders of the 1911 Chinese Revolution, used part of the Confucian aphorism '天下為公' ('all-under-heaven becomes public') as a banner for his revolutionary ideas. However, this notion of the 'public' maintained the historical principals already explained as Sun Yat-Sen emphasized collective responsibilities and obligations as ideals of society (Gregor 1981: 65).

In China, both spheres are intertwined, so it is hard to see where public authority ends and where the public sphere begins. This is contrary to what happened in Western countries, where public authority and the public sphere were gradually de-attached from each other to the point that the two are mutually counterweighted (Habermas 1989: 14–26). I call this plexus the 'Chinese public sphere'. The end of the Chinese Civil War period and the foundation of the People's Republic of China did not change what 'public' means in terms of political organization. As Fewsmith (1991: 46) points out, '公 [the public] was to be embodied in neither state nor society, but in the party. [...] The seamless web between public authority and private interest would be maintained by the party's supervision of both state and society'. This has resulted in 'paradoxical' forms of tight state control in contexts of a highly autonomous civil society, a situation that produces the particular form of a 'consultative authoritarianism' (Teets 2013) based on 'deliberate differentiation' (Sun 2019), or the outsourcing of responsibilities for the provision of public goods.

Public authority is the faculty of the State to govern a territory based on its political power and legitimacy (Sassen 2006: 76–82). Furthermore, in the Chinese context public authority implies the absence of autonomous public spheres but the existence of autonomous social and political actors and forces. Therefore, for the purposes of this chapter, 'public authority' means a faculty and a result of a historical process of consolidation of power and legitimacy based on the control of the public sphere and on autonomous local actors that help in the provision of public good, amongst other outcomes.

It is possible to infer that the 'public good' concept in the Chinese context acquires a different connotation than in a Western context given the historical process of the formation of the public authority. It is important to remember that a 'public good' is a nonmarket good that has four main features: (1) common provision, (2) nonexclusivity, (3) indivisibility of benefits, and (4) impossibility of appropriation (Head 1972). Being a nonmarket good, traditional academic related sources such as Samuelson (1947: 253) recognize the necessity of a monopoly capable of paying the provision of these goods.

The intellectual history of the 'public goods' concept shows the 'public-private divide' as stated by Sassen (2006: 184–185), a situation characterized by a public political realm embodied in governments and the State, on the one side, and an apolitical economic realm embodied in the market on the other side. As Sturn (2006: 43, 48) argue, the concept of 'public goods' is a key ingredient for the general justification of the public sector, including the determination of tasks and institutional boundaries in front of the private sector. In this situation, the State becomes a necessary and a complementary institution for private property as it is limited to regulate private activities, eminently economic activities. In addition to this, some scholars entail the coercive role of the State with the free-rider issue, recalling the 'Hobbesian' identity of the State[2] in order to maximize social well-being and to contain the 'natural human tendency of satisfying its own interest' (Fausto 2006: 69; Mazzola 1958 [1890]: 46). In other words, in the Western tradition, and in a public good context, the public authority has the important role of limiting or solving problems that are a result of free-riders. However, this is always being made considering the 'public-private divide' as the role of State is at the same time relatively bound by the Habermasian public sphere in the form of civil society.

In contrast to the aforementioned, in China, the public good concept is not related to the 'public-private' dichotomy that was produced in the West and, as a consequence, nor does it cause the 'public authority' to be converted into a complement actor of the private property. As I already stated, the 'Chinese public sphere' was revitalized after the Chinese Revolution and became an absolute factor of the social and political organization with the foundation of the People's Republic of China in 1949. In terms of public goods' provision, Marxists theories and ideology not only contributed to maintaining the prevalence of the 'public' in China, but also suggest how to use market mechanisms in order to efficiently provide public goods, and fundamentally they helped to eliminate the notion of the market as a decisive factor of economics (Hu & Jia 2008). For this reason, some Chinese scholars criticize the Western theory of public goods for being too 'market-oriented' (Yang 2016); as Qin (2006: 80) put it: 'non-exclusivity and non-rivalry are technical characteristics of public goods under market economy, [while] common needs of society is the essence of public goods under social ethics…'. The notion of 'common needs of society' (社会共同需要) has even become a cornerstone of a hypothetical Chinese theory of public goods (Liu 2000), and it has been used in some official economic-related discourses and positions (Fan 2018; Tang 2019).

In this conjuncture, public authority in China was revitalized too. As many studies show, one of the main problems for the Chinese Communist Party (CCP) is to maintain political control over society, and taking advantage of its control of the Chinese public sphere, the CCP constructs its political power and legitimacy from an efficient provision of public goods, a situation that is possible through a disciplined decentralization of public management and social disposition for cooperation, which is ultimately a historical path-dependency factor (Dickson et al. 2016; Li 2014).

To sum up, the Western public sphere was formed in opposition to Western public authority during the modern era. This may be better characterized as the Habermasian bourgeois public sphere versus the Hobbesian Leviathan, a situation that symbolizes the 'Western State'. However, in China the public sphere and the authority sphere were not separated during the modern era, a situation that is explained by the absence of a bourgeois social class and the existence of a historical strong State. This situation formed the Chinese public sphere, in which both the public and the authority are intertwined, and consequently the equivalent of the Hobbesian Leviathan without a counterweighting sphere is formed, the Kun (鯤)[3] or 'Chinese State'. Due to the 'public-private divide', in the West the provision of public goods is made because it is a market's necessity, and the public authority is confined to financially provide public goods and to limit the free-rider problem. In contrast, in China the provision of public goods is made because is a social and a political necessity, so the public authority has a greater role than in the West in the provision of public goods, because it coordinates and assures a proper and efficient provision for the sake of the consolidation of its own authority and legitimacy.

The nexus between world power and provision of global public goods

So far, I have explained the relation between public authority and public goods' provision in the context of the State. Nevertheless, how is this situation manifested in the international context? Three elements of Western theories of national public goods were adopted to explain international public goods: (1) the solution to the problem of world free-riders through *coercion*, (2) the need for *someone* to assume financial costs, and (3) the demand for collective action. In a first phase of theorization, authors such as Ruggie (1972) and Russett and Sullivan (1971) argue about international cooperation and world organizations as the best forms of providing international public goods.

Nevertheless, these analyses could not explain how to solve the free-rider problem in the international context, and neither could they offer theories to explain optimal financing for international public goods' provision in the absence of a monopoly that could afford costs. As a consequence, a second phase of theorization emerged with the hegemonic stability theory, whose proponents affirm the necessity of hegemonic State that enables a 'hegemonic governance' based on four factors: (1) victory in the aftermath of a hegemonic war, (2) capacity to provide public goods and to create international regimes, (3) serving as 'lender of last resort' in order to prevent an economic crisis and to maintain stability in international markets, and (4) promoting common international values in order to obtain international legitimacy (Gilpin 1981; Kindleberger 1986; Spiezio 1990).

After many criticisms of the hegemonic stability theory, one of the most important being that the theory does not explain why there can be international regimes even without hegemonic sponsorship (Keohane 1982), a third phase of theorization surged with scholar contributions that again defend international cooperation as the best way to provide public goods in the international arena. Unlike the first phase, these contributions not only omit the necessity of a world leader that is able to limit the free-rider problem, but they condemn it as they value self-management and self-organization. In addition to this, authoritative studies consolidated the concept of the 'global public good' in order to explain world disorders. On the one side, for Ostrom (1990: 41) the 'free-rider' issue is a theoretical fixed variable that justifies the existence of the Leviathan, and this may not exist in empirical situations.

In line with this argument, Keohane & Ostrom (1995: 1) affirm '[n]either modern States nor small farmers in remote areas of poor countries can appeal to authoritative hierarchies to enforce rules governing their relations with one another'. On the other side, Kaul, Grunberg, and Stern (1999a: 488, emphasis added) state that '*[o]ne danger* of relying on the best-shot approach for an expanded range of goods is that *it can easily be turned into a hegemonic model of public good provision*.' Lastly, Barrett (2002: 50) sustains that '[i]n the horizontal world of international governance, there can be no third party enforcement'.

Precisely the contribution of Kaul, Grunberg, and Stern (1999b), along with Kaul et al. (2003) and Ferroni and Mody (2002) form part of the authoritative analyses that have shaped the contemporary concept of the global public good. Their main features are that they (1) were supported by traditional international organizations, such as the United Nations Program for Development and the World Bank, (2) value international cooperation for supplying global public goods, and (3) offer a definition and, most notably, a typology of a global public good.

The turn to valuing international cooperation and to condemning hegemonic provision of global public goods is the global manifestation of the national consolidation of the private sphere. It is vital to recall that from the 1970s onwards neoliberal capitalism started to spread around the globe, and with it a hegemonic ideology, economic thought and political programs, which in turn represent a reaction against Keynesian government interventionism[4] of the 1950s and 1960s (Centeno & Cohen 2012). The Thatcherian adage 'there is no such thing as society' was globalized in a manner that consolidated the bourgeois public sphere in Western countries, and again 're-feudalised' the public sphere, where '[...] power and decisions are presented to the public, not developed by the public' (Gripsrud et al. 2010: 114). In this sense, and according to Sassen (2006: 187–203), in the neoliberal era the private sphere has set the standards for governance and market operation, which causes the 'public good' to become a façade for the private good to be assured within a capitalist dynamics. This is related with the logic of the United Nations discourse around global public goods, which follows the Coxian principle of the theory being made for someone and for some reason, and in this case, it seeks to legitimate the forces of globalization at work (Long & Woolley 2009).

In summary, during the 20th century the consolidation of the hegemony's world power followed relatively speaking the principles of the consolidation of the Hobbesian State's authority, legitimacy and political power. Thus, to provide public goods in the international arena meant to reproduce such world power. With the advent of neoliberal capitalism and the Postmodernity, the provision of global public goods helped to consolidate transnational forces of the private sphere, and indirectly helped to maintain US hegemonic status due to its structural power.

The Belt and Road Initiative discourse as a global public good

China proposed to restore the Silk Road in the 1990s during the visit of then minister Li Peng to Central Asia, almost parallel to the appearance of the global public good concept. Just as in the case of the IR discipline in China (Zhang & Chang 2016), the knowledge around the global public good was introduced gradually to the Asian country. It is possible to witness three phases in knowledge-building around the global public good concept: (1) theoretical learning and adaptation, (2) theoretical formulation, and (3) policy prescription. The Belt and Road Initiative (BRI) falls into this last phase.

The first phase is characterized by eminently scholarly studies about the features of the Western theories of public goods, both from economics and IR; that is international cooperation as the best way of providing global public goods, but also the link between world hegemony and global public goods supply (Liu 2000; Wang 2002). The second phase is characterized by the formulation of global public goods' provision as an instrument for the Chinese diplomacy to contribute to international development, but also it recognizes China's lack of major commitment or incapacities to supply global public goods (Cai & Yang 2012; Mofcom 2012) The participation of some officials in the public debate is noteworthy.

The third phase is the utilization of the global public goods concept as a foreign policy prescription. This has resulted in a major step towards the configuration of a Chinese diplomacy as the Chinese conception of the global public good entails much of the nature of the Chinese public sphere. In the case of the BRI, this phase implies providing public goods 'to pave a way for an emerging world order with Chinese characteristics' (Li 2019: 16), to recede from the traditional model of hegemonic provision of public goods and to enact a new form of provision based on 'the participation of all countries' (Cai 2019: xix), and to complement the consolidation of Xi Jinping's core foreign policy concept 'community with a shared future for mankind' (Liang & Zhang 2019: 21).

To begin with, there is a perception in China of a lack of adequate provision of global public goods, which in turn provokes an 'international leadership deficit' and an important international demand of global public goods for international development (Chen & Zhang 2020: 12; Meng & Yang 2018). As I wrote in the introduction, the Chinese government presented the BRI as a public good precisely in a 'context of need'; as Wang (2015) affirms, 'the contradiction between the increasing demand of international public goods and low supply capacity is the driving force of the BRI'.

It has been considered that the promotion of the BRI as a global public good serves to Chinese soft power and public diplomacy. On the one side, allegedly this soft power is not the 'traditional' soft power considered by Nye (1990), but a Chinese soft power that implies guidance, norms, rules, and innovative mechanisms for international cooperation (Wang 2015). On the other side, the allusion of the public good 'BRI' as a tool for Chinese public diplomacy entails the monopoly of the direction of foreign policy, the acquisition of a responsible world power status and a form to promote a 'great-power' diplomacy (He & Dai 2018; Zhao 2017). That is to say, the BRI as a global public good involves the establishment of a new framework in which the Chinese government has a wide but a relative control of international actions. Ultimately, the BRI is also the sign of China's turn from a passive global stakeholder to an active global player (Chu 2017; Li 2016).

One of the cornerstones of the BRI is its euphemistic 'collective identity': the BRI is for everybody, and everyone can participate. In fact, this is a main reason why the Chinese government presents the BRI as a public good. As He (2018: 86) accurately put it, 'the global public goods narrative is profound for it hits the very core of the BRI: coordinating collective actions to solve common problems.' In this line, the Chinese foreign minister Wang Yi (2016), as well as the Chinese ambassador to the United Nations Liu Jieyi (2016), characterized the adherence of the BRI to the principles of 'extensive consultation, joint construction and shared benefits.' The question here is not whether everyone can participate, but how, and the knowledge around the Chinese public sphere offers some insights.

The pattern of establishment of BRI projects highlights the principles mentioned. In the Western sphere the investment in infrastructure, or setting financial cooperation initiatives, usually would lie in the entirely autonomous economic actors in such a way that investors only will have to wait for economic dividends. However, in the Chinese sphere, it is usual for investments or financial projects to be accompanied by Chinese firms that will aim to establish joint-ventures or to bring workforce, technology or know-how that is nonexistent or nonsufficient in the host country. This action is strengthened by China's main economic objective of continuing its development strategy, and by its main political purpose of consolidating a world power status, as well as promoting its legitimacy and political ideology.

For example, in Pakistan the China Gezhouba Group Corporation (CGGC) was contracted in December 2017 to build the first and second sections of the 'E35 Expressway' that links the Islamic country's north-south traffic artery of Peshawar-Karachi Expressway, but also it 'greatly upgrades transportation and connectivity between the China-Pakistan border area' (Zhang 2019a: 571). In another case, in January 2018 a transborder optical fiber link came into commercial operation in Kathmandu, Nepal, with the joint venture of China Telecom and Nepal Telecom; it is noteworthy that this optical fiber not only reduces Nepali network delays for accessing internet services through China to Europe, Central Asia and the greater Asia-Pacific region, but moreover it represents 'the first direct network route between Nepal and China' (Zhang 2019a: 572). Both projects have contributed to infrastructure development in the host countries, no doubt. Nevertheless, they have also contributed to major Chinese economic and foremost political goals, particularly if it is Pakistan and Nepal who are in charge of maintaining the public goods provided in these situations.

Cases about production capacity cooperation, trade and investment facilitation, as well as financial cooperation are interesting in respect of terms and actions. For example, in December 2017 the governments of China and Ukraine signed the 'China-Ukraine Agricultural Investment Cooperation Plan', among whose core principles are that the plan should '[be] led by government, operating on market basis and the enterprises [be] the main players' (Zhang 2019b: 578). These principles refer only to the Chinese model of a socialist market economy, which combines the 'visible hand' of the government with the 'invisible hand' of the market (Zhou 2019: 5), and which also may not be as familiar to Ukraine as it is supposed. There is a similar case with the establishment of the China-Central, Eastern Europe (CEE) InterBank Consortium on November 2017, given that this follows the principles of 'self-management, independent decision making and risk taking'. While China promotes these banking principles in BRI country members, the official position is to pay attention to BRI country's risks, but also to 'provide risk compensation for overseas investment', and 'to ensure financial security of regional member states' (Liang & Zhang 2019: 122). Thus, according to Andornino (2017), China's promotion of a 'connective leadership' aims to bind transregional connectivity to its own national development strategy by 'outsourcing' some responsibilities to maintaining public goods provision in the BRI without eliminating the fact that China is the new Eurasian leader.

Taking advantage of Eurasia's huge infrastructure demand, China has promoted connectivity building, production capacity cooperation, trade and investment facilitation, financial cooperation, and people-to-people exchanges. The collective action in consolidating these actions in the context of the BRI follows the principles of the Chinese public sphere in the sense that (1) it fulfills social and political necessities in both China and BRI countries, and (2) it helps to coordinate and to assure a proper and efficient provision of public goods for the sake of the consolidation of Chinese global authority and legitimacy. For this, the BRI shapes non-autonomous public spheres in countries that participate in the project, but independent enough to autonomously maintaining the BRI.

Conclusions

The Belt and Road Initiative has emerged in a crucial deglobalization context, where neoliberal capitalism has faced important challenges due to its own contradictions and a profound economic global interdependence. As I wrote before, in this context the provision of global public goods has aided in consolidating transnational forces of the private sphere. Therefore, these transnational forces have failed to deliver adequate global public goods, and the consequences have been embodied in crises of several kinds: financial, humanitarian, security, and so on.

China has been trying to face deglobalization challenges with the BRI. Nevertheless, before a full materialization of the project, the Chinese government is well aware of the risks of an improper discourse and presentation of the BRI (Research Center for Theoretical System of Socialism with Chinese Characteristics CASS 2016). This is why it has constructed a complex discourse in which the BRI is presented as a global public good. Moreover, China has constructed the idea of the BRI as a global public good in order to construct a power of shaping opinions and perceptions, which ultimately aims to consolidate China's world power and will enable China to provide global public goods.

However, as this chapter tried to set forth, the construction of the Belt and Road Initiative as a global public good implies many characteristics of the Chinese notions of the 'public' and 'public authority'. To answer the main research question, it may be safe to argue that China constructs the BRI in order to shape a globalization and a hegemony with Chinese characteristics. It is erroneous to assume that China is a neutral globalization force, or that it will restore neoliberal capitalism globalization. It is possible to consider the BRI as the first step towards a new type of globalization (Liu, Dunford, & Gao 2018), in which there are not autonomous public spheres represented by civil societies, or in which responsibility of local forces is upgraded but only in reference of what the global public authority indicates. To put it in a more figurative way, China's emergence as a hegemonic power, or at least as a global power, does not mean the revitalization of a global Leviathan that can promote neoliberal capitalism globalization. It means the emergence of a global Kun (鯤) that would promote globalization with Chinese characteristics.

Notes

1 For purposes of the chapter, I define 'Habermasian public sphere' as the area conceived by Habermas (1989) in which individuals engage in discussions for political actions, and which results in the formation of civil society guided by bourgeoisie ideas.

2 For purposes of the chapter, I define 'Hobbesian Leviathan' or 'Hobbesian State' (here they are used indistinctly) as the State defined by Hobbes, in which public authority maintains a huge amount of political power and holds the monopoly of violence for its political objectives. See Newey (2008).

3 The equivalent of the Western Leviathan, as stated in the Zhuangzi: '[...] in the bare and barren north there is the dark and vast ocean, the 'Pool of Heaven'. In it there is a fish, several thousand *li* in breadth, while no one knows its length. Its name is the Kun' (Legge 1891, in Chinese Text Project 2020).

4 Here I just define 'Keynesian government interventionism' as the economic policies inspired in the work of John Maynard Keynes, which core feature is the management of market economy by the private sector but with an important active role of governments.

References

ADB (2014) *2014 Annual Report*. Manila: Asian Development Bank. Available at: https://www.adb.org/sites/default/files/institutional-document/158032/adb-annual-report-2014.pdf (accessed April 8, 2020).

Andornino, G.B. (2017) 'The Belt and Road Initiative in China's Emerging Grand Strategy of Connective Leadership', *China & World Economy* 25(5): 4–22.

Barrett, S. (2002) 'Supplying International Public Goods: How Nations Can Cooperate', In M. Ferroni and A. Mody (eds.) *International Public Goods. Incentives, Measurement, and Financing*. London: Kluwer Academic Publishers & The World Bank, pp. 47–80.

Brucan, S. (1971) *The Dissolution of Power: A Sociology of International Relations and Politics*. New York: Knopf.

Cai, F. (2019) 'Foreword', In C. Fang and P. Nolan (eds.) *Routledge Handbook of the Belt and Road*. New York: Routledge, pp. xviii–xx.

Cai, T. and Yang, H. 蔡拓，杨昊 (2012) '国际公共物品的供给: 中国的选择与实践' (Provision of International Public Goods: China's Choices and Practices), 世界经济与政治 *(World Economy and Politics)* 10: 95–115.

Centeno, M.A. and Cohen, J.N. (2012) 'The Arc of Neoliberalism', *Annual Review of Sociology* 38: 317–340.

Chen, Z. and Zhang, X. (2020) 'Chinese Conception of the World Order in a Turbulent Trump Era', *The Pacific Review*, 1–31.

China News Service中国新闻网 (2015) '王毅：'一带一路'构想是中国向世界提供的公共产品' (Wang Yi: The 'Belt and Road Initiative' Concept Is the Public Good That China Provides to the World, 中国新闻网 *(China News Service)*, 23 March. Available at: http://www.chinanews.com/gn/2015/03–23/7151640.shtml (accessed February 3, 2020).

Chu, Y. 储殷 (2017) "一带一路'倡议从项目推进到制度构建' (The Belt and Road Initiative, from Project Advancements to System Construction), 中华人民共和国商务部 *(Ministry of Commerce of the People's Republic of China)*, 28 February. Available at: http://cafiec.mofcom.gov.cn/article/tongjipeixun/201702/20170202524265.shtml (accessed January 13, 2020).

Dickson, B.J., Landry, P.F., Shen, M. and Yan, J. (2016) 'Public Goods and Regime Support in Urban China', *The China Quarterly* 228: 859–880.

Fan, H. 范恒山 (2018) '全面深化改革要着力处理好若干重大关系' (Comprehensively Deepening Reforms Must Focus on Handling Several Important Relationships), 中国共产党新闻 *(Chinese Communist Party News)*, 5 December. Available at: http://theory.people.com.cn/n1/2018/1205/c40531–30443714.html (accessed November 18, 2019).

Fausto, D. (2006) 'The Italian Approach to the Theory of Public Goods', *The European Journal of the History of Economic Thought* 13(1): 69–98.

Ferroni, M. and Mody, A. (eds.) (2002) *International Public Goods. Incentives, Measurement, and Financing*. London: Kluwer Academic Publishers & The World Bank.

Fewsmith, J. (1991) 'The Denguist Reforms in Historical Perspective', In B. Womack (ed.) *Contemporary Chinese Politics in Historical Perspective*. Cambridge: Cambridge University Press, pp. 23–52.

Gilpin, R. (1981) *War and Change in World Politics*. Cambridge: Cambridge University Press.

Gregor, A.J. (1981) 'Confucianism and the Political Thought of Sun Yat-Sen', *Philosophy East and West* 31(1): 55–70.

Gripsrud, J., Moe, H., Molander, A. and Murdock, G. (eds.) (2010) *The Idea of the Public Sphere*. United Kingdom: Lexington Books.

Habermas, J. (1989) *The Structural Transformation of the Public Sphere*. Cambridge: MIT Press.

He, C. (2018) 'The Belt and Road Initiative as a Global Public Good: Implications for International Law', In W. Shan, K. Nuotio and K. Zhang (eds.) *Normative Readings of the Belt and Road Initiative. Road to New Paradigms*. Cham: Springer, pp. 85–104.

He, H. 黄河 and Dai, L. 戴丽婷 (2018). "一带一路'公共产品与中国特色大国外交' ('The Belt and Road Initiative', Public Goods and Great Power Diplomacy with Chinese Characteristics), *Pacific Journal* 26(8): 50–61.

Head, J.G. (1972) 'Public Goods and Public Policy', In C.K. Rowley (ed.) *Readings in Industrial Economics. Volume Two: Private Enterprise and State Intervention*. London: Palgrave, pp. 66–87.

Hu, J. 胡钧 and Jia, K. 贾凯君 (2008) '马克思公共产品理论与西方公共产品理论比较研究' (Comparative Studies between Marx's Public Good Theory and Western Public Good Theory), 教学与研究 *(Teaching and Research)* 2: 9–15.

Kaul, I., Conceição, P., Le Goulven, K. and Mendoza, R.U. (eds.) (2003) *Providing Global Public Goods. Managing Globalization*. New York: Oxford University Press & The United Nations Development Programme.

Kaul, I., Grunberg, I. and Stern, M.A. (1999a) 'Global Public Goods: Concepts, Policies, and Strategies', In I. Kaul, I. Grunberg and M.A. Stern (eds.) *Global Public Goods. International Cooperation in the 21st Century*. New York: United Nations Development Programme & Oxford University Press, pp. 450–508.

Kaul, I., Grunberg, I. and Stern, M.A. (eds.) (1999b). *Global Public Goods. International Cooperation in the 21st Century*. New York: United Nations Development Programme & Oxford University Press.

Keohane, R.O. (1982) 'The Demand for International Regimes', *International Organization* 36(2): 325–355.

Keohane, R.O. and Ostrom, E. (1995) 'Introduction', In R.O. Keohane and E. Ostrom (eds.) *Local Commons and Global Interdependence. Heterogeneity and Cooperation in Two Domains*. London: SAGE, pp. 1–26.

Kindleberger, C.P. (1986) 'International Public Goods Without International Government', *The American Economic Review* 76(1): 1–13.

Legge, J. (1891) *The Writings of Chuang Tzu*. Oxford: Oxford University Press, in Chinese Text Project (2020) '莊子-Zhuangzi'. Also Known as: '南華真經'. Available at: https://ctext.org/zhuangzi (accessed December 25, 2019).

Li, W. 李伟建 (2016) "一带一路'视角下构建合作共赢的国际话语体系' (Building a Win-Win International Discourse System from the Perspective of 'The Belt and Road Initiative'). Shanghai Institute for International Studies. 05 October. Available at: http://www.siis.org.cn/Research/Info/2398 (accessed October 5, 2019).

Li, X. (2019) 'China's Pursuit of the 'One Belt, One Road' Initiative: A New World Order with Chinese Characteristics?', In L. Xing (ed.) *Mapping China's 'One Belt One Road' Initiative*. Aalaborg: Palgrave, pp. 1–28.

Li, Y. (2014) 'Downward Accountability in Response to Collective Actions. The Political Economy of Public Goods Provision in China', *Economics of Transition* 22(1): 69–103.

Liang, H. and Zhang, Y. (2019) *The Theoretical System of Belt and Road Initiative*. Beijing: People's Publishing House.

Liu, J. 刘结一 (2016) "一带一路'唱响联合国舞台（大使随笔）' (The Belt and Road Initiative Sings on the United Nations Arena (Ambassador's Essay), 人民网 *(People's Daily)*, 07 August. Available at: http://world.people.com.cn/n1/2016/1208/c1002–28933405.html (accessed December 5, 2019).

Liu, W., Dunford, M. and Gao, B. (2018) 'A Discursive Construction of the Belt and Road Initiative: From Neo-liberal to Inclusive Globalization', *Journal of Geographical Sciences* 28(9): 1199–1214.

Liu, Y. 刘晔 (2000) '社会共同需要论与公共财政论的比较及分析' (Comparison and Analysis of the Social Common Needs Theory and the Public Finance Theory), 当代经济科学 *(Contemporary Economic Science)* 22(1): 38–43.

Long, D. and Woolley, F. (2009) 'Global Public Goods: Critique of a UN Discourse', *Global Governance* 15(1): 107–122.

MacKinnon, S.R. (1997) 'Toward a History of the Chinese Press in the Republican Period', *Modern China* 23(1): 3–32.

Mazzola, U. (1958 [1890]) 'The Formation of the Prices of Public Goods', In R.A. Musgrave and A.T. Peacock (eds.) *Classics in the Theory of Public Finance*. London: St. Martin's Press & Palgrave, pp. 37–47.

Meng, Y. 孟于群 and Shudong, Y. 杨署东 (2018) '国际公共产品供给：加总技术下的制度安排与全球治理' (International Provision of Public Goods: Institutional Arrangements and Global Governance under Aggregate Technology), 澎湃新闻 *(The Paper)*, 14 June. Available at: https://www.thepaper.cn/newsDetail_forward_2070338 (accessed March 6, 2020).

Mofcom中华人民共和国商务部 (2012) '中国对非洲援助的'战略平衡'问题' (The 'Strategic Balance' of China's Aid to Africa), 中华人民共和国商务部 *(Ministry of Commerce of the People's Republic of China)*, 13 July. Available at: http://www.mofcom.gov.cn/aarticle/i/dxfw/gzzd/201207/20120708228080.html (accessed January 3, 2020).

Newey, G. (2008) *Routledge Philosophy Guidebook to Hobbes and Leviathan*. London: Routledge.

Nye, J.S. (1990) 'Soft Power', *Foreign Policy* 80: 153–171.

Ostrom, E. (1990) *Governing the Commons. The Evolution of Institutions for Collective Action*. Cambridge: Cambridge University Press.

Qin, S. (1998) 'Tempest Over Teapots: The Vilification of Teahouse Culture in Early Republican China', *The Journal of Asian Studies* 57(4): 1009–1041.

Qin, Y. 秦颖 (2006) '论公共产品的本质 兼论公共产品理论的局限性' (On the Essence of Public Goods and the Limitations of the Public Goods Theory), 经济学家 *(The Economist)* 3(3): 77–82.

Rankin, M.B. (1993) 'Observations on a Chinese Public Sphere', *Modern China* 19(2):158–182.

Research Center for Theoretical System of Socialism with Chinese Characteristics CASS中国社会科学院中国特色社会主义理论体系研究中心 (2016) '提高我国在全球经济治理中的制度性话语权' (Improvement of our Country's Institutional Discourse Power in Global Economic Governance), 求是网 *(Qiushi)*, 15 February. Available at: http://theory.people.com.cn/n1/2016/0216/c40531–28128274.html (accessed September 25, 2020).

Ruggie, J.G. (1972) 'Collective Goods and Future International Collaboration', *American Political Science Review* 66(3): 874–893.

Russett, B.M. and Sullivan, J.D. (1971) 'Collective Goods and International Organization', *International Organization* 25(04): 845–865.

Samuelson, P.A. (1947) *Foundations of Economic Analysis*. Cambridge: Harvard University Press.

Sassen, S. (2006) *Territory Authority Rights. From Medieval to Global Assemblages*. Princeton: Princeton University Press.

Scalapino, R.A. and Schiffrin, H. (1959) 'Early Socialist Currents in the Chinese Revolutionary Movement: Sun Yat-sen Versus LiangCh'i-ch'ao', *The Journal of Asian Studies* 18(3): 321–342.

Spiezio, K.E. (1990) 'British Hegemony and Major Power War, 1815–1939: An Empirical Test of Gilpin's Model of Hegemonic Governance', *International Studies Quarterly* 34(2): 165–181.

Sturn, R. (2006) 'Subjectivism, Joint Consumption and the State: Public Goods in *Staatswirtschaftslehre*', *The European Journal of the History of Economic Thought* 13(1): 39–67.

Sun, T. (2019) 'Deliberate Differentiation by the Chinese State: Outsourcing Responsibility for Governance', *The China Quarterly* 240: 880–905.

Tan, S. (2009) 'Huang, Junjie, and Jiang Yihua, eds., New Explorations of Public and Private Spheres: Comparison of East Asian and Western View Points 公私領域新探:東亞與西方觀點之比較 Taipei 臺北: National Taiwan University Press 國立台灣大學出版中心, 2005, (xxxvi+) 303 pages', Review. *Dao* 8: 221–224.

Tang, K. 唐凯麟 (2019) '人的需要的伦理审视' (An Ethical Review on Human Needs), 求是网 *(Qiushi)*, 5 August. Available at: http://www.qstheory.cn/llwx/2019–08/05/c_1124837419.htm (accessed November 20, 2019).

Teets, J.C. (2013) 'Let Many Civil Societies Bloom: The Rise of Consultative Authoritarianism in China', *The China Quarterly* 213: 19–38.

UNSC (2017) *S/RES/2344*. Adopted by the Security Council at its 7902nd Meeting, 17 March 2017.

Wong, R.B. (2019) 'Coping with Poverty and Famine: Material Welfare, Public Goods, and Chinese Approaches to Governance', In M. Tanimoto and R.B. Wong (eds) *Public Goods Provision in the Early Modern Economy. Comparative Perspectives from Japan, China, and Europe*. Berkeley: University of California Press, pp. 130–145.

Wang, Y. 王义桅 (2002) '从注定领导到注定合作. 国际书评：《美国力量的悖论》评介' (From Doomed Leadership to Doomed Cooperation. International Book Review of: 《The Paradox of American Power》), 人民网*(People's Daily)*, 11 April. Available at: http://people.com.cn/GB/guoji/24/20020422/714646.html (accessed November 21, 2019).

Wang, Y. 王义桅 (2015) '王义桅：'一带一路'为何如此受欢迎?' (Why is the Belt and Road Initiative so Popular?), 中国日报网 *(China Daily)*, 10 December. Available at: https://world.chinadaily.com.cn/2015–12/10/content_22682375.htm (accessed January 25, 2020).

Wang, Y. 王毅 (2016) '王毅：'一带一路'倡议提出以来已经取得显著进展' (Wang Yi: Significant Progress Has Been Made Since the 'Belt and Road Initiative' Was Put Forward), 今日中国杂志社

(China Magazine Today), 08 March. Available at: http://www.chinatoday.com.cn/ctchinese/lianghui/2016–03/08/content_716044.htm (accessed December 11, 2019).

Xinhuanet 新华网 (2018) '习近平：努力开创中国特色大国外交新局面'. (Xi Jinping: Work Hard to Create a New Situation in Major-Country Diplomacy with Chinese Characteristics), 新华网 *(Xinhuanet)*, 23 June. Available at: http://www.xinhuanet.com/politics/2018–06/23/c_1123025806.htm (accessed December 18, 2019).

Yang, J. 杨静 (2016) '从'社会共同需要'思想到'共需品'理论——对西方'公共产品'理论的批判性超越' (From 'Social Common Needs' to the Theory of 'Common Needs': A Critical Transcendence of Western Public Good Theory), 教学与研究 *(Teaching and Researching)* 3: 42–49.

Zhang, Y. and Chang, T.-c. (eds.) (2016) *Constructing a Chinese School of International Relations. Ongoing Debates and Sociological Realities*. London: Routledge.

Zhang, Z. (2019a) 'Case Studies of Infrastructure Connectivity Building', In C. Fang and P. Nolan (eds.) *Routledge Handbook of the Belt and Road*. New York: Routledge, pp. 571–576.

Zhang, Z. (2019b) 'Case Studies of Production Capacity Cooperation', In C. Fang and P. Nolan (eds.) *Routledge Handbook of the Belt and Road*. New York: Routledge, pp. 577–581.

Zhao, K. (2017) 'China's Public Diplomacy for International Public Goods', *Politics & Policy* 45(5): 706–732.

Zhou, F. (2019) 'The Historic Contribution of China's Reform and Opening Up to the World', In C. Fang and P. Nolan (eds.) *Routledge Handbook of the Belt and Road*. New York: Routledge, pp. 3–9.

5

The Chinese model of development

Substances and applications in and beyond China

Yu-Wen Chen and Obert Hodzi

Introduction

Scholars in and outside of China have sought to decipher the China model (中国模式) but there remain variegated interpretations and findings, making it impossible to determine what the China model is. In most (but not all) cases, the term 'China model' refers specifically to the developmental model of the People's Republic of China (PRC). Exactly when the term 'China model', which generally speaking refers to economic growth without political pluralism, came into being is unknown, but terms such as 'China's economic development model' or 'China's economic development path' appeared in Chinese and Western academic literature after Deng Xiaoping's Southern Tour in the 1990s (Yip 2012: 16; Qin 2016: 141–142). Because PRC scholars are usually more linked to the Chinese government than scholars in the West, it is difficult to distinguish the academic from the state's political position. This is also clearly reflected in their writings. For instance, Wang Huning (王沪宁) (1995), a scholar at China's Fudan University (and later one of China's top political leaders), declared that Deng Xiaoping has found a development model that is more suitable for China.

On the other hand, academic debates in the West on the China model started in earnest with publication of Joshua Cooper Ramo's 'Beijing Consensus' (北京共识) in 2004, in which the former *Time* magazine editor and the then-Tsinghua University professor asserted that China has found a distinct path of modernization. Since then, the 'China model' concept, whether the model exists or not, and what it really entails, has been debated not only in scholarly literature in the fields of contemporary Chinese studies, International Relations (IR), and development studies, but also among policymakers in and beyond China.

In practice, China's economic and political footprint is increasing in Asia, Africa, Latin America, and some parts of Europe. Increasingly, leaders in developing countries, such as Cambodia, Sri Lanka, South Africa, Kenya, Ethiopia, and Zimbabwe are looking up to China for an alternative development model. It may not be difficult to understand why. In less than four decades, China has grown from being the 'sick man of Asia' to a global power,

DOI: 10.4324/9780429059704-7

seeking more influence and say in global governance commensurate with its new global power status.

The Belt and Road Initiative, the Asian Infrastructure Investment Bank, and the China-Africa Development Fund are examples of recent China-led projects mainly focused on infrastructure development, thus strengthening Beijing's footprint in developing countries. In themselves, these initiatives as pointed out by some scholars may not prove the existence of a China model. The Chinese government has also in the past denied the existence of a China model, let alone advocate for its global adoption. Yet more recently, Chinese president Xi Jinping's 'China Dream' has boldly admitted and advocated the uniqueness of the China model in stark contrast to Western values – suggesting that there is some sort of a China model.

Based on the above background, this chapter offers a timely and comprehensive overview of waves of debates on the substance of the China model by the model's promoters, opponents, and even imitators. Furthermore, this chapter provides an overview of scholarly views on whether the China model is successful and sustainable or not. Success is defined as China's ability to reach economic growth without political reform to change regime or liberalize society. This chapter is structured around four main questions that have been heatedly debated among scholars and policymakers. The first question is whether there is a China model. Second, what are defining characteristics of the model if it exists? Third, what is the prospect of the China model in terms of its success and sustainability? Fourth, can the China model be replicated outside of China? The next two sections tackle the first and second questions.

Is there a China model?

Is there a China model and what are the defining characteristics of the model if it exists? The term 'model' requires a bit of focus because various scholars have interpreted the term in varied ways. Sometimes it is used to mean a developmental path, or specific developmental guidelines, principles, strategies or policies with distinct characteristics (Fang 2016: 3; Qin 2016: 143; Yu 2016: 124). Others understand it as a kind of Chinese experience or Chinese case (Qin 2016: 144). In most literature, the term 'model' is meant to generalize China's overall development and modernization, but rarely is it used to denote China's development in a specific sector or region (Qin 2016: 148). For instance, Yu Keping, Deputy Director of the Compilation and Translation Bureau of the Central Committee of the Chinese Communist Party (CCP) and Peking University professor, defines the China model as both a strategic choice that China undertakes to achieve modernization in the context of globalization as well as a set of developmental strategies and governance patterns that the country has gradually crafted during reforms and opening up (Yu et al. 2006; Yu 2016: 124).

Yip (2012: 15–16) in his review of existing literature on the China model discerns the Western School and the Chinese School of thought – representing the ideas of Chinese scholars. Yip's categorization of Western and Chinese schools of thought gives a useful summary of all the variants of debates on the China model. The Chinese School is mainly comprised of scholars of Chinese politics and IR, the most notable ones being famous scholars like Zhang Weiwei and Pan Wei (Yip 2012: 19; Pan 2009). These Chinese School scholars generally agree that there is a China model, that the model is adapted to the unique circumstances of China, and that it explains China's economic development trajectory.

The Western School, however, questions the existence and uniqueness of the China model (Chen 2010; Horesh 2013; Yip 2012: 27). Scholars in this school are mostly economists or libertarians who have received Western education (Chen 2010; Yip 2012: 27). They argue that China has mostly borrowed experiences, principles, and values from Western economic theories to undertake its reform – hence what is being referred to as the China model is actually a cocktail of East Asian development model components and aspects of the Washington Consensus. Famous scholars such as Chen Zhiwu (2010), for instance, have contended that the China model never existed because China adopted and adopts 'universal values'. Even though some (e.g., Qin Hui, a historian at Tsinghua University) in the Western School agree that China has its own development path or model, they do not necessarily believe that the model can sustain China because Chinese people desire greater freedom and welfare than what the China model can provide (Qin 2010; Horesh 2013: 341–342). In a nutshell, scholars in the Chinese School tend to examine the China model in the context of China's unique circumstances (or the so-called Chinese civilization) while those of the Western School look at the China model in the framework of universal values (Chen 2010; Yip 2012: 27).

Beijing Consensus and the China model

Despite a diversity of interpretations of the China model, the kernel of the various versions is the model's authoritarian foundation and state-led market economy characteristic (Ambrosio 2012: 382). In this regard, most scholars focus on the evolution of China's governance and its goals, strategies and approaches to enhancing governance (Bell 2015; Chen & Naughton 2017; deLisle 2017). The push for an academic conceptualization of the China model, however, comes from scholars based outside of China – the foremost being Joshua Cooper Ramo's 2004 proposal of the so-called 'Beijing Consensus'. In his description of the Beijing Consensus, Ramos argues that China found a unique development strategy, which he contrasted with the Western, neoliberal 'Washington Consensus' model.

In contrasting the two models, Ramo (2004) contends that China's (1) technological innovation, (2) pursuit of equitable and sustainable economic growth, as well as (3) insistence on self-reliance and refusal to accept Western intervention define the Beijing Consensus. The impact of Ramo's Beijing Consensus proposition is that several other scholars have in their writings often conflated the term China model with Beijing Consensus (Qin 2016: 147). However, scholars such as Pang Zhongying argue that the Beijing Consensus is distinct from the China model. For him, the Beijing Consensus merely summarizes China's experiences (Pang 2004). He therefore argues that there is a need to research the essence of the China model. In the next section of this chapter, we will, as argued by Pang further explore the essence of the China model.

Ramo's Beijing Consensus elicited criticisms from scholars in and out of China. Breslin (2011) and Kennedy (2010) are known for their critiques of Ramo's Beijing Consensus. They contend that claiming technological innovation is the main driver of China's economic growth is misleading (Kennedy 2010: 469; Breslin 2011: 1332) as China has been borrowing innovations from elsewhere to undertake economic reforms (Kenney 2010: 470–471; Dickson 2011: 43). It might be more accurate to say that China aspires to have more 'indigenous innovation' as well as equitable and sustainable economic growth than to claim that China already has these achievements (Kennedy 2010: 469; Breslin 2011: 1325; Dickson 2011: 43). Scholars also commented that strong state involvement in a country's development is normal throughout history. One cannot consider the state-led development in China as unique and exceptional (Breslin 2011: 1323).

While the term 'consensus' denotes widely acknowledged or agreed solutions (Yu 2016: 124), Breslin (2011: 1328) questions how one could identify agreed solutions for China's development since there is a 'huge diversity of developmental trajectories within China itself' (Breslin 2011: 1328). Literature that focuses on articulating the China model at the subnational/regional level or in a specific sector exist but is comparatively fewer. The majority of writings on the China model or Beijing Consensus tend to generalize China's overall experience in development.

Despite criticism of the Beijing Consensus and the absence of consensus on what the China model really entails, the topic still is popular among China scholars. This has led some scholars to reason that the China model's popularity as a subject of study is not just because of a global drive to understand China's rise, but motivated by the increasing insecurity of Western Europe and North American policymakers and intellectuals. The West, broadly defined, is concerned that the China model, however it is conceptualized, challenges their own system and values that are globally dominant (Horesh & Lim 2017).

Waves of the China model discourse

The China model discourse has several waves of development. Zhao Suisheng identifies three waves of the China model discourse. He argues that if Ramo's Beijing Consensus and its critiques are the first wave of scholarly contention over the China model, the second wave of debate arose in conjunction with China's 2008 Beijing Olympics achievements (Zhao 2017). After Beijing's successful hosting of the Olympic Games and that it largely remained unscathed by the 2008 global financial crisis, literature on the China model proliferated (Zhao 2017; Yip 2012: 3). Since then, the term has been used in discussions on 'the rise of China' (中国崛起) and 'the miracle of China' (中国奇迹) (Zhao 2017). However, the Hu Jintao-Wen Jiabao administration hesitated to endorse such a discourse for fear of raising concerns of a China threat in the global arena (Zhao 2017).

The third wave of the China model discourse began in 2012 when Xi Jinping assumed the presidency of the PRC. His domestic and foreign policy was hinged on the great national rejuvenation, which prompted a resurgence of the China model debate. Unlike previous leaders of China, Xi is more confident of China's major power status and is vocal in elaborating on the China model. His main assertion is that the China model is not just a result of China's economic achievements but a consequence of the Communist Party of China's leadership, which steered the country toward prosperity. Xi's version of the China model also emphasizes Chinese uniqueness and pits itself against Western norms.

Propelling Xi's national rejuvenation project are scholars such as Zhang Weiwei (张维为), the founding director of Fudan University's China Development Model Center. His book *The China Shock: The Rise of a Civilizational State*, published in 2011, explains the China model and was recommended by Xi Jinping. Published in both Chinese and English, the Chinese version is written in a more patriotic, if not nationalistic tone. The book's main premise is that China is the only civilizational state (文明型国家) still existing in the contemporary world (Zhang 2011). Its sheer size, huge population, superlong history, and abundantly rich culture make its developmental path unique and inapplicable, even incomparable to other countries. Emphasizing China's exceptionalism, he argues (as does Xi Jinping) that other countries' rules cannot be used as a yardstick to measure China. As put by Shaun Breslin, this kind of Chinese exceptionalism discourse has 'far more than semantic importance':

> It not only feeds into understandings of China's place in the world but also has important domestic uses and consequences. It explains why China does not have to follow

> anything – including any path that sees democratization as an inevitable consequence of economic liberalization.
>
> *(Breslin 2011: 1341–1342)*

Among other Western proponents of the China model is Daniel Bell, professor at Shandong University in China. For him, what defines the China model is meritocratic elite governance by which Chinese leaders are selected on the basis of their good performance at lower levels of government (Bell 2015). Their ascension to national level governance is based on their ability to deal with crises and spur economic development, which is usually contrasted with the 'messy' nature of electoral democracy (Bell 2015). At the core of the China model is the performance-derived-legitimacy that Chinese leaders and the CCP have to continue ruling (Bell 2015). On that basis, China's model of development is underpinned by a unique model of governance, which cannot be replicated elsewhere.

Substances and effectiveness of the China model

Is the China model effective and sustainable? Essential to answering this question is some sort of agreement on what constitutes the China model. However, such consensus does not exist, judging from the existing literature. Nonetheless, most scholars agree that the China model is silhouetted in a system of the market economy allied to the one-party rule system. Also, several scholars have referred to Chinese pragmatism and gradualism traits in steering the country toward modernization. Those traits are usually contrasted with the Washington Consensus' 'shock therapy' and one-solution-fits-all approach (Hsu, Wu, and Zhao 2011; Chen and Naughton 2017: 19). Arguably, Western-bred democracy theories are built on the premise that economic growth should lead to modernization, liberalization, and democratization. Francis Fukuyama's (1992) 'End of History' thesis summaries this view on mankind's ultimate path to democracy.

China and Singapore are often raised as counterexamples of countries that achieved modernization with limited democratic development. The explanation is that what makes China and Singapore's regimes sustainable is their ability to offer performance legitimacy. It is this performance legitimacy that underpins the China model. Accordingly, supporters of the model insist that good governance, mostly in the economic domain, gives the CCP legitimacy to remain in power.

Reliance on raw economic growth to sustain the regime is in the ultimate, as argued by some scholars, both flawed and unsustainable (Zhao 2017; Dickson 2011). Fault-lines in the China model's emphasis on preeminence of economic growth include environmental degradation, corruption, exploitation of labor, nonobservance of labor rights, inequality and social unrest (Kennedy 2010; Dickson 2011: 46; Zhao 2017; DeLisle 2017). Notably, as people's basic needs are met, it has proved that they start demanding other rights, such as protection of their environment, transparency, accountability and redress of social and economic inequalities. It therefore follows that a regime, whose legitimacy exclusively depends on economic reforms rather than political reforms will in the end unravel, and the problem is acute in times of economic recession (Thornton & Thornton 2018: 215).

It is in this vein that scholars outside China mostly agree that the China model cannot be a substitute of the Western model of development, in which democracy and market economy develop in tandem (Halper 2010; Zhao 2017). Instead, the China model can become a brand in itself and compete with the Western neoliberal model (Halper 2010). Some scholars seem dissatisfied with such a development and have called for China's democratization in order to balance its state power, 'like what happened in several other East Asian countries' (Zhao 2017: 17).

To sum up, discussions on the China model, whether by Chinese or non-Chinese scholars have often led to a dichotomized way of looking at the matters: the West vs. China, and democratization vs. authoritarianism as illustrated above. To some extent, there is nothing wrong in discerning differences in practices and values. But the constant dichotomization of the matters can be 'potentially dangerous' if the knowledge that the debates produce becomes too simplified – fueling 'zero-sum' conflict between the West and China in their approaches to human development and governance. Scholars, such as Callahan (2013) and Mulvad (2018), have cautioned the danger of such ideological cleavage in contemporary debates on China.

Applications of the China model beyond China

Can the China model be replicated elsewhere and how?

The China model is usually defined by what it is compared to – the Washington Consensus – rather than what it is. Ian Taylor, a professor at St Andrews University, notes that the China model or the Beijing Consensus 'draws its meaning and appeal not from some coherent set of economic or political ideas … but from its intimation of an alternative pole, from which those opposed to Washington and, by extension "the West", can draw inspiration' (Taylor 2014: 115). The implication is that to understand what the China model offers to developing countries, the focus is not what the China model is, but what it is not in relation to the Washington Consensus. Such a comparative approach to defining the China model influences its geographical application beyond China. Because the China model is framed as an alternative to, and sometimes as a competitor of the Washington Consensus, its application is limited to developing countries in the Global South. He Yafei, China's Vice Minister of Foreign Affairs, opined in the *China Daily*, that the Chinese model 'offers other developing countries an option different from the 'American model' for economic development' (He 2018). This is contrary to the near-universal application of the Washington Consensus, which He Yafei refer to as the 'American model'.

There is no doubt that the two models differ on mechanisms of their application and replication in other countries. The main difference is on the nature of the Chinese and American states and their respective positions on promotion of development abroad. Unlike Washington DC, Beijing's official position is that developing countries are free to choose elements of the China model that are applicable in their contexts. Beijing's position has been parroted by government officials, scholars, public intellectuals, and Chinese journalists such as Wang Wenwen. In 2018, Wang published an op-ed in the *Global Times* reiterating that:

> China does not want African countries to copy its model. Rather, by lending its development experiences, China hopes that these countries can explore their own development path and become another young global economic locomotive and world factory.
>
> *(Wang 2018)*

More than a template for development and modernization, the China model, as further argued by Xi Jinping is a new option for other countries that need to speed up their development while preserving their independence and sovereignty. Rhetoric and reality are often blurred in China's foreign policy positions, especially in relation to the China model. The rhetoric is that the China model should not be replicated abroad; the reality however is complex – states can pick and choose elements of the China model that they can replicate, which suggests that the model is replicable. Naughton (2010) argues otherwise – a model is to be taken as a whole. If only elements are taken on board it is by definition not a model, but a series of useful elements. It can therefore be argued what is referred to as the China model in other countries is actually a series of elements of the model being implemented.

Selecting elements of a development model applicable to a country's context is not an option for developing countries wanting to implement the Washington Consensus – as is the case for countries opting for the China model. The differentiating factor as identified by Francis Fukuyama is the nature of the United States and its global outlook. Unlike China, the United States bilaterally and multilaterally impose principles and values of the Washington Consensus on countries in the Global South – forcing them to institute economic and political reforms and implement the Washington Consensus in its totality. China seemingly imposes no such conditions. Neither does it impose political and economic reforms on other countries or seek to institute regime change in cases where its model is resisted (Hodzi 2018). In line with its denial of hegemonic ambition, China appears reluctant to encourage replication of the China model abroad. But the United States has imposed sanctions and unilaterally intervened to enforce its values on other countries. As a result, the Washington Consensus, as put by Rita Abrahamsen (2010: x), 'has been accepted by the vast majority of multilateral and bilateral donors, and there is general agreement on the desirability of both economic liberalism and liberal democracy'.

The 'general agreement on the desirability of both economic liberalism and liberal democracy' need to be historicized. In the Global South, especially in Africa and Latin America, countries that required financial assistance after the Cold War had no choice but align with economic liberalism and liberal democracy. The imposition of conditions tied to aid and development assistance by the World Bank, International Monetary Fund (IMF), and the Organisation for Economic Co-operation and Development (OECD) countries ensured that the liberal development paradigm and its liberal democracy became universal and unchallenged. The 'forced' application of the Washington Consensus on developing countries in the form of Structural Adjustment Programmes of the 1980s failed to 'deal with Africa's unsustainable debt and economic decline … [and they failed] to rekindle economic growth on the continent' (Abrahamsen 2010: 37). The same happened in Latin America. For China, a non-Western power self-identifying as a noninterventionary power, there seem to be no possibility of the China model becoming universal for as long as China does not seek to impose it on other states or is not a global hegemony shaping the world in its image.

Nonetheless, the transferability and replicability of the China model in other countries has been a subject of both academic and policy debate. With limited existing literature on whether the China model is transferable or replicable, much of the existing knowledge is derived from statements by political leaders and opinions in media outlets – making it difficult to distinguish between rhetoric and reality. Scholars differ on whether the China model is transferable or not. Some, such as Zhang Weiwei, who are focused on China's exceptionalism contend that it is hard for others to follow China's development path (Zhang 2012). With the China model intricately underpinned by the Communist Party of China, Margaret Lewis (quoted in Weiss 2019) argues that 'China's Party-state structure is rooted in a particular history that does not lend itself to an easy copy-and-paste abroad'. Andrew Nathan (2015: 161) summed it up when he stated, 'it is rare to find an argument, even by pro regime independent intellectuals, that portrays the Chinese experience as a universal model that should be adopted everywhere'. As argued earlier, Nathan's assertion reflects the complexities of China's foreign policy – that on one hand promotes the rhetoric that the model cannot be adopted elsewhere, but on the other urges that it is an alternative for developing countries seeking to speed up their modernization and development. The denialism is also part of China's strategy against the 'China threat' thesis. Thus, China is keen on being seen as a noninterventionist and nonhegemonic power with no ambition of promoting its development guidelines and blueprints abroad.

In the few cases that Chinese officials have alluded to the existence of the China model, they have hastily argued that it is not universal but that other countries can draw lessons and implement elements that fit their contexts. This argument should be understood for what it is – a diplomatic offensive on the West. 'China denounces the idea of 'universal values' as a form of Western subversion of states that try to protect their autonomy from Western influence' (Nathan 2015: 158). The Washington Consensus has often been criticized for trying to offer 'one-size-fits-all' solutions to other countries problems. If the China model is aimed to be different from the Washington Consensus, then it cannot similarly offer 'all-purpose' solutions (Breslin 2011: 1337). Yet, scholars such as Shaun Breslin use this to argue that the China model is more of a metaphor than a reality – hence there is no such thing as a model that can be applied elsewhere (Breslin 2011: 1328, 1337–1338). But metaphorically, the concept of the China model, by its refusal to be a one-size-fits-all, and insistence that countries can pick aspects of China's path to development that work for them, resembles the freedom and sovereignty over development that the model has come to be known for in Africa and other regions of the developing world. The China model is therefore a symbol that every country can find its own developmental path relevant to its context.

Sovereignty to choose one's own path to development fits into the idea that China is offering the developing world an alternative model to development. Xi Jinping stated in his 19th CPC National Congress report that:

> the path, the theory, the system, and the culture of socialism with Chinese characteristics have kept developing, blazing a new trail for other developing countries to achieve modernization. It offers a new option for other countries and nations who want to speed up their development while preserving their independence; and it offers Chinese wisdom and a Chinese approach to solving the problems facing mankind.
>
> *(Xinhua 2017)*

Appeal of the China model in developing countries

By strategically not presenting the China model as a rival to existing development paradigms, but as one of the options, the desirability of the China model in Africa has increased. In principle, it offers African countries the opportunity to choose between the neoliberal development models of the West and China's model of development, however they conceptualize it. Linked to that is China's push to be recognized as a developing country that is altruistic enough to be an alternative economic collaborator for poor regions of the world. The result has been popularity of the China model of development in authoritarian states burdened by conditionalities imposed by the United States, European powers, and the Bretton Wood institutions. To those countries, China provides economic benefits with relatively fewer but deceptively conditional strings attached (e.g., the One-China policy) and no demands for democratic reforms and respect for human rights (Breslin 2011: 1337–1338; DeHart 2012: 1362). As put by Naidu and Davies (2006: 80), most governments see China as a 'refreshing alternative to the traditional engagement models of the West …

[in particular] African governments see China's engagement as a point of departure from Western neocolonialism and political conditions'. It is in that vein that outside of China, political leaders in developing countries such as Sri Lanka, Cambodia, Costa Rica, Ethiopia, Kenya, and Zimbabwe have alluded to a China model of development that inspires their own development trajectories.

Anchored on nonconditionality, sovereignty and freedom of states to choose their own path to development, the China model seems more desirable for developing countries, mostly in Africa. Speaking at the Belt and Road Initiative (BRI) conference in Beijing, Monica Mutsvangwa, Zimbabwe's Minister of Information, Publicity and Broadcasting Services said: 'We are heartened by the offering of a more diverse and competitive global financial architecture beyond the IMF-World Bank of the Bretton Woods System. ... The BRI summit is a shining example of how China wants to generously and selflessly share out its experience with all nations' (The Herald 2019). Such profiling of China as a responsible global power able to provide public goods and contributing to international development has enhanced China's status in the Global South. In addition, the inception of infrastructure development projects such as the BRI and the growth of China as the biggest trading partner of countries in the Global South and financier of development projects has added to the attractiveness of the China model of development. Hence, China is constantly cited as a model of development and poverty reduction.

In Ethiopia, especially under the leadership of the late Meles Zenawi, the China model was preferred because it challenged the neoliberal assumption that development is linked to democratic governance. In declaring that Ethiopia needs to strengthen its development autonomy, Zenawi said: 'I think it would be wrong for people in the West to assume that they can buy good governance in Africa. Good governance can only come from inside; it cannot be imposed from outside. That was always an illusion. What the Chinese have done is explode that illusion. It does not in any way endanger the reforms of good governance and democracy in Africa because only those that were home-grown ever had a chance of success' (Zenawi 2007). As aptly put by He Yafei 'given a choice between market democracy and its freedoms and market authoritarianism and its growth, stability, improved living standards, and limits on expression – a majority in the developing world and in many middle-sized, non-Western powers prefer the authoritarian model' (He 2015: 129). Even after Zenawi, Ethiopia's development and industrial strategies are closely aligned with China's special economic zones, industrial parks, and public investment in major infrastructure development projects. Ethiopia is however not alone. 'States as disparate as Ethiopia, Rwanda, Kazakhstan, and Bolivia seek to replicate China's economic transformation' (Kaplan 2018).

Beyond Africa, the China model of development has had increased traction in Southeast Asia. According to Kurlantzick (2013), surveys on political values in Southeast Asia suggest that 'people in many Southeast Asian countries share a willingness to abandon some of their democratic values for higher growth, and the kind of increasingly state-directed economic system that many of these countries had, in their authoritarian days, and that China still has today'. Thitinan Pongsudhirak (2018), director of the Institute of Security and International Studies at Chulalongkun University in Thailand, argues that across Southeast Asia, particularly in Cambodia, Brunei, Laos, and Vietnam, increased authoritarianism in those countries 'is crucially underpinned by China's successful system of centralized control combined with economic dynamism'. The result is that as China's economic dominance over the region increases and the countries become more dependent on China. There is a 'shift of the center of regional economic gravity from Japan to China' and 'authoritarianism remains a fierce competition to democracy in East Asia' because 'China is seen as having demonstrated a viable path of growing out of a planned economy and as showing how sequencing political and economic change makes possible a transition from communism to postcommunist authoritarianism' (Chu et al. 2008: 9–10).

The China model was framed along the developmental state discourse (Knight 2014). The emphasis is on a strong state that intervenes in the economy, promotes industrialization, and exercises autonomy and sovereignty in determining its development trajectory. As put by Nathan, 'by demonstrating that advanced modernization can be combined with authoritarian rule, the Chinese regime has given a new hope to authoritarian rulers elsewhere in the world' (Nathan 2015: 158). However, the China model is no longer just appealing to repressive authoritarian regimes but has increased its 'leverage over democracies in the developing world and made Beijing's model of development more attractive even in freer nations, places where there has already been some degree of democratic transition' (Kurlantzick 2013). Thus, as put by Wibowo, 'the attraction to the China model is unconscious – a silent admiration of the spectacular rise of China' (Wibowo 2004: 217).

In the view of opposition political parties in Zimbabwe and Ethiopia, the implementation of the China model by ruling parties in the two countries is meant to mask human rights abuses, suppress political dissent, and consolidate political power. Tendai Biti, vice president of the Movement for Democratic Change Alliance Party in Zimbabwe, argues that:

> Mnangagwa clearly does not know a lot of things. He probably wants to take the Beijing model, which has liberalisation of business while there is absolute closure of political space. … He envies Xi's position where he has effectively made himself life president. China is not a socialist state, but practices state capitalism where everything is run by central government, but still projects the characteristics of a capitalist society. There is a state capitalism in China. When Mnangagwa says he wants to copy the Chinese model he wants to be president for life chosen not by the people, but by the politburo while the country trades with everyone.
>
> *(The Standard 2018)*

Similarly, the former Chair of the Oromo people's Congress in Ethiopia said:

> Really, Meles wants the Chinese model because staying in power is his sole, ultimate goal. … As far back as 1994, 1995, Meles sent a delegation to China, to look very closely at the way China is developing, and especially how to deal with diversity the Chinese way and how to effectively use democratic centralism … he sent the number two, number three [most senior] people to China.
>
> *(Chair of Oromo People's Congress quoted in Fourie 2015: 299)*

The focus of the two opposition political parties is not on the economic and developmental aspects of the China model, but the political system that it represents. Accordingly, the applicability of the China model in Africa is interpreted differently by local actors according to their economic and political interests.

In sum, regardless of developing countries claiming to follow the China model of development, there is scholarly consensus that the China model is yet to be fully developed and that people view it differently. Each of the different countries is following specific elements of China's development experience – which on their own are not the China model. Naughton (2010) concurs that because both the Beijing Consensus and the China model do not accurately describe China's development trajectory, no country can claim to be following the model, although they can derive lessons. As it appears from Ethiopia, Zimbabwe, and other countries, political leaders are seeing the China model as providing them with an opportunity to choose and define their countries' path of development rather than the predefined path imposed by the Washington Consensus. Although this preference may be due to the political leaders' selfish aims as alleged by the opposing parties, this level of development autonomy and the extraordinary economic success of China, is attracting more countries including Hungary that are increasingly showing preference for 'the economic and political approach of China, a model of state capitalism in which the state steers production and the economy' (Moyo 2018: 112).

Conclusion

The China model eludes a concise definition – scholars, policymakers and journalists continue to disagree on the existence of the model, and among those that agree there is a China model, there is no consensus on what it is. The conflicting signals from the government of China add to the complexity of conceptualizing the China model, let alone its application beyond China. Yet, as shown in this chapter, there have been three waves of debates on the substance of the model by the model's promoters, opponents, and even imitators outside of China. As China becomes more comfortable with defining its global role as a major power, there is likely to be a fourth wave of debate on the China model. Xi Jinping's 'China Dream', Belt and Road Initiative and China's alternative multilateral financial institutions such as the Asian Infrastructure Investment Bank (AIIB) suggest a China gearing for more expressions of its global ambitions. With China becoming a financier of development projects and infrastructure development projects in Asia, Africa, and Latin America, the role of China as a model of development or as Xi Jinping puts it, a 'new option' is becoming more illuminated. Countries seeking to derive material benefits from China, and those genuinely attracted to China's development success are increasingly drawing lessons from China and applying aspects of China's development paradigm in their own contexts. The COVID-19 global pandemic manifested China's assertiveness and claim to being a model in effectively dealing with global pandemics. From being the first to announce the testing of possible COVID-19 vaccination to donating the much-needed medical supplies and expertise to both developed and developing countries, China showed its global influence and indispensability. However, there have been criticisms of China's handing of COVID-19. For instance, the United States and other Western countries such as the United Kingdom, France, and Germany accused the Chinese government of hiding the truth in the beginning of the outbreak while other countries have complained about the defective nature of medical equipment donated by China. Regardless, the crisis gave China a good opportunity to demonstrate the effectiveness of its authoritarian governance and exposed the weakness of a plethora of liberal democratic governments. One can say that the 2020 pandemic is a game changer for China to further promote the comparative, if not absolute advantage of its model in the world. The fourth wave of debate should therefore focus on the variants of the China model in the different countries where aspects of the China model are being implemented, with or without China's knowledge. The next question will not be whether China has a model of development, but what variants of the China model exist beyond China.

References

Abrahamsen, R. (2010) *Disciplining Democracy: Development Discourse and Good Governance in Africa*. London: Zed Books.

Ambrosio, T. (2012) 'The rise of the 'China Model' and 'Beijing Consensus': Evidence of authoritarian diffusion?', *Contemporary Politics* 18(4): 381–399.
Bell, D. (2015) *The China Model: Political Meritocracy and the Limits of Democracy*. Princeton: Princeton University Press.
Breslin, S. (2011) 'The 'China model' and global crisis: From Friedrich List to a Chinese mode of governance?', *International Affairs* 87(6): 1323–1343.
Callahan, W.A. (2013) *China Dreams: 20 Visions of the Future*. Oxford: Oxford University Press.
Chen, L. and Naughton, B. (2017) 'A dynamic China model: The co-evolution of economics and politics in China', *Journal of Contemporary China* 26(103): 18–34.
Chen, Z. 陳志武 (2010) 沒有中國模式這回事*! (China Model Never Exists!)*. New Taipei City: 八旗文化 (Baqi Wenhua Publishing).
Chu, Y.H., Diamond, L., Nathan, A.J. and Shin, D.C. (2008) 'Introduction: Comparative perspectives on democratic legitimacy', in Y.-H. Chiu, L. Diamond, A.J. Nathan and D.C. Shin (eds.) *Hoe East Asian View Democracy*, New York: Columbia University Press, pp.1–38.
DeHart, M. (2012) 'Remodelling the global development landscape: The China model and South-South cooperation in Latin America', *Third World Quarterly* 33(7): 1359–1375.
DeLisle, J. (2017) 'Law in the China model 2.0: Legality, developmentalism and Leninism under Xi Jinping', *Journal of Contemporary China* 26(103): 68–84.
Dickson, B.J. (2011) 'Updating the China model', *The Washington Quarterly* 34(4): 39–58.
Fang, N. (2016) 'The political model of China's development', in J. Zhao and B. Wu (eds.) *The Theory of China Model and the Rise of China*. Reading: Paths International Ltd. pp. 3–13.
Fourie, E.E. (2015) 'China's example for Meles' Ethiopia: When development 'models' land', *Journal of Modern African Studies* 53(3): 289–316.
Fukuyama, F. (1992) *The End of History and the Last Man*. New York: Free Press.
Halper, S. (2010) *The Beijing Consensus: How China's Authoritarian Model Will Dominate the Twenty-First Century*. New York: Basic Books.
He, L. (2015) 'The Chinese model of development and its implications', *World Journal of Social Science Research* 2(2): 128–138.
He, Y. (2018) 'Will China and US enter a new 'Cold War'', *China Daily*, 9 July. Available at: http://usa.chinadaily.com.cn/a/201807/09/WS5b42a4f8a3103349141e16d7.html (accessed June 12, 2019).
The Herald (2019) 'Belt, road initiative spawns learning opportunity', *The Herald*, 26 April. Available at: https://www.herald.co.zw/belt-road-initiative-spawns-learning-opportunity/ (accessed April 26, 2019).
Hodzi, O. (2018) 'Does China have the power to change governments in Africa?', *Africa Is a Country*, 3 March. Available at: https://africasacountry.com/2018/03/does-china-have-the-power-to-change-governments-in-africa (accessed June 29, 2019).
Horesh, N. (2013) 'In search of the 'China model': Historic continuity vs. imagined history in Yan Xuetong's thought', *China Report* 49(3) 337–355.
Horesh, N. and Lim, K. (2017) 'The 'China model' as a complicated developmental trope', *China: An International Journal* 15(2): 166–176.
Hsu, S., Wu, Y. and Zhao, S. (eds.) (2011) *In Search of China's Development Model: Beyond the Beijing Consensus*. New York: Routledge.
Kaplan, S.D. (2018) 'Development with Chinese characteristics', *American Interest*, 3 January. Available at: https://www.the-american-interest.com/2018/01/03/development-chinese-characteristics/ (accessed June 24, 2019).
Kennedy, S. (2010) 'The myth of Beijing Consensus', *Journal of Contemporary China* 19(65): 461–477.
Knight, J.B. (2014) 'China as a developmental state', *The World Economy* 37(1): 1335–1347.
Kurlantzick, J. (2013) 'Why the 'China Model' isn't going away', *Atlantic*, 21 March. Available at: https://www.theatlantic.com/china/archive/2013/03/why-the-china-model-isnt-going-away/274237/ (accessed June 29, 2019).

Moyo, D. (2018) *Edge of Chaos: Why Democracy if Failing to Deliver Economic Growth – and How to Fix It*. New York: Basic Books.

Mulvad, A.M. (2018) 'China's ideological spectrum: a two-dimensional model of elite intellectuals' visions', *Theory and Society* 47: 635–661.

Naidu, S. and Davies, M. (2006) 'China fuels its future with Africa's riches', *South African Journal of International Affairs* 13(2): 69–83.

Nathan, A.J. (2015) 'China's challenge', *Journal of Democracy* 26(1): 156–170.

Naughton, B. (2010) 'China's distinctive system: Can it be a model for others?' *Journal of Contemporary China* 19(65): 437–460.

Pan, W. 潘维 (ed.) (2009) 中国模式: 解读共和国的六十年 *(The China Model: A New Interpretation of Sixty Years of the People's Republic)*. Beijing: 中央编译出版社 (Central Compilation and Translation Press).

Pang, Z. 庞中英 (2004) "中国特征的全球化'与'北京共识" ('Globalization with Chinese characteristics' and 'the Beijing Consensus')', 当代世界与社会主义 *(Contemporary World and Socialism)* 5: 15–16.

Pongsudhirak, T. (2018) 'Authoritarianism is accelerating in Southeast Asia', *Nikkei Asian Review*, 1 January. Available at: https://asia.nikkei.com/Editor-s-Picks/Looking-ahead-2018/Authoritarianism-is-accelerating-in-Southeast-Asia (accessed June 14, 2019).

Qin, H. 秦晖 (2010) '中国模式既低自由又低福利 不认为有什么优越性' (China model has low freedom and low welfare: It has no superiority)', 鳳凰網 ifeng.com, 6 April, http://finance.ifeng.com/opinion/xzsuibi/20100406/2014124.shtml (accessed June 28, 2019).

Qin, X. (2016) 'A probe into the concept of China model', in J. Zhao and B. Wu (eds.) *The Theory of China Model and the Rise of China*. Reading: Paths International Ltd, pp. 141–149.

Ramo, J.C. (2004) *Beijing Consensus*. London: Foreign Policy Center.

The Standard (2018) 'Mnangagwa's Chinese dream invites scorn, sparks 'dictatorship' fears', *The Standard*, 8 April. Available at: https://www.thestandard.co.zw/2018/04/08/mnangagwas-chinese-dream-invites-scorn-sparks-dictatorship-fears/amp/ (accessed June 27, 2019).

Taylor, I. (2014) *Africa Rising? BRICS – Diversifying Dependency*. Suffolk: James Currey.

Thornton, W.H. and Thornton, S.H. (2018) 'Sino-globalisation: the China model after dengism', *China Report* 54(2): 213–230.

Wang, W.W. (2018) 'West has no grounds for criticizing China model in Africa', *Global Times*, 27 August. Available at: http://www.globaltimes.cn/content/1117305.shtml (accessed June 27, 2019).

Wang, H. 王沪宁 (1995) 政治的人生 *(Political Life)*. Shanghai: 上海人民出版社 (Shanghai People Publishing House).

Weiss, J.C. (2019) 'A world safe for autocracy? China's rise and the future of global politics', *Foreign Affairs*, July/August. Available at: https://www.foreignaffairs.com/articles/china/2019–06–11/world-safe-autocracy (accessed June 29, 2019).

Wibowo, I. (2004) *Belajar Dari Cina (To Learn from China)*. Jakarta: Penerbit Kompas.

Xinhua (2017) 'Socialism with Chinese characteristics enters new era: Xi', *Xinhua*, 18 October. Available at: http://www.xinhuanet.com/english/2017–10/18/c_136688475.htm (accessed June 29, 2019).

Yip, K. (2012) *The Uniqueness of China's Development Model, 1842–2049*. Singapore: World Scientific.

Yu, K., Shuguang, H.P.X. and Jian, G. 俞可平, 黄平, 谢曙光, 高健 (eds.) (2006) 中国模式与北京共识—超越华盛顿共识 *(The China Model and the Beijing Consensus: Beyond the Washington Consensus)*. Beijing: 社会科学文献 (Social Sciences Press).

Yu, K. (2016) 'Reflections on the China model', in J. Zhao and B. Wu (eds.) *The Theory of China Model and the Rise of China*. Reading: Paths International Ltd, pp. 124–129.

Zenawi, M. (2007) 'FT interview: Meles Zenawi, Ethiopian Prime Minister', *Financial Times*, 6 February. Available at: https://www.ft.com/content/4db917b4-b5bd-11db-9eea-0000779e2340 (accessed June 29, 2019).

Zhang, W. 张维为 (2011) 中国震撼：一个'文明型国家'的崛起 *(The China Shock: Rise of a Civilizational State)*. Shanghai: 上海人民出版社 (Shanghai People Publishing House).

Zhang, W. (2012) *The China Wave: Rise of a Civilizational State*. New Jersey: World Century Publishing Corporation.

Zhao, S. (2017) 'Whither the China model: Revisiting the debate', *Journal of Contemporary China* 26(103): 1–17.

6

China's Central Asia policy

Beijing's doctrines of active defense, Belt and Road, and peaceful coexistence

Liselotte Odgaard

Introduction

This chapter argues that in Central Asia, China pursues policy coordination and conflict prevention to facilitate its emergence as a leading Central Asian economic and security actor. China's approach is modeled on three doctrines: Active defense, the Belt and Road Initiative (BRI), and peaceful coexistence. China is a newcomer to the Central Asian region consisting of Kazakhstan, Kyrgyzstan, Tajikistan, Uzbekistan, and Turkmenistan, and has not established itself as a regional hegemon projecting its values on to others. However, China sees the development of close ties with the Central Asian states and Russia as intrinsic to growth and security in the country's Far West. The view that Chinese growth and security are entwined with Central Asia has engendered a comprehensive Chinese presence in the military-strategic, economic, and political sphere. Beijing's agenda of promoting its economic and security role in Central Asia is attempted realized by policies on the use of force, on economic development, and on multilateral institutions.

Great power politics in Central Asia is often portrayed as a great game with external great powers pursuing national interests in an uncoordinated fashion. Existing studies of China's engagement in Central Asia often focus on its participation in a regional great power game. Zhao (2016) describes Central Asia as unique in the sense that all great powers converge in the region and work bilaterally in a complex pattern without a major cooperative framework. Akiner (2011) highlights that Central Asia is perceived as an arena for great powers seeking advantage and influence and participating in regional strategic competition. Swanström (2014) emphasizes the importance of Chinese–Russian relations for order in Central Asia, arguing that growing rivalry rather than cooperation characterizes the relationship.

This chapter aims to contribute to the debate on China's influence in Central Asia by examining whether Chinese doctrines on military strategy, economic development, and foreign policy shape China's pursuit of its economic and security interests in Central Asia and influence Central Asian objectives and practices. This study does not take the great game metaphor of the nineteenth-century British–Russian political and diplomatic confrontation in Central Asia and Afghanistan as a starting point, since it is based on the assumption that Central Asia's order is characterized by a zero-sum game (Author's interview 2018a).

DOI: 10.4324/9780429059704-8

Instead, the interplay between Chinese doctrines and Beijing's approach to Central Asia is investigated to assess whether China's growing presence is based on efforts to accommodate the regional aspirations of Russia and Central Asian elites.

The chapter uses China's military, economic, and diplomatic historical doctrines (rather than international political theory) to investigate Beijing's Central Asia policy, to emphasize the elements of continuity in China's approach to its neighborhood, and to highlight how its domestic development trajectory and past interaction with other countries shape current regional policies. This approach is derived from analyses of great power behavior within the international society approach, which is also called the English school (Butterfield & Wight 1968; Wight 1978).

The chapter adopts a qualitative rather than a quantitative methodology, relying on semistructured anonymous interviews with open-ended questions. A well-known problem in China and Central Asian studies is the tendency for the regimes to manufacture data for public consumption. Open-ended interviews allowing for a discussion with the interviewees produce knowledge on sensitive issues where official data are either missing or highly unreliable.

The following three sections examine China's Central Asia policy and doctrines regarding the use of force, economic development, and foreign policy. The first section, on China's military-strategic doctrine, outlines the central concept of active defense and how this doctrine influences Chinese approaches to the use of force in Central Asia. The second section, on the economic development doctrine, describes the BRI and examines its impact on China's approach to economic development as a vehicle for advancing its Central Asian interests. The third section, on the foreign policy doctrine, traces the origins of the core concept of peaceful coexistence and its influence on Beijing's institutional preferences in Central Asia. The conclusion discusses whether China's approach to Central Asia advances its own regional interests.

Active defense and the use of force in China's Central Asia policy

China's doctrine of active defense originates from Mao (1936). He used the term 'active defense' to describe China's war against Japan in which a weaker force confronted a more powerful enemy. Active defense was defined as defense for the purpose of counterattacking and taking the offensive. Over the decades, active defense has remained the organizing concept for Chinese military strategy.

Active defense is a self-defensive strategy based on responding to armed provocations to China's national security interests. However, Beijing may act first if an enemy signals the strategic intention to violate China's sovereignty. The aggressor is the side that has taken, or is about to take, action which violates another country's sovereignty at the strategic level; it does not necessarily require shots to have been fired or forces to have moved to occupy another's territory (Academy of Military Science 2013: 48, 144).

Deterrence is a fundamental component of active defense aimed at dissuading, not coercing, an opponent from taking certain actions (Academy of Military Science 2013: 48–49, 107, 145). Deterrence is based on three elements: First, possessing an adequate deterrent force; second, having the will to use that force; and third, ensuring the opponent understands China's capabilities and will (Academy of Military Science 2013: 134–137, 141–145). The will to use military strength is demonstrated through a variety of means, including parades, exercises, exchanges, visits, and equipment tests (Academy of Military Science 2013: 112, 119).

In Beijing's view, Central Asia engenders threats against China from political Islamist groups. China's 2015 defense white paper lists separatist forces for East Turkestan independence as having inflicted serious damage, particularly by escalating violent terrorist activities by the so-called 'East Turkestan independence' forces (Information Office of the State Council 2015). China argues that the Uyghur Muslim minority in China and Central Asia are a main recruiting base for separatists that aim to establish an independent Eastern Turkestan based on Turkish ethnicity. This development is defined by China as a core threat against national sovereignty and unity. Beijing has cooperated with Russia and Central Asian elites on increasing its security and military presence in Central Asia to crack down on peoples that are considered collaborators of separatist terrorists (Author's interview 2018b,c).

Rather than targeting radicalized Uyghurs, China targets the Muslim population as a whole. China has established a reeducation camp system in Chinese Xinjiang and tight surveillance targeting Uyghurs, Kazakhs, Kyrgyz, and Huis, forcing them to abandon the Islamic religion and culture (Ramzy & Buckley 2019). Systematic Chinese surveillance and persecution of ethnic Muslims has been termed a scary engineering project carried out to create uniform human beings loyal to the Chinese Communist Party (Özcan 2019). Uyghurs live primarily in Xinjiang in northwestern China and in Kyrgyzstan, Kazakhstan, and Uzbekistan. China has defined the Uyghurs as key to terrorism and separatism in China's northwest and in Central Asia (Author's interview 2011a). On 10 March 2017, Chinese President Xi called for a 'great wall of iron' facing Central Asia to protect Xinjiang (Pannier 2017).

China's policy on the use of force outside its borders and the areas which it claims is designed to deal with a threat-scenario encompassing terrorist activities, ethnic, religious, border and territorial disputes, and small-scale wars in China's northwestern Central Asian neighborhood (Information Office of the State Council 2015). China's overarching concept for using the military to meet these threats is active defense. The 2015 version of this concept emphasizes that Beijing's pursuit of active defense takes place in the context of a regional framework for security and cooperation (Information Office of the State Council 2015). Consequently, Chinese counterterrorist operations prioritize coordination with Central Asian counterterrorist forces familiar with local conditions. Active defense also involves operating outside of China's territorial borders with governmental consent from the countries that host terrorists. This updated network version of active defense is intended to keep the enemy away from the Chinese heartland by coordinating operations with neighboring states.

Between 2002 and 2019, more than 20 joint antiterrorist exercises have been carried out by China, Russia, Uzbekistan, Kyrgyzstan, Kazakhstan, and Tajikistan, either within or outside the regional institutional Shanghai Cooperation Organization (SCO) framework. The Chinese–Kyrgyz 2002 counterterrorist exercise was the first time China conducted a military exercise with another country (Scobell et al. 2014: 38–40). In 2016, Chinese troops trained with Tajik troops along Tajikistan's eastern border with Afghanistan. The People's Liberation Army (PLA), the People's Armed Police (PAP), and intelligence and security forces participated in multilevel exercises in remote areas where terrorists operate both inside China and in neighboring states (Wallace 2014).

China's attitude toward joint counterterrorist activities in Central Asia became proactive in the 2010s, focusing on military assistance and exercises with Central Asian states. The growing frequency and scale of military assistance and joint exercises can partly be explained by the security vacuum arising from the winding down, from 2012, of the US presence in Central Asia and the International Security Assistance Force (ISAF) in Afghanistan. China has supplied Kyrgyzstan with military equipment since 1999; Kazakhstan has received military assistance since 2002, and Tajikistan since at least 2003. Turkmenistan and Uzbekistan have acquired weapons systems from China (Pannier 2017). In 2016, China established an antiterror grouping encompassing Tajikistan, Pakistan, and Afghanistan (Kucera 2016a).

In 2015, China passed a law that allows the PLA to operate abroad on counterterrorism missions (Martina 2015). China can undertake joint counterterrorist missions in its near abroad on condition of consent from the governments of target states (Author's interview 2015a). In particular, deteriorating socioeconomic welfare combined with rising militant Islamism in the Ferghana Valley poses a threat to unity and security in Kyrgyzstan, Uzbekistan, and Tajikistan. A similar situation applies to Afghanistan and Tajikistan, linking the Central and South Asian theatres together.

This threat is enhanced by the rise of Daesh, which has grown in neighboring Afghanistan and throughout Central Asia while its position in Syria and Iraq has been challenged. According to Russia and China, Daesh has links to Islamists in Central Asia and China, and constitutes a threat to national sovereignty and unity (Author's interview 2018d; Kousary 2017). Although China's military-strategic influence in Central Asia has risen, Russia remains the dominant power. Russian initiatives include Moscow's 2014 pledge to reinforce the combat potential of the Russian airbase in Kant and to supply modern weaponry to Kyrgyzstan's armed forces (*Reuters* 2014). Moreover, in 2015 Russia announced plans to bolster the Afghan–Tajik border with additional helicopters, increasing Russia's military presence in Tajikistan. Russia's largest base outside of Russia is near the capital city of Dushanbe (Putz 2017).

China has grown increasingly concerned about the ability of Central Asian governments to provide security against terrorists. In 2016, a Uyghur suicide bomber rammed the gates of the Chinese embassy in Bishkek, blowing himself up inside the embassy's compound and injuring three people. The incident was seen by China as evidence that Kyrgyz authorities do not provide sufficient protection against terrorist attacks. The terrorist threat has prompted China to assist Kyrgyzstan with border patrols, but also to cooperate more closely with Russia since Moscow is the dominant security provider in the region (Author's interview 2018b, c). In the event of serious destabilization in Central Asia, a possible scenario is a joint Russian–Chinese intervention. A joint intervention can be envisaged for three reasons: First, Russia is reluctant to get involved unilaterally in conflicts between its partners that might create an unwanted image of partiality. Second, China and Russia are both concerned with avoiding spillover from Central Asia into their sovereign territory. Third, Russia needs a partner to help pay for a prolonged intervention (Author's interview 2016a).

Joint exercises between China and neighboring states do not only provide training for the participants, but also aim to intimidate local insurgents and their supporters. This is in line with the active defense doctrine which advocates putting psychological pressure on the opponent and demonstrating willingness to use military strength by means such as visible military exercises. For example, in September 2016, a few weeks after the terrorist attack on the Chinese embassy in Bishkek, the joint Peace Mission SCO exercise kicked off with an antiterror exercise involving much heavier firepower than is usually employed against terrorists. Chinese helicopters practiced using air-to-air missiles (Kucera 2016b). Chinese authorities conducted large military parades in major cities in Xinjiang as a reminder of Chinese strength as a deterrent against Uyghur uprisings (Pannier 2017).

The active defense doctrine emphasizes that military instruments must be coordinated with other social and economic instruments. For instance, the neglection of education and economic redistribution are considered root causes of terrorism (Author's interview 2011b).

China views Central Asia as a region that needs economic development to eradicate terrorism and ethnic violence; this has facilitated growing Chinese economic engagement. The major spheres of cooperation between China and Central Asian elites are investments, high tech industry, transportation, infrastructure, energy, and agriculture (Author's interview 2015b). A focus on these sectors of communication, technology, and resources implies that Beijing is concentrating on expanding China's strategic position by economic means, allowing it to secure a long-term dominant regional role. China has become an important trade partner for Kazakhstan, Uzbekistan, Kyrgyzstan, and Russia.

China's growing military engagement falls on fertile ground in Central Asia. China sees terrorism as a more serious problem than the local Central Asian governments (Author's interview 2018a). The so-called three evils of terrorism, separatism, and religious extremism were not a concern in Central Asia until China became a major regional power (Author's interview 2018d). Nevertheless, authoritarian regimes would like to see more Chinese involvement rather than less because China applies a broad strategy by combining military and nonmilitary instruments, seeking to deter militant Islamists that threaten to delegitimize Central Asian governments within their own population. China's linkage of its national security with the survival of neighboring regimes enhances the likelihood of effective deterrence and, if necessary, prospective warfighting efforts. These initiatives assist the Central Asian governments in building their own military and security forces. Due to their status as former Soviet republics, these capacities have formerly been neglected. China's provision of economic projects in return for enhanced security help fund indigenous capacities, although Beijing tends to provide tangible nonlethal goods such as tents rather than the cash or weapons preferred by Central Asian governments (Author's interview 2018a,c).

China's initiatives help the incumbents remain in power in circumstances where their socioeconomic development remains inadequate to provide improved living standards and hence legitimacy. One example of this is Uzbekistan, where counterterrorist measures have entailed restrictions on freedom of expression in civil society, but have only led to negligible popular protests. This is at least partly due to the extensive power and reach of the security services, and because a few activists' stand is unlikely to generate a snowball of protest that would cause the authorities to withdraw from strong repression (Stevens 2010: 369).

Thus, traditional Soviet-era suspicions of Chinese plans to dominate Central Asia without consideration for indigenous interests have, over a period of 15 years, gradually been supplemented, although not replaced, by recognition among Central Asia's political leaders that China assists the regimes in regaining legitimacy and in preventing any viable opposition to their power from developing (Peyrouse 2016).

BRI and economic development in China's Central Asia policy

The BRI is China's development, communication, and infrastructure strategy for how to establish interregional networks promoting economic growth, peace and stability, and Chinese interests. With the BRI, China plans to link more than 60 countries stretching from Beijing to Europe, through Central Asia, the Middle East, and Africa, in a modern version of the onshore and offshore Silk Roads. The strategy puts China at the center of a global network of interconnections (Guidetti 2015: 43).

The BRI is a major initiative of China's Xi administration. It is a long-term project not intended to have a grand launch (Author's interview 2015c). The main objectives of the BRI include creating an alternative to the liberal free trade projects of Western states and institutions, expanding China's overseas markets, increasing Chinese sources of energy supplies, and promoting financial stability by defining principles of conduct at a time when China is increasingly exposed to financial risk (Think tank scholar 2015). The BRI encompasses private market-driven projects and economic development projects, with the latter type dominating the Central Asian part of the initiative. The objective of political and military stability to protect authoritarian regimes against armed unrest is key to China's willingness to allocate resources to economically unviable regional projects.

The BRI has been criticized for not having a clear set of rules to guide activities and clarify its purpose, objectives, and instruments (Think tank scholar 2015). Other voices have pointed out that BRI is a label for ongoing projects rather than grand new projects (Author's interview 2015d). While this may be true, labelling matters because it holds China accountable for contributing to economic growth and development. Thereby, the BRI clarifies the standards to use when assessing whether China performs as a responsible power. Even without elaborate principles, China still needs to demonstrate its commitment to implementing BRI projects in order to attract market and state actors.

In Central Asia, the BRI encompasses the establishment of railways, roads, communication facilities, and other infrastructure projects. The projects help to strengthen the control of regimes over their territory and peoples, and promote economic development. The initiative constitutes a political superstructure to China's global economic role, presenting governance Chinese-style as a tool to promote peace and stability and not just China's national interests. Central Asia is the part of the continental silk road where China has the most strategic freedom of action due to a low level of military-strategic US involvement and cordial relations with Russia, allowing China to operate in the region without serious challenges to its initiatives.

The test cases of the BRI are Pakistan and Kazakhstan. They are safe choices because China already has considerable interaction with these two neighboring states. Moreover, these cases help promote an important Chinese BRI interest, which is to advance economic development in China's weakly developed Western region, including Xinjiang. The flagship project of the Pakistani BRI initiative is the China Pakistan Economic Corridor (CPEC), a plan that was first on the drawing board in the 1950s. The objectives of development, economic growth, and stability are pursued by building transport, developing energy and communication infrastructure such as fiber optic cables and satellites, and promoting economic interaction and trade. The main projects are the expansion of the port in Pakistani Gwadar and Pakistan's energy, road, and railway infrastructure (Markey & West 2016).

The other test case, Kazakhstan, is where Chinese President Xi announced the onshore part of the BRI in 2013. Kazakhstan is currently China's biggest trading partner in Central Asia. Almost three decades ago, China National Petroleum Corporation (CNPC) had already begun investing in oil fields in Kazakhstan. CNPC is now a dominant foreign producer in Kazakhstan, accounting for about one-quarter of the company's overseas production of 2.46 million barrels of oil as of 2014. In addition, in cooperation with KazMunaiGaz, CNPC constructed China's first cross-border pipeline which opened in 2006. China uses pipelines to access oil from Kazakhstan and areas near the Caspian and Black Seas. China increasingly invests in natural resources, infrastructure, and communications, such as hydropower, gas, uranium, and copper ore (Brown 2015: 76; Downs 2015).

China and Central Asia both have large stakes in developing mutual economic relations. Uzbekistan, which was initially reluctant about Chinese economic interaction, was quick to embrace Chinese investments. A similarly reluctant Turkmenistan has become the largest supplier of gas to China (Zhao 2016: 179). China has invested in all Central Asian countries to establish the infrastructure and communication needed to realize the BRI's aim of linking Xinjiang and Europe via railways and roads in Central Asia. However, China has also invested in areas such as the neglected banking sector. The economies are complementary rather than competitive since China can import natural resources and export consumer products at low prices that are suitable both for the majority, with low living standards, and for the rising consumption of the middle and upper classes in Central Asia (Peyrouse 2016). Not surprisingly, trade between China and Central Asia is on a fast-growing trajectory, rising from US$527 million in 1992 to US$40 billion in 2011 (Alam 2014: 24–25).

China's swiftly growing role in Central Asian economies has profound implications for regional economics and politics. One issue is rising competition between Russia and China, as relatively expensive Russian products become unaffordable for many Central Asians. Russia has reservations about the BRI and its consequences for Russia's dominant regional status. Russia has its own economic integration pet project, the Eurasian Economic Union (EEU) which was established as a free market initiative in 2014 by Russia, Kazakhstan, and Belarus. The EEU now also encompasses Armenia and Kyrgyzstan. China and Russia have agreed to coordinate the activities of the BRI and the EEU. This agreement has mostly yet to be implemented. However, Russia's economy has also experienced significant structural problems. Moscow recognizes that Chinese economic activities benefit an ailing Russian economy unable on its own to bring Central Asia on a positive development trajectory and secure regional peace and stability, particularly as militant Islamist threats grow. Hence, Moscow increasingly views China's BRI as economic opportunity (Author's interview 2016b, c; Trenin 2015).

The Central Asian economies have embraced the BRI as an economic opportunity despite uncertainty as to whether China's economic engagement will benefit them rather than China itself. One issue is water shortages in Central Asia. China is an upstream country for many Asian rivers. Economic development in Xinjiang has increased China's diversion of water from the Irtysh and Illy Rivers, engendering water shortages in Kazakhstan (Chugh 2017). Chinese economic development projects in Central Asia indirectly contribute to water conflicts because they change the need for supplies such as electricity. Cheap Chinese products influence the economic structures in Central Asia because local produce is increasingly unable to compete with Chinese imports. Capital- and labor-intensive sectors are challenged while those in the energy industry benefit (Brown 2015: 78). Adding to these concerns is the worry that Chinese investments in transportation infrastructure will mainly bring economic benefits to Europe whereas Central Asia might end up primarily as a transit route (Putz 2017). Moreover, China's economic influence means that approximately half the external debt of Central Asian countries is owed to China, making them prospective dependents on Beijing (Author's interview 2018a). Furthermore, Chinese BRI initiatives influence the regional balance of power, unintentionally encouraging revivals of regional rivalries, for example between Kazakhstan and Uzbekistan. Kazakhstan holds a special place in the BRI, whereas Uzbekistan and Kyrgyzstan push for the inclusion of projects such as the stalled China–Kyrgyzstan–Uzbekistan railway network (Putz 2017). Relations between Kazakhstan and Kyrgyzstan have taken a downward turn due to trade quarrels. The conflict peaked in late 2017, when Kyrgyzstan rejected US$100 million in aid from Kazakhstan intended to help Kyrgyzstan update its trade standards to EEU level. Moreover, Kyrgyzstan accused Kazakhstan of interfering in its presidential elections. Kazakhstan responded by adopting strict border controls (Author's interview 2018c).

Traditional fears of Chinese migration and its potential influence on Central Asia's demography have been ameliorated in recent years, although concern about Chinese immigration is deeply rooted in the region. In ancient times, China's coming to Central Asia was seen as the end of the world. During the tsar and Soviet periods, the borders with China were closed (Author's interview 2018e). This prolonged isolation from China has fostered fears of the large neighbor. At times, anti-Chinese sentiments are aired in public. For example, it is very difficult for Chinese nationals to get visas to Central Asia compared to the visa process for nationals of other neighboring countries such as Japan (Author's interview 2018d). The 2016 land reforms in Kazakhstan, allowing foreigners to buy land in the country, spurred anti-Chinese protests against the prospects of a growing permanent Chinese presence. However, these protests are at least as much directed against corrupt Kazakh government officials unable to enforce rules about issues such as pesticide control and employment (Author's interview 2018f). China's rise in Central Asia comes not just with economic opportunities, but also with more corruption and inequality (Author's interview 2018d). However, China is mainly considered an opportunity for development in a region where it is the only major trade and investment alternative to Russia. China's heavy investments in Xinjiang combined with its BRI have a spillover effect on investments in Central Asia which makes China the most important economic power in the region.

The BRI is already an integrated part of Central Asia's economies, with many completed or ongoing infrastructure projects and with numerous Central Asians going to China to study (Author's interview 2018f). China is cultivating a pro-Chinese elite of well-educated influential Central Asians to protect Chinese investments (Author's interview 2018g), but is cautious not to appear as a dominant power. For example, in contrast to Russia, China presents its development projects as offers which you are welcome to join rather than forced to take part in (Author's interview 2018h). Adding to the increasingly positive image of China is the experience that most Chinese do not settle in Central Asia to any great extent, making people-to-people interaction evasive and temporary. As living standards rise in China, this tendency becomes even more pronounced. Even if many Central Asians remain skeptical of China, they still focus on their children learning Mandarin, which opens the door to economic opportunity (Author's interview 2018e, f, i; Korolev 2015).

As is the case with its military-strategic engagement, China's expanding role as a source of trade and investments in Central Asia is increasingly considered a force for socioeconomic development that is indispensable. This is despite the growing corruption, environmental problems, and inequality that comes with Beijing's involvement, as well as reservations about the extent to which Central Asia will benefit from the BRI. Overall, complementary economies and agreement between Chinese and Central Asian elites that economic development is a precondition for long-term stability have engendered a predominantly positive outlook on China's regional economic engagement.

Peaceful coexistence and institutional preferences in China's Central Asia policy

Peaceful coexistence is China's grand strategy concept in the sense that it defines China's position in the world and the role of other actors in Beijing's pursuit of its national interests. Beijing defines peaceful coexistence as mutual respect for sovereignty and territorial integrity, mutual nonaggression, noninterference in each other's internal affairs, equality and mutual benefit, and peaceful coexistence in developing diplomatic relations and economic and cultural exchanges with other countries (Constitution of the People's Republic of China 1982). In China's diplomatic practice, these principles have entailed the promotion of international institutional frameworks that are able to accommodate similar and different interests and outlooks. This emerges in practical politics as policy coordination founded in absolute sovereignty and noninterference. Beijing's institutional approach facilitates states focusing on pursuing national interests derived from individual development models rather than on extensive multilateral cooperation (Odgaard 2012: 75–83).

Following the establishment of the People's Republic of China in 1949, Chairman of the Chinese Communist Party Mao based his concept of peaceful coexistence on Lenin's belief that it was possible to establish a third force in the international system that could challenge the dominance of the Eastern and Western Blocs (Tsou & Halperin 1965). On this basis, Premier Zhou launched the Five Principles of Peaceful Coexistence in 1953 (Tzou 1990: 30; Adie 1972). Gradually, the principles became cornerstones of Chinese foreign policy.

During the Cold War, peaceful coexistence came to define an alternative Chinese version of world order that set it apart from the United States and the Soviet Union. At the time, China was not a great power able to contribute to, or alter, world order in any fundamental way (Yahuda 2011: 62). By contrast, after the Cold War China has gradually become sufficiently influential that it attempts to implement its coexistence version of world order. Since 1998, peaceful coexistence has been included in all Chinese government white papers on national defense. The principles of peaceful coexistence are also the basic elements of China's 'peaceful rise' and 'peaceful development' used to characterize Beijing's foreign policy vision in less confrontational terms (Wang 2006).

China sees the UN system as fundamental for providing legitimacy to state actions. According to Beijing, the identification of international security threats and how to address these threats must comply with the UN system. China encourages regional and functional organizations, such as the Shanghai Cooperation Organization (SCO), to play leading roles in determining when there is a threat to international peace and security and the course of action to take when threats are identified (Odgaard 2013). In addition, China has reservations about using force, either in the form of sanctions or armed force, without consent from target states, especially under the UN Charter's Chapter VII. If some form of external intervention to address a global security issue cannot be averted, China advocates making use of nonmilitary means of dialogue and negotiation based on governmental consent. According to Beijing, it is detrimental to stability if states are excluded from international interaction due to their domestic political systems. Instead, the international community should work with the political institutions of target states, however weak or flawed these institutions may be, to help engender economic development. In China's view, economic development is a precondition of stable political institutions. China is reluctant to adopt punitive measures against target states and supports the adoption of measures meant to assist the target government in conflict management, stabilization, and development initiatives (Foot 2016: 940–941).

Central Asia is an important region for China's peaceful coexistence diplomacy because the authoritarian regional governments are looking for means of enhancing their legitimacy despite their flawed record regarding human rights and democracy. China is seen as a model that they can learn from because it has managed to become a key influence in multilateral institutions despite its refusal to implement the basic civil and political rights of the UN Charter. China legitimizes this behavior by arguing that stability should be prioritized over civil and political rights to protect the long-term welfare of peoples. China's policy on regional territorial dispute settlement has provided a chance to demonstrate that stability is a top priority, and that stability requires working with existing political institutions on the basis of mutual respect for sovereignty and territorial integrity, nonaggression, and mutual regime consent. In line with these principles, China refrained from taking advantage of the implosion of the Soviet Union by negotiating dispute settlements in its favor. China's border agreement with Kazakhstan gave China 22% of disputed areas, and its border agreement with Kyrgyzstan resulted in Chinese jurisdiction over 32% of disputed areas. In the 1999 and 2002 agreements with Tajikistan, China received only 4% of the 28,430 square kilometers under dispute (Fravel 2005: 79; Fravel 2008: 160–166). Between 1997 and 2005, China settled its border disputes with Russia, roughly dividing the territory 50-50 (Akihiro 2004: 97; *Xinhua* 2005).

Chinese Premier Li enunciated the principles of peaceful coexistence as the framework governing border negotiations between China and Central Asia in 1994 when he visited Uzbekistan, Turkmenistan, Kyrgyzstan, Kazakhstan, and Mongolia. The border settlements that were negotiated in subsequent years formed the basis for creating the Shanghai Five, an institutional framework to build confidence in the military sphere along the borders of the participating countries that held its first summit in 1996. In addition to China, it included Russia, Kazakhstan, Kyrgyzstan, and Tajikistan. Apart from providing a platform for bilateral border negotiations, the Shanghai Five also included a joint pledge to oppose the three forces of separatism, terrorism, and Islamic extremism. China succeeded in linking Chinese security interests in Xinjiang with those of Russia and Central Asia; this has legitimized a regional crackdown on Uyghurs, which China considers the predominant source of the three security threats (Yahuda 2011: 200–201; Cheng 2011: 634–635). In 2001, the framework became the SCO, and Uzbekistan became a member state. The SCO vowed to embed its work in the UN framework and its principle of noninterference in the domestic affairs of other states, transforming itself into a treaty-based institution (Declaration by the Heads of the Member States of the Shanghai Cooperation Organization 2002). By June 2017, India and Pakistan had become SCO member states, and Afghanistan, Belarus, Iran, and Mongolia are observer states.

The SCO's principal usefulness is as a flexible platform for policy coordination. Policy coordination is not an instrument for enhanced multilateral cooperation; instead, it keeps a lid on potential interstate conflicts and facilitates bilateral agreements. The SCO provides a good example of peaceful coexistence that involves defining the principles of right and wrong international conduct and establishing limited multilateral policy coordination to contain conflicts and facilitate bilateral agreements. Peaceful coexistence allows states to focus on pursuing national interests, but the doctrine stops short of encouraging extensive cooperation. Even in the area of terrorism, which is a priority for all member states, very little cooperation has emerged. The SCO Regional Anti-Terrorist Structure (RATS) has not encouraged much activity (Author's interview 2018a).

Beijing has attempted to steer the SCO's activities toward increasing economic cooperation. However, Moscow continues to stress security, military, and geopolitical aspects. A major reason for this is that Russia and the Central Asian states have no desire to become economic dependents on China.

At the same time, Russia's and Central Asia's political leaders are aware that China invests less than it promises, or at least is slow to deliver on promises (Putz 2017). This is one reason that progress regarding the economic aspect of SCO has been negligible. Moreover, Moscow has established its own institutional arrangements. Apart from the economic free trade institution (the EEU), Moscow has created a mutual defense arrangement, Collective Security Treaty Organization (CSTO), which encompasses Russia, Armenia, Belarus, Kazakhstan, Kyrgyzstan, Tajikistan, and, until 2012, Uzbekistan. Moscow has extended security guarantees to most of Central Asia since 2003. Despite a Rapid Reaction Force of around 4,500 soldiers, the notion of a distinct CSTO military capability is a fiction. Nevertheless, CSTO has allowed Moscow to promote its military and security agenda in

Central Asia, thereby facilitating Russia's continued military-strategic regional dominance (Gvosdev & Marsh 2014: 184–185).

At the bilateral level, China and Russia signed a military cooperation agreement for 2017–2020 in June 2017. Russia has made a similar agreement with India, which is increasingly on a collision course with China on regional economic, strategic, and border delimitation issues. Moscow cooperates with Beijing while demonstrating that it has alternative strategic partners to China. Russia is hedging against China, determined not to become a junior partner but remain on equal footing by avoiding becoming too dependent on Beijing.

Despite Russia's guarded approach to China, seen from a Central Asian perspective the strategic partnership between Beijing and Moscow is on an upward trend, increasingly enabling them to dominate the region – as long as they manage to coordinate their policies to avoid a relationship dominated by their rivalry. The Russian–Chinese partnership raises concerns in Central Asia about an emerging quasi-alliance within the SCO between the two regional great powers focused on control over local elites rather than on building a partnership focused on regional development (Peyrouse 2016). Moscow and Beijing divert the SCO agenda away from economic development cooperation and toward the Chinese–Russian concern about regional security (Author's interview 2018c). Central Asian leaders see Russia's alternative institutional arrangements and alignment with partners outside of Central Asia as their best bet for avoiding too much asymmetrical dependency on China (Torbakov 2016: 262). Such dependency would result in the dominance of China's preference for using institutions as platforms to establish cooperation outside of the multilateral framework. Beijing's institutional approach is to the advantage of the stronger power rather than the weaker Central Asian states.

The SCO has been useful as a platform for policy coordination on counterterrorism and for establishing cooperation between the member states and affiliates outside of the SCO framework. This approach is in line with China's peaceful coexistence approach of policy coordination, with a view to using institutions as platforms for pursuing interests and relationships outside of the institutional framework. Although increasingly influential, China's institutional approach does not dominate Central Asia; this is primarily because Russia provides alternative institutions, allowing Moscow to continue to set the regional agenda alongside Beijing.

Implications of Chinese-style military, economic, and foreign policy doctrines for Central Asian order

China has successfully positioned itself as a leading economic and security actor, making Chinese interests a main Central Asian concern. Beijing has achieved this objective by adopting flexible approaches that facilitate deterrence, connectedness, and policy coordination, contributing to a regional environment in which Chinese interests are central. However, China's approaches do not address fundamental issues affected by its policies, including a changing regional balance of power engendering growing strategic conflict, mounting inequality issues detracting from regime legitimacy, and institutional rivalry over the central frameworks and methods for regional cooperation and conflict management.

China's doctrines of active defense, BRI, and peaceful coexistence primarily establish the preconditions for cooperation, rather than actually facilitating engagement in extensive cooperation. Whether these doctrines establish deterrence capabilities, regional connectivity, or policy coordination, they are highly flexible regarding the scope and range of interaction with the other states involved in their implementation. This characteristic explains, at least in part, why it has been comparatively easy for the traditional Central Asian power, Russia, to accommodate the growing influence of China and adopt a largely positive attitude toward China's approaches to military, economic, and political regional engagement: China's doctrines allow for the existence of supplementary approaches without necessarily producing rivalry. Similarly, the doctrines are suitable for indigenous Central Asian powers and their considerable Soviet legacy, allowing regimes to remain focused on Russia as the principal source of military, economic, and political governance. China's flexible approaches, focusing on providing preconditions rather than requiring integration with other actors, have allowed Beijing to implement its own approaches to the region alongside those of Russia, inviting Central Asian states to participate without limiting their access to alternatives. For example, Turkmenistan has only scantly embraced China's initiatives, preferring to look to states such as Iran and Russia for extensive foreign relations.

One major downside to China's regional imprint is that its approach to Central Asia facilitates the persistence of potentially dysfunctional structures and patterns. For example, civil society continues to be stifled by authoritarian regimes that are reluctant to use popular feedback as a source of policy adjustment and long-term legitimacy. Arguably, this unwillingness to support civil society enhances the ability of militant and separatist Islamists to recruit followers among dissatisfied groups, who are encouraged to see violence and independent political authority as the only feasible approach to political influence. In addition, China's ability to accommodate Russian approaches to Central Asia engenders the possibility of their comanagement of the region, and with that comes a tendency to protect their interests rather than those of the Central Asian states. This tendency produces a risk that Central Asia might end up as a transit route, rather than a focal point for economic development. It also risks leaving Central Asian states with no means of addressing issues such as water shortages, environmental degradation, human rights violations, and socioeconomic inequality, as these concerns do not significantly affect Chinese and Russian interests.

The 2020 COVID-19 pandemic underscored the asymmetrical dependency of Chinese–Central Asian relations. Developments such as falling hydrocarbon prices and the economic downturn resulting from the global lockdowns to control the pandemic have pushed regional states such as Turkmenistan, Tajikistan, Kyrgyzstan, and Kazakhstan further into the Chinese economic orbit. For example, in April 2020 Kyrgyzstan asked China for debt relief as it struggled with the economic costs of the pandemic. In the same month, Kazakhstan protested an article published on a Chinese website stating that Kazakhstan is located on territories that historically belong to China. The incidents demonstrate that Central Asia is likely to face increasingly coercive and China-centric policies from Beijing as China's economic and political power in the region continues to grow.

References

Academy of Military Science (2013) *The Science of Military Strategy*, 2nd edn. Beijing: Military Science Press.

Adie, W.A.C. (1972) '"One World" Restored? Sino-American Relations on a New Footing', *Asian Survey* 12(5): 365–385.

Akihiro, I. (2004) 'An Inquiry for New Thinking on the Border Dispute: Backgrounds of "Historic Success" for the Sino-Russian Negotiations', *Slavic Eurasian Studies* 6: 95–114.

Akiner, S. (2011) 'Silk Roads, Great Games and Central Asia', *Asian Affairs* 42(3): 391–402.

Alam, M.M. (2014) 'China's Changing Strategic Engagements in Central Asia', *The Journal of Central Asian Studies* 21(1): 13–36.

Author's interview (2011a) Chinese Think Tank Personnel, Beijing, P.R.China, May.

Author's interview (2011b) Chinese Authorities in the Counterterrorism Field, Beijing, P.R.China, May.

Author's interview (2015a) High-Ranking PLA Officer, Beijing, P.R.China, January and October.

Author's interview (2015b) Chen Yurong, China Institute of International Studies, Beijing, P.R.China, October 13.

Author's interview (2015c) University Scholar, Beijing, P.R.China, October 15.

Author's interview (2015d) PLA Officer, Beijing, P.R.China, October 19.

Author's interview (2016a) Vasily Kashin, National Research University Higher School of Economics, Moscow, Russia, April 7.

Author's interview (2016b) Arkady Dubnov, Political Analyst and Central Asia Expert, Moscow, Russia, April 4.

Author's interview (2016c) Alexander Gabuev, Carnegie, Moscow, Russia, April 5.

Author's interview (2018a) Kemel Toktomushev, University of Central Asia, Bishkek, Kyrgyzstan, January 15.

Author's interview (2018b) Emil Dzhuraev, The American University of Central Asia, Bishkek, Kyrgyzstan, January 12.

Author's interview (2018c) Joldosh Osmonov, Center for Political and Legal Studies, Bishkek, Kyrgyzstan, January 12.

Author's interview (2018d) Nargis Kassenova, KIMEP University, Almaty, Kazakhstan, January 9.

Author's interview (2018e) Azhar Serikkaliyeva, Al-Farabi Kazakh National University, Almaty, Kazakhstan, January 10.

Author's interview (2018f) Yevgeniy Khon, International Office for Migration, Almaty, Kazakhstan, January 8.

Author's interview (2018g) Dossym Satpaev, Risks Assessment Group, Almaty, Kazakhstan, January 8.

Author's interview (2018h) Kairat Moldashev, Narxoz University, Almaty, Kazakhstan, January 8.

Author's interview (2018i) Liga Rudzite, Tallinn University of Technology, January 13.

Brown, R. (2015) 'Where Will the New Silk Road Lead? The Effects of Chinese Investment and Migration in Xinjiang and Central Asia', *Columbia University Journal of Politics & Society* 69–91. Accessed February 17, 2020. https://doi.org/10.7916/D8KH0N9C.

Butterfield, H. and Wight, M. (eds.) (1968) *Diplomatic Investigations: Essays in the Theory of International Politics*. Cambridge, MA: Harvard University Press.

Cheng, J.Y.S. (2011) 'The Shanghai Co-operation Organisation: China's Initiative in Regional Institution Building', *Journal of Contemporary Asia* 41(4): 632–656.

Chugh, N. (2017) 'Will Central Asia Water Wars Derail China's Silk Road?', *The Diplomat*, March 24. Accessed February 22, 2018. http://thediplomat.com/2017/03/will-central-asia-water-wars-derail-chinas-silk-road/.

Constitution of the People's Republic of China (1982) 'Preamble', December 4. Accessed February 22, 2018. http://en.people.cn/constitution/constitution.html.

Declaration by the Heads of the Member States of the Shanghai Cooperation Organization (2002) June 7, St. Petersburg, Russia. Washington, DC: Cross-Strait Security Initiative, Center for Strategic and International Studies. Accessed July 25, 2017. file:///regional_2002_shanghaicooperationstatement%20(1).pdf.

Downs, E. (2015) 'Mission Mostly Accomplished: China's Energy Trade and Investment Along the Silk Road Economic Belt', *China Brief* 15(6), March 19. Accessed February 22, 2018. https://jamestown.org/program/mission-mostly-accomplished-chinas-energy-trade-and-investment-along-the-silk-road-economic-belt/.

Foot, R. (2016) 'The State, Development, and Humanitarianism: China's Shaping of the Trajectory of R2P', in A.J. Bellamy and T. Dunne (eds) *The Oxford Handbook of the Responsibility to Protect*. Oxford: Oxford University Press, pp. 932–947.

Fravel, M.T. (2005) 'Regime Insecurity and International Cooperation: Explaining China's Compromises in Territorial Disputes', *International Security* 30(2): 46–83.

Fravel, M.T. (2008) *Strong Borders, Secure Nation: Cooperation and Conflict in China's Territorial Disputes*. Princeton: Princeton University Press.

Guidetti, A. (2015) 'Confront or Accommodate? The Maritime Silk Road Will Test US–China Rivalries', *Global Asia* 10(3): 42–47.

Gvosdev, N.K. and Marsh, C. (2014) *Russian Foreign Policy: Interests, Vectors, and Sectors*. London: SAGE.

Information Office of the State Council (2015) *China's Military Strategy*. Beijing. Accessed February 21, 2018. http://eng.mod.gov.cn/Database/WhitePapers/2015–05/26/content_4586688.htm#.

Korolev, A. (2015) 'The Strategic Alignment Between Russia and China: Myths and Reality', *The ASAN Forum*, April 30. Accessed February 22, 2018. http://www.theasanforum.org/the-strategic-alignment-between-russia-and-china-myths-and-reality/.

Kousary, H. (2017) 'The Growing Threat from Non-State Actors: Cooperation between Afghanistan and Pakistan as an Effective Counter-Military Measure', speech delivered at the RDDC-RPI Joint Seminar on Bilateral Reconciliation: Opportunities and Challenges, Kabul, Afghanistan, May 16–17.

Kucera, J. (2016a) 'China Proposes New Central Asian Military Alliance', *eurasianet.org*, March 21. Accessed February 21, 2018. http://www.eurasianet.org/node/77896.

Kucera, J. (2016b) 'SCO Starts First Ever Military Exercises in Kyrgyzstan', *eurasianet.org*, September 19. Accessed February 21, 2018. http://www.eurasianet.org/node/80566.

Mao, Z. (1936) *Problems of Strategy in China's Revolutionary War*. Shensi: Red Army College. Accessed February 21, 2018. https://www.marxists.org/reference/archive/mao/selected-works/volume-1/mswv1_12.htm.

Markey, D.S. and West, J. (2016) 'Behind China's Gambit in Pakistan', *Expert Brief*, New York: Council on Foreign Relations, May 12. Accessed February 22, 2018. https://www.cfr.org/expert-brief/behind-chinas-gambit-pakistan.

Martina, M (2015) 'Draft Chinese Law Paves Way for Counter-Terror Operations Abroad', *Reuters*, February 27. Accessed February 21, 2018. https://www.reuters.com/article/us-china-military/draft-chinese-law-paves-way-for-counter-terror-operations-abroad-idUSKBN0LV0PN20150227.

Odgaard, L. (2012) *China and Coexistence: Beijing's National Security Strategy for the Twenty-First Century*. Washington, DC: Woodrow Wilson Center Press/Johns Hopkins University Press.

Odgaard, L. (2013) 'Peaceful Coexistence Strategy and China's Diplomatic Power', *The Chinese Journal of International Politics* 22(82): 233–272.

Özcan, G.B. (2019) 'E-Otokrasi ve Çin'in Toplama Kampları' [E-autocracy and China's Concentration Camps], *Birikim*, May 18. Accessed December 19, 2019. https://www.birikimdergisi.com/guncel-yazilar/9514/e-otokrasi-ve-cin-in-toplama-kamplari#.XekmHeg3mUl.

Pannier, B. (2017) 'A New Chinese Interest In Central Asian Security', *Radio Free Europe Radio Liberty*, March 30. Accessed February 21, 2018. https://www.rferl.org/a/china-central-asia-security-uyghurs-russia/28400327.html.

Peyrouse, S (2016) 'Caught Between Two Big Powers? Central Asia Under the Weight of Russian and Chinese Influence', *The Asan Forum*, December 16. Accessed February 22, 2018. http://www.theasanforum.org/caught-between-two-big-powers-central-asia-under-the-weight-of-russian-and-chinese-influence/.

Putz, C. (2017) 'Russia's Putin Finds Time for Central Asia Amid Birthday Celebrations', *The Diplomat*, May 17. Accessed February 21, 2018. http://thediplomat.com/2017/05/whats-next-for-the-belt-and-road-in-central-asia/.

Ramzy, A. and Buckley, C. (2019) 'The Xinjiang Papers: "Absolutely No Mercy": Leaked Files Expose How China Organized Mass Detentions of Muslims', *The New York Times*, November 16. Accessed December 19, 2019. https://www.nytimes.com/interactive/2019/11/16/world/asia/china-xinjiang-documents.html.

Reuters (2014) 'Russia to Beef Up Military Presence in Kyrgyzstan – Defense Minister', February 4. Accessed February 21, 2018. https://www.rt.com/politics/russia-kant-kyrgyzstan-military-628.

Scobell, A., Ratner, E. and Beckley, M. (2014) *China's Strategy Toward South and Central Asia, Research Report*. Washington, DC: Rand.

Stevens, D (2010) 'Osama or the Georges: Shifting Threats and State Policy Towards Civil Society in Uzbekistan', *Development and Change* 41(2): 355–374.

Swanström, N. (2014) 'Sino-Russian Relations at the Start of the New Millennium in Central Asia and Beyond', *Journal of Contemporary China* 23(87): 480–497.

Think tank scholar (2015) Speech, Beijing, P.R.China, October 12.

Torbakov, I. (2016) 'Managing Imperial Peripheries: Russia and China in Central Asia', in T. Fingar (ed) *The New Great Game: China and South and Central Asia in the Era of Reform*. Stanford: Stanford University Press, pp. 240–272.

Trenin, D. (2015) *From Greater Europe to Greater Asia: The Sino-Russian Entente*. Moscow: Carnegie.

Tsou, T. and Halperin, M.H. (1965) 'Mao Tse-Tung's Revolutionary Strategy and Peking's International Behavior', *American Political Science Review* 59(1): 80–99.

Tzou, B.N. (1990) *China and International Law: The Boundary Disputes*. New York: Praeger.

Wallace, T. (2014) 'China and the Regional Counter-Terrorism Structure: An Organizational Analysis', *Asian Survey* 10(3): 199–220.

Wang, J. (2006) 'Peaceful Rise: A Discourse in China', talking points, public speech, Cold War Studies Center: The London School of Economics and Political Science, London, U.K., May 8. Accessed July 25, 2017. http://www.lse.ac.uk/IDEAS/EVENTS/Past/events2006.aspx?from_serp=1.

Wight, M. (1978) *Power Politics*. Leicester: Leicester University Press.

Xinhua (2005) 'China, Russia Solve All Disputes Along Shared Border', June 2, reprinted in *People's Daily Online*, June 3. Accessed February 22, 2018. http://en.people.cn/200506/03/eng20050603_188218.html.

Yahuda, M. (2011) *The International Politics of the Asia-Pacific, 1945–1995*, 3rd edn. London: Routledge.

Zhao, H. (2016) 'Central Asia in Chinese Strategic Thinking', in T. Fingar (ed) *The New Great Game: China and South and Central Asia in the Era of Reform*. Stanford: Stanford University Press, pp. 171–189.

7

The role of context in Chinese HUMINT (human source collection) intelligence

Jim Schnell

The role of context in cross-cultural interactions

This report will stress the role of context in cross-cultural interactions. This will be used as the foundation for conveying the theoretical underpinnings for what context is, why it is relevant and how China and the United States differ regarding context. Throughout this development the reader should consider how this holds importance for the HUMINT (human source collection) activities conducted by China and the United States. That distinction will be further developed later in this report. The exchange of meaning in China, involving an American, poses unique challenges for both the US and Chinese perspectives. It requires not only understanding the particular phenomenon being addressed but also the cultural context within which the topic exists. In *Chinese Perspectives in Rhetoric and Communication*, Ray Heisey (2000: xix) stresses how the interaction of Eastern and Western communication perspectives should emphasize an understanding of the cultures within which these communicative practices exist. Such a stress can initially consider the relevance of language.

Devito (1986: 148) states that language is 'a social institution designed, modified, and extended (some purists might even say distorted) to meet the ever changing needs of the culture or subculture'. The element of context is important in this understanding. White (1984: 276) explains:

> As we grow up in the world, our experience is formed by the language in which it is presented and talked about, and this language becomes so much a part of the mind as to seem a part of nature.

Ochs emphasizes this degree of context more strongly in saying that 'language is the major vehicle for accomplishing communication, language functions both *in* context and *as* context, simultaneously constructing and being constructed by the social occasion' (1979: 206).

Chinese people, and the Chinese language which reflects the culture, are less likely to communicate ideas in a direct manner in comparison to people in the United States. Murray posits that 'within Chinese conversational style is a tendency to respond in terms of expectations, goals, even models rather than mundane facts' (1983: 13). The important

 DOI: 10.4324/9780429059704-9

role of context cannot be overstated when the aforementioned is paralleled with the system of government in China. Murray further states, 'China's governance involves both the overt system of public institutions with whose members we interact rather easily and the more shadowy system of political and security organs whose work is not open …' (1983: 10). This process is defined as high-context communication.

Hall (1984) states that high-context cultures must provide a context and setting and let the point evolve. Low-context cultures are much more direct and to the point. Andersen (1987: 23) explains that 'languages are some of the most explicit communication systems but the Chinese language is an implicit high context system'. Andersen goes on to explain that 'explicit forms of communication such as verbal codes are more prevalent in low context cultures such as the United States and Northern Europe' (1987: 24). So, in consideration of the aforementioned, it should be clear that the Chinese tend to operate using a high-context perspective for conveying and receiving meaning. Conversely, it should be clear that Americans tend to operate using a low-context perspective for conveying and receiving meaning. As such a foundation exists for significant confusion and conflict, not just for advancing differing objectives, but for even achieving a common understanding of what the issues are.

I offer a minor footnote to the previous paragraph. The reader should observe I indicated that the Chinese and Americans 'tend' to operate in such ways. It should be understood that there are exceptions. That is, this is not a pure science. There are some Americans that lean toward high-context approaches and there are some Chinese who lean toward low-context approaches. The point is that, for the most part, Chinese (and the Chinese government) will practice high-context approaches and Americans (and the US government) will practice low-context approaches. This is a fundamental premise of this chapter in that it is offered as a foundation for understanding, not just differences between US and Chinese perspectives for communicating, but also differences between US and Chinese approaches for conducting HUMINT operations. As such, it is imperative that the reader grasps this fundamental distinction. It is a simple distinction but it has complex ramifications regarding the differing world views that are a foundation for this distinction and the differing world views that emanate from this distinction.

There are contextual factors that impact this fundamental premise. Reality, and perceptions of that reality, seem to be equally important when seeking to define and understand the US–China relationship. A fairly fundamental and revealing depiction can be recognized in global maps that are produced in each country. Hoffman reveals that 'Maps sold in the US depict North America at the center, with Europe to the east and Asia to the west. Those sold in China have Eurasia to the fore, North America on the periphery' (2008: 9). This is a subtle difference, but it does represent a distinct difference between one that sees the United States as being the center of the world and one that sees China as being the center of the world. Such a disparity provides an explanation for the respective expectations that other countries should fall in line with the lead of the central country. When such adherence does not happen it opens the door for distrust, perceived justification for espionage, preparation for armed conflict, further efforts to destabilize the other and ultimately seeking control of the other.

This premise has relevance for understanding US–Chinese cross-cultural exchanges on the interpersonal, group, organizational, societal, mass communication, and cyberspace levels. As I present the following illustrations, the reader should consider how paralleled situations in his/her own life could exist if confronted with similar kinds of phenomena. What is true for interpersonal encounters also holds true for group behavior. Context is still key.

China is very much a collective society. That is, people tend to function in groups and this group functioning further reinforces their collective nature. The United States, on the other hand, is much more of an individualistic society. That is, we tend to be more independent of each other and think nothing of going our separate ways if our objectives necessitate a change of direction away from family and friends. Groups are obviously the foundation for organizational composition and, as such, US–Chinese cross-cultural exchange reflects the high-context/low-context distinction on the organizational level. Organizational behavior reflects the behavioral norms of the individuals who comprise it.

One can readily find McDonald's fast food in Beijing. McDonald's will seek busy intersections to place their restaurants much as they do in the United States. The intersection of Chang'an Avenue and Wangfujing Street is much like Broadway in New York City. Chang'an Avenue is a main east–west thoroughfare that runs through the heart of Beijing and Wangfujing Street has been a primary shopping district in downtown Beijing for many years. Thus, their intersection is a busy and fashionable crossroads. I observed that there was a very large McDonald's at that intersection and periodically ate there during my many visits to China. Then, during one of my work trips at the US Embassy, I noticed the McDonald's was gone and there was no other McDonald's in the immediate area. This struck me strange, that McDonald's would give up such a prized location, and I asked about it at the US Embassy.

The explanation I received was that McDonald's had contractually arranged control of the property, good for 30 years, so they could run their restaurant there. However, when a developer proposed more lucrative plans for that location, the government decided they wanted to dissolve the contractual relationship. McDonald's declined to break the agreement. The government acknowledged that McDonald's could, in fact, keep the property as stipulated contractually but there was no guarantee that the city of Beijing could provide them with water. That is, they could operate their restaurant at that location but they would need to do so without water. McDonald's then voluntarily vacated the agreement. This situation with McDonald's reflects how understanding of the larger organizational interaction context was essential for McDonald's to function in Beijing. With the United States being a low-context detail-oriented culture, the specified details would serve as foundation for the larger main idea regarding what was agreed upon. Whereas in China, a more high-context social order, the specific details were relevant only insofar as their relationship with the larger backdrop and overall meaning that was intended by the Chinese government officials.

This episode can be seen as illustrating how the state agenda has precedence over individual/private interests and how the rule of law is secondary to that context. It can be seen as illustrative of a high-context society when one understands that the role of context exists on a continuum, with high-context being at one end of the continuum and low-context being at the other end. One could conversely argue that McDonald's would accept this request to vacate the premises as fait accompli, in which case it would reflect acceptance of the specific social reality and power differential involved.

This kind of authoritarian management style has parallels with scenarios where the role of the individual is clearly subordinate to the larger society. It is just the opposite in the United States. Consequently, Chinese individual rights are only understood within the larger context of what best addresses the interests of society. I observed an example of this soon after my arrival in Beijing during my first visit in 1987. I was out for a walk and, as I crossed at a busy intersection, I saw some large poster photographs. I first thought they were advertisements but ruled that out because, at that time, free enterprise was practically nonexistent in China. I looked closer and saw five unusually gory illustrations, depicting various kinds of accidents, that seemed to be designed to serve as warnings to pedestrians that they needed to exercise caution when crossing the street. China was just starting to get more cars on the road and the public, which until that time typically used bikes or walked, was getting used to vehicular traffic.

As I looked more closely at the photographs I was impressed at how realistic they looked. These gory illustrations depicted children who had been run over by cars and trucks, their bodies smashed and bloodied. I was intrigued by how they could so realistically have models pose in such ways and create such effects. Then, all of a sudden, I realized these were actual photographs of children who had been killed at that intersection. The pictures were so graphically realistic. Blood, guts, smashed heads, and anguished faces. I was horrified. It seemed so cruel to the victims to have these actual images posted this way. And then I thought of the families who probably lived nearby and had to see their loved ones depicted in such a manner. The pictures clearly conveyed the desired message – that being anyone crossing the street needed to exercise due caution or else they run the risk of losing their lives in such a manner.

The next day in class I asked some of my older graduate students about the use of such photographs in relation to the rights of the victims and their families. They acknowledged that such photographs are, indeed, gory and unpleasant to look at but their use was necessary for them to have the desired effect. That is, the benefit to the larger social order (possibly saving lives by encouraging due caution) justified the inconvenience to the victims and families. Thus, the larger cultural context was primary over the rights of the individuals. In the United States, such photographs would never be utilized in such a manner. It would infringe on individual rights too much – thus the specific low-context details associated with the individual take precedence in the United States.

The following example offers illustration for how contextual HUMINT operations can manifest themselves with the Chinese social order. I was in Beijing in the summer of 2000, in my role as an Assistant Air Force Attaché at the US Embassy, to assist with Secretary of Defense Cohen's visit to China. Secretary Cohen had departed Beijing and I had been at a 'wheels up' social gathering at Colonel Kevin Lanzit's apartment earlier that evening. He was my supervisor and hosted a dinner and drinks event to celebrate our performance of duties in support of the Secretary of Defense (SECDEF) visit. The beer flowed freely. The Jianguo Hotel was located across Changan Boulevard from his apartment so I drank an extra beer knowing it was a short walk to my room. Upon return to the Jianguo Hotel, which was only a few blocks from the US Embassy, I showered and was preparing for bed when the phone rang and a warm voice conveyed, 'Sir, would you like your evening massage service?' I was startled by the question and paused. She followed up by saying 'It is complimentary for our valued guests'. I was still startled. I had been to Beijing numerous times and this had never happened. I guessed it to be a prostitute and, in a mildly disdainful voice, responded 'No, I will not be needing the massage service tonight or any night. Please remove my name from your call list' and hung up abruptly.

It occurred to me that I might have been targeted for such a call by the Chinese HUMINT (human source collection) agency but I could not know for sure. I assumed Colonel Lanzit's apartment was bugged with listening devices and that my evening of alcohol consumption was duly noted. I also observed that the room I occupied appeared to be the same room where I had stayed on an earlier visit or at least in the same area of the building on the same floor. It seemed easy to speculate about the aforementioned but it was too vague of an occurrence to come to any firm conclusion regarding intent.

I sat down at my desk and flossed my teeth. My eyes drifted to some materials on my desk and night stand that were provided by the hotel. One freestanding card, that appeared to be commercially produced, conveyed a message about the massage service that is offered by the hotel. That was about my twelfth visit to China and I had never experienced such a thing before. It struck me as odd. I went to bed, slept soundly, and did not think much more about it. The next morning I went down to the restaurant for a lengthy breakfast and did some reading while I was eating. I thought about the massage offer incident and decided to report it at the embassy. When I returned to my room I reached for the aforementioned massage offer card, so I could take it to work as part of the reporting process, and it was gone. I could not find it anywhere.

About five years earlier, while doing a duty tour as an Air Force Attaché in Washington, DC, I had met Nicholas Eftimiades. He worked for the Defense Intelligence Agency (DIA) as an expert on China intelligence practices and had authored a book titled *Chinese Intelligence Operations*. I had taken a look at his book and remembered it addressed the aforementioned type of scenario. I did a closer read of his book and Eftimiades specifically mentions the Jianguo Hotel as a location that has surveillance equipment installed to snoop on inhabitants (1994: 45). Eftimiades also lists the Jianguo Hotel as a location that houses intelligence facilities and runs intelligence operations (1994: 2).

I concluded that it was a pretty safe bet that I had been targeted by the Chinese intelligence apparatus. Living and working in China, as a US government employee, put me in other types of related situations that seemed to indicate paralleled conclusions, but such phenomena were difficult to prove for sure in that the evidence was sketchy at best. Thus, I learned that context was very important for dealing with all kinds of situations. I found it very helpful, almost a requirement, to have my contextual radar turned on when in China or when dealing with Chinese in the United States. I came to appreciate how different this must be for them, dealing with Americans, as well. It was not a quaint cultural difference. I found it could be a blunt showstopper if I proceeded in my attaché duties without this sense. Conversely, I found such awareness to be a lubricant for moving issues toward desired resolution.

Understanding context as a variable between US and Chinese HUMINT operations

US and Chinese HUMINT (Human Source Collection) operations have significant differences and these differences are reflective of the contextual themes that are stressed in each culture. That is, China is a high-context culture that focuses more on nuance and indirect meanings and the United States is a low-context culture that focuses more on direct and explicitly stated meanings. Thus, as will be illustrated in the following pages, Chinese HUMINT operations are less direct and rely heavily on generalized contextual meanings and US HUMINT operations are far more explicit and goal-directed. Ultimately, what HUMINT is understood to be differs in each culture and what it means to be human is ultimately called in to question.

Students of the intelligence community will see frequent reference to an illustration that exemplifies a primary unique aspect of Chinese intelligence operations in contrast with other countries such as the United States and Russia. It focuses on intelligence gathering in relation to a sandy beach. According to this explanation, Russian forces would arrive in the dead of night via a submarine loaded with a small highly armed contingent of special forces soldiers who would make their way ashore, promptly fill five buckets with sand from the beach and retreat into the darkness from whence they came. The United States would send a Navy Seal unit in, commensurate with the aforementioned Russian approach, and the extraction would be accomplished. Backup would be accomplished via a Marine commando team landing from the air via helicopters and accomplishing a similar type of sand extraction. Planning and execution of this strategy would be enhanced with National Security Agency satellites providing real-time visuals of the beach area. The Chinese would use a vastly different approach. They would enlist the support of 10,000 beach-goers (families with children etc.) with instructions to go to the beach on a given sunny afternoon, engage in standard beach recreation activities and then return to their place of lodging. These Chinese 'collectors' would then shake off the sand that had accumulated to their towels, sandals, clothing and body into a small pile and these many piles would be collected into one single pile that would be larger and more diverse than the total of what was collected by the Russian and US efforts (Wise 2011: 11; Stober & Hoffman 2001:133; Hoffman 2008: 7).

The point being that the Chinese would use a much more broadly conceived approach that is subtle and far less intrusive. This approach would be vague in conception and practically undetectable in execution. It would draw heavily from the general contextual orientation that is common for such a beachfront. The Cox Committee (US House Select Committee, 1999) develops this type of scope of operations more fully in their report about Chinese intelligence operations. The exceedingly high number of people that can be utilized for Chinese intelligence operations puts the impressive volume of what can be collected, considering size and scope, in an entirely different realm regarding operations that are conceived and strategies that are employed. Eftimiades (1994: 113–114) explains,

> It is, however, not the quality but the sheer number of their operatives that enable a portion of them to succeed. The number of clandestine intelligence operations conducted by the PRC (People's Republic of China) overwhelms Western counterintelligence and law enforcement agencies.

Their focus on many concurrent operations, with particular targeting of ethnic Chinese, has benefitted Chinese intelligence objectives. Stober and Hoffman (2001: 132) reveal:

> China's spying method is enormously inefficient, slow, and piecemeal. So, China works the numbers. The approaches are massive in scale, but the primary targets are the people who appear most likely to hear China's plea for help … primarily ethnic Chinese.

Although ethnic Chinese tend to be the most successful target, having such a large number of operatives allows China to pursue other constituencies as well.

The following example with an American professor offers such an illustration. The Chinese intelligence machine has a record of targeting visiting scholars. Xu Maihong was a People's Liberation Army (PLA) officer who posed as a university student and sought to report on an American professor. Eftimiades reports that Xu Maihong later reported, 'Their responsibilities were to learn English and to keep track of the activities of American scholars and students, in preparation for assignment overseas' (1994: 58). Thus, the concepts of size, scope, and patience could be seen as serving the Chinese intelligence process well. Thus, over time, it becomes clear the high-context Chinese culture operates a HUMINT operation system that seemingly casts large indirect nets as a strategy for meeting intelligence gathering objectives. Conversely, the low-context US culture operates a HUMINT operation system that focuses more directly on the targeting of fewer domains, sources and topics of interest. That is, the HUMINT operations conducted by both countries parallel their respective styles of communication.

Most Chinese intelligence operations fall under the auspices of the MSS (Ministry of State Security). Lowenthal (2012: 351) clarifies the dual functions of internal security activities against dissidents and foreign intelligence operations:

> There are five bureaus within the MSS that focus primarily on HUMINT intelligence operations: the Second Bureau (intelligence collection abroad), Fourth Bureau (technology development for intelligence gathering and counterintelligence), Sixth Bureau (counter intelligence, primarily Chinese communities overseas), Tenth Bureau (economic, scientific & technical intelligence) and Foreign Affairs Bureau (foreign intelligence liaison).

In addition to the MSS, the Military Intelligence Department (MID) of the PLA also engages in espionage outside of China. As such one can recognize the thinking of Sun Tzu, the Chinese military theorist who authored *The Art of War* in about 400 BCE. One chapter, titled 'Employment of Secret Agents', describes five categories of spies: agents in place (who are native to the targeted area), double agents, deception agents, expendable agents (who may be sacrificed) and penetration agents. Wise shares that use of all five types of agents was governed under the central theme of 'know the enemy and know yourself and you can fight a hundred battles with no danger of defeat' (2011: 9–10). This emphasis on Sun Tzu is unique to China in some respects but less so in other ways. The five categories of agents could be replicated in varied forms in other countries. The guiding principles of Chinese intelligence, as stressed by Sun Tzu, could have parallels with approaches, goals, and modus operandi of intelligence operations in other countries. The notions of a high-context orientation certainly exist in China but can also exist elsewhere.

China uses a unique approach to intelligence gathering that generally does not involve paying sources. A common scenario is for a foreign target, visiting China, to participate in a long day of sightseeing, followed by a dinner with alcohol consumption and then being bombarded with varied forms of queries designed to draw information of intelligence value from him/her. Rather than cultivate intelligence sources Wise reports 'China develops general relationships with people that may have an intelligence dimension. Instead of recruiting agents, the MSS often relies on informal contacts to collect intelligence. … China doesn't so much try to steal secrets as to try to induce foreign visitors to give them away' via subtle manipulation (2011: 12–13).

The aforementioned sightseeing/dinner/pressure technique is described in better detail by the FBI. Stober and Hoffman (2001: 77) report the approach of

> Surprise them with a hotel room visit or a banquet at the end of a long, tiring day. Put them off balance, flatter them, surround them, press them for information. For some scientists, there was the added emotional pitch: We're a poor country, struggling to modernize, to catch up. Help us; it won't hurt America.

This type of approach obviously rests on wearing the source down and playing off his/her sense of reciprocity and interactive protocol. Wise (2011: 15–16) conveys that the FBI recognizes three rules that are common in Chinese intelligence operations:

> 1) First, China does not, in most cases, offer money in exchange for information; 2) China does not accept typical walk-in cases because of the possibility that such

> 'volunteers' are being dangled as bait by an opposition intelligence service ... ; 3) China collects information from good people, people who don't have financial problems, don't have emotional problems, who are not motivated by revenge, not unsuccessful in their lives.

The concept of 'guanxi' is recurrent with Chinese HUMINT strategies and it is a uniquely Chinese phenomenon. It refers to relationship networks that are maintained by individuals, groups, and organizations. In the United States it would be more of a bartering club rather than a network of friends. Hoffman explains the guanxi networks that one maintains is correlated with how well he/she can get things done. Guanxi relationships imply reciprocation of favors and a strong sense of obligation. Thus, in the world of intelligence gathering, guanxi does not mean you are dealing with an intelligence source, rather, it is 'a social relationship with an intelligence dimension' (2008: 34, 107–108). Given that guanxi is a vividly Chinese concept it is far more effective with ethnic Chinese since they are more familiar with this practice. Many Chinese intelligence operations generally target, and are more effective with, ethnic Chinese populations but are far less effective with later generations that have been born and raised outside of China and don't speak Chinese. Wise clarifies that 'They are no more likely to commit espionage than any other American' (2011: 17–18).

The expression 'Kindred Spirit' is commonly heard among those who study the Chinese intelligence gathering system. Stober and Hoffman (2001: 122) explain it implies the importance of relationships and the obligations inherent in relationships.

> If you're from the homeland, these guys will say, 'we found your grandmother lives on the third floor of the apartment building. We can get her on the first floor,' producing a profound sense of obligation in the visiting scientist.

The guanxi variable can be recognized in such scenarios and can specifically encourage reciprocation from ethnic Chinese. These distinct Chinese characteristics are worth noting in that they can strike a strong chord within the cultural core that most people maintain within their sense of self. People growing up in China are consistently exposed to varied forms of propaganda that can leave strong impressions well into adulthood. This exemplifies a collective mindset of people ruled in China. The Lei Feng campaigns offer such an example. Lei Feng was a PLA soldier who died while working on a random project in support of Chinese society. He was a random individual, who had a random job and died a random death. Chairman Mao held him up as an example for the Chinese masses to emulate. The Chinese spy Katrina Leung, who was code named 'Parlor Maid', spoke of Lei Feng in her work as a Chinese agent. Wise quotes Leung as saying 'You probably think I am too young to remember Lei but I do and I remember the song that was written about him. She then proceeded to sing a few bars of the lyrics' (2011: 112). His existence as a Chinese icon underscores a theme that resonates within Chinese society that can be manipulated toward desired ends.

These kinds of themes, while recognizable for ethnic Chinese, can pose problems for US officials seeking to uncover common symptoms that reflect wrongdoing. There typically is not a smoking gun that could serve as evidence in a courtroom. Stober and Hoffman (2001: 132) explain

> PRC spies tend to deliver science and technology intelligence in China through a conversation with a scientist in the same field ... spying looks like a social gathering ... The social aspect of it puts up a huge smoke screen.

Hoffman further clarifies that 'the Chinese method of gathering intelligence doesn't even look like espionage' (2008: 7). Thus the guanxi concept, with so many subtleties and reciprocation expectations, exemplifies a cultural influence theme that permeates Chinese intelligence gathering activities aimed at ethnic Chinese. Sometimes referred to as 'ASKINT', as opposed to HUMINT or SIGINT (names for standard intelligence approaches), the guanxi theme does indeed build upon the idea of seeking desired information by creating a context that permits asking for it. Stober and Hoffman convey that one layer worth noting in the guanxi process is that one must not necessarily produce the desired information. To have tried can cover the reciprocation debt – at least temporarily. But, at the same time, it implies that a debt to provide desired information is still at large (2001: 94).

What has been conveyed thus far focuses on intelligence processes. Concrete detection and prosecution present another category of challenge. There are fine lines that exist between what is open-source information, which is legally obtained, and protected information. A Chinese saying – 'The are no walls which completely block the wind' – comes to mind. Two Chinese intelligence analysts published a book, *Sources and Techniques of Obtaining National Defense Science and Technology Intelligence*, that addresses how secret information can be procured in the United States. Wise (2011: 242) shares:

> Most intelligence can be collected from open sources, the authors explained, although about 20 percent must be obtained by 'special means' … But, by mining the vast amount of public materials and accumulating information a drop at a time, often it is possible to basically reveal the outlines of some secret intelligence.

This open-source searching is much more in the realm of library research rather than James Bond 'cloak and dagger' images. Regarding this gathering of this information, Stober and Hoffman (2001: 133) explain:

> The greatest volume by far comes from open publications – newspapers, magazines, TV news, and scientific literature. The Chinese specialize in archiving, then disseminating these to its scientists. A Chinese spying manual reads like a librarian's dissertation.

In this situation, what makes us uncomfortable regarding collection may many times be within the letter of the law but outside of the spirit of the law.

One can observe how the Chinese intelligence system commonly engages in a more broadly conceived information collection approach than is practiced in the United States. It is far less common in the United States because it would be very time consuming and involve a significant number of work hours. The Chinese intelligence apparatus has the workers available for such endeavors. The case of Wen Ho Lee offers insight regarding how this kind of prosecution can go astray and have very unsatisfactory results that fly in the face of what the US democracy purports to be. Lee was jailed under harsh conditions for 278 days in relation to accusations by the FBI and Department of Justice indicating he had engaged in spying against the United States of the worst order. During the court proceedings it became apparent that there were no legitimate grounds for his prosecution. When Lee was dismissed from his detention, he quotes Federal Judge Parker as stating:

> I believe you were terribly wronged by being held in custody pretrial in the Santa Fe County Detention Center under demeaning, unnecessarily punitive conditions … I

> was led astray last December by the executive branch of our government through its Department of Justice, by its FBI, and by its US attorney for the district of New Mexico.
>
> *(Lee 2001: 2)*

These kinds of travesties of justice make prosecutors and the court system exceedingly cautious about such issues.

Eftimiades explains that 'for prosecutive purposes, you are looking at an individual collecting one small part one time, and you don't have the quality of case that our country will take to prosecute as far as espionage' (1994: 27). At the same time, this situation exists within the larger backdrop of many Chinese visiting the United States as students, on business, varied forms of delegations, diplomats, and commercial representatives, and in relation to a large ethnic Chinese community. Ohio State University has roughly 50,000 students. Of that number, 6,000 are students from China. This is not to imply that the aforementioned should not be in the United States. It is meant to stress there is a large volume of traffic between the United States and China and that this will present challenges for deciding what, if any, monitoring needs to be done and how this task is to be addressed. This emphasis on Chinese students in the United States can be interpreted as fear-mongering but it is intended to be so. Granted it is speculative. It is merely presented in a nonjudgmental and objective manner. It can be argued that US citizens who visit China could pose a security threat to China. It makes sense to recognize that possibility. However, far more Chinese visit the United States than the number of Americans visit China.

Cyberspace represents another relevant area that is evolving and poses unique challenges as well. The potential for cyberspying allows for spying to occur without having a physical presence involved. The challenge for detection and prosecution is significant and promises to redefine the notion of context, protocol, and fair play. For instance, a destructive program called 'Ghost Rat' allows the attacker to take full control of an external computer, download files and operate microphones and webcam devices. This would allow for eavesdropping. On a larger scale, in 2009 the *Wall Street Journal* reported that cyberspies could gain access to the power grid in the United States. Wise quotes former CIA director James Woolsey as stating, 'Taking down the grid for months comes as close to a nuclear attack with many weapons on the United States as anything could. You'd have mass starvation and death from thirst and all the rest' (2011: 229). In a similar vein, the 'Cox Committee' congressional report conveyed that cyber-attacks on the United States

> might even include cyber-attacks on the US homeland that target the US financial, economic, energy and communications infrastructure ... if it (China) can acquire niche weapons systems that are relatively inexpensive and that can exploit US vulnerabilities, it stands a chance of deterring or defeating the US in a limited engagement.
>
> *(US House Select Committee 1999: 8)*

One can clearly see that the stakes could be incredibly high if the United States were the victim of a large-scale cyberattack.

Evidence of Chinese government involvement with cyberspying against the United States surfaced from the 2011 WikiLeaks episode. Wise explains that among these leaks was a message from the US Embassy in Beijing, to Washington, DC, indicating 'hacker attacks against Google were directed by the Politburo, the highest level of China's government. The cable stated: "A well-placed contact claims that the Chinese government coordinated the recent intrusions of Google systems"' (2011: 235). Thus, one can see that suspicions about

China's anti-US cyberspace intentions do have some foundation. The obvious question has to do with how extensive such intentions might be and what effects they might have?

The cybersecurity threat can be observed to be associated with a high-context framework when one considers the stealth with which Chinese entities can access US digital domains without being detected. This scenario is continually evolving and is relevant to any discussion of intelligence collection efforts. All of what is conveyed in this chapter must be understood within the larger picture of Chinese modernization and what it represents to the Chinese people. Economy (2017: 141) reports:

> On November 15, 2012, the day he became general secretary of the Chinese Communist Party, Xi Jinping stood onstage at the Great Hall of the People, in Beijing, to reflect back on his country's 5,000 years of history. After citing China's 'indelible contribution' to world civilization, Xi called for 'the great revival of the Chinese nation'.

Thus, it is clear Xi is heralding a return to a glorious mythical past of China. This vision parallels US President Donald Trump's call to 'Make America Great Again'. The 20th century is often seen as a century of shame for China. The 21st century can be a century of redemption.

Conclusion: Acknowledging the complex nature of China-US relations

The US–China relationship is complex. There are historical trends to be considered. At present, there is a bond in the business realm. China relies on the United States to buy its exports as a means to shore up its industries and US businesses are continually seeking to market products in the exceedingly large (and growing) Chinese market. There is reason for optimism in this type of 'trading partner' relationship. However, US claims of corporate espionage committed by the Chinese litter this relational landscape and weaken the relational foundation. It is also worth considering the overall historical context that provides a backdrop for such a relationship. There is considerable depth to appreciate with regard to what has happened in the past, what is going on in the present, what this means for the future and the implications of varied perceptions of all these angles. One can understand the unease that might exist within the Asian American community toward the US government. Wise (2011: 238) shares that

> For sixty years, beginning in 1882 and lasting into World War II, Chinese were barred from immigrating to the United States by the Chinese Exclusion Act. In 1917 Congress created an Asiatic Barred Zone, prohibiting immigration from much of East Asia and the Pacific Islands (until 1952). Thousands of Japanese Americans were shunted off to internment camps in paranoia after Pearl Harbor …

It is a tainted historical context.

Much of the US–China relationship is a matter of perception. Many of the primary aspects of the relationship are open to interpretation and reinterpretation. These kinds of perceptions are subject to manipulation.

> Beijing also engages in a much softer form of irregular warfare through its perception management operations, both in times of tranquil relations and in times of crisis … because the Chinese Communist Party maintains tight political and media

> controls, Chinese perception management campaigns are more tightly coordinated with diplomacy.
>
> *(US House Select Committee 1999: 8)*

A larger issue to consider is how the nature of espionage and HUMINT efforts will be going through redefinition due to ripple effects in relation to the new communication technologies. Such innovations are stimulating linkages and exposures that we have never had before. Forms of electronic collection, that do not even involve classified information, have the potential to become more prevalent. That is the collection and computerized analysis of open-source information, on a macro scale, has the potential to make standard intelligence collection less relevant. This shift will not happen overnight, but the incremental changes will add up over time.

References

Andersen, P. (1987) 'Explaining Intercultural Differences in Nonverbal Communication', Paper presented at the 1987 meeting of the Speech Communication Association, Boston, MA.

Devito, J.A. (1986) *The Interpersonal Communication Book.* New York: Harper and Row.

Economy, E. (2017) 'History with Chinese Characteristics: How China's Imagined Past Shapes Its Present', *Foreign Affairs*, July/August: 141–148.

Eftimiades, N. (1994) *Chinese Intelligence Operations.* Annapolis, MD: Naval Institute Press.

Hall, E.G. (1984) *The Dance of Life: The Other Dimension of Time*. Garden City, NY: Anchor Press.

Heisey, D.R. (2000) *Chinese Perspectives in Rhetoric and Communication.* Stamford, CT: Ablex Publishing Corporation.

Hoffman, T. (2008) *The Spy Within: Larry Chin and China's Penetration of the CIA.* Hanover, NH: Steerforth Press.

Lee, W.H. (2001) *My Country Versus Me.* New York: Hyperion Press.

Lowenthal, M.M. (2012) *Intelligence: From Secrets to Policy.* Thousand Oaks, CA: SAGE Press.

Murray, D.P. (1983) 'Face-to-Face: American and Chinese Interactions', in Kapp, R.A. (ed.) *Communicating with China.* Chicago: Intercultural Press, pp. 9–27.

Ochs, E. (1979) 'Introduction: What Child Language Can Contribute to Pragmatics', in E. Ochs and B. Schiefflen (eds.) *Developmental Pragmatics.* New York: Academic Press, pp. 201–214.

Stober, D. and Hoffman, I. (2001) *A Convenient Spy: Wen Ho Lee and the Politics of Nuclear Espionage.* New York: Simon & Schuster.

US House Select Committee on US National Security and Military/Commercial Concerns with the People's Republic of China (Cox Committee) (1999) 3 vols., 105th Congress, 2nd session.

White, J.B. (1984) *When Words Lose Their Meaning: Constitution and Reconstitutions of Language, Character, and Community.* Chicago: University of Chicago Press.

Wise, D. (2011) *Tiger Trap: America's Secret Spy War with China.* Boston: Houghton Mifflin, Harcourt.

Part II

China's political system and governance

8

Dynamic dictators

Elite cohesion and authoritarian resilience in China

Elina Sinkkonen

Authoritarian resilience

There is a need to improve concepts and research frameworks on authoritarianism and authoritarian resilience. Democratization used to be the dominant trend from the 1980s until roughly 2007, which drove scholars to study regime changes, leaving stable authoritarian regimes poorly studied (Freedom House 2019; Geddes et al. 2018). Yet authoritarian resilience should be puzzling if we assume that lack of electoral representation significantly weakens regime legitimacy. Dickson argued in 2016 that 'much of the recent literature on the survival of authoritarian regimes has limited applicability to China' (Dickson 2016: 5).

Currently the number of liberal democracies is in decline and the third wave of autocratization is here, creating new interest in authoritarian practices (Lührmann & Lindberg 2019). Autocratization does not happen only in democracies, although such processes have recently received most attention. Autocratization also takes place in already authoritarian countries. In order to form a comprehensive understanding of quality of governance globally, it is important to better conceptualize and study deepening authoritarianism in authoritarian regimes and how variation in authoritarian practices may be related to authoritarian resilience.

This chapter aims to demonstrate with Chinese empirical examples that authoritarian regimes are not static. On the contrary, it is precisely the adjustments dictatorships make all the time that keep these regimes in power. To paraphrase Acemoglu and Robinson (2019), authoritarian governance takes place in a narrow corridor. Staying in that narrow corridor requires a right balance of control: There has to be enough control to avoid revolutions and coup attempts, but not too much control which might prevent economic activities. Balance maintenance entails a red queen effect, meaning pressure to adapt faster to changing conditions. Democratization is only one alternative for a particular type of authoritarian rule, as a party-based authoritarian system can become a military junta for example, or an authoritarian regime might simply change their top leaders. Regime stability, be it democratic or autocratic, signifies that the leadership has at least for the time being found a political equilibrium.

To make authoritarian dynamism visible, the starting point of research should be factors that tend to vary among authoritarian regimes, meaning that authoritarianism

DOI: 10.4324/9780429059704-11

should not be approached only as lack of democratic traits. If we wish to understand authoritarian resilience, we need to give up the idea that we could meaningfully place all regimes on a one-dimensional continuum, with democratic governments in the one end and authoritarian governments in the other end. Analytic tools developed for studying democracies are not sufficient to account for the variance of governance relevant variables in authoritarian regimes.

New research provides partial responses to three gaps on the research agenda of authoritarian regimes. First, we should embrace equifinality and focus on the combination of causes and their interactions rather than effects of individual causes when studying authoritarian resilience. In this respect, research conducted by Geddes, Wright, and Frantz (2018) provides the so far most ambitious explanation of authoritarian resilience. Geddes et al. (2018) acknowledge that factors affecting authoritarian resilience are likely to involve interacting causal variables that are not independent of each other.

Second, Geddes et al.'s research findings help to understand ways in which economic factors affect different types of authoritarian regimes and their resilience. Empirical evidence shows that the relationship between wealth and regime type is not simple. As the level of development rises, authoritarian regimes, like democratic ones, become more stable (Geddes 2003: 83). Londregan and Poole (1990) have found that the best predictor of coups in all regimes is poverty. By studying the effects of economic downturns in combination with regime types, Geddes et al. (2018: 190) conclude that economic downturns increase likelihood of collapse in dictatorships that lack extensive party networks. Put the other way around, extensive party networks stabilize authoritarian regimes even when the regime is faced with economic crises.

Furthermore, existing comparative research analyzing the economic origins of regime types tends to attach only positive attributions to economic growth acquired via industrial activities and innovations, and reserve the innovative and industrious growth model to Western democracies. Yet, as Zuboff (2015) argues, data has become a new form of capital and authoritarian regimes may have a comparative advantage in extracting large amounts of it; therefore, our understanding of authoritarian toolkits needs to be updated. Digital revolution and digital capitalism bring with them transnational elements which will transform politics in democracies and autocracies alike.

Third, Geddes et al.'s (2018) research sheds light on the connection between authoritarian resilience and the increase in authoritarian governance practices. Their findings help to clarify that stabilizing factors are regime dependent and deepening authoritarianism does not automatically increase regime resilience. Geddes et al. (2018: 85) report that dictators who score high on personalism scale during their first three years in office are much more likely to stay in power than dictators with low early personalism scores. Yet their overall finding is that personalization decreases regime durability in party-based regimes, while it increases regime durability in military-based regimes (Geddes et al. 2018: 198). In other words, leaders of party-based regimes would increase their chances of staying in power if they would share power after having made it through the difficult regime consolidation phase, which in China often takes a few years. During this consolidation phase, the new regime is especially vulnerable to elite struggles, which increases the likelihood that the regime will resort to their repressive toolkit (Zheng 2010: 71–97).

In literature concentrating solely on China, the relationship of power concentration and regime durability is hotly debated. Researchers disagree whether increased power concentration is a sign of regime strength or weakness. In 2003 Nathan argued that the CCP demonstrated important signs of institutionalization as the leadership managed to create peaceful, timely and stable leadership succession when Hu Jintao became the general secretary of the CCP in November 2002. Others who have found significant evidence of system adaptability include Yang (2004) and Shambaugh (2008).

For Nathan (2003), gradual institutionalization has contributed to regime resilience in China. Nathan's position would align with Geddes et al.'s (2018) finding that power-sharing would be a wise strategy in party-based regimes. Later, Fewsmith and Nathan (2019) argued that party institutionalization has been 'considerably overstated'. For Fewsmith, the authoritarian model has proven resilient due to a return to a hierarchical model in which the execution of rules is personalistic on all levels and the leadership avoids giving too much power to the bureaucracy, not because of institutionalization. While Fewsmith's stance would seem to be in contradiction with the above-mentioned general finding of Geddes et al. we might have to conclude that the jury is still out to decide whose description is more accurate. If we take into account that in social sciences it is not often possible to find general laws holding despite changing historical circumstances, it may be that both Nathan and Fewsmith are partly right. The dataset Geddes et al. (2018) used in their study ends in the year 2010, which is unfortunate given that in many countries' authoritarian tendencies have intensified since then. Yet, despite China's deepened autocratization, CCP is still in power and there are no signs of any credible resistance to its rule. There is recent empirical evidence to support Fewsmith's position, which finds the source of resilience in increased control and personalism. Kendall-Taylor, Frantz, and Wright (2020) state that popular protests have become a more significant challenge to authoritarian regimes between 2001 and 2017. Consequently, the relative weight in effective strategies of political survival might have shifted to societal factors, and keeping the elite satisfied by power-sharing has perhaps lost some of its relevance. If the Chinese regime has studied these same trends, they may have changed their tactics and improved the likelihood of remaining in power. In order to better understand the changes that have taken place in China since 2010, it is useful to delve deeper into different aspects of power concentration.

Measuring power concentration

Understanding variation in key sectors of authoritarian rule will help in answering to the puzzling question of what explains authoritarian resilience and how the regime might find political equilibrium.

There is a great deal of variation in the level and style of authoritarianism between the Jiang Zemin (1989–2002), Hu (2002–2012) and Xi (2012–) regimes. Shambaugh (2016) divides Chinese regimes since 1985 into four types of authoritarianism ranging from neototalitarian to softly authoritarian. The so-called fang-shou cycle (放收周期) of political opening and tightening characterizes Chinese politics (Shambaugh 2016: 98). On a very general level, trends of authoritarian control in China suggest that after the Tiananmen Incident (1989) domestic control increased and started to gradually get lighter again after 1992. The Hu regime preceding Xi was generally characterized as much more consultative than earlier regimes and repression was less visible on the societal level. Hu experimented cautiously with a more consultative approach by promoting intraparty democracy and expanding the number of official actors influencing leadership decisions on foreign policy, which as a policy area has been strictly restricted (Jakobson & Knox 2010; Shirk 2018: 32; Sinkkonen 2014). During the Xi regime China has returned to harsher control with clear concentration tendencies of political rule (Shirk 2018).

While it is useful to grasp the overall trend of authoritarianism in China over the years, we need to delve deeper into characteristics of authoritarian governance if we wish to improve our understanding of how political equilibrium enabling authoritarian resilience might be found. As the first step towards forming such an understanding, elements of authoritarian governance have to be described in detail and measured if possible. Aspects of authoritarian rule that tend to vary according to scholars of authoritarian regimes include power concentration within the elite and domestic repression (Geddes 2003; Geddes et al. 2018; Lührmann and Lindberg 2019; Slovik 2012). Deepening autocratization would thus be a process of increasing either power concentration or domestic repression or both.

Figure 8.1 summarizes measures authoritarian leaders can take with regards to elites and the wider society. It is notable that there can simultaneously be policies increasing and decreasing autocratization, meaning that not all aspects that can vary will necessarily move in the same direction at the same time. On the elite level, authoritarian leadership can increase or decrease power concentration, which can be measured with personalization, administrative centralization, and state control over economic assets. Some scholars of authoritarian regimes have defined cooptation as one tool to maintain authoritarian stability (Gerschewski 2013; Schmotz 2015; Svolik 2012). In what is discussed below, parts of the often used cooptation measures are included in the personalization index (security apparatus), administrative centralization, and state control over economic assets (capital, labor, and land ownership). As the role of the economy in regime maintenance is broader than buying off powerful groups, it is not enough to talk about cooptation.

On the societal level, authoritarian leadership can increase or decrease repression. Repression is costly and increasing repression risks angering apolitical people (Dickson et al. 2017). This is why nondemocratic regimes try to build regime legitimacy and to have

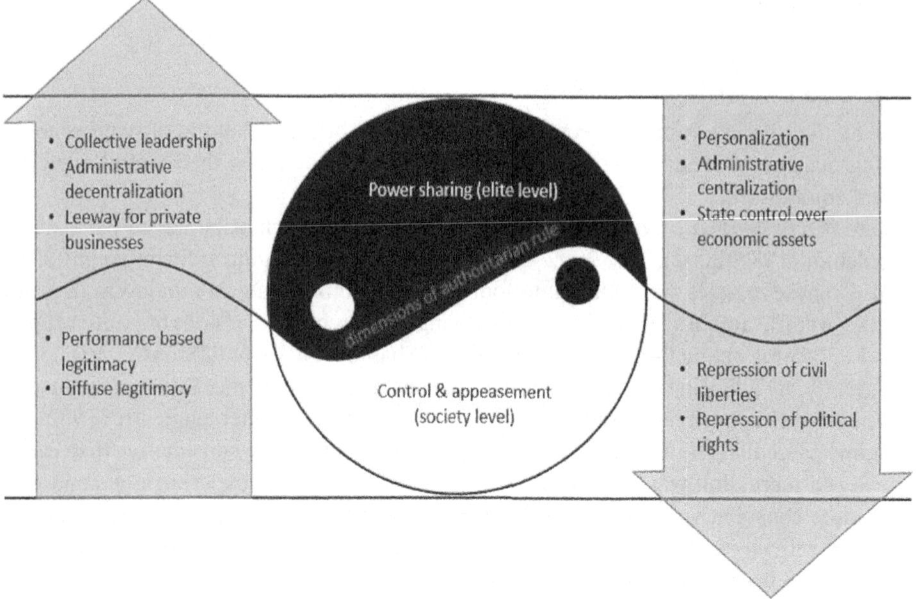

Figure 8.1 Dimensions of authoritarian rule and autocratization.

active consent, rule obedience or sometimes mere toleration for their rule within the population (Gerschewski 2013: 14; Maerz 2020). Leaders can increase public support by building legitimacy through measures enhancing in-group coherence and applying welfare policies.

This chapter concentrates on power concentration on the elite level. I will present below three areas of power concentration which are relevant in the Chinese case and likely to be applicable to also other authoritarian contexts: personalization, administrative centralization, and state control over key economic assets.

Personalization

A dictator wants the minimum support needed to survive, but no more, as he has to compensate support either by sharing power or giving out resources (Geddes et al. 2018: 78; de Mesquita et al. 2003: 100). Thus, he has incentives to concentrate power in his own hands as much as possible. While personalization can sometimes refer to building of a personality cult of some sort, here personalization signifies measurable features of power concentration. Geddes et al.'s (2018: 79–80) measurement for personalization includes:

> dictator's personal control of the security apparatus, creation of loyalist paramilitary forces, dictator's control of the composition of the party executive committee, the party executive committee behaving as a rubber stamp, dictator's personal control of appointments, dictator's creation of a new party to support the regime, dictator's control of military promotions, and dictator's purges of officers.

In their research, Geddes et al. calculate a yearly personalism score for each regime making it possible to show variation during a single dictator's tenure. Before this, 'personalization has never been so carefully and consistently measured across regimes and across time' (Pepinsky 2019).

Drawing from Geddes et al.'s definition above, I discuss personalism in China from the perspective of institutional arrangements in existing institutions, innovation of new institutions, and purges of opponents. In the party-state system, the most powerful position, general secretary of the Communist Party of China, is accompanied by the state presidency and Central Military Commission (CMC) chairmanship (Wang 2017: 5). A new leader's power position in China can be assessed in part based on when they are named as chairman of the CMC (Miller 2014: 9; Nathan 2003), as that does not always happen at the same time as assuming the other two positions. Xi was able to get all top positions at once in comparison to his predecessors Hu and Jiang, who both had to wait for the CMC chairmanship. Composition and size of the Politiburo Standing Committee can also offer clues on the number of supporters a leader has managed to promote there. In 2002, the size of Politburo Standing Committee was expanded from seven to nine members because Hu wanted to enhance collective leadership. In 2012 when Xi came to power, the Politburo Standing Committee was reduced back to seven members and internal security as a policy sector was dropped altogether (Miller 2015: 66–68). In 2018 China rearranged its ministries and diminished the total amount of ministerial-level bodies by eight and vice ministerial-level by seven (Xinhua 2018). As the most telling example of increased personalism, the National People's Congress abolished term limits for the president in March 2018, which indicates that Xi might be planning to stay in power after 2022 (Shirk 2018: 32).

In addition to ensuring support in the party and state organizations, securing the loyalty of the military is one of the most important tasks of Chinese leaders. If the military gets too powerful, it will get political leverage which can be used against the leadership. The People's Liberation Army (PLA) is overviewed by the CMC, which is chaired by the general secretary of the CCP, and there are also other mechanisms to secure power balance. PLA has, for example, political commissars and party committees, which should play a role in all key decisions (Saunders & Wutnow 2016). Since 1992, there has been a limitation of maximum two PLA representatives in the Politburo, to make sure that the general secretary is not using the PLA members as his power base (Miller 2015: 73). In the more influential Politburo Standing Committee, there has been no PLA officer since 1997 (Li 2015: 120). In addition to these administrative forms of party control, Xi has promoted his followers to top positions and frequency of post rotation in the PLA has intensified during the Xi era, arguably to prevent plots (Kou 2017: 878–879). As PLA officers do not have job security, and their evaluation process is perceived as somewhat unfair and being based on personal likes and dislikes (Ledberg 2018), they are vulnerable to intensified political control.

Xi started the biggest military reforms since 1949 in 2015. PLA reform had multiple motivations including military modernization and ensuring more functional chains of command. Yet the personalistic power concentration aspect of the reforms is clear. The tangible changes include reduction of the number of military districts from seven to five, reforms of the military command structure, strengthening Xi's role within the CMC by emphasizing the so-called chairman responsibility system (军委主席负责制) which highlights final say of the chairman and slimming down the CMC from eleven to seven members in 2017 (Mulvenon 2016, 2018; Kou 2017: 866–867). Finally, a prominent feature during the Xi era has been the promotion of his public image as a strong military leader. This trend has been visible in the great number of visits he has made to garrisons (Kou 2017: 873).

Xi has also been active in institutional innovation. He started his term by creating new political bodies, such as the National Security Commission (NSC, 中央国家安全委员会) in January 2014. Xi's aim in establishing the NSC, which supervises both foreign and domestic security issues, was to concentrate power in his own hands and to improve policy coordination (Lampton 2015). You (2016: 183) sees Xi's establishment of NSC during his first year at office as a clear sign of Xi's strong power position. While the need to improve coordination and establishing NSC had been talked about for decades, Hu did not even try such a move and Jiang failed to do it during his years in office. Xi also leads several other new central committee or central commission level decision-making bodies that have been upgraded from the leading small groups existing before 2017 (Wu 2018).

In China, it is common for leaders to start anticorruption measures in the beginning of the term. Anticorruption measures are useful for authoritarian leaders to remove opponents from powerful positions. When anticorruption gets politicized, it is more common to target the opponent's support network, usually mid- to low-level officials, rather than the main competitor himself (Zhu and Zhang 2017: 1190). The armed forces have usually been left out of such maneuvers, with a few notable exceptions. In the beginning of Jiang's term, his power in the PLA was constrained by the so-called 'Yang family clan'. In 1992, Jiang managed to purge the Yang brothers Yang Baibing and Yang Shankun from their military positions with the help of Deng Xiaoping. Moreover, Jiang reshuffled more than 300 senior officers and 1000 regional commanders throughout the country to establish his authority (Gilley 1998: 196).

Yet, Xi took anticorruption measures to a whole new level when compared with his predecessors (Chen 2020: 143). Xi launched the anticorruption campaign in late 2012. Not only did the campaign target exceptionally numerous high-level officials or 'tigers', it also reformed the institutional structures of anticorruption work. In 2014 Xi broke the unwritten rule of not going after former Politburo Standing Committee members by purging Zhou Yongkang, former standing committee member, who was sentenced to life imprisonment for corruption. (Liu 2019: 51–55). In late 2017, the CCP Central Discipline Inspection Commission, headed by Xi's close ally Wang Qishan, had punished almost 1.4 million party members including 17 Central Committee members and two sitting Politburo members (Shirk 2018: 24). The width and breadth of the campaign in the PLA was also unprecedented. The two former vice chairmen of the CMC, Xu Caihou and Guo Boxiong, were both ousted. In the early 2015, Chinese leadership announced investigations of 30 senior military officials on serious corruption charges. While the main objective of the campaign was evidently to remove any officers who were close to Xu and Guo, there has been some moderation as no princeling was targeted. Also, the majority of highest-ranking officers accused had retired whereas those faced with corruption charges while in active service have been mostly at the deputy army level (Chen 2020: 150–151; Kou 2017: 876–878).

Finally, the party established the National Supervision Commission in 2018 as part of a wider reform of the anticorruption system. In these reforms the party aimed for a single anticorruption agency system instead of a dual-track system, in which discipline inspection subbranches at provincial, municipal, county, and township levels were under dual leadership of the local party branches and their higher-level anticorruption organs. While the legal side of anticorruption work was also reformed, the key de facto outcome of the reforms is that central CCP's control was consolidated and local party leadership's role diminished (Chen 2020; Deng 2018). National Supervision Commission can also stretch the anticorruption measures to state employees, meaning that the politicized anticorruption campaign does not concern only party members (Shirk 2018: 24).

Administrative centralization

While personalism is certainly a key aspect of power concentration in authoritarian regimes, it is not the only one. There is also variation regarding power-sharing between regional administration and the central government. Hess (2013: 36–37) argues that 'modern authoritarian cases might be disaggregated into centralized and decentralized types'. Hess (2017: 21) defines decentralization as the transfer of state authority and resources from national governments to the subnational level. For a numeric measurement for decentralization, it is possible to use the International Monetary Fund's cross-national Fiscal Decentralization Dataset from which one can track the percentage of revenues controlled by subnational governments (IMF 2019).

Authoritarian regimes are generally reluctant to decentralize. However, there are a few notable exceptions such as China and Kazakhstan. The logic behind decentralization is that by granting local officials greater authority within their jurisdiction, the centre avoids blame for local authorities' official misdeeds and their use of repression. Relative to their more centralized counterparts, decentralized regimes often exhibit higher levels of durability in the face of popular challenges (Hess 2013: 37; Landry 2008: 9–10). It is part of CCP's deliberate strategy to blame local governments for general problems and enjoy support at the top. According to public opinion surveys, support and trust in the leadership is indeed polarized: Chinese tend to support the central government more than local leadership (Dickson et al. 2017: 131–134). History of cultural revolution era intensified fear of chaos in Chinese society adding credibility to the CCP's claim that one-party rule is most appropriate to maintain stability (ibid. 124).

China has decentralized a great deal in the past decades, as thanks to fiscal decentralization, subnational expenditures jumped from 45% in 1981 to 85% in 2013. This is exceptional among nondemocracies where government expenditures at the subnational level tend to be below 18% (Hess 2017: 21–22; Landry 2008: 6). Yet, centralization and decentralization go in tides. Decentralization has had clear advantages as it contributed to economic performance since the early 1980s (Hess 2013: 33). In the late 1980s and early 1990s China's fiscal reforms led to institutional development labelled local state corporatism which merged state and economy (Oi 1992). The Hu-Wen administration launched a rural development program, 'Building a New Socialist Countryside', abolished agricultural tax in 2006, and applied fiscal transfers from wealthier provinces to the less developed areas (Ahlers et al. 2015). During Xi's regime from 2012 onwards China has recentralized its administration and the anticorruption campaign has constrained local level initiative (Hess 2017: 28). The centralization tendency has also been strengthened by provincial debt crisis, to which central authorities have responded by initiating reforms which considerably limit financial resources available for local governments (Naughton 2015). Despite changing levels of decentralization, Ahlers et al. (2015) emphasize that including the local level in the analyses of Chinese authoritarian resilience remains essential.

State control over economic assets

In many authoritarian regimes, it is not enough for the leaders to control the security apparatus. Often economic elites need to be controlled as well. Authoritarian leaderships have to balance between supporting economic growth in their country and avoiding opposition forces, which can form around powerful economic actors. The relationship economic factors have with authoritarian resilience depends on regime type, as in resource-rich autocracies it is possible to buy off citizens with generous welfare benefits and low taxation. Some resource-poor party-based regimes such as North Korea rely essentially on other counties' assistance in providing sustenance (Smith 2015: 294–311) and can use harsh coercion to suppress any emerging opposition. Large party-based regimes such as China do not have the option of expecting economic assistance from others, which is why economic growth has been and continues to be important in building regime legitimacy.

The Chinese economic model has enabled decades-long economic growth without regime change. While there is a lively debate on what the 'China model' is and whether it even exists (Zhao 2010), according to Breslin (2011: 1341) China model discourse provides backing for CCP's leadership, as the idea about Chinese exceptionalism 'explains why China does not have to follow anything – including any path that sees democratization as an inevitable consequence of economic liberalization'.

When China started its reform and opening up period in 1978, new policies were adopted gradually and first in special economic zones. Gallagher (2002) argues that maintaining political control over timing and sequencing of liberalization of foreign direct investments is the key in understanding why economic growth has not led to regime change in China. From the 1990s until 2012, China's GDP growth averaged around 10% yearly, leading to rising prosperity especially in the Eastern provinces (World Bank). Although the middle class is seen as a key social agent for democratization, in China's case emergence of a middle class has not shaken CCP rule. There is ample public opinion research showing that the Chinese middle class demonstrates a remarkably high-level support for the regime (Chen & Dickson 2010; Dickson 2016). Dickson (2016) states that under Xi's leadership economic growth is no longer a reliable source of popular support and the party's survival strategy has become more diversified. Family income predicts regime support better than GDP growth: if family income rises, the regime can maintain support despite declining GDP figures. Perhaps these dynamics have contributed to the current leadership's decision to continue poverty alleviation measures initiated during Hu's regime. Poverty alleviation through development was added on the government's working agenda in 2014 (Xinhua 2014).

China's development model has many features ensuring party control. Tsai and Naughton (2015: 18–19) list seven characteristics of Chinese state capitalism: direct central control of strategic sectors, state control over finance, market foundation, industrial policy, party control of personnel, regulatory fragmentation and layering, and a dualistic welfare regime. Of these, the first five are especially relevant in building an understanding of China's economic model which has enabled both authoritarian resilience and economic growth. Strategic sectors include telecommunications, electricity, petroleum, defense industries and finance (ibid.: 18). Pettis (2013) argues that a considerable share of China's GDP growth over the years has been accomplished by a consumption-repressive investment-driven model, which is not sustainable in the long run. In China's growth strategy, state control over finances has played a key role: interest rates have been kept low, wage growth remained moderate for a long time, and currency undervalued. These factors have forced the savings rate up, providing the state fuel for its lavish investment policy (Pettis 2013). The banking sector has been strictly regulated and the state owns the majority of shares in the five biggest commercial banks (Stent 2017: 10). This strategy has been changing slowly and the state has tried to increase the domestic consumption share of GDP.

While 'most of the economy runs on market principles' and foreign-invested companies play a big role in some sectors (Tsai & Naughton 2015: 18), the share of state-owned enterprises (SOEs) of China's GDP was estimated to be between 23% and 28% in 2017 (Zhang 2019: 10). Yet another matter is that the role of SOEs cannot be understood without taking into account the broader model of state capitalism. Milhaupt and Zheng (2015) argue that the distinction between SOEs and privately-owned enterprises (POEs) has been greatly exaggerated as functionally SOEs and POEs share many similarities. Both can dominate the market, receive state subsidies, have close connections with the CCP, and execute government's policy objectives.

In recent years, China's industrial policy has emphasized support of innovation in strategically important sectors in which certain companies will receive preferential treatment and state subsidies (Kenderdine 2017; Wübbeke et al. 2016). 'Innovation-driven development' has become a key priority in the Xi era, manifested for example in the Made in China 2025 plan (中国制造 2025), which was launched in 2015 (National Manufacturing Strategy Advisory Committee 2015). The plan highlighted ten priority sectors including robotics, information technology, aircraft, aerospace technology, and pharmaceuticals, in which China aims for global dominance by 2025 using a strategy combining import substitution and generous state financing. Xi's industrial policy has not been received well abroad, as can be seen in China's ongoing trade war with the United States and the suspicion many Western actors have about allowing Huawei to construct parts of their 5G networks (Rühlig 2020).

As a cross-sectional feature, the Chinese communist party can control all key nominations including company CEOs and university rectors through its nomenklatura system, making sure that only loyal people can get top positions (Brodsgaard 2012). There is a revolving door mechanism for cadres circulating them between party positions and state-owned business positions, both in order to enhance their experience and to restrain their personal power by making sure that nobody can stay too long in the same entity (Li 2020:

234). Furthermore, the party is integrated in business life as 53% of private and 91% of state-owned enterprises have CCP organizations (Zheng and Gore 2020: 1).

When it comes to power concentration in the economic realm, an information technology driven social credit system (SCS) is probably the most significant new addition to the communist toolkit in ensuring party control. By collecting data from different sources, social credit systems can monitor, assess, and change the behavior of both citizens and companies. At the time of writing, there were multiple coexisting SCSs for different purposes at different administrative levels rather than one coherent system. Individuals and companies have different systems. In addition, some systems concentrate on creating infrastructure for economic and financial activities whereas others are linked more with social governance. The People's Bank of China is in charge of creating a financial social credit system, whereas Beihang Credit is the only commercial company dealing with commercial credit rating services. In the social governance realm, there are both national and municipal blacklist/redlist systems for both individuals and companies (Liu 2019). Punishments for individuals include public webpages listing the names of blacklisted people, blocking their credit card use and access to high-speed trains and airplanes. Rewards include better interest rates for bank loans, discounts from energy bills and renting without deposits (Mistreanu 2018; Liu 2019). The corporate social credit system is more developed than the system designed for individuals, although the sanctioning mechanisms remains somewhat fragmented when it comes to cooperation between local and central level actors. Similarly to individuals, companies are rated and blacklisted entities can be found form the credit system's webpages. Companies that get poor ratings can get penalties and restrictions to market access. The system was supposed to be ready in 2020, but as there are problems of data-sharing between different parts of the system and sanctioning mechanisms remain underdeveloped, the deadline of 2020 does not seem plausible (European Chamber 2019).

Concluding remarks

This chapter has described fluctuating levels of autocratization in China using a framework concentrating on three dimensions of power concentration: personalization, administrative centralization, and state control over economic assets. It has demonstrated that during Xi's reign, there has been a clear tendency of power concentration in all of these three areas. The Chinese case is part of an international trend: Geddes et al. (2018) show, that as part of deepening autocratization, personalism in autocracies has increased significantly since the end of the Cold War. These trends should not be understated, as higher power concentration is associated with both increased war-proneness and domestic repression (Frantz et al. 2020; Weeks 2012).

The relationship between power concentration and regime resilience is not entirely clear as the Nathan–Fewsmith debate illustrates. While elite cohesion has explained authoritarian resilience in the past, it is possible that the factors associated with regime endurance will change their relative weight in the coming years as popular protests have become more significant a challenge to authoritarian regimes (Kendall-Taylor et al. 2020). Chinese government has taken social unrest issues seriously and invested a lot in digital forms of control such as CCTV cameras with automated facial recognition programmes. In Xinjiang, monitoring includes obligatory DNA sampling used for ethnic profiling (Xiao 2019). Xi's regime has built capacity to forecast large-scale popular protests and adapted its political indoctrination to the era of big data by using artificial intelligence (AI) in surveillance and censorship (Zeng 2016).

Furthermore, the COVID-19 pandemic presents both opportunities and challenges for the Chinese leadership. On the one hand, it provides a convenient reason for restricting mass gatherings, as seen in the decision to lengthen Hong Kong's lockdown in 2020 to prohibit June 4 commemoration activities (Tsang et al. 2020). On the other hand, the economic downturn following the epidemic hit the Chinese economy hard. During the two sessions in May 2020, the leadership decided not to set a GDP growth target for 2020 (Xinhua 2020). This is problematic not only for CCP's performance legitimacy, but the annus horribilis of 2020 will not give the CCP's 100-year anniversary in 2021 the kind of background the party hoped for. The pandemic has also paved the way for further mobile surveillance. Chinese citizens have started to become used to such measures thanks to the social credit system. Adding health data to the long list of data the authorities are collecting and using as a basis for limiting freedom of movement or other rights has not caused wide-ranging opposition in China. China's experiences of developing surveillance applications may provide Chinese companies opportunities to sell such applications abroad. However, data can also cause challenges to Chinese authoritarian regime, as it can be used in elite struggles with devastating effects on regime legitimacy (Zeng 2016).

While the power concentration measures applied in this chapter are useful, future research should keep an open mind about the possible ways political equilibrium in China might be formed in the coming years. Dynamism described here demonstrates how adaptive the party-state has been in the past, but nothing is set in stone. Multiple combinations of causes can result in a political equilibrium, and domestic and international conditions change creating a need for constant adaptation for the party-state. For example, crises of democracy in Western countries and the digital revolution influence the Chinese situation. It is likely that the tools used for maintaining an equilibrium will change and the relative weight given to different components in the combination can fluctuate as well. We need a lot of research in the future to understand what kind of conditions trigger changes in the different parameters of power concentration. However, it is already an advancement to be able to name some of the most important factors that vary in authoritarian governance.

References

Acemoglu, D. and Robinson, J. (2019) *The Narrow Corridor: States, Societies, and the Fate of Liberty*, New York: Penguin Press.

Ahlers, A., Heberer, T. and Schubert, G. (2015) '"Authoritarian resilience" and effective policy implementation in contemporary China – A local state perspective', *Duisburg Working Papers on East Asian Studies No. 99/2015*, 7–27. Available at https://www.econstor.eu/handle/10419/107663 (Accessed 15 May 2020).

Breslin, S. (2011) 'The "China model" and the global crisis: From Friedrich list to a Chinese model of governance?', *International Affairs* 87(6): 1323–1343.

Brodsgaard, K. (2012) 'Cadre and personnel management in the CPC', *China: An International Journal* 10(2): 69–83.

Chen, G. (2020) 'Politics of anti-corruption campaign', in Zheng, Y. and Gore, L.L.P. (eds.) *The Chinese Communist Party in Action: Consolidating Party Rule*, New York: Routledge, 137–158.

Chen, J. and Dickson, B. (2010) *Allies of the State: China's Private Entrepreneurs and Democratic Change*, Cambridge, MA: Harvard University Press.

De Mesquita, B.B, Smith, A. Siverson, R. and Morrow, J. (2003) *The Logic of Political Survival*, Cambridge, MA: MIT Press.

Deng, J. (2018) 'The national supervision commission: a new anti-corruption model in China', *International Journal of Law, Crime and Justice* 52: 58–73.

Dickson, B. (2016). *The Dictator's Dilemma. The Chinese Communist Party's Strategy for Survival*, Oxford: Oxford University Press.

Dickson, B., Shen, M. and Yan, J. (2017) 'Generating regime support in contemporary China: Legitimation and the local legitimacy deficit', *Modern China* 43(2): 123–155.

European Chamber (2019) 'The digital hand: How China's corporate social credit system conditions market actors', Available at https://www.europeanchamber.com.cn/en/publications-corporate-social-credit-system (accessed May 15, 2020).

Fewsmith, J. and Nathan, A. (2019) 'Authoritarian resilience revisited: Joseph Fewsmith with response from Andrew Nathan', *Journal of Contemporary China* 28(116): 174–175.

Frantz, E., Kendall-Taylor, A., Wright, J. and Xu, X. (2020) 'Personalization of power and repression in dictatorships', *The Journal of Politics* 82(1): 372–377.

Freedom House (2019) 'Freedom in the world 2019: Democracy in retreat', *Freedom House*. Available at: https://freedomhouse.org/sites/default/files/Feb2019_FH_FITW_2019_Report_ForWeb-compressed.pdf (accessed May 15, 2020).

Gallagher, M. (2002) '"Reform and Openness". Why China's economic reforms have delayed democracy', *World Politics* 54(3): 338–372.

Geddes, B. (2003) *Paradigms and Sandcastles: Theory Building and Research Design in Comparative Politics*, Ann Arbor: University of Michigan Press.

Geddes, B., Wright, J., and Frantz, E. (2018) *How Dictatorships Work: Power, Personalization, and Collapse*, Cambridge: Cambridge University Press.

Gerschewski, J. (2013) 'The three pillars of stability: Legitimation, repression, and co-optation in autocratic regimes', *Democratization* 20(1): 13–38.

Gilley, B. (1998) *Tiger on the Brink: Jiang Zemin and China's New Elite*, Berkeley: University of California Press.

Hess, S. (2013) *Authoritarian Landscapes: Popular Mobilization and the Institutional Sources of Resilience in Nondemocracies*, New York: Springer.

Hess, S. (2017) 'Decentralized meritocracy. Resilience, decay, and adaptation in the CCP's threat-management system', *Problems of Post-Communism* 64(1): 20–31.

IMF (2019) 'IMF fiscal decentralization dataset', *International Monetary Fund*. Available at: https://data.imf.org/?sk=1C28EBFB-62B3-4B0C-AED3-048EEEBB684F (accessed May 15, 2020).

Jakobson, L. and Knox, D. (2010) 'New foreign policy actors in China', *SIPRI Policy Paper* 26: 1–51.

Kendall-Taylor, A., Frantz, E., and Wright, J. (2020) 'The digital dictators: How technology strengthens autocracy', *Foreign Affairs* 99(2): 103–115.

Kenderdine, T. (2017) 'China's industrial policy, strategic emerging industries and space law', *Asia and the Pacific Policy Studies* 4(2): 325–342.

Kou, C. (2017) 'Xi Jinping in command: Solving the principal–agent problem in CCP–PLA relations?', *The China Quarterly* 232(4): 866–885.

Lampton, D. (2015) 'Xi Jinping and the national security commission: Policy coordination and political power', *Journal of Contemporary China* 24(95): 759–777.

Landry, P. (2008) *Decentralized Authoritarianism in China*, Cambridge: Cambridge University Press.

Ledberg, S. (2018) 'Political control and military autonomy: Reexamining the Chinese People's Liberation Army', *Asian Security* 14(2): 212–228.

Li, C. (2020) 'China's central state corporatism: The party and the governance of centrally controlled businesses', in Gore, L.L.P. and Zheng, Y. (eds.) *The Chinese Communist Party in Action: Consolidating Party Rule*, New York: Routledge, 220–239.

Li, N. (2015) 'Top leaders and the PLA: The different styles of Jiang, Hu and Xi', in Saunders, P. and Scobell, A. (eds.) *PLA Influence on China's National Security Policymaking*, Stanford: Stanford University Press, 120–140.

Liu, C. (2019) 'Multiple social credit systems in China', *Economic Sociology: The European Electronic Newsletter* 21(1): 22–32.

Londregan, J. and Poole, K. (1990) 'Poverty, the coup trap, and the seizure of executive power', *World Politics* 42(2): 151–183.

Lührmann, A. and Lindberg, S. (2019) 'A third wave of autocratization is here: What is new about it?', *Democratization* 26(7): 1095–1113.

Maerz, S. (2020) 'The many faces of authoritarian persistence: A set-theory perspective on the survival strategies of authoritarian regimes', *Government and Opposition* 55(1): 64–87.

Milhaupt, C. and Zheng, W. (2015) 'Beyond ownership: State capitalism and the Chinese firm', *UF Law Faculty Publications*. Available at https://scholarship.law.ufl.edu/cgi/viewcontent.cgi?article=1693&context=facultypub (accessed May 15, 2020).

Miller, A. (2014) 'How strong is Xi Jinping?', *China Leadership Monitor* 43. Available at: https://www.hoover.org/sites/default/files/research/docs/clm43am.pdf (accessed May 15, 2020).

Miller, A. (2015) 'The PLA in the party leadership decision-making system', in Saunders, P. and Scobell, A. (eds.) *PLA Influence on China's National Security Policymaking*, Stanford: Stanford University Press, 58–83.

Mistreanu, S. (2018) 'Life inside China's social credit laboratory', *Foreign Policy*, April 3. Available at https://foreignpolicy.com/2018/04/03/life-inside-chinas-social-credit-laboratory/ (accessed July 7, 2020).

Mulvenon, J. (2016) 'China's "Goldwater-Nichols"? The long-awaited PLA reorganization has finally arrived', *China Leadership Monitor* 49. Available at https://www.hoover.org/research/chinas-goldwater-nichols-long-awaited-pla-reorganization-has-finally-arrived (accessed December 28, 2020).

Mulvenon, J. (2018) 'And then there were seven: The new, slimmed-down central military commission', *China Leadership Monitor* 56. Available at https://www.hoover.org/sites/default/files/research/docs/clm56jm.pdf (accessed December 28, 2020).

Nathan, A. (2003) 'China's changing of the guard. Authoritarian resilience', *Journal of Democracy* 14(1): 6–17.

National Manufacturing Strategy Advisory Committee NMSAC (2015) 《中国制造 2025》重点领域技术路线图 (Made in China 2025. Technology roadmap for key areas). Available at: http://www.cae.cn/cae/html/files/2015-10/29/20151029105822561730637.pdf (accessed June 7, 2020).

Naughton, B. (2015) 'Local debt restructuring: A case of ongoing authoritarian reform', *China Leadership Monitor* 47. Available at: https://www.hoover.org/research/local-debt-restructuring-case-ongoing-authoritarian-reform (accessed May 15, 2020).

Oi, J. (1992) 'Fiscal reform and the economic foundations of local state corporatism in China', *World Politics* 45(October): 99–126.

Pepinsky, T. (2019) 'How dictatorships work: Power, personalization and collapse. (book review)', *Perspectives on Politics* 17(2): 594–595.

Pettis, M. (2013) *Avoiding the Fall. China's Economic Restructuring*, Washington: Carnegie Endowment for International Peace.

Rühlig, T. (2020) 'Who controls Huawei? Implications for Europe', *UI Paper 5/2020, Swedish Institute of International Affairs*. Available at: https://www.ui.se/globalassets/butiken/ui-paper/2020/ui-paper-no.-5-2020.pdf (accessed May 15, 2020).

Saunders, P.C. and Wutnow, J. (2016) 'China's Goldwater-Nichols? Assessing PLA organizational reforms', *Institute for National Strategic Studies, Joint Force Quarterly* 82. Available at: https://ndupress.ndu.edu/Media/News/Article/793267/chinas-goldwater-nichols-assessing-pla-organizational-reforms/ (accessed May 15, 2020).

Schmotz, A. (2015) 'Vulnerability and compensation: Constructing an index of co-optation in autocratic regimes', *European Political Science* 14(4): 439–457.

Shambaugh, D. (2008) *The Chinese Communist Party. Atrophy and Adaptation*, Washington: University of California Press.

Shambaugh, D. (2016) *China's Future*, Cambridge: Polity Press.

Shirk, S. (2018) 'China in Xi's "New Era": The return to personalistic rule', *Journal of Democracy* 29(2): 22–36.

Sinkkonen, E. (2014) *Rethinking National Identity. The Wider Context of Foreign Policy Making During the Era of Hu Jintao, 2002–2012*. Doctoral dissertation. University of Oxford.

Smith, H. (2015) *North Korea: Markets and Military Rule*, Cambridge: Cambridge University Press.

Stent, J. (2017) *China's Banking Transformation. The Untold Story*, Oxford: Oxford University Press.

Svolik, M.W. (2012) *The Politics of Authoritarian Rule*, Cambridge: Cambridge University Press.

Tsai, K. and Naughton, B. (2015) 'Introduction', in Naughton, B. and Tsai, K. (eds.) *State Capitalism, Institutional Adaptation, and the Chinese Miracle*, Cambridge: Cambridge University Press, 1–24.

Tsang, E., Leung, K. and Chan, H.-h. (2020) 'Coronavirus: Hong Kong extends social-distancing curbs including gathering ban, compulsory quarantine as four new cluster cases raise "super spreader" fears', *South China Morning Post*, 2 June. Available at: https://www.scmp.com/news/hong-kong/health-environment/article/3087082/coronavirus-four-new-cases-same-housing-estate (accessed June 6, 2020).

Wang, P. (2017) *China's Governance: Across Vertical and Horizontal Connexions*, Cham: Springer.

Weeks, J. (2012) 'Strongmen and straw men: Authoritarian regimes and the initiation of international conflict', *American Political Science Review* 106(2): 326–347.

World Bank. Databank. Available at: https://data.worldbank.org/indicator/NY.GDP.MKTP.KD.ZG?locations=CN (accessed May 15, 2020).

Wu, G. (2018) 'A setback or boost for Xi Jinping's concentration of power? Domination versus resistance within the CCP elite', *China Leadership Monitor*, 1 December. Available at: https://www.prcleader.org/bump-or-speed-up (accessed May 15, 2020).

Wübbeke, J., Meissner, M., Zenglein, M., Ives, J. and Conrad, B. (2016) 'Made in China 2025. The making of a high-tech superpower and consequences for industrial countries Mercator Institute for China Studies', Available at: https://www.merics.org/sites/default/files/2017-09/MPOC_No.2_MadeinChina2025.pdf (accessed June 7, 2020).

Xiao, Q. (2019) 'The road to digital unfreedom: President Xi's surveillance state', *Journal of Democracy* 30(1): 53–67.

Xinhua (2014) 'Full text: Report on the work of the government (2014)', *Xinhua*, 14 March. Available at: http://english.www.gov.cn/archive/publications/2014/08/23/content_281474982987826.htm (accessed July 6, 2020).

Xinhua (2018) 'Proposed list of ministries, commissions of China's cabinet after reform', *Xinhua*, 13 March. Available at: http://www.xinhuanet.com/english/2018-03/13/c_137035291.htm (accessed May 15, 2020).

Xinhua (2020) 'China focus: Key takeaways from "two sessions" in special year', *Xinhua*, 28 May. Available at: http://www.xinhuanet.com/english/2020-05/28/c_139096488.htm (accessed June 6, 2020).

Yang, D. (2004) *Remaking the Chinese Leviathan. Market Transition and the Politics of Governance in China*, Stanford: Stanford University Press.

You, J. (2016) 'China's national security commission: Theory, evolution and operations', *Journal of Contemporary China* 25(98): 178–196.

Zeng, J. (2016) 'China's date with big data', *International Affairs* 92(6): 1443–1462.

Zhang, C. (2019) 'How much do state-owned enterprises contribute to China's GDP and employment?', *World Bank Working Paper*. Available at http://documents.worldbank.org/curated/en/390691565249400884/How-Much-Do-State-Owned-Enterprises-Contribute-to-China-s-GDP-and-Employment (accessed May 15, 2020).

Zhao, Z. (2010) 'The China model: Can it replace the Western model of modernization?', *Journal of Contemporary China* 19(65): 419–436.

Zheng, Y. (2010) *The Chinese Communist Party as Organizational Emperor. Culture, Reproduction and Transformation*, London: Routledge.

Zheng, Y. and Gore, L.L.P. (2020) 'Introduction', in Zheng, Y. and Gore, L.L.P. (eds.) *The Chinese Communist Party in Action: Consolidating Party Rule*, New York: Routledge, 1–10.

Zhu, J. and Zhang, D. (2017) 'Weapons of the powerful: Authoritarian elite competition and politicized anticorruption in China', *Contemporary Political Studies* 50(9): 1186–1220.

Zuboff, S. (2015) 'Big other: Surveillance capitalism and the prospects of an information civilization', *Journal of Information Technology* 30(1): 75–89.

9

Conceptualizing 'meritocracy' as ruling legitimacy in the course of China's history, transformation, and global rise

Li Xing

Introduction: Crisis, transformation, and legitimacy

The US magazine *Time* (November 2, 2017) published a special edition with an eye-catching cover page in both Chinese and English: 'China Won'. This core article admits,

> As recently as five years ago, there was consensus that China would one day need fundamental political reform for the state to maintain its legitimacy and that China could not sustain its state capitalist system. Today China's political and economic system is better equipped and perhaps even more sustainable than the American model.

Other facts the West might have a great deal of difficulty accepting are that (1) the result of the 2018 Edelman Trust Barometer showed that the average rate of trust in institutions among the general population in China was 84%, the highest among countries surveyed and up eight percentage points from 2017; (2) the Ipsos Public Affairs survey in 2017 showed 87% of Chinese people believe that the country was moving in the right direction; and (3) in July 2020 the Ash Center for Democratic Governance and Innovation, Harvard University, released a landmark study (Cunningham et al. 2020) examining Chinese public opinion over a 13-year period. The survey shows that Chinese citizens are satisfied with Chinese authorities, especially with the central government which receives the strongest level of approval, increasing from 86% to 93% between 2003 and 2016. These facts are totally against the conventional wisdom that people do not trust authoritarian systems which are not democratically elected.

One of the puzzling questions facing many scholars of social sciences, be they Western or Chinese, and especially those who have been engaged in Chinese Studies, is how to comprehend and interpret China's historical transformations marked by fundamental changes, failures, and successes (Dirlik & Meisner 1989; Harding 1987; Hinton 1990; Weil 1996, etc.). The revolutionary and dramatic transformations in China in the 20th century and its continuous global rise in the 21st century qualify China to be an ideal 'case study' for development studies and scientific research on political, economic, and social change. Since the

DOI: 10.4324/9780429059704-12

dawn of the 20th century, the world has witnessed theatrical transformations in China that no other countries had experienced and could be compared with.

Politically, the Chinese empire fell disgracefully from a regional hegemonic 'Middle Kingdom' to a semicolonial periphery country, which experienced a republic revolution turning the country from an imperial multiethnicity monarchy to a short-lived republic of quasi-nationalism, and from a disintegrated and contending warlordism to a centralized revolutionary socialist state. From the end of 1970s, when China started to pursue its economic reform, Western liberal wishful thinking about the imminent transformation of China into a democratic, capitalist, market economy did not disappear until recently when Western core powers and their academics and policymakers reluctantly realized 'the gamble has failed' (*The Economist* March 1, 2018).

Economically, China leaped forward from an agrarian state directly to a socialist centrally planned economy after the founding of the new Republic in 1949. Since the end of the 1970s the country has embarked on economic reform, and gradually moved to a market-oriented economy. What puzzles the West is the fact that China's state-led economic success and its global rise in the past four decades does not conform to some of the most basic Western economic fundamentals about what makes nations grow and about the set of mutually dependent relationships between property rights and economic growth, between the rule of law and market economy, between free currency flow and economic order.

Ideologically, Chinese value systems underwent revolutionary transformations from feudal social relationships to socialist class-based political relationships with the establishment of the new socialist republic. Since economic reform started, the Chinese party-state, albeit still officially associating itself with Marxism and socialism in theory, has in practice implemented many market-oriented policies in line with capitalism and individualism. However, 'sinicization' has been the unique characteristic of the party-state's ideological and political embeddedness. The notion of sinicization entails a spontaneous process of absorbing new or foreign ideas while forcing them to be embedded into Chinese native practices within the Chinese political and cultural norms.

Since the Chinese Communist Party (CCP) won state power and became the ruling party in 1949, the party-state has experienced three major periods of 'legitimation crisis' in which the legitimacy of the party faced unprecedented challenges. The first serious crisis refers to the 'crisis of socialism' (1950s–1970s), during which the decade of the Cultural Revolution (1966–1976) was seen as the period of the uttermost political and economic radicalism and social chaos, which brought the entire country to the brink of civil turmoil. The second major crisis refers to the 'crisis of legitimacy' that was associated with market reform after the end of the 1970s. The grave consequences generated by China's marketization development in terms of overemphasizing economic growth and productivity eroded the party-state's own adherence to 'political correctness' based on socialist equality and common prosperity. The third crisis was the 'crisis of liberation', and it was in one way or another connected with the second crisis. It was driven by the student demonstration, calling for political democratization, which led to the tragedy of Tiananmen Square on June 4, 1989. It was widely believed that the party-state would collapse in a way similar to that of its Eastern European counterparts. Such belief was based on the believed incompatibility between the sociopolitical and socioeconomic liberal forces brought about by the market forces and the party-state's illiberalism and political authoritarianism. It has periodically generated various predictions, such as 'China collapse' (Chang 2001), and 'the end of the CCP rule' (Shambaugh 2015).

Surprisingly, despite the fact that the Chinese party-state experienced dramatic historical transformations embedded with major crises (development setbacks, ideological challenges, and a legitimation crisis), today not only has the party-state survived all these crises but also China has, under the leadership of the CCP, lifted half a billion people out of poverty, become the second largest world economy, the world's largest trading country, the largest foreign currency holder, the largest exporter of high-tech manufacturing goods, a new eminent international aid provider, and the world's largest peace-keeping force, and so on. What makes the world, especially the West, curious about China's rise is the political structure that sits at the heart of China's economic success and that has become a key focus of global attention and controversy. It is under this context, the so-called 'Chinese development model', led by its unique governance system, known as political meritocracy, that calls for global attention in order to grasp China's rise to superpower status.

China's economic success and its global impact raises a controversial question on whether China is developing a 'Chinese model' alternative to the Western one. What worries the West most essentially is twofold: the Chinese statist development model is seen as fundamentally incompatible with Western liberal values in terms of freedom, democracy, and individual human rights; and China is successfully exporting its illiberal model globally (Bell 2018). Meanwhile, the world is currently witnessing the fierce competition between the world's two largest economies, and ironically, such competition is often depicted in the Western media as one between an opaque Communist state and a transparent populous democracy. It can be argued that beneath this superficial difference it is a competition between two political models, one based more on meritocratic leadership and the other on popular election (Zhang 2012).

Recently, Kiron Skinner, the head of policy planning at the US State Department, identified China–US conflict as 'a fight with a really different civilization and a different ideology and the US hasn't had that before', and the China challenge represented 'the first time that we will have a great power competitor that is not Caucasian' (Panda 2019). Although such a 'clash of civilization' (Huntington 1993) approach to China–US competition is rejected by both countries and worldwide, the ghost of 'civilization differences' in terms of philosophies, norms, values, sociopolitical system will never die.

Research questions, analytical approach, and objective

In the context that the Chinese party-state has been able to survive from various crises and becoming even larger and stronger, what is the fundamental political, economic and social basis that has been sustaining the ruling legitimacy in China in the course of its development and transformation? What is the essential historical and cultural source of Chinese political legitimacy? Worldwide debates on this question are still going on (Bo 2015; Hung et al. 2015; Li 2018; Pei 2015; Ruan 2015). One common approach by many Chinese researchers to the above questions is to look more at theoretical explanations by Western theories than at Chinese cultural philosophies when confronted with the legitimacy conundrum regarding political and regime legitimacy in China (Zeng 2014).

Discussing political legitimacy, good government, political representation, and consent is always controversial for any political system anywhere in the world. In the past decades, fascination or irritation with China has always influenced Western scholarship and journalism, which often produces abrupt sentiment from extremes of glowing appraisal and unqualified optimism to extremes of unjustified revulsion and deep pessimism. One common mistake in the West when dealing with China is a lack of deep understanding of the fundamental pillar that sustains the Chinese narratives and identity of political legitimacy shaped by historical and cultural tradition.

The author has also studied how the CCP has proved to possess resilient adaptability to maintain its ruling legitimacy from the neo-Gramscian perspectives (Li 2018). This chapter attempts to focus on the 'mechanism' that underlines ruling legitimacy in China. The objective of this chapter is twofold: First, it provides a *framework*, based on 'meritocracy' as an enduring aspect of Chinese sociopolitical order, for identifying, conceptualizing, and interpreting the core historical and cultural source of China's 'state legitimacy' and exploring the Chinese cultural and civilizational source of 'ruling legitimacy'. Second, it demonstrates and analyzes how meritocracy is functioning as a basis for 'leadership legitimacy' in the contemporary party-state's governance system.

Conceptually, the core analytical lens of this chapter is the notion of 'meritocracy'. In studying China politics and Chinese political culture, meritocracy is one of the most important theoretical paradigms, and there is a close compatibility between meritocracy as a research approach and the fundamental realities of Chinese politics (Guo & Zhang 2014). The chapter analyzes and discusses 'meritocracy' in order to uncover how the concept contributes to influencing Chinese postreform economic development and shaping its distinctive political legitimacy in the course of its global rise. The conclusion of this chapter posits that the Chinese system of political meritocracy is historically and culturally unique, and it has to be judged on the basis of its merits and demerits within the Chinese political cultural context in connection with China's global rise in the era of globalization and transnational capitalism.

Although the main purpose of this chapter is to provide a framework for understanding how the Chinese system of meritocracy historically evolved and how the system functions in the contemporary era, the author is aware of the criticism that the centralization of state power and political individuals underlining the meritocracy system also bears serious contradictions in safeguarding some fundamental aspects of society and human life, such as individual freedom and rights, rule of law, freedom of press and expression, as well as political opposition. In other words, the author recognizes the gap between the ideal and the reality. The message the author wishes to convey is that we should not go to the extremes of romanticizing the Chinese political system of meritocracy or demonizing such a system without attempting to understand where it came from and how it functions. In order to understand the implication and impact of the rise of China on the current world order, it is imperative to understand the role of China's internalities in the process of China's historical transformations and its recent resurgence.

Revisiting 'meritocracy' (精英治国) as a state-governing system

The concept was first coined by the British sociologist and politician Michael Dunlop Young in his book the *Rise of the Meritocracy* (1958). Meritocracy is the political philosophy in which political position and influence are assigned largely according to the intellectual talent and career achievement of the individual. Daniel Bell, who is one of best known for his extensive coverage on Chinese political model defines *political meritocracy* as:

> the idea that a political system is designed with the aim of selecting political leaders with above average ability to make informed political judgments. That is, political meritocracy has two key components: (1) the political leaders have above average ability and anticipated virtue; and (2) the selection mechanism is designed to choose such leaders.
>
> *(Bell 2012)*

The core idea of political meritocracy emphasizes that economic goods and/or political power should be vested in individual people on the basis of talent, effort, and achievement. Advancement in such a system is based on performance, as measured through examination or demonstrated achievement. The fundamental idea of meritocracy is designed with the aim of choosing political leaders and government elites with superior leadership ability and governance experience. The importance of choosing the right leaders is understood by Bell:'the quality of life in any society is determined, in considerable measure, by the quality of leadership. A society that does not have its best men at the head of its leading institutions is a sociological and moral absurdity' (Bell 2015: 2).

The Confucian meritocratic order

The prevailing sustainability of the Chinese political system lies in the belief that power should be invested on the basis of political loyalty, professional capability, and manageable achievement, and the legitimacy of a system must be assessed on the basis of competence and performance. Meritocracy has been both the historical and cultural source of Chinese political legitimacy, and it is one of the fundamental and unique pillars that underline the Chinese political system and ruling legitimacy.

The ideology of meritocracy in China originated in the ancient Chinese philosophy of Confucianism. The Chinese 'Confucian order' was a 'civilization state order'[1] that predetermines (1) the acceptance of a mono moral and sociopolitical arrangement, in which the imperial state (government and elites) enjoyed 'absolute' power and 'natural' authority, and it permitted no challenge; and (2) the strength and durability of a unique political culture which was centered around the Confucian ethics of order, hierarchy, loyalty, obligation, and obedience. Such a political culture explains that 'the overpowering obligation felt by Chinese rulers to preserve the unity of their civilization has meant that there could be no compromises in Chinese cultural attitudes about power and authority' (Pye 1990: 58). The state was perceived as the guardian, custodian, and embodiment of Chinese civilization. The duty of the state is to protect imperial China's unity and integrity – political unity and ideological monolism coexisting with sociocultural pluralism is the condition of its existence. The state obligation and legitimacy was to provide people and society with order, security, and peace. If not, the state then lost the 'Mandate of Heaven'[2] to rule. Even when the imperial system broke down in the early 20th century after the Republic Revolution (1911–1912), which unleashed a great deal of cultural iconoclasm in Chinese society, it was still very rare to find anarchist defenders of self-interested individualism. It was commonly accepted that the state granted rights and determined their limits (Ferdinand 1991: 166).

The Chinese system of meritocracy was historically founded on and connected withinterrelated and two-layer societal structures, and the Chinese-language expression for 'country' or 'nation state' consists of two words 'Guo Jia' (国家, 'state and family'), referring to the two-layer structure: (1) at the top 'Guo' level, it was the imperial governance of various administrative levels; and (2) at the bottom 'Jia' level, it was family- and kinship-based extended society and social networks. Corresponding to the two-layer societal structure, the Chinese meritocratic system also had a two-layer structure. The first layer at the top is 'ruling meritocracy', that is, political meritocracy. Ruling meritocracy is the general principle based on which governing leaders are selected and appointed. As discussed above, the criteria for selection and appointment of leaders are primarily on the basis of their 'competency' including education, work experience, and concrete accomplishment, while the emphasis of competency evaluation is individual ability, experience, capability, and capacity. The second layer at the bottom includes social, occupational, or educational meritocracy, through which every individual is ideally presumed to be able to pursue his or her potential and suitable career. One key aspect to guarantee meritocratic equality is equal access to education, which provides differentiated opportunities for professional advancement.

The 'common sense', which underlines the system of meritocracy, and which has been internalized in China and other Asian societies, is well depicted by Boden (2016: 6) in a nutshell:

> [P]eople are not considered equal, but are ranked hierarchically according to their merits. One has to 'merit' one's position in society. By studying hard, working hard and persistence one can climb up. Those who succeed in building more 'merits' than others 'deserve' to be on a higher scale of the social ladder. Social status is linked to moral power obtained by personal development, talents and competence. Moral behavior means that a person acts according to his or her role in the hierarchy of people in each specific situation.

The Chinese system of meritocracy and its contemporary aspects

Meritocracy was abandoned during the Cultural Revolution (1966–1976), during which 'class struggle', in terms of family root, political inclination, and party internal fraction, replaced meritocracy to became a means of selecting leaders through the party-state structure, and during which ruling legitimacy was transformed from professional 'expert' to political 'red'.[3] Following the implementation of economic reform since the late 1970s, the emphasis on leadership legitimacy changed back from 'red' to 'expert'. Meritocracy in its current form has gone through the economic marketization process and has its manifestation imprinted in the 'Chinese model'.

Economic marketization has fundamentally changed the social basis of the Chinese party-state, and new bases and sources for the legitimacy of the party-state must be constantly regenerated and renegotiated through ideological adjustments and intraparty reforms (Sausmikat 2006). The party-state has adopted a very pragmatic strategy of 'performance legitimacy' (Zhu 2011) since China began its reform. It means that the government relies on accomplishing concrete goals such as economic growth, social stability, strengthening national power, and 'good governance' (governing competence and accountability) to retain its legitimacy. While it is able to attain considerable domestic support by implementing this strategy, it has no particular interest in pursuing democratization. But the flaw of overemphasizing and overrewarding market-based 'professionalism' and 'elitism' caused serious backfire on the 'crisis of legitimacy' brought about by a number of socioeconomic and sociopolitical contradictions, such as social disparities and economic inequalities, corruption, social security decay, environmental degradation. Actions were taken under Xi Jinping's government that initiated nationwide anticorruption and poverty alleviation campaigns in order to improve regime legitimacy. Despite different international opinions on Xi Jinping's regime and on Xi himself, the recent survey of Chinese public opinion mentioned before by the Ash Center at Harvard University (Cunningham et al. 2020) shows that Beijing is 'enjoying greater legitimacy than any Western state' (*South China Morning Post*, July 19, 2020).

China's success in transforming itself from a plan-economy owned and controlled by the state to a market-economy supervised and regulated by the state in combination with the market mechanism has been coined as the 'Chinese model'. This concept has even been paradigmatically raised to the normative level as the 'Beijing Consensus'. The notion of the 'Chinese model' is embedded with specific historical dimensions, unique cultural elements and assertive ideational beliefs, and it is becoming increasingly attractive to developing countries. It is particularly attractive to many developing countries in terms of how to manage state-market-society relations and an international political economy. Thomas Friedman, a *New York Times* foreign affairs columnist, openly admits the affectivity of the Chinese political system according to which 'one party can just impose the politically difficult but critically important policies needed to move a society forward in the 21st century' (Friedman 2009). Even John Williamson, one of the main architects of the 'Washington Consensus', acknowledged in an essay in 2012 that the Beijing Consensus seems to be gaining global recognition at the expense of the Washington Consensus (Kurlantzick 2013).

The manifestation of the Chinese party-state meritocratic system

Historically and culturally, meritocracy at the highest level of the central party-state leadership is less about specific technocratic and administrative skills, but more about charismatic attraction, possession of firm faith and courage and appealing personality, capacity for national organization and mobilization, characteristics of resilient shrewdness to carry out historical mission and national objective, and so on. It is a strong-man level of politics where the recognition as the 'core leader' is not granted but earned by his/her individual abilities in controlling leaders at the provincial level and in the army as well as in uniting fractions within the party-state (Guo 2019). Today in a globalized modern China, some new qualification factors are becoming indispensable, such as age, education level, governing experience, and so on.

For the past four decades of China's economic reform and global rise, the Chinese party-state has strengthened its ruling legitimacy due to its role both in consolidating societies in developmental flux and in creating entrepreneurial classes to compete on the world market. Chinese elites and mainstream intellectuals see authoritarian government as a useful expedient for effective policymaking in the face of political instability and global crises. Most Chinese policymakers do not regard Western liberal democracy on its own as a political system that will necessarily lead to development. From their point of view, what a country needs in facing development challenges and global crises is discipline and governance more than democracy.

Figure 9.1 shows the 'party + state' dual leadership system. Theoretically, there is a division of labor between government and party structures, but in practice, they often perform similar functions with different emphasis. Under all circumstances, the party structure in the form of 'party committees' exercise 'leadership status' over parallel government structures playing a 'guardian' role. The figure also presents a mixture of a three-layer Chinese model which Bell describes as 'democracy at the bottom, experimentation in the middle, and meritocracy at the top' (Bell 2015: 178), and which he regards as the optimized solution for China.

The three-layer stratification also explains how the mechanism of meritocracy functions in the current Chinese political system (Figure 9.2). The bottom layer of township and village is the place where the experiment of deliberative democracy with various Chinese characteristics is practiced, such as elite-public deliberation, village committees/assemblies, and deliberative polls (He 2014; He & Warren 2011). At this level, the emphasis is on 'social harmony' and 'social stability'. This level also provides a space where the 'seed' of local candidates for future local leaders is to be discovered, and where existing individual cadres

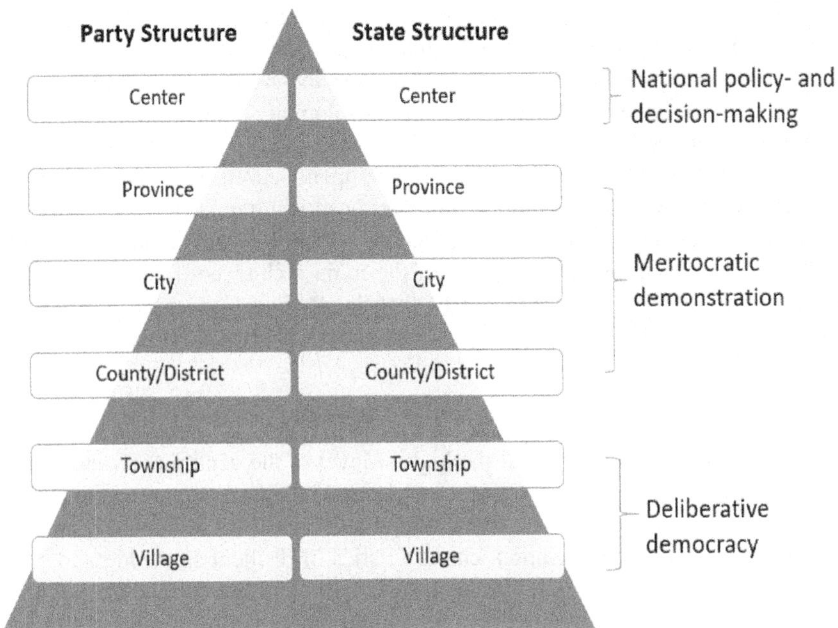

Figure 9.1 The three-layer structure of the Chinese party-state dual leadership system.

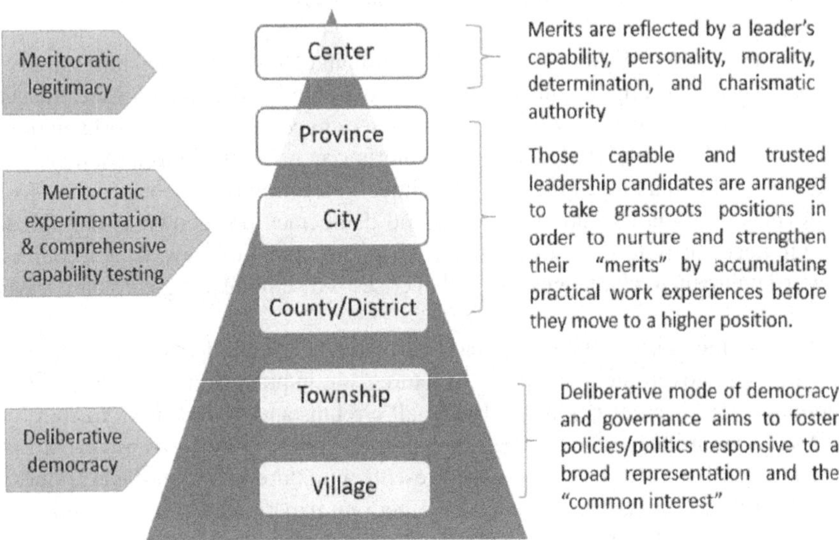

Figure 9.2 The three-layer model of the Chinese meritocratic system.

('干部')[4] can unleash their leadership potentials to demonstrate their merits in fulfilling the targeted objectives in terms of promoting economic development, maintaining local harmony and stability.

At the middle layer of county-city-province, the appointment of party and state official positions is based on candidates' multifaceted 'merits'. The qualification assessment process at this layer consists of a mixture of merit-measuring procedures depending on the nature of the positions, such as 'democratic nomination' (民主提名), 'democratic assessment' (民主测评), 'public opinion' (民意调查), 'analysis of actual achievements' (实绩分析), 'individual interview' (个别谈话), and 'comprehensive deliberation' (综合评价) (Li & Gore 2018: 88). All posteconomic reform Chinese presidents had provincial party-state governor positions before their entrance into the central party-state structures. A good example is the current Chinese President Xi Jinping, who has built a rich career that he has developed across the three levels for four decades (see the Appendix).

The source of Chinese authoritarian resiliency and its self-correcting mechanism

Figure 9.2 shows that the bottom layer of deliberative democracy is one of the key sources that make the Chinese political system resilient. Contrary to the conventional wisdom that authoritarian systems are inherently fragile because of weak legitimacy, overreliance on coercion, overcentralization of decision making, and the predominance of personal power over institutional norms (Nathan 2003: 6), Nathan developed the concept of 'authoritarian resiliency' (2003) in which he describes the resilient capacity associated with the particular Chinese authoritarian system.

One of the features of the resilient capacity of the Chinese political system is 'deliberative mode of governance', also called 'deliberative Democracy'. Accordingly, it is a unique combination of deliberation and democracy. As He and Warren point out (2011: 269),

> Democracy involves the inclusion of individuals in matters that affect them through distributions of empowerments such as votes and rights. Deliberation is a mode of communication involving persuasion-based influence. Combinations of non-inclusive power and deliberative influence – authoritarian deliberation – are readily identifiable in China.

The deliberative mode of governance is one of the crucial sources of the self-correcting mechanism of the Chinese political system.

Figure 9.3 shows the central features of Chinese self-correcting mechanism. They can be characterized as a kind of 'responsive governance', that is, responding efficiently and effectively to societal problems and people's real needs through anchoring policies, strategies, programs, activities and resources. Since the Chinese meritocratic system is based on 'upward accountability', contrary to Western electorate democracy's 'downward accountability', the party-state is aware of the indispensable imperative to be responsive to public opinion. Very often, public opinion and grassroot reaction are generating and regenerating government 'policy cycles', that is, policymaking – policy withdrawal – policy remaking. In other words, the policy cycles also point to another feature of the Chinese self-correcting mechanism – 'experimental governance'. In retrospect, the success of the Chinese development model has been based on a 'trial-test-implementation' process. For example, multiple 'economic zones' in different parts of the country function as a test ground before a policy extends to nationwide implementation.

Guanxi or meritocracy – two sides of the same coin

It is reasonable to claim that all bureaucratic systems in the world including Western democracies cannot avoid a mixture of merit and patronage with different countries prioritizing the former or the latter. Likewise, it also needs to emphasize the phenomenon that Chinese

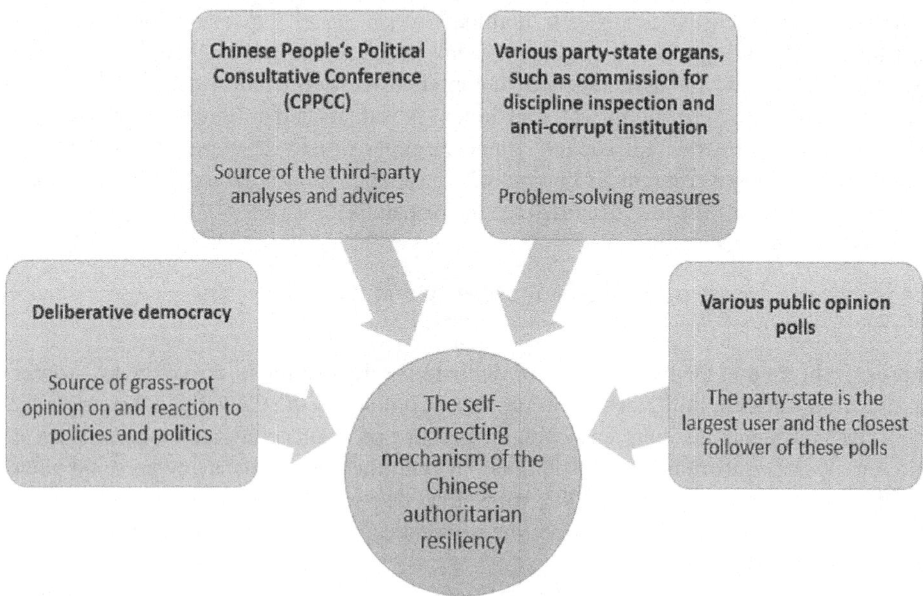

Figure 9.3 Sources of self-correcting mechanism in the Chinese political system.

meritocracy, seen from a deep-seated sociocultural and sociopolitical level of mechanism, is sometimes mixed with 'merit-based patronage' than what is ideally defined as 'meritocracy' (Li & Gore 2018: 88). In other words, meritocracy is only one side of the coin; and the other side is relationship (guanxi关系).

Guanxi is broadly understood as 'the lifeblood of all things Chinese – business, politics, and society' (Luo 1997: 45). Seen from a political perspective, *guanxi* is defined as 'one of the most fundamental aspects of Chinese political behavior' (Pye 1995: 35). To put it in a practical context, *guanxi* is interpreted by a number of scholars as the 'establishment and maintenance of an intricate and pervasive relational network engendered by the practice of unlimited exchange of favors between its members and bound by reciprocal obligation, assurance, and mutuality' (Kavalski 2018). The author needs to point out that it is the 'logic of relationality' (Qin 2016) or 'logic of guanxi' (Kavalski 2018) that is adjusting the 'logic of meritocracy'. For example, a critical research result shows that although both merit and guanxi are important indictors in the Chinese cadre promotion system, nevertheless, 'recognition and appreciation from superiors is sometimes more important than merit' (Li & Gore 2018: 98).

However, since the new Chinese government under Xi Jinping came to power, the anti-corruption campaign has targeted widespread corruption in Chinese officialdom. Rampant corruption deteriorated income inequality and damaged the legitimacy of the party-state. The anticorruption aimed at narrowing the gap between the ruled and the ruling. Many measures to address the problem of 'more patronage than merit' have been installed as part of a self-correcting mechanism. Many meritocratic procedures in state and public institutions are further reinforced in which 'merit evidence' (education, examination, competence, experience, career record) must be prioritized as the central criteria in civil service employment and cadre career promotion.

Meritocratic mechanism for upward mobility – the examination system

The Confucian philosophy and the Confucian social order, as mentioned earlier in the chapter, advocated that a state should be ruled by men of ability and virtue, and state rulers and public servants should be selected and appointed through a competitive selection system. The main method of selection was the examination system (the *Keju* system, 科举制). In Chinese history, such a system became widely applied as a legitimate 'fair' means to select capable civil servants to serve the imperial empire. Ever since its maturity in the Tang Dynasty (618–907), and until its abolition in 1905, the examination system was a crucial competitive mechanism in selecting competent civil servants.

The basic principle of the examination system is to recruit persons on the basis of merit rather than on the basis of family wealth or political connection. Since success in the examination could lead to the improvement of personal prestige and privilege as well as family social status, examination-oriented education was considered as the key to success in the system. Therefore, education was highly regarded in traditional China and intellectuals was ranked the highest in the Chinese social stratifications. The type of 'merits' that the examination system attempted to seek was neither technical and scientific expertise, nor economic bookkeeping, but knowledge of the classics and literary style that promoted shared values and cultures. It was assumed that these ideational 'commons' – philosophical and ideological unification – could help to unify the empire under a ruling legitimacy supported by shared 'merits'. Therefore, the examination system played the function as sociocultural glue and connected various aspects of premodern Chinese culture, history, politics, society, and economy (Cheng et al. 2009).

Meritocracy is also a basic value in modern Western bureaucratic organization, and it is one of the seven factors that Weber (1947) identified as classical attributes of Western bureaucracy: rules, specialization, meritocracy, hierarchy, separate ownership, impersonality, and accountability. In line with Weber, meritocracy rests on the idea that recruitment, promotion, and hierarchies should be determined by an individual's knowledge and skills. Noticeably, Weber, in his *The Protestant Ethic and the Spirit of Capitalism* (2005) [1930], argued that Protestantism fostered a culture that interpreted economic success as a sign of election and salvation, and suggested that meritocracy grew and developed out of a religious worldview and spirit. Following the migration of European Protestants to America, the meritocratic ideology was tightly coupled with the spirit of capitalism, equal opportunity and individual pursuit of success, which are the fundamental components of the concept of the 'American Dream'. With regard to government and legitimacy, Weber's notion about administrative bureaucratic structure (civil service), which truly reflects the key aspects of meritocracy: (a) power concentration in the state apparatus, (b) ruling legitimacy, (c) centrality of leadership groups, and (d) the professional capacity of these elite groups as cohesive power actors, is clearly traceable in his writings (Weber 1972, 1978).

Civil service examination and recruitment

Today, the 'civil service examination system' (公务员考试制度) is still one of the basic mechanisms for the Chinese party-state to find and select candidates for serving party and state administrations at various levels. Literally, the 'civil service' examination aims to recruit 'civil servants' for the party-state bureaucracy. The post-Mao 'civil servant employment system' was initially established in 1989 and it has become a fully mature system for human

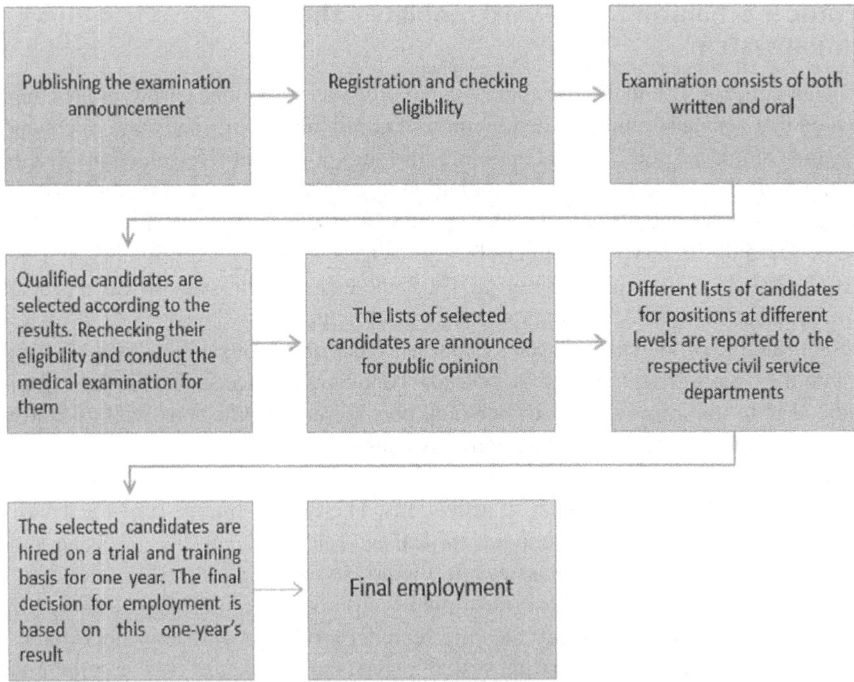

Figure 9.4 The procedure of the Chinese civil service examination and employment.

resource recruitment. Through the examination-employment procedures (see Figure 9.4), the best individuals with strong merits (knowledge, capability, capacity, etc.) are supposed to be discovered. Yet, the procedure is also criticized as being rather complicated and costly both for the state and individuals.

The civil service examination system together with the Civil Service Law ratified in 2005 was a major representative measure for the reform of the Chinese political system since China's reform and opening up. It has fundamentally abolished the 'tenure system of cadres' and has largely improved the efficiency of government. The current 'national civil service system' clearly stipulates that it is necessary to pass a strict and fair examination procedure in order to enter the civil service, thus ending the prereform noninstitutional, nonprocedural, and arbitrary nature of civil servant selection.

Meritocratic self-correcting mechanism for performance evaluation

The above discusses the role of examination as a mechanism for upward mobility especially in selecting and recruiting civil service personnel to serve the party-state. Then, what is the evaluation system to assess the party-state civil service performance? Unlike Western countries where voting and poll are used as mechanisms to assess performance and legitimacy of state and government, the Chinese party-state employs a unique internal adaptive system called the 'cadre evaluation system (CES)' (干部考核制度). It is also understood as the 'cadre responsibility system', which is one of the most important components of meritocratic performance criteria.

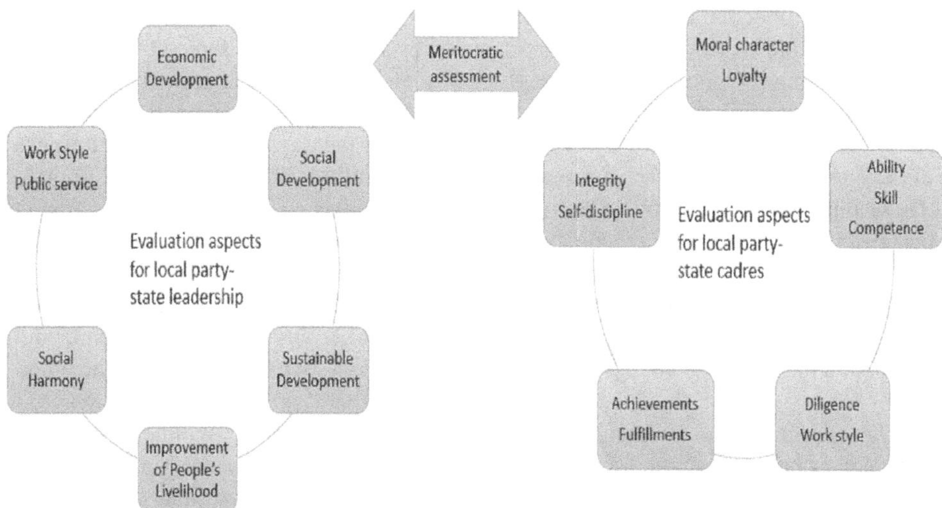

Figure 9.5 The aspects of the cadre evaluation system for local party-state organizations and individual cadres.

Figure 9.5 shows the different aspects of criteria adopted by the cadre evaluation system in assessing the performance of officials at various levels. These aspects help to understand the incentives that are embedded in specific performance criteria. These criteria, also termed as 'performance targets' (Aken 2013) are becoming less politically and ideologically oriented, but more professionally and practically targeted in connection with the planned goals to be achieved by governments of various levels. Taking a retrospective comparison, Whiting pointed out that the current cadre evaluation system is 'moving away from what were seen as subjective evaluations of political attitudes toward specific, measurable, and quantifiable indicators of performance' (Whiting 2004: 103). This kind of merit assessment system motivates and enables local cadres of different levels to do their best to achieve those policy goals that respond to the main concerns of the governments of different levels. As a result of the effect generated by the cadre evaluation system, the collective commitment of cadres to the local and national socioeconomic agendas reinforces the resilience and durability of the party's ruling legitimacy.

Meritocratic governance and the Chinese developmental state

How does the system of Chinese meritocratic governance play a role in the course of China's economic development and global rise? In order to explore China's economic success and its global rise, it is indispensable to study the central features of the Chinese party-state that is capable of shaping national consensus on modernization and maintaining overall political and macroeconomic stability, pursuing wide-ranging domestic reforms and fostering economic growth. There are a few unique characteristics of 'the Chinese development state'[5] that are the result of the effect of its meritocratic civil service system. The system shapes a party-state structure (Figures 9.1 and 9.2) that consists of civil servants capable of maintaining a unique embedded integration of state-market-society relations. In this connection, it is important to point out that one crucial contributing factor to the Chinese economic success is that the disembedded forces of marketization and commodification brought about by the integration in the world economy were balanced by the embedded forces of the Chinese sociocultural and sociopolitical structure (Li 2016). The notion of structural 'embeddedness' implies that state civil servants (policymakers) and institutions are engaged in policymaking and objective-setting activities by closely incorporating factors related to cultural aspects, political uniqueness, social relations, and distinctive institutional forms. The incorporated relationships characterized by patron-client networks between state and market – 'market clientelism' – symbolize the dynamism of China's economic success and 'Chinese model' (Wank 1999). Here are a few dynamic features of state-market embeddedness in China in which the party-state bureaucracies at various levels, guided by the meritocratic promotion system, are playing a central role in fully unleashing market forces, on the one hand, while initiating an innovative grinding-in process of state-market-society relations, on the other:

1 The party-state's overarching planned objective of social and economic development is understood, shared, and implemented by its dual party-state leadership system at all levels. The achievement of the objective is assessed by defined meritocratic evaluation criteria. Such a governance system assisted by a unique official selection and promotion mechanism gives little space to liberal ideologies to diversify the national consensus while limiting the development of political pluralism that might challenge its development goals. The system creates social stability and political predictability in fostering, guiding, and ensuring economic growth and technological modernization over the long term.
2 The system's bureaucratic elites such as policymakers and policy-implementers, who are recruited through the examination procedure, are highly intellectual, competent, and internationally oriented. They are eager to learn and absorb worldwide development experiences while preserving their own policymaking sovereignty as to when, where and how to adopt foreign ideas.
3 The bureaucratic elite, empowered by the party-state's meritocratic norms, is capable of administering the management of state affairs without subjecting them to the influence by various private interest groups. Since the Chinese political system requires that party-state elites are heads of business associations and other major types of growth-promoting associations, these associations maintain close relationships with the party-state of various levels, which effectively shapes the relationships in an arrangement known as 'state corporatism' (Unger & Chan 2015). As a result, economic policymaking processes involve close government-business collaborations in order to correctly receive and respond to market signals. While economic and financial elites attempt to utilize the positive effective generated by state-market embeddedness, social and cultural elites endeavor to resolve dislocations brought about by market disembedded forces.
4 The bureaucratic system, in which civil servants are inspired by their own merit-acquiring procedure and standard, sets up an infrastructure of meritocratic productive forces and labor markets which technically and professionally targets at the global market so that China's export-oriented economic growth is sustainable on a long-term basis. In this connection, the meritocratic examination-based education system is also designed to serve economic growth and global competition.

The above explains one of the crucial factors that contribute to Chinese economic success: economic marketization does not lead to the weakening of the guanxi/client relationship as neoliberal theories would argue, but rather, it leads to the emergence of a new commercialized or performance-based form of clientelism – 'institutional clientism'. The concept denotes an integrating process in which the political power of state institutions and elites is incorporated into economic calculations and business activities that promote local economic growth (Wank 1999). Since economic growth has become the new 'merit' in cadre's evaluation system, state corporatism has two advantages: On the one hand, it can avoid market distortion by 'politicizing the market' (politics in command), while on the other hand, it also can escape from 'marketizing politics' (autonomous business and civil forces) that can challenge the party-state power and legitimacy.

Concluding remarks

How do we understand the puzzling fact that China has achieved a great economic success under a single-party political system? And how do we comprehend the unimaginable coexistence between China's vibrant and innovative market forces and its rigid state politics? The West is much perplexed by the plausible explanations to the survival of the political legitimacy of the Chinese party-state in an era of globalization and market capitalism.

One general conclusion is that China's economic success and its global rise together with the infallible ruling legitimacy of the Chinese party-state and broad public support are due to the outcome and effect of the Chinese meritocratic system that promotes government responsiveness to public demand, that is, performance targets account for that responsiveness (Aken 2013; Li 2016). Other aspects of the resilient capacity of the Chinese political system include the internal self-correcting mechanism within its party-state structure, the constant adaptations through trial and test processes, policy cycles (making, correcting, remaking) and persistent adjustments to internal and external changes, and so on.

Finally, it needs to be pointed out that China's political system of meritocracy is historically and culturally unique, and it is not duplicable or transferable despite its economic success and global rise. Beijing has consistently shown an unwillingness to promote the so-called 'Chinese model' abroad. A general consensus reached both inside and outside China is that while the Chinese meritocratic political system is not a substitute to replace the Western model of electoral democracy, it also indicates that a non-Western alternative does exist. In other words, on the one hand, the Chinese experiences and lessons do not generate and legitimize any universal significance; on the other hand, the Chinese model is a tempting option that bears a great deal of ideational inspiration and influence if we also recognize the limit of Chinese meritocracy in terms of safeguarding individual political and human rights.

Notes

1 The notion of 'China as a civilization state' (文明型国家) was first coined by Lucian Pye (1990).
2 The 'Mandate of Heaven' (天下) is an ancient political-social philosophy that serves as the basic explanation for the success and failure of imperial dynasties. Whenever a dynasty fell, the reason invariably offered by the Mandate of Heaven philosophy of fate was that the ruler had lost the moral right to rule which is given by Heaven alone. In this context, 'Heaven' did not mean a personal god but a cosmic all-pervading power. In today's expression, it simply means 'political legitimacy'.
3 During the Cultural Revolution, 'expert' refered to meritocratic and professional elites and technological specialists.
4 The term 'cadre' in Chinese (Gan Bu干部) refers to an official (civil servant) holding a managerial position in all party-state administrations at all levels and in all spheres including the Chinese military.
5 'Capitalist Developmental State' is a notion that was first coined by Chalmers Johnson (1982) to refer to Japan, the country considered by him as being focused on economic development and taking necessary policy measures to accomplish that objective through far-sighted planning and intervention by bureaucrats.

References

Aken, T.V. (2013) 'China's Secret? Performance Targets', *The Diplomat*, June 27. Available at https://thediplomat.com/2013/06/chinas-secret-performance-targets/.

Bell, D.A. (2012) 'Political Meritocracy Is a Good Thing (Part 1): The Case of China', *Huffpost*, August 21. Available at https://www.huffpost.com/entry/political-meritocracy-china_b_1815245.

Bell, D.A. (2015) *The China Model: Political Meritocracy and the Limits of Democracy*, Princeton: Princeton University Press.

Bell, D.A. (2018) 'China's Political Meritocracy Versus Western Democracy', *The Economist*, June 12. Available at https://www.economist.com/open-future/2018/06/12/chinas-political-meritocracy-versus-western-democracy.

Bo, Z.Y. (2015) 'The End of CCP Rule and the Collapse of China', *The Diplomat*, March 30. Available at http://thediplomat.com/2015/03/the-end-of-ccp-rule-and-the-collapse-of-china/.

Boden, J. (2016) *Democracy Versus Meritocracy How Can Europe and China Cooperate?* Belgium: ChinaConduc.

Chang, G.G. (2001) *The Coming Collapse of China*, New York: Random House Inc.

Cheng, L.S. et al. (2009) *Berkshire Encyclopedia of China*, Massachusetts: Berkshire Publishing Group.

Cunningham, E., Saich, T. and Turiel, J. (2020) *Understanding CCP Resilience: Surveying Chinese Public Opinion Through Time*, Cambridge, MA: Ash Center for Democratic Governance and Innovation, Harvard University.

Dirlik, A and Meisner, M. (eds) (1989) *Marxism and the Chinese Experience*, New York: M E Sharpe.

Economist (2018) 'How the West Got China Wrong', March 1. Available at https://www.economist.com/leaders/2018/03/01/how-the-west-got-china-wrong

Ferdinand, P. (1991) 'Socialism and Democracy in China', in D. McLellan and S. Sayer (eds.) *Socialism and Democracy*, London: Macmillan Academic and Profession Ltd, pp. 164–177.

Guo, W. and Zhang, L. 郭巍青, 张磊 (2014) '精英政治: 研究回顾与理论应用' (Elite Politics: Research Review and Theoretical Application), 求索 *(Seeker)* 5: 10–15.

Guo, X.Z. (2019) *The Politics of the Core Leader in China: Culture, Institution, Legitimacy, and Power*, Cambridge: Cambridge University Press.

Harding, H. (1987) *China's Second Revolution: Reform after Mao*, Washington, DC: Brookings Institution.

He, B.G. (2014) 'From Village Election to Village Deliberation in Rural China: Case Study of a Deliberative Democracy Experiment', *Journal of Chinese Political Science* 19(2): 133–150.

He, B.G. and Warren, M.E. (2011) 'Authoritarian Deliberation: The Deliberative Turn in Chinese Political Development', *Perspectives on Politics* 9(2): 269–289.

Hinton, W. (1990) *The Great Reversal: The Privatisation of China 1978–1989*, New York: Monthly Review Press.

Hung, H.F. et al. (2015) 'When Will China's Government Collapse?', *Foreign Policy*, March 13. Available at http://foreignpolicy.com/2015/03/13/china_communist_party_collapse_downfall/.

Huntington, S. (1993) 'Clash of Civilizations?', *Foreign Affairs* 72(3): 22–49.

Johnson, C. (1982) 'MITI and the Japanese Miracle', *The Growth of Industrial Policy, 1925–1975*, Stanford, CA: Stanford University Press.

Kavalski, E. (2018) *The Guanxi of Relational International Theory*, London: Routledge.

Kurlantzick, J. (2013) 'Why the "China Model" Isn't Going Away', *Atlantic*, March 21. Available at http://www.theatlantic.com/china/archive/2013/03/why-the-china-model-isnt-going-away/274237/.

Li, H. and Gore, L.L.P. (2018) 'Merit-Based Patronage: Career Incentives of Local Leading Cadres in China', *Journal of Contemporary China* 27(109): 85–102.

Li, X. (2016) 'Understanding China's Economic Success: "Embeddedness" with Chinese Characteristics', *Asian Culture and History* 8(2): 18–31.

Li, X. (2018) 'The Endgame or Resilience of the Chinese Communist Party's Rule in China: A Gramscian Approach', *Journal of Chinese Political Science* 23(1): 83–104.

Nathan, A.J. (2003) 'Authoritarian Resillience', *Journal of Democracy* 14(1): 1–17.

Panda, A. (2019) 'A Civilizational Clash Isn't the Way to Frame US Competition With China: Race and Civilization Are the Wrong Framing for the US–China Competition', *The Diplomat*, May 20. Available at https://thediplomat.com/2019/05/a-civilizational-clash-isnt-the-way-to-frame-competition-with-china/.

Pei, M.X. (2015) 'The Twilight of Communist Party Rule in China', 11(4). Available at http://www.the-american-interest.com/2015/11/12/the-twilight-of-communist-party-rule-in-china/.

Pye, L. (1990) 'Erratic State, Frustrated Society', *Foreign Affairs* 69(4): 56–74.

Pye, L. (1995) 'Factions and the Politics of Guanxi', *China Journal* 34(2): 35–53.

Qin, Y.Q. (2016) 'A Relational Theory of World Politics', *International Studies Review* 18: 33–47.

Ruan, L.Y. (2015) 'The Chinese Communist Party and Legitimacy: What Is the Chinese Communist Party's Official Discourse on Legitimacy?' *The Diplomat*, September 30. Available at https://thediplomat.com/2015/09/the-chinese-communist-party-and-legitimacy/.

Sausmikat, N. (2006) 'More Legitimacy for One-Party Rule? The CCP's Ideological Adjustments and Intra-Party Reforms', *ASIEN* 99: 70–91.

Shambaugh, D. (2015) 'The Coming Chinese Crackup', *Wall Street Journal*. Available at http://www.wsj.com/articles/the-coming-chinese-crack-up-1425659198.

South China Morning Post (2020) 'Beijing Enjoys Greater Legitimacy Than Any Western State', July 19. Available at https://www.scmp.com/comment/opinion/article/3093825/beijing-enjoys-greater-legitimacy-any-western-state.

Time (2017) 'How China's Economy Is Poised to Win the Future', November 2. Available at https://time.com/5006971/how-chinas-economy-is-poised-to-win-the-future/.

Unger, J. and Chan, A. (2015) 'State Corporatism and Business Associations in China: A Comparison with Earlier Emerging Economies of East Asia', *Journal of Emerging Markets* 10(2): 178–193.

Wank, D.L. (1999) *Commodifying Communism – Business, Trust and Politics in a Chinese City*, Cambridge: Cambridge University Press.

Weber, M. (1947) *The Theory of Social and Economic Organization*, translated from German by A.M. Henderson and Talcott Parsons, revised and edited, with an introduction by Talcott Parsons, London: Edinburgh.

Weber, M. (1972) [1919]) 'Politics as a Vocation', in H.H. Gerth and C.W. Mills (eds) *From Max Weber*, New York: Oxford University Press, pp. 77–128.

Weber, M. (1978) *Economy and Society*, edited by G. Roth and C. Wittich. Berkeley: University of California Press.

Weber, M. (2005 [1930]) *The Protestant Ethic and Spirit of Capitalism*, Routledge, London.

Weil, R. (1996) *Red Cat, White Cat: China and the Contradictions of 'Market Socialism'*, New York: Monthly Review Press.

Whiting, S.H. (2004) 'The Cadre Evaluation System at the Grass Roots: The Paradox of Party Rule', in B.J. Naughton and D.L. Yang (eds) *Holding China Together: Diversity and National Integration in the Post-Deng Era*, New York: Cambridge University Press, pp. 101–119.

Young, M. (1958) *The Rise of the Meritocracy 1870–2033: An Essay on Education and Society*, London: Thames and Hudson.

Zeng, J.H. (2014) 'The Debate on Regime Legitimacy in China: Bridging the Wide Gulf between Western and Chinese Scholarship', *Journal of Contemporary China* 23(88): 612–635.

Zhang, W.W. (2012) 'Meritocracy Versus Democracy', *The New York Times*, November 9. Available at https://www.nytimes.com/2012/11/10/opinion/meritocracy-versus-democracy.html.

Zhu, Y.C. (2011) '"Performance Legitimacy" and China's Political Adaptation Strategy', *Journal of Chinese Political Science* 16(2): 123–140.

Appendix: An overview of Chinese President Xi Jinping's political career

2018–	Chairman, Central Military Commission of the PRC ***(Reelected March 17, 2018)***
2018–	Deputy, 13th NPC
2018–	President, People's Government People's Republic of China ***(Reelected March 17, 2018)***
2017–	Director, CPC, Central Committee, Central LSG for Internet Security and Informationization
2017–	Director, CPC, Central Committee, Central LSG for Finance and Economy
2017–	Chairman, 19th CPC, Central Committee, Central Military Commission
2017–	General Secretary, 19th CPC, Central Committee
2017–	Secretary-General, 19th CPC, National Congress
2017–	Member, 19th CPC, Central Committee, Politburo, Standing Committee
2017–	Member, 19th CPC, Central Committee, Politburo
2017–	Member, 19th CPC, Central Committee
2017–	Delegate, 19th CPC, National Congress
2017–	Director, CPC, Central Committee, Central Commission for Integrated Military and Civilian Development
2017–	Director, CPC, Central Committee, Central Foreign Affairs Commission
2017–	Director, CPC, Central Committee, Central LSG for Taiwan Affairs
2014–	Head, Central Military Commission of the PRC, Leading Group for Deepening Reform on National Defense
2014–	Director, CPC, Central Committee, Central National Security Commission
2013–2018	President, People's Government People's Republic of China
2013–2018	Chairman, Central Military Commission of the PRC
2013–	Director, CPC, Central Committee, Central LSG for Comprehensively Deepening Reform
2012–2017	Member, 18th CPC, Central Committee, Politburo, Standing Committee
2012–2017	General Secretary, 18th CPC, Central Committee
2012–2017	Member, 18th CPC, Central Committee, Politburo
2012–2017	Chairman, 18th CPC, Central Committee, Central Military Commission
2012–2017	Member, 18th CPC, Central Committee
2012–2017	Secretary-General, 18th CPC, National Congress
2010–2012	Vice Chairman, 17th CPC, Central Committee, Central Military Commission
2010–2013	Vice Chairman, Central Military Commission of the PRC
2008–2013	Vice President, People's Government People's Republic of China
2007–2012	Member, 17th CPC, Central Committee, Politburo
2007–2012	Vice Chairman, 17th CPC, Central Committee, Central LSG for Taiwan Affairs
2007–2012	Member, 17th CPC, Central Committee, Politburo, Secretariat
2007–2012	President, CPC, Central Committee, Central Party School
2007–2012	Member, 17th CPC, Central Committee, Politburo, Standing Committee
2007–2012	Member, 17th CPC, Central Committee
2007–2007	Secretary, CPC, Municipal Committee Shanghai Municipality
2007–2012	Chairman, 17th CPC, Central Committee, Central LSG for Party-Building
2003–2007	Chairman, Provincial People's Congress, Standing Committee Zhejiang Province
2002–2007	Member, 16th CPC, Central Committee
2002–2007	Secretary, CPC, Provincial Committee Zhejiang Province
2002–2002	Deputy Secretary, CPC, Provincial Committee Zhejiang Province
2002–2003	Acting Governor, People's Government Zhejiang Province
2002–2007	First Secretary, PLA, Regions, Nanjing Military Region, Zhejiang Military District CPC, Party Committee Zhejiang Province
2002–2003	Director, PLA, National Defense Mobilization Committee, Provincial-Level Zhejiang Province

(*Continued*)

2001–2002	Member, CPC, Provincial Committee, Standing Committee Fujian Province
2000–2002	Governor, People's Government Fujian Province
1999–2000	Acting Governor, People's Government Fujian Province
1999–2002	Director, PLA, National Defense Mobilization Committee, Provincial-Level Fujian Province
1999–2003	Deputy Director, PLA, National Defense Mobilization Committee, City-Level Jiangsu Province, Nanjing City
1998–2002	Student, Tsinghua University, Humanities Department Beijing Municipality
1998–2003	Deputy, 9th NPC
1997–2002	Alternate Member, 15th CPC, Central Committee
1996–2000	1st Political Commissioner, PLA, Services and Arms, Reserve Artillery Division Fujian Province
1995–2002	Deputy Secretary, CPC, Provincial Committee Fujian Province
1993	***(Won national award for contributions and work for the elderly)***
1992–1997	Delegate, 14th CPC, National Congress
1990–1996	First Secretary, PLA, Regions, Nanjing Military Region, Fujian Military District CPC, Party Committee Fujian Province
1990–1995	Chairman, City People's Congress Fujian Province, Fuzhou City
1990–1996	Secretary, CPC, City Committee Fujian Province, Fuzhou City
1988–1990	First Secretary, PLA, Regions, Nanjing Military Region, Fujian Military District Fujian Province ***(Ningde Military Subarea Command)***
1988–1990	Secretary, CPC, Prefectural Committee Fujian Province, Ningde Prefecture
1985–1988	Executive Vice-Mayor, People's Government Fujian Province, Xiamen City
1985–1988	Member, CPC, City Committee, Standing Committee Fujian Province, Xiamen City
1983–1985	1st Political Commissar, Chinese People's Armed Police Force Hebei Province, Zhengding County
1983–1985	Secretary, CPC, County Committee Hebei Province, Zhengding County
1982–1983	Deputy Secretary, CPC, County Committee Hebei Province, Zhengding County
1982	***(Served as Secretary to Geng Biao)***
1979–1982	Secretary, Central Military Commission of the PRC, General Office
1979–1982	Secretary, General Office of the State Council
1975–1979	Student, Tsinghua University, Chemical Engineering Department Beijing Municipality
1974	Joined, CPC
1969–1975	Cultural Revolution, Sent to do manual labor Shaanxi Province, Yanchuan County

(*Source*: http://www.chinavitae.com/biography/Xi_Jinping/career)

10

Managing public opinion in crisis

Weibo and the Wenzhou high-speed rail crash of 2011

Patrick Gorman

Reporting of the accident is to use 'in the face of great tragedy, there's great love' as the major theme. Do not question. Do not elaborate. Do not associate. No reposting on microblogs will be allowed!

– Central Propaganda Department directive, July 2011

Introduction

The death of Dr. Li Wenliang from COVID-19 ignited much sorrow and anger online toward Chinese authorities. Dr. Li, who had been reprimanded by Wuhan authorities for warning others of a mysterious new illness that would later be known worldwide as COVID-19, succumbed to the same illness while treating patients of the virus (Huang 2020). Pent up frustration toward the government, and toward its control of information in particular, appeared to explode as the hashtag 'We want freedom of speech' trended on the social media platform Sina Weibo, gathering over 2 million views before content was deleted and the hashtag censored (Feng 2020). After an explosion of open discussion, dissent was again silenced. To longtime observers of the Chinese internet, and to many Chinese netizens, the cycle of crisis and online anger followed by censorship is a familiar one. Also familiar was the role of private online media companies, such as Tencent WeChat and Sina Weibo, acting as censors on behalf of the state. This relationship between company and state has shaped internet controls in China since the beginning.

Yet despite the central role played by these private companies, it is often eclipsed by research focusing on the importance of state policy on the one hand, or netizen resistance on the other. A key characteristic of the Chinese state since the early days of economic reform has been adaptation. Key to adapting to the 'socialist market economy' has been the state's ability to coopt and manage the rise of new groups within the capitalist economy. Applying licensing restrictions and third-party liability for internet companies, the government has been able to outsource censorship and surveillance to private companies. The question remains how these platforms balance the business of social media with their political obligations.

With the goal of achieving a deeper understanding of how this relationship is realized, this project utilized the work logs of one of the most influential social media platforms in

DOI: 10.4324/9780429059704-13

China, Sina Weibo. This project asks how the platform navigates between satisfying its online users by providing a place for discussion and entertainment, and the state by filtering content and surveilling problematic users and content.

This primary research data was obtained from an ex-employee of Sina Weibo who worked in Weibo's censorship office in Tianjin between 2011 and 2014. The ex-employee kept copies of the daily shift logs he received while at work outlining the censorship directives for each shift. The source of these logs provided the material to the Committee to Protect Journalists in 2016, where several reports discussing some of the files have been published, and where an interview with this source has also been published (Wang 2016a, 2016b). The source agreed to provide the files for this project.

This chapter looks at one of the most important cases in this study, the Wenzhou high-speed train crash of 2011. The crash occurred during what is considered a high-water mark for the influence of Sina Weibo in Chinese society, when many looked to accounts on Weibo first for unfiltered news about important events. Like the crisis surrounding the Li Wenliang/ COVID-19 affair, the case also involved a disaster that, in addition to leading to many lost lives, also touched on political grievances, in particular prioritizing the control of information over the lives of citizens.

While the logs reveal difficulty in containing discussion within the bounds of acceptable 'mainstream discussion' as the state prefers, it also reveals how Weibo's management was required to respond quickly to changing official requests, to evolving netizen discussion, and to countless threads and posts across the platform to subdue discussion and bring it back within the bounds preferred by the state. In assessing its failures during this crisis, Weibo increased its hiring of censorship personnel and adopted new measures making censorship less apparent, learning from the crisis that obvious censorship is a liability, turning users off the platform and laying bare the oppressiveness of the government's censorship network (Wang 2016b).

At the time of the crisis, censorship directives found in the work logs list content to be deleted 删除 [shanchu] or directed as 见到私密 [jiandao simi, 'see private'], 私密处理 [simi chuli, 'private handling']. 'Private handling', 'make private', 'see private' all refer to blocking the visibility of the content to other users without deleting it. Many of the censored posts were 'made private', as the work logs show. Netizens knew their content was being censored because they received a notification that their content was problematic and had been blocked. Sometime after the crisis, Weibo ceased sending notices to users that their content was being made 'private'. In effect, making censorship invisible.

The crash

On July 23, 2011, a crash occurred between two high-speed trains on the Yongwen rail line outside the city of Wenzhou. The first train had reportedly stopped after being struck by lightning and was then struck by the second train. Signaling equipment on the second train had failed to notify the crew of the stopped train ahead, leading to a collision and derailment that killed at least 40 people and injured many more (Jiang 2011; LaFraniere 2011).

News of the collision was breaking as it occurred, in sporadic posts on Sina Weibo by people at the scene of the crash, and from at least one outside witness at the scene just before the crash occurred, who wondered, 'after all the wind and storm, what's going on with the high-speed train? … It's crawling slower than a snail. I hope nothing happens to it' (ibid. 2011). Another post cried out, 'Help us! Bullet Train D301 has derailed in a place not far from the Wenzhou South Railway Station! Children are crying in the train! No train attendant has managed to get out! Help us! Hurry up!' (*People's Daily* 2011).

The crash became a major topic for news media and internet discussion. According to the Communication University of China's Internet Research Institute, as of 10:00 AM on July 28, there were 17,595 reports directly discussing the crash on 468 websites. There was a total of 2,845,626 comments on these reports. It was estimated that around 26 million messages were posted on Sina and Tencent Weibo by this date (ibid.; *EastSouthWestNorth* 2011).

Allegations of corruption and cover ups were made at the Ministry of Railways, especially after footage of the rescue effort and recovery of the trains was released. The government had announced that all survivors were recovered after five hours of rescue operations, yet a toddler was pulled out alive 20 hours after the accident, leading many to believe that rescue efforts were rushed and careless. Netizens also questioned why the train cars were being buried at the site and not taken to a facility to be analyzed. When a spokesman for the ministry, Wang Yongping, held a press conference, he appeared dismissive of concerns. When asked why the cars were buried on site, he said, 'They told me they buried the car to facilitate the rescue effort and I believe this explanation'. When questioned about whether the rescue efforts had been rushed after the discovery of the toddler, Wang dismissed this as an exception 'that was a miracle' (Jiang 2011).

State guidance

The initial directives are typical directives covering sensitive topics or news in China, specifically that media contain the story and refrain from posting any but the official narrative. The request that the media follow '"in the face of great tragedy, there's great love" as the major theme. Do not question. Do not elaborate. Do not associate', shows how the propaganda department desired to control the story and spin the coverage toward more 'positive' discussion. However, given the flood of critical commentary online and the very open coverage of the disaster, it seems demanding that 'No reposting on microblogs will be allowed!' was hopeful at best. The entire record of the leaked directives for the first week can be found below. They were issued by the Central Propaganda Department and State Council Information Office. The directives were leaked by journalists and workers at these companies and websites and have been compiled by *China Digital Times*.

Between July 23 and 25

Central Propaganda Department: In regard to the Wenzhou highspeed train crash, all media outlets are to promptly report information released from the Ministry of Railways. No journalists should conduct independent interviews. All subsidiaries including newspaper, magazines and websites are to be well controlled. Do not link reports with articles regarding the development of high-speed trains. Do not conduct reflective reports.

Additional directives for all central media: The latest directives on reporting the Wenzhou high speed train crash: 1. Release death toll only according to figures from authorities. 2. Do not report on a frequent basis. 3. More touching stories are to be reported instead, i.e. blood donation, free taxi services, etc. 4. Do not investigate the causes of the accident; use information released from authorities as standard. 5. Do not reflect or comment.

Reminder on reporting matters: All reports regarding the Wenzhou high speed Train accident are to be titled '7.23 YongWen line major transportation accident'. Reporting of the accident is to use 'in the face of great tragedy, there's great love' as the major theme. Do not question. Do not elaborate. Do not associate. No reposting on microblogs will be allowed! Related service information may be provided during news reporting. Music is to be carefully selected!

(Severdia 2011; Fu 2011)

State media, *Xinhua* and *People's Daily*, responded by reporting on the official causes of the crash. Articles in *Xinhua* from July 23 to 25 acknowledge what has already been widely discussed online, the crash and the official explanation, but also release statements from the central government outlining that rescue efforts are a high priority, that the crash will be investigated and that negligent officials will be held to account. 'Every effort should be made to save the lives of the injured and provide counseling and aid for the relatives of the dead', Vice premier Zhang Dejiang was quoted as saying. According to the *People's Daily* article published July 25, as a result of the crash and investigation,

> the Ministry of Railway earlier confirmed that three railway officials, including Long Jing, head of the Shanghai Railway Bureau; Li Jia, head of the bureau's Communist Party of China (CPC) Committee, and He Shengli, a deputy chief of the bureau, were removed from their posts.
>
> *(Xinhua 2011)*

Other coverage by the official press followed the official theme of 'in the face of great tragedy, there's great love', by focusing on the participation of netizens in sharing information about the rescue operations and updating the list of missing persons (*People's Daily* 2011).

The tone of the official media shifted later in July, with a withering of media coverage on the crash as the government more tightly restricted coverage. Updates and features about the Wenzhou crash were reportedly scrapped at the last moment under pressure from the government (Bandurski 2011). The following directives from July 29 to 30 show how the government directed all media, including subordinate newspapers (those tabloids owned by Party organs, where reporting is often more open than the official mouth pieces), to 'cool off' reporting on the issue, as well as to restrict any reports linking the signal device that failed with the same technology used on the Beijing subway (Xin 2011):

July 29

From the Central Propaganda Department: Due to the increasing complexity of the domestic and foreign public opinion on the 7.23 Wenzhou high speed train crash, all media outlets including all subordinate newspapers and news websites are to immediately cool off on reporting the accident. No additional reports will be allowed except positive ones or information released by authorities. Do not publish any commentaries.

(Fu 2011)

July 30

From the Propaganda Department of the Beijing Municipal Party Committee:

Attention to all Beijing media outlets and the Office of Internet Police:

Regarding the signal system of Beijing Subway, which is said to be developed by the same company involved in Wenzhou high speed train crash, no reports or comments are allowed. The Beijing Internet Administration Office is responsible for regulating public opinion on cyberspace.

(ibid.)

With much of the public outrage expressed on Weibo and other websites, and with much of the story breaking on Weibo, how did Weibo management implement state directives to 'cool off' the Wenzhou story and to restrict reposting?

Weibo management

The following directives were recorded in the daily shift logs for Weibo censors. Italics have been added to the user content to differentiate it from the directives written by Weibo management. The logs were recorded between July 23 and August 5, 2011. Due to the large volume of directives related to the Wenzhou high-speed train crash, the directives have been divided by different categories for clearer analysis and discussion.

Incitement to action

The priority for Weibo management immediately following the crash was to prevent the spreading of any messages inciting action – mass gatherings, marches or protests. Directives related to incitement to action during the crisis include – make private, hide or 'resolutely delete'. The importance of timeliness of the response by censors as well as the severity of the filtering are evidence of the sensitivity of these posts. Weibo censors are instructed to deal with these kinds of posts before responding to other state and propaganda directives. Examples of incitement to action following the Wenzhou train crash include public mass displays of mourning, especially those connected to government or government ministries such as the Ministry of Railways.

> ***July 23–28***
> Regarding the train crash, currently only deal with attacks on the party and calls to go to hold a memorial at the entrance of the Ministry of Railways. First stop and hide the protest content, the general transmission of provincial and municipal propaganda directives [you] do not need to deal with yet.

An example of 'incitement to action' which censors are instructed to immediately 'clean up' 清理下 [qingli xia] encourages public marches to government offices to voice discontent over the handling of the crash:

> ***July 23–28***
> *Every major accident will have a spontaneous memorial to the people, every carnation is placed with mourning; invite the people of Beijing on Monday afternoon at Two O'clock to spontaneously proceed to the Ministry of Railways big main gate to hold a citizens memorial to commemorate the Wenzhou train accident; 1. Pay homage to the dead pray for the injured but living to get well soon 2. Tell the big leaders public opinion 3. hope that the price of blood is exchanged for scientific progress rather than bloody development! No way to escape! Regarding not going on the Internet not going on Weibo with regard to this the big leaders, the information is screened, letting the leaders only attach value to the core. Beijing and Wenzhou students should carry forward the spirit to Shanghai Jing'an District to collect flowers to mourn the innocent victims; Beijing Location: Ministry of Railways; Wenzhou Location: City Hall; tomorrow afternoon two o'clock; only relying on Weibo is useless.*

Similar to the above call by netizens to go to the Ministry of Railways if found immediately clean it up.

While directives are insistent that calls to action must be dealt with quickly and firmly, a later clarification is issued to make sure censors only apply this directive to posts that are linked to organizing. Mourning is acceptable; public gatherings marching to government offices are not.

> ***July 28–August 5***
> Now regarding the top seven things about the train, only deal with action. Offline what the organization does at a specific time and place. Online Weibo release activities, calling to change the portrait, calling to change the signature, don't care about others.
>
> The core is: wanting to organize, calling to [organize]. Without this layer of meaning, do not count it as an action, do not go too far implementing this.

> ***July 28–August 5***
> Set the day of national mourning, the flag at half mast, 'commemorate the 7.23 accident'. [content] like this should be made secret or deleted?
>
> This kind of content, does not need to be handled, agitating offline action resolutely delete, online mourning in general this can be allowed to pass.

Bottom line

The bottom line of the Party, the line between what can be accepted in public discussion and what cannot, is outlined in detail throughout these logs. For the most part, posts that 'attack the government, the system' are crossing the line and are filtered. However, because of the complexity and variety of content and the shifting Party line related to the crash, Weibo management issued some notices instructing what content 'can pass' and what content crosses the line and should be filtered. The initial notices list any attacks on the government, including those that 'request the Minister of Railways step down' as unacceptable content that should be made private.

> ***July 23–28***
> http://news.ifeng.com/mainland/special/wzdongchetuogui/content-3/detail_2011_07/23/7898933_0.shtml D301 and D3115 in Wenzhou rear-end section 6 car off-line.
>
> Content should be careful not to attack the government, the system, request the Minister of Railways step down, accountability and so on. If discovered, make private.

An exception to the above notice soon appears however, as the official narrative evolves, and the Ministry of Railways comes under the scrutiny of the central government and the official media, criticism of the ministry 'can be allowed to pass'. However, 'Attacking the Central Committee' is still unacceptable. Criticism of specific officials in the ministry is to be distinguished from attacks on the Party and members of the central government. The latter remain very much off limits.

> ***July 23–28***
> Content regarding the train crash, condemning the Ministry of Railways, requesting the minister to step down, can be allowed to pass. No need to make private.
>
> Attacking the Central Committee or contacting some members of the Standing Committee is still private treatment.

Directives in the logs also outline what is acceptable content but also where censors need to pay attention, since an acceptable post may have antigovernment content. The following notices show how posts and messages related to mourning and commemoration of the crash are permitted, but that censors need to make sure they don't attack the government.

> ***July 28–August 5***
> [During the] Zhangbei music festival, Wang Feng called on fans to point a finger to the night sky and observe a minute and a half of silence on behalf of the high-speed rail victims, in general this content can be left. Attacking, provocative remarks, deal with them.
>
> Today the Chinese Football Association's moment of silence for the victims of the 723 incident, related content watch out.
>
> Pictures of the Hong Kong people and the Broadcasting University commemorating the high-speed rail event are relatively numerous, in general [you] do not have to deal with them. Using the opportunity to attack or express provocative opinions, deal with them.

Negative content

The logs also contain requests to remove content that can be classified as broadly 'negative'. This content is negative in the sense that it casts the government in a negative light, or it is content that can be used toward ends that are problematic for the government. This content is the opposite of the propaganda theme 'in the face of great tragedy, there's great love', and was ordered to be deleted or made private by management.

One example of such negative content is the pictures referencing the rumors of the brutal 'rescue' effort which may have led to the deaths of survivors who had yet to be rescued from the wreckage (Figure 10.1):

> ***July 23–28***
> [*Please give me back my head.*]
>
> Make Private

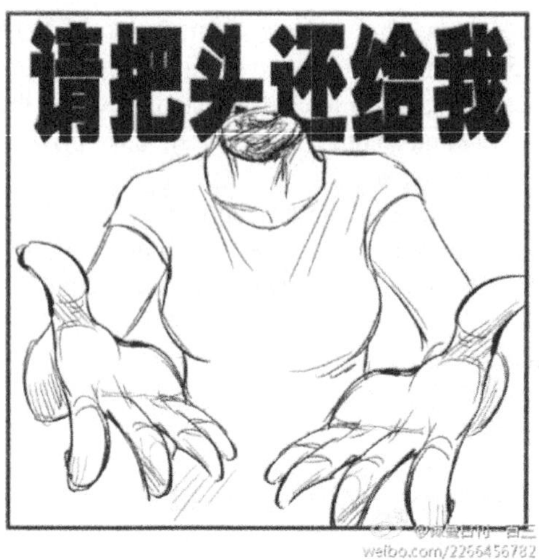

Figure 10.1 Please give me back my head.

Similar negative content below, labeled 'false content' and also made private, depicts the heartlessness of authorities when dealing with families of the victims.

> ***July 28–August 5***
> [*How much power do you have in your hands... Open your rotten claws!!! She just lost a family member (s)*]
> False content make private.

Not all negative content targeted for filtering is labeled false or is opinion. The example below of Wenzhou authorities reportedly banning lawyers from representing the families of victims, was a news item. Censors are instructed to curtail the discussion by making related posts with a high number of reposts private.

> ***July 28–August 5***
> Wenzhou to ban lawyers from serving the families of the victims. There is news of this, at night make private [those with a] high number of reposts.

Included in these examples of negative content to be removed is also content that is not antigovernment per se, but which could undermine opinion guidance in other areas. An example of such content is the photo of a Japanese news anchor who was said to have laughed about the Wenzhou train crash. Perhaps wishing to prevent the feeding of anti-Japanese nationalism, it is directed to be made private:

> ***July 23–28***
> This image make private

Figure 10.2 The photo of a Japanese news anchor.

News of a negative nature is also filtered if it receives too many reposts, as the example below shows:

July 28–August 5

Members of the Hong Kong Association for Democracy and People's Livelihood (ADPL) were rumored to have gone to the Liaison Office by the Western Police Station this morning to ask the Central Government to conduct a comprehensive investigation of the Wenzhou train accident. These images private, stop text with a high number of reposts. train incident, microblogging mentioned in the Propaganda Department ban, those matching the higher authorities' requirements of withdrawal, forbidden reports, and the like are made private.

Every two hours make a report counting the number related to the ban.

By the second week, the amount of negative content is enough that management suggested dealing with this content, if the number was too large, by first auditing 审核 [shenhe] the users and content and then filtering it together.

July 28–August 5

Strengthen the control of this subclass of microblog, in general delete train accident related negative content, If a lot first audit then [delete].

Discussion of censorship

As a result of the widespread discussion of the crash, censorship touched a very large group of netizens, many of whom were part of the core of Weibo's 'mainstream opinion,' rather than fringe activists. Evidence of censorship of the media also showed up in content that was to be filtered. Interestingly, because of the nature of the crisis, discussion of censorship itself became a major category of content to be censored on Weibo.

July 23–28

Just forwarded, Zhejiang Propaganda Department ordered [that] the news units can only use the Xinhua News Agency draft in an instant smothering it. Shit! Get lost! Now we do not know the cause of the accident. Just want to know what ordinary people can do for those who need help. What use is waiting for an announcement. Fuck

This content about the propaganda department prohibition, make private.

[*Just now a radio friend told me that the work unit has received a notice from ZX Department, requesting 'Wenzhou train accident, every media must report in a timely manner the information released by the Ministry of Railways, do not send reporters to investigate, especially from journals and websites, do not include hyperlinks to High Speed Rail development related information, do not do reflective reports'.*] Make private.

Logs from this period continue to feature examples of posts critical of government censorship of the media and online content, the content of these posts are often sarcastic or angry. Weibo censors are directed to filter them:

Figure 10.3 A page from the newspaper *The Economic Observer*. July 28–August 5: [A page from the newspaper, 经济观察报 *The Economic Observer* has a page with a photo of the Wenzhou crash site with the logo of the Ministry of Railways and a picture of a train falling with the text: *Break up the Ministry of Railways.* A note posted to the right of the newspaper article reads: *Xinhua News Agency: 7.23. You don't have the guts to write, do you have the guts to see?*] [Request that] This picture be deleted.

The following account's detailed and sarcastic description of the fallout of the accident as a cycle of 'cover ups' and censorship is flagged to be made private:

> ***July 28–August 5***
> *RT@CorndogCN: accident → microblogging discussion → ZF[government] try to cover up → microblog crazy discussion → traditional media follow-up → microblog rumors everywhere → Li Chengpeng issued document→ Hanhan issued document→ Weibo wants lively revolution→ movies stars come, arrive late→ Weibo expresses thanks for Premier Wen's hard work → harmony, harmony, harmony → microblog for the Premier to collect 65535 blessings → constellation Encyclopedia of words subordinates → next accident*
> Make Private

The understanding that the news is being controlled leads to distrust toward the media and government and the proliferation of conspiracy theories and rumors about journalists being censored or who are in danger while working to reveal the truth about the crash. Both examples below were ordered to be filtered by making private:

July 28–August 5
Chai Jing, has already disappeared from the people's view, and has taken over an independent investigation of the Wenzhou train accident, promised to give all the Chinese [people] the truth. She is not only honest, more valuable is that she is willing to pay everything for this: If I am killed because of the investigation of this matter, my family will find the information I have published.[1]
The above false content is to be made private

July 28–August 5
Reliable news, Shanghai 'Youth Daily' deputy editor Jin Chao (@ Jin Chao 1976) has been removed from office, the reason might be on July 29, the first page was left blank to commemorate the train incident. Related content make private

Perhaps an indication of the desperation experienced by Sina managers at the time, the directive below asks censors to watch out for the possible consequences to Sina management reaching out to Weibo VIP users to cooperate with the propaganda department to 'work together' on the high-speed train incident. That Sina management reached out to VIP users for help in managing the online discussion indicates the influence which these VIP users have as 'opinion leaders' as well as the adaptive moves used by Weibo to manage the crisis.

July 28–August 5
Today, Sina gave a group of VIP users who do not cooperate with the Propaganda department on the high-speed train incident, a telephone call to request them to work together. If someone [VIP User] posts the contents of this phone call, if the user has lots of fans, make the content private, if the user has fewer fans, directly delete the content.

Discussion of 'politics' and attacks on leaders

Although coverage in the media begins to 'cool off' as directed toward the end of the first week, Weibo management appears to have difficulty bringing the discussion back within acceptable limits during this time. As the source of these logs mentioned in his published interview with the *Committee to Protect Journalists*, 'The sheer volume of content generated by users created enormous pressure on Weibo's censorship team. We didn't know what to do for a moment' (Wang 2016b).

July 28–August 5
Please strengthen the audit process to place and block users, especially those who only talk about politics. [Those with] a number of fans of about 10,000, also V [verified user], all can be handled, do not be lenient. Especially the kind that is full of vicious attacks on our party content microblogs. Starting immediately, every hour report the number of times. To one o'clock in the early morning. Tomorrow at eight o'clock reply, [until then] do not stop blocking.

The above directive indicates the volume of antigovernment content that censors are attempting to filter. The notice requests censors to pay particular attention to posts attacking the Party.

Other content that attacks officials is deleted, with the content and users reported to the head office:

> ***July 23–28***
> Delete the poll on whether the Minister of Railways should resign, the contents of the audit related to the poll send to Beijing.

Another large subgroup of negative content with numerous examples for filtering in the logs during this period is content about officials in the central government, in particular Wen Jiabao, who is criticized for not appearing at the crash site sooner. The officials are described as heartless and uncaring. These posts are directed to be made private and cleaned up.

> ***July 23–28***
> Http://weibo.com/1618051664/xgej1zrEt clean up comments, no cursing of Hu Wen [General Secretary Hu Jintao and Premier Wen Jiabao], Zhang Dejiang [Vice Premier]
>
> ***July 28–August 5***
> [Content] questioning Zhang Dejiang, saying he requested that the scene [of the accident] be cleaned up as soon as possible, make private.

The log below instructs censors to remember to fill in their report when cleaning up content attacking leaders:

> ***July 28–August 5***
> Urgent notice: Online rumor 7.23 is Zhang Dejiang sent the order to clean up the scene as soon as possible, now immediately all content must be completely cleaned up, then fill out the contents of the form, if there is one, report one, please treat it with a high degree of importance, send the report as soon as possible,
>
> Zhang Dejiang, Sheng Guangzu and other train incident related leaders are set to automatic private, touching on blame, requesting [someone] step down etc. negative information clean up all of it.

The discussion of whether Wen Jiabao was too sick to visit the crash site became a major point for attacking the premier and was listed as a topic to filter. As was his response in general to the crash.

> ***July 28–August 5***
> *Hong Kong Journalists Association issued a statement calling on Premier Wen to personally follow up the incident, asked the XX department to withdraw the order, let the truth be made public, so that we can learn the lesson, so as not to repeat the same mistakes.*
>
> This content is private
>
> Xinhua News Agency report about Wenzhou and Premier Wen Jiabao: 'I am sick for 11 days, cannot leave the hospital' has been reported wrong. The actual situation is 'I am sick for 11 days, cannot travel' stop discussion of this on Weibo.

> ***July 28–August 5***
> Premier goes to Zhejiang content, news conference has already ended, ridiculing, criticizing, insulting the premier [content] is made private, the standard is still slightly strict. For example: Actor, Cheat, Performer. This general guideline, specific post, deal with it according to the circumstances of every post's content.

Earlier directives regarding attacks on Wen Jiabao instruct users to stop the discussion and make private. Later directives begin to request that these comments are directly 'deleted' and to report 'important users' involved to management. 'Important users' 重要用户[zhongyao yonghu] refers to sensitive users who have been flagged for posting sensitive content.

> ***July 28–August 5***
> To call into question whether Wen Jiabao was sick, latest content about his journey, immediately delete, report important users to him.
> [this content deal with] according to the make private handling.

Many examples of posts attacking the premier can be found, including one which management describes as 'relatively large'. The criticism of Wen Jiabao as an 'actor' 影帝 [yingdi] is prevalent and serious enough for Weibo management, that the keyword is added for automatic filtering:

> ***July 28–August 5***
> Serious offenses are all committed by Wen Jiabao, the size of this topic is relatively large, but the boss requests a review by tomorrow night.
> actor [added as sensitive keyword] has been made automatically private to 2:00 am, remind Beijing comrades at night to add actor to [trigger] automatic stop.

Earlier directives had intended to direct online criticism toward the ministry responsible for the high-speed train infrastructure, and which had been reported as under investigation, but examples of posts with expansive lists of those to hold accountable continued to show up in the logs for this period, including the example below, which Weibo management ordered to be deleted. Political discussion involving attacks on leaders in the central government are among some of the most numerous examples of posts to be censored in these logs; they are also the most strongly filtered.

> ***July 28–August 5***
> [Figure 10.4. Top left: *Sheng Guangzu (The Ministry of Railways murders for money)*
> Top right: *Zhang Dejiang (The Vice Premier kills people like cutting grass)*
> Bottom left: *Zhou Yongkang (The Ministry of Public Security destroys evidence)*
> Bottom right: *Li Changchun (The Propaganda Department blocks the truth)*]
> Delete, this picture doesn't go up

Even posts that target the minister can be problematic when they touch on deeper issues of systemic corruption and nepotism. Despite the log's description of the post below as 'false information', the fact that the story 'rings true' may be more important. The widespread perception that corruption is a serious systemic problem in China makes these posts problematic.

Figure 10.4 Photos of four leaders in the central government.

> ***July 28–August 5***
> *Hello Mr. Wang Yongping, Minister of Railways, your eldest daughter Wang Xiaoying is the director of the Finance Department of the Ministry of Railways, your eldest son Li Gekui is the deputy director of the Beijing Municipal Bureau of Transportation, your second daughter Wang Xiaoxia is the head of the Beijing Municipal Bureau of Family Planning, Beijing Central Hospital Vice President, your younger son Wang Xiaofei is the Ministry of Railways Quality Control Section chief, your daughter-in-law Zhang Ning is the city women's association director, your grandson is Beijing experimental primary school vice president Wang Xiaoshuai,*
>
> False information, delete, do not make private.

Conclusion

The open atmosphere, both online and in the media in the early days of the crash, made it difficult for the government to control public discussion. This was especially true in the case of Weibo, where discussion of the crash first appeared, and where angry posts and accusations aimed at officials continued well after media coverage had 'cooled off'. The logs demonstrate the difficulty in dividing the 'negative' fringe discussion from 'mainstream public opinion' in the case of a tragedy such as the Wenzhou crash that the public can be directly affected by, especially when deaths may have been caused by systemic problems. The initial notices to allow discussion of the official reports, and then criticism of local mismanagement, while also filtering attacks on the Party, central leaders, or the government, became difficult to manage. Differentiating between acceptable demonstrations of mourning and incitement to action was apparently difficult for censors, as the repeated examples and distinctions in the logs demonstrate.

A 'Disaster and Response Crisis', this case not only included antigovernment posts but also comments on the local responses, attempts to commemorate those lost, and questions about the safety of China's high-speed rail network. The crash was widely known and reported, and the content being posted fell between the acceptable and the clearly forbidden, posing a significant challenge to management.

Broadly deleting all Wenzhou-related content might stop the spreading of sensitive material, but it would also likely kill activity on the platform. The response was a concerted effort, as demonstrated by the directives in the logs, to manage the crisis by standardizing responses to different kinds of content and clarifying where the bottom line was. Looking at these categories gives an idea of what kinds of content was most problematic and what was most sensitive.

Both incitement to action and political content attacking the Party and central government are revealed as most sensitive by the logs. Incitement to action is the content that is set as the priority for cleanup by Weibo in the first days after the event, with other content put aside for later scrutiny. After this, content attacking leaders through criticism and the spreading of rumors, such as the large amount of content attacking Wen Jiabao, is also a priority for cleanup. This shows that negative content not linked to group formation can also be a priority for filtering. In fact, this negative content attacking leaders is among the few that is targeted for clear deletion and the reporting of those responsible for the content to Weibo management in Beijing.

The scale of the crisis is illustrated by the growth in the number of categories, sensitive keywords, such as 'actor' 影帝 [yingdi], which trigger the hiding of content for auditing, as well as the setting aside of some user privileges. The status or popularity of the users does not necessarily protect content. When filtering the large amount of antigovernment content, censors are instructed, 'block users, especially those who only talk about politics. [Those with] a number of fans of about 10,000, also V [verified user], all can be handled, do not be lenient'.

One of the telling aspects of the inability to contain the crisis, was the way in which censorship of the topic became a sensitive yet widely discussed topic in itself. Censorship in the media and online merely fueled netizen resentment, disbelief in the Party line, and the proliferation of rumors. Roughly cutting out netizens who posted critically on the topic failed to stem the flow of sensitive posts.

The source of these logs maintains that the Wenzhou crash was a major crisis for Weibo management. They had been unprepared for the sheer scale and complexity in managing the fallout from the crash. According to the source, 'the rail crash led to the censorship department accelerating its recruitment and co-operating with the government more closely' (Wang 2016b). The source also believes that the change in censorship procedure, to send a notification to users when making their content private, was implemented sometime after the incident:

> Don't know when they stopped sending a warning, probably after the High-speed Train Incident [Wenzhou Train Crash] when the incident of a big pressure large scale deletion of posts began? Everything is top secret, including the auditors they also do not know, but this is 'reasonable', right?

The failure of Weibo management to maintain 'mainstream public opinion' in line with state expectations during the crisis would have likely called into question some of the control methods. The visibility of censorship, especially when it touches large groups of netizens usually comfortably inhabiting the 'mainstream' of Weibo discussion, is problematic for both the state and Weibo, exposing the fiction of an open space for public discussion. The failure of hard visible forms of censorship, such as deletions and blocking with notices sent to users to filter negative content and the failure of censors to stay ahead of the crisis and to 'direct' the flow of discussion back toward the mainstream, appears to have provoked an upgrade in the number of censors and capacity of Weibo's censorship department as well as a movement toward less visible and more comprehensive forms of censorship in the period following the crisis.

The stress of serving these two purposes requires creative adaptation by the company to meet the requirements of the state. The Wenzhou crash revealed weaknesses in the company's capacity to filter, but also the strength in outsourcing the work to private companies with the capacity to identify strategic weaknesses and to adapt to better manage the demands of the state. This adaptive form of censorship and surveillance, supported, and managed by private companies such as Sina Weibo, and directed by the state, defines the system of outsourced content filtering and surveillance that characterizes the Chinese internet.

Note

1 柴静 Chai Jing was a journalist working at CCTV at the time of this log as a host and investigative reporter. Chai Jing's 2015 documentary 'Under the Dome' investigated the causes of China's air pollution.

References

Bandurski, D. (2011) 'Chinese Media Muzzled After Day of Glory', *China Media Project*, http://cmp.hku.hk/2011/07/31/chinese-media-muzzled-after-day-of-glory.

EastWestNorthSouth (2011) 'Everything You Want To Know about the Wenzhou Train Crash', http://www.zonaeuropa.com/20110730_1.htm.

Feng, E. (2020, February 8) 'Critics Say China Has Suppressed and Censored Information in Coronavirus Outbreak', *NPR*, https://www.npr.org/sections/goatsandsoda/2020/02/08/803766743/critics-say-china-has-suppressed-and-censored-information-in-coronavirus-outbrea.

Fu, S. (2011) 'Directives from the Ministry of Truth: July 5–September 28, 2011', *China Digital Times*, http://chinadigitaltimes.net/2011/10/directives-from-the-ministry-of-truth-july-5-september-28-2011/.

Huang, C. (2020, March 31) 'Online Wailing Wall': How Chinese Netizens Continue to Honor Li Wenliang', *COVID-19 Whistleblower, SupChina*, https://supchina.com/2020/03/31/chinese-netizens-continue-to-honor-li-wenliang-covid-19/.

Jiang, S. (2011, July 26) 'Chinese Netizens Outraged Over Response to Fatal Bullet Train Crash', *CNN*, http://www.cnn.com/2011/WORLD/asiapcf/07/25/china.train.accident.outrage/index.html.

LaFraniere, S. (2011, August 16) 'China's Troubled Railway Ministry Fires Spokesman', *The New York Times*, http://www.nytimes.com/2011/08/17/world/asia/17trains.html?src=recg.

People's Daily (2011, July 27) 'Microblogs Unite Rescuers in Wenzhou Train Disaster', http://en.people.cn/90001/90776/90882/7453443.html.

Severdia, S. (2011) 'Directives from the Ministry of Truth: Wenzhou High-Speed Train Crash', *China Digital Times*, https://chinadigitaltimes.net/2011/07/directives-from-the-ministry-of-truth-wenzhou-high-speed-train-crash/.

Wang, Y. (2016a, March 3) 'The Business of Censorship: Documents Show How Weibo Filters Sensitive News in China', *Committee to Protect Journalists*, https://cpj.org/blog/2016/03/the-business-of-censorship-documents-show-how-weib.php.

Wang, Y. (2016b, March 3) 'Read and Delete: How Weibo's Censors Tackle Dissent and Free Speech', *Committee to Protect Journalists*, https://cpj.org/blog/2016/03/read-and-delete-how-weibos-censors-tackle-dissent-.php.

Xin, D. (2011, July 26) 'Unanswered Questions Over Rail Dispatch System', *China Daily*, http://www.chinadaily.com.cn/china/2011-07/26/content_12979921.htm.

Xinhua (2011, July 25) 'Ministry Spokesman Apologizes for Deadly Crash; Says High-Speed Railway Still Faces Challenges', https://web.archive.org/web/20111204072458/http://news.http://xinhuanet.com/english2010/china/2011-07/25/c_131006463_2.htm.

11

A review of the research and practice of e-government in China

Jesper Schlæger

Introduction

In the early 1990s, rules of administrative case processing were considered state secrets, and citizens had little way of knowing how to prepare for an application. Rules could be changed or made up along the way, and personal contacts – often complemented by bribes – would be required to get anything done, such as opening a business. Cadres abused their privileged rights and contact networks to get ahead in society, flaunting their ill-gotten gains. The legitimacy of the CCP was already strained to its limits, and among senior leaders, there was agreement that the corruption had gotten out of hand. However, vested interests in the bureaucracy resisted change. With the adoption of electronic government, later renamed e-government, new digital technologies were approached by the central government as a means to force the bureaucracy into line and provide better services to garner public support.

The phenomenon of e-government can be broadly defined as the use of information and communication technology (ICT) in public administration (Schlæger 2013). The technology involved could be, for example, a government app, a government website, a network of surveillance cameras, or an intranet connecting a ministry and its subsidiaries. The study of e-government deals with the interplay between these technologies, ideas about how they could or should be used, and the existing institutions, including policy and organizations. This paper argues that the purpose of e-government in China has been to consolidate and strengthen the rule of the CCP. We propose that e-government can change governance in two main ways: (1) e-government can enhance party-state control (a) internally, over government organizations, and (b) externally, over society; and (2) e-government can improve the delivery of public services thereby creating output legitimacy. Accordingly, to analyze e-government we need to examine both sides of the coin: control and service provision. The empirical focus is, therefore, how the government organizes its activities through the adoption of new technologies as reflected in government policy. The emphasis is not on the content of the curated public discourses, or the citizen satisfaction with public services, but rather on the organizational setup that shapes these outcomes.

Every year for the last three decades, tens – and later hundreds – of billions of Chinese taxpayers' renminbi have been spent on e-government (Wang et al. 2019: 82). The technical

DOI: 10.4324/9780429059704-14

innovations are easy to spot by the ubiquitous presence of surveillance cameras and computers in government organizations. However, the organizational consequences require us to take a closer look at changes in, for instance, administrative transparency and rule-by-law to consider the consequences in government and for the citizens. On the one hand, citizens have benefitted from more efficient service provision and less petty corruption due to the digital monitoring of government employees. On the other hand, the public has experienced more control in the form of social management and the shaping of online discourses (Schlæger & Jiang 2014; Zhang & Wang 2019). Taken together, these elements contribute to enhanced stability, legitimacy, and resilience of the CCP and the party-state (Göbel 2016). In a rapidly changing, and, at times, very hostile, environment, the ability of the party-state to adapt through the use of e-government to protect its governing core is one of the most significant feats of the comprehensive deepening of the long-term reform agenda through e-government.

The remainder of this chapter examines how Chinese e-government has been studied in academia and how the implementation of e-government has unfolded in practice. Finally, we discuss recent developments in theory and practice.

Academic research on e-government in China

For majors in public administration in Chinese universities, e-government is a well-established course and there are dozens of textbooks on the topic. Furthermore, specialized journals such as *E-Government* (电子政务) cover the area supplemented by articles in public administration journals. For instance, *Chinese Public Administration* (中国行政管理) often publishes pieces on informatization in government.

A search for the term 电子政务 (e-government) in the China National Knowledge Infrastructure (CNKI) database of Chinese Social Science Citation Index (CSSCI) journals resulted in 3,040 articles in total. The publication curve for e-government research peaked in 2012 and has since been receding in steps until reaching a steady production of around 100 articles per year (see Figure 11.1).

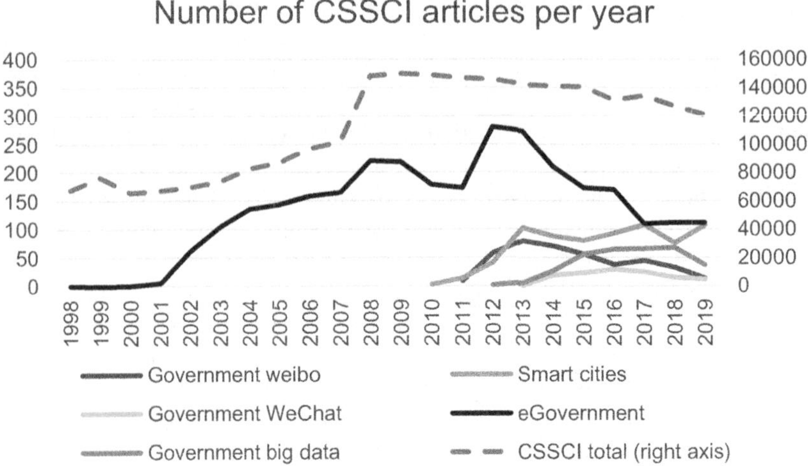

Figure 11.1 Development trend of topics related to e-government 1998–2019
Data source: CNKI-database accessed on 11 May 2020, limited to CSSCI-indexed journals.

In addition, subfields have emerged over time mainly responding to the invention of new technologies. Figure 11.1 illustrates several such fields. Articles related to smart cities (智慧城市) appeared around 2010 and through the next years grew to a reasonably stable state around 100 publications per year. The field has established its dedicated readership and theoretical interests related to digital urban planning and management. Then, in 2011, the first CSSCI articles on government microblogging (政务微博) were published. The microblogs enabled the government to engage in everyday communication with the public, and the research interest peaked in 2013. The next wave of exploration started at the top of interest of microblogging with the first article on government – WeChat (政务微信) published in 2013. The fascination topped in 2016, after which research paid less attention to government social media. Reflecting government use of new analytical techniques and the ability to process large amounts of data in real-time, government big data appeared in works from 2013 and capped in 2016. The interest in the topic has been more persistent than WeChat and research output has been quite stable lately. Other subfields include open government data and information openness, echoing the increased importance of online data in the economy and society (Zheng 2015).

The type of articles in the field of e-government has changed over time. This shows in the analysis below of the 100 most cited articles and all the available articles from 2019 and until May 2020. Of the former, five articles were omitted because they were unrelated to the field, for instance, purely technical papers. Figure 11.2 illustrates how the type of articles have changed from the most cited articles, that are generally older, and to the newest articles that were published in 2019–2020.

The sources were coded as either review, conceptual, or empirical articles. Most of the reviews are either policy or literature reviews. Among the literature reviews, there is consensus that the most important trend in e-government studies has been from conceptual pieces and reviews toward empirical studies, which signals a maturation of the field (Yang & Xu 2010; Zhang & Wang 2019).

Among the conceptual articles, we find studies without data collection that are not systematic reviews either. The conceptual studies are therefore a diverse group including

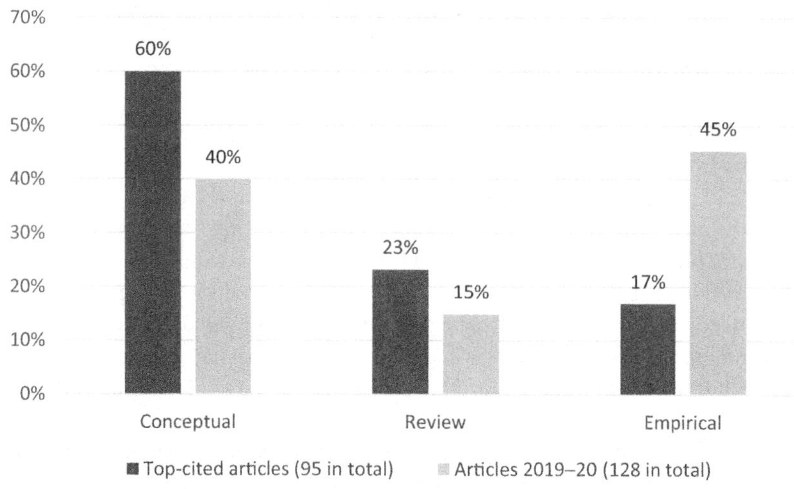

Figure 11.2 Type of inquiry in Chinese articles on e-government
Data source: CNKI-database accessed on 11 May 2020, limited to CSSCI-indexed journals.

theoretical work on the one hand, and opinions, thought pieces, or political statements on the other. The authors often grapple with defining and make typologies of the many new phenomena in e-government, such as smart cities, government WeChat, or open government data (Wang and Wang 2006; Zheng 2015). Every time a new technology is introduced, the literature tries to make sense of it, and find out what the consequences of adoption might be. In general, the articles focus on the official policy and practice of e-government. The importance of policy can be seen by the fact that the most cited article in the search for e-government is a summary and explanation of the political concept of Internet Plus (互联网+) which is the official strategy for expansion of the use of the internet into all spheres of the economy, extending beyond government to include the private sector (Ning 2015). In addition, not only academics but also political figures publish in academic journals. They thereby shape the academic discourse, for instance, by using certain terms and directing academic inquiry in the direction deemed appropriate by the government, as by connecting e-government explicitly to administrative reform and administrative innovation (Wen 2004).

Concerning empirical articles, they contain some form of data collection, most often through surveys, but there are also examples of qualitative case studies with interviews. Case studies of e-government outside China are also counted as empirical, even though the data collection may not be systematic. In this group of works, research methods spanning most of the conventional social science toolbox are applied with much of the work being quantitative. One approach is to use second-hand statistical data to examine, for example, the main factors determining how e-government innovations spread (Ma 2012). Another way is to conduct surveys, which has been used to find out, among other things, what people use government WeChat for, how e-government affects anticorruption, or how e-government affects the satisfaction with public service (Wang & Zhang 2014; Zhang & Ni 2020; Zhang et al. 2020). Thanks to their representative sampling, these studies can say something more general about e-government in the larger perspective of government reforms. Sometimes, other types of contextualized knowledge are needed. A smaller number of articles use case-study designs employing time-consuming qualitative interviews, organizational observations, and field visits. They examine, for instance, how to reduce the administrative burden of citizens or other concrete issues of policy-implementation related to local implementation of e-government (Ma 2019; Shanggong & Hou 2019). Such studies would mainly focus on social mechanisms rather than correlation or causality, thereby linking to certain strands within organization theory.

In terms of theory, academic work on e-government is quite cross-disciplinary. However, the theories of stages of e-government maturity, and institutionalization of technology stand out as central to the field. With foundational importance, the stages theory asserts that e-government progresses through continuously more advanced levels starting from posting information, one-way interaction, two-way interaction, to full online transactions (Dang & Zhang 2003). The stages-approach has been important in shaping the construction of e-government because it has been used as a normative template for policy and as evaluative criteria used to benchmark government websites globally (Wang 2019). Academics have competed about launching the authoritative version, and government departments have scrambled to make their websites comply with the requirements of the benchmarking schemes, an important part of their key performance indicators. In this literature, there is often talk about barriers to e-government construction, such as the digital divide, legal framework, budgets, and leadership engagement (Qiu & Hachigian 2005). Indeed, from a practitioner's perspective, these aspects are important to consider. For example, it makes little sense that the government puts services online if citizens do not have access to the internet. Whereas the logic behind the stages-approach is seductively clear, empirical research has, nevertheless, failed to validate the stages, and in practice, they are rather 'elements' of which some are more fundamental than others (DeBrí & Bannister 2015).

Another important theory addresses the phenomenon that when e-government is adopted in an organization, a process of institutionalization follows. The new technology is enacted in an institutional context rather than being a neutral tool that works identically everywhere (Zhang 2003). Thus, the implementation of new technology does not simply lead to the same results in all organizations. This implies that both institutional rules and procedures and the information systems must be adapted to reach any desired results, and e-government, therefore, is not purely a technical matter but an organizational one as well. The institutional influence is even stronger when cross-agency information systems are concerned because there are several institutional contexts in play. The theory about the institutionalization of technology has provided important insights about interorganizational sharing of information which again is important for the integration of services to reach the higher stages of maturity (Fan 2008).

In sum, the above literature review draws the main outline of the field of e-government in China characterized by its high degree of policy orientation. Over the last decades, the field has become established with stable output and turned from conceptualizations toward empirical questions. Even though the studies tend to borrow much of their theory from adjacent fields, the stages of maturity and the institutionalization of technology provide theoretical points of reference throughout most of the literature.

Main policies and practices of e-government in China

This section examines the policies and practices of e-government to establish how control and service elements play out in practice. More specifically, we investigate e-government-related policies from 2012 to 2017 as collected in the *E-Government Yearbooks*, an official publication (Yearbook 2013, 2014, 2015, 2016, 2017, 2018). The policies illustrate the transition from the previous administration to the current one. In total, 107 policy documents were analyzed. Additionally, the analysis includes descriptions of projects and practices from the *E-Government Yearbooks*. For the years before 2012, academic studies complement the data from the yearbooks. The first topic is internal control, then external control, and finally, service provision.

Creating control internally in government

To eradicate corruption and bureaucratism in the Chinese government, the first line of attack is through establishing internal control mechanisms. By first building up an information infrastructure, then adopting rules on transparency the central government has tried to rein in the administrative bureaucracy.

Infrastructure construction

In China, e-government was inaugurated based on a commercial impulse but the government quickly adapted it to serve political interests. China Telecom pitched the idea of e-government to central ministries and created a coalition to initiate the digitization of the public administration. The state council bought into the idea and made sure to establish a top-level design (顶层设计) controlling the overall development of e-government so that it would serve the government interests (Liou 2007). The basic infrastructure construction for e-government was attained through a series of 'golden' projects (金字工程) commenced in 1993 (Qiu & Hachigian 2005). The projects were a foundation for control (Kluver 2005). They cover the areas of customs, taxation, financial auditing, public security, and many more. The projects all aim at building up a basic network infrastructure with clear standards and centralized control. For instance, the golden card project enabled nationwide credit card payments and permitted monitoring of where cadres spent government money. The golden tax project created databases of tax collection giving the central government a new tool to make sure local governments were not hiding any income for themselves. Apart from these projects concentrating on hardware, the software side has witnessed progress as well. A whole ecology of e-government websites have been set up, increasingly centralized and standardized (Yearbook 2016: 29). Lately, the standardization of tax and trade information, for instance, has also become an export item promoted to the countries around the Belt and Road Initiative (Yearbook 2018: 185). The infrastructure construction thus lays a foundation for control in China and beyond.

Government transparency and internal monitoring

Previous studies have shown that to control a corrupt and ineffective bureaucracy one way is to introduce *transparency* in the administration to stop arbitrary wielding of government power. If the public knows the rules they are subject to, the opportunity for bureaucrats to arbitrarily come up with new requirements is removed. Clear rules and process descriptions posted online opens the black box of government case processing to enable rule-by-law (Wang & Wang 2006). Government policy acknowledges that information openness allows 'governing in the sunlight' and is hence the basis for rule-by-law (Yearbook 2017: 6). A major problem in Chinese public administration is the overlapping and unclear areas of authority. This precludes the development of clear administrative processes and is, therefore, a barrier toward e-government construction. Various policies have been adopted to solve this issue. In 2015, several bureaucracies were selected as trial sites for the adoption of the lists of mandates (权力清单) that indexes exactly what the single bureaucratic organizations have the power to do (Yearbook 2017: 36). Government information openness covers policymaking, implementation, management, service, results, and special focus areas, such as large government projects (Yearbook 2017: 13–14). As a point of departure, all government information should be accessible to the public, except for the items on a negative list (负面清单), a register of the policies that cannot be made public, such as those relating to public security, social stability, and economic security (Yearbook 2017: 15). If not actively published online, citizens can still request other information by applying. Increased openness is a way of rethinking the relations between citizens and the state, and the Chinese government has taken important steps. Nevertheless, many processes of governance are still beyond the scope of government openness, for instance, the criteria applied for internal decision making in policy formulation or urban zoning.

Research has also identified another element of the internal control, namely, *monitoring* of the bureaucrats to ensure they follow the rules. Inside the administration, disciplinary authorities have routinized the monitoring of government employees. Frontline-employee behavior can be tracked via security cameras, GPS, and through the case-processing systems implemented in most government organizations (Schlæger & Wang 2017). The information asymmetry between supervisors and the street-level bureaucrats is thus reduced, and the result is less shirking and petty corruption. So, the monitoring technologies enhance state stability by ensuring that citizens experience less corruption and more efficiency at the point-of-contact with local administrations.

Creating external control

Apart from stepping up control inside the administration to reduce corruption, the government has also developed a comprehensive system of online discourse management and censorship. The techniques and the results are beyond the scope of this chapter. In the following, we discuss how the organization of censorship tends to over-enforce, and how organizational dynamics have shaped the social credit system, originally mainly intended to control cadres and commercial entities, to become instead a social control mechanism.

Discourse management

A cornerstone of social management is the control of public discourses attained through censorship of information transfer on the Chinese internet (Paltemaa et al. 2020). In practice, this censorship is carried out by internet service providers on behalf of the government. Censorship works in different ways. One is through IP-blocking preventing users from accessing particular websites or internet services based on their internet address. Another way is control of the information transported on the internet, for instance, blocking messages on social networks if they contain certain keywords. The implementation which rests on internet service providers means that the lists of blocked keywords and blocked websites may differ from province to province and even between the various providers.

Xi Jinping said in a speech that 'Most of the netizens are ordinary people from all over the place. They have different experiences and opinions. We cannot ask them to see all problems so accurately and speak correctly. We should be more tolerant and patient' (Yearbook 2017: 5, author's translation from Chinese). There is, however, a long chain of implementation from the center to the local internet service providers. A speech such as the once mentioned is open for various interpretations of the limits of expression. These limits are first discussed in the Propaganda Department that issues a guideline to the provincial propaganda departments, and further downstream local propaganda departments will make their amendments before, finally, the internet service providers are presented with an interpretation of the guideline. The final list is made on the ground level. On each level, decision makers stay on the safe side, which implies that when the censorship is finally implemented it is much more constraining than what one would believe if just reading the central-level policy. We, therefore, see how the organization in many layers leads to what we can call overimplementation. In addition to censorship, government websites are designed to provide services on one hand and a platform for discourse management on the other (Yearbook 2018: 63). The websites are regulated to enhance broadcasting ability, among others through using the clusters of government websites to transmit news (Yearbook 2015: 40).

Social credit system

Recent research has explored another means of social control instituted with the social credit system (社会信用体系) (Kostka 2019). The system (actually, systems, because there are several locally developed ones) use big-data analysis to predict whether people are creditworthy. Many countries have credit rating companies that help banks and businesses determine whether they can trust a person with a loan or if the person tends to default on credit.

Scammers and loaners who do not repay their debt hurt the economy. However, China does not have any unified credit-score system. The social credit system is an attempt to innovate in this area. It uses an exceptionally broad range of personal data collected for other purposes, such as information about bank-accounts, online consumption, online gaming, and contacts on social networking sites. The resulting credit score divides people in a red and a blacklist, and people who have been blacklisted are constrained, for example, from getting loans or travelling on flights and trains. Due to the broad scope of personal data and the wide-ranging sanctions, the system could be used to exert social and political pressure on people. However, according to survey data shows that this concern is overruled by the perceived benefits such as access to faster granting of credit, lower interest rates on loans, or fast-tracked check-ins in hotels and airports (Kostka 2019: 1585).

The work on the social credit system started two decades ago as an attempt to create the trust necessary to support a market economy (Yearbook 2015: 17–22). Originally, the system was not only a digital project but a legal and cultural venture as well and the control was primarily directed toward the administration and business companies (Yearbook 2015: 19–20). It was supposed to prevent government abuse of power and regulate businesses to stop all kinds of illegal practices such as market distortion, fake commercials, and bribery. However, the focus has changed over time. The social credit system illustrates a tendency to solve the easiest problems first. In this case, monitoring the public is relatively easy because the information systems are already to a large extent present. However, inside government – except for the areas of case processing taking place on the e-government network–monitoring and data collection is less mature, and it touches the core of the vested bureaucratic interests. Accountability can be unpleasant for someone with things to hide, for instance, a bureau chief who favors friends or connections in a public procurement tender. The mechanisms for balancing of interests within the bureaucracy may also not be suitable for public scrutiny if political deals are based on personal interests rather than on a consideration of the common good. So, the easier task of citizen surveillance is implemented, whereas the difficult accountability dimension – which was originally considered more important – is postponed.

Providing public services

Through e-government, the control internally in the administration and the control externally of society have been supported to limit petty corruption and shape the online discourse. This implies that more constraints have been introduced. However, as the flip side of control, e-government has contributed to more efficient provision of public services.

The government online project

To leverage the ICT for public service provision, the government needs to establish websites and make sure the public has access to the internet. The Government Online Project was adopted in 1998, mandating all government organizations to construct websites and establish e-government networks during the following year (Qiu & Hachigian 2005). The project was led by Premier Wen Jiabao in front of the informatization leadership group (信息化领导小组). The group struggled with coordinating the network development which was driven by local-level experiments leading to compatibility problems (信息孤岛). Another barrier was the low internet penetration rate. It has, until very recently, been a concern for the government in terms of a transition to online services that part of the population did not have access to the internet. The yearly internet-coverage statistics from the Chinese Internet Network Information Centre (CNNIC) have thus been a returning point of focus in both research and practice. The inauguration of government websites, although symbolic at first, added an element necessary for government transformation, namely a window to the virtual state.

One-stop-shopping

One-stop-shopping government affairs service centers were adopted in many Chinese local administrations from the early 2000s. The centers are physical buildings where all the government organizations are represented by employees. By going to the center, a citizen can handle all affairs in one place to save the trouble of running around between different offices. By virtually linking up government organizations both horizontally and vertically, e-government supports the reforms to delegate power, streamline administration, and optimize government services (放管服改革) (Yearbook 2016: 11–12). In particular, by simplification of rules, the administration tries to make life easier for businesses (Yearbook 2017: 81). The centers are widely touted for their efficiency. Reductions in case-processing time were enabled by computer systems that allowed several bureaus to work on the same case in parallel. In Zhejiang, the slogan 'run once at most' (最多跑一次) signaled that previously convoluted processes had been simplified so the public could experience genuine one-stop-shopping. To some extent, the efficiency is make-believe that looks impressive on TV, for instance, reducing the time for case processing from 40 to 3 days. However, the government accounts and evaluations do not mention any resource consuming prerequirements (前置条件). To the applicant, a case often begins with a lengthy process of gathering, for instance, health declarations or property assessments, but these necessary documents are invisible in the government accounts of time consumption (Shanggong & Hou 2019). In the literature there are no reliable pre-, post-test research designs to tell us what kind of effect the computer systems had on case processing and whether the processes are more efficient seen from the citizens' point of view. Even so, considered an overall improvement in service quality, the one-stop-shopping has become a staple of Chinese government administration.

Online services

From the early 1990s until around 2009, e-government concentrated on building intranets and reforming the internal work processes (Yearbook 2013: 84). Although the administration used websites these were merely tools for information dissemination. Over the last decade, more interactive websites, process improvements, mobile services, have been steps toward online services. As a way of reforming the user experience, the provision of online services has shown to lead to an increase in public satisfaction and a sense of gain (获得感) (Zhang et al. 2020: 51). However, other research has asserted that online processing is still unavailable in many cases of administrative approvals and applications, and information about process requirements is often insufficient and unclear (Zhang & Ni 2020: 64). The way to a fully online government is still long and the pace of transition to online applications is relatively slow. One explanation for the lack of interactive services is that the user-focus remains inadequate. Various policies state that user-needs should be the cornerstone of e-government construction, and hence local governments measure user satisfaction. However, the surveys set the bar very low. For instance, Haozhou City reports a satisfaction-rate of 99.99% for their e-government hall (Yearbook 2018: 767). If a government gets a perfect score there is no incentive to improve. Furthermore, the policy lacks clear mechanisms to ensure accessibility options for websites. As it were, rules mandate the inclusion of basic functionalities to help people with disabilities to access government online services. However, the rules are vague and rely on local governments to experiment and develop new standards (Yearbook 2017: 112–115). Providing there is no central mandate and standards the user-focus and online services are likely to remain rudimentary.

Another way of bringing services closer to the citizens is through *mobile media*. For instance, a service can be accessed on a mobile app instead of going to a government office. China has a high uptake of mobile internet, and the mobile government services placed on the WeChat, Weibo, and Alipay platforms have all been well-researched. The platforms have different characteristics and where microblogging is particularly well-suited for information dissemination, WeChat and Alipay include payment and personal identification functions, and so, can solve issues of public service provision that require these forms of interactivity (Wang & Zhang 2014). Payment of utility bills, for instance, can be done conveniently online instead of going to a physical office every month to pay. Citizens can file their tax returns through an app, and they can apply for business certificates online. Apart from that, the mobile service provision is still sketchy.

In theory, the administration can increase online *responsiveness* to gain legitimacy and enhance the resilience of the political regime. However, studies find that the government is highly selective about which types of public affairs they put their effort to resolve (see review in Qiaoan & Teets 2020). Research has shown that the administration responds more comprehensively to the kinds of grievances that have the potential to threaten social stability and government legitimacy than to other kinds of citizen contacts (King et al. 2013). Another area of research has documented how the party-state tries to respond to citizen grievances through the adoption of leader's mailboxes where the public can circumvent lower-level cadres that try to obstruct their case (Hartford 2005). The mailboxes, inaugurated from the early 2000s, were later complemented with online townhalls with high-ranking officials including President Hu Jintao and Premier Wen Jiabao allowing people to pose questions about public policies.

Data management

The government can improve service and policy through *data analysis* to deliver personalized services and improving decision making. The centralization of databases is a foundation for big-data analysis to enable the government to predict what a user requires. Although it is a technical question of how to build databases, in practice one of the main barriers to the sharing of data resources is institutional and organizational limitations (Li 2008). For instance, some departments may use data as a bargaining chip to get benefits from their peers rather than simply share it. Additionally, concerns that other organizations may not be able to guarantee data security may affect the decisions of bureaucracies to hesitate from sharing personal and potentially sensitive information.

The implementation of data sharing is difficult, however. First, the government financial departments do not reimburse the data producers, and, therefore, there is no incentive to share the data (Yearbook 2016: 32). Secondly, data sharing is based on agreements between the relevant departments which means that the organizations lack a clear mandate from above (Yearbook 2016: 32). The e-government coordinated construction opinion in 2014 provided an introduction with a remarkably negative tone, stating the 'the capacity to serve the general public is relatively low, and it is quite far away from the requests of the leading comrades and the needs of the masses' (Yearbook 2015: 43). In particular, the database construction did not sufficiently support decision making. The frustration is noticeable, as the document calls for the various departments to coordinate the construction of e-government. Without a clearer mandate and an attractive funding mechanism, this was no easy task and, expectedly, data sharing did not work without limitations. Even today, there are problems of coordination and data sharing, which is a stumbling block for the integration of government services.

Discussion

The above analysis focuses on control and service, but it does leave out other sides of e-government. For example, the political economy of e-government integrates governance reforms with commercial interests and the forging of an e-government industry. Chinese government explores how to use and capitalize on the vast amounts of data stored in the bureaucracy through big-data analysis and open government data (Yearbook 2016: 47). Additionally, the government has formulated a cloud-based e-government strategy to establish China as a world leader in cloud computing (Yearbook 2013: 1026).

This paper addresses the Chinese party-state on its own premises. In the literature, and in practice, when we talk about the implications of e-government for ordinary citizens there seems to be an acceptance of the autocratic rule, focusing on the benefits, such as improved public services, rather than costs of authoritarianism, in terms of individual freedom and privacy (Kostka 2019). A discussion of the democratic implications of e-government warrants a paper in itself and is beyond the scope of this chapter (see, e.g., Kluver 2005). The aim here has been to maintain a balanced discussion and critique of policy and practice.

New directions in research and practice

The COVID-19 crisis increased the uptake of mobile e-government applications. Already in 2016, the use of big-data analysis of health data was adopted along with the construction of shared databases making data available for commercial use in health apps (Yearbook 2017: 49). The crisis spurred the exploitation of these capabilities in the mandatory use of health codes that everybody had to download to their mobile phones. The apps would generate a bar-code in green, yellow, or red categorizing the holder as healthy or potentially contaminated, based on automated assessment of self-reported data combined with information about location and visits to medical facilities. Based on this code, people were free to move or would be quarantined, respectively.

The crisis exemplified the importance of private service providers. Instead of requiring registration on a government-run software application, most localities operated their health codes on WeChat or Alipay where most people already have a verified identity. As a government big-data office director is quoted for saying, 'If we ask them [the citizens JS] to register on another platform, would they agree? If we use WeChat or Alipay login, this problem is solved' (Luo 2020). Possibly, the government chose to rely on private service providers to save precious time during the epidemic. Additionally, if the citation above can be taken generally, it shows how the government carefully avoids creating an unnecessary hassle for citizens and thereby tries to evade negative publicity.

In research and practice, e-government will be at the center of attention because it augments the control capacities of government both internally and externally. In the aftermath of the crisis, the Chinese government – for the first time since the reform and opening-up – faces austerity which may lead to threats to political stability. During the COVID-19 crisis, the government has instated more invasive surveillance and control than ever. Some localities, for instance, Hangzhou, contemplated the possibility of making their health code a permanent feature of social management. However, this suggestion was immediately met with a strong public pushback. This illustrates the importance of exploring the privacy issues related to increased use of personal data, including re-use for other purposes than originally intended. Moreover, the balance between control and service warrants further discussion, as do the relations between the state and the private service providers in the e-government industry.

Conclusion

The Chinese government administration today is different from the one 30 years ago due to the increased adoption of ICT. As one side of the coin, the party-state control of the public administration has become stronger and more centralized. It has become increasingly difficult for frontline employees to engage in corruption because their actions leave digital trails, and lists of mandates allow the public to hold them accountable. On their side, the citizens are subject to increased surveillance embodied in the social credit system and the health codes during the COVID-19 crisis. Moreover, the party-state strictly censors the information available on the internet. As the other side of the coin, digital systems have improved the provision of public services. ICT has accelerated case processing, particularly, for items requiring cross-bureaucratic interaction. The citizens now enjoy the benefits of government websites offering some degree of online services and one-stop-shopping facilitating administrative applications. Nevertheless, the main structure of the public organizations and the power relations between them – seen from a vantage point – remain unchanged, or even reinforced. The purpose of e-government thus remains to modernize the governance capacity and strengthen the rule of the party-state.

References

Dang, X. and Zhang, X. 党秀云, 张晓, 2003. 电子政务的发展阶段研究 (Research on e-government development stages). 中国行政管理 *(Chinese Public Administration)*, 211 (1), 21–23.

DeBrí, F. and Bannister, F. 2015. E-government Stage Models: A Contextual Critique. *IEEE*, 2222–2231.

Fan, B. 樊博, 2008. 跨部门政府信息资源共享的推进体制、机制和方法 (The system, mechanisms and methods of information sharing among public sector organizations). 上海交通大学学报*(哲学社会科学版) (Shanghai Jiaotong University Journal (Philosophy and Social Sciences))*, 16 (2), 13–20.

Göbel, C. 2016. Information technology and the future of the Chinese state: How the Internet shapes state-society relations in the digital age. *Comparativ*, 26 (2), 56–74.

Hartford, K. 2005. Dear Mayor online communications with local governments in Hangzhou and Nanjing. *China Information*, 19 (2), 217–260.

King, G., Pan, J., and Roberts, M.E. 2013. How censorship in China allows government criticism but silences collective expression. *American Political Science Review*, 107 (2), 326–343.

Kluver, R. 2005. The architecture of control: A Chinese strategy for e-governance. *Journal of Public Policy*, 25 (1), 75–97.

Kostka, G. 2019. China's social credit systems and public opinion: Explaining high levels of approval. *New Media & Society*, 21 (7), 1565–1593.

Li, W. 李卫东, 2008. 政府信息资源共享的原理和方法 (Principles and methods of government sharing of information resources). 中国行政管理 *(Chinese Public Administration)*, 271 (1), 65–67.

Liou, K.T. 2007. E-government development and China's administrative reform. *International Journal of Public Administration*, 3 (1), 76–95.

Luo, J. 罗婧姝, 2020. 健康码遭层层'加码'，互认真的这么难吗？ (The result of health codes is that each level adds a code, is common recognition really that difficult?) [online]. Available from: https://ishare.ifeng.com/c/s/v002gQnN-_vvioCPgbpDQUwECBtPfJJIdqlmqFbgNX3-_-_22I__ [Accessed 30 May 2020].

Ma, L. 马亮, 2012. 政府创新扩散视角下的电子政务发展—基于中国省级政府的实证研究 (The development of e-government from the perspective of government innovation diffusion: An empirical study on Chinese provincial governments). 图书情报工作 *(Library Information Work)*, 56 (7), 117–124.

Ma, L. 马亮, 2019. 政务服务创新何以降低行政负担:西安行政效能革命的案例研究 (How do administrative service innovations alleviate administrative burden: A case study of administrative reform in Xi'an). 甘肃行政学院学报 *(Journal of Gansu School of Administration)*, 2019 (2), 4–11, 126.

Ning, J. 宁家骏, 2015. '互联网+'行动计划的实施背景、内涵及主要内容 (The execution background, meaning, and key contents of the Internet plus action plan). 电子政务 *(E-Government)*, 2015 (6), 32–38.

Paltemaa, L., Vuori, J.A., Mattlin, M., and Katajisto, J. 2020. Meta-information censorship and the creation of the Chinanet Bubble. *Information Communication & Society*, online first. doi:10.1080/1369118X.2020.1732441.

Qiaoan, R. and Teets, J.C. 2020. Responsive authoritarianism in China – A review of responsiveness in Xi and Hu administrations. *Journal of Chinese Political Science*, 2020 (25), 139–153.

Qiu, J. and Hachigian, N. 2005. *A New Long March: e-Government in China*. Paris: OECD.

Schlæger, J., 2013. *E-Government in China: Technology, Power and Local Government Reform*. London: Routledge.

Schlæger, J. and Jiang, M. 2014. Official microblogging and social management by local governments in China. *China Information*, 28 (2), 189–213.

Schlæger, J. and Wang, Q. 2017. E-monitoring of public servants in China: Higher quality of government? *Journal of Chinese Governance*, 2 (1), 1–19.

Shanggong, L. 上官莉娜 and Hou, Y. 侯寓栋, 2019. 当前我国行政服务'简约化'治理的实践与困境—以北京市海淀区为例 (Contemporary Chinese administrative 'simplification' governance practice and predicaments – The case of Haidian District in Beijing). 中南民族大学学报*(人文社会科学版)* *(Journal of South-Central University for Nationalities (Humanities and Social Sciences))*, 39 (2), 131–137.

Wang, Y. 王益民, 2019. 全球电子政务发展现状与趋势—《2018年联合国电子政务调查报告》解读之一 (Global e-government development and directions – '2018 United Nations e-government survey report' analysis part one). 行政管理改革 *(Administration Management Reform)*, 2019 (1), 44–50.

Wang, F. 王芳 and Wang, X. 王小丽, 2006. 基于电子政务的信息公开服务 (Information openness service based on e-government). 图书情报工作 *(Library Information Work)*, 2006 (8), 76–81.

Wang, F. and Zhang, L. 王芳, 张璐阳, 2014. 中国政务微信的功能定位及公众利用情况调查研究 (Survey on the functions and public use of Chinese government-WeChat). 电子政务 *(E-Government)*, 142 (10), 58–69.

Wang, W., Wang, J., and Yin, J. 王伟玲, 王晶, 尹静, 2019. 我国电子政务产业发展对策研究 (Research on the Chinese e-government industry development recommendations). 行政管理改革 *(Administration Management Reform)*, 2019 (5), 81–85.

Wen, J. 温家宝, 2004. 深化行政管理体制改革 加快实现政府管理创新 (Deepening reform of the administrative management, accelerate the realisation of government management innovation). 国家行政学院学报 *(Journal of the National School of Administration)*, 2004 (1), 4–8.

Yang, K. and Xu, X. 2010. E-government in Mainland China. In: E. Berman, M. Moon, and H. Choi, eds. *Public Administration in East Asia*. Boca Raton, FL: CRC Press, 165–192.

Yearbook 电子政务理事会, 2013. 中国电子政务年鉴（*2012*）*(Chinese E-Government Yearbook (2012))*. 北京 Beijing: 社会科学文献出版社 Social Sciences Academic Press.

Yearbook 电子政务理事会, 2014. 中国电子政务年鉴（*2013*）*(Chinese E-Government Yearbook(2013))*. 北京 Beijing: 社会科学文献出版社 Social Sciences Academic Press.

Yearbook 电子政务理事会, 2015. 中国电子政务年鉴（*2014*）*(Chinese E-Government Yearbook(2014))*. 北京 Beijing: 社会科学文献出版社 Social Sciences Academic Press.

Yearbook 电子政务理事会, 2016. 中国电子政务年鉴（*2015*）*(Chinese E-Government Yearbook(2015))*. 北京 Beijing: 社会科学文献出版社 Social Sciences Academic Press.

Yearbook 电子政务理事会, 2017. 中国电子政务年鉴（*2016*）*(Chinese E-Government Yearbook(2016))*. 北京 Beijing: 中国社会出版社.

Yearbook 电子政务理事会, 2018. 中国电子政务年鉴（2017）(Chinese E-Government Yearbook(2017)). 北京 Beijing: 社会科学文献出版社 Social Sciences Academic Press.

Zhang, C. 张成福, 2003. 信息时代政府治理:理解电子化政府的实质意涵 (Information age government governance: Understanding the real meaning of electronic government). 中国行政管理 *(Chinese Public Administration)*, 211 (1), 13–16.

Zhang, J. and Ni, X. 张军, 倪星, 2020. 控权问责、服务提升与电子政务的清廉效应—基于中国282个地级市调查数据的实证分析 (Administrative control, service improvement and the effect of e-government on anti-corruption—An empirical analysis based on the survey data of 282 prefecture-level cities in China). 中国行政管理 *(Chinese Public Administration)*, 417 (3), 59–66.

Zhang, L., Tang, Z., and Zeng, Z. 张龙鹏, 汤志伟, 曾志敏, 2020. 技术与民生：在线政务服务影响公共服务满意度的经验研究 (Technology and livelihood: An empirical study on the impact of online government services on citizen satisfaction with public service). 中国行政管理 *(Chinese Public Administration)*, 416 (2), 45–53.

Zhang, R. and Wang, Y. 张锐昕, 王玉荣, 2019. 中国政府上网20年:发展历程、成就及反思 (Chinese government online 20 years: Development history, attainments and reflections). 福建师范大学学报*(哲学社会科学版) Fujian Normal University Journal (Philosophy and Social Science Edition)*, 2019 (5), 43–50, 168.

Zheng, L. 郑磊, 2015. 开放政府数据研究:概念辨析、关键因素及其互动关系 (Study on open government data: Definitions, factors and interactions). 中国行政管理 *(Chinese Public Administration)*, 365 (11), 13–18.

12

Cultural heritage politics in China

Christina Maags

Introduction

Understanding cultural heritage politics in China means grasping the multiple ways in which the party-state employs the Chinese past to achieve its objectives in the present. China's cultural heritage is frequently associated with the large-scale destruction of temples, ancestor halls and antiques during the Mao era, particularly the Cultural Revolution, when many 'material' forms of culture as well as local traditions and beliefs were forbidden (Silverman & Blumenfield 2013: 3). After the Reform and Opening Period commenced in 1978, the Chinese Communist Party's (CCP) stance toward cultural heritage has changed considerably. Since then, 'cultural heritage' has been 'revitalized' and become a resource for various political, economic, and social objectives such as enhancing national unity and economic development domestically as well as fostering the PRC's national image internationally.

Yet, why has the party-state 'revitalized' China's traditional culture after decades of neglect and repression? And how was it able to do so in practice? This chapter looks into the reasons, processes and effects of the 'revitalization' of Chinese cultural heritage by conducting a comparative case study of 'intangible cultural heritage' (ICH) protection on the ground – in urban Nanjing and rural Lancang County. I argue that the party-state has adopted a UNESCO[1]-inspired heritage regime to revitalize China's cultural heritage to enhance its political legitimacy. This heritage regime allows the party-state to gain control of interpreting and exploiting the Chinese past at the expense of local communities. While, on the one hand, China's cultural heritage has thus been 'revitalized' – allowing Chinese people to reconnect with the past which was cast aside during the early 20th century – on the other hand, it enables the party-state to exploit this process to the extent of offsetting the positive gains made by this cultural revitalization process.

Conceptions of Chinese cultural heritage over time

An important step in establishing a 'heritage regime' in China, as for any other country, was the adoption of the notion of 'heritage'. Originating in 'the West' (Vecco 2010), no similar

DOI: 10.4324/9780429059704-15

concept existed in China until the turn of the 20th century. As Lai (2016) notes, with increasing contact with the West many terms were adopted that we consider to be part of a nation's 'heritage' today, such as 'as 'guwu' 古物 (ancient objects), 'shiji' 史跡 (historic sites), 'guji' 古跡 (ancient sites), 'mingsheng' 名勝 (famous sights), 'wenwu' 文物 (cultural relics), and 'guobao' 國寶 (national treasures)' (2016: 50). Many of these terms were only introduced when China was 'learning from' and 'catching up' with the West (Lai 2016). Chinese traditional culture was soon identified as the reason for China's backwardness vis-à-vis the Western imperial powers, resulting in criticism of Chinese culture, particularly during the May Fourth Movement of 1919. This criticism marked a turning point for the role and protection of Chinese cultural heritage, as it would lead to its repression and in part destruction of over the course of the 20th century, not least during the Cultural Revolution (Silverman & Blumenfield 2013: 3).

With China's opening to the international community after 1978, however, China's framing and attitude toward its cultural heritage changed. After ratifying the World Heritage Convention in 1985, the party-state began to adopt global concepts and norms (Maags 2018a), such as 'cultural heritage' (文化遗产), replacing the notion of 'cultural relics' that had been employed during the Mao era. Whereas 'material' heritage was 'revitalized' rather soon after 1978, the party-state was less eager to reframe and revitalize traditional cultural practices formerly deemed as 'superstitious' until its ratification of the UNESCO Convention for the Safeguarding of Intangible Cultural Heritage (hereafter: ICH Convention). Soon after, UNESCO's notion of 'intangible cultural heritage' (非物质文化遗产) would come to replace the Chinese concept of (ethnic) 'folklore' (民间民族文化). Overall, with the adoption of the notions of (material) 'cultural heritage' and 'intangible cultural heritage' the Chinese government established a multilevel heritage regime, which is linked to and interacts with the international realm (Yan 2018; Zhu & Maags 2020). As the next sections will demonstrate, it is this adoption of concepts and best practices from the international realm which enables the party-state to extend its control over the interpretation and exploitation of the past.

Governmental objectives behind cultural heritage protection in China

The party-state's willingness to adopt international concepts and best practices for the sake of 'revitalizing' China's heritage is a result of its search for ways to enhance its political legitimacy. With the decline in socialist values and the rapid modernization and globalization of China during the Reform and Opening Period, the Chinese party-state was facing a '"crisis of faith" which was not merely a loss of faith in communism but a loss of faith in Chinese culture and tradition as well' (Guo 2003: xi). To counter this crisis, the party-state started promoting a specific interpretation of China's history and culture in, for instance, the education system[2] (Dirlik 2011), museums (Denton 2005) and patriotic education campaigns (Zhao 1998), to actively foster cultural nationalism across different segments of society (Guo 2003: 1). In this specific interpretation of China's past, the historic achievements of the Chinese civilisation are strategically linked to those of the CCP, for instance, by promoting narratives how the Communist Party saved China by ending the century of national humiliation and establishing a New China (Callahan 2006). While using different methods of disseminating this narrative, including the media, public holidays, the education system and the like, 'Beijing has creatively used history education as an instrument for the glorification of the party, for the consolidation of the PRC's national identity, and for the justification of the political system of the CCP's one party rule' (Wang 2008: 784).

The party-state's strategic interpretation of the past is moreover aimed at countering nationalist and separatist movements among ethnic minorities by promoting pride in a single Chinese nation. While acknowledging ethnic differences in its official narrative of the Chinese 'multi-ethnic nation state' (Silverman & Blumenfield 2013: 6; Gorfinkel 2012), the party-state simultaneously 'insists that all are members of a large nation that binds them together by the Communist state' (Zhao 1998: 291). In listing traditional buildings and cultural practices as 'national heritage', for instance, the party-state demonstrates its sovereignty and control over territories with large ethnic minority populations. Since these national sites and cultural practices, such as the Tibetan Potala Palace, are recognized by the UNESCO as 'Chinese heritage' (Shepherd 2009), the party-state has used international heritage lists to bind ethnic minority territories and groups more closely to the state – thereby receiving international legitimacy for ruling over ethnic minority territories.

Through international heritage lists and domestic protection of its heritage, the party-state, not only receives international recognition but is moreover able to enhance its soft power worldwide. To date, the PRC has listed the largest amount of 'World Heritage Sites' (55 sites) at the UNESCO (UNESCO 2020a) – together with Italy – and the largest number of items (40) on the 'Representative List of the Intangible Cultural Heritage of Humanity', which focuses on traditional cultural practices (UNESCO 2020b). Both lists are used by the party-state to present China as a 'civilised country with a rich history, ethnic unity and cultural diversity' (Inkster 2018) and thus promote cultural soft power internationally.

In addition to supporting Chinese nation-building and soft power, the revitalization of China's cultural heritage is used as a tool to foster economic development. As elsewhere, the listing of a building or site as a UNESCO 'World Heritage Site' results in a marked increase in domestic and international tourists visiting the site, and thus in the development of the tourism industry (Sofield & Li 1998). As Chau (2005) and Liang (2013) have observed, in addition to heritage sites, traditional festivals have been turned into tourist attractions – despite them being based on local 'superstitious' beliefs and religions. Heritage and tourism policies are used as a civilizing and modernization project to develop rural and ethnic minority areas' local economies (Wang 2017). To attract tourists, the party-state has moreover fostered the rebranding of entire cities along particular heritage themes. The city of Xi'an, which is known for its Terracotta Army, for instance, has been revived through a strategic reconstruction of its built environment that highlights its Tang dynasty history (Zhu 2017).

The revitalization of China's cultural heritage thus supports the pursuit of many political and economic objectives that are all interlinked: Both the promotion of national unity under CCP rule as well as the pride in China's cultural achievements and international recognition thereof facilitate the spread of cultural nationalism that celebrates the party-state as the leader and protector of the Chinese nation and culture. China's rapid economic development, in turn, further supports this state-led nationalism as the Chinese populace's pride in the past is linked to its prosperity and achievements today. Together, the nationalist interpretation of and economic exploitation of the Chinese past via the heritage regime thus support the ruling legitimacy of the party-state.

Multiple layers of cultural heritage politics

The main tool to control the interpretation and exploitation of the past is China's heritage regime, which is influenced by developments on the international, national and local level. The PRC is State Party to UNESCO Conventions on heritage protection and thereby vows to protect and promote heritage within its borders. To do so, the central government has issued laws and policies on heritage protection which are implemented by local governments. These three levels combined determine heritage politics on the ground.

The international level: UNESCO

In ratifying and implementing the UNESCO World Heritage Convention of 1972 (UNESCO 1972) and the ICH Convention (UNESCO 2003) – in short establishing a heritage regime domestically – the party-state has voluntarily agreed to protect domestic heritage via laws and policies, governmental agencies and programs, promoting research and raising public awareness. In return, the party-state may nominate heritage sites to the World Heritage List, or intangible cultural heritage (ICH) practices such as traditional dances and songs to the Representative List of the Intangible Cultural Heritage of Humanity. Both activities, protecting heritage domestically and listing it internationally facilitates China's international prestige and recognition, and thus soft power.

As cultural heritage is a key resource to promote the party-state's economic and political objectives, the PRC has become a key player within the UNESCO. While in the 1980s and 1990s, the party-state was still wary of international organizations and less integrated within UNESCO internal groups (Meskell 2014: 224), it is now increasingly making pacts with other BRICS[3] countries to pursue its objectives on the international stage. The PRC today has the largest UNESCO delegation, engages in lobbying and hands in the largest number of nomination files to support its international objectives, resulting in the highest success rate of heritage inscriptions at the UNESCO (Meskell et al. 2015) as evident in the data number of inscriptions listed above.

The Chinese party-state's savvy use of UNESCO Conventions and programs to pursue its political and economic interests, however, has also resulted in tensions with its neighbouring countries. One prominent case concerns the PRC's listing of archival materials related to the 'Nanjing Massacre' to the UNESCO's 'Memory of the World' Programme – a program which seeks to foster global remembrance of wars and atrocities of the past. As Japan rejects China's stance toward Japan's actions in Nanjing during the Second World War, this inscription enhanced existing tensions in Sino-Japanese international relations. In response, the Japanese government halted its financial contributions to the UNESCO (Nakano 2018). Through such actions, and listings of ethnic minority heritage on UNESCO heritage lists, the party-state seeks to substantiate its sovereignty and interpretation of the past more strongly in the international realm.

The national level: Central government

The Chinese party-state's actions within the UNESCO are strongly shaped by its domestic cultural heritage regime and vice versa. In contrast to the Mao era, the PRC today has established an elaborate domestic system of identifying, listing and managing heritage sites and cultural practices (Zhu & Maags 2020), which is strongly influenced by UNESCO guidelines on heritage protection. For instance, just as on the international level, Chinese government actors and experts use the instrument of 'heritage lists' to manage heritage on the ground. Through listing ICH practices on four government levels, the domestic heritage regime produces a four-level hierarchy of 'Chinese heritage' which provides the basis for subsequent listings at the UNESCO: Whereas national government agencies select from provincial heritage lists, provincial governments choose from municipal-level heritage lists.

County-level lists, in turn, are the source for municipal lists and thus provide the backbone of Chinese heritage regime (Maags & Trifu 2019). Similarly, heritage sites are listed on national inventories and categorized for tourism purposes according to a five-tier ranking system, which ranges from 1A (A) to 5A (AAAAA) (Shepherd & Yu 2013: 53).

By including certain cultural sites, objects, and practices on 'lists', the party-state is able to take control over the interpretation, valorization, and management of China's cultural past. Not only can the government decide what is to be identified as 'Chinese heritage', and what is to be discarded as unworthy of protection or 'superstition', its classification via lists moreover adds different kinds of value to the heritage sites and ICH practices inscribed. On the one hand, the inscription on different levels creates a hierarchy of values – as in being of international, national, provincial, or local value (Maags 2018b). On the other hand, as Zhu and Maags (2020) explain, identifying a reminiscent of the Chinese past as 'heritage' turns it into a public good for the display in museums and into a private good for commercial gain. As the party-state is able to monopolize on the narratives told at as well as on the economic profit made from heritage exhibitions and sites (Denton 2005; Yan 2015) it can determine how China's past is interpreted and used.

There are numerous bureaucratic actors in charge of protecting China's cultural heritage who use the Chinese heritage regime to interpret and exploit China's past in practice. While the State Administration of Cultural Heritage is responsible for preserving archaeological excavations and heritage sites, the Intangible Cultural Heritage Department within the Ministry of Culture and Tourism is responsible for all work related to safeguarding ICH practices (Bodolec 2012; Maags & Trifu 2019). Together they are tasked to oversee the implementation of heritage laws and policies across China, by supervising their superordinate agencies on the provincial, municipal, and county level (Shepherd & Yu 2013).

Similar to nomination processes within the UNESCO, government agencies on each level are supported by 'expert committees' who gather material on each heritage site and practice, evaluate them and make recommendations on which to enlist. Moreover, as experts are handpicked by the government, heritage-making is a process directed by 'symbiotic government-scholar networks' (Maags & Holbig 2016) who mutually support and benefit from each other. While the party-state includes selective nonstate actors in the decision-making process, government officials have the final say in what to identify as 'Chinese heritage' and how to exploit it to pursue its political and economic objectives.

Members of the community who have cared for historical sites or practiced cultural practices for centuries are not included in this decision-making process. Whereas in countries such as Germany or France, NGOs, associations, and individuals are able to make proposals for their country's nominations to the UNESCO's 'Representative List of the Intangible Cultural Heritage of Humanity', and thus have a say in what should be regarded as 'national heritage' and receive government protection, in China this is not the case. The party-state, supported by experts, defines what heritage is and how it is to be used (Maags & Trifu 2019). Therefore, in contrast to liberal democracies, in China, there is very limited space for local communities, ethnic minority groups and individuals to influence what is to be regarded as Chinese heritage. For instance, as Greazer Bideau and Yan (2018) show in their analysis of Beijing's traditional neighbourhoods called Hutongs, local communities are not consulted in deciding which historical buildings are to be protected and thus valorized, but instead forcefully relocated to the outskirts of the city. The party-state not only singlehandedly determines which material heritage to protect but also how to interpret and market it for tourist consumption, often ignoring ethnic or religious beliefs associated with natural and cultural heritage – as in the case of a Tibetan village in Yunnan described by Laukkanen (2018).

As public participation in decision making is limited, Chinese people have developed alternative ways to commemorate their past or have resorted to openly contesting official discourses and heritage practices (Yu 2015; Cui 2018; Zhu & Maags 2020). As Guo (2003) argues, members of the Chinese populace are 'contesting the meaning of the same signifiers that the party-state wants to hegemonize, such as patriotism, "national interest", "national tradition", "national spirit", "national harmony" and "Chineseness"' (2003: 1). Thus, while the Chinese heritage regime appears to be a holistic machinery designed to control and exploit the Chinese past for the sake of enhancing political legitimacy, in practice heritage politics are much more complex, involving constant negotiation and contestation.

The local level: Local governments, businesses, and communities

Contestations around how to interpret, valorize, and use China's cultural heritage mainly unfold on the local level. On the one hand, the party-state's revitalization of cultural heritage has created opportunities for local communities to reconnect with and economically gain from their past. For example, much has been written about the ways in which local governments have used the central government's change in attitude toward heritage as an opportunity for urban rebranding (Xie & Heath 2017; Zhu 2017) and developing the local economy, particularly the tourism (Sofield & Li 1998; Shepherd & Yu 2013) and cultural industries (O'Connor & Gu 2014; Chen et al. 2016). After the central government declared the tourism industry as 'a new key area of growth for the national economy' in 1998, heritage has become a valuable economic resource to attract domestic and international tourists (Nyíri 2008). Consequently, many local governments, businesses, and members of the community have sought to profit from the rapidly growing tourism sector (Zhu 2018). Municipal governments adopt tourism policies to enhance local economic growth (Yan & Bramwell 2012) and set up tourism companies to manage and profit from tourism development (Zhu & Li 2013). The increasing development of China's cultural heritage-based tourism sector has resulted in the greater internationalization of China's 'World Heritage Sites' (Wang 2010), which has brought economic opportunities to local communities as well as enhanced their pride in China's cultural heritage.

Therefore, in some areas, the revitalization of cultural heritage has been gauged to be a positive development. The promotion of ethnic tourism practices, for instance, has supported a 'cultural revival' (Oakes 1993) and raised living standards (Kang 2009: 250). Increased state attention to heritage protection, moreover, opened the door for more community-led practices of celebrating and protecting the past (Svensson 2018), resulting in the revitalization of cultural practices, which were at the verge of extinction (McLaren 2010). Therefore, as Gao (2013) notes, particularly the state's recognition and support of 'intangible cultural heritage' safeguarding has allowed the Chinese people to reconnect with their past and overcome the century-long critique of its traditional culture embodied in the May Fourth Movement.

However, more often than not, local communities have contested this commodification and valorization of heritage due to their exclusion from this 'revitalization' process. For instance, after the historic city center of Lijiang (Yunnan province) was turned into a tourism hot spot, many members of the local Naxi ethnic group had to relocate to the city outskirts, to make way for state and private tourism developers (Su & Teo 2009). While the question of who manages and who economically benefits from local heritage is often the basis of contention, at times struggles occur over the right of interpreting the past (Yan & Bramwell 2012). As mentioned above, the official narratives and discourses presented at historical sites often run counter to vernacular understandings and interpretations of local culture, leading to resistance and contestation (Yu 2015). In addition, as heritage listings and narratives recognize certain heritage sites and cultural practices as being of value, struggles of recognition unfold over who or what is recognized as 'official heritage' and who/what is not (Maags 2018b). The main reason for contestations is thus the exclusion of local communities from interpreting and economically benefitting from 'their' past, which – due to the extensive Chinese heritage regime – has become a monopoly of the party-state. However, as local communities are the 'bearers' of culture (people whose ancestors have erected historical buildings and who perform traditional cultural practices), their exclusion from the interpretation and use of 'their' cultural heritage risks undermining what should be the purpose of the Chinese heritage regime: the protection and promotion of Chinese historic past for future generations.

Case study: 'Intangible cultural heritage' in China

A closer look at China's safeguarding of ICH practices exemplifies the tensions between simultaneously (commercially) promoting and protecting heritage. With its ratification of the ICH Convention in 2004, being the sixth country worldwide (UNESCO 2020c), the party-state embarked on a mission to safeguard its 'intangible cultural heritage'.[4] To protect China's ICH, the Chinese heritage regime – which was largely based on protecting material forms of culture such as heritage sites, historic buildings, and antiques – first had to be extended to also enable the 'safeguarding' of traditional cultural practices such as songs, dances, handcrafts, and folktales.

Implementing the UNESCO ICH Convention in China

Similar to the adoption of the World Heritage Convention, the party-state implemented the ICH Convention by adopting regulation (SC 2005, 2011) and establishing a new ICH Department (Bodolec 2012: 525; Maags & Holbig 2016), which is supported by a second-tier ICH Safeguarding Centre (IHChina.cn 2018a). The main tool to manage ICH, as mentioned above, are heritage lists. In China, ICH departments create two different 'ICH lists' which complement each other: The first list represents an inventory of cultural practices officially recognized as 'ICH practices' at that particular administrative level (county, municipal, provincial, or national), whereas the second list pairs these practices with respective 'ICH inheritors' – the bearers of the cultural practice. The party-state's 'revitalization' of traditional culture has had certain positive effects: These two lists enhance the visibility and awareness of ICH practices by officially recognizing and linking them to state safeguarding projects, while also supporting the maintenance and transmission of the traditional knowledge needed to perform the ICH practice itself (Maags & Trifu 2019). In addition to the title 'ICH inheritor', these officially recognized cultural practitioners receive an annual stipend and (in some cases) other in-kind state support, in return for teaching students and taking part in state-organized ICH events such as ICH museum exhibitions, expos, festivals, or 'cultural heritage days' (Maags 2018b).

As these two lists are adopted across China on four different administrative levels, the party-state recognizes and supports several tens of thousands of ICH practices and cultural practitioners. To date, on the national level alone, the four 'national ICH lists' (2006, 2008, 2011, and 2014) include 1372 ICH safeguarding projects that are associated with 3145 ICH practices (IHChina.cn 2018b). Given that only a few decades ago many cultural practices and traditions were repressed, the extensiveness of the Chinese ICH regime is even more astonishing. Indeed, as Rees (2012) notes, '[t]he treatment of intangible cultural heritage in the People's Republic has (thus) undergone a remarkable transformation. China may have come late to the party, but the liveliness and number of ideas, concepts, policies and plans are startling' (2012: 25). However, while the party-state has been innovative in creating ICH safeguarding practices, its control of the interpretation and exploitation of ICH has resulted in ambiguous, often negative, side effects on the ground.

Ambiguous effects of ICH policy implementation

In the following, I will briefly illustrate two cases from my fieldwork – Nanjing City (Jiangsu province) and Lancang County (Yunnan province) – to showcase these effects of the ICH safeguarding regime across different provinces, administrative levels as well as socioeconomic, ethnic, and cultural contexts.

Drawing on international and national best practices for ICH safeguarding, Jiangsu's provincial government quickly established an extensive provincial ICH regime. It was among the first to adopt provincial-level policies on ICH safeguarding, it has listed comparatively many ICH practices and inheritors on its 'ICH lists' (Maags & Holbig 2016; Zhu & Maags 2020) and it has promoted the establishment of ICH museums and exhibitions. Jiangsu is well known for its traditional practices, which are predominantly associated with Han Chinese high (imperial) culture (Britannica 2020). In Nanjing, the capital of rich and prosperous Jiangsu province, the provincial museum, for instance, houses a very successful ICH exhibition. This exhibition introduces the visitor to the notion of ICH, Jiangsu province's ICH lists, and a selection of ICH practices by offering ICH inheritors the opportunity to showcase their ICH practice – mostly handcrafts – to the visitor. The visitor can 'browse through' Jiangsu province's ICH by stopping at different stands, talking to ICH inheritors and by purchasing an ICH-related product such as embroidery, hand-painted masks, or shadow puppets. A similar concept is employed at another museum, the ethnic folk culture museum, which is located in a historical building complex of the Qing dynasty, thereby linking and simultaneously showcasing material and intangible heritage of the province.

The ICH museum exhibitions successfully support the transmission of ICH practices. First, they raise awareness among museum visitors of regional cultural traditions and the need to protect them. This strengthens the visitors' cultural identity and pride in the cultural achievements of the province or China as a whole. In addition, particularly members of younger generations may become interested in learning to perform this cultural practice, thereby supporting its transmission to the next generation. Second, the 'stands' function as workshop space for ICH inheritors which is given to them free of charge by the provincial government. In my interviews with ICH inheritors many emphasized how the opportunity to sell their products to visitors has supported them in earning a living – something they had previously struggled with as renting a shop is expensive and the museum guarantees a continuous stream of visitors.

However, Nanjing's ICH safeguarding approach has also resulted in negative side effects. For instance, the museum exhibition only represents traditional handcrafts, neglecting other forms of ICH practices such as traditional folk literature or performing arts. Similarly, due to limited space, only a dozen, mostly provincial-level ICH inheritors obtain the opportunity to showcase their culture. Both processes result in a 'selection' of cultural practices and people for official state recognition and support which causes envy and contestation among ICH inheritors (Maags 2018c). In other words, contestations occur because state museums display a specific selection and thus interpretation of ICH practices as well as determine which cultural practitioner can benefit (and conversely who cannot). One might argue that due to practical reasons a selection is necessary and that it is better to showcase a few ICH practices and inheritors than none at all. This is certainly the case. Yet as the state makes this selection, who and which ICH practice is represented is a political question and will be influenced by the political and economic objectives mentioned above.

The state's objectives and priorities are visible in the province's approach toward ICH-related products in tourism areas. Although the government has provided workshop space near the Nanjing's famous Fuzi Temple, it does not police or punish nearby commercial vendors from selling 'fake' ICH goods (goods which are mass produced by machines, not hand-made) which carry the official governmental ICH logo on their packaging. As the ICH regime identifies certain traditional cultural practices as 'ICH', this has added value to associated goods. Consequently, ICH inheritors need to compete with vendors which sell the same type of goods at a much lower price. As a result, cultural practitioners suddenly need to compete with fake goods illegally making use of the 'ICH brand'. The party-state's ICH regime thus has intervened in the local market environment for handcrafts, changing its dynamic. However, as it prioritizes the development of the tourism sector over ICH safeguarding, its support for ICH inheritors is in part offset by its lack of action against the illegal selling of 'fake' ICH tourist products.

In comparison, in Lancang County – a rural and impoverished area in Southern Yunnan province – ICH safeguarding has taken a different form (Maags 2018d). As the county is largely inhabited by members of the Lahu ethnic group, the county is designated as 'autonomous' (FMPRC 2014). Being situated in a mountainous region at the border to Myanmar, the county is rather far from municipal centers such as Pu'er or Xishuangbanna. Despite its rather remote location and limited fiscal resources, however, the Lancang County government has put a lot of effort into developing and implementing ICH policies locally. It has sought to use the central government's attention toward ICH safeguarding to have its local ICH practices inscribed at higher ICH lists so as to receive superordinate government levels' financial support (Interview 42/2015). The Lancang County government's efforts have paid off. Lancang managed to have two of its local ICH practices, the Mupamipa legend and the Lusheng dance, inscribed on China's first national ICH list in 2006 and was designated a 'model county' for ICH safeguarding.

Lancang County's strategy to safeguard ICH practices differs greatly to that of Nanjing. In Lancang, there is no ICH museum or exhibition at which ICH inheritors could perform their practice and earn a living. As very few 'outsiders' visit the County, this would not be a suitable model. Moreover, local ICH inheritors are commonly farmers with very little or no education (including the ability to speak Mandarin Chinese) and the ICH practices they represent belong to the category of 'performing arts'. To preserve local ICH, the county government has stipulated that each village is to have its own cultural performance group and a cultural center at which students can study local traditional cultural practices free of charge.

In addition, the county seat has been rebranded according to the local Mupamipa legend. Since the legend tells the story of the God Exia forming the first Lahu people out of a calabash, the streets of the county seat, particularly the central square, are decorated with figures of the calabash. The county government has moreover used the Mupamipa legend as a theme in the local 'Lahu Traditional Garden', a newly created tourist attraction, where the visitor can learn about local culture by looking at the statues depicting scenes of the legend or listening to performing arts presented at the open-air stage. Overall, due to the establishment of the ICH regime in China, the county government has been able to revitalize practices formerly deemed as 'superstitious' and received state funds to support community-based safeguarding of local Lahu performing arts.

While this strategy is directed at safeguarding and preserving ICH practices of the Lahu people, as an ICH official explained, it is also an effort to develop the local tourism industry so that 'visitors can learn about Lahu culture'. As in Nanjing, governmental ICH safeguarding is thus linked to economic objectives. This strategy, however, has been in conflict with higher-level objectives of turning Lancang and neighbouring counties into a 'Tea Origin Culture Park' (Yunnan gov. 2015). Lancang lies within the historic 'Ancient Tea Horse Road' (Sigley 2010) – an ancient trade route spreading from Nepal and Tibet across Yunnan and Sichuan province, forming a part of the 'Southern Silk Road'. However, as the local ICH official noted, Lahu culture is not related to tea at all. As Lancang County has little means to counteract provincial-level decisions, its attempt to brand itself along Lahu culture may be overpowered by provincial interests in promoting Yunnan as a historic landscape of the 'Southern Silk Road' (Sigley 2010: 535). While the ICH regime has enabled the Lancang County government to revitalize Lahu culture, it has also paved the way for different administrative levels to compete over who can interpret and manage ICH on the ground for the sake of economic gain. This has resulted in an exclusion of local communities from this process and potential negative side effects for the sociocultural environment ICH needs to survive.

As these brief case studies demonstrate, China's creation of an ICH regime has had profound impact on the ground, albeit in different ways. Most significantly, the party-state has set up an extensive system which encourages and financially supports the safeguarding of traditional culture – many of which would have been labeled 'superstitious' in the past. This has, on the one hand, meant that China's heritage, after decades of repression, has been revived as a foundation of local and national identities. On the other hand, however, the regime enables the party-state to intervene on unprecedented scale in the interpretation, management, and control of cultural practices. The ICH regime resulted in the appearance of 'fake' ICH goods (Nanjing) and governmental competition over how to interpret and exploit Lahu ethnic culture for the tourism industry (Lancang), with the potential of undermining the very basis of its existence. In both cases, individual cultural practitioners and local communities are excluded from the 'revitalization' process, as it is the state who identifies and interprets 'Chinese heritage' for promotion and who makes the decision as to who can economically benefit from it and how.

Conclusion

With the Reform and Opening Period, China's cultural heritage has become a key resource for the party-state to foster its political legitimacy. The Chinese heritage regime, based on UNESCO concepts and best practices, has enabled the party-state to gain control of the interpretation and exploitation of the Chinese past. It has used this regime to foster cultural nationalism and economic development domestically, as well as soft power internationally.

For the Chinese people, this 'revitalization' process has had mixed consequences. On the one hand, after almost 100 years, the Chinese populace has been 'allowed' to reconnect with its historical past. Consequently, the party-state's shift to officially embracing cultural heritage has created many opportunities ranging from increased government recognition and financial support to the ability to once again make a living off of cultural goods and performances. As the brief case studies of Nanjing and Lancang demonstrate, however, the 'revitalization' process has also had negative side effects. While being the 'bearers' of tradition and culture since ancient history, with the establishment of the Chinese heritage regime, the party-state has now taken over control and effectively excluded local communities from the interpretation and use of 'their' heritage. While in Lancang the local government is forced to change the interpretation and practice of local culture because it better suits higher-level political objectives to promote the 'Southern Silk Road', in Nanjing, the local government enables the overcommercialization of ICH products to foster economic development. In both cases, the party-state risks exploiting Chinese heritage to the extent of offsetting the positive gains of the revitalization process in the first place.

Whereas many governments across the globe use cultural heritage to pursue their interests, the party-state, an authoritarian government, differs from liberal democracies in certain ways. First, it has more power to determine when to allow the 'revitalization' of traditional culture. In contrast to liberal democracies where there is more space for bottom-up activities and contestation of the state, in China, it only became possible to promote ICH practices after the formal 'go ahead' of the party-state. Second, and related to the former point, the party-state has significant power to determine what heritage is, and what it is not. This differs in democratic systems. While not all liberal democracies include communities in the decision-making process (for instance in Japan), in many cases NGOs, community groups, or professional associations have a say in what constitutes 'their' cultural heritage (Maags & Trifu 2019). In this way, the party-state is able to manipulate the meaning of cultural heritage in a way that it emphasizes the CCP-preferred interpretation of Chinese history and culture. In so doing, it seeks to use heritage to promote its ruling legitimacy domestically and its soft power internationally to serve its global ambitions. Finally, the party-state's significant administrative reach and power has produced a comprehensive heritage regime which can intervene in the protection and transmission of traditional culture down to the community-level. Nevertheless, despite the overwhelming power of the state, contestation and circumvention of central state policies and objectives persists – by actors within and outside of the party-state. It is in these acts of contestation and resistance where Chinese cultural heritage politics unfolds in multifaceted ways.

Notes

1 The United Nations Educational, Scientific and Cultural Organisation.
2 Examples include 'Study of the Nation' (Guoxue or 国学) classes in Chinese schools and universities (Dirlik 2011).
3 BRICS is an acronym for five emerging national economies, Brazil, Russia, India, China, and South Africa, which have become significant regional powers.
4 According to the ICH Convention, ICH can be defined as 'practices, representations, expressions, knowledge, skills – as well as the instruments, objects, artefacts and cultural spaces associated therewith – that communities, groups and, in some cases, individuals recognize as part of their cultural heritage' (UNESCO 2003).

References

Bodolec, C. (2012) 'The Chinese Paper-Cut: From Local Inventories to the UNESCO Representative List of the Intangible Cultural Heritage of Humanity', in Regina F. Bendix, Aditya Eggert, and Arnika Peselmann (eds.), *Heritage Regimes and the State*. Goettingen: Goettingen University Press, 249–264.

Britannica (2020) 'Jiangsu', https://www.britannica.com/place/Jiangsu/Resources-and-power (accessed December 13, 2019).

Callahan, W. (2006) 'History, Identity, and Security: Producing and Consuming Nationalism in China', *Critical Asian Studies*, 38(2): 179–208.

Chau, A.Y. (2005) 'The Politics of Legitimation and the Revival of Popular Religion in Shaanbei, North-Central China', *Modern China*, 31(2): 236–278.

Chen, J., B. Judd, and S. Hawken (2016) 'Adaptive Reuse of Industrial Heritage for Cultural Purposes in Beijing, Shanghai and Chongqing', *Structural Survey*, 34(4/5): 331–350.

Cui, J. (2018) 'Heritage Visions of Mayor Geng Yanbo. Re-creating the City of Datong', in C. Maags and M. Svensson (eds.), *Chinese Heritage in the Making. Experiences, Negotiations and Contestations*. Amsterdam: Amsterdam University Press, 223–244.

Denton, K. (2005) 'Museums, Memorial Sites and Exhibitionary Culture in the People's Republic of China', *The China Quarterly*, 183: 565–586.

Dirlik, A. (2011) 'The National Learning Revival Guoxue/National Learning in the Age of Global Modernity', *China Perspectives*, 1: 4–13, https://journals.openedition.org/chinaperspectives/5371.

FMPRC (Foreign Ministry of the PRC) (2014) 'The Lahu Ethnic Minority', https://www.fmprc.gov.cn/mfa_eng/ljzg_665465/3584_665493/t17896.shtml (accessed January 6, 2020).

Gao, B. 高丙中 (2013) '中国的非物质文化遗产保护与文化革命的终结 (China's Intangible Cultural Heritage Protection and the End of the Cultural Revolution)', *Open Times* (开放时代), 5: 143–152.

Gorfinkel, L. (2012) 'From Transformation to Preservation. Music and Multi-ethnic Unity on Television in China', in K. Howard (ed.), *Music as Intangible Cultural Heritage: Policy, Ideology, and Practice in the Preservation of East Asian Traditions*. London: Routledge, 99–112.

Greazer Bideau, F. and H. Yan (2018) 'Historic Urban Landscape in Beijing. The Gulou Project and Its Contested Memories', in C. Maags and M. Svensson (ed.), *Chinese Heritage in the Making. Experiences, Negotiations and Contestations*. Amsterdam: Amsterdam University Press, 93–120.

Guo, Y. (2003) *Cultural Nationalism in Contemporary China. A Search for National Identity under Reform*. London: Routledge.

IHChina.cn (2018a) '中国非物质文化遗产保护中心 (China's Intangible Cultural Heritage Safeguarding Centre)', http://www.ihchina.cn/jigou_desc_details/175.html (accessed December 8, 2019).

IHChina.cn (2018b) '国家级非物质文化遗产代表性项目名录 (National-level List of Representative Intangible Cultural Heritage Projects)', http://www.ihchina.cn/project#target1 (accessed December 8, 2019).

Inkster, N. (2018) 'Chinese Culture and Soft Power', https://www.iiss.org/blogs/analysis/2018/03/chinese-culture-soft-power (accessed May 30, 2020).

Kang, X. (2009) 'Two Temples, Three Religions, and a Tourist Attraction: Contesting Sacred Space on China's Ethnic Frontier', *Modern China*, 35: 227–255.

Lai, G. (2016) 'The Emergence of "Cultural Heritage" in Modern China: A Historical and Legal Perspective', in A. Matsuda and L.E. Mengoni (eds.), *Reconsidering Cultural Heritage in East Asia*. London: Ubiquity Press, 47–85.

Laukkanen, S. (2018) 'Holy Heritage. Identity and Authenticity in a Tibetan Village', in C. Maags and M. Svensson (eds.), *Chinese Heritage in the Making. Experiences, Negotiations and Contestations*. Amsterdam: Amsterdam University Press, 195–219.

Liang, Y. (2013) 'Turning Gwer Sa La Festival into Intangible Cultural Heritage: State Superscription of Popular Religion in Southwest China', *China: An International Journal*, 11(2): 58–75.

Maags, C. and H. Holbig (2016) 'Replicating Elite-Dominance in Intangible Cultural Heritage Safeguarding: The Role of Local Government-Scholar Networks in China', *International Journal of Cultural Property*, 23: 71–97.

Maags, C. (2018a) 'Disseminating the Policy Narrative of "Heritage under Threat" in China', *International Journal of Cultural Policy*, doi:10.1080/10286632.2018.1500.

Maags, C. (2018b) 'Struggles of Recognition: Adverse Effects of China's Living Human Treasures Program', *International Journal of Heritage Studies*, doi:10.1080/13527258.2018.1542330.

Maags, C. (2018c) 'Creating a Race to the Top. Hierarchies and Competition within the Chinese ICH Transmitters System', in C. Maags and M. Svensson (eds.), *Chinese Heritage in the Making. Experiences, Negotiations and Contestations*. Amsterdam: Amsterdam University Press, 121–143.

Maags, C. (2018d) 'Cultural Contestation in China: Ethnicity, Identity, and the State', in J. Rodenberg and P. Wagenaar (eds.), *Cultural Contestation, Palgrave Studies in Cultural Heritage and Conflict*. Cham: Palgrave Macmillan, 13–36.

Maags, C. and I. Trifu (2019) 'When East Meets West: International Change and Its Effects on Domestic Cultural Institutions', *Politics & Policy*, 47(2): 326–380.

McLaren, A.E. (2010) 'Revitalisation of the Folk Epics of the Lower Yangzi Delta: An Example of China's Intangible Cultural Heritage', *International Journal of Intangible Heritage*, 5: 30–43.

Meskell, L. (2014) 'States of Conservation: Protection, Politics, and Pacting within UNESCO's World Heritage Committee', *Anthropological Quarterly*, 87(1): 217–243.

Meskell, L., C. Liuzza, and N. Brown (2015) 'World Heritage Regionalism: UNESCO from Europe to Asia', *International Journal of Cultural Property*, 22(4): 437–470.

Nakano, R. (2018) 'A Failure of Global Documentary Heritage? UNESCO's "Memory of the World" and Heritage Dissonance in East Asia', *Contemporary Politics*, 24(4): 481–496.

Nyíri, P. (2008) 'Between Encouragement and Control: Tourism, Modernity and Discipline in China', in T. Winter, P. Teo, and T.C. Chang (eds.), *Asia on Tour. Exploring the Rise of Asian Tourism*. London: Routledge, 153–169.

Oakes, T.S. (1993) 'The Cultural Space of Modernity: Ethnic Tourism and Place Identity in China', *Environment and Planning D: Society and Space*, 11: 47–66.

O'Connor, J. and Gu, X. (2014) 'Creative Industry Clusters in Shanghai: A Success Story?' *International Journal of Cultural Policy*, 20(1): 1–20.

Rees, H. (2012) 'Intangible Cultural Heritage in China Today: Policy and Practice in the Early Twenty-First Century', in K. Howard (ed.), *Music as Intangible Cultural Heritage: Policy, Ideology, and Practice in the Preservation of East Asian Traditions*. London: Routledge, 23–54.

SC (State Council of the PRC) (2005) '国务院关于加强文化遗产保护的通知 (State Council's Notice on Strengthening Cultural Heritage Protection)', http://www.gov.cn/gongbao/content/2006/content_185117.htm (accessed December 10, 2019).

SC (State Council of the PRC) (2011) 'Intangible Cultural Heritage Law of the People's Republic of China', http://english.www.gov.cn/archive/laws_regulations/2014/08/23/content_281474982987416.htm (accessed December 10, 2019).

Shepherd, R. (2009) 'Cultural Heritage, UNESCO, and the Chinese State. Whose Heritage and for Whom?' *Heritage Management*, 2(1): 55–80.

Shepherd, R.J. and L. Yu (2013) *Heritage Management, Tourism, and Governance in China: Managing the Past to Serve the Present*. New York, NY: Springer.

Sigley, G. (2010) 'Cultural Heritage Tourism and the Ancient Tea Horse Road of Southwest China', *International Journal of China Studies*, 1(2): 531–544.

Silverman, H. and T. Blumenfield (2013) 'Cultural Heritage Politics in China. An Introduction', in H. Silverman and T. Blumenfield (eds.), *Cultural Heritage Politics in China*. New York, NY: Springer.

Sofield, T.H.B. and F.M.S. Li (1998) 'Tourism Development and Cultural Policies in China', *Annals of Tourism Research*, 25(2): 362–392.

Su, X. and P. Teo (2009) 'Tourism Politics in Lijiang, China: An Analysis of State and Local Interactions in Tourism Development', *Tourism Geographies*, 10(2): 150–168.

Svensson, M. (2018) 'Managing Affective Engagements with the Local Heritage in Taishun', in Christina Maags and Marina Svensson (eds.), *Chinese Heritage in the Making. Experiences, Negotiations and Contestations*. Amsterdam: Amsterdam University Press, 269–292.

UNESCO (1972) 'Convention Concerning the Protection of the World Cultural and Natural Heritage', https://whc.unesco.org/en/conventiontext/ (accessed August 27, 2019).

UNESCO (2003) 'Convention for the Safeguarding of the Intangible Cultural Heritage 2003', http://portal.unesco.org/en/ev.php-URL_ID=17716&URL_DO=DO_TOPIC&URL_SECTION=201.html (accessed August 27, 2019).

UNESCO (2020a) 'Properties Inscribed on the World Heritage List', http://whc.unesco.org/en/statesparties/CN (accessed August 27, 2019).

UNESCO (2020b) 'Elements on the Lists of Intangible Cultural Heritage', https://ich.unesco.org/en/state/china-CN?info=elements-on-the-lists (accessed August 27, 2019).

UNESCO (2020c) 'Convention for the Safeguarding of the Intangible Cultural Heritage. Paris 17 October 2003', http://www.unesco.org/eri/la/convention.asp?KO=17116&language=E (accessed December 13, 2019).

Vecco, M. (2010) 'A Definition of Cultural Heritage: From the Tangible to the Intangible', *Journal of Cultural Heritage*, 11: 321–324.

Wang, C. (2017) 'Heritage as Theatre: Reconceptualizing Heritage-Making in Urban China', *China Information*, 31(2): 195–215.

Wang, D. (2010) 'Internationalizing Heritage: UNESCO and China's Longmen Grottoes', *China Information*, 24(2): 123–147.

Wang, Z. (2008) 'National Humiliation, History Education, and the Politics of Historical Memory: Patriotic Education Campaign in China, *International Studies Quarterly*, 52: 783–806.

Xie, X. and T. Heath (2017) *Heritage-led Urban Regeneration in China*. London: Routledge.

Yan, H. (2015) 'World Heritage as Discourse: Knowledge, Discipline and Dissonance in Fujian Tulou Sites', *International Journal of Heritage Studies*, 21(1): 65–80.

Yan, H. (2018) *World Heritage Craze in China. Universal Discourse, National Culture, and Local Memory*. New York, NY and Oxford: Berghahn.

Yan, Y. and B. Bramwell (2012) 'Heritage Protection and Tourism Development Priorities in Hangzhou, China: A Political Economy and Governance Perspective', *Tourism Management*, 33: 988–998.

Yu, H. (2015) 'A Vernacular Way of "Safeguarding" Intangible Heritage: The Fall and Rise of Rituals in Gouliang Miao Village', *International Journal of Heritage Studies*, 21(10): 1016–1035.

Yunnan gov. (Yunnan Provincial Government) (2015) '普洱茶祖文化公园 (Pu'er Tea Origin Cultural Park)', http://pelc.yninvest.gov.cn/InvestDetail.aspx?id=3374 (accessed December 19, 2016).

Zhao, S. (1998) 'A State-Led Nationalism: The Patriotic Education Campaign in Post-Tiananmen China', *Communist and Post-Communist Studies*, 31(3): 287–302.

Zhu, Y. (2017) 'Uses of the Past: Negotiating Heritage in Xi'an', *International Journal of Heritage Studies*, 24: 181–192.

Zhu, Y. (2018) *Heritage and Romantic Consumption in China*. Amsterdam: University of Amsterdam Press.

Zhu, Y. and N. Li (2013) 'Groping for Stones to Cross the River: Governing Heritage in Emei', in T. Blumenfield and H. Silverman (eds.), *Cultural Heritage Politics in China*. New York, NY: Springer, 51–71.

Zhu, Y. and C. Maags (2020) *Heritage Politics in China – The Power of the Past*. London: Routledge.

13

Population ageing and social policies in China

Challenges and opportunities

Huoyun Zhu and Alan Walker

Introduction

Population ageing is a remarkable global demographic trend that will intensify during the 21st century, especially in the less developed countries. For the first time in human history people aged 65 and over are about to outnumber children under the age of five. As the country with the greatest number of older people, China faces considerable challenges in establishing social protection for older people at the same time as transforming its economy and traditional social structure. China experienced two baby booms during the 1950s and 1960s resulting in two ageing peaks in the 2010s and 2020s (Chen 1999). As reported by the National Bureau of Statistics, more than 2 million babies were born in China in 2018, lower than in 2017, and fewer had been born in 2017 than in 2016.

In light of the increasing economic power of China how it is dealing with this societal challenge is attracting global attention. Beyond being anxious about a potential crisis, as many in the West seem to be (*The New York Times* 2019), domestic researchers are seeking ways to overcome the challenge and turn it to an opportunity. This endeavor has introduced successful approaches to societal ageing from Canada, Japan, the United Kingdom, and other developed countries, which have experienced rapid ageing over the last three decades and developed innovative theories and pragmatic approaches to 'active ageing'. Others are involved in putting forward proposals for policy reform based on the history, current status, and future trends of China.

Population ageing has also attracted the focus of the Chinese government. The government established a committee to participate in the First Assembly on Ageing in Vienna, early in 1982, when China was not an aged state according to the UN's classification, which was reorganized, in 1999, as the Office of National Commission on Ageing. China has always been present at UN Assemblies on Ageing, which indicates a positive attitude to population ageing. The first law primarily referring to older people, the Law of the People's Republic of China on the Protection of the Rights and Interests for Older People, was issued in 1996, and a social welfare system for this population group has been gradually built up under its guidance. As a result the Chinese government was awarded the Second International Social Security Association Medal in 2016, with praise from the former president of the ISSA:

DOI: 10.4324/9780429059704-16

> China has made unprecedented progress in the development of its social security in the past decade and has successfully extended pension, health and other forms of coverage for the benefit of its population through a combination of sustained government commitment and significant administrative innovations.
>
> *(International Social Security Association 2016)*

To introduce the issue of ageing in China, we present a comprehensive discussion on population structure, crisis, and social goods and services for older people in this chapter. It consists of five sections: first we describe the ageing trend and its characteristics with consideration of the changes in Family Planning Policy; then the most important challenges to social welfare provision for the old are outlined with an emphasis on both family and government; thirdly social welfare provision system in China for older people since the Reform and Opening up is summarized; then we outline relevant ageing theories on a timeline from the ageism to active ageing; finally with a view to protecting the human rights of older people, we propose social policies to respond to the challenges of population ageing in the light of theories and practices both from China and abroad, especially the active ageing paradigm which is promoted in both theoretical and practical terms in Europe.

China's ageing population

By the end of 2018, the total population had risen slightly to 1.395 billion with a 5.3 million increase over 2017. 2018 was the second consecutive year of decrease in newborns following the first fall from 17.86 million in 2016 to 17.23 million in 2017, after the implementation of the universal two-child policy on January 1, 2016. This went against the expectations of demographers and provoked a heated discussion among both experts and citizens' groups. The latter criticized the inaccurate expectations of the government. Zhai Zhenwu, the president of China Population Association (CPA) predicted in an authoritative journal that there would be a significant increase in the birth rate with a peak value of up to 49.95 million babies per year (Zhai et al. 2014). The gap between theoretical prediction and reality confirms once again the difficulty of policy intervention in this field and, therefore, the inevitability of ageing. The CPA claimed that the reduction in the birth rate was caused by the interaction of many complex factors.

China's population trend has been labelled as 'two highs and three larges'. The 'two highs' means a high speed of population increase and a high proportion at the advanced ages, while the 'three larges' includes a large number of older people, a large dependency ratio, and significant regional disparities (Zeng 2001). Older people aged 65 and over have increased from 63.68 million in 1990 to 166.58 million in 2018, at an annual rate of plus 5.5%. This compares with the 27 European Union countries that saw an increase to 100.27 million at a rate of 1.6% per year, from 1990 to 2018. Many statements concerning China's population challenges were widely spread among the academic community before 2009 when the country's GDP was lower than that of Japan (ranking third in the world) and the per capita GDP was $3,830, slightly lower than the $3,896 which was the lower limit of 'middle-income' countries according to the World Bank. The two most cited statements in the literature were 'ageing before affluence' and 'ageing without preparation'.

Population ageing results from a combination of declining fertility and rising longevity. On the one hand, China has experienced a remarkable decline in the total fertility rate (TFR) during the past four decades, from 2.61 to 1.18, far below the replacement level (2.1). In addition to the decline in fertility resulting from modernization as with other ageing societies, the major causes were the one-child policy and rapid economic growth. Birth control was regarded as a basic state policy and added to the Constitution in 1982, which set 1.2 billion as the upper limit of population by the end of the 20th century. To achieve that goal, the central government issued an act, 'Decision on strengthening family plan and strict controlling population', in which the leadership responsibility system was established. Leaders who were responsible for birth control would be severely punished if it went out of control, which was called the 'one vote veto'. The 'one vote veto' policy was expanded to all workers in the public sector at the end of the 1980s. They were deprived of promotion and awards, and could be fired for dereliction of duty. Almost all families did not dare to transgress except for some disguised pregnancies in rural areas, which made up 90% of the excess births (Yang 1992). Economic growth not only results in the transition to low fertility but also raises the financial childcare burden for all families, which also affects the birth rate. The cost of supporting a child from birth to 16 years old reached 83,000 CNY in 1998, including 67,000 CNY from the family and 16,000 CNY from the government (Zhang 2000). The annual cost of 5,188 CNY increased to 22,500 CNY per year in 2013, more than 75% of the per capita disposable income (Li 2016). At the same time life expectancy has increased continuously as a result of improvements in medical technology and public health. The average life expectancy reached 77.3 years in 2019, almost ten years more than that in 1981, and is expected to rise to 79 by 2030. This means that the number of older people aged 60 and over will reach 364 million consisting of one-quarter of the total population in 2030 (United Nations 2019).

Population challenge to social welfare provision system

The establishment of welfare states assumed that people would spend their early years in education and then go on to a long period in work followed by a short period in retirement, but this pattern no longer matches reality (Doyle et al. 2009). Many media commentators argue that ageing populations pose a fundamental threat to the sustainability of welfare states. Before taking steps to accommodate ageing populations, without abandoning the social solidarity that has prevailed in the postwar period, we have to objectively face up to the challenges they pose to the social welfare system.

First of all, population ageing results in financial constraint on the resources distributed to social welfare for older people. The scale of public expenditure on social welfare rises in step with population ageing. Thus the correlation coefficient between dependency and the size of the welfare state reached 0.8 to 0.9 according to the empirical data from 21 OECD countries (Disney 2007), and was 0.8 in China based on the official statistics. In the absence of preventative measures ageing tends to increase the share of beneficiaries of the two most extensive welfare programs: pensions and health care. Public expenditure on social security and health care accelerated to 2.7 trillion CNY and 1.6 trillion CNY in 2018, with, on average, a 16% and 20% annual growth rate, respectively.

Meanwhile, ageing is accused of being harmful to economic growth, which is a key foundation of social welfare. The relationship between population ageing and economic growth has also been fully discussed in the academic literature. Globally, ageing tended to slightly limit GDP per capita at an average 0.09 percentage points of growth per annum during the first half of this century (Bloom et al. 2011) and 0.2% in the welfare capitalist countries (Martins et al. 2005). In China the equivalent figure was 1.23% (Zheng et al. 2014). This dilemma has been attracting attention from sociologists, economists, and gerontologists who characterize it as 'ageing before affluence' (Cai 2012).

The second challenge to the social welfare system is the decrease in labor force participation (a major contributor to funding the social welfare system). Ageing not only amplifies public expenditure on older people but also diminishes the contributions from active workers and employers. As argued by many economists, the negative impact of population ageing on economic growth is mainly driven by decreased labor participation (Wang & Ma 2012). On the one hand, the working-age population has slightly decreased with on average 0.1 to 0.2 percentage points per annum since 2015, which is expected to speed up since 2030; on the other hand, the labor participation rate has decreased from 86.95% in 1980s to 77.37% in 2010 and is expected to continuously decline to 73.42% in 2050 (Tong 2014). The dependency ratio (older people aged 60 and over to those aged between 16 and 59) approximately doubled from 15.7 in 1999 to 27.8 in 2018, and is expected to rise to over 40 in 2029 and 50 in 2036 (Zhai et al. 2016). This is likely to be an underestimate when we take the following two factors into consideration. First, the legal retirement age for women workers is 50, and for women cadre it is 55, both of which are far below 60. As reported by many researchers, the average actual retirement age is as early as 52 years, even when including men (Zhu 2017). The second factor is that a large portion of the population within the 'working-age' category is out of work, including the disabled, homemakers, students, the unemployed, and other inactive groups, which equal 16.3% of the economically active population according to the available data in 2015. The dependency ratio of actual retired people to the employed population surged to 46% in 2015, which means that nearly two workers support every one retired person.

The third challenge lies in the sustainability of pensions and benefit inequities among subgroups. Rapid ageing is seen as one of the crucial factors driving expenditure on pensions, which here refers to contributory pensions. China established a contributory pension scheme for urban enterprise workers (workers old-age insurance, WOI) in 1997. It is the first social insurance pension for combining social pooling and individual accounts that is based on contributions from both employees and employers and is independent of the public finances. However, the ageing trend posed a challenge to the financial balance of the WOI. The former deputy director of the Social Security Department of the Ministry of Finance, Lu and Du (2000), predicted that insurance funds would experience a deficit period from 2028 until 2050. The implicit pension debt (IPD) has been actuarially estimated, ranging from 1.1 to 6.7 trillion CNY, equivalent to 33 to 71% of GDP (Wang et al. 2001). Under the pressure of IPD, many people contested that the individual account, on the one hand, increases the burden on workers, while, on the other hand, it cannot meet the financial demands of older people at the ageing peak. The best way to reform, as argued by many scientists, lies in either changing to a Nominal Defined Contributory (NDC) system or by eliminating the individual accounts (Zheng 2003).

The pension gap between different social groups is becoming a severe problem when pensions have reached a peak as well as providing effective coverage. For largely historical reasons the state provides a stratified pension system generally according to occupation (Zhu & Walker 2018a). Rural residents, including farmers and rural migrant workers in cities, lie at the bottom of the pension system, and a disproportionate proportion of older people reside in rural areas. There are also pension gaps among geographical areas. Due to the large labor migration from west to east, proportions of the ageing population in western and middle provinces are higher than those in eastern ones, while both benefit levels and the pension reserves of the former are much lower than those of the latter. How to combat the potential financial crisis in pensions as well as inequalities in provision are urgent challenges for the government.

The fourth challenge is social services provision for older people. The family is the major provider of social care for older people, even in present day China. Although the central government initiated a strategy of 'social welfare socialization' in the 1990s, responsibility for social care provision was still pushed back to the family and individuals, particularly women, due to the absence of government responsibility and the deficiencies of the market mechanism and voluntary organizations (Zhu & Walker 2018a). Historically men are more likely to provide direct financial support to older parents, while daughters and daughters-in-law are more likely to provide direct personal support (Xu 2015). However, this traditional system is challenged by changes on both the demand and supply sides. On the one hand, China is facing increasing demand for eldercare services as a result of demographic shifts. The latent demand (actual demand, regardless of affordability) for long-term care services will increase from 309 billion CNY to 4 trillion CNY from 2014 to 2050, and the effective demand (demand taking account of affordability) is predicted to increase from 117 billion CNY to 2 trillion CNY (Hu et al. 2015), which is conservatively predicted to be 6.8% of GDP in 2050 (Zeng et al. 2012). On the other hand, the trend towards smaller family size due to the one-child policy and cultural transitions towards greater gender equality, which have challenged the traditional division of domestic labor, and new work and life opportunities for women outside the family sphere due to industrialization and urbanization, have reduced the supply of potential informal caregivers in China (Luo & Chui 2019). As reported by the CHARLS, a comprehensive national survey of middle-aged and older people, only 15% of interviewees took care of their older parents or parents-in-law, with the figure being 5% higher in urban areas than rural ones. The government has placed most attention on financial support to older people, with establishing a universal pension system, while the eldercare services insufficiency is relatively more severe, especially in the rural areas where both informal and formal services are commonly absent. The major residential circumstance of older people was an 'empty nest', at over 60% in 2014, which is expected to increase in the future. Of those, over 75% lived in rural areas, a total of over 40 million in 2011 (Liu 2012). It is a huge challenge to achieve the equalization of basic public services between urban and rural areas by 2020 based on the current highly unequal distribution.

Social welfare provision for older people

Here we summarize the social welfare provision system for older people from two aspects which reflect the policy practice over the past four decades in China: Material welfare and social services.

Since the new country was established in 1949 China followed the Soviet Union and established an employer-based social protection system until the middle of the 1980s when the economic system shifted from a planned economy to a market-oriented one, which is the foundation of the original social welfare system. Policy makers focused on pensions for workers in enterprises while pensions for the rest, such as civil workers and farmers as well as other social welfare items such as social services for all older people, have remained unchanged as a result of the stratified pension system (Zhu & Walker 2018a). Taking into account the national and international context, a mixed new pension model combining social pooling and individual accounts, the Enterprise Employee Basic Old-age Insurance (EEBOI), was designed for enterprise workers in 1995 and was unified at the national level in 1997. According to the No. 38 Act issued by the State Council in 2005, pension benefit levels depended both on individual contributions and on the social average wage. While public servants had benefited from the most generous pensions, with an approximately 90%

replacement rate and without their own contributions during the whole work-life until 2015, when it was shifted to a new scheme to be consistent with the EEBOI. Meanwhile, the majority of residents living in rural areas and those in urban areas excluded from the above two schemes, had no pensions until 2009, when the Resident's Old-age Insurance (ROI) was piloted in selected rural areas, which consisted of 10% of the total counties.

Although the mixed model combining social pooling and an individual account was used by the three main schemes, there are essential diversities among those schemes in terms of benefits. First of all, the three schemes are operated independently. Funds, information, and the management of each scheme belong to different systems. Second, the benefits for public servants are the highest among the three schemes due to having highest contribution bases and an additional compulsory occupational annuity, which, however, is voluntary for enterprises. By the end of 2018 there were 87,400 enterprises having established annuities which covered 23.88 million workers, equivalent to 6% of workers covered by the EEBOI. Moreover, the actual contribution bases of the EEBOI are much lower than worker's wages, which is further lower than that of the public sector. Third, pensions from social pooling accounts in the ROI are paid by a combination of central and local governments, at extremely low levels and being characterized by regional diversity. The ratio of benefit levels among the three social pensions was 20:14:1 in 2015. In terms of benefits, the stratified pension system takes the shape of an inverted pyramid. At the top are civil servants with the most superior social pensions; below them are employees in state-owned enterprises (SOEs) with mid-upper social pensions and considerable occupational pensions; in the middle of the pyramid are workers in private companies, the self-employed and some ordinary residents with relatively high income both in rural and urban areas; the mid-lower class is the majority of urban and rural residents who are only covered by the ROI and without a commercial pension; the lowest class are those without any pensions (Zhu & Walker 2018a).

Despite there still being large room for improvement China has made considerable efforts in pension coverage and benefit levels. The legal coverage (the extent to which existing legal frameworks offer legal entitlements) of pensions reached 100% in 2012 when the ROI was extended to the whole country; while the effective coverage (the effective implementation of the legal framework) was 90% and constituted 942.92 million people at the end of 2018 with an average annual increase of 19% (International Social Security Association 2016). Of those, more than one-half, 523.92 million, were covered by the ROI. Referring to benefits, the most important policy is the annual benefit adjustment of the EEBOI initiated in 2005 to offset the decrease of its replacement rate since 1997. The central government has compulsorily improved its levels at the rate of 10% every year since 2005, 8% in 2016, 5.5 in 2017, and 5% in 2018 and 2019 with the increase of average levels from 770 CNY per month to 3,153 CNY. Before the reform, pension levels for public servants adhered to the wage of working staff, keeping a relative stable replacement rate. In contrast the benefit level of the ROI is characterized as having a low starting point and an absence of an institutional benefit adjustment mechanism. In 2009, the starting year, every older person entitled to the ROI received a public pension valued at 55 CNY per month subsided by the government and this remained unchanged until to 2015 when it increased to 70 CNY in 2015, and to 88 CNY in 2018. Taking the subsidies by local government voluntarily and individual account pensions into consideration, older people received 152 CNY per month on average in 2018.

Another universal income security scheme for older people is the Old-age Allowance (OA) operated at province level, which was promoted by the Ministry of Civil Affairs in 2009. The OA benefits people aged 80 and over, covering 29.7 million in 2018 and provides progressive allowances with the age increases according to the local standard. Due to the lack of a unified policy at the national level, although the Ministry of Civil Affairs had promised to do so in 2014, there are vast differences among provinces in terms of both ages and benefits. As reported by the Ministry of Civil Affairs in 2016, the majority of provinces provided universal OA to all older people aged 80 and over, but Qinghai and Shannxi set the entitlement age at 70 years, and Tianjin reduced it to 60, while several provinces such as Shanghai, Henan, Guizhou included only centenarians. Benefit levels range from 60 CNY per month to 1,200 CNY determined by the age of the beneficiary and region. Another two schemes established at the provincial level in 2015 are income compensation for the service expenditure and the nursing care allowance both for disabled older people living in poverty. The former covered 5.2 million beneficiaries and the latter 0.7 million in 2018.

Social service systems for older people had given way to income security for a very long time, until 2006, when there was a vital shift from institutional to home-based care. Overall, China has experienced a three-stage development path. Between its establishment and the Reform and Opening up, older people were divided into three groups, those employed by the public sector or enterprises depended on their employers; those without formal occupations depended on their families; while the poorest 'three Nos' older people were protected by the government. Since the Reform and Opening up in 1978, a majority of SOEs and collective enterprises have been privatized, so many retired workers depending on them previously fell into poverty. In response to this problem, the Ministry of Civil Affairs launched 'social welfare socialization' in the 1990s but ended with 'social welfare familization' due to the premature retreat of the government responsibility when the market and voluntary organizations were too weak to act as independent providers (Zhu & Walker 2018b). At this stage, from the 1980s to the 1990s, the government was only responsible for the 'three Nos', while the vast majority were left to their families. Since the turn of the century, social service provision has reemphasized the dominant responsibilities of the family, accompanied by enhancing the responsibility of other sectors. In view of the failure of 'social welfare socialization', policy makers initiated a strategy called 'home-based, community service-reliant and institutional care-supplemented', founded on the principle of guiding by policy, supporting by government, organizing by society, and promoting by the market in 2006. To implement this strategy, over 30 policies were issued during the first 15 years of the 21st century, and this has been further intensified recently. Macro-social policies, such as the Report of the 19th National Congress of the Communist Party of China, Annual Report on the Work of Government, the Five-year Plan for Old-age Programs Development, Health China 2030, place more attention on social services for older people. The latest national plan, especially the one for ageing issued on November 22, 2019, National Medium and Long-term Plan for Responding Actively to the Population Ageing, provides a strategic, comprehensive guide to the challenges of population ageing during the future 30 years until 2050. Active ageing was accepted by policy makers as an essential part of this strategy.

There has been a remarkable enhancement of social service provision. According to the available data from the Ministry of Civil Affairs, public expenditure on social services has increased from 12.2 billion in 2007 to 54.4 billion in 2016, at an annual average rate of 18.1%; aged care beds have increased from 3.1 million in 2010 to 7.4 million in 2017, but slightly decreased to 7.3 million in 2018; and community service stations have increased from 50,000 in 2007 to 147,000 in 2018. It is surprising that the numbers of community-based facilities for older people in rural areas are greater than those in urban ones, which should be attributed to the efforts of the government in recent years. The mutual happiness house, a form of collective ageing in place, initiated by a small village, Qiantun Cun in

Hebei province, was officially praised by former president Hu Jintao in 2011 and by the former director of the Ministry of Civil Affairs, Li Liguo, in 2012. Since then, it has been extended rapidly to many provinces such as Fujian, Hubei, Shandong, and covered 82,000 people in 2018. Self-help and mutual aid are perceived as a practical choice to respond to the ageing challenge in the context of China, which was said to conform to the traditional filial piety culture (Gao & Zhang 2016).

From ageism to active ageing

Gerontology is a comparatively 'young' science concerned with the study of ageing. It consists of a number of different perspectives dominated by biology and medicine, followed by psychology, sociology, and their combination, such as the social-psycho model and biomedicine. These differences in uses, approaches, definitions, and emphasis, together with the interdisciplinary overlaps, indicate the complexity of the field. Each perspective, in fact, is supported by distinguished theories and paradigms as a result of the diverse approaches to ageing. The biological and medical approaches to ageing are concerned with how the passage of time affects physiological systems, which view the ageing as a normal and internal process occurring in the postreproductive phase (also called 'third phase') of life accompanied by a decrease in the ability of the body to maintain homeostasis (Strehler 1962). The psychological approach concentrates upon examining personality, mental function, and notions of self and identity. Like the biological approach, the psychological one focuses on the negative impact, decline, and loss of older people with ageing from mental illness and subjective cognition. As criticized by the social gerontological perspective, both biological and psychological approaches confuse the distinction between age-related changes and diseases, which attributes responsibility to individuals. The social gerontological approach is concerned with using sociological perspectives to understand ageing, which tries to comprehensively understand the ageing at least from three perspectives (individual, social, and societal) and at two levels (microscale and macroscale) (Victor 2005). In contrast the social gerontological perspective views ageing positively, resulting from a series of extrinsic factors including diet, occupation, and cultural and economic transformation. For example, one of the often-cited explanations of ageing, life course theory, emphasizes the plasticity and heterogeneity determined by the interaction between individual lives and social structures. Scientists have created a variety of scientific theories based on those diverse paradigms giving us rich insights to understand the ageing process (Walker 2015).

Disengagement was the first explicit social theory that was concerned with ageing (Cumming & Henry 1961). This theory argues that ageing involves a gradual but inevitable withdrawal or disengagement from the interaction between the individual and his/her social context which implies a triple loss for the individual: a loss of roles, a restriction of social contacts and relationships, and a reduced commitment to social customs and values (Victor 2005). From the viewpoint of disengagement, old age is seen as a social problem and older people as a social burden. It was a dominant theory interpreting the ageing phenomenon within the academic community until the mid-1980s when other newer theories arose while disengagement was viewed as outdated.

Successful ageing was a replacement of the disengagement perspective (Rowe & Kahn 1997). It argued that research on ageing has emphasized average age-related losses and neglected the substantial heterogeneity of older people. Instead, it emphasized the importance of social and environmental factors on the physiological and mental development of ageing individuals. As a consequence, there is a vital shift from age-intrinsic to age-extrinsic and from treatment to prevention (Bülow & Söderqvist 2014). However, what is successful ageing and how to operationalize this concept remain inconsistent. Although Rowe and Kahn (1997) further tried to operationalize it with three criteria: a state of low probability of disease; good physical and mental functioning; and active engagement with life, this concept did not include every older person because of the fact that the advanced ages are inevitably far from those criteria, so it tends to be confined to the young-old.

Affected by neoliberalism, this concept resurfaced in the United States in the 1990s in the guise of 'productive ageing' (Walker 2002). Researchers had begun to shift the focus of ageing research from older people to the process of human development over the life course. Mainly due to the fact that cohort reaching old age is increasingly well-educated, healthy, and economically secure, one might expect that they would continue to make productive contributions to the society such as paid work, volunteerism, education, advocacy consumerism, and political action. The concept challenges the persistent 'myth of unproductivity' and adheres to the assumption that the skills, expertise, and experience of those in later life are presently inefficiently employed and can be used better. Proponents of productive ageing, therefore, take an interest in the actual and potential market contributions of older adults (Cole & Macdonald 2015).

Most of the variants of productive ageing are focused narrowly on the production of goods and services and, thereby, tend to be instrumental and economistic (Walker 2002). However, on the one hand, like the successful ageing paradigm, the oldest old are destined to be excluded from the productive group due to their disability and incapability; on the other hand, the ideological imagination making maximum use of the older people's potential did not appear to be happening. Opportunities and incentives for older persons to engage in productive social activities have declined (Uhlenberg 1992). Reflecting the new science of ageing (Walker 2015), active ageing promoted by the WHO embraces a richer meaning rather than focusing exclusively on contributions of older people to the family, community, and society. Active ageing refers to the process of optimizing opportunities for health, participation, and security in order to enhance the quality of life as people age (World Health Organization 2002). It allows people to realize their potential for physical, social, and mental well-being throughout the life course and to participate in society according to their needs, desire, and capacities while providing them with adequate protection, security, and care when they require assistance beyond their instrumental values to the society. Moreover, active ageing gives more emphasis to the close relationship between older people and public policy (Walker 2009; Walker 2018). It deconstructs the popular ageist stereotypes which see the older people as the passive recipients of pensions and welfare dependents since the post–Second World War era, while reconstructing a new connection with a positive perspective (Walker 2015). The thinking behind the new approach is expressed perfectly in the WHO dictum, 'years have been added to the life, now we must add life to the years'.

Other concepts such as healthy ageing, radical ageing, conscious ageing, and harmonious ageing have been put forward by researchers in an attempt to place a specific focus on the ageing agenda. One of the many challenges confronting gerontologists is to be able to integrate these different approaches to enhance and develop our understanding of ageing and later life.

Toward an active social policy on ageing

Population ageing first seen in the European welfare states and Japan at the beginning of the last century is now a global trend and will be intensified over the coming decades in China. Theories and experiences applied in the developed countries, as well as practices in

China, together provide valuable lessons for future social policies. Before outlining some proposals, we should be clear that population ageing is a challenge but also an opportunity, the outcome of which will be determined by our attitudes to it and the social policies we adopt. Going beyond traditional gerontological theories, active ageing takes a fresh look at older people and sees them as neither a social burden nor an instrument of economic development, but rather as one section of humanity who may need help from society but also contribute to it. Guided by this approach, policy makers in China should focus on the following aspects designed to progress a comprehensive active ageing strategy.

First, it is essential to recognize the substantial heterogeneity within older people. Most mass media and statistical reports tend to use a single index of the impact of ageing, such as the proportion of older people aged 65 and over to the total population, but at the expense of neglecting their diversities. Yet empirical research has demonstrated that those posing the greatest challenge to Chinese society, in fact, are actually a minority of the very elderly with a disability. The probabilities of disability in older people aged 60 and over in China, based on a national sample survey, range from 8% to 15% (Zhang & Wei 2015). Another study based on the sixth population census in 2010 reported that the proportion of disabled among older people is 2.95%, or 5.23 million people (Lin 2015). A majority of the young-old are faced with lower disability risks and would normally be engaged in economic and social activities. As shown in Figure 13.1, however, the average employment rate of older people is low and decreases with age from 30% among 60-year-olds to no more than 6% in 75-year-olds and above. Of those, 90% are engaged in agriculture. Older people who live in rural areas and small towns are excluded from mandatory retirement age and opt to work longer until disability prevents them from doing so, which accounts for their high statistical employment rate. In urban areas, only 7.2% of older people return to economic activity despite the fact that their capacity is higher than their counterparts in rural areas. Hence, what China should do is urgently shift attention from the scare-mongering about the ageing challenge towards tailored social policies for different age groups to meet their individual needs.

Second, it is important to develop social policies facilitating social participation among younger older people. Employment is potentially one of the foundations of well-being.

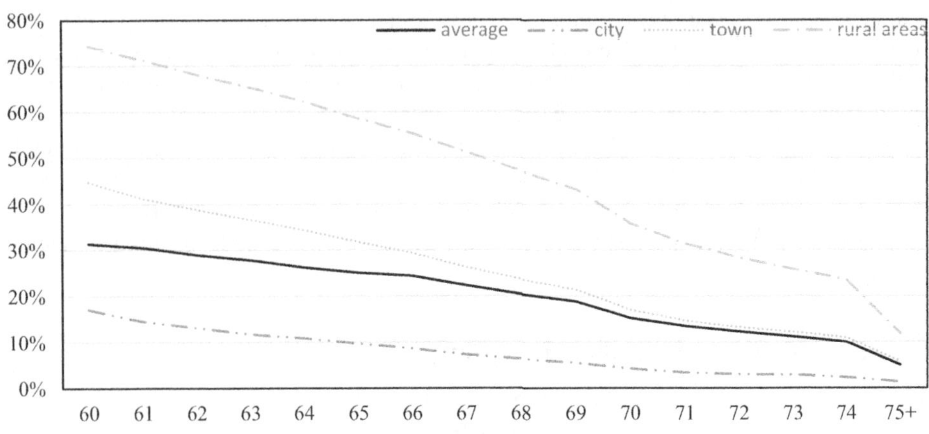

Figure 13.1 Employment rates of older people according to age and region.

Mandatory retirement age, which was designed in the 1950s, needs to be postponed in the context of present increases in average life expectancy. There is an average of 25 years between actual retirement age and life expectancy. Many Chinese researchers have discussed a wide range of plans to postpone retirement and there are two policy consensuses. One is that the statutory retirement age should be postponed to what has been implemented in most developed countries because of the narrowing gap in life expectancy between them and China. The other is that flexible retirement and pension benefits would be good for China. Early in 2012, the Ministry of Human Resources and Social Security initiated a demonstration of postponing retirement but confronted many difficulties. Employment is not the only way to social participation. Unpaid activities like volunteerism, education, advocacy consumerism, and political action highlighted by the active ageing approach, but ignored in practice in China, should be given more attention. The mutual happiness house mentioned above is a positive direction to social participation. Both in rural and urban areas, older people living alone or with their partners is a widespread status in China. Mutual aid among older people may be a right choice for the challenge of the social service gap. Nevertheless, it is also crucial that the government should undertake its duty to sustain it with a 'shared care' policy, including subsidies for the younger older people providing social services.

Thirdly, social policies should be aimed at risk prevention. Ageing is inevitable but also malleable. Evidence from the major UK New Dynamics of Ageing (NDA) Programme, alongside other international evidence, suggests that it is possible to modify the ageing process at earlier stages of the life course so that the outcomes in old age are less restricting both physically and mentally (Walker 2018). As we propose, policy makers could implement social policies in both the short and long terms. In the short term, higher taxes on particular health hazard goods such as tobacco and alcohol, a national program of physical exercise, long-term calorie restriction, and a healthy diet are beneficial choices to prevent most age-associated chronic diseases. In the longer term, it is essential to match the scale of the ageing challenge with an ambitious and comprehensive response. The life course approach is at the core of the active ageing concept but is often overlooked in policy and practice, where old age alone is spotlighted. Active ageing from the perspective of the life course embraces all activities and age groups at all levels, including the individual, organizational, and societal levels in all ways, including upstream as well as downstream ones (Walker 2018).

Fourthly, it is essential to provide adequate income security and treat all people more equally. Before pension provision intergenerational transfers were the dominant income for older people but are still important. China is likely to see further decreases in family provision, financial and social, as a consequence of development. Enhancing the proportion of social welfare expenditure on GDP is on the agenda. It is essential also to discuss and design a scientific regular benefit adjustment method. A key consideration of the adequacy of pensions is their ability to retain their purchasing power and real value. Conventions No. 102 and 128 from the ILO both call for levels of benefits in payment to be reviewed following substantial changes in the level of earnings or of cost of living, while recommendation No. 131 explicitly stipulates that benefit levels should be periodically adjusted to take into account changes in the general level of earnings or cost of living. Looking at indexation methods across countries, there are four primary ones, including price indexation, wage indexation, mixed indexation, and *ad hoc*. Wage indexation was more popular in the past, but nowadays an increasing number of schemes guarantee, at best, only adjustments in line with cost of living increases (International Labour Organization 2017). In consideration of a huge gap in pensions between groups of older people, a combination of regular and *ad hoc* adjustment is an acceptable option. At the first stage, for pensioners such as retired civil servants, price indexation methods are able to guarantee their current living standards; for older people retired from enterprises with moderate pensions, a mixed price and wage indexation method would allow them to keep pace with economic development. For those covered by the ROI, an *ad hoc* method is urgently needed to prevent pension erosion and protect them from poverty, while further narrowing the gap with other more advantaged classes of pensioner, for the sake of equality. Then, when the gaps among subgroups are narrowed to an acceptable level, considering a unified method of indexation for all pensions would be a sound policy option.

Conclusion

This chapter has reviewed one of the biggest social and economic challenges facing China – its rapid population ageing. We described the remarkable ageing trend; outlined the most important challenges to social welfare provision posed by population ageing; summarized the design of the social protection system; contextualized the debate about ageing within the major theories of gerontology; and, finally, advanced some recommendations for policy reform based on the concept of active ageing, which China itself has adopted. The pursuit of this strategy in a comprehensive way would mean that the challenge of population ageing can not only be met but also that greater opportunities can be opened up for millions of Chinese older people to participate widely in society.

References

Bloom, D.E., Canning, D., & Fink, G. (2011) *Implications of Population Aging for Economic Growth.* Working Paper No. 16705.

Bülow, M. & Söderqvist, T. (2014) Successful ageing: A historical overview and critical analysis of a successful concept. *Journal of Aging Studies*, 31: 139–149.

Cai, F. (2012) "Ageing before affluence" and China's sustainable economic growth. *International Economic Review*, 1: 82–95.

Chen, J. (1999) An analysis of living resources of older person reserved by themselves. *Population Journal*, 5: 17–23.

Cole, M.B. & Macdonald, K.C. (2015) *Productive Aging: An Occupational Perspective.* Thorofare, USA: SLACK Incorporated.

Cumming, E. & Henry, W.E. (1961) *Growing Old: The Process of Disengagement.* New York, NY: Basic Books.

Disney, R. (2007) Population ageing and the size of the welfare state: Is there a puzzle to explain? *European Journal of Political Economy*, 23(2): 542–553.

Doyle, Y., McKee, M., Rechel, B., & Grundy, E. (2009) Meeting the challenges of population ageing. *British Medical Journal*, 339: b3926.

Gao, H. & Zhang, A. (2016) Traditional mutual aid form among older people and its values in Chinses folk. *Shandong Social Sciences*, 4: 42–46.

Hu, H., Li, Y., & Zhang, L. (2015) Estimation and prediction of demand for Chinese elderly long-term care service. *Chinese Journal of Population Science*, 3: 79–89.

International Labour Organization (2017) *World Social Protection* Report 2017–19*: Universal Social Protection to Achieve Sustainable Development Goals*, Geneva.

International Social Security Association (2016) *The Government of China Receives International Social Security Award.* World Social Security Forum, Panama.

Li, P. (2016) Analysis of influencing factors of the direct economic cost of child-rearing in a family. *Journal of Fujian Administration Institute*, 5: 103–112.

Lin, B. (2015) An analysis of the status and trend of the elderly population without self-care ability in China. *Population & Economics*, 4: 77–84.
Liu, X. (2012) The situation and path selection of China's social support system for the elderly. *Population Research*, 36(5): 104–112.
Lu, H. & Du, Z. (2000) Prediction about payment balance of basic old-age insurance. *Economic Theory and Business Management*, 2: 56–59.
Luo, M.S. & Chui, E.W.T. (2019) Trends in women's informal eldercare in China 1991–2011: An age-period-cohort analysis. *Ageing & Society*, 39(12): 1–20.
Martins, J.O., Gonand, F., Antolin, P., et al. (2005) *The Impact of Ageing on Demand, Factor Markets, and Growth*. OECD Economics Department Working Paper, No. 420, OECD Publishing, Paris.
Rowe, J. & Kahn, R. (1997) The new gerontology. *Science*, 278(5227): 367.
Strehler, B.L. (1962) *Time, Cells and Aging*. New York, NY: Academic Press.
The New York Times (2019) China is not having enough babies. 26 February 2019.
Tong, Y. (2014) Changes and challenges of labour supply in China in the context of population ageing. *Population Research*, 38(2): 52–60.
Uhlenberg, P. (1992) Population aging and social policy. *Annual Review of Sociology*, 18: 449–474.
United Nations (2019) *World Population Prospects 2019*, online edition, Rev. 1. New York, NY: Department of Economic and Social Affairs.
Victor, C.R. (2005) *The Social Context of Ageing: A Textbook of Gerontology*. Oxon: Routledge.
Walker, A. (2002) A strategy for active ageing. *International Social Security Review*, 55(1): 121–139.
Walker, A. (2009) Commentary: The emergence and application of active ageing in Europe. *Journal of Aging and Social Policy*, 21(1): 75–93.
Walker, A. (2015) *The New Science of Ageing*. Bristol: Policy Press.
Walker, A. (2018) Why the UK needs a social policy on ageing. *Journal of Social Policy*, 47(2): 253–273.
Wang, L. & Ma, W. (2012) Population ageing and actual labour supply changes in China: A new approach of four-dimensional perspective. *Chinese Journal of Population Science*, 6: 23–33.
Wang, Y., Xu, D., Wang, Z., & Zhai, F. (2001) The implicit debt, transition cost, reform forms and the influence of China's pension system. *Economic Research Journal*, 5: 3–12.
World Health Organization (2002) *Active Ageing: A Policy Framework*. Madrid: Spain.
Xu, Q. (2015) Sons or daughters? Who is caring for ageing parents: A comparative gender study of the Chinese family. *Chinese Journal of Sociology*, 35(4): 199–219.
Yang, S. (1992) Factors and strategies for avoiding fetuses. *Population Journal*, 16(1): 57–60.
Zeng, Y. (2001) The main features of population aging and policy consideration in China. *Population & Economics*, 5: 3–9.
Zeng, Y., Chen, H., & Wang, Z. (2012) Analysis on trends of future home-based care needs and costs for the elderly in China. *Economic Research Journal*, 47(10): 134–149.
Zhai, Z., Chen, J., & Li, L. (2016) Ageing in China: General trends, new characteristics and corresponding policies. *Journal of Shandong University (Philosophy and Social Sciences)*, 3: 27–35.
Zhai, Z., Zhang, X., & Jin, Y. (2014) Demographic consequences of an immediate transition to a universal two-child policy. *Population Research*, 38(2): 3–17.
Zhang, W. & Wei, M. (2015) Disability level of the Chinese elderly: Comparison from multiple data sources. *Population Research*, 39(3): 34–47.
Zhang, Y. (2000) A survey on the cost of childcare age from birth to 16 in Zhengzhou. *Marketing Research*, 6: 35–37.
Zheng, B. (2003) Nominal defined contributory: A rational selection of pension system reform in China. *Management World*, 8: 33–45.
Zheng, W., Lin, S., & Chen, K. (2014) Characteristics and trend of population aging in China and its potential impact on economic growth. *The Journal of Quantitative & Technical Economics*, 8: 3–20.

Zhu, H. (2017) *Income Redistribution Effect of Pension*. Peking: Economic Science Press, p. 81.
Zhu, H. & Walker, A.C. (2018a) Pension system reform in China: Who gets what pensions? *Social Policy & Administration*, 52(6): 1410–1424.
Zhu, H. & Walker, A.C. (2018b) The gap in social care provision for older people in China. *Asian Social Work and Policy Review*, 12(1): 17–28.

14

A place-specific approach to environmental governance in China

The Protean Environmental State

Nick Hacking and Andrew Flynn

Introduction

The national government in Beijing has long faced serious difficulties with its national waste management strategy. Rapid urbanization, population growth, and industrialization continue to produce unprecedented increases in waste generation. In 2018, China produced a total of 228.02 million tons of municipal solid waste (MSW) (National Bureau of Statistics of China 2019). This material surrounds two-thirds of nearly 680 cities. Typically, it is transported to the hinterlands of urban areas to be disposed of in landfill sites. It is in this context that many Chinese cities, most particularly Beijing, have long been referred to as being under a 'garbage siege' or 'waste siege' (Li et al. 2011) and the volume of MSW produced annually will increase faster for the foreseeable future. Affordable, effective and truly sustainable waste management is therefore a key point for the development of urban areas in China. Sustainable waste disposal practices can reduce health risk, protect the environment, conserve natural resources, and provide energy recovery. In the face of dwindling options as accessible urban landfill sites filled up (Schonberg 2014), the country committed itself from the 2010s to a large-scale construction programme of energy-from-waste (EfW) plants to incinerate the waste instead. EfW plants are justified by the national government in Beijing as a way of breaking the waste siege and overcoming waste management problems. The national government supports the technological claims made by developers and engineers that newer EfW facilities are more sustainable than the previous generation of incinerators as they can reclaim energy from burning unrecoverable MSW. Delivery of this new waste infrastructure, however, remains well behind schedule in the face of contested claims for sustainability between developers, environmental nongovernmental organizations (NGOs) and dissenting members of affected communities.

The seemingly intractable policy and research challenges facing waste management in China mean that we need to reexamine the evolution of key approaches to environmental governance in the context of the centralized and authoritarian Chinese state's waste policies. We present a novel and dynamic approach to Chinese environmental governance:

DOI: 10.4324/9780429059704-17

the 'Protean Environmental State' (Flynn & Yu 2019). According to Flynn and Yu (2019, 451), this model is based upon a 'reconceptualisation of the local state from being one that is almost wholly development oriented to one that recognises environmental imperatives' based in part on the trials of strength between actors in opposing networks (cf. Latour 1987).

To begin the chapter there is, first, a critique of the neoliberal ecological modernization (EM) approach to environmental governance as it applies to the sustainability of Chinese local economic development (see Mol & Carter 2006; Zhang et al. 2007; Li & Lang 2010; Carter & Mol 2013). Here, EM and its vision of the 'environmental state' are found to be wanting in their analysis of transitional change and the evidence on the ground for a hoped-for environmental state no longer matches the theory: EM is essentially aspatial.

Second, another approach to environmental governance is critiqued: 'Chinese governmentality', or the *ways* in which the centralized Chinese state practices government; in other words, its attempts to maintain control over its territorial space (cf. Foucault 1991; Dean 2010; Sigley 2006; Jeffreys & Sigley 2009, 2014). This Foucauldian approach to governance suggests that, to achieve more sustainable policy ends, top-down compliance is required from a range of peripheral actors, such as planning and environmental enforcement officers, operating in networks at geographical distance from Beijing in a very rigid institutional space. However, while Chinese governmentality does this reasonably well, this approach has relatively poorly developed notions of dissenting actors and networks who operate from the bottom up in a much more flexible and informal institutional space where horizontal, rootlike 'rhizomic' links are made (cf. Murdoch 2006; Deleuze & Guattari 1987). This is witnessed with case study evidence of localized trials of strength, i.e. temporal 'hot spots' where the top-down imposition of waste policies from Beijing reaches its limit (Hacking & Flynn 2018).

Third, we use the theoretical discussion to make the case for a new, place-specific approach to better understand efforts to promote more sustainable waste management in China: the 'Protean Environmental State' (PES). This model is advanced to theorize China, at least in the more developed East and coastal areas of the Country, as shifting from being a development-oriented state toward one that has several faces of governance depending upon localized circumstances, i.e., it is currently simultaneously trying to take account of economic *and* environmental governance via regulatory, recovery, and resource management dimensions. A PES further spatializes asymmetries of power via individuals in local areas (Harvey 1989). The Chinese state is therefore a PES with many faces depending upon local institutional and development circumstances (cf. Flynn & Yu 2019).

These points are highlighted in a case study of Gao'antun on the eastern outskirts of Beijing. Here we examine how the Chinese policy of building EfW plants faces serious difficulties in its implementation. With dwindling options for landfill over recent decades, Beijing committed itself in 2011 (Twelfth Plan) to a major construction programme involving 125 newer, more sustainable EfW plants by 2015. These facilities reclaim energy from the burning of unrecoverable MSW, and they typically do so more efficiently and more cleanly compared to the previous generation of waste incinerators. Delivery of this new waste infrastructure, however, remains well behind schedule (now going into the Thirteenth Plan and beyond). We document efforts to tackle China's urban 'waste siege' in a more sustainable way than simple landfill and/or incineration, while corporate and local state claims for EfW sustainability continue to be heavily contested by dissenting members of affected communities and/or environmental NGOs (Johnson 2013a).

Ultimately, our analysis suggests that the top-down implementation of a national waste policy can be theorized – up to a point – in terms of EM and Chinese governmentality.

However, the limitations of these approaches are shown by their inability to satisfactorily explain spatial relations and overt and/or covert dissent, respectively. Opposition to EfW plants is witnessed in specific places – which have their own histories and development potentials (i.e., place-based characteristics) as trials of strength, with actor networks (such as developers and protestors) drawing on a variety of resources to advance or defend their case. In questioning the national government this suggests bottom-up processes of civic, rootlike 'rhizomic resistance' are also occurring (Hacking & Flynn 2018). This Deleuzoguattarian conception of local, place-specific dissent – which we link to the PES approach – points to the limits of the effectiveness of the way national waste policy is being rolled out. Our focus on waste policy provides new insights into the pragmatic adaptation over time of the Chinese central state's mode of environmental governance from an economic to a partly environmental one.

Ecological modernization (EM)

The EM approach to environmental governance suggests that economic growth and environmental protection can be decoupled by actors in networks, i.e., made more environmentally sustainable (Mol 1995). Mol (1995: 37) explains that EM 'indicates the possibility of overcoming the environmental crisis while making use of the institutions of modernity and without leaving the path of Modernisation'. This occurs, it is suggested, by 're-embedding' ecology into economic modernization through actors 'ecologising the economy' and 'economising the ecology' (cf. Huber 1982, cited in Mol 1995, 30). This redirection and transformation of market capitalism is said to occur 'in such a way that it less and less obstructs, and increasingly contributes to, the preservation of society's sustenance base' (Mol & Janicke 2009: 24).

EM is both a commentary on the way in which states integrate environmental issues into previously narrowly dominated economic arenas and a prescription for further reform, for example, in political institutions and regulatory frameworks. For the proponents of EM, it is at heart an optimistic model of relations between the environment and development (Mol 1995, 2006). Rather than rejecting globalization, the task for EM advocates is attacking 'certain elements or forms of a globalizing world while strengthening others' (Mol 2001: 10). So, while Mol and colleagues reject some neoliberal solutions for networked actors, they do not embrace antiglobalization strategies either. Instead, a state-centred analysis is pursued with EM to help answer current environmental problems and challenges. EM involves networked actors pursuing technological innovation and institutional change, the adoption of market-based and voluntary policy instruments and the promotion of corporate and consumer-responsible self-regulation (Sonnenfeld & Mol 2002). There is the expansion of arenas for public reasoning and consultation of citizens and NGOs as well (Pellizzoni 2011). Called the 'environmental state' (Mol & Buttel 2002; Mol 2007), this approach to environmental governance covers 'that part of the state system involved in and focused on environmental protection' (Mol 2006: 214).

Despite its aspatial approach, one specific context for Mol and colleagues' interest in an environmental state is China (Zhang 2002; Mol 2006; Carter & Mol 2007). This is because of the country's relatively recent shift from a developing to a more advanced economy, especially in the coastal areas and East of the country, with its concomitant commitments to improvements in environmental protection. Moreover, the authoritarian governing context of China rather than the neoliberal economic context of Western case studies provides an alternative setting in which to explore EM (Mol & Carter 2006; Zhang et al. 2007; Carter

& Mol 2013). Perhaps the most notable contributions to current understandings of EM in China come from the report by the influential Chinese Academy of Sciences (CAS) in 2007 (China Centre for Modernisation Research 2007). The CAS report highlights the role of technology in EM thinking, but gives less emphasis to reform of social institutions (e.g. decision-making processes). A less inclusive approach to decision making, along with the country's top-down delivery mechanism, may mean that ecological reforms to protect the environment and stimulate green economic development can be more quickly and widely diffused than in more democratic societies (Zhang et al. 2007; Li & Lang 2010). In China, there is a growing recognition at both national and local levels that EM ideas are informing policy development and practice (e.g. China Centre for Modernisation Research 2007; Zhang et al. 2007; Mol 2006) and need to be considered when analyzing policy (Flynn & Yu 2019).

In summary, EM seeks to recast the traditional zero-sum game between growth against environmental protection as one of win-win. At the local level, though, there are numerous examples of environmental protection continuing to be marginalized. As a result, EM's adequacy for analysis is questioned (Christoff 1996; Foster 2002; York & Rosa 2003; Li et al. 2011). For example, in comments directed toward Western advocates but that are equally relevant to the Chinese case, York and Rosa (2003) point out that EM provides technocratic solutions to environmental problems. Unless strengthened in their reflexivity, state planners will continue to fail to recognize the more deep-rooted conflicts in institutions that help to undermine ecological progress. Subsequently, more attention has been paid to how the state, market, and society interact (Buttel 2000), and to exploring the different ways in which EM may take root in different societies.

In the next section, we analyze another perspective, Chinese governmentality, practitioners of which are interested in how state and markets interact and so examining what it means for the greening of environmental governance.

Chinese governmentality

Foucault's concept of governmentality involves the top-down, noncoercive techniques of government of a centralized Western state (Dean 2010: 17). However, it has been transposed to a non-Western, illiberal context with literature on 'Chinese governmentality' (see, for example, Sigley 2006; Jeffreys & Sigley 2009, 2014). This approach to governance 'at a distance' suggests that, to achieve more sustainable policy ends, a relatively more coercive top-down approach to compliance must be exercised with a range of actors operating in networks. These networks are at a physical distance from Beijing and include state actors, e.g., the Communist Party; nonstate actors, e.g., environmental NGOs; and a range of 'technologies' of measurement at work over a number of administrative levels (Hacking & Flynn 2018). These technologies include accounts, policies, audits, and targets, and can be fruitful for gauging the strength of the national government's centralized networks of power used to impose rules, regulations, and plans upon geographically distant actors in waste management networks.

China has liberalized its economy to some degree since the 1980s. The country's political transition from socialist plan to market socialism has involved reconfiguring state governance from Beijing along the lines of 'scientific social engineering and socialist planning combined with neo-liberal strategies of governing from a distance' (Jeffreys and Sigley 2009: 1). Foucault (1991) argues that the increasing institutionalization of professional expertise is a key part of the process of governing modern central states. In China's case,

Beijing's plans have involved economic rationalization and marketization programs in employment, education, sustainability, and health, amongst others (Dutton 1992, 2008; Greenhalgh & Winckler 2005). The development of the socialist market economy in the 1990s in China has thus encouraged a new form of authoritarianism for the market, one that has many similarities with the notion of 'good governance' within advanced liberal societies and global institutions. The establishment of a socialist market economy, however, has not signaled a retreat of the state. Rather, a socialist market economy requires a powerful government that continues to intervene but often in different, more subtle ways. From the 1980s, Beijing has further incorporated a range of expertise into its ambitious plans for social engineering.

In China, according to Hindess (1996), there are neither distinctly socialist nor liberal Foucauldian technologies of government. Instead, both political traditions point towards the central state's realization of a community of individuals who can largely regulate their own activities. Nevertheless, the 'prevailing discourse on government in China continues to approach the task of government in a distinctly Chinese ... and ... "socialist" manner' (Sigley 2006: 495). The neoliberal roll back of the central state, for example, is certainly not being pursued in China as it is in the West. Instead, Beijing is intervening in different ways, combining both neoliberal and socialist, facilitative, and authoritarian, strategies (Bray 2006; Jeffreys & Sigley 2009). Crucially, the Communist Party of China remains important and necessary as the ruling party in this one-party state (cf. Dean 2010).

In summary, Chinese governmentality acknowledges that state actors do not govern through Western neoliberal notions of 'freedom' and 'liberty'. Instead, the ways in which Chinese state actors choose to govern – operating as they do at different levels from Beijing down to the communities – is evidenced via distinct economic planning and administrative rationalities. As in the West, Chinese approaches to governance rely on a body of technical expertise whose growth has been sponsored by the state. We argue below, however, that there are limits to the top-down approach of Chinese governmentality. In the case of waste governance, Chinese citizens who mistrust the government and government-appointed experts have developed their own health risk expertise particularly in terms of environmental toxicology. Since the 2000s, Chinese citizens have demanded to be more involved in decision making via the national planning system. This development of an incipient civil society is directly linked to the emergence of some 'open government' initiatives including attempts at public participation in policymaking (People's Republic of China 2019). The governmentality approach suggests such evidence from the Chinese national planning system permits new insights into the nature of Chinese governmentality in terms of relational 'topologies of power', i.e., how, when, where and why technologies of measurement and control are deployed (cf. Allen 2016; Collier 2009).

To summarize the situation so far: EM is helpful in pointing to the growing importance of environmental imperatives in state activities but is weak in understanding how these relations may unfold in particular places; meanwhile, a governmentality perspective seeks to explain how governing of different places will take place but has shown only limited interest in environmental issues. As a result, governmentality underplays the dissent that can arise from the grassroots as people's awareness of their individual and collective environmental interests clashes with state policies. In other words, both EM and governmentality are typically concerned with nation-state activities, but we believe that the discretion within the Chinese system of governance means that we should pay more detailed attention to the local environmental state. In the next section, we outline a new way of looking at evolving environmental governance: the PES.

The Protean Environmental State (PES)

The developing Chinese state has pragmatically adapted and evolved its mode of environmental governance over time and we recognize this shift as being at the heart of another new approach called the Protean Environmental State (PES) (Flynn & Yu 2019). A PES perspective draws on Harvey's (1989) focus on place, power, and individuals. Municipal governments now have some capacity to act to improve local environmental conditions. Moreover, municipal governments are being assisted to some extent in their rethinking of environment–economy relations by a central government policy agenda that is moving from an overwhelming preoccupation with development to taking on board welfare and environmental concerns. This situation demands a reconceptualization of the local state from being one that is almost wholly development-oriented to one that recognizes environmental imperatives. The PES is therefore a 'more nuanced analysis of the multifaceted nature of environmental governance' than that provided by advocates of ecological modernization or Chinese governmentality (Flynn & Yu 2019: 443). In a local context with waste and resources, analysis is made of how industrializing cities in China are facing up to the waste produced by the polluted Chinese environment and how they are seeking to steer activity toward a new, more ecologically friendly development pathway.

At the level of localized development initiatives, the concern for place reveals the nature and impacts that growth has. This includes an appreciation of the enablers of, and constraints to, economic and environmental possibilities. Individuals, meanwhile, may have the power to readily shape the nature of development (Harvey 1989). In the Chinese context, Flynn and Yu (2019) point to city and/or provincial leaders who can knit together a wide-ranging state apparatus to direct and deliver change. In addition, the links between state and market actors are much closer in China than those of liberal market economies providing a further mechanism to steer change.

The complex nature of environmental problems allied to the breadth of state interventions in China enables the emergence of a multifaceted local environmental state. One long-standing state activity is the regulation of pollution by companies. There are, though, a set of other local state activities that are part of environmental governance. These include state-led initiatives to recover the environment by improving degraded spaces. This might be cleaning up waterways or tackling spoiled landscapes. In addition, the state can act to enhance the environment by seeking to replace 'dirty' industries with cleaner ones. Another area of local state environmental activity is in relation to resource management (such as forests). Importantly, the nature of the environmental state is connected to development opportunities and environmental challenges. We have termed the different facets of the PES, regulatory, recovery, resource, and enhancement. These terms reflect the multifaceted, multidimensional nature of state environmental activity and how it is in a constant state of flux. At any point in time, the PES can present one or more feature to different audiences. Moreover, these are not hard-edged features but blur into one another.

By conceptualizing the state in this more flexible way, we can begin to better understand how particular spaces are governed (e.g., in a regulatory or a recovery manner or a mix of both). It also helps to appreciate which of the different facets of the environmental state might be to the fore (or marginalized) and why. We can also examine how different facets of the PES complement or are in tension with one another (for example, efforts to recover polluted waterways might be undermined if the regulation of waterside firms is lax; see also Walker 1989: 32).

Ultimately, Flynn and Yu (2019) found that a more nuanced approach is necessary with analyses of the local environmental state. In reconceptualizing the local state, it is argued that attention needs to be given to local development histories, the interplay between national and local policy agendas, and crucially the more flexible and multifaceted ways that environmental governance occurs. Regulatory activities provide high profile and visible evidence of efforts to curb the activities of polluting firms. Commitments to a cleaner environment, enable investment in environmental enhancements and increase the potential to attract low carbon and high-tech firms. This can further accelerate the transformation of the local economy. The development of the PES marks a significant advance on existing approaches to the local state, at least as they apply to the more economically developed areas of China.

The way in which the PES engages with the national government suggests likely tensions in the latter's drive to improve the environment (Flynn & Yu 2019). For example, national governments want pollution regulation at the local level to be strictly enforced. Central government's interest in regulation for environmental quality – where data is relatively easy to measure, monitor (and manipulate) – results in much greater accountability for both local political leaders and officials. There is, though, a contradiction at play here: central government interventions and oversight of local government may provide reassurance to citizens that government is taking pollution seriously, but such actions also undermine the credibility of local regulatory activities. Flynn and Yu (2019: 460) suggest that:

> The Protean Environmental State will need to continually reinvent itself to demonstrate its worth. In doing so, its flexibility is helpful: regulation can be tightened or relaxed, or alternative emphases can be presented to the same or different audiences, or the focus of investments can switch between air, water or waste.

Or, we might add in the case of waste, resource management.

The lack of public participation in the Chinese planning system can be linked to overt and/or covert dissent in the past in specific places. However, currently no overt dissent is permitted by Beijing. We theorize earlier dissenting activity as 'rhizomic resistance': Localized, dissenting bottom up, and civic (cf. Deleuze & Guattari 1987). The terms rhizome and rhizomic are part of a powerful notion borrowed from biology. It is a metaphor for the unlimited horizontal growth of root systems. When applied to analysis of past events, the rhizomic approach is characterized by 'ceaselessly established connections between semiotic chains, organizations of power, and circumstances relative to the arts, sciences, and social struggles' (Deleuze & Guattari 1987: 7). As Semetsky (2003: 18) indicates, a rhizome, or network of dissenting actors '[multiplies] its own lines and establishing the plurality of unpredictable connections in the open-ended … smooth, space of its growth'. Smooth or 'fluid space' is irregular, open, and heterogeneous. This is contrasted with the striated space of state power which has rigid schemata and fixed points ordered by hierarchical power (Allen 2016; Deleuze & Guattari 1987; Murdoch 2006; Semetsky 2003). Rhizomic resistance supports the focus we adopt on better understanding the local environmental state and enables us to advance the PES by exploring whether, from the perspective of Beijing and Chinese civil society more widely, it can successfully advance different 'faces' to quell local dissent or, if it increasingly adopts commitments to environmental protection, including those voiced by residents, that enable it to operate to at least some extent as an autonomous environmental state.

In the next section, an EfW case study is outlined illustrating how events switch from a local state developmental approach to an environmental approach. However, moves toward improved sustainability are undermined by a lack of transparency and poor public participation via the planning system.

Case Study: EfW in Gao'antun, Beijing

In this section, we critically evaluate the Chinese policy of building a significant number of new EfW plants. Beijing's hope is that this policy will deal with the country's long-standing waste disposal crisis – the so-called 'garbage siege' in which cities in the 2000s and 2010s have been running out of landfill space – with a greener, more sustainable set of technologies that can encourage recycling and reuse of certain materials and recover renewable energy from the incineration of unrecoverable waste material. For this case study, methods were pursued in line with data collection for Hacking and Flynn (2018).

Two EfW facilities are currently located side-by-side at Gao'antun, a site 20 km to the northeast of Beijing on the East Fifth Ring Road beside a landfill site. In terms of conceptualizing what has gone on at this site, the shortcomings of the EM and Chinese governmentality approaches, described above, are revealed. Similarly, how the three dimensions linked to the PES approach – regulatory, recovery, and resource management – are illustrated as offering a more nuanced view of events.

The material on the Gao'antun EfW plant also shows that there were distinct preexisting and localized sensitivities to an environmental hazard in the area. These sensitivities included the presence of the major landfill site. The numbers of local residents grew rapidly from 2004 and they began complaining ever increasingly to local government bodies about smells. When nothing changed, trust in the local authorities was lost.

In terms of localized rhizomic resistance to Beijing's top-down imposition of its EfW waste policy, the incoming residents in Gao'antun were mainly middle class and young. They were encouraged to locate there thanks to upmarket apartment developments. These individuals were not particularly united given their status as a new community, nor were they very persistent with their complaints to the authorities. Also, these community dissenters were relatively less well connected – to more experienced activists in the one Chinese city with more distinct freedoms, i.e., Hong Kong, which is 2,000 km to the south (Johnson 2013b). The Beijing community dissenters were, however, reasonably well connected with certain local members of the media and the legal professions.

Regulatory dimension

EfW via incineration was being advocated by the central state in Beijing from the mid-1990s because of the rapidly growing waste problems, specifically lack of landfill capacity. Top-down governance on this issue began with the Law on Prevention and Control of Environmental Pollution Caused by Solid Waste. This law also established a monitoring, inspection, and enforcement regime for solid waste disposal. Fines of up to 500,000 yuan (£58K in 1996 prices) could be imposed for illegal breaches.

It was in 1999 that the Chinese Environmental Protection Agency (SEPA) first approved an Environmental Impact Assessment (EIA) for an incinerator to be built by the Environmental Engineering Group next to the Gao'antun landfill site near Beijing. Construction was then delayed for several years before this facility received another approval from SEPA in 2004 (Johnson 2013a). This occurred after the publication of the Chinese central state's 2003

White Book on waste disposal that encouraged the technological selection of a newer generation of incinerators that Western multinational engineering firms had also been marketing in Europe, North America, and Australasia.

In November 2005, the first EfW plant began construction based on German technology. The site was within 2 km of some commercial premises. Local residents were not made aware of the plans for an EfW plant. Residents only first mobilized in a bottom-up sense as construction neared completion in 2007. Residents from the Home Defence Action Group (HDAG) framed their opposition in legal terms and undertook some public protests. At the time, plainclothes police warned HDAG members against protesting. In mid-2007, HDAG twice faxed SEPA asking to see the incinerator's 2004 EIA report. Residents eventually saw an abridged version in October but could not photocopy it.

That same month, HDAG filed an administrative review application with SEPA claiming the Administrative Review Law was broken as SEPA lacked evidence to support its decision. HDAG also claimed public participation was absent and residents' rights were ignored. SEPA released its administrative review decision and upheld the legality of the 2004 EIA decision. A local council appeal was also rejected on the grounds that the full report contained 'company secrets' and could not be disclosed.

By early 2008, many residents became resigned to the incinerator's existence and started to give up their campaign. After the Beijing Olympics, HDAG organized protest 'strolls' including blocking a waste vehicle's route. This action highlighted opposition to the incinerator and the landfill smell and helped win concessions from Chaoyang District Government (CDG). A month later, CDG formally apologized to residents promising to resolve the smell within 20 days. Officials met residents to discuss the incinerator but officials claimed not to have heard of 'dioxins' and lost credibility in the eyes of community dissenters. In 2008, Gao'antun resident Zhao Lei filed a lawsuit against the waste operators after suffering from respiratory problems allegedly linked to the waste site. Zhao later lost the case and subsequently sold her property and moved away.

From 2009, the first incinerator began burning waste mostly from the Chaoyang district, having moved from the construction to the operational phase. Gao'antun EfW officials confirmed that the plant continues to operate at a reduced level (i.e., below 1,600 tonnes of waste per day). Wang Weiping, the municipal government's chief incineration engineer, nevertheless said more dioxin was produced from 'grilling a single lamb kebab' (Johnson 2013a). In September 2009, Beijing Municipal Commission of City Administration and Environment announced plans to expand the city's daily waste treatment capacity to 17,000 and 30,000 tonnes by 2012 and 2030, respectively. In March 2010, a giant display screen was erected at Gao'antun for real-time data of emissions of sulfur dioxide and nitrogen oxide, but no figures were given for dioxins. Issues of trust and odor remain problematic for residents. Beijing's vice mayor, Ji Lin, confirmed on March 18, 2010, plans to build an industrial waste treatment plant later in 2010 that will focus more on recycling waste and less on burning it. In 2011, approval was granted for the second Gao'antun incinerator plant to be built, this time with a capacity of 1,800 tons/day (Johnson 2013a, 2014).

Recovery dimension

As stated, the significant shift of the Chinese state toward EfW as a waste siege solution represents a generally more sustainable approach to waste management at least when and where the technology in the plants is closely monitored and effectively regulated. More specifically, there is a recovery dimension to the work in which existing landfills close, are slowly drained of methane and their boundaries are kept resilient. The land ultimately can later be returned to more productive use. Similarly, beyond their energy production, EfW plants give the option of separating and sorting recoverable materials which, typically with further treatment, can and need to become resources for other production processes in a sustainable industrial ecology or 'circular economy' (Feng & Yan 2007; McDowall et al. 2017). There is a potential policy conflict here because EfW plants need to burn a minimum amount of waste material in order to run efficiently. This means a long-term commitment to EfW – currently around 20 years – runs counter to a progressive commitment to the recovery of more and more resources through reuse and recycling (as part of a stated commitment to developing a more circular economy at a range of scales). Thus, EfW, as a quick technical fix for the problem of the garbage siege, has since been questioned in some quarters – usually environmental NGOs – for its long-term appropriateness and not just in China but around the world.

Resource management dimension

With the Gao'antun EfW plant's announcement in 2004, the health risk perceptions of the by-now-mistrustful local residents shifted to focus on the imposition of the risks of incineration on their local area. This included concerns about the potential toxic impacts of dioxins, furans, and heavy metals, amongst other potential air pollutants (Johnson 2013a, 2013b).

In terms of more sustainable resource management, public participation in the decision making on incineration technology and the siting of the Gao'antun EfW plant was extremely limited. The national Chinese planning and environmental regulatory systems did not entertain meaningful opportunities for engagement. Trust in the national agency, SEPA, was lost in 2007 when campaigners learned that they had not been consulted in 2004 for the plant's EIA (which was undertaken in secret). Instead, with their lower incomes, less networked power and no access to local media or legal advice, the views of 50 nearby rural residents were considered more malleable by the authorities for the EIA. This institutional context, and the central Chinese state's top-down approach to incineration policy, did provoke rhizomic resistance amongst the local community in the Gao'antun community, however. These dissenters were most concerned about the objectivity of the scientific approach in EPA's EIA undertaken in 2004 (and that was not released). These dissenters opted to challenge the city authorities via persistent persuasion and citizen science. They deployed their own counterexpertise regarding perceived environmental health risks:

> [They] demonstrated a good understanding of technical and legal issues related to waste incineration … [and] claimed that public participation was lacking and that SEPA [now MEP] had 'not only harmed our environmental rights and interests, but had also violated national laws'.
>
> *(Zhou et al. 2007, cited in Johnson 2013b: 115)*

Gao'antun residents failed to prevent the incinerator from operating. In the end, they were unable to obtain sufficient network support. Opportunities for public participation after the licensing decision remained poor. The community dissenters inevitably found they were much less able to fight the project once it had been constructed.

Overall, the trial of strength in Gao'antun involved residents who are middle class, not predominantly working class. They were poorly connected and politically disunited but had some media contact (Johnson 2013b). Gao'antun residents demonstrated a good understanding of technical and legal issues related to waste incineration. They claimed that public participation was lacking and that this was the responsibility of the environmental regulator, SEPA (later MEP, now MEE – Ministry of Environment and Ecology). Community dissenters in Gao'antun failed to prevent the EfW plant from operating because their network was weaker than the state's network. Opportunities for public participation after the licensing decision remained poor. This all suggests a significant disconnect between national environmental policies about participation, transparency, EIA, and so on, and the activities of local and regional state bodies who actually have to weigh up conflicting laws, priorities, and resources and act on the ground. The open manifestations of dissent over EfW seen at Panyu in Guangzhou Province (Hacking & Flynn 2018) and Panguanying, Hebei Province (Johnson et al. 2018), for example, depend in large part, on the ways those decisions are taken by the local state, i.e., relatively less consensually, and the strength, and coherence of the countervailing political momentum of the local population. Where flare ups of resistance to EfW policy have occurred, Beijing's (and hence the local state's) tokenistic approach to public participation in planning, whether pre- or post- a plant's licensing decision, was central to the rejection of the state's expertise by community members, chiefly in its framing of health risk (cf. Hacking & Flynn 2017). This rejection of expertise underpins the dissenters' trials of strength or rhizomic resistance. Their collective agency in a more 'fluid space' than that in which state institutions operate in supports campaigns of persistent persuasion, media attention, citizen science, and/or direct action. Such events then trigger further attempts by an embarrassed local state (relative to the Party in Beijing) to crack down harder and/or concede ground while further justifying the top-down approach to waste policy delivery (Hacking & Flynn 2018).

In terms of the shift toward more sustainable waste policy and practice that China's central state is trying to achieve in a relatively short period of time, this case study evidence suggests that a PES approach to governance – one which better recognizes the unique locational and historical circumstances of individual communities and modifies national policies accordingly – is much needed. The multiple and overlapping PES dimensions – with their associated regulatory, recovery, and resource management activities – were all witnessed at Gao'antun but shifts between them were not coordinated in a more unified and context-specific way by the authorities.

Conclusions

This chapter has examined the evolution of several approaches to environmental governance in the context of the Chinese state's waste policies. Initially, there was a critique of the neoliberal EM approach as it applies to the sustainability of Chinese local economic development (Mol & Carter 2006; Zhang et al. 2007; Li & Lang 2010; Carter & Mol 2013). EM and its vision of the 'environmental state' were found to be wanting in their analysis of geographical space in transitional change. Another approach, 'Chinese governmentality' (Sigley 2006; Jeffreys & Sigley 2009, 2014), was similarly critiqued for its relatively basic development of relational space most evident with case study evidence of localized trials of strength where the top-down imposition of waste policies from Beijing reached the limit of their effectiveness (Hacking & Flynn 2018). Instead, we have made the case for a new, place-specific approach toward more sustainable waste management in China: the PES. This model is advanced to theorize China as shifting from being a development-oriented state toward one that has several 'faces' depending upon localized circumstances, i.e., it is currently simultaneously trying to take account of economic *and* environmental governance. A PES further spatializes asymmetries of power in local areas both geographically and relationally as per Harvey (1989) (cf. Flynn & Yu 2019).

These points were highlighted in a case study of the Chinese policy of building EfW plants. Efforts to tackle Beijing's 'waste siege' in a more sustainable way than simple landfill and/or incineration were outlined but corporate and local state claims for EfW sustainability continued to be heavily contested by dissenting members of affected communities and/or environmental NGOs (Johnson 2013b). The use of a Deleuzoguattarian conception of local, place-specific dissent – which we link to the PES approach – points to both limits the effectiveness of the way this particular national waste policy is being rolled out in particular places (but also the storing up of localized grievances and a sense of political illegitimacy for the specific piece of infrastructure in question).

In the case of moves toward more sustainable waste management in China, our case study suggests that there is much to be gained from thinking of the local state's environmental activities as 'Protean' or changing over time from the inflexible and very authoritarian government of the Maoist period to the more liberalized era from Deng Xiaoping (premier 1978–1992) to the present. In that time frame, waste management efforts – directed by Beijing but played out at the local state level – have attempted to be more sustainable in parallel with, but not as fully free-market as, the neoliberal environmental management efforts arising in more developed countries (cf. Birch 2017; Biebricher 2018). In this context, we see much stronger than expected parallels between localized dissent in relation to waste infrastructure planning in China and in Western nations. The PES model, we feel, is able to show how deep asymmetries of power between opposing actors underpin trials of strength in the context of the social relations based on environmental governance. In this way, the PES offers a useful way of analyzing the behavior of civic actors involved in the local environmental state particular when adding the notion of rhizomic resistance to characterize trials of strength with dissenting actors. Ultimately, these heuristics in combination provide a new, more flexible way of seeing sustainable change taking place from competing perspectives over time.

Acknowledgements

Interviews in China were conducted by Dr. Linjun Xie of Nottingham University Ningbo.

References

Allen, J. 2016. *Topologies of Power: Beyond Territory and Networks*. Oxford: Routledge.

Biebricher, T. 2018. *The Political Theory of Neoliberalism*. Stanford, CA: Stanford University Press.

Birch, K. 2017. *A Research Agenda for Neoliberalism*. Cheltenham, UK: Edward Elgar Publishing.

Bray, D. 2006. Building 'community': New strategies of governance in urban China. *Economy and Society*, 35, 530–549.

Buttel, F.H. 2000. World society, the nation-state, and environmental protection: Comment on Frank, Hironaka, and Schofer. *American Sociological Review*, 65, 117–121.

Carter, N. and Mol, A.P. 2013. *Environmental Governance in China*. Abingdon, UK: Routledge.

China Centre for Modernisation Research 2007. *China Modernisation Report 2007: Study of Ecological Modernisation*. Beijing: Beijing University Press.

Christoff, P. 1996. Ecological modernisation, ecological modernities. *Environmental Politics*, 5(3), 476–500.

Collier, S.J. 2009. Topologies of power: Foucault's analysis of political government beyond 'governmentality'. *Theory, Culture & Society*, 26, 78–108.

Dean, M. 2010. *Governmentality: Power and Rule in Modern Society*, 2nd Edition. London, Thousand Oaks, CA, and New Delhi: SAGE.

Deleuze, G. and Guattari, P.F. 1987. *Thousand Plateaus: Capitalism and Schizophrenia*. Minneapolis, MN: University of Minnesota Press.

Dutton, M.R. 1992. *Policing and Punishment in China: From Patriarchy to "The People"*. Cambridge: Cambridge University Press.

Dutton, M.R. 2008. Passionately governmental: Maoism and the structured intensities of revolutionary governmentality. *Postcolonial Studies*, 11, 99–112.

Feng, Z.J. and Yan, N.L. 2007. Putting a circular economy into practice in China. *Sustainability Science*, 2, 95–101.

Flynn, A. and Yu, L. 2019. The Protean Environmental State in Dongguan: Reconceptualising the local state and ecological development in China. *Environment and Planning C: Politics and Space*, 38, 443–463.

Foster, J.B. 2002. *Ecology Against Capitalism*. New York, NY: NYU Press.

Foucault, M. 1991. Governmentality. In: Foucault, M., Burchell, G., and Gordon, C. (Eds.), *The Foucault Effect: Studies in Governmentality*. Chicago, IL: University of Chicago Press.

Greenhalgh, S. and Winckler, E.A. 2005. *Governing China's Population: From Leninist to Neoliberal Biopolitics*. Stanford, CA: Stanford University Press.

Hacking, N. and Flynn, A. 2017. Networks, power and knowledge in the planning system: A case study of energy from waste. *Progress in Planning*, 113, 1–37.

Hacking, N. and Flynn, A. 2018. Protesting against neoliberal and illiberal governmentalities: A comparative analysis of waste governance in the UK and China. *Political Geography*, 63, 31–42.

Harvey, D. 1989. *The Urban Experience*. Baltimore, MD: Johns Hopkins University Press.

Hindess, B. 1996. *Discourses of Power from Hobbes to Foucault*. Oxford: Blackwell.

Huber, J. 1982. *The Lost Innocence of Ecology: New Technologies and Superindustrial Development*. Frankfurt am Main: Fisher.

Jeffreys, E. and Sigley, G. 2009. Governmentality, governance, and China. In: Jeffreys, E. (Ed.), *China's Governmentalities: Governing Change, Changing Government*. Abingdon, UK: Routledge.

Jeffreys, E. and Sigley, G. 2014. Government, governance, governmentality and China: New approaches to the study of state, society and self. *Journal of Chinese Studies*, 18, 129–146.

Johnson, T. 2013a. The health factor in anti-waste incinerator campaigns in Beijing and Guangzhou. *China Quarterly*, 214, 356–375.

Johnson, T. 2013b. The politics of waste incineration in Beijing: The limits of a top-down approach? *Journal of Environmental Policy & Planning*, 15, 109–128.

Johnson, T. 2014. Good governance for environmental protection in China: Instrumentation, strategic interactions and unintended consequences. *Journal of Contemporary Asia*, 44, 241–258.

Johnson, T., Lora-Wainwright, A., and Lu, J. 2018. The quest for environmental justice in China: Citizen participation and the rural–urban network against Panguanying's waste incinerator. *Sustainability Science*, 13, 733–746.

Latour, B. 1987. *Science in Action: How to Follow Scientists and Engineers Through Society*. Cambridge, MA: Harvard University Press.

Li, V. and Lang, G. 2010. China's "Green GDP" experiment and the struggle for ecological modernisation. *Journal of Contemporary Asia*, 40(1), 44–62.

Li, Y.W., Miao, B., and Lang, G. 2011. The local environmental state in China: A study of county-level cities in Suzhou. *The China Quarterly*, 205, 115–132

McDowall, W., Geng, Y., Huang, B., Bartekova, E., Bleischwitz, R., Turkeli, S., Kemp, R., and Domenech, T. 2017. Circular economy policies in China and Europe. *Journal of Industrial Ecology*, 21, 651–661.

Mol, A.P. 1995. *The Refinement of Production: Ecological Modernisation Theory and the Chemical Industry*. Utrecht: International Books.

Mol, A.P. 2001. *Globalization and Environmental Reform: The Ecological Modernisation of the Global Economy*. Cambridge, MA: MIT Press.

Mol, A.P. 2006. Environment and modernity in transitional China: Frontiers of ecological Modernisation. *Development and Change*, 37, 29–56.

Mol, A.P. 2007. 10. Bringing the environmental state back in: Partnerships in perspective. In: Glasbergen, P., Biermann, F., and Mol, A.P. (Eds.), *Partnerships, Governance and Sustainable Development: Reflections on Theory and Practice*. Cheltenham, UK: Edward Elgar Publishing.

Mol, A.P. and Buttel, F.H. 2002. The environmental state under pressure: An introduction. In: Mol, A.P. and Buttel, F.H. (Eds.), *The Environmental State Under Pressure*. Bingley, UK: Emerald Insight.

Mol, A.P. and Carter, N.T. 2006. China's environmental governance in transition. *Environmental Politics*, 15(02), 149–170.

Mol, A.P. and Janicke, M. 2009. *The Origins and Theoretical Foundations of Ecological Modernisation Theory*. Abingdon: Routledge.

Murdoch, J. 2006. *Post-structuralist Geography: A Guide to Relational Space*. London, Thousand Oaks, CA, and New Delhi: SAGE Publications Limited.

National Bureau of Statistics of China 2019. 8–18 Collection, transport and disposal of consumption wastes in cities by region (2018). In: NBSC (Ed.), *China Statistical Yearbook 2019*. Beijing: Author.

Pellizzoni, L. 2011. Governing through disorder: Neoliberal environmental governance and social theory. *Global Environmental Change*, 21, 795–803.

People's Republic of China 2019. *The Civil Code of the People's Republic of China* (full text of the official version) (effective from 1 January 2021). http://www.elawcn.com/rule/2019/1217/524.html?utm_source=chinadialogue+newsletter+%E2%80%93+bilingual&utm_campaign=9bc6ef8e26-EMAIL_CAMPAIGN_2019_05_23_03_03_COPY_01&utm_medium=email&utm_term=0_5db8c84b96-9bc6ef8e26-46411770&mc_cid=9bc6ef8e26&mc_eid=5e45f28620 (accessed July 29, 2020).

Schonberg, A. 2014. China's landfills are closing: Where will the waste go? *Collective Responsibility* [Online Think Tank], https://www.coresponsibility.com/shanghai-landfills-closures/ (accessed May 19, 2020).

Semetsky, I. 2003. Deleuze's new image of thought, or Dewey revisited. *Educational Philosophy and Theory*, 35, 17–29.

Sigley, G. 2006. Chinese governmentalities: Government, governance and the socialist market economy. *Economy and Society*, 35, 487–508.

Sonnenfeld, D.A. and Mol, A.P. 2002. Ecological modernisation, governance, and globalization: Epilogue. *American Behavioral Scientist*, 45, 1456–1461.

Walker, K.J. 1989. The state in environmental management: The ecological dimension. *Political Studies*, 37, 25–38.

York, R. and Rosa, E.A. 2003. Key challenges to ecological modernisation theory: Institutional efficacy, case study evidence, units of analysis, and the pace of eco-efficiency. *Organization & Environment*, 16, 273–288.

Zhang, L. 2002. *Ecologizing Industrialization in Chinese Small Towns*. PhD Thesis, Wageningen University.

Zhang, L., Mol, A.P., and Sonnenfeld, D.A. 2007. The interpretation of ecological modernisation in China. *Environmental Politics*, 16(4), 659–668.

Part III

Chinese culture and history

15

Martial legacies

Strategic culture, ethnic conflict, and the military in modern Chinese history

Eric Setzekorn

Throughout China's past, warfare and military campaigns have been critically important to political development, social change, and cultural life. Beginning with the massive conflicts during the Warring States period over 2,000 years ago, through the fall of the Qing dynasty in the early 20th century and continuing after the establishment of the communist People's Republic of China (PRC), military conflict has been deeply embedded in the Chinese historical experience. In the 20th century alone, millions of Chinese were killed in internal conflict and wars with neighboring countries, and the legacies of war continue to impact the foreign relations and ethnic divides in the PRC. This chapter cannot cover the entirety of such a vast and important topic and will instead focus on aspects of Chinese military history that have continuing relevance throughout the modern era (1800–present). In addition, this section will highlight how new scholarship is increasingly making military history and conflict a central element of the Chinese historical tradition.

More specifically, this chapter will examine areas of military history that are being hotly debated and reassessed because of new perspectives and issues of contemporary relevance. In the early 20th century, three critical areas of Chinese military history have been central to public debate, as well as Chinese foreign and domestic policy. First, the role of military power in China's strategic culture has profoundly shaped how China's role in an increasingly globalized world is viewed, either as a benign neighbor, or an aggressive conqueror. Second, historical legacies of Chinese imperialism have important implications for both territorial disputes in East Asia, as well as the PRC's turbulent ethnic relations. Lastly, recent debates have examined patterns of political control of military forces, with the PRC remaining a global outlier by relying on a military force loyal not to a nation, but to a political party, the Chinese Communist Party (CCP).

Military power and Chinese strategic culture

In the past 30 years, academic perspectives that emphasized the role of nonmilitary civilian elites in East Asian civilization, particularly China, has been displaced by a more nuanced assessment that highlights a central role for force and armed conflict. For military historians, this intellectual shift has had several major effects. First, it has dramatically increased the

DOI: 10.4324/9780429059704-19

importance of military affairs for Asian history. Chinese military power and civil-military relations are now seen as core elements of the historical narrative. This shift in how Chinese 'strategic culture' is viewed has made military affairs an active driver of larger historical trends, rather than a lagging indicator of social or economic developments. Second, recent works have destabilized the narrative of peaceful Chinese territorial expansion, based on cultural achievements and a spread of a Han or Confucian 'civilization', instead suggesting an aggressive and expansionary state that successfully used military conquest to expand its territory. In particular, younger historians have shifted the focus of academic discussion away from concepts of a 'unique' Chinese civilization and are increasingly demonstrating, through innovative and provocative historical research, the similarity of Chinese military and government policy with that of other colonial and imperial systems (Perdue 2009; Hostetler 2001; Hevia 1993; Larsen 2008). Lastly, this chapter will highlight how the military as an organization has been developed and controlled by political power.

Military power and the decision to use military force to defeat or coerce an opponent, are profoundly shaped by the cultural environment of the conflict initiator. Over time, civilizations and nations develop traditions and patterns about what constitutes proper military behavior, what is a just war, and how conflicts should be ended. In the past 20 years, historical research has reevaluated Chinese historical patterns of military power and political control. New scholarship has highlighted the 'imperial' nature of the Chinese military and political traditions, as well as conflicted territorial and ethnic legacies. These recent changes to the historical narrative of the Qing empire and its use of military power have also promoted a larger debate on the nature of Chinese strategic culture. Strategic culture can be thought of as the enduring conceptions about the utility of war and force in political affairs. In effect, states have a number of critical factors shaping their environment, such as their formative history, philosophy, values, or composition of elite decision makers. The strategic culture of a group, country or state, gives these factors meaning and tends to constrain behavior into a narrower range of outcomes than a purely objective policymaker might choose. Analysis of strategic culture itself is relatively new, growing rapidly in the 1970s and 1980s, as scholars became frustrated by game-theory models of strategic calculations, which lacked the ability to evaluate contextual and qualitative factors shaping decisions. New perspectives have brought into focus ethnic differences between the ethnically Manchu-led Qing dynasty (1644–1912) and earlier Han dominated dynasties, such as the Ming (1368–1644). Regardless of which ethnic or political group was preeminent, Chinese imperial states were rooted in similar concepts of a unipolar world order that was supported by expansive military campaigns to conquer or coerce any rivals.

For much of the 20th century, academic assessments of Chinese strategic culture and the role of conflict in Chinese civilization were shaped by historical sources prepared by Han Chinese civil administrators that emphasized the ideological correctness of imperial rule. This profound source bias played a role in shaping a one-sided conception of Chinese strategic culture as defensive. An indicative example of this paradigm was the eminent historian John King Fairbank's assessment of Chinese expansion, 'It also followed that expansion through wen [culture], the arts of peace and especially the sagehood of the ruler, was natural and proper, whereas expansion by wu [violent conflict], brute force and conquest, was never to be condoned' (Fairbank & Kierman 1974). Understandably, this view of Chinese expansion and conquest as somehow natural and proper was flattering to Chinese, but from the perspective of Koreans, Vietnamese, or other groups that fought and often defeated Chinese aggression, this view is inherently biased and overlooks Chinese aggression.

Contemporary scholars have now largely abandoned, or heavily modified Fairbank's assessment to highlight the presence of two strategic cultures: One a peaceful, idealized, and symbolic Confucian system that exists on paper, and the other a realpolitik operational culture reliant on military power that is evident throughout Chinese history. Alastair Iain Johnston's groundbreaking work *Cultural Realism: Strategic Culture and Grand Strategy in Chinese History* argued that Chinese emperors had a clear conception of themselves as a dominant power with a central place in the world, a rationale that intellectually legitimizes expansion and domination (Johnston 1995). Johnson contends that Chinese dynasties created a highly structured and rigid hierarchy that encompassed some elements of the ritual and 'tribute' diplomacy that John King Fairbank emphasized but was also supported by military might and war. In the past 15 years, Johnson's provocative assessment has provided the basis for scholarly reassessments. Yale University historian Peter Perdue has solidified this assessment, noting strong strategic culture patterns that pushed Chinese to create an ordered environment, motivating Qing Emperors to take extreme measures, such as 'pulling up the roots entirely' by which he meant ethnic cleansing of groups found to be recalcitrant (Perdue 2005). Peter Lorge has similarly identified an impulse to dominate going back through at least the Song period, when leading Chinese political and military leaders sought to 'establish the real or ritual dominance of the Song dynasty over every polity with which it was in contact' (Lorge 2008). A critical element of this reorientation of Chinese strategic culture is because scholars are increasingly reading between the lines of Chinese source material. For example, Yuan-Kang Wang's 2010 work, *Harmony and War: Confucian Culture and Chinese Power Politics*, illustrates the disingenuous language tropes used by Chinese rulers, who insisted they did not invade, but merely 'recovered' territory, even if that territory had never been theirs (Wang 2011). In summary, the understanding of Chinese strategic culture and the willingness to use military power aggressively is now more impartial, with improved research and demonstrable case studies that have replaced generalized cultural stereotypes.

Military conflict and Chinese imperial traditions

The impact of Johnson's provocative and influential argument, as well as subsequent studies, has been to stimulate historical integration of an activist strategic culture into a broader understanding of Chinese colonialism and empires. As a result, historians of China have moved away from Sino-centric explanations of the 'unique' Chinese civilization and stressed the commonality of Chinese practices with other colonial and imperial states (Perdue 2009; Hostetler 2001; Hevia 1993; Larsen 2008). Focusing on the modern era, post-1800, recent works on the Qing empire have highlighted connections between imperial practices and broader currents of 'Chinese' strategic culture. In many ways, the military history of the Qing state corresponds to Chinese imperial practices dating back thousands of years. First, despite the Manchu dominance of court politics, Qing imperial campaigns were financed, supplied, fought, and led by Han Chinese. Second, like other dynasties, the Qing strategically resettled Han farmers on disputed land, supported expensive military outposts to control key border positions, and undertook preemptive military expeditions against potential threats. Lastly, there was no fundamental difference in the strategic objectives, or the willingness to use military power, between the Qing and their predecessors.

Historical research into the complexity of Chinese military affairs and its relationship to larger questions of imperialism corresponds to broader academic scholarship which argues imperialism was not unique to European states. In the words of historian Emma Teng, 'Like

European imperialisms, Qing imperialism was a complex and dynamic convergence of strategic, economic, political, cultural, and ideological interests' (Teng 2004). Like other empires, Chinese military and political leaders were especially sensitive to control of potentially volatile border and frontier areas, and used military forces for territorial control and punitive campaigns. Recent scholarship has emphasized the secret to the Qing empires vast territorial scope of control was a mixture of raw military power, supported by sophisticated logistics operations, decentralized government in sparely populated non-Han regions and a network of cultural ties, especially with Central Eurasian peoples (Crossley et al. 2006). Prior to the 2000s, the dominant paradigm for understanding Chinese territorial expansion was through Han population migration and the slow process of 'sinification'. The military campaigns of the first imperial state, the Qin Dynasty (221–206 BCE), the subsequent Han Dynasty (206 BCE–220 CE), the Tang Dynasty (618–907 CE), all steadily expanded the empire, reaching the borders of modern-day Vietnam and deep into Central Asia. Later dynasties, such as the Song (960–1279 CE), and Ming (1368–1644 CE), faced military competition from the Mongols, who formed the relatively brief Yuan dynasty (1279–1368 CE) and the Qing dynasty (1644–1912 CE), respectively, but even if defeated militarily, the sinification concept suggested an eventual long-term cultural victory for the Han. In this conception, 'barbarians' were transformed by more advanced Han Chinese language, culture and political structures, but Mongol and Manchu 'barbarians' also appear to have adopted Chinese imperial models of state power and territorial conquest. Recent works have emphasized the central role of Qing military power and the pursuit of geostrategic and economic interests as a crucial driver of imperial expansion (Perdue 2005; Teng 2004; Giersch 2006). This new research has not been accepted easily by some scholars, and some have viewed these new academic conclusions as destabilizing and politically motivated. For many traditional scholars, military histories that highlight a more militaristic and aggressive past are politically dangerous. Peter Lorge, a distinguished scholar of Chinese military history has argued persuasively that there is a 'political and cultural agenda behind the de-militarization of imperial China, and the emphasis on violent, predatory foreigners' (Lorge 2005). This is especially important because the presentation of 'China' as a victim of Western and Japanese imperialism has been a core tenet of nationalist groups during the Republican period (1911–1949) and after 1949 under Chinese Communist Party rule (Callahan 2004). Moreover, scholars studying the military conquest of areas of Central Eurasia and Tibet have drawn attention to the short duration, and often tenuous Qing and later Chinese control over these areas, a conclusion that is anathema to current CCP leaders.

After conquering the Ming dynasty and gaining power in 1644, the ethnic Manchu people established the Qing dynasty, which had almost two centuries of consistent battlefield success. The tremendously successful campaigns of Qing forces in Central Asia, South China, and Tibet expanded the territory controlled by a 'Chinese' dynasty to its greatest extent. The Qing military was a hybrid police/military force made up of Han Chinese, Manchu, and Mongol elements. This structure was organizationally complicated but successfully maintained large military forces at relatively low cost throughout the dynasty. The hybrid structure also prevented internal Manchu opposition to the imperial family or large-scale revolts by ethnic Han military commanders. Qing imperial forces fought a series of large-scale campaigns to expand the empire far beyond the Ming borders. They launched campaigns against the 'Jinchuan' people, living in modern Sichuan from 1747 to 1749 and 1771 to 1776, initiated four invasions of what is now Burma in the 1760s and attacked Vietnam in 1788 (Theobald 2013; Dai 2009). The northern and western borders of the Qing empire were areas of special concern because of the possibility of attacks from Central Asia or Mongolia. The Qing empire used a variety of techniques, including supporting local client rulers, appointing military governors, ethnic cleansing, and political integration in an attempt to keep tenuous control over the huge region. Despite the logistical difficulties for military forces operating in arid Central Eurasia, historians are in agreement that of all areas of Qing imperial expansion, this region was the most challenging and fully demonstrates the Qing imperial prowess. Nicola Di Cosmo writes,

> Both the territorial expansion and bureaucratic apparatus of Qing rule in Inner Asia had no precedent in Chinese history: the Qing 'pacification' of independent territories to the north, west, and south of China proper was, in magnitude, one of the largest expansions in seventeenth and eighteenth-century world history.
>
> *(Di Cosmo 1998)*

A prime historical example of the Qing imperial decisiveness and ruthlessness was the campaign begun by the Emperor Qianlong against the ethnically Turkic Zunghar people. Qing diplomacy isolated the Zunghars from potential Mongol, Tibetan, and Russian allies while a formidable logistics apparatus was developed to support military expeditions into the desolate region. Ultimately, a series of scorched earth campaigns eliminated 80% of the Zunghar population and displaced them as an independent political and military power (Perdue 2005). After the initial brutality of the conquest, Qing military domination of the region rested on an often generous and respectful devolvement of authority to local leaders backed by large Qing military garrisons. Qing military and political leaders hoped indirect rule would enable a cost-effective approach to maintaining imperial power and influence without requiring large military garrisons.

After the initial conquests, animosities lingered, and heavy fighting on the borders of the Qing Empire also took place from 1850 to 1877 due to ethnic and territorial conflict. These mid-19th-century military campaigns in Yunnan, Guizhou, Shaanxi, Gansu, and Central Asia resulted in the deaths of millions, but linked these disputed areas more firmly to the Qing state. These historical conflicts form the historical basis for contemporary geographic and ethnic disputes between the PRC and local populations. In each case, the Qing armies were led by Han Chinese Generals and composed of Han Chinese troops (Kessler 1969). The death toll of these campaigns totaled between 12 and 15 million people: 5 million in Yunnan, 1.5 million in Shaanxi, 4.5 million in Guizhou, 3 million in Gansu, and about 100,000 in Central Asia, with the casualties predominantly composed of non-Han ethnic groups (Atwill 2006; Ma 1993; Gillette 2008; Dillon 1999; Chang 1987; Lu 2003; Hou 1997; Jenks 1994).

The Dali Sultanate in Yunnan was the most stable independent government that emerged from the 19th century anti-Qing rebellions. This intellectually vibrant, multiethnic state had broad support from the diverse local population (Atwill, 2006). Yunnan had been loosely controlled by the Qing, but ethnic disputes emerged after 1800 as increasing numbers of Han immigrants moved into Yunnan (Giersch, 2006). The integration of Yunnan into the Qing economy led to tensions between Han immigrants and local Hui people (ethnically Han but religiously Muslim) over land and mining rights, resulting in hundreds of deaths in fighting. During these clashes few Han perpetrators were punished, and officials turned a blind eye to the formation of Han militias, which attacked Hui villages, massacred the inhabitants, and destroyed property. In 1856, believing their actions to be condoned by the Qing administration, Han militias operating openly in the provincial capital of Kunming killed over 8,000 Hui (Atwill, 2003). The non-Han population of Yunnan rallied around

Hui militias for protection, and opposition forces slowly formed a government in the city of Dali, under Hui leader Du Wenxiu. Du Wenxiu's government was multiethnic, with people from non-Hui groups given key positions, but the new 'Pingnan' state had 'an undeniably strong Islamic hue' (Atwill 2006: 146). At its height, the Pingnan government had over 200,000 soldiers, and controlled the majority of Yunnan. Qing forces rallied, bringing in troops from other provinces to fight a war of attrition. Between 1869 and 1874, the Dali Sultanate was slowly crushed as Han Chinese military forces and Qing bribes gradually reduced the Pingan territory and ground down its military. Eventually, Qing armies reached Dali and despite the surrender of Du Wenxiu, they massacred the entire Hui population, ending the rebellion through a scorched earth policy.

Mid-19th-century ethnic tensions also flared in the neighboring province of Guizhou, as fighting between the local Miao population and Han erupted (Herman 2007; Weinstein 2014, Sutton 2003). Like in Yunnan, a wave of Han immigration between 1750 and 1850 saw almost 4 million immigrants enter Guizhou, displacing the native Miao population from their ancestral lands. In 1854, a poor harvest, long-standing grievances between the Han and Miao communities, and the charismatic leadership of Buddhist monk Yang Yuanbao combined to produce a minor rebellion of roughly 2,000 men. Although this band was quickly defeated by Qing forces, the survivors splintered and fled throughout the province to encourage further revolts. By late 1855 much of the province had driven off Qing military forces, and was governing itself in small collectives, headed by ethnic or religious leaders. With the Qing government focused on the massive Taiping rebellion in the Yangtze river valley, no significant reinforcements or funding arrived for over a decade, and only in 1868 did Qing military forces begin a reconquest. The Qing reconquest in 1868 relied on a solid logistical network to sustain armies in the field for long periods of time, a method that enabled them to outlast many of the local forces but left them vulnerable to tropical diseases. Like in Yunnan, the campaign was devastating for much of the local population, and the total death toll was 4.9 million people out of a province population of 7 million in 1854 (Jenks 1994). While only a small percentage of this number was killed in direct combat, the forcible relocation of ethnic minorities, along with outbreaks of disease and food shortages, claimed many lives.

New historical assessments of Chinese imperialism have direct connections to contemporary political disputes in the PRC region of Xinjiang (or East Turkestan). Sustained opposition to Han Chinese rule in the region led a recent *Economist* magazine article to label the region 'China's Chechnya' (*Economist* 2014). This area had been brought under Qing control in the 1780s and 1790s with the defeat and destruction of the Zunghar people (Perdue 2005). A widespread revolt erupted in June 1864, which seized the key cities of Kucha, Urumqi, Yarkand, and Kashgar. By 1873, Yaqub Beg had created a new government that stretched from Gansu province to the Hindu Kush in Afghanistan. Yaqub Beg had also created a standing army of 35,000–40,000 men and used diplomatic connections to obtain military assistance from the Ottoman Empire. Despite this large military force, Beg was unable to oppose the methodical Qing advance in the summer of 1877, and the sudden death of Yaqub Beg in July 1877 (most likely due to stroke) shattered the nascent East Turkestan state. The Qing armies reached Kashgar by the end of the year.

Yet another part of the Qing imperial state attempted to break way when the Hui communities in Shaanxi and Gansu rose up in revolt during the 1860s. Responding to a familiar pattern of imperial misgovernance and rising animosity because of growing numbers of ethnic Han, the Hui were successful in seizing control of much of Shaanxi and Gansu. Between 1862 and 1876, Qing imperial forces conducted a series of brutal military campaigns to reestablish control. During the fighting, over 91% of the pre-1850 Hui population was killed or displaced (Lu 2003).

Assessing the historical legacies of Chinese military history, the imperial traditions of territorial expansion, ethnic conflict, and military conquest very clearly continue to resonate. After the fall of the Qing dynasty in 1912, political leaders in the subsequent Republic of China (ROC) in power from 1912 to 1949, and People's Republic of China (PRC), in power since 1949, have insisted on maintaining the full extent of territory conquered by their imperial predecessors.

Chinese military structures and political control

During the Qing dynasty, a complex network of personal loyalties and cultural connections ensured military obedience, but not always competence. During the mid-19th century, Qing military institutions began to reform and professionalize their recruitment, training and tactics, and this effort led in large part to the overthrow of the dynasty by young military officers in 1912. The influence of military officers during the early 20th century, and the complex, fractured political environment of the post-1912 era led to new patterns of controlling military power, and models of civil-military relations that are still present 100 years later. Political leaders in the Nationalist (KMT) party, the dominant political party in the ROC from 1912 to 1949, and later the CCP, the sole political party in the PRC period from 1949 to the present, began to develop their own military forces as part of a larger party organization. KMT and CCP military forces owed their existence not to the nation, but to a political party. This policy continues to be used in the PRC, which lacks a national army in the traditional sense, and military force remains under the control of the CCP.

The core of Qing military strength was the 'Bannermen', descendants of the original 24 units (banners) that had been formed in the early 17th century by Manchu leader Nurhaci. Banner forces were instrumental in conquering the Ming dynasty and establishing the Manchu ruled Qing dynasty in 1644. The 24 banner units were ethnically subdivided into eight Manchu, eight Mongol, and eight Han Chinese units (Elleman 2001). All Manchu were officially enrolled in one of the eight Manchu banners with recruitment being hereditary (Elliott 2001). Supporting the Bannermen was the 'Green Standard Army', which was originally formed by the ethnic Han Chinese that had switched sides in 1644 to support the Manchu. Although the Green Standard Army theoretically numbered over 300,000 soldiers, these troops were dispersed in small garrisons and operated as a police or paramilitary force rather than a conventional military organization (Kuhn 1970).

By the mid-19th century, the banner organization had degenerated so much that a visiting American general reported,

> The bannermen are seldom required to drill, and, when they are called out, muster with rusty swords, bows, spears, and weapons of various descriptions. ... As soldiers they have long since ceased to be useful, and until reorganized and disciplined, they must remain but profitless pensioners of the Government.
>
> *(Upton, 1878)*

The inability of Qing military forces to defeat British or French forces in 1842 and 1860 embarrassed the dynasty but these sporadic engagements did not undermine the economic or political foundations of Manchu rule or threaten civilian control of military forces. A much more central threat was the Taiping rebellion, which began in 1850, and quickly led not only to the loss of the economically vital Yangzi River valley to the Qing state but also challenged the ideological system that legitimized Manchu rule (Spence 1996). The military necessity for Qing forces to provide a defense against Taiping rebels who appealed to the peasantry led to the formation of militia forces that were organized and led by ethnic Han elites at the local level. The militias expanded as commanders drew on local and regional networks of the Chinese 'gentry' officials in the Yangtze region for officers (Kuhn 1970). Training for these regional military forces depended on the skill and initiative of the officers, many of whom had little military experience. A small but innovative component of the forces raised by Li Hongzhang was a mixed foreign/Han Chinese brigade of 5,000 men formed in the summer of 1861. Dubbed the 'Ever Victorious Army' after a series of battlefield successes, the force sought to utilize imported organizational structures, create a small staff system, and introduce foreign weapons (Elleman 2001).

After the Taiping rebellion was suppressed, Li continued to modernize his military forces and created new patterns of military education and weapons development, separate from established Qing methods of cultural and political control. Li established a military academy in Tianjin to instruct officer candidates on mathematics, military drill, military engineering, surveying, which was a radical change from Manchu traditions that emphasized physical ability or Han Chinese emphasis of Confucian literary examinations (Smith 1978). As the technical skills of his forces grew, Li began the systematic importation of large amounts of weapons from foreign arms manufacturers, primarily Krupp artillery, to increase the firepower of his forces (Bell 1884). In spite of the promising reforms initiated by Li, the battlefield performance of the Qing military in the Sino-Japanese war of 1894–1895 was poor. Weak leadership by senior officers and weak battlefield discipline among Chinese forces revealed a lack of coordination in military policy between political leaders and military forces (Fung 1996). The defeat of Chinese army and naval forces by Japan in 1895 spurred the Qing War Council to create a new military force in North China that would incorporate foreign military innovations in organization, weapons, and tactics. A young officer, Yuan Shikai, was selected as the commander of this force, and he was a strong supporter of wholesale military change, remarking: 'If we do not make a drastic reorganization adopting western methods and introducing a system of thorough military training; then, I would really shudder to face any further repetition of our early reverses …' (Liu, 1951a).

Improving the military education and self-discipline of officers and men was a major component of Yuan's program. Obsolete Manchu physical tests, such as shooting a bow for officer recruits were abolished in 1901. Ending of Confucian-based civil examinations in 1905 further broadened the pool of potential officer recruits and aligned military requirements with technical skills being taught in Qing schools (Dreyer 1995). To train officers in specialized military skills and inculcate a professional military identity, Yuan established a military academy in the city of Baoding, 100 miles away from the intrigue and politics of the capital, Beijing (Powell 1955; Zheng & Zhang 2005, Zhu & Xuefang 1990). The shifting of military identity and loyalty from ethnic and personal ties toward a focus on the state was also reflected during the last decade of the Qing dynasty, as martial values were encouraged by the Qing state and anti-Manchu Han nationalists. Young men were exhorted to see military service to the state as a responsibility that was shared by all, and respected because the soldier served the people. One textbook, the 1904 'New National Reader', stated clearly, 'soldiers are the foundation of a strong country', and repeatedly linked national greatness to military valor and courage (Fung 1980).

Despite these reforms, the last decade of the Qing dynasty saw the increasing divergence of senior Manchu leaders from the new military forces, which were almost exclusively ethnically Han. The Wuchang Uprising in October 1911 by ethnic military Han officers initiated a series of military revolts and political maneuvers that eventually led to the end of the Qing dynasty on February 12, 1912 (Esherick 1976; McCord 1993; Sutton 1980; Fung 1980). The end of the Qing dynasty and the short-lived national government of Yuan Shikai as president of the newly formed Republic of China was a confusing time for Chinese military forces because they now lacked a clear chain of command or sense of loyalty to a defined political organization. The period from 1912 to 1927, often called the 'warlord era', was characterized by military governments in a politically divided China. In this period of transition from empire to republic, military organizations were often the most cohesive part of the government, and military officers moved into positions of political leadership as a result of both opportunism and in response to weak and divided civilian political systems. The confusing and decentralized political situation after 1912 and the role of military leaders in government was harshly criticized by contemporary observers as a perversion of the ideals of civilian control of the military. The 'solution' to the problems of warlord rule was the creation of military forces loyal to political parties, not the country as a whole.

The creator of the enduring 'Party-army' (*dangjun*) model of Chinese military identity was the Kuomintang (KMT), which quickly became the leading national political party after 1911 under the leadership of Sun Yat-sen. During the January 1913 National Assembly election, the KMT won a plurality of seats in both the lower house and the Senate, but the National Assembly was disbanded by Yuan Shikai in 1914 (Chien 1970). The KMT was able to restart its political efforts in southern China during 1916 and 1917, but without military power it was vulnerable to local warlords. Sun noted that political power in China was founded on military strength, observing that 'unless we [the KMT] appeal to the force of arms there is no way to settle the present national crisis' (Liu 1956b). During the late 1910s and early 1920s, Sun was also impressed with the glowing reports coming from Russia, where the Bolsheviks had created the 'Red Army' during its Civil War (Bergere 1998). In 1921, Sun signed agreements to create an independent KMT military academy in Guangdong using Soviet instructors and equipment.

On May 1, 1924, the Nationalist Party of China-Army Officer Academy, officially opened, and the KMT was able to attract large numbers of applicants to the academy (Yuan & Huang 1971; Chen 2007; Landis 1969). Known as the 'Whampoa Academy' because of its location in Whampoa, in Guangdong province, the school combined Soviet military ideas about an ideologically motivated and politically controlled military with tactical instruction by Chinese instructors who were trained at Baoding or the Japanese Military Academy. Although during its brief period of operation only several thousand officers received training at Whampoa, the school was the incubator of Sun's new 'Party Army' concept in China. Coordination of Soviet and Chinese instructors was difficult due to language differences, limiting teaching to basic infantry tactics, such as suppressive fire and basic flanking maneuvers (Cherepanov 1982). The Whampoa Academy curriculum included a large amount of political and ideological indoctrination, and classes and instruction given to officer cadets emphasized loyalty and obedience to party leaders and revolutionary principles (Liu 1947). To ensure the loyalty of military officers to the KMT, Soviet military and political instructors helped established a Political Department within the military. This organization used techniques that had been created by the Soviet Red Army, including the use of ideological education, extensive anti-imperialist propaganda, and emphasizing deference to party authority (Gillespie 1971).

To further cultivate the loyalty of military personnel and ensure obedience, a network of 'political officers' was installed throughout the newly created KMT military, and political officers had several tasks within a unit to ensure party loyalty (Feng 1972). First, they were to develop the party organization, which meant creating party cells within the military and recruiting important military personnel such as almost all officers and many noncommissioned officers into the party. In addition, the political officer worked to indoctrinate military personnel on the concept of Party supremacy through education, cultural activities, and personal interactions. Finally, the political officer was responsible for the welfare of the soldiers, many of whom were very young, poorly educated, and far from home. Throughout this process, the political officer continually sought to encourage discipline and unity with the KMT army, as well as obedience to party leadership. Many of these tasks conflicted with traditional notions that a military commander had sole authority over his soldiers, and political officers had to ensure that political mandates did not stifle military effectiveness.

An important aspect of the political officer role was a separate chain of command, with political officers being responsible only to party leaders, not their military counterpart. This organizational structure limited the power of military officers over political officers, and it ensured that political officers were evaluated only by the next higher level within the Political Department. The creation of a separate chain of command provided the means by which the central Political Department headquarters could maintain operational and ideological control over their political officers, and through them, ensure that military forces were obedient to party guidance.

Conclusion

In conclusion, recent studies of Chinese military history have raised very provocative questions and significantly increased our understanding of Chinese strategic culture, imperialism, and political control of the military. As the PRC has become a regional, and in many ways a global power, enduring, historical patterns of strategic culture have reemerged after the uncertainty and ideological conflicts of the Maoist period (1949–1976). A clear example of the return to a more activist, hegemonic Chinese military culture is the conflict with Vietnam that began in 1979. The PRC attacked Vietnam in a limited 'punitive expedition' because of Vietnamese attacks on Khmer Rouge forces in Cambodia. In Chinese discussions of the conflict, the fighting is referred to as a 'defensive counterattack' or a 'preemptive counterattack', a clear indication that in the Chinese mentality a regional neighbor, Vietnam, was not allowed to take action against a Chinese client. This example highlights a return to an energetic and active military posture that was prevalent in the Qing period, where Chinese forces are used to coerce neighbors and demonstrate power.

In another similarity with historical patterns of military expansion and empire, the strategic culture demonstrated by the PRC highlights a willingness to use military forces to define borders, expand government control, and solidify governmental powers in frontier areas. As of 2019, the PRC has territorial disputes with 23 nations, and does not recognize judgments by the United Nations (UN), preferring unilateral military solutions. In the South China Sea, the PRC has built military bases on artificial islands despite a 2016 UN Court of Arbitration ruling that China had no legal basis for any territorial claims. Another area of expansion is along the border with India, with the PRC continuing to administer areas seized during a brief 1962 war, and continuing to dispute areas of Arunachal Pradesh. In 2017, this border dispute was exacerbated by Chinese military construction and patrolling in a disputed area of Doklam, raising tensions between India and China. PRC attempts to intimidate Taiwan, a self-governing island that is claimed by the PRC, further highlights the willingness to use military power for territorial expansion.

Moreover, the ethnic conflicts that emerged because of Qing imperialism, and which were so destructive to the mid-19th-century Qing dynasty continue to radiate through the current PRC. The PRC has 55 officially recognized minority groups, in addition to the majority Han, and tensions over religious practices, Han immigration into minority areas, and conflict, although localized, has been enduring. In Tibet, a heavy military presence by the People's Liberation Army (PLA) and the destruction of numerous religious sites during the past 50 years has led to occasional riots and ethnic fighting. In the central Asian province of Xinjiang, PLA military forces were used to develop the oil and gas industry, and large garrisons have been permanently stationed in the area. Ethnic conflict between Han immigrants and the local Uyghur population has been fueled by economic inequality and discrimination, resulting in occasional conflict, and heavy military surveillance of the civil population, and the detention of hundreds of thousands of people in what the PRC government refers to as 'vocational education' camps.

Lastly, the PRC, like the Qing dynasty, has developed a unique military structure that is responsible to a small select group rather than the population. Although the military structures of banner forces have long evaporated, the 'Party-Army' concept first developed in China by Sun Yat-sen, continues to be the template used by the CCP to control its own military force, the PLA. Despite the creation of the People's Republic of China government in 1949, the PLA has maintained its role as a party military force, with CCP political officers embedded in military formations and the Central Military Commission (CMC) of the CCP exercising command and control. During the 1990s and 2000s the PLA began a modernization program designed to improve the firepower and mobility of PLA units, particularly in a local regional conflict, but any notion of moving the PLA under Chinese government authority, rather than party control, was resisted by the CCP. Since the elevation of Xi Jinping as General Secretary of the Communist Party in 2012, he has moved to bolster ideological indoctrination of military forces and solidify loyalty to the CCP rather than the PRC. The Qing dynasty demonstrated that establishing military forces linked by cultural and economic ties to Beijing rather than the people can succeed, and for the foreseeable future, the PLA will likely remain loyal to the party, rather than the national government.

This chapter has sought to highlight three vital threads of military history that have relevance throughout the modern era (post-1800): strategic culture, Chinese imperialism, and political control of the military. As new scholarship continues to expand our understanding of the military history of China, the academic, political and cultural debates will continue to assess how we view the impact of past conflicts. The three aspects of military history discussed in this chapter will continue to be shaped by legacies of the past and maintain their importance as China moves into an uncertain future.

References

Atwill, D.G. (2006). *The Chinese Sultanate: Islam, Ethnicity and the Panthay Rebellion in Southwestern China, 1856–1873*. Stanford, CA: Stanford University Press.

Atwill, D.G. (2003). 'Blinkered Visions: Islamic Identity, Hui Ethnicity, and the Panthay Rebellion in Southwest China, 1856–1873'. *Journal of Asian Studies*, Vol. 62, No. 4, pp. 1079–1108.

Bell, M. (1884). *China: Being a Military Report on the Northeastern Portions of the Provinces of Chih-Li and Shan-Tung; Nanking and its Approaches; Canton and its Approaches; etc*, Vols. I and II. Simla: Government Central Branch Press.

Bergere, M.-C. (1998). *Sun Yat-sen*. Stanford, CA: Stanford University Press.

Callahan, W. (2004). 'National Insecurities: Humiliation, Salvation, and Chinese Nationalism'. *Alternatives*, Vol. 29, pp. 199–218.

Chang, H.Y. (1987). 'The Hui (Muslim) Minority in China: An Historical Overview'. *Journal of the Institute of Muslim Minority Affairs*, Vol. 8, No. 1, pp. 62–78.

Chen, J.H. 陈建华 (ed.). (2007). 黄埔军校研究. Guangzhou: Zhongshan daxue chubanshe.

Cherepanov, A.I. (1982). *As Military Advisor in China*. Moscow: Progress Publishers.

Chien, T.-S. (1970). *The Government and Politics of China, 1912–1949*. Stanford, CA: Stanford University Press.

Cosmo, N. Di (1998). 'Qing Colonial Administration in Inner Asia'. *The International History Review*, Vol. 20, No. 2, pp. 287–309.

Crossley, P., H. Siu, and D. Sutton (eds.). (2006). *Empire at the Margins: Culture, Ethnicity and Frontier in Early Modern China*. Berkeley, CA: University of California Press.

Dai, Y. (2009). *The Sichuan Frontier and Tibet, Imperial Strategy In the Early Qing*. Seattle, WA: University of Washington Press.

Dillon, M. (1999). *China's Muslim Hui Community: Migration, Settlement and Sects*. Surrey: Curzon Press.

Dreyer, E. (1995). *China at War, 1901–1949*. London: Routledge.

The Economist (9 August 2014). 'China's Far West: A Chechnya in the Making'. https://www.economist.com/leaders/2014/08/09/a-chechnya-in-the-making (accessed August 22, 2019).

Elleman, B. (2001). *Modern Chinese Warfare, 1795–1989*. London: Routledge Press.

Elliott, M. (2001). *The Manchu Way: The Eight Banners and Ethnic Identity in Late Imperial China*. Stanford, CA: Stanford University Press.

Esherick, J. (1976). *Reform and Revolution in China: The 1911 Revolution in Hunan and Hubei*. Berkeley, CA: University of California Press.

Fairbank, J.K. and F. Kierman (eds.). (1974). *Chinese Ways in Warfare*. Cambridge, MA: Harvard University Press.

Feng, S. 馮紹焜. (1972). 國軍政戰史. Taipei: Zhengzhi zuozhan xuexiao bianying.

Fung, A. (1996). 'Testing the Self-Strengthening: The Chinese Army in the Sino-Japanese War of 1894–1895'. *Modern Asian Studies*, Vol. 30, No. 4, pp. 77–78.

Fung, E. (1980). *The Military Dimension of the Chinese Revolution*. Vancouver: University of British Columbia Press.

Giersch, C. P. (2006). *Asian Borderlands: The Transformation of Qing China's Yunnan Frontier*. Cambridge, MA: Harvard University Press.

Gillespie, R.E. (1971). *Whampoa and the Nanking Decade, 1924–1936*. PhD Dissertation, American University.

Gillette, M. (2008). 'Violence, the State, and a Chinese Muslim Ritual Remembrance'. *The Journal of Asian Studies*, Vol. 67, No. 3, pp. 1011–1037.

Herman, J.E. (2007). *Amid the Clouds and Mist: China's Colonization of Guizhou, 1200–1700*. Cambridge, MA: Harvard University Press.

Hevia, J. (1993). *Cherishing Men From Afar: Qing Guest Ritual and the Macartny Embassy of 1793*. Durham, NC: Duke University Press.

Hostetler, L. (2001). *Qing Colonial Enterprise: Ethnography and Cartography in Early Modern China*. Chicago, IL: University of Chicago Press.

Hou, C. 侯春燕. (1997). '同治回民起义后西北地区人口迁移及影响'. *Shanxi daxue xuebao*, Vol. 1997, pp. 68–72.

Jenks, R.D. (1994). *Insurgency and Social Disorder in Guizhou: The 'Miao' Rebellion, 1854–1873*. Honolulu, HI: University of Hawaii Press.

Johnston, A.I. (1995). *Cultural Realism: Strategic Culture and Grand Strategy in Chinese History*. Princeton, NJ: Princeton University Press.

Kessler, L.D. (1969). 'Ethnic Composition of Provincial Leadership during the Ch'ing Dynasty'. *Journal of Asian Studies*, Vol. 3, No. 28, pp. 489–511.

Kuhn, P. (1970). *Rebellion and Its Enemies in Late Imperial China: Militarization and Social Structure, 1796–1864*. Boston, MA: Harvard University Press.

Landis, R.B. (1969). *Institutional Trends at the Whampoa Military School*. Unpublished PhD Dissertation, University of Washington.

Larsen, K. (2008). *Tradition, Treaties and Trade: Qing Imperialism and Chosen Korea, 1850–1910*. Cambridge, MA: Harvard University Press.

Liu, F.F. (1951a). *The Nationalist Army of China: An Administrative Study of the Period 1924–1946*. PhD Dissertation, Princeton University.

Liu, F.F. (1956b). *A Military History of Modern China, 1924–1949*. Princeton, NJ: Princeton University Press.

Liu, Z. 劉峙. (1947). 黃埔軍校與國民革命軍. Nanjing: Duli chubanshe.

Lorge, P. (2005). *War, Politics and Society in Early Modern China: 900–1795*. London: Routledge.

Lorge, P. (2008). 'The Great Ditch of China and the Song-Liao Border'. In Don J. Wyatt (ed.), *Battlefronts Real and Imagined: Wars, Border and Identity in the Chinese Middle Period*. New York, NY: Palgrave.

Lu, W. 路伟东. (2003). '清代陕西回民的人口变动'. *Huizu Yanjiu*, Vol. 52, pp. 71–77.

Ma, C. 马长寿 (ed.). (1993). 同治年间陕西回民起义历史调查记录. Xian: Shaanxi renmin chuban she.

McCord, E. (1993). *The Power of the Gun: The Emergence of Modern Chinese Warlordism*. Berkeley, CA: University of California Press.

Perdue, P. (2005). *China Marches West: The Qing Conquest of Central Eurasia*. Cambridge, MA: Harvard University Press.

Perdue, P. (2009). 'China and Other Colonial Empires'. *The Journal of American-East Asian Relations*, Vol. 16, pp. 85–103.

Powell, R.L. (1955). *The Rise of Chinese Military Power, 1895–1912*. Princeton, NJ: Princeton University Press.

Smith, R. (1978). 'The Reform of Military Education in Late Ch'ing China, 1842–1895'. *Journal of the Hong Kong Branch of the Royal Asiatic Society*, Vol. 18, pp. 15–40.

Spence, J.D. (1996). *God's Chinese Son: The Taiping Heavenly Kingdom of Hong Xiuquan*. New York, NY: Norton and Co.

Sutton, D. (1980). *Provincial Militarism and the Chinese Republic: Yunnan Army, 1905–1925*. Ann Arbor, MI: University of Michigan Press.

Sutton, D. (2003). 'Violence and Ethnicity on a Qing Colonial Frontier: Customary and Statutory Law in the Eighteenth-Century Miao Pale'. *Modern Asian Studies*, Vol. 37, No. 1, pp. 41–80.

Teng, E. (2004). *Taiwan's Imagined Geography: Chinese Colonial Travel Writing and Pictures, 1683–1895*. Cambridge, MA: Harvard University Press.

Theobald, U. (2013). *War Finance and Logistics in Late Imperial China: A Study of the Second Jinchuan Campaign*. Leiden: Brill, 2013.

Upton, E. (1878). *The Armies of Asia and Europe*. Portsmouth: Griffin and Company.

Wang, Y.-K. (2011). *Harmony and War: Confucian Culture and Chinese Power Politics*. New York, NY: Columbia University Press.

Weinstein, J.L. (2014). *Empire and Identity in Guizhou: Local Resistance to Qing Expansion*. Seattle, WA: University of Washington Press.

Yuan, S. 袁守謙 and J. Huang 黄杰. (1971). 黃埔建軍. Taipei: Unknown Publisher.

Zheng, Z. 郑志廷 and Q. Zhang 张秋山. (2005). 保定陆军学堂暨军官学校史略. Beijing: Renmin chubanshe.

Zhu, B. 朱秉一 and Y. Xuefang 楊學房. (1990). 陸軍大學沿革史. Taipei: Sanjun daxue.

16

History of international law and China

Eurocentrism, multinormativity, and the politics of history

Maria Adele Carrai

Introduction

After what has been defined by Chinese elites as 'the century of humiliation', China has reclaimed the central stage in international affairs. Especially now that it has re-emerged as a great power, capable of shaping international norms in its own interests, new questions about the nature, history, and resilience of the so-called 'international rule-based order' and international law continue to surface. Although there exists a gap between the written norms and their application and international law has been increasingly contested, the latter has continued to orient states and other nonstate actors in their international behaviors. While its fragmented and politicized nature has been widely exposed (Koskenniemi 2011, 2013; Krasner 1999; Roberts 2017), international law and its institutions – aimed at preserving sovereign equality, self-determination, and peace under the law – still constitute the backbone of international society. If one looks at the way China has been portrayed with regard to international law in many Western historical accounts, but also the way it is often characterized today, it continues to be considered partly as an outsider, a norm breaker, a noncompliant state, an exception, although historically it has increasingly integrated and become an active participant in the international legal forum (Johnston 2019). At the same time Chinese accounts of their country and the history of international law have been politicized and tend to perpetuate the narrative of the century of humiliations and support the current rhetoric of China's unique historical trajectory toward great rejuvenation. The roots of this perceived exceptionalism can be found on the one hand in the way the history of international law has been constructed (Koskenniemi et al. 2017), and on the other hand on China's modern history and its gradual familiarization with international law in the course of the 19th and 20th centuries and its emergence as a great power in the 21st century.

In recent decades, scholarship on the history of international law has attracted the attention of a growing number of academics and lawyers. Its shortcomings, reported by the jurist Lassa Oppenheim at the beginning of the 20th century but then ignored by several generations of functionalists, seem to have at last been eliminated by the so-called historiographical turn (Craven 2006; Galindo 2005). This new interest in international legal history is

DOI: 10.4324/9780429059704-20

related to the current time of crisis, exacerbated by the recent pandemic. The sense of uncertainty generated by the collapse of the Cold War order, and the emergence of new actors like China (that defies current liberal paradigms with its millennial history and current illiberal system) are profoundly challenging the supremacy of the cosmopolitan project of international law. Historians and jurists have therefore started to look at the history of international law to find causes and possible responses to current issues, or to read events in continuity with a new liberal teleology aimed at transforming the international legal and political order into a global one, where the classic sovereignty paradigm is outclassed by humanitarian progressivism (Koskenniemi 2004). The most recent historiographies of international law recognized and attempted to address some of the major issues of the more traditional historiographies that affect also the way the history of international law in Asia has been narrated and constructed. The limitations can be summarized in its Eurocentrism, its teleological-linear vision of history, a hierarchical approach that disregarded encounters with low-level players and regular persons (Cogan 2020; Benton 2019), and legal orientalism (Ruskola 2013). At the same time, Chinese scholars influenced by Xi Jinping's Great Rejuvenation rhetoric, that roots the bright future of the Chinese nation in its millennial history, have also begun to put a new emphasis on the history of the humiliating encounter between China and Western international law as a way to justify the current and future redemption of China as a great power able to rewrite some of the rules of international law, deemed too tied to Western history and experience.

Eurocentrism and legal orientalism characterize much of the histories of international law in Asia. The two are related: While the former is an attitude of Western scholars who look at the world from a European perspective that assumes the superiority of European culture, the latter treats other political entities – in this case China – as an object of study by a cognitively superior West that tends to deny the existence of modern legal institutions in other contexts. Both Eurocentrism and legal orientalism are embedded within a teleological vision of history that views modern international law and sovereignty as values in and of themselves and the final telos of history. State sovereignty, besides being essential for international law and its history, became necessary also for the definition of modernity, which – conceiving the sovereign nation-state as a value in itself – tended to treat it as the final end towards which the linear history of the various forms of power organization come gradually to conform with. International law in this vision became also part of the final telos of history, seen as a natural end point of the normative order that regulated sovereign states. Another limitation of the past historiographies of international law is their focus on nation states and key international actors (leading lawyers, jurists, and diplomats). This has translated into a positivistic and formalistic vision of international lawmaking that limits our understanding of how international law has evolved outside of where law is expected to reside – not only in non-Western contexts but also among low-level officials, nonlawyers, and regular people (Cogan 2020).

In the past decades, in response to these deficiencies, new approaches have been developed that attempted to dismantle colonial epistemologies and broaden the history of international law to include places and people often neglected. The new approaches developed to overcome the general limitations of the historiographies of international law include the Third World approaches to international law (TWAIL), postcolonial histories (whose critic is based on the premise that law is deeply intertwined with power), Critical Legal Studies, global histories of international law that focus on non-Western countries and contextual, cultural, and social histories. Authors adopting a postcolonial perspective tend to challenge the traditional scholarship that saw international law as a progressive science and intrinsically as a European project. Taking into account the colonial and imperial legacies these writers rethought the history of international law as something more fragmented and less scientific, pointing out the relationship between what was considered a science and the ideological apparatus that underpinned it. The Third World approaches to international law are an important example of a postcolonial turn within the history of international law (Mutua & Anghie 2000). The TWAIL critiques neoliberal international law and its homologous narrative of progress, aiming to expose what lies beyond the rhetoric of humanitarian cosmopolitanism while legitimizing alternative approaches and histories of international law, namely those of Third World countries. Particularly, it emphasizes the experiences and histories of colonized people, and the way in which international law was used as an instrument of power and subjugation by Western countries.

In light of the various scholarship developments of the past decade, this chapter provides an overview of the different approaches to the history of international law in China, highlighting their values and shortcomings. The first part presents the legacies of Eurocentrism in the historiographies that look at China's encounter with the West and international law in the course of the 19th century, seeing such an encounter as necessary for China's modernization. If on the one hand, these historiographies tend to dismiss the agency of Chinese actors, on the other hand, Chinese accounts tend to read such encounter as part of China's bitter historical trajectory that after a century of humiliations is leading it toward a brighter future of great power, finally able to rewrite international rules and take back what it considers to be its rightful place in the world. The second part introduces the global histories of international law that attempt to overcome Eurocentrism by expanding the history of international law to other temporalities and non-Western spaces. The scholarship that argued for the existence of international law in ancient China belongs to this group. Despite the good intention to be more inclusive and pluralistic, such scholarship involuntarily falls prey to the opposite, forcing categories that would not be, per se, necessarily universal into other histories. The third part introduces the studies that started to look at Chinese appropriation of international law, focusing on the agency of Chinese diplomats and jurists and the fourth part discusses legal pluralism and multinormativity as new fruitful alternatives to study the history of international law in China. The conclusion, while exposing the politics of history behind most of the historical constructions, provides some general remarks about these different methodologies and suggests unexplored areas that deserve further study.

International law in China: Eurocentrism and the encounter with the West

Over the course of the 19th and 20th century, modern international law, as a worldview based on sovereign equality among states and a set of rules that guided diplomatic intercourse among the Christendom, gradually became a technique for empire capable to legally justifying the submission of other non-Christian/European polities. It has come to regulate and define the current international system. While international law has claimed to be universal since its birth as a modern science in the 18th century (Vec 2012), not only has it reflected entrenched power dynamics and imperial aspirations of European countries, but many polities have been left behind from its practice and history, as they were deemed uncivilized and not part of the family of Christian nations. China was not an exception and was considered as an outsider to the international legal order in the 18th and 19th centuries.

Despite the cravings of the British and foreigners to open up China to mercantilism and their profitable illegal sale of opium, the Qing empire (1644–1911) was closed off from foreign trade and Christian missionaries. It did not practice international law or its diplomatic protocols, and it did not embrace an international law worldview. Before its entrance into the family of nations and the adoption of modern international law in its foreign relations over the course of the late 19th and 20th century, China used to have its own normative order, based on the so-called tribute system, *chaogong tixi* 朝贡体系 (Fairbank 1968). It was based on the assumption of Chinese superiority, from which it derived a nonegalitarian and hierarchical system of foreign relations centered on the supreme figure of the emperor. Despite the great limitations of the tribute system as a tool of historical analysis (Hevia 1994; Hamashita 2008: 12–26; Carrai 2019: 44–45), it is still a valid theoretical framework that helps underline the difference between the Western and Chinese normative orders before the globalization of international law.

The 1842 Treaty of Nanking marked the beginning of the Western imperial project in China, which granted foreign powers the application of their own law in Qing territory and exemption from local jurisdiction. This extraterritorial system created a suspension not only of international law as it was practiced among Western sovereign states, but also of the legal subjectivity of China, deemed an aberration by the European family of nations and thus defined as semisovereign. To become a full member of the international society, a country was expected to comply with the standards of civilization, particularly modern legal institutions. Due to the power dynamics of the new world order dominated by the systems of Western sovereign states, China suddenly found itself no longer at the center of the world, but at its margins, and Chinese intellectuals and literati from the end of the 19th century started to promote profound reforms of their own system to accommodate the new international situation and to appropriate international law.

Passages of international law codes were translated into China only during the First Opium War (1839–1842), when Lin Zexu (1785–1850), the Guangdong governor appointed by the Qing government to deal with its opium trade-related controversies with Great Britain, asked the imperial interpreter Yuan Dehui to translate passages from Vattels' *Le Droit des gens*. The translation, not yet systematic, was included in Wei Yuan's influential *Haiguo Tuzhi* (Atlas and Description of the Countries beyond the Seas), published in 1847 (Masini 1993). It was only after the Second Opium War (1856–1860) that the first systematic translation of international law in Chinese, made by the American protestant missionary William Alexander Parsons Martin, was introduced to China; Chinese diplomats started to adopt its conceptual and linguistic framework as a reference (Martin 1998). Following the Opium Wars, Chinese diplomats and political figures did not merely come to terms with international law and the notion of sovereignty through which the Western order was predicted. They also began to use it in their struggles to be part of international law and its history, contribute to shaping it, and for a new representation of the world in which they projected China's own power and justified legitimacy to both defend itself from Western encroachment and for its own imperial aspirations predicted within a new legal language and framework.

It is largely within this historical context of China 'encountering the modern West' that histories of international law in China have been written. As a consequence, studies on the history of international law in Asia have focused primarily on the Western encounter, especially during the 19th century. While there is a rich area of studies and literature that describe the social and political evolution in East Asia before Western models arrived, the research on these processes from a legal perspective remains lacking. This period has often been neglected in the field of the history of international law. For some international legal scholars, who have been accustomed to assessing non-Western states' politico-legal structure and their patterns of foreign relations by reference to the modern international law system in the West, it is difficult to find a reasonable explanation for this lengthy period in East Asian history in the discourse of Western international law (Kroll 2019). Consequently, whenever it comes to issues concerning the East Asian region and international law, scholars tend to focus on how the late Qing, Republican China, the Meiji regime of Japan or the late Joseon Dynasty, reacted to and were assimilated into the Western international legal system against the backdrop of conflicts between the West and the East from the middle of the 19th century to the early 20th century (Kroll 2019). These historiographies tend to assume the classical periodization that saw, for example, the starting point of modern international law in the Peace of Westphalia, and its teleological narrative based on the notion of national sovereignty. China thus would enter modernity and international law only once it translated international law and once it was accepted by the members of the civilized family of nations.

Within these lenses, China's modernization is seen as a process of transformation of a universal empire, based on the idea of *tianxia*天下 into a sovereign state within an international legal order. For instance, John Fairbank, in his analysis of the Chinese tribute system of the 1960s, described the transformation of China from being a cultural-based empire into a modern nation-state (Fairbank 1968; Fairbank & Ch'en 1941). The historian Joseph Levenson distinguished between a premodern Chinese universal empire, *tianxia*, understood as a regime of values, and a modern country, *guo* 國, conceived as a regime of power (Levenson 1965: 98). Although for Levenson, *guo* and *tianxia* coexisted in China until its modernization, this last one was realized through a process of complete transformation of *tianxia* into the modern *guo*. In his *After Empire,* Peter Zarrow identified Chinese modernization with the replacement of the belief in the emperor as the final source of authority with new ideas of statism, nationalism, and sovereignty at the end of the 19th century (Zarrow 2012).

National sovereignty not only became a necessary requirement for admission to the realm of history, but it was also necessary to enter the family of nations and the world of legality. The lack of national and sovereign history corresponded to a lack of civilization, and quintessentially to a lack of legality as European jurists gradually framed an idealized European rule of law in contrast with the image of non-European lawlessness. This approach has been identified with the term 'legal orientalism' (Ruskola 2013). China, under the lens of legal orientalism, becomes an inanimate object to be studied by a cognitively superior West, which dictates its own version of law, defining its subject and deciding who is in the legal/civilized club and who is not – in other words, who is sovereign and who is not. China becomes 'an antimodel and stands for everything that we would not wish to be – or admit being' (Ruskola 2013: 44). This attitude can be seen not only in the study of Chinese law, which according to legal orientalists is absent in China, but also can be found in what is believed to be the original lack of the concept of sovereignty and international law in China in the 19th century. From this orientalist belief derives the obligation of China to introduce the new legal system, adapt to it and its terms, and be judged accordingly. These historiographies thus tend to focus on 'China's reaction' to modern international law and its inevitable advancement and progress. They fail to see the rich normative realm in which international law was introduced and the agency of Chinese actors that contested it, appropriated it, and used in their own interests, contributing to its development and globalization.

Chinese accounts of the history of international law also focus on the encounter between the Qing empire and the imperialist West in the 19th century, seen as a painful but necessary step toward China's modernization (He 2019; Tian 2001; Yang 2001). However, the way this encounter is contextualized and used by Chinese international lawyers and historians is different. Chinese accounts tend to expose the imperial nature of international law and how it was imposed upon the Qing empire through the unequal treaties, extraterritoriality, and legations that gave rise to the so-called century of humiliations (Zhang 2016). They also emphasize how the establishment of the People's Republic of China in 1949 finally ended the humiliations and placed China in a new trajectory, where China has gradually become a norm shaper, that might culminate with the realization of Xi Jinping's Dream of China's Great Rejuvenation (He 2019). In the Chinese accounts, the humiliations and the pain suffered by China due to the encounter with Wester imperialists in the 19th century becomes a political device that while promoting a nonnegotiable nationalism justifies China's journey of redemption and resistance, embodied by the successes of the People's Republic of China under the leadership of the Chinese Communist Party (Lai 2011; He & Sun 2015).

Global histories and ancient Chinese international law

The current attempts to globalize international law can be seen as a way to overcome its Eurocentrism. One recent example is Fassbender and Peters (2012), which sets out an example of how to construct a global history of international law by going beyond those narratives that conceived international law as a mere *droit public européen*. The global turn supported by the book is meant to be an answer to the denunciations expressed by the postcolonial turn. It is conceived as a way not only to broaden the scale of history by including voices and experiences that are often neglected, but also as a way to stress the connections across broad spaces and how these eventually contributed to the development of international law, going beyond the traditional forms of container-based paradigms, in particular that of the nation-state (Conrad 2017: 4). Although the handbook seeks to expand the history of international law both temporally and spatially by including non-European experiences narrated in the form of 'encounter', what the authors look for in non-Western experiences are the categories and the dogmas of modern international law as it was originally born and as it was developed in Europe. In other words, the risk is that Europe remains the main subject of such a history, being the place where international law finds its origin – while other experiences and histories, including the Chinese, seem to be simple variations of a European grand narrative. This serves to legitimize a cognitive horizon that seemed to have become universal over the course of the 19th century and that remains deeply influenced by what Lorca defined 'the center'; this was and continues to be identified with the liberal West and some of its categories, such as today's rule of law, democracy, human rights, capitalism, and so forth. The history of international law, no matter how global, appears at least in part condemned to take on a Eurocentric perspective, especially if – in a global space and time – the meeting between international law and other realities is something taken for granted, or as part of an inevitable process of integration of these non-Western experiences with the history of progress of international law.

One articulation of global history of international law that looks for categories of international law in the Chinese past are the historiographies that argued for the existence of international law in ancient China. While this starts with good intent – to legitimize China in international law – once again, it does not question the very Eurocentric categories of international law. Several authors have spoken of the presence of an international law *guojifa* 国际法 in the Warring States and the Spring and Autumn period of the Western Zhou Dynasty (770–256 BC) (Hong 1939; Sun 1999; Huai & Sun 2000; Xu 1931; Yi 2014). In these instances, the history of international law is detached from the history of Europe and forced to become universal through a lack of historical accuracy, projecting into different times and spaces categories that are more specific to European history. Consequently, we can find international law in ancient China and potentially anywhere. It was outside the current debates on global history that the American missionary W.A.P. Martin (1827–1916) at the end of the Qing period originally suggested the existence of international law in ancient China (Martin 2012). This idea was quickly supported by other important jurists during the Republican period, such as Zhou Gengsheng and, more recently, Wang Tieya and Xue Hanqin, in their handbooks of international law (Wang 1995, 1990, 1991; Xue 2011; Zhou 1976, 1929). This can be read as an attempt to validate China's role in the history of a normative order that was foreign to her until quite recently, an order that was initially imposed upon China. The cost of this strategy appears to be a wholesale rewriting of history, which ends by perpetuating legal orientalism. It is in fact an act of 'self-orientalism', in that it attempts to force the complex history of China and its premodern normative order into Western categories that are not themselves questioned and are instead validated and assumed to be necessary. Recently, the Cambridge legal historian Stephen Neff has embraced this approach. In his attempts to write a global history of international law, he ascribed to China and the Warring States period the origin of international law, in that it is in this period that there was the first systematic writing of international relations, hence the first appearance of international law as an intellectual discipline. If China contributed to this almost mythical origin of international law, then the rest of history, at least until recently, has been driven by European powers (Neff 2014: 21). However, Neff, together with other scholars that in good faith try to include the Chinese past within the history of international law, instead achieves the opposite, inadvertently constraining categories that are not quite universal into other histories. This would be like trying to find the origin of the tribute system as an intellectual discipline and a diplomatic practice in Europe.

In many Chinese accounts that argue for the existence of international law in ancient China, one of the main objectives, besides legitimizing China as an equal actor of international society, was to universalizing Confucianism through the history of international law (Carrai 2020). As Rune Svarverud has noted,

> the very fact that an indigenous system of international law may be identified in these sacred writings, at the time of Confucius himself, and in the sacred tradition of the golden age of the ancient Zhou, has given these ideas high prestige in Confucian circles in China and in East Asia.
>
> *(Svarverud 2007)*

It served to create a sense of self-confidence for Chinese diplomats and intellectuals in international affairs, going well beyond Martin's original intentions. While Martin thought that a system that worked well for China was useful as a way to find commensurability with international law and deserved study, he did not advocate export of ancient Chinese legal institutions abroad (Carrai 2020). Chinese intellectuals, however, used Martin's idea not only to frame China's emerging international identity, but also to universalize Confucius in order to enlighten and correct what they considered being the limits and hypocrisies of international law as translated from Western languages. Chinese Ancient international law of the spring and autumn period could make up for the shortcomings of current international law. In their historical reconstruction of an ancient Chinese international law it was therefore imperative to not emphasize the uniqueness of the Chinese tradition, but to restructure a new world picture, using the internal context of Confucianism as a basis to establish a universalist worldview and public law (Zeng & Wang 2004).

Beyond the West–East encounter: China's agency and the appropriation of international law

Although much of the research on the history of international law in Asia remains dominated by the studies of the diffusion of European international law and the encounter between China and the West and how this has prompted China's modernization and its joining or being accepted within the family of nations (Gong 1984), in the past decade, new scholarship has emerged that started to focus on the translation and adaptation of international law by local Chinese actors (Svarverud 2008), and on the agency of Chinese counterpart. This new perspective explores the processes of the transplantation of norms by looking at adaptation and contestation and the active role of local actors (So & So 2018; Zhao & Ng 2017). Adaptation is far from being a passive form of reception, but rather appropriation for strategic purposes (Kroll 2016; Becker Lorca 2014). In order to assert Chinese subjectivity, relativizing the universality of an international law understood as a mere *droit public européen,* authors have focused on the process of hybridizing the meaning of some key concepts of international law once these have been transplanted into China. This scholarship opposes those who viewed China as a passive object of Western domination; it emphasizes China's role as an agent able to influence and complicate the meaning of the transplanted legal concepts. Even if in the longer term this leads to a socialization of foreign norms, this is something quite different from the mere transplantation or imitation of European normative patterns (Shogo 2009). This is also illustrated by the emergence of indigenous approaches to international law, as seen through Chinese discourses on the unequal treaties of the early 20th century (Wang 2003, 2005). During the past decades, the history of these unequal treaties and extraterritoriality has been revisited. It has become much clearer now that the translation and adaptation of European international law was not just a process of passive reception but was initiated and executed by local elites who aimed at reforming their polities in order to make them more resilient to foreign influences (Kroll 2019).

There are several authors that have looked at the way in which Chinese scholars appropriated the language and the conceptual framework of international law and at the role played by Chinese lawyers and diplomats in the development of international law from the late nineteenth century. This is in line with the work of Rune Svarverud and Lydia Liu. By looking at the language of international law, they have emphasized how translation was by no means a neutral process; it is an active appropriation, in which the gradual legitimization of a new word and concept in a given host language takes place in an arena where there are constant struggles of a political and ideological nature to assert different interests. Thus, the meaning of a translated term is a hybrid within the host language rather than a perfect equivalence between the two languages (Liu 1995: 26). In these narratives, Chinese jurists and internationalists, far from being passive recipients of European standards, appear to be active players in the forums in which international law was created, such as at the early Hague Conventions, often providing a different understanding and interpretation of European standards and contributing to a real internationalization and universalization of international law. Here it is worth mentioning the historian Tang Qihua and Deng Ye. Both have tried to shed new light on the Republican period – previously reduced by much of the historiography to a chaotic period of division – by focusing on the role of Chinese lawyers in the formation of the League of Nations and later of the United Nations (Tang 2010, 1998, 2005; Deng 1986). Tang Qihua and Deng Ye emphasized how, in the Republican period, Chinese jurists gave a different interpretation of international law, promoting the interests of the nascent Republic of China. The historians Lin Xuechong and Tian Tao work along similar lines of enquiry. They have published work that deals with the introduction of international law at the end of the Qing Dynasty, highlighting the role of Chinese thinkers and reformers in the process of the hybridization of newly introduced Western concepts. Tian Tao, for instance, provides a conceptual history of key concepts of international law, noting not only how they deviated from Western formulations but also how there were variations among Chinese authors (Lam 2009; Tian 2001; Jin 2010).

As part of the scholarship that focuses on the hybridization and adaptation, belongs those historiographies that looked at international law as a framework that can be used to support different, if not opposing, claims. One example lies in the unequal treaties. On one hand, the Western powers legitimized the unequal treaties and subsequently limited the sovereignty of China on the basis of an interpretation of international law grounded on the standard of civilization. On the other hand, the Chinese jurists used international law as a platform to assert China's new international subjectivity, emphasizing the principles of equality and sovereignty. For instance, Liu Wenming has criticized how Western powers projected the standard of civilization onto international law. This, he lamented, in line with Gerrit Gong's previous work *The Standard of Civilization in International Society*, created a hierarchy that placed European powers in a superior position, so as to justify their imperialistic behavior in China (Liu 2014; Gong 1984). Similarly, in his recent book Wang Jianlang emphasizes how the Chinese use of international law differed from its Western counterparts. In particular, the unequal treaties have affected the reception of international law in China and its history, influencing current Chinese behavior in international society (Wang 2015; Liu 2010; Wang 2004). In the 1990s, the Chinese jurist Wang Tieya adopted this strategy in essays that appeared in the *Collected Courses of The Hague Academy of International Law*. In it, he legitimizes the Chinese historical contribution to the development of international law by examining the Chinese use of international law, focusing in particular on the Five Principles of Peaceful Coexistence – mutual respect for each other's territorial integrity and sovereignty, mutual nonaggression, mutual noninterference with each other's internal affairs, equality and mutual benefit, and peaceful coexistence – which Wang considers the greatest Chinese contribution to international law. Wang is a major point of reference in Chinese legal scholarship and he strongly influenced, for example, important Chinese jurists such as Xue Hanqin and Jia Bingbing (Wang 1991). While the PRC has prided itself for noninterfering in the internal affairs of other countries and for not imposing conditionalities in its foreign aid and investments, the principle of mutual noninterference and sovereignty has been used as a shield against foreign criticisms and possible intervention in its domestic abuses of human rights, especially in those areas like Xinjiang, Tibet, Inner Mongolia, Hong Kong, and Taiwan where the legacies of history and the unsettled territorial questions are still lingering.

Legal pluralism and multinormativity: An account of autochthonous 'international law' in China

The notion of legal pluralism has been used by scholarship to address the normative institutions in East Asia. For instance, Cassel's works on extraterritoriality in China and Japan in the 19th century, relying on previous work of the German Chinese Studies scholar Dorothea Heuschert, has led the discussion on legal pluralism (Cassel 2012). Scholarship on legal pluralism has further developed and become much more diversified. However, one drawback of legal pluralism is that despite its attempts to take into account different legal orders, it still tends to prioritize the law as it is currently understood and does not do justice to other types of normativity. The idea that the pluralism has to be 'legal' and related to a certain definition and understanding of the law inevitably promotes a centrality of the law and tends to dismiss other normativities as nonlaw (Duve 2016). In order to avoid a new asymmetry that sees the law above other normativities, recently legal historians introduced the notion of 'multinormativity' (Duve 2016; Kroll, 2019). This allows the exploration of other modes of normativity that are not necessarily structured by a certain idea of law. The approach of multinormativity allows also to focus on the 'vernacular' law, looking beyond state practice, legal theory, and the decisions of international courts and tribunals and to explore the role of low-level officials and nonlawyers. As part of the multinarrative approach applied to the history of international law in China, authors focused on the normative orders that preceded the introduction of international law in China. They tended to oppose the view that, before the introduction of international law, the Chinese tribute system was the very opposite of a 'proper' or 'modern' legal and political culture. Modern international law represents the fruit of the West and its encounters with other polities and its globalization in the course of the 19th and 20th century. In this sense, the work of Timothy Brook is quite exemplary. He broadens the categories of international law and provides historical accounts of international relations in Asia from the 13th to the 20th century (Brook et al. 2018).

Some of the scholarship that gives credit to the Chinese normative system before the introduction of international law shows how China, within the universal normative order of the *tianxia* and of the tribute system, was not peripheral or semiperipheral. Rather, the rest of the world was peripheral to China. This strategy does partly break away from the view according to which even the most critical analysis of modern international law from a global historical perspective cannot escape the parochialism of European categories. It is the strategy used by those scholars, such as the IR scholar Zhao Tingyang, who are recovering the *tianxia* system as alternative for the global order. According to Zhao, instead of adopting what he considers as a narrow Westphalian view that starts from the sovereign state, one should adopt the global perspective of *tianxia,* in that its point of departure is the world, not the state. In this vision the problem of difference can be resolved through the transformation (*hua* 化) of the many into one. Through its Confucian-Leninist elite, China would initiate and guide this transformation of the world into one. If Zhao's project has been criticized for lacking textual foundation, it has largely been received with enthusiasm in China. International relations professor William Callahan points out that Zhao's rhetoric of *tianxia* is fundamentally based on an absolute distinction between a moral China and an immoral West, and that it is an attempt to justify China's new hegemonic project. *Tianxia* seems to correspond to China and ultimately to the Chinese Communist Party, which can no longer count on the sacredness of *tian* for legitimation and cannot provide cosmological or metaphysical depth to Chinese national claims (Carrai 2019: 224). As Callahan argues, *tianxia*'s ostensible inclusiveness ignores the possibility that not every state may want to participate. Thus, Zhao's theory becomes guilty of the very behavior that he criticizes Western thought for: universalizing a worldview (Callahan 2008). Second, it also worth noting that *tianxia* seems to be present a utopian ideal of world peace without providing an explicit pathway to get there. Zhao's notions of 'common imitation' and 'Confucian improvement' rely on the shaky assumption that all nation states will somehow come to agree upon a set of common interests more important than individual aims (Zhang 2010).

While Zhao' s system is more a utopia of difficult realization, there are also Chinese international jurists that attempted to recover the normative value of the *tianxia* worldview and the tribute system before the introduction of international law and translate them into practical terms producing a risky expansion of sovereign claims of China to its imperial borders. This is the case, for instance, of Jia Bingbing and Gao Zhiguo, who, in order to support the historical sovereign right of China in the South and East China Sea, point to the value of the ancient relationship between China and its neighboring countries prior to 1935 and Chinese 'sovereign' activities in the Sea. Such rights are grounded in the belief that the history of the tributary relationship between China and the tributary states is a valuable source of normativity, functionally equal to that established through international law (Gao & Jia 2013). The risks of some of these accounts of the history of international law in China that exalts the autochthonous normative orders before the introduction of international law include the instrumentalization and politicization of history and new forms of Sinocentrism. If one discusses the *tianxia* or tribute system, it is difficult to discuss the history of 'tributary' relations independently of the role and experience of China and Chinese actors. Thus, also in this context, it is important to eschew a centric analytical perspective to realize the goal of an 'inclusive, pluralist, global history of international law' (Lesaffer 2017) and avoid a risky politicization of history. It is crucial not to regard certain concepts of the 'tributary system' a priori as universal for the East Asian system of interpolity relations, but to open up the perspective for adaptations and contestations also here. The risk otherwise is to move from a type of Eurocentrism to another in the form of Sinocentrism. The latter would promote a selective re-reading of Chinese history in order to justify the current global leadership of the Chinese Communist Party and play down the role in international society of human rights, rule of law, democracy and other values that are too 'Western' and do not conform to the official re-reading of Chinese history.

Conclusion

The histories and strategies used by some of the authors presented here represent only a fraction of a complex and thick plot of authors that contribute to tracing the contours of the nonlinear history of international law in China and the normative orders that preceded the translation of international law in the Middle Kingdom. As China is not a monolithic entity – but rather a country shaped by the myriad of cultures, dialects, and ethnic groups that inhabit it – the same applies for the histories of international law in China, which varied from the center to the periphery of the vast multiethnic and multinormative empire, in which the elite was composed by Manchu, Chinese, Korean, Mongols, Turkic, and Tungstic people, among others. We have observed the risks of Eurocentrism, which presumes the superiority of European culture and effectively alienates any system that does not conform to Western legal institutions, ultimately limiting a genuine understanding of other temporalities and geographies. Akin to the risk of Eurocentrism in research on international law in the 18th and 19th centuries, research on international law in Asia before colonialism is subject to the danger of Sinocentrism and the politicization of the history by Chinese scholars under the new imperatives of China's Great Rejuvenation. While the PRC promotes sovereignty and noninterference, given its global rise and its new interests and investments abroad, this attitude could well change. Not only China has already become more assertive in international forums, like the United Nations, where it has promoted a relativization of human rights, placing the right to development above civil and political liberties, but it could gradually export its model of development, including its authoritarianism abroad. For instance, what used to be the resource-rich backyard of Europe, Africa, will be increasingly under the influence of Beijing. As Rolland has described, the development of new digital infrastructures created around a 5G mobile network provided by Chinese State-Owned Enterprises (SOEs), such as China Mobile and China Unicom, could lead to the creation of a digital market in which data are controlled by Chinese government using standards that incentivize censorship and that limit freedom of speech. In such a world, we could expect people to buy Chinese goods through Unionpay using as a currency the renminbi and adopting the Silk Road e-commerce platform, such as Alibaba's Tmall.com or Jindong's JD.com. The world leading universities could be Chinese and could train on socialism with Chinese characteristics rather than freedom of expression and democracy. The dispute-resolution and arbitration systems could be based in China and independent from the International Center for Settlement of Investments Disputes and could operate without complying with the standards of due process. Google, Twitter, WhatsApp, or Facebook would be replaced by Chinese counterparts and their censorship (Rolland 2017: 142–148). These are just a few examples that allow us to imagine the possible extreme and not completely unrealistic repercussions of Chinese growth on some of the key principles that underpin the so-called liberal world. From a historical perspective, it is central not to regard certain concepts of the 'tributary system' a priori as universal for the East Asian system of interpolity relations in its historical past or in the current attempt to resuscitate them in the present, but to open up the perspective for adaptations and contestations. Moreover, the past does not lead inevitably to the present. Especially in the light of the manipulation and politization of history under the rhetoric of China's dream of great rejuvenation, it should be emphasized that the historiographies of international law in China are not unilinear, in the sense that they emerged from a contingent historical context that can lead to completely different results.

Legal pluralism and multinormativity offer new methods of analysis to study Asian normative past in a way that is more detached from categories that belong to the European public law. As the increased reflection on Eurocentrism in contemporary international law studies, it is necessary to scrutinize and reassess the system of international relations created by non-Western states before modern times and do justice to the way different polities regulated their relations – not only to how norms were created and functioned, but also how they were contested and vernacularized by the 'periphery'. Peripheries are special places of legal transformation where important normative questions are re-negotiated, and normative practices emerge. To promote the development of scholarship that critically reexamines different normative sources and practices, legal, political, religious, and cultural, which have so far hardly been discussed in the context of international relations and international law, it is important to rely on sociolegal scholarship and cultural history that are more detached than jurists from legal categories. Cultural historians often had better answers to this historiographical dilemma than legal historians or international lawyers that attempt to write histories of international law in China having already in mind what they are looking for – rather than allowing history to speak for itself.

Bibliography

Becker Lorca, A. (2014) *Mestizo International Law 1842–1933*, Cambridge: Cambridge University Press.

Benton, L. (2019) 'Beyond Anachronism: Histories of International Law and Global Legal Politics', *Journal of the History of International Law* 21(1), 7, 12.

Boltjes, M., Brook, T., and van Walt van Praag, M. (2018) *Sacred Mandates: Asian International Relations since Chinggis Khan*, Chicago: University of Chicago Press.

Brook, T., M. van Walt van Praag, and M. Boltjes, eds. (2018) *Sacred Mandates: Asian International Relations since Chinggis Khan*, Chicago: University of Chicago Press.

Callahan, W.A. (2008) 'Chinese Vision of World Order', *International Studies Review* 10, 749–761.

Carrai, M. (2019) *Sovereignty in China. A Genealogy of a Concept since 1840*, New York: Cambridge University Press.

Carrai, M. (2020) 'The Politics of History in the late Qing Era: W.A.P. Martin and a History of International Law for China', *The Journal of The History Of International Law / Revue D'histoire Du Droit International* 22, 2–3.

Cassel, P.K. (2012) *Grounds of Judgment: Extraterritoriality and Imperial Power in Nineteenth-Century China and Japan*, Oxford: Oxford University Press.

Chan, P. (2014) *China, State Sovereignty and International Legal Order*, Leiden: Brill Nijhoff Publishers.

Chen, L. (2009) 'Law, Empire, and Historiography of Modern Sino-Western Relations: A Case Study of the Lady Hughes Controversy in 1784', *Law & History Review* 27(1), 1–53.

Chen, L. (2011) 'Universalism and Equal Sovereignty as Contested Myths of International Law in the Sino-Western Encounter', *Journal of the History of International Law* 13(1), 75–116.

Chen, L. (2012) 'Legal Specialists and Judicial Administration in Late Imperial China, 1651–1911', *Late Imperial China* 33(1), 1–54.

Chen, L. (2016) *Chinese Law in Imperial Eyes: Sovereignty, Justice, and Transcultural Politics*, New York: Columbia University Press.

Cogan, J. (2020) 'A History of International Law in the Vernacular', *Journal of the History of International Law* 2–3, pp. 205–217.

Conrad, S. (2017) *What Is Global History?* Princeton, NJ: Princeton University Press.

Craven, M. (2006) 'Introduction: International Law and its Histories', in Matt Craven and Malgosia Fitzmaurice (eds.), *Time, History and International Law*, Leiden: Brill, pp. 1–25.

Deng, Ye. 邓野 (1986) *Bali hehui Zhongguo juyue wenti yanjiu* 巴黎和会中国拒约问题研究 [An Analysis of Issue of the Chinese Rejection of the Treaty at the Paris Conference], Zhongguo shehui kexue 中国社会科学, 2: 131–146.

Duara, P. (1995) *Rescuing History from the Nation: Questioning Narratives of Modern China*, Chicago: University of Chicago Press.

Duve, T. (2016) 'Global Legal History – A Methodological Approach', Max Planck Institute for European Legal History Research Paper Series No. 2016–04.

Fairbank, J.K. (1968) *The Chinese World Order, Traditional China's Foreign Relations*, Cambridge, MA: Harvard University Press.

Fairbank, J.K., and Ch'en, T. (1941) 'On the Ch'ing Tributary System', *Harvard Journal of Asiatic Studies* 6(2), 135–246.

Fassbender, B., and Peters, A. (2012) *The Oxford Handbook of the History of International Law*, Oxford: Oxford University Press.

Galindo, B., and Rodrigo, G. (2005) 'Martti Koskenniemi and the Historiographical Turn in International Law', *The European Journal of International Law*, 16, 3.

Gao, Z., and Jia, B. (2013) 'The Nine-Dash Line in The South China Sea: History, Status, And Implications', *The American Journal of International Law* 107, 98.

Gong, G. (1984) *The Standard of Civilization in International Society*, Oxford: Oxford University Press.

Guantao, J. 金观涛 (2010) *Guannianshi yanjiu: Zhongguo xiandai zhongyao zhengzhi shutu de xingcheng,* 观念史研究：中国现代重要政治术语的形成 [A Research in Conceptual History: The Formation of Important Political Terms in China], Beijing, Falü Chubanshe.

Hamashita, T. (2008) *China, East Asia and the Global Economy: Regional and Historical Perspectives*, London: Routledge.

Hanqin, X. (2011) 'Chinese Contemporary Perspectives on International Law: History, Culture and International Law', *Recueil des cours/ Académie de droit international* 355: 41–234.

He, L. 何力 (2019) 人类命运共同体视角下的国际法史与文明互融 [Evolution of International Law and Fusion of Civilizations from the Perspective of the Community with a Shared Future for Mankind], Journal of Xiamen University 厦门大学学报, 6.

He, Z., Sun, L. 何志鹏, 孙璐 (2015) 中国的国际法观念:基于国际关系史的分析 [The Notion of International Law of China: An Analysis Based on the History of International Relations], Journal of International Relations and International Law (国际关系与国际法学刊), 5.

Hegel, G., and Sibree, J. (1900) *The Philosophy of History*. CADAL, New York: Colonial Press.

Hevia, J. (1994) 'Sovereignty and Subject: Constituting Relationships of Power in Qing Guest Ritual', in Angela Zito and Tani E. (eds.), *Body, Subject and Power in China*, Barlow. Chicago: University of Chicago Press, chap 7.

Hong, J. 洪鈞培 (1939) *Chun qiu guo ji gong fa* 春秋國際公法, Shanghai, Zhonghua shu ju.

Huang, P. (1996) *Civil Justice in China: Representation and Practice in the Qing*, Palo Alto: Stanford University Press.

Huang, P. (2001) *Code, Custom, and Legal Practice in China: The Qing and the Republic Compared*, Palo Alto: Stanford University Press.

Johnston, A. (2019) 'China in a World of Orders: Rethinking Compliance and Challenge in Beijing's International Relations', *International Security* 44(2), 9–60.

Koskenniemi, M. (2004) 'International Law and Hegemony: A Reconfiguration', *Cambridge Review of International Affairs* 17(2), 197–218.

Koskenniemi, M. (2011) 'Histories of International Law: Dealing with Eurocentrism', *Rechtsgeschichte – Legal History* 2011(19), pp. 215–240.

Koskenniemi, M. (2013) 'Histories of International Law. Significance and Problems for a Critical View', *Temple International and Comparative Law Journal* 27(2), 215–240.

Koskenniemi, M., Rech, W., and Jiménez Fonseca, M. (Eds.) (2017) *International Law and Empire. Historical Explorations*, Oxford: Oxford University Press.

Krasner, S. (1999) *Sovereignty. Organized Hypocrisy*, Princeton: Princeton University Press.

Kroll, S. (2016) 'Zooming in on Norm Research. Towards a Suitable Scale for the Shanghai Mixed Court', *Global Constitutionalism* 5(3), 383–404.

Kroll, S. (2019) 'International Orders in Late Imperial Period.' Paper presented at the Conference 'Legal Pluralism in Asia and Global Histories of International Law(s)' on September 2019, Harvard University.

Lai, J. 赖骏楠 (2011) 误读下的新世界:晚清国人的国际法印象 [The Misread New World: Impression of International Law of the Chinese in Late Qing Dynasty], Tsinghua Discourses on Rule of Law (清华法治论衡), No. 1.

Lam, H.-C. 林學忠 (2009) *Cong wanguo gongfa dao gongfa waijiao* 从万国公法到公法外交 [From the Law of Nations to International Diplomacy], Shanghai, Shanghai Guji Chubanshe.

Lesaffer, R. (2017) *The Cambridge History of International Law, General Outline*, Cambridge: Cambridge University Press.

Levenson, J. (1965) *Confucian China and Its Modern Fate*, Vol. 3, London: Routledge & Kegan Paul.

Liu, L. (1995) *Translingual Practice, Literature, National Culture and Translated Modernity – China, 1900–1937*, Stanford: Stanford University Press.

Liu, L. 刘利民 (2010) *Bu ping deng tiao yue yu Zhongguo jin dai ling shui zhu quan wen ti yan jiu* 不平等条约与中国近代领水主权问题研究, Changsha, Hunan ren min chu ban she.

Liu, W. 刘文明 (2014) *19 shijimo ouzhou guojifa zhong de 'wenming' biaozhun 19* 世纪末欧洲国际法中的'文明'标准 [The Civilization Standard of International Law in 19th Century Europe], World History, Shijie lishi 世界历史, 1.

Mutua, M., and Anghie, A. (2000) 'What Is TWAIL?' *Proceedings of the Annual Meeting American Society of International Law* 94, 31–40.

Martin, W.A.P. (1998) *Wan guo gong fa* 《萬國公法》, Taibei, Zhongguo guo ji fa xue hui.

Martin, W.A.P. (2012) 'Traces of International Law in Ancient China', *Chinese Recorder and Missionary Journal* 13–14.

Masini, F. (1993) *The Formation of Modern Chinese Lexicon and Its Evolution toward a National Language: The Period from 1840 to 1898*, Berkeley, CA: Project on Linguistic Analysis.

Neff, S. (2014) *Justice among Nations: A History of International Law*, Cambridge, MA: Harvard University Press.

Ping, Y. (2014) 'The View of Early 20th Century Chinese Intellectuals on Ancient China's International Law', *Peking University Law Journal*, 2, 2.

Roberts, A. (2017) *Is International Law International?* Oxford: Oxford University Press.

Rolland, N. (2017) *China's Eurasian Century? Political and Strategic Implications of the Belt and Road Initiative*, Seattle, WA, and Washington, DC: The National Bureau of Asian Research.

Ruskola, T. (2013) *Legal Orientalism: China, the United States, and Modern Law*. Cambridge, MA: Harvard University Press.

Shogo, S. (2009) *Civilization and Empire. China and Japan's Encounter with European International Society*, London and New York: Routledge.

So, K. and So, S. (2018) 'Commercial Arbitration Transplanted: A Tale of the Book Industry in Modern Shanghai', in *Chinese Legal Reform And The Global Legal Order: Adoption And Adaptation*, Cambridge: Cambridge University Press, pp. 238–256.

Sun, Y. 孙玉荣 (1999) *Gu dai Zhongguo guo ji fa yan jiu* 古代中国国际法研究, Beijing Shi, Zhongguo zheng fa da xue chu ban she.

Svarverud, R. (2007) *International Law as World Order in Late Imperial China: Translation, Reception and Discourse*, 1847–1911, Leiden: Brill.

Svarverud, R. (2008) *International Law as World Order in Late Imperial China. Translation, Reception and Discourse*, 1847–1911, Leiden: Brill.

Tang, Q. 唐启华 (1998) *Minguo chunian Beijing zhengfu xiuyue waijiao zhi mengya* 民国初年北京政府' '修约外交' 之萌芽, *1912–1918*, [The Origin of the Treaty Revision Diplomacy of the Beijing Government at the Beginning of the Republican Period, 1912–1918], Wenshixue bao 文史学报 28: 118–143.

Tang, Q. 唐启华 (2005) *Qingmo min chu zhongguo dui haiya baohe hui zhi canyu* 清末民初中国对'海牙保和会'之参与 [Chinese Attitude toward the Hague Conferences in the Period Between the End of the Qing and the Beginning of the Republican Era], Guoli zhengzhi daxue lixue bao 国立政治大学历史学报, 23: 45–90.

Tang, Q. 唐启华 (2010) *Bei feichu bu pingdeng tiaoyue zhebi de beiyang xiu yue shi* 被'废除不平等条约'遮蔽的北洋修约史(*1912–1928*)[The Abrogation of Unequal Treaties: The Obscured History of the Diplomacy of Treaty Revision of the Beijing Government (1912–1928)], Beijing, Shehui kexue wenya chuban she.

Tian, T.田涛 (2001) *Guo ji fa shu ru yu wan Qing Zhongguo* 国际法输入与晚清中国, Jinan Shi, Jinan chu ban she.

Vec, M. (2012) 'Universalization, Particularization, and Discrimination. European Perspectives on a Cultural History of the 19th Century International Law', *InterDisciplines* 2, 79–101.

Wang, D. (2003) 'The Discourse of Unequal Treaties in Modern China'. *Pacific Affairs* 76(3), 399–425.

Wang, D. (2004) *China's Unequal Treaties: Narrating National History*, New York: Lexington Books.

Wang, D. (2004) 'Redeeming A Century of National Ignominy: Nationalism and Party Rivalry Over the Unequal Treaties, 1928–1947', *Twentieth-Century China* 30(2), 72–100.

Wang, D. (2008) *China's Unequal Treaties, Narrating National History*, New York: Lexington Books.

Wang, H. (2008) 'The liberation of the Object and the Interrogation of Modernity, Rethinking the Rise of Modern Chinese Thought', *Modern China* 34(1), 114–140.

Wang, J. (2015) *Unequal Treaties and China*, Beijng: SilkroadPress.

Wang, T. 王铁崖 (1991) *International Law in China: Historical and Contemporary Perspectives*, Recueil des cours 2 (1990): 195–370; Wang Tieya, *Zhongguo yu guojifa-lishi yu dangdai* 中国与国际法一历史与当代 [China and International Law: Past and Present], Zhongguo guoji baokan 中国国际法报刊 70.

Wang, T. 王铁崖 (1995) *Guojifa* 国际法 [International Law], Beijing, Falü Chuban she.

Wang, T., and Wei, M. 王鐵崖, 魏敏 (1995) *Guojifa* 國際法[International law]. Beijing: Falv chuban she.

Xiaofeng, H., and Sun, Y. 懷效鋒, 孫玉 (2000) *Gu dai Zhongguo guo ji fa shi liao* 古代中國國際法史料, Beijing, Zhongguo zheng fa da xue chu ban she.

Xu, C. 徐傳寶 (1931) *Xian Qin guo ji fa zhi yi ji* 先秦國際法之遺跡, Shanghai, Xu Chuanbao.

Xu, J. (许纪霖) 'Xin tianxia xhuyi – shijie lishi de zhongguo shike 新天下主义 – 世界历史中的中国时刻' [New Tatungism – The China Era in World History] available at http://www.chinalecture.com/lecture/play9786.html.

Xu, J. 许纪霖 (2014) *Guojia renting yu jia guo tianxia* 国家认同与家国天下 [National Identity and National Tianxia], Huadong shifan daxue xuebao zhe sheban 华东师范大学学报哲社版4.

Xu, Z. 许章润 (2015) *Lun 'jiaguo tianxia' – duiyu yi weida gudian hanyu xiuci yili neihan de wenhua zhengzhi xue chanfa*, 论 '家国天下' – 对于这一伟大古典汉语修辞义理内涵的文化政治学阐发 [On the 'jiaguotianxia' – An Explanation of the Cultural and Political Elements of the Connotation of this Great Classical Chinese Rhetorical Principles], Xueshu yuekan 学术月刊.

Xue, H. (2011) 'Chinese Contemporary Perspectives on International Law: History, Culture and International Law', *Recueil des cours/Académie de droit international* 355(2011), 41–234.

Yang, Z. 杨泽伟(2001) 宏观国际法史 [Macro-History of International Law], Wuhan University Press (武汉大学出版社).

Yi, Ping 易平(2014) 被遗忘的话语 – 20世纪初期中国学者严重的中国古代国际法, 中国国际法年刊.

Zarrow, P. (2012) *After Empire: The Conceptual Transformation of the Chinese State, 1885–1924*, Stanford, CA: Stanford University Press.

Zeng, T., and Wang, H. 曾涛, 汪晖 (2004) Xiandai Zhongguo Sixiang de xingqi 现代中国思想的兴起, Vol 1 (Sanlian shudian).

Zhang, F. (2010) 'The Tianxia System: World Order in a Chinese Utopia', *China Heritage Quarterly* 21. http://www.chinaheritagequarterly.org/tien-hsia.php?searchterm=021_utopia.inc&issue=021

Zhang, Y. 章永乐 (2016) 从萨义德到中 国《法律东方主义》的一种读法 [From Said to China: A Reading of 'Legal Orientalism'], *Zhongguo falu pinglun* 中国法律评论. 4.

Zhao, Y., and Ng, M. (Eds.) (2017) *Chinese Legal Reform and the Global Legal Order: Adoption and Adaptation*, Cambridge: Cambridge University Press.

Zhou, G. 周更生(1929) *Guojifa dagang* 国际法大纲 [A Manual of International Law], Shanghai, Shangwu yinshuguan faxing.

Zhou, G. 周更生(1976) *Guo ji fa* 国际法 [International Law], Beijing, Shang wu yin shu guan.

17

Marx in China

William Leon McBride

Introduction

In a certain sense, Karl Marx is virtually everywhere in today's world. His presence is certainly felt strongly in China. Separate Schools of Marxism are to be found in Chinese universities. Textbooks teaching an approved version of that philosophy are legion. 'Marxism' remains an approved name for the official ideology of the government. In the course of its evolution in China, Marxism has undergone a process of Sinicization, which a Chinese colleague of mine ideally defines as 'the organic combination of the basic principles of Marxism and the reality of China'. And so, reciprocally, a very large statue of Marx was donated by the Chairman of the People's Republic of China, Xi Jinping (习近平), to the city of Trier, Marx's birthplace, on the occasion of the two hundredth anniversary of his birth in 2018 and accepted, although not without dissent among members of the city council.

But there is a paradoxical aspect to this whole state of affairs. After all, Marx himself, while very much a scholar of history, knew comparatively little about the history of China. His sociopolitical and philosophical theory made use of a European philosophical approach to reality known as 'dialectics', especially indebted to his near-contemporary fellow German, Hegel, and directed above all to the rigorous criticism of the ascendant Western economic system known as capitalism. How is it that the spirit and thinking of Marx have come to occupy such pride of place in 21st-century China? An excellent question.

The present contribution to this handbook will be divided into, roughly, three main parts. The first will aim briefly to recount the early years of the history of Marx in China, a history whose principal roots date back scarcely more than half of the two centuries before 2018. The second part will concentrate on the adoption of Marx's thought by Communist China's most colossal figure and long-time ruler, Mao Zedong (毛泽东). And the third and longest will consist of an honest effort to try to answer a question that plagues and to some extent puzzles both Chinese intellectuals and outside observers: Just what place do Marx and Marx's thought *really* occupy, beyond labels and slogans, in contemporary China?

DOI: 10.4324/9780429059704-21

The early years of Marx in China

At the beginning of the 20th century, as far as scholars can ascertain, not a single text of Marx's had been published in Chinese translation. *The Universal Communiqué*, published in Shanghai in 1899, contained the first known introduction of Marx to China. Ling Quichao (梁启超), who had participated in the Reform Movement of 1898, published an article introducing Marx's thought in 1902. Two years later, a translated citation appeared in print from a rather anodyne portion of *The Communist Manifesto*, the section in which it is said that, while different policies will need to be implemented in different countries, certain policies (e.g., free elementary education for all, centralization of the means of communication and transport in the hands of the state) will be generally applicable. By the time of the beginning of World War I, when the revolution that ended the Chinese empire had taken place, some more of Marx's writings were in print in Chinese translation, but still relatively few. Some Chinese intellectuals were able to read Japanese, and much more of Marx's work was available in that language. By the time of the 'official' founding meeting of the Chinese Communist Party in July 1921, there were also some who read Russian. The two individuals whom historians generally regard as most important in that founding (neither of whom, ironically, was present at the actual meeting), Chen Duxiu (陈独秀) and Li Ta-Chao (李大钊), had both spent brief periods of time in Japan and had presumably become more aware of Marx's growing global influence while there.

The 'teen' years of the 20th century were extremely chaotic both politically and intellectually in China, so that no simple, straightforward account of just how Marx rose to ascendancy is possible, but it is safe to say that Peking University played an important role in this process: During brief periods of time, Chen Duxiu served as Dean of its School of Arts and Letters, and Li Ta-Chao was the university librarian. During an even briefer period, the winter of 1918–1919, Mao Zedong was an assistant in that library and participated in formal discussions of political texts, including especially those of Marx, with the director and others.

What appears to have motivated Li and especially Chen to embrace Marxism, however, was not so much the intellectual attractiveness of Marx's thought relative to other competing theoretical orientations that were abroad at the time – anarchism, liberalism, versions of social democracy, and so forth – but rather, above all, the success of the October (1917) Revolution in Russia. Chen, who identified himself with the 'New Youth' (新青年), announced his conversion to Bolshevism and his consequent commitment to what came commonly to be called 'Marxism-Leninism'. At the same time, and indeed throughout the earlier and later reorientations revealed in his extensive essay writings, he retained a deep sense of rootedness in Chinese tradition and a sense of the historical uniqueness of China. In fact, it would have been difficult for any of the young Communist intellectuals of the time (Chen was older than most of this group) to disregard the need to adapt their actions and their ideology to the special situation of China. In other words, 'socialism [or Communism] with Chinese characteristics' was built into the reception of Marx in China from the beginning.

Another very important historical event of the end of the 'teen' years was the movement of May 4, 1919, in which people gave expression to their pent-up fury over the effects on China of Western imperialism and disillusionment with the West, a disillusionment that was intensified by the Treaty of Versailles, which gave considerable recognition to Japan but virtually none to China. The seeds had been sown for Marx's appearance in China. The first full Chinese translation of *The Communist Manifesto*, by Cheng Wangdao (陈望道), appeared in August 1920, and important secondary works about Marxist theory soon began to appear, as well, notably *Historical Materialist Interpretation, Marx's Economic Theory,* and *Overview of Social Issues*, all translated by Li Da (李达).

Given the importance of the Russian Revolution as a model in this context, it should not be surprising that ideological issues and disputes dominating the new Russian landscape began almost immediately to be taken up within the still very small milieu of Chinese Communists, geographically divided for a time mainly between a northern group centered in Beijing – Zhou Enlai (周恩来) organized a Consciousness Society in nearby Tianjin – and a southern group centered in Shanghai, where the official inaugural meeting, consisting of just 13 representatives, was actually held in July 1921. (As I have already mentioned, neither Chen Duxiu nor Li Ta-Chao was able to attend; Mao Zedong was one of the 13.) The problem of whether a party that called itself, in accordance with Marxian analysis, the 'party of the proletariat', could legitimately rule over a country like Russia that was far behind Western countries in industrial capacity and portion of its population engaged in factory work became even more acute when applied to China, the greatest part of the population of which, far vaster than that of Russia, consisted of peasantry and other individuals engaged in preindustrial or nonindustrial types of work.

The question of whether China needed, in accordance with what Marx was thought to have regarded as necessary historical sequence (even though, in fact, in a letter to a Russian newspaper he had disavowed such rigid thinking), China would have to pass through a period of bourgeois dominance before undergoing a proletarian revolution soon became linked with the practical issue of how the Communists should relate to the Kuomintang, the party of Sun Yat-Sen (孙中山). A delegate of the Comintern (International) sent from Russia to China, who went by the pseudonym of Maring, put pressure on Chen, as the Party's First Secretary, and the others to form a united front (统一战线) with the Kuomintang (which was itself highly factionalized), and they agreed, albeit in Chen's case reluctantly. The growing tensions in Russia itself between Stalin and Trotsky, which eventually resulted in Trotsky's departure for exile in Mexico, included a disagreement over China policy: Trotsky opposed the 'united front' idea. Within a few years, Chen began openly to assert strong pro-Trotskyite views and was expelled from the Communist Party that he, more than any other single individual, had founded. He lived for some years thereafter without exerting any serious influence on his country's affairs. Meanwhile, the Guomintang itself, under the leadership of Chiang Kai-Shek, ended the united front by turning violently on its erstwhile Communist partners in 1927.

Mao Zedong and Marx's philosophy

While Chen's grasp of Marxist theory was apparently never very profound or extensive, one hesitates to make the same assertion regarding the person who gradually became the embodiment of Chinese Marxism-Leninism, Mao Zedong. Mao was an avid reader of the Marxist classics, which in his early adult years he regularly discussed with his comrades. Among the most notable of these was the scholar Li Da, who was to serve for 13 years as President of Wuhan University. Mao, himself from a peasant background, found no difficulty with the idea of a peasant revolution carried out in Marx's name. The story of the eventual triumph of the Communists under Mao's leadership – their near defeat in the early 1930s, the heroic 'Long March' (长征) across the country, from southeast to northwest, in 1934, the reuniting of the enemies during the long period of Japanese occupation of most of China, and the renewed warfare leading to the flight of the Guomintang to Taiwan and the proclamation of the People's Republic on the Mainland – is interesting in its own right, although its connection with Marx is, at best, indirect and tenuous. Can the same be said concerning some of the major policy initiatives undertaken by Mao during the many years of his rule, most notably the 'Great Proletarian Cultural Revolution' of Mao's later years, which caused so much upheaval and resulted in great hardship for so many? I doubt it; I cannot imagine that Marx, if he had been alive, would have applauded that initiative of Mao's. Yet Mao himself put enormous stress on the very close connection between theory and practice, and so it may be useful to make a few remarks about Mao as theoretician, by way of background to the question of Marx's place in China in recent years up to the present.

Mao Zedong was especially intrigued by the dialectical method as key to both theory and practice. The ability to think dialectically, that is, in terms of contradictions and their overcoming at a new level, seems to have been very helpful to him in developing strategy. His strategy was not always successful, of course, but this affinity for dialectics seems to have contributed to his understanding both of past history and of current society, as well as to his vision of the future. In addition, the underlying spirit of Marx, which above all sought to unmask and end exploitation, certainly motivated Mao strongly throughout his long career, even though, once again, his actions were not always faithful to that spirit. Mao understood very well that Marx had seen himself as a child of his own times and society, a keen analyst, but not a purveyor of supposed eternal truths in the style of both Western and Eastern classical philosophers. He insisted, throughout his career, on the importance of studying Marx's works – always with a view to applying them in practice, not simply in order to learn the theory better – and he was known to lament the decline, at least at one time, of interest in Marx in China, regretting that Marx's thought was no longer so fashionable.

Can Mao be said to have interpreted Marx's philosophy in such a way as to add to and/or alter it? I would say 'yes and no'. For one thing, Mao thought of Marxism as being Marxism-Leninism, and he wrote, somewhat indifferently, about the philosophy in its hyphenated and unhyphenated versions. (One can even find the more hyphenated version, 'Marxism-Leninism-Stalinism', in Mao's writings, but less frequently.) In keeping with Mao's strong interest in contradiction, he developed a distinction, not to be found (to the best of my knowledge) in Marx, between antagonistic and nonantagonistic contradictions (that is, contradictions between hostile forces as distinct from contradictions within the Party and movement). Given the force of circumstances in Mao's life, he devoted considerable attention to analyses, not to be found anywhere in Marx's work, of the military, in which Mao emphasizes the importance of mutual respect both between officers and ordinary soldiers – not so common as one would have wished in the armies of his day – and between the army and the people. In discussing the need for such respect he did not hesitate to use the language of democracy. He accepted the Leninist idea, to which I shall return later, of democratic centralism (民主集中制), combining an insistence on the importance of discussion and an equally strong insistence on adhering to the views of the majority once a decision has been reached. He also, at one point, famously launched the notion of 'letting a hundred flowers bloom', referring both to diverse artistic styles and schools in science, about which there are no close parallels in Marx. (But of course Marx was never in a position, as Mao was over so many years, of initiating cultural or social policies.) So much for some of the topics that are not to be found in Marx upon which Mao dwelled in his writings.

Nevertheless, Mao's continued adherence to Marx appears, at least from his writings, to have been sincere enough, and this seems to be best borne out by his equation of Marxism with objectivity and by his commitment to what he once called Marxist philosophy's two great characteristics, practicality (the interconnection of theory and practice) and class nature. Mao developed and elaborated on different class conceptions, based on the structure of Chinese society (e.g., poor peasants, middle peasants, and rich peasants), beyond Marx's standard class opposition of bourgeoisie and proletariat, but he always returned to the importance of class struggle. This is well illustrated by a late-in-life reflection on the ascendancy of Nikita Khrushchev in the Soviet Union after Stalin's death: as far as Mao was concerned, Khrushchev was a revisionist, contributing to the re-emergence of the bourgeoisie in that country, and he warned against the emergence of a similar revisionism in China. He presciently foresaw a bright future for China as an advanced industrial society. To summarize, Mao regarded himself as a Marxist, one for whom Marxism was a living reality, not a mere abstract theory. (He denounced as 'liberals' those who thought that Marxism was simply a set of interesting dogmas.) However, one may still ask the question, of interest to Marx scholars if to no one else, as I have with respect to the Cultural Revolution, as to how much Marx would have seen himself in Mao's writings and policies. This leads us to the further questions, which by their nature must, for different reasons, remain somewhat open-ended, 'What would Mao think about Marx's place in China today?' and 'What are we to say about it?

Marx in contemporary China

Perhaps a story about a personal encounter of mine would be a good way of beginning my outsider's analysis of Marx in China today. Early in the period of China's opening up to Western visitors, I had the privilege of leading a small group of American philosophers on a trip that combined tourism with academic encounters. One of our stops was at a Confucian center which had recently reopened. In the middle of our discussion, one of the Chinese scholars suggested that perhaps we foreign colleagues could help resolve a major theoretical problem: how to reconcile Marxism, Confucianism, and free market economics. He and his teacher, who was also present, then began to argue about whether, as one put it, it was possible to accept a 180-degree change of perspective. Needless to say, we colleagues had no immediate solution to offer.

The question was, and remains, very appropriate within the intellectual atmosphere of contemporary China, although it is usually not stated quite so bluntly. And the intellectual atmosphere is of greater importance, perhaps, than in most countries, both because China has such a long, though one cannot say uninterrupted, history of respect for learning and because adherence to Marxism, however that is to be understood, has been central to the Chinese Communist Party since its inception. It is not insignificant in this regard that the flag of the CCP resembles the national flag except that, in place of the stars on the latter, the hammer and sickle symbol is displayed. This symbol, developed at the time of the Russian Revolution, is an apt reminder of the fact that the peasantry, the sickle-wielders, was considered an important element in Communist revolutions from the start, even though neither Marx nor his colleague Engels put much stock in its potential to abet revolutionary change. (In fact, as Marx noted and endeavored to explain in his account of mid-19th-century France, *The Eighteenth Brumaire of Louis Bonaparte*, a sizable portion of the peasantry at that time was politically reactionary.)

So the capacity to adapt Marxism to different times and circumstances goes back to the beginning. It is a bit ironic, in this regard, that, as I have said, the first Marxian text to be published in Chinese translation was a passage in *The Communist Manifesto* listing certain policy principles that were said to be generally applicable despite the fact that the political situations of different countries were such as to call for different measures in different places. The *Manifesto* itself had at one point been supposed to be written in dogmatic, catechetical style, which had apparently been Engels' preference. But the more rhetorical approach, in some ways dogmatic but in other ways open-ended, that was eventually employed was undoubtedly far more persuasive and, I believe, more in keeping with the spirit of Marx's thought.

However, the spirit of dogmatism crept early into the Communist Party tradition as it evolved. It can be seen to some extent already in Engels' own later work, in the polemics within the German Social Democratic Party, and certainly in the writings of Lenin. Lenin had the remarkable quality of making numerous contributions, if that is what they are to be called, to Marxist theory (in epistemology, the reflection theory of cognition; in practical strategy, the idea of the Vanguard Party; and so on) and at the same time insisting on strict adherence to the truths emanating from the texts of Marx. A very important part of this achievement in the domain of practice was Lenin's elaboration of the doctrine of 'democratic centralism', which, at least in principle, encouraged discussion of the line to be taken by the party and then, once a decision was made, demanded unwavering adherence to that decision. Over the decades that followed in the Soviet Union under Stalin, the dogmatic ideology (well, the meaning of 'ideology' as I am using it here is not entirely in keeping with Marx's own usage of the term, but that is another story) that came to be known as dialectical materialism, or 'diamat' for short, became entrenched in the textbooks of the Soviet Bloc. This self-styled 'orthodox Marxism' sclerosed, as Jean-Paul Sartre aptly expressed it.

Now, as a general point, no complex philosophy or other systematic theory (e.g., a religion) is capable of surviving across decades, much less centuries, without being subjected to diverse and usually competing interpretations and emendations – I can at least be dogmatic in making this assertion. So it was inevitable that Marx, upon his entry into China and subsequent residence therein, would take on new characteristics, especially Chinese characteristics. But of course what is meant by 'Chinese characteristics' is by no means univocally understood, either. With this in mind, I would like to consider, in turn, three major areas in which Marx's thought and spirit can be brought to confront the China of today, the China of the beginning of the third decade of our twenty-first century: religion, the free market, and relations with the outside world. The focus of this analysis will be primarily conceptual and intellectual, with historical events serving as necessary backdrop.

Whether Confucianism should be considered, strictly speaking, a religion is a debate that I leave to specialists in religious studies. In any case, it as well as other ethical and spiritual movements, such as Buddhism (in which early-20th-century Chinese intellectuals, notably Chen Duxiu, took considerable interest in their youth), certainly played a central role in the history of Chinese culture. Marx himself obviously believed, as his early writings, which were unknown to the founders of Chinese Communism, show very clearly, that the practice of religion would die away in a socialist society of the future. (While Marx, at least in his theoretical works and contrary to what some scholars continue to insist, did not try to present a definitive prediction of future events and refused to offer a blueprint for the society of the future, believing that that society would need to be shaped by its members, he did have certain expectations concerning aspects of present-day society that would be absent from it.) His most famous characterization of religion, which is to be found in these early writings, is that it is 'the opium of the people' – meaning, as Marx explained it, that religion served as a balm and defense against a cruel world for ordinary human beings in the way that opium, which was quite expensive at the time, served for the wealthy. (Marx's very infrequent references to China do include allusions to the Opium Wars.) Stalin, a former seminarian, was fiercely hostile to religion and decreed the destruction of many churches, although his hostility was not enough to obviate a religious revival in Russia after the Soviet Union collapsed. What, then, about religion in China today, especially in light of the continued importance of Marx?

I cannot offer a really comprehensive account of the role of religion in contemporary China, for that would require an essay in itself. I am aware of recent efforts by the Vatican to negotiate the possible restoration of its ties with Chinese Catholics who practice their religion in separation from it, I have visited a Protestant seminary west of Shanghai and a Buddhist seminary in Xiamen, and I know from many sources that religions of various sorts are practiced by many Chinese, some to the strong disapproval of the authorities and some with their (at least grudging) consent. I do, however, want to suggest a link, one that is by no means a secret or a mystery, between China's Marxist heritage and the revival of Confucianism that has taken place with varying degrees of approval by those same authorities. This approval has waxed and waned over relatively brief periods of time in recent years, and will no doubt continue to wax and wane. I will not attempt to enter into the details of this process, because, to repeat, my interest here is in the intellectual relationship to the spirit of Marx. One development that is at least symbolically significant in this process and that bears noting is the creation of so-called 'Confucian Institutes', funded by the Chinese governments, affiliated with non-Chinese universities worldwide. The faculties of some universities have objected to the at least partial control over appointments to these institutes that this practice concedes to their donor, and some have been closed, but this is not my concern here, either. My single question is, why the Confucian revival in Marx's China?

One obvious answer to this question is that the sayings and thought of Confucius, brought into and adapted to the realities of the modern world (e.g., the advocacy of greater respect for the role of women), are a powerful intellectual achievement that deserves to be preserved and studied. (Among recent writers in China, Tu Weiming (杜维明) has been an especially important advocate of this idea, the idea of 'Neo-Confucianism'.) At the same time, however, many who care about Chinese culture, including but not only those in government, have expressed grave concern over the new form of 'materialism', to wit, strong consumerism, that has become a deeply ingredient part of contemporary Chinese society. Perhaps the slogan, 'Enrich yourselves', should never have been uttered, but it is too late now: there are too many millionaires in contemporary China. So there is a strong desire, on the part of well-meaning people in China, to instill a greater sense of ethical principles especially in the younger generation, and the figure of Confucius serves as a powerful model.

But where does this leave our Sinicized Marx? It is fair to say that Marx never wrote an ethics, and that he and Engels were both highly skeptical of claims about the existence of objective eternal ethical truths. It would be terribly wrong, though, to assert that Marx had no ethical perspective. No serious person who has read carefully through the pages of *Capital*, for example, long footnotes and all, can avoid the realization that Marx had a profound sense of the evil, the inequities, of the system that he analyzed, reinforced by the often outrageous defenses of it by economists and others whom he cites. Marx himself was an extremely hard-working individual, saved from possibly dire poverty by the help of his better-off colleague Engels, a person whose real though deliberately open-ended vision of a better future society can be deployed to reinforce the kinds of ethical perspectives that, whether one calls them 'religious' or not, the Confucian revival is meant to convey and inculcate. This is a task to which some Chinese philosophers of education, particularly elementary and secondary education, have set themselves.

The reconciliation of Marx with free market capitalism is a larger challenge than that of reconciling him with Confucianism, or at least Neo-Confucianism; in fact, when expressed straightforwardly, it is impossible. But, while many observers claim that China's contemporary economic system is fundamentally capitalist, fewer would be comfortable with the 'free market' part of this designation, given the extent to which regulation by the government is ultimately overriding. *The Communist Manifesto* contains one paragraph in which 'free buying and selling' are mentioned as bourgeois slogans. There it is said that, if these words mean anything, they may be applicable to the difference between buying and selling within capitalism and the limited, highly controlled conditions of buying and selling under feudalism. On the other hand, it says, 'free buying and selling' mean nothing when applied to a future society in which buying and selling are themselves abolished. To put it mildly, this has not yet occurred in China, as the previously-mentioned concern over consumerism makes abundantly evident.

On the other hand, I am not at all sure just what the abolition of buying and selling means, and I suspect that many scholars, both inside and outside China, would be equally baffled if asked to explain it. In the West, there are strong and persuasive advocates of what is called 'market socialism', and among them are many who claim to take their inspiration from Marx, even though market socialism was never his expressed ideal. The broader context of the *Manifesto* paragraph in question is Marx's (and Engels') insistence on the hypocrisy and manipulation involved in the assertion, by the defenders of capitalism, that 'freedom' and individualism are the hallmarks of a system that is in fact extremely exploitative of individuals, favoring the wealthy few over the mass of the population. This is a dominant theme in virtually all of his writings. If resurrected in today's China, Marx would undoubtedly be pleased to know that that country's tens of thousands of serious scholars of his ideas continue, at least for the most part, to recognize and accept this fundamental element of his critical theory. Whether he would be equally pleased with official China's endorsement of what many have called a system of 'state capitalism', one that is market-oriented but subject to fairly rigorous controls, much less with its participation in the world trade system as it is currently constructed, is a very serious question. (The thorny issue of 'free trade' roiled Marx's England and occupied his attention throughout his adult years.)

This brings me to the third of the areas of Marx's thought that I wish to consider in light of today's China, namely, international relations. I am forced once again to turn to *The Communist Manifesto* to bring out the best-known of Marx's statements on this subject. There, it is said that the workers of the world have no country, and the document's ringing conclusion calls for the workers of the world to unite. Marx himself, of course, lived the bulk of his life in England, far from Trier, and spent short periods of time in Paris and (even shorter) Belgium. He was a true cosmopolitan, in many senses of the term. He was a correspondent for a New York newspaper until the American Civil War forced a suspension of this activity, and he wrote extensively on the condition of India under British rule. It was from a newspaper review in Saint Petersburg, Russia, that he took such encouragement as to make it the focus of his important Afterword to the Second German Edition of *Capital*. As I have pointed out, the Russian Revolution and the so-called 'International' that was established in the Soviet Union in the aftermath of that revolution played a highly significant role in the history of the founding and the early years of the Chinese Communist Party. But, as everyone knows, the reality of socialist internationalism often fell far short of the ideal, and there were many tensions and conflicts between and among socialist countries, notably between China and the USSR, over the years. China was not a member of the postwar Warsaw Pact. During a period after the collapse of that alliance and then the breakup of the Soviet Union itself, it was not uncommon to hear Russian scholars, or indeed ordinary Russian people, express envy of the People's Republic of China, which has now lasted longer as a political institution than the USSR itself did, for its comparative prosperity. In short, the world of today, despite the World Trade Organization and the vast interdisciplinary literature of recent decades examining the phenomenon of 'globalization', a phenomenon that suffuses much of Marx's work *avant la lettre*, remains much more of a Westphalian world, a world of nation-states and often accompanying nationalisms, than might have been imagined when the PRC was proclaimed three-quarters of a century ago.

Equally unimaginable to most observers back then (perhaps not including Mao Zedong) was the preeminent role that China now plays in this world. My concern here, however, is less with great power politics than it is with the extent to which the world-outlook of the Chinese people, if one can speak of such a thing, retains any element of Marx's thought with respect to the other peoples on this planet. (There is also the special issue of ethnic minorities in China and their world-outlook, but it would not be possible, out of considerations of space, to explore this adequately in the current discussion of Marx in China.) At the height of Mao Zedong's power and influence, there was an insistence on ideological conformity (not that everyone actually conformed, of course) that resulted in a highly paradoxical Chinese Marxist provincialism. Mao himself, however, always insisted that Chinese patriotism and Communist internationalism should go hand-in-hand. The opening to the world that followed in the years after Mao's death was not merely geographical, with many visitors coming to China and Chinese beginning to travel abroad in substantial numbers, but also intellectual: a living Marx would have begun to think of himself as less unique in China than in the earlier days when his name was constantly invoked but used in very unaccustomed ways. Marx scholarship, not just the rote teaching of a few basic 'principles', flourished, and Marx scholars from other countries began to feel welcome in China. If a professional philosopher's bias may be allowed to display itself here, I like to think of the 2018 quinquennial World Congress of Philosophy, held in Beijing and hosting a record number of participants, in virtually equal quantities, both from China and from the rest of the world, as a quintessential moment of this intellectual opening. Marx was of course celebrated in many sessions of the Congress, especially given the significance of his two hundredth birthday year, but so were many other Eastern and Western philosophers alike. The final plenary session, at the end of the week, featured a tribute to Marx by an American philosopher, myself, speaking about 'Marx at the World Congress and in the World'. Whatever the underlying tensions, which are always there, the interconnected nature of the world, very much in the spirit of Marx, was emphasized and accepted at this Congress.

At the time of the writing of this paper, the effects of the insidious COVID-19 virus, which originated in Wuhan, are being strongly felt almost everywhere, with ruinous consequences for domestic economies and for world trade as well as for world health. It would be foolish to devote much effort to imagining how Marx would have reacted to these events, except to note that he was an unwavering materialist, with a strong belief in the power of nature, as well as a sufferer from physical problems in his later years, and so he would have accepted the tragic reality of the current situation calmly and without resorting to superstition or wild conspiracy theories. As far as the pandemic's longer-range effects on China itself and the entire international order are concerned, one can only speculate at this point, but my guess is that they will be profound. It is difficult to be precise at this stage as to how much the thought of Marx is relevant to this state of affairs, but it is at least important to note that that thought militates against the ultraindividualism evinced by vocal minorities in Western countries, particularly the United States, who, invoking the spirit of a certain conception of capitalism, have denounced emergency regulations to lessen the danger as assaults on their freedom, and therefore unacceptable – with very deleterious results.

However, the longer-term issue concerning Marx in China, which is playing out against the backdrop of the existence of many flourishing Schools of Marxist Philosophy at the universities and much first-rate Marx scholarship that I mentioned at the outset of this essay, is the tendency of the teaching of Marxism at less exalted levels to become dogmatic in the way in which that teaching became in the Soviet Bloc, with textbooks too often giving canned answers, curtailing teachers' desire to innovate and, to put it bluntly, boring students to death. The spirit of Marx, as I have always understood it, was more closely linked to real history than that of any other major Western philosopher before him, and an important aspect of that linkage was Marx's recognition that his writings were inextricably connected with their time and place – from which it should follow that Marx would have welcomed reinterpretations of his thought in light of new circumstances. The relative success of Marx's thought in China, while due in part to peculiarities of the early twentieth century world, mentioned earlier, in which China was a subordinate and subordinated player, was also due to the inherent flexibility and adaptability of that thought. If it should begin to become a mere slogan without really believable content, then, however great China's future may be, Marx himself will no longer be a 'living' resident of it.

Bibliography

Feigon, Lee. *Chen Duxiu. Founder of the Chinese Communist Party*. Princeton: Princeton University Press, 1983.

Mao Zedong. *Selected Works of Mao Tse-Tung*. Beijing: Foreign Languages Press. https://www.marxists.org/reference/archive/mao/selected-works/index.htm

Marx, Karl. *Capital, Vol. 1: A Critique of Political Economy*, tr. B. Fowkes. London: Penguin Books, 1976.

Marx, Karl, and Engels, Friedrich, *Manifesto of the Communist Party*, in R. Tucker, ed., *The Marx-Engels Reader*, 2nd ed. New York: W. W. Norton & Co., 1978, pp. 469–500.

Meisner, Maurice. *Li Ta-Chao and the Origins of Chinese Marxism*. Cambridge, MA: Harvard University Press, 1967.

18

Chinese correlative cosmology

A Chinese view of the world?

William Matthews

Introduction

'Correlative cosmology' describes a view of the cosmos based on the relationships between different cosmic forces and perceptible phenomena, such as directions, colors, flavours, organs, animals, and so on (Nylan 2010: 410–414 provides a helpful overview of usage of the term). This idea underlies practices including Daoism and popular religion, Chinese medicine, 气功 *qigong* exercises and other martial arts, many forms of Chinese divination (such as 八字 *bazi* horoscopy and techniques using the 易经 *Yijing* or *Book of Changes*), 风水 *fengshui*, changing fortune in relation to the lunar calendar, and historically the ideology and rituals of the imperial Chinese state. Although the imperial state no longer exists to promote this cosmology, it continues to be of huge importance in the day-to-day lives of people in China. Through practices like *fengshui* and divination, it helps people decide when to move house, how to resolve family conflicts, whether their child's partner is a suitable match, and so on. Through Chinese medicine and *qigong* it guides people's decisions about maintaining good health, how they exercise, and what to eat. It also fosters comparisons with modern science, allowing traditional knowledge and practices to endure and flourish even in the context of advanced technology and modernization. That is, correlative cosmology exists alongside other cosmologies, or theories of the universe, in China today. These include the modernist, scientific, atheistic worldview promoted by the Chinese Communist Party and the state in Taiwan, as well as the cosmologies of Buddhism, Islam, and Christianity. Indeed, it is possible for people to adhere to ideas and practices from several of these cosmologies simultaneously, and this was no less true historically (even though modern scientific cosmology was unknown).

While correlative cosmology's importance in people's lives today, let alone through China's premodern history, makes it an important subject for understanding Chinese society, correlative cosmology has also been a long-term focus for understanding 'China' in the abstract. From scholars emphasizing conceptual counterpoints to European philosophy, to discourses of popular nationalism in China, to political punditry and popular books on doing business in China, correlative cosmology continues to be invoked to explain a unique 'Chinese' way of thinking, or even a distinctive 'Chinese' mind. This is usually one which

DOI: 10.4324/9780429059704-22

focuses on relationships rather than the self, is holistic rather than analytic, stresses the collective over the individual, and so on. A key emphasis of this chapter is instead on the historical contingency of correlative cosmology and the fact that all of these contrasts, where they are warranted at all, are about differences in explicit emphasis rather than in kind. All of the examples mentioned risk veering into orientalist depictions of China, as well as occidentalist depictions of the West, but the primary reason they should be questioned is because they do not match with the facts, either of Chinese history and society, or what we know about human thought and culture in general. As this chapter demonstrates, 'correlative cosmology' is not timeless and unchanging, involves as much 'analytic' thinking as any other form of thought, and exists in contexts which also embrace science and modernity. This is especially important to emphasize at a time when China's rise provokes increasing attention, and inaccurate culturalist stereotypes or claims to unbroken millennia of cultural continuity pose an increasing risk both to the wellbeing of individuals and to developing an adequate understanding of the intentions of the Chinese state.

In China today, while not everyone 'believes in' the view of the world described by correlative cosmology, one would be hard-pressed to find someone who has never engaged with it, or does not know someone who has. The key concepts that lie at the heart of correlative cosmology – 气 *qi*, 阴 *yin* and 阳 *yang*, the Five Phases (五行 *wuxing*) of metal (金 *jin*), wood (木 *mu*), water (水 *shui*), fire (火 *huo*), and earth (土 *tu*), the Heavenly Stems (天干 *tiangan*) and Earthly Branches (地支 *dizhi*), and the trigrams (卦 *gua*) of the *Yijing* – are common knowledge and part of everyday discourse in the People's Republic and Taiwan, even if many people do not engage closely with the details of their cosmological significance. An adequate understanding of the practices described and many of the key systems of ideas so crucial in Chinese history, from Confucian ethics (gender, family, and political roles such as ruler and subject understood in terms of *yin* and *yang*) to health (Chinese medicine) to the reckoning of time (correlating the seasons, Five Phases, colors, and so on), requires some familiarity with correlative cosmology. This chapter introduces key concepts and their underlying logic, followed by an account of their historical development and the question of how far they represent a distinctively 'Chinese' way of thinking. Correlative cosmology began to be consolidated in the Warring States period (475–221 BCE), developing into a shared coherent understanding of the cosmos based on *qi* (matter-energy) during the former Han period (206 BCE–9 CE). The early period of its development has been of particular interest to sinologists and is arguably most important for understanding how the ideas fit together, and is accordingly granted attention here. This is followed by a discussion of later developments, including changing attitudes in the context of encounters with Western imperialism from the mid-19th century, and attempts to combine correlative cosmology with science. The final section of the chapter also addresses the question of correlative cosmology's uniqueness. While there are important differences of emphasis between correlative cosmology and other accounts of the world, these relate to a certain level of reflection and should not be taken to indicate deep differences in perception or ways of thinking – that is, despite its unique content Chinese correlative cosmology does not mark out a distinctive 'Chinese mind'.

What is correlative cosmology?

This section introduces key concepts of correlative cosmology: *qi* (the basic energy and substance of the universe), (the basic energy and substance of the universe), the Five Phases, *yin* and *yang*, the Heavenly Stems and Earthly Branches, and the trigrams of the *Yijing*. The section describes how they are linked together, and what this means for how the cosmos is understood. The section is intended as a general reference and introduction to the concepts.

A cosmos of qi

According to correlative cosmology as understood today, everything in the universe (including thought and emotion) is composed of *qi*, an energy and substance, which flows according to constant principles of transformation. These are described by Five Phases, which interact with one another in various ways, most importantly through generating (生 *sheng*) and overcoming (克 *ke*) relationships as illustrated in Figure 18.1. As Geoffrey Lloyd points out (2014: 23), these Phases are best understood in processual terms, fire 'flaming upwards' and water 'soaking downwards', for example, in comparison with classical Greek ideas of the four elements (see Table 18.1). They express the relationships between different beings and phenomena with which they are correlated, with different kinds of correlates having

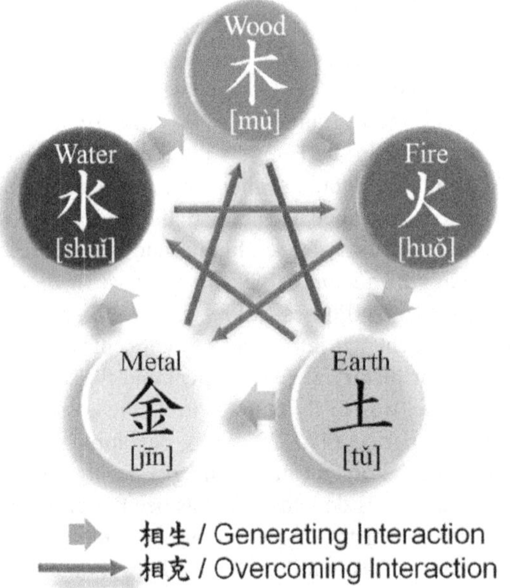

Figure 18.1 The Five Phases, showing cycles of generating (*sheng*) and overcoming (*ke*). Image by Parnassus – Own work, CC BY-SA 3.0, https://commons.wikimedia.org/w/index.php?curid=28500461.

Table 18.1 Correlates of the Five Phases found in the *Hongfan* chapter of the *Shangshu*, discussed below, based on Nylan's translation (1992)

Phase	*Water*	*Fire*	*Wood*	*Metal*	*Earth*
Processual Quality	Soaking and descending	Blazing and ascending	Curving and straightening	Malleability and changeability	Seeding and harvesting
Flavour	Saltiness	Bitterness	Sourness	Acridity	Sweetness

Table 18.2 The Five Phases correlated with the Eight Trigrams in the Former Heaven sequence

Trigram	Qian 乾☰	Dui 兌☱	Li 離☲	Zhen 震☳	Xun 巽☴	Kan 坎☵	Gen 艮☶	Kun 坤☷
Phase	Metal 金 *jin*	Metal 金 *jin*	Fire 火 *huo*	Wood 木 *mu*	Wood 木 *mu*	Water 水 *shui*	Earth 土 *tu*	Earth 土 *tu*

greater salience in different cosmological practices; these include organs of the body (key to Chinese medicine), cardinal directions (as in *fengshui*), and dates via correlations with the (Heavenly) Stems and (Earthly) Branches (干支 *ganzhi*), as used in the traditional calendar, as well as types of animal, weather patterns, emotions, and so on. They also correlated with the eight trigrams (卦 *gua*, three-line diagrams) found in the *Yijing* (Table 18.2), a classical divination text which played a key role in the development of correlative cosmology and is still widely used for divination and as a source of wisdom in its own right (see Redmond and Hon 2014; Smith 2008; Zhu 1995 for accounts of the *Yijing's* history and reception; and Li 2019; Matthews 2016 for its contemporary use).

Balancing correlates of time and space

The 10 Stems and 12 Branches together generate cycles of 60 (the sexagenary cycle). They are similarly correlated with the Five Phases, meaning that days, months, and years are associated with particular kinds of *qi*. Because different directions, activities, and so on are also correlated with the Phases, one can select more or less auspicious times and places for action based on whether the Phases of a time, place, and activity interact productively or destructively. This logic underlies the descriptions of suitable activities for different days included in traditional almanacs, as well as the diagnoses and predictions identified in many divination techniques (Bruun 2003; Feuchtwang 1974; Homola 2013; Matthews forthcoming). The same logic holds for any practice based on correlative cosmology – in Chinese medicine, for example, different foods or meteorological influences will variously affect the health of different organs based on the relationship between their respective Phases of *qi*. The total number of correlates is huge, as are various other forms of relationship between the Phases; rather than exhaustively document them here, the reader is referred to Stephan Feuchtwang's (1974) study of correlative cosmology as used in *fengshui* (geomancy, orienting space to maximize positive *qi*), to Manfred Porkert's (1974) of its use in Chinese medicine, and William Matthews (2016, 2018) on *Yijing* divination, for detailed catalogues of the relationships between the Phases and their correlates.

This logic gives rise to the idea that such practices are concerned with 'balance' or 'harmony', which can perhaps be more intuitively understood by someone unfamiliar with correlative cosmology as 'optimization'. What all of these practices aim to do is to maximize exposure to auspicious *qi*, which will have positive effects, and minimize the influence of harmful *qi*. Because everything in the cosmos is *qi*, and as such at any given moment is influenced by a particular Phase, great attention is paid to the context of action and the relationships involved (some examples are discussed in the following sections). The cosmos thus envisaged is one in which all phenomena mutually influence one another, but do so in ways that are predictable according to the principles of the Five Phases and their correlates.

Relativity and scale

These ideas rely on the concepts of yielding *yin* and active *yang*, more widely known beyond the Chinese context. These are relational terms – something is always *yin* or *yang* with respect to something else, so for example in Confucian gender ethics, women are *yin* in relation to men who are *yang*, but an unequal relationship between two women will involve one who is relatively *yin* and one who is relatively *yang*. This extends to the Five Phases and other correlates, which can be seen in terms of *yin* and *yang* and the cycle between them, made explicit in the famous 太极 *taiji* (supreme ultimate) symbol ☯. As *yang* wanes, *yin* waxes, and vice versa; as the symbol indicates, *yin* and *yang* contain each other within themselves (represented in the symbol by the small dots). Thus, they produce change in the cosmos as described by the Five Phases and other correlates. For example, the trigrams of the *Yijing* consist of solid lines, denoting *yang*, and broken lines, denoting *yin*, and are held to describe change through the waxing and waning of the two. They are considered to refer to eight basic configurations of the cosmos, and can be combined to produce the 64 hexagrams, or six-line diagrams, of the *Yijing* which describe specific types of situations. The trigrams can thus be arranged in sequence according to the flow of *yin* and *yang*, as they transform into each other, in the 'Former Heaven' (先天 *xiantian*) sequence shown in Table 18.2 (Feuchtwang 1974: 75).

In the *Yijing* we find a good example of correlative cosmology from the late Warring States period, in the commentary 'Explaining the Trigrams' (说卦 *shuogua*). This text predates clear evidence of correlative cosmology being thought of in terms of universal *qi* and the Five Phases (see Nylan 2010 for a discussion), but gives a good idea of how the system works (and today it is understood in terms of *qi*). In this text, the eight trigrams are systematically correlated with natural forms, actions, cardinal directions, relational qualities, animals, body parts, and family members. This results in, for example, the trigram 艮 *gen* being correlated with mountains, restraint, the northeast, cessation, dogs, hands, and youngest sons (Matthews 2018: 53). This kind of grouping has long provoked characterizations of correlative cosmology as relying on categories that are not based on shared essence but are rather relational in character (Hall & Ames 1995; Ziporyn 2012). For example, Brook Ziporyn argues that particular beings or phenomena are correlated with trigrams based on their relationship to other members of their natural group – so, for *gen*, dogs are positioned in relation to other animals in the same way that hands are to other body parts, or youngest sons to other family members. In this reading, it is an example of a highly systematized mode of *bricolage* (Lévi-Strauss 1974), a way of thinking based on groupings that go well together conceptually through various forms of analogy. However, as Feuchtwang (2014a) points out in relation to correlative cosmology more generally (though he does not use that label), this way of thinking is also concerned with relations across scales, from the micro- to macro-level. Matthews (2018) argues that accordingly, the categories in *Explaining the Trigrams* can also be read in terms of shared essences – from a cosmological perspective, the 'natural categories' of animals, directions, and so on, can be understood as different scales on which the particular cosmic forces denoted by the trigrams are manifest.

This dual character, of relational significance and shared underlying cosmic principles, is crucial for practices that make use of correlative cosmology. If the sets of correlates associated with a trigram or a Phase were only based on analogous relational properties, they could not be employed to make predictions or diagnoses. Consider the example of choosing a good time for action – this is based on a causal relationship between different Phases (of destruction or production) that works across scales. For example, the Earth Phase overcomes the Water Phase and can have this effect regardless of whether or not the two operate on the same scale. So a person with a Water fate, based on their date of birth, should exercise caution in years correlated with Earth, but also in relation to any other Earth phenomena (food, animals, etc). This is due to interactions between cosmic forces (two types of *qi*), which cause particular kinds of effect regardless of the scales on which, or between which, they occur. At the same time, an Earth year can be understood as having the same relation to a Water year as an Earth planet (Saturn) to a Water planet (Mercury). Strictly speaking, then, rather than relying on analogy correlative cosmology is a system of homologies, in which similar properties and relationships on different scales indicate common underlying causes in the form of cosmic principles (Matthews 2017a). Nonetheless, the extent to which the description so far characterizes pre-Han correlative thinking remains subject to debate – the next section describes some aspects of how correlative concepts eventually developed into *qi*-based cosmology.

The development of correlative cosmology in early China

Most debates on the nature of correlative cosmology concern its development up to and including the period of China's first empires, the Qin and Han. This is true both of scholarship and of more general discussions of it as an example of 'Chinese thought', which often point to its long history but do not necessarily acknowledge its evolution over time. Some understanding of its development is key to asking further questions concerning both correlative cosmology in its own right, and comparisons with other polities. While the latter has been considered extensively from a humanistic perspective in relation to classical Greece, often in terms of early Chinese thought more generally (Jullien 2000; Lloyd 2002, 2004, 2014; Lloyd & Sivin 2002; Raphals 2013), such comparisons are also of interest from the point of view of comparative social science, particularly in terms of the relationship between cosmology and sociopolitical structure (Descola 2013; Feuchtwang 2014b; Puett 2015). In particular, examining the historical context of the emergence of correlative cosmology provides groundwork for investigation into the causal relations between state formation, empire, popular knowledge traditions, the spread and standardization of writing, and the substantive content of official and popular belief systems. As discussed here, correlative cosmology became extremely important in the Qin and Han dynasties as justification for dynastic succession and rule, which was presented as following a natural sequence of cosmic principles. This was linked to Confucian ethics, in turn providing a normative justification for the paternalistic rule of the emperors, and their role as mediators between Heaven and Earth.

Early origins (Shang and Western Zhou)

The Shang kings (c. 1600–1046 BCE) seem to have employed correlative thinking in their imagination of the state in relation to other polities associated with the 'Four Corners' (四方 *sifang*), each of which was correlated with a cardinal direction and a particular wind (Wang 2008: 29), but this was quite different from the cosmology described above. Following the Zhou victory over the Shang, and over subsequent centuries, the concept of the Four Quarters became attached to the idea of the 'Mandate of Heaven' (天命 *tianming*). Referring to the legitimacy of political rule and its extent, this was used to justify the Zhou conquest based on correlating celestial movements, particularly of the five visible planets, with patterns of dynastic change (Pankenier 2015). Hence, even at this early stage certain correlative principles were a key part of establishing state legitimacy, though as David Keightley describes (1988, 1999), the Shang cosmology rested on a fundamental division between the human world and the divine rather than a continuous cosmos based on *qi*, which remained true into the Zhou dynasty (Puett 2004: 54–79).

Development and systematization from the Eastern Zhou to Han

This began to change during the Eastern Zhou period, following the Zhou being forced from their capital in 771 BCE and the collapse of their practical authority, leading to a shift in the focus of political cosmology from the person of the King directly to Heaven (天 *tian*) (Wang 2008). Over the centuries leading to the Warring States period, the concept of *tian* shifted from one of a personal deity to an increasingly naturalistic idea of a cosmic force, interacting with Earth (地 *di*) and Humanity (人 *ren*), marking an important shift towards a conception of an ontologically continuous cosmos. However, the development of this cosmology was not limited to questions of political legitimacy. The proliferation of schools of thought during the Warring States period coincided also with the further spread of writing beyond the field of religion, including writings associated with 'natural experts' (Harper 1999: 813), such as diviners, medical specialists, writers of almanacs, and musicians. Cosmological knowledge was no longer primarily the preserve of the ruler, but of literate specialists on whom rulers often depended (Wang 2008: 78–79).

From the fourth century BCE onwards, that key elements of correlative cosmology became established, including the idea of *qi*, increasingly associated with *yin* and *yang*, as the 'basic stuff of human life and of other things in nature' (Harper 1999: 861), even as the concept continued to hold different meanings in other contexts (Graham 1986: 71–72; Nivison 1999: 775–776). By the third century BCE, correlative sets of five, although not yet part of a single standardized system as today, were prevalent (Wang 2008). Good examples of correlative cosmology from the late Warring States period include the 洪范 *Hongfan* ('Great plan') chapter of the 尚书 *Shangshu*, extremely influential on Han correlative cosmology, which describes the Five Phases as processes with explicitly causal relations with flavours as shown in Table 1; for example, Water, by soaking downwards, 'makes for' (作 *zuo*) saltiness (Nylan 1992: 15–16). Another example comes from the 吕氏春秋 *Lüshi Chunqiu* ('Springs and Autumns of Master Lü'), which presents the relations of 'mutual overcoming' (相克 *xiangke*) between the Five Phases (Graham 1986: 80–81; Harper 1999: 865), which remain central to cosmological practices today. This is presented in the context of dynastic succession, correlating the mythic Yellow Emperor with Earth, Emperor Yu with Wood, King Tang of the Shang with Metal, and King Wen of the Zhou with Fire; Water logically follows, associated with Qin – thus the system of mutual conquest justifies the rise of the Qin state to preeminence (see Knoblock & Riegel 2000: 282–284 for the relevant passage and English translation).

In Han dynasty texts we find even clearer demonstrations of these ideas, and explicit characterization of the causal relations between correlates in terms of what Robert Sharf translates as 'sympathetic resonance' (感应 *ganying*) (Sharf 2002). These texts include the idea that cosmic principles can be manipulated in the interests of governing human affairs, as in writings attributed to scholar-official 董仲舒 Dong Zhongshu, which link Confucian ethics to correlative cosmology and argue that *yin* and *yang qi* can be manipulated to effect change (Puett 2004: 290–291). As John Henderson puts it, '[c]orrelative cosmology reached its high-point of development' under the Han, notably represented by texts such as the 淮南子 *Huainanzi* and 春秋繁露 *Chunqiu fanlu* (Henderson 2010: 182; though Puett 2000 argues that even in such texts, correlative cosmology was a claim rather than a basic assumption). The idea of being able to manipulate the world through an understanding of cosmic principles also characterized forms of divination (a pervasive element in state and popular practice; Kalinowski 2010) developed in the period, including the integration of the *Yijing* and its trigrams and hexagrams with *qi*-based correlative cosmology. As the *Yijing* became part of the official 'Five Classics' (五经 *wuijing*) on which Han state ideology was based in 136 BCE, correlative cosmology became increasingly integrated. It formed the basis for a coherent, normative conception of the cosmos and the role of the state in maintaining balance between Heaven and Earth, through ritual and the regulation of the human realm.

What should be noted is the relative lateness of these Han-era conceptions of a unified correlative cosmology with respect to the correlative systems they integrated; the textual record does not allow us to unambiguously infer the existence of such a system any earlier (Nylan 2010). The complex threads of intellectual history prior to the Han warn against an anachronistic conception of correlative cosmology as a timeless, constant expression of a 'Chinese' way of thinking, as discussed below. At the same time, viewing this history from the point of view of post-Han *qi*-based cosmology risks the impression of that system's inevitable development. That is a question for large-scale comparisons of the relationship among sociopolitical change, imperial expansion and consolidation, and cosmological ideas. While the evidence we have might suggest that already-existing ideas of correlation of dynastic change with astronomical observations and other changes made their increasing use and development more likely, observations of such correlations are far from unique to Chinese history. The question of why correlative cosmology became a conceptual foundation for the first Chinese empires, rather than say a pantheon of divinities as in Rome, remains a subject for future research.

Correlative cosmology as a way of thinking

Changes and external influences

Although most work on 'correlative cosmology' has concentrated on early China, it is worth pointing out that the integration of this system in the Han did not simply mark an endpoint of its development. Constraints of space prevent anything approaching a comprehensive account of post-Han developments, but the continued development and transformation of correlative cosmology should be acknowledged, in particular in relation to the impact of external approaches to cosmology, most notably Buddhism from the Eastern Han (25–22 CE) onwards, and Western science from the arrival of the Jesuits in the Ming (1368–1644) and especially from the late 19th century under the influence of European imperial expansion. John Henderson (1984) provides an extensive account of post-Han developments up to the late Qing period, focusing in particular on periods of returns to correlative cosmology as a topic of enquiry among the literati during the Eastern Han, Song, and Ming dynasties, and especially increasing scepticism of Han ideas among certain early Qing scholars. It should be noted though that what Henderson describes as a 'decline' in correlative cosmology among the literati does not extend to the multifarious technical practices which continued to rely on it (such as medicine, *fengshui*, and so on), and even among the sceptics did not amount to a wholesale rejection of ideas like *qi*.

Robert Sharf (2002) demonstrates that correlative cosmology had a major influence over how Buddhism was interpreted in China from the Eastern Han onward, correlative principles being drawn on as a primary idiom for understanding the new concepts. Indeed, as can be seen by popular religious practice in China today, Buddhist ideas and worship of Buddhist deities are routinely held alongside beliefs and practices of Daoist origins, and explicit understandings of correlative cosmology, the role of Heaven (*tian*), and conceptions of the realm of gods and ancestors as analogous to the imperial bureaucracy (Feuchtwang 2004). That is, various cosmological traditions have historically influenced one another and continue to do so – though the extent to which ideas from particular traditions, be they correlative cosmology or Buddhism, are held by individuals of course varies.

Indeed, the relationship and interaction between correlative cosmological ideas and practices and those with origins in other cosmologies is indicative of the fact that, like any system of thought, these are constituted by historically varying chains of transmission between different individuals and groups. This is particularly clear in the case of the relationship between correlative cosmology and modern scientific ideas, which began exerting a huge influence over China's intellectual landscape from the mid-19th century, and far more than Buddhism were seen as constituting a direct challenge to the foundations of Chinese culture. By the late 19th century, the impact of Western imperial power, and increasingly that of Japan, was sorely felt in China, provoking a range of responses among the governing elite and literati, from resistance to foreign ideas, to compromise as in the 体用 *tiyong* formula (Chinese wisdom for basic principles, Western knowledge for practical use), and wholesale rejection of Chinese traditions and practices (see Duara 1997; Jenco 2015 for overviews).

Following the overthrow of the Qing in 1911, the Republican government and many intellectuals adopted an aggressively modernizing, science-oriented attitude (see Goossaert & Palmer 2011 for a comprehensive account of religion and politics in China up to the present). Correlative cosmology, in which the imperial administration had been rooted, could not serve as the basis for a new China as a modern nation-state, and thus became increasingly marginalized. It continued as the basis of technical practices, but many of these, such as popular religion, divination, and *fengshui*, were condemned as 'superstition' (迷信 *mixin*). In parallel to similar movements in Buddhism and Daoism (Nedostup 2010), the latter likewise rooted in correlative cosmology, adherents of divination and related practices based ultimately on the Han conceptions of the cosmos increasingly searched for parallels between correlative cosmology and modern science (Li & Lackner 2018), including the scholar Liu Zihua's attempt to predict the assistance of a planet using the cosmology of the *Yijing* (Homola 2014).

While many practices rooted in correlative cosmology were subject to heavy repression in mainland China under Mao (with notable exceptions such as Chinese medicine) (Taylor 2005), and periodic repression into the Reform era, practices such as *qigong* (Palmer 2007), *fengshui* (Bruun 2003), and divination (Li 2019; Matthews 2017b) have experienced major revivals. The transmission of these techniques through teaching and publication is frequently characterized by developing apparently scientific justifications for correlative cosmological claims, often through drawing analogies between correlative cosmology and physics, such as parallels between *qi* and matter-energy or electromagnetism (for detailed examples, see Billioud & Thoraval 2015 on popular Confucianism; Chau 2006: 98–108 on the efficacy of local temples; Matthews 2017a, 2017b on *Yijing* divination; and Palmer 2007 on qigong). While the Chinese state today is far removed from that of the imperial dynasties, and no prospect of its own practical adoption of correlative cosmology exists, in the People's Republic the revival of popular interest in these practices, and correlative cosmology more generally as a branch of 'national studies' (国学 *guoxue*) is accompanied by increasing rhetorical support from the state. This is particularly so given the increasing prominence of nationalism as a legitimating ideology, beginning with a significant shift away from Marxist ideology with the Patriotic Education Campaign in the early 1990s (Zhao 1998) but gaining significance in the 2000s and especially under Xi Jinping – including the inclusion of correlative cosmology as part of the 'Chinese Citizen Science Quality Benchmark' for popularizing science (Xu 2017).

Cultural change and cultural difference

If the early history of correlative cosmology demonstrates its mixed origins, post-Han developments and, particularly, its history over the last two centuries, indicate the endurance of certain concepts through adaptation. In contemporary practices we find references to the same concepts consolidated under the Han, but considered in relation to scientific and political ideas unimaginable to those early cosmologists. Most important of all in understanding the implications of correlative cosmology for understanding the relationship between culture and cosmological imagination, though, is not the acknowledgement of a catalogue of influences or thinkers but recognition that the notion of 'correlative cosmology' as a particular set of ideas is a convenient shorthand. While we might debate the philosophical merits of particular correlative concepts, in terms of historical and social scientific scholarship what is most important is the fact that correlative cosmology exists in the minds of individual human beings who hold different kinds and degrees of understanding and have their own histories of learning; 'correlative cosmology' is thus a useful label for an aggregate of understandings within groups of people over history.

If we view correlative cosmology in these terms, then we can appreciate both the multiple perspectives and theories so far discussed, and the evolutionary trajectories of the concepts transmitted and received by different individuals through radically different historical contexts. While a *fengshui* consultant today might draw on the concepts described in Warring States and Han sources, they may also have a scientific education, and operate in a polity far removed from one justified according to correlative cosmic principles. This raises a second important point. Not only is correlative cosmology properly considered in terms of the transmission of aggregate individual understandings, but it is also one dimension of experience among many on the part of adherents. That is, while individuals might make use of correlative cosmology in certain practices, or on reflection consider phenomena in the world from a correlative cosmological point of view, as with any cosmology or 'worldview' we should not mistakenly imagine that it comprehensively guides perception and experience. It is an explanation of the world that pertains to moments of reflective consideration rather than something that guides intuitive assumptions (Boyer 2010). A similar point has been made forcefully by Edward Slingerland (2018), who demonstrates that, contrary to the arguments of some sinologists, early Chinese conceptions of the heart-mind (心 *xin*) rested on a foundation of intuitive mind-body dualism, as indicated both from textual evidence and findings from the cognitive sciences which demonstrate such dualism to be a universal feature of human psychology.

Like the erroneous argument that the concept of *xin* indicated a thoroughly holistic perception of mind-body unity on the part of the early Chinese (inevitably contrasted with the perennially dualist West), arguments have been made for a fundamental cognitive gulf between China and Europe on the basis of correlative cosmology. This can be traced to the arguments of Marcel Granet (2012 [1934]), to the effect that correlative thinking was a property of the 'Chinese mind', drawing on the work of social scientists such as Émile Durkheim and Marcel Mauss on 'primitive' classification (Durkheim & Mauss 2009 [1903]). It should be noted that Durkheim and Mauss' work acknowledges that such systems of thought are more widespread than China (they compared Chinese correlative cosmology with classification systems used in Aboriginal Australia and among the Zuñi and Sioux). Indeed, correlative systems were a key part of premodern 'Western' societies, from the classical period (Lloyd 2002, 2014) to the Renaissance and beyond (Henderson 1984), and can be found elsewhere (Descola 2013; Farmer et al. 2000).

However, approaches including those of Needham (1956), Graham (1986), Hall and Ames (1995), and Jullien (1995), focus in particular on contrasting correlative thinking with 'analytic' or 'causal' thinking, even when they acknowledge correlative thinking in Western traditions. In some cases, such as Graham's arguments, this amounts to an acknowledgement that 'correlative' (or analogical) thinking is universal, but distinctive in style from the analytic thought that characterizes modern science (demonstrating the influence of structuralism on his thinking); for Graham, both modes of thought are universal but one more expressed in premodern China and the other more in the modern West. Drawing on Graham's approach, Hall and Ames argue for a more fundamental distinction between correlative thought and linear causal thought, coupled with heavy emphasis on an opposition between process (in China) and substance or permanence (the West). In this view, analogical thinking is opposed to causal thinking, and the kind of understanding of correlative categories set out in the first section of this chapter, of underlying shared cosmic principles, is apparently impossible. Such views are taken to an extreme, and advanced with far less rigour, in the work of Jullien, who effectively treats all Chinese thinkers as part of a single homogenous bloc and relies on linguistic determinism to argue, among other things, that the Chinese had 'scant interest in causal explanation' (1995: 219–221; see Matthews Forthcoming; Slingerland 2018 for critiques).

Such strong opposition of correlative/analogical and causal/analytic thinking has significant problems. In a critical assessment of Granet, Needham, Graham, and Hall and Ames, Fung (2010) argues that they provide little evidence for such a distinction, and that correlative thinking is itself analytic. Indeed, as demonstrated above, correlative cosmology can easily be read in terms of causation, and in many of the key early Chinese sources is presented in explicitly causal terms (consider the example from the *Hong Fan*). Moreover, the close comparisons drawn between correlative cosmology and physics by modern-day diviners, for example, demonstrate the ready compatibility (and structural similarities) of both (Matthews 2017a). The notion of cosmic *qi* is thoroughly causal, and analytic – *qi*-based cosmology presents ideas of constant principles which can be applied to different contexts in order to explain them and make predictions. This does involve an emphasis on dynamic process rather than substance per se, but nonetheless relies on a conception of *qi* as a substance being transformed. It is far more accurate to consider differences between correlative cosmology and other cosmological accounts differences of conceptual content rather than differences in mode of thought, which also helps avoid obviously ludicrous claims such as 'the Chinese' having no theory of causation (Jullien 1995). Many of the problems of such orientalist depictions of correlative cosmology stem from a baseline assumption of radical difference (as Fung argues), or from taking the shorthand of 'correlative cosmology' too seriously, replacing the history of individual human understandings with reified, fixed ideas. This has the effect of treating the ideas in isolation, and forgetting the necessities of everyday life engaged in by the writers concerned and the collectives of which they were part.

Conclusions

Correlative cosmology remains at the heart of many systems of thought and practice that make up Chinese culture, even though it no longer forms the basis of state governance. While the core concepts of this understanding of the world, such as *yin* and *yang*, *qi*, and the Five Phases, have endured as shared concepts, they have also evolved over time. From the beginning, correlative cosmology developed through the transmission of ideas between individuals, as a reflection on the nature of the cosmos and the place of humans and other phenomena within it. While its core concepts are part of a distinctive Chinese intellectual heritage, that does not mean that it reflects a uniquely 'Chinese' way of thinking, or manifests 'analogical' thinking in opposition to Western 'analytic' thinking. Rather, it is best understood in terms of a historically particular chain of cultural transmission between individuals, more or less shared at different points in its history or based on shared practices, which relies on universal human capacities to think in terms of analogy and causation and reflect on the structure and processes of the cosmos.

References

Billioud, S. & J. Thoraval 2015. *The Sage and the People: The Confucian Revival in China*. Oxford: Oxford University Press.

Boyer, P. 2010. Why Evolved Cognition Matters to Understanding Cultural Cognitive Variations. *Interdisciplinary Science Reviews* **35**, 376–386.

Bruun, O. 2003. *Fengshui in China: Geomantic Divination Between State Orthodoxy and Popular Religion*. Honolulu: University of Hawaii Press.

Chau, A. Y. 2006. *Miraculous Response: Doing Popular Religion in Contemporary China*. Stanford: Stanford University Press.

Descola, P. 2013. *Beyond Nature and Culture*. Chicago: University of Chicago Press.

Duara, P. 1997. *Rescuing History from the Nation: Questioning Narratives of Modern China* (New edition). Chicago: University of Chicago Press.

Durkheim, E. & M. Mauss 2009. *Primitive Classification (Routledge Revivals)*. Abingdon: Routledge.

Farmer, S., J.B. Henderson & M. Witzel 2000. Neurobiology, Layered Texts, and Correlative Cosmologies: A Cross-Cultural Framework for Premodern History. *Bulletin of the Museum of Far Eastern Antiquities* **72**, 48–90.

Feuchtwang, S. 1974. *An Anthropological Analysis of Chinese Geomancy*. Taipei: Southern Materials Center, Inc.

Feuchtwang, S. 2004. *Popular Religion in China: The Imperial Metaphor*. Richmond: RoutledgeCurzon.

Feuchtwang, S. 2014a. Coordinates of Body and Place: Chinese Practices of Centring. In *Framing Cosmologies: The Anthropology of Worlds* (eds) A. Abramson & M. Holbraad, 116–133. Manchester: Manchester University Press.

Feuchtwang, S. 2014b. Too Ontological, Too Rigid, Too Ahistorical but Magnificent. *HAU: Journal of Ethnographic Theory* **4**, 383–387.

Fung, Y. 2010. On the Very Idea of Correlative Thinking. *Philosophy Compass* **5**, 296–306.

Goossaert, V. & D.A. Palmer 2011. *The Religious Question in Modern China*. Chicago: University of Chicago Press.

Graham, A.C. 1986. *Yin-Yang and the Nature of Correlative Thinking*. Singapore: The Institute of East Asian Philosophies.

Granet, M. 2012. *La Pensée chinoise*. Paris: Albin Michel.

Hall, D.L. & R.T. Ames 1995. *Anticipating China: Thinking Through the Narratives of Chinese and Western Culture*. Albany: State University of New York Press.

Harper, D. 1999. Warring States Natural Philosophy and Occult Thought. In *The Cambridge History of Ancient China: From the Origins of Civilization to 221 BC* (eds) M. Loewe & E. L. Shaughnessy, 813–884. Cambridge: Cambridge University Press.

Henderson, J.B. 1984. *The Development and Decline of Chinese Cosmology*. New York: Columbia University Press.

Henderson, J.B. 2010. Cosmology and Concepts Of Nature In Traditional China. In *Concepts of Nature: A Chinese-European Cross-Cultural Perspective*, 181–197. Leiden: Brill (available online: https://brill.com/view/book/edcoll/9789004187511/Bej.9789004185265.i-566_007.xml, accessed May 18, 2020).

Homola, S. 2013. Pursue Good Fortune and Avoid Calamity: The Practice and Status of Divination in Contemporary Taiwan. *Journal of Chinese Religions* **41**, 124–147.

Homola, S. 2014. The Fortunes of a Scholar: When the Yijing Challenged Modern Astronomy. *The Journal of Asian Studies* **73**, 733–752.

Jenco, L. 2015. *Changing Referents: Learning Across Space and Time in China and the West*. New York: Oxford University Press.

Jullien, F. 1995. *The Propensity of Things: Toward a History of Efficacy in China* (trans J. Lloyd). New York; London: Zone Books.

Jullien, F. 2000. *Detour and Access: Strategies of Meaning in China and Greece* (trans S. Hawkes). New York: Zone Books.

Kalinowski, M. 2010. Divination and Astrology: Received Texts and Excavated Manuscripts. In *China's Early Empires: A Re-appraisal* (eds) M. Nylan & M. Loewe, 339–366. Cambridge: Cambridge University Press.

Keightley, D.N. 1988. Shang Divination and Metaphysics. *Philosophy East and West* **38**, 367.

Keightley, D.N. 1999. The Shang: China's First Historical Dynasty. In *The Cambridge History of Ancient China: From the Origins of Civilization to 221 BC* (eds) M. Loewe & E. L. Shaughnessy, 232–291. Cambridge: Cambridge University Press.

Knoblock, J. & J. Riegel 2000. *The Annals of Lü Buwei: A Complete Translation and Study*. Stanford: Stanford University Press.

Lévi-Strauss, C. 1974. *The Savage Mind*. London: Weidenfeld and Nicolson.

Li, F. & M. Lackner 2018. Contradictory Forms of Knowledge? Divination and Western Knowledge in Late Qing and Early Republican China. In *Coping with the Future: Theories and Practices of Divination in East Asia* (ed) M. Lackner, 451–485. Leiden: Brill (available online: https://brill.com/view/title/34845, accessed May 19, 2020).

Li, G. 2019. *Fate Calculation Experts: Diviners Seeking Legitimation in Contemporary China*. New York: Berghahn Books.

Lloyd, G.E.R. 2002. *The Ambitions of Curiosity: Understanding the World in Ancient Greece and China*. Cambridge: Cambridge University Press.

Lloyd, G.E.R. 2004. *Ancient Worlds, Modern Reflections: Philosophical Perspectives on Greek and Chinese Science and Culture*. Oxford: Oxford University Press.

Lloyd, G.E.R. 2014. *Being, Humanity, and Understanding: Studies in Ancient and Modern Societies*. Oxford: Oxford University Press.

Lloyd, G. & N. Sivin 2002. *The Way and the Word: Science and Medicine in Early China and Greece*. New Haven: Yale University Press.

Matthews, W. Forthcoming. Reducing Uncertainty: Six Lines Prediction in Contemporary China. In *The Other Yijing* (ed) T.-K. Hon. Leiden: Brill.

Matthews, W. Forthcoming. Getting Our Ontology Right: A Critique of Language and Culture in the Work of Francois Jullien. *Theory, Culture & Society*.

Matthews, W. 2016. The Homological Cosmos: Ontology, Epistemology, and Ethics in Yi Jing Prediction. PhD Thesis, University College London, London.

Matthews, W. 2017a. Ontology with Chinese Characteristics: Homology as a Mode of Identification. *HAU: Journal of Ethnographic Theory* **7**, 265–285.

Matthews, W. 2017b. Making 'Science' from 'Superstition': Conceptions of Knowledge Legitimacy among Contemporary *Yijing* Diviners. *Journal of Chinese Religions* **45**, 173–196.

Matthews, W. 2018. Encompassing the Horse: Analogy, Category, and Scale in the Yijing. *Journal of the British Association for Chinese Studies* 8, 32–61.

Nedostup, R. 2010. *Superstitious Regimes: Religion and the Politics of Chinese Modernity*. Cambridge, MA: Harvard University Press.

Needham, J. 1956. *Science and Civilisation in China, Vol. 2, History of Scientific Thought*. Cambridge: Cambridge University Press.

Nivison, D. S. 1999. The Classical Philosophical Writings. In *The Cambridge History of Ancient China: From the Origins of Civilization to 221 BC* (eds) M. Loewe & E. L. Shaughnessy, 745–812. Cambridge: Cambridge University Press.

Nylan, M. 1992. *The Shifting Center: The Original 'Great Plan' and Later Readings*. Sankt Augustin: Institut Monumenta Serica.

Nylan, M. 2010. Yin-yang, Five Phases, and Qi. In *China's Early Empires: A Re-appraisal* (eds) M. Nylan & M. Loewe, 398–414. Cambridge: Cambridge University Press.

Palmer, D. A. 2007. *Qigong Fever: Body, Science, and Utopia in China*. New York: Columbia University Press.

Pankenier, D.W. 2015. *Astrology and Cosmology in Early China*. Cambridge: Cambridge University Press.

Porkert, M. 1974. *Theoretical Foundations of Chinese Medicine: Systems of Correspondence*. (New edition edition). Cambridge, MA: MIT Press.

Puett, M. 2000. Violent Misreadings: The Hermeneutics of Cosmology in the Huainanzi. *Bulletin of the Museum of Far Eastern Antiquities* **72**, 29–47.

Puett, M. 2015. Ghosts, Gods, and the Coming Apocalypse: Empire and Religion in Early China and Ancient Rome. In *State Power in Ancient China and Rome* (ed) W. Scheidel, 230–259. Oxford; New York: Oxford University Press.

Puett, M.J. 2004. *To Become a God: Cosmology, Sacrifice, and Self-Divinization in Early China*. Cambridge, MA: Harvard University Press.

Raphals, L. 2013. *Divination and Prediction in Early China and Ancient Greece*. Cambridge: Cambridge University Press.

Redmond, G. & T.-K. Hon 2014. *Teaching the I Ching*. Oxford: Oxford University Press.

Sharf, R.H. 2002. *Coming to Terms with Chinese Buddhism: A Reading of the Treasure Store Treatise*. Honolulu: University of Hawaii Press.

Slingerland, E. 2018. *Mind and Body in Early China: Beyond Orientalism and the Myth of Holism*. New York: Oxford University Press.

Smith, R.J. 2008. *Fathoming the Cosmos and Ordering the World: The Yijing (I Ching, Or Classic of Changes) and Its Evolution in China*. Charlottesville: University of Virginia Press.

Taylor, K. 2005. *Chinese Medicine in Early Communist China 1945–63: A Medicine of Revolution*. London: RoutledgeCurzon.

Wang, A. 2008. *Cosmology and Political Culture in Early China*. Cambridge: Cambridge University Press.

Xu, B. 徐蓓 2017. 听講|"陰陽五行"為什麼能被寫入《中國公民科學素質基準》 Listen to a Talk: Why '*Yinyang wuxing*' Can Be Written into the 'Chinese Citizen Science Quality Benchmark'. 搜狐 *Sohu* (available online: http://www.sohu.com/a/148073229_119707, accessed June 13, 2017).

Zhao, S. 1998. A State-Led Nationalism: The Patriotic Education Campaign in Post-Tiananmen China. *Communist and Post-Communist Studies* **31**, 287–302.

Zhu, B.朱伯崑 1995. *Yixue zhexue shi* 易学哲学史 *[A History of the Philosophy of the 'Changes']*. Beijing: Huaxia chubanshe.

Ziporyn, B. 2012. *Ironies of Oneness and Difference: Coherence in Early Chinese Thought; Prolegomena to the Study of Li*. New York: State University of New York Press.

19

Philosophical hermeneutics and Chinese metaphors

Joshua Mason

Introduction

This chapter brings together three strands of academic study: metaphor theory, hermeneutics, and Chinese philosophy. They come together when we focus on the interpretation of philosophically significant metaphors in the Chinese tradition.

Chinese philosophy overflows with metaphors: the way is like water; human nature is a sprout; society should be harmonious. Our collective interpretations of these metaphors deliver the depth, enrichment, and truth of Chinese thought and culture.

Metaphors[1] can speak to our hearts in an instant, yet at the same time present challenges to interpretation and understanding. Scholars of Chinese philosophy have given explicit attention to many particular metaphors, as well as the general use and function of metaphor in Chinese discourse, generating a growing field of research with broad implications. To further this work, I recommend the insights developed in the discipline of hermeneutics, the philosophy of interpretation. Hermeneutics has traditionally been a methodology for making sense of texts from across temporal, linguistic, and cultural distances. Philosophical hermeneutics, as it has developed through the influences of phenomenology and existentialism in the 20th century, shifts from methodology to ontology, aiming to reveal the fundamental conditions of human understanding that enable us to encounter the truth and meaning of being. By attending to the insights of hermeneutic philosophers into the existential situation of human understanding, our interpretations of Chinese philosophy's key metaphors can be more responsible to the traditions we belong to and can open greater possibilities for knowing truth and meaning. Careful reflection on our processes of interpretation can clarify our understanding of philosophically loaded metaphors and open up new horizons.

The broad conclusion of this chapter is that conceptual metaphor use is an existential condition that shapes our foundational philosophical interpretations. This makes Chinese metaphor studies a legitimately philosophical mode of cross-culture pursuit of truth and meaning. It also suggests that understanding the truths of Chinese philosophical metaphors – such as *dao* (道) and *yin-yang* (阴阳) – through a fusion of horizons is a transformative experience that can change our way of being in the world.

DOI: 10.4324/9780429059704-23

This chapter starts with a brief review of conceptual metaphor theory. It follows with a critique of traditional metaphor theory as applied to Chinese philosophy, then highlights six areas of interest in Chinese philosophy (iconology, paronomasia, correlative cosmologies, arguments by analogy, borrowed entailments, and philosophical frameworks) in which a theory of conceptual metaphor provides a new lens on significant ideas. After this survey of conceptual metaphors in Chinese philosophy, it moves on to lay out the processes of interpretation theorized in Heidegger's and Gadamer's hermeneutics. Finally, the conclusion explores some of the implications that hermeneutics and metaphor theory together have for Chinese studies.

Metaphor studies

Classical theories of metaphor stemming from Aristotle described metaphor as the substitution of one literal term for a metaphorical term, which was thought to share some similarity with the literal term, but which was not literally true. This traditional distinction between literal and metaphorical language casts metaphors as ornamental and inessential. As flowery rhetorical devices, metaphors can be aesthetically pleasing, but philosophical reason pursues the truth, and literary metaphors are literally false: Juliet is not, in fact, the sun; human nature is not, in fact, a bean sprout. Since metaphors do not deliver truth, they were not supposed to have important roles in the theoretical sciences of math and philosophy.

Across the philosophical upheavals of the 20th century, metaphor theory grew in new dimensions. Strands of inquiry that stand prominently in contemporary theories of metaphor took shape in the wake of George Lakoff and Mark Johnson's 1980 book, *Metaphors We Live By*, which showed how metaphors are not just occasional literary embellishments, but are part of our conceptualization of existence and experience of life. We cannot think or speak without relying upon them to give meaning to our most important concerns.

A basic definition of conceptual metaphors is understanding one domain of experience in terms of another. Metaphors create cross-domain mappings, which transfer the structures, relationships, and meanings we associate with a concrete 'source domain' to an abstract 'target domain'. Our primary metaphors draw upon embodied experiences of, for example, visual fields, or locomotion, or objects interacting, and apply the physical schemas of experience to the target domain. The best way to recognize these structural correspondences is with an example, such as ANGER IS FIRE. Zoltán Kovacs (2017) reminds us that our everyday way of talking about anger is full of words having to do with fire:

That *kindled* my ire.
Those were *inflammatory* remarks.
Smoke was coming out of his ears.
She was *burning* with anger.
He was *spitting fire*.
The incident *set* the people *ablaze* with anger.

Then he outlines the systematic correspondences that make sense of why we think about anger and fire in the same terms.

the fire = the anger
the cause of fire = the cause of anger
causing the fire = causing the anger

the thing on fire = the angry person
the intensity of fire = the intensity of anger[2]

These correspondences show why a word like 'inflammatory' makes sense in a statement about anger, which literally has nothing to do with producing flames. It takes a common experience, the visual and tactile encounter with fire, and uses elements of this experience to conceive the more abstract emotional process. This kind of metaphorical transference is most often implicit and goes unnoticed, but has a powerful effect on fundamental concepts. Philosophical examples include KNOWING IS SEEING, TIME IS SOMETHING MOVING TOWARDS US, PURPOSES ARE DESTINATIONS, MORALITY IS CLEANLINESS, and so forth. Once we start looking for them, examples are pervasive and unavoidable.

The theories of conceptual metaphors created a multidisciplinary wave of interest that continues to generate fresh research in linguistics, cognitive science, neuroscience, mathematics, politics, and beyond. Evidence of conceptual metaphors and elaboration on the way they work has grown dramatically (Gibbs 2011). As a broad and productive field of inquiry, theories of conceptual metaphor have made a compelling case that metaphors structure the way that all humans think and act in the world, and are ever-present in human discourse.

This dramatic shift in recognizing the role of metaphor in cognition sets up challenges to prominent strands of philosophy, such as correspondence theories of truth (Johnson 2008: 51). Philosophy's long-standing pursuit of a purely rational conceptualization that literally represents true reality is threatened by a theory of cognition and language that is fundamentally metaphorical and embodied. While universal features of human embodiment – such as moving forwards more easily than moving backwards – provide some invariant structures of experience that appear to provide universally available metaphors, these common experiences receive variable emphasis and carry different meanings and implications that depend on cultural traditions (Fusaroli & Morgagni 2013; Yu 2008, 2015). Conceptual metaphor theory leads us to rethink the goals and methods of philosophy, and to reconsider the roles of the body and culture in our pursuit of truth and meaning.

Metaphor's place in Chinese philosophy

There is a long and complex history of metaphor's role in Western reflection on Chinese thought and language. Below is a brief review and critique of this tradition, following which we turn to the productive possibilities of recognizing conceptual metaphor in Chinese philosophy.

Metaphor and the status of Chinese philosophy

Early on, sinologists recognized the importance of metaphor to Chinese philosophy. However, Chinese texts were initially approached from the perspective of 'classical' metaphor theory, which was often used to condemn Chinese thought as not really philosophical. Primed by the influence of G.W.F. Hegel's *History of Philosophy*, which cast China as a primitive civilization, and Max Weber's notion of 'rationalization', which left China stuck in the irrational past, early sinologists deemed Chinese thought to be underdeveloped, unable to make the transcendental breakthrough of pure reason. China's traditional written characters were believed to represent 'picture thinking', and their authors stuck in images that did not rise to the level of pure reason. The more extreme versions of this become the chauvinist view that Chinese philosophy is not really philosophy, because it does not seek the transcendent truth, but only aesthetic and pragmatic values as appear in rhetoric. The flip side of chauvinism was the enthusiastic orientalism that saw Chinese metaphoricity as a great antidote to the stifling scientism of the west. Akin to the romantic reaction to the enlightenment, metaphorical China was still contrasted with the literalist west, but the order of priority was reversed. Whether positively or negatively charged, the metaphoricity of Chinese philosophy was defined in contrast with Western rationality and its claims to scientific truth.

There is no need to posit this kind of essentialism to Eastern or Western thinking, or hierarchy between them. Logical thinking and metaphorical thinking are both present anywhere there are human beings. Human cognitive capacities are broadly similar across cultural differences. The essential opposition of the 'oriental mind' to the 'occidental mind' is obsolete, and the contemporary theories of cognitive metaphor have been part of the movement carrying us beyond that view.

This opposition of Eastern and Western cognitive capacities has been overcome, not by putting an end to the view that metaphoricity is deep in the character of Chinese thought, but by challenging Western philosophy's self-claimed mantle of 'literal' truth (Slingerland 2011: 6). Everybody thinks in metaphors. This is the way people engage with truth and reality. It is not oriental or occidental, but simply human. All philosophy is fleshed out in metaphor, putting Chinese traditions on a par with any that would claim to be doing true philosophy. One implication of this is that studying Chinese metaphors should be recognized as a reasonable way to inquire rigorously into the deepest and most important truths. Metaphors line the path for any lover of wisdom.

Working with metaphor in Chinese philosophy

Below we will briefly consider some areas of Chinese philosophy in which a theory of conceptual metaphor can shed new light on important ideas. For now, we can gesture towards some topics where further reflection on metaphor use might be fruitful: (1) the iconology of some traditional written characters, (2) paronomasia in the definitions of words, (3) correlative cosmologies, (4) arguments by analogy, (5) borrowing entailments across domains, and (6) conceptual frameworks of core philosophical ideas.

1. Iconology

Chinese literature is recorded as characters, *hanzi* 汉字. The iconic and symbolic portrayals of these characters invites metaphorical interpretation. For millennia, people have tried to understand the meaning of certain words by interpreting the images of character components.[3]

To be clear, only a small subset of characters are iconographic representations, while many more have combined elements to symbolize a further idea, and a large part of them have abstract meanings that cannot be discerned at all from the imagery of the characters. Only in those characters that do have an image resembling something in the world, or a combination of images to suggest something further, can we attempt to follow the mapping from the images to the ideas they represent.

Let's take a familiar example. The component radicals of the word *hao* 好, meaning 'good', shows a woman and child. This maternal image gives us a source of positive feelings that connect to objects of positive evaluation. The embodied memory of family affection feeds the emergent meaning and enriched connotation of *hao*. We can also see that *hao*'s meaning as 'good' is derivative of its ancient usage, where it is often a verb meaning 'to be fond of', 'to like', or 'to love'. There is fondness and love when mother and child are there together. This is a source from which the more abstract evaluation, 'good', gets its positive connotations. This metaphor – GOODNESS IS MOTHER AND CHILD – evokes the deep remembrance of warmth, safety, and nourishment we receive from those who mother us. A family-centric, relational sense of goodness is built into our emotional and ethical memory, and colors the meaning of the term 'good'. This is a particular kind of goodness, embodied in the warmest embrace between a child and its mother.

Another example is the character for *zheng* 正, meaning right, correct, straight, positive, main, just, and more. At first glance, its image of clean right angles may seem to be an excellent example of straightness, justified, and correct. However, when we look at the written styles of ancient characters and try to interpret their symbolic representation, we see something much different.

Here we see more directly an image of a foot, placed below (or in front) of a circle or a square or a line. What does this image represent? In my interpretation, the foot indicates where one stands. I see it as showing the position a subject takes in relation to the circle/square/line.

The single horizontal line, 一, is the character for 'one' 'identity' 'unity'. It is often a synonym for the *dao*, the way of the cosmos. It also simply represents a boundary, like a line in the sand. The square and circle could simply be undefined objects, but we might also note that in Chinese cosmology earth is considered 'square' and heaven is 'round'. Furthermore, I have heard suggestions that the square could represent an altar, or that the circle could represent the sun. None of these speculations can be definitive and our assumptions about what the line/alter/sun could be are subject to revisitation, but my interpretation is that to be 'correct' is to be properly placed in relation to the way, nature, and the sacred. When a person stands before the altar, or beneath the sun, or on the right side of the line, this gives us an embodied sense that everything is aligned and in place. This sense of being 'correct' has much different implications than a philosophy that holds 'correctness' to be accurate representation of reality in the mind. This subtle iconographic etymological influence on our concepts calls for interpretation of the connotations provided by their characters' visual imagery.

2. Paronomasia

One way that words acquire definition and meaning in the Chinese tradition is through a process called 'paronomasia', which is to connect terms through their homophonic pronunciation. This is akin to punning. Often in Chinese language, the similar pronunciation of two words is based on a shared phonetic radical in the written character. This phonetic element serves as the similarity that connects two written terms. This association through paronomasia uses the similar sound or shared written elements of two words to provide the bridge by which aspects of one concept are mapped on to the other.

For example, the Confucian notion of *ren* 仁 (humane) is glossed by the words *ren* 訒 (careful speech), and *ren* 人 (human). To the ear, being humane is connected to being respectful in speaking and with being fully human. Similarly, the word *zheng* 政 (governance) is associated with the word *zheng* 正 (correction). The shared written radical and the auditory similarity among terms sets up a connection that can stimulate creative metaphorical exploration. Given the phonological linkage, we are moved to seek other connections that show how *zheng* 政is like *zheng* 正, as in exercising self-control, bringing order, or putting things in their proper place. *Zheng* 政 is not literally *zheng* 正, but in sounding them out they mutually redound with meaningful associations. Of course not all of the meanings and implications and polysemy of *zheng* 正 can map to *zheng* 政, a fact noted in CMT's notion of partial mapping, but it does provide enough connections to resonate significantly.

We find this way of imputing meaning to terms in the early Chinese lexicons. The *Shiming* (釋名), an ancient glossary of terms, uses puns – called either 'voice explanations' (*shengxun* 聲訓) or 'sound explanations' (*yinxun* 音訓) – throughout to give meaning to the characters that it addresses. Each character is matched with another character that has a similar pronunciation, followed by a comment that ties the meaning of the two words together and shows why the rhyming definition is apropos.

While the *Shiming* was explicitly using the homophonic connection to transfer meaning, this is a species of the broader technique of association. Roger Ames describes this process of paronomasia as 'knowing better by tracing out relevant associations'. This tracing is akin to 'mapping correspondences'. An example of this process appears in the *Shuowen Jiezi*, China's greatest classic dictionary, as it attempted to provide a record of the meaning and character derivation of written words. It was the first lexicon to categorize characters according to their radicals, which provides another route for characters to be associated. More directly, its entries for characters take the form: AB 也. This kind of statement is typically translated as 'A is B', making the grammatical particle *ye* 也 seem like a marker of identity. However, this *ye* is not so much a marker of strict identity or predication, but of affirmation and additional linkage. This is reflected in its modern use as the word for 'also', which is an association rather than an equation. For example, the *Shuowen* says: 'correctness is being so' (*zheng shi ye*正是也). Here *zheng* (correct) is associated with *shi* 是 (what is). How does the *Shuowen Jiezi* define *shi*? It says: being so is straightness (*shi zhi ye* 是直也). And what is straightness? Straightness is correct seeing (*zhi zheng jian ye* 直正见也). That puts in question the definition of 'correct' in 'correct seeing', which leads us to circle back around this loop again. The *Shuowen* does not give us an analytical definition or an exhaustive account of *zheng* 正or *shi* 是or *zhi* 直. Instead, it indicates that there are associations between being correct, what is the case, and straightness. The definitions are left at that, and we are left to map out the relevant similarities among the concepts. An affirmative judgment (*shi*) is not literally 'straightness' (*zhi*), but there is something about 'straightness' that metaphorically informs the concept of affirmation. This suggestive association is an entry into meaning, but not an exhaustive or essential definition.

Ames writes that 'we discover that terms are not as much defined analytically and etymologically by appeal to essential, literal, putatively 'root' meaning, as they are generally explained metaphorically or paronomastically by semantic and phonetic associations' (2008: 39). Instead of analyzing concepts by identifying their essential definitions, paronomasia is a metaphorical process of knowing one idea by referring to another. Seeing one term as partially defined by the content carried by another term is a metaphorical mapping of meaning. Tracing the meaning of a word through its homophonic, radical, and definitional associations is a way of accounting for it without recourse to a literal phrase that might substitute for it. Rather, it relies on the productivity of metaphorical transference to extend meaning through paronomasia.

3. Correlative cosmology

The correlative cosmology characteristic of classical Chinese philosophy is a vast system of cross-domain mappings across diverse categories. Explanations of correlative cosmology are typically given in terms of *yin-yang* characteristics, or the five phases (earth, air, water, wood, and fire), or the 64 hexagrams of the *Book of Changes*. These systematic conceptions set up broad categories (*lei* 类) in which diverse phenomena are associated with the lead cosmological characteristic and with each other. In investigating these categorical schemes, we can see that 'Metaphor is a central organizing component of correlative thinking, of making productive associations, and of the activity of philosophy in early China' (Mattice 2014: 12).

The following abbreviated chart of two of the phases and several categories helps reveal the way these correlating concepts are organized.

Phenomena within the same cosmological category were said to be mutually resonant (*ganying* 感應). This subtle vibratory connection and amplification, like the sympathetic resonance of instrument strings, is the route by which meaning crosses from one domain to the other. The phenomena in a category take on metaphorical transferences in meaning implied by the elemental phase (wood, fire, earth, metal, water). They also have a presumption of similarity with each of the other categories associated with the same phase. This scheme provided organization for the Chinese worldview, and mapped the complexity of worldly phenomena in a comprehensible order.

The most general correlative framing is in terms of *yin* and *yang*. These dynamic forces lend their conceptual connotations to the myriad things. The characteristics of *yin* and *yang* are themselves metaphorically borrowed from concrete experiences of sunny and shady, light and dark, hot and cold, rising and falling, growing and shrinking, and so forth. There is *ganying*, mutual resonance, between *yin* and *yang* and their correlates, such that they contribute to each other's connotations and character.

Some of the basic correlative transferences are obvious and invoke primary metaphors with a sensual basis, such as the *yin* association that threads through dark, cold, wet, depths, valleys, and voids. As more categories are introduced in the Five Phases and 64 hexagrams systems, sometimes the threads of metaphorical mappings seem tenuous. Just what is it about wood that mutually resonates across mutton, eyes, stringed instruments, and Jupiter? While tracing the intracategory resonances can take a bit of imagination, in the long tradition of the five phases they have become correlated with each other through their expression of various wooden qualities, making a fairly coherent order out of the 10,000 things.

The metaphors that take shape in correlative cosmology are not transferring meaning across radically dissimilar domains, but rather across correlates that have a natural association: 'the Chinese metaphor does not try to establish a parallelism between two domains, but rather wants to show that there is a *convergence* between them' (Reding 2004: 136). This correlative understanding of phenomena provides systematic linkages in a world that coheres through mutual resonance. This way of relational definition gives correlates meaning through their resonances, mapped from one cosmological category to another.

4. Arguments by analogy

Analogy is a kind of mapping that says a similarity in one aspect of the domains under comparison implies similarities in other aspects.[4] Analogy's practical role in argumentation is

Table 19.1 Sample categories of the five phases cosmology

Phase	*Color*	*Planet*	*Sense Organ*	*Season*	*Smell*	*Animal*	*Crop*	*Music*
Wood	Green	Jupiter	Eyes	Spring	Musty	Goat	Wheat	Strings
Water	Black	Mercury	Genitals	Winter	Putrid	Pig	Millet	Chimes

widely employed, but in formal logic, argument by false analogy can lead away from truth. Despite their failure to guarantee truth, good analogies can offer strong probable evidence and inductive reasons to assent. They connect one idea to another and carry metaphorical implications across domains. Many arguments by analogy are persuasive because they transfer not only logical entailments, but emotional and bodily ones too.

Ancient Chinese philosophers developed the logic of analogies, particularly in the Mohist and School of Names traditions. Jana Rosker describes analogy's place in this Chinese logic:

> In this framework, analogy depends upon the mapping or alignment of elements in the source and target, which regard not only objects but also relations both among objects and among relations. Hence, this mode of analogical reasoning was determined by the structure of such relations, and the fabric of this structure was tightly connected to language and meaning.
>
> *(2017: 843)*

Systematic criteria of similarities (and differences) unite entities into *lei* 类 (kinds or categories), which make it possible to analogize relations across categories. Practices of *zhengming* 正名 (proper naming) in accordance with *li* 理 (structural patterns) coherently organize the concordances of similar kinds and enable the transfer of assumptions from one domain to another. Early Chinese logicians used these conceptual tools of analysis – categorization, rigid designation, patterning – in systematic efforts to map the corresponding similarities of analogous relations.

Zhuangzi argued against this rigid categorical logic of analogy, but used his own analogical reasoning to great effect. For instance, he argued with the logician Huizi about the happiness of fish in the River Hao, claiming that his own not knowing the fish's happiness was analogous to Huizi's not knowing Zhuangzi's knowing. He uses the power of analogy to spin the logician around, until we arrive at knowledge of fish happiness by analogy to Zhuangzi's own experience, there by the River Hao.

While Chinese philosophy has been denigrated for its limited use of deductive logic in argumentation, good analogies can provide very strong inductive evidence for arguments, and Chinese philosophers used them with powerful effects. For example, David Wong (2015) analyzes the Mencius-Xunzi debates over human nature and ethics and demonstrates the persuasiveness of analogical argumentation. In describing the process of ethical self-cultivation, we see two different analogies with different implications. When Mencius suggests that self-cultivation is to human nature as adornment is to a beautiful face, this inclines us to see moral practices differently than if we, with Xunzi, see that self-cultivation is to human nature as craft is to a recalcitrant material. They each use the further implications of these analogies to justify their preferred methods of ethical cultivation: subtle supplementation or harsh correction, respectively. These philosophers invoked the underlying implications of these metaphors to persuade us towards effective self-cultivation. These are among the most persuasive arguments in Chinese history, built upon the capacity of analogy to impart metaphorical implications.

5. Borrowed entailments

The direct application of conceptual metaphor theory to the Chinese tradition has focused on the implications of particular metaphorical mappings on philosophical topics. I will outline just a few of these efforts.

Ted Slingerland has been expanding awareness of conceptual metaphor in Chinese studies. In an early example of this (2004), he identifies several metaphors that contribute to the notion of the 'self' in the *Zhuangzi*. These include SELF AS SUBJECT, SELF AS CONTAINER, SELF AS ESSENCE, SELF AS OBJECT OF MANIPULATION, and SELF AS OBJECT UNDER CONTROL. These conceptualizations all contribute to the Zhuangzian understanding of the self. By showing how these metaphors structure the conception of self in both Chinese and Western philosophical traditions, he points to the similarities in the available metaphors that arise out of similar conditions of human embodiment.

Erin Cline (2008) presented another metaphor of self, SELF AS MIRROR. While showing how this metaphor makes sense of human experience of the world, she also cautions against expecting underlying similarities in analyzing metaphors from different cultures. While both Chinese and Western philosophers employ the mirror metaphor and draw on similar concrete experiences of looking in reflective surfaces, the processes of mirroring and the meaning of the metaphor seem to show distinct differences. Western thinkers, like Kierkegaard and Rorty, typically conceive of mirroring as accurate representation, while Zhuangzi and Xunzi conceive it as responsiveness. This suggests that certain embodied experiences and metaphorical processes may be common cross-culturally, but the meaning communicated by the metaphors may still be culturally conditioned.

While humans everywhere have ears that recognize harmony, the roots of Western harmony theory in Pythagorean mathematics generates a different set of implications than the Chinese harmony theory rooted in the *Book of Changes*. The Chinese concept of harmony also draws on the sense of taste, which provides an additional flavor to the metaphor. Mason (2018) argues that these different cultural conceptions of harmony provide the basis for divergent political ideals when envisioning a goal of 'social harmony'.

The culturally refined practices and skills of archery, one of the six classical arts, lend themselves to understanding ethical and epistemological domains. James Behuniak (2010) has unpacked Confucian ethical concepts that are conceived in terms of pulling the bow and aiming an arrow to hit the center of a target. He connects the ethical meaning of these archery metaphors to the social aspect of Chinese shooting competitions. Rina Marie Camus (2017) takes aim at the same metaphor, showing how archery implies an ethics of ritual propriety when invoked by Confucius, and a teleological ethics when invoked by Aristotle.

Ning Yu (2015) has analyzed a host of metaphors applying cognitive linguistics to Chinese language. Yu's primary discipline is linguistics, but his choices of metaphors to explore have carried this scholarship deep into philosophical territory, revealing the metaphorical structures that contribute to Chinese notions of time, selfhood, morality, happiness, the heart, and more. This work gathers evidence from language use to reveal the conceptual metaphors that contribute meaning to our philosophical concepts.

6. Philosophical frameworks

Our fundamental ways of understanding and interpreting the world we live in are shaped by deep metaphorical structures. Certain metaphors provide the architecture of our philosophical frameworks.

Sarah Allan writes, 'we must begin by exposing the metaphors that underlie the Chinese terminology and imbue it with meaning' (1997: 18). First, she shows how water provides a model for understanding such pervasive philosophical ideas as *dao* 道 (way), *wuwei* 无为 (doing nothing), *xin* 心 (heart/mind), and *qi* 气 (breath, vapor, vital energy). These concepts follow the model of water in various forms – flowing, draining, pooling, flooding – and so

Chinese philosophy would not make sense without a sense of how water makes its way in the world. The entailments of the water metaphor provide an experiential basis for conceiving Chinese theories of the cosmos, the mind, and human behavior.

Allan's second core metaphor is about how plants grow. This kind of agricultural image shows up in Mencius's famous claim that human nature is like a sprout. Allan writes, 'the principles of plant growth are extended from plants to an understanding of all living things, including humans' (1997: 96). The implication of such a metaphor are dramatic, especially in contrast with the traditional Western imagery: 'Thus, people are not 'reasoning animals' but living things which have a certain potential for growth when they are nurtured properly' (Allan 1997: 96). This agricultural metaphor informs the broad conception of human nature.

Slingerland's (2003) conception of *wuwei* uses conceptual metaphor theory to reveal the embodied schemas shaping China's philosophical discourse. He argues that the experience of effortless action feeds many strands of Chinese thought and he aims to 'present a systematic account of the role of the personal spiritual ideal of *wuwei* or 'effortless action' in Warring States Chinese thought, showing how it serves as a common ideal for both Daoists and Confucians, and also contains within itself a conceptual tension that motivates the development of Warring States thought' (2003: vii). His elaboration of that tension and its effects suggests the power of conceptual metaphors in guiding our theoretical discourse and ethical ideals.

Because the *xin* 心is the human connection to the cosmos, the organ of all thought and feeling, and the ruler of behavior, our understanding of it affects our conceptions of Chinese metaphysics, epistemology, and ethics. Yu (2009) surveys the metaphors of *xin*, situating it within both ancient philosophy and modern discourse. While cataloging the language used in reference to the *xin*, he provides an account of the philosophical and cultural situation in which the concept is used and elaborated. Yu's empirical account of metaphors that feed our understanding of *xin* reveals a Chinese framework of interpretation that does not radically separate cognition from emotion.

When the *Daodejing* begins by saying, 'The *dao* that can be spoken is not the eternal *dao*', it denies the possibility of literal representation of this reality, and so we are pushed towards metaphor to understand this most important Chinese philosophical concept. Forced to give some expression to this obscure notion, Chinese philosophy has settled on the metaphor of a path, a course, a way. This gives us the sense of a *dao* as a directional heading that guides the forward movement of the cosmos as it advances through time. This fecund metaphor lends itself to myriad conceptualizations, from cosmic evolution, to the seasonal progression, to proper human behavior. In its comprehensive breadth and depth, *dao* provides a philosophical framework that has implications for all other aspects of existence. There is no area of Chinese philosophy that is not touched by this guiding metaphor.

Hermeneutics

In all encounters with Chinese metaphors, we are engaged in interpretation. This is the domain of hermeneutic theory. Across history, Chinese philosophy has been fundamentally a hermeneutic discipline: Confucius read, interpreted, and commented on the Rites of Zhou; Mencius read, interpreted, and commented on Confucius; Zhu Xi read, interpreted, and commented on all three of these, and many more. The great Chinese lineage of the *daotong* 道統 is a dialog about the proper interpretation of the *dao*.

The Western tradition of hermeneutic theory – from Aristotle, to biblical studies, to jurisprudence, to history – has developed thoughtful and careful methods for interpreting texts from far away and long ago. There are richly elaborated theories about the best practices for comprehending meaning communicated through written language. The image of the hermeneutic circle, cycling endlessly from part to whole and from whole to part, headlines this methodology, and there are detailed canons of interpretation that can be brought to bear in our reading of Chinese philosophy. These resources are instructive when it comes to deciphering the meaning of literary metaphors we encounter in texts, but here we will focus on the modern turn in philosophical hermeneutics. The field underwent a shift in the 20th century, creating a broad historical division between the period from Aristotle to German Romanticism – where the focus was methodology in specialized fields – and the Post-Nietzschian period with the turn to phenomenology, existentialism, and ontology.

The field turned philosophical primarily through the work of Martin Heidegger and Hans-Georg Gadamer.[5] In trying to understand the world as given in experience, they brought fundamental questions of human existence into focus. They claimed that human experience of the world is always conditioned by pregiven understandings, which are shaped by our circumstances, traditions, and languages. Human existence is embedded in physical, social, and historic contexts that enable us to encounter the world meaningfully, but not fully objectively or autonomously. The transformation of hermeneutics from a discipline of methodology to one that aims at ontology – the study of being and existence – brought these constitutive features of human understanding to the foreground.

What Heidegger calls the 'hermeneutic situation' is expressed by the 'fore-structures' of understanding: 'fore-having', 'fore-sight', and 'fore-conception' (1996: 140–141). These ideas describe the way we encounter a world always already structured by our anticipations and prejudgments. In any experience, we come with a background of presuppositions and assumptions about the world, as well as an unspoken orientation towards what is meaningful and of concern, and a scheme of conceptualization that organizes and makes sense of whatever we might encounter. We address the world with intentionality, and find ourselves thrown into a meaningful world beset with our particular concerns and conceptualizations.

For Heidegger, only when these fore-anticipations are disrupted and we can no longer leave background understanding in the background do we explicitly interpret the world in which we exist. When we interpret, we work with the 'as' structure of understanding. We do not confront pure sense data or an uninterpreted field of experience; rather, the objects and events that call our attention have 'the structure of *something as something*' (Heidegger 1996: 139). We *see* the world *as* we've been led to expect it to be, made possible by the categories and words afforded us by our upbringing.[6] Heidegger showed how humans interpret in the midst of an environment addressed through our concerns and our fore-given frameworks and vocabularies. These guide our descriptions of the world and our judgments about what we experience. We encounter the world in the mode of constituting things as they make sense to us – seeing a hammer as a hammer, a mountain as a mountain, a smile as a smile.

Expanding on Heidegger's insights, Gadamer (2004) emphasizes that finitude, historical situation, belongingness to tradition, and speaking a language are unavoidable conditions of human understanding. Every person operates with what Gadamer calls a 'horizon', which suggests both the magnificent vistas one can experience and the limits of one's vision. Those limits are dynamic and expand as one achieves higher vantage points through life's experiences, but they seem to be structurally insurmountable for human consciousness. There is no way to step outside of one's concrete embodiment in language and traditions to see the world from a neutral standpoint. We have the concerns that our familial, cultural, educational, economic, historical, and linguistic surroundings have delivered over to our conscious lives. These underlie our ability to understand in any sense, and while they are limitations, they are also indispensable.

It is from within one's horizon that one encounters the claims of another. This kind of hermeneutic 'fusion of horizons' is an experience of the truths of another human through art, history, and language. This kind of truth is not from matching up a proposition to an objective reality, but an experience that transforms one's way of being in the world. Gadamer vehemently opposed the importation of a scientific model of methodology in pursuit of objectivity into the humanistic sciences. Instead, he argues that an experience of profound truth changes the way we experience the world ever after it. These transformative experiences become part of our guiding assumptions about the world. In this way, truth is an advancement that corrects or refines our fore-anticipations. While we cannot escape the conditions that both limit and enable our understanding, we can reflect upon and improve our assumptions and prejudgments.

Hermeneutics is this kind of reflective discipline. Confronted with what it would mean to experience the truth of Being fore-conceived through the metaphors of 'the way' and 'the reversions of *yin* and *yang*', we have to re-address familiar expectations carried through Western philosophy, such as 'reality and appearance', 'mind and body', so on. As part of this reflective practice, we remain open to encountering truths expressed by others that might have something to say to us, something true and transformative.

As a methodological discipline, hermeneutics brings a rigorous inquiry to bear on meaningful texts, seeking to reduce our distorting biases and prejudices, so that greater comprehension can stand forth. As an ontological discipline, hermeneutics is the human participation in the truths of being, and especially being as expressed by humans to one another. In any approach to interpreting meaningful texts, hermeneutic practices will be operative; in approaching classical Chinese metaphors, the exquisite hermeneutic challenge of interpreting across distances of time, language, and culture reaches its greatest extent.

Hermeneutics and metaphor and Chinese philosophy

Gadamer early on recognized the 'the fundamental metaphoricity of language', and the 'fundamental metaphorical nature [of] … verbal consciousness' (2004: 428–429). While he did not develop these ideas, they gesture toward the insights of conceptual metaphor theory. As described above, the contemporary view puts metaphor at the heart of cognition and discourse, shaping our concepts and the frameworks in which our conceptions arise. This makes conceptual metaphor an inescapable feature of understanding. It is what Heidegger calls an unavoidable '*existentiale*' of human being in the world. By the time we are able to speak and understand, we are already approaching the world through fore-structures imparted to us by our community. Through language acquisition and social enculturation, we come to speak of the world in the vocabulary and categories that our family and neighbors do. In this way, we unconsciously adopt the metaphors that make shared sense of our shared world. Our traditions direct our conception of experience and the truths experienced. As Gadamer might put it, particular metaphors are part of our prejudgments – our prejudices – about the world. These become our fore-metaphors.

Like the rest of our prejudices, implicit fore-metaphors and their implications can be raised to awareness and put at risk. Cross-cultural philosophy provides an opportunity to do just this. Mattice (2014) gives an example of this by showing the metaphorical entailments of the prevalent PHILOSOPHY IS COMBAT metaphor, and proposing alternatives drawn from hermeneutics and Chinese philosophy, namely PHILOSOPHY IS PLAY and

PHILOSOPHY IS AESTHETIC EXPERIENCE. This demonstrates how the metaphors we use are part of our hermeneutic situation, yet are subject to hermeneutic revision.

We always undertake our explicit interpretations of metaphors from within a horizon. In some cases, especially when approaching a Chinese metaphor from an English-speaking academic background, the limits of our horizons are painfully apparent because the metaphors do not accord with our fore-anticipations of meaning. For example, when we read in *Daodejing* chapter five that 'heaven and earth treat the ten thousand things like straw dogs', the metaphor of 'straw dogs' should make most readers pause because there is no immediate flash of insight about just what the analogy is pointing to. We are, as Gadamer says, 'drawn up short' by unfamiliar ideas. At other times though, a metaphor may strike us as perfectly apt, full of pregnant meaning, and obviously true. On these occasions too, we must remain vigilant for the possibility of projection, overwriting, and cultural imperialism in our assumption that the classical Chinese texts have univocal meanings and are obviously in accord with our own understanding of the world.

Reflection on our hermeneutic situation guides us to be circumspect in thinking that others must understand the world like we do, and that metaphors that draw from our common embodiment must therefore have a common meaning. For instance, the metaphor LIFE IS A PATHWAY[7] appears in both biblical and Daoist sources.[8] Matthew 7:13–14 gives us the image of two paths a life can take – the broad road through the wide gate, or the straight road through the narrow gate. Zhuangzi tells us that 'the way is made in walking'. These sources each draw upon our common physical experience of traveling on a pathway but have different underlying conceptions and connotations: the biblical path has a fixed destination; the Daoist path is free and easy wandering. Although each speaks of paths and our manner of traveling, they are not saying the same thing, and to assume that a path is a path is a path can lead us in the wrong directions.

Although we may begin with different assumptions, nonetheless, we can make some sense of each other's favored metaphors, even across the gulfs of culture and language. In practice, translated works often do make foreign ideas intelligible. These translations can never be literal representations, but they can reinscribe the meaning developed in open dialog through the encounter of linguistic and cultural traditions. Although some metaphorical resonances will not survive translation, it is possible – provisionally, contingently, and incompletely – to bring the subject matter at hand to shared understanding.

Although there are different dominant metaphors that shape the fore-conceptions of reality in Chinese and Western traditions, sorting through the meanings of these metaphors gives us a greater interpretive vocabulary and a further opening to new experiences of truth. As Gadamer says of transformative experience: 'The truth of experience always implies an orientation toward new experience' (2004: 350). In trying to see the world as metaphors of *dao* and *yin-yang* structure it and as metaphors of waterways and sprouts reveal it, we open and extend our horizons of meaning. To take these metaphors seriously is not bad science or illogic, but rather the way to get in touch with and be transformed by ideas with deep ethical value that have given human lives their beauty, meaning, and truth. Cross-cultural metaphor study makes possible a fusion of horizons.

Of course, the 'fusion of horizons' is itself a metaphor. It is not literally what is happening when you read and understand words on a page. Nonetheless, it suggests something meaningful about how we experience an encounter with the truths of human existence. When we encounter the philosophies of a Confucius or a Laozi, we may have to alter our conceptual boundaries and see the world with an augmented perspective. While there may be no literal visual 'horizon' and no melting 'fusion', these metaphors provide a mapping of what it is like to be transformed in the experience of truth available through China's philosophical metaphors.

Notes

1 'Metaphor' here is an umbrella term to capture many ways in which we associate features of one concept with those of another, such as simile, analogy, metonymy, blends, and such. This broad scope covers any kind of cross-domain substitution, transfer, correlation, or mapping of meaning.
2 For comparison of this metaphor in Chinese, see Yu 1995.
3 As critics of Heidegger have objected, explicating etymologies is a creative enterprise, liable to our projections and biases. That is true, and is also a concern for etymology through iconology. Nonetheless, this can still be a speculative way of mining characters for meaning rooted in and carried forward by tradition.
4 This is a more narrow form of analogizing than is sometimes meant, as in the contrast of analogical thinking to logical thinking (Hall & Ames 1995).
5 Paul Ricoeur's *Rule of Metaphor* is a monumental work in hermeneutics and metaphor, but primarily addresses the question of literalness, and so isn't my focus here.
6 In Heidegger-speak: *Dasein* speaks as *Das Man* speaks.
7 Linguistically, this conceptual metaphor shows up in the ethical fear of *slipping*, *stumbling*, *deviance*, becoming a *wayward* soul, and so forth, and in Chinese conceptions of *guo* 过, and *xing* 行.
8 Also in the 1990s rock song, 'Life is a Highway,' which bespeaks another embodied metaphor of speed and adventure.

References

Allan, S. (1997) *The Way of Water and Sprouts of Virtue*, Albany, NY: State University of New York Press.

Ames, R. (2008) 'Paronomasia: A Confucian Way of Making Meaning', in D. Jones (ed) *Confucius Now: Contemporary Encounters with the Analects*, Chicago: Open Court, pp. 37–48.

Behuniak, J. (2010) 'Hitting the Mark: Archery and Ethics in Early Confucianism', *Journal of Chinese Philosophy* 37 (4): 588–604.

Camus, R. (2017) 'Comparison by Metaphor: Archery in Confucius and Aristotle', *Dao: A Journal of Comparative Philosophy* 16 (2): 165–185.

Cline, E. (2008) 'Mirrors, Minds, and Metaphors', *Philosophy East and West* 58 (3): 337–357.

Fusaroli, R. and Morgagni, S. (2013) 'Introduction: Thirty Years After', *Journal of Cognitive Semiotics* 5 (1/2): 1–13.

Gadamer, H.G. (2004) *Truth and Method*, J. Weinsheimer and D. Marshall (trans), Second Revised Edition, London: Continuum.

Gibbs, R. (2011) 'Evaluating Conceptual Metaphor Theory', *Discourse Processes* 48 (8): 529–562.

Hall, D. and Ames, R. (1995) *Anticipating China: Thinking Through the Narratives of Chinese and Western Culture*, Albany: State University of New York Press.

Heidegger, M. (1996) *Being and Time*, J. Stambaugh (trans), Albany, NY: State University of New York Press.

Johnson, M. (2008) 'Philosophy's Debt to Metaphor', in R. Gibbs (ed) *The Cambridge Handbook of Metaphor and Thought*, Cambridge: Cambridge University Press, pp. 39–52.

Kovaces, Z. (2017) 'Conceptual Metaphor Theory', in E. Semino (ed) *The Routledge Handbook of Metaphor and Language*, New York: Routledge.

Lakoff, G. and Johnson, M. (1980) *Metaphors We Live By*, Chicago: University of Chicago Press.

Mason, J. (2018) 'Generalization, Cultural Essentialism, and Metaphorical Gulfs', *Dao: A Journal of Comparative Philosophy* 17 (4): 1–19.

Mattice, S. (2014) *Metaphor and Metaphilosophy*, Lanham, MD: Lexington Books.

Rosker, J. (2017) 'Structural Relations and Analogies in Classical Chinese Logic', *Philosophy East and West* 67 (3): 841–863.

Slingerland, T. (2003) *Effortless Action*: Wu-*wei as Conceptual Metaphor and Spiritual Ideal in Early China*, Oxford: Oxford University Press.

Slingerland, T. (2004) 'Conceptions of the Self in the "Zhuangzi": Conceptual Metaphor Analysis and Comparative Thought', *Philosophy East and West* 54 (3): 322–342.

Slingerland, T. (2008) 'Metaphor from Body and Culture', in R. Gibbs (ed) *The Cambridge Handbook of Metaphor and Thought*, Cambridge: Cambridge University Press, pp. 247–261.

Slingerland, T. (2009) *The Chinese HEART in a Cognitive Perspective: Culture, Body, and Language*, New York: Mouton de Gruyter.

Slingerland, T. (2011) 'Metaphor and Meaning in Early China', *Dao: A Journal of Comparative Philosophy*, 10 (1): 10–30.

Slingerland, T. (2015) 'Embodiment, Culture, and Language', in F. Sharifian (ed) *The Routledge Handbook of Language and Culture*, London: Routledge, pp. 227–239.

Wong, D. (2015) 'Early Confucian Philosophy and the Development of Compassion', *Dao: A Journal of Comparative Philosophy* 14 (2): 157–194.

Yu, N. (1995) 'Metaphorical Expressions of Anger and Happiness in English and Chinese', *Metaphor and Symbolic Activity* 10 (2): 59–92.

20

Poetry and emotion in classical Chinese literature

Chen Xia

Chinese poetry lies close to the heart of the Chinese cultural tradition and is an important component of classical Chinese literature. Expressing emotions has widely been believed to be the essence of classical Chinese literary culture. A modern, historically influenced, interpretation of this tradition was first put forward by the Chinese thinker Liang Qichao (梁啟超, 1873–1929), who placed the notion of 'emotion' at the core of the classical Chinese poetry tradition, inspired by the Enlightenment and the emergence of European modernity in the 18th century (Zhang 2012). From European antiquity, and later integrated with the ideas of Christianity, the relation between body and mind was regarded as a unity, shaped as a particular balance derived from the cosmological pattern of the four natural 'humors' penetrating the universe in various transformations. According to this holistic thinking, emotions are the result of external forces disturbing the natural balance of any human being, and, according to Stoicism in particular, it is the task of all humans to protect their mental and bodily equilibrium by combatting extreme emotions through an act of reason. Stoicism began in the third century BCE and continues as an active philosophy in European thinking until today (Nussbaum 2010). In the mid-18th century, the period in which Liang Qichao found inspiration, this cosmologically based conception of emotions was turned around by the thinking of David Hume (1771–1776) and Adam Smith (1723–1790) among others. Within the horizon of European individualism emotions were individualized as a mental force which, from within, defined personal identity. Emotions were seen as individually and socially edifying forces – quite opposite to earlier periods. From this perspective, emotions were not integrated with a universal pattern of basic feelings, but always occurred as an individual blend and cluster of feelings – some of a social nature, like love, moral feelings etc., and some of a disruptive nature, like extreme passion, obsessions etc. Yet even the latter were endowed with some positive qualities because of their role in forming individual identity.

Combining Confucianism, Buddhism, and Western aesthetics, Liang Qichao believed that in classical Chinese poetry emotion was the main driver of poetic creation and viewed as the key to educating people. According to Liang Qichao's emotional poetics, through the process of literary creation and appreciation of classical Chinese poetry people can freely explore and improve their own personalities, acquire empathy and resonance with others in the most comprehensive way through emotional engagement, and it is also emotions

DOI: 10.4324/9780429059704-24

that can organically integrate the aesthetic and moral experience of poetry (Zhang 2012). Inspired by Liang Qichao, this chapter explores a number of concepts and examples in order to demonstrate the historical embodiment of emotions in the literary tradition of classical Chinese poetry and the way it is disseminated.

Poetry and the expression of emotion as a tradition

As the guiding principle of ancient Chinese literature, the concept of the 'poetic incentive' (詩言志) is inherent in the earliest recorded classical literature (Cao 1996). This is quite a different category from the notion of 'emotion' in Liang Qichao's poetics in a literal sense. The meanings of 'poetic incentive' have been discussed and elaborated in different historical periods. It is believed that the core component of the concept of Zhi (志), meaning 'incentive', 'will', 'ambition', has experienced a highly diverse and complex evolution. From the earliest periods of poetry as ritual, music and sacrifice, the 'poetic incentive' was a kind of sacrifice to the gods, that is, a yearning for the unity of divine and human. In the Spring and Autumn Period (770–476 BCE), when the rites of the Zhou Dynasty collapsed, so-called 'Poetry Diplomacy' (詩賦外交) gained momentum, emphasizing a view of the 'poetic incentive' as also applied to diplomatic contexts. In *The Poetic Exposition on Literature* (文賦, 266–316, in Jin Dynasty) by Lu Ji (陸機, 261–303), it is made clearer that 'the poem follows from the affections and is sensuously intricate' (詩緣情而綺靡, Owen 2019: 143–145), and that the aesthetic characteristics of poetry in a gradually maturing style rely on the way the 'poetic incentive' unites emotion and volition. In *Ts'ang-lang's Remarks on Poetry* (滄浪詩話, 1228–1233/1241–1252, in the Southern Song Dynasty) by Yan-yu (嚴羽, 1192～1197–1241～1245), he proposes that poetry is 'to sing what is in the heart' (吟詠性情) (Owen 2019: 524–525), highlighting the singular and incomparable capacity of poetry to touch the inner feeling world of readers, and underlines how this effect is channeled by the poet's emotion and personality. This has gradually become the concept of ancient Chinese literary theory recognized and appreciated by later generations. Thus, the 'poetic incentive' of classical Chinese literature evolved over time, through generations of poets and literary critics, and came by the beginning of the 20th century to form a consensus very close to Liang Qichao's emotional poetics.

Before the Han Dynasty (202–220) all of Chinese poetry was contained in *The Book of Songs* (詩經, 1046–256 BCE) and *The Songs of Chu* (楚辭, 475–221 BCE), which are the 'forefathers' of Chinese poetry (Lv 2018: 276). The 'Guo Feng' (國風) in *The Book of Songs* is the source of the realist tradition in classical Chinese poetry, while Qu Yuan's 'Li Sao' (離騷), in *The Songs of Chu,* created a romantic style for ancient Chinese literature.

As advocated by Confucius and following the tradition of *The Book of Songs,* the type of poetry found in the 'Guo Feng' laid the ground for the realist function of social education, politics and diplomacy, with the best emotional expression defined as 'expressive of enjoyment without being licentious, and of grief without being hurtfully excessive' (樂而不淫, 哀而不傷) (Legge 2016a: 91–92), which is derived from Confucian aesthetics. Here is an example of the realist style from *The Book of Songs* (小雅·采薇):

昔我往矣,
楊柳依依。
今我來思,
雨雪霏霏。

English translation by James Legge:

> At first, when we set out,
> The willows were fresh and green.
> Now, when we shall be returning,
> The snow will be falling in clouds.
>
> *(Legge 2016b: 158–161)*

Four sentences from the poem perfectly embody the notion of 'expressive of enjoyment without being licentious, and of grief without being hurtfully excessive' and, known as one of the best verses in *The Book of Songs* (Zhou 2014: 15), have influenced a history of interpretation for more than 1,500 years, since the Southern Dynasties (420–589). One interpretation has it that this poem was more likely written in the time of King Xuan of Zhou and the work of soldiers returning to the army. The poem sings of their hard life and feelings of yearning for home. In the Zhou Dynasty, the Northern Nation (玁狁, later Xiongnu) was very powerful and often invaded the Central Plains, bringing disaster to the lives of Northern people. There are many historical records of Zhou Tianzi sending troops to defend border areas. The poem is like a picture, expressing the unspoken suffering of soldiers far from home.

According to literary theory originating from *The Analects of Confucius* (論語·陽貨, Spring and Autumn Period; Warring States Period, 770–221 BCE), the social functions of ancient Chinese poetry are fourfold. '*The odes*', Confucius writes, serve to 'stimulate the mind (xìng興)', 'be used for purposes of self-contemplation (guān觀)', 'teach the art of sociability (qún群)', and 'show how to regulate feelings of resentment (yuàn怨)' (Legge 2016a: 634). The 'odes' mentioned here refers to *The Book of Songs*. Known in the pre-Qin period (before 221 BCE) as *Three Hundred Poems* (詩三百), it was collated by Confucius in the Spring and Autumn Period (770–476 BCE). Emperor Wu of the Han Dynasty respected this collection of poems as a classic and named it *The Book of Songs,* which means 'poetry classic'. Confucius gave a clear and concrete exposition of the significance of *The Book of Songs*, of which two examples are given below.

> '不學詩，無以言。'(論語·季氏)
>
> 'If you do not learn the Odes, you will not be fit to converse with'
>
> *(Legge 2016a: 607–608)*
>
> '誦《詩》三百，授之以政，不達；使于四方，不能專對；雖多，亦奚以為？' (論語·子路)
>
> 'Though a man may be able to recite the three hundred odes, yet if, when entrusted with a governmental charge, he knows not how to act, or if, when sent to any quarter on a mission, he cannot give his replies unassisted, notwithstanding the extent of his learning, of what practical use is it?'
>
> *(Legge 2016a: 446–447)*

Here, '言 [yán]' refers to diplomatic language, while '專對 [zhuān duì]' refers to the meaning of diplomatic negotiation and response. The meaning of these two paragraphs is: if you do not understand *The Book of Songs* or you cannot write or use poems, you cannot participate in diplomatic activities; also, if you do not understand the 300 pieces of *The*

Book of Songs, you cannot negotiate independently, and it will be useless for you to read more poems. This is the so-called 'poetry diplomacy', which originated in the Western Zhou Dynasty and prevailed among princes in the Spring and Autumn Period. It refers to a kind of diplomatic discourse in which fragments of *The Books of Songs* seem to suggest that the diplomatic intentions of one's country and the exploration of those of other countries are best articulated and understood through the 'poetic incentive' typical of each country (Piao 2012: 149–163). The tradition persists to this day: Chinese leaders often recite poems to demonstrate their solemnity and diplomatic friendship during major state visits.

It is believed that the poem 'Li Sao' by Qu Yuan (屈原, about 340–278 BCE), began the romanticism of expressing personal feelings of sadness and indignation in poetry, while 'Li Sao' itself is also a masterpiece full of political implications. *The Songs of Chu,* represented by 'Li Sao', was a product of the Yangtze River civilization. In the field of poetics, according to Yang (2012), Qu Yuan brought the Yangtze River civilization into the general development of Chinese civilization, extending the development of poetic civilization to Hunan and regions to the south which were still at that time regarded as remote and less civilized. In 'Li Sao', Qu Yuan expresses his ideas through a series of metaphors and other literary devices intended to enhance the 'Xing' of poetry – according to Confucius its capacity to concentrate on the subject of the poem. Flowers and herbs are used to describe the noble and virtuous gentleman, foul-smelling things to denote the treacherous villain, and the wearing of herbs symbolizes the poet's moral cultivation. No less than 34 different herbs are mentioned, some in general terms and others by their proper names. Qu Yuan was the first in Chinese literature to explicitly use 'beauty' as a symbol of perfect politics (美政, a perfect government or an esteemed monarch). Although this ideal of perfect politics was to be repeatedly frustrated in reality, as a poetic tradition his metaphor of fragrant grass and beauty (香草美人) became a model for Chinese literati when expressing their will and emotion with regard to politics.

The Book of Songs symbolizes a poetic tradition favoring emotions of gentleness and restraint, while *The Songs of Chu* shows a liberation of emotions and creation of a new, vigorous and powerful poetic style with more space for intense and self-forgetful emotions. The realist spirit of *The Book of Songs* is mainly embodied in the folk songs included in 'Guo Feng', which reflect the social reality of its time. By comparison, 'Li Sao' borrows materials from Chu's mythology and religious culture of Wu (巫, an ancient regional characteristic culture, with astrology and divination as the main form, and salt culture and medicine culture as the main content), and began a magnificent tradition of the romantic in classical Chinese poetry. *The Book of Songs* is a collection of poems without named 'poets', basically a mass collective creation with little expression of individuality, while 'Li Sao' in *The Songs of Chu* can be read as a long 'personal biography of a political career', embodying the poet's personal ideals and experience, his pain and all his enthusiasm for life, which mark the poems with the distinct personality of the first poet-author in the history of ancient Chinese literature (Lv 2018: 276–279). 'Li Sao' from *The Songs of Chu* and 'Guo Feng' from *The Book of Songs*, together referred to as 'Feng-Sao' (風-騷), exercised a profound influence on the poetic creations of later generations.

Poetry and emotion as literary and aesthetic categories

In the aesthetic philosophy genres and institutionalized forms of classical Chinese poetry, Wind and Bone (風骨), Li-Qu (理趣) and Jing-Jie (境界), all revolve around the relationship between poetry and emotion. Liu Xie (劉勰, 465–532)'s concept of Wind and Bone emphasizes the critical importance of the strong and sincere emotions from which poetic expression is created. Under the influence of Neo-Confucianism, Song Dynasty poetry advocates Li-Qu, paying attention to the meaning and delight contained in ordinary life. According to the theory of Jing-Jie, as integrated by Wang Guo-Wei (王國維, 1877–1927) and further interpreted by Zhu Guang-Qian (朱光潛, 1897–1986), a core idea is the creative blending of Qing (情) – emotions rooted in reality – and Jing (景) – scenery.

Wind and Bone: Emotion and expression

The concept of Wind and Bone was first introduced to character evaluation during the Wei and Jin Dynasties (220–420). Later, calligraphers and painters used it to describe a certain style of calligraphy and painting. Liu Xie, a famous literary theorist of the Northern and Southern Dynasties (420–589), integrated the literary theory of Wind and Bone into his *Wen-hsin tiao-Lung* (文心雕龍, completed in 501–502), the first literary theory monograph with a systematic theory, strict structure and detailed discussion, which established Liu Xie's position in the history of ancient Chinese literature and criticism.

As a category of literary criticism and aesthetic philosophy, the construction of Wind and Bone as a concept involves rhetorical devices of metaphor. Wind (風) comes from the natural wind, and then refers to the literary tradition originating from *The Book of Songs*. In Liu Xie's literary theory, this concept of Wind emphasizes that emotion in poems should be sincere and strong, so as to ensure that the work embodies a moving artistic appeal. Bone (骨), originally related to the physical structure of human beings, in Liu Xie's literary criticism means that the content of poems should be fully conveyed in vigorous language and an energetic style of expression. When poems strive to convey an earnest and abundant emotion, with vigorous expression, this is 'the wind clear and the bone splendid' (風清骨峻, Owen 2019: 257–258), as described by Liu Xie (Tong 1999). Gibbs points out that Liu Xie tried to integrate previously various meanings of Wind, to form a more comprehensive and powerful concept. Through Liu Xie's work, Wind and Bone was established as a literary phenomenon and an internal impulse of poets to influence readers, whereby the author aspires to stimulate a resonance of emotion in their hearts through specific ways of writing (Gibbs 1972). Liu Xie's creative conceptualization poses a problem for translation: 'Wind and Bone' as a literal translation of '風骨' has been not only criticized extensively by overseas English scholars, but also constantly questioned by domestic scholars. However, no appropriate alternative has been proposed (Liu 2009).

Cao Cao (曹操, 155–220), the founder of the Cao Wei regime in the Three Kingdoms (220–280), was an outstanding statesman, strategist, writer, and calligrapher of the late Eastern Han Dynasty (184–220). His poems give expression to his own political ambition and reflect the miserable life of the people at the end of the Han Dynasty. Cao initiated and flourished in the Jian'an (196–220) literary mode. As a military commander, he climbed Jieshi Mountain on his way home after a victory on the Northern expedition, and wrote the poem 'The Blue Sea' (觀滄海).

東臨碣石，以觀滄海。
水何澹澹，山島竦峙。
樹木叢生，百草豐茂。
秋風蕭瑟，洪波湧起。
日月之行，若出其中；

星漢燦爛，若出其裡。
幸甚至哉，歌以詠志。

On the East Hill I stand, O'er looking the blue sea.
The waters far expand; The isle juts up like T.
The trees grow upon trees; The grass sprawls on so lush.
Now soughs an autumn breeze; That spurs the waves to rush.
O Sun, o Moon, so light, Have you risen from there?
O Milky Way, so bright, Have you taken their glare?
How happy, o hurray! I sing, sing up this lay.

Tr. Zhao Yanchun (Zhao 2015)

Jieshi Mountain is located in Hebei Changli. It is said that both the first emperor of the Qin Dynasty (221–207 BCE) and Emperor Wu of the Han Dynasty (202 BCE – 220) detoured to this mountain and carved stones overlooking the sea. In the Autumn of 207 Cao passed this way on his triumphal return from a critical battle in his great plan for unification of the North. Ascending the summit of Jieshi, Cao embraced the magnificent view of the sea. The emotion is vigorous and conveyed through description of the scenery rather than through words and phrases of literal emotion. This poem is a representative work in the Jian'an mode, 'with the wind clear and the bone splendid'.

Li-Qu: Emotion and reason

Generally speaking, Tang and Song poetry are regarded as the two most canonical types of Chinese poetry, each with its own distinct features. Poets of the Tang Dynasty (618–907) paid more attention to extraordinary feelings, while those of the Song Dynasty (960–1279) acknowledged that life was mainly ordinary and so were the feelings expressed in their poems. The lyricism of Tang poetry is particularly prominent, with narration, description and discussion usually introduced as auxiliary to lyricism. In Song poetry this is not the case. Poets of the Song Dynasty often deliberately expand the composition of narration, description and discussion, and reduce the lyrical element. Therefore, Song poetry often feels more like a rhymed text than a poem (Lv 2019: 88–111). The poetry of the Song Dynasty as a whole presents a free and elegant artistic merging with Neo-Confucianism, which is different from the more individualized variety of emotions in Tang poetry (Zhou 2019: 3–100).

Shen De-Qian (沈德潛, 1673–1769), minister, poet and scholar of the Qing Dynasty, said in his collection of poems of that Dynasty (清詩別裁集): 'Poetry cannot be separated from Neo-Confucianism. This, the philosophic inspiration from Neo-Confucianism is valued higher than poetic language' (詩不能離理，然貴有理趣，不貴有理語) (Shen 1998).

Su Shi (蘇軾, 1037–1101) was a writer, calligrapher and painter of the Northern Song Dynasty (960–1127), a literary star who achieved great things in all domains of art and writing. His poems are characterized by a unique style, broad themes, and fresh and vigorous feelings, with a use of metaphors and exaggerations. When Su Shi was 'relegated' from Huangzhou to Ruzhou in May 1084 he passed the Jiujiang River and visited Lushan Mountain. The magnificent landscape inspired him to complete a number of travel poems about Lushan Mountain, including 'Written on the Wall at West Forest Temple' (題西林壁), which has remained popular with succeeding generations.

橫看成嶺側成峰，
遠近高低各不同。
不識廬山真面目，
只緣身在此山中。

From the side, a whole range; from the end, a single peak:
Far, near, high, low, no two parts alike.
Why can't I tell the true shape of Lu-shan?
Because I myself am in the mountain.

Tr. Burton Watson (Wei 2013)

From shifting directions and distances, Lushan Mountain assumes different shapes, since the observer's view is always limited. This is not only a picturesque scenery poem, but also a philosophical poem. It alludes to Su Shi's perception of his own political experience. After beginning his career as a civil servant at court, he was involved in the struggle between Conservatives and Reformists and these shifting shapes of Lushan in his poem can be seen as depicting the complicated political situation. Meanwhile, simple and unadorned, the poem also has an immediate appeal to the reader beyond the metaphorical political context. In addition to the beautiful image of the mountain, from a historical perspective this poem stands out as a representative work of Neo-Confucian poetry of the Song Dynasty, beautifully integrating mild emotion, external scenery and philosophical thinking (Qian 2012: 72).

Jing-Jie: Emotion and scenery

'Jing-Jie' is the aesthetic of artistic practice, 'Jie' (界) meaning skills and 'Jing' (境) a landscape to be related to or become immersed in. Poetry creates an infinite aesthetic effect with limited imagery, and this is expounded in the Jing-Jie genre. The literary term Jing comes originally from Buddhism. The concept of Jing in poetry dates from the Tang Dynasty, while Wang Guo-Wei used the concept of Jing-Jie to integrate Eastern and Western aesthetic philosophy. According to Zhu Guang-Qian's further interpretation, the pursuit of Jing-Jie in the creation and appreciation of poetry means an integration of Qing and Jing, a harmonious unity between subject and object, meaning and image, text and acceptance, as shaped in and by the text (Zhu 2012: 46–49).

Wang Wei (王維, 701–761/699–761), known as the 'Buddhist Poet,' is a representative poet of the prosperous Tang Dynasty. He was proficient in Buddhism, greatly influenced by Zen, famous for his poems, calligraphy and painting, versatile and particularly proficient in music. In his landscape poems, many images of Zen are introduced. One perfect example is to be found in the poem 'At My Villa in Zhongnan' (終南別業), written about 758 BCE in the Tang Dynasty, during his later and personally difficult years.

中歲頗好道，晚家南山陲。
興來每獨往，勝事空自知。
行到水窮處，坐看雲起時。
偶然值林叟，談笑無還期。

Midway on life's journey I believed in Tao,
Now that I'm old I dwell near mountains green.
I loiter there alone whenever in the mood,
And enjoy without a companion the quiet scene.
Sauntering along till the end of the brook,
I take a rest and watch the clouds appear.
Casually encountering an old neighbor,
I forget to return, chatting in good cheer.

Tr. Sun Liang (Xu, Lu, & Wu 1988: 55)

Zhu Guang-Qian interpreted Wang Guo-Wei's concept of 'Jing-Jie' as a blending of images (意象) and feelings (情趣) (Zhu 2012: 46–49). The typical images in this poem are of 'the end of a stream or fountain' and 'rising clouds', and the feeling is the thoroughness of Zen. Having climbed the mountain to the source of the stream, the poet sits at his ease, with no worries, and contemplates the view of the clouds rising over the mountain. The two sentences '行到水窮處，坐看雲起時' have been highly appreciated by poets of later generations because of the richness of Zen ideas. Moreover, they are as picturesque as any landscape painting. It was Wang Wei's images of Zen blending with peaceful mood that won him the title of Buddhist Poet.

Poetry and emotion in global dissemination

Max Weber analyzed *modernity* from the perspective of a *disenchantment* of the world, proposing that *disenchantment* had affected all aspects of life in politics, the economy, culture, ideas and the whole of modern society. With the disenchantment and deconstruction of a traditional system of civilization, as Weber observes, modernity triggers people's existential anxiety, as defined by Søren Kierkegaard (1813–1855), a pioneer of existentialism in the 19th century. According to the work of Rollo May, one of the founders of existential psychology, further developed by American contemporary humanistic psychologist James Bugental, existential anxiety is produced by natural or manmade disaster or disease imperils an individual's survival, loss of important spiritual beliefs, ideals or values (Chen & Wang 2009). In a period when global modernity is impacting human society, classical Chinese poetry offers a peaceful platform for softening existential anxiety.

Hanshan's poems and the Beat Generation

Hanshan (寒山), whose years of birth and death, like his given name, are not known, gave himself the name of Hanshan or Hanshanzi (寒山子), because he lived for many years in seclusion on Cuiping Mountain (also known as Hanyan or Hanshan Mountain) in Tiantai. While some hold that he was born in the early Tang Dynasty, others believe he lived during the middle Tang Dynasty. The image of Hanshan as a poor, crazy wild man was fixed by later generations. Now accepted as one of the most important writers of the Tang Dynasty Vernacular Poetry School, Hanshan did not exercise a substantial social influence in his own time; his poems were circulated only in Buddhist temples. During the Song Dynasty, his poetry found a small readership among the educated elite. The content and style of Hanshan's poems are consistent with Song Dynasty thought (Xiang 2019: 1–17).

Here is one of Hanshan's poems, 'Cold Mountain with Hidden Wonders' (寒山多幽奇), with a translation by Gary Snyder:

寒山多幽奇, 登者皆恒慑。
月照水澄澄, 风吹草猎猎。
凋梅雪作花, 枯木云充叶。
触雨转鲜灵, 非晴不可涉。

Cold Mountain has many hidden wonders,
People who climb here are always getting scared.
When the moon shines, water sparkles clear.
When wind blows, grass wishes and rattles.
On the bare plum, flower of snow
On the dead stump, leaves of mist.
At the touch of rain it all turns fresh and lives
At the wrong season you can't ford the creeks.

Tr. Gary Snyder (1965)

The faith embodied in Hanshan's poems combines ideas of Confucianism, Taoism, monastery life and everyday reality. But most of his work precisely embodies the spirit of Buddhism, as in this poem, where images of home and scenery are described in Buddhist spiritual terms such as 'deep and serene' (幽深) and 'Vivikta' (空寂, 'open and quiet'). The artistic style is also diverse, generally describing emotion directly, free from the rules and regulations of ancient Chinese poetry and both down-to-earth and elegant. Later generations called this 'Hanshan's style' and these poems long failed to gain a place in the canonical literary history of China. By contrast, Hanshan's poetry has enjoyed a more advantageous fortune abroad (Xiang 2019: 1–17). In the past hundred years, it has been highly valued and respected in Japan; and it was Gary Snyder who led Hanshan's poetry on a legendary cross-cultural literary journey, as one of the 'texts without borders' during globalization (Larsen 2020: 5), and entered the landscape of American literature (Zhao 2013: 71–74). In the 1950s and 1960s, the youth generation in the United States, known as the *Beat Generation*, worshipped Hanshan as a spiritual idol after reading the American Zen poet Gary Snyder's powerful English translations of his poems. Members of the Beat Generation grew up in the economic crisis that began in the late 1920s in the United States, experienced the devastation of World War II, and then lived with the Cold War and nuclear threat. Their pursuit of *Vision* (meaning scene, vision, and illusion, and the experience of transcending and entering the eternal realm), defined the spiritual world of the Beat Generation. Buddhism, jazz, sex and drugs were all ways for them to live this *Vision*, which they found reflected in Hanshan's poems (Ye 2015). A prominent representative of this generation, Jack Kerouac, wrote an influential book, *The Dharma Bums* (2006), in which he invited Hanshan, the poet monk, to return to life on the podium of the 'backpack revolution', giving the poems a new life in the West (Chen 2020).

Classical Chinese poetry and Chinese anxiety

In recent decades, contemporary Chinese society has experienced an accelerated modernization through globalization and urbanization. Most Chinese have enjoyed the benefits of modern civilization, but have also been exposed to a new existential anxiety almost on a daily basis, triggered by a pluralism of values and an intensified identity crisis on both personal and social levels. Research by social psychologists suggests that, as Chinese people are faced with contemporary existential anxiety, nostalgia and national elements have become fashionable themes for the cultural industries (Zhou et al. 2019). In this context, traditional classical Chinese poetry may help contemporary Chinese to reshape their traditional cultural identity and cope with the ubiquitous anxiety activated by experience of modernity. For example, in 2016, the classical Chinese Poetry Show (中國詩詞大會), a nation-wide TV cultural program, became extremely popular and inspired a surge in people's interest in Chinese poetry. Likewise in 2018 another large-scale TV cultural program, the Classic Chant Spread (經典詠流傳), achieved high ratings and public acclaim. Through this program, which combined ancient Chinese poems with modern pop music, the poem 'Moss' (苔) by Yuan Mei (袁枚, 1716–1797), which had not been a popular poem for nearly 300 years, moved hundreds of millions of Chinese people to tears in the first few days of Chinese New Year 2018.

白日不到處，青春恰自來。
苔花如米小，也學牡丹開。(也 一作：亦)

In places daylight doesn't reach,
that's where, in spring, the green appears —
the moss-flowers, small as rice-grains,
learn to open from the peonies.

Tr. Will Buckingham[1]

Yuan Mei was a poet and essayist of the Qing Dynasty (1636–1912) and one of the representative poets of the Qianjia period (1736–1820). This little poem is an ode to vitality. Moss is an often ignored plant that lives in dark and humid places, but also has its own instinct and intention to persist. It will not lose the courage to grow because of a hostile environment, even in an unsuitable place where daylight does not reach. Moss grows green and vividly shows the vitality of Spring, successfully breaking through the obstacles of its environment to bloom as fully as a peony, even though its flowers are as small as grains of rice – a victory for life itself. This poem was performed on the TV show by volunteer teacher Liang Jun (梁俊) and his students. In 2013, Mr. Liang and his wife went to the poor and remote mountain village of Shi-men-kan in Guizhou Province to volunteer at the local school. He found that it was difficult for the children in those mountains to learn the Chinese language properly, so he composed music for ancient Chinese poems and played them with his guitar in class. Unexpectedly, the children passionately embraced this way of learning poems. In two years, Liang helped the students to learn more than 100 poems and encouraged them to write poems of their own. Liang said that children in such remote mountains were similar to moss-flowers, when compared with their counterparts in cities, so they should learn from the peony and bravely open up. He not only helped the students to learn their language but through the singing of ancient Chinese poems also inspired them and stimulated their sense of a meaning in life. Liang expressed as his firm belief that 'reading ancient Chinese poetry can make a better modern Chinese' (Amy 2018).

Poetry and global anxiety in the COVID-19 epidemic

Globalization has offered opportunities for the rapid development of global human connectivity. At the same time, it has not only led to a pluralism of values and a threat to traditional spiritual beliefs, but resulted in global crises in economy, political conflicts, environment and public health. In the early spring of 2020, the COVID-19 epidemic first attacked mainland

China, and then began to ravage the entire globe, with frequent diplomatic crises targeting China, while racial discrimination and threats against overseas Chinese (even Asian Americans) were frequently reported in the press. In early April, the BBC launched *Du Fu* (杜甫, 712–770), a historical TV documentary praising one of China's greatest poets (Wang 2020). This documentary evoked warm historical collective memories among Chinese experiencing great existential anxiety and aroused an expression in overseas social media of people's yearning for classical Chinese poetry.

The BBC documentary was hosted and directed by historian Michael Wood, who as a young man studied English translations of Tang poetry in China in the 1980s, using English translations adapted from William Hung (洪業)'s versions produced for his 1952 biography of Du Fu. The film also features the young British guitarist Ian McClain and the popular Shakespearean actor Ian McKellen, who interprets 15 of Du Fu's poems with tunes from Shakespeare's time. The TV audience was moved by Du Fu's poems and his moral emotions and conscience. The program can be seen as an attempt to establish cross-cultural communication, bridging the differences between the traditions of English poetry and classical Chinese poetry (Chen & Zhou 2018). On the program the American sinologist Stephen Owen, participating together with Zeng Xiang-Bo of Beijing, and Liu Tao-Tao of Oxford, paid tribute to Du Fu:

> 'We have not only Dante, Shakespeare, but also Du Fu.'

Du Fu was a great Tang realist poet and regarded by later generations as a 'Poet Sage'. His more than 1,400 poems have been preserved and continued to have a far-reaching influence. Unlike Li Bai (李白, 701–762), whose achievements were recognized widely before his death, Du Fu's fame was not established until 30 or 50 years after he died (Chen 2019: 276). Born in a family embracing Confucianism, he experienced war, exile, poverty and illness for most of his life, but always expressed greater care for people and country than for himself, embodying traditional Chinese moral values. Du Fu's poems are known as 'Historical Poetry', a term referring to poetry that reflects social realities and major events of a historical period, so possessing historical value. With the political corruption in the later Tang period under Emperor Xuanzong, Du Fu witnessed rebels occupying the capital and floods and famine destroyed the whole country, and was forced to flee. These tribulations formed a large part of the subject matter of Du Fu's poems in his later years, regarded by Stephen Owen as the voice of the Chinese people at that time.

Du Fu wrote, probably in his last year of life, a poem in the style of a Jueju (絕句，a poem of four lines each containing five or seven characters, with a strict tonal pattern and rhyme scheme), which has been seen as a masterpiece, one of his best 'seven-character Jueju', and highly praised during later dynasties. This poem, 'On Meeting Li Guinian in Jiangnan' (江南逢李龜年), was probably written in 770, when Du Fu was in Changsha.

岐王宅裡尋常見，
崔九堂前幾度聞。
正是江南好風景，
落花時節又逢君。

In prince Qi's home,
I saw you often;
in Cui Jiu's halls,

I heard you many times.
Now south of the river,
the scenery is lovely —
it is the season of falling petals,
and again we meet.

Tr. Will Buckingham

In only four sentences, Du Fu summarizes all the vicissitudes of his times, the dramatic social changes and huge personal loss of the whole Kaiyuan period (713–741). As Haun Saussy's insightful description of the Jueju (Saussy 2019), this poem of Du Fu is to see the world in a grain of sand, with plain language but richness of feeling and infinite implications. Nonetheless, its evocation of historical context with the names of Prince Qi and of Cui Jiu and metaphorical references like 'south of the river' and 'the season of falling petals' may require some explanation.

Prince Qi (岐王), the younger brother of Emperor Xuanzong of the Tang Dynasty, was fond of socializing with talented musicians. Among these was Li Guinian (李龜年), who is the 'you' of the poem but apparently no longer present. A famous musician in the Kaiyuan and Tianbao years of the Tang Dynasty, he was favored by Emperor Xuanzong and very popular for a time, but after a rebellion by An-Shi led an wandering life of poverty. Cui Jiu (崔九) served as a supervisor in the palace and was also a favorite of the emperor. Cui was a prominent family name at that time, showing that Li Guinian was highly appreciated by the upper class. Regions 'south of the [Yangtze] river' (江南), in this poem refers to the area of today's Hunan Province. In peaceful times, the beautiful region south of the Yangtze River was where poets yearned to go for a pleasant trip. The 'season of falling petals' (落花時節), late Spring, usually refers to the third month of the lunar calendar. There are many implications of references to late Spring in ancient Chinese poetry: surrounding aging and/or lost people, or social corruption and chaos.

Stephan Owen praises Du Fu for his ability to cover a wide range of subjects and to master a variety of poetic genres. Liang Qichao regards Du Fu as a 'saint of emotion' because, no matter how his life turned to disarray, he always had the strength to express warm feelings for the ruined country and its suffering people. In his poems, Du Fu integrated his personal feelings with a profound empathy for society and people. When his little son died of hunger, he was deeply grieved, yet at the same time he still expressed his sympathy with the pains of people poorer, more desperate and more grief-stricken than himself and his family. When his thatched cottage was damaged by the wind, he still acknowledged his duty to help poor, homeless people in the same situation to find a shelter. Despite his own misery, Du Fu's affection for the poor never ceased to flow. As John Donne (1572–1631) wrote in a sermon (1623), 'no man is an island entire of itself'; in Du Fu's poetic world the emotional equivalent of this is the sentiment that any man's death diminishes himself. In his poetry he achieved a blend of his aesthetic and moral feelings which has caused his poems to reach new readers ever since, among Chinese and foreign translators alike. Du Fu's political ideal of helping to give people better lives has never been realized; but his poems, charged with an overflow of empathetic emotions, have inspired and moved the Chinese nation for generations.

Coda

It is necessary to point out that the basic concept of emotion differs across cultures and history. We know that there are different emotions, that different cultures and periods favor different emotional qualities and also that people do not similarly evaluate the same emotions as positive or negative (Lehman, Chiu & Schaller 2004). For instance, in the Spring and Autumn Period (770–476 BCE), under the cultural system of the Yellow River Basin represented by *The Book of Songs*, Confucius had already advocated 'expressive of enjoyment without being licentious, and of grief without being hurtfully excessive'. In contrast, in the Period of Warring States (475–221 BCE), the emotion overflowing in 'Li Sao' from the Chu culture was unrestrained and intense, charged with the individual courage and dignity of Qu Yuan and embodying the Sublime so highly praised by Immanuel Kant (Kant 1964: 84–107; Bai 1985: 31–37), but intriguingly controversial among later literary theorists who embraced Confucianism.

Shared or different evaluations or expressions of emotion notwithstanding, emotional resonance is easily accomplished in literature. While John Keats (Keats 1899: 314) proposed the notion of Negative Capability to elaborate upon that talent of poets to withstand uncertainty intellectually or confusion philosophically, in the tradition of ancient Chinese poetry creativity is mainly associated with empathy. This originally referred to the psychological ability to make less distinct the differences between self and other, and to produce emotional resonance with others (Hall & Schwartz 2018). Confucianism highly respects moral values such as 'not to do to others as you would not wish done to yourself' (己所不欲,勿施於人---論語·顏淵, Legge 2016a: 399), as contained in Du Fu's masterpieces and characterized by his profound empathy with the misery of others. Moreover, through recourse to the concept of empathy, Zhu Guang-Qian further interpreted Wang Guo-Wei's poetic category of Jing-Jie, expanding the mechanism of empathy to include the ability to blend one's internal subjective emotional experiences with objects or external scenery.

Acknowledgements

Acknowledgement is due to Will Buckingham's contributions of cowriting of proposal, translations of poems, and inspiring discussions; to editor Chris Shei's insightful comments encouraging re-framing; to Svend Erik Larsen's professional academic editing, and essential contributions and inspirations in the sections on concepts of emotion, giving a new life to this chapter; and to Jean Morris' meticulous linguistic assistance including full-text proofreading. This research was financially supported by Sichuan University (grant skqx201505). Chen Xia, the author, is responsible for all mistakes and omissions.

Note

1 Will Buckingham's translations were provided for this chapter; see Acknowledgements.

References

Amy (2018) '《经典咏流传》梁俊: 白日不到处, 青春恰自来' (Liang Jun in the Classic Chant Spread (經典詠流傳): In Places Daylight Doesn't Reach, that's Where, in Spring, the Green Appears), 意林: 少年版 (Yilin Magazine: Youth Edition) 11: 12–12.

Bai, D.-R. 白敦仁 (1985) '《略论屈原赋的崇高美》' (On the Sublime Beauty of Qu Yuan's Fu), 成都大学编印《白敦仁论文六篇》 (in Six Essays by Bai Dun-Ren, edited by Chengdu University) 31–37.

Cao, S.-Q. 曹顺庆 (1996) '东方文论选' (Selected Works of Oriental Literary Theory), 成都: 四川人民出版社 (Chengdu: Sichuan People's Publishing House).

Chen, J. 陈杰 (2020) '从狂欢之路走向沉默, 这就是"垮掉的一代"的真实面孔' (From Carnival to Silence, this is the True Face of the Beat Generation), 《新京报·书评周刊》2020.7.5.B01版～B05版专题《'垮掉的一代' ——旅程与误解》(The Beijing News: Book Review Weekly (2020.7.5.b01–b05): The Beat Generation: Journey and Misunderstanding).

Chen, J. and Wang, D.-Y. 陈坚, 王东宇 (2009) '存在焦虑的研究述评' (A Review of Research on Existential Anxiety), 心理科学进展 (Journal of Advances in Psychological Science) 17(1): 204–209.

Chen, S.-J. 陈尚君 (2019) '李杜齐名之形成' (The Process of Equal Popularity of Li Bai and Du-Fu), 陈尚君编选: 《花舞大唐气象新》 (in Chen Shang-Jun (eds) New Atmosphere of Tang Poetry), 北京: 商务印书馆 (Beijing: The Commercial Press). pp. 276–295.

Chen, X., and Zhou, J. (2018) 'English translation of classical Chinese poetry', *Orbis Litter* 73: 361–373.

Gibbs, D.A. (1972) 'Notes on the Wind: The Term *Feng* in Chinese Literary Criticism', in Buxmaum, David C. & Frederic W. Mote (eds) *Transition and Permanence: Chinese History and Culture*, Hong Kong: Cathy Press Limited. pp. 285–293.

Hall, J., and Schwartz, R. (2018) 'Empathy present and future', *Journal of Social Psychology* 00224545.2018.1477442: 1–19.

Kant, I. (Tr. Zong, Bai-Hua) [德] 伊曼努尔·康德 (宗白华译) (1964) '《判断力批判》上卷' (The Critique of Judgement: Volume I), 商务印书馆 (The Commercial Press). pp. 84–107.

Keats, J. (1899) *The Complete Poetical Works and Letters of John Keats* (Cambridge ed.), Boston, MA: Houghton, Mifflin & Company.

Larsen, S.E. (Tr. Zhuang, Pei-Na) [丹麦] 斯文德·埃里克·拉森 (庄佩娜译) (2020) 无边界文本: 文学与全球化 (Texts Without Borders: Literature and Globalisation), 成都: 四川大学出版社 (Chengdu: Sichuan University Press).

Legge, J. [英] 理雅各 (2016a) 论语(英译) (Confucian Analects in English), 沈阳: 辽宁人民出版社 (Shenyang: Liaoning People's Publishing House).

Legge, J. [英] 理雅各 (2016b) 诗经: 英汉对照 (The Book of Songs in English), 郑州: 中州古籍出版社 (Zhengzhou: Zhongzhou Ancient Books Publishing House).

Lehman, D.R., Chiu, C.Y., and Schaller, M. (2004) 'Psychology and Culture', *Annual Review of Psychology* 55(1):689–714.

Liu, Y. 刘颖 (2009) '从《文心雕龙》"风骨"英译及阐释看关键词的重塑和话语秩序的建立' (On the Reconstruction of Key Words and the Establishment of Discourse Order from the English Translation and Interpretation of Feng-Gu in Wen-hsin tiao-Lung), 中外文化与文论 (Cultural Studies and Literary Theory) 1:49–60.

Lv, Z.-H. 吕正惠 (2018) 楚辞: 泽畔的悲歌 (The Songs of Chu: The Elegy of the Riverside), 北京: 九州出版社 (Beijing: Kyushu Publishing House).

Lv, Z.-H. 吕正惠 (2019) 第二个经典时代: 重估唐宋文学 (The Second Classic Era: Reassessment of Literature of Tang and Song Dynasties), 北京: 生活·读书·新知三联书店 (Beijing: SDX Joint Publishing Company).

Nussbaum, M. (2010) *Upheavals of Thought. The Intelligence of Emotions*, Cambridge: Cambridge University Press.

Owen, S. (Tr. Wang, Bai-Hua and Tao, Qing-Mei) [美] 宇文所安著 (王柏华, 陶庆梅译) (2019) 中国文学思想读本: 原典·英译·解说 (Readings in Chinese Literary Thought), 北京: 生活·读书·新知三联书店 (Beijing: SDX Joint Publishing Company).

Piao, Z.-J. 朴钟锦 (2012) '中国"诗赋外交"的起源及近代发展' (The Origin and Modern Development of Poetry Diplomacy in Ancient China), 国际政治研究(季刊) (International Political Studies: Quarterly) 1: 149–163.

Qian, Z.-S. 钱钟书 (2012) 宋诗选注 (The Selected Notes on Song Poetry), 北京: 人民文学出版社 (Beijing: The People's Literature Publishing House).

Saussy, H. (2019) 'Jueju', *New Literary History* 50(3): 453–456.

Shen, D.-Q. et al. (清) 沈德潜等 (1998) 历代诗别裁集 (A Collection of Poems of Different Dynasties), 杭州: 浙江古籍出版社 (Hangzhou: Zhejiang Ancient Books Publishing House).

Snyder, G. (1965) *Riprap & Cold Mountain Poems*, San Francisco: Grey Fox Press.

Tong, Q.-B. 童庆炳 (1999) '《文心雕龙》"风清骨峻"说' (On the Theory of 'the Wind Clear and the Bone Splendid' in Wen-hsin tiao-Lung), 文艺研究 (Journal of Literature and Art Research) 6: 31–41.

Wang, X. 王鑫 (2020) '寻找沟通中西方观众的"理、事、情"' (Looking for Reason, Matter and Emotion to Communicate with Chinese and Western Audiences), 中国青年报(文化观察) 2020.6.8.02版 (China Youth Daily: Cultural Observation, 2020.6.8.02).

Wei, H.-X. 魏红霞 (2013) '从深层结构探讨《题西林壁》的翻译' (On the Translation of Ti-Xi-Lin-Bi from the Perspective of Deep Structure), 外国语文研究 (Foreign language research) 1: 155–164.

Xiang, C. 项楚 (2019) 寒山诗注: 附拾得诗注 (Notes to Han Shan's Poems: with the Notes to Shi De's Poems Attached), 北京: 中华书局 (Beijing: Zhonghua Book Company).

Xu, Y.-C., Lu, P.-X., and Wu, J.-T. 许渊冲, 陆佩弦, 吴钧淘 (1988) 英汉对照唐诗三百首新译 (New English Translations of Three Hundred Tang Poems), 中国对外翻译出版公司与商务印书馆(香港)有限公司合作出版 (Beijing, China: China Translation & Publishing Corporation; Hong Kong, China: The Commercial Press (Hong Kong) Limited).

Yang, Y. 杨义 (2012) '屈原诗学的人文地理分析' (An Analysis of Qu Yuan's Poetics from the Perspective of Cultural Geography), 北方论丛 (The Northern Forum) 4: 1–15.

Ye, L. 叶理 (2015) '加里·斯奈德翻译寒山诗的创造性叛逆' (Gary Snyder's Creative Treason in Translating Han Shan's Poems), 南京师范大学文学院学报 (Journal of Chinese Language and Culture School Nanjing Normal University) (03): 168–171.

Zhao, Y.-C. 赵延春 (2015) http://blog.sina.com.cn/s/blog_698085bf0102vk9i.html.

Zhao, Y.-H. 赵毅衡 (2013) 诗神远游: 中国如何改变了美国现代诗 (The Muse from Cathay: How Has China Changed Modern American Poetry), 成都: 四川文艺出版社 (Chengdu: Sichuan Literature and Art Publishing House).

Zhang, G.-F. 张冠夫 (2012) '梁启超1920年代的"情感"诗学研究' (Research on Liang Qi-chao's Poetics of Emotion in 1920s), 清华大学中国文学博士学位论文 (Dissertation Submitted to Tsinghua University for the degree of Doctor of Philosophy in Chinese Literature).

Zhou, X.-T. 周啸天 (2014) '诗的产生到四言诗---原始歌谣和《诗经》' (The Origin of Poetry Comes from the Four Character Poem: The Original Ballad and The Book of Songs), 中国分体文学史. 诗歌卷/赵义山, 李修生主编 (In Zhao Yi-Shan and Li Xiu-Sheng (eds) The History of Chinese Split Literature: Poetry Volume), 上海: 上海古籍出版社 (Shanghai: Shanghai Classics Publishing House). pp. 1–23.

Zhou, X.Y., Tilburg, W.A.P., Mei, D.M., Wildschut, T., and Sedikides, C. (2019) 'Hungering for the past: Nostalgic food labels increase purchase intentions and actual consumption', *Appetite* 140: 151–158.

Zhou, Y.-K. 周裕锴 (2019) 宋代诗学通论 (On Poetics in Song Dynasty), 上海: 上海古籍出版社 (Shanghai: Shanghai Classics Publishing House).

Zhu, G.-Q. 朱光潜 (2012) 诗论 (On Poetry), 桂林: 漓江出版社 (Guilin: Lijiang Publishing House).

21

The advocacy of cultural change through translation

The rhetoric of Chinese sutra translators

Weixiao Wei and Hui Shi

Introduction

Has China ever had a translation theory? Some insisted that there was no real existence of translation theory in China until the introduction of Eugene Nida in the late twentieth century. Ma (2019), for one, suggested that there was neither original translation theory nor internationally recognized translation theorists in China. Shei and Gao (2018) thought that there was no systematic account of translation theory in the Chinese history and the relatively few discussions were mostly abstract and impressionistic in nature. Wang (2009) observed that Chinese translation theory was mostly based on subjective experiences and lacking in scientific analysis. At the other end of the pole, some researchers seriously entertain the idea that translation theory had existed in China. Wang and Gao (2017), for example, openly denounced Chinese researchers' exercise of overemphasizing Western translation theory at the expense of indigenous theory. They thought that the practice of Buddhist sutra translation and the thoughts generated from the activities had laid a solid foundation for the formation of Chinese translation theory in Ming and Qing dynasties and modern China. Wu (1998) considered Chinese translation theory fairly practical and embodying a well-grounded humanistic approach. Wei (2020: ix) suggests that Chinese translation is currently at the last of the three phases of translation theory formation: translating, discoursing about translation, and developing translation theory. Thus, it is important work at the current stage to systematically study the Chinese discourses on translating and reorganize and rebuild them into theoretical models that represent solid and coherent modern translation theory. By deciphering the monk translators' discourses on translation, we return to their context of translating and are able to see the effect of their personality, enthusiasm, and eloquence on the intended receivers of the translation. As we do so, we find their translation not only incorporates techniques and considerations in translating but also their personality and passion for the religious truths they believed in. This is when the Rhetoric Model of Translation comes in, which sees translating as a rhetorical act expressing the translator's ideal and passion in the hope of winning the audience's recognition. The rhetoric of translation is expressed both covertly in the target text itself and overtly in the translator's discourse about translating. A similar idea of reconceptualizing translation in light of rhetoric was provided

DOI: 10.4324/9780429059704-25

in Gonzales' Revised Rhetoric of Translation model which sees translation not as 'a static, mechanical activity that is disassociated from cultural and historical motivations' but as an activity 'tied to the broader goals and objectives of people and organizations' (2018: 57). Gonzales' model gives us a good start to build a Rhetoric Model of Translation across the two disciplines of Rhetoric and Translation Studies, combining relevant concepts and theory usefully to produce new theoretical framework to analyse existing problems and generating new insights. In this article, we explore a few renowned monk translators' rhetoric in light of the proposed framework with a view to demonstrating the continued existence of Chinese translation theory and setting an example for further exploration of historical recourses of Chinese translation.

The Rhetoric Model of Translation

To date there has been little effort in connecting rhetoric to translation studies. France (2005) was a notable exception who offered to see translating from the rhetorical point of view. France thought that some debates in translation such as literalism vs. adaptation, foreignization vs. domestication etc. could be resolved by linking the act of translating to the use of rhetoric in context. According to France, '[w]hat matters is not to prolong the pointless debate about the 'correct' method of translating, but to become aware of the way in which the translator, like the orator, negotiates between a subject and an audience, seeking out a rhetoric adequate to the situation' (2005: 267–268). This view was echoed by Collombat, who introduced the 'translator as a rhetorician' concept where the role of the translator as a rhetorician is to '[find] arguments in the target culture that are equivalent to those contained in the source text' (2017: 3). For Collombat, 'the rational empathetic attitude of translators leads them to reconstruct a rhetorical environment, to transpose the rhetorical universe of the source text onto the target culture' (ibid.). Using the terminology of translation studies, Collombat then started to associate this rhetorical function of the translator to the purpose of translation (*skopos*) and to translation strategies applicable for different text types. However, Collombat's proposal was essentially an equivalence-based model working at the level of text, not very different from Nida's dynamic equivalence (Nida 2004). Only a different name is used (i.e. *rhetoric*) as a conceptual header to subsume the linguistic operations carried out through the process of translating. The same idea was captured by Károly (2013) who prospectively implemented Collombat's (2017) model by calculating the shifts of relational propositions as a Rhetorical Structure in Hungarian-English news translation. In the current Rhetoric Model of Translation proposed by us, in contrast, we go beyond the function of text and include in the equation the character and behaviour of the translator involved in the production of the translation. As Figure 21.1 shows, what we envisage is a comprehensive network consisting of the translator as a rhetorician who uses all three principles of rhetoric (*ethos*, *pathos*, *logos*) to express and implement their ideals achievable through their translation and commentaries. In this chapter, we use four prominent Chinese monk translators to illustrate how their success in achieving ideals and ambitions could best be explained by the model, where the product of translation is only part of a greater picture. The translator's personality, including their knowledge and reputation and their character and passion in implementing the translation projects and related goals, are equally important in attaining overall success. More importantly, the model also connects back to existing research in translation studies, maintaining a close relationship with concepts and theory such as translation ethics, skopos theory, and text types.

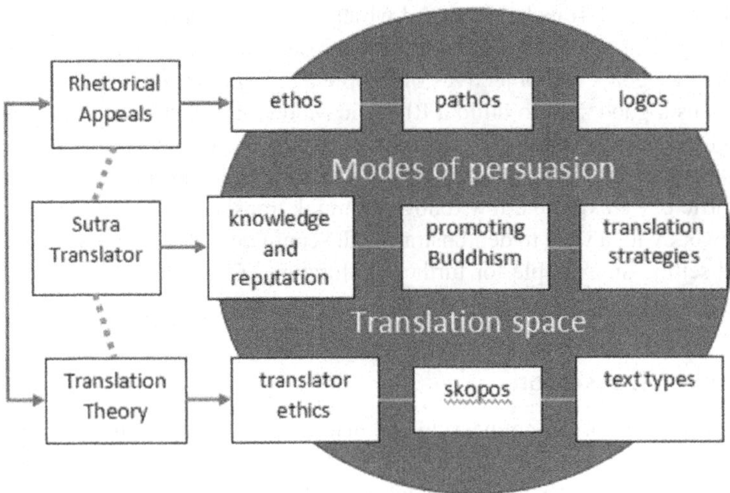

Figure 21.1 The rhetoric model of translation: Translating as an art of persuasion.

Aristotle's well quoted distinction between three modes of persuasion runs as follows:

> Of the modes of persuasion furnished by the spoken word there are three kinds. The first kind depends on the personal character of the speaker; the second on putting the audience into a certain frame of mind; the third on the proof, or apparent proof, provided by the words of the speech itself.
>
> *(Aristotle, 350 BCE)*

These three modes of persuasion or rhetorical appeals are usually concisely represented by the three Greek words listed below:

- ethos: 'Persuasion is achieved by the speaker's personal character when the speech is so spoken as to make us think him credible'
- pathos: 'Secondly, persuasion may come through the hearers, when the speech stirs their emotions'
- logos: 'Thirdly, persuasion is effected through the speech itself when we have proved a truth or an apparent truth by means of the persuasive arguments suitable to the case in question' (Aristotle, 350 BCE).

In this article, we contend that Aristotle's three modes of rhetoric are fully realized in Chinese sutra translators' works and their discourses about translation. These translators were religious leaders with advanced knowledge in Buddhism, high official ranks and great reputations. Their good characters (*ethos*) and their religious passions (*pathos*) created a favorable backdrop for their rhetorical appeals (*logos*) to pan out with the audience. The powerful thrust delivered by these monk translators in their acclaimed translations were a combination of knowledge and reputation, religious passion and translation skills. Thus, in the Rhetoric Model of Translation currently proposed, France's (2005) resolution of 'a rhetoric adequate to the situation' is realized in two ways: the 'micro level rhetoric' manifested as translation strategies used by the translator in rendering the target text, and the 'macro level rhetoric' residing in the translator public image including their scholarly reputation and their translation discourse uttered in the public sphere as a personal statement of their translation, often imbued with religious enthusiasm and a desire to spread Buddhist gospel. In the following four sections, we retrace the rhetoric of four renowned sutra translators in the Chinese history to illustrate how the Rhetoric Model of Translation works and to show how this newly contrived analytical framework can rejuvenate Chinese translation theory by assigning new meanings to existing materials. It should be noted that ancient monk translators' discourses are mostly out of reach due to language barrier and accessibility problems. In this regard, the widely acclaimed resource book published by Martha Cheung in 2014, *An Anthology of Chinese Discourse on Translation* (Volume 1), provided a helping hand. Most of the monk translators' putative speeches have been quoted from this book.

Dao An (道安): Translation criticism

Dao An (312–385) was a highly esteemed monk living in the Six Dynasties (222–589). He became a monk at the age of 12 and surprised his mentors and colleagues with high intelligence in learning sutras and eloquence in explaining Buddhist philosophy early on despite his unsightly appearance. He became a religious leader and a well-established Buddhist scholar later in his life and was known to have interpreted Buddhist concepts with classic Chinese terminology without violating the tenets of Buddhism so that Buddhism can be integrated into the Chinese culture (see, e.g., Wang 2017). Dao An himself did not know Sanskrit or translate any sutras but he did compile a directory of translated sutras entitled *A Comprehensive Catalogue of the Sutras* (综理众经目录) which was considered one of the four great achievements of Dao An by Ma (1982). That catalogue not only established Dao An as a grand master of Buddhist scholarship but also demonstrated his unique insights into the theory of translation and translation criticism. The following excerpt from the Preface to the Taoxing Sutra quoted from Cheung (2014) shows Dao An's surprising insights on how one can 'get lost in translation' and fail to grasp the meaning of the source:

> When attempting to explain this sutra …, one who analyses it at the level of the words to get at the point will blur the theme, while one who examines it sentence by sentence to check the meaning will lose the message. Why should that be so? Analysing the text at the level of the words restricts one's understanding to the verbal constructs of contrasts and similarities, and examining the text sentence by sentence ties one's attention to the notions and ideas one will want to abstract from them. Concentrating on the words detracts from the final theme, while concentrating on the sentences makes one lose sight of the original purpose. If one can grasp the original purpose and carry it right through to the final interpretation, or if one can forget about the words and get the substance [*zhì* 質] of the text as a whole, then one can understand the mystery of great wisdom …
>
> *(Cheung 2014:, 71–72)*

Given the time of writing of the above excerpt (i.e., approximately 1,600 years ago), one has to admit the sound reasoning behind the rhetoric and seriously consider Dao An's compelling view that 'substance' in translating is more important than any embellishment created by vocabulary and sentence structures. However, being a well-learned and relatively open-minded Buddhist scholar, Dao An did not confine himself to any single rendering of a given sutra or any uniquely recommended translation method. Instead, Dao An often critically engaged different versions of translated sutra and making observations and recommendations to the general public. For example, in the face of two different translations of the same sutra, Dao An suggested that '[i]t is best to study the *Guangzan* Sutra and the *Fangguang* Sutra together. The two translations throw light on each other, and one can obtain from such a study a great deal of understanding and revelation' (quoted from Cheung 2014: 75). This is a sensible suggestion and one that goes well with the image of a high-profile monk and an erudite scholar. By far the most significant contribution of Dao An to the history of Chinese translation studies, however, was not only his initiation of a likely discipline, but also his proposal of the 'five instances of losing the source' (五失本), which had since become the source of inspiration and the topic of discussion for ensuing debates on Chinese translation theory. Dao An articulated this translation theory in prose but the five points can be summarized as follows:

In translating from Hu-language to Chinese, five cases of losing the source can occur:

1. when the original word order is reversed to conform to that of Chinese
2. when the original text is embellished to please the Chinese reader
3. when the elaborated and detailed sutras are trimmed to make 'less boring'
4. when the repetitions and hymns are omitted from the original sutra
5. when the ST makes useful digressions that are removed from the TT (see, for example, Wang 2017: 41–42)

As previously mentioned, Dao An was a glorified religious leader who contributed substantially to the ease of Buddhism into the Chinese culture. In doing so he had to modify the Buddhist terminology to some extent in accordance with the Chinese tradition, using compatible vocabulary within Chinese culture, literature, and philosophy. One example was given in Lin (2016) where the Sanskrit word *prajna* ('wisdom') was referred to in Dao An's discourse in Daoist terms such as *benwu* ('root void') and so on. However, the five points proposed as a warning for prospective sutra translators not to lose the source, showed Dao An's fear of skewing Buddha's original teaching when translators freely made structural and textual adjustments. To add further supplements to his proposed principle of translation, Dao An further raised the issue of 'three difficulties in translating' which went as follows:

(Buddha's wisdom is expounded in the sutras and has to be reinterpreted as times go by. Three difficulties are involved in doing so:)

First, the antiquated elegant features of the sutras have to be removed and readjusted to the fashion of the present time;

Second, the translator has to make the many subtle and profound words from a millennium ago understandable to the general public;

Third, the arhats used to be cautious about the editing of the sutras, but the ordinary mortals seem to be reckless while editing the texts.

(adapted from Cheung 2014: 79)

Dan An's concerns about losing the source and about the difficulties of maintaining the feasibility and authenticity of the target text, generated plenty of ensuing research and discussions about translation strategies to meet the stringent requirements of translation depicted in Dao An's discourses. Liu and Lan (2019), for example, usefully divided Dao

An's translation criticism model into two layers: the objective domain and the subjective domain. The first two items of the five instances of losing the source reflect the objective differences between the source language and the target language. The last three items and all three translation difficulties mentioned by Dao An engage the translator's subjective perception, that is, how they see the source text and what effect they desire from the translation reader. Liu and Lan then went on to discuss different ways of pursing the source under different contexts: Simplifying the source (约本), combining the sources (合本), following the source (案本) and correcting the source (正本). In the past, Dao An's contributions to Chinese translation theory had been felt but not correctly or fully conceptualized. Seen from the perspective of the Rhetoric Model of Translation, we are now able to combine Dao An's erudition in Buddhism, his passionate ideals about the source and the teaching of the religion, and his proposed guidelines for sutra translating, all in one powerful rhetorical package. Only by doing so can we start to appreciate Dao An's discourses about translation and their relevance to and influence on the development of Chinese translation theory.

Kumārajīva (鸠摩罗什): Untranslatability and translation ethics

Kumārajīva (344–413) was born to a noble family in Kutsi (龟兹), an ancient country at the Western Regions of China, became a monk and learned Buddhist scriptures at very young age. He learned Buddhism from different masters in different countries and achieved great fame. He was also proficient in both Sanskrit and Chinese. At around 40 years of age, a Chinese emperor conquered Kutsi and captured Kumārajīva. Working for the Chinese emperor and in charge of several state-sponsored Buddhist sutra translation projects, Kumārajīva translated at least 39 sutras amounting to 313 currently available fascicles (see Yao 2017) and created an unprecedented wealth of Buddhist literature for China. As a result, Kumārajīva's scholarly work and his contributions to the dissemination of Buddhist culture and philosophy in and beyond China have been extensively studied, including a conference on the influence of Kumārajīva's sutra translation on the Buddhist culture of China and Japan held in Xi'an in 2004, and another conference held in New Delhi in 2011 on Kumārajīva 'as a philosopher and seer' (Zhang 2015). According to Wang (2018), Kumārajīva created the first team translation method where a Presiding Translator (主译) explained the Sutra written or memorized in Sanskrit; while one or more Interpreters (度语) orally translated the contents of sutras and any explanations into Chinese (which was especially desirable when the Presiding Translator had no Chinese); and finally a Recorder (笔受) wrote down what had been said in formal Chinese. This team translation effort not only manufactured a large quantity of sutra translations, but also provided a great opportunity for participating monks to learn from the great Buddhist masters. As a result of his erudition in Buddhism, his devotion to the religion, his great proficiency in both Sanskrit and Chinese and his extensive translating experiences, several strands of translation theory have been attributed to Kumārajīva including the untranslatability of Buddhist scriptures, the emphasis on the refinement (文) rather than the substance (质) of translation, the 'pledge of honesty' by the dying translator, the relinquishment of the *geyi* (格义) translation method (equivalent to the 'domestication' strategy), and the advocacy for concise target text (Wang 2018:, 173). Cheung (2014) suggested that a deep dissatisfaction on the part of Kumārajīva over his own translations of the sutras probably caused his reticence on translation as a subject, in the sense that he did not comment a lot on the issue of translating in the same way that Dao An did. Indeed, all that were shown in Cheung's anthology were two short excerpts believed to be said by Kumārajīva in his whole career of translating amidst the massive outputs he had produced. The two short discourses, however, did portray Kumārajīva's as a very powerful rhetorician describing the problems of translation and his own devotion to the work in very graphic terms. In the first excerpt supposedly recorded by another monk Hui Rui, Kumārajīva referred contemptuously to translating Sanskrit odes into Chinese based on meaning while sacrificing the original beauty of the sound.

> But when the *Fàn* [Sanskrit] sutras are translated into Chinese, the beauty of form and the colour and verve are lost. The meaning can generally be conveyed, but in a form very different from the original. It is like giving someone rice that you have chewed; he will find it not just tasteless, but downright disgusting.
>
> *(from Cheung 2014: 94)*

In this short discourse, Kumārajīva conjured up a vivid and repulsive image of a person feeding chewed rice to someone else, which became a powerful metaphor and a rhetoric device to push forward his idea of the untranslatability of Buddhist sutras into another language when the acoustic beauty of the sutra sung in Sanskrit could not be maintained. Contrary to the general presumption that he was an advocator of refinement of target text, Kumārajīva here apparently used the 'chewed rice' metaphor to convey the untranslatable nature of the source and the undesirability of digressing from it. Despite his mastery of Buddhist philosophy and his proficiency in both Sanskrit and Chinese, Kumārajīva seems to convey a pessimistic message about translating from a tormented soul which struggled to maintain the original beauty of the language while doing anything necessary to promote his beloved religion. As Cheung (2014: 95) usefully summarized,

> Kumārajīva's thorough grasp of the source language, his encyclopaedic knowledge of the Buddhist canon, and his own personal cultural affinities also made him feel that he was not doing full justice to the sutras he had translated. Hence his sense of dissatisfaction, almost of disgust.

Hence, Kumārajīva's rhetoric to the general public through the 'chewed rice' metaphor was one to convey a deep pessimism about translating and of the translator's retroflection, self-denial, and even guilt in the face of the impossible challenge of producing an acceptable target text despite all the challenges. Such being the case, no wonder Kumārajīva nevertheless felt that as a translator he had done everything he could to produce at least passable translations throughout his lifetime. This conviction was affirmed by Kumārajīva's alleged final words to fellow monks on his deathbed as recorded in *A Biography of Kumārajīva* (鸠摩罗什传) which was anthologized in *A Collection of Records on the Emanation of the Chinese Tripitaka* (出三藏记集), quoted below from Cheung (2014: 109):

> We have met in the teaching of the Buddha, in the work of which I have not done as much as I had wished. Now we have to part and go our separate ways; I have no words for my sadness. I have tried in my inadequate way to serve as a translator. If I have not transgressed the truth in my translations, let my tongue not be destroyed in my cremation.

In ancient China, an official interpreter was called a 'Tongue-man' (舌人) among other names; therefore, the tongue was symbolic of the professional identity of a translator in Kumārajīva's times. Notwithstanding his disillusionment about translating, Kumārajīva apparently believed in his own honesty and the credibility of the translations he produced. This sense of self-confidence and devotion prompted him to vow on the deathbed that his tongue would not be burned during the cremation process, as the ultimate proof of the symbolic value of his integrity and his work. The legendary outcome of Kumārajīva's prediction was affirmative – that his tongue was indeed not burned according to his posthumous autobiography. But what is more important is the alleged deathbed vow which conveyed the belief that a translator could still produce usable translations in the face of seemingly insurmountable difficulties. Despite the paucity of translation discourses attributed to Kumārajīva, his reticence makes a lot of sense in the Rhetoric Model of Translation currently being proposed. This is because the model looks at the translator and the translation as a whole which together output a rhetorical package to convince the reader of the value of the translation and the deed. The translator persuaded the audience not only with the micro level rhetorical devices – the target text created by their translation competency and strategies, but also by the macro level rhetorical means – by their personal credentials and by putting the audience in a certain emotional state with their translational discourse. Aristotle's three rhetorical appeals are in full force thanks to the historical profile of the sutra translator presented in the form of his lifetime achievements in Buddhist learning and teaching, his discourse about translating and all the sutras translated under his supervision.

Yan Cong (彦琮): The importance of source

Yan Cong (557–610) was another Buddhist prodigy who became a monk at the age of ten and was invited to give lectures on religious matters in the court by the time he was 14. Throughout his life, Yan Cong was highly respected and well treated by the emperors of his time, given the responsibilities of organizing, translating and teaching the Buddhist scriptures. Before his early death at the age of 54, Yan Cong saw the completion of 23 sutras (Cheung 2014: 136) and wrote a very important treatise on translation: *On the Right Way* (辩正论). The latter was recognized as the first relatively complete and systematic theory about translation in China's history (Fu 2011); while the contents of the treatise have been extensively studied by Chinese researchers (Huang 2011, 2013, 2014) in recent years. Huang (2011), for example, summarized Yan Cong's thoughts about sutra translation in four ways as expressed in his treatise. Firstly, Yan Cong set the aim of the essay as an attempt to establish the norm for sutra translation and the way to promote the religion. Secondly, Yan Cong recapitulated Dao An's 'five instances of losing the source' and the 'three difficulties in translation' as principles of translation to be closely followed, and proposed his own idea of respecting the source while translating. Thirdly, and most importantly, Yan Cong proposed the Eight Prerequisites for Translators (八备) as guidelines for fostering future translators to accomplish the sacred mission of sutra translation. In the fourth part of the essay, Yan Cong concluded the treatise with a Q&A session to emphasize the importance of learning Sanskrit to benefit directly from Buddha's original teaching. The Eight Prerequisites for Translators proposed by Yan Cong are summarized below:

First, a monk translator must love the Buddhist Dharma and be devoted to helping others by spreading the Buddhist truth.

Second, he must closely follow the precepts and rules and abstain from worldly influences to attain the Buddhahood.

Third, he must be well learned in both Mahayana and Hinayana Buddhism and not be deterred by the difficulties presented in Buddhist cannons.

Fourth, he must study the Chinese classics and be well versed in letters so that his translations will not be clumsy and inelegant.

Fifth, he must be kind-hearted, humble, open-minded and good at communication, and must not be stubborn or biased.

Sixth, he should master every method and technique for sutra translation, be indifferent to fame and riches and harbour no desire to show off.

Seventh, he must work hard on Sanskrit and learn the correct methods of translating so that he will not lose the meaning of the doctrines.

Eighth, he must also acquaint himself with the vocabulary of ancient Chinese writings and the different styles of Chinese script.

(adapted from Huang 2014: 130–131 and Cheung 2014: 142)

As can be seen, most of the eight prerequisites Yan Cong proposed for worthy translators were related to the translator's faith and scholarship in Buddhism and their devotion and competence in disseminating the religion. From this point of view, it seems Chinese translator's ideology and behaviour can best be explained by the Rhetoric Model of Translation we propose, which looks at the act of translating in a rich context of variables including the environment and the audience and, notably, the translator's own personality, inclination and passion while doing or discoursing about the translation. In the case of Yan Cong, not only did he emphasize what kind of character and emotional state a good translator should possess and be in, but, more significantly, he also highlighted the inevitable distance between the target text and Buddha's original teaching and the importance of approaching the source by observing the rules of the religion (the second prerequisite), learning the original contents (the third prerequisite) and the language (the seventh prerequisite) of the religion. This point is further emphasized in Yan Cong's discourse about the importance of the source quoted from the same work (i.e. *On the Right Way*) below:

> When Buddha was alive, people could listen to his teaching and amazing power was bestowed from his words. The disciples' spiritual growths were connected to Buddha's spiritual insights. But nowadays we no longer live where Buddha used to live and we cannot listen to his golden words. Even if we have texts explaining his ideas we cannot fully understand. … Sutras were used to explain Buddha's speeches but the translated sutras are further away from Buddha's original teaching. … I for one will steer clear of interpreting Buddha's ideas based entirely on the superficial words.
>
> *(adapted and translated from Fu 2011: 23)*

In this excerpt Yan Cong vividly described the discrepancy between Buddha's original teaching and what could be transcribed on the source text (and eventually translated into the target text). This untranslatability of Buddha's teaching then allowed Yan Cong's proposed prerequisites for translators to make more sense since all is not dependent on translation skills or familiarity with the text. Background learning and true appreciation of the source are all the more important in helping the translator to arrive at a feasible translation. This respect for the source, the impossibility of a perfect translation, and the alternative means of approaching the source, were reiterated in Yan Cong's concluding paragraph to his famous treatise:

> Now that we are studying Buddhist scriptures from distant countries, we have accepted a completely different way of living. While worshipping the Buddha, we should be

> ashamed of not knowing the source of the Buddhist script. We should concentrate on absorbing the teaching of Buddha and be ashamed of only pursuing the interest of Buddhist text. If we fill the reader's eyes with scripture text, we cannot increase people's respect for Buddhism. It is like encountering a Buddhist monk without feeling any admiration but outrage only. … The era of the Buddha will pass, but the truth of the Dharma will be inherited. However, inheriting the Dharma by means of text translation is really a reluctant option.
>
> *(adapted and translated from Fu 2011: 23)*

Yan Cong's discourse and the embedded rhetoric in it shows how important it is to evaluate a Chinese sutra translator's works in the overall context of their ideology, personality and emotional state. If we simply scrutinize the target text without getting to know the background of production, we fail to see the translator's reasons for selecting certain translation strategies and appreciate their struggles in undertaking the translation project.

Xuan Zang (玄奘): Translation projects and terminology management

Another renowned sutra translator was born nearly three hundred years after Dao An. With a large number of sutras translated by them in a limited lifetime, Xuan Zang (602–664) was hailed together with Kumārajīva as two of the four great sutra translators in China's history, the other two being Zhen Di (449–569) and Bu Kong (705–774). Bearing a certain degree of similarity with Kumārajīva, Xuan Zang had travelled extensively across a huge number of countries on religious pilgrims (including India) and acquired a large quantity of sutras. When he finally returned to Chang'an, the capital of Tang dynasty, and established himself in large temples sponsored by the state, he completed a staggering number of 75 sutras translations consisting of 1335 fascicles (Cheung 2014). Sun (2012) was one of the many authors who recommended Xuan Zang as the most accomplished Buddhist master and scholarly translator in Chinese history. For one thing, Xuan Zang was responsible for organizing the largest Translation Assembly (译场) in history where as many as a dozen posts were created to see to the interpreting, verification, recording, annotating, embellishing, editing, monitoring, and other tasks related to the project during the process of translating – see, for example, Zhang (2014), Luo (2014), Bao (2017). The translation infrastructure of such grandness, commitment, and intellectual creativity continued for nearly 20 years and created an unprecedented number of solidly translated sutras. Shi and Lu recommended that 'Xuan Zang's translations reached the peak in the history of Chinese Buddhist scriptures in terms of quantity and quality, representing the highest level of translation of ancient Buddhist scriptures in China' (2013: 43, our translation from original Chinese publication).

Despite their remarkable accomplishments in translation, Xuan Zang followed Kumārajīva's example and did not leave a legacy of theory or teaching related to sutra translation. However, his 'five no-translation' (五不翻) strategy concerning the treatment of Buddhist terminology in translating and his relevant position in seeing Buddhism as a distinct discipline (as separate from Daoist philosophy, for example) are forceful reminders of the translation theory implicitly connected to his rhetorical position as the leading sutra translator in his time. Cheung (2014, p. 157) provided an apt English translation of the five kinds of terms in Buddhist sutras which Xuan Zang insisted should not be translated by meaning but should be transliterated with Chinese characters representing similar sounds:

1. If a term partakes of the occult
2. If a term has multiple meanings
3. If the object represented by a term does not exist in this part of the world
4. If a past rendering of a term has become established and accepted
5. If a term elicits positive associations

According to Hou (2014), Xuan Zang's five no-translation principle can be attributed to two motivations: first, to serve as an overarching guideline for terminology treatment to a large translation team; second, to overcome the weaknesses of the *geyi* (格义) method inherited from traditional sutra translation machinery which dictated that Buddhist terminology be converted to Daoist terms in the hope of making Buddhism more understandable to the general public. Yan (2017) asserted that Xuan Zang's insistence on keeping the original sounds of the five kinds of Buddhist terms signified his respect to the original Sanskrit language and culture, existing translation scholarship, and the religious conventions of Buddhism, an early manifestation of the concept of translator's ethics. According to Chen and Zhang (2006), Xuan Zang's proposed norm for sutra translation was a direct result of his Buddhist learning and his intellectual capacity. The undisputed identity of Buddhism held in his mind was vehemently expressed in the form of a defence of Buddhism as an individual discipline and against the assimilation of Daoist cultures, as recorded in a biography of Xuan Zang included in a historical document anthologized in Cheung (2014: 159):

> Xuan Zang said, 'Buddhism and Taoism are two separate religions. They are completely different in nature; why should Buddhist terms be linked up with Taoist meanings? A thorough examination of the development of Buddhist terms shows that they are original terms and are not derived from elsewhere.'

In another excerpt quoted from Cheung (2014), Xuan Zang was shown to explain why once upon a time it was necessary and useful to translate Buddhist sutras with Daoist terms but as Buddhism matured in the Chinese culture there was no longer need to do so. Xuan Zang's eloquence as an orator showed his unquestionable erudition in Buddhism and the clear logic and confidence in his words as he refuted the proposal of mingling Buddhist concepts with Daoist terms:

> When Buddhism was first preached, its profound meaning was still concealed under heavily-clustered language. Taoist metaphysical expressions could be unobtrusively tagged onto the words of Buddha. Seng Zhao, in his treatises, merely employed Taoist terms and expressions as analogies [*liánlèi* 联类] to facilitate understanding of his teaching. How could a mere figure of speech used for teaching be taken as the ultimate link between Buddhism and Taoism? There are now many Buddhist classics and treatises; they all have their own direction and focus.
>
> *(Cheung 2014: 160)*

In this excerpt, Xuan Zang was seen to conceptualize the initial use of Daoist terms to introduce Buddhist concepts as a rhetorical move to ease the new religion into the minds of the general public. When Buddhism became entrenched in the Chinese culture, the original aim had been achieved and the method of analogy was no longer needed. In other words, it was time for Buddhist philosophy to be absorbed in their original form. When he was later asked by a Tang emperor to translate *Laozi* (a Daoist scripture) into Sanskrit in order to disseminate Daoism into the Western countries, Xuan Zang also showed great respect to Daoism as a distinct religion. When a fellow translator proposed that a preface to *Laozi* be included in the translation which was likely to bend the philosophical work into a work on health and wellbeing, Xuan Zang refused to do so. When a minister from the court asked how advanced the Western countries were in scientific studies, Xuan Zang gave the following answer:

> As for writings about the four elements constituting the physical existence of the world, or writings about the six categories of the primal properties of the self and the world, they deal with subjects that have not even been mentioned here in the East. If I really translated a preface for *Laozi*, I fear the countries in the Western Regions might see it as a joke.
>
> *(Cheung 2014: 160)*

With consistent academic rigor, Xuan Zang insisted on translating *Laozi* using Daoist terms (instead of mingling it with Buddhist terminology as other team members suggested) and keeping the philosophical nature of the work instead of downgrading it to a medical handbook. Xuan Zang's rhetoric and his translations showed his erudition in religion, skills in translating and eloquence in defending his positions. As observed by Yu (2017: 30), many great religious figures have appeared in China, India, and the world but with the passage of time, the scholarly monk Xuan Zang has become more visible than before and gained ever more attention and admiration. Many of Xuan Zang's achievements in sutra translation were original, for example, the meticulous translation infrastructure created for his translation projects and the terminology management principles he proposed. The few discourses about translation Xuan Zang left for us showed his rhetorical ability and intellectual integrity, on the other hand. When we see Xuan Zang's lifetime achievements within the Rhetorical Model of Translation, we realize how his legendary reputation and increasing popularity make sense. As a sutra translator, like many of his outstanding predecessors, Xuan Zang convinced the audience of the value of his work not only by his translation products but also by his character, his reputation and his discourse about translation and the background ideology.

Concluding remarks

When examined from a rhetorical point of view, the connections between variables of translation such as time period, political backdrop, culture setting and the readership, motivation for and purpose of translation, selection of source texts, translation methods and the inherent restrictions and so on, become clear and what the translators do and claim make sense in the overall environment they work in. For such a large and ancient civilization with relatively stable sovereignty but a turbulent history, China's translation activities usually tied in closely with some political mandate, social demand, cultural motivation, and intellectual thinking. In the case of sutra translation, Chinese emperors were usually the ones who initiated the top-down approach, hoping to engage the commoners in religious thoughts and create a harmonious society for easy ruling. Sutra translators were usually monks with highly renowned monk scholars serving as heads of translation projects. There was a complicated web of relationships between the religious beliefs held by the monks, the political motivation of the sponsoring emperors, the translation infrastructure officially implemented and the available means and resources for translating. If we only look at the target texts produced by the translators, analyse their translation strategies, or even study the discourses they presented about translation, without interpreting all these variables as rhetorical package occurring in a certain context with a targeted audience in mind, then we miss the overall significance of the translation act.

In this chapter, we have examined four prominent sutra translators' religious beliefs and their ideas about translating, among other things. Although a systematic account of monk translators' discourses on sutra translation has so far not been carried out, Cheung (2014) offered a good start for further attempts at consolidating monk translators' commentaries and formulating a translation theory based on their rhetoric and translations. According to Cheung, discourses about sutra translation came in various forms including 'remarks, comments, longer and more sustained discussions, and treatises, but never settling into something with a boundary clear enough to be called a genre' (Cheung 2014: 9). That being said, if we look closely, some of the monk translators' ideas about translation and their strategies were actually precursors of contemporary translation theory in the West. According to Wang (2018: 168), for example, translators prior to Kumārajīva had used Taoist terms to translate Buddhist concepts to make them more acceptable to the home culture. However, Kumārajīva started the trend of remaining faithful to the source and adding translator's explanations to facilitate understanding. These two opposite strategies in cultural orientation during translating were subsequently termed 'domestication' vs. 'foreignization' by Lawrence Venuti approximately 1350 years later. In retrospect, monk translators a thousand years ago were already keenly aware of the differences between taming the Buddhist terms in Sanskrit with Chinese indigenous philosophical jargons and preserving the original sounds and rhythms while acclimatizing the audience to Buddhist language and pronunciation. Conceivably, if more Chinese discourses on translation are studied and further developed into analytical patterns and conceptual models, a systematic account of Chinese translation practice and theory will soon be in the making. Hadley and McElduff (2018: 129), for one, noted that 'it appears that research on the rhetorical mechanics of the Chinese Buddhist translation project constitutes a very substantial source of research data that is currently under-researched or un-researched, especially in scholarship in European languages'. The Rhetoric Model of Translation arguably presents a most viable analytical framework to rediscover the monk translators' ideology, strategies and contributions to the collective endeavour of sutra translation in Chinese history.

A Rhetorical Model of Translation can better explain why a certain translation method is used against a given historical background than, say, the polysystem theory proposed by Even-Zohar in some respect. According to Munday's interpretation of the polysystem theory, 'if translated literature is secondary, translators tend to use existing target-culture models for the TT' (2016: 173). More specifically,

> If translated literature assumes a secondary position, then it represents a peripheral system within the polysystem. It has no major influence over the central system and even becomes a conservative element, preserving conventional forms and conforming to the literary norms of the target system.
>
> *(Munday 2016: 172)*

This, however, does not explain why Kumārajīva and Xuan Zang adopted a foreignization method when translated literature was practically nonexistent. The Rhetorical Model of Translation, on the other hand, adequately explains why Kumārajīva and Xuan Zang deliberately violated the existing norm of sutra translation (i.e. the *geyi* method) and insisted on translating Buddhist terms with original sounds due to their profound understanding of and respect for the source. When looking at the picture as a whole, the polysystem theory has neglected translator's subjectivity and their free choice in the literary environment they find themselves in. Sutra translator such as Kumārajīva challenged the protocol and used his own rhetoric means in translating to express his own ideology and devotion to the subject of translation. A Rhetorical Model of Translation clearly illuminates the problems of individual translator's behaviours and concerns against their ecological systems by involving factors like translators' character and ideals while analyzing factors like source text and translation strategies and purposes. The Rhetorical Model of Translation is not only capable of explaining the phenomenon of sutra translation, it can also be used to predict the rhetoric and translation strategies of translation activisms in other areas such as translation of political systems, human rights, climate control, indigenous cultures and so on.

An important function of translation theory in the West is, according to Baker (2011), to draw from modern linguistic theory to 'provide a basis for training translators and can inform and guide the decisions they have to make in the course of performing their work.' (Baker 2011: 4). In China, no systematic analysis and consolidation of individual translator's ideas had appeared until the introduction of Western translation theory near the end of the 20th century. Currently, Chinese academics in translation studies are vigorously copying research examples from the West and attempting to formulate Chinese translation theory anew without referring back to the great wealth of rhetoric and translation of Chinese translators. Wei (2020), for example, briefly introduced two of China's 'home made' translation theories that have attracted some followers: the so-called Eco-translatology (生态翻译学) and the 'translation variation' theory (变译理论), neither of which draw substantially from the wealth of rhetoric and translation from the Chinese tradition. With the research framework introduced in this article and the demonstration of how to make sense of Chinese monk translators' contributions with the help of this theoretical model, we hope to shed new light to the increasingly invigorated research on Chinese translation studies and to the creation of new translation theory based on the unique characteristics of Chinese translation.

References

Aristotle (350 B.C.E) *Rhetoric*. Retrieved 11/01/2020 from: http://classics.mit.edu/Aristotle/rhetoric.1.i.html.

Baker, M. (2011) *In Other Words: A Coursebook on Translation*. Abingdon, OX and New York, NY: Routledge.

Bao, B. 包布赫 (2017) 浅析玄奘的翻译观及其佛经翻译 (A brief comment on Xuanzang's view on translation and his sutra translation). 文学教育(Literature Education). 2017(12): 1.

Chen, L. and Zhang, C. 陈琳, 张春柏 (2006) 从玄奘与哲罗姆的比较看中西翻译思想之差异 (The difference between Chinese and Western mentalities on translation: a comparison between Xuan Zang and St. Jerome). 外语研究 (Foreign Languages Research). 2006(01): 61–65+80.

Cheung, M.P.Y. (2014) *An Anthology of Chinese Discourse on Translation (Volume 1): From Earliest Times to the Buddhist Project*. Abingdon, OX and New York, NY: Routledge.

Collombat, I. (2017) 'Skopos Theory as an Extension of Rhetoric'. *Poroi*. 13(1): 1–10.

Frances, P. (2005) 'The Rhetoric of Translation'. *The Modern Language Review*. 100: 255–268.

Fu, H. 傅惠生 (2011) 彦琮《辩正论》对我国译论的历史贡献 (The contribution of Yan Cong's *Dialectic of the Right Way* to the history of Chinese translation theory). 中国翻译 (Chinese Translators Journal). 2011(01): 19–23.

Gonzales, L. (2018) *Sites of Translation: What Multilinguals Can Teach Us about Digital Writing and Rhetoric*. Ann Arbor, MI: University of Michigan Press.

Hadley, J.L. and S. McElduff (2018) 'Rhetoric, oratory, interpreting and translation'. In Kirsten Malmkjær (Ed.) *The Routledge Handbook of Translation Studies and Linguistics*. London and New York: Routledge. pp.121–132.

Hou, G. 侯国金 (2014) 浅论玄奘'秘密故'不翻之翻 (A brief discussion on the 'occult reason' of Xuan Zang's five no-translation). 外国语言文学 (Foreign Language and Literature Studies). 2014(2): 108–118+143.

Huang, X. 黄小芃 (2011) 再论隋释彦琮《辩正论》的翻译思想 (More on the translation ideology of Shi Yan Cong's *Dialectics of the Right Way*). 西南民族大学学报(人文社会科学版) (Journal of Southwest University for Nationalities(Humanities and Social Science)). 2011(2): 183–186.

Huang, X. 黄小芃 (2013) 隋释彦琮《辩正论》的佛教思想及与翻译思想的关系 (The relationship between Yan Cong's Buddhist ideology and translation ideology in *Dialectics of the Right Way*). 天府新论 (Tianfu New Idea). 2013(04): 141–146.

Huang, X. 黄小芃 (2014) 隋释彦琮《辩正论》'八备'与翻译 (Translation of 'Babei' in the treatise *On Right Way* by monk Yan Cong in Sui Dynasty). 外国语文(Foreign Language and Literature). 2014(1): 127–131.

Károly, K. (2013) 'Translating Rhetoric: Relational Propositional Shifts in Hungarian-English Translations of News Stories'. *The Translator*. 19(2): 245–273.

Lin, J. 林继红 (2016) 构建与交往:佛典汉译的话语意义——以释道安汉译佛典为例 (Constructing and interacting: the discourse meaning of Chinese translation of sutra – taking Shi Dao An translated sutras as example). 福建论坛(人文社会科学版) (Fujian Tribune). 2016(9): 208–213.

Liu, P. and Lan H. 刘朋朋, 蓝红军 (2019) 佛经翻译方法论 (Translation methodology in Buddhist Sutra translation). 中国文化研究 (Chinese Culture Research). 2019(1): 133–143.

Luo, C. 罗长斌 (2014) 玄奘大师佛经翻译的价值和启示 (Values and enlightenments from Xuan Zang's translation of Buddhist Scriptures). 广东外语外贸大学学报 (Journal of Guangdong University of Foreign Studies). 2014(3): 75–79+83.

Ma, H. 马会娟 (2019) 走出'西方中心主义'基于中国经验的翻译理论研究 (Exloping the Feasibility of Decentering Eurocentrism in Chinese Translation Studies). 上海大学学报社会科学版 (Journal of Shanghai University (Social Science)). 2019 (2): 104–113.

Ma, Z. 马祖毅 (1982) 我国最早研究翻译理论的释道安和彦琮 (The earliest researchers on translation theory in China: Shi Dao An and Yan Cong). 中国翻译 (Chinese Translators Journal). 1982(5): 28–30.

Munday, J. (2016) *Introducing Translation Studies: Theories and Applications*. Abingdon, OX and New York, NY: Routledge.

Nida, E. (2004) 'Principles of Correspondence'. In Lawrence Venuti (Ed.) *The Translation Studies, Reader*. New York: Routledge, pp. 153–167.

Shei, C. and G. Zhaoming (2018) 'Editors' introduction'. In Chris Shei and Gao Zhaoming (Eds.) *The Routledge Handbook of Chinese Translation*. London and New York: Routledge, pp. xviii–xx.

Shi, X. and Lu, X. 石小梅, 路晓红 (2013) 玄奘术语翻译理论的创新性及其现代意义 (The innovation of Xuan Zang's translation theory and its contemporary meaning). 民族翻译 (Minority Translators Journal). 2013(2): 43–49.

Sun, Q. 孙清祥 (2012) 论玄奘对翻译的贡献 (On Xuanzang's contribution to translation). 南昌高专学报 (Journal of Nanchang College). 2012(02): 52–54.

Wang, D. 汪东萍 (2018) 回归翻译本质：解读鸠摩罗什的翻译思想 (Return to translation essence: Interpret Kumarajiva's translation thought). 学术研究 (Academic Research). 2018(12): 168–173+178.

Wang, X. 王小琴 (2009) 中西译论对比研究 (A comparative study of Chinese and western translation theories). 语文学刊:外语教育与教学 (Journal of Language and Literature). 2009(2): 85–87.

Wang, X. 王向远 (2017) '不易'并非'不容易'——对释道安'三不易'的误释及其辨正 (A note on misunderstanding of SHI Dao-an's key principle in translation). 北京师范大学学报(社会科学版) (Journal of Beijing Normal University (Social Sciences)). 2017(04): 41–51.

Wang, X. and Gao Y. 王小琼, 高玉卉 (2017) 中国古代佛经译论发展之管窥: 从支谦、道安至玄奘 (Origin of Chinese translation theory from Zhi Qian，Dao An to Xuan Zang). 蚌埠学院学报 (Journal of Bengbu University). 2017(05): 162–165.
Wei, W. (2020) *An Overview of Chinese Translation Studies at the Beginning of the 21st Century: Past, Present, Future*. London: Routledge.
Wu, Y. 吴义诚 (1998) 中西翻译理论的比较 (A comparison between Chinese and western translation theories). 外国语 (Journal of Foreign Languages). 1998(3): 48–52.
Yan, C. 闫常英 (2017) 以玄奘为例分析译者的翻译伦理 (An analysis of translator's translation ethics with Xuan Zang as an example). 北京印刷学院学报 (Journal of Beijing Institute of Graphic Communication). 2017(07): 71–73.
Yao, X. 姚旭 (2017) 鸠摩罗什及其翻译于今人的三点启示 (The three inspirations given by Kumārajīva and his translation). 中国高校科技 (Chinese University Science & Technology). 2017(S1): 156–157.
Yu, L. 郁龙余 (2017) 伟大玄奘对于当今世界的意义 (The meaning of the great Xuan Zang to the contemporary world). 湖南科技学院学报 (Journal of Hunan University of Science and Engineering). 2017(01): 30–35.
Zhang, K. 张开媛 (2015) 1995年以来国内鸠摩罗什研究综述 (The Literature Review of Kumarajiva in China since 1995). 邯郸学院学报 (Journal of Handan College). 25(1): 107–116.
Zhang, R. 张茹娟 (2014) 玄奘翻译成就探析 (Analysis of Xuanzang's achievements in translation). 文教资料 (Wen Jiao Zi Liao). 2014(2): 30–31.

22

Shaolin, the cradle of Chan

Lu Zhouxiang

Introduction

Buddhism was introduced to China during the Han dynasty (206 BCE–220 CE) by monks from India (Fang 2010). Together with the rise and fall of Chinese dynasties, various schools of Buddhism developed in China, with 禅 (Chan), 律 (Vinaya), 华严 (Huayan), 净土 (Pure Land), 天台 (Tiantai), and 密 (Vajrayana) the most popular forms (Fo & Ming 2003). 少林寺 (Shaolin Monastery or Shaolin Temple) at 嵩山 (Mount Song) in Dengfeng, Henan Province, is considered the cradle of the Chan school of Buddhism. It is also famous for its martial arts tradition. From the early 20th century, Chinese scholars began to study Shaolin. Book chapters and monographs were published to this end, most of which focus on Shaolin kung fu due to its overwhelming popularity. Tang Hao's *A Study of Shaolin and Wudang* (1930), which investigates the origins of Shaolin kung fu, is considered the most important pioneer work at the time. It was not until the 1980s that historians in China started to examine Shaolin in the context of Chinese history, culture, and religion, with Xu Changqing's *Shaolin Monastery and Chinese Culture* (1993), Wen Yucheng's *Explore the History of Shaolin* (1999), and Lu Hongjun's *Shaolin Monastery at Mount Song* (2001) being the most comprehensive works of this kind. In the past two decades, an increasing number of books on the topic of Shaolin have also been published in the West, introducing the theory, philosophy, and practice of Shaolin kung fu to martial arts fans. For example, Meir Shahar's *The Shaolin Monastery: History, Religion, and the Chinese Martial Arts* (2009) was the first scholarly work in English to offer in-depth analysis of the history of Shaolin and Shaolin kung fu in dynastic China. While most of the current studies on Shaolin focus on its martial arts tradition, this chapter takes a different approach and presents a brief overview of Shaolin's role in the history of Chan Buddhism.

The birth of Shaolin

The Northern and Southern dynasties era (420–589) marked the first golden age of Buddhism in China. It was during this period that Shaolin was born. The monastery was built around 496 by Emperor Xiaowen (467–499) of the Northern Wei (386–534) for the Indian monk

DOI: 10.4324/9780429059704-26

跋陀 (Batuo), who had traveled to China to spread Buddhist teachings (Cai 2000: 98). Led by Batuo, Shaolin grew into 'a major center for translation, scholarship and meditation' (Johnston 2000: 1159). Following in the footsteps of Batuo, the Indian monk Bodhidharma (?–mid-530s), also known as 达摩 (Damo), arrived in China around the 470s to teach Chan Buddhism (Shi 2014: 565–566). He traveled around the country for decades and stayed in Shaolin (Wen 2009: 31). Legend has it that he faced the wall and practiced meditation in a cave on top of Wuru Peak, northwest of Shaolin Monastery, for nine years.

Bodhidharma's Chan teachings were primarily based on the 楞伽经 (Laṅkāvatāra Sūtra) which centers on the concept that all forms of objects and experience are nothing but projections of the mind and that 'the knowledge of this is something that must be realized and experienced for oneself and cannot be expressed in words' (Red Pine 2012: 303). Based on these theories, Bodhidharma developed the doctrine of 二入四行 (Two Entrances and Four Practices). The two entrances refer to the two basic approaches to entering the Buddhist path and achieving enlightenment: 理入 (Entry by Principle) and 行入 (Entry by Practice). 'Entry by Principle' advocates the idea that 'all sentient beings have a Buddha nature, and that one's own Buddha nature can be revealed by 壁观 (wall contemplation)'. According to this doctrine, 'Enlightenment is in fact the moment of revelation, when one understands the true nature of phenomenal reality and comes to a realization of one's own purity' (Bowring 2008, 293). The 'Four Practices' include retribution of enmity; recognizing and following causes and conditions; seeking nothing and eliminating greed; practicing in accordance with the dharma.

The *Laṅkāvatāra Sūtra* and Bodhidharma's 'Two Entrances and Four Practices' laid the theoretical foundations for Chinese Chan Buddhism. Although Chan Buddhism had been introduced to China as early as the second century, Bodhidharma is remembered as 'the first Chan patriarch in the Chinese Chan lineage' (Li 2012: 261), and Shaolin is regarded as 禅宗祖庭 ('The cradle of Chan').

After the establishment of the Sui dynasty (581–618), Emperor Yang Jian (541–604) was eager to build up his image as a divinely ordained Buddhist ruler and use the shared Buddhist faith of people in the south and the north to consolidate the unity of the newly established empire (Tang 2016). Shaolin developed accordingly and was hailed by the emperor for bringing peace and harmony to the world (The Shaolin Monastery Stele of 728). During the Tang dynasty (618–907), against the background of a rise in cosmopolitanism, Chinese monks traveled to the birthplace of Buddhism to collect Buddhist texts and seek enlightenment. These exchange activities helped Chinese Buddhism to develop its unique characteristics. Various schools of Buddhism based on Indian counterparts, but with unique Chinese characteristics, started to develop (Tang 2016). As Buddhism continued to grow in popularity as a religion and philosophy of life, Shaolin enjoyed royal patronage and gradually developed into a center of Buddhist studies (Wen 2009).

Bodhidharma died in the early 530s (Hu 2012: 71). His disciple Shi Huike (487–593) is considered the second patriarch of Chinese Chan Buddhism (Hu 1993: 207). Huike transmitted the dharma to Shi Sengcan (?–606) and confirmed him as the third patriarch of Chan. In 593, Shi Daoxin (580–651) became a disciple of Sengcan. He studied with him for years and became the fourth patriarch of Chan. In 624, Daoxin established Zhengjue Monastery underneath Mount Poe in Huangmei County, Hubei (Shi 2014: 807). He lived the rest of his life there and developed the theory of 一行三昧 (One Practice Samadhi), which advocates that Chan meditation can be practiced at any time and on any occasion, as the cultivation emphasizes understanding the mind (Shi 2010: 319).

Unlike the previous Chan patriarchs, who had traveled around the country and only passed on Chan teachings to a few disciples, Daoxin settled down to teach and introduce

Chan to a wider audience (Yang 1999: 70). Daoxin transmitted the dharma to his disciple Shi Hongren (602–675), who established a monastery in Huangmei County in 654 and founded the 东山法门 (East Mountain Teaching) (Zhao 2003: 30). By the mid-seventh century, Hongren's disciples had developed Chan into two branches: the 北宗 (Northern School), headed by Shi Shenxiu (606–706), and the 南宗 (Southern School), led by Shi Huineng (638–713).

The Northern School of Chan centers on the concept that an enlightened person's mind is as clear as a mirror. Constant and gradual cleaning of the mirror is required to keep the dust away. It upholds the idea that enlightenment is a gradual process and that spiritual cultivation is a purposeful activity, one which requires detachment from the phenomenal world and emphasizes the importance of seeing the ultimate truth, namely nonbeing or emptiness. The cultivation of the mind is a long and difficult process involving arduous physical and mental exertion, self-discipline, and self-restraint (Lai 2008: 263). The Northern School's teachings and ideas won the appreciation of Empress Wu Zetian (624–705) and her successors (Du & Wei 1993: 214).

Huineng, creator of the Southern School, promoted his Chan teachings in Baolin Monastery in Shaozhou, Guangdong (Johnston 2000: 614–15). Huineng and his disciples advocated the 金刚经 (Diamond Sūtra) and promoted the ideas of 直指人心 (Directly Pointing to the Heart/Mind) and 见性成佛 (Seeing Nature and Becoming a Buddha) (Hong 2013: 269). They claimed that everyone possessed a Buddha nature and thus could be 'enlightened at once without lengthy, arduous study by using formless precepts and unfettered meditation' (Johnston 2000: 615). In general, the Southern School significantly lowered the threshold for Chan practice and allowed Chan to be introduced to a wider audience (Hao 2004: 22).

Shenxiu and Huineng were widely regarded as the joint sixth Chinese patriarchs of Chan. The fifth Chan patriarch Hongren's prime disciple, Shi Faru (638–689), is traditionally thought to have received dharma transmission from Hongren and was therefore also honored as the sixth Chan patriarch. Faru joined Shaolin in 683. His arrival in Shaolin marked the revival of the Chan tradition after the second patriarch, Huike, had left the monastery more than a century previously. Unlike Huineng and Shenxiu, who had actively promoted their own Chan sects, Faru practiced orthodox Chan teaching in Shaolin and helped to reinforce the reputation of Shaolin Monastery as the cradle of Chan (Wen 1999: 102–103).

In the second half of the ninth century, the Northern School declined and the Southern School developed into the Five Houses: 沩仰 (Weiyang), 临济 (Linji), 曹洞 (Caodong), 法眼 (Fayan), and 云门 (Yunmen) (Tang 2016: 189). Shaolin Monastery, which used to be a center of the Northern School of Chan, began to advocate the Southern School.

Leading the development of Caodong Chan

After the fall of the Tang dynasty, its territory was shared by the Northern Song dynasty (960–1126), the Liao dynasty (907–1125) and the Western Xia dynasty (1038–1227) (Bai 1980). The Song rulers sought to improve the bureaucratic system with new forms of religion and philosophy. Both Buddhism and Daoism received support from the imperial court. Buddhist and Daoist doctrines were incorporated into the framework of Confucianism. The Five Precepts of Buddhism were amalgamated into the Five Constant Virtues of Confucianism. Daoism was used to explain the inherent principle of the universal order in neo-Confucianism. This was called 三教合流 (Unity of the Three Teachings) and laid the theoretical foundation for the following dynasties' social-ethical values.

A distinctive feature of the development of Buddhism against the background of the Unity of the Three Teachings was the dominance of the Chan sect (Liang 2011: 9). After more than three centuries of development, Huineng's Southern School had integrated Buddhist doctrines with Daoist and Confucian philosophies and thoroughly reformed Indian Chan into Chinese Chan (Dong 2001: 21). By the thirteenth century, of the five houses of the southern Chan sect, the Linji school and Caodong school had become the most influential. This was referred to as 临天下, 曹一角 ('Linji dominates the world, Caodong holds its own').

The Linji school was founded by Shi Yixuan (?–867) from Linji Monastery in the Zheng region of Hebei (Du and Wei 1993: 309). It was centered on the idea that 'True Nature is the Mind; the Mind is the Buddha; the Buddha is the Dharma' (Liu 1999: 411). Linji masters' methods of teaching were associated with harsh encounters with students, such as shouting and beating with sticks, and seemingly nonsensical answers to students' questions as a means to evoke a direct, experiential enlightenment. The teaching and practice were also based on the study of 公案 (public case or precedent), collections which recorded the masters' discourses, sayings and stories. (Keown & Prebish 2010: 210).

The Caodong school was founded by Shi Liangjie (807–869) in Mount Dong, Yifeng County, Jiangxi. It centered on the doctrine of the 五位 (Five Ranks), a form of dialectical analysis that sought to explain the Buddhist doctrine of the two truths: 'relative/commonsensical truths' and 'absolute/ultimate truths'. This doctrine was also used to illustrate the process of Chan practice and different stages of enlightenment or awakening (Fang 2014: 100). Sitting in meditation was the major practice to achieve enlightenment. From the early twelfth century, the method of 默照禅 (Silent Illumination) was employed by Caodong Chan master Shi Zhengjue (1091–1157) to help practitioners to maintain 'original purity of the mind by simply sitting silently in meditation' (Buswell Jr & Lopez Jr 2013: 166).

From the late eleventh century, Shaolin started to adopt Caodong Chan. It was also during this period that two major temples of Shaolin, the 初祖庵 (First Patriarch Temple) and the 二祖庵 (Second Patriarch Temple), were built to commemorate Bodhidharma and his dharma heir Huike, and to reinforce Shaolin's status and influence in the Buddhist world (Lu 2001: 169). In addition, as a renowned center of Buddhist studies, Shaolin Monastery played its part in the Unity of the Three Teachings. This is illustrated by the Shaolin stele of 1209, entitled 'Saints of the Three Teachings' which shows Confucius and Laozi bowing to the Shakyamuni Buddha. Inscriptions on the stele read: 'They achieved the highest level of enlightenment. They are all our teachers' (The Shaolin Monastery Stele of 1209).

In 1115, the Liao Empire was overthrown by a nomadic tribe called the Jurchen. The Jurchen also declared war against the Song in 1125 and forced the Song court to retreat and establish the Southern Song dynasty (1127–1279) (Bai 1980: 160). The Jin rulers adopted the Han bureaucratic system, and promoted Buddhism, Daoism and Confucianism (Zhang 1997: 297). In this context, Chan Buddhism continued to flourish and Shaolin Monastery developed accordingly.

In the early 13th century, led by Genghis Khan (1162–1227), the Mongols conquered the Jin and the Southern Song and reunified China. The Mongol-Jin War and the Mongol conquest of the Song had only a limited negative impact on Buddhism. In the early 13th century, Shi Xingxiu (1166–1246), an eminent dharma heir of the Caodong lineage, rose to become a leading figure in the religious sphere. He was respected by both Emperor Zhangzong of Jin (1168–1208) and Ögedei Khan (1186–1241) of the Mongol empire (Yang 2014: 50). Xinxiu's disciple Shi Zhilong (1217–1223) served as abbot of Shaolin during the reign of Emperor Xuanzong of Jin (1163–1224) between 1215 and 1222 (Lu 2001: 514–515).

Through his efforts, the Shaolin Pharmacy Bureau was established to provide medical services to monks and local residents (Yuan 2015: 6–7).

After the Mongols took over Yanjing, Shi Deren (1197–1266), another disciple of Xingxiu, was made abbot of Shaolin around the late 1230s and served the monastery for nine years. He was awarded the title of Grand Chan Master of Zhengzong Xingjiao by the imperial court (Zhou 2006: 377). In 1245, Xingxiu's dharma heir Shi Fuyu (1203–1275) was appointed abbot of Shaolin (Lu 2001: 518). In the context of the Unity of the Three Teachings, Fuyu introduced a Confucian patriarchal clan system to Shaolin and composed a poem from which the following generations of Shaolin monks would derive their names. Since the late Eastern Jin dynasty (317–420) era, following a reform carried out by the eminent monk Shi Daoan (312–385), every Buddhist monk/nun or disciple in China has been given a three-character dharma/clerical name. The first character, the surname, is always Shi (释) for Shakyamuni Buddha, the founder of Buddhism. The second two characters are the given name. The given name usually contains a specific meaning related to Buddhist ethics and virtues. The poem by Fuyu consists of 70 Chinese characters which starts from 'Fu' (福), the first character of Fuyu's given name. The remaining 69 characters of the poem are the generational names (the first character of the given name) of future Shaolin generations. For example, Shi Yongxin, the current abbot of Shaolin, is the 23rd generation of Fuyu's Shaolin clan. His dharma/clerical name starts with the 23rd character of the poem, 'Yong' (永).

In 1253, Fuyu was appointed Head of the General Administration of Buddhist Affairs and was given the title of Head of Buddhist Affairs by Möngke Khan (1209–1259) (Wen 2009: 129). He retired to Shaolin in 1274 and died there in 1275 (Tang 2015: 127). As the dharma heir of the Caodong lineage, Fuyu helped Shaolin to establish its position as the center of Caodong Chan and one of the leading religious institutions in the Mongol empire. Supported by royal patronage, Shaolin entered a new golden age. Many of the major buildings of the monastery were constructed during this period (Lu 2001: 36–39). At the same time, Shaolin established and acquired 下院 (Affiliated Monasteries) around the country (Ye 2014). By the 1330s, it owned over 30 affiliated monasteries (Ye 2010: 32). In addition, subsidiary temples based on the Confucian clan system invented by Fuyu began to emerge (Ye 2015: 175). These temples were built around the Monastery and called the 门头房 (Lineage House). Each temple represented a lineage created by a Chan master from Shaolin and normally accommodated two to three generations of monks and lay disciples. By the late Yuan dynasty, Shaolin accommodated more than 200 monks, excluding branch temples and affiliated monasteries (The Shaolin Monastery Stele of 1318). It drew followers not only from China but also from Japan, Korea, and other Asian countries.

Entering the Ming dynasty (1271–1368), thanks to supportive government religious policies and a stable social environment, Buddhism enjoyed a long period of steady development (Shan 1997). Shaolin firmly held its position as the center of Caodong Chan throughout the 15th century. However, the monastery's influence in the Buddhist world started to decline in the 16th century, when dharma heirs of the Caodong Chan lineage left Shaolin and spread their teachings into eastern and southern China. Starting with Abbot Shi Zongshu (1500–1567)'s dharma heirs, Shi Changrun (1514–1585) and Shi Changzhong (1514–1588), the Caodong school of Chan further developed into three branches: (1) Changrun was made abbot of Shaolin, and his dharma heir Shi Zhengdao (1592–1609) became his successor and carried on the Caodong lineage in the monastery; (2) Changrun's other disciples traveled to eastern China and established the 云门系 (Yunmen Branch). They employed the theory and practice of Pure Land Buddhism to complement Caodong Chan. (Wei 2013: 298–299); (3) Changzhong traveled to Mount Linshan and transmitted the dharma to Shi Huijing (1548–1618), who started the 寿昌系 (Shouchang Branch) in Shouchang Monastery, Lichuan County, Jiangxi Province. Huijing and his disciples focused on the 看话禅 (Kanhua Chan) practice.

By the mid-16th century the Caodong lineage was mainly carried on by the Shouchang and Yunmen branches (Du & Wei 1993: 539). In the context of social unrest and widespread rebellion, the promotion of Buddhist studies was no longer the sole concern of Shaolin. Shaolin monks served the Ming government as a loyal military force against rebels in central and western China and pirates in eastern China.

In the Qing dynasty (1644–1911), the Manchu government openly supported Buddhism and Confucianism as instruments of an Inner Asian policy to win the allegiance of the Manchu, Mongols, Tibetans and Han Chinese (Jiang 2010: 270–278). Favored by Manchu rulers and Han scholars, Chan still dominated the Buddhist world (Wei 2013: 359–360). Shaolin enjoyed favorable treatment from the Qing court. In 1658, Shi Haikuan (1596–682) was officially appointed by the government as the abbot of Shaolin. Thanks to donations from government officials, a major renovation project was carried out on the monastery between 1652 and 1653 (Fu 1997: 150). In the following years, more temples, halls, and Buddha statues were repaired and restored. In 1704, the Kangxi Emperor (1654–1722) wrote tablet inscriptions for the monastery. The 少林寺 (Shaolin Monastery) tablet was put on top of the newly constructed 山门 (Main Gate) in 1735. (Ye & Jiao 1997: 89). In 1750, the Qianlong emperor (1711–1799) visited Shaolin and composed poems and couplets for Shaolin. In one poem, Qianlong comments on the legend of Bodhidharma, the first patriarch in the Chinese Chan lineage:

> Among the eminent monks in the world,
> There was Bodhidharma with green eyes.
> After facing the wall for nine years,
> He vanished without a trace.
> Sonyun met Bodhidharma in Mount Congling,
> Chan developed after him into five schools …

The Manchu emperor's visit greatly boosted the reputation of Shaolin as the cradle of Chan Buddhism. Throughout the 18th and 19th centuries, Shaolin maintained a good relationship with the Qing government and enjoyed a peaceful time.

The decline of Buddhism and the fall of Shaolin

The Qing dynasty saw the decline of the Buddhist faith due to various reasons such as competition from local religious organizations, secret societies, and the cults of innumerable divinities (Wright 1959); the abolishment of the ordination certificate system (Ch'en 1972: 452–453); and the rapid expansion of Christianity in China (Shi 1984: 49). In 1843, inspired by Christian missionaries, Hong Xiuquan (1814–1864) and his associates founded the 拜上帝会 (God Worshipping Society), launched the Taiping Rebellion (1850–1864), and established the 太平天国 (Heavenly Kingdom of Peace). The rebels intended to overthrow the Qing government and make Christianity the state religion. Therefore, a massive number of Buddhist and Daoist monasteries, Confucian clan temples, and folk shrines were destroyed (Tarocco 2007: 48). The rebellion caused further damage to an already declining Buddhism (Shi 1984: 67).

Following the collapse of the Qing dynasty in 1911, the newly established Republic of China (ROC) was carved up by warlords. In the context of the social unrest and economic hardship caused by warlordism, Shaolin struggled to revive itself. As it had in the past, Shaolin maintained a good relationship with the authorities. Head monk Shi Henglin (1865–1923) was appointed Head of Dengfeng County Buddhist Registry in 1912. Under his leadership, Shaolin monks allied with the local authorities to protect the monastery, and they assisted in dozens of small battles in the Mount Song region and defeated various groups of bandits (Wen 2001: 13). In order to build up its defence, Shaolin allied with the warlord Fan Zhongxiu (1888–1930), but this led to disaster. In 1928, the monastery was torched by Fan Zhongxiu's opponent Shi Yousan (1891–1940), subordinate general of the famous Christian Warlord Feng Yuxiang (1882–1948). This destruction was not merely an act of revenge, but a product of the anti-Buddhist persecution launched by Feng Yuxiang. After the Northern Expedition of 1927, Feng's pro-Christian policy was adopted by the newly established Nanjing government. A campaign was launched by the government in 1928 to transform Buddhist monasteries/temples into schools. (Xue 2005: 21) Decrees were issued to extend state ownership to Buddhist institutions, resulting in the further decline of Buddhism (Shi 1984: 346) Discouraged by the government's anti-Buddhist religious policy, Shaolin never recovered from the destruction of 1928.

Following the establishment of the People's Republic of China (PRC) in 1949, the atheist government carried out reforms to eliminate feudal elements in all religions; in other words, to end private land ownership and reduce the clergy's power and influence. The main task was to confiscate the land of religious institutions. As one of the biggest landowners in the Mount Song region, Shaolin Monastery became a prime target (Dengfeng County Records Office 1988: 16). All the land owned by Shaolin was confiscated and distributed to local farmers. Fewer than 20 monks chose to stay, and they were allocated less than five acres of land (De 2005).

However, the PRC's religious policy was not all hostile. Decrees were issued to protect famous Buddhist monasteries regarded as major cultural and historical sites. As one of China's most famous Buddhist monasteries, Shaolin received favorable treatment from the government. Between 1951 and 1963, the state provided funding on several occasions to repair the monastery's main buildings, pagodas, and wall murals. The monastery was also visited by influential politicians, intellectuals, and artists.

During the Cultural Revolution (1966–1976), people were encouraged to declare war on feudalism by abandoning the 四旧 (Four Olds) – old ideas, old culture, old customs, and old habits. Religion came to be regarded as a major symbol of the Four Olds that should be totally abandoned. Most religious venues were closed down, statues and relics were destroyed, and religious scriptures were burned. Monks, nuns, priests, and imams were subjected to mass struggle sessions, and many were forced to return to lay life (Laliberte 2011: 197). Shaolin Monastery was affected by the political turmoil and the monks were forced to stop performing rituals or wearing Buddhist robes (Zheng 1997). Despite this, they tried their best to save religious artefacts and relics (Yue 2011: 28). Thanks to the monks' efforts and also due to its remote location, Shaolin became one of the few religious institutions lucky enough to survive the Cultural Revolution.

The revival of Shaolin

Since the launch of reform and opening-up in the late 1970s, China has experienced rapid development and profound changes. The government finally recognized the importance of religion in society and sought to more openly ensure the prosperity of mainstream religions to serve the purposes of social stability and interethnic harmony. Consequently, monasteries, temples, churches, and mosques resumed religious services. Religious educational institutions began to recruit students. By the 1980s, mainstream religions had revived and were thriving. At the same time, in line with the new economic policies, which focused on commercialization and marketization, renowned Buddhist and Daoist monasteries were turned into tourist attractions to boost local economies. As one of the most influential Buddhist monasteries in China, Shaolin entered a period of revival. State-funded renovations were carried out in the late 1970s and the 1980s to restore Shaolin's historic appearance. In 1983, Shaolin was named a National Key Buddhist Monastery by the State Council (Han 2006: 383). One year later, Shaolin monks regained control over the monastery from the government (Shi 2013: 21–22). By the end of the 1980s, nearly all the existing buildings, temples, and pagodas had been renovated. Most of the buildings and Buddha statues that had been destroyed in 1928 had been rebuilt. (See Figure 22.1)

From the early 1990s, Shaolin monks began to make increasing efforts to lead the development of Chan Buddhism. In 1999, the Shaolin Culture Research Centre was established to conduct research on Shaolin and Chan Buddhism. One year later, the Buddhist Association of China (BAC) resumed the ordination certificate system, which had been abolished by the Qing government in 1774. Subsequently, Shaolin hosted a 传授三坛大戒法会 (Three Ordination Platform Precept Transmission Ceremony) between May and June 2007. Buddhist novices from around the country participated in the event, and 730 of them were ordained by the BAC (Hou 2007). The monastery hosted another four ceremonies in 2010, 2013, 2016, and 2019, during which more than 2,000 Buddhist candidates had been ordained. These ceremonies have helped Shaolin to consolidate its central position in China's Buddhist community.

Figure 22.1 The main gate of Shaolin Monastery. Photo by the author (2019).

In 2005, Shaolin hosted the 禅七法会 (Chan Seven Assembly), a 49-day Buddhist retreat during which the clergy conduct intense meditation practice to seek enlightenment. It has since become one of Shaolin's most important annual religious events. Each year, the Assembly is attended by over a hundred monks, nuns, and Buddhist candidates from China and abroad. During the assembly, the monks are not allowed to leave the Meditation Hall and have to cast aside matters of life and death. Each meditation session lasts for the duration of the burning of 12 sticks of incense, followed by a walking session that lasts for the same amount of time. During the 49 days, group leaders discuss practitioners' feelings, experiences and achievements with them three times, and give them guidance.

In 2006, Shaolin hosted its first 少林问禅 (Shaolin Chan Inquiry), a forum for the Buddhist community and the general public to discuss and study Chan Buddhism. The forum features debate on 公案 (Public Case/Precedent) stories, calligraphy shows, photo exhibitions, public lectures, pilgrimages, and prayer assemblies. The 机锋辩禅 (Ji Feng Chan Debate) is the prime event of the forum. Contestants debate topics selected from classic public cases in front of the audience and a group of judges determine the winners. For example, the topics of the 2015 Ji Feng Chan Debate included: 'How to deal with delusion?'; 'The fifth patriarch stated: it would be useless to study the dharma if one does not realize his/her conscience. What is conscience? How to realize conscience?'. By 2015, Shaolin had held ten Chan Inquiries, each attracting hundreds of monks, lay disciples and celebrities from various fields. These events have successfully introduced Chan Buddhism to a wider spectrum of society. From 2013, in response to the growing demand from lay disciples, Shaolin began to build up a network of Chan halls in major cities in China, which offers venues for people to study Buddhist sutras and conduct medication, further boosting the revival of Chan Buddhism.

Conclusion

The rise and fall of Shaolin depends on the social and economic environment and the ruling regime's religious policy, and the development of Shaolin has always followed the pattern of the dynastic cycle. Throughout history, Shaolin has enjoyed prosperity when the country is unified and at peace, but has rarely escaped the destruction and chaos brought about by political turbulence. Today, after decades of revival, Shaolin is widely recognized as one of the most influential religious institutions in China and has also become a well-known symbol of Chinese culture. In 2010, Shaolin was named a World Cultural Heritage Site by UNESCO (Shaolin Temple 2010). In June 2013, the State Council declared Shaolin a Key Historical and Cultural Site Protected at the National Level (Pei 2013). As the cradle of Chan and epicentre of Caodong lineage, Shaolin is now playing an important part in the development of Chinese Buddhism. Stemming from Chan doctrines and assisted by Shaolin kung fu, the monastery has created a legacy of remembrance for the Chinese nation.

Acknowledgment

Some parts of this chapter are taken from my monograph *A History of Shaolin: Buddhism, Kung Fu and Identity* (Routledge 2019). To meet the publication requirements, they have been reorganized and rewritten.

References

Bai, S. 白寿彝 (1980) 中国通史纲要 (An outline history of China), Shanghai: Shanghai People's Press.

Bowring, R. (2008) *The Religious Traditions of Japan 500–1600*. Cambridge: Cambridge University Press.

Buswell Jr., R. and Lopez Jr., S. (2013) *The Princeton Dictionary of Buddhism*. Princeton, NJ: Princeton University Press.

Cai, R. 蔡日新 (2000) 中国禅宗的形成 (The formation of Chinese Chan Buddhism), Taipei: Yunlong Press.

Ch'en, K. (1972) *Buddhism in China: A Historical Survey*. Princeton, NJ: Princeton University Press.

De, Q. 德虔 (2005) '素喜: 少林至尊 7' (Suxi: the hero of Shaolin 7), 精武 (Pure Martial) (8): 46.

Dengfeng County Records Office 登封县志办公室, (ed.) (1988) 新编少林寺志 (New records of Shaolin Monastery), Beijing: China Tourism Press.

Dong, Q. 董群 (2001) 慧能与中国文化 (Huineng and Chinese culture), Guiyang: Guizhou People's Press.

Du, J. 杜继文 and Wei, D. 魏道儒 (1993) 中国禅宗通史 (History of Chinese Chan Buddhism), Nanjing: Jiangsu Guji Press.

Fang, L. 方立天 (2010), 中国佛教与传统文化 (Chinese Buddhism and traditional culture), Beijing: China Renmin University Press.

Fang, L. 方立天 (2014) 方立天讲谈录 (Fang Litian's collection), Beijing: Jiuzhou Press.

Fo, Y. and Ming, X. 佛源, 明向 (eds.) (2003) 大乘佛教与当代社会 (Mahayana Buddhism and contemporary society), Beijing: East Press.

Fu, J. 傅景星 (1997) '重修少林寺记' (Rebuild Shaolin Monastery), in Ye, Feng and Jiao, Qinchong叶封, 焦钦宠 (eds.) 少林寺志 (Records of Shaolin), Yangzhou: Jiangsu Guangling Ancient Classics Press.

Han, X. 韩欣 (ed.) (2006) 中国名园 (Famous gardens in China), vol. 2, Shanghai: East Press.

Hao, R. 郝润华 (2004) 鉴真评传 (Biography of Jianzhen). Nanjing: Nanjing University Press.

Hong, X. 洪修平 (2013) 中华佛教史: 隋唐五代佛教史卷 (History of Chinese Buddhism: Sui, Tang and Five dynasties), Taiyuan: Shanxi Education Press.

Hou, Y. 侯亚媚 (2007) '少林寺300年来再次举行封坛受戒600人度入佛门' (Hosted its first ordination ceremony in 300 years. 600 Buddhist candidates ordained), 河南商报 (Henan Business Post), 25 May.

Hu, S. 胡适 (1993) 胡适说禅 (Hushi explains Chan), Beijing: East Press.

Hu, S. 胡适 (2012) 禅学指归 (Studies on Chan Buddhism), Beijing: Beijing United Press.

Jiang, W. 蒋维乔 (2010) 中国佛教史 (The history of Chinese Buddhism), Beijing: The Commercial Press.

Johnston, W.M. (ed.) (2000) *Encyclopedia of Monasticism*. Abingdon: Routledge.

Keown, D. and Prebish, C. (eds.) (2010) *Encyclopaedia of Buddhism*. London and New York: Routledge.

Lai, L. (2008) *An Introduction to Chinese Philosophy*. Cambridge: Cambridge University Press.

Laliberte, A. (2011) 'Contemporary Issues in State-Religion Relations', in D. Palmer, G. Shive and P. Wickeri (eds.) *Chinese Religious Life*. Oxford: Oxford University Press, 192–208.

Li, P. (2012) *A Guide to Asian Philosophy Classics*. Peterborough: Broadview Press.

Liang, Q. 梁启超 (2011) 中国近三百年学术史 (China's academic history in the past 300 years), Beijing: Commercial Press.

Liu, Z. 刘泽亮 (1999) 黄檗禅哲学思想研究 (Study of Huangbo's Chan Doctrine), Wuhan: Hubei People's Press.

Lu, H. 吕宏军 (2001) 嵩山少林寺 (Shaolin Monastery of Mount Song), Zhengzhou: Henan People's Press.

Pei, L. 裴蕾 (2013) '河南少林寺，曹操墓古迹入选重点文物保护单位' (Henan's Shaolin monastery and Cao Cao's tomb declared major historical and cultural sites), *Zhengzhou Evening Post*, 6 May.

Red Pine (trans.) (2012) *The Lankavatara Sūtra*. Berkley: Counterpoint Press.

Shahar, M. (2009) *The Shaolin Monastery: History, Religion, and the Chinese Martial Arts*. Honolulu: University of Hawaii Press.

Shan, X. 山锡之 (1997) '重装佛像碑纪略' (Rebuild the Buddha Statues), in Ye, Feng and Jiao 叶封, 焦钦宠 (eds.) 少林寺志 (Records of Shaolin), Yangzhou: Jiangsu Ancient Classics Press.

Shaolin Temple (2010) 'Cradle of Chinese Kung Fu, Shaolin Temple Kicks Its Way into UNESCO heritage list', 2 August. Available at: http://www.shaolin.org.cn/templates/T_newS_list/index.aspx?nodeid=294&page=ContentPage&contentid=2874 (Accessed 28 March 2017).

Shi, D. 释东初 (1984) 中国佛教近代史 (A history of Buddhism in modern China), Taipei: Dongchu Press.

Shi, D. 释道宣 (2014) 续高僧传 (Further biographies of eminent monks I), edited by Guo, Shaolin 郭绍林, Beijing: Zhonghua Book Company.

Shi, H.Y. (2010) *The Rabbit's Horn: A Commentary on the Platform Sūtra*. Los Angeles: Buddha's Light Publishing.

Shi, Y. (2013) *Shaolin Temple in My Heart*. Beijing: China Intercontinental Press.

Tang, H. (1930) 少林武当考 (A study of Shaolin and Wudang), Nanjing: Zhongyang guoshu guan.

Tang, Y. 汤燕 (2015) 少林寺庆公功行碑考释 (A study of Shaolin Monastery Stele: 'Biography of Master Qinggong'), in Shi, Yongxin 释永信, (ed.) 少林学论文集 (Shaolin studies essay collection), Beijing: Religious Culture Publisher.

Tang, Y. 汤用彤 (2016) 隋唐佛教史纲 (History of Buddhism in Sui and Tang dynasties), Beijing: China Book Company.

Tarocco, F. (2007) *The Cultural Practices of Modern Chinese Buddhism: Attuning the Dharma*. Abingdon: Routledge.

The Shaolin Monastery Stele of 728 '唐皇嵩岳少林寺碑' (The Emperor Tang Songyue Shaolin Temple Monument).

The Shaolin Monastery Stele of 1209 '三教圣象' (Saints of the Three Teachings).

The Shaolin Monastery Stele of 1318 '少林禅寺第十代妙严弘法大禅师古岩就公和尚道行碑铭并序' (Biography of the tenth generation of Shaolin abbot Chan Master Guyan Jiugong).

Wei, D. 魏道儒 (2013) 中华佛教史-宋元明清佛教史卷 (History of Chinese Buddhism: Song, Yuan, Ming and Qing dynasties), Taiyuan: Shanxi Education Press.

Wen, Y. 温玉成 (1999) 少林访古 (Explore the history of Shaolin), Tianjin: Hundred Flowers Literature Press.

Wen, Y. 温玉成 (2001) '少林寺历史概述' (A brief history of Shaolin Monastery), in Shaolin Culture Research Centre 少林文化研究所 (ed.) 少林文化研究论文集 (Shaolin culture studies essay collection), Beijing: Religious Culture Press.

Wen, Y. 温玉成 (2009) 少林史话 (Book on history of Shaolin Temple with illustrations), Beijing: Gold Wall Press.

Wright, A.F. (1959) *Buddhism in Chinese History*. Stanford: Stanford University Press.

Xue, Y. (2005) *Buddhism, War, and Nationalism: Chinese Monks in the Struggle against Japanese Aggression* 1931–1945. Abingdon: Routledge.

Yang, Z. 杨曾文 (1999) 唐五代禅宗史 (Chan Buddhism in the Tang and Five dynasties era), Beijing: China Social Sciences Press.

Yang, Z. 杨曾文 (2014) '金末元初万松行秀和北传曹洞宗' (Wansong Xingxiu and the development of the Caodong school in northern China during the late Jin and early Yuan Dynasties), in Yi, Xue 怡学 (ed.) 元代北京佛教研究 (The Development of Buddhism in Beijing in the Yuan Dynasty), Beijing: Gold Wall Press.

Ye, D. 叶德荣 (2010) 宗统与法统 (Clan transmission and Dharma transmission: Shaolin Monastery at Mount Song), Guangzhou: Guangdong People's Press.

Ye, D. 叶德荣 (2015) '论汉地僧人宗统结构-以嵩山少林寺为例' (The clan system of Han Buddhist monks: The case of Shaolin at Mount Song), in Shi, Yongxin 释永信 (ed.) 少林学论文集 (Shaolin studies essay collection), Beijing: Religious Culture Publisher.

Ye, F. and Jiao, Q. 叶封, 焦钦宠 (1997) 少林寺志 (Records of Shaolin), Yangzhou: Jiangsu Guangling Ancient Classics Press.
Ye, X. 叶宪允 (2014) '蒙元前期都城"哈剌和林"城的北少林寺考' (Northern Shaolin Monastery in Karakorum in the early Yuan era), 世界宗教研究 *Studies in World Religions* 146 (6): 51.
Yuan, H. 元好问 (2015) '少林药局记' (Records of the Shaolin Pharmacy Bureau), in 遗山先生文集, 卷35 (Collection of Mr Yishan, vol. 35), Beijing: National Library of China Publishing House.
Yue, X. 岳晓锋 (2011) '当代少林十讲之六' (Ten lectures on Shaolin in modern China, 6), 少林与太极 (Shaolin and Taichi) (12): 28.
Zhang, S. 张声作 (ed.) (1997) 宗教与民族 (Religion and ethnicity), Beijing: China Social Sciences Press.
Zhao, J. 赵金桃 (2003) 西山四祖 (The fourth patriarch), Beijing: Religious Culture Press.
Zhen, B. 甄秉浩 (1997) 少林中兴之祖 (The masters who revived Shaolin), Tianjin: Tianjin Ancient Classics Press.
Zhou, S. 周绍良 (2006) 周绍良先生纪念文集 (Collection of Mr Shaoliang Zhou), Beijing: Beijing Library Press.

Part IV

Chinese people and society

23

Embracing the middle class

Wealth, power, and social status

David S.G. Goodman

Introduction

Since 2002 the Chinese Communist Party (CCP) has targeted growing the middle class as a central part of its social policy goals and domestic political strategy. The objective has been to highlight increased prosperity (and thereby to increase legitimacy) and to encourage social harmony. Scholars both inside and outside China have reacted to the challenge of this ideological departure in a number of different ways. Some, particularly those in the Institute of Sociology at the Chinese Academy of Social Sciences [CASS], have welcomed the usefulness of the concept of the middle class and that Institute has developed a social stratification model to explain the change. Others, including voices within China, have rejected this idea and the model of social structure in whole or in part. Still others have argued that while there is a middle class, it is not the middle class identified by the Party itself, or even by CASS. A substantial number of commentators now argue that the CCP's embrace of the middle class is in practice more concerned with the advantages of the political discourse than with the development of a social structure (Zhou 2005).

The middle class has not been a precise term in the social sciences generally, or indeed for that matter as applied to China. Its definition has changed over time and with context, ranging from the owners of capital (the bourgeoisie) to the supporters and servants of capital (the managerial and professional classes). Importantly though for some time the literature on the middle class in other countries at earlier times (particularly writings by Barrington Moore and Samuel Huntington) has suggested that they are likely to be the drivers and carriers of regime as well as social change, especially as they grow in numbers and influence. More recently in the last two decades, scholars outside the People's Republic of China [PRC] (notably Anthony Giddens and Erik Olin Wright) have generally adopted an approach to the middle class identified in terms of the professional, managerial, and entrepreneurial middle classes, derived from their access to knowledge, skills, and expertise, and their experience in the exercise of authority over the subordinate classes within the elite's system of economic and political control.

While the potential of the middle class to bring political change has been at the heart of research on the topic, almost all the recent literature on China challenges that possibility

DOI: 10.4324/9780429059704-28

(Wright 2010; Goodman 2015; Rocca 2017). In the first place, while it is accepted that the middle classes have certainly expanded with economic growth since 1978, that growth remains limited (Goodman 2014). Reference to the term 'middle' in this context cannot be read, as would be the case in many Anglophone countries, as referring to the majority, middle-income sectors of society. China's self-described middle class are more usually at most the top 15% in terms of the country's income distribution, and more realistically the top 12%.

Secondly, research suggests that unlike their counterparts in other countries, the attitudes and actions of China's middle class are more likely to be regime-reinforcing rather than regime-changing. The dominant explanation is that while in other countries the emergence of a middle class is often held to be characterized by its independence from the state, this is not the case in China where the middle class are not only not independent of the Party-state, but a substantial proportion of the professional and managerial middle classes still work within and under the auspices and with the support of the Party-state (Chen 2013).

The majority of the entrepreneurial middle classes have emerged from within the Party-state. Those entrepreneurs who did not emerge from within the Party-state with its economic reconstruction in the reform era, have been brought into the fold of the Party-state's political processes by the CCP in a number of ways. These include not simply being able to join the CCP, but also being appointed to government positions, serving in advisory positions, and working closely together with the CCP and the Party-state institutionally, as well as associationally (Dickson 2003). In both cases, their success as entrepreneurs to a considerable extent depends on the maintenance of close working relations with the Party-state. At the same time though it is clear that members of the middle classes generally are nonetheless often critical of Party-state policy, and as will be seen, are prepared to act in defense of their economic interests when those are threatened (as for example in housing development schemes) or to speak out about some of the perceived injustices that have come with economic growth and economic inequality (Tang & Unger 2013; Rocca 2013).

The idea of the middle class

Before 1978 the CCP's class analysis first focused on the political opposition of the proletariat and peasantry to the old ruling class, and later the possibility of the recrudescence of a capitalist class. As a result, the middle class was not a term of political usage to describe any aspect of socioeconomic development in the PRC. The change in the PRC's economic development strategy in the late 1970s and its success have led to external speculation that there might be the rise of a new Chinese middle class and consequences for political development. The focus of attention during the 1990s was the new entrepreneurial class engendered by the CCP's new approach to development. While some commentators, such as Glassman, argued that a democratic revolution was almost certain to follow others were more cautious. There were essentially two counterarguments. One was that the new entrepreneurs were so closely connected to the Party-state that there was no alternative critical position for the new entrepreneurs to occupy (Dickson 2003). The second counterargument was that the new entrepreneurs were in fact less a new middle class than a new bourgeoisie because they to some extent owned or controlled capital (Goodman 1992).

The middle class became part of the political discourse in the PRC for the first time after 1949 during the first few years of the 21st century. The starting point was 2002 when General Secretary of the CCP, Jiang Zemin, in his valedictory speech to the 16th National Congress made the middle class the focus of the Party's social policy, even while maintaining the

CCP's ideological commitment to the working class and the peasantry. The goal would now be to 'control the growth of the upper stratum of society, expand the middle, and reduce the bottom' (Jiang 2002). The immediate cause of this pronouncement was the management of inequality, which had been growing so dramatically through the 1990s that by 2000 the Party-state had thought it more desirable to stop publishing details of the PRC's Gini Coefficient – a standard index of income inequality. The longer-term genesis of this policy departure was the drive for economic growth and prosperity, centered to some extent on a notion of individual economic wealth, especially in the form of private entrepreneurs, also now encouraged to join the CCP and afforded respectability.

Jiang's comments were followed by both an academic substantiation (from the CASS Institute of Sociology) and considerable public debate. Under the leadership of Lu Xueyi (at CASS) a series of reports detailed both the extent of the middle class and emphasized the importance of its growth for China's future (Lu 2002, 2004, 2010). In this view, an expanding middle class leads to prosperity, ensures greater equality and social harmony, and provides equality of opportunity for all. Each report detailed the increasing size of the middle class, which by 2007 was said to have reached 22–23%, on its intended way to becoming the dominant class (Lu 2012). The reports also adopted a ten stratum schema of Chinese society, in which the entire working population is classified according to four criteria: relationship to the means of production, position in the authority structure, the possession of skills and expertise, and (in an obvious acknowledgment of the role of the Party-state in the determination of occupations and life chances) whether individuals were within or outside the Party-state's formations. Though the ten social categories are called 'strata', according to Lu Xueyi the 'theoretical meaning of the term "stratum" is close to that of the term "class" in English' (Lu 2005: 419). The distinction has been made in order to differentiate current understandings from those of class and class conflict as they had been previously understood by the CCP before 1978.

Though the CASS Institute of Sociology took the lead in this regard there were also other academic voices raised to comment on the emergence of a middle class. These included Li Qiang and Sun Liping at Tsinghua University, both of whom are well-known academics and social commentators. Others include Zhou Xiaohong (Nanjing University), Li Youmei (Shanghai University), Li Lulu (Renmin University), as well as Lu Hanlong (Shanghai Academy of Social Sciences), and Liu Xin (Fudan University.) These scholars generally agreed that the middle class were those employed in specific high-status occupations, especially those associated with the Party-state. The middle class are managers and supervisors, generally higher education graduates, and self-identified to a high degree by their consumption and lifestyle. In particular, as Zhou Xiaohong emphasizes, car purchase and homeownership not only bring status recognition but also assist in creating a 'new notion of consumption' (Zhou & Chen 2010: 94).

While there is a high degree of agreement that there is a middle class, there is considerable disagreement amongst PRC commentators about which social categories constitute the middle class as well as its size. Lu Xueyi's initial class categorization of Chinese society allowed for every one of the ten recognized strata except for the unemployed to be capable of contributing to or becoming part of the middle class. Other interpretations have been less inclusive. One central issue lies in whether entrepreneurs should be included in the definition of the middle class. Zhou Xiaohong has excluded all entrepreneurs (because in his view they are part of the dominant class) but includes the managers of private, foreign-funded, state-owned enterprises and town and village enterprises, alongside professional and technical staff (Zhou 2008). For her part, Li Chunling includes all private entrepreneurs and business people. She identifies four middle classes: the capitalist middle class (in her view, since the PRC is a socialist market economy it cannot have a fully formed capitalist class); the professional and managerial middle class; the self-employed and small-scale business people; and white-collar workers (Li 2010: 144–145).

It has become normal practice for commentators both PRC-based and otherwise to include all business people in any definition of the middle class (Li 2013; Yang 2013) though clearly, this is controversial in terms of the wider social sciences. Very-large-scale private entrepreneurs are more likely to be part of the elite than the middle class. Some private entrepreneurs may be middle class, but not because of the scale of their enterprise so much as their restricted access to capital and the development of their social position through experience and the use of specific skills, knowledge, and expertise. A few of the self-employed and small-scale business people might conceivably be middle class, because of their supervisory and managerial roles, but the vast majority are likely to be part of the subordinate classes: individual petty traders, itinerant artisans, stallholders, and small shopkeepers.

In the PRC there was some adverse reaction to the new embrace of the idea of an expanding middle class. This is not surprising given the lack of a role for the middle class in Marxist-Leninist ideology, and some of the opposition even denied the existence of a middle class at all. There was a negative reaction to Lu Xueyi's predictions that the middle class would become the dominant class not least from those who were more conservative ideologically. An article in the *Global Times* reported 'the so-called middle class in China is no more than a myth invented by media reporters and scholars' (Cai 2004). Within China, three lines of criticism were articulated. First, it was said that ideologically there could be no middle class, and if there were to be one, then it could not possibly become dominant (Liu 2006). Second, the expansion of the middle class to dominance has been rejected. One such objection proceeded from the observation that since two-thirds of the workforce are either industrial workers, migrant workers, or agricultural workers and peasants, the possibility of the middle class ever becoming the majority was seen as unlikely (Chen 2005). Another resulted from the observation that the growth of the wealthy has hampered the expansion of the middle class (Sun 2006). Third, while there might appear to be a single middle class, the heterogeneity of the middle classes was emphasized, each with its own specific agenda but no common values (Shen 2005).

Understandably, given the various different definitions, there is little agreement about the size of the Chinese middle class in the literature, either in the writings published in China or elsewhere. As of 2007, the CASS Institute of Sociology estimated the Chinese middle class as 22–23% of the working population but the relationship between this figure and the CASS ten stratum schema is completely unclear. Zhou Xiaohong estimated the middle class at 11.9% in 2004 (Zhou 2008). The National Bureau of Statistics provided a figure of 5% in 2005, based on income alone; Li Chunling's estimate in 2006 was 10–12% (Li 2010). Chen Jie has estimated the middle class at 24.4% in 2007–2008 based on occupational identification (Chen 2013), and later the Boston Consulting Group used an estimate of 28% (2011) based on consumption patterns (Silverstein et al. 2012) and management consultants McKinsey a figure of 14% for the upper-middle class and 54% for the 'mass middle class' in 2012 (McKinsey 2013).

Any society can generally be described in terms of three broad classes. A dominant class that occupies their position in the hierarchies of wealth, social status, and power by virtue of their ownership and dominance of the economy, and their political position. The middle classes whose class position is determined by their possession of knowledge, skills, experience and expertise. And a series of subordinate classes determined by their reliance on their own manual labor (Giddens 1973; Wright 1997). In these terms, it is estimated that the current Chinese middle classes constitute no more than about 12% of the total working population (Goodman 2015: 9). This is derived as follows:

- The entrepreneurial middle class: no more than 1%
- Middle-class office workers: about 1% or 2%
- Professionals: 6%
- Cadres and managers: 3% or 4%

In contrast, the OECD estimated (2019) that in most economically developed countries on average the middle classes were about 61% of the population, although in the United States this proportion had fallen to 52%, and 58% in both Australia and the United Kingdom (OECD 2019).

The middle-class lifestyle

Uncertainties about the precise social structure(s) to be identified as either the middle class or the middle classes have led many authors to focus on issues of lifestyle and consumption. Li Chunling has highlighted that there are three separate views of the middle class in China: those of the public, the government, and social scientists. The public focus on commodities and consumption: a middle class of 'business people, managers, and intellectual elites with very high incomes and consumer habits'. The same is true of government which seeks to increase people's material standard of living and in the process to reduce the potential for social instability. It is only the social scientists who see the middle class as not necessarily the wealthy but more a question of occupation and employment (Li 2010).

Zhou Xiaohong has argued that the middle class is defined by its consumption and is without political impact. In his view, the impact of China's accession to the WTO and the globalization of its economy has meant that the middle class has become 'the vanguard of consumption and the rearguard of politics' (Zhou & Chen 2010). This is a view shared by many others, acknowledging that for most people the middle class implies houses, cars and aspirations especially for the young. In this interpretation, the middle class is more a cultural than a social construct (Miao 2016; Goodman 2015; Tang 2017).

There can be no gainsaying the strength of the state-sponsored discourse of the middle class. The State Council's Development Research Center, in its 2012 report with the World Bank, stated that the explicit goal is to emulate the experience of other industrial countries in ensuring 'a large middle class that acts as a force for stability, good governance, and economic progress'. The message has certainly been publicized within the Party-state. A handbook for cadres and officials (from China's Police Academy) states that the middle class is 'the political force necessary for stability ... the moral force behind civilized manners ... the force necessary to eliminate privilege and curb poverty. It is everything' (Tomba 2011). Generally speaking, it is clear through widespread and general social surveys undertaken regularly that most people regard themselves as either middle class or aspirational middle class (Bian 2002; Bian et al. 2005).

Authors outside China (such as particularly Anagnost and Tang) have certainly focused on lifestyle and consumption in analyzing the discourse of the middle class and its consequences. Research has highlighted not only the role of private automobiles and private housing in identity formation, but advanced technology purchases; shopping in malls with international brands; eating out two-thirds of the time; consuming foreign food and drink; spending leisure time in activities such as golf, sauna, teahouses; learning and speaking foreign languages; engaging in tourism and foreign travel; and providing foreign education for one's child (Silverstein et al. 2012). All of these have resonances with middle-class activities elsewhere but there are also some particularly Chinese characteristics. The Chinese consumer is considerably more brand conscious than consumers elsewhere, 70% preferring to purchase a branded rather than a nonbranded product, compared to 30% in the United States. At the same time, foreign brands are preferred for clothing and consumer articles, but domestic brands for home appliances, presumably because foreign brands carry higher status and must be seen, whereas domestic brands even if as reliable are cheaper and less on public display.

University education has been a particular focus of study. Student numbers have expanded dramatically, especially after 1997, from just over 2 million to 32 million in 2013; the number of institutions of higher education has doubled; and state investment has increased from 33.4 billion *yuan* to 290.2 billion *yuan* in 2011. CASS researchers, amongst others, have heralded this as increasing access to and expanding the middle class. Others have also seen the opportunities for the previously under-represented, especially women, rural residents, and minority nationalities, and rural women in particular (Lin & Sun 2010; Hu et al. 2012). However, the evidence is that these hopes have not been realized. As Teresa Wright has pointed out higher education expansion has only benefitted the already financially privileged (Wright 2010). Research on four leading universities in three poor provinces during 2009 confirms that women, rural residents and national minorities are significantly under-represented in enrolments. Poor, rural women from minority nationality groups were found to be the most excluded of all. As the researchers concluded: 'College is still a rich, Han, urban and male club' (Wang et al. 2013: 469).

Housing has been another focus of study. Homeownership, like higher education, is a symbol of social standing, though since almost everyone owns their own house it is also clearly differentiated by wealth and status. The gated community, providing security and other services is characteristic of middle-class living. Some gated communities can be extremely luxurious, with detached villas but there are many more gated communities with more modest blocks of apartments and townhouses. Homes in these lesser-ranked gated communities are bought on the open market by private purchasers or supplied by state agencies and enterprises to their employees as subsidized housing (Tomba 2004). Anagnost's study of a gated community in Chengdu found that the realtor defined the middle class for a potential purchaser, reassuring them that they too 'belonged' in terms of income, car ownership, demeanor, leisure time activities and interests (Anagnost 2008).

The entrepreneurial middle class

Research generally has emphasized the fragmented and heterogeneous character of the middle classes in China; a variety of entrepreneurial, professional and managerial classes. The continuation of a ruling Communist Party-state means that the relationship between the middle class and the state is close. Many of the professional and managerial middle class are either state officials or state sector employees (including large numbers in the education, communications and health sectors) and many of the entrepreneurial middle class have close institutional and associational relations with the Party-state.

The PRC had no entrepreneurial class outside the Party-state between 1955 and the early 1980s. In the post-1978 reemergence of China's business classes, 1992 was a clear watershed. Those who were business people before that date were considerably less educated than those who came later, and their links with the Party-state were almost nonexistent. After 1992 business people increasingly came from the same social background as middle-level cadres, where indeed they had not served in those roles themselves beforehand. They were well educated, many as graduates of higher education, and often either experienced managers, the children of cadres, or both. In both cases, they were largely natives of the localities in which they became entrepreneurially active.

The entrepreneurial middle class is relatively small and closely connected to the Party-state. The Party-state still plays a role in the economy beyond the state-owned sector. It is estimated that about a quarter of designated private enterprises are owned by State Owned Enterprises (SOE), while an undetermined number of additional enterprises are hybrid public-private concerns. Entrepreneurs have either come from the institutions of the Party-state or been accommodated within them, once their enterprises are established. In 2006-7 one survey found that 51% had previously been employed in the state sector, 19% had been a cadre; and 37.8% were CCP members. Almost all entrepreneurs were members of local government-organized Chambers of Commerce and business associations (Chen & Dickson 2010).

The key question examined by external researchers about the entrepreneurial middle classes in China is whether their growth will lead to mobilization for political change. Barrington Moore's comment on European development that 'no bourgeoisie, no democracy' has become the starting point for further examination (Moore 1967). There are those who see a necessary connection in China between the entrepreneurs' growing economic strength and their desire to set the political agenda in the same way. It is also argued that democratization must come because the Party-state cannot manage the increased complexity resulting from economic growth.

The dominant view of researchers in study after study is that entrepreneurs do not speak with one voice, or have a single view on anything (Tsai 2005). Nor is there any evidence of their push for a competitive electoral system to replace the Party-state (Tang et al. 2009). Instead, the weight of evidence is that there is a close, symbiotic relationship between the new entrepreneurs and the Party-state, variously described as 'socialist corporatism', in terms of 'allies' or otherwise. Kellee Tsai (and Teresa Wright) have argued that 'capitalists have never had better access to the political system in PRC history' (Tsai 2007).

Research to date suggests strongly that the rise of entrepreneurs in China will not lead of itself to pressure for liberal democracy. It has been argued that the widening of the elite to encourage and support the development of private entrepreneurs is itself a form of democratization (Li 2009). It is also argued that the growth of a nonpublic sector of the economy has brought additional categories of people from different social backgrounds, who had not previously engaged in economic entrepreneurialism, into positions of economic leadership and political influence, thereby also enlarging the political and the economic elite (Goodman 2014).

The professional and managerial middle classes

The numbers of those in the professional and managerial middle classes has grown considerably since 1978, probably doubling as a proportion of the workforce. Certainly, this was fueled by the growth of the nonstate sector, but the state sector itself, both state administration and sectors such as communications and education, has also increased. In the process, the range of occupations has expanded to include professions previously excluded (notably lawyers but also a range including market research, management consultants and services) or that did not exist (information technology).

The resultant professional and managerial classes have been variously conceptualized by scholars outside the PRC. Wang and Davis through an analysis of the China Household Income Project [CHIP] data for 1995 and 2002 differentiated elements of the professional and managerial middle class according to education and occupation. They identified cadres; an upper middle class of managers and professionals with a college education; and a lower middle class, comprising ordinary white-collar workers, and noncadre managers and professionals without a college education (Wang & Davis 2010); Chen Jie saw the middle class in urban China as comprising self-employed laborers, managers, professionals, and ordinary office workers (Chen 2013). Teresa Wright concentrated on the range of different professions: intellectuals, lawyers, accountants in particular (Wright 2010).

From the CHIP data for 2002, Wang and Davis found that cadres were 6% of the urban working population, the upper middle classes in their definition were 8%, and the lower middle classes were 44%. From data for 2004, Chen Jie calculates that managers were 1.5% of the population, professionals were 5.1%, and 4.8% were ordinary white-collar workers.

Wang and Davis are very clear about the differences between the upper- and lower-middle classes. Indeed, they suggest that those identified as lower-middle class are more aspirant than those in the middle class. The upper middle classes are better educated, have larger incomes, more financial assets, better housing, and are healthier. During 1995–2002 (the period studied by Wang and Davis) upper-middle-class salaries grew faster, and actually grew faster than those of cadres and workers. Wang and Davis highlight the central role of the middle class in the Party-state system. In 2002, more than 80% of the middle classes were working in the Party-state, including not only white-collar workers in the state administration and the SOEs, and managers and professionals in the state sector of the economy, as well as a sizeable number of professional and technical staff in the state utilities and service agencies.

There were two separate recruitment channels for the professional and managerial middle classes before 1978: cadres were selected on the basis of political reliability; professionals according to educational qualifications (Walder et al. 2000). This dualism remained after 1978, even though cadres were now also required to have qualifications in higher education. Qualifications from higher education are clearly the most important determinant of the professional and managerial classes in the PRC, although family influence remains considerable (Gong et al. 2010). Access to a professional or managerial appointment comes mainly from higher education, and access to higher education is a function of direct parental influence, not least because of the variable quality of the high school system. Professional employment practice reinforces this trend: there is a high level of inheritance in the professions with children usually following their parents.

There is a wider literature about the professional and managerial middle classes elsewhere in the world that highlights their role in bringing about liberal democracy (Huntington 1991). One obvious objection to this model of middle-class mobilization is that the professional and managerial middle classes are so fragmented that they can have no common values and attitudes. Moreover, the various component parts of the professional and managerial middle classes differ in their social and political attitudes and their propensity to action. They may share some general values and a common approach to change, though there is a general lack of desire for regime change, even where there is a commitment to reform and improvement.

It is generally clear that the professional and managerial middle classes owe their position and standing to the Party-state. Proximity to the Party-state is the determinant of each element of the professional and managerial middle classes' support for the current regime. Repeated surveys have demonstrated that the closer members of the middle class are to the institutions of the Party-state the more those individuals do not wish to see regime change. To quote Chen Jie on the politics of the PRC's middle class: 'the value and material bonds between the middle class and the state significantly affect the orientation of the middle class toward democratic change' (Chen 2013).

The Party-state has also acted to ensure a closer relationship with those elements of the middle classes that might otherwise present challenges to the regime. The experience of the entrepreneurial middle classes has already been noted. Tang and Unger provide another excellent example through their study of policy towards university teachers (Tang & Unger 2013). At the start of the reform era, university teachers were rapidly becoming dissatisfied. Compared to others with similar educational and social backgrounds their salaries seemed to be going backwards, and many were forced to take second jobs. A small but vocal minority was involved in reform activity during the 1980s that stepped beyond the Party-state's acceptable limits. In the wake of the events of 1989 in Beijing, that involved both students and academic staff in leadership positions, the government moved to improve salaries and conditions for university teachers. Particularly during the late 1990s when university staff, as members of the state sector, were privileged through the processes of housing reform, a new relationship with the Party-state was established. As Tang and Unger conclude from their survey of university teachers during 2007–2009:

> The Chinese educated middle class has, as a whole, become a bulwark of the current regime. As a consequence, regime change or democratization should not be expected any time soon. The rise of China's educated middle class blocks the way.

Of course, it would be naïve to think that no university academics would prefer regime change, but the majority appear to be regime-supporting. Many desire to obtain positions of various kinds in government and Party agencies, and others campaign for political reform within the current regime.

Many authors have described the various ways in which the various components of the professional and managerial middle classes have been active in defense of their own interests and even to some extent critical of wider issues, such as social policy, government accountability, and the role of the state sector in economic development. There have been many studies of homeowners' movements looking at the development of gated communities and the new and complex relationships that have emerged amongst real estate developers, local governments, homeowners, and contractors involved in the construction and maintenance of housing. Rocca argues from his study of homeowners' movements that these changes may well be more significant for political change in China than any attempt to create a liberal-democratic revolution since they help develop and express political interests from the bottom up (Rocca 2013). Political change in this context is then to be seen maybe not in terms of overthrowing the current regime but certainly influencing the way it reacts to public opinion, especially from its middle-class supporters.

Research into (in)equality and its reception suggests that those who see themselves as having benefitted from the changes of the last three decades also see the resultant distribution as fair. All the same, there are exceptions to this: the professional and managerial middle classes in particular have developed a concern with the extent of inequality, and a desire for greater social justice. Beibei Tang quotes an interview with a retired official:

> Under Chairman Mao, workers' pensions and medical care were the same as cadres. Everything was guaranteed. But today, you see, cadres have got everything, cars, a house, and money. What do the laid-offs have today? No wonder they feel left out.
>
> *(Tang 2013: 66)*

In a very large-scale survey undertaken during the first decade of the 20th century, there were criticisms of the 'unfair' distribution of wealth from the more educated (Han & Whyte 2009). This was a finding reinforced by Ching Kwan Lee's research among the professional and managerial middle classes in Beijing, who additionally criticized the imbalances resulting from the exercise of political power, even when they were the main beneficiaries (Lee 2009).

The potential future middle class

As of now, China's middle class is though heterogeneous, still fairly small, and almost inherently bound to the Party-state. This observation highlights an obvious paradox in the regime's stated desire to bring about a dominant middle class. The precise meaning of dominance in this context is unclear – domination might be by weight of numbers, political clout, or wealth. Nonetheless, it remains clear that the growth of the middle class remains for the moment at least tied not simply to its relationship with the Party-state, but limited to its position within those structures. There is a nascent private sector of the economy, but as a series of top-level Party-state meetings have announced since 2013, even when reemphasizing the continuation and furtherance of the reform agenda the private sector is to play a secondary role to the dominant public sector, even if the former produces a greater share of GDP.

The growth of China's middle classes beyond their current boundaries of wealth, status, and power depends on a more open political economy, greater consumption, and the opening up of the domestic market. The expansion of the domestic market is particularly important. The middle classes are not evenly distributed across China. The wealthier areas – the Pearl River Delta; the Lower Yangtze Delta (Shanghai, Southern Jiansgu, Northern Zhejiang); Beijing; Qingdao – have high standards of living, high GDP per capita, and relatively large middle classes. Elsewhere, the middle class is much less visible, other than as a euphemism for those with wealth, status and power.

Apart from regional differences of this kind, the system of household registration is a further check on the growth of the middle class. In China, household registration is determined by one's mother's birthplace. It ensures access to state welfare provision (notably education, housing and medical treatment) is only readily available to the individual in that location. The new migrant working class has been the largest social category to emerge from three decades of economic reform, far larger than the increase in the middle class, yet precisely because of their migrant status the children of these workers are denied access to the educational and employment opportunities which are a necessary (if not sufficient) condition for entry to the middle classes. This too is then a major brake on the continuing expansion of China's middle class.

The prospect of an expanding middle class appears then remote, as does its potential in this context for bringing about dramatic political change as is sometimes imagined by commentators outside of the PRC (Glassman 1991). One key reason for that conclusion is that China's middle class is much more a junior partner and subordinate part of the dominant class than an independent sociopolitical entity. This is of course one major explanation for the paradox of a communist party embracing the middle class. The other is that middle-class aspiration plays a central role in the regime's formulation of the 'China Dream' encouraging everyone to work hard and produce a prosperous and stable society.

References

Anagnost, Ann (2008) 'From 'class' to 'social strata': Grasping the social totality in reform-era China' in *Third World Quarterly* 29, 497–519.

Bian, Yanjie (2002) 'Chinese social stratification and social mobility' in *Annual Review of Sociology* 28, 91–116.

Bian, Yanjie, Ronald Breiger, Deborah Davis and Joseph Galaskiewicz (2005) 'Occupation, class, and social networks in urban China' in *Social Forces* 83, 1443–1468.

Cai, Zhenfeng (2004) 'China's middle class has not taken form yet' in *Global Times* 28 January.

Chen, Jie (2013) *A Middle Class Without Democracy: Economic Growth and the Prospects for Democratization in China*, New York: Oxford University Press.

Chen, Jie and Bruce J. Dickson (2010) *Allies of the State: China's Private Entrepreneurs and Democratic Change*, Cambrdige, MA: Harvard University Press.

Chen, Yiping 陈义平 (2005) '分化与组合：中国中产阶层研究' (Separation and coherence: Research on China's Middle Class) 广州：广东人民出版社 (Guangzhou: Guangdong renmin chubanshe).

Dickson, Bruce J. (2003) *Red Capitalists in China: The Party, Private Entrepreneurs, and Prospects for Political Change*, Cambridge: Cambridge University Press.

Giddens, A. (1973) *The Class Structure of Advanced Societies*, London: Hutchinson.

Glassman, Ronald M. (1991) *China in Transition: Communism, Capitalism and Democracy*, New York: Praeger.

Gong, C. H., Leigh, A. and Meng, X. (2010) 'Intergenerational income mobility in urban China', IZA DP No. 4811.

Goodman, David S. G. (1992) 'China: The state and capitalist revolution' in *The Pacific Review* 5, 4.

Goodman, David S. G. (2014) *Class in Contemporary China*, Cambridge: Polity Press.

Goodman, David S. G. (2015) 'Locating China's middle classes: Social intermediaries and the Party-state' in *Journal of Contemporary China* 25(97), 1017.

Han, Chunping and Martin King Whyte (2009) 'The social contours of distributive injustice feelings in contemporary china' in Deborah Davis and Wang Feng (ed) *Creating Wealth and Poverty in Postsocialist China*, Palo Alto: Stanford University Press, pp.193–212.

Hu, Jianguo, Li Chunling and Li Wei (2012) 'Social class structure' in Lu Xueyi (ed) *Social Structure of Contemporary China*, Singapore: World Scientific Publishing, pp.397–436.

Huntington, Samuel P. (1991) *The Third Wave: Democratization in the Late Twentieth Century*, University of Oklahoma Press.

Jiang, Zemin 江泽民 (2002) '全民建设小康社会，开创中国特色社会主义事业新局面 – 在中国共产党的第十六次全国代表大会上的报告'在11月18日人民日报 (Build a Comprehensive Xiaokang Society and Create a New Order of Socialism with Chinese Characteristics: Report to the 16th Congress of the CCP) in *Renmin ribao* [The People's Daily] 18 November).

Lee, Ching Kwan (2009) 'From inequality to inequity: Popular conceptions of social (in)justice in Beijing' in Deborah Davis and Wang Feng (eds) *Creating Wealth and Poverty in Postsocialist China*, Stanford University Press, pp.213–231.

Li, Cheng (2010a) (ed) *China's Emerging Middle Class*, Washington: Brookings Institution Press.

Li, Cheng (2010b) 'Chinese scholarship on the middle class: From social stratification to political potential' in Cheng Li (ed) *China's Emerging Middle Class*, Washington: Brookings Institution Press, pp.55–83.

Li, Chunling (2010c) 'Characterizing China's middle class: Heterogeneous composition and multiple identities' in Cheng Li (ed) *China's Emerging Middle Class*, Washington, DC: Brookings Institution Press, pp.135–156.

Li, Chunling (2013) 'Sociopolitical attitude of the middle class and the implications for political transition' in Minglu Chen and David S G Goodman (eds) *Middle Class China: Identity and Behaviour*, Cheltenham: Edward Elgar, pp.12–33.

Li, Linda Chelan (2009) *Towards Responsible Government in East Asia*, Abingdon: Routledge.

Lin, Jing and Xiaoyan Sun (2010) 'Higher education expansion and China's middle class' in Cheng Li (ed) *China's Emerging Middle Class*, Washington: Brookings Institution, pp.217–242.

Liu, C. 刘长江 (2006). '"中产阶级"研究：疑问与探源'在社会' ("Zhongchan jieji" yanjiu: yiwen yu tanyuan' [Studies of the middle class: questions and origins] in *Shehui* [Society]) 4: 43–56.

Lu, Xueyi 陆学艺 (2002) (ed) '当代中国社会阶层研究报告' (Report on Research into Social Stratification in Contemporary China) 北京：社会科学文献出版社. (Beijing: Shehui kexue wenxian chubanshe).

Lu, Xueyi 陆学艺 (2004) '当代中国社会流动' (Social Mobility in Contemporary China) 北京：社会科学文献出版社 (Beijing: Shehui kexue wenxian chubanshe).

Lu, Xueyi (2005) *Social Mobility in Contemporary China*, Montreal: American Quantum Media.

Lu, Xueyi 陆学艺 (2010) '当代中国社会结构' (The Social Structure of Contemporary China) 北京：中国社会科学文献出版社 (Beijing: Zhongguo Shehui kexue wenxian chubanshe.).

Lu, Xueyi (2012) (ed) *Social Structure of Contemporary China*, Singapore: World Scientific Publishing.

McKinsey (2013) 'Dominic Barton, Yougang Chen and Amy Jin 'Mapping China's Middle Class' in *McKinsey Quarterly* 3, June.

Miao, Ying (2016) *Being Middle Class in China: Identity, Attitudes and Behaviour*, Abingdon: Routledge.

Moore, Barrington (1967) *Social Origins of Dictatorship and Democracy: Lord and Peasant in the Making of the Modern World*, Boston: Beacon Press.

OECD (2019) *Under Pressure: The Squeezed Middle Class*, Paris: Organization for Economic Cooperation and Development.

Rocca, Jean-Louis (2013) 'Homeowners' movements: Narratives on the political behaviours of the middle class' in Minglu Chen and David S. G. Goodman (eds) *Middle Class China: Identity and Behaviour*, Cheltenham: Edward Elgar, pp.110–134.

Rocca, Jean-Louis (2017) *The Making of the Chinese Middle Class: Small Comfort and Great Expectations*, Palgrave Macmillan.

Shen, Hui 沈晖 (2005) '中产阶层的认同及其构建' ('Middle class identity and structure') 在周晓虹主编《中国中产阶层调查》中 (in Zhou Xiaohong (ed) Survey of the Chinese Middle Class) 20–61. 北京：社会科学出版社 (Beijing: Shehui kexue chubanshe).

Silverstein, Michael J., Abheek Singhi, Carol Liao and David Michael (2012) *The $10 Trillion Prize: Captivating the Newly Affluent in China and India*, Harvard Business Review Press.

Sun, Liping 孙立平 (2002) '90年代中期以来中国社会结构演变的新趋势' ('New Trends in China's Social Structural Evolution since the Mid-1990s') 当代中国研究 (Research on Contemporary China) 3: 1–20.

Sun, Liping 孙立平 (2006) '断裂：20世纪90年代以来的中国社会' ('Fracture: China's social structure since the 1990s') 在李友梅、孙立平、沈原主编'当代中国社会封层：理论与实证' (in Y Li, L Sun and Y Shen (ed) Social Stratification in Contemporary China: Theory and evidence) 1–35北京：社会科学文献出版社 (Beijing: Shehui kexue wenxian chubanshe).

Tang, Beibei (2013) 'Urban housing status groups: Consumption, lifestyles, and identity' in Minglu Chen and David S. G. Goodman (eds) *Middle Class China: Identity and Behaviour*, Cheltenham: Edward Elgar, pp.54–74.

Tang, Beibei (2017) *China's Housing Middle Class*, Abingdon: Routledge.

Tang, Beibei and Jonathan Unger (2013) 'The socio-economic status, co-optation and political conservatism of the educational middle class: A case study of university teachers' in Minglu Chen and David S. G. Goodman (eds) *Middle Class China: Identity and Behaviour*, Cheltenham: Edward Elgar, pp.90–109.

Tang, Min, Dwayne Woods and Zhao Jujun (2009) 'The attitudes of the Chinese middle class towards democracy' in *Journal of Chinese Political Science* 14, 81–95.

Tomba, Luigi (2004) 'Creating an urban middle class: Social engineering in Beijing' in *The China Journal* 51, 1–26.

Tomba, Luigi (2011) 'Who's afraid of China's middle class' in *East Asia Forum* 25 August 2011.

Tsai, Kellee S. (2005) 'Capitalists without a class: Political diversity among private entrepreneurs in China' in *Comparative Political Studies* 38, 1130–1158.

Tsai, Kellee S. (2007) *Capitalism without Democracy: The Private Sector in Contemporary China*, Cornell University Press.

Walder, Andrew J., Li Bobai and Donald J. Treiman (2000) 'Politics and life chances in a socialist regime: Dual career paths into the urban Chinese Elite, 1949–1996' in *American Sociological Review* 65, 191–209.

Wang, Jianying and Deborah Davis (2010) 'China's new upper middle classes: The importance of occupational disaggregation' in Cheng Li (ed) *China's Emerging Middle Class*, Washington, DC: Brookings Institution, pp.157–176.

Wang, Xiaobing, Chengfang Liu, Linxiu Zhang, Yaojiang Shi and Scott Rozelle (2013) 'College is rich, Han, urban, male club' in *The China Quarterly* 214, 456–470.

Wright, Erik Olin (1997) *Class Counts: Comparative Studies in Class Analysis*, Cambridge: Cambridge University Press.

Wright, Teresa (2010) *Accepting Authoritarianism: State-Society Relations in China's Reform Era*, Stanford University Press.

Yang, Jing (2013) 'Understanding entrepreneurs' in Minglu Chen and David S. G. Goodman (eds) *Middle Class China: Identity and Behaviour*, Cheltenham: Edward Elgar, pp.149–168.

Zhou, Xiaohong周晓虹 (2005) '中国中产阶层调查' (*Survey of the Chinese Middle Classes*) 北京：科学文献出版社(Beijing: Shehui kexue wenxian chubanshe).

Zhou, Xiaohong (2008) 'Chinese middle class: Reality or illusion?' in Christophe Jaffrelot and Peter van der Veer (eds) *Patterns of Middle Class Consumption*, London: Sage.

Zhou, Xiaohong and Qin Chen (2010) 'Globalization, social transformation, and the construction of China's middle class' in Cheng Li (ed) *China's Emerging Middle Class*, Washington: Brookings Institution, pp.84–103.

24

Labor migration and rural development in China

Elise Pizzi

Introduction

Since economic reforms introduced in the mid-1980s, migration has transformed China. As more than 230 million migrants have moved from rural areas to find off-farm work, major cities, regional urban centers, and the rural countryside have changed dramatically. Most scholarship has focused primarily on the consequences from an urban perspective. This chapter adds to the scholarship by addressing what we know about the impact of migration on development in rural origin communities.

Migration trends have changed over time as the economy has grown and the experience and expectations of migrants and their families have adjusted to new social and economic realities. While early migrants were mostly young men who moved to the cities to work in factories and construction, rural Chinese increasingly expect that most young people will go to the city to work, at least temporarily. Both government policy and left behind family members help migrants maintain strong ties to rural communities. Remittances to these family members have helped lift migrant-sending communities out of poverty and distributed the economic benefits of China's booming economy.

In addition to remittances, return migration has helped bring expertise and capital to help develop rural areas. Increasingly, however, migrants return to their home regions to be close to their families but do not move back to their home villages. Instead, the current trend is to return to regional cities and urban centers close to their families so they can enjoy the culture of their home region and proximity to their family while also enjoying the convenience of urban public services, opportunity, and lifestyle. The growth and development in sending regions are now primarily focused on urban centers.

It's important to note the wide variation across families, villages, and regions. I generalize in my discussion of trends and outcomes but every individual, family, village, and region has had slightly different migration experiences. This chapter primarily relies on a review of previous literature and has been informed by my own fieldwork in rural China to try to capture the way broad trends have shaped development in rural communities.

The chapter begins by exploring migration trends in China. I then turn to the strong ties between migrants and source communities. The third section discusses migrant settlement

DOI: 10.4324/9780429059704-29

trends and intentions. The last section discusses the overall effects of migration on rural China and highlights the way migration has shaped and been shaped by changes in economic growth and development patterns.

Migration trends

Labor migration has boomed in China as workers moved from poor and rural areas to the wealthier cities and coastal regions in search of work and opportunities. Between 1980 and 2010, the urban population grew from less than a fifth of the total population to more than half (Zhang 2012). China as a whole is now more urban than rural, and the effects of migration on rural communities are particularly stark. By 2000, nearly 20% of the rural labor force had migrated for work (De Brauw & Rozelle 2008), and more than half of all rural households had at least one migrant (Du, Park, & Wang 2005). As movement has become easier, networks became established, and migration normalized, the numbers of both temporary and permanent migrants have grown. Today, nearly a third of China's rural peasants are considered migrants, either because they have settled in the cities for the long term or because they are part of the 'floating' population of temporary migrants (Ye et al. 2013).

The main driver of this vast wave of migration is economic inequality between the sending communities and destinations (Zhang, Yi, & Ha 2009; Zhang & Song 2003). Following major economic reforms in the early 1980s, cities in coastal regions grew quickly while rural areas and interior provinces were left behind. More recent efforts to boost growth in rural areas and interior provinces have been successful, but they still have not caught up with coastal cities. Even as villages and rural areas have grown richer, labor is more productive in the cities and wages are higher, so migration continues.

Migration is considered a household decision in the New Economics of Labor Migration (NELM) literature (Taylor, Rozelle, & De Brauw 2003; Mendola 2012). Migration is a way for the household to diversify income sources. In order to take advantage of the benefits of migration, families send the member who is most likely to be successful in the city labor market and thus most likely contribute the most cash to overall household income (Zhang, Yi, & Ha 2009; Taylor, Rozelle, & De Brauw 2003; Mendola 2012). Therefore, migrants are typically young adults, relatively educated, and able to work. Since marginal labor productivity on rural farms is rather low, added incomes from city migrants easily compensate for lost farm labor (Zhu & Luo 2010).

Labor migrants can continue to support family income by returning regularly. Worldwide, most labor migration is temporary and circular, and Chinese laborers are no exception (Mendola 2012). While almost half of migrants relocated temporarily in 1990, by 2000 almost 75% of migrants were temporary (Fan 2008). Most migrants stay away from home between nine months and five years (Zhao 1999; De Brauw & Rozelle 2008). Migrants often return home during planting and harvesting seasons or during other periods where extra labor is required for farming. Almost one in five migrants leaves home seasonally, and nearly one in three stays at home for at least three months each year (Zhang, Yi, & Ha 2009). Other migrants, including those who move from city to city rather than rural areas to cities, return to their home communities for family holidays. These regular visits help maintain extended family ties and reinforce connections between rural and urban areas.

While inequality drives migration, distance and initial family income are important for migrants to access city labor markets. The poorest regions tend to be farthest away from the coastal cities, making migration costly and access to these economic opportunities more difficult. Households that are closer to bus stations or the county capital are more likely to participate in labor migration (Zhu & Luo 2010). Most migrants are from central provinces and move to the richer coastal areas, while the poorest counties are in the far west of the country, too far to easily access the labor market (Ye et al. 2013). Even within regions, the poorest families cannot necessarily afford the initial costs of migration and therefore are less likely to send a family member to the cities for work (Du, Park, & Wang 2005). Poor villages tend to send fewer migrants than nonpoor ones (De Brauw & Rozelle 2008).

Most migrants move to cities that are relatively close to their homes, at least for their initial move (Zhang & Song 2003). Many migrants start by moving to regional cities or to places where fellow villagers have established networks. In a study of migrants to Tianjin, a large and relatively wealthy coastal city, Li (2006) found that most migrants were from close regions and that most had lined up jobs through networks or through recruiters before they even moved to the city. These networks are vital to finding work, but also important means of recruitment for companies and businesses trying to find labor outside the city. The networks also provide a support system to migrants in the cities and reinforce ties to sending communities.

Ties to rural communities

Migrants tend to maintain strong ties to their home communities. First, Chinese policy ties migrants to their home location. The *hukou* or household registration system ties individuals to a specific location within China and limits access to social benefits and public services based on their *hukou* classification and location. Second, migrants often leave their families behind to look after farmland and maintain land rights, or because city living is too expensive for extended families. Migrants make up part of the household economy, which typically remains rooted in sending communities. The decision to leave family behind is influenced by the *hukou* policy and by land policies that require at least one person to continue farming land in order to maintain land use rights. Children often remain behind to be looked after by grandparents because of restrictions on school access in the city. Together left behind family and *hukou* policies strengthen ties with origin communities and reinforce the cross-national trend toward circular and temporary labor migration.

The hukou *system*

While migration patterns in China mirror the labor migration trends in other countries, internal migration policies are unique. The *hukou* system reinforces trends of temporary and circular migration and creates additional hurdles to permanent and family migration. The h*ukou* system assigns all citizens a location and a classification – either 'residents' (*jumin*) or 'peasants' (*nongmin*). Individuals can only have one permanent residence and must get approval to change the location and type of classification. The location of registration identifies where individuals can receive social benefits while the classification identifies the level and type of benefits available (Biao 2007; Fan 2008; Chan & Buckingham 2008; Zhang 2012). Social benefits such as housing subsidies, healthcare, and free education are tied to *hukou* status and location. Migrants who want to access free education or to visit a public hospital for free can only do so in their home location, where they are registered, not the city where they work. Other *hukou* benefits can include permission for more than one child, access to land for farming, subsidized housing, and preferential hiring for state jobs.

The *hukou* system was established in 1958 and modeled after the *propiska* system of the Soviet Union (Chan & Buckingham 2008; Wang 2004). At the time, the main function was to limit rural–urban migration so that grain prices remained low enough to support industrialization (Biao 2007). Economic reform in the 1980s included more freedom of movement and sparked mass migration to the cities. Migration and urbanization have been critical for China's economic boom, but growing inequality – including between rural and urban residents and between regions – is a major concern for the Chinese Communist Party (CCP) (Whyte 2010). The *hukou* system is not fully to blame but does create clear hierarchies of belonging and reinforce status differences.

Recent reforms to the *hukou* system, partly to address potential social inequality, have been largely decentralized and therefore uneven in their implementation and effectiveness (Chan & Buckingham 2008; Zhan 2011; Zhang 2012). In 1997, almost 400 small cities eased access to urban *hukou* status for anyone with a steady job, stable income, or regular place to live (Zhan 2011). These reforms were extended to all small cities in 2001 and may be expanded to more medium-sized cities in the future. Most migration has been to large cities and large cities continue to have more economic opportunities and therefore appeal to migrants more than small- or medium-sized cities. As a result, the *hukou* reforms may have limited effect on broad interregional trends and migration to large cities but may reinforce the current trend toward urbanization and the growth of small and medium-sized cities.

Reforms have reduced the importance of certain aspects of *hukou* classification. For example, the distinction between agricultural and nonagricultural classification was more important when grain rations were provided only to those with nonagricultural status. Some places have even gone so far as to eliminate rural–urban distinctions altogether (Zhan 2011). Still, since benefits vary by location, local *hukou* is now more important than urban status. In more urbanized settings such as Guangzhou and the Pearl River Delta, those with rural *hukou* status can enjoy benefits such as land rights and extra birth allowance even while living in an urban setting (Chan & Buckingham 2008). Thus, despite ongoing reforms and even reports that China is abolishing the entire system, most scholars still agree that the *hukou* system is "alive and well" (Wang 2004: 129).

Cities are reluctant to reform their local *hukou* policies if they will have to fund added social services and public benefits for rural migrants and new residents (Zhang 2012; Zhan 2011). Some cities have implemented strict points-based conversion criteria to only provide services to a select set of new residents while others have coupled the loosening of restrictions with severe reduction in *hukou*-related benefits. Where cities do provide social services to nonlocals, the quality is typically inferior (Zhang & Treiman 2013). Access to the public benefits associated with *hukou* status is extremely important for migrants and potential migrants in deciding where they will move (Pizzi & Hu 2019). Migrants who cannot get public benefits where they work must return home if they get sick or pay for private provision of services like education and health care.

Clearly, the difficulty of changing official status and getting government approval for permanent residence in a new city has not dissuaded millions of migrants from moving to the cities. Some migrants would prefer not to transfer their *hukou* even if they could (Zhu & Chen 2010). More often migrants calculate that other benefits – income opportunities, primarily – must outweigh access to a coveted *hukou* status. Even though *hukou* conversion is the most difficult in the largest cities, they remain the most popular destination for migrants (Chan & Buckingham 2008; Li, Li, & Chen 2010; Xing & Zhang 2017). Major cities like Shenzhen and Shanghai continue to draw migrants even without offering any hope of *hukou* conversion. As a result, the total number of migrants and the share of the population without local status continue to grow. Instead of dissuading migrants, the *hukou* system simply reinforces the common cross-national trend toward circular and temporary labor migration.

Left behind families

Labor migration in China has resulted in split families, as older adults and young children remain in rural communities while working-aged adults move to cities. The primary reasons families remain behind are the limitations on access to social services created by the *hukou* system, agricultural land policies in the villages, and migrant intentions to return to their roots. Split families strengthen ties to the rural community and mean that rural development is particularly important, even for migrants.

For households to effectively split their labor between the rural communities and the cities, the family members who can earn the most off-farm income move to the cities. These migrants then send remittances to family members who remain in their home village (Zhang & Song 2003; Zhu & Luo 2010). These remittances improve family incomes and sometimes village inequality (Taylor, Rozelle, & De Brauw 2003; Du, Park, & Wang 2005; De Brauw & Rozelle 2008).

While the most skilled young adults typically leave to find work, those left behind are typically the very old and the very young, or those who cannot work due to limited skillsets or other responsibilities in the villages. Labor migration has transformed village demographics, as some 58 million children, 47 million wives, and 45 million elderly have been left behind (Ye, Wang, Wu, He, and Liu 2013). Rural village populations can be referred to as the "'38–61–99 Army': '38' for the left behind wives (March 8, Women's Day), '61' for children (June 1, Children's Day), and '99' for old people (September 9, the day honoring the elderly in China)" (Biao 2007, 180).

Children are left behind in the care of grandparents in part because they cannot necessarily attend schools in the cities. Children inherit the *hukou* status of their parents and only have full access to free public education where their *hukou* is located. Local governments have been required to provide education for migrants since 2001, but migrant children are often required to pay higher school fees than locals while receiving education of inferior quality (Chan & Buckingham 2008). Local *hukou* registration for children is difficult to obtain. Children of migrant mothers are less likely to be registered at all, further limiting access to government services and protections (Vortherms 2019).

In addition, agricultural policies encourage split families. In China, the state owns all land and natural resources, not farmers. If villagers leave the countryside and do not actively work their land, they can lose farming rights (Taylor, Rozelle, & De Brauw 2003; Zhao 1999; Du, Park, & Wang 2005; Ye et al. 2013; Fan 2011). Most families try to retain rights to their land as a safety net, a source of food and income, and a place to return if work in the cities becomes scarce. To maintain access to land rights, someone in the family must remain behind and actively farm. Most migrants don't actually want to change their family's *hukou* location, especially if they would have to give up land (Zhu & Chen 2010). Still, sometimes having some family members in the village is not enough. Village leaders can reallocate land to households that will use it productively. When villagers expect land reallocations to take place, they are less likely to migrate (Giles & Mu 2017). The threat of losing land in this way is enough to keep migrants from leaving to find work and to keep them in in the village at critical times.

Migrant settlement and return migration

Strong ties to home communities are simultaneously shaped by migrant intentions and shape migrant intentions. Most labor migrants in China, as in most developing countries, tend to relocate on a temporary basis and intend to eventually return to their rural communities (Zhu & Chen 2010; Mendola 2012; Ye et al. 2013; Fan 2016). However, trends have changed over time. While the first wave of migrants returned to their rural villages, there are now more migrants staying in the cities or returning to their home regions but not to their home villages.

The first migrants moved on a short-term basis, frequently returning home to visit left-behind families. Still, they repeatedly left to find work, making the split household and migrant employment into long term practice (Fan 2015). A second and even third generation of villagers has grown up with the expectation that most of them will migrate to for work, at least temporarily. These newer migrants typically leave their villages immediately after completing school and often have no experience as farmers.

Xu, Liu, and Liu (2017) identify four main waves of return migration. While the first wave of return migration was driven by economic opportunity in the villages, the second wave was driven by reduced employment opportunities in the cities. Starting around 1990, the first wave of migrants began to return to their home villages. These returnees were the earliest migrants, mostly young men who had left their wives and children behind or did not yet have young families. Some of these early return migrants had grown older and no longer wanted to work in factories and cities. Rural areas also become more appealing for entrepreneurs as local governments promoted the rapid development of Township and Village Enterprises (TVEs). The new opportunities in villages needed human capital rather than just remittance or savings, and those who had experience in the cities could contribute knowledge and skills gained during their experience outside the village (Ma 2001). They could also invest in new entrepreneurial activities, so local governments actively tried to attract return migrants in the hope that they would help boost growth and employment at home (Murphy 2002; Démurger & Xu 2011).

Rural communities also provided a safety net to wait out economically challenging times for the second and third waves of return migrants. The second wave of return migrants responded to a change in economic policy that promoted the private sector (Solinger 2002). State promotion of the private sector led to dramatic changes to employment opportunities and unemployment policies in the cities. Beginning after 1997, urban workers were laid off as the government reformed or closed State Owned Enterprises (SOEs) in the city (Xu, Liu, & Liu 2017). Migrant workers were often the first to be fired and faced discrimination in urban areas, so they returned to their families, villages, and rural labor, at least for a time.

The third wave came after the 2008 global financial crisis but was relatively short-lived. Migrants lost jobs in factories and cities but could find work in rural areas because the government was investing heavily in major construction and infrastructure projects in an effort to promote rural development. During economic downturns, migrants typically return to rural communities where life is less expensive and they have family and farm obligations to occupy their time (Lu 2014). Once economic opportunities are more abundant, many plan to return to the cities. In a survey in Guizhou, a poor interior province, return migrants reported their intention to return to the cities once economic opportunities improved. In this case, the economy rebounded by 2010, and migrants returned in vast numbers.

The most recent and ongoing wave of return migration is perhaps the most complex. Beginning in the 2010s, migration trends started to show signs of change as economic opportunities shifted. Factories have been relocating to interior provinces, which have boosted the local economies and fostered an economic climate more favorable for new businesses (Xu, Liu, & Liu 2017). Migrants no longer go only to coastal regions or major cities. Instead, western and central regions – once the source of migrants – have become migrant destinations, even for those who plan to move permanently. The 2010 census showed that 92% of migrants remained in the province where they were born and 83% still lived in the same county (Guo 2014).

Return intentions, as with the makeup of migrants, seem to be evolving over time. While the earliest migrants intended to return, increasingly migrants want to stay in the cities (Li 2006). In 2002, Zhu and Chen found that 45.7% of migrants wanted to return home, but by 2006, only 40.2% did (2010). Other surveys have also reliably found that between 30 and 40% of migrants intend to remain in the city, although between 15 and 30% are undecided about their plans (Fan 2011). Typically, intentions reflect the constraints and status of family. If family members are also in the city, and if jobs and wages are steady, migrants are more likely to want to stay. Of course, actual actions may not directly reflect settlement intention and preferences. The challenges to settling in cities, including *hukou*, family obligations, and wage stability may not allow migrants to stay in the cities even if their survey answers suggest they prefer city life (Zhu & Chen 2010; Fan 2011). In addition, as cities become increasingly expensive, crowded, competitive, and polluted, and as rural areas improve their economic opportunities and public goods provision, migrants are returning (Zhao 2018).

Part of the new trend in migration and return migration is that migrants are now moving within provinces rather than across them. Return migrants no longer have to return to farms or to underdeveloped regions with difficult living conditions. Instead, migrants prefer to move to urban areas closer to home. Survey results suggesting that migrants increasingly want to 'remain' in cities may reflect this 'return' migration to urban centers near origin communities. Especially migrants with less farming experience, returning to village life can be challenging. Once they are used to the amenities of city living, rural and remote communities lose their appeal. Instead of returning to their home communities, migrants increasingly prefer to move to the county seat or township center (Xu, Liu, & Liu 2017; Zhu & Chen 2010). The growth of services and infrastructure has made life in second- and third-tier cities more palatable, and economic opportunities – the primary reason for migrants to leave their villages – have expanded across the country. As small cities proceed to relax *hukou* policies or eliminate *hukou* categories altogether, the barriers to urbanization will continue to fade. The government also is trying to promote "return" migration from major cities to regional urban centers and even initial rural–urban migration to regional cities rather than to the megacities that were traditional migrant destinations (Zhao 2018). The latest wave of migration and return migration thus shifts the primary focus of development from rural to urban communities in rural and underdeveloped regions.

Consequences for rural China

The overall effects of labor migration on rural China are difficult to generalize. Most of the studies cited in this chapter provide analysis based on a case study of a single region, migration route, or even village. Those that do compare multiple locations typically find variation not only in the patterns and trends of migration but in its impact on rural communities. Variations in destinations, time spent in the cities, origin circumstances, remittances, and household consumption and investment behavior make generalizing the effects on communities especially challenging. The impacts have likely changed over time along with migration patterns and community and local government responses. Still, with full acknowledgement of the variation, this section explores the main trends in the impact of migration on rural development.

First, migration has been overwhelmingly positive for those who have migrated and their families. Migrants are better off in terms of the amount of money rural households can spend on food, healthcare, and education. However, migration has led to a sense of abandonment by those left behind and disillusion and isolation among those who migrate (Ye et al. 2013; Li 2006). Left behind children are particularly vulnerable to neglect and a sense of abandonment. Still, the reduction in poverty and improved standard of living continue to motivate more migrants to move to the cities.

Second, in terms of inequality and economic wellbeing, migration has generally had a positive impact. After all, the primary reason most migrants leave is to find better economic opportunities. The remittances they send back to families have been particularly beneficial for rural consumption (De Brauw & Rozelle 2008). Income per capita among those who are left behind typically rises, although estimates of the boost in income range between 8.5% and 43% (Taylor, Rozelle, & De Brauw 2003; Du, Park, & Wang 2005). At the same time, the overall effects are complex and uneven. Poorer households benefit less than wealthier ones, in part because lost agricultural labor makes up a larger share of their income and because their migration opportunities are constrained. Indeed, the very poorest households are less likely to be able to migrate to the cities at all, which means that migration may not have an equalizing effect within villages and may not be as effective in alleviating real poverty as it is at boosting average village incomes.

Third, while migration has clear benefits for the households with migrants, the effects on communities overall are more ambiguous. Out-migration of the most capable and motivated villagers can hinder collective action and community sentiment, although the extent varies by region (Ye et al. 2013). Village leaders often complain that they want to organize public works, but only those too old or too young to work are left to contribute. However, research in Sichuan Province shows that out-migration does not hinder participation in community activities (Qin & Flint 2012). Instead, in cases where communities collectively act to provide public goods, the lack of participation by migrants can be replaced by financial contributions. The additional investment and substitution of capital for labor as well as government attention to villages unable to independently provide public goods without additional state investment can actually lead to better provision of geographically concentrated services like drinking water (Pizzi 2018).

The impact of out-migration depends in part on prior systems of governance and village relations. In one of the few studies to explore the effect of out-migration on rural governance, Lu Jie finds that the effect of out-migration on public services depends on the form of village governance institutions (2014). Village governance can rely primarily on rule-based institutions, i.e. elections for local officials, or on informal systems such as solidarity groups. While other research has shown that solidary groups positively influence public goods provision (Tsai 2007), Lu shows that the disruptive effects of migration are greater on those communities that depend on low-cost access to information about community behaviors and social sanctions, i.e. village governed by relations-based institutions. Rural communities in China differ widely in their ability to cooperate for public goods provision, their economic circumstances, and natural and social conditions, so it seems intuitive that the effect of out-migration would be at least partly shaped on prior conditions. Moderate levels of migration are less disruptive to public goods provision if villages rely on elections and other formalized rules-based institutions. Still, very high levels of migration can be disruptive to every type of governance institutions.

The effect of migration also varies by the type of public good and migration patterns, however. While water can be provided locally with minimal external expertise and support, education and healthcare require different types of investment. Temporary and circular migration may bring more remittances, taxes, and fees to their local communities, but permanent out-migration does not. Villages that are likely to see a return on their investment in education may continue to provide schools, but where the most educated leave permanently, villages reduce their investment in education (Guo 2014). School consolidation and closure is, in turn, one of the primary reasons migrants cite for abandoning their villages and moving to townships and urban centers (Wang et al. 2019). In an effort to improve the efficiency of public goods, the government has started to consolidate schools in township centers rather than have one school per village. The effect is urbanization not only of those who are moving for work, but children and family members who move to regional urban centers to care for them. These trends reinforce each other – migrants want to move to places with public schools and the act of migration reduces the incentive to provide schools in remote villages. The result is village abandonment rather than development.

Urbanization, development, and public goods provision emerge together in rural China. Like the consolidation of schools, it is more efficient to provide some other public services like hospitals, security, and transportation where the population is more concentrated. One of the reasons return migrants are moving to urban centers near their home villages is the lifestyle benefits, including things like access to reliable electricity, better schools, and other amenities (Xing & Zhang 2017). While rural development strategies certainly vary by region (Donaldson 2009), the current trend seems to focus on improving social services, economic opportunities, and quality of life in regional urban centers rather than the remaining rural communities. Development in regions that were previously the sources of labor migration primarily takes the form of urbanization and development in township centers and county seats rather than in truly rural villages or remote areas. If all small cities eliminate *hukou* requirements and distinctions entirely, we are likely to see even more fluidity of populations between rural and small urban areas and more concentration of development efforts in county seats, township centers, and other currently underdeveloped urban areas.

Future migration

Going forward, how will migration shape rural development and regional governance? Trying to predict the Chinese path forward is challenging at the best of times, but given the ongoing trade tensions with the United States, the slowing domestic economy, aging population, and the impact of COVID-19, it seems particularly difficult. That said, current trends and past waves of migration and return migration shed some light on likely developments.

During past crises and major changes in economic policies, migrants to the cities have tended to return to their home villages and regions to wait out uncertain times. It is likely that we will see similar responses to the disruptions caused by COVID-19. Many families remain split between home regions and urban centers with more opportunities for laborers. Since factories have closed and urban economies slowed, there is less demand for labor, including migrant labor. Migrants are typically the first to be laid off and often the last to be rehired, so it is likely that migrants will return in their home communities and remain there until demands for labor increase again. Rural and potential migrant households will likely continue their strategies of dividing labor between farms and cities, seeing diverse sources of income, and flexible living arrangements.

When the economy does open again and laborers are free to move, we can expect that the trend toward urbanization in the regions and the growth of small cities will accelerate. Even before COVID-19 struck, the trend has been toward urbanization and the growth of urban centers that are geographically accessible and maintain close social and economic ties to rural communities. These are the first places potential migrants can look for work and can find opportunities while living at home or close to extended families. For the government, urbanization of these regional centers provides an opportunity for organization, streamlined public goods provision, and governance. Attracting skilled officials, ensuring policy implementation, and generally improving the quality of government is easier in centralized urban centers than in rural areas or remote villages. Modernizing the governance system is likely to spread first to regional centers before any efforts to expand to truly rural areas. For potential migrants, opportunities have been expanding in regional centers. Those with exposure to urban lifestyles and little experience in farming are often loth to return to the countryside. These cities increasingly provide educational opportunities and public services that are not available in rural areas and not accessible due to *hukou* policies in larger urban centers. Smaller cities are also less expensive and more accessible than the megacities, adding to their appeal in economically uncertain times. Thus, while it is difficult to predict China's future, we can expect development to focus on township centers and county seats – smaller cities that are accessible and closely tied to rural communities – and for those small cities to be the center of migration and development once economic and movement restrictions are loosened and potential migrants are able to start moving again.

Conclusion

While rural China is better off than it was 30 years ago and the Chinese economy is now the second largest in the world, large rural–urban disparities and development challenges remain. This chapter has explained the circular and temporary patterns of Chinese labor migration, the strong ties between migrants and source communities, and the changes in return migration trends. Through a review of the literature, I have tried to highlight the ongoing benefits of migration for rural communities, and the current trend toward regional development. Even so, rural development lags behind the focus on provision of public goods and services, economic opportunity, and social change in urban centers.

Overall, migration and return migration provide clear benefits to rural China, including remittances, human capital, investment, and business opportunities. Certainly, without the opportunity for labor migration, rural China – and China as a whole – would be much poorer today. Still, there is wide variation in the migration experience and outcomes for individuals, families, and whole villages. The latest wave of migration and return migration does offer some hope for broader development in regions that were previously left behind. Regional urban centers that were once the source of migrants are now benefiting from migration moving in rather than out and from return migration. These growing small cities in less developed areas offer hope of better economic opportunities, social services, and quality of life. Certainly, rural China is more developed in terms of both economic well-being and access to opportunity than it was before mass labor migration.

References

Biao, Xiang. 2007. "How Far Are the Left-behind Left behind? A Preliminary Study in Rural China". *Population, Space and Place* 13 (3): 179–91.

Chan, Kam Wing, and Will Buckingham. 2008. "Is China Abolishing the Hukou System?" *The China Quarterly* 195: 582–606.

De Brauw, Alan, and Scott Rozelle. 2008. "Migration and Household Investment in Rural China". *China Economic Review* 19 (2): 320–35.

Démurger, Sylvie, and Hui Xu. 2011. "Return Migrants: The Rise of New Entrepreneurs in Rural China". *World Development* 39 (10): 1847–61.

Donaldson, John A. 2009. "Why Do Similar Areas Adopt Different Developmental Strategies? A Study of Two Puzzling Chinese Provinces". *Journal of Contemporary China* 18 (60): 421–44.

Du, Yang, Albert Park, and Sangui Wang. 2005. "Migration and Rural Poverty in China". *Journal of Comparative Economics* 33 (4): 688–709.

Fan, C. Cindy. 2008. "Migration, Hukou, and the City". In *China Urbanizes: Consequences, Strategies, and Policies*, Directions in Development, eds. Shahid Yusuf and Tony Saich. Washington, DC: The World Bank, 65–89.

Fan, C. Cindy. 2011. "Settlement Intention and Split Households: Findings from a Survey of Migrants in Beijing's Urban Villages". *China Review* 11 (2): 11–41.

Fan, C. Cindy. 2015. "Migration, Remittances and Social and Spatial Organisation of Rural Households in China". In *Transnational Labour Migration, Remittances and the Changing Family in Asia*, eds. Lan Anh Hoang and Brenda S. A. Yeoh. New York: Springer, 194–226.

Fan, C. Cindy. 2016. "Household-Splitting of Rural Migrants in Beijing, China". *Trialog: A Journal for Planning and Building in a Global Context* 116/117: 19–24.

Giles, John, and Ren Mu. 2017. "Village Political Economy, Land Tenure Insecurity, and the Rural to Urban Migration Decision: Evidence from China". *American Journal of Agricultural Economics* 100 (2): 521–44.

Guo, Gang. 2014. "Domestic Migration, Benefit Spillovers, and Local Education Spending: Evidence from China 1993–2009". *Asia Pacific Journal of Education* 36 (4): 1–17.

Li, Bingqin. 2006. "Floating Population or Urban Citizens? Status, Social Provision and Circumstances of Rural–Urban Migrants in China". *Social Policy & Administration* 40 (2): 174–95.

Li, Limei, Si-ming Li, and Yingfang Chen. 2010. "Better City, Better Life, but for Whom?: The Hukou and Resident Card System and the Consequential Citizenship Stratification in Shanghai". *City, Culture and Society* 1 (3): 145–54.

Lu, Jie. 2014. *Varieties of Governance in China: Migration and Institutional Change in Chinese Villages*. Oxford: Oxford University Press.

Ma, Zhongdong. 2001. "Urban Labour-Force Experience as a Determinant of Rural Occupation Change: Evidence from Recent Urban-Rural Return Migration in China". *Environment and Planning A* 33 (2): 237–55.

Mendola, Mariapia. 2012. "Rural Out-Migration and Economic Development at Origin: A Review of the Evidence". *Journal of International Development* 24 (1): 102–22.

Murphy, Rachel. 2002. *How Migrant Labor Is Changing Rural China*. Cambridge: Cambridge University Press.

Pizzi, Elise. 2018. "Does Labor Migration Improve Access to Public Goods in Source Communities? Evidence from Rural China". *Journal of Chinese Political Science* 23 (4): 563–83.

Pizzi, Elise, and Yue Hu. 2019. "Are Strict Rules a Deterrent? Political Restrictions and Migration in China". Presented at the American Political Science Association, Washington, DC, August 29.

Qin, Hua, and Courtney G. Flint. 2012. "The Impacts of Rural Labor Out-Migration on Community Interaction and Implications for Rural Community-Based Environmental Conservation in Southwest China". *Human Organization* 71 (2): 135–48.

Solinger, Dorothy J. "Labour Market Reform and the Plight of the Laid-Off Proletariat". *The China Quarterly* 170 (2002): 304–26.

Taylor, J. Edward, Scott Rozelle, and Alan De Brauw. 2003. "Migration and Incomes in Source Communities: A New Economics of Migration Perspective from China". *Economic Development and Cultural Change* 52 (1): 75–101.

Tsai, L. L. 2007. *Accountability without Democracy: Solidary Groups and Public Goods Provision in Rural China*. Cambridge: Cambridge University Press.

Vortherms, Samantha A. 2019. "China's Missing Children: Political Barriers to Citizenship through the Household Registration System". *The China Quarterly* 238: 309–30. https://doi.org/10.1017/S0305741018001716.
Wang, Chengchao, Yaoqi Zhang, Yusheng Yang, Qichun Yang, and Jing Hong. 2019. "What Is Driving the Abandonment of Villages in the Mountains of Southeast China?" *Land Degradation & Development* 30 (10): 1183–92.
Wang, Fei-Ling. 2004. "Reformed Migration Control and New Targeted People: China's Hukou System in the 2000s". *The China Quarterly* 177: 115–32.
Whyte, Martin. 2010. *Myth of the Social Volcano: Perceptions of Inequality and Distributive Injustice in Contemporary China*. Stanford, CA: Stanford University Press.
Xing, Chunbing, and Junfu Zhang. 2017. "The Preference for Larger Cities in China: Evidence from Rural-Urban Migrants". *China Economic Review* 43: 72–90.
Xu, Zhihua, Yungang Liu, and Kaizhi Liu. 2017. "Return Migration in China: A Case Study of Zhumadian in Henan Province". *Eurasian Geography and Economics* 58 (1): 114–40.
Ye, Jingzhong, Chunyu Wang, Huifang Wu, Congzhi He, and Juan Liu. 2013. "Internal Migration and Left-behind Populations in China". *Journal of Peasant Studies* 40 (6): 1119–46.
Zhan, Shaohua. 2011. "What Determines Migrant Workers' Life Chances in Contemporary China? Hukou, Social Exclusion, and the Market". *Modern China* 37 (3): 243–85.
Zhang, Junsen, Junjian Yi, and Wei Ha. 2009. "Inequality and Internal Migration in China: Evidence from Village Panel Data". *Human Development Research Paper* (2009/27).
Zhang, Kevin Honglin, and Shunfeng Song. 2003. "Rural–Urban Migration and Urbanization in China: Evidence from Time-Series and Cross-Section Analyses". *China Economic Review* 14 (4): 386–400.
Zhang, Li. 2012. "Economic Migration and Urban Citizenship in China: The Role of Points Systems". *Population and Development Review* 38 (3): 503–33.
Zhang, Zhuoni, and Donald J. Treiman. 2013. "Social Origins, Hukou Conversion, and the Wellbeing of Urban Residents in Contemporary China". *Social Science Research* 42 (1): 71–89.
Zhao, Litao. 2018. "Massive Return Migration Emerging in China". *East Asian Policy* 10 (03): 75–86.
Zhao, Yaohui. 1999. "Leaving the Countryside: Rural-to-Urban Migration Decisions in China". *American Economic Review* 89(2): 281–86.
Zhu, Nong, and Xubei Luo. 2010. "The Impact of Migration on Rural Poverty and Inequality: A Case Study in China". *Agricultural Economics* 41 (2): 191–204.
Zhu, Yu, and Wenzhe Chen. 2010. "The Settlement Intention of China's Floating Population in the Cities: Recent Changes and Multifaceted Individual-level Determinants". *Population, Space and Place* 16 (4): 253–67.

25

Chinese nationalism in comparative perspective

Luyang Zhou

Chinese nationalism: A comparative perspective

With China's economic and military power rapidly expanding, interest in Chinese nationalism is arising, within and outside of academia. As research methods advance and empirical knowledge accumulate, studies of Chinese nationalism have moved from China-single-case-based approach to international and interregional comparative perspective. This chapter engages in this move. It reviews existing literature that compares Chinese nationalism to others and suggests how such a comparative perspective should be advanced in the future.

Nationalism seeks the congruence between cultural and political boundaries, which means each nation should have its state (Gellner 1983). Under this general concept, nationalism can be defined in numerous ways. This article provides a roughly defined dichotomy: the efforts to integrate and homogenize a society from inside; the efforts to defend a nation from external intrusion and expand the nation's international influences. Neither face of nationalism carries essential features. While early generations of scholars equalized nationalism with aggression, xenophobia, and irrationalism, scholars since World War II have taken nationalism more as a multifaceted complex. Nationalism can be evil, by encouraging discrimination, ethnic cleansings, war crimes and undermining cultural diversity. Nationalism can also be good, though – spreading literacy and enlightenment, overthrowing despotism and colonialism, and forging a common market and strong state to promote development. Given the enormous variations within nationalism, a comparative perspective will be able to tell when nationalism is good and when it is evil.

The main body of this chapter reviews three debates in comparative studies of Chinese nationalism. First, was premodern China a unique polity that had become a quasi-nation-state long before its adoption of the Western idea of the nation-state? Second, over the nearly two centuries since the 1840s, how was the formation of Chinese nationalism similar and dissimilar to nation-building in other parts of the world? Third, does contemporary China, the state as well as the populace, bear an aggressive nationalism that threatens to challenge the world order? Based on the reviewed scholarship, the author suggests four future topics for comparisons: How does China's historical legacy shape its modern nation-building, especially the capacity to respond to a global public crisis? How does the history of modern Chinese

DOI: 10.4324/9780429059704-30

revolution shape the current Chinese state's capacity in containing populist nationalism? How to draw methodologically rigorous comparative analyses between China and those historical rising powers? How is the secessionist nationalism at Hong Kong, Taiwan, Tibet, and Xinjiang similar and dissimilar to the separatist movements in historical colonial empires?

This chapter maximizes regional and methodological representation. It reviews the scholarship that compares China with other regions, both present and in the past – ancient empires, colonies, former communist states, fascism, Middle East and Africa, the West, and societies faced with the challenge of separatism. The review covers most methods in use – comparative historical analysis, transnational survey, text analysis, ethnography, and, when a topic is at the emerging stage, journalistic writings. Because of the word limit, this review only includes English-language literature, though readers may find the most updated Chinese sources in the cited works' bibliographies. Lastly, research based on China as the single case is not reviewed.

Was premodern China a nation-state?

Sociologists have long debated whether or not nationalism is particular to modernity. Modernists argue that nationalism takes shape only when the structural conditions, such as industrialization, the spread of printing and mass literacy, communication, etc., are met. Primordial scholars, by contrast, contend that nationalism has premodern origins, engendered by ethnic conflicts or alien rule. China, because of its incomparably long history of homogeneous culture and political unity, has been an ideal case for this debate for a long time. Major discussions revolve around three topics: cultural homogeneity, 'introverted' foreign behaviors, and incomparable longevity.

A primordial nation-state?

Most sociologists agree that ethnic homogeneity eases nation-building. However, when it comes to China, debate arises surrounding whether China's long history of cultural unity facilitated or impeded the transition to the modern nation-state. Levenson's dichotomy of 'culturalism' and 'nationalism' (1968) has been widely accepted. His theory suggests that China's premodern cultural unity was different from and against the spirit of modern nationalism. According to Fairbank (1983: 99–101), unlike the post-Charlemagne France and Germany, which developed their own national cultures based on shared Christianity, the ancient Chinese state was ideally coterminous with the entire culture. This enabled universal kingship, used by Mesopotamia, Egypt, India, and pre-Columbian America – to persist in China until modern times.

Against this conventional thesis, recent sociological literature highlights China's unique linguistic foundation for nation-building. This theory suggests that China's common written script, that had existed for two millenniums, made Chinese culture more homogenous than any other ancient civilization. Such homogeneity bred resiliency towards political unity and prevented competing elites from fragmenting along ethnic lines as occurred in many multiethnic societies. This enabled China to avoid the trajectories of most modern empires, which have disintegrated along ethnic and linguistic lines, especially Russia and the Soviet Union (Wimmer 2018).

Along with this conventional thesis, Weberian scholars insist that China's seemingly homogenous culture was a barrier rather than a facilitator to modern nationalism (see Lash 2020). Unlike European states, provinces in China failed to achieve 'vernacularization', which would have destroyed the Confucian cultural hegemony and the Heavenly Principle. In this sense, the empire was too strong to let in the nation-state. The lack of vernacularization partially stemmed from the fact that Chinese is not a 'grammatological' language (unlike India) nor does it have a root in ritual or morphological purity. The Confucian hegemony was shaky in the Song period, threatened by Buddhism, but survived through Zhu Xi's reformation. Similarly, the lack of commitment to value-oriented action led to more unity and stagnancy, preventing the rise of the European-style nation-state system (Kalberg 2014).

Scholars comparing civilizations suggest that China was in an 'in-between' situation. Political unity became the source of legitimacy, but the technological capacity to maintain unity remained insufficient (Creel 1970). The lack of capacity on the center side and the absence of coordination on the periphery side made any qualitative social transformation unlikely to occur (Eisenstadt 2003: 300–301). Moreover, in comparison with Christianity and Islam, China lacked transcendent religion as its dominant ideology. It also had less reference to a foreign mode of thought, or indeed anything of ultimate or spiritual quest (Mann 1986: 343–344).

'Peace-loving' tradition?

A second dimension to analyze ancient China's resemblance to nationalism is its foreign behaviors. The literature associated with or based on China's domestic (official and popular) discourse conveys the notion that China was an introverted state since the unification by Qin in 221 BCE (Zhao 2015: 961–962); however, the official and popular discourses lack comparison to other civilizations and over-rely on data in Chinese (see Yu 2014). Academic writings depict China as an 'all-under-heaven' international system that only pursued peaceful coexistence and reciprocal trade (Bell 2017). Alongside this thesis, another analysis examines China's military culture, highlighting its emphasis on 'justice' 'human' and 'stratagem' compared to Western culture's emphasis on 'interest' 'weapon' and 'strength' (Zhang & Yao 1996).

Scholarship against the 'peace-loving' thesis introduces more comparisons to show similarities between China and colonial powers. It argues that China's tribute system was unstable and ritual, coexisting with a malign face of aggression (Kim 2018: 142–143). The Han-dominated central dynasties bullied small nations such as Korea and Vietnam (French 2017). The nomad-established dynasties, like Qing, shared the element of expansionism with colonial empires such as France, Ottoman, Russia, and Mughal (Perdue 2015). It is also argued that Qing's conquest into Central Asia and Tibet, like the European adventurists, involved playing the religious card, though the motivation was mixed, ranging from practical considerations to real personal beliefs (Perdue 1998). Underneath these similarities, specific differences are also revealed. When Ming China's attack on Mongolian nomads is compared with Muscovy Russia's expansion into Siberia, it is argued that the central government's control on border activities was firmer in China than in Russia (Perdue 2005).

Research that involves systematic comparisons suggests an 'introverted' (although not 'peace-loving') China. Moving beyond aggregating resemblances, scholars reveal that China did have 'significant' differences compared to other empires. A quantitative comparison shows that the China-led tribute system did have fewer wars with neighbors (not including border skirmishes) (Kang 2010). While China did possess advanced maritime technologies, it generally lacked nationwide adventurist convention and competitive economy to support overseas expansion (Deng 1997). Nor was China a naval power, except for the short-lived voyage of the 15th century (Pantucci & Petersen 2012).

More theoretical comparisons seek the economic, political, geopolitical, and religious reasons behind China's introverted behaviors. China followed the general rule that the balance of burden and technological capacity determines how far expansion may go, which was contextualized by China's geographic limits (Elvin 1973). Unlike most polities, China achieved political unification within a vast geographic space, despite its primitive infrastructural power. Against the endless struggle to maintain 'great unity', most dynasties refrained from expanding outside the 'internal region' where universal legitimacy was claimed (Pines 2012). In terms of geopolitics, unlike Mediterranean and European empires, China, isolated from the Eurasian amass, rarely faced serious and viable rivalries (Zhao 2015). Finally, a strict comparison on state-religion relations that covers major empires of human histories ranks China's Confucian-legalist regime as the least expansionist and assimilationist, only second to the Mongolian, Archimedean, and Parthian Empires (Zhao & Sun 2019).

Long duration of history

The making of nationalism takes time. In this regard, China has a unique 'advantage'; the length of its duration spanning over three millenniums is incomparable to most civilizations. Thus, works that compare the effect of historical length are rare. As Finer says, in terms of historical endurance, China was only comparable to the Eastern Roman Empire (1999). Comparisons to Byzantium arise, but while it shared political structure and ideological continuity with China, it differed from the latter on foreign competition and dynastic succession (Lattimore 1970: 6). However, though many leading historical sociologists have emphasized the two polities' comparability, very few compare them (Arnason 2010). One exception is Graff (2016), who argues that China and Byzantium shared similar military culture because they responded to common foes on the Eurasian steppe.

Scholars who engage in comparison attempt to break down 'longevity' through the growth and death of 'civilization'. To Toynbee (1935), the Chinese civilization retained momentum through periodic divisions and foreign conquests, preventing it from death like other ancient entities. By contrast, Fairbank (1983: 100–105) dissects China's longevity as a dynastic circle, which, absent in other ancient civilizations, reproduced the identical imperial political structure and ideological identity over millennia. To Huntington, 'civilization' denotes to the transformation of longevity into cultural characteristics that 'are less mutable and thus less easily to be compromised and resolved by political and economic ones' (Huntington 1993: 27). This transformation paves the way for the conflict between Confucian-Islamic civilizations and the West.

The recent rise of the concept 'civilizational state' started with Pye's (1998) reference to China as 'a civilization pretending to be a state'. After the Cold War, China, Russia, and other states identified themselves as 'civilization states' with cultural identities and political institutions different from the model of Western nation-states (Pabst 2019). By highlighting civilization instead of nation, China disseminates a discourse of diversity and noninterventionism (the 'Harmonious World') while at the same time alludes cultural essentialism and exceptionalism. Within this category, China is unique in two ways. First, China was the sole state that almost monopolized control over the historical civilization's territory. This control differs from states, besides Iran (Kuo 2018), that either descended from the dead civilizations or only share part of existing ones. Second, the incomparable long history shaped strong resilience. Unlike in the West, China's political legitimacy was derived from the relationship between state and civilization with unity, integrity, and coherence being the highest priority (Jacques 2009).

How was modern Chinese nationalism different from others?

Although it is debatable whether premodern China was once a primordial nation-state, it is clear that from the 1840s onward, there was a continuous process of 'growth'. This growth involved coalescing the masses into a political community, through warfare, revolution, and modernization. This reality relates Chinese nationalism to a second theoretical theme: how it resembled and differed from other models. In this strand, scholars try to explain how the unique social dynamics – latecomer to modernization, semicolony, and, most importantly, revolutions – shaped modern Chinese nationalism.

Latecomer to modernization

Because China was a latecomer to modernization, the broadest comparison situates its nationalism, 'Eastern', against 'Western' (Kohn 1944). Chinese nationalism, unlike Western Europe ones rooted in individuals' fight for their own concrete rights, was a forced response to foreign invasion. Not undergirded by mass literacy and modern communication, it was invented by a small group of intellectual elites who lacked channels and capacities to impose their ideas on society. Not rooted in a total social transformation, it retained many historical components, despotism, xenophobia, internal hierarchy, racism, and a general nostalgia of the culture's past (Arnason 2006).

In terms of responding to Western challenges, Chinese nationalism, though not as efficient as Russian and Japanese ones, was able to overcome nostalgia, discard old traditions, and adjust to modern values. In this sense, it showed less resistance than most anticolonial ones (e.g., Islam) (Eisenstadt 2000: 17–20; Westad 2012: 14). However, as Moore (1966) has argued, due to extreme insufficiency of agricultural commercialization and the absence of an agricultural capitalist class, China failed to generate a fascist nationalism, unlike Germany and Japan.

Comparison with Japanese nationalism is compelling. In general, East Asia accepted nationalism, which differed from the Middle East where Arabic nationalism was superseded by a transnational Islamic movement in pursuit of reviving a unified Caliphate (Tønnesson 2016). Within East Asia, Chinese nationalism was largely a response to a Japanese one, although in both societies popular nationalism was absorbed by the state to pursue state-building and development. The military modernization in response to Western imperialism adopted state-centralization in Japan and decentered approach in Qing China, making Chinese nationalism a fragmented conglomerate (Hevia 2012). Meanwhile, in both cases, state nationalism created alienation – in Japan because of the close ties with the United States and in China because of non-Han minorities' exclusion by the Hans' connection with diaspora (Duara 2008). China is distinct from Japan as it lacks a long-existing and transcendent system of Tenno as the cornerstone of modern nation-building. The Chinese emperor had involved so profoundly in the imperial history that it had to be negated in the Revolution of 1911 (Greenfeld 2019: 119–120).

Semicolonial experiences

Since Lenin (2004), Chinese nationalism has been explored in comparison with other anticolonial movements. Recent comparison situates postimperial Chinese nationalism to Wilsonism. The fall from high expectation to deep disappointment, also seen in Egypt, India, and Korea after the Great War, led to anticolonial nationalism and then a switch to Bolshevik leftism (Manela 2007).

Comparisons with India show that Chinese nationalism is more determined to embrace modernity. China struggled but had fewer zigzags than India. Prior to the end of World War II, the National Congress and the KMT cultivated an alliance based on the mutual appreciation of promoting cultural conservatism, though disagreement emerged as Congress preferred anti-British movement to fighting the Japanese (Tsui 2013). After the foundation of the PRC, both Nehru and Mao moved toward a 'Third-Worldism'. However, there was a difference consistent throughout the KMT and the CCP periods: because of the absence of intense religious obsession and direct confrontation with British colonialism (Deepak 2010), Chinese nationalism did not have figures like Gandhi, who not only proposed an alternative to Western modernity but also generated a massive anticolonial movement based on that (Duara 1995).

Broader comparison with colonial and postcolonial world suggests that Chinese nationalism was shaped by China's status as 'semicolony'. China, like the Ottoman, was weak but large enough to avoid full conquest or partition (Duus 1989). After the Boxer Rebellion, China became a 'contact zone', where external powers maintained a balance of power through competition (Yang 2019). Except for Britain and Japan, powers did not occupy formal colonies, but rather exerted influences through local collaboration, missionary presence, and military intimidation (Osterhammel 1986: 300–306). This unequal treaty system not only prevented China from becoming full colonies like Poland, Korea, and India (Goodman & Goodman 2012) but also gave Chinese nationalism extra power. The power gap between Chinese authorities and colonial powers was constantly changing, which allowed the Chinese to be flexible and attempt multiple alternatives to protect their own legitimacy (Osterhammel 1986: 306). Moreover, under a formal Chinese government and sovereignty, societal nationalists could assert requests through mass protest on behalf of an existent 'nationhood', which was unavailable in India (Reinhardt 2018).

Communist revolution

A third unique trajectory is the communist revolution, whereby China is often compared to Russia. It has long been argued that the Bolshevik revolution lacked fusion with Russian nationalism, as Russia itself had been a colonizer and imperialist power (Friedman 2015; Smith 2008; Wright 1961). Both Russia and China used Marxism to bridge empire with nation-state but had different agendas. Whereas Moscow agitated anticolonial movements creating a constellation of Asian nation-states, China, since Sun Yat-sen of the 1920s, generally resisted Moscow's internationalism but tended to view the organizational model of Leninism as an instrument to empower the KMT movement (Liu 2004). Recently, a growing literature probes the ethnic backgrounds of the two revolutions: while the Bolsheviks approached Marxism as a negation of nationalism to overcome ethnopolitics, Chinese communists' nationalism was a Han-dominated revolution concerned less with multiethnicity than domestic social justice (Zhou 2019).

Derived from the China–Russia comparison is the most compelling question: how did the communist revolution and state-building shape Chinese nationalism? It is argued that due to overall underdevelopment, China could not breed a powerful nationalism like Germany or Japan's, which compelled certain elites to incorporate the antinationalist ideology, communism (Zhou 2018). Regarding this paradox, comparative scholars have articulated several distinctions of China. First, Chinese nationalism has been based on 'mass mobilization' since the CCP revolution. In terms of an organizational basis, it thus differs from nonmobilizational nationalism and elite nationalism in many postcolonial societies (Slater & Smith

2016). It is also argued that Chinese nationalism has demarcated a fourth route apart from ethnic, civic, and plural nationalisms, class nationalism, which defines citizenship by individuals' class ascription (Tønnesson 2009).

Second, in the economic realm, by adopting 'national socialism', Chinese nationalism bears a similarity with most 'catch-up' states, such as Latin America, South Korea, Southeast Asia and India. In this model, state, whether or not carrying a socialist ideology, plays a dominant role in coordinating and commanding economic development (Duara 2008; Szporluk 1991). Third, China, like most communist states, adopted a national model in-between federalism and assimilationism, embodying the ideal of combining 'proletarian dictatorship' and communist internationalism. Ethnic minorities are recognized as 'nations' (*minzu*) and given autonomic regions without sovereignty. Meanwhile, minorities, at least in the official narrative, are encouraged to develop their native languages and culture as long as they do not challenge 'international solidarity' (Connor 1984).

The comparison most relevant to the present is with postcommunist states. Post-1976 China falls into the category 'post-totalitarian regime', retaining a delicate ideology after marketization (Linz & Stepan 1996). Within this category, Chinese nationalism differs from Russia's in that it continues to build formal institutions rather than rely on personalistic and cryonicist relations to maintain elite unity (Chen 2016). Chinese nationalism also differs from Eastern European ones (e.g., Russia, Romania, and Hungary) by showing resistance to both extreme ethnic nationalism and liberal nationalism (Chen 2007).

Is Chinese nationalism 'aggressive'?

Since the 1990s, the West has vigilantly watched 'the rise of Chinese nationalism'. Scholarly and policy discussion on Chinese nationalism involves three concerns. First, the rapid economic development created a mismatch with China's relative inferiority in the international system, potentially breeding anti-Western hawkish nationalism among the popular and state elites. Second, China, as a rising power, may seek to displace or replace the present hegemon, the United States, through military means. Third, as Marxist-Leninist ideology fades, the CCP state strengthens the 'Chinese' face of its political program, leading to intervention, assimilation, and repression against China's peripheral peoples. This section reviews the literature on these three topics.

Nationalism in public opinions and state propaganda

One of the most comparative traditions in the study of Chinese nationalism is on public opinions, based survey methods. Since the mid-1990s a number of surveys conducted by universities, think tanks, and survey companies, target multiple regional populations and social groups to inquire about their level of nationalist attitude (see Weiss 2019). Some questions surround opinions on international affairs, such as 'do you agree that China relies too much on military strength?' or 'do you agree that China spends too much on defense?', and ask for group responses regarding territorial disputes on the South China Sea.

The 2003 National Identity Survey, which covers respondents from 35 countries, suggests that the strength of Chinese national identity ranked in the top ten, alongside the most developed societies such as Japan and Canada and above postcommunist Eastern and Central European countries (Tang & Darr 2014). A quantitative analysis of popular protests (Gries et al. 2011) suggests that unlike in the United States, in China 'patriotism' and 'nationalism' are distinct. While patriotism is a benign internationalism, nationalism is a blind and malign patriotism sensitive to the perceived US threats. Callahan (2017) argues that both the 'China Dream' and 'America Dream' involve the pursuit of the perfect nation; 'American Jeremiad', a move toward a multiethnic concept of the American nation, and Chinese 'patriotic worrying' which probed socialism and 'Chinese civilization'. Similarly, based on textual analysis of the opening ceremonies of the Beijing and London Olympics, Lee and Yoon (2017) depict a Sinocentric new nationalism versus a civic-based multicultural nationalism. As for the most sensitive anti-Japanese nationalism, He Yinan's comparison of Sino-Japanese and Pole-German relations suggests that China's and Japan's reluctance in deep de-mythification of the Sino-Japanese War has prevented a full normalization unlike the successful Pole-German relation (He 2009).

Comparison with rising powers in history

One way to explore China's potential to become an expansionist hegemon is to compare it to rising powers in history. This approach has three streams. The first engages the debate on whether China is a new imperialist-colonialist power by comparing China's ongoing presence in the developing world. Lee (2018) argues that China's state capital in Africa differs from its global capital by its profit-optimization approach, orientation for physical production, and culture of collective aestheticism. Martinez (2018) emphasizes that China lacks the elements to develop Lenin-defined imperialism: seeking territorial occupation and political domination, securing economic interests by military means, and being indifferent to local development. However, there is also concern that that comparison of China with old imperialism may be misleading, in that 'traditional imperialism' has enormous internal variation and China's investment in mass media cannot find an equivalent with old colonial powers (French 2014).

The second stream concerns whether China will become a challenger to the US- and West-led international order. Such concerns started as early as the success of the CCP Revolution. Rostow (1955) argues that China would be a more dangerous power than the Soviet Union in exporting revolution, in that the CCP's experiences of peasant nationalism was more attractive than the Bolshevik model for Asia and Africa. Recently, discussion has shifted to whether China can wage a Cold War against the United States. Existing comparisons agree that China fundamentally differs from the Soviet Union of the Brezhnev era. Beijing not only lacks interest in bringing back Maoist diplomacy but also has a deep interdependency with the world economy (Westad 2019). Moreover, there is also little power vacuum awaiting intervention. China is circumstanced by Japan, India, Russia, and Korea, which differs from the Soviet Union of 1945, the free-rider of global decolonization (Leffler 2019).

A broad comparison of 15 cases over the past 500 years suggests that rising powers have been less likely to war with hegemons (Allison 2015). Comparisons with imperial Germany and Japan are popular. Some argue that China is unlikely to become a second pre–World War II Japan, in that the international order facilitates China's rise and the technological change has prevented offensive warfare (McKinney 2017). Yet, as China is not warring with any states, this comparison remains limited – comparison with imperial Germany shows that China hitherto has shown the faces of both Bismarck and Wilhelm II (Moore 2018), whereas Chong and Hall (2014), drawing comparisons with pre-1914 British–German relations, show that despite many similar pitfalls, Sino-US contest is curbed by a deeper spatial buffer, the taboo of using nuclear weapons, and a nonsocial-Darwinist culture. Comparison of naval nationalism suggests that China has somewhat repeated the trajectories of France and Germany, in the sense that its naval expansion is driven more by mass nationalism and leaders' personal commitment than by geopolitical threats (Ross 2018).

Offensive against the periphery?

Apart from the West, the other significant subject of Chinese nationalism are the minorities at China's peripheries, which the central regime seeks to assimilate or integrate. The policies and positions toward these minorities have drawn comparative interest. In general, the CCP's multiculturalism, like that of most Asian states, carry an assimilative and authoritarian character, distinct from the Western liberal constitutional multiculturalism (Kymlicka & He 2005). Although China's nationality system was an imitation of the Soviet Union's ethnoterritorial federalism, there were two significant distinctions. First, unlike 'Soviet internationalism' of the USSR, the CCP cultivated a supranationality 'Sino-Celestial Nation' (*zhonghua minzu*). Second, China's ethnic demarcation is based primarily on historicity and free will than on 'objective' ethnogenesis (Matsuzato 2017).

This literature focuses on the varied reach of state and societal Chinese nationalism. A comparison of Western China with other regions suggests that ethnic conflicts between the Han population and local minorities have been limited within Xinjiang and Tibet (Leibold 2016). Yet, a fuller historical comparison covering Inner Mongolia, Manchuria, and Xinjiang and spanning the past century suggests that these regions are unlikely to remove the Hans control even if a collapse of China's central regime occurs, in that Han population or Han-led local regime retained superiority in military strength (Chung 2018). In terms of difference, a comparative analysis of China's counterinsurgency strategies shows that in Tibet, because of the broad transnational connections, China is more restrained from the outside. Whereas in Xinjiang, China can overcome this barrier by joining the US-led anti-Taliban operation and by coordinating the Russia and Central Asian state within the SCO framework (Odgaard & Nielsen 2014). There are also comparisons that relate the West to China's southeastern peripheries. It is argued that Chinese nationalism incorporates Guangdong by integrating local elites into central administration while excluding Xinjiang by keeping local elites outside (Wang 2001). It is also indicated that Tibetan nationalism encounters greater difficulties in reconciliation with Beijing because it lacks the economic integration, cultural and ethnic convergency with mainland China as, for example, Taiwan has (Sun 2011; Yu & Kwan 2013).

A comparison of other countries such as Tibet and Kashmir reveals that China and India, despite disparities in regime types, share the pattern of 'postcolonial informal empire', seeking to transform peripheral peoples into culturally different but politically subservient subjects (Anand 2012). Comparison of Tibet with Sri Lanka suggests that the mechanism of economic liberalization exacerbates ethnic hatred by favoring nonlocal settlers who are more familiar with the law of market (Alling 1997). Comparison of Uyghur and Sikh reveals that secular central nationalism, regardless of ideological orientations, makes accommodation to linguistic claims in exchange for minorities' concessions on religious rights (Reny 2009). A recent China–Russia comparison finds that in Ürümqi, Ungurean language is used more in everyday conversation but lacks a salient presence in formal document; this differs from the use of Tartar in Kazan (Tsakhirmaa 2019).

Comparison centered on Taiwan, Hong Kong and Macau demarcates a distinct stream of literature, given the escalation of anti-Chinese movements. Most scholars agree that Taiwan possesses the most solid condition to resist Chinese nationalism. Taiwan nationalism is most politically mature, in comparison with Hong Kong's and Okinawa's, because Taiwan has a well-developed statehood based on a long-term process of social integration since the 16th century and an institutional accumulation of state-building projects (Wu 2016). In comparison with Hong Kong, Taiwan is not located under Beijing's direct control, limiting Beijing's ability to destruct the local civil society, the basis of vibrant protests (Lee & Sing 2019). Taiwan's textbook and education system, though facing the same contradiction between civil value and nation-building as in Hong Kong, stably moves toward cultivating Taiwanese identity against Chinese nationalism and global citizenship (Hughes & Stone 1999; Law 2004). State-led Chinese nationalism has a different reach to Hong Kong and Macau, which reflects China's attitudes toward 'large' and 'small' colonial states. In Hong Kong, it highlights national dignity against the British rule, whereas the Portuguese colonial history is concealed in Macau's posthandover museum exhibition (Law 2014).

Scholars also indicate a comparison of Hong Kong's umbrella movement, Taiwan's Sunflower movement with the Arab Spring, Turkey's Taksim Square Occupation, and the Occupy Wall Street movement. These protests are similar in that they did away with formal mobilization, snowballed in response to state repression, and shared nonhierarchical, decentralized leadership (Lee & Sing 2019). A comparative approach is valuable in that similar cases in history help to compensate information insufficiency in ongoing dynamics. A recent example, which regards Hong Kong's 'Anti-Extradition' protest starting in summer 2019, is Wasserstrom's (2020) comparison of Hong Kong with dissident movements in colonial empires' peripheries as well as heroic protests in modern Chinese, which implies a moral inspiration to encourage protesters in Hong Kong. The author emphasizes at the end of the book that drawing historical analogues should carry care.

Evaluations and suggestions for future research

Based on the three groups of existing scholarship reviewed, I suggest developing present comparisons three directions, all of which commonly requests a 'so-what' answer on how the uniqueness of Chinese nationalism may shape China's current nation-building and foreign policies. First, the debate on whether or not pre-modern China was a proto-nation-state should be furthered to answer the question of how the relative cultural homogeneity and stable political identity shaped China's transition from empire to modern nation-state. Put it more generally, how did a polity's premodern legacy shape its ability in building an inclusive nation that is legitimate to multiple social and ethnic groups (for definition, see Wimmer 2018)? This discussion can be laid in a comparative Eurasian context, mainly, through comparison with the other three major successors of the Mongolian empire: Russia, Ottoman Turkey, and Iran. These four actors shared similar backgrounds: state legacy left over by Mongolians, multiethnicity, geopolitical pressure from the West, and historical longevity that crossed premodern and modern periods. These four cases also differed on ethnic composition, colonial experiences, and cultural values of empire building. China's distinction for homogeneous population, status of semicolony, and Confucian universalism would help explain the important question of why some nations hold together while others fall apart. In this regard, some efforts have been drawn (Arjomand 2019: 308–09; Lupher 1996; Zarakol 2011), but an integrative research project is still absent. As the COVID-19 pandemic is spreading to the developing world and emerging economies, how the historical base of nation-building shapes these nations' responses can be of great interest.

Second, the current discussion on China's unique experiences in generating modern nationalism can be furthered to probe the relationship between authoritarian and nationalism, and, more broadly, the intertwining complication between power struggle and nationalist sentiment which may overwhelm any political actor in China. The status of semicolony prevented a full-coverage and direct rule by any colonial power, which left Chinese nationalists with ample political space to adhere to domestic power competition. To win such a competition, during the War with the Japanese, both the CCP and the KMT had developed sophisticated skills of maneuvering and disciplining nationalism. These skills enabled them to control internal nationalist sentiment, popular or elite, and channel it to attack domestic rivalries rather than to engage hopeless confrontations with the Japanese. Does the current Chinese state still retain such a historical capacity? More explicitly, will the current CCP state be able to go against domestic populist sentiment against the US superpower and Taiwan? To answer this question, further comparisons should be drawn with the historical regimes which had wanted to make use of nationalism but bore tensions with the latter, such as traditional dynastic states in pre–Great War Europe – Spain, and Austria-Hungary. For these old regimes, nationalism was a nondirectional bomb, which could boost authoritarianism as well as burn them, through disenchanting their ruling ideologies and arousing separatist ethnopolitics. During the COVID-19 pandemic, the CCP faces a severe challenge in this regard. If Beijing cannot cool down the domestic popular anti-US nationalism it has aroused, economic disasters, the recession of technology development, and backfire from the export industry and overseas Chinese may become the immediate consequences.

Third, the scholarship on whether Chinese nationalism is as aggressive as the Nazi and Imperial Japanese ones needs far more rigorous analysis as well as broader comparison. Relative to the first two approaches, this stream of compassion is at the emerging stage – most writings are authored by journalists, activists, diplomats, and politicians. As scholars have pointed out, though China's behavior today has many resemblances with imperial Germany, Japan, and the Soviet Union, there are also significant differences (Luce 2019). Crude analogies are not only empirically imprecise but also politically dangerous, as a self-fulfilling prophecy to lead to destructive conflicts. To better understand China's behavior through a comparative perspective, I suggest a multiple-point comparison. The comparison should be broadened to as many cases, rather than confined to a few expansionist powers of the 20th century. For instance, in some aspects, China does resemble imperial Germany, Japan, and the Soviet Union, whereas, in other aspects, similarities can be found with the pre-1914 United States, Austria-Hungary, Ottoman, and Iran. By the same token, the Sino-US relation should not be the sole focus either, as this relation is subject to the dynamics of China's relations with other nations. At present, comparisons should especially draw on historical conditions that were similar to COVID-19 pandemic, which plagued most members of the international community and had a special destructive force to more developed social systems. A crisis may shift international order, but how shift occurs depends on the character of the crisis.

A fourth suggestion goes to Chinese nationalism at the former empire's peripheries: Hong Kong, Taiwan, Xinjiang, Tibet, as well as Inner Mongolia and Macau. Existing scholarship mainly focuses on comparisons between different areas, showing that the capabilities and wills to resist Beijing's control vary enormously. My suggestion is to extend this logic to historical and present colonial empires, namely, to the secessionist movements at these empires' peripheries. Currently, such analyses are limited, most of which are more juxtaposition than comparison. Likewise, comparisons should follow the multiple-point approach suggested. For example, Hong Kong's local resistance to Beijing's increasing interference should be compared to not only successful cases such as Eastern Europe of 1989, but also frustrated ones, like Poland of 1863. A comparative historical analysis that involves diverse enough cases can tell the future of these movements. By the same token, cases sharing historical backgrounds similar to COVID-19 pandemic deserve special attention. Crisis sometimes eased power integration while sometimes check it. To understand what occurs we need a comparative perspective.

References

Alling, Greg. 1997. "Economic Liberalization and Separatist Nationalism: The Cases of Sri Lanka and Tibet". *Journal of International Affairs* 51(1):117–45.
Allison, Graham. 2015. "The Thucydides Trap: Are the US and China Headed for War?" *Atlantic* September 14.
Anand, Dibyesh. 2012. "China and India: Postcolonial Informal Empires in the Emerging Global Order". *Rethinking Marxism* 24(1):68–86.
Arjomand, Said Amir. 2019. *Revolution: Structure and Meaning in World History*. Chicago: The University of Chicago Press.
Arnason, Johann. 2006. "Nations and Nationalisms: Betweeen General Theory and Comparative History". pp. 44–56 in *The SAGE Handbook of Nations and Nationalism*, edited by Gerard Delanty and Krishan Kumar. London: SAGE Publications Ltd.
Arnason, Johann P. 2010. "Byzantium and Historical Sociology". in *The Byzantine World*, edited by Paul Stephenson. London; New York: Routledge, 491–504.
Bell, Daniel A. 2017. "Realizing Tianxia: Traditional Values and China's Foreign Policy". pp. 129–48 in *Chinese Visions of World Order*, edited by Ban Wang. Durham; London: Duke University Press.
Callahan, William. 2017. "Dreaming as a Critical Discourse of National Belonging: China Dream, American Dream and World Dream". *Nations and Nationalism* 23(2):248–70.
Chen, Cheng. 2007. *The Prospects for Liberal Nationalism in Post-Leninist States*. University Park, PA: Pennsylvania State University Press.
Chen, Cheng. 2016. *The Return of Ideology: The Search for Regime Identities in Postcommunist Russia and China*. Ann Arbor: University of Michigan Press.
Chong, Ja Ian, and Todd H. Hall. 2014. "The Lessons of 1914 for East Asia Today: Missing the Trees for the Forest". *Quarterly Journal: International Security* 39(1):7–43.
Chung, Chien-peng. 2018. "Comparing China's Frontier Politics: How Much Difference did a Century Make". *Nationalities Papers* 46(1):158–76.
Connor, Walker. 1984. *The National Question in Marxist-Leninist Theory and Strategy*. Princeton, NJ: Princeton University Press.
Creel, Herrlee G. 1970. *The Origins of Statecraft in China: Volume One: The Western Chou Empire*. Chicago; London: The University of Chicago Press.
Deepak, B. R. 2010. "The 1857 Rebellion and the Indian Involvement in the Taiping Uprising in China". pp. 139–49 in *India and China in the Colonial World*, edited by Madhavi Thampi. New Delhi: Social Science Press.
Deng, Gang. 1997. *Chinese Maritime Activities and Socioeconomic Development, c. 2100 B.C.–1900 A.D.* Westport, CT: Greenwood Press.
Duara, Prasenjit. 1995. *Rescuing History from the Nation: Questioning Narratives of Modern China*. Chicago: University of Chicago Press.
———. 2008. "The Global and Regional Constitution of Nations: The View from East Asia". *Nations and Nationalism* 14(2):323–45.
Duus, Peter. 1989. "Introduction". in *The Japanese Informal Empire in China, 1895–1937*, edited by Peter Duus, Ramon H. Myers, and Mark R. Peattie. Princeton, NJ: Princeton University Press, xi–xxix.
Eisenstadt, S. N. 2000. "Multiple Modernities". *Daedalus* 129(1):1–29.
———. 2003. *Comparative Civilizations and Multiple Modernities*. Leiden; Boston: Brill.
Elvin, Mark. 1973. *The Pattern of the Chinese Past*. Stanford: Stanford University Press.
Fairbank, John K. 1983. *The United States and China*. Cambridge, MA: Harvard University Press.

Finer, S.E. 1999. *The History of Government from the Earliest Times Volume 2: The Intermediate Ages*. Oxford: Oxford University Press.

French, Howard W. 2014. *China's Second Continent*. New York: Alfred Knopf.

French, Howard W. 2017. *Everything under the Heavens: How the Past Helps Shape China's Push for Global Power*. New York: Alfred A. Knopf.

Friedman, Jeremy Scott. 2015. *Shadow Cold War: The Sino-Soviet Competition for the Third World*. Chapel Hill: University of North Carolina Press.

Gellner, Ernest. 1983. *Nations and Nationalism*. Ithaca: Cornell University Press.

Goodman, Bryna, and David S. G. Goodman (Eds.). 2012. *Twentieth-Century Colonialism and China: Localities, the Everyday, and the World*. London: Routledge.

Graff, David A. 2016. *The Eurasian Way of War: Military Practice in Seventh-Century China and Byzantium*. New York: Routledge.

Greenfeld, Liah. 2019. *Nationalism: A Short History*. Boston: Brookings Institution Press.

Gries, Peter Hays, Qingmin Zhang, H. Michael Crowson, and Huajian Cai. 2011. "Patriotism, Nationalism and China's US Policy: Structures and Consequences of Chinese National Identity". *The China Quarterly* (March):1–17.

He, Yinan. 2009. *The Search for Reconciliation: Sino-Japanese and German-Polish Relations since World War II*. Cambridge; New York: Cambridge University Press.

Hevia, James L. 2012. "Western Imperialism and Miiitary Reform in Japan and China". *Frontiers of History in China* 7(3):404–14.

Hughes, Christopher, and Robert Stone. 1999. "Nation-Building and Curriculum Reform in Hong Kong and Taiwan". *The China Quarterly* 160(December):977–91.

Huntington, Samuel P. 1993. "The Clash of Civilizations?" *Foreign Affairs* 72(3):22–49.

Jacques, Martin. 2009. *When China Rules the World: The Rise of the Middle Kingdom and the End of the Western World*. New York: Penguin.

Kalberg, Stephen. 2014. "Max Weber's Sociology of Civilizations: The Five Major Themes". *Max Weber Studies* 14(2):205–32.

Kang, David. 2010. *East Asia before the West: Five Centuries of Trade and Tribute*. New York: Columbia University Press.

Kim, Youngmin. 2018. *A History of Chinese Political Thought*. Cambridge, UK: Polity Press.

Kohn, Hans. 1944. *The Idea of Nationalism: A Study in Its Origins and Background*. New York: Macmillan Co.

Kuo, Kaiser. 2018. "Kuora: On The Idea That China Is A Civilization, Not A Nation-State". in *Supchina*.

Kymlicka, Will, and Baogang He (Eds.). 2005. *Multiculturalism in Asia*. Oxford: Oxford University Press.

Lash, Scott. 2020. "The Literati and the Dao: Vernacular and Nation in China". pp. 376–91 in *The Oxford Handbook of Max Weber*, edited by Edith Hanke, Lawrence Scaff, and Sam Whimster. New York, NY: Oxford University Press.

Lattimore, Owen. 1970. *History and Revolution in China*. Lund: Studentlitteratur.

Law, Kam-yee. 2014. "The Red Line over European Colonialism: Comparison of the Macao Museum and Hong Kong Museum of History after Their Return to China". *International Journal of Heritage Studies* 20(5):534–55.

Law, Wing-Wah. 2004. "Globalization and Citizenship Education in Hong Kong and Taiwan". *Comparative Education Review* 48(3):253–73.

Lee, Ching Kwan 2018. *The Specter of Global China: Politics, Labor, and Foreign Investment in Africa*. Chicago: University of Chicago Press.

Lee, Ching Kwan, and Ming Sing. 2019. "Take Back Our Future: An Eventful Sociology of the Hong KongUmbrella Movement". pp. 1–33 in *Take Back Our Future: An Eventful Sociology of the Hong KongUmbrella Movement*, edited by Ching Kwan Lee. Ithaca: Cornell University Press.

Lee, Jongsoo, and Hyunsun Yoon. 2017. "Narratives of the Nation in the Olympic Opening Ceremonies: Comparative Analysis of Beijing 2008 and London 2012". *Nations and Nationalism* 23(4):952–69.

Leffler, Melvyn P. 2019. "China Isn't the Soviet Union. Confusing the Two Is Dangerous". in *Atlantic*.
Leibold, James. 2016. "Interethnic Conflict in the PRC: Xinjiang and Tibet as Exceptions?" pp. 223–50 in *Ethnic Conflict and Protest in Tibet and Xinjiang: Unrest in China's West*, edited by Ben Hillman and Gray Tuttle. New York: Columbia University Press.
Lenin, Vladimir. 2004. *The Awakening of Asia*. London: University Press of the Pacific.
Levenson, Joseph R. 1968. *Confucian China and Its Modern Fate: A Trilogy*. Berkeley; Los Angeles: University of California Press.
Linz, Juan J., and Alfred C. Stepan. 1996. *Problems of Democratic Transition and Consolidation: Southern Europe, South America, and Post-Communist Europe*. Baltimore: Johns Hopkins University Press.
Liu, Xiaoyuan. 2004. *Frontier Passages: Ethnopolitics and the Rise of Chinese Communism, 1921–1945*. Washington, DC: Woodrow Wilson Center Press.
Luce, Edward. 2019. "The Reckless Analogy between China and Nazi Germany". in *Financial Times*.
Lupher, Mark. 1996. *Power Restructuring in China and Russia*. Oxford: Westview Press.
Manela, Erez. 2007. *The Wilsonian Moment: Self-Determination and the International Origins of Anticolonial Nationalism*. Oxford: Oxford University Press.
Mann, Michael. 1986. *The Sources of Social Power: A History of Power from the Beginning to A. D. 1760*. Cambridge: Cambridge University Press.
Martinez, Carlos. 2018. "Is China the New Imperialist Force in Africa?" in *Invent the Future* https://www.invent-the-future.org/2018/10/is-china-the-new-imperialist-force-in-africa/.
Matsuzato, Kimitaka. 2017. "The Rise and Fall of Ethnoterritorial Federalism: A Comparison of the Soviet Union (Russia), China, and India". *Europe-Asia Studies* 69(7):1047–69.
McKinney, Jared. 2017. "China: The New Imperial Japan?" *The National Interest*, January 3.
Moore, Barrington. 1966. *Social Origins of Dictatorship and Democracy: Lord and Peasant in the Making of the Modern World*. Boston: Beacon Press.
Moore, Gregory J. 2018. "Bismarck or Wilhelm? China's Peaceful Rise vs. Its South China Sea Policy". *Asian Perspective* 42:265–83.
Odgaard, Liselotte, and Thomas Galasz Nielsen. 2014. "China's Counterinsurgency Strategy in Tibet and Xinjiang". *Journal of Contemporary China* 23(87):535–555.
Osterhammel, Jorgen. 1986. "Semi-Colonialism and Informal Empire in Twentieth-Century China: Towards a Framework of Analysis" in *Imperialism and After: Continuities and Discontinuities*, edited by Wolfgang J. Mommsen and Jürgen Osterhammel. London; Boston: Allen & Unwin, 290–314.
Pabst, Adrian. 2019. "China, Russia and the Return of the Civilisational State". in *New Statesman*.
Pantucci, Raffaello, and Alexandros Petersen. 2012. "China's Inadvertent Empire". *The National Interest* 122(November/December):30–39.
Perdue, Peter C. 1998. "Comparing Empires: Manchu Colonialism". *The International History Review* 20(2):255–62.
Perdue, Peter C. 2005. *China Marches West: The Qing Conquest of Central Eurasia*. Cambridge, MA: Belknap Press of Harvard University Press.
Perdue, Peter. 2015. "The Tenacious Tributary System". *Journal of Contemporary China* 24(96):1002–14.
Pines, Yuri. 2012. *The Everlasting Empire: The Political Culture of Ancient China and Its Imperial Legacy*. Princeton, NJ: Princeton University Press.
Pye, Lucian. 1998. *International Relations in Asia: Culture, Nation, and State*. Washington, DC: Sigur Center for Asian Studies.
Reinhardt, Anne. 2018. *Navigating Semi-Colonialism: Shipping, Sovereignty, and Nation-Building in China, 1860–1937*. Cambridge, MA: Harvard University Press.
Reny, Marie-Eve. 2009. "The Political Salience of Language and Religion: Patterns of Ethnic Mobilization among Uyghurs in Xinjiang and Sikhs in Punjab". *Ethnic and Racial Studies* 32(3):490–521.
Ross, Robert S. 2018. "Nationalism, Geopolitics, and Naval Expansionism: From the Nineteenth Century to the Rise of China". *Naval War College* (Autumn):17–50.

Rostow, W. W. 1955. "Russia and China Under Communism". *World Politics* 7(4):513–31.

Slater, Dan, and Nicholas Rush Smith. 2016. "The Power of Counterrevolution: Elitist Origins of Political Order in Postcolonial Asia and Africa". *American Journal of Sociology* 121(5), 1472–1516.

Smith, S. A. 2008. *Revolution and the People in Russia and China: A Comparative History*. Cambridge: Cambridge University Press.

Sun, Yan. 2011. "The Tibet Question through the Looking Glass of Taiwan: Comparative Dynamics and Sobering Lessons". *Asian Ethnicity* 12(3):337–53.

Szporluk, Roman. 1991. *Communism and Nationalism: Karl Marx Versus Friedrich List*. New York; Oxford: Oxford University Press.

Tang, Wenfang, and Ben Darr. 2014. "Chinese Nationalism and its Political and Social Origins". Pp. 1–16 in *Construction of Chinese Nationalism in the Early 21st Century: Domestic Sources and International Implications*, edited by Suisheng Zhao. New York: Routledge.

Tønnesson, Stein. 2009. "The Class Route to Nationhood: China, Vietnam, Norway, Cyprus—and France". *Nations and Nationalism* 15(3):375–95.

Tønnesson, Stein. 2016. "Will Nationalism Drive Conflict in Asia?" *Nations and Nationalism* 22(2):232–42.

Toynbee, Arnold J. 1935. *A Study of History*. London: Oxford University Press.

Tsakhirmaa, Sansar. 2019. "Comparative Institutionalised Bilingualism in Kazan, Russia and Ürümqi, China". *Europe-Asia Studies* 71(9):1532–61.

Tsui, Brian Kai Hin. 2013. "China's Forgotten Revolution: Radical Conservatism in Action, 1927–1949". Doctoral dissertation at the department of East Asian Language and Cultures. New York: Columbia University.

Wang, Yuan-Kang. 2001. "Toward a Synthesis of the Theories of Peripheral Nationalism: A Comparative Study of China's Xinjiang and Guangdong". *Asian Ethnicity* (2):177–95.

Wasserstrom, Jeffrey. 2020. "Vigil: Hong Kong on the Brink". in *Columbia Global Report*.

Weiss, Jessica Chen. 2019. "How Hawkish is the Chinese Public? Another Look at "Rising Nationalism" and Chinese Foreign Policy". *Jessica Chen Weiss* 28(119):679–95.

Westad, Odd Arne. 2012. *Restless Empire China and the World since 1750*. New York: Basic Books.

Westad, Odd Arne. 2019. "The Sources of Chinese Conduct: Are Washington and Beijing Fighting a New Cold War?" *Foreign Affairs* 98(5), 86–95.

Wimmer, Andreas. 2018. *Nation Building: Why Some Countries Come Together while Others Fall Apart*. Princeton; Oxford: Princeton University Press.

Wright, Mary C. 1961. "A Review Article: The Pre-Revolutionary Intellectuals of China and Russia". *The China Quarterly* (6):175–79.

Wu, Rwei-Ren. 2016. "The Lilliputian Dreams: Preliminary Observations of Nationalism in Okinawa, Taiwan and Hong Kong". *Nations and Nationalism* 22(4):686–705.

Yang, Taoyu. 2019. "Redefining Semi-Colonialism: A Historiographical Essay on British Colonial Presence in China". *Journal of Colonialism and Colonial History* 20(3):DOI: https://doi.org/10.1353/cch.2019.0028.

Yu, Fu Lai Tony, and Diana S. Kwan. 2013. "Social Construction of National Reality: Tibet and Taiwan". *Journal of Chinese Political Science* 18:259–79.

Yu, Haiyang. 2014. "Glorious Memories of Imperial China and the Rise of Chinese Populist Nationalism". *Journal of Contemporary China* 23(90):1174–87.

Zarakol, Ayse. 2011. *After Defeat: How the East Learned to Live with the West*. Cambridge; New York: Cambridge University Press.

Zhang, Junbo, and Yunzhu Yao. 1996. "Differences between Traditional Chinese and Western Military Thinking and their Philosophical Roots". *Journal of Contemporary China* 5(12):209–21.

Zhao, Dingxin, and Yanfei Sun. 2019. "Religious Toleration in Pre-modern Empires". pp. 240–61 in *States and Nations, Power and Civility: Hallsian Perspectives*, edited by Francesco G. Duina. Toronto: University of Toronto Press.

Zhao, Suisheng. 2015. "Rethinking the Chinese World Order: The Imperial Cycle and the Rise of China". *Journal of Contemporary China* 24(96):961–82.

Zhou, Luyang. 2018. "Boosting Nationalism with Non-Nationalist ideology: A Comparative Biographical Analysis of the Chinese Communist Revolutionaries". *Nations and Nationalism* 24(3):767–91.

Zhou, Luyang. 2019. "Nationalism and Communism as Foes and Friends: Comparing the Bolshevik and Chinese Revolutionaries". *European Journal of Sociology* 60(3):313–50.

26
Populism in China

He Li

Introduction

The start of the 21st century saw the resurgence of populism, which has been the subject of intense reflection and debates among the Chinese intellectuals. Yet, up to this point, most treatment on the topic has mainly done by the Chinese scholars (Gao 2018; Lin 2007; Ma 2016; Sun 1994; Tang 2016; Xiao 2012; Ying 2020; Zhang 1994; Zhao 2008; Zang 2010). International discussions have remained considerably less well-informed about the rise and spread of populism in China. As of this writing, when 民粹主义 ('populism') as used as a keyword in a search of papers in http://www.nssd.org [National Social Science Database], 1,104 journal articles were found, most were published since the beginning of the twenty-first century. A Baidu (the largest search engine in China) search of 民粹主义 registered more than 25 million hits. Clearly, the discussion of populism is far more widespread than has been recognized.

Most liberal thinkers agree that the surge of populism could undercut long-term economic growth and endangers the rule of law. Some even fear that the growing populism might produce a breakdown in the political process and lead the country into chaos (Ma 2016). Through a close textual analysis of the works by leading Chinese scholars and other primary materials, this chapter explores the Chinese discourse on populism and its implications. This chapter will proceed as follows. We begin by discussing what the term actually means in China. Next, I will turn to the origins of the reemergence of populism in China. The third section reviews the Chinese discourse on populism. The last one examines the implications of the debates.

What is populism? What does the term actually mean?

Populism is a rather complex system of ideas and comes in various national, political, and ideological forms. Carothers (2018) considers populism as a political movement rooted in the idea of outsiders challenging established norms. Gidron and Bonikowski (2013) define populism as an ideology, a discursive style, and a form a political mobilization. Because of the thin ideology, populism is compatible with different ideologies and in different historical

 DOI: 10.4324/9780429059704-31

and geographical economic contexts. Beyond that, they can take any shape. For instance, Juan Perón of Argentina is a populist. So is Donald Trump. Both of them sold their agenda as a struggle of the masses against a powerful, corrupt establishment that cares only for its own self-preservation at the expense of common people. Generally speaking, populism remains poorly understood and vaguely defined. In this study, Chinese populism is defined as a discourse that champions the rights of the common people against that of the elite and global capitalism.

In fact, populist politics emerged in different historical periods. According to Mencius' idea of people-based governance (*minben*), for instance, the legitimacy of the ruling strata can only be established if they are seen to be reflecting and acting upon the people's will (Lee 1995). Conversely, popular revolt can be legitimized if the rulers are seen to have failed to carry out their paternalistic duty. Both the idea of Mandate of Heaven and Mencius' *minben* legitimized the people's attempts to revolt when their needs went unfulfilled by the ruling elites (Ling & Shih 1998).

Townsend (1977) notes that populism in contemporary China has drawn on traditional sources. The first source is the great rebellions such as the Taiping movement of the mid-19th century. The next one is the reform movements since the late 19th century, such as the May Fourth Movement, which introduced into China many social and political ideas that contribute to the ideological foundations of populism. The third source is the major ideal that Mao drew from the Marxist-Leninist legacy.

Maoism is considered as a form of populism. The Chinese Communist Party (CCP) came to power by mobilizing and unifying diverse groups of marginalized and discontented segments of the population (Ma 2016). Populism has been frequently used by the Communist Party leaders to shore up their support. Populist appeals have been inherent to the discourse of the CCP ever since its foundation. The CCP leaders from Mao Zedong to Xi Jinping have used populist narratives to bolster their credentials as the leaders of the country.

For many years, the CCP has been adept at using populist language to mobilize those who were at the bottom of society, which happened to be the Nationalist Party's weakest link. It is noted that the Nationalist Party proved capable of mobilizing only the middle class and the elites thereby leaving the lowest level of society entirely to the CCP. The mass line (*qunzhong luxian*) is a powerful weapon of the CCP as it struggled to seize and consolidate power. Rong Jian (2013) finds that the CCP's ruling elites used 'the principle of the masses' to mobilize large groups of people. During the period of the Cultural Revolution (1966–1976), Mao also mobilized the masses to achieve his political objectives. The mass line implies that the CCP should work for and rely on the 'masses', and that method should be the instrument and tool of the party-state and the 'cadres' of the party-state must remain part of the public and to be continually attentive to its desires. The concept of the 'mass line' remains an important doctrine of the CCP to this day,

Populism is lauded by some, reviled by others, and has sparked a variety of critical responses. In the minds of some Chinse intellectuals, populism and democracy are two sides of the same coin, regardless of whether their discourse systems originated in China or the West (Gui et al. 2020). After simmering for years, populism, which pits the people against the elite, has gained traction in China. The recent years have seen the liberals *(ziyou pai*) and populists constantly clashed over both the strategies and outcome of the reform launched by Deng Xiaoping in the late 1970s.

It is worth noting that in the Chinese discourse, populism has a negative connotation. In fact, the concept of 'populism' has been translated into different terms like 平民主义, 人民党主义, 民粹主义, 庶民主义, 大众主义, and 民众主义. From the perspective of the orthodox Marxists, populism must be reactionary, because its analysis focuses on the 'people' rather than classes. The propaganda of the Communist Party tends to repeat the cliché that populism is simply a snare and delusion calculated to undermine the party leadership and could result in social instability. It avoids direct class-based appeals and claims instead to act in the interest of the people and nation as a whole. It is important to note that while numerous people in China support the populist sentiment, very few populists identify themselves as populists.

Origins of the reemergence of populism

Zang (2010) finds that political populism is an emerging conservatism that is going currency in China today and the rise of populism in China signals a deepening of its political crisis in general, and China's hinterlands in particular. Many Chinese people are attracted to populism out of frustration, anger, and fear about poverty, misery, and lack of opportunity. In this section, I answer the question: What accounts for the comeback of populism in China?

To begin with, the root course of populism is the substantial increase of income polarization. Enormous growth since the late 1970s has produced obscene wealth for the few and left many in poverty and insecurity. China has moved from being an equal country in the 1970s to being one of the most unequal countries. The research from the Hurun Report, finds China minted 206 billionaires in 2017, taking the country's total to 819 billionaires 40% more billionaires than in the United States. On the other hand, a significant part of the Chinese population is economically disadvantaged. As Premier Li Keqiang pointed out in May 2020, China has over 600 million people whose monthly income is barely 1,000 yuan (about US$140) and their lives have further been affected by the coronavirus pandemic. China's Gini index, a widely used measure of income dispersion across a population, has risen more steeply over the last decade than in any other country. Here is the great extraordinary irony: China, a so-called communist country, is the only major economy in the world that still has neither property tax nor inheritance tax. Some inequality is to be expected with industrialization, but in China, it has happened at a staggering pace.

In addition to a wide wealth gap, China has a severe divide between rural and urban areas. Hu Angang, professor at the Chinese Academy of Sciences and Tsinghua University, coined the phrase 'One China, Four Worlds' (*yi ge zhongguo, si ge shijie*) depicting the regional disparity in China. Home prices in China's major cities have risen far beyond the average family's budget. *Fangnu* (house slave), a popular term, emerged in recent years. *Fangnu* refers to those locked into jobs they may not like in order to meet their mortgage payments. The weak and vulnerable groups feel betrayed by the reform and open-door policy. More importantly, they are anxious and sensitive to the perceived lack of social mobility.

Since the start of the economic reform, few workers enjoy stable employment. 'Iron rice bowl' refers to an occupation with guaranteed job security, as well as steady income and benefits no longer exits. The low-income people have become marginalized; China's entry to the World Trade Organization (WTO) has benefited the skilled workers and vested interests drastically. The weak and vulnerable groups also known as 'lower strata' such as peasants, migrant workers, and the urban poor feel left behind. In the reform era, millions of migrant workers came to the cities with few legal protections. More importantly, they are anxious and sensitive to the perceived lack of social mobility. Indeed, there is strong resentment against the market-oriented reform.

Second, the voice of populist people is also the product of the deteriorating US–China relations. The Trump administration has declared China a strategic competitor and escalated a trade dispute into a multifront conflict. The trade discord has become a fertile ground for populists to cultivate. The pandemic also heightened the rivalry between China and the West. For the United States, 2020 is very different from 2008, the year the global financial crisis erupted. The attitude toward China has changed dramatically. Under Trump, the recognition that cooperation with China is necessary to manage global development has given way to protectionism and hostility. The populists consider the conflict with the United States as the cause of economic hardship that afflicted the 'ordinary people'.

Liberal scholars believe that meeting Mr. Trump's demands was beneficial for China's own long-term growth and stronger tie with the West is in the long-term interests of the country. Quite a few of them hope the trade war would force the government to reinvigorate 'reform and opening'. But the US intensification of tariffs and arrest of a Huawei Technologies executive undermine their case 'because it looks like you're capitulating to US pressure' (Ip 2019). For years, the Chinese middle class eyed the United States with envy and admiration; now many of them look on with despair. COVID-19 is reinforcing the enmity between the United States and China. To make the matter worst, President Donald Trump called the coronavirus the 'Chinese virus' repeatedly, setting off a wave of anti-American sentiment.

China's populism goes hand in hand with nationalism. National populism is reflected in one of the most frequent statements of the CCP, the original intention of the CCP is 'to seek happiness for the people and rejuvenation for the nation'. Instead of seeking support through elections, the CCP is increasingly relying on national populist appeals. The Beijing leadership emphasizes China's 'century of humiliation' and its historic destiny. Popular reactions against the US help explain the convergence of nationalism and populism. A growing number of Chinese are convinced that the United States started the current conflict to thwart China's rise. They identify the US under Trump an enemy of 'the people'.

Third, populism is also a response to growing injustice. Exposures of corrupt officials, brutal police officers, and the super-rich are often their trigger points. The economic reform initiated by Deng intends to free the market from politics. Yet, in the eyes of populists, it was turned into an arena for predatory politicians and greedy business people. Deng Xiaoping's suggestion of 'allowing some people to become wealthy first' is considered an elitist view. They also believe the market-oriented reform has replaced socialism with crony capitalism, generating wealth for the new rich and sadness for the rest.

Fourth, social media has played an important role in spreading the populist message. Under strict control, most, if not all, in China are hesitant to discuss the sensitive political issues publicly. They only talk about these issues among family members and close friends. Chinese intellectuals, in general, do not endorse the one-party rule but they do not publicly express this view. To some extent, social media has changed this significantly. Populists have benefited from social media and the internet, which has allowed them to connect directly with others. The cyberspace and new media technologies have indeed opened up spaces for increased contestation. The rise of social media in China has enabled debates on a variety of hot button issues to go viral. Social media has transformed an area once monopolized by official ideology and traditional media. With the emergence of new media platforms like WeChat, public media's monopoly by the CCP is over. Nowadays, populists can reach ordinary people without passing through the Party hierarchies or winning favor from the official media. Any person with a Weibo or WeChat account can disseminate their own ideas on politics and social issues to a wider audience than was previously possible. As Tang (2016) sees it, the internet can play a significant role in the spread of populism because it forces the government to recognize and respond to whatever issues the netizens are deeming unjust, in the absence of more robust intermediary legal institutions. In other words, netizens can now harness online resources to ignite popular uproar about issues from the legal domain, making it easier to fuel bigger disturbances into outcomes that are more favorable to them.

Populists hold a grassroots position to stand for the interests of the weak and underprivileged and advocate safeguarding national interests. Why did some Chinese intellectuals embrace populism? Zheng Yefu (2004), a sociology professor at Peking University, suggested that after the Chinese intellectuals accepted the idea of equality, they developed an awareness of their original sin. They felt responsible for the social inequality that denigrated the masses. In the political campaign following the founding of the new China in 1949, the intellectuals denied themselves while idealizing the masses as embodying the highest morals. Burdened by their guilt, they rejected the existing education and culture, abandoned their mission as enlightened intellectuals, and proposed leaning from the masses. They did not hesitate to replace their flawed and unequal modern culture with the impractical culture and the masses. The feeling of original sin weakened the character of the intellectuals and contributed to the growth of populism. Moody (2007), on the other hand, maintains that in the reform era, the Chinese intellectuals no longer depend as much upon the state, but many have nothing to offer that is valued on the market. Such frustrated intellectuals may become available to mobilize, articulate, and lead populist discontent. In brief, populism is a reaction against the growing income polarization and social injustice as well as China's resentment to 'arrogance' of the West in general and the United States in particular. The populists see themselves, by and large, in opposition to the elites.

Polemics between liberals and populists

The Chinese populists have employed an 'us-them' strategy to help the vulnerable group focus on a common enemy as the source of their suffering, typically the elite at home and abroad. They tap into people's anger by appealing to their sense of social justice and calling for tougher regulation of business and corrupted government officials. Their discourse emphasizes the social and economic rights of the vulnerable group. This section explores the Chinese discourse on populism, in particular, that between the proponents of liberalism and populists. Their debates focus on issues including Mao and the Cultural Revolution, nationalism vs. globalism, and 'big democracy' vs. the rule of law.

Rethink Mao and the Cultural Revolution

Soon after Mao's death, he was judged '70 per cent correct and 30 per cent wrong' by the CCP leadership. The overwhelming majority of the Chinese intellectuals rejected Maoism. He was denounced and his legacy blemished. Such assessment of Mao's blunders during the Cultural Revolution was challenged by the populists. In the eyes of the populists, despite some failings and setbacks, it is an inescapable historical conclusion that the Maoist era was the time of China's modern political, agricultural, and industrial revolutions. Mao was praised for his contribution to building a new China. Popular sayings such as 'Long live Chairman Mao!' and 'Long live the Cultural Revolution!' are evidence of the return of populism. It should be noted that the current regime under Xi recast Mao as a respectable, great political leader and not a tyrant who pushed China into turmoil and brought the country's economy on the verge of bankruptcy.

Since the beginning of the millennium, the populists and New Leftists joined forces calling for rethinking the Cultural Revolution and Mao. They are nostalgic about the

Cultural Revolution. Their narratives resonated strongly with peasants, laid-off workers, and some former government officials under Mao's era. For them, Mao is remembered for his mobilization of the people, for his efforts to provide them with a better life and a sense of social worth (Townsend 1977). For the vast majority of Chinese intellectuals, the Cultural Revolution is a period that evokes painful memories since it brought about a complete annulment of whatever legal system had been built by the time. Many of them were tortured during the Cultural Revolution. In fact, China was described as a populist society during the period of the Cultural Revolution.

The populists share common people's concern about pervasive official corruption and the huge gap between the haves and have-nots. They advocate socialism because it makes workers the 'masters of the country'. Like many other populists, Fan Jinggang, manager of Utopia, a Chinese internet forum noted for its strong support of Maoism, talks of the forgotten casualties of the market-oriented reform. For instance, privatization of state-owned enterprises (SOEs) saw tens of millions laid off and the country's wealth controlled by powerful elites; health care and education 'changed from a fundamental citizen welfare to an industrialized commodity'. Today, access to all three poses 'major problems for mid- to low-income individuals and families' (Hunwick 2013). In addition, housing allocation under socialism was abolished.

Fang's arguments were echoed in the works of other populists. Sima Nan, a journalist known for his anti-Western values, defends the country's Maoist legacy. Sima Nan has expressed frustration at growing corruption in the government and the widening social and economic inequalities that post-Mao economic reforms have produced. For him, only a return to Maoist political ideals of the sort once championed by Bo Xilai, former mayor of Chongqing, can save China from political and moral collapse. The years following Bo's fall from power have put Sima Nan in the awkward position of continuing to champion Bo's so-called 'Chongqing Model' of neo-Maoist governance while disavowing any connection to the man himself. That model seeks to combine state economic intervention, crackdown on crime and corruption, and nostalgic Maoist populism to better the lives of the Chinese workers and peasants who have benefited little from China's 'market socialism'.

There is a broad consensus among the populists that the state should play a leading role to protect the interests of the low-income class. Wang and Hu (1993) called for the build-up of the increased 'state capacity', viewing the state as the ultimate defense to protect the national interests. The liberals rejected the idea that the Chinese state could really be as weak as what Wang and Hu had claimed. They maintain that, in any case, the state should withdraw from the economy in favor of a free market.

The populists frequently eulogize the era of Maoist rule, when the Chinese people still spoke of their country as a socialist state based on an alliance between workers and peasants. A growing number of low-income Chinese yearn for egalitarianism (equal outcome) under Mao. They trace widening income disparity and corruption to the process of economic liberalization. As they see it, China's market reform has not brought greater equality and prosperity for all Chinese citizens. They hold that there is a great need to strengthen the power of the state to protect the interests of the poor.

The advocates of liberalism are typically the victims of the Cultural Revolution. They are staunch supporters of the economic reform. They acknowledge the limitations of liberalism especially following the outbreak of the global financial crisis of 2008 and the upswing of populism in the West in recent years. However, they deem that reviving Maoist-era policies could lead to a return to the chaos of the Cultural Revolution. They view the Great Leap Forward 'great swollen version of populist egalitarian thought' and the Cultural Revolution 'the result of a populist paranoia of the rise of capitalism' (Moody 2007). Moreover, the liberals are fed up with the endless 'mass campaigns' (*qunzhong yundong*) and 'socialist revolution'. They express concern about the resurgence of Maoism in China. In the liberal discourse, the post-Mao China has seen phenomenal economic success and the Chinese people are having the best time in their history both historically and comparatively (Li 2010).

Nationalism versus globalism

Populism and nationalism have been closely correlated, both empirically and conceptually (De Cleen 2017). Tang and Darr (2012) find that the level of nationalism in China is one of the highest in the world. Xenophobic populist discourse pits 'the common people' against the 'elite' and global capitalism. Nationalist sentiment among the public provided potential grounds for protest against the elite who failed to defend the interests of the country.

Escalating tensions with the United States and impacts of the global pandemic have in turn created some appeals to populism. Under such circumstance, national populism has become an expedient unifying force in China. Trump's pressure tactics have angered a growing number of Chinese. Populism and nationalism are on the march across China. The Chinese populists are associated with the nationalists on the right and the Maoists on the left. They present themselves as 'outsiders' fighting the 'social injustice' and global capitalism. The populists tend to blame foreigners for hardship and wrenching problems China faces today. They hold the West responsible for most of the country's ills. They see themselves the victims of the trade confrontation and regard President Trump's economic war as further evidence that China ought to rebuild a dynamic socialist system that safeguards the interests of the people. A number of national populists proclaim that with the age of Western global dominance coming to an end, it is China's time to shine.

The liberals tend to be more optimistic about the future of globalization. They see free trade as a net plus rather than a net minus for the country, Liberal scholars, represented by Li Xiao, an economics professor at Jilin University, pointed out in 2018, 'Do we continue to calmly recognize our huge gap with the US and humbly learn from them, or insist on walking a populist path of anti-Americanism?' They see the trade tussle with America is a strategic gift for China and hope the US strategy of sustained pressure to induce further economic and political reforms. They believe the two countries are not natural partners, but they are not inevitable enemies either. With the increasing tensions with the West, they vent discontent with President Xi and his policies.

Pro-market liberals view the free trade policies would permanently improve China's relationship with its trading partners. To them, the United States is helping China to liberalize foreign access to the financial sector. Huang Qifan, a distinguished professor at Fudan University, pointed out, 'China should champion the world trade order by promoting its opening up on the basis of zero tariffs, zero subsidies, and zero barriers'. His speech drew widespread attention and became the representative voice of the market reform school. In the view of the scholars in this camp, the benefits of zero tariffs for China's manufacturing, agriculture, energy, and consumer sectors would outweigh the risks. Zero barriers would greatly improve China's investment climate and help the Chinese firms expand their overseas footprint. Zero subsidies would not only help China's structural reforms but also wean state-owned enterprises (SOEs) off government support while easing trade frictions with foreign countries and reducing opportunities for rent-seeking by vested interests (Li 2019).

The liberals argue that China needs to fight against crony capitalism by restraining the administrative power of the government and gradually phasing out administrative interventions in macroeconomic activities, and by transforming the government to a service-oriented model. The liberal scholars reckon that isolation policy could seriously undermine the Chinese economy and (Li 2020). If history is any guide, the closed-door policy (also known as self-reliance) failed to promote growth and alleviate poverty. Zhu Xueqin, a prominent liberal scholar, pointed out that 'nationalism was the most dangerous force in modern Chinese history. We should enter the world system at top speed, because globalism was much, much better than nationalism' (Wang 2003). Liberal scholars believe nationalism is a double-edged sword. Sometimes nationalism acts as an adhesive agent, unifying the populace to resist foreign humiliation and safeguarding the legitimate rights and interests of the nation. Other times, it is a drug driving the users into a frenzy and causes division, war, and regression. Not surprisingly, national populism could engender negative consequences (Ma 2016).

To a large extent, the arguments between supporters of the state-led model and market-oriented reformists (or between open-minded innovators and independent innovators) run in continuity with the debate between Justin Yifu Lin and Zhang Weiying, two Peking University economists, on industrial policy. While Lin believes that, as a latecomer, China needs an industrial policy to catch up with developed countries, Zhang made it clear that what China most needs is market-oriented reform, and suggests that government intervention into industrial development should be restricted (Lin 2016).

The liberals are upset by the retreat of academic freedom and *guo jin min tui* (advance of the state sector, retreat of the private sector) in recent years. The huge, inefficient, and uncompetitive SOEs have always weighed down China's economy, as the state ignores market demand and directs huge amounts of capital into selected industries for its own reasons. They doubt the protective policies will work in the long run. In their view, a better strategy would be to focus on structural reform as it will deter populist upheaval and its damage to society.

The liberals contend that the Beijing leadership should continue to reduce barriers to trade and investment by foreign firms in China, including by following through on the announced relaxation of restrictions on foreign financial firms operating in the country. Such measures would raise Chinese households' real income by enhancing their purchasing power while strengthening the competitiveness of the country's corporate sector by putting pressure on less efficient domestic firms. China's own experience following its accession to the WTO suggests that greater openness ultimately brings more prosperity to its households.

The liberal thinkers reckon that China must give greater sway to market forces and shrink the state, warning that not doing so will lead to economic stagnation and stoke tensions with the West. They were of the view that the fundamental problem plaguing China is its existing systems. That is the cause of many of its social and economic woes. They believe further structural reform, not state protectionism, is the answer to the challenges China faces. If the state continues to dominate the process of resource allocation, it will distort the market and stifle incentives for innovation (Li 2015; Tang & McConaghy 2018) The liberal reformers provided two prescriptions to deal with the China–US trade war: deepening opening-up and acceleration of domestic market-oriented reform.

The liberal scholars see the slowdown of the economy as largely due to domestic factors, not trade tension between China and the United States. From the perspective of the scholars in the camp of liberalism, crony capitalism not competition results in inequality. The existing political system is causing the unfair distribution of wealth and the governing system allows certain actors to exploit loopholes on an uneven playing field created for their own advantage. In addition, a number of government officials exchange power for money. They worry that without deep reform of the existing system, another revolution like that in 1949 could happen. The liberals, in general, contend that China needs to work closely with the West instead of confrontation. In contrast, the national populists oppose globalization and market-oriented reform. They regularly accused the liberals of being agents for the West and advocate of the greedy rich.

Big democracy versus the rule of law

The populists desire for more widespread political participation. They aim at empowering people by providing them with opportunities of active political participation as they had during the Cultural Revolution. One of the most important tenets of the Chinese populists is big democracy (*daminzhu*, also known as 'great democracy') which means direct mass democracy. They distrust representative democracy and are cynical about liberal democracy and elections in the West. They play loose with established law and woo the population to simplistic solutions to complex problems. For them, 'To rebel is justified'. This slogan was used by the Red Guards during the Cultural Revolution. During the Cultural Revolution, Mao symbolized the people when 'big democracy' without a systematic basis became a new secular religion or political liturgy that was based on crowd action. Such political populism provided an instrument of social control rather than the emancipation of the masses (Xu 2001). While the mob dictatorship of the Cultural Revolution, still etched in many people's memories, has left the Chinese people more aware than most of the potential outcome of such upheavals.

In the minds of the populists, 'big democracy' was a great training school and provided four big freedoms (*si da zi you*) for the Chinese people. These 'freedoms' refer to speaking out freely (*da min*), airing views fully (*da fang*), great debates (*da bianlun*), and writing big-character posters (*da zibao*). The 'Four Big Freedoms' was written into the constitution in 1969 but abolished after Mao's death. People's rights to exercise these freedoms were never clearly defined and guaranteed. In reality, so-called 'big democracy' allowed the ignorant mob to humiliate thousands of members of the political and intellectual elites.

The populists advocate that the masses should take part fully in politics as much as possible and should hold the greatest power. In their view, big democracy would expand people's political rights and allow them a voice in important decisions that concerned the interests of the whole nation. They see politics as a contest between 'the people' and the 'elite,' a characterization common to populism on the left and the right. Their ire was directed mainly at the rich and powerful. However, their views on big democracy were criticized by liberals as heretical. The liberals assert that emphasizing big democracy risks unleashing another Cultural Revolution and that stressing mass participation may lead to social upheavals.

Many Chinese liberal intellectuals embrace the West especially the United States enthusiastically and endorse liberal and democratic values (Lin 2020). Tremendous efforts have been made by the liberals to promote the concept of the rule of law, in which everyone, the government officials in particular, is subject to the law, and the power of the government is limited by law, with the result that individual rights are effectively protected by the law against the abuse of the government in particular. In their view, the main challenge China confronts today is the lack of the rule of law and the CCP is above the law. Only democratic accountability can reduce many of man-made disasters in China. This conception may help explain why the liberal thinkers are arguing that the establishment of the socialist legal system with Chinese characteristics is only the first step in a long march of ten thousand miles. As Tang (2016) puts it, the continuing ideology of mass line, weak institutionalization and direct government response suggest that the country might be moving towards populist authoritarianism as its mode of rule.

Ma (2016) demonstrates that in modern China, public interest is often violated by the government, and nongovernmental organization (NGO) activities are restricted. Because legal channels are blocked, populism leans toward extremism and violence. That could be a disaster for China. For instance, in the case of Yang Jia murdering police officers, the Shanghai High Court did not make public the trial and evidence. Yang Jia, who murdered six Shanghai police officers with a knife, became an internet hero. This and many other political process problems sparked the explosive growth of populism. Thus, to mitigate the effects of populism, the proper path is to implement legal reforms for a transparent and just system.

In the minds of the populists, Deng Xiaoping's suggestion of allowing some people to become wealthy first is an elitist view. One of the greatest changes to the Chinese reform was replacing populism under Mao with free market and competition, leading to fast economic growth. Yet, without the rule of law and equal opportunity for all, the 'unfettered market' could bring about populist movement. The liberals maintain that political reform is necessary because problems in the Chinese society, such as rampant abuse of power, a deficient legal system, and economic malaise have reached the point of no return (Li 2020; Lin 2020; Cheek, Ownby, & Fogel 2019).

Implications

While China's populism and populism in other parts of the world may look similar, the content of the two is not quite the same. It is difficult to compare China's populism with that typically found in Latin America, Europe, or other parts of the world. There is no sign of populist movement nor parties in China as the CCP cracks down on any sign of collective organization and action.

Liberal scholars played key roles in advancing social and economic change through defining and defending citizen rights, developing civil society, promoting market reform and democratic changes (Li 2015). As a reaction against the unanticipated consequences of globalization and market-oriented reform, which accelerated in the early 1990s, liberalism has lost some of its appeals and the intellectual discourse in China is flooded by the national populist narratives. In the minds of the populists and policymakers in Beijing, the liberals merely echo Western ideas or repeat Western concepts without a deep understanding of the reality of China. They are often referred to as *dailudang* – that is, people who guide invading foreign armies. In contrast, the populists enjoy greater latitude for political expression than do liberals. The liberal scholars worry about the spread of populist ideology. They consider populism is pushing aside liberal democratic values and beliefs by drawing on people's fear and disillusionment with market-oriented reform. Nonetheless, the tenets of populism such as fairness, justice, protection of national interests, and anti-corruption are gaining traction in China.

The return of populism has tremendous implications. First, there is a widening gulf among the Chinese intellectuals (Fewsmith 2012; Cheek, Ownby, & Fogel 2019). Xi Jinping, who is seen as a hero of fighting corruption, defender of national interests, and fighter for the poor, has become well-liked by the weak and vulnerable groups, but derided by the liberal intellectuals and private entrepreneurs. There is little doubt that a large number of people in China have become suspicious of and hostile toward the elite and the establishment. Even the critics of the Chinese populist rhetoric seldom deny that it addresses real problems, but it offers the wrong solutions. In the words of Ma (2016), a well-known liberal writer, although the populists make case for combating social injustice and widespread corruption, the methods advocated by the populists to resolve these problems are destructive. Populism finds little resonance among the intellectuals and private entrepreneurs. Some of them fear that China might swing back to a strongman style of political leadership, and shift towards a more autocratic political system.

With the start of the trade war and slowdown of the economy, populism and nationalism are increasingly used by the Party apparatus to unite the country and boost the control. Given the populist backlash against globalization, it is only a matter of time before the ordinary people begin to organize to react to the consequence of the economic decoupling. Ever since the 1989 Tiananmen Square protests, which shook the CCP to its core and resulted in a government crackdown on dissent, the CCP has ceaselessly exploited national populist sentiment to shore up its legitimacy of the regime established after 1949. In the event of decoupling and latent economic stagnation, the CCP is likely to bolster those efforts.

Carothers (2018) finds that the Chinese policymakers are unsettled by nationalist and anti-globalization sentiments that often accompany populist movements and run counter to national interests. Nationalism appeals to those who feel left out by the market-oriented reform and the trade war, the danger is that it might contribute to a demagogic populism. It seems fair to say that in the first stage of the Chinese reform, the United States stood very high in the Chinese public opinion. At present, America probably is seen as antagonistic. Under the Trump administration, Washington has used sanctions to cut China out of global supply chains. Many in China posit that America's decoupling with China is designed to hinder China's rise. American current involvement in Taiwan and Hong Kong is considered meddling in internal Chinese domestic affairs. After the collapse of the former Soviet Union and the subsequent decline of Russia, a large number of the Chinese public come to realize that the top leadership in Beijing made a better choice. A critique of global capitalism and attempt to maintain a state-led development model carry more weight in China's populism than in many other societies.

Meanwhile, the CCP also takes pains to limit the rise of populism to assure that things do not get out of hand. There is always the chance that discontent against the wealthy and the West could easily turn to disgruntlement against those in power. Since 2012, the fifth-generation leadership under Xi has gradually departed from the pro-business policies implemented during the initial period of the economic reform and pursued a state-led strategy and pro-poor approach in order to accumulate their political capital. The party-state has given tacit recognition to nationalism as a source of regime legitimacy. At the same time, the Beijing leadership worries about the populist and nationalist sentiments that run counter to China's ambition to lead the next phase of globalization.

Conclusion

On the major issues facing the nation today, the populists found common ground with the New Left and nationalists. For instance, they all claim to represent the weak and underprivileged groups against the 'elite' and global capitalism, and construct their political demands as representing the will of 'the ordinary people'. While the spread of populism has generated intense debates, it has also been manipulated to promote fear, wreak devastation, and divide the nation and infringe on individual rights. So far, populism in China remains as an online movement of 'netzens' without a clear leader. However, rising income disparity, rampant official corruption, and soaring tensions with the West have sown the seeds for the populist movement.

References

Carothers, T. (2018) 'The Rise of populism and implication for China', available at https://carnegieendowment.org/files/Episode_105-_The_Rise_of_Populism_and_Implications_for_China.pdf.

Cheek, T., Ownby, D., and Fogel, J. eds. (2019) *Voices from the Chinese Century, Public Intellectual Debate from Contemporary China*, New York, NY: Columbia University Press.

De Cleen, B. (2017) 'Populism and nationalism', in Cristóbal Rovira Kaltwasser, Paul Taggart, Paulina Ochoa Espejo and Pierre Ostiguy (eds) *Handbook of Populism*, Oxford: Oxford University Press, pp. 342–62.

Fewsmith, J. (2012) *China since Tiananmen: The Politics of Transition*, New York: Cambridge University Press.

Gao, Y. 高扬 (2018) '警惕民粹主义危害 防范民粹主义风险' (Watch out for the dangers of populism and prevent the risks of populism)，学习时报 available at http://www.studytimes.cn/zydx/DDSJ/HUANQLW/2018-07-15/13394.html.

Gidron, N., and Bonikowski, B. (2013) 'Varieties of populism: Literature review and research agenda', Weatherhead Working Paper Series, no. 13–0004.

Gui, Y., Huang, H., and Ding, Y. (2020) 'Three faces of the online leftists: An exploratory study based on case observations and big-data analysis', *Chinese Journal of Sociology* 6(1): 67–101.

Hunwick, R. (2013) 'Utopia website shut down: An interview with Fan Jinggang', available at https://www.thechinastory.org/key-intellectual/fan-jinggang-%E8%8C%83%E6%99%AF%E5%88%9A/.

Ip, G. (2019) 'Has America's China backlash gone too far?' *Wall Street Journal*, available at https://www.wsj.com/articles/has-americas-china-backlash-gone-too-far-11566990232.

Lee, T. (1995) 'Chinese culture and political renewal', *Journal of Democracy* 6(4): 3–8.

Li, H. (2010) 'Debating China's economic reform: Liberals vs. new leftists', *Journal of Chinese Political Science* 15(1): 1–23.

Li, H. (2015) *Political Thought and China's Transformation: Ideas Shaping the Reform in Post-Mao China*, New York: Palgrave Macmillan.

Li, H. (2020) 'The Chinese discourse on good governance: Content and implications', *Journal of Contemporary China* 29(126): 824–37.

Li, W. (2019) 'Towards economic decoupling? Mapping Chinese discourse on the China-US trade war', *The Chinese Journal of International Politics* 12(4): 519–56.

Lin, H. 林红 (2007) 民粹主义：概念、理论与实证 (*Populism: Concept, Theory, and Empirical Practice*), 中央编译出版社，Beijing: Central Compilation and Translation Press, 2007.

Lin, J. Y. 林毅夫 (2016) '产业政策与我国的经济发展–新结构经济学的视角' (Industrial policy and China's economic development: A perspective on new structural economics), available at https://www.guancha.cn/LinYiFu/2016_09_14_374342.shtml.

Lin, Y. (2020) 'Beaconism and the Trumpian metamorphosis of Chinese liberal intellectuals', *Journal of Contemporary China*, available at https://doi.org/10.1080/10670564.2020.1766911.

Ling, L., and Shih, C. (1998) 'Confucianism with a liberal face: The meaning of democratic politics in postcolonial Taiwan', *The Review of Politics* 60(1): 55–82.

Ma, L. 马立诚 (2016)当代中国八种社会思潮 (*Leading Schools of Thought in Contemporary China*), Beijing: 社会科学文献出版社 Social Sciences Academic Press.

Moody, P. (2007) 'Conservative populism', in Moody, P. (ed) *Conservative Thought in Contemporary China*, Lanham, MD: Rowman & Littlefield, pp. 125–50.

Rong, J. 荣剑 (2013) '没有细想的中国' (A China bereft of thought) originally published in 2013 on the website www.21.ccom.net, which has since been shut down, available at https://www.thechinastory.org/wp-content/uploads/2017/02/Rong-Jian-%E8%8D%A3%E5%89%91-%E6%B2%A1%E6%9C%89%E6%80%9D%E6%83%B3%E7%9A%84%E4%B8%AD%E5%9B%BD.pdf.

Sun, L. 孙立平 (1994) '平民主义与中国改革' (Populism and China's reform), 战略与管理 (Strategy and Management), no. 5, pp. 1–11.

Tang, W. (2016) *Populist Authoritarianism: Chinese Political Culture and Regime Sustainability*, New York: Oxford University Press.

Tang, W., and Darr, B. (2012) 'Chinese nationalism and its political and social origins', *Journal of Contemporary China* 21(77): 811–26.

Tang, X., and McConaghy, M. (2018) 'Liberalism in contemporary China: Questions, strategies, directions', *China Information* 32(1): 121–38.

Townsend, J. (1977) 'Chinese populism and the legacy of Mao Tse-Tung', *Asian Survey* 17(11): 1003–15.

Wang, H. (2003) 'The new criticism,' in Chaohua Wang (ed) *One China, Many Paths*, London: Verso, p. 79.

Wang, S. 王绍光 and Hu, A. 胡鞍钢 (1993) '中国国家能力报告' (*A Report on China's State Capacity*), Shenyang: Liaonin rennin chubanshe.

Xiao, G. 萧功秦 (2012) 超越左右 (*Beyond Left and Right Radicalism*), Hangzhou: Zhejiang University Press.

Xu, B. (2001) 'Chinese populist nationalism: Its intellectual politics and moral dilemma', *Representations* 76(1): 120–40.

Ying, M. (2020) 'Can China be populist? Grassroot populist narratives in the Chinese cyberspace', *Contemporary Politics*. DOI: 10.1080/13569775.2020.1727398., p. 79.

Zang, D. (2010) 'Rise of political populism and the trouble with the legal profession in China', *Harvard China Review* 6(1): 79–99.

Zhang, X. 张祥平 (1994) '启蒙–民粹–大民主的历史反思' (Reflections on the history of enlightenment, populism, and grand democracy), 战略与管理 (Strategy and Management), no. 5, pp. 15–19.

Zhao, D. 赵鼎新 (2008) '民粹政治， 中国冲突性政治的走向' (Populism in China: Origins, manifestations, and political implications), 领导者 (Leader) no. 2.

Zheng, Y. 郑也夫 (2004) 知识分子研究 (*Study of Intellectuals*), Beijing: Zhongguo qingnian chupanzhe.

27

Social transformations of Chinese society in the focus of modern sociological science

Pavel Deriugin, Liubov Lebedintseva, and Liudmila Veselova

Introduction

Sociology as a science that studies the social world in all its diversity and complexity emerged in China at the beginning of the 20th century and has since experienced a series of ups and downs, crises, and periods of prosperity. According to Chinese scholars, the history of sociology in China can be divided into several stages: 1891–1910 – the emergence of sociology; 1911–1918 – the 'first sprouts' of Chinese sociology; 1919–1927 – the 'young shoots' of sociology; 1927–1949 – the growth of sociological science; 1949–present – the development of uniquely Chinese sociology (*30 Years of Chinese Sociology* 2008: 104). The historical development of sociology in China embodies the larger dramatic changes which occurred in Chinese society in a span of over 100 years. The initial emergence of sociology in China coincided with a period of deep crisis caused by defeat in the wars of the late 19th century (Liu 2006: 71–74). Progressive-minded reformers in China launched a movement as a way to spread and promote the social sciences, as they believed that knowledge in these fields would serve as the theoretical basis for reforms. A young generation of Chinese scientists educated abroad – in Japan, Russia, the United States, and some European countries – imported sociology from the outside as a way to help China at a time when the country lacked qualified and experienced specialists.

The achievements of European sociology in the context of China faced with centuries-old traditions of Confucian understanding of sociality and society, as well as Taoism and Buddhism, in explaining social values and interpretation of the facts of social psychology. The specific approaches of Confucianism in understanding society in its integrity and unity, harmony with nature and the human spirit, as well as in-depth attention to chaos and numerous interconnections in social phenomena, was not consistent with many axiomatic provisions of modern European sociology. A characteristic of the Chinese understanding of sociality is the comprehension of harmony and unity of all elements in the universe, the search for a 'golden mean', and recognition of the decisive role of humanity and moral in the interaction between people, the concept of 'people-base', and so forth. The central idea of the whole system of social values in China was recognized as filial piety. Hierarchy of relations and traditions were formed on the basis of this concept. The repetition of the ritual creates the foundation of a stable and inertly developing state.

DOI: 10.4324/9780429059704-32

The development of society through the prism of scientific development: The 'one step back–two steps forward' of sociology in China

Chinese interest in sociology emerged at the end of the 19th century and into the Xinhai revolution of 1911. Neo-Confucian reformers played an active role in this development, but so too did the general need to modernize China. At this time, the first translations of classical works of Western sociology appeared. In 1903 the Chinese philosopher and public figure, Yan Fu (严复) (1854–1921), translated Herbert Spencer's *The Principles of Sociology* (3 vols., 1876–1896), which in Chinese was translated as *The Study of Sociology* (群学肄言). The first two chapters of the book were published in 1898 in the Tianjin journal, *Country News Compilation* (国闻汇编). Yan Fu also translated Thomas Huxley's *Evolution and Ethics* (1901–1902) and Adam Smith's *The Wealth of Nations* (1902). Yan Fu focused largely on positivist sociology, which had a significant influence on Chinese thinkers of the time. Yang Fu accomplished a difficult task: he explained the evolutionist concept of world development and conveyed the concepts of 'evolution', 'struggle for existence', and 'natural selection' using the vocabulary of traditional science. Yan Fu's translations were unique in that he provided commentary of his own, such as in his translation of Spencer's interpretation of Darwinism (Osipova 2013: 52).

Meanwhile, another well-known Chinese philosopher and enlightener, Zhang Binlin (章炳麟) (1869–1936), translated the book *Sociology* by the Japanese scientist, Kashimoto Nomura. In his book, Nomura introduced the concepts of Herbert Spencer and other leading American sociologists (Lu 2000: 37–84). Chinese translations of these works introduced the public to Western and Japanese ideas about society. In 1902 Zhang Binlin translated from Japanese Spencer's *Foundations of Sociology* in which he used the Japanese term '社会学' ('shehuixue') for the first time to refer to the concept of 'sociology'. It should be noted that the words 'society' (社会) and 'sociology' (社会学) were introduced into Chinese from Japanese, also spreading to other Asian countries, such as Korea and Vietnam. Before the 1870s, the Japanese used various characters to explain the term 'society' – '社交", 交际', ' 世间', and '世态'. In the late 1870s, writers mostly used '社会' and '世态', and by the 1880s, most scholars began to use only '社会' (Giri 2018: 318–321).

The Chinese authorities criticized and persecuted nearly all progressive scholars of sociology since sociological knowledge contradicted the centuries-old traditions of monarchical rule. During the 'One hundred days of reform' in 1989, for example, Chinese historian, philosopher, and politician, Liang Qichao (梁启超) (1873–1929), along with another well-known Chinese reformer, Kang Youwei (康有為) (1858–1927), actively participated in the creation of the Society of National Preservation (保国会). Liang Qichao became one of the leaders of the party of reformers called the Society of National Preservation. The authorities eventually crushed the party, and many of its members were convicted and executed. In his works, Liang Qichao tried to rethink Confucianism and the traditional Chinese system of interpreting and understanding society. He agreed with Buckle, Montesquieu, and Rousseau about the idea of a 'citizen of the country', the values of independence, personal freedom, and self-reliance. In answering the question about the mechanisms needed for the progressive development of Chinese society, Qichao noted that the main reason behind the superiority and glorification of the West was the ability of Europeans to actively defending their own interests.

In 1906, thanks to the efforts of a few extraordinary individuals, the so-called 'doctrine of society', a precursor to sociology in China, started being taught at St. John's University in Shanghai (上海圣约翰大学). Beginning in 1910, the sociology curriculum was supplemented by industrial and social policies. According to rules of the time, a degree in higher education granted its bearer the right to become a government official without the need to pass an examination. Since few sociological works had been translated into Chinese, sociology was taught using books from the West. Western missionary-scholars played an active role in institutionalizing sociology in China. In 1908 one of the first foreign sociologists, American Arthur Monn, began to teach a course on sociology in Shanghai at St. John's University. There, in 1913, American professor, Daniel Kulp II, founded China's first sociology department. Sociology departments began attracting scholars who studied and defended their dissertations abroad (in Japan, the United States, and Western European countries). One of the first doctoral dissertations in sociology defended by a Chinese student Zhu Yuyu in 1911 at Columbia University was dedicated to the topic of 'Charity in China'. After returning to China, Zhu Yuyu began teaching at St. John's University in Shanghai (Lu 2000: 38–39).

Sociology as a science gradually began to spread to neighboring countries. Yet it should be noted that nearby Asian countries did not play a critical role in the development of sociology in China. For various reasons, in many of the countries surrounding China, sociology arose later, following an even more difficult and thorny path of development. Many Asian countries, being colonies of other states, were unable to pursue their own paths in sociological research and theory. After World War II, American sociological traditions greatly influenced the development of sociology in Hong Kong, the Philippines, and Taiwan. While Singapore, Malaysia, and India, being colonies of Great Britain, more closely followed European traditions in both science and education.

Because of the strong influences that American specialists had on the development of sociology in China, some researchers even characterized early sociology in China as 'American missionary sociology' (Chen 2018: 11). In general, the US government paid a great deal of attention to the changes happening in China's educational system. With the understanding that younger generations of Chinese would be the country's future decision-makers, the United States was interested in attracting Chinese students to study in the United States, and at the same time, in preventing them from studying in Japan and Europe. Having reduced the amount of 'boxing' indemnity that China was required to pay the United States and several European countries following the 'anticolonial' Boxer Rebellion (1899–1901), the United States allocated financial support to the Chinese government, which eventually became a fund for developing cultural activities in China. With the help of this funding, Tsinghua University was founded. Likewise, a number of future Chinese scholars were able to study in the United States, including Sun Benwen (孙本文), Li Jinghan (李景汉), Wu Wenzao (吴文藻), Wu Jingchao (吴景超), Wu Zelin (吴泽霖), and others (Pang 2009: 132).

One of the first signs that sociology as a science began taking root in China was the launch of sociology lectures in 1912 at one of the country's most advanced universities, Peking University. Among the first Chinese sociology professors in the 1920–1930s were Kang Xinfu (康心孚) (1884–1917), Zhang Binlin, Liang Qichao, and Yan Fu (Porter et al. 2003: 500). In the 1920s sociology as an academic discipline started to appear in the curriculum of other Chinese universities. Over time, leading sociological schools and academic departments were established: 1922 – in Beijing University; 1925 – in Fudan University; 1926 – in Guanghua in Shanghai and Tsinghua in Beijing; and 1927 – at the National Central University in Nanjing and Jinan in Guangzhou. In 1928 a sociology department was established at Dongbei University, and then in 1929 at the Shanghai University of Labor. Due to the fact that foreign missionaries managed these universities, training in new sociology departments was religious in nature. According to Chinese sociologist, Sun Benwen (孙本文) (1892–1979), by 1930 sociology departments had already been established at 11 universities in China. At some universities, sociology departments were combined with departments of history, political science, and anthropology (Zheng & Yingsheng 2003: 67). During the 1920–1930s, books on sociological topics started being published in China. During this ten-year period, over 75 books on sociological topics were published annually.

The experience of Western sociology was significant not only for sociological theory, but also for the formation of Chinese applied sociology. At first, many of those who received a professorship did not know how to conduct sociological research. They simply lacked field research experience (Arkush 1981: 27). At the beginning of the 20th century, foreign scholars carried out small sociological studies of Chinese society. For example, in 1914–1915 the American sociologist, John Stuart Burgess, investigated the lives of Chinese rickshaw workers, and then in 1921, together with another American sociologist, Sidney D. Gamble (1890–1968), published the study 'Peking: A Social Survey', a large-scale survey of a Beijinger's social life (Arkush 1981: 27). The methodology and methods used in conducting these and other empirical studies at the time was an important moment in the development of applied sociology in China.

It should be noted that some organizations interested in sociological studies in China started to appear in the United States. In 1898 the organization, Princeton in Asia (PiA), organization was founded in China. In 1908 one of the first foreign sociologists, American Arthur Monn, served as a bridge between the United States and China. Arthur Monn as a member of the Princeton in Asia organization brought his knowledge and expertise to China (Princeton in Asia). In 1928 The Harvard-Yenching Institute was founded. Its main goals were to conduct research on Chinese culture and society. It also helped to develop and maintain educational institutions in China (History of the Harvard-Yenching).

In 1930 Chinese sociologists, including Sun Benwen, Wu Jingchao, and Wu Zelin, formed the Chinese Sociological Society. Its foundation was a testament to the growing number of professional sociologists in China. The members of the Chinese Sociological Society actively participate in the development of the sociological studies in Chinese education. At the same time, the Journal of Sociology (社会杂志) began to be published in China, with Sun Benwen serving as chief editor (Pang 2009: 131). Among the Chinese Sociological Society's objectives was the development of a standard sociology curriculum in universities and creating a complete list of sociological terms to be translated into Chinese, which the Ministry of Education would then publish.

As a result of the nationalist government's (1925–1948) reforms in higher education, more students in China started to enroll at sociology departments. In 1934 more than 450 university students studied sociology. Sociology became such a popular subject that it was ranked fifth after Chinese literature, Western literature, history, and education (Chen 2018: 19). Due to political instability in the country, as well as the war with Japan (1937–1945), the training of sociologists was discontinued in China. At the time, no one questioned whether or not this measure would be only temporary (Lu 2000: 40). Following the victory over Japan, universities reopened and sociological training resumed. According to Sun Benwen, at this time 144 sociology instructors worked universities, meanwhile, 107 out of 134 Chinese sociology teachers were educated abroad and subsequently returned to China. Three years later, in 1948, 21 sociology departments were opened at Chinese universities, enrolling more than 600 students total (Lu 2000: 40).

With the foundation of the People's Republic of China (PRC) in 1949, a new era of centralized higher education began, where the Ministry of Education controlled the activities of universities, which included decided which subjects were taught. China's newly established central authority seemed capable of controlling practically any innovative and progressive knowledge. At first, the government supported the development of sociology and other social sciences with curricula that included, for example, 'Selective Reading of Famous Works of Marx and Lenin', 'Political Economy', 'The New Democratic Doctrine', 'The History of the Development of Sociology', and others (Lu 2000: 40–41). However, this did not last for long, and sociological education in China faced another wave of suppression amidst the revolutionary transformations led by Mao Zedong. At this time, many young people joined a revolutionary and anti-intellectual movement, which led to lower attendance numbers at universities, the closure of sociology departments, and ultimately, the cancellation of sociology courses altogether. Starting in 1949, sociology was criticized as a 'bourgeois science', an attitude which not only hindered the development of sociology, but also caused avoidable social problems. A classic example was the rejection of the ideas of Malthus and his book *The New Theory of Population*, which analyzed uncontrolled population growth, a kind of 'demographic inflation' (Liu 2006: 71–72). By 1952 there were only ten sociology departments left in China, with an enrollment of approximately 472 students (Lu 2000: 40–41). Later, sociology was banned outright. Sociologists were deprived of the opportunity to engage in scientific work, and those who received an education abroad, in particular those who studied in the United States, were criticized and accused of bourgeois views. Following the ban on sociology, only a few sociologists were able to continue their scientific research. This included sociologists such as Professor Pan Guangdan (潘光旦) (1899–1967), who investigated the problems of Chinese families, his student, Fei Xiaotong (费孝通) (1910–2005), who investigated villages in the Jiangsu province, and Li Jinghan (李景汉) (1895–1986), who investigated life in villages in the suburbs of Beijing (Lu 2000: 41). However, these individual cases were exceptions rather than the rule.

Among the main reasons as to why sociology was banned in China are as follows:

- In the 1950s the entire country was inspired by the idea of building socialism, with the standards of the USSR help up as a model. Sociology was thus declared a 'bourgeois pseudoscience'
- It was thought necessary to study the basic ideas and methods of social development from the point of view of historical materialism
- Problems inherent in capitalist societies were thought to be absent in China's new socialist society (Lu 2000: 41)
- The personal factor: Mao Zedong had a negative attitude toward sociology, calling it 'vulgar', 'opposing class struggle' (Zheng 2000: 177)

The intensified class struggle in Chinese society blurred the lines between science and politics. The party elite began to view sociology as a conspiracy to restore capitalism, meanwhile, scientists who tried to engage in sociological work were again criticized. In August 1957 *The New Construction Magazine* published an article titled 'Discussing the Reactionary Character of Bourgeois Sociology' (谈资产阶级社会学的反动性) (Wang 1989: 2). Head of the state security organs of the PRC, Kang Sheng (康 生) (1898–1975), oversaw this critique of sociology, where he closely analyzed the work of the Ministry of Education and the subjects of academic disciplines. By Sheng's order, some social science disciplines were replaced with a 'course of socialist education', which had students read the works of Chairman Mao (Usov 2004: 173). At a meeting on August 20, 1957, Kang Sheng criticized sociology, characterizing sociologists as criminals and the scourge of Chinese society. Many scholars were subsequently repressed, their works were banned, and more than 1,000 books on various social issues were placed on 'blacklists'.

Later, the course of sociology's development in China changed yet again. This occurred after the VIII Congress of the Communist Party of China (CPC) (1958) when Mao Zedong put forward the idea of the intelligentsia's active participation in the political life of the country. The CPC launched the new campaign under the slogan 'Let a hundred flowers bloom, let a hundred schools compete' (百花齐放, 百家争鸣). Well-known sociologists from Peking University, such as Chen Da (陈 达) (1892–1975), Wu Jingchao (吴景 超) (1901–1968), and Fei Xiaotong, had the chance to express their views about the restoration of sociology in newspaper publications and at meetings of the Political Advisory Council (Wang 1989: 1). On February 20, 1957 the Hong Kong newspaper, *Wen Wei Po* (文汇报), published an article by Fei Xiaotong entitled 'A Few Phrases About Sociology' (关于社会学, 说几句话). Xiaotong described the ban on sociology as a serious mistake, calling for the speedy restoration of sociology as a scientific discipline (Zheng & Yingsheng 2003: 178). A new surge of interest in sociology was made possible in part thanks to the possibility to publish articles in the scientific-periodical journal *New Construction* (新建设). The journal began printing invitations to Beijing sociologists to discuss prospects and new approaches in the development of sociology in China. The Social Research Working Committee (社会调查工作委员会) was soon thereafter formed, chaired by Professor Chen Da (Wang 1989: 2). In the 1950–60s official social studies, infused with Marxist-Leninist ideology, began with the aim of opposing 'bourgeois sociology'.

The years of the Cultural Revolution (1966–1976) nearly brought Chinese sociology to a standstill. Yet some sociologists during this period continued to conduct research informally, without receiving permission from the government. Chinese sociologists addressed demographic issues, family and marriage problems, ethnic groups, and crime statistics. These studies were later reconducted following the rehabilitation of sociology (Lu 2000: 43). The Cultural Revolution was a dramatic period in Chinese history due to the assault on the education, which saw many young specialists forcibly sent to villages, as well as a number of professors and scientists jailed and even killed. Some scholars managed to emigrate to Europe and the United States.

The death of Mao Zedong in 1976 had a profound effect on the political and social stability of the country. The Gang of Four, one of the most powerful radical political elite in China, and the main driver of the Cultural Revolution, lost what remained of their power and were imprisoned. The country had entered a new era. The year 1978 became an important moment for the entire country, but for Chinese sociology in particular. At the plenary meeting of the Central Committee of the CPC, sociology was officially restored. The new party elite decided to reassess Mao Zedong's political decisions. Likewise, state propaganda was eased as a way of encouraging independent and active thinking among citizens, the result of which would be an 'orientation to facts', in other words, focusing on that which could be measured and observed rather than strictly adhering to Marxist-Leninist ideology. Chinese reformer and politician, Deng Xiaoping (邓小平) (1904–1997), considered the restoration of the natural and social sciences to be of great importance. Xiaoping laid out his framework of 'Four modernization'(四个现代化). In a report entitled 'Firmly adhere to the four basic principles', Xiaoping emphasized the fact that research in the field of sociology has been neglected in China for a significant period of time, and that efforts were necessary in order to restore it. This was the first time that sociology was officially mentioned in the documents of the CPC Central Committee (Lu 2000: 45). From that point onward, with the support of the state, sociology began its rapid development in China.

In March 1979 President of the Chinese Academy of Social Sciences, Hu Qiaomu (胡乔木), announced the beginning of sociology's restoration in China, as well as the creation of the National Planning Office for Philosophy and Social Sciences (全国哲学社会科学规划会议筹划 备处). However, the future of sociology as a science was still uncertain because, by this time, sociology departments at Chinese universities had been completely dismantled. Likewise, many scholars, still frightened by the horrors of the Cultural Revolution, were suspicious of the government's new proposals for restoring sociology (Wang 1989: 3). The primary goal of the forum was to answer the question of how sociological research was to be carried out in modern China. Speaking at the conference, Hu Qiaomu outlined the key challenges that sociology faced at the time:

- How to couple historical materialism and sociology
- How to study and borrow the theories and approaches of Western sociologists
- How to support research teams and encourage them to create sociological research centers
- How to reopen sociology departments
- How to develop talent and retain specialists
- How to attract students who could further development sociology (Lu 2000: 44)

At the conclusion of the sociology forum on March 18, 1979, the Chinese Sociological Study Association (中国社会学研究会) was established, signaling sociology's new rise in China. The Association's committee consisted of 50 people, a number of places for sociologists from Taiwan were reserved, and the famous sociologist, Fei Xiaotong, was appointed chairman (Wang 1989: 5). In 1982 the Association was renamed to the Chinese Sociological Association (中国社会学会) (Chinese Sociological Association 2012a). The main goals of the Chinese Sociological Association (CSA) were to coordinate academic events, develop sociological teaching and research, publish books, as well as represent China in local and international conferences (Chinese Sociological Association 2012b). It should be noted that the CSA shared strong ties with the state. The establishment of a professional sociological association in China encouraged sociologists from other cities to open their own local associations, such as in Beijing, Tianjin, Hubei, Shanghai, Jiangsu, Jilin, and Heilongjiang.

In the 1980s China's education system again underwent significant changes, largely due to the fact that the country lacked qualified and experienced professionals. The older generations of sociologists were no longer aware of the modern developments in sociology, meanwhile, the new generation of sociologists still had much to learn. Many students switched from studying philosophy, as well as other disciplines, and began to undergo intensive training in sociology. These students were to become a new generation of talented sociologists who would go on to teach and conduct research. The training of these students was provided financial support from different American foundations (Chen 2018: 32). The sociology curriculum was intended to have at least six core disciplines: general information about sociology, methods of social research, social psychology, economic sociology, comparative sociology, and theory of Western sociology (Lu 2000: 46). In many ways, Fei Xiaotong sided with Western sociologists and their work, believing it necessary to learn from the West and that sociology in China should consciously model American sociology. At this turbulent period in Chinese history, sociologists sought to depart from theories of class struggle, which explains why Max Weber's theory of stratification became popular.

Over a period of six years, 11 universities in China saw their sociology departments reopened. In December 1979, on the basis of the US–China agreement on scientific exchange, an American delegation to China was met by Yao Yilin, Deputy Secretary General of the Central Committee of the Communist Party of China. The delegates exchanged their scientific knowledge and expertise with their Chinese colleagues and cooperated in research projects (Wang 1989: 6).

On January 18, 1980, with the support of the PRC Academy of Social Sciences, the Institute of Sociology of the Chinese Academy of Social Sciences (CASS) was founded, and Fei Xiaotong was appointed its director. The core scientific research aims of the CASS included: China's socialist modernization construction, studying topics of great theoretical and practical significance in the development of Chinese society, discussing general laws of social development, as well as laws of social development particular to China; exploring social strata, groups, organizations, communities, social structures, and social mobility. Thanks to the efforts of several generations of sociologists, CASS has since become a sociological research institution with a wide range of sociological disciplines and the largest staff of sociologists in China. In 2009 the CASS has a total of ten laboratories, one editorial department, two functioning sociology departments, two national societies, three college-level research centers, and five institute-level research centers (Institute of Sociology 2010).

Sociological institutions gradually started to open in other major cities. In 1980–81 sociology seminars were held in Beijing, with more than a hundred attendees. In 1980 Shanghai University became the first educational institution which reopened its sociology department. By 1989 already 22 sociology departments could be found in the country, where more than 2,000 sociologists were trained and more than 200 professors worked (Lu 2000: 48–49).

In 1982 the Chinese Sociological Society published the textbook *General Information on Sociology* under the editorship of Professor Fei Xiaotong. This provided the impetus for the further publication of books on sociology. Scientific teams, individual scientists, and even private individuals began to write books on sociology, which included works such as *Methods of sociological research*, *History of sociology in China*, and *History of sociology in the West* (Lu, 2000: 49). Likewise, in the 1980s new periodicals started to appear, such as *Society* ('社会'), *Journal of sociology* ('社会杂志'), *Sociological Research* (社会学研究), *Sociological Information* (社会学通讯), and *Reference Materials on Foreign Sociology* (国外社会学参考资料). The sociology departments of large universities played an active role in this process by publishing their own journals (Lu 2000: 52–53). Meanwhile, the range of topics which interested Chinese sociologists widened significantly. Research topics came to include problems of fundamental sociology, the history of Western sociology, the theory of modernization, problems of urban residents, social structure and social transformation of Chinese society, social stratification, the relationship between the state and society, problems of workers and peasants, and more. Economic reforms in the 1980s gave rise to new social issues requiring careful study, for example, issues of migration from rural areas to cities and the emergence of the middle class.

In the 1980–1990s, nearly all universities in China were reopened and most sociology departments were reopened: in 1989 – 12 departments; in 1999 – 33. In 2006, 80 institutions offer a bachelor's degree in sociology, 115 offer a master's degree, and 25 offer a doctoral degree (Chen 2018: 35). In an article dedicated to the 50th anniversary of Chinese sociology, the famous sociologist, Lu Xueyi, outlined the seven key issues of interest to Chinese sociologists in 1980–90:

1. Social problems of small cities
2. Family and marriage issues. In 1983, under the leadership of Professor Lei Zetsong (雷洁琼),theproject,'StudyingFamilyandMarriageinfiveCitiesofChina',(中国五城市结婚家庭研究) was launched. The project's findings were published in a series of articles, including 'A Study of Family and Marriage Issues in China' (中国婚姻家庭研究) and 'Marriage and Family in Chinese Cities' (中国城市婚姻与家庭). The articles covered issues such as living expenses in urban Chinese families, fertility problems in cities, educational work with families, and elderly care
3. Theory of social transformation. Research dedicated to this issue resulted in a number of works, for example, 'From Traditional Chinese Society to Society. In the process of dynamic transformation' (从传统向现代快速转型过程中的中国社会), written by Beijing People's University professor, Zheng Hansheng (郑杭). The transformation of Chinese society was unique in many ways. The most burning research questions included the gap between rich and poor, destruction of the traditional family, increased divorce rates, and changes to traditions and customs in society
4. Theory of modernization. This issue closely examines the features of modernization in China, opportunities and barriers to modernization, and strategic steps to strengthen modernization. At present, professor of Peking University, Sun Liping (孙立平), and professor at Chinese Academy of Social Sciences, Zhang Zhuo (张琢), actively study this issue
5. Rural society and village development. This area of research focuses on issues of marriage and family in rural areas, grassroots organization, township and rural municipality enterprises, construction of small towns, clans and clan members, social stratification, and consumption systems
6. System of social indicators. In China, the study of social indicators began only in the 1980s. In 1985 *Statistical Materials on Chinese Society* (中国社会统计资) was first published. The study of social indicators was a priority for Chinese sociologist, Zhu Qingfang (朱庆芳), and his colleagues, who first conducted a comparative analysis on the standard of living in China, comparing it with the living standards of other countries
7. Methods of analysis and predicting social trends. The rapid changes occurring in China at the end of the 20th century required control and analysis in order to avoid mass protest and social unrest. In 1993 so-called Blue Books began being published annually in China. This is a series of publications devoted to the social problems of modern China (Lu 2000: 58–62)

In the 1980s Chinese sociologists pursued a path of 'specialization' and 'professionalization'. For young scholars, sociology was not just a tool for solving social problems but also a scientific discipline which had its own rules and standards. All of this was linked to a weakening of ideological control, which also led to changes in sociological vocabulary once dominated by Marxist phraseology (Merle 2004). Around this time, Chinese scholars began to produce professional textbooks, including, for example, *Introduction to Sociology Trial Edition* (社会学概论), which was published in 1984 and whose chief editor was Fei Xiaotong (Chen 2018: 43).

In 1991 the CPC Central Committee established a new organ called the National Planning Office of Philosophy and Social Sciences (全国哲学社会科学规划办公室), which was controlled by Philosophy and Social Science Planning Group, which became the highest body in the Chinese social sciences. Within the framework of the National Planning Office of Philosophy and Social Sciences, the National Social Science Fund

(NSSF) was founded. The NSSF also manages the National Social Sciences Database and runs annual research funding programs indicating which research topics will be funded in each discipline. Beginning in 1992, more subfields began to appear in sociology and more and more research was conducted. Thanks to the economic reforms, sociological case studies became more meaningful and applied (Lu 2000: 45–46). The NSSF became the main source of state funding for social scientific research, which led to an increase of sociological research. During the 1990s, some of the main areas of research included socioeconomic development, changing social stratification, state-society relations, and economic sociology. At the same time, the Chinese government launched programs to support scholars in their work. The government also turned its attention to bringing back Chinese scientists who had immigrated abroad, especially those who had moved to the United States.

In 1994 the Hundred Talents program (百人计划) was launched with the aim of attracting scholars under the age of 45 from abroad. Within the program, each scholar is awarded a grant of two million yuan (Hundred Talents Program). The mission of the program was to return Chinese scientists from the United States who might otherwise contribute to the further development of science in China. It was programs like this that further played a role in strengthening US influence on Chinese sociology. The Thousand Talents Program became yet another successful program (千人计划). It was launched in 2008 by the State Council of China, and it separates its Fellows into several categories:

- University professors, employees of world-famous companies and start-ups, and inventors whose technologies or patents are internationally recognized (under 55 years old)
- 'Young professionals' (under 40 years old)
- 'International experts' (under 65 years old) (Thousand Talents Program)

Furthermore, the government began to support R&D and publications of Chinese scientists. In 2016 Chinese authors ranked first place in the Scopus database of international scientific journals. In 2000 China's share of articles was 4%, but in 2016 that number had reached 18.6 %. One of the main reasons behind this level of publishing activity was the need to publish research as a way to fulfill a KPI from universities and institutions. Researchers from some of the most prestigious universities in China began publishing more and more in the English language so that their work would reach a larger audience (Xie & Freeman 2019: 1–6).

Up until the end of the 20th century, Chinese universities lacked a standard curriculum in sociology. However, in July 1999 at the Joint Meeting of National Higher Education Sociology Teaching Steering Committee and Heads of Sociology Departments, ten core subjects for a degree in sociology were identified: introduction to sociology, social research, foreign sociological theories, history of Chinese social thought and sociology, social statistics, introduction to social work, introduction to community studies, social psychology, economic sociology, and social development (Chen 2018: 42).

By the end of the 20th century, around 40 sociology departments operated throughout the country, with departments consisting of more than 3,000 people, as well as more than 400 researchers at various scientific institutions in the country. In 2000 an updated sociology department was opened at Beijing Tsinghua University. In May 2000 the department began to publish the journal, Tsinghua Sociological Review (清华社会学 评论), which raises issues such as the relationship between the state and society in rural China, as well as social transformations in Chinese society. In September 2006 the Research Center for Social

Sciences of China at Peking University was opened, which engages in the study of social issues in Chinese society.

Over time, the scientific interests of Chinese scholars also changed. In the *Chinese Sociological Yearbook 2007–2010*, the following social issues were highlighted: uneven income distribution in China, the income gap between rich and poor, issues of education and medical care, social security and social well-being and the influence of socioeconomic factors on inequality and social injustice (Chen 2011). Based on the data presented in the *Chinese Sociological Yearbook 2011–2014*, it can be said that most of the studies that were conducted at this time were devoted to social stratification and mobility, social ties and social capital, social work and research on consumer society, youth issues, and family and marriage issues (*Chinese Sociology Yearbook 2011–2014* 2016). Also, researchers began to dedicate themselves to studying economic sociology, and in 2014 the first periodical on economic sociology, the yearbook *Studies on Economic sociology in China* (经济社会学集刊), began publication.

In 2016 Xi Jinping delivered a speech urging Chinese scholars to 'accelerate the construction of philosophy and social sciences with Chinese characteristics' (加快构建中国特色哲学社会科学), as well as to renew the long-standing opposition between Western and Chinese social sciences inherited from postcolonial studies. This meant that Chinese researchers were expected to understand the scientific contributions of other countries, but at the same time, remember the legacy of Chinese scientists and implement their contributions through the lens of Marxism (Accelerate the construction 2018). It should be noted that the Chinese government actively supports science and research in China. According to statistics provided by the Organization for Economic Co-operation and Development (OECD), in 1991 China's R&D spending accounted for just 0.72% of its annual GDP. In 2015 this number increased to 2.07%, and by 2020 the government aimed to reach 2.5% R&D spending of GDP (China Power Team 2018).

Today, scholars of Chinese society are interested in a wide range of topics. In order to learn which sociological issues are most important in modern China, one should consult the works published by Social Science Literature Press (社会科学文献出版社). Its most well-known publications are yearbooks, so-called 'Blue Books', which cover social, political, and economic issues relevant in China today. Some of the latest publications include works on social security in China, global warming and greening of urban areas, the consumption model of Chinese society, the relationship between various ethnic groups, rural modernization, gender issues, and social management.

Conclusion

Globalization is pushing scientists to intensively search for a common understanding of modern sociology, its tasks and directions of development. In sociological circles, the notion that the content of sociology is universal and free from the influence of the history and culture of individual countries is becoming increasingly prevalent. The global community of sociologists mainly relies on the contribution of Western scholars, and the core of sociological knowledge is based on categories developed by scholars in the West. Nevertheless, it is incorrect to view the history and achievements of sociology in China only within the context of Western sociocultural tradition. After all, sociology is always connected with the society to which it belongs and which it actively studies. Chinese society is unique and diverse, with a long history and deep traditions. For this reason, Chinese sociology has taken its own path of development, acquiring unique characteristics and qualities along the way.

Note

This research is funded by the Russian Science Foundation under Grant No. 19–18–00246.

References

30 Years of Chinese Sociology 1978–2008 (中国社会学30年(1978–2008)) (2008)/Editor of Zheng, Hangsheng(郑杭生主编), Beijing, China Social Sciences Press (中国社会科学出版社), 2008.

Accelerate the construction of philosophy and social sciences with Chinese characteristics(加快构建中国特色哲学社会科学). Official web-site of the CPC. [Electronic resource]. URL: http://theory.people.com.cn/n1/2018/0103/c416126–29743631.html.

Arkush, R.D. (1981) *Fei Xiaotong and Sociology in Revolutionary China*. Cambridge and London: Harvard University Press.

Chen, G. 陈光金 (2011) 2007–2010年中国社会公平壮况经验研究 (2007–2010 Empirical Research on the State of Social Equity in China), 中国社会学年鉴: 2007–2010 (Chinese Sociology Yearbook: 2007–2010), Beijing, Institute of Chinese Academy of Social Sciences, Social Science Literature Press.

Chen, H. (2018) *Chinese Sociology. State-Building and the Institutionalization of Globally Circulated Knowledge*. London: Palgrave Macmillan.

China Power Team. (2018) Is China a Global Leader in Research and Development? *China Power*, [Electronic resource]. URL: https://chinapower.csis.org/china-research-and-development-rnd/.

China spends $ 279 billion on R & D in 2017 (2018) Science Minister. *Reuters*, [Electronic resource]. URL: https://www.reuters.com/article/us-china-economy-rd/china-spends-279-bln-on-rd-in-2017-science-minister-idUSKCN1GB018.

Chinese Sociological Association (2012a). Major Events in 1982. (中国社会学会。1982年大事记). [Electronic resource]. URL: http://csa.cssn.cn/dsj/201208/t20120813_1966461.shtml.

Chinese Sociological Association (2012b). Constitution of Chinese Sociological Association. (中国社会学会。中国社会学会章程) [Electronic resource]. URL: http://csa.cssn.cn/gyxh/zctl/.

Chinese Sociology Yearbook: 2011–2014 (中国社会学年鉴: 2011–2014) (2016). 中国社会科学院研究所编 (Edited by Institute of Chinese Academy of Social Sciences), Beijing, Social Science Literature Press.

Giri, A.K. (Ed.) (2018) *Social Theory and Asian Dialogues: Cultivating Planetary Conversations*. London: Palgrave Macmillan.

History of the Harvard-Yenching Institute. [Electronic resource]. URL: https://harvard-yenching.org/history.

Hundred Talents Program ('百人计划'简介). Chinese Academy of Sciences.中国科学院. [Electronic resource]. URL: http://www.cas.cn/ggzy/rcpy/brjh/.

Institute of Sociology, Chinese Academy of Social Sciences. 中国社会科学院社会学研究所. 2010. [Electronic resource]. URL: http://sociology.cssn.cn/jgtt/yjjg/201010/t20101027_1977790.shtml. Accessed 17 June 2017.

Liu, D. (2006) From the History of Sports Sociology in China. Vestnik NSU. Seriya: Istoriya, filologiya [Vestnik NSU. Series: History, Philology]. Vol. 5, No. 4. pp. 71–74. (In Russ.)

Lu, X. 陆学艺 (2000). 新中国社会学五十年 (50 Years of Sociology in New China), 中国社会学年鉴(1995–1998) (Chinese Sociology Yearbook (1995–1998)), Beijing, Social Science Literature Press, pp. 37–84.

Merle, A. (2004) *Towards a Chinese Sociology for 'Communist Civilisation': China Perspectives*, [Electronic resource]. URL: http://chinaperspectives.revues.org/801.

Osipova, N.G. (2013) Sociology in the Countries of Asia, Africa and Latin America: Key Figures. Vestnik Moskovskogo universiteta. Seriya 18. Sotsiologiya i politologiya [Moscow State University Bulletin. Series 18. Sociology and Political Science]. No. 4. pp. 37–59. (In Russ.)

Pang, D. (2009) History of sociology in China. *Sociological Studies*. Russian Academy of Science. No. 4 (300). pp. 130–136 (In Russ.)

Porter, R., Porter, T., and Ross, D. (eds.) (2003) *The Modern Social Sciences/The Cambridge History of Science: Volume 7*. Cambridge: Cambridge University Press.

Princeton in Asia (PiA). About us. *Mission*, [Electronic resource]. URL: https://piaweb.princeton.edu/about-us.

Thousand Talents Program ('千人计划介绍'). Official web-site of Thousand Talents Program.千人计划网. [Electronic resource]. URL: https://web.archive.org/web/20190605134918/http://www.1000plan.org/qrjh/section/2.

Usov, V.N. (2004) *Chinese Beria Kang Sheng*. Moscow: OLMA-Press. (In Russ.)

Wang, K. 王康 (1989) 中国大陆社会学的重建. 庆祝中国大陆社会学恢复重建十周年 (Reconstruction of Sociology in Mainland China. Celebrating the 10th Anniversary of the Reconstruction and Reconstruction of Sociology in Mainland China), 中国社会学年鉴1979–1989 (Chinese Sociology Yearbook 1979–1989), Beijing, China Encyclopedia Press.

Xie, Q., and Freeman, R.B. (2019) Bigger Than You Thought: China's Contribution to Scientific Publications and Its Impact on the Global Economy, *China & World Economy*. Vol. 27, No. 1. pp. 1–27.

Zheng, H., and Yingsheng, L. 郑杭生，李迎生 (2003) 中国社会学史新编 (New Edition of the History of Chinese Sociology), Beijing, Higher Education Press.

28

The differential cosmopolitan Chineseness in Australia's Chinese ethnic media

Fan Yang

Introduction

Media have long been identified as a potent factor in national and cultural identity construction. According to Anderson (1983), print capitalism plays a key role in unifying people in the imagined community of the nation-state, through the way of forging a sense of nationhood, a collective memory, and national identity. With the intensified process of globalization and *human flows*, media are of critical importance in the maintenance and reconfiguration of this process (Subervi-Vélez 1986; Appadurai 1990). People in transnational movements carry with them a collective memory of their homeland to the host society. While settling down in their new home, migrants maintain their ties with their homeland through transnational economic, social, cultural, informational, and political participation enabled by legacy media and new information and communication technologies, ranging from newspapers, traditional telephony to satellite TV and TV boxes, internet and social media platforms (Sinclair & Cunningham 2000, Cunningham 2001; Sun 2002; Shi 2005; Couldry & Dreher 2007; Yin 2015; Martin 2018). Ethnic media which are generally defined by media produced by and serve ethnic migrant communities, therefore, are often thought of as quaint services for nostalgic migrants, which are responsible for the maintenance of ethnic identity through segregating the media sphere from mainstream media ecology, and thus bridge ethnic culture transnationally through various ways of media representation and storytelling (Hall 1996; Aragrande 2018: 76).

Chinese ethnic media studies are normally discussed while being situated in the context of broader Chinese migrant communities. Developed from an ongoing research project which focuses on the content production practice of digital Chinese-language media, this chapter particularly concerns about the construction of Chineseness in Chinese ethnic media in Australia. Specifically, it explores the very question of 'Chineseness', which has normally been taken for granted in many academic inquiries into Chinese-language media. It asks how the concept of Chineseness has been constructed and represented in the course of Chinese-language media development. The analysis is informed by the data coming from two sources, including the review of literature on Chinese-language media in Australia, and the analysis on the first-generation Chinese newspaper in Australia which was established in the 1850s in Victoria during the Gold Rush.

DOI: 10.4324/9780429059704-33

Started in the 1850s, Chinese ethnic media or Chinese-language media (transliterated as *huaren meiti*) in Australia is contingent on the way in which large scale of migrants who identify themselves as Chinese cultural ancestry established their new homes in Australia and have been historically recognized as part of Australia's ethnic minority communities. Despite the increasing diversities in demographic compositions within Chinese migrant communities, people of Chinese ancestry, or even broadly Asian ancestries, are normally generalized as 'Chinese' migrants. This singular English word 'Chinese' cannot fully capture its diverse cultural meanings, and political and ideological connotations that are defined by migrant communities and may even cause confusion in the sense of what being Chinese stands for.

In Chinese, in both the spoken and the written language, many terms are used to describe racial, cultural, regional, ethnical, and national varieties of people from China, for example, *zhongguoren* (Chinese people), *zhonghua minzu* (Chinese ethnicity), *huaren* (Chinese), *huaqiao* (people of Chinese ancestry living in non-Chinese countries), *tangren* (people of southern Chinese), *hanren* (Han Chinese) and so on (Wu 1991: 159). One singular term cannot grasp the complexities of Chinese identity. Therefore, suggested by many scholars who demonstrate their interest in researching on the nuance of Chinese identities, the understanding of Chineseness should be situated in the context of political histories inside and outside China (Wu 1991; Ang 1994; Chun 1996). While the objective of this chapter is not centred on the idea of Chineseness in general, it is more interested in discussing the situation of Chineseness in the context of Chinese ethnic media in Australia, which is drawn upon and reflects on the Chinese identities embedded in Australia's Chinese ethnic groups.

By referring to the general recognition of ethnic media, contemporary Chinese ethnic media in Australia are here defined as media produced within Chinese migrant groups to serve media consumption needs and commercial interest of Chinese ethnic communities in Australia. Specifically, they include Chinese-language newspapers, broadcasting services, films, television programmes, news websites and most recently WeChat Official Account which is the information broadcasting function on WeChat that is taken up to disseminate news stories. Most of them were established by Chinese media entrepreneurs in order to provide news information and commercial opportunities to diasporic communities in Australia. This definition of Chinese ethnic media is not uncontested. The concept of ethnic media can be easily interchangeably used with terms such as diasporic media, ethnic minority media, minority media, and alternative media. In some circumstances, non-English programmes in the West such as the British Broadcasting Corporation (BBC) and Australia's Special Broadcasting Service (SBS) can be classified into the broader category of ethnic media. Second, the idea of Chinese has been vaguely defined. It has been used to indicate the ethnicity and cultural heritage whereas political connotations have been overlooked. In this chapter we discuss the aspect of Chineseness that is constructed by Chinese ethnic media by teasing out how Chineseness has been developed and shaped through the historicization of Chinese-language media in Australia.

To follow this research agenda, we examine the development of Chinese ethnic media from the first documented Chinese-language newspaper *The English and Chinese Advertiser* to the recently popularized WeChat Official Accounts. This documentation of its development trajectory demonstrates how Chinese ethnic media influence the passing-on of ethnic identity from self-identified Chinese to non-Chinese for an entire ethnic group in Australia. On the premise of this, this chapter intends to respond to the series of questions: What is the Chineseness in Chinese ethnic media in Australia? How has Chineseness been constructed throughout its development? And what are the factors that contribute to the construction of Chineseness in the media sphere?

I contend that the idea of Chineseness in Chinese ethnic media is inherently a contested, historically 'malleable' field and is increasingly dictated by commercial and political imperatives due to its precarious nature. It is not a static concept but rather dynamic and inevitably various. It has been driven by Chinese ethnic media organizations in responding to their media consumers, media makers, advertisers, and institutions that provide financial sponsorship outside Australia. At the very beginning of its development, to include as many consumers and advertisers as possible, Chinese media organizations have constructed, what I hereby adopt the term 'cosmopolitan Chineseness' (Yue 2012: 104; Goh 2015; Sun & Yu 2016). Later, with the arrival of migrants coming from mainland China, the financial sponsorship provided by Beijing and the recent expansion of Chinese social media WeChat, cosmopolitan Chineseness changes its meaning and is destabilized by Chinese cultural chauvinism. Many Chinese-speakers have been absorbed into a homogeneous Chinese ideology through media technologies, despite their diverse cultural backgrounds.

To further explicate this argument, this chapter is organized according to the historical development of Chinese ethnic media in Australia. The timeline is classified into four stages which are marked by significant structural changes in both China and Australia. I start with the history of Chinese ethnic media by tracing back the first Chinese-language newspaper during Gold Rush. The second phase of its development indicates Chinese ethnic media in the period from the 1970s to the early 2000s with the abandonment of White Australia policy along with the establishment of multiculturalism, China's Reform and Open-up policy in 1978 and Tiananmen Square incident in 1989. In this period, Australia witnessed a boom in Chinese-language newspapers, broadcasting services, bullet board system, and news websites. The third stage is marked by the timeframe from early 2000 to early 2010 thanks to China's media 'Go Out' policy (transliterated as *Zouchuqu Zhanlve*) proposed in 1999 walking hand in hand with the increasing recruitment of international students as skilled migrants in Australia since the mid-1990s to the present. This shifted the paradigm of Chinese ethnic media towards their content and financial reliance on the media in mainland China. The fourth stage is characterized by the recent global expansion of Chinese social media substantiated by China's Internet Plus policy in 2013, and it signposts another change in the paradigm when Chinese ethnic media intersect with social media platform developed in mainland China.

It should be noted that the chronological development of the argument does not suggest the linear evolvement of Chinese ethnic media because some media forms can coexist with each other. Neither does it imply the technological advancement of some media forms is meant to replace the previous one. Through the historicization, the intention is to understand how Chineseness has been shaped by ethnic media organizations and what are the factors that tend to shape this pliable field. Ultimately, this chapter hopes to invite us to think reflexively on the differential politics of Chineseness when we discuss Chinese ethnic media or generally Chinese diasporic communities overseas.

The beginning: Chinese-language newspapers during the Gold Rush in Victoria

The first Chinese-language newspaper emerged under the circumstances when Chinese communities in Ballarat, a region in a British settler colony, Victoria, that used to be famous for its gold wealth during the 1850s, were treated with resentment, suspicion, and violence from the host society (Reeves & Mountford 2011: 112). Chinese gold miners were generally perceived as a great threat by the British colonial government and the European miners. This hostility walked hand in hand with policy disadvantages against Chinese gold miners. At that time, Chinese migrants were burdened with mining taxes, Chinese head taxes, protection tickets, and business licenses. These actions were purposed to confine the future emigration from China (Byrans 2013: 127; Wang & Ryder 1999: 300).

With the initial intention of assisting Chinese gold miners to adapt to the new life in Ballarat and thus integrating them in the European community, Robert Bell who was a scientist and linguist from Britain with Chinese-language capacity founded one of the earliest documented Chinese-language newspapers in Australia and initially named it *The Chinese Advertiser* (transliterated as *Tangren Xinwen Zhi*, and later *Fan Tangren Xinwen Zhi*) in April 1856 (Wang & Ryder 1999). The name of the paper was later changed to *The English and Chinese Advertiser*, transliterated as *Yingtang Zhaotie* in Chinese, marking the shift from a Chinese-language newspaper to an English-Chinese bilingual newspaper, in the hope of promoting cross-cultural understanding between the Chinese and the broader European community (Wang & Ryder 1999: 300).

This paper was published on a weekly basis and was placed in local grocery stores free for access. Due to the lack of people who had language proficiency and literacy, Bell acted as a manager, editor, interpreter, and also printer of the newspaper. Following the research trajectory of Wang and Ryder in 1999, I paid a visit to the State Library of Victoria in Melbourne in February 2019, where two copies of the original paper are stored.

Figures 28.1 and 28.2 give us some insights into the earliest Chinese-language newspaper in Australia. It is documented that *The Chinese Advertiser* changed its names three times from 唐人新文纸 (*Tangren Xinwen Zhi*) to 番唐人新文纸 (*Fan Tangren Xinwen Zhi*) and finally settled as 英唐招贴 (*Yingtang Zhaotie*) whose English name was ultimately changed to *The English and Chinese Advertiser* in accordance. It is interesting to see what Robert Bell was attempting to achieve through the name changes. *Tangren*, the indication of people from the Tang dynasty, was a conventional use by southern Chinese emigrants sailed from mainland China and engaged in business and export industry in Southeast Asian countries (Kuhn 1997). Therefore, *Tangren* designated Hokkien and Cantonese dialect groups and was later used to label overseas Chinese coming from Canton, Fujian and southeast Asian countries who later settled in the West including countries such as the United States and Australia. *Fan Tangren* is a more specific indication of *Tangren* resettled at foreign states. *Fan* (番) used to indicate the perceived culturally inferior barbarians such as *Hufan* (胡番) since ancient times by the Chinese. This was informed by the traditional view of Chinese being located at the centre of the universal existence, which was surrounded by barbarians at peripheries, the *Yi* (夷) in the east, the *Di* (狄) in the west, the *Rong* (戎) in the north and the *Man* (蛮) in the south (Wu 1991: 161). This has always been an important aspect of being Chinese, from which it is believed the name of China, the middle kingdom, was derived. This anthropocentric view is based on a deep-rooted sense of belonging to a unified civilisation that boasts several thousands of years of uninterrupted history. *Fan Tangren* reinforces the image of a certain group of Chinese – one who is Chinese but partly alienated from China and often associated with the West or associated with Southeast Asian countries. Such a sense of unity and continuity was common in Gold Rush among Chinese gold miners who moved overseas to settle among non-Chinese people (Wu 1991: 160). By changing the name from 唐人新文纸 (*Tangren Xinwen Zhi*) to 番唐人新文纸 (*Fan Tangren Xinwen Zhi*), this indicated an attempt to form a more specific, inclusive and strong

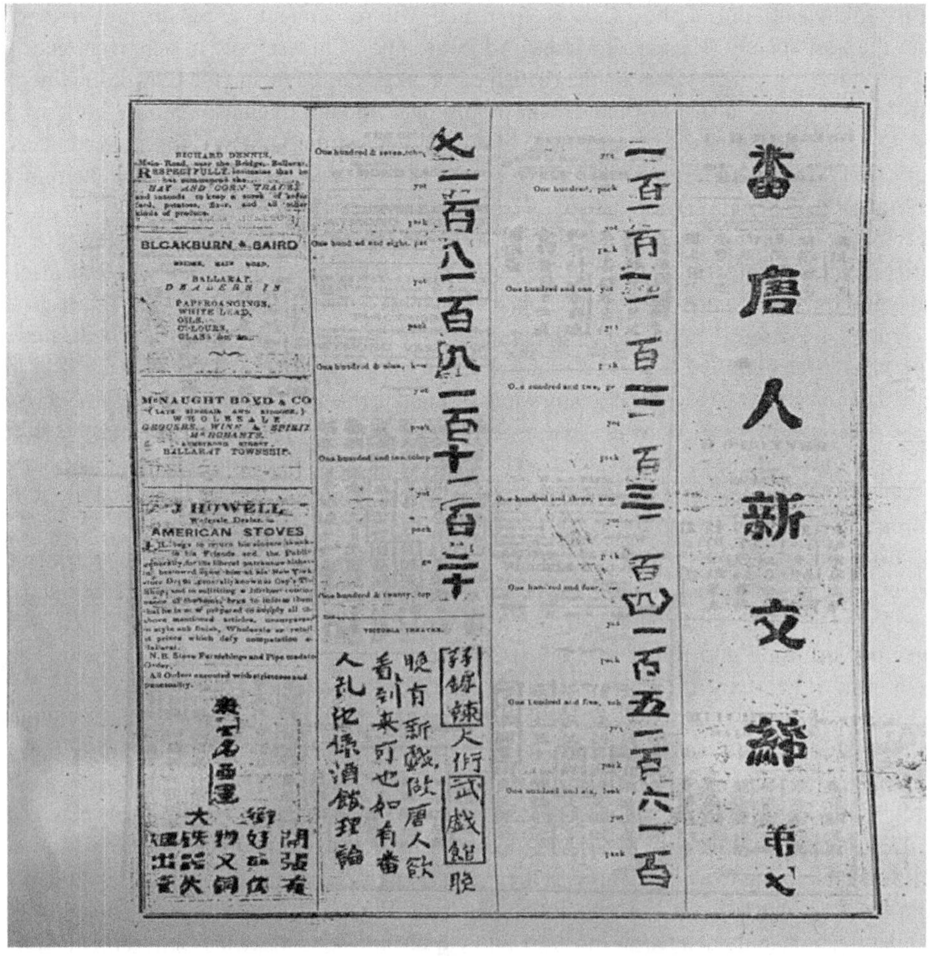

番唐人新文紙

第七

One hundred, pack

One hundred and one, yut

One hundred and two

One hundred and three

One hundred and four

One hundred and five

One hundred and six

One hundred & seven

One hundred and eight

One hundred & nine

One hundred and ten

One hundred & twenty

VICTORIA THEATRE.

RICHARD DENNIS,

Main Road, near the Bridge, Ballarat,

RESPECTFULLY intimates that he has commenced the

HAY AND CORN TRADE

and intends to keep a stock of hay, potatoes, flour, and all other kinds of produce.

BLACKBURN & BAIRD

BALLARAT,

DEALERS IN

PAPERHANGINGS,

WHITE LEAD,

OILS,

COLOURS,

GLASS &c. &c.

McNAUGHT BOYD & CO

WHOLESALE

GROCERS, WINE & SPIRIT

MERCHANTS,

BALLARAT TOWNSHIP.

J. HOWELL,

Wholesale Dealer in

AMERICAN STOVES

N.B. Stove Furnishings and Pipe made to Order.

All Orders executed with despatch and punctuality.

Figure 28.1 One of the first issues of *The Chinese Advertiser*. This photocopy was taken by the author at the State Library of Victoria.

Chinese-oriented identity outside the home country when encountering challenges coming from European communities.

The intention of operating a Chinese-language newspaper oriented from helping Chinese gold miners adapt their lives to the new host society to commercializing Chinese migrant communities. This transformation was indicated by the name and content change that laid its emphasis on the ‘advertising’. To accommodate more Chinese newcomers in the second half of the 1850s and European communities into this Chinese ethnic economic sphere, the reception scale of *The Chinese Advertiser* needed to be expanded beyond Chinese communities. This was marked by a transformation in its English name shifting towards *The English and Chinese Advertiser* (transliterated as *Yingtang Zhaotie*, 英唐招贴). This action of name-change symbolized a broadening Chinese market in Ballarat and the ever-increasing commercial opportunities that the European began witnessing and exploiting. Since then, European merchants and businesses were included in Chinese ethnopolis.

The English and Chinese
ADVERTISER.

英唐招帖

3RD. YEAR — NO. 87 SATURDAY JUNE 5 1858 GRATIS

THOMAS SLATER

J. R. GRUNDYS

R. DAVIDSON

Figure 28.2 The English and Chinese Advertiser. This photocopy was taken by the author at the State Library of Victoria.

Based on the remaining original copies of the paper and the online digital archives, *The English and Chinese Advertiser* printed content can be classified into three genres including marketing materials and advertisements that occupied most of the space in the paper, news and policy announcements, and educational and informational content. For marketing purpose, *The English and Chinese Advertiser* predominantly served for the demand for horse selling, timber, gold, clothes, groceries, tobacco, opium, and currency exchange service. They also displayed a small number of translations of government notices and transportation notices from English to Chinese and other informational content such as Bible learning and English learning to accommodate Chinese migrants into the British colonial society. The readthrough of *The Chinese Advertiser* and *The English and Chinese Advertiser* led to the realization that it was the pan-Chineseness or the 'cosmopolitan Chineseness' that was created by the first Chinese-language newspaper. It bridged the gaps among different regional, linguistic, generational, and socioeconomic sub-Chinese groups. It, to some extent, demonstrated the founder, Robert Bell's desire to meet all the needs of different generations, ages and cultural subgroups. The emergence of Chinese ethnic media, as a cultural broker or intermediaries between the European and the overseas Chinese, was purported to bridge and monetize the cultural difference by mediatizing the European business enterprises with the Chinese enclave market sphere. The discursive and original mission of the first Chinese-language paper – integrating Chinese migrants, was premised upon the commodification of the Chinese communities in Ballarat.

In August 1858, *The English and Chinese Advertiser* stopped issuing its weekly passes due to the lack of financial incomes and the decline of Chinese gold-seekers in Ballarat caused by a series of restrictive immigration policies imposed by the colonial government (Zhang 2019). Notoriously known as the White Australia policy, the elimination of immigration, primarily Chinese and Pacific Islanders, to Australia led to a significant slowdown of the development of Chinese ethnic media.

Structural changes: Multiculturalism, Open-up and Reform policy

Until the 1940s, the Chinese migration substantiated by the Colombo Plan in Australia continued at a small scale (Yue 2012: 35). The White Australia policy was ended at the end of the 1960s and people who self-identified with the Chinese ancestry were given permission to their migration from Vietnam and Cambodia to Australia. Since then, multiculturalism has been institutionalized and Australia has always been considered to be one of the Anglo-Saxon countries with a high level of sensitivity to multiculturalism and integration.

While recognizing that First Nations people had established their multicultural histories 60,000 years ago prior to the British colonization in the 17th century, there had been more than 380 indigenous tribes and 250 distinct languages in Australia. The governmental presentation of multicultural policies in a speech entitled 'A Multi-Cultural Society for the Future' delivered by the Minister for Immigration Al Grassby in 1973 recontinued the multicultural framework and symbolized the institutionalization of multiculturalism in Australia. Later in December 1978, with the introduction of *Open-up and Reform Policy*, the paradigm of Chinese migrant communities in Australia started being changed. In the aftermath of 1989, the Tiananmen amnesty migration enabled the first large group of new Chinese migrants from mainland China to come to Australia and obtained their right to stay in the country (Gao 2006; Yue 2012: 35; Ang 2014: 1187). More and more people from mainland China embarked on their journey to Australia. Therefore, Chinese migrant communities in Australia have been exposed to more diversities and more dynamic nature in terms of cultural identifications in the group of Chinese migrants. The dynamic nature existing in Chinese migrant identity echoes Jia Gao's (2006) argument in his research on Chinese students in Australia in the post-Tiananmen era. There has been a 'strategic identity formation' of the students coming from mainland China in the relevant period, argued by Gao. The students not only negotiated the changing stance of the Australian government toward asylum seekers in order to meet its criteria for obtaining the residency in the country but also coped with a series of transformation including numerous changes happening in China that can have an impact on their perceptions of their own identities. The demographic features of Chinese migrant communities continued evolving. From the 1980s onward, new waves of migrants from Hong Kong, Taiwan, Singapore, Malaysia and Indonesia brought different strata of Chinese-identified migrants into Australia (Ang 2014: 1187). This new demographic features within the broader Chinese communities imposed a new challenge on Chinese ethnic media regarding the tailoring of content to cater to the diverse interests of their readers. The variegated backgrounds and trajectories of migrants define the diverse ranges of people who self-identify as 'Chinese' today. Groups of Chinese people from different regional and cultural backgrounds put in the demand for an exponential growth of Chinese ethnic media in Australia.

Chinese ethnic media from the 1970s to the early 2000s

While historicizing Chinese ethnic media in relation to Chinese migrant communities in Australia, Yue (2012: 27) demonstrated an interesting fact that there was a strongly unified news consumption tendency of Chinese communities in Australia that showed a sense of belonging to a 'cosmopolitan Chineseness' despite the distinct Chineseness that migrants from different cultural and political backgrounds enjoyed. Cosmopolitan Chineseness from the 1970s to the early 2000s indicated an international community where Chinese identity was shared by the broader Chinese community globally (Yue 2012). This Chineseness was constructed within their communal networks but beyond their host countries (Sun & Yu 2016: 3). It connoted the imagination of tolerance, openness and hospitality within the Chinese community on top of the cultural and ideological nuances. This happened especially when being confronted with the challenges and injustice coming from the mainstream society such as biased representations of the Chinese migrant community in Australian mainstream media and the exclusion of the Australian job market. The idea of cosmopolitan Chineseness was similar to the pan-Chineseness that was constructed in the Chinese-language newspaper during the Gold Rush. The only difference would be the scale of cosmopolitan Chineseness that could be more extensive than pan-Chineseness which indicated Chinese communities coming from Fujian and Canton regions. The concept of cosmopolitan Chineseness at this stage laid its emphasis on the rise of transnational networks of migrants who were resettled in global cities, post-national social formations created by migrants and diasporic flows.

Since the 1970s, Australia has been a home for multicultural media established by migrant communities and indigenous communities. Under such circumstance, all sorts of Chinese-language media with different ideological and political orientations mushroomed. Some empirical research conducted by Wanning Sun and her colleagues in 2011 has revealed that Chinese migrants in Australia consumed news from various sources and channels, to name a few, *Xin Yimin* (*New Migrants*), *Xingdao Ribao* (*Singtao Daily*), *Hualian Shibao* (*The United Chinese Times*), *Shang Quan* (*Business Circle*), *Dayang Shibao* (*The Great Ocean Times*), *Huaxia Shibao* (*The Chinese Weekly*), and *3CW Chinese Radio*, and so forth (Sun et al. 2011). Beginning in the mid-1990s, Chinese ethnic media engaged with the networked capacity of the internet once left to magazine, newspapers and broadcasting service. A wide range of Chinese-language websites sprang up in order to cater to the needs of diverse niche communities. For example, while Chinatown.com focuses on broadcasting news and information to general Chinese-language users, other information websites have narrower target audiences. Yumcha.com serves business professionals and yeeyi.com has a specific focus on Chinese international students (Sun et al. 2011: 520). The ideological varieties embedded in Chinese-language media represented a scene that can be concluded as 'a hundred flowers bloom and a hundred schools of thought contend' (*Bai Hua Qi Fang, Bai Jia Zheng Ming*). Despite being exposed to various media forms, Chinese-language newspapers still play a critical role in migrant communities and remained intensely competitive in the ethnic media market.

Chinese ethnic media had historically been playing the role of cultural broker or intermediary which pointed the arrow of Chinese migrant communities towards Australia mainstream society. This can be attributed to at least three factors including the diverse demographic features of the audience, the perception of multiculturalism in migrant communities gravitating toward cultural assimilation and adaptation, and the digital disconnection from the media sphere in the host country. Under the multicultural framework where cultural assimilation was advocated, news stories published by Australian media outlets tended to be more appreciated by Chinese-language media organizations. It was disclosed by the research participants who used to work for Chinese-language newspapers that news translation from English media into simplified Chinese or traditional Chinese, was a primary component of their daily work. Materials that were translated normally spoke to a critical stance on issues in relation to China. For example, *Singtao Daily*, a newspaper established in Hong Kong and launched in Melbourne in the 1980s. The reportage of Tiananmen Square incident oriented toward an anti-Beijing stance (Sun 2005). In the context of ethnic media, translation can always be strategically used by media practitioners in the negotiation of their identity with the Western ideology (Aragrande 2018). It is argued by Aragrande (2018) that while they did not completely agree with the agenda set by the host society, translation became their articulation of how a media worker with a different perspective made sense of an event by re-expressing words in their native language. Therefore, localizing and personalizing the attitude of news reports was peculiar to the news discourse and news translation. This was how strategic identity transformation and nuanced Chineseness were exhibited in Chinese news reports through news translation.

Chinese-language media after the 2000s

Ethnic media have always been struggling with their survival financially. To cut the cost, the news is normally translated from English media outlets; staff members are recruited from new migrant groups who might not have professional experience in journalism and thus are not recognized as journalists by mainstream media. In 2001, as part of the Chinese media 'Go out' strategy (*Zou Chuqu Zhanlve*), China has been using media to promote its view and vision to the wider world and to counter negative images in the West-dominated international media by making a significant investment in Chinese-language media overseas and promoting its own official channel such as China Global Television Network (CGTN) in the West (Edney et al. 2019). This opened new financial opportunities to Chinese-language media overseas. In Australia, Chinese ethnic media have been heavily influenced by China's self-promotion strategy since then. While being sponsored by Chinese government, thereby a close relationship has been formed, most of those Chinese-language media organisations and publications started to shift their news preferences towards Chinese state-sponsored newspapers or are dedicated to reporting issues from the perspective of People's Republic of China (PRC). Some of these Chinese-language media also demonstrate their close connection with Chinese government bodies and engage with activities organized by the embassy of the PRC and state-owned companies (Sun et al. 2011: 142–143). As a consequence, there has been a lack of variety of voices in Chinese-language newspapers in Australia's media sphere. A uniform idea of Chineseness orienting toward the ideology of CCP has since been formulated among Chinese migrant communities.

In the meantime, a series of policies in Australia functioning as a pull factor in migration movements has perpetuated to attract people from mainland China to resettle, work and study. For example, the industrialization of Australia's high education sector worked conjunctively with Australia's skilled migration and its economic needs. The reduced governmental funding to the universities pushed academic institutions to shift the cost burden onto students. While Australian domestic students formed a relatively smaller market, reaching out to the international market helped Australian universities fill this economic void (Welch 2014: 23). In order to gain its competence in terms of the higher education sector among Organisation for Economic Co-operation and Development (OECD) countries especially among those traditional immigration destination states such as the United Kingdom, the United States, and Canada, a loose skilled immigration policy proposed by John Howard government in 1997 (Hugo 2006: 107; Wright 2014) had offered some support to fill the financial gap occurring in the privatization process and gain it competency in the higher education sector. With the promise of settling down through studying, Australia has witnessed a dramatic increase of the enrolment of international students in migration professions such as accounting, Information Technology, engineering, architecture and education, etc (Poyrazli & Grahame 2007; McDowall & Jackling 2010). Driven by the conjunctional forces of education commercialization and skilled migration scheme, students from the People's Republic of China joined the third tide of overseas study (*Liuxue Chao*)[1] after the establishment of new China in 1949 (Yao 2015). Studying a migration profession in Australia has been considered as a pathway for their later settling down in this country. As a consequence, people from mainland China have formed the second-largest migrant community in Australia after the United Kingdom, equivalent to 8.5% of Australia's overseas-born population and 2.5% of Australia's total population, according to the census in 2016 (Australian Government Department of Home Affairs 2019).

The idea of cosmopolitan Chineseness has been destabilized by the changed demographic features of Chinese migrant communities and the Chinese government's self-promotion strategies since then. Chinese ethnic media have reflected this change and generated another new layer of meaning of Chineseness within the media. Compared with the paid propagandistic content offered by the Chinese government with financial sponsorship, advertising was no longer an imperative attraction for some Chinese-language media organizations or potent force to maintain the ideological liberty of Chinese ethnic media in Australia. When making advertising choices, advertisers evaluate both the size and the composition of the readership of the target media outlet. Most of the Chinese-language media had had trouble in presenting themselves as profitable media entities because of the perceived revenue-generating capacity of the target audience (Husband 2005: 467) and make them less attractive to potential patron clients. This financial precarity aspired them for contributing to the vitality of political party or institutions and conveyed news that represented the perspective of mainland China.

Chinese-language media in Australia since then have functioned as a pathway through which Chineseness constructed by PRC was disseminated. The new cosmopolitan Chineseness granted by Chinese ethnic media after the 2000s carried the connotation of modern patriotism or nationalism, making Chinese migrants feel a connectedness with the fate of China as a nation (Wu 1991: 160). The ideological boundary of Chineseness in the media sphere had thus been established through the way that Chinese ethnic media operated and sustained themselves. This revealed the contradictory nature of the cosmopolitan Chineseness, i.e., how can cosmopolitanism be maintained if nationalism was strongly suggested? In actuality, there has been a recognition that cosmopolitanism itself is rooted in cultural particularity (Nussbaum 1996). Cosmopolitan Chineseness, rooted within CCP's propaganda strategy, at that stage did not negate openness to cultural difference or regional difference but form a universalist ideological consciousness, an extension of the national unity, and a sense of moral responsibility that goes beyond the Chinese nation-state (Wu 1991). For example, it is uncovered in Wanning Sun's report in surveying the development of Chinese ethnic media in Australia that in covering the Tibetan issues in 2008, Chinese-language newspapers in Australia predominantly followed the CCP's ideology (Sun 2009). Cosmopolitan Chineseness in the context of Chinese ethnic media since the 2000s gestures towards an ideological movement for building the modern Chinese nationalism, which was sparked by the challenge from the Western world and was later used by the CCP to serve the grand communist revolution narrative and practical needs of the national modernization and civilisation project.

Chinese-language media in the era of WeChat (after 2011)

The expansion of WeChat/Weixin (微信), one of the primary social media platforms developed in Shenzhen, China, extends the scale of cosmopolitan Chinese and consolidates this idea in Australia through its transnational platform governance. Before we understand how WeChat, as a sociocultural medium, inserts ideological impact on Chinese ethnic media, it is necessary to grasp some brief knowledge on how WeChat functions overseas as a platform being regulated in China.

WeChat is one of the primary social media platforms in mainland China, owned by Tencent Holdings. It converges functions including messaging, social networking, user-generated content, financial transactions and services, gaming, short videos and mini-programmes. Growing out of a messaging application, WeChat is now an all-in-one digital infrastructure. The focus of this research is on WeChat Official Accounts (hereafter WOAs, *Weixin Gongzhong Hao*), also known as WeChat Subscription Accounts or WeChat Public Accounts, which is the information broadcasting function on WeChat serving media entities, institutions, governments, individuals, and businesses to disseminate their information. Official Accounts serve a diverse range of users – from relatively well-established traditional media groups, to non-professional and amateur individual bloggers and small-to-medium enterprises and to business enterprises. Like those public accounts on YouTube or Facebook, each of these participants approaches WeChat with their own purposes and aims.

WeChat is now one of the primary sources of news and information not just in mainland China but among Mandarin-speaking communities globally. According to a survey, 97.5% of the Chinese international students in Australia are reported to check WeChat several times a day (Martin et al. 2019: 29). With the capacity of circulating content and influence globally, WOAs provide a new opportunity for Chinese-language media to reach out to broader readership. For most Chinese migrants, in spite of being exposed to various media platforms and channels and enjoying a relatively high level of digital literacy, most of them in Australia continue their news-sourcing habits in China and prefer to access news particularly through WOAs (Martin 2018: 11). Although there is no official estimation of the amount of WOAs focusing on news production and consumption of Chinese migrant communities, the figure is likely to be in the hundreds due to the low threshold to entry.

With an abundant number of groups and individuals engaging in the content production on WeChat, the platform engendered a specific genre of WOAs – news-focused WOAs, that involve in translating news stories published by Australian media outlets from English to Mandarin and disseminating news stories among groups of subscribers who are mostly migrants from mainland China. Their function seems to be familiar to Chinese ethnic media in terms of news translation and circulation among Chinese migrant groups. However, they occupy a tricky emerging space in both local and transnational media ecologies – they are located at the intersection between Chinese ethnic media in Australia and social media in China. While being operated in Australia, news-focused WOAs are influenced by media regulations and ideological forces on WeChat, driven by the Chinese government, with limited attention or influence from the Australian side.

On the Australian side, as opposed to the mainstream media whose practices are monitored by national and regional media regulatory frameworks, these news-focused WeChat Official Accounts tend to escape from Australian Commonwealth media regulation largely due to the language barriers to Australian authorities (Martin 2018). This ignorance is also helped by the hierarchy that is inherently embedded in the relationship between mainstream media and ethnic media. Reporters who work at ethnic media organizations are not normally considered as 'professional journalists'; instead, writers or copywriters are normally the labels that they use to address their professional identity. News information coming from migrant media is not recognized as legitimate sources and sometimes they are being cited without being credited. Because these news-focused WOAs do not work according to detailed protocols in Australia (Martin 2018: 10), they enjoy a significant level of autonomy in terms of setting the stage for commercial initiatives and news production. However, without being supervised by the Australian side, these small media organizations are far from being neutral. China's state censorship of content applies so that even though they are operated in Australia, content producers are aware of self-censorship and tend to avoid publishing topics that are unfavoured by the Chinese authority such as the more recent tension between the United States and Huawei technology company and protests in Hong Kong in 2019.

One may argue that as a platform, WeChat is well known for its "one platform with two memberships" or "one app, two systems" (Ruan et al. 2016) where users located outside China can be out of the regulation loop. WeChat draws its own boundary by segregating their users into 'Chinese users' and 'non-Chinese users' according to the way in which their accounts are registered. This is what I refer to as the "platform citizenship" designated by WeChat. Platform citizenship has less to do with territory, nationality or citizenship in a modern state sense. It is the platform which defines and sketches out its territory of regulation and governance.

For individual or organizational users who register their WeChat Official Accounts with a valid Chinese ID card or a Chinese business license, they are classified into the category of users based in China, regardless the nationality of the user. They must obey platform regulations established for 'Chinese users' which include the restriction of the right to freedom of information. For those who register their account with a non-Chinese business license, they are as assigned a non-Chinese membership. More application fee and a lengthy process of registration can be applied. They are also restricted to a relatively limited amount of readership. The content that they published can only be visible to non-Chinese users who connect their WeChat user account with their non-Chinese mobile number. The exclusivity of WOAs to non-Chinese platform users leads to the fact that most of the Chinese ethnic media in Australia borrowed business licenses from mainland China to make their content accessible to their broader Chinese platform users, despite being located in Australia.

The dominance of Chinese-language media has been taken over by WeChat since 2014 when more and more small-to-medium-sized media organizations and individuals engaged with WOAs. As a consequence, Chineseness is complicated by the crossover between Chinese ethnic media and the transnational platform and skews towards the cosmopolitan Chineseness constructed by mainland China. A new term 'ethno-transnational media' (Martin 2018) has been coined to signpost this encounter between ethnicity and transnationality. Transnationality comes along with the transnational nature of platform and internet, which allows WOAs to organize and distribute content across space and time. It does not simply entail tearing down spatial barriers but also connotates the rescaling of the state governance (Sassen 2006: 345–347). Different from the perception of social media platforms in the West, in which social media are conceived as being independent of the government to serve the public, media platforms in China are perceived as the extension of the authoritarian regime. That is to say, instead of leaning toward liberty, WeChat indicates an obvious state-bounded cosmopolitan Chineseness inscribed in the platform, most visibly, China's system of internet censorship and surveillance.

According to the interviews with media workers with work experience in the industry of news-focused WOAs, to negotiate with reader's interest and the ideology of the platform, issues related to Chinese politics and social affairs are not normally discussed or are translated through the lens of pro-Beijing. Touching on any content that might displease Beijing can cause their accounts to be suspended for months, and thus distance themselves away from commercial opportunities coming from businesses. For most advertisers, the decision of their investment in particular accounts is informed by the speculation and projection of a stable statistics on the readership, clicks, and comments. Commercial imperatives align news-focused WOAs tightly with the Chineseness constructed by WeChat, influenced by mainland China, not only in a political sense but also ethically and morally. Published content must strictly follow the socialist core values (*Shehui Zhuyi Hexin Jiazhiguan*) which are all tightly bound to the CCP's ideology, even though the values can be dynamic and vaguely defined to some extent. For example, in the coverage between Hong Kong and Beijing intensions since April 2019, news-focused WOAs chose to either ideologically align with Beijing or keep silent if they adopted a pro-Hong Kong attitude. The existing connotation of cosmopolitan Chineseness is still in its process of evolving as media workers – Chinese migrants who experience strategic identity transformation – negotiate their own Chineseness, the Chineseness imposed by the platform and the Chineseness inherited from the historical development of migrant communities.

Conclusion

For centuries, the meaning of the Chineseness in Chinese-language media seemed simple and definite. This chapter hopes to bring into attention that Chineseness contains much ambiguity when used to refer to an identity, an ethnicity or a culture. Instead of viewing Chineseness as a homogeneous and essentialist concept, it should be considered as a hybrid identity that is constructed differently in different contexts, and by diverse groups, individuals, and social institutional processes (Kuhn 2006; Wang & Zhan 2019). My discussion focused on the construction of the meaning of Chineseness in Chinese ethnic media in Australia and demonstrates how Chinese ethnic media can be influenced and shaped, and therefore, pass on ethnic identity from Chinese to non-Chinese and from the Chinese government to people settling overseas. I compared the differential politics of Chineseness designated by Chinese ethnic media through the way they are established and identified themselves, the demographic features of their readership, sponsorship and structural forces coming from China and Australia sides. The changes of Chinese ethnic media have reflected the fact that the Chineseness of Chinese ethnic media has been amalgamating, restructuring, reinventing and reinterpreting itself. The seemingly static Chinese identity constructed by Chinese-language media has been in a continuous process of assigning important new meanings about being Chinese overseas.

Acknowledgment

Special thanks to Dr. Luke Heemsbergen for his question at my confirmation and Dr. Robbie Fordyce for always inspiring conversations.

Note

1 Tides of overseas study: the first tide is marked by studying in the former Soviet Union in the 1950s and the second wave is marked by the implementation of Open-up and Reform policy in 1979.

References

Anderson, B. (1983) *Imagined Community: Reflections on the Origin and Spread of Nationalism*, London: Verso.

Ang, I. (1994) 'The Differential Politics of Chineseness', *Southeast Asian Journal of Social Science* 22 Cultural Studies in the Asia Pacific (1994): 72–79.

Ang, I. (2014) 'Beyond Chinese Groupism: Chinese Australians between Assimilation, Multiculturalism and Diaspora', *Ethnic and Racial Studies* 37(7): 1184–1196. DOI: 10.1080/01419870.2014.859287.

Appardurai, A. (1990) 'Disjuncture and Difference in the Global Cultural Economy', *Theory Culture Society* 7: 295–310.

Aragrande, G. (2018) *Multilingual Journalism, News Translation and Discourse: Converging Methods, Converging Theories*. Doctoral Dissertation. Bologna: University of Bologna.

Australian Government Department of Home Affairs (2019) 'Country Profile—China', retrieved from https://www.homeaffairs.gov.au/research-and-statistics/statistics/country-profiles/profiles/china (accessed January 21, 2020).

Bryans, D. (2013) 'A Tolerable Interpreter: Robert Bell and the Chinese on the Ballarat Goldfields', *La Trobe Journal* 92(December):126–143.

Chun, A. (1996) 'Fuck Chineseness: On the Ambiguities of Ethnicity as Culture as Identity', *Boundary 2* 23(2): 111–138.

Couldry, N. & Dreher, T. (2007) 'Globalisation and the Public Sphere', *Global Media and Communication* 3(1): 79–100. DOI: 10.1177/1742766507074360.

Cunningham, S. (2001) 'Popular Media as Public "Sphericules" for Diasporic Communities', *International Journal of Cultural Studies* 4(2): 131–147.

Edney, K., Rosen, S. & Zhu, Y. (2019) 'Introduction', in K. Edney, S. Rosen & Y. Zhu (eds) *Soft Power with Chinese Characteristics: China's Campaign for Hearts and Minds*, Abingdon: Routledge, pp. 1–20.

Gao, J. (2006) 'Migrant Transnationality and Its Evolving Nature: A Case Study of Mainland Chinese Migrants in Australia', *Journal of Chinese Overseas* 2(2): 193–219.

Goh, D.P.S. (2015) 'Elite Schools, Postcolonial Chineseness and Hegemonic Masculinities in Singapore', *British Journal of Sociology of Education* 36(1): 137–155. DOI: 10.1080/01425692.2014.971944.

Hall, S. (1996) 'Introduction: Who Needs Identity', in S. Hall and P. du Gay (eds) *Questions of Cultural Identity*, London: Sage, pp. 1–17.

Hugo, G. (2006) 'Australian Experience in Skilled Migration', in C. Kuptsch & E. F. Pang (eds) *Competing for Global* Talent, Switzerland: International Institute for Labour Studies, pp. 107–154.

Husband, C. (2005), 'Minority Ethnic Media as Communities of Practice: Professionalism and Identity Politics in Interaction', *Journal of Ethnic and Migration Studies* 31(3): 461–479. DOI: 10.1080/1369183050058802.

Kuhn, P.A. (1997) 'The Homeland: Thinking about the History of Chinese Overseas', *The Fifty-Eighth George Ernest Morrison Lecture in Ethnology 1997*.

Kuhn, P.A. (2006) 'Why China Historians Should Study the Chinese Diaspora, and Vice-Versa', *Journal of Chinese Overseas* 20(2): 163–172.

Martin, F. (2018) 'Iphones and "African Gangs": Everyday Racism and Ethno-Transnational Media in Melbourne's Chinese Student World', *Ethnic and Racial Studies*. DOI: 10.1080/01419870.2018.1560110.

Martin, F., Qin, C., Douglass, C.C., Lim, M. & El-Hayek, C. (2019) *Intimate Attitudes, Knowledges and Practices: Chinese-Speaking International Students in Australia*, Melbourne, Australia: Burnet Institute: Medical Research, Practical Action.

McDowall, T. & Jackling, B. (2010) 'Attitudes towards the Accounting Profession: An Australian Perspective', *Asian Review of Accounting* 18(1): 30–49.

Nussbaum, M. (1996) 'Patriotism and Cosmopolitanism', in J Cohen (ed) *For Love of Country? Debating the limits of patriotism*, Boston: Beacon, pp. 155–162.

Poyrazli, S. & Grahame, K.M. (2007) 'Barriers to Adjustment: Needs of International Students within a Semi-Urban Campus Community', *Journal of Instructional Psychology* 34(1): 28–45.

Reeves, K. & Mountford, B. (2011) 'Sojourning and Settling: Locating Chinese Australian History', *Australian Historical Studies* 42(1): 111–125. DOI: 10.1080/1031461X.2010.539620.

Ruan, L., Knockel, J., Ng, J.Q. & Crete-Nishihata, M. (2016) 'One App, Two System: How WeChat Uses One Censorship Policy in China and Another Internationally', *The Citizen Lab*, retrieved from https://citizenlab.ca/2016/11/wechat-china-censorship-one-app-two-systems/ (accessed January 6, 2020).

Sassen, S. (2006) *Territory, Authority, Rights: From Medieval to Global Assemblages*, New Jersey: Princeton University Press.

Shi, Y. (2005) 'Identity Construction of Chinese Diaspora, Ethnic Media Use, Community Formation, and the Possibility of Social Activism', *Continuum: Journal of Media and Cultural Studies* 19(1): 55–72. DOI: 10.1080/1030431052000336298.

Sinclair, J. & Cunningham, S. (2000) 'Go with the Flow: Diasporas and the Media', *Television & New Media* 1(1): 11–31. DOI: 10.1177/152747640000100102.

Subervi-Vélez, F.A. (1986) 'The Mass Media, Ethnic Assimilatino and Pluralism: A Review and Research Proposal with Special Focus on Hispanics', *Communication Research* 13(1): 71–89.

Sun, W. (2002) *Leaving China: Media, Migration, and Transnational Imagination*, Maryland: Rowman & Littlefield Publishers, Inc.

Sun, W. (2005) 'Media and the Chinese Diaspora: Community, Consumption, and Transnational Imagination', *Journal of Chinese Overseas* 1(1): 65–86.

Sun, W. (2009) 'Mission Impossible? Soft Power, Communication Capacity, and the Globalisation of Chinese Media', *International Journal of Communication* 4: 54–72.

Sun, W., Gao, J., Yue, A. & Sinclair, J. (2011) 'The Chinese-Language Press in Australia: A Preliminary Scoping Study', *Media International Australia* 138: 137–148.

Sun, W. & Yu, H. (2016) 'Digital/Social Media and the Chinese Community in Australia', *Media Asia* 43(3–4): 165–168. DOI: 10.1080/01296612.2016.1277826.

Wang, J. & Zhan, N. (2019), 'Nationalism, Overseas Chinese State and the Construction of "Chineseness" among Chinese Migrant Entrepreneurs in Ghana', *Asian Ethnicity* 20(1): 8–29. DOI: 10.1080/14631369.2018.1547875.

Wang, Y. & Ryder, J. (1999) 'An "Eccentric" Paper Edited for the Unwelcome Aliens: A Study of the Earliest Australian Chinese Newspaper, The Chinese Advertiser', *Australian Academic & Research Libraries* 30(4): 300–312. DOI: 10.1080/00048623.1999.10755103.

Welch, A. (2014) 'Be Careful What You Wish For: Pending privatisation of Australian Higher Education', *International Higher Education* 77(Fall): 22–24.

Wright, C.F. (2014) 'How Do States Implement Liberal Immigration Policies? Control Signals and Skilled Immigration Reform in Australia', *Governance: An International Journal of Policy, Administration, and Institutions* 27(3): 397–421.

Wu, D.Y. (1991) 'The Construction of Chinese and Non-Chinese Identities', *Daedalus* 120(2): 159–179.

Yao, S. 姚蜀平 (2015) '中国现代化历程中的十次留学潮' (Ten Waves of Study Overseas in China's Modernisation History), 科学文化评论 (Science and Culture Commentary) 2: 43.

Yin, H. (2015) 'Chinese-Language Cyberspace, Homeland Media and Ethnic Media: A Contested Space for being Chinese', *New Media & Society* 17(4): 556–572. DOI: 10.1177/1461444813505363.

Yue, A. (2012) 'Mobile Intimacies in the Queer Sinophone Films of Cui Zi'en', *Journal of Chinese Cinemas* 6(1): 95–108.

Zhang, C. 张冲天 (2019) '【口述历史】巴拉瑞特的华人故事（二十六）' (Oral History: The History of Chinese in Ballarat (26)), retrieved from http://www.au123.com/literature/cities/20190614/490031.html (accessed December 26, 2019).

29

The cultural meanings of home ownership for China-born migrants in Australia

Christina Y. P. Ting, Iris Levin, and Wendy M. Stone

Introduction

In many Western countries, home ownership is entrenched in policy and cultural narratives as a means of securing both a home and a financial asset base (Arundel & Ronald 2020). Owning a home is not only about the possession of a physical object but also the experience of home ownership. For the past two decades, studies have examined various home ownership differences and similarities in diverse countries (e.g., Azevedo et al. 2016; Burke et al. 2020; Wind & Dewilde 2018), or the effect of culture on home ownership experiences of various communities living in one country (e.g., Marcen & Morales 2020; Zorlu et al. 2014). Yet, there is inadequate literature on the cultural meanings of home ownership and what home ownership means for people who live in one country and then migrate to another.

Australia is a nation of home ownership, with 67% of residents owning a home, including many migrants (ABS 2017a). In 2018, migrants made up 29% of Australia's population of just under 25 million. Out of 7.3 million migrants, the 651,000 migrants from China made up the second-largest group of overseas-born residents (2.6%) (after England at 4%) (ABS 2019). About 64% of China-born migrants owned their home in Australia (23% outright and 41% with a mortgage) (id. 2016). In 2016, Melbourne had 156,000 migrants from mainland China, comprising 3.5% of Melbourne's population of almost 5 million (ABS 2018a). Within this context, we aim to explore these questions: What are the cultural meanings of home ownership for China-born migrants in Melbourne, Australia? Have these meanings changed before and after migration?

Following the introduction, we draw on scholarship on cultural capital to understand the cultural meanings of home ownership of China-born migrants before and after their migration to Australia and settlement in Melbourne. We then present the context of migration from China to Australia and the settlement of these migrants in Australia and in Melbourne. The methods section describes the two datasets we draw on in this chapter, which are taken from two separate research projects. In the findings section, we unravel the cultural meanings of home ownership for China-born migrants before migration in China and after migration to Australia, as understood through the lens of Bourdieu's concepts of cultural capital and habitus. In our conclusions we discuss the importance of the findings for policy and options for further research in a COVID-19 context.

 DOI: 10.4324/9780429059704-34

The cultural meanings of home ownership

Home ownership has been studied extensively in many countries around the world, with research examining local and global trends, as well as drivers and barriers that shape the reach and distribution of home ownership in various societies, often in comparative studies (e.g., Azevedo et al. 2016; Yates & Bradbury 2010; Wind & Dewilde 2018; Wood et al. 2017). Several studies have examined the intersection of migration, culture, and home ownership, including, for example, disparities in home ownership for different ethnic groups in the Netherland (Zorlu et al. 2014), the effect of culture on home ownership in the United States (Macren & Morales 2020), the impact of migration status on home ownership in Australia (Chua & Miller 2009), and home ownership as a measure of migrant integration in the United States (Schoenholtz 2005).

Yet, very few studies have examined the cultural meanings of home ownership for migrants before and after migration. An exception is Pulvirenti (1997), who focused on the home ownership significance for Italian migrants in Australia. In her study, Pulvirenti revealed that before migrating to Australia, the desire for home ownership was linked to participants' family homes in Italy. Family homes belonged to their families for generations, and represented family values, unity, self-sufficiency, and independence, although for the younger generations living in them, those who later migrated to Australia, they represented a lack of privacy, lack of independence, and overcrowding. After migration, home ownership represented for participants their ability to provide for their own families and gain independence from their families back in Italy. As Pulvirenti elegantly explains (1997: 33):

> This examination of the experiences of housing shows that home ownership rates can be at least in part, attributed to culture. But it is not a culture that emerges from some innate 'Italian-ness' transported from Italy through international migration. Rather, it is a culture which was and is continually created and recreated through the every-day experiences of that migration and the settlement process that follows it.

To our knowledge, there has been little focus on the cultural meanings of home ownership for migrants from China, the second-largest migrant group in Australia. Following Pulvirenti, and to reveal the cultural meanings of home ownership for migrants in this study, we draw on Bourdieu's theory of practice and his concepts of cultural capital and habitus. Understanding these concepts in this context can help expose the hidden meanings of practices around home ownership among China-born migrants in Australia.

Bourdieu's concepts of cultural capital and habitus

Over many years, French philosopher and sociologist Pierre Bourdieu has developed a theory of practice in which he coined the terms *habitus* and *symbolic capital* (1977, 1984, 1990, 2005). His development of the habitus as 'a system of durable and mostly unconscious bodily dispositions' which shapes human behaviors has been a significant contribution to the analysis of social practices (Noble 2013: 343). For Bourdieu, habitus is 'a system of predispositions acquired through the process of socialization' (Tabar et al. 2010: 17), in which the symbolic capital operates and which leads to the internal embodiment of social structures such as class, gender, and race (Levin 2018). The social field is the arena in which the symbolic capital and habitus operate.

Symbolic capital, as developed by Bourdieu, includes economic capital, social capital, and cultural capital, all of which can change form and convert from one to the other. *Cultural capital* itself can exist in three forms of capital: embodied capital, referring to the 'long-lasting dispositions of the mind and body' (e.g., accent, bodily behaviors); objectified capital, referring to cultural assets (e.g., dress, accessories, cars, an art collection); and institutional capital, referring to educational qualifications (Bourdieu 1984: 47).

According to Bourdieu (1977: 83), habitus represents 'a past which survives in the present and tends to perpetuate itself into the future by making itself present in practices structured according to its principles' (from Silverstein 2004: 557). Bourdieu (2000:161) later put forward that:

> habitus changes constantly in response to new experiences. Dispositions are subject to a kind of permanent revision, but one which is never radical, because it works on the basis of the premises established in the previous state. They are characterized by a degree of constancy and variation.

Noble (2013: 343) calls this 'migrating the habitus'. He explains that habitus is not simply the embodiment of sociocultural location (in terms of class, gender, ethnicity). It also has the ability to improvise and change behaviors, speech, and manners as social contexts change. Noble further argues that the 'habitus offers a tool for exploring the interdependence of social determination and human agency, and the relationship between the field-specific nature of competence and the fact that bodies travel across diverse contexts' (cited in Noble 2013: 344).

Cultural capital and habitus in migration studies

Although Bourdieu has never focused on migration or migrants as his subject of study (Erel 2010), his work has been applied to the study of migration in various fields. For example, habitus has assisted geographers to understand the participation of migrants in the Canadian labor market (Romanowski 2003; Bauder 2005; Kelly & Lusis 2006), and the concepts of cultural capital and habitus have been applied to understand practices of migrant families from Hong Kong who send their children to study in Canada (Waters 2006; Zhu 2019) and the social transformation of migrant youth in Australia (Jakubowicz et al. 2014). For example, Ong (1999) studied the importance of cultural capital for Hong Kong migrants in California. She found that migrants from Hong Kong used objectified capital (e.g., expensive clothes and accessories, cars) and institutional capital (e.g., university credentials) to establish themselves in their global networks. Similarly, focusing on experiences around the home, Levin (2018) has applied a cultural capital lens to examine a house owned by migrants from China in suburban Melbourne. She concluded that the house can be understood as a global-middle-class house, as a subcategory of the migrant house.

Cultural scholars have used the concept of habitus to examine practices of migrants expressed through bodily differences, speech and language expressions (Noble 2013; Abdel-Fattah 2016). Noble (2013: 343), for instance, examined the embodied linguistic capacities of an Australian-Lebanese academic through Bourdieu's work on habitus and field, suggesting that through resettlement in a different country, the migrant forms a new set of bodily capacities which, sometimes, never quite become similar to dispositions of those who are native by birth. Similarly, in the study of Lebanese-Australian youth, Tabar et al. (2010) defined 'ethnic habitus' as aspects that refer to the embodied, performative, and affective dimensions, shaping what it means to be a Lebanese-Australian in Australia.

The key aim of this paper is to reflect on Bourdieu's concepts of cultural capital and habitus when examining the meanings of home ownership for China-born migrants in Australia. We aim to show how such meanings have changed between China and Australia, through the lens of what Noble (2013: 343) aptly describes as 'migrating the habitus'.

Context: Migration from mainland China to Australia

Since British settlement, Chinese migrants have been an integral part of Australia's history, arriving for labor-intensive work during the Gold Rush in Victoria (1850s) and NSW (1860s). However, due to the 'White Australia' policy, the number of Chinese immigrants declined from around 37,000 by end of the 1880s to 6,404 in 1947 (Ip et al. 1992; Jupp 1991). When this policy ended in 1973, Asian migration to Australia increased. Immigration from China continued, and by the 1990s, there were approximately 450,000 people of Chinese background in Australia (La Trobe 2019). During the 1990s, the immigration program changed to favour skilled and business migrants (Dharmalingam & Wulff 2008). This led to a large proportion of migrants from China arriving as business migrants who came with capital for investment in Australia. These Chinese migrants also had higher educational qualifications and incomes than the Australian average (Jupp 2002). In the 2016 Census (ABS 2018a), migrants from China were the largest migrant group from a non-English-speaking background (NESB), with 509,555 China-born people living in Australia (2.2%), an increase from 142,780 (0.8%) in 2001. In 2016, migrants from China were relatively young, with a median age of 34, as university students made up 22% of all China-born people in Australia (ABS 2018b).

In 2016, Melbourne had a population of 4,485,221, including an overseas-born population of 1.5 million (40.2%), second to Sydney's (ABS 2018a). There were 155,998 (3.5%) residents who were China-born in Melbourne. Most of these China-born migrants concentrated in the eastern suburbs of Box Hill, Doncaster, and adjoining suburbs.[1]

Methods

In this chapter, we aim to explore the cultural meanings of home ownership for China-born residents in Melbourne and whether these meanings have changed before and after migration. To answer these questions, we combined data from two separate research projects and datasets.

The first dataset (DS1 hereafter) used for this chapter was a survey with 61 China-born migrant participants undertaken in 2010 and 2011. The researcher had face-to-face interviews with the participants using two questionnaires in one sitting. The questionnaires focused on the participants' home ownerships, dwelling contexts such as dwelling size, dwelling type and tenure, and location prior to their migration to Australia and after settling in Australia. Both questionnaires, the letter to residents and the consent form, were available in English and Chinese. The duration of the interviews with the China-born participants ranged between 45 minutes and one hour. The criteria used to assess the participants' eligibility was: country of birth must be mainland China; the year they left China was 1995 or after; aged 18 years or older; and they lived within the eastern suburb of Box Hill, approximately 15 kilometers from Melbourne's CBD. The emphasis on post-1995 migration was to focus on the cohort associated with the major surge in migration of China-born people to Australia. There were 13 male and 48 female participants. Most of the participants were of the 18–44 years age group (48%), 36% of the 45–64 years age group, and 16% 65 years and over.

Various methods were used to recruit the 61 China-born participants, including letter-box drops and approaching multicultural societies, various community clubs, and religious organizations that had connections with China-born residents within the survey areas (see Ting et al. 2018 for a previous publication based on this research).

The second dataset used for this chapter was a set of 12 in-depth interviews (DS2 hereafter) with migrants from mainland China who migrated to Australia and settled in Melbourne during the 1990s and the 2000s. The interviews were conducted in 2007 and 2008. Of the 12 China-born migrants interviewed, nine were women and three were men, and all were married to another migrant from China. Five migrated to Australia during the second half of the 1990s and seven migrated in the first half of the 2000s. Participants were recruited through connections at work and a snowballing process. All the participants were middle-class professionals in their 30s and 40s when they were interviewed, all of them were married and most had children. They all lived in the eastern suburbs of Melbourne around Box Hill.

The interviews took place in participants' homes, which they owned, and lasted for around an hour each. During the interviews, we asked participants about the meanings of their current home for them in Australia, and the meanings of their past homes back in China. We were taken on a tour of the house and yards and took photos. We asked participants to draw their past home in China and explain what made it a home. The questions thus revolved around the feeling of being at home in the house and the settlement process in Australia (see Levin 2012, 2016 for previous publications based on this research).

This study had some limitations. First, the two datasets used for the analysis are from 2007 to 2008 and 2010 to 2011. However, the data is still relevant to the focus of this chapter, as social practices are very slow to change. Second, the data has been collected from a sample of 73 China-born migrant participants. This is by no way a representative sample of China-born migrants in Melbourne. As explained above, participants in the two datasets were recruited through various methods. For DS2 participants, this included the snowball method, meaning some participants shared the same networks. These participants came from a middle-class background, which led to some specific cultural meanings of home ownership.

Findings and discussion: The cultural meanings of home ownership of China-born migrants before and after migration

In this section, we discuss findings from the two datasets regarding home ownership and housing, first in China before migration to Australia, and then after migration, when participants lived in Melbourne. These findings are examined from the perspective of Bourdieu's theory of practice (2000: 161) and his ideas of habitus changes, or as Noble (2013: 343) puts it, 'migrating the habitus'.

Before migration: The cultural meanings of home ownership in China

In China, the preference for home ownership is due to its long tradition of owning one's home. Home ownership is a complex issue in China due to the rapid social and institutional changes from its socialist system to a postsocialist society (Fu 2016). Since its housing reforms in the 1980s, China has become a nation of homeowners. It has one of the world's highest rates of home ownership, with more than 90% now owning their home. Home ownership has become the symbol of success and a mark of adulthood, showing that one is ready for a family. It is now the quintessential Chinese dream (Parkash & Smyth 2019). Owning a home is seen as a 'positional good' for young men, boosting their competitiveness in China's marriage market (Cui et al. 2015; Hu 2013: 952). For Chinese internal migrants and urban locals, owning a home indicates 'their economic, social, and psychological assimilation', thereby impacting on the 'urban residential landscape' (Cui et al. 2015: 188).

Participants in our datasets (DS1 and DS2) lived in large- and medium-sized cities before migrating to Australia. Most lived in the Central Business District (CBD) or in newer suburbs (41.0% and 44.3%, respectively, for participants in DS1). Almost all these participants (93.4%) lived in an apartment in China, and only one participant came from a rural area. Most of the participants in DS1 (26.2%) lived in a home with an area of 100–150 square meters, while 21.3% lived in 50–100 square meters and 14.8% in 250 square meters or larger. In total, more than 60.6% of these participants lived in an area of 150 square meters or less.

In DS2, all 12 participants had lived in apartments; 10 of the 12 participants lived in apartments owned by the workplace or themselves (if it was owned by the workplace, they could buy it later at a lower price), and two others lived in university dormitories. They all appreciated the location of their apartments, their proximity to amenities and services, and liked the centrality and urban nature of their living environments.

Participants who took part in DS1 also shared the same sentiments regarding the convenience of shops within walking distance and the ease and accessibility of public transport to travel from one place to another while living in China. These were indicative in their response to how they travel to shops and services in China. For instance, the majority (41%) walked to shops and services, compared to 16.4% who drove and 16.4% who took public transport.

Most of the participants in DS2 emphasized the lack of space in their apartments in China, whether it was workplace-owned or owned by them. Participants agreed that their former apartments in China were small and inadequate for their family needs. This could be explained by the fact that participants in DS2 were young and at the beginning of their professional careers in China. Moreover, a third of the participants (31.1%) in DS1 indicated that they were living with extended family, due to the common practice of filial piety (i.e., being good to one's parents), an aspect of Chinese culture.

Coming from a communist housing market that has been privatized since the 1980s, participants in DS2 described the practicalities of home ownership in China. Hui[2] described her experience of home ownership back in China:

> in the past few years there has been a reform in housing so everyone can buy a house, apartment, sorry, we have very few houses in China. ... I still lived in an apartment allocated by my work unit. We lived there permanently; we bought it at a price lower than the market price, mm, yes, so we were still in that small apartment. It was too small for us.

Jin explained how, as a young couple, she and her partner bought their apartment in a coastal city in northeast China:

> We did a bit of renovation there ... we bought the house in 1996 I think, that apartment, back then while you purchase a property it's like very plain, very rough, so you have

> to do the renovation by yourself, so we put tile, we put the tile in the bathroom, right so we bought all the appliance like the kitchen stuff, and we bought all the furniture so … so my husband and I did it together, we rearranged the living area, we bought a TV, fridge, everything, is similar to what we did here [in Melbourne].

Jin and her husband did not have spare money to invest in their newly owned apartment, so they fixed it by buying products and materials that were cheap and not of high quality. Jin liked her apartment in China and felt it was suitable for their needs at the time as a young couple. She felt it was 'spacious' with its 74 square meters, was well-located and close to the beach. Jin felt that they had made the apartment their home as they decorated themselves and did the interior design and decorations.

These findings show that for participants in the two datasets, all of whom have left China around the late 1990s and early 2000s, home ownership has become a cultural goal. As postsocialist China has become a nation of homeowners due to the societal and cultural changes in the postsocialism period (Prakash & Smyth 2019; Cui et al 2015), owning a home has become a symbol of objectified cultural capital. The accumulation of cultural capital is done both to gain cultural appreciation in the form of status symbolism, and to be able to convert it to economic capital.

This pursuit of home ownership is portrayed by China-born migrants who have migrated to Australia, reflecting Bourdieu's (1977: 83) notion of habitus that represents the 'past which survives in the present and tends to perpetuate itself into the future'. So, the question remains whether China-born migrants' habitus and practice persisted or changed after their migration to Australia. This question is examined in the next section.

After migration: The cultural meaning of home ownership in Melbourne

Historically, home ownership in Australia has been high compared to other developed countries, facilitated particularly by policies of nation-rebuilding following World War II (Andrews & Caldera Sánchez 2011; Burke et al. 2020). At the 1986 Census, the home ownership rate (both owned outright or owned with a mortgage) was 70.4% at its highest. Since 1986, the home ownership rate has gradually decreased and in the 2016 Census it was 67.1% (Parliament of Australia 2017). The significance of home ownership in Australia is encapsulated in the Australian Dream idea – owning a detached house in the suburbs on a quarter-acre block (Davison 1997; Wiesel et al. 2013). This aspiration was, and still is, prevalent in Australian society, despite it being almost out of reach for many young Australian-born households as well as recently arrived immigrants, due to the unaffordable housing market (Burke, Stone, & Ralston 2014). Most Australian dwellings still include detached housing (73%), despite a recent increase in semidetached, townhouses and apartments (26%) (ABS 2017b).

Upon migrating to Australia, China-born migrants who participated in both DS1 and DS2 settled in established urban areas of the eastern middle-ring suburbs of the Melbourne metropolitan area, where there is a large population of China-born residents. These suburbs are well-connected to the CBD and other suburbs by a freeway and public transport services. These are also middle-class suburbs with good public schools and other amenities (ABS 2018c; Butt 2018).

Cultural capital in the choice of the home

The majority of DS1 participants (62.3%) owned a home, with 29.5% owning a home outright and 32.8% owning a home with a mortgage. Sixty-two percent lived in a detached house and the rest in semidetached houses[3] and apartments. All the participants in DS2 owned their home (80% with a mortgage), as this was a condition to participate in the study. Ten participants lived in detached houses and two lived in semidetached houses. The homes of participants from both datasets were larger in size than their homes in China. This was indicated by 80% of DS1 participants whose homes included a garden. The increase in the size of their living space in Australia was also due to more bedrooms (29.5%) and bathrooms (39.3%). This is matched with DS2 participants' experiences regarding the size of their Australian homes. Here the concept of habitus has changed in the new living environment through its migration. The small apartments participants lived in when in China seemed too small for participants when they were interviewed in Melbourne. The feeling that their homes in China were limited in size seems to have influenced DS2 participants' decisions regarding their housing in Australia.

Both groups shared similar reasons to settle in the eastern suburbs, which included social networks, proximity to services, and access to work. For all 12 participants in DS2, the neighborhood and the surrounding environment were extremely important. Participants in DS2 carefully considered their settlement suburb of choice, based on advice from networks of other China-born friends who lived in the area and recommended it to them. The main factors influencing the choice of suburb were good education facilities in walking distance from the house, proximity to shopping centers, and proximity to the highway to easily reach the city centre, which has the majority of workplaces in Melbourne. Only after these conditions have been met was the house itself considered. The location of the house in a 'good suburb' is also a form of an objectified cultural capital – a house that can later on convert to economic capital with an increased value.

Hui said about her choice of the suburb:

> Yeah, we were told we are very fussy, and because we want first public transport, so we have a bus stop just outside the garden, we need a primary school within a walking distance, we need a shopping centre nearby, and we need to be a double storey house. So with all these requirements, and around the price range, ah, yes, so it's not easy at all (laughs).

This fussiness was also shared by the DS1 participants, who tended to compare the services to those in China, despite the presence of good public transport services in their suburbs. Although they chose to live among other China-born migrants and prefer living in these suburbs over living in inner-city suburbs, some participants found the services inconvenient and expensive. Three other participants shared that they now had to drive more often. The changes in their commuting patterns could be due to the spread of services and shops within the sprawling suburbs of Melbourne, compared to the high-density cities in China.

Despite the recent densification of most Australian capital cities, and in particular Sydney and Melbourne, the majority of Australian residents still live in detached houses, considering it ideal for raising children, in contrast to an apartment. These cultural practices and expectations of owning a home in a convenient location were aptly portrayed by DS2 participants. Lily explained:

> so finally, after about half a year of hunting, finally we found the house here so this is the current house, so this is quite a good house that meets our requirements. Like close to public transportation and quiet and nice area and house you know with plan quite generous with land size and the house itself not so big, 3 bedrooms, but still quite ok

> for us because we are still a couple here, so yeah, in the near future it still fits our needs so that's why we chose that.

The house serves Lily's current needs, but she and her husband already planned for raising a family in the suburb. Despite coming from a cultural norm of apartment living in China, or perhaps because of that background, most China-born participants in both DS1 and DS2 embraced the Australian way of life, choosing to settle in detached houses in the suburbs.

Hui further elaborated on the importance of home ownership in Chinese culture and how that affected her and her husband when searching for a house in Australia:

> in Chinese concept a house is an important part of home, if you have no house you have no root … just to own a house, that was what my husband was thinking about so we started looking for a house as soon as we arrived here, and for many Chinese people to buy a house, even a unit or an apartment is the most important thing for settling down.

The above quote highlights the continuous importance of home ownership in Chinese culture. Thus, what does 'migration of the habitus' mean for these China-born migrants? They have settled in a new host society that allowed them to transfer their past experiences and cultural practices into their adjusted new habitus. They found themselves in the new environment where their aspiration to live in a large, detached house in Australia came true, something that was beyond their reach back in China.

Perhaps their expectations of homes were due to their lived experiences in China and where their previous homes were. These comparisons of their habitus from the past to the current illustrates the 'migration of the habitus' (Noble 2013: 343). Like many other groups migrating to Australia before them, as well as Australian-born residents (Davison 1997; Levin & Fincher 2010; Easthope et al. 2017), China-born participants felt they need to establish themselves and become more 'Australian' through home ownership and living in a big house in the suburbs. This has enabled them to fully integrate into Australian society.

Cultural capital and habitus inside the homes

Migrants from China who participated in DS2 turned their houses into homes in various ways. Mostly, they used the interiors of their houses to make it a home, rather than the external facades. Participants wanted their houses to look 'Australian', without any representations of Chinese culture visible to passers-by, but were happy to represent their culture inside their homes. One source of discontent was the open-space kitchens. Some participants thought that an enclosed kitchen is best for Chinese cooking, but others preferred the modern design they associated with Australia. Shu said:

> many houses have open kitchens but people adapt their habits and don't heat the oil so much. This is what I do – and then keep the open plan. The kitchens here got more space than in China. People normally install a powerful range hood that takes the smell out like in China. But I guess most of the people adapt themselves to the environment, because open kitchens look nicer to them than the closed ones.

This quote demonstrates how China-born participants have changed their habitus and practices in order to adjust to the 'Australian' way of living. But small adjustments and keeping cultural practices in the making of the home was relatively easy since it did not involve major changes to the house construction or design.

There were some common features that were present in all or most of the homes. For example, many participants hung red knots on door frames and handles, as well as Chinese calligraphy or Chinese-style illustrations of landscapes on the walls. All participants had a piano standing in the lounge, with formal family photographs of educational milestones of the children displayed on it. Education and the proximity to educational facilities are extremely important for Chinese families. The piano, thus, has come to symbolize discipline and culture in these homes, both important features of education for Chinese families (Waters 2006). These displays showcase the family's pride and achievements in the academic and financial status to maintain the Confucian practice of '*mien-tzu*' or 'save face' (Wong & Ahuvia 1998). '*Mien-tzu*', a core element of the Chinese thought process, stands for a 'reputation achieved through getting on in life, through success and ostentation' (Hu 1944: 45; Zhang & Baker 2008). That practice is an institutional form of cultural capital through education achievements, as Ong (1999) demonstrates in her study of Hong Kong migrants in California. Another cultural practice migrated to Australian homes was the shoe-stand at the entrance of all houses, as both residents and guests are expected to take off shoes when entering the house.

Most of these items were displayed in the privacy of the homes, while the external facades have not changed much except for a satellite dish connecting to Chinese television, which was present on some of the roofs. These interior physical displays are how the migrants retain their cultural and past experiences of home within the new habitus. The structural buildings of home have embraced the changed habitus of China-born migrants in Australia, adopting the Australian Dream of having a home in the suburbs.

Conclusions

This chapter has shown that the cultural meanings of home ownership for China-born participants in Melbourne have not changed dramatically after migration. Despite the vast differences in the housing forms and locations of China-born migrants before and after migration, the value they have placed on home ownership and the making of the home have not significantly changed. Participants felt that having a home in Melbourne was extremely important for their social and economic integration into Australian society, as a form of objectified cultural capital, while retaining their Chinese culture and values through the adaptation of their habitus. Home ownership has preserved its cultural meanings through the changing of contexts, urban landscapes, and housing markets. Participants had to change their habitus to adapt to living in Australia, through the changing of housing and neighborhood preferences. They have placed importance on home ownership as a form of accumulating cultural capital, which can be converted into both social and economic capital. This is a form of what Noble (2013: 343) called 'migrating the habitus'. In a similar way to Lebanese-Australians who use their bodily manners and performative acts as their 'ethnic habitus' (Tabar et al. 2010), China-born migrants have used the ownership of their homes as a way to preserve their habitus in a changed context.

Our findings have also shown that the importance participants placed on home ownership is a continuation of their practices in China that are part societal and part cultural practices of status, wealth, and maintenance of Chinese culture. These practices of habitus are preserved in Australia. The perpetuation of pursuing the Chinese way of living in their new habitus distinctively shows that these migrants, despite living in a new host society, to a large extent preserve their Chinese cultural practices. This chapter has also shown that their attainment of the Australian Dream somewhat enables them to preserve their cultural practice of '*mien-tzu*'.

Since cultural meanings of home ownership are found to be preserved with the move to a new country by China-born migrants, Australian housing policy will do wisely to harness these cultural practices for its benefit, strengthening home ownership as a tool for this migrant group to integrate into Australian society. An important emerging question for future research into the integration of Chinese migrants to countries such as Australia is how an overall decline in home ownership-opportunity, related to housing affordability pressures, will affect the home ownership pathways for future migrant generations. Further research could examine the links between the cultural meanings of home ownership for China-born migrants and their housing needs within the unaffordable Australian housing market.

With the outbreak of the COVID-19 pandemic recently, the local housing market and economy have been drastically affected. At the global level, international travel has also been impacted by the COVID-19 pandemic, and the political sensitivities over international travels, including those between China and Australia, may have repercussions on international migration. This is shown by the slump in building plans which was at its lowest level in 2020 since early 2013. This slump was predicted to be due to a major drop-off in demand for new dwellings, with immigration having dried up during the COVID-19 pandemic (Janda 2020). It would be interesting to see to what extent the COVID-19 pandemic will impact international migration in general, and specifically, migration from China to Australia, with these migrants' unique cultural capital and habitus.

Notes

1 In Australia, neighborhoods are referred to as suburbs, regardless of their distance from the city center.
2 Names are pseudonyms.
3 This is a house attached to other houses on the same block, usually with a shared driveway and other common areas.

References

Abdel-Fattah, R. (2016) '"Lebanese Muslim": A Bourdieuian 'Capital' offence in an Australian Coastal Town', *Journal of Intercultural Studies* 37(4): 323–338.

ABS. (2017a) 'Snapshot of Australia.' *2071.0—Census of Population and Housing: Reflecting Australia—Stories from the Census, 2016.* Viewed on 27/12/2019 at https://www.abs.gov.au/ausstats/abs@.nsf/Lookup/by%20Subject/2071.0~2016~Main%20Features~Snapshot%20of%20Australia,%202016~2.

ABS. (2017b) *6523.0—Household Income and Wealth, Australia, 2015–16.* Viewed on 09/07/2020 at https://www.abs.gov.au/AUSSTATS/abs@.nsf/DetailsPage/6523.02015–16?OpenDocument.

ABS. (2018a) *2016 Census QuickStats.* Viewed on 08/08/2019 at https://www.abs.gov.au/websitedbs/D3310114.nsf/Home/2016%20QuickStats.

ABS. (2018b) *Media Release: ABS Reveals Insights into Australia's Chinese Population on Chinese New Year.* Viewed on 08/08/2019 at https://www.abs.gov.au/ausstats/abs%40.nsf/mediareleasesbyCatalogue/D8CAE4F74B82D446CA258235000F2BDE?OpenDocument.

ABS. (2018c) 'Socio-economic advantage and disadvantage', *2071.0—Census of Population and Housing: Reflecting Australia—Stories from the Census, 2016.* Retrieved from https://www.abs.gov.au/ausstats/abs@.nsf/Lookup/by%20Subject/2071.0~2016~Main%20Features~Socio-Economic%20Advantage%20and%20Disadvantage~123.

ABS. (2019) *Australia's Population by Country of Birth, 3412.0—Migration, Australia,* 2017–18. Viewed on 19/2/2020 at https://www.abs.gov.au/ausstats/abs@.nsf/lookup/3412.0Media%20Release12017–18.

Andrews, D. and Caldera Sánchez, A. (2011) 'The evolution of home ownership rates in selected OECD countries: demographic and public policy influences', *OECD Journal: Economic Studies*, 2011/1.Viewed no 27/12/2019 at http://dx.doi.org/10.1787/eco_studies-2011–5kg0vswqpmg2.

Arundel, R. and Ronald, R. (2020) 'The false promise of homeownership: homeowner societies in an era of declining access and rising inequality', *Urban Studies*. DOI:10.1177/0042098019895227.

Azevedo, A. B., López-Colás, J. and Módenes, J. A. (2016) 'Home ownership in Southern European countries: similarities and differences', *Portuguese Journal of Social Science* 15(2): 275–298.

Bourdieu, P. (1977 [1972]) *Outline of a Theory of Practice*. Cambridge: Cambridge University Press.

Bourdieu, P. (1984 [1979]) *Distinction: A Social Critique of the Judgement of Taste* (R. Nice, Trans.). Cambridge, MA: Harvard University Press.

Bourdieu, P. (1990 [1980]). 'Appendix: The Kabyle house or the world reversed', in *The Logic of Practice* (pp. 271–283). Cambridge: Basil Blackwell.

Bourdieu, P. (2000 [1997]) *Pascalian Meditations*. Stanford, CA: Stanford University Press.

Bourdieu, P. (2005) 'Habitus', in J. Hillier & E. Rooksby (eds), *Habitus: A Sense of Place* (2nd ed. ed., pp. 43–49). Aldershot: Ashgate.

Butt, C. (2018) *Melbourne's Richest and Poorest Suburbs: How Does Your Area Compare?* Viewed on 20/11/2019 at https://www.theage.com.au/national/victoria/melbourne-s-richest-and-poorest-suburbs-how-does-your-area-compare-20180327-p4z6hi.html.

Burke, T., Nygaard, C. and Ralston, L. (2020) *Australian Home Ownership: Past Reflections, Future Directions*, Australian Housing and Urban Research Institute Final Report No. 328.

Burke, T., Stone, W. and Ralston, L. (2014) *Generational Change in Home Purchase Opportunity in Australia*, Australian Housing and Urban Research Institute with Swinburne University, Final Report no. 232.

Chua, J. and Miller, P. W. (2009) 'The impact of immigrant status on home ownership in Australia', *International Migration* 47(2): 155–192. DOI:10.1111/j.1468–2435.2008.00504.x

Cui, C., Geertman, S. and Hooimeijer, P. (2015) 'Access to home ownership in urban China: a comparison between skilled migrants and skilled locals in Nanjing', *Cities* 50: 188–196.

Davison, G. (1997) 'The great Australian sprawl', *Historic Environment* 13(1): 10–17.

Dharmalingam, A. and Wulff, M. (2008) 'Chinese settlement in Melbourne', *Around the Globe* 4(3): 42–45.

Easthope, H., Stone, W. and Cheshire, L. 'The decline of 'advantageous disadvantage' in gateway suburbs in Australia: the challenge of private housing market settlement for newly arrived migrants', *Urban Studies* 55(9): 1904–1923. DOI:10.1177/0042098017700791

Erel, U. (2010) 'Migrating cultural capital: Bourdieu in migration studies', *Sociology* 44(4): 642–660.

Fu, Q. (2016) 'The persistence of power despite the changing meaning of homeownership: an age-period-cohort analysis of urban housing tenure in China, 1989–2011', *Urban Studies* 53(6): 1225–1243.

Hu, F. (2013) 'Homeownership and subjective wellbeing in Urban China: does owning a house make you happier?' *Social Indicators Research* 110: 951–971.

Hu, H. C. (1944) 'The Chinese concepts of "Face"', *American Anthropologist* 46(1): 45–64.

.id—The Population Expert (2016). *Are Australia's Migrants Home Owners?* Viewed on 26/12/2019 at https://blog.id.com.au/2016/population/demographic-trends/are-australias-migrants-home-owners/

Ip, D., Bethier, R., Kawakami, I., Duivenvoorden, K., and Tye, L. C. (1992). *Images of Asians in multicultural Australia*, A report submitted to the Toyota Foundation.

Janda, M. (2020) 'Coronavirus house price slide worsens, but first home loan deposit scheme attracts new buyers', *Australian Broadcasting Corporation (ABC) News*, 2 July 2020. Viewed on 10/07/2020 at https://www.abc.net.au/news/2020–07–01/house-price-slide-accelerates-as-coronavirus-pandemic-drags-on/12409166

Jupp, J. (1991) *Immigration*. Sydney: Sydney University Press.

Jupp, J. (2002) *From White Australia to Woomera: The Story of Australian Immigration*. Cambridge: Cambridge University Press.

La Trobe University. (2019) 'Asian studies program: Chinese Australia', *Brief History of the Chinese in Australia*. Viewed on 08/08/2019 at https://arrow.latrobe.edu.au/store/3/4/5/5/1/public/education/history.htm#b1

Levin, I. (2012) 'Chinese migrants in Melbourne and their house choices', *Australian Geographer* 43(3): 303–320.

Levin, I. (2016) *Migration, Settlement, and the Concepts of House and Home*. New York: Routledge.

Levin, I. (2018) 'A global-middle-class house? Cultural capital, taste, and kitsch', *Home Cultures* 15(2): 155–179. DOI:10.1080/17406315.2019.1612565.

Levin, I. and Fincher, R. (2010) 'Tangible transnational links in the houses of Italian immigrants in Melbourne', *Global Networks* 10(3): 401–423.

Marcén, M. and Morales, M. (2020) 'The effect of culture on home-ownership', *Journal of Regional Science* 60(1): 56–87. DOI:10.1111/jors.12433

Noble, G. (2013) 'It is home but it is not home': Habitus, field and the migrant', *Journal of Sociology* 49(341–356). DOI:10.1177/1440783313481532

Ong, A. (1999) *Flexible Citizenship: The Cultural Logics of Transnationality*. Durham, NC: Duke University Press.

Parliament of Australia. (2017) *Trends in Home Ownership in Australia: A Quick Guide*. Viewed on 26/12/2019 at https://www.aph.gov.au/About_Parliament/Parliamentary_Departments/Parliamentary_Library/pubs/rp/rp1617/Quick_Guides/TrendsHome ownership.

Prakash, K. and Smyth, R. (2019). 'The quintessential Chinese dream'? Homeownership and the subjective wellbeing of China's next generation', *China Economic Review* 58: 101350. DOI:https://doi.org/10.1016/j.chieco.2019.101350

Pulvirenti, M. (1997) 'Unwrapping the Parcel: an examination of culture through Italian Australian Home Ownership', *Australian Geographical Studies* 35(1): 32–39.

Romanowski, Michael H. (2003) 'Cultural capital of migrant students: teachers' and students' perspectives and understandings', *Rural Educator* 24(3): 40–48.

Schoenholtz, A. I. (2005) 'Homeownership and the Integration of Immigrants in the United States', in Guild, Elspeth, Selm, Joanne van. (eds) *International Migration and Security: Opportunities and Challenges* (pp. 191–216), New York: Routledge.

Tabar, P., Noble, G. and Poynting, S. (2010) *On being Lebanese in Australia: Identity, Racism and the Ethnic Field*. Beirut: Lebanese American University Press.

Ting, C. Y. P., Newton, P. W. and Stone, W. (2018) 'Chinese migration, consumption, and housing in twenty-first century Australia', *Geographical Research* 56(4): 421–433. DOI:10.1111/1745–5871.12316

Waters, J. (2006) 'Geographies of cultural capital: education, international migration and family strategies between Hong Kong and Canada', *Transactions of the Institute of British Geographers* 3(1): 179–192.

Wiesel, I., Pinnegar, S. and Freestone, R. (2013) 'Supersized Australian dream: investment, lifestyle and neighborhood perceptions among "Knockdown-Rebuild" owners in Sydney', *Housing, Theory and Society* 30(3): 312–329. DOI:10.1080/14036096.2013.782890

Wind, B. and Dewilde, C. (2018) 'Home-ownership and housing wealth of elderly divorcees in ten European countries', *Ageing and Society* 38(2): 267–295. DOI:10.1017/S0144686X16000969

Wong, N. and Ahuvia, A. C. (1998) 'Personal taste and family face: luxury consumption in Confucian and Western societies', *Psychology and Marketing* 15: 423–441.

Wood, G. A., Smith, S. J., Cigdem, M., and Ong, R. (2017) 'Life on the edge: a perspective on precarious home ownership in Australia and the UK', *International Journal of Housing Policy* 17(2): 201–226. DOI:10.1080/14616718.2015.1115225

Yates, J. and Bradbury, B. (2010) 'Home ownership as a (crumbling) fourth pillar of social insurance in Australia', *Journal of Housing and the Built Environment* 25(2): 193–211. DOI:10.1007/s10901–010–9187–4

Zhang, H. and Baker, G. (2008) *Think like Chinese*. Sydney: The Federation Press.

Zhu, Y. (2019) 'Mobilizing mothering: Chinese migrant mothers and transnational cultural capital', *Canadian Ethnic Studies Journal* 51(3): 75–93.

Zorlu, A., Mulder, C. H. and van Gaalen, R. (2014) 'Ethnic disparities in the transition to home ownership', *Journal of Housing Economics* 26: 151–163.

30

Dating and mate selection in contemporary China

Examining the role of gender and family

Sampson Lee Blair

Introduction

Young adults in contemporary China often find themselves dealing with the same basic maturational process which their counterparts around the globe also face – finding an intimate partner. In the case of young men and women in China, however, they are doing so in a decidedly unique time in their country's history, a time in which modernization and economic change have dramatically altered the larger culture. In the context of traditional Chinese culture, becoming married and having children, thereby continuing the family's lineage, has been a core expectation (Qi 2014). Throughout its long history, mate selection has largely involved parental control, wherein mothers and fathers would choose a partner whom they considered appropriate and suitable for their daughter or son to marry. This cultural practice endured for many centuries, yet recent shifts over the past several decades, involving not only modernization, but also a tendency toward materialism and individualism (Schwartz 2004), have changed the expectations, perceptions (Chen 2015), and practices within mate selection to a significant degree. From a developmental perspective (Thornton 2001), societal modernization is often accompanied by substantial change in familial structures and familial aspirations (Thornton 2005). Among young adults, modernization may increase individuality, social mobility, and freedom of individual expression (Cheung & Kwan 2009; Qi 2014), all of which may affect dating and mate selection. This chapter will examine these changes and will focus particularly upon contemporary forms of mate selection in China, along with an emphasis upon how gender roles and family influence may be changing the manners in which young adults approach dating and mate selection.

Gender and intimate relationships

Throughout most of its history, Chinese culture has maintained an emphasis upon traditional family structures and behaviors, and particularly the continuity of family lineage, along with firmly patriarchal beliefs concerning gender and gender roles. Much of these beliefs are based upon Confucian ideologies, which steadfastly proposed that all young adults were expected to marry, and to do so at a younger, rather than later, age (Wei et al.

DOI: 10.4324/9780429059704-35

2013). Of course, traditional Chinese culture is collectivist in its nature, supporting the contention that the needs of individuals are secondary to those of the family and, thereafter, the larger society (Han 2008). As such, the initiation of intimate relationships by the young adults, themselves, was relatively uncommon throughout most of China's history. Instead, the selection of an eventual spouse was left almost entirely under the control of parents, who would choose someone whom they considered to be a suitable and appropriate partner for their adult child. From the 16th century through the establishment of the People's Republic of China in 1949, marriages were typically arranged by parents (Wolf & Huang 1980). Daughters and sons were expected to wholly respect the choices of their parents, and thus had little, if any, opportunity to express their own preferences. The basis for this practice is again partially grounded in Confucianism, which posits that parents should instill respect and obedience in their children and steer them away from becoming independent or autonomous (Chao 1994). This form of parent-controlled mate selection is certainly not unique to China and is often evident within agrarian societies (Goode 1970).

The practice of parent-controlled mate selection was brought to an end in 1950, with the passage of the New Marriage Law. This legislation fundamentally altered the existing practice of parental control over daughters' and sons' choice of marriage partner and stipulated that all persons had the right to choose their own spouse. Within the context of a patriarchal culture, this was a considerable shift and, understandably, was not immediately popular. One of the inherent goals of the New Marriage Law was to establish a legal and, eventually, cultural foundation for equality between the sexes. Overall, the law served as a formal rejection of the traditional ideologies concerning marriage and promoted substantially more progressive and egalitarian ideologies. With this change, young adults were free to select their own partners, seemingly apart from the control of parents and the constraints of traditional cultural expectations (Blair & Madigan 2019). However, while the introduction of the new law provided a legal opportunity for the free choice of an intimate partner, young adults were nonetheless left to contend with the still salient cultural expectations and, among those, the prevailing gender ideologies of past generations.

Young men and women faced distinctly separate sets of expectations within the larger culture, and particularly so with regard to mate selection. Within the tenets of traditional Confucianism, women were expected to accept and adhere to a submissive set of roles, while the roles of men were granted considerable authority over women (Yu & Chau 1997). The secondary status of women extended throughout their lives, as Confucian philosophy stipulated that women be obedient in three specific regards: (1) prior to becoming married, women should obey their fathers and brothers; (2) once married, women should obey their husbands; and (3) in widowhood, women should obey their adult sons (Chia et al. 1997; Yang 1968). The patriarchal quality of these expectations extended into a variety of realms in the lives of women and men. Prior to marriage, women were expected to maintain their virginity, as a necessary quality for marriage. Men, on the other hand, were allowed considerably more discretion in matters of sexual behaviors, thus making sexual intercourse acceptable for unmarried men, but forbidden for unmarried women (Higgins et al. 2002). In conjunction with the double standards concerning sexual behavior, traditional family norms were patrilocal, creating the expectation that newly married couples should move in with (or at least near) the parents of the husband (Lui 2016). This practice was strongly linked to the expectation that the new bride would provide domestic assistance and physical care to the parents of her husband. For young wives, then, the traditional expectation was that they be subservient to both their husbands and the parents of their husbands.

While the patriarchal ideologies of traditional Chinese culture seem quite incompatible with the modernized culture of contemporary China, several studies have offered evidence that traditional gender expectations may yet persist. With regard to domestic responsibilities, research has shown the division of household chores among contemporary married couples to be skewed, such that wives perform a significantly disproportionate share of housework (Cook & Dong 2011). Not surprisingly, this same pattern is evident with regard to childcare, wherein mothers of young children perform the vast majority of duties associated with the instrumental care of children (Rosen 1992). The relative standing of women and men within the familial context thus seems to still reflect, to a significant extent, the traditional gender ideologies of Chinese culture. Following the revolution, women were to be treated as equals of men and to have the same opportunities and responsibilities of men. Although women's occupational and educational attainment did increase, as a consequence, the anticipated shift in gender ideologies did not necessarily occur in its entirety. In the interweaving of family and occupational roles, for instance, men are still expected to occupy the provider role (Chia et al. 1997).

With its rapid pace of modernization over the last half-century, China has experienced considerable change, and especially so with regard to its economy. Economic changes, in turn, may be bringing about a concurrent shift in terms of gender ideologies, and also with regard to how young people perceive marriage and family life. Over the last several decades, educational attainment has increased dramatically, with the highest increases shown among young women (Nakano 2016). Chinese colleges and universities have experienced a steady increase in the proportionate representation of women on their campuses, such that female students far outnumber their male counterparts. With increasing rates of female educational attainment, and particularly in terms of achieving college degrees, female occupational attainment has followed a similar path, resulting in higher rates of labor force participation among younger women (Yu & Xie 2015). Seemingly, higher levels of educational and occupational attainment would elevate the status of women, thereby resulting in increasing equality and parity with men, but the success of women has also resulted in other forms of gender bias. Women who are college educated, employed, but have not married by the time they have reached their 30s are often labeled as '*sheng nu*', which roughly translates as 'leftover women'. Such women are regarded as having placed their own individual fortunes ahead of those of their families and the larger society, and these women are looked upon with disdain by many (Gaetano 2010). The negative connotation of this label places considerable pressure upon such women to find a husband (Nakano 2016), yet no comparable labels or stereotypes are applied to well-educated unmarried men, thus maintaining yet another double standard concerning gender and gender roles.

Given the steady increase of economic modernization and coupled with an increase in materialism and the growth of the middle class, it is certainly logical to assume that ideological change will result. Economic independence theory (Willis 1987) proposes that increased social capital among women, especially in terms of educational and occupational attainment, may lessen the appeal of conventional marital and parental roles. Hence, women's desire for marriage may be lessened by their opportunities to obtain greater educational and occupational successes. The decline in marriage rates, in conjunction with rising divorce and cohabitation rates, may support this notion, and may also have implications for the very nature of intimate relationships in China. However, the relative influence of parents over the lives of their young daughters and sons, and particularly with regard to issues involving intimate relationships, remains quite tangible.

Parental control

Within Chinese families, filial piety has long been the foundation upon which all family relationships are based. Filial piety is embodied in the respect which children are expected to give to their parents, but the expectations go well beyond simple respect. Given the influence of both Buddhism and Confucianism, children are taught from birth onward to respect not only their mothers and fathers, but their entire lineage (Yeh & Bedford 2003), involving both living and deceased members of one's family. As mentioned previously, traditional Chinese culture is regarded as collectivist, wherein greater emphasis is placed upon the needs of the family (and larger society), rather than the individual. The mandate of filial piety is both consistent and supportive of this collectivist quality of the larger culture, as it helps to instill a sense of obligation in children (to respect their parents) and enhance children's respect for their ancestors (Chao 1994). Children are expected to develop a strong sense of family obligation, and to place greater priority upon the needs of the family, and particularly their parents, rather than their own individual needs.

In order to fully comprehend the nature of filial piety, along with how it may affect mate selection in contemporary China, it is necessary to examine its origins. The expectations associated with filial piety arose with the beginnings of Confucianism, in the Spring and Autumn periods (approximately 770 BCE and 476 BCE). Confucianism spread steadily across China, and received the endorsement of Emperor Wu (156–87 BCE), who officially proclaimed it to be the ideology of the state (Jinbo & Huihua 2012). At this time, the expectations of filial piety were clearly established, and a hierarchical authority was promoted within families. Within this hierarchy, men were labeled as the authority figures within families, whereas wives and children were expected to be obedient and subservient (Qi 2014). This hierarchical authority system also stretched across generations, with elderly parents still being able to exert considerable control over their adult children. Indeed, the notion of 'fumu zai, bu yuanyou' arose from these ideologies, stipulating that adult children should not only obey their aging parents, but also provide them with financial and instrumental support.

When the People's Republic of China was created, one of the core aims of the new government was to establish the state as the true authority within society, and thus supersede the family as the entity to which individuals should commit their loyalty and obedience, thus challenging the tenets of filial piety which had been in place for many centuries. On many levels, filial piety and family authority not only continued, but were also eventually woven into law (Yeh et al. 2013). As previously mentioned, the New Marriage Law of 1950 was initially intended to create a formal registration system for marriage, but it also focused upon the abolishment of arranged marriages, placing the choice of marriage partners squarely in the hands of individuals. With a growing elderly portion of the population, the government amended the law in 1980, thereafter requiring individuals to attend to the needs of their families (Fei 1992). In terms of the pragmatic aspects of the law, the core of this amendment was the requirement that adult children look after the needs of their elderly parents, which is consistent with traditional ideologies concerning filial piety.

The interconnected nature of laws and ideologies concerning filial piety has continued. During the 1980s, Family Support Agreements were introduced, which were intended to enforce the support of aging parents by their adult children. These agreements were more commonly used in rural areas, due to the frequent situation wherein daughters and sons moved away from their parents' home, often relocating in urban areas which were quite distant. The design was straightforward – daughters and sons would sign a legally binding agreement wherein they agreed to support their parents in their later years. Within the bounds of filial piety, such support should be expected, but the introduction of this legal component was not always welcomed, as many felt that such agreements may have actually disrupted the normative and affective components of filial piety (Chou 2011).

Over many centuries, and coupled with the numerous forms of societal change that have transpired, the construct of filial piety, itself, has transformed and evolved (Han 2008), leading scholars to address its complicated nature. To this end, researchers have recognized the multiple forms which filial piety may take on within familial relationships. In the dual filial piety model (Yeh & Bedford 2003), the construct is regarded as having two distinct elements: (1) authoritarian filial piety and (2) reciprocal filial piety. These elements come into play at various points across the life course of a daughter or son but are regarded as being continually present and having a significant impact upon parent-child relationships. Authoritarian filial piety is often associated with the childhood years, when children are still living at home, going through their childhood and adolescent years, and are expected to completely and absolutely comply with their parents' wishes. From birth onward, children are taught to recognize their parents as the clear authority in their lives (Chao & Tseng 2002). This expectation of compliance with parents is present throughout the lives of children, even as they mature and enter adulthood. The second element, reciprocal filial piety, involves both the affective expectations placed upon parents – to love and care for their children- and the gratitude which children should freely feel and express toward their parents (Yeh et al. 2013). This element of filial piety thus pertains to both parents and children, simultaneously, and requires that each fulfill their respective obligations. For parents, this particularly involves the provision of affection, while for children, they essentially need to display their sincere gratitude for the same (Lum et al. 2016). During childhood, daughters and sons can express their gratitude through the display of affection, stating their sincere thanks, and in other manners which will convey their appreciation. During adulthood, though, the reciprocal element of filial piety is more readily conveyed through taking care of aging parents. Indeed, the concept of filial piety is represented through '*xiao*', the Chinese character of which visually represents a child with an elderly man on her/his back (Han 2008).

The broad interpretation of *xiao* as filial piety is accurate but does not fully express the complicated nature of parental authority within traditional Chinese culture. Again, the hierarchical structure of authority, along with the patriarchal gender attitudes of the larger culture, places fathers in the role of provider for the family (*yangjia*), while daughters and sons are expected to be obedient and complaint (*shunfu*) toward their parents. On the surface, such cultural expectations seem decidedly patriarchal, and may lead to the assumption that fathers are strict, demanding, and controlling figures within families. However, an additional expectation, *guanjiao*, involves both parental control and parental affection. This notion is actually twofold, involving *guan* –the supervision of children – and *jiao* –the advice and expectations of parents. During the childhood years, *guan* might be displayed through parental monitoring of school grades and performance, while *jiao* might be conveyed through parents' expression of concern about the same. Clearly, this creates a rather complicated set of expectations for parent-child relationships, but both elements are regarded as being equally necessary (Bush et al. 2002).

The changing nature of dating and intimacy

During the adolescent years, schools strongly discourage students from being in romantic relationships, and parents typically oppose such activities by their own daughters and sons (Chen et al. 2009; Wu 1996). With the modernization of China, coupled with a rising emphasis upon individualism and materialism, as well as greater exposure to Western notions of romance, young people are increasingly pursuing dating relationships. For a society in which parental control over relationships has long been the practice, the introduction of individual choice and dating has, nonetheless, evolved. In the contemporary form, young adults often 'meet' online, through various websites and cellphone apps. Indeed, a growing number of such apps have greatly improved young adults' prospects for finding that 'special someone'. The notion of love within dating relationships, though, is still evolving. Despite having perceptions of love and romance which are quite distinct from those of their parents' generation (Lange et al. 2015), many young adults view dating in a more pragmatic manner, regarding it as an opportunity to have fun, to socialize, or to have sex. The evolving perceptions of romance have, to some extent, been woven together with traditional beliefs, albeit in the name of commerce. The Qixi Festival, which is based upon the legend of two lovers who yearned for one another but were unable to be together except for one day each year (the seventh day of the seventh lunar month), has now become Chinese Valentine's Day. Similar to its Western counterpart (celebrated on February 14), it has become a day wherein young couples should express the affections toward one another, and preferably so through the giving of flowers, candies, jewelries, and other gifts. Such materialist displays of love are rapidly becoming the norm, and even continue as couples move toward marriage itself, as weddings often become overly elaborate affairs in which everything from bridal gowns to flowers to wedding photos must be of the highest, and most expensive, quality (Sun 2017).

The expression of romantic feelings, once a dating relationship has begun, has similarly evolved over recent years. Public displays of affection, including the holding of hands and kissing, have become increasingly common, yet these must also be recognized as a substantial departure from previous generations (Yang 2011). Beyond holding hands and kissing, young couples often engage in behaviors which are intended to announce their relationship to others, such as dressing alike, eating in the front windows of small cafes, where they can be seen by others. Despite their seemingly progressive approach to dating relationships, young adults' preferences with regard to physical intimacy may be somewhat conservative (Higgins et al. 2002). Whereas high schools are environments wherein dating relationships are discouraged, colleges are often regarded as 'love havens', where young women and men can more openly express themselves, often far from the supervision of their parents (Xia & Zhou 2003). Although estimates vary, some studies have suggested that over one-third of college students will become sexually active (Lei 2005; Pan 2007). Colleges and universities often attempt to discourage sexual behaviors through the use of policies and educational programs (Aresu 2009), yet the preferences of college students strongly indicate their desire to become sexually active (Blair & Scott 2019). However, a double standard exists in terms of sexual behavior, as young men support the practice of premarital intercourse, yet still prefer that their eventual brides be virgins at the time of marriage (Pan 2004).

Before dating begins, though, young women and men typically give careful consideration as to what, precisely, they are seeking in a prospective partner. While such preferences are often gender-typed within many other cultures, China's modernization and accompanying culture change makes preferences in dating partners a relatively new, and evolving, dimension of intimate relationships. Given the patriarchal nature of Chinese culture, it is somewhat understandable that certain gender-typing does exist. Young men often express a preference for women with attractive physical features, while young women often focus more on the intelligence and wealth of men (Xia & Zhou 2003). Stereotyped perceptions of young men and women persist, with women being regarded as quiet, gentle, and shy, while men are regarded as serious, ambitious, and powerful (Jankowiak & Li 2017). Recent studies have shown that such stereotyped preferences still continue, with young women expressing concern about the financial standing of men, while young men are more concerned about the physical appearance of women (Blair & Madigan 2016). Although young adults in China may seem to seek their individual preferences, parents have been shown to exert substantial influence over both dating and marriage partner selections (Gui 2017).

Examining current patterns of dating

In order to better understand how gender, parental control, and changes in the larger culture may be affecting dating, this chapter now turns to an examination of current trends. Data of this study includes survey responses from students attending five public universities in four provinces in China, during 2019. Students were randomly invited to participate in a survey concerning dating and mate selection. Of those invited to participate, approximately 86% agreed to participate. After checking for missing or incomplete responses, 47 cases were removed, resulting in 918 females and 609 males. A more complete description of this data, and its accompanying methodologies, may be found in Blair and Scott (2019). The young adults included in this sample range in age from 18 to 25 years of age. Among the females, approximately 45% were currently in a dating relationship, while approximately 48% of the males reported likewise.

Table 30.1 presents the mean levels of dating and marriage preferences among young women and men. As shown, the majority of both females and males actively desire to be in a dating relationship. Approximately 54% of both sexes express a clear preference for such relationships. Certainly, it does raise the question of why the preference for dating isn't higher, but this may be linked to the nature of the sample. College students, while perhaps having greater autonomy and independence (particularly in terms of parental supervision), may also be directing their time and energy toward their studies, such that intimate relationships simply are not a top priority at this point in their lives. The young women and men in the sample do, though, express a clear preference for marriage. In response to the statement, 'I would like to marry, one day', approximately 70% of females, along with 73% of males, responded in the affirmative. Indeed, less than 10% of each sex responded to this statement in the negative, thus suggesting that the expectation of marriage remains quite strong among young adults. While the desire to marry is certainly strong, the timing of marriage is yet another issue to consider. Within this sample, women express the desire to marry at approximately 27 years of age, with men preferring to marry just shy of 28 years of age. Obviously, the timing of marriage is constrained somewhat by law, but with a sample of college students, many of the respondents may be choosing a preferred time which occurs well after the completion of their degrees.

As previously discussed, females and males often have distinct expectations concerning intimate relationships. This can encompass a wide variety of traits concerning dating and relationships, but one distinction which is present from the very beginning of dating concerns what each sex is looking for, respectively, in a partner. To that end, Figure 30.1 presents the desired partner characteristics, as ranked by each respondent across a seven-point scale (with the higher score indicating a greater preference for that particular characteristic). Across the 13 characteristics, it is readily apparent that females and males do, in fact, have considerably different preferences in a prospective partner. Given the stereotypes which are often applied to each sex, it is understandable that such stereotypes also exist with regard to mate preferences. Males, as the stereotypes suggest, are primarily interested in the physical features of a woman. Is she pretty? Does she have an attractive body? Is her hair nice? Of

Table 30.1 Mean levels of dating and marriage preferences among young Chinese women and men

	Females	*Males*
Want to Date	3.52	3.53
	(1.01)	(1.05)
Strongly Agree	17.0%	18.9%
Agree	37.7	35.6
Unsure	29.0	29.4
Disagree	13.3	12.2
Strongly Disagree	3.1	3.9
Want to Marry	3.87	3.89
	(0.94)	(0.96)
Strongly Agree	26.5%	27.4%
Agree	43.7	45.3
Unsure	22.2	18.6
Disagree	5.3	5.9
Strongly Disagree	2.3	2.8
Preferred Age at Marriage	26.95	27.76
	(2.51)	(3.01)
20 and younger	0.6%	1.2%
21 to 25	29.8	22.4
26 to 30	66.4	67.6
31 to 35	2.9	8.8
36 and older	0.2	0.3
N	918	609

Note: Standard deviations shown in parentheses.

course, stereotypes similarly exist with regard to women's preferences. The long-standing stereotype applied to women is that they are primarily seeking a man who can provide for them financially. Is he wealthy? Can he provide me with a nice home, as well as a nice car?

As shown in Figure 30.1, women and men appear to have relatively distinct preferences when it comes to a prospective dating partner. With regard to stereotypes of women, there may be some evidence to support such beliefs. As compared to men, women place a substantially greater premium upon their partners being: (1) ambitious, (2) successful, (3) wealthy, and (4) well-educated. These traits, particularly when taken into consideration as a collective set of characteristics, would certainly support the notion that women actively seek men whose financial standing and/or prospects thereof are sufficiently high. Simply, having more money may make a male more attractive, given these findings. In terms of the stereotypes concerning males, men are shown to place a higher premium upon a woman being: (1) sexy and (2) affectionate. These two differences do provide some, albeit only meager, support for the existing stereotype that men are primarily interested in a woman's physical appearance. The overall patterns shown, however, suggest that women express higher preferences across the majority of desired characteristics in a prospective partner. Aside from those traits associated with financial concerns, women also place a high preference for men who are considerate, kind, and loving. In the relative regard, these desired preference actually suggest that women are placing a greater premium upon personality traits,

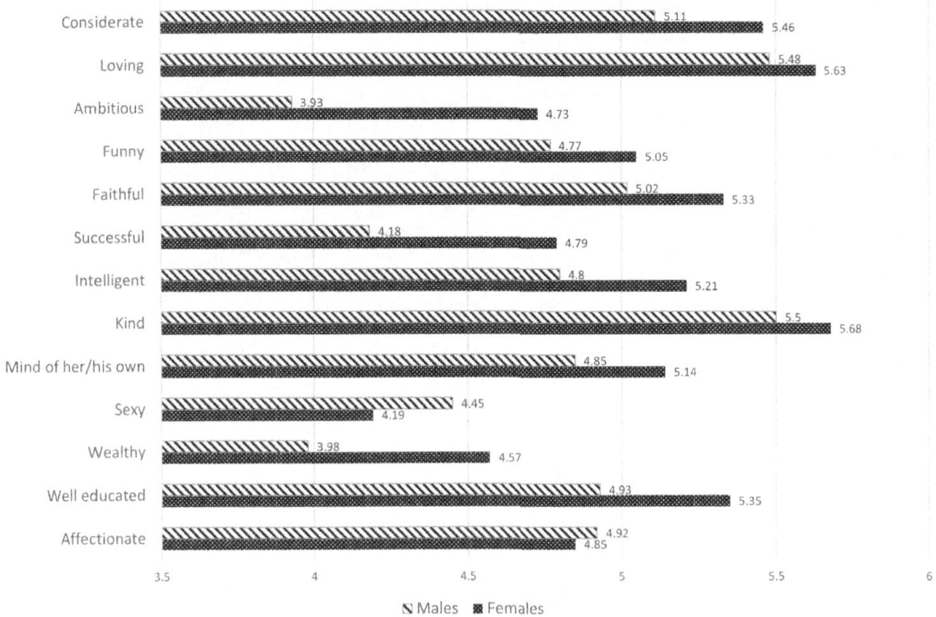

Figure 30.1 Desired partner characteristics, by sex.

and particularly those which are linked to qualities associated with caring and emotional sensitivity. It should also be noted that women place a higher preference for faithfulness, as compared to men. This may be interpreted as a desire for sexual exclusivity, but also likely pertains to emotional exclusivity, as well.

Given the extent of parental control over mate selection throughout much of China's history, this study also examined to what extent such parental influence still remains. Table 30.2 presents the mean levels of parental control among young women and men. As shown, the willingness of young adults to go against the wishes of their parents varies, both by the sex of the young adult and the nature of the intimate relationship. With regard to dating, over one-third of daughters report that they are willing to date someone without the approval of their parents. By comparison, slightly more than half of sons are willing to date without parental approval. This difference may result from the lingering aspects of patriarchy within Chinese families, such that daughters are given less freedom of choice, as compared to sons. It is equally plausible, though, that the reality of the dating market, and particularly the skewed sex ratio leads sons to exercise more freedom of choice, so as to increase their chances of finding a partner. Interestingly, the willingness of both sons and daughters to go against their parent's wishes is substantially less when it involves the selection of a spouse. Among daughters, only about one-fifth (20.3%) state that they are willing to marry someone without the approval of their parents. Among sons, 38.9% are willing to marry without parental approval, which is considerably more than the percentage of sons who would not marry without parental approval (28%). These patterns strongly suggest that, while societal and cultural change may be contributing to greater individualism among young adults, parental influence and, perhaps, outward parental control, is still having an impact upon the choice of both dating partners and eventual spouses.

Table 30.2 Mean levels of parental control among young Chinese women and men

	Females	*Males*
Willing to date without parental approval	3.05 (1.02)	3.42 (0.99)
Strongly Agree	5.9%	13.0%
Agree	29.6	37.1
Unsure	19.0	13.8
Disagree	13.3	12.2
Strongly Disagree	8.5	3.4
Willing to marry without parental approval	2.64 (1.05)	3.12 (1.05)
Strongly Agree	3.9%	7.9%
Agree	16.4	31.0
Unsure	35.4	33.0
Disagree	28.4	21.0
Strongly Disagree	15.8	7.1
N	918	609

Note: Standard deviations shown in parentheses.

As previously mentioned, the nature of dating in China has changed considerably over recent decades, with greater individual choice, the expression of sexuality, and the influence of peer culture. In order to provide a more complete understanding of contemporary patterns of dating in China, Table 30.3 presents the mean levels of dating characteristics among young adults. As shown, peer pressure may be a factor in encouraging young adults to pursue and maintain dating relationships. Among young adult females, 36.9% report that the majority of their friends are in dating relationships, while a comparable percentage (40.9%) of young adult males report the same. During the young adult years, as individuals are becoming more independent of their parents, peers will increasingly influence patterns of behavior in terms of appearance, behaviors, and beyond. It is quite reasonable to assume that the same can be said of intimate relationships, where peers represent significant role models for other young adults. Hence, the influence of peers, in the young adult years, may even begin to surpass the influence of parents.

A final element of dating relationships which should be considered herein is the sexual behaviors within dating. Respondents were asked to respond to two separate queries, asking whether they would be willing to kiss or have sex on a first date. Within many other cultures, the notion of engaging in physical intimacy on a first date would not necessarily be regarded as out of the ordinary. However, in the context of contemporary China, wherein young adults are expressing their individuality, while respecting the traditions of previous generations, the physical element of relationships may require greater nuance and discretion. With regard to kissing on a first date, only about one-fifth (25.8%) of young women were willing to do so. Not surprisingly, considerably more young men (43.2%) were willing to kiss on a first date. Kissing, however, is not necessarily going to shock anyone, at least when expressed in a private context. Sexual intercourse, on the other hand, represents a substantially greater shift away from traditional cultural norms concerning the behaviors of unmarried couples. Among young adult females, only about one out of ten (10.3%) stated that they were willing to have sexual intercourse on a first date. By comparison, the

Table 30.3 Mean levels of dating characteristics among young Chinese women and men

	Females	*Males*
# of Friends Dating	2.91	2.78
	(1.08)	(1.06)
All or almost all	8.5%	18.9%
More than half	28.4	29.4
About half	35.9	35.5
Less than half	18.0	17.2
Only a few or none	9.1	6.4
Willing to kiss on first date	2.70	3.29
	(1.13)	(1.14)
Strongly Agree	4.2%	16.1%
Agree	21.6	27.1
Unsure	33.9	34.3
Disagree	21.1	14.4
Strongly Disagree	19.2	8.0
Willing to have sex on first date	1.88	2.71
	(1.11)	(1.28)
Strongly Agree	3.1%	11.0%
Agree	7.2	15.9
Unsure	16.9	30.0
Disagree	21.1	19.2
Strongly Disagree	51.7	23.8
N	918	609

Note: Standard deviations shown in parentheses.

overwhelming majority (72.8%) of young women stated that they would not have sex on a first date. Among young men, about one-fourth (26.9%) stated that they would be willing to have sexual intercourse on a first date. While this may leave the impression that young men, at least as compared to young women, are particularly interested in the sexual dimension of a dating relationship, it is worth noting that fully 43% of young men stated that they would not be willing to have sex on a first date. Hence, while young men do seem more eager to engage in the physical aspects of a dating relationship, as compared to young women, the conservative and traditional expectations concerning such relationships still seem to permeate young adults' perceptions of how dating relationships should be.

Conclusions

Modernization theories posit that as societies undergo significant change, the various norms concerning social institutions will also begin to change (Thornton 2005). In the case of the social institution of the family, one of its necessary components concerns how individuals find a suitable partner, typically with the eventual goal of becoming married and forming their own new family. In China, recent decades have been witness to a wide-ranging variety of change, particularly including economic change. The rapid growth of the middle class, along with increased emphases upon materialism and individualism, have brought about a very different context in which mate selection occurs. Over recent decades, marriage rates have decreased, divorce rates have risen dramatically, and cohabitation and singlehood are increasingly regarded as acceptable alternatives to traditional marriage. From the generational perspective, young adults are encountering a radically different social context in which to find a potential partner. The manners in which older adults found a spouse may seem rather quaint and outdated through the eyes of young adults, today. Long-standing practices of parental control, coupled with a decidedly public form of mate selection, have given way to such practices as finding a partner online, not for the purpose of emotional involvement, but rather, often purely for the goal of having sexual intercourse. The norms and expectations concerning dating and mate selection, likely so many others in contemporary China, have changed dramatically over recent decades, and continue to evolve before our eyes.

Although considerable differences exist between the dating practices of contemporary youth and their older counterparts, there are, nonetheless, several key elements which have not changed much over time. As shown in the results from the survey discussed herein, along with other recent research, young women and men strongly prefer to both date and, eventually, become married. Understandably, increases in educational attainment have brought about a concurrent increase in the timing of marriage, with women and men marrying at later ages. In terms of their ultimate goals, though, it does appear that the majority of young adults are seeking the same relationship structures as those of their own parents.

Mate selection, and the inherent qualities of dating itself, seems to have a combination of both traditional and progressive elements. Some of the traditional stereotypes concerning what women and men, respectively, are seeking in partner do appear to have valid support. Contemporary women do appear to have an elevated preference for men who can provide substantial financial support (i.e., 'He's rich!'), while men still seem to have a strong preference for women's physical appearance (i.e., 'She's beautiful!'). Among young men today, the pursuit of 'bai fu mei' (white, rich, and beautiful) is a common aspiration, while young women seek male partners who are 'gao fu shuai' (tall, rich, and handsome). The emphasis upon materialism and individualism, coupled with the manners in which the media upholds many of these gendered stereotypes, may be associated with the preferences of young women and men. Indeed, the search for partners with these stereotyped traits seems quite consistent with the broader societal shifts toward individualism and materialism. While it seemingly makes both sexes seem rather shallow, it is difficult to envision when these gender differences will, if ever, fade away. The portrayal of young women as being somewhat materialistic in their partner preferences is even supported by the older generations. In 'marriage markets' around the country, aging parents often advertise their adult sons not by their charming personalities, but rather, by their income and the size of their home.

Young adults do appear, on the surface, to be more independent and willing to chart their own course for their future lives. While young adults were a bit more willing to forego their parents' wishes in terms of dating partners, substantially fewer were shown to be willing to go against their parents when it came to choosing a spouse. These patterns suggest that many young adults may find themselves in a difficult quandary – wanting the freedom to choose their own partners, free of parental control, yet still having to accept the cultural expectation that their parents do, in fact, have the ability to exert such control over their personal lives. In late 2019, COVID-19 struck, resulting in a societal lockdown, wherein residents were largely restricted to their homes. Understandably, such circumstances would seem to pose a considerable obstacle to young adults' pursuit of intimate relationships. However, in many ways, the virus and its ensuing travel restrictions may have actually increased the pursuit of intimacy, as young adults simply heightened their use of online interaction, through the use of social media and social/dating apps. In most instances, parents are quite unaware of their daughters' and sons' online activities and, even if they were curious, it is highly unlikely that young adults would voluntarily share such intimate information with their parents. While the long-term effects remain to be seen, it is conceivable that the coronavirus situation may lead to new patterns of dating and mate selection.

As China continues to change, it is certainly plausible that generations of young adults will become increasingly independent and autonomous, and particularly so with regard to intimate relationships. However, the norms associated with filial piety have existed for thousands of years, and the enduring impact of such norms is not likely to quickly dissipate, even in the face of modernization. A multitude of factors, ranging from demographic issues (e.g., the sex ratio) to changes in gender roles (e.g., the educational attainment of women) will continue to change the nature of dating and mate selection. The modernization of China, after all, will continue and, as such, the ways in which young women and men find a partner will continue to change, as well. Even the goals of dating and mate selection will continue to change, as traditional marriage may effectively come to compete with other options – singlehood, cohabitation, or some variation which has yet to evolve.

References

Aresu, A. (2009) 'Sexuality education in modern and contemporary China: Interrupted debates across the last century', *International Journal of Educational Development*, 29: 532–541.

Blair, S. L. and Madigan, T. J. (2016) 'Dating attitudes and expectations among young Chinese adults: An examination of gender differences', *The Journal of Chinese Sociology*, 3(12): 1–19.

Blair, S. L. and Madigan, T. J. (2019) 'Dating, marriage, and parental approval: An examination of young adults in China', *Social Science Quarterly*, 100(6): 2351–2368.

Blair, S. L. and Scott, C. L. (2019) '"It started with a kiss": The initiation of sexual intimacy among young adults in China', *Sexuality & Culture*, 23(4): 1147–1166.

Bush, K. R.; Peterson, G. W.; Cobas, J. A.; and Supple, A. J. (2002) 'Adolescents' perceptions of parental behaviors as predictors of adolescent self-esteem in mainland China', *Sociological Inquiry*, 72: 503–526.

Chao, R. K. (1994) 'Beyond parental control and authoritarian parenting style: Understanding Chinese parenting through the cultural notion of training', *Child Development*, 65: 1111–1119.

Chao, R. and Tseng, V. (2002) 'Parenting of Asians', in M. H. Bornstein (ed), *Handbook of Parenting: Vol. 4, Social Conditions and Applied Parenting (pp. 59-94)*, Mahwah, NJ: Lawrence Erlbaum.

Chen, R. (2015) 'Weaving individualism into collectivism: Chinese adults' evolving relationship and family values', *Journal of Comparative Family Studies*, 46(2): 167–179.

Chen, Z.; Guo, F.; Yang, X.; Li, X.; Duan, Q.; Zhang, J.; and Ge, X. (2009) 'Emotional and behavioral effects of romantic relationships in Chinese adolescents', *Journal of Youth and Adolescence*, 38: 1282–1293.

Cheung, C., and Kwan, A. Y. (2009) 'The erosion of filial piety by modernization in Chinese cities', *Ageing & Society*, 29: 179–98.

Chia, R. C.; Allred, L. J.; and Jerzak, P. A. (1997) 'Attitudes toward women in Taiwan and China', *Psychology of Women Quarterly*, 21: 137–150.

Chou, R. J. A. (2011) 'Filial piety by contract? The emergence, implementation, and implications of the 'Family Support Agreement' in China', *The Gerontologist*, 51(1): 3–16.

Cook, S. and Dong. X. (2011) 'Harsh choices: Chinese women's paid work and upaid care responsibilities under economic reform', *Development and Change*, 42: 947–965.

Fei, X. (1992) *From the Soil: The Foundations of Chinese Society*. Berkeley, CA: University of California Press.

Gaetano, A. M. (2010) *Single Women in Urban China and the 'Unmarried Crisis'*. Lund: Centre for East and South-East Asian Studies, Lund University.

Goode, W. J. (1970) *World Revolution and Family Patterns*. New York, NY: Free Press.

Gui, T. (2017) "Devalued' daughters versus 'appreciated' sons: Gender inequality in China's parent-organized matchmaking markets', *Journal of Family Issues*, 38(13): 1923–1948.

Han, J. (2008) *Chinese Characters*. Beijing: China Intercontinental Press.

Higgins, L. T.; Zheng, M.; Liu, Y.; and Sun, C. H. (2002) 'Attitudes to marriage and sexual behaviors: A survey of gender and culture differences in China and United Kingdom', *Sex Roles*, 46: 75–89.

Jankowiak, William and Xuan Li. (2017) 'Emergent conjugal love, mutual affection and female marital power', in Goncalo Santos and Stevan Harrell (eds) *Transforming Patriarchy: Chinese Families in the Twenty-First Century* (pp. 146–162). Seattle: University of Washington Press.

Jinbo, L. and Huihua, N. (2012) 'Confucian filial piety, economic growth, and divergence among civilizations', *Social Sciences in China*, 4(November): 69–88.

Lange, R.; Houran, J.; and Li, S. (2015) 'Dyadic relationship values in Chinese online daters: Love American style?', *Sexuality & Culture*, 19: 190–215.

Lei, Y. (2005) *Love and Reason in the Ivory Tower: Report on Investigating Issues Concerning Dating and Love Among Contemporary College Students*. Zhenzhou: Henan University Press.

Lui, L. (2016) 'Gender, rural-urban inequality, and intermarriage in China', *Social Forces*, 95(2): 639–662.

Lum, T. Y. S.; Yan, E. C. W.; Ho, A. H. Y.; Shum, M. H. Y.; Wong, G. H. Y.; Lau, M. M. Y.; and Wang, J. (2016) 'Measuring filial piety in the 21st century: Development, factor structure, and reliability of the 10-item contemporary filial piety scale', *Journal of Applied Gerontology*, 35(11): 1235–1247.

Nakano, L. (2016) 'Single women and the transition to marriage in Hong Kong, Shanghai, and Tokyo', *Asian Journal of Social Science*, 44: 363–390.

Pan, S. 潘绥铭 (2004) 当代中国人的性行为与性关系 (Sexual behavior and relation in contemporary China). 中国北京(Beijing, China): 涩会科学文献出版社(Sekai Scientific Literature Press).

Pan, S. M. (2007) *The Incidence of Chinese College Students, Beijing, China: Chinese People's Sexual Behavior and Sexual Relationship: Historical Development 2000–2006*. Retrieved from http:/blog.sin.com.cn/s/blog_4dd47e5a010009j2.html.

Qi, X. (2014) 'Filial obligation in contemporary China: Evolution of the culture-system', *Journal for the Theory of Social Behavior*, 45(1): 141–161.

Rosen, S. (1992) 'Women, education, and modernization', in R. Heyhoe (ed), *Education and Modernization: The Chinese Experience* (pp. 255–284), Exeter: Pergamon.

Schwartz, S. H. (2004) 'Mapping and interpreting cultural differences around the world', in H. Vinken, J. Soeters, and P. Ester (eds), *Comparing Cultures, Dimensions of Cultures in a Comparative Perspective*. Leiden, the Netherlands: Brill.

Sun, W. (2017) 'Bridal photos and diamond rings: The inequality of romantic consumption in China', *The Journal of Chinese Sociology*, 4(15): 1–17.

Thornton, A. (2001) 'The Developmental Paradigm, Reading History Sideways, and Family Change', *Demography*, 38: 449–65.

Thornton, A. (2005) *Reading History Sideways: The Fallacy and Enduring Impact of the Developmental Paradigm on Family Life*. Chicago, IL: University of Chicago Press.

Wei, Y.; Jiang, Q.; and Basten, S. (2013) 'Observing the transformation of China's first marriage pattern through net nuptiality tables: 1982–2010', *Finnish Yearbook of Population Research*, 48: 65–75.

Willis, R. (1987) 'What have we learned from the economics of the family?', *American Economic Review Papers and Proceedings*, 77: 68–81.

Wolf, A. P. and Huang, C. S. (1980) *Marriage and Adoption in China*. Stanford, CA: Stanford University Press.

Wu, D. Y. H. (1996) 'Chinese childhood socialization', in M. H. Bond (ed), *The Handbook of Chinese Psychology* (pp. 143–154). Hong Kong: Oxford University Press.

Xia, Y. R. and Zhou, Z. G. (2003) 'The transition of courtship, mate selection, and marriage in China', in Hamon and Ingoldsby (eds), *Mate Selection Across Cultures* (pp. 231–246). Thousand Oaks: Sage.

Yang, M. C. (1968) *A Chinese Village: Taitou, Shantung Province*. New York: Columbia University Press.

Yang, R. (2011) 'Between traditionalism and modernity: Changing values on dating behavior and mate selection criteria', *International Review of Modern Sociology*, 37(2): 265–287.

Yeh, K. H. and Bedford, O. (2003) 'A test of the dual filial piety model', *Asian Journal of Social Psychology*, 6(3): 215–228.

Yeh, K. H.; Yi, C.; Tsao, W.; and Wan, P. (2013) 'Filial piety in contemporary Chinese societies: A comparative study of Taiwan, Hong Kong, and China', *International Sociology*, 28(3), 277–296.

Yu, J. and Xie, Y. (2015) 'Changes in the determinants of marriage entry in post-reform urban China', *Demography*, 52(6): 1869–1892.

Yu, S. W. K. and Chau, R. C. M. (1997) 'The sexual division of care in mainland China and Hong Kong', *International Journal of Urban & Regional Research*, 21: 607–619.

31

Reconstruction of gender and youth identities

A study of online gaming communities in Shanghai

Andy Xiao Ping Yue and Eric Ping Hung Li

Introduction

Owing to the economic reforms proposed by Deng Xiaoping in the late 1970s, mainland China has experienced a dramatic transformation in its sociocultural environment (Naughton 2008). The 'market socialist' mechanism has not only created a new market environment for Chinese and international businesses but has also exposed Chinese consumers to different global brands, communication technologies, and consumer ideologies (Cayla & Eckhardt 2008; Dong & Tian 2009; Zhao & Belk 2008). Online gaming, for instance, is one of the most popular entertainment activities in China and has played an important role in shaping the 'Chinese youth culture'.

The dramatic rise of online gaming in China is now regarded as a subset of popular culture that influences the sociocultural environment of Chinese society. The internet has opened up tremendous networking opportunities for today's Chinese youth,[1] who are significantly more technologically advanced than earlier generations that relied on face-to-face interactions (Chin 2011; Li 2006; Wang et al. 2009). As Belk (2013) aptly put it, new communication technologies and devices are becoming consumers' second or third skin, allowing them to connect to others and convey their thoughts, opinions, and identity to a broad range of users across the globe.

While many view these changing social interactions and consumption patterns as beneficial, they in fact present new challenges to the Chinese society. Boellstorff (2008) argues that virtual worlds reconfigure selfhood and sociality, but this is only possible because they rework the virtuality that characterizes a human being in the actual world. The blurring boundary between online gaming and real life has created a new cultural pattern for Chinese citizens. New types of friendships, gender relationships, identities, and social dynamics are forged in this 'synthetic world' (Castronova 2008).

As these are relatively novel phenomena, this investigation focuses on online gaming, as one of the most popular entertainment activities in mainland China, and its role in the development of 'Chinese youth culture' in metropolitan cities like Shanghai. Building on the

DOI: 10.4324/9780429059704-36

theoretical foundations of liminality (Van Gennep 1960) and performativity (Butler 2002), the aim of the research presented here is to elucidate how online games affect the everyday lives of youth in mainland China, as well as how online gaming activities intersect the discourses of gender and identity.

As a part of our empirical study, we examined how Chinese online gamers construct and convey their desired identities to their peers in the online world by, for example, adopting a new persona that distances them from the real world, or creating avatars that represent their personalities in online games. As the online gaming market in China is largely male-dominated, the reconstruction of gender identity and gender relationships in this online space is also explored.

The rise of digital self and online communities

The emerging 'digital self' phenomenon is considered as an outcome of the widespread popularity of digital technologies (e.g., Belk 2013; Schau & Gilly 2003; Zhao 2005). Agger (2004) was the first to use this term to refer to 'the person connected to the world and to others through electronic means such as the internet, television, and cell phones' (1). Zhao (2005) subsequently defined 'digital self' as an internet-mediated self-construction that is '(1) inwardly oriented, (2) narrative in nature, (3) retractable, and (4) multiplied' (395). More recently, Belk (2015) employed Cooley's (1992) notion of 'looking-glass self' to describe the co-constructive nature of the digital self. He argued that consumers' self-identity is driven by others' responses to their online behaviors, such as online tagging, comments, and endorsements.

The digital world also offers new spaces for community-building. In their study on the Apple Newton brand community, Muniz and Schau (2005) found that consumers were engaged with each other and developed a collective shared mythology accentuating the unfair abandonment of their brand, its amazing abilities, and its possible revival in the system of a rumored newer model.

Early in the 1990s, Castells (1996, 1997) recognized the importance of social networks in the infancy of the internet, arguing that members of the young generation obtain information and inspiration from global sources. Since then, consumer researchers similarly opine that modern youth have the tendency to put the 'self' at the very center of their discourse (e.g., Kjeldgaard & Askegaard 2006; Wooten 2006). In their view, youth treat identity development, realization, or affirmation as the ultimate source of their consumption needs and desires. As a result, their consumer behaviors are determined primarily by their 'lifestyle choices' and decision-making rather than by structural factors like age, sex, and class. According to Arvidsson (2001), young consumers seem to be 'a priori socially displaced', prompting them to adopt a more dynamic role in their identity construction.

In addition to providing new spaces for the reconstruction of youth identity, the online communities also serve as a new arena for gendered performativity. Butler (2002) argued that our identities, gendered and otherwise, do not signify the authentic inner 'core' self but are merely a dramatic *effect* (as opposed to the cause) of our performances. Yet, the rapid growth of social media and online community that has taken place in recent decades is changing the construction of gender identity. For example, findings yielded by previous studies on internet usage indicate that certain activities, such as online gaming, tend to be more popular among male users (Condis 2018). However, the recent rise of female gamers would seem to indicate a change. Although Williams et al. (2009) argued that not many women would consider gaming an attractive pastime, partly because this would imply deviation from traditional gender activities and roles, nearly two decades ago, Kidder (2002) already noticed certain gender-specific behaviors in the cyberworld. He found that men were encouraged to be 'heroic' and portray competitiveness, aggressiveness, and ambition while female gamers were expected to be more caring and nurturing. More recently, Kaye and Pennington (2016) found that the 'girls can't play' stereotype greatly impacted female online gamers' performance and social identities. These findings demonstrate that the existing gender identities and expectations are also adopted or even exaggerated in cyberspace. However, we argue that there is a need to further explore the impact of online games on gender identities and social relationships.

Research methods

In the present study, an ethnographic approach was adopted to examine the reconstruction of youth identity and gendered relationships within online gaming communities. To better understand the interactions among members of online game communities, the first author immersed himself into one online gaming community by participating in social activities and attending different gaming events. The aim was to explore the paradoxical rhetoric of online gaming and better understand how online gaming communities are structured in mainland China. This approach was guided by the hypothesis that online gaming communities are a reflection of the sociocultural environment in which the youth in mainland China is being raised. By studying the changes in the nature of online games and their impact on gamers' lifestyle and sense of self, the goal of this investigation was to unpack the dialectic relationship between gender and identity in this emerging economy.

Field site – online gaming in Shanghai

Online gaming is one of the fastest-growing consumer markets in mainland China. According to a report published in China Briefing (Koty 2020), the Chinese online game revenue exceeded USD36.5 billion in 2019. Online gaming is an important segment of the youth-oriented market in China. A Statista report further indicates that the majority of online gamers in China are aged 18–25 years (Thomala 2020). In 2017, the number of mobile gamers in China reached 554 million and most of these individuals reported spending one to two hours per day playing online games. According to Millward (2014), males comprise 73% of the Chinese gaming population, confirming that the online game market is both male-dominated and youth-oriented.

To examine this phenomenon further, the research reported here was conducted in Shanghai, mainland China. Shanghai was chosen as the field site because the city is the consumption center of China and is home to many well-educated and wealthy young consumers. In addition, as the birthplace of China's online gaming industry, which has grown steadily over the years, Shanghai is the ideal place to conduct this ethnographic research. In 2017, the Shanghai municipal government announced that it would develop the city into a cultural and creative center with international partners by 2035. At the same time, the municipal government promised to improve the city's public services for the animation and gaming industry to attract investors to develop Shanghai as a global animation and game production base (Hu 2017).

Data collection procedure

To gain insight into the online gaming phenomenon in mainland China, we employed the existential-phenomenological approach (Thompson et al. 1989) to capture the lived experiences of online gamers in Shanghai. The data for this study was gathered via 19 in-depth

Table 31.1 Descriptions of research participants

Name	*Age*	*Gender*	*Occupation*	*Role in the Gaming Community*	*Years in Gaming Community*
Liao Rao	23	M	Graduate student	Gamer	10
Jiao Zhu	20	M	Undergraduate student	Gamer	8
Sui Ku	24	M	Banker	Gamer	6
Miao Miao	22	F	Teacher	Girlfriend of gamer	2
Shu Shao	25	M	Undergraduate student	Gamer	7
Chen Hong	24	M	Unemployed	Gamer	n/a
Shen Shen	21	M	Hotel management	Friend of gamer	n/a
Xu Rong	23	M	Graduate student	Gamer	11
Tang Yao	22	M	Undergraduate	Friend of gamer	2
Tan Tao	25	M	Entrepreneur	Gamer	13
Xiu Lo	25	M	Secretary	Gamer	5
Lu Lou	25	M	Official assistant	Gamer	n/a
Chen Shao	24	M	Administrative assistant	Gamer	10
Liu Jei	34	M	Military	Parent of gamer/Gamer	n/a
Yao Juan	23	M	Government intern	Gamer	n/a
Jing Chen	25	M	Realtor	Gamer	11
Ming Hao	24	M	Works for family business	Gamer	8
Da He	25	M	Automotive	Gamer	n/a
Hen Jing	24	M	Administrative clerk at a fashion firm	Gamer	9

interviews in Shanghai. Majority of our informants were male gamers aged 18 to 24 years, who were either university students or working-class members (Table 31.1). During the interviews – which were conducted in gaming cafés, university dormitories, informants' homes, libraries, and other venues – common themes of youth identity, gender relationships, and online game consumption in diverse localities of Shanghai were explored. All interviews were audiotaped and their duration ranged from 45 to 60 minutes.

Each interview began with some 'grand tour' questions (McCracken 1988) about the participant's personal background before delving into his/her online gaming[2] experience. In addition, participants were asked to provide a definition of youth identity and share their thoughts on their relationships with others around them and on gender relationships in particular. They also discussed masculinity and femininity ideals in online gaming, as well as the importance of bonding and teamwork.

We also conducted participant observations in gaming cafés, the China Joy Digital Entertainment Exposition (Figure 31.1) and key consumption sites for online gamers, such as Wen Miao Lu (文庙路), which is often referred to as the 'otaku street' or 'animanga street' in Shanghai (Figure 31.2). As a part of this research phase, we were able to compete with and learn various new games from our informants. At other times, we watched them compete with others online or against each other in gaming cafés (Figure 31.3).

Internet cafés are common in Shanghai, where middle- to high-end venues usually offer clean and smoke-free environments and provide various perks for members, along with food and drinks. These cafés are open 24 hours a day, seven days a week, and are typically divided into various sections, including those designated for couples (allowing additional privacy), group gaming, and other options, and the prices vary accordingly.

Figure 31.1 Tencent Inc. company booth and stage at the China Joy Digital Entertainment Exposition.

Figure 31.2 Wen Miao Lu, the 'otaku street' or 'animanga street' in Shanghai.

Figure 31.3 Interior of an internet café in Shanghai.

In addition to observing gaming behavior in gaming cafés, we had many opportunities to observe gaming participants' activities in at-home settings. We noticed that many of our informants used the software YY (www.yy.com), a widely accepted voice-chat system in the gaming world of China, to communicate with others during gameplay.

Data analysis

Consumption patterns and identity narratives of individual informants were examined through qualitative data analysis. Prior to commencing thematic analysis, each interview was transcribed and translated from Chinese to English by the first author. The data analysis commenced by categorizing interview segments according to the normative influences that were examined: relationships among gamers, those with friends and family, and with market agents. Next, the team investigated the formation and dynamicity of gender construction within the online game community. Finally, the research team categorized codes according to individual or communal issues, such as how online gamers redefine the notions of youth culture and gender ideals.

Findings

Our aim was to elucidate why online gaming is so attractive to Chinese youth and determine the role online games play in their everyday lives. Our findings show that gamers view online games as a means for releasing the stress of everyday life and achieving satisfaction through the gaming experience, as well as via the social interactions related to gaming activities. Data analysis further revealed that online gaming allows gamers, especially young ones, to experience a sense of control and empowerment in the highly hierarchical and competitive society of mainland China. For many gamers, online games are not merely a form of entertainment, but are also lived experiences that shape their present and future sense of self. In the following sections, we present the three themes that emerged from the study data, which respectively pertain to the gamer identity construction, gender construction in the gaming communities, and the development of the new online gaming culture.

Online gaming as a space for identity reconfiguration

The concept of 'gamer' is polysemous. Our findings show that the term 'gamer' as an identity refers not only to the excitement of a particular leisure activity or hedonic consumption (Hirschman & Holbrook 1982) but also to one's self-conception and group bonding/affiliation (Scimeca 2014).

Even though online gaming is becoming increasingly acceptable in mainland China, negative connotations associated with this lifestyle remain an obstacle for the young generations. For the majority of youth born and raised in mainland China, filial piety is crucial and obedience to one's parents is still expected despite considerable advances in other social domains. Rao (M 23), for instance, shared that until he left home to attend college, his parents had controlled his entire life by hiding his computer accessories, limiting his playing time, or not giving him money to hang out with his friends. As a result, Rao resorted to spending more time online and found that online gaming empowered him in many ways, as he was able to control the actions of the game characters, as well as create his own profile and form his own social networks. He pointed out:

> I want to control the aspects of my life from here on. In online games, I can customize my own avatar's skin, which makes me stand out from the rest. Unless my computer or Internet [is] down, my hero in the game will always obey me; it is a matter of how I control [the action] to win.

Rao's narrative shows a typical mindset of Chinese youth, many of whom believe that online gaming provides a space to escape from parents and a way to gain a sense of control and empowerment. Rao displays his enthusiasm for online gaming through the ability to make and execute his own choices. His avatar is very much like his second skin in the virtual community (Belk 2013). Controlling online game characters and various avatars also gives online gamers a temporary sense of empowerment, as online gamers can exert total control of their virtual 'lives' and activities, beyond the influence of the parents and societal factors that govern their everyday activities in the real world. For most young people, socializing in the virtual world is part of their everyday lives, and this extends to the gaming environment.

However, spending most of one's time online can be viewed as toxic, as reflected in the derogatory term '*zhai nan*' (translated as 'stay-at-home male computer geeks'). Similar to the Japanese term 'otaku' and English term 'geek', the Chinese youth labeled as '*zhai nan*' are perceived as socially inept due to which they choose to remain within their own bubble.

Gender reconstruction in online gaming communities

As mentioned earlier, Chinese online gaming community comprises of mostly young males, who forge and strengthen their relationships through collaboration, sharing, information exchange, and working as a closed group. To compete with other male gamers, they strive to increase their individual skills, acquire powerful virtual weapons, and demonstrate strong leadership and execution techniques, but also form strategic relationships with other gamers. Many online games feature characters or avatars imbued with great physical strength, further emphasizing the masculine traits of the gaming environment. According to our informants, gamers typically develop a masculine representation in the games to convince others that they would be strong teammates. The superiority of the male figures and the macho image have become the dominant drivers in shaping gender norms in contemporary Chinese society. Many of our informants believe that if they were born female, their parents would strictly prohibit them from partaking in online gaming because the older generation still perceives online games as 'a man thing'.

Yet, wealthy females aged 18–30 are becoming increasingly active in the online gaming community, prompting changes to the long-established community dynamics. According to Ku (M 24), this new trend in the gaming realm or internet cafés has created a sense of excitement for males. He says:

> When I notice a few girls playing one particular online game that I play, either online or at gaming cafés, I feel positive about the game's future growth and potential. Meeting them would definitely be great; however, without common friends, it may be a bit awkward as these girls are definitely something extraordinary.

Based on the observations conducted by the first author and his direct involvement in the online gaming community, female players tend to play online games mainly for social reasons such as connecting with friends and meeting new friends.

Given this newly developed admiration for female traits, male gamers sometimes portray themselves as females online. Some even use photos of their female friends as a way to receive special treatment from other gamers. Some male gamers that took part in this study, however, indicated that this is simply their way to experience the female power and uniqueness within the Chinese society. This practice shows the vast scope of the online world for enacting one's desires and aspirations. On the other hand, it is also an indication of how far Chinese gamers are willing to go to obtain certain virtual items and benefits to succeed in this highly competitive environment. Unfortunately, these new perceptions of females have introduced a new set of social issues and new forms of gender discrimination among the Chinese youth which have to be examined in conjunction with the ongoing commoditization of female body within the online game community by marketers, as gaming is still viewed as a predominantly male pastime.

In the online gaming industry, marketers frequently use female characters to attract and excite male gamers. As a result, the way young, attractive females are portrayed in the online game community by Chinese gamers is rather controversial. According to our participants, in-game expressions can sometimes be taken to extreme levels that include profane and sexist language, threats, and bullying. Hong (M 24), for instance, shared that the 'majority of the female characters in online games are sexually portrayed both to entertain the male gamers and redefine the beauty standard for females'. Similarly, Shao (M 25) expressed that a new beauty standard is being defined by the appearance of the gaming character or avatar, as 'the less the female (game character) wears, the more attractive she looks, with accessories such as stockings and high heels'.

This portrayal could be viewed as a reflection of the stereotype and the expectation for young females in contemporary Chinese society to be physically appealing to their male counterparts. The gaming industry further exploits such expectations through game design and marketing strategies. For market agents, the female body represents a gateway to hypersexuality in the minds of Chinese men. By developing scantily dressed and light-skinned female characters that act and speak provocatively, marketers are able to attract more male gamers. However, this over-sexualized portrayal of women in the virtual realm may create unrealistic expectations of females in real life. In response to this new phenomenon, some Chinese women have recently started exploiting their sexuality, signifying that outward appearance and money is increasingly given precedence over other cultural values such as gender equity and respect.

The hypersexual representation of females in the marketplace also challenges the conventional conceptions of family and gender relationships. For instance, Lou (M 25) commented that long-lasting relationships are no longer of great cultural importance in affluent Chinese cities such as Shanghai and Beijing. Attractive upper-middle-class young females have thus become the ideal image for females in Chinese society, characterized as '*bai fu mei*' (white, wealthy, and pretty). Even though some argue that this is not a sign of degradation of social and moral norms, the negative connotations of high expectations and bossy attitudes that these affluent young women typically adopt as a part of their overall image indicates that there is a great need for reform.

'Brotherhood': The development of a new digital youth culture

While gamers seek to tap into the feeling of hypermasculinity in the online environment by exerting power and dominance over other gamers, they also engage in activities to reinforce the sense of 'brotherhood' by bonding with other males. Brotherhood in China is often referred to as '*tie ge men*' (literally translated as 'steel brother men') and has become an extended form of '*guanxi*' (relationship) in a male-dominated space. Our informants believe that playing online games together is a way to build trust.

Many of our informants are of the view that, in the intrinsically complex Chinese society, true friendships cannot be developed in the business context, but are rather forged in other social settings. Prior to the advent of the internet, computer games developed for the Chinese market aimed to promote courage and power derived from the rich Chinese history and culture. These aspects are also embraced in online gaming platforms, allowing gamers to show respect toward friends by gifting them with virtual products. According to our informants, these are fairly common practices in developing *guanxi* amongst gamers. As gaming is becoming increasingly popular pastime activity for young Chinese males, they also see online communities as spaces where they can develop friendships and social networks. As a result, relationships formed in virtual worlds are gradually taking precedence over those with real friends and family. In most cases, the clans and teammates youth interact with in the online game setting are their real friends, but their bond is strengthened by the joint activities in the virtual domain, whereby they are often seen as 'honorary' family members. It is thus not surprising that changes in the perception of family and gender relationships, as well as the notion of 'brotherhood', were some of the emerging themes identified in the context of online gaming and youth culture.

Social interactions among online gamers are not limited to the virtual world. For instance, the China Joy Expo in Shanghai is one of the homecoming events for '*zhai nan*' within China. This event is similar to the annual fandom expo, Comic-Con, in San Diego. Gaming fans would line up for hours during China Joy to purchase gaming merchandise and gear, many of them taking photos with showgirls. Similar to Comic-Con, where organizers publicize hashtags (words or phrases preceded by #, allowing users to find others with similar interests) (Jenkins 2012), China Joy attendees actively publicize the event through

Figure 31.4 Showgirls at the China Joy Exhibition.

tweets on Weibo, flooding social media with the news of China Joy during that particular weekend.

In China Joy, there is a clear distinction between performers and participants, whereby the latter are mainly '*zhai nan*' gamers, while the former are showgirls connected to gaming companies. Cosplay is not uncommon in the China Joy arena, hypersexualized showgirls were staged to entertain the '*zhai nan*' participants (Figure 31.4). Instead of being a networking event like Comic-Con or Mardi Gras in New Orleans, China Joy is more of a consumption event and an exhibition venue for online gamers.

While China Joy is considered a temporal communal space for online gamers, the recent development of the 'animanga street' in Wen Miao Lu, Shanghai, signifies spatial transformation of the city based on the increasing popularity of online gaming. Stores with anime merchandise located in this area not only cater for gamers wishing to acquire the accessories or collectables connected to their favorite online games and/or animation, but the street is a great after-school/work gathering place for gamers and their peers.

Discussion: The online gaming community as a liminal space for Chinese Youth

Findings yielded by the current study point toward a pervasive culture of identity- and community-building in the online gaming subculture in China. In extant research in this domain, 'computer geeks' or 'otaku' are commonly used terms to describe males interested in video games, anime, and manga – a fascination widely viewed as perverse. Owing to this prevalent stereotype, many youths look down on 'otaku' as of a lower class, as they perceive their lifestyle and taste as degraded, which leads to social ostracism. Our research gives an alternative perspective on '*zhai nan*' in the field of youth online gamers. Even though it is rather derogatory term amongst the youth in China and has some connection to 'moe' (Slater 1997), it is not as negative as 'otaku'. Online gamers tend to perceive the 'youth-only' communities as a safe space for freely expressing themselves and re-creating their (online) identity, as their parents have no or minimal control of their 'virtual' lives.

Our findings show that Chinese youth are experiencing three intertwined self-construction and community-building processes. First, as they are experiencing the transition from childhood to adulthood, they are learning how to behave and act like 'adults' in both online and real-life settings. Second, Chinese youth are acculturating to the new online communities. As the 'born digital' generation, young gamers are both creating and adapting a new culture. Finally, Chinese youth are reconfiguring gender identities and gender relationships in 21st-century China. By partaking in the online gaming community, Chinese gamers are given an opportunity to recreate gender ideals as well as develop new rules and norms for social interactions.

In China, as a result of the One-Child Policy,[3] young generations have grown up without biological siblings and have to forge stronger bonds with their schoolmates to compensate for the lack of close peer relationships within the family unit. As boys age, their play behaviors are transferred to online games that may shape the development of masculinity. According to our informants, the feeling of traditional brotherhood has been transferred to online battles and quests that strengthen the ties within an imagined community.

This new representation of brotherhood exhibits a form of hypermasculinity and is interplayed among various imagined communities that operate online, with leaders and members remaining close and ready to help out each other continuously. This results in the formation of various identities and fandom groups critical to this generation of young males. Online gaming culture can thus be seen as an important element of Chinese adolescents' growth and maturation process. It also draws on some traditional Chinese values, such as collectivism, which is encouraged on a social level, but is also promoted in the context of virtual communities.

Our study on online gaming in China has revealed that gender identity and relationships among youths have started to change. Our findings offer an alternate perspective on masculinity related to domesticity through the perception of the virtual space as both antagonist and protagonist to masculine identities. In the Chinese society that remains steeped in tradition, young males feel restricted in their ability to partake in physical activities typically associated with a strong and brave male image. The general hegemonic theorizations of masculinity and consumption in the man-of-action hero model (Holt & Thompson 2004) in the arena away from home brings these young players into the virtual space where masculinity is conveyed through skill levels, battles, and performance.

Online games in China originally targeted and promoted the stereotypical image of muscular men of great strength. Even though young females are increasingly attracted to this form of entertainment, online games are still designed for male audiences. In online gaming, there is a need to empower individuals by giving them a feeling that they can perform extraordinary actions, as well as forge strong bonds with other players. Thus, findings yielded by the present study both align with and challenge previous theoretical representations of masculinity and consumption practices. Many men in China, especially more affluent ones, still perceive women as an inferior social group. As mentioned earlier, in order to conform to this prevalent view, young male gamers tend to use gaming as a means of attaining a sense of control over the opposite gender by acting through female avatars in the virtual realm, given that they typically lack social skills to interact with girls in the physical world. This unique experience of role-playing as the opposite gender can provide an alternate form of perceived hypermasculine control and empowerment. Such observations are in line with Yee's (2006) finding that men were seven to eight times more likely to play as female characters in WoW (World of Warcraft) than women.

While it is generally accepted that online gaming provides space for forging connections and community-building, many also believe that online gaming is also the cause of discord among couples and conflicts among family members. Our analyses indicate that conflicts are not limited to parents, as many gamers' girlfriends and spouses do not condone gaming as an acceptable pastime. This is aptly surmised by one of our informants who noted, 'If he (my boyfriend) is so in love with online games, why does he need me? Just have a relationship with the virtual world; you can fantasize about whoever whenever you want' (Miao Miao). Clearly, how to maintain a balance between online gaming and dating is an ongoing challenge for many online gamers in China.

Our findings show that the popularity of online gaming provides a distinctive identity marker for many Chinese youths. The young generation sees online gaming as a form of rebellion, as it allows them to exert their independence from their parents' control and monitoring. For many young adults in China, online games provide a sense of control and empowerment. The absence of parents or members of an older generation in the online gaming community creates a new 'youth-only' social space.

Conclusion

Even though online gaming is often referred to as a new 'digital opium' that threatens the spiritual and cultural development of Chinese youths (Leibold 2011), our findings indicate that the new digital culture has empowered the young generation in multiple ways. For instance, youth in China are actively reconstructing their identity and redefining gender and gender relationship through new technologies and 'youth-only' social spaces such as online games. Due to the limited opportunities for dating and entertainment activities, online gamers resort to the promotion of masculinity and materiality in the virtual world as a tool in the creation of a new social order in the contemporary Chinese youth culture.

Findings yielded by the present study have shown that online gaming is perceived by many Chinese youths as a way of asserting their identity and forging social bonds that may remain elusive in the real world. Youth in Shanghai are actively creating 'youth-only' social spaces and see online gaming as a means of attaining a sense of control and empowerment. For young males, games provide opportunities for bonding and displaying masculinity just as drinking did for the younger generation in the past. As a result of the One-Child Policy introduced by the PRC government in the late 1970s, Chinese youth have been deprived of sibling relationships and thus perceive gaming community as 'brotherhood' that imbues them with the much-needed sense of belonging. The emergence of '*zhai nan*' label in recent decades, however, indicates that online gamers are still stigmatized by the broader society. Our analyses further reveal that gender identity and relationships have also been reconstructed and are continually negotiated within online game communities.

The contribution of this study is twofold. First, our findings are aimed to prompt a critical discussion on the reconstruction of gender and youth identities at the intersection of the consumerism and digital worlds in a cosmopolitan city of Shanghai. Second, we have identified the key factors influencing or mediating the construction of digital youth culture among the middle-class consumers in Shanghai. In this work, we have drawn on a number of theoretical perspectives to explore the construction of Chinese youth culture through the investigation of the development of online gaming communities. This ethnographic study shows that online gaming is not merely a popular leisure activity for young adults, as it in fact plays an important role in shaping and reconstructing gender identity and relationships in contemporary Chinese society. Acting through various identities, young males see gaming as a form of escape from the confines of Chinese society. The formation of online communities and the representation of masculinity and 'brotherhood' also redefine the male identity among the young generation. The practice of gender-switching when playing online games is another very intriguing aspect of the gaming community.

Our findings can also benefit policymakers entrusted with the future development of education programs and regulations. For instance, the study of online gaming should not be limited to addictive behaviors, as focus must also be given to intergenerational conflict, gamers' perception of self and the government, and social relationships in virtual and real-world settings.

Gender-related issues in online gaming are another key topic that policymakers should explore further. In a male-dominated popular culture like online gaming, female bodies have become a commodity, whereby hypersexual female in-game characters and showgirls employed in public events such as China Joy are deliberately styled that way to appeal to male consumers. Hence, greater regulation of gender stereotypes and negative connotations is the key responsibility of policymakers who must find the means to monitor and control market agents' abuse of female bodies to ensure that online gaming is a 'clean' environment for Chinese youth of both genders.

Authors of future studies in this domain can also explore the sociality of female gamers and their views of materiality and hypermasculinity in the online gaming community. This may include both hardcore gamers as well as those partaking in light mobile gaming, the popularity of which has boomed in the emerging economies such as India, Brazil, and Russia across the globe. Last but not least, as a part of future investigations, researchers can conduct a cross-cultural analysis among online gamers and their construction of masculinity and materiality in the virtual world. In conclusion, our study has revealed that online gaming behaviors are culturally bounded. Gamers are living at the intersection of traditional Chinese culture and global consumer culture, while also striving to navigate the intergenerational expectations and societal norms at the crucial time in their development as they transition from childhood to adulthood.

Notes

1 We followed the United Nations' (2013) definition of 'youth' pertaining to persons aged 15–24 years.

2 We recognize that there are many categories of online games (e.g., board games, first-person shooting, arcade games, action and adventure games, card games, sports games, etc.) and acknowledge that online games could be played via different devices (desktop/laptop computers, mobile phones, and tablets). However, the primary focus of this investigation was on massively multiplayer online role-playing games (MMORPGs) typically played using desktop or laptop computers.

3 Even though the PRC government relaxed its One-Child policy in 2014 and reimplemented the Two-Child Policy in 2016, the country's birth rate declined gradually between 2016 and 2018 (Leng, 2019).

References

Agger, B. 2004. *The virtual self: A contemporary sociology*. Malden, MA: Blackwell Publishing.

Arvidsson, A. 2001. From counterculture to consumer culture: Vespa and the Italian youth market 1958–78. *Journal of Consumer Culture* 1: 47–71.

Belk, R. W. 2013. Extended self in a digital world. *Journal of Consumer Research* 40: 477–500.

———. 2015. Co-construction of the digital self. In *NA—Advances in Consumer Research* Volume 43, ed. K. Diehl and C. Yoon 111–16. Duluth, MN: Association for Consumer Research.

Boellstorff, T. 2008. *Coming of age in second life: An anthropologist explores the virtuality human.* Princeton, NJ: Princeton University Press.

Butler, J. 2002. *Gender trouble*. London: Routledge.

Castells, M. 1996. *The rise of the network society, the information age: Economy, society and culture Vol. 1*. Malden, MA: Blackwell Publishers.

———. 1997. *The rise of the network society, the information age: Economy, society and culture Vol. 2*. Malden, MA: Blackwell Publishers.

Castronova, E. 2008. *Synthetic worlds: The business and culture of online games*. Chicago: University of Chicago Press.

Cayla, J. and Eckhardt, G. M. 2008. Asian brands and the shaping of a transnational imagined community. *Journal of Consumer Research* 35: 216–30.

Chin, Y.-L. 2011. 'Platonic relationships' in China's online social Milieu: A lubricant for banal everyday life? *Chinese Journal of Communication* 4: 400–16.

Condis, M. 2018. *Gaming Masculinity: Trolls, Fake Geeks, and the Gendered Battle for Online Culture*. Iowa City, IA: University of Iowa Press.

Cooley, C. H. 1992. *Human nature and the social order*. New Brunswick: Transaction Publishers.

Dong, L. and Tian, K. 2009. The use of Western brands in asserting Chinese national identity. *Journal of Consumer Research* 36: 504–23.

Hirschman, E. C. and Holbrook, M. B. 1982. Hedonic consumption: emerging concepts, methods and propositions. *Journal of Marketing* 46: 92–101.

Holt, D. B. & Thompson, C. J. 2004. Man-of-action heroes: The pursuit of heroic masculinity in everyday consumption. *Journal of Consumer Research* 31: 425–40.

Hu, X. 2017. Shanghai to thrive in animation, gaming industries. *China Daily*, December 19. https://www.chinadaily.com.cn/a/201712/19/WS5a38d7eca3108bc8c6735e07.html (accessed June 03 2020).

Jenkins, H. 2012. Superpowered fans: The many worlds of San Diego's Comic-Con. *Boom: A Journal of California* 2: 22–36.

Kaye, L. K. and Pennington, C. R. 2016. 'Girls can't play': The effects of stereotype threat on females' gaming performance. *Computers in Human Behavior* 58: 202–9.

Kidder, D. L. 2002. The influence of gender on the performance of organizational citizenship behaviors. *Journal of Management* 28: 629–48.

Kjeldgaard, D. and Askegaard, S. 2006. The glocalization of youth culture: The global youth segment as structures of common difference. *Journal of Consumer Research* 33: 231–47.

Koty, A. C. 2020. How to enter China's online gaming market. *China Briefing*, April 14. https://www.china-briefing.com/news/entry-strategy-chinas-online-gaming-market-opportunities-license-compliance/ (accessed May 17 2020).

Leibold, J. 2011. Blogging alone: China, the Internet, and the democratic illusion? *Journal of Asian Studies* 70: 1023–41.

Li, E. P. H. 2006. "Let's go online': A contextual review of the consumption of Internet in mainland China. *Asia-Pacific Advances in Consumer Research* 7: 317–24.

Leng, S. 2019. China's birth rate falls again, with 2018 producing the fewest babies since 1961, official data shows. South China Morning Post, January 31. https://www.scmp.com/economy/china-economy/article/2182963/chinas-birth-rate-falls-again-2018-producing-fewest-babies (accessed May 20 2020).

McCracken, G. 1988. *The long interview*. Thousand Oaks: Sage.

Millward, S. 2014. Let's take a look at China's $13.5 billion online gaming industry (INFOGRAPHIC). https://www.techinasia.com/china-online-gaming-industry-2013–2014-infographic/ (accessed August 25 2019).

Muniz, A. M. and Schau, H. J. 2005. Religiosity in the abandoned Apple Newton brand community. *Journal of Consumer Research* 31: 737–47.

Naughton, B. 2008 A political economy of China's economic transition. In *China's great transformation*, ed. L. Brandt and T. G. Rawski, 91–135. Cambridge: Cambridge University Press.

Schau, HoH. J. and Gilly, M. 2003. Are We What We Post? Self-Presentation in Personal Web Space. *Journal of Consumer Research* 30: 385–404.

Scimeca, D. 2014. Why I can't call myself a gamer anymore. Salon. January 2. http://www.salon.com/2014/01/02/why_i_cant_call_myself_a_gamer_anymore/ (accessed August 20 2019).

Slater, D. 1997. *Consumer Culture and Modernity*. Oxford, UK: Polity Press.

Thomala, L. 2020. Age distribution of video gamers in China H1 2019. Statista.com. April 20. https://www.statista.com/statistics/1104459/china-video-player-age-distribution/ (Accessed December 28 2020)

Thompson, C. J., Locander, W. B. and Pollio, H. R. 1989. Putting consumer experience back into consumer research: The philosophy and method of existential phenomenology. *Journal of Consumer Research* 16: 133–46.

United Nations 2013. Definition of youth. (January 23). https://www.un.org/esa/socdev/documents/youth/fact-sheets/youth-definition.pdf (Accessed May 23 2020).

Van Gennep, A. 1960. *The Rites of Passage*. Chicago: University of Chicago Press.

Wang, J., Zhao, X. and Bamossy, G. 2009. The sacred and profane in on-line gaming, In *Virtual Social Identity and Social Behavior*, ed. M. Solomon and N. Wood 109–24. Armonk, NY: ME Sharpe.

Williams, D., Consalvo, M., Caplan, S. and Yee, N. 2009. Looking for gender: Gender roles and behaviors among online gamers. *Journal of Communication* 59: 700–25.

Wooten, D. B. 2006. From labeling possessions to possessing labels: Ridicule and socialization among adolescents. *Journal of Consumer Research* 33: 188–98.

Yee, N. 2006. The demographics, motivations, and derived experiences of users of massively multi-user online graphical environments. *Presence: Teleoperators and Virtual Environments* 15: 309–29.

Zhao, S. 2005. The digital self: Through the looking glass of telecopresent others. *Symbolic Interaction* 28: 387–405.

Zhao, X. and Belk, R. W. 2008. Politicizing consumer culture: Advertising's appropriation of political ideology in China's social transition. *Journal of Consumer Research* 35: 231–44.

Part V
Oppression and opposition

32

Nonviolent revolution in China

Past and prospects

John J. Chin

Introduction

Over the last three decades, Western observers have regularly predicted the end of the Chinese Communist Party (CCP) regime.[1] Some scholars focus on *when* regime change will likely occur. Optimists predict a 'short march' to democracy within a few years (e.g., Rowen 2007; Gilley 2004; Liu & Chen 2012; Pei 2016), while others argue that China's 'long march' to democracy could be derailed or delayed (e.g., Chin 2018). Others focus on *how* any regime change in China may occur (e.g., Gilley 2004; Pei 2007), and whether political change will involve top-down reform or a bottom-up revolution by disaffected Chinese masses (e.g., Cheng 2013; Huang 2013).

For over a decade after the end of the Cold War, triumphalist belief in the 'end of history' led some observers to assume that the rising global tide of the 'third wave' of democratization since the 1970s would inexorably raise all democratic boats (e.g., Rowen 1995). With modernization theory predicting a tight linkage between economic development and democracy, and with East Asia being one of the most economically dynamic regions in the world, it has been natural to assume that East Asia is poised to lead the 'fourth wave' of democratization (Diamond 2012). China's unprecedented record of economic development in the 'reform and opening' era since the late 1970s led some observers to assume that China's leaders would be forced to pursue an elite-led process of gradual political liberalization or 'creeping democratization' (Pei 1995). To facilitate a soft landing economically, China would have a 'soft democratic takeoff' politically.

But China has confounded these expectations, showing little improvement in core democratic rights, according to virtually all cross-national measures of democracy from Freedom House to the Varieties of Democracy (V-Dem) project. Experiments with local-level democracy and 'inner-party democracy' have either disappointed or have not been scaled up (Fewsmith 2013). The CCP regime's ability to confound prior predictions of collapse and fragmentation (e.g., Chang 2001, 2011) gave rise to very lively literature on the sources of China's 'authoritarian resilience' (e.g., Nathan 2003; Wright 2010). Some even argued that a meritocratic but nondemocratic 'China model' may be sustainable and that a 'Beijing consensus' may enable China to thrive in an increasingly authoritarian twenty-first century (e.g., Halper 2010; Jacques 2009).

DOI: 10.4324/9780429059704-38

An alternative possibility is that China's current regime still carries within it the seeds of its own destruction. Though single-party regimes, including those led by communist parties, have proven to be among the longest-lived authoritarian regimes in the world since World War II (Magaloni & Kricheli 2010), no prior party regime has proved to be immortal. The Communist Party of the Soviet Union (CPSU) and Mexico's Institutional Revolutionary Party (PRI) were the prior longest-lived such regimes and each managed to rule no more than about 70 years. This naturally leads many to wonder to what extent the CCP can set new records for authoritarian endurance.

A major approach in the comparative literature on the survival of communist regimes analyzes whether the CCP exhibits signs of institutional atrophy or adaptation (e.g., Shambaugh 2008). Though some observers have been impressed with the CCP's ability to recruit talent, maintain loyalty within its ranks, and promote economic growth (McGregor 2010), others see clear signs of atrophy, scandal (e.g., the Bo Xilai affair), and factionalism that could undermine party unity (Cheng 2012). Some further argue that endemic corruption will become a drag on the economy, and that as China's economy inevitably cools, corruption will become less tolerable to China's growing middle class. To avoid capital flight, the CCP must 'democratize or die' (Huang 2013).

The optimism of the 1990s that the CCP would take the path of gradual political reform has thus slowly but surely been replaced with optimism among some that the party's failure to do so will lead to the path of revolution. Having said 'goodbye to gradualism' (Wang 2013), some now assume that political change in China could come very quickly and unexpectedly (Nathan 2013). One lesson of the 'surprising' revolutions of 1989 in communist Europe is that regimes that appeared highly stable due to 'preference falsification' of the population can quickly fall once a revolutionary tipping point leads more people to join protests (e.g., Kuran 1991). A middle class that accepts authoritarianism today could be on the streets tomorrow if a political opportunity arises. China, this line of thinking goes, is a 'fragile superpower' (Shirk 2007), one that may be a single spark away from a prairie fire, to recall Mao's famous dictum on revolution.

Indeed, some prominent observers currently believe that the CCP may be on its last legs. In 'The Coming Chinese Crackup', veteran China scholar David Shambaugh (2015) warned in the pages of the *Wall Street Journal* that the 'endgame of communist rule in China has begun'. He added 'Communist rule in China is unlikely to end quietly. A single event is unlikely to trigger a peaceful implosion of the regime. Its demise is likely to be protracted, messy, and violent. I wouldn't rule out the possibility that Mr. Xi will be deposed in a power struggle or coup d'état'. In 'China's Coming Upheaval', Minxin Pei (2020) argued that an increasingly rigid CCP has been weakened by the spread of the coronavirus and the CCP could face 'cataclysmic change'.

Is China in fact ripe for the outbreak of a (non)violent pro-democracy revolution? If so, would a 'Tiananmen II' movement be any more successful than previous major episodes of resistance? In a necessarily preliminary effort to probe these questions, this chapter briefly surveys the causes of the onset and failure of prior abortive nonviolent pro-democracy revolutions in modern China since 1949. The chapter then concludes by reflecting on structural politico-economic trends in contemporary China – including rising personalism under Xi Jinping – that may make China more or less ripe for any successful nonviolent democracy revolutions in the future.

Before proceeding, it is worth mentioning what this chapter does *not* do due to space limitations. First, although protest has become more frequent on China's periphery from Tibet (Dorjee 2015) to Hong Kong (e.g., 2014 Occupy Movement and 2019 anti-extradition bill protests), this chapter focuses on protest led by mainland China's ethnic Han majority. Second, China has seen much nationalist and social protest in recent years over a litany of policy grievances concerning housing, labor rights, pollution, and the like. Yet much of this protest has had limited demands and targeted local/provincial governments. This chapter limits its focus on pro-democracy campaigns that seek 'maximalist' political reform or regime change in Beijing. Finally, this chapter intentionally does not focus on 1989 but other lesser well-known revolutionary episodes.

China's record of nonviolent revolution since 1949

Protests are an everyday occurrence across China and have become more frequent over the last three decades. Chinese authorities use the ambiguous term 'mass incident' (群体性事件) to refer to large demonstrations (of at least 100 protestors) that 'have the potential to develop into violent stand-offs between crowds of demonstrators and the authorities, or violent attacks on government organs, factories, or other property' (Tanner 2010). Mass incidents 'take various forms, from peaceful small-group petitions and sit-ins to marches and rallies, labor strikes, merchant strikes, student demonstrations, ethnic unrest, and even armed fighting and riots'. According to official statistics from the Ministry of Public Security (MPS), the number of mass incidents increased from 8,700 in 1993 to 32,000 by 1999, with most of the growth coming after 1997 (Tanner 2004). In 2006, MPS reported 87,000 'public-order disturbances' in 2005. Although MPS has since stopped publicizing data on mass incidents, academic and activist sleuthing suggests that the trend of rising protest has only continued (*Economist* 2018). One estimate claims there were 187,000 mass incidents in 2010 (Shambaugh 2016).

Although international media cite the presumed high number of 'mass incidents' as proof that China is a cauldron of social discontent, most 'mass incidents' are small-scale and localized events (Freeman 2010). A study of 871 mass incidents by the China Academy of Social Sciences (CASS) in 2014, for example, found that about two-thirds of mass incidents involve over 1,000 people but only 1% involve more than 10,000 protestors. Less than half of mass incidents actually target government officials (Hou 2014). A study of mass incidents in 2015 found that two-thirds concerned economic grievances (e.g., wages) and were concentrated in coastal manufacturing hubs such as Guangdong, Shandong, Shenzhen, and in major factory cities. However, 'bigger concerns such as regime change are generally off the table' in most mass incidents. For one thing, protestors may think regime change would not benefit them. Second, since large gatherings 'hostile to China's socialist system' are illegal under China's constitution, many protestors use smaller-scale tactics to avoid repression (Headley & Tanigawa-Lau 2016).

All nonviolent revolutions are 'mass incidents', but only a few 'mass incidents' over the last 70 years could become revolutions. Maximalist resistance campaigns are rare events (Chenoweth & Ulfelder 2017). Yet they are arguably the most consequential for macro-level political outcomes such as electoral democracy (e.g., Celestino & Gleditsch 2013; Bayer et al. 2016). These are the 'prairie fires' that could actually shake the CCP regime to its core. According to my Nonviolent Episodes and Violent Episodes of Resistance (NEVER) dataset (Chin 2020), there have been no more than a half dozen revolutionary 'sparks' in China since 1949.

Hundred Flowers Movement (1957). In the wake of Nikita Khrushchev's secret speech against Stalin in early 1956, Mao Zedong proposed to 'let a hundred flowers bloom, let a hundred schools of thought contend'. There was an outpouring of criticism by China's intellectuals over five weeks after May 1, 1957. Much of the criticism to CCP rule was ambiguously revolutionary insofar it was mainly couched in terms of loyal opposition to bureaucratic despotism and targeted cadres below Mao. Taken aback by the scale of the criticism, Mao blessed a crackdown in June 1957. By the end of 1957, over 300,000 'rightist' intellectuals were jailed, sent to labor camps, or 'sent down' to the countryside in the antirightist campaign (Spence 1999). With democratic forces thoroughly demobilized, it would be nearly two decades – following the turmoil of the Great Leap Forward (1958–1960) and Cultural Revolution (1966–1976) – until another primarily nonviolent mass movement seemingly emerged to challenge the regime.

The April Fifth Movement (1976). The revolutionary spark was the death of Zhou Enlai in January 1976. When Jiang Qing and the Gang of Four, widely resented for the most extreme policies of the cultural revolution, criticized Zhou and tried to ban public memorials of the dead premier, protests broke out in Nanjing on March 26 (Dong & Walder 2014). Word of the 'Nanjing Incident' spread, and by April 4, the eve of the annual Qingming festival, a traditional day for 'sweeping the graves' to pay homage to one's ancestors, up to a million people visited Tiananmen Square to honor the legacy of Zhou Enlai. The next day, mass protests broke out after authorities removed the memorials overnight. As in 1957, protests were ambiguously revolutionary insofar as they demanded only a return of 'genuine' Marxism-Leninism (Baum 1996). In any event, Mao suspected that Deng Xiaoping – who had opposed the thrust of the Cultural Revolution for months – was behind the April 5 incident (Teiwes & Sun 2004). Thousands of protestors were arrested, Deng was denounced as a new Imre Nagy (reformist leader of the 1956 Hungarian uprising) and purged from the CCP leadership, and Mao appointed Hua Guofeng premier and his heir apparent. Some argue that the April Fifth Movement was 'the first time average Chinese people directly challenged' the CCP's authority (Sullivan 2007).

The Democracy Wall Movement (1978–1979). In November 1978, the CCP Beijing Municipal Committee reversed its verdict on the April Fifth Movement (1976) and called it a 'completely revolutionary action'. Sensing a new tolerance for political dissent, thousands of Beijing residents began to post big-character posters (*dazibao*, 大字报) along 'democracy wall' located on Chang'an avenue west of Tiananmen Square. By December 1978, the movement had spread to all of China's major cities. The movement's leading voice was Wei Jingsheng, an electrician-turned-activist and socialist who wrote passionately about democracy as 'the fifth modernization' (第五个现代化). The posters and underground journals published by Wei and fellow dissidents mark the first unambiguous revolutionary call for democracy in modern China (Goldman 1999), one that he argued was necessary for the success of the 'four modernizations' that the CCP officially sought, including economic development (Wei 1979). Although Deng Xiaoping (now rehabilitated) initially promoted the movement (to weaken his rival Hua Guofeng), he authorized a crackdown on the movement in 1979 (Brodsgaard 1981). Wei and many others were arrested and given long jail sentences. In September 1980, at Deng's suggestion, the National People's Congress removed the constitutional right to display posters.

The NPC Direct Election movement (1986–1987). In December 1986, student protests broke out in Hefei and Wuhan against electoral manipulation denying student candidates a chance to sit in local-level city and university congresses. Their slogans and posters echoed the 1979 Democracy Wall Movement. Student protests quickly spread to Beijing, Shanghai, and other major cities. Some professed support for Deng Xiaoping; a few posters (perhaps planted by the regime itself) called for the overthrow of the CCP. When the crackdown came in January 1987, the reformist secretary-general of the CCP, Hu Yaobang, was made a scapegoat for failing to prevent the protests and forced to resign in favor of Zhao Ziyang, another protégé of Deng Xiaoping. Fang Lizhi, an astrophysicist and vice president of the University of Science and Technology in Hefei, who was seen as a moral leader of the protests as a leading critic of intolerance and proponent of freedom of speech and thought, was purged from the CCP (Kwong 1988; Schell 1988).

The Tiananmen Square movement (1989). The trigger (but not the fundamental cause) for the largest nonviolent revolution in China to date was the death of Hu Yaobang on April 15, 1989. As with those who mourned Zhou Enlai's passing in 1976, those who saw Hu as a symbol of liberalization mobilized, first to offer memorials and then to protest. Over seven weeks until the crackdown of June 4 (*liusi*, 六四), millions of people participated protests in over 130 major cities, including Beijing and 27 of 30 provincial capitals (Tong 1998; Unger 1991), even eclipsing the visit of Mikhail Gorbachev in Beijing in mid-May. Images of the 'Goddess of Democracy' (Tsao 1994) and 'Tank Man' (Burgan 2014) remain ingrained in the west's cultural memory of China's first televised revolution. Detailed histories of this movement have been told elsewhere (readers unfamiliar with this literature would do well to start with excellent books by Calhoun 1994; Brook 1998; Zhao 2004; Lim 2014). Deng sided with Li Peng and hard-liners who ordered the final brutal crackdown that left hundreds or more dead. Zhao Ziyang, sympathetic to the protests, was forced to resign as CCP secretary-general, just as Hu Yaobang was forced to do in 1987. The 'Tiananmen Papers', compiled by the pseudonymous Zhang Liang (Nathan & Link 2001), Zhao Ziyang's journals made while under house arrest (Zhao et al. 2009), and the 'New Tiananmen Papers' (Nathan 2019; Nathan & Wu 2019) all give a glimpse into the internal regime struggles during and immediately after the protests.

The post–Cold War nonrevolutions. None of the aforementioned nonviolent revolutions succeeded in achieving major democratic reform; if anything, they all led to a period of conservative backlash and heightened regime repression. Still, the period 1976–1989 represents the most contentious period of CCP rule to date, with an average of one revolutionary episode every four years. Although 'doomed' (Pei 2013), the 1989 revolution came closer to success than any before or since. The Tiananmen mothers' movement – reminiscent of the Mothers of La Plaza de Mayo in Argentina in the late 1970s – has received no answers or justice for those killed in the massacre. If anything, as China's economy has taken off in the wake of Deng's 1992 'southern tour' and 2001 entry into the World Trade Organization, China has successfully managed to employ nationalism (Gries 2004) and 'performance legitimacy' to coopt potential opposition, even coopting entrepreneurs and the private sector (e.g., Dickson 2003, 2008).

Since 1989, the CCP has prevented mass incidents from escalating into a serious revolution and has successfully crushed every movement that potentially could threaten its monopoly on political power. Three examples should suffice to highlight this trend. First, seizing on the apparent thaw following Deng Xiaoping's death and the Hong Kong handover in 1997, activists led by 1989 student leader Wang Youcai attempted to create a genuine opposition political party, the China Democracy Party (CDP). By 1999, however, nearly all of the CDP leaders were jailed (Wang was sentenced to 11 years) and party members were driven underground or overseas (Wright 2002; Goldman 2005). Second, the Falun Gong movement founded by Li Hongzhi shocked Jiang Zemin and CCP leaders when 10,000 of its adherents unexpectedly staged a peaceful protest outside of Zhongnanhai on April 25, 1999. The group was banned as an 'evil cult' three months later and crushed over the next few years (Tong 2009). Third, in December 2008, 303 civil society leaders signed a 'Charter 08' manifesto – inspired by the 'Charter 77' manifesto by Czech dissidents – demanding independent courts, respect for human rights, and an end to one-party rule. Many signatories were soon jailed (Cunningham & Wasserstrom 2011), including Liu Xiaobo, a leading Beijing-based literary critic and supporter of the 1989 protests (Liu 1994), who went on to win the Nobel Peace Prize in 2010.

China's prospects for nonviolent revolution

Why Chinese dissidents failed to break the wheel of repression and have not successfully launched another attempted democratic revolution after 1989 is a crucial and still unresolved empirical puzzle, one which has a direct bearing on China's prospects for nonviolent revolution. Though many factors are no doubt in play, we can briefly discuss three main factors here.

Autocratic learning and diffusion-proofing. During the 1989 protests, China's fear of contagion and suffering the same fate of communist parties in Hungary and Poland was a critical factor pushing Deng to authorize the bloody crackdown (Sarotte 2012). After 1989, to keep western-backed 'peaceful evolution' at bay, the CCP sponsored postmortems of the causes of post-Tiananmen mass protest in China (e.g., Sun 2002), the causes of the collapse of other communist parties in Eastern Europe and Soviet Union (Shambaugh 2008: ch. 4), and the causes of the East European 'color' revolutions' (Shambaugh 2008: ch. 5; Chen 2010). Chinese leaders' obsession with avoiding the same fate as these other regimes led the CCP to seek to actively 'diffusion-proof' the regime from possible spillover of democratic revolutions (Koesel & Bunce 2013). To contain 'internal chaos, external aggression' [*nei luan wai huan*], Chinese leaders formulated dual strategies to promote a 'harmonious society' at home and China's 'peaceful rise' within a 'harmonious world' abroad. As a result, although protest spread to many countries during the Arab Spring, there was no Jasmine revolution in China in 2011 (Dickson 2011; Kennedy 2012).

Preemptive repression. Investments in China's internal security apparatus have also played a straightforward role in facilitating preemptive repression ('stability maintenance' operations) that has prevented the emergence of organized political opposition and the escalation of mass incidents into revolutionary upheaval (on China's security state, see Guo 2012). The People's Liberation Army (PLA) remains the last line of defense for internal security (Tanner 2009), although since 1989 the PLA has actively sought to avoid internal policing deployments (Fravel 2011; Tanner 2010). In most cases, 'thugs-for-hire' (Ong 2018), local police, and the People's Armed Police (PAP) (Cheung 1996) are the regime's front line of defense against 'internal chaos'. Although China's security spending was not historically unprecedented as late as 2012 (Greitens 2017), internal security spending since has exceeded spending on external defense. Rising worker resistance as well as efforts to formally adjudicate a growing number of labor disputes across China helps explain increases in PAP spending (Elfstrom 2019).

China has also stepped up efforts to police political education since 2013 (Tiffert 2019). To nip unrest in the bud, China has sought to prevent urban concentration (Wallace 2014) and made major investments in a surveillance network (Mitchell & Diamond 2018) with 200 million video cameras in public places (Economy 2019). China has so far also confounded techno-optimism in prior decades that the internet would undermine CCP rule. Strategic censorship of internet activism is designed not so much to silence all antigovernment criticism but to prevent dissidents' collective action (King et al. 2013). What's more, China strategically engages in more preemptive repression (e.g., detentions) prior to potential 'focal events' on dissidents' calendars, such as the anniversary of Tiananmen on June

4 or the PRC's founding on October 1 (Truex 2019). Such repression is strategic since the odds of protest are over one-third higher during anniversaries of the aforementioned failed pro-democracy movements (Carter & Carter 2019).

Performance legitimacy. One of the most common triggers of pro-democracy protests are economic crises (Brancati 2014); conversely, economic growth tends to be associated with political stability in dictatorships, in the same way that economic growth is seen to favor incumbents in democracies. The basic conceit of China's growth strategy in the 'opening and reform' era was that a rising economic tide would 'lift all boats'; that is, there would be 'reform without losers' (Lau et al. 2000). Although China's economic growth record over the last three decades is historically unprecedented, there have indeed been economic 'losers' as economic inequality has risen. However, much public opinion polling data seems to suggest that rising economic inequality has not necessarily undermined the CCP's legitimacy or led to a 'social volcano' upon which revolutionary pro-democratic grievances might erupt (Whyte 2010; Chen 2013). Nevertheless, inequalities of power within China may still prove to be an active 'social volcano' that could generate revolutionary grievances despite economic growth (Whyte 2016). The 'dark side' of performance legitimacy, from the perspective of China's ruling regime, is that any precipitous worsening economic performance in China would undermine the CCP's legitimacy, and ipso facto, could invite challenges to its 'mandate of heaven' (Zhao 2009).

What then are we to make about China's prospects for nonviolent revolution? Could a mass movement like Tiananmen 1989 happen again in the near future? The CCP's success in preventing 'Tiananmen II' for the last 30 years might inspire confidence that China had successfully adapted and may be able to maintain such control of its population indefinitely. At present, some prominent observers think a Tiananmen II is 'unthinkable' (Nathan 2019). Yet we must remember that nonviolent revolutions are rare events in general, occurring in only 3.8% of years under autocratic rule, according to the NEVER dataset. If China were no different than the average autocracy, then we might suspect that China is just about due for a nonviolent revolution (given one occurs approximately once every 26 years on average). In arguing that Tiananmen II is in fact quite possible, some have noted that 'dissent is not dead' among intellectuals, environmentalists, women's groups, etc. (Economy 2019). 'Rapacious land seizures, widespread official corruption, and choking environmental problems are creating pockets of discontent among people who feel that they have little left to lose' (Lim 2014), including a growing army of 'the young and the restless' in China's third-tier cities (Gilley 2019).

What could trigger Tiananmen II, if anything? The trigger events for some revolutions appear sui generis and fully unpredictable. For example, who could have predicted that the self-immolation of a Tunisian street vendor in late 2011 would spark the Arab Spring? Nevertheless, some revolutionary triggers stand out as relatively more common, especially certain kinds of elections with international monitors and fraud (Tucker 2007; Beaulieu 2014) and, as mentioned before, economic crises. At present, an electoral revolution in China is highly improbable, if only because there is no organized opposition to mobilize against electoral fraud (recall the crushing of the CDP in the 1990s). Although electoral protest like that of 1986 may be possible, it seems unlikely that China would be caught up in a wave of 'color revolutions' such as the one that occurred in Eastern Europe in the wake of Serbia's 2000 Bulldozer Revolution. An economic crisis could be the biggest risk factor that could predict future nonviolent revolution in China, as in 1989, when the adoption of price reform in 1988 led to a doubling of inflation (Pei 2013).

As of this writing, whether or not the economic and political fallout from the spread of the coronavirus (COVID-19) will accelerate the CCP's demise remains to be seen. The domestic political consequences of the coronavirus for China will likely depend on how well the CCP is seen as responding compared to the west. Pei (2020) argues that the coronavirus has revealed Xi Jinping's fragile strongman rule, exposed gaps in the censorship regime, and could lead to more mass disaffection. Yet despite anger at the initial cover-up in Wuhan (Xu 2020; Economy 2020), the CCP may in fact emerge stronger in the short run to the extent that Chinese citizens 'rally around the flag' and see Xi as providing international leadership lacking by the United States (Chen 2020). The long-run implications of COVID-19 are even murkier. The 2020 pandemic will no doubt be remembered as a historically important turning point, but whether it marks the beginning of the end for the CCP is debatable. The pandemic could act like Mexico's major 1985 earthquake, undermining the ruling party's legitimacy and providing a spark to opponents. Or the pandemic could consolidate the CCP's international standing (Campbell & Doshi 2020).

Finally, the 20th CCP National Congress in 2022 might be a focal point for unrest to the extent that there is the potential for elite instability or a succession crisis. Since becoming CCP general secretary and CMC chairman in November 2012 and president in March 2013, Xi Jinping quickly consolidated his personal authority over the party and armed forces, in part by launching an anti-corruption campaign that many saw as a way to purge rival regime elites (Char 2016). As early as 2014, some were calling Xi an 'imperial' president (Economy 2014). The trend toward personalization has only continued. In 2017, Xi began his second five-year term. Xi Jinping Thought was enshrined in the CCP charter, and he broke precedent from Jiang Zemin and Hu Jintao in not naming a successor. In March 2018, Xi engineered revisions to the 1982 constitution removing the two-term limit for president, fueling speculation he intended to rule past 2022. In 2022, Xi will be 69 years old. The norm, in place since the 1990s, has been that politburo members must retire at the age of 68. His continued rule would thus clearly violate party norms that have attempted to ensure rotation of leadership after Mao (Womack 2017). More than one nonviolent revolution worldwide has been triggered by executive power grabs.

Yet research on personalization and technologies of rebellion finds that personalist regimes are more likely to collapse by violent means than nonviolent means, and thus are less likely to transition to democracy (Geddes et al. 2018). For example, high levels of personalism, especially within the security forces, are associated with an increased risk of assassination attempts against incumbent dictators (Chin et al. 2020a) but a reduced risk of mass uprisings (Chin et al. 2020b), in part because personalist dictators' ability to select more loyal security agents increases preemptive repression and expectations among would-be revolutionaries that security forces will follow orders to shoot. Security force personalization has certainly been increasing under Xi. With the PAP now placed firmly under the PLA, as chairman of the Central Military Commission, Xi Jinping now 'has direct control over all of China's primary instruments of coercive power. This represents the highest degree of centralized control over China's paramilitary forces since the Cultural Revolution' (Wuthnow 2019). In the short run, then, rising personalism under Xi should be expected to make Tiananmen II less likely.

Any predictions about the evolution of protest politics in China is compounded by uncertainty over how quickly China's phenomenal economic growth may slow down in the years ahead.

Economic crises would be likely to increase the chances for mass mobilization against the CCP. What's more, nonviolent revolution tends to be more likely in more educated

(Dahlum 2019), wealthier, older, and more urbanized countries with higher penetration rates of information and communication technologies (Chenoweth & Ulfelder 2017) with high levels of manufacturing (Butcher & Svensson 2016). In contrast to personalism trends, China's continued economic modernization therefore should make mass uprisings more likely in China in the years ahead. In the past, Chinese universities acted as 'free spaces' within which a 'culture of opposition' grew (Nepstad 2011). To the extent that the internet is not truly a 'free space' in China today, where organized opposition will emerge in China is unclear. Like protestant churches in East Germany, perhaps underground churches in China could one day become such 'free spaces' (Tao 2019).

Conclusion

Would a future nonviolent pro-democracy revolution in China have any chance of success? Generally speaking, nonviolent revolutions with large, cleavage-cutting coalitions are more likely to succeed than violent campaigns (Chenoweth & Stephan 2011), suggesting that the level of nonviolent discipline present in any potential revolution in China may be important for campaign success. For any future nonviolent revolution in China to succeed, it would have to generate elite defections from within the regime. Deputies in the National People's Congress (NPC) joined protesters twice, first during the Hundred Flowers Movement and a second time when hundreds of NPC deputies signed a petition during Tiananmen in 1989. Truex (2016) surmises that NPC will likely play a key role in any future successful popular democratic movement. Odds are the behavior of security forces will be even more decisive. Despite the hesitation of a few commanders to carry out orders to repress in 1989 (Scobell 2003), the PLA has heretofore proved to be loyal to the CCP leader's orders to repress (Barany 2016). In 1989, some argue that it was the institutionalized nature of the CCP regime that bred military loyalty. More personalized security forces might be more likely to fracture during nonviolent revolutions, making security force defections and a democratic pact more likely (Lee 2014). That is, Xi's personalist rule might make revolution less likely in the short run, but if revolution were to break out, the chances of the success of Tiananmen II might be higher than for Tiananmen I.

Although the history of China's nonviolent revolution is written, its future will only be revealed in the fullness of time. Given China's contentious internal security environment, neither China's 'authoritarian resilience' nor its 'coming collapse' are assured (Wedeman 2019). Contingency and chance will play a role. If the CCP's regime continues down the repressive path of 'hard authoritarianism', China's 'social volcano' may become more and more active (Shambaugh 2018). Despite the failure of all prior nonviolent revolutions in China, given the CCP's monopoly on the use of force, peaceful resistance remains 'the only pragmatic strategy available' to those in China who seek political democracy (Goldman 2009). With the 30th anniversary of Tiananmen having passed relatively quietly in 2019, we would do well to remember: the arc of modern Chinese political history is long but bends toward revolution.

Note

1 An early version of this work was presented at the Political Science Workshop at Carnegie Mellon University (CMU) in the fall of 2019. Many thanks to my CMU colleagues Ignacio Arana, Daniel Hansen, Dan Silverman, and Dani Nedal, as well as to Chris Shei and anonymous reviewers, for helpful feedback. The author alone is responsible for any remaining errors.

References

Barany, Z. D. (2016). *How armies respond to revolutions and why*, Princeton, NJ: Princeton University Press.

Baum, R. (1996). *Burying Mao: Chinese politics in the age of Deng Xiaoping*, Princeton, NJ: Princeton University Press.

Bayer, M., Bethke, F. S. and Lambach, D. (2016). 'The democratic dividend of nonviolent resistance', *Journal of Peace Research* 53 (6): 758–771.

Beaulieu, E. (2014). *Electoral protest and democracy in the developing world*, New York: Cambridge University Press.

Brancati, D. (2014). 'Pocketbook protests: Explaining the emergence of pro-democracy protests worldwide', *Comparative Political Studies* 47 (11): 1503–1530.

Brodsgaard, K. E. (1981). 'The democracy movement in China, 1978–1979: Opposition movements, wall poster campaigns, and underground journals', *Asian Survey* 21 (7): 747–774.

Brook, T. (1998). *Quelling the people: The military suppression of the Beijing democracy movement*, Stanford, CA: Stanford University Press.

Burgan, M. (2014). *Tank man: How a photograph defined China's protest movement*, North Mankato, MN: Compass Point Books.

Butcher, C. and Svensson, I. (2016). 'Manufacturing dissent: Modernization and the onset of major nonviolent resistance campaigns', *Journal of Conflict Resolution* 60 (2): 311–339.

Calhoun, C. (1994). *Neither gods nor emperors: Students and the struggle for democracy in China*, Berkeley, CA: University of California Press.

Campbell, K. M. and Doshi, R. (2020). 'The coronavirus could reshape global order', *Foreign Affairs*, March 18.

Carter, E. B. and Carter, B. L. 2019. 'Protests and focal moments in autocracies: Evidence from China'. *Working Paper*. University of Southern California.

Celestino, M. and Gleditsch, K. (2013). 'Fresh carnations or all thorn, no rose? Nonviolent campaigns and transitions in autocracies', *Journal of Peace Research* 50 (3): 385–400.

Chang, G. (2001). *The coming collapse of China*, New York: Random House.

Chang, G. (2011). 'The coming collapse of China: 2012 edition', *Foreign Policy*, https://foreignpolicy.com/2011/12/29/the-coming-collapse-of-china-2012-edition/.

Char, J. (2016). 'Reclaiming the party's control of the gun: Bringing civilian authority back in China's civil-military relations', *Journal of Strategic Studies* 39 (5–6): 608–636.

Chen, D. (2020). 'China's coronavirus response could build public support for its government', *Washington Post*, March 27.

Chen, J. (2013). *A middle class without democracy: Economic growth and the prospects for democratization in China*, New York: Oxford University Press.

Chen, T. C. (2010). 'China's reaction to the color revolutions: Adaptive authoritarianism in full swing', *Asian Perspective* 34 (2): 5–51.

Cheng, L. (2012). 'The end of the CCP's resilient authoritarianism? A tripartite assessment of shifting power in China', *The China Quarterly* 211: 595–623.

Cheng, L. (2013). 'Top-level reform or bottom-up revolution?', *Journal of Democracy* 24 (1): 41–48.

Chenoweth, E. and Stephan, M. J. (2011). *Why civil resistance works: The strategic logic of nonviolent conflict*, New York: Columbia University Press.

Chenoweth, E. and Ulfelder, J. (2017). 'Can Structural Conditions Explain the Onset of Nonviolent Uprisings?', *Journal of Conflict Resolution* 61 (2): 298–324.

Cheung, T. M. (1996). 'Guarding China's domestic front line: The People's Armed Police and China's stability', *The China Quarterly* 146: 525–547.

Chin, J. J. (2018). 'The longest March: Why China's democratization is not imminent', *Journal of Chinese Political Science* 23 (1): 63–82.

Chin, J. J. 2020. 'Recounting nonviolent campaigns: Introducing the Nonviolent Episodes and Violent Episodes of Resistance (NEVER) Dataset', *Working Paper*.

Chin, J. J., Escribà-Folch, A., Song, W. and Wright, J. 2020a. 'Reshaping the threat environment: Personalism, coups, and assassinations', *Working Paper*.

Chin, J. J., Song, W. and Wright, J. 2020b. 'Personalization of power and mass uprisings in dictatorships', *Working Paper*.

Cunningham, M. E. and Wasserstrom, J. N. (2011). 'Interpreting protest in modern China', *Dissent* 58 (1): 13–18.

Dahlum, S. (2019). 'Students in the streets: Education and nonviolent protest', *Comparative Political Studies* 52 (2): 277–309.

Diamond, L. (2012). 'The coming wave', *Journal of Democracy* 23 (1): 5–13.

Dickson, B. J. (2003). *Red capitalists in China: The party, private entrepreneurs, and prospects for political change*, New York: Cambridge University Press.

Dickson, B. J. (2008). *Wealth into power: The Communist Party's embrace of China's private sector*, New York: Cambridge University Press.

Dickson, B. J. (2011). 'No 'Jasmine' for China', *Current History* 110 (737): 211–216.

Dong, G. and Walder, A. G. (2014). 'Foreshocks: Local origins of Nanjing's Qingming demonstrations of 1976', *The China Quarterly* 220: 1092–1110.

Dorjee, T. (2015). *The Tibetan nonviolent struggle: A strategic and historical analysis*, Washington, DC: International Center for Nonviolent Conflict.

Economist 2018. 'Masses of incidents', *The Economist*, London: The Economist Intelligence Unit.

Economy, E. (2014). 'China's imperial president: Xi Jinping tightens his grip', *Foreign Affairs* 93: 80.

Economy, E. (2019). '30 years after Tiananmen: Dissent is not dead', *Journal of Democracy* 30 (2): 57–63.

Economy, E. (2020). 'The coronavirus is a stress test for Xi Jinping', *Foreign Affairs*, February 10.

Elfstrom, M. (2019). 'Two steps forward, one step back: Chinese state reactions to labour unrest', *The China Quarterly* 240: 855–879.

Fewsmith, J. (2013). *The logic and limits of political reform in China*, New York: Cambridge University Press.

Fravel, M. T. (2011). 'Economic growth, regime insecurity, and military strategy: Explaining the rise of noncombat operations in China', *Asian Security* 7 (3): 177–200.

Freeman, W. (2010). 'The accuracy of China's 'mass incidents''. *Financial Times*, March 2.

Geddes, B., Wright, J. and Frantz, E. (2018). *How dictatorships work*, Cambridge: Cambridge University Press.

Gilley, B. (2004). *China's democratic future: How it will happen and where it will lead*, New York: Columbia University Press.

Gilley, B. (2019). '30 years after Tiananmen: The young and the restless', *Journal of Democracy* 30 (2): 50–56.

Goldman, M. (1999). 'The twentieth anniversary of the democracy wall movement', *Harvard Asia Quarterly* 3 (3). https://www.worldlymind.org/demmerl.pdf.

Goldman, M. (2005). *From comrade to citizen: The struggle for political rights in China*, Cambridge, MA: Harvard University Press.

Goldman, M. (2009). 'The 1989 demonstrations in Tiananmen square and beyond: Echoes of Ghandi', In: Roberts, A. and Garton Ash, T. (eds.) *Civil resistance and power politics: The experience of non-violent action from Gandhi to the present*. New York: Oxford University Press.

Greitens, S. C. (2017). 'Rethinking China's coercive capacity: An examination of PRC domestic security spending, 1992–2012', *The China Quarterly* 232: 1002–1025.

Gries, P. H. (2004). *China's new nationalism: Pride, politics, and diplomacy*, Berkeley, CA: University of California Press.

Guo, X. (2012). *China's security state: Philosophy, evolution, and politics*, New York: Cambridge University Press.

Halper, S. A. (2010). *The Beijing consensus: How China's authoritarian model will dominate the twenty-first century*, New York: Basic Books.

Headley, T. and Tanigawa-Lau, C. (2016). 'Measuring Chinese Discontent: What Local Level Unrest Tells Us', *Foreign Affairs*, March 10.
Hou, L. (2014). 'Report identifies sources of mass protests', *China Daily*, April 9.
Huang, Y. (2013). 'Democratize or Die', *Foreign Affairs* 92 (1): 47–54.
Jacques, M. (2009). *When China rules the world: The end of the western world and the birth of a new global order*, New York: Penguin Press.
Kennedy, J. J. (2012). 'What is the Color of a Non-Revolution? Why the Jasmine Revolution and Arab Spring Did Not Spread to China', *The Whitehead Journal of Diplomacy and International Relations* 13 (1): 63–74.
King, G., Pan, J. and Roberts, M. E. (2013). 'How censorship in China allows government criticism but silences collective expression', *American Political Science Review* 107 (2): 326–343.
Koesel, K. and Bunce, V. (2013). 'Diffusion-proofing: Russian and Chinese responses to waves of popular mobilizations against authoritarian rulers', *Perspectives on Politics* 11 (3): 753–768.
Kuran, T. (1991). 'Now out of never: The element of surprise in the East European revolution of 1989', *World Politics* 44 (1): 7–48.
Kwong, J. (1988). 'The 1986 student demonstrations in China: A democratic movement?', *Asian Survey* 28 (9): 970–985.
Lau, L., Qian, Y. and Roland, G. (2000). 'Reform without losers: An interpretation of China's dual-track approach to transition', *The Journal of Political Economy* 108 (1): 120–143.
Lee, T. (2014). *Defect or defend: Military responses to popular protests in authoritarian Asia*, Baltimore: Johns Hopkins University Press.
Lim, L. (2014). *The People's Republic of Amnesia: Tiananmen revisited*, New York: Oxford University Press.
Liu, X. (1994). 'That Holy Word, 'Revolution'', In: Wasserstrom, J. and Perry, E. (eds.) *Popular protest and political culture in China: Lessons from 1989*. Boulder, CO: Westview Press, pp. 309–324.
Liu, Y. and Chen, D. (2012). 'Why China will democratize', *The Washington Quarterly* 35 (1): 41–63.
Magaloni, B. and Kricheli, R. (2010). 'Political order and one-party rule', *Annual Review of Political Science* 13: 123–43.
Mcgregor, R. (2010). *The party: The secret world of China's communist rulers*, New York: Harper.
Mitchell, A. and Diamond, L. (2018). 'China's surveillance state should scare everyone', *The Atlantic*.
Nathan, A. J. (2003). 'Authoritarian resilience', *Journal of Democracy* 14 (1): 6–17.
Nathan, A. J. (2013). 'Foreseeing the unforeseeable', *Journal of Democracy* 24 (1): 20–25.
Nathan, A. J. (2019). 'The new Tiananmen papers: Inside the secret meeting that changed China', *Foreign Affairs* 98 (July/August): 80–91.
Nathan, A. J. and Link, E. P. (2001). *The Tiananmen papers*, New York: Public Affairs.
Nathan, A., and W. Yulun. (2019). 最後的秘密 ： 中國十三屆四中全會"六四"結論文檔 (The Last Secret: The Final Documents from the June Fourth Crackdown). Hong Kong: 新世紀出版及傳媒有限公司 (New Century Press).
Nepstad, S. E. (2011). *Nonviolent revolutions: Civil resistance in the late 20th century*, New York: Oxford University Press.
Ong, L. H. (2018). 'Thugs and outsourcing of state repression in China', *The China Journal* 80 (1): 94–110.
Pei, M. (1995). '"Creeping Democratization" in China', *Journal of Democracy* 6 (4): 65–79.
Pei, M. (2007). 'How will China democratize?', *Journal of Democracy* 18 (3): 53.
Pei, M. (2013). 'China: The doomed transitional moment of 1989', In: Stoner, K. and Mcfaul, M. (eds.) *Transitions to democracy: A comparative perspective*. Baltimore: Johns Hopkins University Press, pp. 378–399.
Pei, M. (2016). 'Transition in China? more likely than you think', *Journal of Democracy* 27 (4): 5–19.
Pei, M. (2020). 'China's coming upheaval: Competition, the coronavirus, and the weakness of Xi Jinping', *Foreign Affairs* 99 (3): 82–95.
Rowen, H. S. (1995). 'The Tide underneath the "third wave"', *Journal of Democracy* 6 (1): 52–64.
Rowen, H. S. (2007). 'When will the Chinese people be free?', *Journal of Democracy* 18 (3): 38–52.

Sarotte, M. E. (2012). 'China's fear of contagion: Tiananmen square and the power of the European example', *International Security* 37 (2): 156–182.

Schell, O. (1988). *Discos and democracy: China in the throes of reform*, New York: Pantheon Books.

Scobell, A. (2003). *China's use of military force: Beyond the Great Wall and the long march*, New York: Cambridge University Press.

Shambaugh, D. (2008). *China's Communist Party: Atrophy and adaptation*, Berkeley: University of California Press.

Shambaugh, D. (2015). 'The coming Chinese crackup', *Wall Street Journal*, March 7.

Shambaugh, D. (2016). *China's Future*, Malden, MA: Polity.

Shambaugh, D. (2018). 'Contemplating China's future', *Journal of Chinese Political Science* 23 (1): 1–7.

Shirk, S. L. (2007). *China: Fragile superpower*, New York: Oxford University Press.

Spence, J. D. (1999). *The search for modern China*, New York: WW Norton & Company.

Sullivan, L. R. (2007). *Historical dictionary of the People's Republic of China*, Lanham, MD: Scarecrow Press.

Sun Liping. 孙立平. 2002. 我们在开始面对一个断裂的社会? (Are We Starting to Face a Fragmented Society?) 战略与管理 (*Strategy and Management*), 2 (9): 9–14.

Tanner, H. M. (2010). 'The People's Liberation Army and China's internal security challenges', In: Kamphausen, R., Lai, D. and Scobell, A. (eds.) *The PLA at Home and Abroad: Assessing the Operational Capabilities of China's Military*. Carlisle Barracks, PA: US Army War College Strategic Studies Institute.

Tanner, M. S. (2004). 'China rethinks unrest', *The Washington Quarterly* 27 (3): 137–156.

Tanner, M. S. (2009). 'How China manages internal security challenges and its impact on PLA missions', In: Kamphausen, R., Lai, D. and Scobell, A. (eds.) *Beyond the Strait: PLA Missions Other Than Taiwan*. Carlisle Barracks, PA: US Army War College Strategic Studies Institute, pp. 39–98.

Tao, Y. (2019). 'Protest and religion: Christianity in the People's Republic of China', In: Thompson, W. R. (ed.) *Oxford Research Encyclopedia of Politics*. Oxford: Oxford University Press, https://doi.org/10.1093/acrefore/9780190228637.013.685.

Teiwes, F. C. and Sun, W. (2004). 'The first Tiananmen incident revisited: Elite politics and crisis management at the end of the Maoist era', *Pacific Affairs* 77 (2): 211–235.

Tiffert, G. (2019). '30 years after Tiananmen: Memory in the era of Xi Jinping', *Journal of Democracy* 30 (2): 38–49.

Tong, J. (1998). 'The 1989 democracy movement in China: A spatial analysis of city participation', *Asian Survey* 38 (3): 310–327.

Tong, J. (2009). *Revenge of the forbidden city: The suppression of the Falungong in China, 1999–2005*, Oxford: Oxford University Press.

Truex, R. (2016). *Making autocracy work: Representation and responsiveness in modern China*, New York: Cambridge University Press.

Truex, R. (2019). 'Focal points, dissident calendars, and preemptive repression', *Journal of Conflict Resolution* 63 (4): 1032–1052.

Tsao, T.-Y. (1994). 'The birth of the goddess of democracy', In: Wasserstrom, J. and Perry, E. (eds.) *Popular Protest and Political Culture in Modern China*. Boulder, CO: Westview Press, pp. 140–147.

Tucker, J. A. (2007). 'Enough! Electoral fraud, collective action problems, and post-communist colored revolutions', *Perspectives on Politics* 5 (3): 535–551.

Unger, J. (ed.) 1991. *The Pro-democracy Protests in China: Reports from the Provinces*, New York: M.E. Sharpe.

Wallace, J. (2014). *Cities and stability: Urbanization, redistribution, and regime survival in China*, New York: Oxford University Press.

Wang, T. (2013). 'Goodbye to gradualism', *Journal of Democracy* 24 (1): 49–56.

Wedeman, A. (2019). 'Unrest and regime survival', In: Wright, T. (ed.) *Handbook of Protest and Resistance in China*. Cheltenham, UK: Edward Elgar Publishing, pp. 12–26.

Wei, J. (1979). 'The fifth modernisation: Democracy', *Index on Censorship* 8 (5): 9–11.
Whyte, M. K. (2010). *Myth of the social volcano: Perceptions of inequality and distributive injustice in contemporary China*, Stanford, CA: Stanford University Press.
Whyte, M. K. (2016). 'China's dormant and active social volcanoes', *The China Journal* 75 (1): 9–37.
Womack, B. (2017). 'Xi Jinping and continuing political reform in China', *Journal of Chinese Political Science* 22 (3): 393–406.
Wright, T. (2002). 'The China Democracy Party and the politics of protest in the 1980s–1990s', *The China Quarterly* 172: 906–926.
Wright, T. (2010). *Accepting authoritarianism: State-society relations in China's reform era*, Stanford, CA: Stanford University Press.
Wuthnow, J. (2019). *China's other army: The People's Armed Police in an era of reform*, Washington, DC: National Defense University Press.
Xu, Z. (2020). 'Viral Alarm: When Fury Overcomes Fear', *Journal of Democracy* 31 (2): 5–23.
Zhao, D. (2004). *The power of Tiananmen: State-society relations and the 1989 Beijing student movement*, University of Chicago Press.
Zhao, D. (2009). 'The mandate of heaven and performance legitimation in historical and contemporary China', *American Behavioral Scientist* 53 (3): 416–433.
Zhao, Z., Bao, P., Chiang, R., Ignatius, A. and Macfarquhar, R. (2009). *Prisoner of the state: The secret journal of Zhao Ziyang*, New York: Simon & Schuster.

33

Studying the Chinese political opposition in exile

Jie Chen

Introduction

This chapter studies the Chinese political opposition in exile, commonly known as the overseas Chinese democracy movement (OCDM, or 海外民运, *haiwai minyun*), an enduring struggle mounted by the dissidents since the era of China's reform started. The chapter first presents a historical context to define and profile the fluctuating movement. Second, it reviews the state of research. Third, it explores areas to enrich and update the research.

The movement

The OCDM consists of the organizations, networks, and campaigns of those mainland Chinese political activists or dissidents in exile, mostly in the West but particularly in the United States (US). Through lobbying, publicity, conferencing, training, protests, and many other contentious activities, they advocate liberal democratic values to systematically expose the fundamental flaws and human rights abuses in the party-state of the People's Republic of China (PRC) and struggle for the ending of the regime. The term 'exiles' is used as a broad reference to the active participants in the OCDM. They include not only those well-known dissidents who fled China from various rounds of political persecution or were involuntarily sent abroad by the authorities. They also include those people who, regardless of how and when they left China, chose to become proactive in the overseas political opposition, such as the people who became politicized while studying or living or visiting abroad. Some came to the West as students, some as migrants, and some even members of official delegations. In this sense, 'exile' mainly indicates that all leading activists have been barred from re-entry in the homeland due to their 'anti-China' activities abroad.

An organized opposition movement overseas against the PRC has its genesis in the state's own reform and open-door policy. Part of this policy was to dispatch students and scholars to the West from 1979. To continue the struggle of the suppressed Democracy Wall movement in Beijing (1978–79), a group of students and scholars abroad inaugurated a dissenting magazine *China Spring* in 1982 and founded the Chinese Alliance for Democracy (CAD) in 1983, both in New York. The momentum created by this first overseas political opposition

DOI: 10.4324/9780429059704-39

organization of China since 1949 expanded dramatically with the Tiananmen Square massacre of pro-democracy demonstrators by the People's Liberation Army in Beijing in June 1989. The violent crackdown caused a mass exodus of student leaders, liberal intellectuals and free trade unionists from both Beijing and the various provinces. Wuer Kaixi, Chai Ling, Yan Jiaqi, and Han Dongfang were among the most prominent ones. Under the global media spotlight, these star exiles established the Federation for Democratic China (FDC) in Paris in late 1989. Numerous other groups also emerged, though attracting fewer members compared to the many thousands active in CAD and FDC headquarters and their expanding global branches. Broadly, ranks of the OCDM were inflated by a large number of Chinese students and visitors who came to the Western countries earlier but stayed on due to the Beijing massacre. After the mid-1990s, the Chinese government picked up a few prominent activists still in jail, including Democracy Wall veteran Wei Jingsheng, and Tiananmen icons Wang Dan and Wang Juntao, and expelled them to the overseas dissident community in the name of medical parole as a diplomatic trade-off with the US. In this century, more and more human rights lawyers and dissident intellectuals left China to join the exiles, particularly during the more totalitarian Xi Jinping administration.

The movement has not been expanding in unity. In fact, overall its public profile and influence over the host states' China policies have declined compared to its moral and politico-diplomatic peak achieved during the first half of the 1990s. At the time, various organizations held grand global membership meetings and staged mass protest rallies worldwide frequently, with leading exiles seen by followers as poised for historic roles in a future postcommunist regime at home. Dissidents effectively leveraged the annual US congressional debate over China's Most Favoured Nation trade status to present their proposals to force tangible changes in China's human rights practices as a condition to retain this status – a status which China, as a poor developing economy, sorely needed. Exiles also conducted similar lobbying in other Western states. Meanwhile, exiles' presentations were able to swing the votes at the UN Commission on Human Rights in Geneva, which had become a key forum where member states frequently debated China's political repression, often forcing the regime into a vulnerable position. However, these promising developments in much of the decade were to peter out. Internal feuds among the leading exiles and between the proliferating organizations, largely caused by financial scandals and personal egos, has fragmented the movement. More importantly, conjunction of external factors from the late 1990s ushered in a rapidly deteriorating operational environment for the exiles. The movement suffered from the loss of much of the crucial sympathy and support from the Western states, Taiwan, and the overseas Chinese community. The Western states became far less willing to promote democracy in China or raise the issue of human rights abuses with Beijing, due to their surging stake in pursuing major economic and trade interests in the thriving Chinese economy. Official support from Taipei, which was the biggest financial sponsor of the exile movement during the 1980s–1990s, dwindled after it lost interest in the traditional ideological crusade against Beijing due to Taiwanization or de-Sinification defining the island's own political democratization. Meanwhile, more and more people in the Chinese diaspora community, the main grassroots of OCDM, started to become increasingly lured to the economic and career opportunities in China, thus no longer willing to be seen to associate with 'anti-China forces'.

The aforementioned arduous circumstances have largely remained to the present except that the US' developing attacks on the PRC's political regime since 2018 has given the exiles fresh hope. As a result, the dissident circles commonly see their movement in the first two decades of this century as evolving in a low tide, fighting a tough uphill battle against

Beijing's rising global power. A major setback is that most of the traditional membership-based organizations, such as CAD, FDC, and a host of political parties including Social Democratic Party, Democracy Party, Republican Party, and Labour Party, have seen their rank and file shrinking. Measured by organizational membership, the number of active participants in the movement has sharply dropped from close to 10,000 around the mid-1990s to about 300–400 today, as estimated by some leading activists in correspondence with this author. Some prominent exiles have left the movement for other careers.

However, the rise and fall of a few famous exiles and their organizations is not the full story of the movement. New trends have emerged over the recent decade or so, reshaping and recharging the movement. Deteriorating operational environment compelled many activists to reflect on its dilemma and seek sustainable tactics to survive, develop – and help the domestic comrades and their activism in niche and diverse ways. This eventually recreated some democracy veterans and more significantly bred tightly structured professional and specialized groups, cosmopolitan and media-savvy activists, novel tactics, broader activities, and intense use of information technology and social media. Thus, though the movement remains fragmented, it is not about more organizations and activities of the same kind. Since it is impossible to fully list such new type of groups and their priorities, one can only present a small number of major cases here. Initiatives for China (Washington, DC) and China Aid (Midland, Texas) have become widely reported in the mainstream media as professional lobby and public relations institutions. Humanitarian China (San Francisco) and Support Network for the Persecuted in China (Sydney) specialize in assisting the persecuted domestic activists and their families, including help in escape and resettlement and cash aid to those still in China. Tiananmen Democracy University and New School for Democracy are two online educational platforms operated by exiles based in San Francisco and New York respectively, with the help of Taiwanese and Hong Kong activists in the latter case. Mingjing Huopai (Mirror Live, New York) is one of those proliferating YouTube-based live-streamed broadcasts (accessible via online search, Twitter and Facebook) which are systematically operated by dissident intellectuals with routinized programs to counter Beijing's Grand External Propaganda blitz. Featuring many well-known political exiles, it boasted a total of 283k subscribers by February 2020 according to its own website. The Institute for China's Democratic Transition (Princeton, New Jersey) is one of the emerging dissident think tanks but specifically studying and conferencing on potential paths of regime change at home and feasible roadmap for opposition forces. Liberty Sculpture Park (Los Angeles), with its artworks and a Tiananmen Massacre Museum for public education, is a leading example of the creative work done by more and more politically conscious artists, writers and composers. Collectively they keep international memory of Tiananmen alive and educate the audience (Western and Chinese) on the brutal history of political movements of the PRC from the Mao years.

The OCDM as a whole is shifting from sloganeering towards the more practical endeavours. The movement has developed well beyond state lobbying and expanded into the social, cultural, educational and informational fields or the so-called civic politics. It is true that the movement has not revived its momentum achieved during the period from 1989 to mid-1990s. However, that was the period defined by post-Tiananmen and post-Soviet hyperexcitement, and China's economic significance to the West was yet to reveal. Thus it makes little sense to overuse the OCDM's momentum at the time to measure its progress afterwards. What can be argued is that the movement has been gradually recreating itself and moving from the bottom of its low tide over the past ten years or so. It can even be posited that a new and more diverse movement is making its debut. It is more like a promising social movement or civil society sphere than a bunch of demoralized and struggling political opposition parties (or similar traditional groups) chased out of the homeland. In particular, as will be discussed later, the exile activism has demonstrated a fresh uplift in the US in the recent two years. The OCDM has played a supporting role in China's cause of democratization. Now it is arguably functioning as the main front for the cause, considering that the heightened totalitarian repression in the homeland, characterized by high-tech surveillance and media control, has made the domestic struggle extremely difficult to wage.

State of research

Literature on the Chinese exiles has been intermittent, particularly on the movement which the individual exiles/organizations have all along claimed they are part of, although the state of research has gradually developed in recent years. This can be seen from a chronological review. The historic founding of *China Spring* and CAD's initial growth attracted little academic interest. Attention was fixated with the initial decade of China's own unfolding economic reform. The Tiananmen exodus triggered excitement in the exile politics. Zhang (1990) presented a basic informational account of CAD and its magazine, and listed their activities supporting the Tiananmen movement. Nathan (1992) postulated on the roles of the leading intellectuals fresh in their exile. Ma (1993) borrowed basic concepts in Albert Hirschman's seminal model of 'exit and voice' used to describe the evolving relationship between consumers and products of deteriorating quality. Thus he defined the sentiment of political exiles in terms of three essential elements of exit, voice, and struggle for return, and examined how each of these characterized the Chinese exile politics. This initial intuitive excitement over the Tiananmen exiles was to diminish. Over the ten years after 1993, three works were published. He (1997) studied the functions and impacts of some exile organizations as part of Chinese civil society, not fully part of international civil society. In an investigative volume consisting of personal interviews, Buruma (2001) explored the life, experiences and thoughts of some leading exiles. Finally, as if to read positively the downhill-going movement, Beja (2003) examined the activities of a small number of burgeoning lobbying and research organizations or what he called émigré Chinese NGOs such as Laogai Research Foundation (Washington, DC), a harbinger of what was to develop and expand during the second decade of this century. He focused on their potentials to influence the US' relations with China.

On the other hand, reflecting a sentiment that the movement was declining and becoming unimportant, there were more than ten years of silence in the literature after 2003, before the 25th anniversary of the Tiananmen event (2014) saw three works published on the subject. Thus, in an oral history, Rowena He (2014) interweaved her own experiences with the accounts (from childhood to exile) of three student leaders exiled from China in the aftermath of the military crackdown in Beijing. Junker (2014) presented a quantitative analysis comparing the tactical dispositions of two Chinese movements overseas: The OCDM and the Falun Gong, a religious community forced into exile in 1999. He concluded that the OCDM was mainly continuing a Confucian tradition where scholars and students were supposed to voice criticisms against despotic authorities out of moral conscience. This does not fully capture the developing and diversifying dynamics of the exile activism by that point of time since Junker's analysis of forms of the OCDM activism was based on data from 1989 to 1991, which is relatively easy to access since they are recorded in the magazines published by CAD and FDC. The last publication in 2014 was by Chen, which focused on the newly emerging trends from about 2010, namely the proliferating new organizations and their activities as described earlier. Based on this evidence, Chen (2014) critically engaged a wide-spread doom and gloom verdict on the exile activism. Chen continued to discuss the subject in two more works published in more recent years. One analyzed the developmental patterns of dissident activities by adaptively deploying the theory of diaspora politics. This theory posits that the operational environment of diaspora politics, of which the OCDM is a form, is conditioned by the diaspora activists' relations with the host land and homeland, and by intradiaspora relations. Thus the OCDM's low tide could be attributed to a deteriorating operational environment which was caused by the China-engaging Western nations' sidelining of the exiles, China's increasingly sophisticated tactics to divide and destroy the exiles, and the Chinese diaspora's distancing from the exiles (Chen 2018). In his volume published at the 30th anniversary of the Tiananmen event (Chen 2019), Chen explored the impact of the evolving and diverse exile movement comprehensively by using the idea of world civic politics and theoretical insight from the general literature on the exile politics of the world. He compellingly argued that efficacy of the Chinese exile politics must be judged not just by their ability to outright change the political regime or influence the host states' China policies but also their much broader attempts to inform and influence public opinion, develop new ideas and lend support for domestic activists in various ways. This debunked the received perception that the movement had become irrelevant just because the Tiananmen exiles were still in remote wildness far from the homeland, failing to return to influence the regime change while the party-state was thriving with strategic partnerships with major Western powers.

Literature on the OCDM usefully forms part of the broad literature on the exile politics of the world. During the Cold War exile, political movements against repressive home regimes were common, targeting the party-states in the Soviet bloc behind the Iron Curtain, Latin American juntas, and authoritarian or colonial regimes in East Asia, Africa, and Southern Europe. Some were defined by revolutionary violence, but more were peaceful. Some were governments in exile but more social movements (Shain 2005). As a result, academic works on exile politics are voluminous, mostly historical narratives based on individual national cases either as origins or hosts (Goddeeris 2007). In some case studies, such as postwar exile politics of Poland, extensive research has continued well after the movement was over (Paweł 2015). On the other hand, the literature on the Chinese case is just a small part of the tremendous and expanding literature on the postwar exile political campaigns in the world and their contributions. More should be done from multiple disciplines, considering the influence of China as well as the OCDM's historic significance. Symbolically, the OCDM has persevered as China's only political opposition movement and the world's leading living example of exile politics against a party-state. The Chinese exiles are, after all, among the nation's best intellectuals, students, scientists, social activists, and rights lawyers. Sacrificing what could have been potentially lucrative career and business opportunities in the homeland and/or host countries, they chose exile to become the first cohort of PRC citizens to experiment with real democratic practices and systematically campaign for the political liberalization of their homeland. The comparative paucity of research of their struggle may be mainly due to three reasons. First, mainstream China scholars in the West, including the ethnic Chinese academics, may have found the subject politically too sensitive and risky in terms of their career-important relations with China. Scholars researching the ongoing Cuban exile politics have little to lose. Second, comprehensive research of the OCDM is very challenging even though the researcher may not have a language barrier, since data collection must rely on a multitude of primary sources and extensive fieldwork. Primary sources refer to the memoirs of democracy veterans, literature, and reports generated by the movement itself through its own online media outlets and many online thematic discussion forums, a host of self-broadcasting platforms accessible on YouTube, and independent international Chinese language media such as Radio Free Asia and Voice of America. Field research entails interviewing the major dissidents and their international supporters and funders, and observing a number of organizations' activities, mainly in the US, Taiwan, and Australia. Thirdly, scholars inherently deploy a state-centric approach to study the OCDM, as reflected in some of the listed works. Consequently they only took the exiles seriously when they were seemingly poised to return and participate in the shaping of a new regime in Beijing in the immediate post-Tiananmen or post-Soviet years when the days of the party-state seemed numbered or when they displayed potentials to influence the major Western states' China policies. Little attention has been paid to the increasingly diverse forms of activism in the civic political realms which have become the mainstay of the Chinese exile politics in the recent decade. The OCDM should be judged as a civil society community or social movement, not a collection of serious political opposition parties in exile, and certainly not a rival government-in-exile. In fact, few works on exile politics of the world would have been written if the judgement of the activists' effect must always be whether they were the main forces which brought down or replaced the home regime, or decisively swayed the host state's relations with the home regime.

The following sections try to enrich and update the literature on OCDM by observing the movement from three angles. First, I will elucidate the uniqueness of the OCDM by locating the movement in the world exile politics against authoritarian regimes. Second, I will cast light on the rise of a distinct transnational campaign sphere or a loose coalition unifying all exile and activist communities from a Greater Chinese Region. Third, I will explore whither the OCDM goes since the commencement of a kind of China containment strategy by the Trump administration which seems to give the exile movement a new lease of life.

Comparative uniqueness of the OCDM

This section illuminates the distinct features of the OCDM as a form of exile political activism by comparing and contrasting it with other similar movements targeting authoritarian states, including the exile politics of the Soviet bloc, Latin America and East Asia (Mikkonen 2012; Torres 1999; Angell & Carstairs 1987; Shain & Thompson 1990; Oo 2006; Lee 1987). This task is long overdue since the literature on the OCDM and the works on other exile cases including those of general and theoretical nature have never developed a dialogue. For a brief comparative exercise, two important benchmarks can be deployed. The first is geopolitical parameters which condition the operation of exiles. The second is the function of the diaspora factor since all exile groups are grounded in their own émigré communities.

In the heyday of the Cold War, the US wholeheartedly used the Soviet and East European exiles in political and psychological warfare against the Soviet bloc. The US Central Intelligence Agency (CIA) mobilized these exiles with lavish funding and strong organizational support from the State and Defence Departments. A Cold War framework persisted as an unmistakable basis for the collaboration. The US enthusiasm in coopting the exiles from an ally of the Soviet Union for its own foreign policy needs was even reflected in the CIA's training and arming of numerous Cuban émigrés for raids on the Cuban coast. In comparison, the Chinese exiles have always had an ambiguous operational environment in terms of interacting with the host states. From Sino-US rapprochement in the early 1970s to the Soviet disintegration in 1991, the Chinese party-state was a useful partner, though not a formal ally, of the US in its Cold War campaign against the Soviet Union. Despite nominal criticism by the US of some events of political repression in China, the OCDM could not expect to enjoy the sort of favourable support from the Western states as the Soviet bloc exiles did. The Western host states started to become receptive to the OCDM only after June 4, 1989, yet without having ever developed a comprehensive political and psychological warfare program to proactively mobilize the exiles.

Compared to the clear-cut operational environment of the Soviet bloc exiles, their Chinese counterparts share more commonalities with fellow travellers from those countries which had authoritarian regimes allied to the US during the Cold War and had all along integrated with Western capitalism. Starting from different years, political exiles from South Korea, the Philippines, Chile and Taiwan campaigned against home regimes without necessarily always receiving unambiguous support in the US, since Washington often must ignore domestic repression of these allies. However, exiles from these 'small' countries enjoyed a far more favourable international and domestic environment to exert political influence at home than their Chinese counterparts can imagine. First, their diplomatically and economically dependent home regimes were considerably more susceptible to influence by political forces in the US when they could be mobilized by exile lobbyists. Second, political systems in those authoritarian allies of the US were overall more liberal and open than the PRC has ever been – there were some elections openly contested by opposition forces in South Korea, the Philippines, Chile and Taiwan. This made it easier for the exiles to integrate their struggle with legal opposition forces at the home front. In fact, many of them were already leading opposition figures in the mainstream system and enjoyed solid mass support before they were forced out of the homeland. Some, including East Timorese exiles, eventually returned to become national officials in the new regimes, with strong backing from the West, a most unlikely scenario for the current cohort of Chinese exiles.

So far as the diaspora factor is concerned, the mobilizational base of the OCDM in that regard is among the smallest and least solid compared to other cases. This is so despite the sheer large number of the loosely defined overseas Chinese population. Compared to many other national diaspora communities based in the West, the ethnic Chinese community – even when one just looks at the migrants from the PRC – lacks a sustainable rallying call suitable for political mobilization. Some national diaspora communities were almost synonymous to exile communities per se in substance, at least during the early stage of exile politics. That is because the origin of the formation of these communities was largely associated with a single political or military crackdown which caused violent mass demographic dispersion or fleeing in fear. In such cases, the whole or large part of diaspora communities formed in the West was politically conscious, creating a fertile ground for the core activists to mobilize for their campaigns by invoking collective memory or a common narrative. Examples of émigré communities of critical mass being formed due to one single event or a series of closely connected events include the cases of Cuba, Chile, Vietnam, Tibet, Tamils, East Timor, Burma, and the post–Second World War emigration from the Soviet Union. Correlation in the forming of diasporic and exile communities laid a broad foundation for exile political mobilization.

Compared to all the above cases, the Chinese exile movement has faced the least favourable ethnic mobilizational ground since its inception in the 1980s, due to a comparative lack of an evident collective political identity in the diaspora in favour of the exile cause. The Chinese diaspora community in the West is the most diverse of all migrant communities. They came from numerous countries including the PRC. Their common identity is based literally just on ethnicity and some broadly defined cultural traditions. The PRC-originated Chinese migrant community, which came into critical mass from the late 1990s and is most relevant to the OCDM, has not been formed by mass exodus caused by one single political or military event. It is true that the Tiananmen exodus in 1989 and the Western states' mass granting of permanent residence to tens of thousands of Chinese students and visitors for humanitarian reasons at the time were crucial in the expansion of Mandarin-speaking mainland Chinese community in the West. However, their numbers were soon to be overwhelmed by the wealthy Chinese migrants who benefited from the post-1989 reform and left China through normal migration or study schemes. The Chinese diaspora as it stands today is just a function of economic and sociocultural globalization who are likely to support the regime as bona fide beneficiaries of the system. In short, far from equating exile community to diaspora community as seen in the other cases, one can only see the OCDM as a very small segment of the diaspora.

Thus compared, the OCDM is arguably the most difficult exile experience. As a challenger to a communist party regime, it has never received the sort of strong support the exiles of the Soviet Union and its allies received from the US and some West European states. To the extent that exiles try to influence the host state's policies towards the homeland and general political affairs in the latter, the OCDM's task is more challenging than that of the exiles from those small Third World allies of the US. Furthermore, the OCDM is comparatively least representative of the sentiment of the broad diaspora except arguably for a few years after 1989.

Transnational collaboration of the Greater Chinese Region: Peripheral solidarity against the center

The national unity across multiethnic and multireligious communities which the PRC regime has largely failed to achieve thanks to a *Han* Chinese-centered nationalist narrative, the exiles are achieving it through the shared upholding of universal values of human rights and democracy. There has emerged a distinct transnational campaign sphere. The term 'the Greater Chinese Region' is tentatively used for want of a better word. It by no means implies that the component groups all identify with Chinese nationalism – certainly not the brand propagated by the regime. These components of an emerging, albeit still loose, coalition include the OCDM, Tibetan exiles, Xinjiang Uighur exiles, Falun Gong exiles, Hong Kong's young democracy activists and some social activists in Taiwan who have developed interest in the mainland's human rights conditions. In opposition to the common political enemy, they have been converging and supporting each other over the recent decade, by way of dense communication, coordinated campaigns and joint lobbying. A major institutional example is the expansion and salience of the annual InterEthnic/InterFaith Leadership Conference, one of the signature projects operated by Initiatives for China (IC). With the venues rotating between the US, Japan, Taiwan, and India, participants in this large-scale forum include Uighurs, Tibetans, Mongolians, Falun Gong practitioners, Christians (all hailing from respective exile communities) as well as secular activists from Hong Kong, Taiwan and the mainland exile community. Apart from interfaith dialogue, an international normative trend post-9/11, many other themes are also debated including a future federal or confederal structure of China, Beijing's policies in the ethnic minority regions, and general sociopolitical conflicts in China and their impacts on peripheral regions.

This partnership is both important and natural for the OCDM. The world of exile politics started to shrink rapidly since the 1990s, with activists from the Soviet bloc, East Asia and Latin America returning to their transitioning or democratizing homelands. The Chinese exiles were only able to forge perfunctory comradeship with the remaining fellow travellers from Cuba, Vietnam and Laos. However, new and more useful partners came in this century, from an expanding overseas sphere of the Greater Chinese Region. Collaboration was first developed with the Falun Gong exiles. The OCDM circles appreciated that the spiritual movement's campaigns evolved from defending the human rights of its practitioners to a wholesale crusade against the party-state. Dissidents particularly benefited from Falun Gong's global multimedia platforms. Individual OCDM activists' dialogue with representatives of the Tibetan government-in-exile, based in Dharamshala, India, started in the 1990s. However, serious exchanges with the Dalai Lama and his activist followers started after the Lhasa unrest in March 2008. This was largely initiated by the government-in-exile. The Chinese diaspora's common support for Beijing's crackdown in the Autonomous Region compelled the Dalai Lama to see the importance of dialogue between the Tibetans and Chinese in order to advance mutual understanding between the two peoples. A practical start was to open regular forums between the Tibetan and Chinese exiles. The OCDM's collaboration with the Uighur exiles also evolved in the same way. The July 2009 Urumqi riots in Xinjiang, and the resultant need for Muslim Uighurs and *Han* Chinese to empathize each other free of Beijing's dominant chauvinistic narrative, facilitated closer ties between the OCDM groups and the World Uighur Congress and the leading exiles such as Rebiya Kadeer (a former Xinjiang businesswoman expelled to the US in 2005). Collaboration with minorities has benefited the Chinese exiles in a number of ways. First, the latter have enhanced their movement's moral legitimization by being seen to enjoy the blessing from holy figures like the Dalai Lama. Second, since the Tibetan and Uighur exile groups all enjoy sympathy and funding support from mainstream America, the OCDM's solidarity with them helps in maintaining the movement's own standing. Third, the OCDM embodies the first bunch of *Han* Chinese intellectuals and activists in the PRC's history to have both the opportunity and desire to understand those ethnic peoples and shake off prejudices adopted in their early political education. This is useful in their intellectual endeavour to design a future democratic federation of China.

As for the Taiwan component in the Greater Chinese Region activist coalition, it mainly reflects a binary development of the island so far as China's human rights and democracy is concerned. The government has continued to be lacklustre in supporting the cause of Chinese democracy, due to the impact of twin factors of economic and trade interests and political de-Sinification, though these two factors weigh differently for the Kuomintang and Democratic Progressive Party administrations. However, while the Taiwanese in general are emotionally increasingly detached from the mainland politics as long as it does not directly interfere with the island, some social activists have developed interest in campaigning for Chinese democracy and human rights during this decade. Free of the traditional 'one China' sentiment, their main position is that a repressive PRC regime is the single most serious menace to Taiwan's own vibrant democracy and the island's quest for independent statehood. They focus on China also from the perspective of promoting universal values, arguing that campaign for the mainland's democratization is a way to project Taiwan's status as a responsible international citizen. Thus protecting a democratic way of life in an independent Taiwan itself and promoting universal values both necessitate improving the prospects of democratization across the strait – at least for some Taiwanese social activists. As a result, relevant campaign groups have been established over the recent decade by activists who are usually pro-independence. They include the Taiwan Association for China Human Rights, the Taiwan Support China Human Rights Lawyers Network, and the Taiwan Students Working Committee to Facilitate China's Democratization. They have actively lobbied the government on issues such as passing a coherent refugee law to handle the mainland asylum seekers based on international conventions on political refugees. This new momentum has offered the Chinese dissidents a fresh opportunity to recapitalize on Taiwan, if only largely at the societal level. Taiwanese civil society has provided the Chinese exiles with solid space to disseminate their views through media and conferencing, train themselves in social activism, and influence both Taiwanese and mainland students. Also, the island has become a useful gathering ground in the Greater Chinese Region campaign coalition in that it has hosted events attended by all the components of this coalition in such close range of the PRC. This is epitomized by the annual memorial service at the Liberty Square in Taipei to commemorate the Tiananmen event. Initiated by Taiwan's own activists and some mainland exiles of Tiananmen genre in 2011, the rallies have attracted Tibetan, Uighur, and Chinese exiles travelling from afar, and joined by Hong Kong democracy activists in recent years. In addition to keeping international memory of Tiananmen from being erased, the annual rallies have been forming a symbolic Greater Chinese Region solidarity championing universal values against the practice of 'one country, two systems'. This theme has been mostly inspired by the democracy activists in Hong Kong since the Umbrella Movement of 2014. This movement, the antiextradition protests in 2019 and imposition of a new National Security Law in Hong Kong in 2020 have highlighted the unreliability of Beijing's commitment to this formula, variant of which was first imposed in Tibet and Xinjiang and is officially intended to hit Taiwan. The emerging young Hong Kong activists have led the mainland exiles to rediscover the value of the former colony. Hong Kong was a strong material support base for students and intellectuals during the Tiananmen movement, as seen in the contributions of Hong Kong Alliance in Support of the Patriotic Democratic Movement in China. Such role, however, waned after the 1997 handover, which made it impossible for the leading mainland exiles to even visit Hong Kong. Meanwhile, political conflicts there started to concentrate more on local issues such as struggling for universal suffrage and against the erosion of residents' existing civic freedom. Though mass protests in recent years are not intended to directly assist the grand vision of China's democratization, the OCDM activists see them as potentially igniting a spark for the rest of the country. Therefore, the mainland exiles have strongly supported the Umbrella Movement and anti-extradition protests. For example, while these protests were unfolding, the former Tiananmen student leaders repeatedly warned the international media and Western governments of a Tiananmen-style massacre if Beijing had a free hand. Those Hong Kong activists fleeing to the West due to the new National Security Law have started to operate closely with the OCDM veterans in the frontier of exile politics.

Transnational coalition of the Greater Chinese Region has served the OCDM and other parties well so far, magnifying each other's voice and beefing up each other's campaigns. However, aside from overseas solidarity against a common target, in the long run it remains uncertain how the spirit of universal values can enable the OCDM activists to reconcile with the sentiment of 'national separatism' of a large number of Tibetan, Uighur, Taiwanese – and even Hong Kong – activists. Simmering disputes over national identity might not be always sidelined.

The US and China postengagement: A turning point for the exile movement?

China engagement practiced by the US and its allies since the late 1990s was the major factor creating an arduous operational environment for the OCDM, since the US has always been the leading host land of exiles. Thus the end of 'panda hugging' in the US' China policy since 2018 has opened a window of opportunity for the movement. The bipartisan China containment started with the Trump administration's trade war and tough military-security gestures, but has expanded into the areas of political systems and values. This reflects the US concern not only with the escalating repression by Xi Jinping's increasingly personalized political regime, as embodied in the Uighur internment camps in Xinjiang and violent crackdown on the anti-extradition protestors in Hong Kong, but also more importantly with Beijing's extending long-arm of political interference in the Western democracies. Through its 'sharp power' campaign, Beijing is seen to try to erode democracy in the heartland of liberal democracy by perforating the information environments in the targeted countries. Under the circumstances, in public statements, for the first time since Nixon, some leading US officials such as Vice President Mike Pence and State Secretary Mike Pompeo have purposely differentiated between the Chinese Communist Party (CCP) and China. Bipartisan support for a hard China policy was also manifested in the swift passing of congressional bills on democracy and human rights in Hong Kong and Xinjiang in December 2019. The 2020 Defence Appropriation Bill signed by President Trump in the same month also castigated China over human rights, and justified the strengthened defence relations with Taiwan in the name of defending democracy.

The exiles have both capitalized on this more fertile sociopolitical environment and strived to fuel its development. The sort of diverse political and civic activities over the past decade as described earlier have achieved more evident impacts in the recent two years. Both at the level of state lobbying and socially oriented information campaign, the exiles' voices have been heard more than any time since the late 1990s. More and more exiles have actively testified at the public hearings of the congressional US–China Economic and Security Review Commission, Congressional-Executive Commission on China, and the European Parliament. They discussed incidents of, and recommended ways to counter, Beijing's propaganda and disinformation operations. Vice President Mike Pence has met and consulted the Chinese exiles many times. To help turn the trade war into broader political and ideological sanctions against Beijing, organizations like IC and China Aid (CA) try to reinforce the perception that as long as the one-party state is not reformed, the US will never enjoy free and fair trade with China. Human rights deficit in the latter is the ultimate cause for the chronic trade deficit suffered by the former. Similarly, the exiles have actively campaigned to counter Beijing's soft power propaganda which capitalizes on its own quick progress in containing the spread of COVID-19 pandemic as evidence of the party-state's political superiority compared to the US, which has underestimated the risks of the outbreak and operated an inequitable health system. The counternarrative from the exiles is that the rapid spreading of Wuhan coronavirus first and foremost owes a lot to the suppression of freedom of speech and whistle-blowers in China. It is a global catastrophe inflicted on the whole world by the very substance of the political regime in the first place, and the regime's self-claimed success in containing the virus should be taken with a grain of salt. They have also warned the international community that the ease with which Beijing has been able to lock down numerous cities and confine several hundred millions of people to their homes through mass surveillance merely shows an alarming scale of its totalitarian reach (Yang 2020).

The OCDM's long-standing campaign against the US-based activities of Beijing's propaganda mouthpieces, as first exemplified by the CAD's unsuccessful defamation suit against *The People's Daily* in DC Superior Court in 1985, has been echoed in the mainstream politics recently. In 2018, IC's legal team made use of the newly extended mandate of the Foreign Agents Registration Act, and effectively lobbied the Justice Department to request the US offices of Xinhua News Agency and China Central Television (CCTV) to register themselves as foreign government agents since they were no more than the CCP's tools (Voice of America 2018). In February 2020, the State Department further announced the treatment of five foremost PRC media agencies – Xinhua, China Global Television Network (CCTV's external organ), China Radio, *China Daily* and *The People's Daily* – as foreign diplomatic institutions, subject to the same rules of monitoring as diplomats stationed in the US.

Another progress in both political lobbying and public education campaign is to follow the US laws to systematically publicize and deter human rights abusers in China. At the beginning of the 2010s, a group of legal professionals active in the OCDM started to urge the US and European Union to use relevant legislation to impose visa bans on those bureaucrats, police officers, judges, prosecutors, prison officers, state security agents responsible for torture and abuses of petitioners, rights lawyers and religious believers. Although public moral shaming was the main intention at the time, this effort has eventually integrated with the Global Magnitsky Human Rights Accountability Act, which was passed by the US Congress in January 2017, authorizing the President to impose financial sanctions and visa restrictions on foreign persons in response to certain human rights violations and acts of significant corruption. The OCDM circles, particularly IC and CA, have been closely involved in nominating the Chinese officials for such sanctions. This campaign has been extended to collect information in order to nominate those public security officials responsible for persecuting the medical whistle-blowers at the early stage of coronavirus outbreak.

In short, exiles are adroitly making piecemeal achievements by taking advantage of an emerging bipartisan political atmosphere and public sentiment in favour of a much harsher China policy since 2018. However, it remains unclear how far the movement will flourish other than becoming a more effective actor in influencing public opinion and political decisions. The message from the US is often mixed, with President Trump himself saying little critical of the political regime in China. Unless using a very stretched definition of the Cold War, a Cold War II between the US and China does not seem in the making so far. China has developed dense social-cultural relations with the US and become an indispensable economic and trade partner for the Western world, all in ways the Soviet bloc never had. Trade war has been fought precisely because of a deep level of enmeshment between the two economies. Perhaps due to similar reasons, the exiles' lobbying in the US allies to adopt their own Magnitsky Act and sanction Beijing's government media have not made significant progress so far, whereas in the Cold War, Washington and its allies acted as one against Moscow on ideological issues. In a nutshell, it is too early, if not pointless, to speculate the likelihood of whether the Chinese exile community would enjoy the sort of support that the key US government agencies lent the Soviet bloc exiles.

Conclusion

Since its emergence in the early 1980s, the OCDM has been a distinct sphere of activism campaigning for a liberal democratic homeland. Sparked by the Democracy Wall movement, the exile community expanded dramatically with mass participation in the aftermath of the Tiananmen crackdown. Organizations proliferated, lobbying activities were effective, and some leading activists imagined they could return home triumphantly soon. Such dynamics started to wane after the mid-1990s. Gradually but unmistakably, support for the split movement from the host states (particularly the US), Taiwan and diaspora diminished. Since the late 1990s, the movement has not been able to regain its peak momentum seen in the period from 1989 to mid-1990s, which materialized under very special circumstances. However, it has been rejuvenating itself over the recent decade. Away from grandstanding and readying itself for imagined regime change, the OCDM has seen more pragmatic activists trying to explore more seriously their niche roles under challenging circumstances. Forms of activism have become more diverse, going beyond the exiles' capacity to sway state policies, into the various civic political realms. The movement is now defined less by famous dissidents' rise and fall, infighting and disrepute, but more by the less historic figures' routine but useful pursuits trying to make the best out of perennial exile. More study of the movement should be conducted. Future research can benefit from critically looking into its unique features compared to other cases of exile politics, investigating the rise of a Greater Chinese Region coalition forged by the mainland Chinese exiles, minority exiles and Taiwanese and Hong Kong activists, and assessing fresh dynamics of the movement amid what looks like a turning towards China containment in the US foreign policy. On the other hand, research remains intrinsically difficult due to China's popularity as an indispensable economic partner to all the host nations of political exiles and in the eyes of its own economically thriving but politically largely indifferent middle class and new generations. Maintaining the legitimacy of research on China's oppression of dissidents continues to be a challenging task.

Acknowledgment

I'd like to thank Dr. Chris Shei (at Swansea University) and another anonymous reviewer for their constructive comments on the draft of this chapter. Their suggestions have improved my analysis.

References

Angell, A. and Carstairs, S. (1987) 'The Exile Question in Chilean Politics', *Third World Quarterly* 9 (1): 148–67.

Beja, J. (2003) 'The Fly in the Ointment? Chinese Dissent and US–China Relations', *The Pacific Review* 16 (3): 439–53.

Buruma, I. (2001) *Bad Elements: Chinese Rebels from Los Angeles to Beijing*, New York: Random House.

Chen, J. (2014) 'The Overseas Chinese Democracy Movement after Thirty Years: New Trends at Low Tide', *Asian Survey* 54 (3): 445–70.

Chen, J. (2018) 'The Chinese Political Opposition in Exile: A Chequered Development', *Europe-Asia Studies* 70 (1): 108–29.

Chen, J. (2019) *The Overseas Chinese Democracy Movement: Assessing China's Only Open Political Opposition*, Cheltenham, UK and Northampton, MA: Edward Elgar Publishing.

Goddeeris, I. (2007) 'The Temptation of Legitimacy: Exile Politics from a Comparative Perspective', *Contemporary European History* 16 (3): 395–405.

He, B. (1997) 'Political Organizations in Exile', in *The Democratic Implications of Civil Society in China*, London: Macmillan Press, pp. 85–105.

He, R. (2014) *Tiananmen Exiles: Voices of the Struggle for Democracy in China*, New York: Palgrave Macmillan.

Junker, A. (2014) 'The Transnational Flow of Tactical Dispositions: The Chinese Democracy Movement and Falun Gong', *Mobilization: An International Quarterly* 19 (3): 329–50.

Lee, S. (1987) 'South Korea: Dissent from Abroad', *Third World Quarterly* 9 (1): 130–47.

Ma, S. (1993) 'The Exit, Voice, and Struggle to Return of Chinese Political Exiles', *Pacific Affairs* 66 (3): 368–85.

Mikkonen, S. (2012) 'Exploiting the Exiles: Soviet Émigrés in US Cold War Strategy',*Journal of Cold War Studies* 14 (2): 98–127.
Nathan, A. (1992) 'Historical Perspectives on Chinese Democracy: The Overseas Democracy Movement *Today*', in Roger Jeans (ed) *Roads Not Taken: The Struggle of Opposition Parties in Twentieth-Century China*, Boulder: Westview Press, pp. 313–27.
Oo, Z. (2006) 'Exit, Voice and Loyalty in Burma: The Role of Overseas Burmese in Democratizing Their Homeland', in Trevor Wilson (ed) *Myanmar's Long Road to National Reconciliation*, Singapore: Institute of Southeast Asian Studies, pp. 231–59.
Paweł, Z. (2015) 'Exiles and the Homeland: The State of Research', *Polish American Studies* 72 (2): 33–48.
Shain, Y. (2005) 'Introduction', in *The Frontier of Loyalty: Political Exiles in the Age of the Nation-State*, Ann Arbor, MI: University of Michigan Press, pp. 1–6.
Shain, Y. and Thompson, M. (1990) 'The Role of Exiles in Democratic Transitions: The Case of the Philippines', *Journal of Developing Societies* 6 (1): 71–86.
Torres, M. (1999) *In the Land of Mirrors: Cuban Exile Politics in the United States*, Ann Arbor, MI: University of Michigan Press.
Voice of America (2018) 'Media War between the US and China', 20 September, available at https://www.voachinese.com/a/voaweishi-20180920-io-full/4579773.html.
Yang, J. (2020), President of Initiatives for China, Essays and Speeches in *China E-Weekly Magazine*, available at http://yibaochina.com/, various issues.
Zhang, J. (1990) 'China Spring and the Chinese Alliance for Democracy', *International Communication Gazette* 45 (1): 3–17.

34

The Chinese Communist Party's control of online public opinion

Toward networked authoritarianism

Wen-Hsuan Tsai

Introduction

Effective control of public opinion is pivotal to the survival of contemporary authoritarian regimes (Krastev 2011; Stern & Hassid 2013), and the key to this control lies in mastering network technology and cyberspace. As several studies have pointed out, citizens of authoritarian countries can sometimes resist their governments and launch democracy movements through association with each other online (Diamond 2010; Iskander 2011). For example, during the Arab Spring of 2011, network technology was significant in enabling the civilian population to connect with each other and bring about the downfall of nondemocratic regimes in Tunisia, Egypt, Yemen, and Libya. In general, the rise of network technology and electronic media seems to have brought about a 'fourth wave' of democratization (Howard & Hussain 2013: 84–87).[1]

However, other studies argue that authoritarian regimes will try to make use of the potential of network technology to enhance their control and turn cyberspace into a mechanism of governance. For example, more and more scholars believe that it is naïve to expect that network technology will drive democratization in mainland China. They admit that it may facilitate liberalization at a local level, but network technology alone cannot promote democratization in its true sense (Zheng 2008: 79–102). These studies echo the claim of Andrew Nathan et al. that the CCP regime is an example of resilient authoritarianism, under which the state is capable of adapting to both economic and social change as well as coping with any new threats to its authoritarian status. Starting from this viewpoint, this chapter seeks to identify the mechanisms the CCP employs to reduce any threat to the stability of its regime posed by network technology, particularly during an emergency situation (Nathan 2003; Brodsgaard & Yongnian 2004: 19).

The CCP as a polity of networked authoritarianism

The degree of importance that the CCP attaches to online public opinion is apparent from the close-knit hierarchical structure of the control systems it has put in place. The key agency for managing online public opinion during emergencies is the Network Bureau of the Central

DOI: 10.4324/9780429059704-40

Propaganda Department (CPD, 中宣部网络局) which was established in 2006. As confirmed in a report written by a CCP insider, the Network Bureau holds weekly public opinion seminars to keep abreast of current social conditions. Prior to 2006, reports on public opinion were submitted to the minister in charge of the CPD, who between 2002 and 2012 was Liu Yunshan (刘云山), and to the then secretary of the Central Political and Legal Affairs Commission, Zhou Yongkang (周永康). Since 2006, reports have been submitted directly to members of the Politburo and its standing committee (Tao 2007).[2] This change in procedures indicates how control of public opinion online has become more important in the eyes of the CCP.[3]

The Network Bureau of the CPD is a mysterious agency that is little known to outsiders. This may be because it has only recently been established and because it deals with matters that are extremely confidential. In an article written by a CCP official for Yunnan Television, it was stated that an official from the Network Bureau of the CPD had called the TV station asking for confirmation of the plans the province had in place to manage emergencies (Ma & Zhang 2009: 19). That does at least prove that the Network Bureau exists. The Network Bureau is in charge of two agencies: the CPD Public Opinion Information Bureau (中宣部舆情信息局) and the Network Research Center of the State Council Information Office (国务院新闻办网研中心). These two agencies are responsible for managing public opinion concerning the Party and the government, respectively. As soon as an unusual event occurs in society, these agencies collect online public opinion concerning the event and report it to the CPD Network Bureau on a daily basis.[4]

The Party agency, the CPD Public Opinion Information Bureau, is responsible for coordinating similar subordinate agencies within the Party, the most important of which are the People's Net Public Opinion Monitoring Office (人民网舆情监测室) and the Xinhua Net Public Opinion Monitoring and Analysis Center (新华网舆情监测分析中心).[5] The former was established on the eve of the 2008 Beijing Olympic Games to collect public opinion about the Games and pass it daily to the various interested departments. An internal publication issued by this agency, *Network Public Opinion* (网络舆情), is circulated among cadres above bureau level (局级). The internal publication issued by the Xinhua Net Public Opinion Monitoring and Analysis Center, *Network Public Opinion Reference* (网络舆情参考), is available mainly to the leaders of organizations dealing with political and legal affairs, society management, the maintenance of social stability, and public security, as well as procuratorial units and the people's courts.[6] Both agencies have established 'information direct reporting points' (信息直报点) in local branches of the *People's Daily* and the Xinhua News Agency. Employees dealing with online affairs in these organizations receive training directly from the CPD.[7]

The Network Research Center of the State Council Information Office supervises the reporting of online public opinion by subordinate departments of the State Council and provincial governments. These departments and governments have all established their own public opinion monitoring centers. For example, the Supreme People's Procuratorate has created its own official website, Justice Web (正义网), which acts as its public opinion monitoring center. The website submits reports on any public opinion it collects on political and legal affairs.[8] In the higher education system, colleges and universities at all levels have set up units for monitoring online public opinion. Any sign of antigovernment discourse or other indications that online opinion may disrupt social stability are immediately reported to the relevant local government and the Bureau of Ideological and Political Work of the Ministry of Education (教育部政治思想工作司).

In addition to the agencies operating at the center, there are public opinion information offices or monitoring centers under the propaganda departments of most provinces, cities, districts, and some counties (Wang 2010: 36). These centers have, in turn, established their own information direct reporting points. These direct reporting points, staffed by specialists, are scattered across schools, enterprises, NGOs and other important social organizations. Once the direct reporting points have collected information about social resistance or dissatisfaction with the government, specialists will immediately report on this through internal channels to the public opinion information offices or monitoring centers, which then promptly submit these reports to relevant departments for processing (Huang 2012). As can be seen from this network of opinion-gathering organizations, the CCP attaches great importance to controlling online public opinion during an emergency. In addition to monitoring expressions of public opinion, the organizations are responsible for employing special means, if necessary, to prevent any escalation of a situation resulting from negative public opinion online.

The life cycle of online public opinion events

Effective control of online public opinion requires the organizations discussed above to act swiftly; otherwise, the regime may face a rapid escalation of social unrest. The intensity of public discussion of major events will rise and fall over time, and the content of the discussion will change. This is termed the 'life cycle' of an event (Rogers et al. 1991).

There are a number of studies that analyze the online discussion of events in society from a life cycle perspective. A study conducted by the People Net's Public Opinion Monitoring Office (PTPOMO) divides the development of online public opinion surrounding an event into four periods: (1) the incubation period (酝酿期), during which the Chinese government often deletes posts to avoid further escalation of public opinion regarding an incident that has just occurred; (2) the development period (发展期) when the state begins to hire people to collect online public opinion and submit it to the relevant leaders; (3) the upsurge period (高涨期) when the state cajoles online opinion leaders, seeks to differentiate between them, and discredits those it cannot win over; and (4) the fallback period (回落期) when online expressions of public opinion about an event die down (PTPOMO 2012: 139–143).

During the incubation period, the regime does all it can to prevent online public opinion from escalating the situation, by, for example deleting posts. As soon as discussion on a network reaches a certain level in the wake of a negative social event, a 'hot incident' (热点) will be declared, such as those involving antigovernment activity, etc. The CCP employs 'network commentators' (网络评论员) to delete posts on official or unofficial online message boards and blogs about a hot incident where necessary.[9] If a hot incident cannot be prevented from escalating in this way, it will enter the development period, during which time any developments in public opinion will be instantly reported to the relevant officials. If the incident reaches the upsurge period, the government must separate antigovernment voices from pro-government ones and try to unite the latter and weaken the former. We will discuss how this is done in the following two sections. Having dealt with all these issues, the CCP must then try to bolster the government's prestige during the fallback period which will shortly ensue.

Development period: Reporting online public opinion through monitoring organizations

Before 2008, the CCP tried to limit the impact of hot incidents through actions such as deleting posts, and this may have achieved some small degree of success. However, since 2008, as more and more people have gained access to the internet, the CCP has found that the old means of controlling public opinion, by covering up, delaying, deleting, or suppressing information, have become less effective. So, in addition to deleting posts, the CCP has developed a range of more sophisticated control techniques. Local propaganda departments have established their own systems for monitoring online public opinion. These departments submit regular reports to their superiors concerning the current situation of public opinion and the degree of concern about the latest hot incident (Huang 2012: 43). The information direct reporting points may submit reports to the relevant leaders.[10] One example is the Hunan Provincial Government's Red Net (红网). The information direct reporting points under the public opinion monitoring centers at the provincial and central departmental levels promptly report any expressions of opinion inconducive to social stability to local propaganda departments and politics and law committees. These reporting points are mostly established in the local branches of the government agencies.[11]

One new development since 2008 is the use of online public opinion analysts (网络舆情分析师) working in the information direct reporting points, collecting and reporting public opinion regarding hot incidents.[12] Initially, these analysts were located in the information direct reporting points of People's Net and Justice Web. From 2010 onwards, academic institutions such as the Communication University of China, Fudan University, and Shanghai Jiaotong University have also employed their own public opinion analysts (Hou 2011). University units are one of the key areas of the CCP's control of public opinion, especially ideological management for youth. Whenever they are required to do so by the units in which they work, the analysts employ scientific methods to collect, sample, and statistically analyze online opinion concerning hot incidents. They also predict future development trends and offer suggestions for coping with them.[13] This is referred to by mainland Chinese insiders as 'reading the network on behalf of leading cadres' (帮领导干部读网). The analysts are required to 'have the accuracy of a weather forecaster in predicting public opinion' (像预报天气一样的预报舆情).[14]

After analysis, the measures employed may be summarized as follows. First, the analysts may suggest that officials deemed to be responsible for the hot incident should be punished.[15] For example, when there was online criticism of an official who had taken his wife on an overseas trip at public expense, the analysts suggested that the head of his unit should be ordered to resign, to avoid tarnishing the image of the unit as a whole.[16] Second, analysts may suggest that officials speak with one voice about any given incident, as this would enhance control over public opinion.[17] Third, analysts may also make suggestions about the choice of words to be used in official reports, thus avoiding further public dissatisfaction being triggered by inappropriate wording. In one example of this, in 2009, the Yunnan Provincial Government ordered that the use of emotive words and phrases which might 'alienate the masses' should be avoided when reporting emergencies. Terms such as 'unruly people' (刁民), 'evil force' (恶势力), and 'the ill-informed masses' (不明真相的群众),[18] were to be left out of speeches, as these words, which are reminiscent of the Cultural Revolution era, convey impressions of class struggle and could easily provoke public dissatisfaction.

Public opinion in ethnic minority areas is particularly complex, so the CCP has also deployed network public opinion analysts there. For example, the Propaganda Department of the Xinjiang Party Committee began recruiting analysts in November 2013 to work in its online public opinion monitoring department on behalf of Party and government organizations dealing with publicity, public petitions, public security, transportation, environmental protection, education, and sanitation, and to submit reports on online public opinion to the relevant leaders.[19] For example, in the event of a major violent incident, the analysts may suggest that the 'truth' be published, in order to soothe an angry public.

However, this will likely be a version of 'the truth' that will play down the authorities' political responsibility.

In targeting hot incidents, the CCP pays particular attention to relationships between cadres and the masses, the police and the public, rich and poor, and other sensitive areas (PTPOMO 2012: 97). Searches are carried out using keywords suggested by public opinion analysts and other experts. For example, the information direct reporting point of a county's public opinion monitoring center will set the name of the county as a keyword. The analysts can then search for any relevant positive or negative posts regarding that county on Baidu and Google and then submit their findings to the county leaders. The leaders attach great importance to any posts suggesting that their cadres are acting against the public interest.[20] This is because in recent years, the CCP has instituted a 'top leader responsibility system' (一把手负责制), under which any dereliction of duty by local cadres will affect the promotion of their leaders (Tsai & Liao 2020: 51–52). The leaders will punish delinquent cadres unless there are any political reasons not to do so. For example, if a leader has close ties with the delinquent cadre, they may suppress public opinion on their wrongdoing, so as not to affect their own careers.

The public opinion analysts then use mathematical tools to produce statistics on hot incidents and rank their sensitivity according to a weighted scoring system. Comments posted by certain opinion leaders, such as media commentators, public intellectuals, sports personalities, or other influential individuals who are very active online, are given higher scores and must be swiftly reported to leaders. In addition, analysts must also assign due weighting to the most important websites, especially major national forums such as People's Net, Xinhua Net, Tianya (天涯),[21] and Utopia (乌有之乡). Once an event occurs, the analysts search for comments on it according to the weighting of the websites on which they are posted (PTPOMO 2012: 96–128).

Online comments are scored according to the influence of the website and the attention paid to it by general users, opinion leaders, the traditional domestic media, and overseas media. The higher the hot incident's score, the more sensitive its implications and the more government attention it attracts. Incidents given a score of between 90 and 100 by the analysts are classified as a 'red alert' (红色警报) which means they require close attention. A score of 80–90 represents orange alert (橙色警报), 70–80 is yellow (黄色警报), and 60–70 is blue (蓝色警报).[22] This scoring system for hot incidents makes it easier for China's leaders to grasp trends in public opinion and decide what measures to adopt to deal with them.

Upsurge period: Splitting antigovernment forces on the internet

If a hot incident continues to escalate, public opinion will enter the upsurge period during which there will be a lot of negative and emotionally charged discussion online. This leads to a build-up of hostility and antagonism toward the rich, law enforcement officials, and the political class. At this stage, the traditional media, experts, scholars, and other organizations will also join the discussion (Zeng 2012: 57). Therefore, it is necessary for the authorities to use more sophisticated methods to control online expressions of public opinion. These methods are detailed below.

Simply put, during this upsurge period, the government's propaganda departments must act boldly to 'catch the flag' (抢旗帜) and create divisions among the online antigovernment forces. This means adopting a uniform government position and, in particular, drawing in pro-government opinion leaders to combat the opposition. What the CCP is trying to do here is to adapt its old 'united front'[23] techniques to the internet age. The CCP fears that if online opinion leaders are allowed to develop antigovernment sentiments based on escalating calls from the public for social justice, this would have a significant negative impact on the regime's ability to govern (Zhu 2009: 139).

The regime's first step in avoiding this negative impact consists of identifying and drawing in online opinion leaders. This is an approach that was proposed by the CCP's United Front Department during the Pilot Work Conference on the Informatization of the National United Front System, held in November 2011 (Wang 2012: 28). In line with this proposal, local government propaganda departments attempt to recruit allies within online communities. These allies are permitted by the CCP to criticize the deficiencies of local governments to a certain extent, in order to steal the thunder of the antigovernment opinion leaders. However, they can only go so far in their criticism – any comments that could be seen as too radical, or as opposing the leadership of the CCP, are not permitted (Zhu 2009: 139). The People's Net Public Opinion Monitoring Office has even prepared a list of 300 online opinion leaders who could potentially be made use of by the regime, based on their degree of activity and influence. This list was submitted to the Propaganda Department so they could target them should a hot incident start to escalate.[24]

If it is impossible to win over opinion leaders, efforts will be made to block or discredit them online. One prominent online commentator said that, when he started out as a reporter, he was very familiar with the CCP's united front techniques. He described how the CCP had shut down his microblog account, thus stopping him from voicing his opinions anywhere online in mainland China.[25] Another means frequently adopted by the CCP in dealing with antigovernment opinion leaders is to damage their reputations by publishing negative coverage of them in the official media. In 2013, one prominent online opinion leader, Xue Biqun (薛必群), was charged with soliciting prostitutes and other sexual misdemeanors. Arrangements were made for Xue to broadcast his 'confession' on the official TV station, China Central Television. Xue explained in the newscast that China is in a stage of social transformation, so the emergence of problems is inevitable. He said the comments he had reposted mocking officials for keeping mistresses, as well as other comments he had made himself, had been exaggerated and had intensified dissatisfaction with the government.[26] This 'confession' was very much in accord with the expectations of the CCP.

Monitoring online public opinion: The case of Li Wenliang, the COVID-19 whistle-blower

In keeping with its characteristics as a networked authoritarian polity, the CCP spares no effort when it comes to controlling public opinion in the event of a serious public incident. In the above discussion, we have identified four periods in the evolution of online public opinion: the incubation period, the development period, the upsurge period, and the fallback period. We will now discuss how the CCP has conducted online monitoring in connection with the COVID-19 pandemic and the death of the whistle-blower, doctor Li Wenliang (李文亮). At the end of December 2019, the Wuhan-based ophthalmologist warned of the outbreak in China of a new, highly infectious disease, becoming one of the first medical professionals to alert the outside world to what became known as COVID-19. The following month, Li was given an official warning by the police for 'publishing false statements on the internet'. As it happened, Dr. Li caught the virus himself at the end of January, and he died at dawn on February 7.

In this chapter, I use the number of posts on one online forum, Tianya Focus (天涯聚焦), part of the well-known Tianya Community (天涯社群),[27] to estimate the online interest in

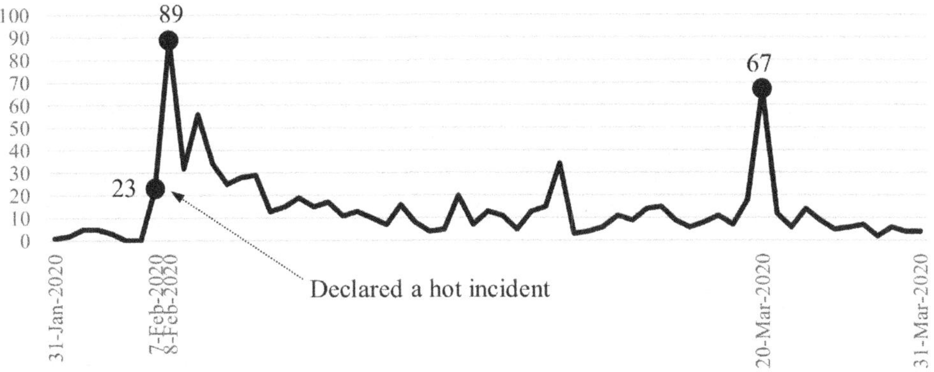

Figure 34.1 The life cycle of public opinion concerning the Li Wenliang incident.

this case. After Li Wenliang was hospitalized at the end of January, the incident entered the incubation period as people began discussing it online. After Li's death on February 7, it entered the development period as discussion surged and it was designated a hot incident. At this point, the CCP requested advice from public opinion analysts. From February 8, as the upsurge period began, online opinion leaders were subjected to cajoling or suppression to weaken criticism of the government. During this period, the intensity of online criticism of Li's treatment fluctuated, demonstrating that the situation was very unstable. On March 19, the CCP began trying to set the tone for the incident by making some positive comments about Dr. Li. The following day, online praise for Li Wenliang reached a peak. Subsequently, the incident entered the fallback period and was no longer the focus of online discussion. The life cycle of online discussion of this incident is shown in Figure 34.1.

We can see from Figure 34.1 that, after February 7, the incident quickly attracted public attention in mainland China and became a hot topic of discussion. In online discussions, it was argued that if the Chinese government had heeded Dr. Li's warning, the disease would not have spread so quickly. The incubation period of this hot incident was brief, and it soon entered the development period. On the evening after Li's death, there were more than seven hundred thousand heated discussions going on online; in one leap, the incident became the most searched for topic on Chinese social media.

During the development period, the CCP appointed a large number of network commentators to delete posts in an effort to prevent this hot incident from receiving further attention. As one anonymous commentator interviewed by Bitter Winter website said, 'Li Wenliang was declared dead at around 9:00 PM, at which time people started fiercely criticizing the government online. Therefore the government asked the hospital to continue their life-saving efforts. However, what's the use of trying to resuscitate a "dead body"!' The same commentator said that at 9:00 PM on February 6, the government requested the hospital to continue to use ECMO (extracorporeal membrane oxygenation) to resuscitate Dr. Li and to announce publicly that he was still alive. From this time onwards, this news was posted in various online communities and reports that Dr. Li was dead and criticisms of the authorities were being deleted. But at 2:28 AM the next day, the hospital gave up its meaningless efforts to save the doctor's life. Although pro-government network commentators continued to emphasize that the government valued Li Wenliang's life and had done their best to save him, they were still unable to suppress the critical voice of public opinion (Li 2020).

After February 7, as the situation continued to intensify, the Chinese government appointed network public opinion analysts to collect information and offer suggestions. According to Taiwanese media reports, a public opinion research firm called the Womin High Tech Wode Online Public Opinion Research Institute (沃民高科沃德网情研究院; hereinafter Womin High Tech) began to submit summaries of online posts relating to Li Wenliang to the relevant departments of the central government. The founder of this company, Dr. Qi Zhongxiang (齐中祥), is head researcher at the Center for Public Opinion, part of the Intelligence Department of mainland China's Ministry of Industry and Information Technology. As such, he has close links with the CCP. Womin High Tech employs newly developed AI technology and big data to help the CCP monitor public opinion (Wu 2020a).

Womin High Tech also suggested how this particular incident should be dealt with. These suggestions included partially admitting Dr. Li's contribution and disciplining cadres for dereliction of duty to quell public anger. Furthermore, the firm advised strengthening censorship of negative online public opinion. Finally, it suggested that the government should release news about the pandemic that had already been vetted, together with information about the government's measures for dealing with it, with the aim of diverting attention away from the Li Wenliang incident.[28]

The incident entered its upsurge period after February 8, and the CCP began their usual campaign to cajole, differentiate, and discredit opinion leaders. Emeritus Professor Ai Xiaoming (艾晓明) of Zhongshan University, Professor Zhang Qianfan (张千帆) of Beijing University, Professor Guo Yuhua (郭于华) of Qinghua University, and scholars such as Xiao Shu (笑蜀) and Guo Feixiong (郭飞雄) issued an open letter in which they demanded that the CCP loosen its grip on public opinion to prevent similar incidents in the future. The CCP went into battle against these eminent opinion leaders, issuing informal warnings, releasing them from employment, or putting them under house arrest (Wu 2020b).

During the upsurge period, the CCP and the protesters competed for space on the internet. In addition to suppressing opinion leaders, local officials and the CCP's propaganda departments started to reshape Li Wenliang's image from that of a person to be 'admonished' to a person to be 'praised'. In mid-February, local officials or social media influencers working for the government began referring online to Li as a 'revolutionary martyr' (革命烈士), and this title obtained recognition in the internet community. The conversion of Li from a 'whistle-blower' to a 'martyr' and a national hero was helpful in inspiring patriotism among the public, thus defusing criticism of the CCP.[29]

By March 19, the National Supervisory Commission published the report of its inquiry into the Li Wenliang affair. This concluded that the police officers who had detained him had acted unlawfully and should be punished. However, the report also emphasized that Li Wenliang was a CCP member and was in no way attempting to overthrow the system or foment public disorder. These assertions were made in the hope that the public would not use the report as an excuse to attack the government.[30] At this point, the Li Wenliang incident was approaching its fallback period.

As a way of conclusion, the CCP's approach to controlling online public opinion can be summarized in Table 34.1. In recent years, the CCP has invested heavily in terms of both hardware and capital to study modes of internet control. One of their most important policies is to apply the government's historical experience of social control to the field of internet technology. This strategy seems to confirm Evgeny Morozov's opinion that authoritarian governments control the internet through a combination of technological and sociopolitical means (Morozov 2011a: 73).

Table 34.1 The CCP's control of public opinion relating to the Li Wenliang incident

Incubation period (Jan 31–Feb 7)	Emphasis: **Avoiding the emergence of a hot incident** 1. Deleting posts, etc.
Development period (Feb 8)	Emphasis: **Reporting online public opinion** 2. Assigning network public opinion analysts to measure online public opinion concerning the hot incident. 3. Suggesting how to deal with the incident.
Upsurge period (Feb 9–March 19)	Emphasis: **Splitting online antigovernment forces** 4. Seeking out and winning over opinion leaders. 5. Differentiating between opinion leaders and discrediting those who cannot be won over. 6. Officials playing the role of opinion leaders to shape public opinion.
Fallback period (March 20–March 31)	Emphasis: **Damage control** 7. Repairing the prestige of the government.

Conclusion: The evolution of a dictatorship

As several scholars have pointed out, many authoritarian states have become aware of the potential threat to their regimes posed by internet technology and are trying to control it and use it for their own ends (Deibert & Rohzinski 2012: 29–34; Deibert et al. 2012). The fact that this is happening goes some way to confirming the pessimistic views of scholars who argue that the internet will not promote democratic transition in authoritarian regimes but may actually strengthen those regimes' ability to govern (Morozov 2011b).

The case of contemporary China is a living example of networked authoritarianism, as the CCP regime seems to be adapting efficiently to new developments in technology. The regime commenced its battle to control cyberspace as soon as the internet was introduced into China (Qiang 2011). As Shan Xuegang (单学刚), deputy secretary-general of the People's Net Public Opinion Monitoring Office, said in 2013, 'the government must understand the internet before controlling it'.[31] It is certainly the case that the CCP regime has indeed equipped itself with more sophisticated network control technology than other authoritarian states.

Notes

1 According to Samuel P. Huntington (1993), the world has gone through three waves of democratization since the beginning of the 19th century. The first wave took place in North America and Europe between 1828 and 1926, the second wave occurred in former colonies from 1943 to 1962, and the third wave (1974–(192) arose first in Portugal, Greece, and Spain, and then overtook the countries of Eastern Europe. Some scholars argue that the outbreak of the Tunisian'Jasmine Revolution'in 2011 marked the beginning of a fourth wave of democratization.

2 It is believed that Tao Xizhe is the pseudonym of a cadre working in a CCP network agency, so the report is deemed to be of uncertain credibility.

3 In 2018, the CCP established the Internet Security and Information Commission (网络安全和信息化委员会) in an effort to integrate the various departments and resources concerned with network control.

4 The Chinese government has established other network administration-related agencies, such as the Network Bureau of the State Council Information Office and the Ministry of Industry and Information Technology (MIIT). However, the former is responsible for reviewing applications for websites, while the latter formulates policies and laws/regulations pertaining to the internet. Neither of them deals directly with the management of public opinion in times of emergency. Interview, January 16, 2014, with a reporter working for an official journal.

5 People's Net and Xinhua Net are managed by the *People's Daily* and the Xinhua News Agency, respectively, the CCP's two most important media organizations. These websites are the most significant official agencies of the CCP responsible for guiding and monitoring public opinion.
6 新华网舆情监测分析中心 [Xinhua Net's Public Opinion Monitoring and Analysis Center], '关于建立网络舆情观察员队伍体系的通知' [Notice on Establishing a Network Public Opinion Observer Team System], 2013, 新华网 [Xinhua Net], http://big5.xinhuanet.com/gate/big5/news.xinhuanet.com/yuqing/2013-10/16/c_125547949.htm.
7 Interview, January 16, 2014, with a reporter working on an official journal.
8 '正义网舆情监测系统概况' [Overview of the Justice Web Public Opinion Monitoring System], 2012, 正义网 [Justice Web], http://yq.jcrb.com/fwtx/201203/t20120301_815159.html.
9 'Network commentators' are network monitoring personnel, appointed on the authority of the CCP, who are mainly responsible for deleting posts (Hung, 2010: 154–159).
10 *Southern Metropolis Daily*, December 22, 2010, Section AII15.
11 Interview with a local cadre, May 12, 2019.
12 Compared to network commentators, network public opinion analysts are trained in emergency management skills. Their primary function is not to delete offending posts, but to predict the development of events and offer suggestions for emergency intervention.
13 *Beijing News*, September 28, 2013, Section B4.
14 *Beijing Morning Post*, 北京晨报, September 9, 2013, Section C6.
15 These analysts are mostly recruited and trained by the propaganda department of the CCP and carry out relevant work according to the instructions of the propaganda department.
16 *Beijing News*, October, 3, 2013, Section A14.
17 *News Express*, October, 21, 2010, Section A11.
18 *Southern Metropolis Daily*, August, 29, 2009, Section A17.
19 '新疆有了首批网络舆情分析师' [Xinjiang Has the First Batch of Network Public Opinion Analysts], 2013, 凤凰网 [Phoenix Net], http://news.ifeng.com/gundong/detail_2013_11/23/31496235_0.shtml.
20 *Beijing Morning Post*, 北京晨报, October 3, 2013, Section A14.
21 Tianya, set up in 1999, is an extremely influential online forum among Chinese communities; the discussions on Tianya are very open.
22 '地方网络应对能力排行榜' [Chart of the Corresponding Capability of Network in Local Government], 2009, 网络舆情 [Network Public Opinion], 83: 7.
23 The principle of the united front is to win over less important enemies to join the fight against major enemies. For related discussion, see Kenneth Lieberthal, *Governing China: From Revolution through Reform* (New York: W.W. Norton, 1995), pp. 72–76.
24 '人民网发布2013年互联网舆情报告' [People's Net Releases Internet Public Opinion Report 2013], 2014, 人民网 [People's Net], http://yuqing.people.com.cn/GB/371947/373066/.
25 Interview, January 22, 2014, with the editor of an official journal.
26 *Ming Pao*, 明报, September 16, 2013, Section A17.
27 The Tianya Community covers a wide variety of content, from society and the economy to fashion, entertainment, and sport. Tianya Focus is a condensed version of the Tianya Community.
28 '武汉肺炎 '吹哨人' 李文亮去世 网曝中共舆情管控引民愤' [The Wuhan Corona Virus 'Whistleblower' Dies; Online Revelations of the CCP's Control of Public Opinion Provoke Popular Indignation], 2020, 新唐人 [Xin tangren], https://www.ntdtv.com.tw/b5/20200208/video/263624.html.
29 Interview with a cadre from a local CCP propaganda department, June 22, 2020.
30 '国家监委：公安对李文亮发训诫书不当 促追究责任' [The National Supervisory Committee: Public Security Services Were Wrong to Issue Li Wenliang with a Formal Warning, Prompting Action to Discipline Those Responsible], 2020, Now新闻 [Now xinwen], https://news.now.com/home/international/player?newsId=384960.
31 *Beijing News*, 新京报, October 3, 2013, Section A14.

References

Brodsgaard, Kjeld Erik and Zheng Yongnian, 2004, 'Introduction: Bringing the Party Back In' in *Bringing the Party Back In: How China is Governed*, eds. Kjeld Erik Brodsgaard and Zheng Yongnian, Singapore: Eastern University Press, 1–21.

Deibert, Ronald and Rafal Rohzinski, 2012, 'Contesting Cyberspace and the Coming Crisis of Authority' in *Access Contested: Security, Identity, and Resistance in Asian Cyberspace Information Revolution and Global Politics*, eds. Ronald Deibert, John Palfrey, and Rafal Rohzinski, Cambridge, MA: MIT Press, 21–41.

Deibert, Ronald, Rafal Rohzinski, and Masashi Crete-Nishihata, 2012, 'Cyclones in Cyberspace: Information Shaping and Denial in the 2008 Russia-Georgia War' *Security Dialogue*, 43(3): 3–24.

Diamond, Larry, 2010, 'Liberation Technology' *Journal of Democracy*, 21(3): 69–83.

George, Cherian, 2007, 'Consolidating Authoritarian Rule: Calibrated Coercion in Singapore' *The Pacific Review*, 20(2): 127–145.

Hou, Wenchang, 侯文昌, 2011, '传媒新角色：舆情分析师的专业素养' (New Media Role: The Specialist Literacy of Public Opinion Analysts) 中国记者 (Chinese Journalist), 9:48–49.

Howard, Philip N. and Muzammil M. Hussain, 2013, *Democracy's Fourth Wave? Digital Media and the Arab Spring*, New York: Oxford University Press.

Huang, Xiaoyan, 黄小燕, 2012, '网络舆情分析：面向政府的决策情报服务'(Network Public Opinion Analysis: Government-oriented Policy-Making Information Service), 现代情报 (Modern Information), 3(32): 43–44.

Hung, Chin-Fu, 2010, 'China's Propaganda in the Information Age: Internet Commentators and the *Weng'an* Incident' *Issues & Studies*, 46(4): 149–180.

Huntington, Samuel P., 1993, *The Third Wave: Democratization in the Late Twentieth Century*, Norman: University of Oklahoma Press.

Iskander, Elizabeth, 2011, 'Connecting the National and the Virtual: Can Facebook Activism Remain Relevant after Egypt's January 25 Uprising?' *International Journal of Communication*, 5:1225–1237.

Krastev, Ivan, 2011, 'Paradoxes of the New Authoritarianism' *Journal of Democracy*, 22(2): 5–16.

Li, Guang 李光, 2020, '中国删帖员：武汉肺炎期间日删万条政府不许可敏感言论' (Chinese Post Deleter: 10,000 Articles are Deleted Every Day during Wuhan's Pneumonia), 寒冬 (Bitter Winter), https://zh.bitterwinter.org/chinas-online-censors-hide-truth-with-governments-lies/

Ma, Jianyu and Zhang Jing, 马建宇、张晶, 2009, '当电视遭遇突然' (When TV Encounters Emergencies), 当代电视 (Contemporary TV), 11:11–19.

Morozov, Evgeny, 2011a, 'Whither Internet Control?' *Journal of Democracy*, 22(2): 62–74.

Morozov, Evgeny, 2011b, *The Net Delusion: The Dark Side of Internet Freedom*, New York: Public Affairs.

Nathan, Andrew, 2003, 'Authoritarian Resilience' *Journal of Democracy*, 14(1): 6–17.

PTPOMO, (人民网舆情监测室如何对应网络舆情), 2012, 如何对应网络舆情 (How to Cope with Network Public Opinion), Beijing: Xinhua Publishing House.

Qiang, Xiao, 2011, 'The Battle for the Chinese Internet' *Journal of Democracy*, 22(2): 47–61.

Rogers, Everett M., James W. Dearing, and Soonbum Chang, 1991, *AIDS in the 1980s: The Agenda-Setting Process for a Public Issue*, University of Austin, Texas: Association for Education in Journalism and Mass Communication.

Stern, Rachel E. and Jonathan Hassid, 2013, 'Amplifying Silence: Uncertainty and Control Parables in Contemporary China' *Comparative Political Studies*, 45(12): 1–25.

Tao, Xizhe, 陶西喆, 2007, '揭开中国网络控制机制的内幕' (Unveiling the Inside Story of China's Network Control Mechanisms), 记者无国界 (Reporters Without Borders), http://rsf-chinese.org/IMG/pdf/China_Internet_Report_in_Chinese.pdf.

Tsai, Wen-Hsuan and Xingmiu Liao, 2020, 'Mobilizing Cadre Incentives in Policy Implementation: Poverty Alleviation in a Chinese County' *China Information*, 34(1): 45–67.

Tsai, Wen-Hsuan, Xingmiu Liao, and Chien-Min Chen, 2019, 'Intermediate Agents in the Resistance Process: Petition Brokers and Social Governance in Contemporary China' *China: An International Journal*, 17(4): 155–167.

Wang, Guohua, 王国华, 2010, '我国舆情信息工作体系建设' (Construction of the Public Opinion Information Work System of Our Country) 图书情报工作(Library and Information Service), 54(6): 36–39.

Wang, Jianguo, 王建国, 2012, '重视发挥网络统战在社会管理创新的积极作用' (Pay Attention to the Positive Role of a Networked United Front in Social Management Innovation), 中国统一战线 (China's United Front), 5:28–29.

Wu, Cishan, 吴赐山, 2020b, '武汉肺炎打 '吹哨者'中国在 '李文亮'事件后这么做' (Wuhan Corona Virus Crackdown on 'Whistleblowers.' This Is How China Did It after the 'Li Wenliang' Incident) New Talk 新闻 (New Talk xinwen), https://newtalk.tw/news/view/2020-02-12/365474.

Wu, Jiesheng, 吴介声, 2020a "吹哨人'李文亮之死：中共如何打压网络逆风舆论？' (The Death of the 'Whistleblower' Li Wenliang: How Does the CCP Crack Down on Unfavorable Public Opinion Online?), 鸣人堂 (Mingren tang), https://opinion.udn.com/opinion/story/120611/4334599.

Zeng, Shengquan, 曾胜泉, 2012, 突发事件舆情应对指南 (Guide to Coping with Public Opinion in Emergencies), Guangzhou: Southern Daily Press.

Zheng, Yongnian, 2008, *Technological Empowerment: The Internet, State, and Society in China*, Stanford: Stanford University Press.

Zhu, Huaxin, 祝华新, 2009, '给地方政府应对网络舆论的10 条建议' (10 Suggestions for Local Governments to Deal with Online Public Opinion), 领导文翠 (Leadership literature), 12:139.

35

In the name of stability

Literary censorship and self-censorship in contemporary China[1]

Kamila Hladíková

Introduction

Postmodern approaches to censorship – the so-called 'new censorship' referred to for example by Burt (1994), Holquist (1994), or Post (1998) – consider censorship a natural part of every speech or discourse. They strive to overcome the traditionally perceived antagonism between writer and censor, 'light' and 'darkness', 'truth' and 'lie'. Already thinkers like Lacan or Foucault started to examine, what is and is not possible to say under certain psychological or historical conditions. According to Bourdieu (1992: 175) all discourses are characterized by a certain tension between expression and censorship. In other words, the attention shifts from the institutionalized censorship leaving blank spaces on pages of printed texts, burning books and punishing writers and/or publishers, toward discursive formations and self-censorship, intentional or unintentional, conscious or subconscious.

For Foucault, power is always productive, constructing knowledge and social practice. Analogically, the 'new censorship' is also described as productive and is characterized as a form of production of speech and meaning always preceding every text (Post 1998: 2). As Butler writes, 'if power is, however, also productive, then it contributes to making the object that it also constrains. [...] the subject who is censored as well as the subject who censors are constituted in part by a restrictive and productive power' (1998: 247). For Butler, censorship aims to regulate the whole domain of socially acceptable and imaginable speeches, i.e., to regulate the discourse. For example, censorship may be used to codify certain version of historic collective memory, as the form of state control over preserving national legacy or as insisting that certain historical events can be narratively represented in a single and unquestionable way (252).

The very nature of censorship is always monologic. As Müller (2004: 13) argued:

> The legitimizing discourses brought forward in defense of censorship depict censorship as a means of protecting the public from allegedly harmful influences, which means that a monolithic subject and common interests are constructed, thus denying legitimacy to diverging interests of particular audiences.

DOI: 10.4324/9780429059704-41

A 'canon', which is (re)constructed by censorship then serves as a tool 'to measure cultural products' (ibid.). This is mentioned also by Fik: 'As censor determines the hierarchy in arts, he [the censor] finally overcomes the role of 'co-author' of a particular work [...] and participates in formation of cultural reality [...] serving as patron of some authors while oppressing others' (2012: 413).

Despite growing pressure on censorship in contemporary PRC, which is, however, focusing mainly on media, social media, and internet, where it permeates into all possible spheres of public or even private life, literary censorship seems to be less actual. There is a general presupposition that after the end of the Cultural Revolution and the death of Mao Zedong in 1976, literary production in the PRC has abandoned strict and binding rules of Maoist discourse and Chinese socialist realism and has gained a certain degree of freedom of expression. Nevertheless, censorship has not disappeared from Chinese literature. It has only become more subtle and sophisticated, or, in words of one of the most renowned contemporary Chinese writers Yan Lianke, has shifted from 'hard censorship' to a 'soft' one (2016: 263), relying mainly on self-censorship. Such a system motivates writers to actively comply with the Party's long-term ideological objectives while at the same time enabling them to insert certain acceptably critical points or even covered hints with subversive potential.

Starting with Mao's 'Talks at the Yan'an Forum on Literature and Arts' delivered in May 1942, for the Communist leadership, literature was considered one of the main tools of propaganda and its aim was officially limited to disseminating key ideological concepts among the broad masses of people. Censorship and (often violently forced) self-censorship have both been natural parts of Chinese literary system established after the founding of the PRC in 1949. The centralized, state-controlled literary establishment was gradually abolished during the post-Mao era, but basic principles in the official Party discourse remain and literature should still to some extent serve to extraliterary objectives. Contemporary literary system retained some of the traits described by Link (2000), and Chinese writers have still not been able to leave the 'velvet prison' of 'resigned agreement' mentioned by Hungarian dissident writer Haraszti (1987), however, many of them learned to enjoy the comfort this 'prison' offers.

Building on Hockx's (1999) adaptation of Bordieu's (1993) concept of the literary field for modern Chinese literature, which is characterized by the addition of 'political capital' to Bordieu's original two-dimensional figure, the present study highlights continuity in the official standpoints and requirements concerning the basic function of literature and arts despite turbulent changes in both politics and society in the PRC during the last 70 years. Hockx linked the 'political capital' to '[writers'] ability to deal with the concept of people', which is still plausible, not only on the official level – as the slogan of 'serving the people' was repeatedly stressed by chairman Xi Jinping on 'Work Forum on Literature and Arts' held in Beijing in 2014 – but also in the everyday reality of each part of the literary field, from writers through editors to publishers and sellers.

The literary field in the PRC is still characterized by the tension between writers' (critical) commitment to 'reality' and the officially formulated (idealistic) aims of literary creation that surfaced back in 1942 in Yan'an as it was described by Goldman (1971). This tension has arisen from the collision between the symbolic and the political capitals, which both need to deal with the growing potential of the economic capital and massive influence of pop culture since the 1990s. Based on case analyses of selected literary works bringing up 'sensitive' topics, some of which have been banned or were subject to official criticism during the last few decades, this study aims to describe the mechanisms and provide a deeper insight into the ideological objectives of contemporary Chinese censorship, which can be summed up by notions of 'maintaining stability' and 'social harmony'.

Censorship in the PRC from history to present

Starting from the 1930s, relations between the CCP leadership and Chinese intelligentsia, nurtured by the liberal spirit of the May Fourth Movement influenced by Western philosophy and values, were tense. The CCP strived to incorporate members of educated elites – in that time mostly recruited from gentry or bourgeoisie – with the left-wing inclinations into the process of formation and dissemination of its ideology, but it lacked the mechanisms how to effectively limit the leftist intellectual and literary discourse to the actual interpretation of Party ideology. Only during the 1940s did the ideology apparatus come up with mechanisms that were for the first time used during the 'rectification movement' in Yan'an. The first 'literary dissent', described in detail by Goldman, foreshadowed the relationship between writers and the CCP elites after 1949. The movement culminated with 'Forum on Literature and Arts', which determined the future position of writers in Chinese socialist literary system and defined the primary function of literature as a tool of propaganda. Literature and art as formulated in Mao Zedong's thought were supposed to serve the people and it was expected from 'revolutionary writers' that they 'collect the raw material based on the life of people and transform it into the ideological form of literature and art serving to the masses' (Mao 1996: 472). In his concluding talk, Mao strongly opposed the standpoint of some writers that literature and arts should remain separated from politics and that it is the writers' obligation to 'equally stress the bright and the dark [sides of reality]' and to 'expose [evil or short-comings]' (479) in the way the founder of modern Chinese literature Lu Xun did in his satirical essays that targeted the Kuomintang government.

The Yan'an campaign became the main model for political movements of the 1950s and 1960s whose aim was usually not simply to eliminate dissenting voices, but rather to 'rectify' them through ideological training and reeducation through labor. The Maoist era ended and in 1978 Deng Xiaoping announced a new policy of 'reforms and opening up', which brought an influx of Western ideas and influences again, after almost 40 years. Emerging literary trends and currents included metafiction, postmodernism or feminist literature, and the Chinese version of socialist realism, a combination of revolutionary realism and revolutionary romanticism introduced by Zhou Enlai and Guo Moruo in the late 1950s' virtually disappeared from the literary discourse. However, Mao's key notions on literature have never been fully revised and the premises of serving the people, being rooted in the real life of the masses, or emphasizing the positive side, are on the official level still plausible as the untouchable guidelines for literary and artistic creation, as it is evident from official materials.

Censorship in the Chinese socialist literary system after the Cultural Revolution

The Chinese socialist literary system of the 1980s was described in Link (2000), where he paid much attention to censorship and self-censorship. Link pointed out that – unlike literary systems in the former eastern bloc in Europe, as analyzed for example by Darnton (1995) or Urbański (2012) – the Chinese system was less institutionalized and was largely based on psychological pressure, stressing the need of ideological education and conscious self-censorship. Link has described it as 'more subtle' and at the same time 'more totalistic' than other systems (2000: 56). He writes:

> Socialist China did not have the kind of formal censorial organs that other autocratic regimes have maintained. Literary control was less mechanical and more psychological than it has been elsewhere. It depended primarily on the private calculation of risks and balances in the minds of writers, editors, and those who supported them.
>
> *(Link 2000: 81)*

In this system, every individual had to negotiate his/her own position before taking any kind of action, regarding the political 'weather', but also his/her personal connections. For Link 'the political-literary weather in socialist China' was highly unpredictable exactly because of 'the primacy of human beings over written documents' (77). Such atmosphere and the enormous pressure of personal responsibility in all spheres of the literary field led naturally to the strengthening of self-censorship. As Barmé (1999) wrote, borrowing Haraszti's metaphor of 'velvet prison': '[...] coercive style of indoctrination was changed into self-imposed acquiescence [...]' (3). Any kind of criticism always had to be indirect and covered, something that seemed quite natural to writers rooted in the two-thousand-years-long tradition of literature and censorship in China. Specific literary means had been developed by generations of traditional Chinese literati – allegories, analogies, fables, metaphors, and so forth, not dissimilar to the modern form of so-called Aesopean language used in the Soviet literature as described by Loseff (1984).

Following the implementation of basic principles of the market economy after 1992, the subsequent commercialization of all kinds of production loosened up the heavily controlled literary system and writers were no longer existentially fully dependent on their 'work unit'. They could earn high provisions from the sales of their books and could even leave the official institutions and 'dive into the sea' of the free market. Nevertheless, even under such conditions, censorship and self-censorship have still been fully employed.

After 'opening up' the Chinese regime faced new challenges and it became more difficult to exercise direct and strict control. Large-scale political campaigns of the 1950s and 1960s, intruding into the lives of virtually all people, were in the 1980s substituted by smaller-scale critical campaigns with more specific targets, but much vaguer in character. Their aim was, on the one hand, to disseminate the actual ideological directives and on the other hand to show selected negative examples of themes and thoughts to be avoided in public discourse. The period of the 1980s saw two major centrally organized campaigns, both of them targeting what was labeled as 'liberalism', a term describing attitudes and behavior generally ascribed to the 'bourgeois capitalist' influences 'from the West'.

The target of the 1980s' campaigns gradually shifted from 'modernism' and 'humanism' to literature (and film) that by their uncritical approach seemed to promote even vaguer categories, like 'selfishness and irresponsibility', and were considered 'decadent'. Already in 1980 the general secretary Hu Yaobang, who was later in 1987 himself criticized for spreading 'bourgeois liberalist' ideas, organized a conference on drama, where he talked about negative 'social effects' of controversial art and called for bigger 'social responsibility' on the side of authors (Barmé 1999: 11). Later he warned against the 'candy artillery shells' sent from the West in the form of 'women, fancy commodities, and lust for money'. On the ideological level, these 'arrows' were represented by notions of 'literary modernism', 'humanism', and 'alienation' (异化) [from the original ideals of Communism] (Link 2000: 63).

One of the key arguments against 'modernism' and in general the new literary techniques inspired by Western modernism and avant-garde literature was 'unintelligibility' and 'obscured' meaning, which were – alongside the 'negative social effects' – seen as the most undesirable features of literary works targeted in critical campaigns. In other words, from the authorities' point of view, literature should not corrupt readers with descriptions of decadent and irresponsible lifestyle, but rather focus on promoting socialist values. To do it properly, literature must be able to convey the meaning in the form, style and language that is understandable to broad masses. Such a requirement clearly resonates with Mao's initial ideas about literature and art pronounced in Yan'an.

As indicated, Chinese literary censorship has been characterized by persistent psychological pressure, self-censorship, risk-balancing, and powerful connections. This kind of system typically targets works only after their publication, which happens in the case that one or more parts of the subtle and highly subjective control mechanism fail. During the 1980s, specific literary and film works were singled out for criticism in official media to illustrate negative examples. These campaigns were mostly limited to a small number of works or authors, writers were rarely imprisoned and use of physical violence typical for the time of the Cultural Revolution was not applied any more. Under market economy conditions, any 'scandal' could, on the one hand, draw the curiosity of readers and bring fame to the author, but, on the other hand, would often lead to loss of state employment, social position or Party membership for everyone involved (often editors, as the author might have been more independent). Some writers even successfully monetized their 'controversial books' in case they complied with the system in past and agreed to do so in future. This kind of social and economic pressure has gradually changed the system from 'hard' to 'soft' censorship and the relation between writers and the state has finally, through decades of ideological education and reeducation, come to the point when writers and editors, incorporated into the system and motivated by the lure of the market, actively participate.

With the loosening of the centralized state literary system and under influence of market economy forces and internet, censorship lost its ultimate power, but was never abandoned completely. The key principles and mechanisms from Yan'an have still been – more covertly – at stake. This fact was confirmed after Xi Jinping came to power in 2012. On October 15, 2014, he gave a talk at the 'Forum on Literature and Art in Beijing', which was immediately compared to Mao's talk from 1942. In his opening talk titled 'Literature and Art cannot Lose the Course in the Waves of Market Economy',[2] Xi stressed the importance of creating such works that 'will not cast any shadows of doubts about our great nation and our great era' (Xi 2014). Targeting primarily commercialized, consumerist, 'fast food' production, he, on the one hand, repeated the idea, originally used by Mao in 1956 and again brought up by Jiang Zemin in 2002, of 'letting a hundred flowers bloom and a hundred schools of thought contend' in a call for a variety of forms and themes, but on the other hand he emphasized that 'the socialist art is primarily the art of the people'. As such, it should 'reflect the voice of the people and persist in serving the people and socialism'. Contemporary literature and art should, similarly to the revolutionary romanticism of the 1950s and 1960s 'combine the spirit of realism with romantic idealism [...] use light to fight the darkness, use beauty to fight ugliness, and show the people glory and hope, tell them that the dream is reachable'. Xi even mentioned the metaphor of the writer as 'engineer of human soul' originally used in 1934 by the father of the Soviet socialist realism of Stalin's era Zhdanov. Finally, he condemned such works that 'ridicule the sublime, skew the classics, turn the history upside down, are not able to differentiate between truth and lie, good and evil, beautiful and ugly, and focus only on the dark sides of the society'. Some works, although not mentioned specifically, were likened to MDMA, others were called 'cultural waste' and even the – at times much-discussed – slogan of 'art for art' did not escape the leader's criticism (Xi 2015).

Although since the 1990s the Chinese literary market is not as strictly regulated as before, even compared to the 1980s, specific strategies need to be applied by writers, editors and publishers in order to survive and succeed. As the 'soft censorship is deliberately flexible and vague' (Yan 2016: 265), self-censorship has been applied more carefully than ever and 'the entire industry has been transformed into one in which everyone is watching everyone else' (267). As Yan pointed out, rather than cutting out problematic parts of texts, more attention has now been paid to 'intent and sentiment' of works. It means that even 'problematic' topics (such as the Cultural Revolution or corruption) are acceptable when handled in a proper way. In general, such works are appreciated that represent the so-called 'major melody' (主旋律), i.e., follow the official master narrative and deal even with negative aspects through the lens of 'positivity' (265). The works, which comply with these requirements are, in accordance with Fik's words quoted above, gaining publicity and awarded important prizes, while those that do not are subject to marginalization and slowly forgotten, rather than banned – a step drawing too much attention in the globalized world connected through internet and social media.

Dealing with 'sensitive topics': Three case studies

There are two main categories of works subjected to a ban after their publication in the PRC during the last 30 years: works labeled as 'pornographic'[3] and those condemned for political reasons. This study has focused on 'political mistakes' (政治错误) rather than on the content labeled as 'pornographic', even though it mostly does have political implications, too. It is a generally known fact that notable political taboos arose around certain historical events (for example the Great Leap Forward or the June Fourth Clampdown in 1989). However, there are much less obvious 'political mistakes' based on perspectives and standpoints that are different from the official master narrative, which are considered more serious than for example setting the plot in a problematic historical period. Yan has complained about how the official literary scene tends to use 'concealment and deception to encourage amnesia and the creation of false memories' (2016: 268).

Contemporary censorship tends to pay special attention to several 'sensitive topics', among which perhaps the most notorious one is the representation of some of China's 55 ethnic minorities, namely Tibetans or more recently Uighurs. Literary works are expected to emphasize the positive representation of their life in 'new China' after 1949. Official propaganda tends to stress their 'backwardness' in the old 'feudal slavery system' in sharp contrast to the progress and flourishment brought to them by the Chinese (i.e., Han) 'civilizing mission'.[4] In general, writers should stay within the frame of stereotypes created by the official propaganda and spread by state authorities. Besides the contrast between 'backward' old societies and progress and wealth brought by the socialist modernity, it allows a positive reflection of certain exotic aspects of native cultures (such as Tibetan 'mysteriousness') and harmonious cohabitation with the Han majority.

A well-known early example of a writer targeted during the campaign against bourgeois liberalization in 1987 was Ma Jian (马建) who was criticized for his negative representation of Tibetan culture. It provided him with a reason to leave the country via Hong Kong and finally to stay in exile after the Tiananmen clampdown in 1989. Ma, who even in exile is known for his brutal naturalistic depictions of all the kinds of cruelty that one human being can cause to another, found inspiration for his stories during an adventurous trip to Tibet in the mid-1980s. Later he published a series of five short stories called *Stick out your Tongue or Everything is just a Void* (亮出你的舌苔或空空荡荡). It appeared in the prestigious official literary journal *People's Literature* (人民文学) with approval of the editor-in-chief, senior writer Liu Xinwu (刘心武), who lost his position after Ma Jian's escape.

The main critical argument against Ma's work was that it depicted Tibetan characters too negatively and not as based on reality. Such representation was said to 'vilify Tibetan culture'. The short stories were subsequently criticized as an example of several aspects of the 'bourgeois liberalism' imported from the West, including open descriptions of sex, violence and death, which proved their 'decadence' and 'negative social effect'. This kind of 'decadence' was at the same time closely related to the author's lifestyle: Ma Jian was not employed in an official *danwei*, lived in a free community of artists in the suburbs of Beijing and – running away from police harassment – spent several months traveling around China and Tibet, as he himself described this period in his nonfiction piece *Red Dust* (红尘, 2001). In his Tibetan series, this lifestyle was reflected in the author-narrator who recorded what he observed, experienced and heard during his travels.

The stories were inspired by the author's personal experiences and perceptions, mixed with oral legends and notorious orientalist stereotypes characterizing Tibet as a 'magical' or 'mysterious' exotic place. Furthermore, the author applied some of the broadly accepted Chinese stereotypes and fantasies about Tibetans and other ethnic minorities, turning around 'savage mind'-like concepts of cultural inferiority, for example, believe in 'feudal superstitions' or – as compared to the strict Confucian morality of the Han – more liberal attitudes to sexual relations and sex (extramarital sex, promiscuity, polygamy, polyandry).[5] While this kind of representation of Tibet and Tibetans would be possible as a criticism of the feudal past, as a depiction of the present state it was ideologically not acceptable.

Shortly after the publication, the forefront *Journal for Literature and Arts* (文艺报) published an official reaction of the Tibetan branch of Writers' Association (Zhongguo zuojia xiehui Xizang fenhui 1987). It opens with a statement that the work 'naturally incited a strong resentment and extreme indignation of the masses of Tibetan people and other brotherly nationalities, as well as of literary circles in general' (2). The author(s) emphasized the need to 'stick to the 'four basic principles'[6] and fight against the 'bourgeois liberalism'' (ibid.) and argued that literature should 'stress support and help of the CCP in the economic development in Tibet' and 'support and protect the equality of all nationalities, their unity, mutual love and help provided by the new socialist relations' (ibid.). The short stories are considered mere reflections of 'the author's fantasies and his impure soul'.

The critique, on the one hand, strives to affirm that Tibet has its own history and rich culture (and thus is not 'uncivilized' or 'barbaric' as Ma has described), but, on the other hand, it strongly emphasized the CCP's key role in 'overthrowing the feudal serf system' after the so-called 'peaceful liberation' and in implementation of what the propaganda calls 'democratic reforms'. Important arguments point out that the author 'fails to describe the real life of Tibetan people', departs from 'his own subjective imaginations and is driven by his own lust and greed for money' (ibid.). Such negative representation allegedly creates a mistaken image of 'hardworking, unpretentious, wise and brave Tibetan people' who 'are depicted as heartless, dull, cruel and immoral, which deeply hurts their feelings and should be considered as severe offense against the ethnic and religious policy of the Party' (3).

Finally, the closing part of the critical text calls to responsibility the editors of *People's Literature*, the original publisher of the work. The author(s) ponder over the critical state of literary and art circles, where the ideas of 'bourgeois liberalism' had already rooted so deeply, and they call for more attention to be paid to the editorial and publishing processes, which should give more space to works that reflect the correct socialist values. In case of ethnic minorities, literature and art are expected to stress the key principle of 'unity' (团结) of all PRC's nationalities and general social and economic progress, which all the 'brother-nationalities' have reached thanks to the CCP. In the longtime perspective, Tibet is one of the most vulnerable territories of the PRC and the government has exerted huge effort and spent endless resources since the 1950s to keep the region stable. With the leaders' emphasis on 'maintaining stability' and 'social harmony', it is not surprising that Tibet has become one of the most sensitive topics in Chinese literature and film, as proved by another well-known censorship incident some 16 years later.

In 2003 a young female poet of mixed Sino-Tibetan origin Tsering Woeser (Weise 唯色, b. 1966) published a nonfiction book called *Notes on Tibet* (西藏笔记). It was a collection of highly subjective essays written as the author's confession about her relationship to Tibet and its cultural and religious tradition. The character of essays ranges from travelogues (or rather informed traveler's observations) through records of history, both written and oral, mythology and legends, to personal ponderings reflecting the author's own search for roots and her intimate meditations inspired by Tibetan Buddhism. Some of the essays were openly polemical and many included references to foreign sources, literary and academic. The work represented Tibet from a perspective that was considerably different from the official Party narrative. Tibetan history in Woeser's essays was not the history of the 'feudal theocracy', 'peaceful liberation', and 'democratic reforms', but a history constructed as based on Buddhist legends, a spiritual history violently disrupted by the incursion of Marxist and Maoist ideology and dialectic materialism. The author was probably aware of the subversive and potentially controversial character of the text and applied certain extent of self-censorship as it is evident from her later uncensored texts published in Taiwan. Already the Taiwanese reedition of *Notes on Tibet* from 2006, published under a new title, *A Poem Called Tibet* (名为西藏的诗; Weise, 2006), included passages that could have never been published in the PRC, namely the parts about the tabooed Cultural Revolution in Tibet and about the two Tibetan religious leaders living in exile, the 14th Dalai Lama and the 17th Karmapa.

In fact, even the original Huacheng edition had many potentially subversive passages that in the end led to the ban of the book in mainland China. For example, in the chapter called 在轮回中永怀挚爱 (Eternal Love in Samsara; Weise 2003: 204) there is a long quote from the 14th Dalai Lama's autobiography *Freedom in Exile* and from the book *Tibet: Its History, Religion, and People* written by the Dalai Lama's elder brother Thubten Jigme Norbu known as Taktser Rinpoche, books that were published in Lhasa in the 1980s as 'internal' material intended for critical evaluation. Woeser used elliptic hints revealing the pressure of self-censorship. For example, the third part of the Chinese edition called 西藏感受 (Tibetan Impressions), includes the author's ponderings about her own troubled identity and about life in contemporary Tibet, suggesting several polemic points, which, however, could not be discussed openly. The last essay, 西藏随想 (A Few Thoughts about Tibet; Weise 2003: 214) only outlines several sensitive or tabooed topics in a lyrically stylized form without getting to the point – a kind of 'Aesopean language' communicable only to the knowing implied readers. Finally, the epilogue raises a question about 'representation of Tibet' in reference to E. Said's book *Orientalism*, which opens with a well-known quote by Marx ('They cannot represent themselves; they have to be represented') as a clear indication of the de-facto colonial relation between China and Tibet.

In an independent documentary *The Dossier* (Zhu 2014) Woeser said she did not expect any problems after the book had already been out, even mentioning how she gave copies as presents to her Party official colleagues. However, exactly her colleagues and superiors from the Cultural Federation (文联) stood up against the book and criticized its 'roundly mistaken political standpoints and opinions', 'bordering with political misdemeanor' (Cchering 2015: 8). The official statement released by the Tibet Writers' Association criticized the 'narrow-minded nationalism' present in the book, drawing it close to 'splittist tendencies' of the 'Dalai Lama clique'. The author was further blamed from 'drowning in nostalgic talks about the old Tibet', 'not sticking to correct political principles' and 'lacking social responsibility' (ibid.) As a result, Woeser lost her job in the official institution along with her income and all social securities and had to leave Lhasa. Her case proves that the official Party rhetoric and vigilance are still not so far from Yan'an. On the contrary, during the last few years, we have been witnessing a new wave of 'cold wind' after the new Party leadership came to power in 2012.

A more recent fiction book by Ning Ken (宁肯) called *Heaven – Tibet* (天·藏) illustrates well the sophistication that an author needs to apply to have a book about Tibet published in China in the 2010s. In a review published on the official website of Chinese Writers' Association, Wang Desong compared the novel to a labyrinth, borrowing the words of senior Tibetan writer and the Tibet Writers' Association chairman Tashi Dawa (扎西达娃), who called the work 'philosophical labyrinth novel'. Tashi Dawa is quoted to have praised the novel as 'a work about Tibet, which transcends Tibet, the first novel after Ma Yuan's (马原) 1980s stories, which *represents* and *discovers* Tibet from a purely literary point of view' (Wang 2010, emphasis added). It may sound strange because the main characters are a Han Chinese intellectual, a French Buddhist monk, and a young woman of mixed Sino-Tibetan origin who grew up in Beijing and studied in Paris. The novel does not say literally anything about the 'real life of Tibetan people', not to say anything about recent Tibetan history. But from a certain point of view Tashi Dawa, one of those Wenlian officials who criticized Woeser in 2003, was right. The novel gives as many hints as is possible and acceptable in present Chinese literary system, building a 'labyrinth' of suppressed, forbidden collective memory.

The main character, Han Chinese intellectual Wang Mojie decided to move to Tibet on purpose, in Wang Desong's words, after he 'experienced the loss of direction common among intellectuals at the end of the 1980s'. Indeed, they are clues hinting that Wang Mojie came to Tibet after what he had personally witnessed on the Tiananmen Square in June 1989, as it is symbolically expressed through his masochist deviation due to which he finds sexual pleasure in being beaten and humiliated by women in police uniforms. Not much is said about what happened in Tibet since the 1950s, but there are indirect references to the Cultural Revolution, for example when an old nun from a nunnery destroyed in 1968 told Weige (the Sino-Tibetan female character) searching for her grandmother: 'We worked together … we cleaned the streets … I wanted to give it [a letter] to her, but I had already lost it. Everything was lost' (Ning 2010: 190). Or at one point the narrator characterized Tibet as 'shadows of faded glory – seemingly, the tradition goes on, but in fact, it is nothing more than an illusion. But even an illusion can become a kind of existence, creating an illusory history' (Ning 2010: 256). Just as the whole story of the novel is an illusion. It celebrates Tibetan Buddhist tradition that was in reality drastically disrupted, and one of the main focuses of the novel, the dialogue between a French Buddhist monk, Mathieu Ricard, personal interpreter of the 14th Dalai Lama, and his father, the French philosopher Jean-Françoise Ravel, in reality could never take place in Drepung monastery in Lhasa. It happened in Kathmandu.

Ning Ken's novel is an example of a new level of sophistication of self-censorship in China. The work fully complies with the official narrative of unproblematic, yet orientalistically mysterious Tibet,[7] leaving numerous blank spaces in its history and the collective memory of Tibetan people, who are not even present, not to say represented, in the novel. But at the same time, the 'mix of realism with modernist and postmodernist narrative techniques' (Wang 2010) allows the implication of meanings that cannot be expressed openly. Only a handful of intellectuals would understand these meanings, such as references to the Cultural Revolution, destruction of monasteries and religious traditions or the so-called Tiananmen 'June 4 Incident', while the general public in China as well as in the West (as proved by the reception of the novel in its Czech translation) can enjoy the Shangrila-like fantasies about Tibetan Buddhist wisdom leading a dialogue with Western philosophy amid the beautiful scenery of the Himalayas.

Conclusion: Literature in service of social stability

As shown by the analysis, censorship and self-censorship are still an integral part of the present Chinese literary system, only the methods shifted from direct force and violence to softer psychological as well as economic pressures. Yan (2016) mentioned a system of 'self-monitoring' based on 'the seduction of power, fame and influence rather than being a product of fear and desperation' (2016: 270). Under such conditions, all parts of the literary field are actively participating in creating a – from the CCP's point of view – harmless meta-discourse of 'social harmony' and 'stability'. Although the concrete ideological objectives, mechanisms and tools, have notably changed over the last three decades, the key premises of literature 'serving the people', now clearly a substitute for the State and the Party, remained. Literature and art still should be, in the words of the Communist leaders, based in the real life of masses and should convey a clear meaning, emphasizing socialist values. Positive depictions of reality are preferred over social criticism and writers should avoid 'decadent' content with 'negative social effect'. Nevertheless, a certain degree of experimentation may be welcome, as it diverts attention from politically sensitive topics.

Building an image of 'harmonious society', literature should contribute to 'maintaining stability' and promote the 'unity of motherland' and all her nationalities. Any deviation from the official narrative, which provides its own ideologically determined complex interpretation of history and culture, is seen as a transgression that cannot be tolerated. Direct censorship may be applied in the case that a published work has instigated discussions in public space, media, or on the internet.[8] The aim of such censorship is to showcase a negative example, which helps to fix the frames of discourse. However, this is the most extreme tool for dealing with works including severe moral or political 'mistakes'. More often, some works simply tend to be made less visible compared to officially promoted literature that gets preferential publicity and makes it to prize lists.

An alternative way of publishing in Taiwan or Hong Kong has become a regular option for mainland authors, possibly opening them the door to Western markets, where 'censored' books are especially welcome and appreciated. Writers thus have a choice of targeted market for their books and apply self-censorship accordingly. In the time of the internet, social media, and digital authoritarianism, literature is no longer the main tool for disseminating Party ideology and literary censorship has different functions and objectives: to avoid social turmoil and 'maintain stability' by setting the positive frame of 'core socialist values' (社会主义核心价值观). The eight decades of political education of Chinese intellectual elites finally resulted in a state that should be highlighted in the conclusion to this chapter.

The present literary system does not need a physical 'censor' or even institutionalized censorship, because the authors, publishers, editors, as well as other parts of the literary field, now including even the broad masses of readers, have been largely incorporated into the official system, have accepted political or academic functions and are motivated to keep within the limits of the system to maintain their social and economic status.

In other words, the original antagonism between author and censor has been in the practice of the Chinese system already overcome and, paraphrasing Butler's words, 'the subject who is censored' has through 'the agency of restrictive and productive power' become one with 'the subject who censors' (1998: 247), which applies even to the recipients of such works. Only a few would transgress the line, and if they do, it is often an intentional, conscious step. For many readers, this kind of 'soft censorship' is almost invisible, because it has become less violent and less obvious. Compared to the 1980s, writers tend to moderate the risks more carefully, also with regard to readers, in a process of constant negotiation. As the analyzed examples show, (self)censorship is applied in every single step of the process of production and reception, from choosing a topic, geographical and historical setting, to characters and particular motives of each work, and all segments of the literary field actively participate. Nevertheless, while in general sticking to the monologic official master narrative affirming their participation in the system, writers frequently use their own forms of 'Aesopean language' to represent the untouchable empty spaces – gaps in personal and collective memories and between personal expression and CCP ideology.

Notes

1 The research for this chapter was supported by European Regional Development Fund within the project Sinophone Borderlands – Interaction on the Edges, reg. no CZ.02.1.01/0.0/0.0/16_019/0000791.
2 Translations from Chinese and other languages into English, if not indicated otherwise, are my own.
3 One of the works criticized for 'pornographic content' was, for example, Jia Pingwa's (贾平凹) *Abandoned Capital* (废都, 1993), which has been compared to the famous classical socially critical novel featuring numerous erotic scenes *Jin Ping Mei*. Similarly, morally motivated censorship was applied to works of the so-called 'writing beauties' (美少女作家) such as Wei Hui (卫慧) or Mian Mian (棉棉).
4 Chinese 'civilizing missions' in the areas inhabited by non-Han ethnics are often compared to the Western colonial endeavor in Asia, Africa, and the Americas. The similarities have been brough up by Harrell (1995).
5 For a more detailed analysis of the short stories, see Hladíková (2013: 70–73).
6 四项基本原则: (1) adherence to the socialist road; (2) adherence to the democratic dictatorship of the people; (3) adherence to the leadership of the Communist Party; (4) adherence to Marxism-Leninism and Mao Zedong Thought; (Barmé 1999: 384, note 41). These 'four principles' were announced in March 1979 in an anti-liberalist campaign against the democratic movement around the 'democracy wall' in Beijing.
7 As argued by Hladíková (2013: 213), the attributed 'mysteriousness' of Tibet and Tibetan religion and culture is one of the manifestations of (Western) orientalist fantasies about Tibet, but at the same time of Chinese 'internal orientalism' (Schein 2000) that gave birth to Tibetan 'magical realism' as a product of the Chinese colonial presence in Tibet. Emphasizing Tibet's 'otherness' and perceived impossibility to modernize can be interpreted as a metaphorical expression of the uneven power relations between the two cultures.
8 In a recent example of much discussed *Wuhan Diary* (武汉日记) by a senior female writer Fang Fang (方方, b. 1955), former high-ranking official of the Chinese Writers' Association, it was not even the authorities who incited the condemnation of the book – a personal diary from the period of Wuhan's coronavirus lockdown – but rather the ultra-leftist nationalist netizens on social media, who blamed the author, saying that she was 'providing bullets to the enemy/the imperialists'.

References

Barmé, G.R. (1999) *In the Red. On Contemporary Chinese Culture*, New York: Columbia UP.

Bourdieu, P. (1992) *Language and Symbolic Power* (transl. by G. Raymond, M. Adamson), Oxford: Polity Press.

———. (1993) *The Field of Cultural Production*, Cambridge: Polity Press.

Burt, R. (1994) 'The "New" Censorship', in R. Burt (ed.) *The Administration of Aesthetics: Censorship, Political Criticism, and the Public Sphere*, Minneapolis: University of Minnesota Press, xi–xxx.

Butler, J. (1998) 'Ruled Out: Vocabularies of the Censor', in R. C. Post (ed.) *Censorship and Silencing. Practices of Cultural Regulation*, Los Angeles: Getty Research Institute for the History of Art and the Humanities, 247–259.

Cchering Özer (Tsering Woeser) (2015) 'Předmluva k českému vydání' (Foreword for the Czech Edition of Notes on Tibet), in K. Hladíková (transl.) *Zápisky z Tibetu* (Notes on Tibet), Praha: Verzone, 7–9.

Darnton, R. (1995) 'Censorship, A Comparative View: France, 1789—East Germany, 1989', *Representations*, 49 (Winter 1995): 40–60.

Fik, M. (2012) 'Censor jako spoluautor' (Censor as Co-author) (transl. from Polish to Czech by M. Havránková), in T. Pavlíček et al. (eds.) *Nebezpečná literatura? Antologie myšlení o cenzuře* (Dangerous Literature? Anthology of Thoughts About Censorship), Brno: Host, 400–415.

Goldman, M. (1971) *Literary Dissent in Communist China*, New York: Atheneum.

Haraszti, M. (1987) *The Velvet Prison: Artists Under State Socialism* (Transl. by K. and S. Landesmann), New York: Basic Books.

Harrell, S. (ed.) (1995) *Cultural Encounters on China's Ethnic Frontiers*, Washington: University of Washington Press.

Hladíková, K. (2013) *The Exotic Other and Negotiation of Tibetan Self. Representation of Tibet in Chinese and Tibetan Fiction of the 1980s*, Olomouc: VUP.

Hockx, M. (ed.) (1999) *The Literary Field of Twentieth Century China*, Honolulu: University of Hawai'i Press.

Holquist, M. (1994) 'Corrupt Originals: The Paradox of Censorship', PMLA, 109(1): 14–25.

Link, P. (2000) *Uses of Literature. Life in the Socialist Chinese Literary System*, New Jersey: Princeton UP.

Loseff, L. (1984) *On the Beneficence of Censorship. Aesopian Language in Modern Russian Literature*, München: Verlag Otto Sagner.

Ma, Jian 马建 (1987) '亮出你的舌苔或空空荡荡' (Stick Out Your Tongue or Everything is Just a Void), 人民文学 (People's Literature) 1, 2. Re-published in 马建 (1988) 你拉狗屎 (You Shitty Dog), 台北：海风出版社 (Taipei: Haifeng chubanshe), 201–250.

Mao, Zedong (1996) 'Talks at the Yan'an Forum on Literature and Arts', in K. A. Denton (ed.) *Modern Chinese Literary Thought: Writings on Literature 1893–1945*, Stanford: Stanford UP, 458–84.

Müller, B. (ed.) (2004) *Censorship and Cultural Regulation in the Modern Age*, Leiden: Brill.

Ning, Ken 宁肯 (2010) 天·藏 (Heaven – Tibet), 北京：十月出版社 (Beijing: October Publishing House).

Post, R.C. (ed.) (1998) *Censorship and Silencing. Practices of Cultural Regulation*, Los Angeles: Getty Research Institute for the History of Art and the Humanities.

Schein, L. (2000) *Minority Rules: The Miao and the Feminine in China's Cultural Politics*, Durham and London: Duke UP.

Urbański, A. (2012) 'Cenzura—kontrola kontroly. Systém sedmdesátých let' (Censorship—Control of Control. The System of the 1970S) (transl. from Polish to Czech by M. Havránková), in T. Pavlíček et al. (eds.) *Nebezpečná literatura? Antologie myšlení o cenzuře* (Dangerous Literature? Anthology of Thoughts About Censorship), Brno: Host, 200–216.

Wang, Desong 王德颂 (2010) '构建精神的高原 – 读宁肯的长篇小说 《天·藏》' (Constructing Spiritual Highland: Reading Ning Ken's Novel *Heaven – Tibet*), 中国作家网 (China Writer Web), July 9. Accessible at: http://www.chinawriter.com.cn/news/2010/2010-07-09/87448.html [quot. 2019.12.17].

Weise 唯色 (2003) 西藏笔记 (Notes on Tibet), 广州：花城出版社 (Guangzhou: Huacheng chubanshe).

———. (2006) 名为西藏的诗 (A Poem Called Tibet), 台北：大块文化出版社 (Taipei: Locus Publishing House).

Xi, Jinping 习近平 (2014) '文艺不能在市场经济大潮中迷失方向' (Literature and Art Cannot Lose the Course in the Waves of Market Economy), *Xinhuanet*, October 15. Accessible at: http://www.xinhuanet.com/politics/2014-10/15/c_1112840544.htm. [quot. 2018.4.19.].

———. (2015) '在文艺工作座谈会上的讲话' (Talk at the Work Forum on Literature and Arts), Xinhuanet, October 14. Accessible at: http://www.xinhuanet.com/politics/2015-10/14/c_1116825558.htm. [quot. 2018.4.19.].

Yan, Lianke (2016) 'An Examination of China's Censorship System', in C. Rochas, and A. Bachner (eds.) *The Oxford Handbook of Modern Chinese Literatures*, Oxford: Oxford UP, 263–74.

Zhongguo zuojia xiehui Xizang fenhui 中国作家协会西藏分会 (Tibet Writers' Association) (1987) '一篇丑化侮辱藏族人民的劣作' (A Depraved Work Vilifying and Humiliating Tibetan People), 文艺报 (Journal for Literature and Arts), March 28: 2–3. Re-published in Ma, Jian马建 (1988) 你拉狗屎 (You Shitty Dog), 台北：海风出版社 (Taipei: Haifeng chubanshe), 251–256.

Zhu, Rikun 朱日坤 (2014) *The Dossier* 档案 (film documentary), Huangniutian Film Group, 128 min. Chinese with English subtitles.

36

The typology of on- and offline collective action in China

Ting Xue and Jacquelien van Stekelenburg

Introduction

According to the Chinese Academy of Social Sciences' blue paper (book) on society, the number of crowd events in China in 1993 was 8,700, which rose to 87,000 in 2005 and exceeded 90,000 in 2006 (Dong 2016). Meanwhile, the popularity of the internet has spawned more types of collective actions in China. The on-and offline collective actions not only reflect the reality of the modern society of China but also influence the ideology of Chinese people and the policies of the Chinese government (Yang 2013; Yu 2006). Especially, the increase of a large variety of collective actions in contemporary China could be a challenge to the Chinese government to maintain stability (King et al. 2013). Therefore, the essential characteristics and potential impact of these collective activities have attracted the attention of scholars and practitioners both in China and abroad (Xue et al. 2016, 2018).

Western researchers usually explain the characteristics of collective actions in China in terms of theories from Western society, which has also been followed by some Chinese researchers. However, as we will argue in this chapter, there are several events with a unique Chinese style that cannot be fully explained by Western models. For example, evidence shows that right-defending motivation is the dominant driver for Chinese people to participate in both on- and offline collective actions (Liu 2004; Yang 2009). In China, people often cannot find reasonable channels for rights protection when their legitimate interests are damaged. Therefore, they have to resort to certain kinds of collective actions to solve the problems (Ma et al. 2017; Yu 2018). Some surveys have proved that issues relating to land acquisition and house demolition, ecological and environmental pollution, labor-management conflicts, income gaps, and corruption have become the main causes of crowd offline events in contemporary China (Zhai et al. 2016). Similarly, information that involves social contradictions, such as social livelihood, social distribution, and social management, is relatively easy to form hot public opinions about on the internet, and can trigger other online and offline collective actions (Li et al. 2017). Xu (2019) summarized the characteristics of Chinese collective action as the goal to safeguard specific rights, not to subvert the social system. The accusation was directed at the local government, not the central government.

DOI: 10.4324/9780429059704-42

Discourse struggles rather than violent actions were frequently used, and passive response rather than proactive power struggle was the most cases.

To understand the various kinds of collective actions in China, specific localized concepts are needed in the equation. Although much effort has been taken, a widely accepted system of definition and categories of collective actions in China has not been established. Thus, we find a chaotic situation in China, where Chinese scholars with diverse disciplinary and/or professional backgrounds use similar concepts to explain different situations, or created different terms to discuss similar events. For example, 'public online opinion' ('网络舆论'), 'hot online event'('网络热点事件'), and 'crowd online event' ('网络群体性事件') are used simultaneously to refer to the same event, such as the case of the 'wives of the official in Zhang Jiagang tour abroad in-group', a tour group composed of eight wives of government officials who spent 246000 yuan in eight days, which concerns or is discussed by millions of netizens in China (Dong et al. 2012). In these cases, it is hard to make a valid and reliable comparison to achieve a solid conclusion on similarities and differences. Therefore, we propose in this chapter a relative comprehensive classification for offline and online collective actions in China, respectively, with the purpose to clarify the relationship among the various kinds of definitions and classifications relevant to collective actions, and to facilitate in-depth analysis of the characteristics and mechanisms of collective actions in China.

Defining and classifying offline collective action in China

As aforementioned, the classical theories of collective actions, collective behaviors, and social movements proposed in the Western context have also become an important basis to explain the phenomenon in China. For example, the definition of collective action proposed by Wright et al. (1990: 995), that is 'a group member engages in collective action any time that he or she is acting as a representative of the group and where the action is directed at improving the conditions of the group as a whole', has been well recognized by Chinese scholars (e.g., Liu et al. 2018). Popenoe (1999) defines collective behaviors as reacting to a common influence or stimulus under relatively spontaneous, unpredictable, unorganized, and unstable conditions, and he defines social movements as a collective effort that mainly relies on noninstitutionalized methods to generate social change. As Popenoe (1999) pointed out, social movements, such as reform, revolution, and resistance, are more purposeful and more organized, and often have a longer duration, compared with collective behaviors. Moreover, he divides collective behavior into two types. First, primary collective behaviors, such as rumors, gossip, propaganda, and public opinion, refer to the ways for people to share information and ideas, which can be viewed as a form of collective behavior or the primary stage of more serious collective behavior, such as panic or riots. Second, mass behaviors, such as panic, mass hysteria, and postdisaster behavior, which often occur in scattered groups, and participants usually do not know each other or have little connection with each other (Popenoe 1999). Although this Western classification of collective behavior could explain part of the group phenomenon in China, it does not get much attention from Chinese scholars and practitioners. In China, society and politics pay usually more attention to collective behaviors with a potential negative impact on social order, such as demonstrations, strikes, illegal gatherings, etc., which do not have a unified term in the Western theories. Consequently, some different concepts have been created by Chinese people, with 'crowd event' as the core concept (Chen et al. 2010).

The terms related to 'crowd event' were born with a negative connotation because their creators were concerned more about the reason why people violated the rule of law and disrupted normal social life. For example, in the document formulated by the Ministry of Public Security in 2000, 'crowd security event' was defined as the collective behaviors implemented by the masses which violate national laws, regulations, and rules, as well as disrupting social order, endangering public security, and infringing citizens' safety, public and private property safety (Chen et al. 2010). While some neutral or even positive point of views came into being, for example, Lv (1989) proposed that, in a more general way, petitions or demonstrations were not necessarily antisocial, people may sign a petition or get together for a demonstration to express their emotion or for other reasonable purposes. Wang (1995) believed that such collective actions could reflect the legitimate interests and aspirations of the public and could even help to develop the social policies more healthily.

A framework of offline collective action in contemporary China

This chapter first proposes a new framework of offline collective action in contemporary China by integrating Popenoe's theory and relevant Chinese research. As Liu (2004) proposed, collective actions in China encompass a continuum from sudden collective behaviors to formal social movements. Thus, in this framework, collective actions consist of collective behaviors and social movements. Since social movements are still seldom in contemporary China, we will only focus on collective behaviors that further include primary collective behaviors, mass behaviors, and crowd events (see Table 36.1). In our framework, we rely

Table 36.1 Defining and classifying offline collective actions in China

			Definition	*Characteristics*	*Examples*
collective action	collective behaviors	primary collective behaviors	It is the way people share information and ideas	nonorganization; no common actions	rumors, gossip, propaganda, public opinion
		mass behaviors	It is a kind of collective behaviors conducted by disparate social groups	nonorganization or little degree organization; no common actions	panic, mass hysteria, popularity, fanaticism
		crowd event	It is a kind of collective behaviors conducted by individuals without a fixed group	unstable organization; a short duration	football hooligans riots, strike, parade
	social movements			more firmly established leadership and organization; a longer duration	reform, revolution, resistance movement, expressive movement

(also see Chen et al. 2010)

on the definition of primary collective behavior and mass behavior as proposed by Popenoe (1999). Crowd event is defined from the general perspective that it may have a negative or positive social impact (Lv 1989). In addition, some examples and characteristics of each kind of offline collective action are also listed. It could be seen that the main difference among these kinds of collective actions lies in the organizational characteristics.

We further integrate relevant categories of crowd events. As aforementioned, Chinese scholars have attempted to divide offline crowd events into positive crowd events and negative crowd events according to their social influence(Lv 1989; Wang 1995). Here we emphasize the categories of the negative crowd events since they still attract much more attention compared to the positive ones. Four kinds of classification and their criteria are described in Figure 36.1. As Zhuang and Chang (1998) have demonstrated, negative crowd events could be divided into 'public security crowd event' and 'political crowd event' based on the social root of the crowd event. Specifically, a 'public security crowd event' refers to collective behavior that may disrupt the social order or threaten people's daily life, such as football hooligan riots and civil disturbance (affray). The 'political crowd event' refers to collective behaviors with the purpose to oppose the Party and the socialist system, or to overthrow the legal government, such as demonstrations and strikes. Meanwhile, Ma (2001) classified the negative crowd event into a 'situational crowd event' and a 'functional crowd event' concerning the nature of the law of the event. That is, the 'situational crowd event' is usually initiated by accidental or occasional reasons, such as football hooligan riots. Though some of them may be relatively chaotic and destructive, they usually neither cause too much trouble to normal life nor destroy the social order. The 'functional crowd event' mainly occurs due to certain social conflicts or political causes and is prone to have a profound effect on social life, such as a petition and demonstration. It is usually observed in specific

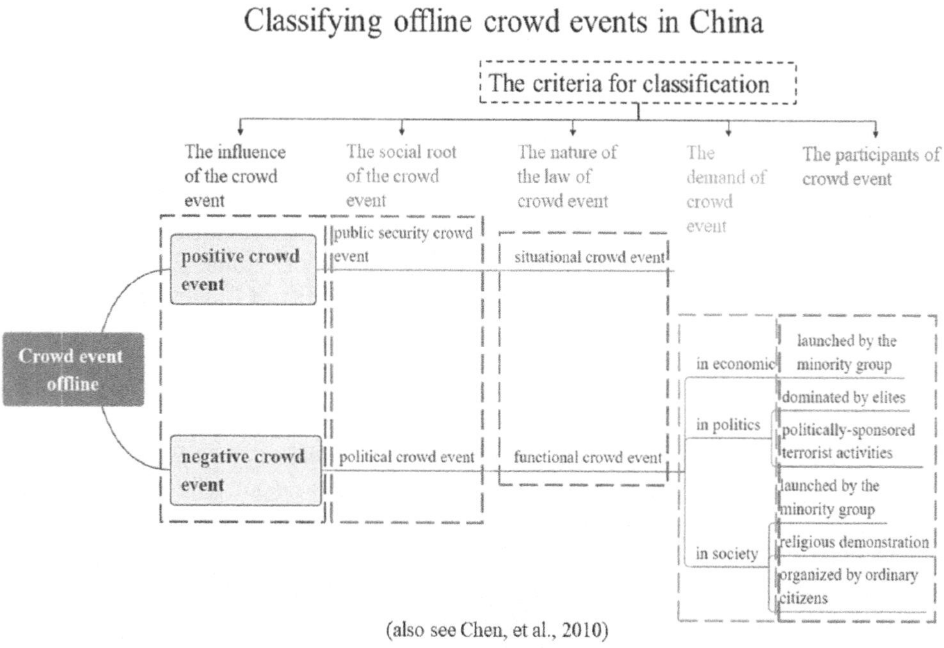

Figure 36.1 Classifying offline crowd events in China.

social contexts or certain stages of social development. As Ma (2001) explained, during the Cultural Revolution in China, the frequent collective action was partly due to the childish political passion of citizens. While, in contemporary China, most of the functional crowd events are rooted in the contradictions in the redistribution of social resources, leading to the damage of some groups' social interest. To summarize, the 'situational crowd event' basically corresponds to the 'public security crowd event', and the 'functional crowd event' corresponds to 'political crowd event', concerning their social roots or political purposes (Chen et al. 2010).

In China, the functional or political crowd events have been widely discussed because they threaten the authority of the government and social stability (Ma 2001). The argument is still ongoing on their characteristics and potential influence. To clarify these questions, some refined classifications have been made. Liu (1989) divided the functional or political crowd event into three subclasses according to the demand motivating the collective behavior. First, the societal crowd event is organized to meet the rights of participants' ingroup. Second, the economic crowd event is often triggered by the impaired economic interest of a group of people. Finally, the political crowd event involves the requirements for government officials or political policies.

Moreover, other scholars differentiated functional crowd events into five subclasses, which happened mainly in urban areas in China, in terms of the composition of participants and their demands. First, the collective action is dominated by elites, and their demands are often politically motivated, such as the protests initiated by intellectuals or university students as an immediate response for international and domestic political events. Second, collective action is organized by ordinary citizens, which often involves demands related to civic life or general human interest, such as environmental protection actions and consumer rights protection. Third, collective action is launched by a minority group, which is usually a type of rights protection. For example, laid-off workers protest for unfair treatment and migrant workers protest for arrears of wages. Fourth, the religious demonstration is motivated by the social need or spiritual demand of specific religious subgroups, such as the Qigong group. Finally, the terrorist activity expresses political demand through extreme behavior, such as political separatism in some areas in China (Liu 2004).

Overall, the contribution of the new categorical framework of collective actions offline in China can be summarized in three aspects. First, it helped to clarify the relationship between the existing concepts and classifications relevant to collective actions or crowd events in China. Second, the refinement of the crowd events reflects the social-psychological motivation as well as the organizational characteristics of certain kinds of collective actions in China. Finally, it partially reveals the social mentality of Chinese people and the major inequalities in contemporary China, such as the gaps between the rich and the poor, between urban and rural, and between different regions (Pan et al. 2018; Zhang et al. 2018). In addition, it also helps to indicate the development of the political participation of Chinese people, both in terms of quantity (amount of activities) and quality (the type of activities). As predicted by scholars, the stimulation of the social conflicts as well as the arousing of the awareness of civil rights of the public in China constitutes a powerful driver for future collective action, especially various types of crowd events. On the other hand, the lax performance of some local officials, the low efficiency of traditional media, and the insufficient supply of institutions in offline political participation would make more and more Chinese people use the internet to defend their rights and express their voice (Ma et al. 2017; Ni 2017; Xu 2019; Xue et al. 2016). Therefore we will proceed by defining and classifying online collective action in China.

Defining and classifying online collective action in China

According to a report by the China Internet Network Information Center (CNNIC 2019), by June 2019, 854 million people in China were using the internet, making up 47.9% of the total population. The number of online users of government service reached 509 million, accounting for 59.6% of netizens as a whole. The internet has gradually become the main venue for Chinese citizens to participate in politics (Xue et al. 2016). Online collective actions not only surge in number and form but also have inextricable relationships with the offline world. Although there have been numerous studies probing online collective actions in China, some concepts and classifications relating to the topics are still not clear. Therefore, to obtaina better understanding of the new forms of political participation and the right protection for Chinese people, this chapter further proposes an integral categorization of online collective action in China (see Table 36.2).

First of all, the basis of the classification is the characteristic of participants, regarding the distinction between 'crowd' and 'group' in social psychology (Yue 2017). Yang (2009) demonstrated that the participants in most online collective actions could be viewed as a type of 'online crowd'. That is digitalized individuals, with common needs or concerns, interact with each other under certain rules and ways. However, there are also some participants in certain online collective actions who meet the conditions for a kind of 'group', that is, they have a common goal and a unified feeling, a relatively clear behavior norm, and ongoing interaction (Yue 2017). In summary, whether the participants of a specific collective activity have common concerns, common beliefs, or common behaviors (including all words and deeds on- and offline) are made as the key criteria to classify online collective actions in the Chinese context. The order of the three criteria is fixed, which reflects the developing direction of the event and the internal mechanisms of various types of online collective actions to some extent.

Secondly, this framework has sorted out the existing classifications in a comprehensive way. Though Chinese scholars from various fields have tried to define and categorize public online behavior based on the understanding of the offline collective action, there are still overlaps among some categories. For example, Du and colleagues (2010: 44) defined 'online collective behaviors' as 'a certain number of unorganized online groups get together on the internet because of a specific theme or stimulating factor from the real world, and their interaction could strengthen their opinion and may make a difference on the real life'. Meanwhile, Yang (2009: 47) defined 'online crowd event' as 'a new special form of crowd event, i.e., a group of netizens use the internet to communicate and organize, and get together in the real world. Their behaviors may disrupt normal social life and harm the social and political stability'. Qiu (2009) has further divided online crowd events into 'online and offline coexisting', 'reality-induced and happen online', and 'reality-induced and extended to offline'. Although this categorization revealed the interaction between online and offline behavior, it does not include other popular online collective behaviors, such as public opinion online, human flesh search, and cyberbullying, which will be improved in our classification (Fei 2016; Wei 2019).

A framework of online collective actions in contemporary China

We can now propose a categorical framework for online collective actions in China by integrating the above classification of offline collective actions and research involving this topic (see Table 36.2). In this framework, the online collective action mainly refers to 'individual

Table 36.2 The classification of online collective actions in China

Classification				*Characteristics*	*Examples*
Online collective actions	online collective actions based on common concerns			have certain common concerns reached by the Netizens but only expressed by discourse explicitly	online rumors, online sentiments
	online collective actions based on common beliefs			have clear goals and practical actions but only limited to online behaviors; spontaneous and unorganized	online public opinion, cyberbullying, online trials
	online collective actions based on common goals	collective activities only happening online		have clear goals; the action extending to the real world; spontaneous and unorganized; last shortly	'human flesh search', *egao* online, online rally
		online crowd events involving behaviors offline	offline collective actions initiated by online dissemination		'human flesh search', flash mob online, anti-Japanese protests in 2012
			offline collective actions enlarged by online communication		Dazhu event in Sichuan Province in 2007,the Wengan event in Guizhou Province in 2008
			offline collective actions mobilized or organized online	have clear goals; have the process of resource mobilization by a certain organization	Anti-PX events in Ximan, the Ruian event in Zhejiang Province in 2012

(also see Yue et al. 2010)

or collective efforts based on a common effect, stimulus or target, which happened on the internet or were influenced by the internet' (Yue et al. 2010: 101). According to the characteristics of the participants and the activities mentioned above, this chapter divided online collective actions into actions based on common concerns, actions based on common beliefs, and actions based on the common goals that are consisted of online collective actions only happening online and online collective action involving collective behaviors offline (that is the so-called 'online crowd event'). Here 'online crowd event' actually refers to a type of offline collective behaviors that are caused by an online stimulus, prompted or deteriorated by online interaction, or mobilized and organized by using online resources. Conceived as such, 'online crowd event' is the key connection between on-and offline collective actions. The concepts and examples of different types of online collective actions will be discussed below. The main characteristics of each kind of online collective action are also summarized in the framework, which not only reflects the developing process of different types of online collective activities but also indicates the social-psychological mechanisms of online collective action, with a systematic and dynamic perspective.

Online collective actions based on common concerns

This kind of online collective action mainly refers to a potential attitude or statement formed among netizens towards a specific event or stimulus in the real world and leaking out from some online behavior or generated immediately online due to the powerful function of the internet in disseminating information, such as online rumors and online public sentiment (Wang 2008). It can be regarded as an independent subcategory of online collective action or as the primary stage of other online collective behavior. There is evidence showing that the online public sentiment not only reflects the stage of certain crowd events but also could take the role of inciting or prompting the event (Xu 2003; Zhang 2009; Zheng et al. 2006). Even as the simplest and the most primary form of online collective action, it reveals the change in the way people access and communicate information in the internet era. Take the online rumor as an example, at the time of writing this chapter, a severe epidemic named COVID-19 had broken out in China. Hubei Province is the most affected area at the moment of writing. By February 5, 2020, the number of cumulative confirmed cases reached 24,433 on the Chinese mainland and 16,678 in Hubei Province, including 493 deaths on the Chinese mainland and 479 in Hubei Province. Since the outbreak, various rumors have been spread on the internet, such as 'multilayer masks can prevent the virus', 'smoking can prevent infection', 'pharmacies and supermarkets in Wuhan (the provincial capital in Hubei Province) will be completely closed in three days', etc. Previously, there was a post titled 'Shuang Huang Lian (Oral Liquid of Chinese patent medicine) can inhibit the new coronavirus'. The topic was reposted more than 60,000 times in 24 hours and received more than 1 million likes. A large number of citizens went to drug stores overnight, lining up to buy the drug.

Online collective action based on common beliefs

The online collective actions based on common beliefs could be described as 'a group of netizens reaches a consensus on specific events or concerns, which usually does not involve collective activities, but they are mainly expressed by voice, such as the public opinion formed and expressed online, some Cyberbullying, and online trials' (Yue et al. 2010: 102). Compared with the online sentiment, public opinion online emphasizes the common belief and attitude of the Netizen to a public event being explicitly expressed on the internet (Wang 2008). In addition to being a typical form of online collective action in China, it could work as a stepping-stone between more elementary forms of online collective phenomena (such as online sentiment) to more complex forms of online collective actions (Wang 2007). For example, during the COVID-19 epidemic in 2020, numerous solidarity posts and support from Chinese netizens have been expressed on various online platforms to support Wuhan and the country. A popular Chinese star posted on Sina Weibo: 'Come on, Wuhan! Come on, China! Strengthen our confidence, walk towards the light, and look forward to spring blossoms'. The post was reposted 881,000 times and liked 823,000 times in just 5 hours.

Cyberbullying and online trails are special expressions of a more Chinese style. Sometimes netizens collectively make offensive or insulting statements to the person or organization involved in a hot event. These behaviors (usually called cyberbullying in China) may cause public opinion pressure or reputation damage on the person or organization (Liang et al. 2009). Or netizens gather online to convict or punish someone by violent language with the purpose to achieve some extent of justice (that is the so-called online trials in China) (Du 2009). For example, on the morning of August 21, 2018, a netizen posted that on the G334 train from Jinan Station to Beijing South Station, a male passenger occupied the window seat reserved by others. When the cabin crew came, he refused to yield his seat in a bad manner. Then the picture of the man was spread on the internet, his personal information was exposed by angry netizens, and the accusations against him dominated the screen till he was punished by the China Railway Administration.

Online collective actions based on the common goals

As mentioned previously, according to the place where the collective behavior occurs, online collective actions based on the common goals can be further divided into collective activities happening only online and collective activities both online and offline (Yue et al. 2010).

a. Collective activities only happening online

This kind of online collective action is usually spontaneous and unorganized, but with a relatively clear goal, such as the 'human flesh search', *egao* (spoof) online, 'killing order online' and online rally, and so forth. Of these examples, 'human flesh search' and *egao* have received the most attention. The process of the 'human flesh search' matches its name very well, that is, netizens make use of the information technology to collaboratively search the truth of an event, or to find the identity of a person. It is a social activity of netizens to some extent (Lu et al. 2008; Yin 2009; Yue et al. 2010). In 2015, a report about a female driver beaten by a male driver was released and disseminated on the internet. Netizens first expressed broad sympathy for the female driver. When the male driver's driving video was made public, they turned to condemn the inappropriate behavior of the female driver and carried out a human flesh search. The woman's previous illegal driving records, home address, and other personal information was exposed online. Finally, the woman was forced to apologize publicly. Moreover, the 'human flesh search' not only includes a large number of collectivities and collective actions on the internet, but also some behaviors extend to real life. Therefore, it could be included in two subcategories of the online collective actions based on the common goals.

The *egao* online has attracted broad attention partly due to its unique Chinese style. Netizens individually or collectively deconstruct pictures, text, films, or television works, with the purpose to subvert the dominant culture. It may be recognized as various forms of online behavior, such as entertaining imitation, cultural criticism, creative show, and malicious infringement (Nie 2009). For example, when a report titled 'Beijing Raised the Red Warning for the Haze' was published on the front page of a newspaper netizens then collectively made similar sentences (such as 'it is hard to differentiate between orange warning and red warning', '橙色预警和红色预警, 傻傻分不清') to make fun, and more importantly, to express their dissatisfaction with this propaganda (Tang 2016).

b. Online crowd events involving behaviors offline

As mentioned above, in this chapter we define all the offline collective action involving the internet as 'online crowd events', which could be divided into three categories. It should be noted that the reality and the virtual world are often closely intertwined in actual situations, making it hard to have a clear distinction. The three subclassifications below are used in particular to emphasize the different roles played by the internet in certain collective actions.

The first one is the collective actions triggered by online communication. That is, some online events as a fuse causes online public opinion formation and online activities first, then upgrades to collective behavior in the real world by online propagation, such as some 'human flesh search' involving activities offline and the anti-Japanese protests in 2012. In 2012, Japan's nationalization of the Diaoyu Islands has aroused the anger of the Chinese people. Although this event came from real life, what ignited the group-based anger was the widely shared posts relevant to the event on the internet. According to the 'Report of China Internet Public Opinion in 2012', the followers of the online posts relating to Diaoyu Island exceeded 100 million, making it the hottest online issue of the year, which in turn triggered a large-scale anti-Japanese march offline in September 2012 throughout China.

The second one refers to collective action caused initially by an issue offline and then escalating into a large-scale crowd event due to some online rumors or extreme views that go viral, such as the Dazhu event in Sichuan Province in 2007 and the Wengan event in Guizhou Province in 2008. On December 30, 2006, a female employee of a hotel in Dazhu County, Sichuan Province, died for an unknown reason. Ten days afterward, the local police still did not give a reasonable investigation report. The relatives of the deceased and some citizens were very angry, causing hundreds of people to gather in front of the hotel and ask relevant departments to find out the cause of death as soon as possible. At the same time, many local netizens continued to report the development of the incident on the internet, mixed with many inaccurate rumors, such as the female employee was killed in the hotel. Numerous live pictures and text comments attracted more and more people to gather around the hotel. In the end, some people rushed into the hotel and set fire to the hotel during the conflict, leading to a serious crowd event.

The last category is collective action mobilized or organized on the internet. In this category, people with specific demands or purposes consciously use the internet as a tool to exchange and disseminate information of certain planned collective action offline and to encourage and instruct more people to join in as well. Compared with the first examples of online collective action involving activities offline which are usually spontaneous, unorganized, and short-lived, this type of collective action usually has clearer organization and social influence, with certain characteristics of resource mobilization. So it can be seen as the most extreme form of online collective action, with the closest relationship to crowd events offline. For example, in October 2012, a PX[1] project was planned to locate in Zhenhai District, Ningbo City, Zhejiang Province. Then discussions about the environmental pollution of the PX project started on the internet. On October 25 and 26, people in Zhenhai District made a large-scale protest, which soon spread to Ningbo on the 27th and 28th with the help of the dissemination and organization on the internet. More attention was attracted and more news from different media was reported. In the end, the Ningbo Government decided to stop the PX project.

Conclusion

In this chapter, we reclassified the off-and online collective actions in contemporary China by integrating research both from China and abroad. It could be used to examine and reanalyze the results of the relevant studies using different terms to define collective actions in China. The typology of on- and offline collective actions in China also indicates the similarities and differences between Chinese and Western collective action. On the one hand, the types of collective offline actions in China can be incorporated into the mature classification system of collective action in the West. The crowd events that have attracted much attention in China seldom happen in the West, but they can be one of the subcategories of collective behavior. The specific classification of the crowd events is helpful for the Chinese and foreign scholars to learn the characteristics of the participants and their motivations to take part in such kind of actions in contemporary China. On the other hand, the international consensus on the characteristics of 'crowd' and 'group' is one of the important foundations of the classification of online collective actions in this chapter. This typology may be helpful for scholars at home and abroad to understand the basic features of China's unique types of online collective action, such as the concerns, beliefs, and goals shared in the 'human flesh search', *egao*, and online crowd events. However, why some types of collective actions are unique or popular only in China need to be answered.

The two frameworks are also systematic and dynamic, that is, each subcategory can both be seen as an independent kind of collective action, and also as the transitional phase of a higher degree of actions. Moreover, the overlap between the two categories of on- and offline collective actions, such as online crowd events, also indicates the close interaction between virtual and real life. For example, with the help of the technology of the internet and the development of the event, some online collective action with common concerns may develop into online collective action with common beliefs and common goals. The influence of a collective activity may in turn trigger the online concerns and discussion when it spreads into the real world. Scholars have pointed out that the close relationship between virtual and real could help to explain the mechanism of online political mobilization in China (Du 2009; Yang 2009). The problems in real life are projected in cyberspace one by one. And netizens with more power begin to use the internet to communicate and mobilize, which may, in turn, expand the effect of the event or even prompt the development of policies (Wen et al. 2018; Zhu 2018). However, the essential feature and mechanisms of these Chinese-style collective actions, as well as the developing regulation and the correlation of different kinds of collective action, such as, how the internet helps to form the common beliefs and common goals in Chinese netizens and what is the role of the internet in mobilizing collective actions offline, still need to be clarified in future studies.

Note

1 PX is a petrochemical industrial chain intermediate product, mainly used to produce PTA (Pure Terephthalic Acid) and DMT (Dimethyltryptamine).

References

Chen, H., Xue, T. and Yue, G.-A. 陈浩,薛婷,乐国安 (2010) '集群行为诸相关概念分类新框架' (A New Categorization Framework for Collective Behavior-related Concepts), 广西民族大学学报: 哲学社会科学版(Journal of Guangxi University for Nationalities(Philosophy and Social Science Edition)), (6), 56–60.

CNNIC 中国互联网络信息中心 (2019). '中国互联网络发展状况统计报告 (第44次)' (Statistical report of Internet development in China (44th)).

Dong, T.-C. 董天策 (2016) '从网络集群行为到网络集体行动——网络群体性事件及相关研究的学理反思' (From the Network Collective Behavior to the Network Collective Actions: Theoretical Reflections on Network Group Events and Related Studies),新闻与传播研究 (Journalism & Communication), (2), 80–99.

Dong, T.-C. and Liang, C.-X. 董天策, 梁辰曦 (2012) '究竟是'网络群体性事件'还是'网络公共事件'抑或其他? ———关于'网络舆论聚集'研究的再思考' (Internet Mass Event, Internet Public Event or Something Else? Rethinking Internet Opinion Gathering), 新闻与传播研究 (Journalism & Communication), 27(1), 87–128.

Du, J.-F. 杜骏飞 (2009) '网络群体事件的类型辨析' (A Study on the Categories of Internet Mass Events), 国际新闻界(Journal of International Communication), (7), 76–80.

Du, J.-F. and Wei, J. 杜骏飞, 魏娟 (2010) '网络集群的政治社会学: 本质、类型与效用' (The Political Sociology of Internet Collective Behavior: Essence, Type and Utility), 东南大学学报(哲学社会科学版) (Journal of Southeast University (Philosophy and Social Science)), (1), 43–51.

Fei, J.-H. 费久浩 (2016) '民粹主义视阈下网络群体性事件的演化机制研究' (Research on the Evolution Mechanism of Network Mass Events from the Perspective of Populism),电子政务 (E-Government), (6), 27–38.

King, G., Pan, J., Roberts, M.E., (2013). 'How censorship in China allows government criticism but silences collective expression.' *American Political Science Review*, 107(2), 326–343.

Li, H.-X., Wang, S.-G. and Li, B.-K. 李红星,王曙光,李秉坤 (2017) '应对网络群体性事件的政策工具分析' (Analysis of Policy Tools for Dealing with Internet Mass Events), 中国行政管理 (Chinese Public Administration), (2), 149–151.

Liang, L. and Lv, R.-C. 梁丽, 吕瑞超 (2009) '传播学视角下网络暴力初探' (The Initial Exploration of Network Violence from the Perspective of Communication), 法制与社会 (Legal System and Society), (12), 238–239.

Liu, B., Li, Y., Xue, B., Li, Q., Zou, P.X., Li, L., (2018). 'Why do individuals engage in collective actions against major construction projects?—An empirical analysis based on Chinese data.' *International Journal of Project Management*, 36(4), 612–626.

Liu, N. 刘能 (2004) '怨恨解释, 动员结构和理性选择——有关中国都市地区集体行动发生可能性的分析' (Interpretation of Resentment, Mobilization Structure and Rational Choice-An Analysis of the Possibility of Collective Action in Urban Areas of China), 开放时代 (Open Times), (4), 57–70.

Liu, S.-L. 刘世林 (1989) '处理'聚众活动'的理论和实践' (The Theory and Practice of Handling 'Gathering Activities'), 公安部公共安全研究所报告 (Report of the Public Security Institute of the Ministry of Public Security), (6), 73.

Lu, C.-L. and Tan, Y.-M. 卢春伶, 谭有模 (2008) '网络'人肉搜索'集群现象浅析' (Simple Analysis on the Cluster Phenomenon of 'Human Flesh Search' in Network), 中国集体经济(China Collective Economy), (3), 120–121.

Lv, S.-M. 吕世明 (1989) '警察对群众事件的应有认识' (Police's Due Understanding of Mass Events), 世界警察参考资料 (World Police Reference), 6(7).

Ma, C.-Q. and Zhao, Y. 马春庆, 赵燕 (2017) ''网络群体性事件'的界定及防治策略' (The Definition and Prevention Strategy of 'Network Mass Events'),东岳论丛 (Dongyue Tribune), (8), 188–192.

Ma, G.-H. 马广海 (2001). '社会转型期功能性集体行为的原因与控制' (The Reason and Control of Functional Collective Behavior in the Social Transition Period).人文杂志 (The Journal of Humanities), (4), 13–17.

Ministry of Public Security 公安部 (2000) '公安机关处置群体性治安事件的规定' (Provisions on Handling Mass Public Security Incidents by Public Security Organs).

Ni, M. 倪明 (2017) '公民网络抗争动员: 从概念建构到关联性议题反思' (Civil Network Protest Mobilization: From Concept Construction to Reflection on Related Issues), 天津社会科学 (Tianjin Social Sciences), (4), 12.

Nie, J.-L. 聂晶磊 (2009) '网络恶搞的特征、原因与对策' (On the Characteristics, Reasons And Countermeasures of Network Kuso), 新闻界(Press Circles), (4), 58–59.

Pan, J., Xu, Y.-Q., (2018). 'China ideological spectrum.' *Journal of Politics*, 80(1), 254–273.

Popenoe, D., (1999). *Sociology*, trans. LiQiang, et al., Beijing: China Renmin University.

Qiu, J.-X. 邱建新 (2009) '为'网络公众舆论'正名——关于'网上群体性事件'概念适当性的思考' (Correct the Name of 'Internet Public Opinion'-Reflections on the Appropriateness of the Concept of 'Internet Mass Events'), 江苏社会科学 (Jiangsu Social Sciences), (6), 97–101.

Tang, J.-T. 汤景泰 (2016) '情感动员与话语协同: 新媒体事件中的行动逻辑' (Emotional Mobilization and Discourse Synergy: Action Logic in New Media Events),探索与争鸣(Exploration and Free Views), (11), 49–52.

Wang, F.-D. 王福德 (1995) '论消极性集合行为发生的心理动因及其控制' (On the Psychological Motivation and Control of Negative Collective Behavior),四川警察学院学报 (Journal of Sichuan Police College), (2), 14–16.

Wang, L.-H. 王来华 (2008) '论网络舆情与舆论的转换及其影响' (On the Transformation and Influence of Internet Public Opinion and Public Opinion), 天津社会科学(Tianjin Social Sciences), (4), 66–69.

Wang, X. 王雪 (2007) '网络舆论、集体行为与社会控制' (Internet Public Opinion, Collective Behavior and Social Control), 探求(Academic Search for Truth and Reality), (1), 57–62.

Wei, H.-T. 魏海涛 (2019) '集体行动的形成:一个文化视角的理论模型' (The Making of Collective Action: A Theoretical Model from Culture Perspective), 社会学评论 (Sociological Review of China), (4),75–83.

Wen, Z.-Q. and Hao, Y.-L. 温志强, 郝雅立 (2018) '大数据环境下群体性事件的智能预警' (Artificial Intelligence Warning of Mass Event in Big Data Environment), 上海行政学院学报(The Journal of Shanghai Administration Institute), 19(002), 80–87.

Wright, S.C., Taylor, D.M., Moghaddam, F.M., (1990). 'Responding to membership in a disadvantaged group: From acceptance to collective protest.' *Journal of Personality and Social Psychology*, 58(6), 994.

Xu, N.-L. 徐乃龙 (2003) '群体性事件中网络媒体的负面影响及其对策' (Negative Influence of Internet Media in Mass Events and Its Countermeasures), 江苏警官学院学报(Journal of Jiangsu Public Security College), (6), 11–14.

Xu, X. 许鑫 (2019) '网络公共事件: 概念辨析及其要素, 特征分析' (Network Public Events：Concept Discrimination and Analysis on Its Elements and Characteristics), 惠州学院学报 (Journal of Huizhou University), 39(004), 84–90.

Xue, T., van Stekelenburg, J., (2018). 'When the Internet meets collective action: The traditional and creative ways of political participation in China.' *Current Sociology*, 66(6), 911–928.

Xue, T., van Stekelenburg, J., Klandermans, B., (2016). 'Online collective action in China: A new integrated framework.', Sociopedia.isa, DOI: 10.1177/205684601661.

Yang, G.-B. 杨国斌 (2013) '连线力：中国网民在行动'(The Power of the Internet in China: Citizen Activism Online), 广西师范大学出版社(Guangxi Normal University Press).

Yang, J.-H. 杨久华 (2009) '试论网络群体性事件发生的模式、原因及其防范' (On the Modes, Causes and Prevention of Network Mass Events),重庆社会主义学院学报 (Journal of Chongqing Institute of Socialism), 11(4), 89–92.

Yin, J. 殷俊 (2009) '从典论喧嚣到理性回归-对网络人肉搜索的多维研究' (From the Uproar of Typical Theories to Rational Regression-A Multidimensional Study of Online Human Flesh Search),四川大学出版社(Sichuan University Press).

Yu, J.-R. 于建嵘 (2006) '集体行动的原动力机制研究——基于H县农民维权抗争的考察'(The Study of the Motivational Mechanism of Collective Action: Based on the investigation of farmers' right defense in H Country)，学海(Academia Bimestris), (2), 28–34.

Yu, Y.-H. 余艳红 (2018) '群体性事件与政治稳定: 一项基于风险模型的新解释' (The Mass Incidents and Political Stability: A New Interpretation Based on the Risk Models), 哈尔滨工业大学学报(社会科学版)(Journal of Harbin Institute of Technology(Social Sciences Edition)), 104(3), 29–35.

Yue, G.-A. 乐国安 (2017) '社会心理学' (Social Psychology),中国人民大学出版社(China Renmin University Press).

Yue, G.-A., Xue, T. and Chen, H. 乐国安, 薛婷, 陈浩 (2010) '网络集群行为的定义和分类框架初探' (The First Exploration on the Definition and Classification Framework of Network Cluster Behavior), 中国人民公安大学学报(社会科学版) (Journal of Chinese People's Public Security University(Social Sciences Edition)), 26(6), 99–104.

Zhai, Z.-K., Lan, Y.-X., Liu, Y. and Liu, B.-Y. 瞿志凯,兰月新,刘媛,刘冰月 (2016) '基于网络舆情信息综合研判的群体性事件预警研究' (Research on Early Warning of Mass Incidents Based on Comprehensive Analysis of Internet Public Opinion Information), 电子政务 (E-Government), (11), 20–30.

Zhang, L. 张亮 (2009) 'Web数据挖掘在群体性事件预警系统中的应用' (The Application of the Web Data Mining in the Alarm System of the Ensemble Event), 光盘技术(CD Technology), (6), 27–28.

Zhang, S.-W. and Xue, Z.-G. 张书维, 许志国 (2018) '行为公共管理学视角下政府决策的互动机制——基于环境型项目的分析' (Interaction Mechanism of Public Decision-making from the Behavioral Public Administration Perspective: An Analysis Based on Environmental Projects), 中国行政管理 (Chinese Public Administration), (12), 59–65.

Zheng, D.-B., Feng, H.-D. and Feng, F.-H. 郑大兵,封海东,封飞虎 (2006) '网络群体性事件的政府应对策略' (The Government's Countermeasures to Network Mass Events), 信息化建设 (Informatization Construction), (11), 34–35.

Zhu, W.-J. 朱婉菁 (2018) '互联网与抗争行动的研究进展与本土化修正——基于文献的阅读和研究现状的反思' (Research Progress and Localization Revision of Internet-based Protests), 宁夏党校学报(Journal of Ningxia Communist Party Institute), 20(2), 73–81.

Zhuang, K.-Y. and Chang, Y.-Q. 庄康义,常宇秋 (1998) '消极性集合行为的心理机制及治安对策' (Psychological Mechanism of Negative Collective Behavior and Security Countermeasures),公安理论与实践 (Theory and Practice of Public Security), (4), 27–30.

37

Personality and contentious participation in China

Ching-Hsing Wang

Introduction

The concept of contentious politics has been widely employed to study social movements over the past decade and denotes the use of noninstitutionalized and disruptive actions to attain political ends or change government policy. Examples of such actions include social movements, demonstrations, riots, strike waves, and even more extreme forms of participation such as civil wars, revolutions, and episodes of democratization. The phenomenon of contentious politics has been observed across the world, such as the Arab Spring that a series of antigovernment protests, uprisings, and armed rebellions spread across Arabic-speaking countries in North Africa and the Middle East in the early 2010s. The recent well-known case of contentious politics is Hong Kong protests that have continued in Hong Kong and were triggered by the introduction of the Fugitive Offenders Ordinance amendment bill by the Hong Kong government. Given the prevalence of contentious politics, there is no exception for China where it is estimated that the number of protests in China doubled between 2006 and 2010 and there were 180,000 reported mass incidents in 2010 (Leung 2015: 34).

The vast number of protests in China might contradict our impressions of China's authoritarian governance and a number of studies have attempted to understand popular protests in China (e.g., Chen 2012; O'Brien 2009; Tong & Lei 2013). However, the majority of studies have placed the focus on institutional explanations of contentious politics in China, such as power structure, resource mobilization, political opportunity, and protest leadership (e.g., Cai 2008; Chen 2012; Li & O'Brien 2008). By contrast, little scholarly attention has been paid to the influence of individual-level factors. While previous studies have investigated the effects of demographic characteristics and political attitudes on contentious participation in China (Ong & Han 2019; Wang et al. 2018), the relationships between psychological predispositions and individual participation in contentious politics have been hardly examined. Given that prior research has identified the effect of personality on individual political participation (e.g., Gerber et al. 2011a; Ha et al. 2013; Mondak & Halperin 2008; Wang 2016), this study aims to examine the relationship between personality and contentious participation at the individual level in China in order to enrich our understanding of the role of personality in Chinese people's participation in contentious politics.

 DOI: 10.4324/9780429059704-43

In the following sections, we first provide a theoretical framework to explain the relationship between personality and contentious participation and proposes some testable hypotheses. Then a section describes the data, measurement of variables, and model specification, followed by a section reporting the empirical results for the effect of personality on various types of contentious participation. The final section concludes by summarizing the key findings and discussing the implications of the results.

Theoretical relationship between personality and contentious participation

The dramatic rise of protests in China since the 1990s has attracted a lot of attention from the media and academics. The number of annual protests in China had steadily risen from 5,000 to 10,000 in the early 1990s to 60,000 to 100,000 by the mid-2000s (Wright 2018) and as mentioned previously, China witnessed 180,000 protests in 2010 alone, that is, on average approximately 500 protests every day. Not all protests are initiated to fight against the Chinese government; instead, they cover a wide range of political, economic, and social purposes, including dissatisfaction with corruption, unpaid wages, human rights abuses, environmental degradation, petitions for religious freedom, and civil liberties, nationalist protests against foreign countries and so on. Some protests have drawn international attention, such as the 1999 demonstration by Falun Gong practitioners, the 2005 anti-Japanese demonstrations, and the 2011 Chinese pro-democracy protests. Particularly, given China's notorious reputation for human rights abuse, in the international media, massive protests in China have raised public concerns about human rights violations under the control of the Chinese Communist Party. On the other hand, many academic works have investigated why there has been a dramatic surge in protests in China from an institutional perspective. For instance, Wallace and Weiss (2015) find that both state-led patriotism and the availability of collective action resources are positively associated with nationalist protests in China, whereas Lorentzen (2017) views China's central government as an institutional designer whose policies on social conflicts shape popular contention. Although the institutional perspective could provide explanatory power for contentious politics in China, we also need to understand what factors motivate Chinese people to participate in contentious politics from the individual-level perspective. For example, Shi (2001) indicates that political trust is negatively associated with all aspects of potential protest participation among Chinese people; Wang et al. (2018) identify the significant relationship between the perception of human rights conditions and individual participation in contentious political activities in China; moreover, in contrast to the positive effect of education found in democratic societies, Ong and Han (2019) find a significant negative association between education level and the likelihood of protest in China, suggesting that the opportunity cost of a higher education level in terms of higher forgone income far outweighs the positive enabling effect. Nonetheless, in comparison with institutional explanations of contentious politics, few efforts have been made to unveil the effects of individual-level factors on Chinese people's contentious participation. Since people play a key role in the protests, there is a pressing need to find out what drives Chinese people to engage in contentious politics at the individual level. Given the close connection between personality and human behavior, this study aims to examine the impact of personality on Chinese people's contentious participation.

Personality can be defined as the intraindividual organization of experience and behavior (Asendorpf 2002) and it is generally acceptable to divide personality into five broad domains, namely the Big Five personality traits: extraversion, agreeableness, conscientiousness, emotional stability, and openness to experience. Specifically, *extraversion* includes the characteristics of being energetic, talkative, and assertive; agreeableness includes the characteristics of being kind, altruistic, and cooperative; *conscientiousness* includes the characteristics of being organized, responsible, and dependable; *emotional stability* includes the characteristics of being calm, cheerful and hopeful; and *openness to experience* (hereafter referred as 'openness') includes the characteristics of being insightful, creative and imaginative (Gosling et al. 2003). Since personality plays an important role in how individuals interact with the political and economic environment and respond to external stimulus, political scientists have employed the concept of personality to account for individual differentiation in political behavior over the past decade. Mondak and Halperin (2008) first offer a clear theoretical framework for the general relationship between personality and political behavior and since then numerous studies have provided empirical evidence in support of the effects of the Big Five personality traits on individual political participation, regardless of institutionalized and noninstitutionalized forms of participation.

In particular, when it comes to the relationship between personality and contentious participation, Opp and Brandstätter (2010) make the first attempt to look at the effects of personality traits on individual protest participation. First, Opp and Brandstätter (2010) contend that people with higher levels of extraversion prefer to interact with people and tend to seek social stimulation and opportunities to engage with others, and protest events allow this kind of people to fulfill their needs for attention and social interaction. Therefore, people who are high in extraversion are expected to be more likely to participate in contentious politics. Second, Opp and Brandstätter (2010) argue that people with higher levels of agreeableness are generally considerate, trustworthy, and willing to compromise their interests with others and thus they would tend to avoid uncomfortable situations that bring them into conflict with others. Accordingly, people who are high in agreeableness are expected to be less likely to engage in contentious politics. Third, the relationship between conscientiousness and contentious politics depends on the type of contentious participation. People with higher levels of conscientiousness are inclined to be self-disciplined and dutiful and comply with social norms. Protest situations provide this kind of people with an opportunity to realize this behavioral tendency, but as indicated by Opp and Brandstätter (2010: 326), 'this is only plausible for conventional forms of protests such as collecting signatures, signing petitions or working in a protest group, but not for disruptive forms of political action'. If protests involve more extreme forms of action such as demonstrations, rallies, marches, or even revolutions, conscientious people will be unwilling to participate in such activities that break the rules of established norms (Ha et al. 2013). Since the current study focuses on contentious participation relevant to boycott, demonstration, strike, and protest, we expect that people who are high in conscientiousness are less likely to participate in contentious politics. Fourth, people with lower levels of emotional stability tend to have sensitive temperaments, experience negative emotions, and view the world as threatening and beyond their control. Since protest situations might bring negative emotions to people with low emotional stability, they will prevent themselves from getting into this kind of event. By contrast, emotionally stable people are better able to manage stress and distress coming from protest participation, so they are more likely to take part in protest events. Consequently, we expect that people who are high in emotional stability are more likely to participate in contentious politics. Finally, people with higher levels of openness are apt to seek new experiences and support social change (Tsai et al. 2019). This kind of people are easily attracted to protest events that could provide the opportunity to obtain new experiences and achieve change. Therefore, people who are high in openness are expected to be more likely to partake in contentious politics.

Past studies have provided empirical evidence to support the relationships between personality traits and contentious participation. Based on a panel survey conducted in East Germany, Brandstätter and Opp (2014) demonstrate that people with higher levels of agreeableness have a lower tendency to protest, but the traits of emotional stability and openness could increase individuals' propensity to protest. Mondak et al. (2011) use the survey data conducted in Uruguay and Venezuela to show that conscientiousness is significantly negatively associated with protest participation in both Latin American countries, but extraversion is only significantly positively correlated with protest participation in Venezuela. Similarly, by focusing on the United States, Weinschenk (2013) reveals that people who are high in extraversion are more likely to protest; however, those who are high in conscientiousness are less likely to protest. Furthermore, Ha et al. (2013) illustrate that agreeableness exerts a negative influence on protest participation, whereas openness has a positive effect on protest participation in South Korea. In light of the above-mentioned theoretical framework and empirical evidence, it is obvious that personality traits matter for individual participation in contentious politics. In the absence of conclusive evidence about the relationships between personality traits and contentious participation in China, the present study makes the first attempt to examine whether dispositional characteristics could affect Chinese people's participation in contentious politics.

In addition to the direct effects of personality traits on contentious participation, many previous studies have also indicated that personality traits could indirectly influence individual political behavior through attitudinal factors, such as civic duty, political interest, political efficacy, strength of partisanship, and so on (e.g., Gallego & Oberski 2012; Wang 2016; Wang et al. 2017). In other words, attitudinal factors could mediate the effects of personality traits on political participation. While several attitudinal factors could play a mediating role in the relationships between personality traits and contentious participation, we would only focus on political interest due to data constraints. Prior research has consistently shown that political interest mediates the effects of personality traits on voter turnout (Gallego & Oberski 2012; Wang et al. 2017). By contrast, insufficient attention has been made to confirm the mediating role of political interest in the relationships between personality traits and contentious participation. To establish the mediation mechanism, two types of relationships must be affirmed. That is, personality traits could influence individual interest in politics and political interest could affect individual participation in contentious politics as well. On the one hand, several studies have identified the linkage between personality traits and political interest. Specifically, people who are high in extraversion, conscientiousness, and openness are inclined to display more interest in politics, whereas those who are high in agreeableness tend to pay less attention to politics (Gerber et al. 2011b; Mondak & Halperin 2008). Consequently, it is evident that extraversion, agreeableness, conscientiousness, and openness influence individual interest in politics. On the other hand, it has been documented that political interest is a significant determinant of protest participation (e.g., Machado et al. 2011; Schussman & Soule 2005). Specifically, people with higher levels of interest in politics are more likely to participate in protest activities because they want to make their voices heard. Thus, it is reasonable to infer that political interest could serve as the mediator of the relationships between personality traits and contentious participation.

To sum up, we argue that personality traits exert not only direct effects but also indirect effects through political interest on Chinese people's participation in contentious politics.

Table 37.1 Theoretical relationships between personality traits and contentious participation

	Contentious participation	
Personality Trait	*Direct effect*	*Indirect effect via political interest*
Extraversion	+	+
Agreeableness	–	–
Conscientiousness	–	+
Emotional stability	+	None
Openness	+	+

Note: "+" indicates a positive association, whereas "–" indicates a negative association.

Table 37.1 summarizes all hypotheses in terms of direct and indirect effects of personality traits on contentious participation.

Data, measurement of variables, and methods

To empirically examine the effects of personality traits on contentious participation in China, we utilize the survey data from the sixth wave of World Values Survey (WVS), a global research project concerning political and social values and beliefs of individuals in 60 countries and societies around the world. For the purposes of this study, only data on China are used to analyze the relationships between personality traits and individual participation in contentious politics. The data on China were collected by the Research Center for Contemporary China at Peking University using face-to-face interviews between November 2012 and January 2013. The Research Center for Contemporary China at Peking University adopted the stratified, multistage probability proportional to size (PPS) sampling method to select the respondents from the population. The respondents covered individuals aged 18 and over in all provinces of Mainland China. A total of 2,300 respondents completed the survey. However, due to missing values in some variables, the effective number of observations is reduced to 1,181 for empirical analysis. The main reason for missing values is because several hundred respondents provided nonresponse answers (i.e., "Don't know" and "No answer") to personality questions. Therefore, we further examined the WVS data to see whether there are systematic differences in demographic characteristics between this analytic sample and the missing observations and found no significant differences in income and gender. Therefore, the missing observations are assumed to be missing at random and the analytic sample is still demographically representative. In addition, the weights are calculated based on strata, age, and gender and are employed to produce estimates that are representative of the intended population. Given that raw data could not be directly used for data analysis to meet the purpose of this study, analytic variables are recoded and generated. The operationalization of analytic variables is explained as follows.

The dependent variable, *contentious participation*, is defined as forms of political participation that employ nonconventional and confrontational means of action in expressing collective interests (Kim 2011). Specifically, we operationalize it as individual participation in four political activities: boycott, demonstration, strike, and protest. In the WVS, the respondents were asked whether they had participated in the above-mentioned contentious political activities, respectively. Their responses are coded as 1 if they have participated or might participate in contentious politics and 0 for those who would never engage in contentious politics under any circumstances. While these four variables of contentious participation are highly related to each other (i.e., correlation coefficients are higher than 0.6), they are still different from each other by nature. Therefore, the current study chooses not to combine them together and uses four dichotomous variables to measure contentious participation.

The key independent variables, *the Big Five personality traits*, are operationalized by the ten-item version of the Big Five Inventory (BFI-44) abbreviated by Rammstedt and John (2007), namely the BFI-10. Rammstedt and John (2007) have demonstrated that the BFI-10 scales retain significant levels of reliability and validity, suggesting that the BFI-10 provides an adequate assessment of personality for research settings in which the participants have limited time to respond to the survey. Specifically, the respondents were asked to indicate how well each personality item described themselves using a five-point scale. Every two items are used to assess each personality trait. The score for each personality trait is obtained by adding, after appropriate recoding, the two items for each particular personality trait, and a higher score means that an individual has a more salient personality trait. Each personality trait is coded to range between 2 and 10. Ludeke and Larsen (2017) contend that the data on the Big Five personality traits from the WVS are extremely problematic because items from the same trait are negatively correlated with each other contrary to the expectation. This study, however, argues that it is not the case for the China data. As demonstrated in Table 37.2, two items measuring the same personality trait are always positively correlated with each other and thus, there is no need to worry about personality measurement in the China data. Besides, Table 37.3 reports the correlations between the Big Five personality traits, showing that they are weakly correlated with each other and hence, they should capture different dimensions of personality.

Although the purpose of the present study is to examine the relationships between personality traits and contentious participation, we also control for some variables relevant to individual participation in contentious politics so as to provide unbiased estimates of the effects of personality traits on contentious participation. First of all, political interest is not

Table 37.2 Correlations among ten personality items

Personality trait	*Personality items*	*Correlation*
Extraversion	Not reserved; outgoing	0.13***
Agreeableness	Trusting; do not find faults	0.08**
Conscientiousness	Not lazy; do the thorough job	0.19***
Emotional stability	Relax; not nervous	0.15***
Openness	Imagination; has artistic interests	0.12***

Note: ***: $p < 0.001$; **: $p < 0.01$.

Table 37.3 Correlations among the Big Five personality traits

	Extraversion	*Agreeableness*	*Conscientiousness*	*Emotional stability*
Agreeableness	−0.06*			
Conscientiousness	0.09**	0.17***		
Emotional stability	0.22***	0.23***	0.14***	
Openness	0.14***	−0.09**	0.06*	0.01

Note: ***: $p < 0.001$; **: $p < 0.01$; *: $p < 0.05$.

only a strong predictor of political participation, but also is expected to play a mediating role in the relationships between personality traits and contentious participation. Political trust is coded to range from 1 to 4 and a higher value indicates a higher level of interest in politics. Second, according to the idea of social capital, social networks play a crucial role in motivating people to participate in politics. A series of questions are used to measure social networks by asking whether the respondents are members of 11 organizations such as labor unions, professional associations, charitable organizations, consumer organizations, recreational organizations, and so on. The number of organizations to which the respondents belong is added to reflect the strength of social networks. It is expected that respondents with strong social networks are more likely to engage in contentious politics. Third, political trust is an important indicator of political legitimacy. Once 7. do not trust the government or cast doubt on the righteousness of the government, they might resort to noninstitutional, even illegal, approaches to fighting against the government. Therefore, we anticipate that people with higher levels of political trust should be less likely to participate in contentious politics. A single question about public trust in the central government is used to measure the individual level of political trust and is coded to range from 1 to 4. A higher value signifies a higher level of political trust. Fourth, economic dissatisfaction could lead to individual participation in contentious politics, especially in an authoritarian country like China (Wang et al. 2018). We contend that people who are more satisfied with their economic situations should be less likely to partake in contentious politics. Economic satisfaction is coded to range from 1 to 10 and a higher value indicates a higher level of satisfaction with personal economic situation. Finally, given the potential effects of sociodemographic factors on contentious participation in China (Zhu & Rosen 1993), we control for income, education, gender, and age as well. A ten-point scale is employed to assess the respondents' income levels and a higher value means a higher level of income; a dummy variable, *college degree or above*, is generated with 1 for the respondents who are in the corresponding categories and 0 otherwise; gender is also treated as a dichotomous variable coded as 1 if the respondents are female and 0 for males; lastly, age is measured by the number of years since birth. Table 37.4 reports the descriptive statistics for all variables used for empirical analysis.

To examine the relationships between personality traits and contentious participation in China, we test two theoretical mechanisms, that is, whether personality traits have direct effects on contentious participation and whether personality traits exert indirect effects on contentious participation via political interest. Since four types of contentious participation are treated as dichotomous variables, we employ the binary logit model and generalized structural equation model to respectively estimate the direct and indirect effects of personality traits on Chinese people's participation in contentious politics. The statistical model used for analysis can be presented as the following equations:

$$\begin{aligned}\ln\Omega(X) = \ln\left(\frac{Pr(y=1 \mid X)}{1-Pr(y=1 \mid X)}\right) &= \beta_0 + \beta_1(Extraversion) \\ &+ \beta_2(Agreeableness) + \beta_3(Conscientiousness) \\ &+ \beta_4(Emotional\ stability) + \beta_5(Openness) \\ &+ \beta_6(Political\ interest) + \beta_7(Social\ networks) \\ &+ \beta_8(Political\ trust) + \beta_9(Economic\ satisfaction) + \beta_{10}(Income) \\ &+ \beta_{11}(College\ degree\ or\ above) + \beta_{12}(Female) + \beta_{13}(Age)\end{aligned} \tag{1}$$

Table 37.4 Descriptive statistics of variables

Variable	*Mean*	*S.D.*	*Min.*	*Max.*
Boycott	0.39	0.49	0	1
Demonstration	0.35	0.48	0	1
Strike	0.31	0.46	0	1
Protest	0.34	0.47	0	1
Extraversion	6.26	1.53	3	10
Agreeableness	6.72	1.30	3	10
Conscientiousness	7.40	1.34	3	10
Emotional stability	6.53	1.41	2	10
Openness	6.09	1.51	2	10
Political interest	2.47	0.92	1	4
Social networks	0.48	1.31	0	11
Political trust	3.30	0.65	1	4
Economic satisfaction	6.31	1.93	1	10
Income	4.40	1.85	1	10
College degree or above	0.13	0.34	0	1
Female	0.47	0.50	0	1
Age	40.74	14.08	18	75
N		1181		

where ln $\Omega(X)$ is the natural logarithm of the conditional odds of engaging in contentious participation relative to nonparticipation; β_0 is the intercept and β_1 through β_{13} are the coefficients for explanatory variables.

$$\begin{aligned} \textit{Political interest} = {} & \gamma_0 + \gamma_1(\textit{Extraversion}) + \gamma_2(\textit{Agreeableness}) \\ & + \gamma_3(\textit{Conscientiousness}) + \gamma_4(\textit{Emotional stability}) \\ & + \gamma_5(\textit{Openness}) + \varepsilon_i \end{aligned} \tag{2}$$

That is, political interest is a linear function of personality traits; γ_0 is the intercept and γ_1 through γ_5 are the coefficients for personality traits; ε_i is the error term.

Empirical results

Table 37.5 shows the effects of personality traits on contentious participation. It is evident that extraversion and openness are consistently associated with all four types of contentious participation, although three out of four coefficients for openness are only statistically significant at the 0.1 level. Specifically, in line with the theoretical expectation, extraversion exerts a positive influence on individual participation in contentious politics. That is, people who score high on extraversion are more likely to engage in contentious collective action such as boycott, demonstration, strike, and protest. However, in contrast to the theoretical expectation, we find that openness is negatively associated with Chinese people's participation in contentious politics. One possible explanation for the observed negative relationship between openness and contentious participation might be that the authoritarian regime in China make Chinese people adjust their behavioral patterns which do not fit their personality feature. While people with higher levels of openness tend to pursue social change, they would worry about repression and punishment in an authoritarian context if they engage in political activities that are not acceptable to the government. Ackermann (2017) argues that the relationships between personality traits and political protest behavior depend on contextual factors. She uses direct democracy to constitutes the political context and operationalizes it using the number of cantonal initiatives giving agenda-setting power to the people. By conducting a subnational comparative analysis of the Swiss cantons, Ackermann (2017) finds that the relationship between openness and protest participation is negatively moderated by the practice of direct democracy. This implies that political context, or regime types, might lead to differentiated relationships between openness and contentious participation in democratic and authoritarian countries. The reason why political context matters more for the relationship between openness and contentious participation and is not so prominent for the other four personality traits is beyond the scope of the current study and future research is needed to address this unsolved puzzle.

Besides, the association of emotional stability with contentious participation is also inconsistent with the theoretical expectation. That is, people who are high in emotional stability are less likely to engage in boycotts and protest perhaps due to the authoritarian context in China. Nevertheless, emotional stability is not associated with Chinese people's participation in demonstrations and strikes. On the other hand, as expected, conscientious people are less likely to engage in demonstrations and strikes, although conscientiousness has no influence on individual participation in boycotts and protests. Finally, different from past studies (Brandstätter & Opp 2014; Ha et al. 2013), the result reveals that agreeableness has nothing to do with contentious participation in China. On the whole, the above results lend some support to the proposition that personality traits have relevance for the prediction of Chinese people's contentious participation.

To demonstrate the substantive effects of personality traits on contentious participation, we compute the average marginal effects of personality traits by holding the other variables in the model constant. As displayed in Table 37.5, on average, a one-point increase in extraversion could increase the probabilities of engaging in boycotts, demonstrations, strikes, and protests by 2.5%, 2.3%, 2.1%, and 2.7%, respectively. By contrast, on average, a one-point increase in openness could decrease the probabilities of participating in boycotts, demonstrations, strikes, and protests respectively by 2.3%, 1.8%, 1.7%, and 1.6%. In addition, on average, a one-point increase in conscientiousness could lead to a 2.7% decrease in the probability of engaging in demonstrations and a 2.1% decrease in the probability of partaking in strikes, whereas a one-point increase in emotional stability could decrease the probabilities of participating in boycotts and protests respectively by 2.6% and 3.0%. Furthermore, we have calculated the predicted probabilities of four types of contentious participation varying by statistically significant coefficients of personality traits. Specifically, the differences in predicted probabilities of four types of contentious participation between people with the highest level of extraversion and those with the lowest level of extraversion range from 16.7% to 21.5%. Moreover, by holding all other variables in the model at their observed values, the higher level of conscientiousness would decrease the predicated probabilities of participating in demonstrations and strikes respectively from 50.1% to 28.1% and from 43.7% to 26.1%, whereas the higher level of emotional stability would decrease the predicated probabilities of engaging in boycotts and protests respectively from 51.0% to 30.4% and from 48.8% to 24.5%. Last but not least, the differences in predicted probabilities of four types of contentious participation between people with the lowest level of openness and those with the highest level of openness range from 12.6% to 18.0%. Based on the above results, it

Table 37.5 Binary logit analysis of contentious participation

	Boycott			*Demonstration*			*Strike*			*Protest*		
	Coef.		*O.R.*	*Coef.*		*O.R.*	*Coef.*		*O.R.*	*Coef.*		*O.R.*
	(S.E.)		*(A.M.E.)*	*(S.E.)*		*(A.M.E.)*	*(S.E.)*		*(A.M.E.)*	*(S.E.)*		*(A.M.E.)*
Extraversion	0.111	*	1.118	0.108	*	1.114	0.103	*	1.108	0.126	**	1.135
	(0.043)		(0.025)	(0.044)		(0.023)	(0.045)		(0.021)	(0.043)		(0.027)
Agreeableness	–0.010		0.990	0.030		1.031	–0.016		0.984	0.052		1.053
	(0.050)		(–0.002)	(0.050)		(0.007)	(0.051)		(–0.003)	(0.050)		(0.011)
Conscientiousness	–0.061		0.940	–0.123	*	0.884	–0.103	*	0.902	–0.059		0.942
	(0.047)		(–0.014)	(0.048)		(–0.027)	(0.049)		(–0.021)	(0.048)		(–0.013)
Emotional stability	–0.115	*	0.891	–0.075		0.928	–0.062		0.940	–0.139	**	0.870
	(0.047)		(–0.026)	(0.047)		(–0.016)	(0.048)		(–0.013)	(0.047)		(–0.030)
Openness	–0.102	*	0.903	–0.085	$	0.918	–0.083	$	0.921	–0.073	$	0.930
	(0.044)		(–0.023)	(0.044)		(–0.018)	(0.045)		(–0.017)	(0.044)		(–0.016)
Political interest	0.365	***	1.441	0.322	***	1.380	0.318	***	1.375	0.121	$	1.128
	(0.073)		(0.081)	(0.074)		(0.069)	(0.075)		(0.066)	(0.073)		(0.026)
Social networks	0.185	***	1.203	0.126	*	1.134	0.054		1.055	0.092	$	1.097
	(0.051)		(0.041)	(0.049)		(0.027)	(0.049)		(0.011)	(0.048)		(0.020)
Political trust	–0.155		0.856	–0.154		0.857	–0.087		0.917	–0.264	**	0.768
	(0.097)		(–0.035)	(0.098)		(–0.033)	(0.100)		(–0.018)	(0.098)		(–0.057)
Economic satisfaction	–0.067	$	0.935	–0.082	*	0.921	–0.039		0.962	–0.043		0.958
	(0.034)		(–0.015)	(0.035)		(–0.018)	(0.036)		(–0.008)	(0.035)		(–0.009)
Income	0.015		1.016	–0.021		0.979	–0.006		0.994	0.020		1.020
	(0.036)		(0.003)	(0.037)		(–0.005)	(0.038)		(–0.001)	(0.037)		(0.004)
College degree or above	0.174		1.190	0.150		1.161	0.156		1.169	0.139		1.149
	(0.190)		(0.039)	(0.193)		(0.032)	(0.195)		(0.032)	(0.191)		(0.030)

(Continued)

Table 37.5 (Continued)

	Boycott			*Demonstration*			*Strike*			*Protest*		
	Coef.		*O.R.*	*Coef.*		*O.R.*	*Coef.*		*O.R.*	*Coef.*		*O.R.*
	(S.E.)		*(A.M.E.)*	*(S.E.)*		*(A.M.E.)*	*(S.E.)*		*(A.M.E.)*	*(S.E.)*		*(A.M.E.)*
Female	0.192		1.212	0.170		1.185	0.323	*	1.381	0.124		1.132
	(0.126)		(0.043)	(0.128)		(0.037)	(0.131)		(0.067)	(0.128)		(0.027)
Age	−0.016	**	0.985	−0.013	**	0.987	−0.016	**	0.984	−0.012	*	0.988
	(0.005)		(−0.003)	(0.005)		(−0.003)	(0.005)		(−0.003)	(0.005)		(−0.003)
Constant	1.124	$	3.077	1.056		2.875	0.558		1.748	1.084		2.957
	(0.670)			(0.680)			(0.695)			(0.676)		
N	1181			1181			1181			1181		
Likelihood ratio test	80.94	***		63.14	***		52.84	***		45.32	***	
Pseudo R^2	0.05			0.04			0.04			0.03		
Log likelihood	−767.34			−749.36			−725.84			−753.64		

Note: 1. ***: $p < 0.001$; **: $p < 0.01$; *: $p < 0.05$; $: $p < 0.10$.

2. O.R.: odds ratio; A.M.E.: average marginal effect in terms of probability change.

is evident that personality traits play a nontrivial role in driving Chinese people's contentious participation.

On the other hand, we also argue that there exists a mediation mechanism of the relationship between personality traits and contentious participation in China. Specifically, political interest is regarded as a mediator in the relationship between personality traits and contentious participation. We have employed the generalized structural equation model to estimate the indirect effects of personality traits on contentious participation in China. As demonstrated in Table 37.6, a one-point increase in extraversion could indirectly increase the probabilities of engaging in boycotts, demonstrations, and strikes, respectively, by 1.0%, 0.9%, and 0.8% through political interest. In addition, a one-point increase in openness could indirectly increase the probabilities of participating in boycotts, demonstrations, and strikes by 0.5%, 0.4%, and 0.4% via political interest respectively. Although openness has a negative direct effect on Chinese people's contentious participation, it could indirectly help individual participation in contentious politics by means of political interest. In addition to extraversion and openness, the other three personality traits do not have an indirect influence on contentious participation through political interest. Moreover, political interest does not mediate the effects of all five personality traits on protest participation. The results lend some support to the mediation hypotheses, but it is noted that political interest only plays a mediating role in the effects of extraversion and openness on some types of contentious participation in China.

Finally, the results also demonstrate that some variables provide explanatory power for individual participation in contentious politics in China. Not surprisingly, political interest is consistently found to exert a positive effect on all four types of contentious participation. That is, people who are more interested in politics have a higher likelihood of participating in contentious politics. In line with social capital theory, social networks are a powerful force to motivate people to engage in contentious politics. Specifically, people who have more social networks are more likely to take part in boycotts, demonstrations, and protests. Contrary to previous research on the relationship between political trust and contentious participation, this study finds that political trust plays a limited role in Chinese people's contentious participation and only has a significant relationship with protest participation.

Table 37.6 Indirect effects of personality traits on contentious participation

	Mediator: Political interest						
	Boycott		*Demonstration*		*Strike*		*Protest*
	Indirect influence	*A.M.E.*	*Indirect influence*	*A.M.E.*	*Indirect influence*	*A.M.E.*	*Indirect influence*
Extraversion	+	1.0%	+	0.9%	+	0.8%	None
Agreeableness	None		None		None		None
Conscientiousness	None		None		None		None
Emotional stability	None		None		None		None
Openness	+	0.5%	+	0.4%	+	0.4%	None

Note: 1. "+" indicates a statistically significant and positive indirect influence at the 0.05 level or less; "none" indicates no significant indirect influence.

2. A.M.E. indicates marginal effect in terms of probability change.

That is, people who are more trusting of their central government have a lower likelihood to engage in protests. Furthermore, economic satisfaction is found to have a significant negative impact on participating in boycotts and demonstrations. In other words, people with higher levels of economic satisfaction are less likely to join boycotts and demonstrations. However, economic satisfaction is not associated with individual participation in strikes and protests. Among sociodemographic factors, age is the only one that exerts a consistent and significant influence on all four types of contentious participation. That is, as people get older, they are less likely to engage in contentious politics in line with previous research that young people are more likely to participate in contentious politics than their older counterparts (Zhu & Rosen 1993). The other sociodemographic factors such as income, education, and gender have nothing to do with contentious participation, implying that sociodemographic characteristics offer weak explanations to Chinese people's contentious participation.

To sum up, the present study provides evidence that personality could provide some explanatory power for individual participation in contentious politics. In addition, given that prior research has identified gender-differentiated effects of personality traits on individual political behavior (Wang 2014), we further investigate whether there are gender differences in the effects of personality traits on contentious participation in China. It was found that compared to women, men not only report higher levels of emotional stability, but also display higher levels of extraversion in China (see Table 37.7). The former is in line with previous research (Schmitt et al. 2008), but the latter is different from the findings of past studies and requires future investigation. Due to gender differences in extraversion and emotional stability, we also looked at whether extraversion and emotional stability have different effects on women's and men's contentious participation by adding the interaction terms to the model. The results reveal no gender-differentiated effects of extraversion and emotional stability on contentious participation. Overall, the effects of personality traits on contentious participation are homogeneous for women and men in China.

Table 37.7 Gender differences in personality traits

	Women	*Men*	
	Mean	*Mean*	*Wald test*
	(S.E.)	*(S.E.)*	
Extraversion	5.99	6.51	*F*-statistic = 28.94
	(0.07)	(0.07)	$p < 0.001$
Agreeableness	6.71	6.73	*F*-statistic = 0.05
	(0.06)	(0.06)	$p > 0.05$
Conscientiousness	7.33	7.45	*F*-statistic = 1.98
	(0.06)	(0.06)	$p > 0.05$
Emotional stability	6.36	6.67	*F*-statistic = 12.67
	(0.06)	(0.06)	$p < 0.001$
Openness	6.07	6.10	*F*-statistic = 0.09
	(0.07)	(0.06)	$p > 0.05$
N	559	622	

Conclusion

It might be surprising to observe the emergence of contentious politics in an authoritarian country like China since public contentious participation might endanger the political stability of an authoritarian regime. Previous studies have provided explanations for why the Chinese government allows people to participate in contentious politics and how it addresses contentious politics. Different from the approaches adopted by previous research on contentious politics in China, this study aims to understand what individual-level factors stimulate Chinese people's contentious participation by centering on personality traits. The empirical evidence demonstrates that personality traits play a pivotal role in contentious participation among Chinese people. Specifically, extraversion consistently has a positive effect on contentious participation, whereas openness consistently exerts a negative impact on contentious participation. That is, people who score high on extraversion are more likely to participate in contentious politics, but those who score high on openness are less likely to engage in contentious politics. In addition, conscientiousness and emotional stability are only negatively associated with some types of contentious participation. While the findings on the associations of extraversion and conscientiousness with contentious participation are consistent with past studies, it is noted that the observed effects of emotional stability and openness on contentious participation are opposite to our theoretical expectations. This might be due to the political context of China that pushes people to change their behavioral patterns as they are supposed to have based on their own personality type. Future research is needed to uncover why extraversion and conscientiousness have the same effects on contentious participation as found in other countries, but it is not the case for emotional stability and openness.

In addition, we also attempt to examine the mediation mechanism of the relationships between personality traits and contentious participation in China. Due to data limitations, we could only investigate whether political interest mediates the effects of personality traits on contentious participation in China. Specifically, only extraversion and openness could exert indirect positive effects on contentious participation through political interest in China. The current study also provides evidence that political interest and social networks matter for Chinese people's contentious participation. Specifically, people who are more interested in politics and have more social networks tend to have a higher likelihood of engaging in contentious politics. It is, however, surprising to observe that political trust plays a trivial role in individual participation in contentious politics in China. This might be because we simply use trust in the central government to operationalize political trust and more dimensions of political trust should be taken into consideration when it comes to contentious politics in China.

Overall, this study provides new insight into contentious participation in China by emphasizing the role of personality. Previous research has indicated that human genetic variation and the external environment could lead to differences in personality traits among individuals (Bouchard et al. 1990; Hopwood et al. 2011). Although genetic characteristics of individuals play a more important part in determining the personality traits of individuals, it is possible that individuals' interactions with the external environment can change their inherited personality traits and even adjust their behaviors that they should have based on their personality characteristics. Therefore, the findings of the present study do not intend to suggest that people with some specific personality traits would necessarily participate in contentious politics. If the government can meet the needs of the people, then there is no reason for people to take to the streets even though their prominent personality traits are connected to contentious participation.

References

Ackermann, K. (2017) 'Individual differences and political contexts—the role of personality traits and direct democracy in explaining political protest', *Swiss Political Science Review* 23(1): 21–49.

Asendorpf, J. B. (2002) 'The puzzle of personality types', *European Journal of Personality* 16(S1): S1–S5.

Bouchard Jr., T. J., Lykken, D. T., McGue, M., Segal, N. L. and Tellegen, A. (1990) 'Sources of human psychological differences: the Minnesota study of twins reared apart', *Science* 250(4978): 223–28.

Brandstätter, H. and Opp, K.-D. (2014) 'Personality traits ("big five") and the propensity to political protest: alternative models', *Political Psychology* 35(4): 515–37.

Cai, Y. (2008) 'Power structure and regime resilience: contentious politics in China', *British Journal of Political Science* 38(3): 411–32.

Chen, X. (2012) *Social Protest and Contentious Authoritarianism in China*, New York, NY: Cambridge University Press.

Gallego, A. and Oberski, D. (2012) 'Personality and political participation: the mediation hypothesis', *Political Behavior* 34(3): 425–51.

Gerber, A. S., Huber, G. A., Doherty, D., Dowling, C. M., Raso, C. and Ha, S. E. (2011a) 'Personality traits and participation in political processes', *Journal of Politics* 73(3): 692–706.

Gerber, A. S., Huber, G. A., Doherty, D. and Dowling, C. M. (2011b) 'Personality traits and the consumption of political information', *American Politics Research* 39(1): 32–84.

Gosling, S. D., Rentfrow, P. J. and Swann Jr., W. B. (2003) 'A very brief measure of the big-five personality domains', *Journal of Research in Personality* 37(6): 504–28.

Ha, S. E., Kim, S. and Jo, S. H. (2013) 'Personality traits and political participation: evidence from South Korea', *Political Psychology* 34(4): 511–32.

Hopwood, C. J., Donnellan, M. B., Blonigen, D. M., Krueger, R. F., McGue, M., Iacono, W. G. and Burt, S. A. (2011) 'Genetic and environmental influences on personality trait stability and growth during the transition to adulthood: a three wave longitudinal study', *Journal of personality and social psychology* 100(3): 545–56.

Kim, S.-C. (2011) 'Participation, contentious', in Bertrand Badie, Dirk Berg-Schlosser and Leonardo Morlino (eds) *International Encyclopedia of Political Science, Volume 1*, Thousand Oaks, CA: Sage Publications, Inc.

Leung, P. P. (2015) *Labor Activists and the New Working Class in China: Strike Leaders' Struggles*, New York, NY: Palgrave Macmillan.

Li, L., and O'Brien, K. J. (2008) 'Protest leadership in rural China', *The China Quarterly* 193: 1–23.

Lorentzen, P. (2017) 'Designing contentious politics in post-1989 China', *Modern China* 43(5): 459–93.

Ludeke, S. G. and Larsen, E. G. (2017) 'Problems with the big five assessment in the World Values Survey', *Personality and Individual Differences* 112: 103–5.

Machado, F., Scartascini, C. and Tommasi, M. (2011) 'Political institutions and street protests in Latin America', *Journal of Conflict Resolution* 55(3): 340–65.

Mondak, J. J., Canache, D., Seligson, M. A. and Hibbing, M. V. (2011) 'The participatory personality: evidence from Latin America', *British Journal of Political Science* 41(1): 211–21.

Mondak, J. J. and Halperin, K. D. (2008) 'A framework for the study of personality and political behaviour', *British Journal of Political Science* 38(2): 335–62.

O'Brien, K. J. (ed) (2009) *Popular Protest in China*, Cambridge, MA: Harvard University Press.

Ong, L. H. and Han, D. (2019) 'What drives people to protest in an authoritarian country? Resources and rewards vs risks of protests in urban and rural China', *Political Studies* 67(1): 224–48.

Opp, K.-D. and Brandstätter, H. (2010) 'Political protest and personality traits: a neglected link', *Mobilization: An International Quarterly* 15(3): 323–46.

Rammstedt, B. and John, O. P. (2007) 'Measuring personality in one minute or less: a 10-item short version of the big five inventory in English and German', *Journal of Research in Personality* 41(1): 203–12.

Schmitt, D. P., Realo, A., Voracek, M. and Allik, J. (2008) 'Why can't a man be more like a woman? Sex differences in big five personality traits across 55 cultures', *Journal of Personality and Social Psychology* 94(1): 168–82.

Schussman, A. and Soule, S. A. (2005) 'Process and protest: accounting for individual protest participation', *Social Forces* 84(2): 1083–08.

Shi, T. (2001) 'Cultural values and political trust: a comparison of the People's Republic of China and Taiwan', *Comparative Politics* 33(4): 401–19.

Tong, Y. and Lei, S. (2013) *Social Protest in Contemporary China, 2003–2010: Transitional Pains and Regime Legitimacy*, New York, NY: Routledge.

Tsai, C., Wang, C.-H. and Weng, D. L.-C. (2019) 'Personality traits and individual attitude toward the independence-unification issue in Taiwan', *Journal of Asian and African Studies* 54(3): 430–51.

Wallace, J. L. and Chen Weiss, J. (2015) 'The political geography of nationalist protest in China: cities and the 2012 anti-Japanese protests', *The China Quarterly* 222: 403–29.

Wang, C.-H. (2014) 'Gender differences in the effects of personality traits on voter turnout', *Electoral Studies* 34: 167–76.

Wang, C.-H. (2016) 'Personality traits, political attitudes and vote choice: evidence from the United States', *Electoral Studies* 44: 26–34.

Wang, C.-H., Weng, D. L.-C., Barnstead, L. and DuMond, G. (2018) 'Disrespect for human rights and contentious participation: evidence from China', *Journal of Chinese Political Science* 23(4): 537–61.

Wang, C.-H., Weng, D. L.-C. and Cha, H.-J. (2017) 'Personality traits and voter turnout in South Korea: the Mediation argument', *Japanese Journal of Political Science* 18(3): 426–45.

Weinschenk, A. (2013) "Cause you've got personality: political participation and the tendency to join civic groups', *SAGE Open* 3(4): 1–12.

Wright, T. (2018) *Popular Protest in China*, Cambridge, UK & Medford, MA: Polity Press.

Zhu, J.-H. and Rosen, S. (1993) 'From discontent to protest: individual-level causes of the 1989 pro-democracy movement in China', *International Journal of Public Opinion Research* 5(3): 234–49.

Part VI

Chinese studies: Scope and methodology

38

Chinese studies in Brazil

History and current perspectives

André Bueno

Introduction

The history of Chinese studies in Brazil followed a peculiar trajectory. As an integral part (1500–1822) of the Portuguese mpire, the country developed an intimate and vivid connection with Afro-Asian civilizations, receiving profound ethnic and cultural influences that guided the formation of Brazilian identity. Brazil was part of an extensive network, which connected Portugal, Macau, Goa, Angola, and Mozambique, receiving several material and cultural inflows from these other regions; and the marks of a discreet, but evident Chinese presence in the country, appeared since the 18th century. (Russell-Wood 1998; Leite, 1999; Freyre 2003). On the other side, the Brazilian academy has not developed a tradition in Sinology like those existing in Europe and the United States, leaving the study of Chinese civilization in the hands of individual initiatives. Only in the beginning of the 21st century, a set of broader actions – opening Chinese-language courses, developing bilateral relations, and increasing trade with China – stimulated the emergence of several research groups, whose theoretical orientations are quite diverse.

But, despite conservative elements of an Asian presence in their culture, inherited from the period between the 17th and 19th centuries, the production of knowledge about Asian civilizations – and specifically about China – still quite limited, and constantly depends on foreign academic contributions. To understand this paradox, we need to review the history of Brazil, its insertion in the global panorama, and how the construction of Chinese studies in the country has become an important epistemological and cultural problem. The development of Sinology in Brazil confronts important challenges, but it can also create an original approach to Chinese studies.

What we intend here, therefore, is to examine the roots of this historical question, and some of its current perspectives. In this article, we will take the following steps: we will examine the history of relations between Brazil and China, highlighting the cultural influences and the first Brazilian sinological discussions in the 19th century; next, we will analyze the Chinese studies before and after the Second World War, and the emergence of the Brazilian theoretical concept of 'China-as-Model'; the opening of the research area at the end of the 20th century; finally, we will discuss the current perspectives for Chinese

DOI: 10.4324/9780429059704-45

studies in Brazil, including the new epistemological possibilities involved in the formation of this field.

Before Sinology: China in Brazil

Between its discovery in 1500, until independence as a nation in 1822, Brazil constituted an important part of the Portuguese empire, being the largest territorial domain and intensely colonized. The country was integrated into a vast network of trade and exchanges, which brought goods, spices, and native products to all the provinces of the kingdom of Portugal, spread across America, Africa, India, and China (Russell-Wood 2001; Antony 2013). In the 16th–17th centuries, Portugal was probably the largest producer of information about Asia (Barreto 1998: 273–274), and the first Chinese-language dictionary for a Western language, launched in 1610, was also made in Portuguese (Ricci et al. 2001). As important as the construction of this knowledge was the question of the cultural and human transit between these vast spaces of the empire. Russell-Wood (1998) revealed that countless travelers, from the most diverse origins, circulated in the network built by Portugal. It was not just Portuguese who traveled: among the available biographies and documents, we see peoples born in Brazil, Africa, and Asia who passed between the provinces, writing important reports to understand the dynamics of the empire. This information is relevant for us to know which Chinese came to Brazil, and which Brazilians also went to China.

Currently, it is still not possible to know, in more precise numbers, how many Chinese came to Brazil in this vast period. However, we can witness its presence in the Brazilian cultural and artistic heritage, marks of Chinese evidence. Gilberto Freyre (2003) proposed that Brazilian colonial society was built with these 'oriental' influences, manifesting profound differences that contrasted with the cultural practices of the Portuguese metropolis. Habits, food, clothing, and architecture had several Asian traits. José Roberto Leite (1999) made an extensive survey of Chinese brands in Brazil, revealing that, in the 17th century, there were already Chinese workers and artists in the country. Many works of art, produced at the time of the Brazilian Baroque (mainly, in the churches of the state of Minas Gerais) showing paintings and sculptures with Chinese patterns, motifs, and styles. More recently, Júlio Bandeira (2018) added new information to this survey, showing other Chinese artistic manifestations in colonial Brazil; and Paulina Lee (2018) expanded this set of evidence, revealing this Chinese presence in several different sources (literature, documents, and reports).

About the Brazilian presence in China, the studies by Carlos Francisco Moura (2012, 2014) represent a fundamental contribution to understanding the circulation of Brazilians in the Chinese world, until the 19th century. Moura showed that a significant group of travelers and adventurers made their way to China in that period, going to serve in the colony of Macau. Some Brazilians even held important positions in the city; and the first official history about Macau was written by José de Aquino Guimarães Freitas (1828), a Brazilian born in the state of Minas Gerais. In 1807, judge João Rodrigues de Brito, proposed to import Chinese labor to Brazil (Brito 1821: 58). This information shows the intense transit between China and Brazil, building a subtle, ancient, and complex relationship.

In mid-years of 1808–1814, Dom João VI, king of Portugal, decided to start a tea plantation in Rio de Janeiro (Sacramento 1825; Andrade 1835), and hired a group of Chinese specialists to develop the project. As a result, Brazil was the first official colony to receive, in all the Americas, a group of workers from China (Moura 2012: 33–43; Lesser 2001: 40–43). Other Chinese colonies later appeared in the United States (1821) and Cuba (1840), but the Brazilian initiative was pioneering (Hui 1992: 29–30, 126–128). This broad and intense movement of cultural exchanges did not mean, however, that Brazilians learned more about Chinese culture. As Kamila Czepula (2017) demonstrated, throughout the 19th century, it was common to make references to the Chinese in Brazilian newspapers; but they appeared assimilated, using Portuguese names. The Chinese were scattered in the country, but without representation. In 1822, when Brazil became independent, it partially disconnected itself from the trade network with Asia: that interest was resumed 30 years later when began again the debates to import Chinese workers. The aim was to replace the slave labor of Afro-Brazilians; and at that moment, Brazilian intellectuals start to get involved with the birth of modern Sinology.

The origins of Sinology and the Brazilian question

The origin of Chinese studies is directly connected with the European expansion over the world, which began in the 16th century. When the Portuguese arrived in Asia, they felt the urgent need to write about Chinese civilization. There was an abundant production of essays, reports, translations, and manuals on China by Portuguese authors in that period (Barreto 1998: 273–292). Many accounts were produced by travelers and geographers, but the main studies on China, up to the 19th century, were produced by Christian missionaries. As Charles Le Blanc (2007: 19–34) proposed, before the second half of the 19th century, practically all sinological materials were produced by clergymen. The central theory that dominated these works was the Christian Catholic view, which explained cultural differences across religions, and intended to evangelize the Chinese. It is a period of fertile production of Portuguese (Aresta 1997: 9–18), Spanish (Álvarez 2007: 1–40), and French (Frèches 1975: 24–33). In the 18th century, France gradually took a leading role in studies of China.

Only in 1812 the French scholar Abel Rémusant (Bougeart 1814: 71–79) create the neologism 'Sinology', meaning a field of study of the Chinese language and culture. In the years that followed, there would be a revolution in European Chinese studies. After the first Opium War (1839–1842), and the consequent race towards China, European academies assumed a monopoly on Chinese studies, transferring research and teaching to universities. As Bony Schachter (2020) pointed out, Sinology has become an enterprise closely linked to the imperialist expansion of the 19th century, becoming an object of interest to Colonialist Nations Following France and England, Germany, Italy, Holland, Belgium, Hungary, Russia, and the United States, among others, promoting the training of specialists in Chinese studies, and creating academic spaces for this field of research.

Initially, Asian studies were contaminated by Orientalist conceptions (Chan 2009) and contributed directly to the construction of various prejudices against the Chinese. The advancement and specialization of research made Sinology gradually become a relatively independent area of study, surpassing many of these views. However, authors like Daniel Vukovich (2012) denounce the contemporary recurrence of Orientalists discourses, in attitudes of prejudice toward Chinese society.

The question of Chinese studies in Brazil is part of this historical context. At the time, Brazil was going through the period entitled 'Segundo Reinado' ('Second Reign' 1840–1889), ruled by Emperor Pedro II. A well-known scholar and orientalist, Pedro II inspired the interest of Brazilian intellectuals in 'Eastern' civilizations. There was a 'Brazilian Orientalism', which combined European theories on linguistics and art with a national ideology of ethnic and cultural diversity, having singular characteristics (Maffra & Stallaert 2016).

This 'Brazilian Orientalism' influenced profoundly the Sinology in the country. The central preoccupation in this period was the problem of Chinese immigration to Brazil, in which Bocaiuva (1868), Pinheiro (1869), Galvão, Macedo and Montmorency (1870) and Moreira (1870) stood out. These authors discussed the feasibility of importing Chinese labor, its economic and cultural impact. The central lines of these works were based on culturalist and eugenic theories, without considering the Chinese viewpoint (Czepula 2020). Occasionally, the Brazilian public also had texts written by Portuguese authors, such as the famous author Eça de Queiróz (1845–1900). He published a series of columns in the newspaper *Gazeta de Notícias* (published in the city of Rio de Janeiro, capital of the Empire), discussing various aspects of Chinese and Japanese culture, criticizing Eurocentrism and defending the migration of Chinese to Brazil (Garmes & Vanzelli 2017). However, none of them were professional sinologists, and they used travelers' testimonies, reports, and imported works to voice their opinions.

After the 'Agriculture Congress – 1878' (Anais 1988), a new project for Brazilian agricultural production was discussed, and the necessity to deepen studies on Chinese immigration became clear. A strong opposition, led by abolitionist Joaquim Nabuco (1879), opposed Chinese immigration, arguing that their exploitation of Chinese people would be a disguised form of slavery. Conversely, Salvador de Mendonça wrote a more specialized sinological study, entitled *Trabalhadores Asiáticos* ('Asian Workers' 1879). This author carried out his research with the Chinese installed in the United States, and read the reports about the Chinese communities in Cuba. His book strongly supported the hiring of workers from China and was considered a key reference on the issue.

The Empire of Brazil encouraged the carrying out of a mission to China, seeking to establish direct contact with the Chinese government (Dantas 2006; Bastos 2010). A friendship and trade treaty was planned, in the same sense as the treaties carried out by European countries. The mission was accomplished in 1880, and produced two important documents; the first is the account of diplomatic discussions held between Brazilian diplomats Eduardo Callado and Artur Motta with Viceroy Li Hongzhang 李鴻章 (Callado & Motta 2012); the second was the book *A China e os chins* ('China and the Chinese' 1888), by diplomat Henrique Lisboa, an historical and anthropological work done directly in China by a Brazilian researcher. The study of H. Lisboa was conscientious with advances in the field of Sinology (mainly from the French School), and its observations were able to overcome many prejudices and misunderstandings, constituting an important defense of Chinese civilization.

Even so, the issue of Chinese immigration remained controversial. Due to the mission of Callado and Motta, the diplomat and trader Tang Jingxing 唐景 星 came to Brazil in 1883, to try a new agreement about Chinese migration. The episode was surrounded by controversy and the attempt proved unsuccessful. Despite the difficulties and conflicts, Brazil managed to gain a special position with the Chinese court and intellectuals. Mao (2007: 1–18) analyzed the projects by Kang Youwei 康有為 (1858–1927) and Fu Yunlong 傅雲龍 (1840–1900) to colonize Brazil as a large Chinese population; on the other hand, an international movement led by English and Brazilian abolitionists, actively fought against Chinese migration (Ré 2018).

All of these projects failed with the overthrow of the Brazilian Empire in 1889; the new republican government maintained an institutional and limited interest in the Chinese empire. In 1908, another Asian colonization project – with Japanese families – eclipsed the idea of Chinese immigration, installing, in Brazil, the largest Japanese colony in the world. The conflicts between Japan and China would be reproduced by Brazilian intellectuals and researchers: in 1931, for example, Lima Figueiredo (1941), military attaché, would accompany the Japanese invasion in China, even fighting alongside the Japanese.

Chinese studies ended up following this trend. Limited to the scope of international relations, the works on China produced in Brazil at the turn of the 20th century were mostly travelers' reports or discussions about diplomatic relations with the country. Following current political guidelines, Chinese studies were limited to individual initiatives, with the exception of specific interest in Confucius' philosophy (Bueno 2018).

Chinese studies in Brazil after the Second World War

The Second World War marked a turning point in the interests of Brazilians in Asia. The Japanese came to be seen as dangerous, due to their alignment with Germany (Dezem 2008), and the government of Brazil turned to China. In 1944, Song Mei Ling 宋美齡, wife of President Chiang Kaishek 蔣介石, was in Brazil to ask for support in the fight against Japanese and Communists. Chinese culture once again attracted the Brazilian public, who eagerly consumed the translations of Lin Yutang's 林語堂 work (1895–1976). This relationship, however, did not last long: in 1949, with the rise of communism in mainland China, the Brazilian government followed the American ideological orientation and recognized Taiwan as a Chinese representative.

This moment was important for Chinese studies: from the official viewpoint of the Brazilian government, investigations on Asia should be restricted to the diplomatic sphere. However, a large number of intellectuals traveled to mainland China to observe the rapid development of society and the economy based on socialist theories. This gave rise to an important Brazilian sinological approach, the 'China-as-Model'. In general, these thinkers proposed the following:

a. China and Brazil would have similar problems of economic underdevelopment, deficient industrial and technological growth, a large rural population, a high poverty rate, and a great inequality in the distribution of money and land
b. The adoption of socialism in China, adapted to the problems of Chinese society, was responsible for rapid economic growth and the 'technological leap' that emerged after the Second World War (this was, at least, the idealized impression that the Brazilian public had about China)
c. China maintained its political independence, building an alternative global power axis to that of the United States and the Soviet Union

Thus, if Brazil adopted a development model inspired by Chinese experiences, it could achieve a new status of power on a world scale. The originality of this approach was to use the Chinese model, but to adapt it to Brazilian cultural characteristics. We can cite some more important texts: the work of Duarte (1956a, 1956b) brought an extensive account of the Chinese reality, and proposed comparisons and adaptations for the Chinese-Brazilian model; and Adolpho Bezerra de Menezes (1956), a diplomat who attended the Bandung conference in 1955, advocated an alternative alignment of postcolonial Afro-Asian and Latin American countries. An approximation between this line of Chinese studies and the Brazilian government took place in the early 1960s, when San Tiago Dantas (2011), Minister of Foreign Affairs, proposed the 'PEI – Política Externa Independente' (Independent Foreign Policy). This theory defended an independent political position in the context of the Cold War, negotiating alternately with the United States, the Soviet Union, China, India, and the countries then classified as 'Third World'. The general conception was to prioritize the interests of the Brazilian State, maintaining a nonaligned ideological stance. In 1961, the Vice President of Brazil, João Goulart, made an official visit to mainland China, reinforcing the idea of the Chinese model as an example for Brazil.

This approximation project with China was interrupted in 1964 when a military government was established in the country (1964–1984). Confirming its support for the United States and the 'western world', the new government combated and persecuted socialists and communists, undermining the development of a sinological community based on the idea of 'China-as-Model'. Even so, this did not prevent independent intellectuals from continuing to follow and defend the Chinese model as ideal for Brazil: Josué de Castro, an intellectual who exhaustively fought against the problem of hunger and poverty, traveled to China in 1957, and considered the experience of Chinese collectivist as one of the most viable solutions for the contemporary world. His main book, *Geopolítica da fome* ('Geopolitics of Hunger' 1957) was even translated into Chinese. He even made, include, an engaged defense of Maoist China (1971), which circulated widely in European circles. Other authors, such as Braga (1982) and Studart (1982) have also done substantial works, continually defending the adoption of structural experiences from China.

The crucial point in all of these studies is that they were not done by professional sinologists; most Brazilian universities did not have regular Chinese-language courses, and most of the translated books and articles were of European origin. Thus, Brazilian scholars had to make tremendous efforts, sharing their travel experiences, and drawing on the sources available in several languages. On the other hand, these intellectuals proposed new interpretations, which combined the Chinese model with Brazilian cultural experiences. We will see, later, that this sinological theory – the 'China-as-Model' – continues to exist in Brazil, reformulated according to political oscillations.

Finally, it is necessary to mention an important intercultural dialogue initiative promoted by Brazilian Catholic clergymen, interested in bringing Chinese socialist ideas closer to Christian thinking. They were based on the ideas of *Liberation Theology*, a theory that advocated a deepening of relations between the church and disadvantaged communities. Actions to combat misery, social inequality, and racism were the main points of this movement of Catholic thought, which has gained considerable representation in Latin America (Gutiérrez 2000). A series of studies promoted by these clergymen defended the view that Chinese communism, based on solidarity, altruism, and simplicity, approached various points of original Christian thought. China, therefore, would be prepared to convert to a noninstitutional (but philosophically authentic) Catholicism. This movement weakened considerably in the late 20th century, with the Chinese economic and political opening, but left some interesting works. Leonardo Boff, the main representative of this line in Brazil, organized and published three representative books on the issue (1979, 1982, 1993); and after retiring from religious life in the Catholic Church, he continued his studies on China, publishing an important and original work on ecology, Chinese thought and the globalized world (Boff 2009).

In parallel with these studies, some Brazilian researchers sought academic and professional expertise in Sinology. Ricardo Joppert is the most notable author of this period: he studied Chinese Language and Art in France and Taiwan, and produced works recognized in Brazil and abroad (1979, 1999). He also contributed to the formation of an important research center, the Center for Afro-Asian Studies at Cândido Mendes University. Joppert's work brought to Brazil an updated and original approach to Chinese philosophical and artistic thinking. He was the first author to present a profound mastery of Chinese intellectual concepts, stimulating a qualitative leap in Brazilian sinological studies.

In 1968, the University of São Paulo (USP) started a regular Chinese-language course ('Mandarin' 普通話), coordinated by professionals from Taipei (Shyu & Jye 2008: 228). The course strengthened academic ties between Brazil and Taiwan, taking several students to complete their training in the country. A nucleus of excellence was formed, which produced important translators and researchers, such as Mário Bruno Sproviero – translator of an original version of *Daodejing* 道德經 into Portuguese (2002) – Antônio Bezerra de Menezes, a scholar of Lusophone translations of Chinese classics (2015) and Ho Yeh Chia, a specialist in Chinese education (1999). Until the Confucius Institute (from the People's Republic of China) came to Brazil in 2008, the Chinese-language course at the University of São Paulo represented the main course that prevails in the country.

The hallmark of these studies is a concern for traditional Chinese culture, and its dialogue with Western ways of thinking. These authors sought to master the language and the guiding concepts of Chinese thought, representing an important alternative view in the context of Brazilian Chinese studies.

From the late 1990s to the beginning of the 21st century, China's political and economic openness was accompanied by growing interest on the part of the Brazilian intellectual public. There were a series of questions about how Chinese Socialism managed to survive, and an attempt to understand the rescue of traditional Chinese culture after years of revolutionary Marxist thinking. Some authors, such as Drummond (1994), Chacon (1995), and Pomar (1987, 2009) sought to accompany these transformations, trying to translate them for the Brazilian public opinion. Chinese studies experienced a new stimulus, mainly in the area of economics and international relations. Severino Cabral (2004) systematically studied and develops strategies for cultural and political dialogue with the new context of bilateral China–Brazil relations.

In the field of Cultural Studies, the emergence of the Projeto Orientalismo (Orientalism Project 1998), organized by André Bueno, represented the first attempt to offer translations and materials on classical Chinese texts, mainly in the area of ancient philosophy and literature. A textual body was built which contained Confucian, Daoist, and other schools' sources, and the project continues to operate today. It was also the first Brazilian and Portuguese-speaking project on the internet for this purpose. The role of Márcia Schmaltz (1973–2018) is worth noting, a specialist in the Chinese language, whose mastery of the language and quality ofthe translations reached prominence in the Chinese study community. His work permeates fundamental discussions on the issue of translation and comparative Chinese-Portuguese literature in Brazil (Schmaltz 2015). Márcia Schmaltz was also the coordinator of a network of Brazilian and foreign sinologists and orientalists, promoting relevant meetings in the cities of São Paulo and Macau.

Current perspectives

Currently, the Brazilian university has a significant number of groups and scholars on Chinese studies. These research centers are still fragmented, without forming a more cohesive network. However, these new Brazilian sinologists have sought to respond to the social and epistemological demands on knowledge in China.

On the other hand, in Brazilian historiography, persistently rooted the conception that Brazil and China would be very similar countries in economic and social terms in the first half of the 20th century. This allowed the idea of 'China-as-Model' continually to be intensely defended by Brazilian socialist intellectuals. In the early 2000s, trade and diplomatic relations with China became a common cause, appropriated by the Brazilian government. Engaged ideological orientations gave rise to the pragmatism of economic and political interests. The 'China-as-Model' concept is very much present in academic and bureaucratic circles, being widely debated.

The central problem of the 'China-as-Model' for Chinese studies in Brazil is its historical and epistemological structure. Like Brazilian intellectuals of the 19th century, many adherents of this theoretical line have an immediate concern with the relations between Brazil and China, but without necessarily deepening their knowledge of Chinese culture. Most of the work in this line continues to use translated materials, mainly North American. Often, they incur into Orientalist practices, analyzing the Chinese context at a distance. Although supporters of 'China as a model' occasionally discuss problems related to China from the Brazilian point of view, it is very common to repeatedly use foreign authors to explain Chinese ideas, to the detriment of Brazilian experts themselves. A clear example of this is the widespread use of the book *On China*, by Henry Kissinger (2013). Kissinger is not a sinologist, but his work is read by many Brazilian intellectuals as a specialized essay on Chinese studies. The 'China-as-Model' also suffers from divergent political orientations related to Brazilian political instability. Some authors seek to be pragmatic and try to adapt to current political contexts, varying the interest of their research. Thus, many scholars involved in this idea of 'China-as-Model' continue, in a way, to reproduce Orientalist stereotypes, believing that they can understand China through literature and theories of Western experts, without needing to learn the Chinese language or analyze the studies done by the Chinese themselves.

The dominant assumption of this theoretical line is that 'China', as an epistemological object, must respond to Brazilian demands in a specific way, without manifesting an active attitude. These stances provoke countless disappointments for the followers of the 'China-as-Model' since occasionally China 'does not behave' according to its forecasts and analyzes. This is an inevitable problem when knowledge acquisition occurs mediated by secondhand studies.

There is a generation of Brazilian researchers who studied directly in China, bringing experiences that can change this scenario. Recently, a Rede Brasileira de Estudos da China – RBChina (Brazilian Network of Chinese studies) was formed, which brings together researchers from the most diverse institutions, and who have a direct experience with the Chinese reality. RBChina members have produced updated studies in the field of politics, economics, and social studies in China, with a focus on the contemporary context. Being multi-institutional, the RBChina does not present a unified theoretical field, but it is methodologically characterized by an 'open mind' approach to Chinese culture, which we could name 'Go-and-Back' strategy. Proposed by the French sinologist François Jullien (2010: 1–20), the 'Go-and-Back' theory consists of interrogating Chinese culture based on Western epistemological and intellectual challenges. Chinese experiences are not just to be copied or refuted, but help to build new comparative knowledge. It is necessary to 'go' to China with our own questions; and 'We came back' from China with diverse and innovative responses. These responses may represent alternatives to traditional Western concepts. They can be the same, or similar; or yet, they may not exist or be less relevant to the Chinese, pointing out different ways of rationalization. In synthesis, François Jullien proposes that we should learn about China in its original contents (language, history, thought, and literature), and use that knowledge as a counterpoint to develop Western sciences and knowledge.

A possible third way is what we call 'Via Sinica'. The 'Via Sinica' is the theoretical line that privileges Chinese sources and authors in the analysis of their own culture. The researchers involved in this theoretical perspective have not abandoned the studies produced in the West, but they propose to establish a new paradigm of understanding about China, based on reading and using Chinese studies. In the same way, the so-called 'Via Sinica' has sought to transpose the epistemological challenges of including the Chinese conceptual and theoretical vocabulary to Brazilian thinking. This methodology has favored the development of a new theory of knowledge, which combines 'Western' (Brazilian) and Chinese experiences. In practice, it intends to concretize the construction of an 'Ecology of Knowledge', as proposed by Boaventura de Sousa Santos (2009: 23–72). The 'Via Sinica' seeks to overcome the limitation of 'understanding' Chinese systems (which maintains a persistent distance) for an 'integration' of them – that is, their broad understanding and use according to the specifics of the problems. This would result in the construction of a new epistemological approach, capable of accessing China itself, but also of analyzing the problems of knowledge in a truly Universalist perspective. The 'East' would constitute one of the last frontiers of human knowledge (Santos 2002: 19–36), completely reformulating the notion of Otherness. Consequently, integrating Chinese wisdom with universal human knowledge is to reformulate its functional and conceptual structure – which is desirable, in the search for an alternative epistemology.

One of the goals for this proposal is the concept of 'Chineseness', proposed by Tu (1991). The recreation of the meanings of 'being Chinese' in different contexts, and in relation to the broader and more general idea of a 'Chinese culture', are fundamental to understanding the adaptations, modifications, and meanings of Chinese knowledge in contact with Brazilian culture. This 'Chineseness' – the search for a Chinese 'conceptual essentiality' – in view of its diverse manifestations, in the most different environments, allows for a multifaceted experience of intercultural dialogue, which refreshes the traditional conception of sinological practice. The work of Ricardo Joppert, previously mentioned, can be characterized as the first initiative in this sense. Joppert's works brought a Chinese conceptual wealth, unprecedented in Brazilian Chinese studies. The analyses of his texts open frontiers in the field of aesthetics, philosophy, and history, constituting a significant contribution in this 'epistemological revolution' that the 'Via Sinica' can represent.

Bueno (2005) has carried out investigations in the field of philosophical dialogues with classical and modern China, notably with Confucianism. Some of his works also intend to discuss the Theory of History and Knowledge (2015, 2020) within the Brazilian academic context. The studies by Bony Schachter (2014) on Daoism is an important highlight, which has reached an important public in Brazil and abroad. An internationally recognized specialist, Schachter is part of a select group of foreign professionals who teach Chinese history and culture at Chinese universities. Another remarkable author is Sinedino, whose versions of *Lunyu* (2012) and *Daodejing* (2016) were recognized as the best scientific translations in the Portuguese-speaking world. These works took the Chinese studies of Chinese classics, in Brazil, to a new level.

It is also necessary to remember the studies by Costa (2019) and Zica (2019) on Daoism in Brazil, and Apolloni (2004) on the culture of martial arts. These specialists have made a great effort to bring Chinese views to the Brazilian public, making them understandable and integrated with the scope of university intellectual conceptions. The principal challenge of the 'Via Sinica' remains, however, the qualification of the researchers, and the difficulties to build more solid capacities. The poorly developed structure of language courses, and the recurrence of prejudices at the university, practiced by professionals with a Eurocentric and colonialist alignment, continues to hinder the creation of a defined space for Chinese studies.

Chinese immigration in Brazil

The concept of 'Chineseness' can also be found in studies on Chinese immigration to Brazil, in which the concepts of Otherness, identity and cultural practices are being widely debated. This area has received special attention, seeing great growth in the last decade. Studies on Chinese immigration in Brazil have revealed facets hitherto little known in Brazilian history; likewise, it is a basis for combating prejudices against Asian ethnicities present in society. In the beginning, the concern of some of these works was to understand historically the Brazilian ideas about the Chinese immigration; however, currently it is sought to perceive the migration process to Brazil as a complex phenomenon, involving visions from both sides, the construction of cultural identities and the rewriting of global history, in which both nations were protagonists.

We have already commented on some studies on the problem of Chinese immigration in the 19th century; the question is being taken up again, in the field of historiography, by several specialists. Dezem (2005) and Lesser (2001) produced indispensables texts on the conflicts that involved the construction of the Brazilian national identity and the Asian presence in the country; Czepula (2017, 2020), analyzes the impact of Chinese immigration on newspapers and periodicals during the time of the Brazilian Empire, resizing the question of the Chinese presence in the country.

Shyu and Jye (2008) did important work on the issue of contemporary Chinese migration to Brazil, tracing a historical trajectory of this recent presence, mainly in the State of São Paulo; Araújo (2015) carried out similar research, revealing the Chinese presence in the State of Rio de Janeiro. Some of these texts show the Chinese adaptation difficulties in Brazil, for the most diverse reasons. These experiences were important to establish a counterpoint with the idea of 'China-as-Model'. Many Chinese have taken refuge in Brazil fleeing the Mao Zedong regime, denouncing the disasters of economic reform projects and political repression. These criticisms surprised the intellectuals who defended 'China-as-Model'; the news released by Chinese immigrants from the continent and Taiwan differed from everything these thinkers preconized. Because of their ideological alignment, they have not changed their concepts about China; but in the texts produced in the 1970s and 1980s, we can perceive, very often, that they sought to contradict the Chinese refugees, trying to justify attitudes and speeches by the Chinese government. In 1981, the intellectual and cartoonist Henfil (pseudonymous of Henrique de Souza Filho 1944–1988) published a book entitled *Henfil na China, antes da Coca-Cola* ('Henfil in China, before Coca-Cola'), in which he made a humorous analysis of the political situation in China, and discussed criticisms and stereotypes related to Chinese culture and society. Although it was not an academic work, the book had a positive impact on the Brazilian imagination, helping to bring balance to the ponderations on the Chinese world. This confrontation of ideas positively stimulated a series of reflections on the real role of Chinese studies in the Brazilian academy. On the other hand, after the re-establishment of diplomatic relations between Brazil and mainland China (1974), a new wave of Chinese immigrants arrived in Brazil in the 1980s, bringing a different and positive view of Chinese communist society. Although the coexistence between the pro-Taiwan and pro-China groups is harmonious in Brazil, specific conflicts have already occurred, revealing the transposition of historical, political, and cultural dilemmas inside this community (Shu 2017).

More recently, Shu (2018) organized important meetings of researchers on Chinese immigration in Brazil, favorably expanding this field, and creating a network of researchers in history, anthropology, economics, and international relations. Machado (2009) also stood out for her profound and revealing work on Chinese immigrants and international trade, bringing an enriching contribution to Brazilian Sinology. Machado is also an active combatant against prejudice in Brazil, actively participating in the media on issues related to discrimination against Chinese and Asians.

Conclusion

The Chinese studies in Brazil followed a singular development. Although in the 19th century Brazilian intellectuals were keenly interested in China, the bankruptcy of the Chinese migration project significantly delayed the development of Brazilian Sinology. The absence of colonial objectives, on the part of Brazil, created a special situation of relationship between the two civilizations. At one point, Brazil was seen as a 'New China', as Kang Youwei dreamed; on the other hand, the Brazilian imagination developed a regular interest in China, although the level of that same interest varied according to the Brazilian political situation.

Despite the strong Eurocentric and Orientalist influences, Brazilian intellectuals sought to develop their own conceptions about cultural problems, which were manifested in Chinese studies. These views can be understood as utilitarian or pragmatic, as in the 'Model view', guided by Brazilian political variations, and having as a starting point a self-centered view; or the 'Via Sinica', based on an epistemological break with the Western cognitive empire, creating the structuring of a new rationality by the inclusion of Asian knowledge. Boaventura de Sousa Santos proposed that contemporary time is the moment for the construction of a new epistemology of knowledge, which he called 'Epistemologies of the South' (2009: 9–21) – and the 'Via Sinica' can be one of his best expressions.

Quantitatively, Chinese studies in Brazil are still far from reaching North American, French, English, or German production; nevertheless, Brazilian works are born multidisciplinary and multilingual, flexibly incorporating new concepts and ideas in the area of Sinology. The consolidation of the field in the country can give rise to a 'New Sinology', as Geremie Barmé (2005) proposed. Chinese studies in Brazil are developing innovative features, using Chinese concepts and ideas in the production of theories and research instruments. For this, however, it will be necessary to avoid the simplest and most immediate solutions, as occasionally occur in the project 'China-as-Model'. The construction of a research field involves investments and resources that vary, according to the interests of the government in Brazil. Even so, some of the individual initiatives presented here show that the community of Brazilian sinologists maintains a productive autonomy, which preserves their freedom of ideological orientation. Chinese studies in Brazil, therefore, represent a unique model of university and institutional research in the Humanities; and from it, a new and original Sinology may emerge soon.

References

Alvarez, José Ramón (2007) 'Esbozo de la sinología española [An Outline of Spanish Sinology]' *Encuentros en Catay*, vol.21: 1–38.

Anais do congresso agrícola do Rio de Janeiro 1 1878. (1988) Rio de Janeiro: Fundação Casa de Rui Barbosa.

Andrade, José Inácio de (1835) *Notícia sobre o chá, sua cultura e manipulação, extraída das 'Cartas escritas da Índia, e da China nos anos de 1815 a 1835'* [Manuscrito]16p. Rio de Janeiro: Biblioteca Nacional.

Antony, Philomena Sequeira (2013) *Relações intracoloniais Goa-Bahia 1675–1825*. Brasília: Funag.

Apolloni, Rodrigo W. (2004) *'Shaolin à brasileira': estudo sobre a presença e a transformação de elementos religiosos orientais no Kung-Fu praticado no Brasil*. Master Thesis in Science of Religions. São Paulo: Pontifícia Universidade Católica.

Araujo, Marcelo (2015) 'Chineses no rio de janeiro: o século xx e a migração em massa' *Revista Encontros*, vol.13, nº25: 68–82.

Aresta, António (1997) 'A Sinologia portuguesa: um esboço breve' *Revista de Cultura do Instituto Cultural de Macau*, vol.32: 9–18.

Bandeira, Júlio (2018) *O Brasil na Rota da China*. Rio de Janeiro: ArtePadilla.

Barmé, Geremie (2005) 'On New Sinology' *Chinese Studies Association of Australia Newsletter*, Nº 31, May.

Barreto, Luis Felipe (1998) 'O Orientalismo conquista Portugal' Novaes, Adauto (org.) *A descoberta do Homem e do Mundo*. Rio de Janeiro: Minc-Funarte/Companhia das Letras.

Bastos, Lúcia; Bessone, Tânia; Guimaraens, Lucia (2010) 'O Império do Cruzeiro do Sul e a Corte Celeste de Tien-Tsin: apontamentos sobre as relações sino-brasileiras no século XIX' *Revista Navigator*, vol.6, nº12: 66–75.

Bocaiuva, Quintino (1868) *A Crise da Lavoura: succinta exposição por Q. Bocayuva*. Rio de Janeiro: Typ. Perseverança.

Boff, Leonardo [org.] (1979) *China e Cristianismo*. Petrópolis: Vozes.

Boff, Leonardo [org.] (1982) *China: Harmonia dos Contrários*. Petrópolis: Vozes.

Boff, Leonardo [org.] (1993) *Há lugar para Cristo na Ásia?* Petrópolis: Vozes.

Boff, Leonardo (2009) *The Tao of Liberation: Exploring the Ecology of Transformation*. New York: Orbis.

Bougeart, Luis (1814) 'Litterature Chinoise: Plan d'um dictionnaire chinoise, par Abel Rémusant' *Mercure Étranger*, tomo III, Paris: Colas: 73–79.

Braga, Humberto (1982) *O Oriente é Vermelho*. São Paulo: Círculo do Livro.

Brito, João Rodrigues (1821) *Cartas Economico-politicas sobre a agricultura e commercio da Bahia pelo Desembargador João Rodrigues de Brito, Deputado das Côrtes*. Lisboa: Imprensa Nacional.

Bueno, André (2005) *A Justa medida em Confúcio e Aristóteles*. Doctoral Thesis in Philosphy. Rio de Janeiro: UGF.

Bueno, André (2015) 'Abolir o passado, reinventar a história: a escrita histórica de Hanfeizi na China do século III a.C' *História da Historiografia: International Journal of Theory and History of Historiography*, vol.8, nº18 (14 set.): 29–42.

Bueno, André (2018) 'Confucius for Brazilians' *International Journal of Latin American Religions*, vol.2, nº1 (Jun.): 117–124.

Bueno, André (2020) 'Sinologia e Orientalismo no Brasil' In Bueno, André (org.) *Sinologia Hoje*. Rio de Janeiro: Proj. Orientalismo/UERJ.

Cabral, Severino (2004) 'O Diálogo Brasil-China: Perspectivas para o Século XXI' In Bellucci, Beluce [org.] Abrindo os olhos para a China. Rio de Janeiro: UCAM.

Callado, Arthur e Motta, Eduardo (2012) 'Documentação Diplomática da Missão à China (1879–1882)' *Cadernos do CHDD*, nº 20. Rio de janeiro: Centro de História e Documentação Diplomática.

Castro, Josué (1968) *Geopolítica da fome: ensaio sobre os problemas de alimentação e de população*. São Paulo: Brasiliense.

Castro, Josué (1971) 'O Ocidente contra a China' In Cautela, Afonso (org.) *A China e o Ocidente—Cadernos do Século, n.10*. Lisboa: Editorial Século: 9–22.

Chacon, Vamireh (1995) *Goa e Macau*. Rio de Janeiro: Bertrand Brasil.

Chan, Adrian (2009) *Orientalism in Sinology*. Palo Alto: Academica Press.

Costa, Matheus (2019) *Daoismo Tropical: A Transplantação do Daoismo ao Brasil*. São Paulo: Fonte Viva.

Czepula, Kamila (2017) *Os indesejáveis 'chins': um debate sobre a imigração chinesa no Brasil Império (1878–1879)*. Master Thesis in History: UNESP: Assis.

Czepula, Kamila (2020) 'La cuestión de los trabajadores 'chinos': ¿salvación o degeneración de Brasil? (1860–1877)' *Anuario Colombiano de Historia Social y de la Cultura*, vol.47, nº1: 303–325.

Dantas, Fábio Lafaiete (2006) *Origem das relações entre o Brasil e a China: a missão especial de 1879*. Recife: Liber.

Dantas, San Tiago (2011) *Política Externa Independente*. Brasília: Funag. (original: 1962)

Dezem, Rogério (2005) *Matizes do 'amarelo': a gênese dos discursos sobre os orientais no Brasil (1878–1908)*. São Paulo: Associação Editorial Humanitas.

Dezem, Rogério (2008) 'Elementos Formadores do Imaginário Sobre o Japonês no Brasil' *Revista de Estudos Orientais*, nº6: 46–59.

Drummond, Carlos (1994) *Viagem a Grande China*. São Paulo: Scritta.

Duarte, Osny (1956a) *A China de hoje*. Rio de Janeiro: Pongetti.

Duarte, Osny (1956b) *Nós e a China*. Rio de Janeiro: Pongetti.

Figueiredo, Lima (1941) *Um ano de observação no Extremo Oriente*. Rio de Janeiro: Americana.

Frechès, José (1975) *La Sinologie*. Paris: Presses Universitaires de France.

Freitas, José de Aquino Guimarães (1828) *Memória sobre Macao*. Coimbra: Real Imprensa da Universidade de Coimbra.

Freyre, Gilberto (2003) *China tropical: e outros escritos sobre a influência do Oriente na cultura luso-brasileira*. Brasília: Editora Universidade de Brasília (First Edition 1936).

Galvão, Ignácio C.; Macedo, Miguel Calmon M. de; Montmorency, Deschamps (1870) *Parecer da seção de colonização e estatística sobre a questão 'Se convirá ao Brasil a importação de colonos chins'* O Auxiliador da Industria Nacional, nº7. Rio de Janeiro, Typ. Laemmert.

Garmes, Helder & Vanzelli, José Carvalho (2017) 'Eça de Queirós, a China e o Brasil' Itinerários, Araraquara, nº44 (jan./jun.): 229–246.

Gutiérrez, Gustavo (2000) *Teologia da Libertação. Perspectivas*. São Paulo: Edições Loyola.

Henfil (1981) *Henfil na China, antes da Coca-Cola*. São Paulo: Círculo do Livro.

Ho, Yeh Chia (1999) *Confúcio e Educação: a antropologia filosófica dos Analectos*. São Paulo: DLO-FFLCHUSP/Mandruvá.

Hui, Juan Hung (1992) *Chinos en América*. Madrid: Mapfre.

Joppert, Ricardo (1979) *O alicerce cultural da China*. Rio de Janeiro: Avenir.

Joppert, Ricardo (1999) *Porcelana chinesa*. Rio de Janeiro: Artmed.

Jullien, François (2010) 'Pensar a partir de um fora (a China)' *Revista Periferia*, vol.2, nº1 (jan.–jun.): 1–20.

Kissinger, Henry (2013) *Sobre a China*. Rio de Janeiro: Objetiva.

LeBlanc, Charles (2007) *Profession Sinologue*. Montréal: Presses de l'Université de Montréal.

Lee, Ana Paulina (2018) *Mandarin Brazil: Race, Representation, and Memory*. Stanford: Stanford University Press.

Leite, José Roberto Teixeira (1999) *A China no Brasil: influências, marcas, ecos e sobrevivências chinesas na sociedade e na arte brasileiras*. Campinas: Editora da Unicamp.

Lesser, Jeffrey (2001) *A negociação da identidade nacional: minorias e a luta pela etnicidade no Brasil*. São Paulo: Editora Unesp.

Lisboa, Henrique Carlos Ribeiro (1888) *A China e os Chins. Recordações de viagem do Ex. Secretário da Missão Especial do Brasil a China*. Montevideo: Typ. Gobel.

Machado, Rosana Pinheiro (2009) *Made in China: produção e circulação de mercadorias no circuito China-Paraguai-Brasil*. Doctoral Thesis in Antrophology. Porto Alegre: UFRGS.

Mafra, Adriana & Stallaert, Christiane (2016) 'Orientalismo Crioulo: Dom Pedro II e o Brasil do Segundo Império' *Iberoamericana*, vol.XVI, nº63: 149–168.

Mao, Haijian 茅海建 (2007) '巴西招募华工与康有为移民 巴西计划之初步考证' In 史林 (History Review) Shanghai: Shanghai Academy of Social Sciences, n.5:1–18.

Mendonça, Salvador de (1879) *Trabalhadores Asiáticos*. New York: Typographia do Novo Mundo.

Menezes, Adolpho Bezerra de (1956) *O Brasil e o Mundo Asio-Africano*. Rio de Janeiro: Pongetti.

Menezes, Antônio Bezerra de (2015) *Joaquim Guerra S.J. (1908–1993): releitura universalizante dos clássicos chineses*. Lisboa: Instituto Internacional de Macau.

Moreira, Nicolau Joaquim (1870) *Convirá ao Brasil a importação de colonos Chins? Discurso pronunciado na sessão da sociedade auxiliadora da indústria nacional em 16 de Agosto de 1870*. Rio de Janeiro: Typ. Laemmert.

Moura, Carlos Francisco (2012) *Chineses e chá no Brasil no início do século XIX*. Macau/Rio de Janeiro: Instituto Internacional de Macau/Real Gabinete Português de Leitura.

Moura, Carlos Francisco (2014) *Brasileiros nos extremos orientais do império: séculos XVI a XIX*. Lisboa / Rio de Janeiro: Instituto Internacional de Macau / Real Gabinete Português de Leitura.

Nabuco, Joaquim (1879) 'Discursos Parlamentares 1879' In *Câmara dos Deputados: Centro de documentação e informação-Coordenação de Publicações*. (1983), Brasília.

Pinheiro, José Xavier (1869) *Importação de trabalhadores chins: Memória apresentada ao Ministério da Agricultura, Comércio e Obras Públicas e Impressa por sua ordem*. Rio de Janeiro: Typ. de João Ignácio da Silva.

Pomar, Wladimir (1987) *O Enigma chinês*. São Paulo: Alfa-Ômega.

Pomar, Wladimir (2009) *China, desfazendo mitos*. Publisher Brasil.

Ré, Henrique Antonio (2018) 'Os esforços dos abolicionistas britânicos contra a imigração de chineses para o Brasil no final do século XIX' *Varia historia*, vol.34, nº66: 817–848.

Ricci, Matteo; Ruggiere, Michele; Witke, John (2001) 葡漢辭典 *Dicionário Português-Chinês*. Lisboa: Biblioteca Nacional de Portugal.

Russell-Wood, Anthony John (1998) *Um mundo em movimento. Os portugueses na África, Ásia e América (1415–1808)*. Lisboa: Difel Editora.

Russell-Wood, Anthony John (2001) 'A dinâmica da presença brasileira no Índico e no Oriente. Séculos XVI-XIX' *Topoi Rio de Janeiro*, vol.2, nº3: 9–40.

Sacramento, Leandro (1825) *Memoria econômica sobre a plantação, cultura e preparação do chá*. Rio de Janeiro: Typ. Nacional.

Said, Edward (1998) *Orientalismo—A invenção do Oriente pelo Ocidente*. Rio de Janeiro: Companhia das Letras.

Santos, Boaventura de Sousa (2002) 'O Fim das descobertas imperiais' In Oliveira, Inês Barbosa & Sgarb, Paulo (orgs.) *Redes culturais, diversidades e educação*. Rio de Janeiro: DP&A:19–36.

Santos, Boaventura de Sousa & Meneses, Maria Paula (2009) *Epistemologias do Sul*. Coimbra: Almedina.

Schachter, Bony (2014) 'Gaoshang Yuhuang benxing jijing (Combined scriptures of the Original Acts of the Exalted and Superior Jade Sovereign): An Annotated Translation and Study of Its First Chapter' *Monumenta Serica—Journal of Oriental Studies*, vol.LXII: 153–212.

Schachter, Bony (2020) 'Introdução a sinologia ao público lusófono' In Bueno, André (org.) *Sinologia Hoje*. Rio de Janeiro: Proj.Orientalismo/UERJ.

Schmaltz, Márcia (2015) *Resolução de problemas na tradução de metáforas linguísticas do chinês para o português: um estudo empírico-experimental*. Doctoral Thesis in Languages. Macau: University of Macau.

Shu, Changsheng (2017) 'Um Estudo Preliminar sobre a Imigração Chinesa no Rio de Janeiro 1812–2012' In Arlete Cavaliere, Antônio Bezerra Menezes (Org.). *Linguagens do Oriente: Contemporaneidade*. 1ed. São Paulo: Paulistana: 119–154.

Shu, Changsheng (2018) '巴西华侨华人研究文献综述与人口统计 (Studies on Chinese Migrants in Brazil: Literature Review and Population Statistics)' *Journal of Overseas Chinese History Studies*, n.1, (March): 30–40.

Shyu, David Jye Yuan & Jye, Chen Tsung (2008) 'Integração Cultural dos Imigrantes Chineses no Brasil' *Revista de Estudos Orientais*, nº6: 206–33.

Sinedino, Giorgio [trad.] (2012) *Analectos*. São Paulo: Ed. Unesp.

Sinedino, Giorgio [trad.] (2016) *Daodejing: Escritura do Caminho e Escritura da Virtude com os comentários do Senhor às Margens do Rio*. São Paulo: Ed. Unesp.

Sproviero, Mário Bruno [trad.] (2002). *Daodejing—Laozi*. São Paulo: Hedra.

Studart, Heloneida (1982) *China—o Nordeste que deu certo*. Rio de Janeiro: Novo Tempo.

Tu, Wei Ming (1991) 'Cultural China: The Periphery as the Center' *Daedalus*, vol.120, nº2, (Spring): 1–32.

Vukovich, Daniel F. (2012) *China and Orientalism: Western Knowledge Production and the P.R.C.* London: Routdledge.

Zica, Matheus (2019) *Daoismo, Estéticas Chinesas & Outras Artes*. Curitiba: Appris.

39

On 'lagging behind' and 'catching-up' – postcolonialism and China

Marius Meinhof

Introduction

The story of China's defeat and oppression by 'foreign powers' is a key narrative for Chinese modern identity today. To many Chinese, it delivers the powerful message that 'the backwards will be beaten' (落后就要挨打). This memory of colonialism is produced in official political speeches and propaganda (Callahan 2006), but also in everyday talk (Meinhof 2018). It goes far beyond the 'anti-western propaganda' (Wang 2012) it is portrayed to be by some Western scholars. For example, it plays an important role in state discourse in the PRC (Callahan 2004) but it equally plays a role in antistate discourses (Chen 1995). Its lesson can be about the evil of the West, but just as often it is read as a lesson about the mistakes and weaknesses of old China. The images of 'the West' derived from it are highly ambivalent (see for example Huang 2017). It seems that for many Chinese, the question of modernity, but also of today's Chinese identity is connected to memories of colonialism.

This idea that colonial history matters for today, that we have to talk about it if we want to understand modernity today, and that we have to trace its heritage into the contemporary lies at the heart of postcolonialist thinking. Postcolonialism comprises a wide range of authors, such as the early anticolonial thinkers in the French empire (Césaire 1972; Fanon 2017), Indian Subaltern and Postcolonial Studies (Chakrabarty 2000; Spivak 1988), the Latin American decolonial theory schools (Escobar 1995; Quijano 2008), and many more. Their works do not necessarily share one specific theoretical position (a 'postcolonial theory'), but rather revolve around a set of shared concerns, of which some are very visible in China today. These are for example concerns to disrupt the lasting impacts of colonialism, to understand the relation between modernity and coloniality and to claim the possibility for the non-Western to articulate own visions of the future and own models of a modern society – and, most significantly, the need to overcome the stigma of centuries of being labeled as backward, uncivilized, inferior, unhygienic, or sick. Beyond a doubt, the 'solutions' for these shared concerns differ greatly between postcolonialism and Chinese official discourse – a critique of coloniality/modernity on the one side, and a proud nationalist insistence to erase colonial humiliation by 'catching-up' on the other side. Postcolonialism attempts to deal with exactly these concerns, and thus is prone to take them seriously as concerns, even

DOI: 10.4324/9780429059704-46

if it rejects the solutions chosen in Chinese nationalist discourse; this alone is already a reason why postcolonialism should be taken more seriously in debates on China.

In the following chapter, I will provide an overview of some postcolonial works on mainland China. So far, such works have regrettably failed to form a consistent theoretical discourse. Thus, my overview will assemble fragmented works on different phenomena and suggest theoretical perspectives they have in common. Therefore, this chapter will organize literature around common theoretical concepts and concerns, not around material objects of research. For example, in one paragraph one may not find works on one single material topic such as religion or family, but works with a common theoretical concept such as 'colonial modernity' or 'colonial temporality'. I hope this encourages other scholars to go beyond the discourse on specific social phenomena and also engage in a theoretical debate on a postcolonial theory on Chinese modernity.

There have been fruitful debates on postcolonialism in China in respect to other places and contexts, for example, Macao and Hong Kong (a recent and great example is Chun 2019), which regrettably cannot be discussed here.

Postcolonialism in China Studies?

Most postcolonial scholarship is driven by the attempt of intellectuals in/from former colonies to understand the incompleteness of decolonization. In the past I have argued that three concerns are fundamental for most postcolonial works (Meinhof et al. 2017): First, postcolonial thinkers theorize the ongoing impact of colonialism on today's world. The 'post' in postcolonial thus does not imply that colonialism is over, but rather that we arrived in a situation that is not quite colonialism anymore, but has also not really left colonialism behind (e.g., Quijano 2008: 181). Second, most postcolonial scholars are concerned with Eurocentric structures in knowledge production today. This includes the famous notion of orientalism (Said 1978) as a discourse constructing the (formerly) colonized as the *Other* of the Western civilization, but it also targets the unequal right to theorize in today's academia, where theory is produced in the West and 'applied' to countries like China, which have to be marked and explained as specific 'local context'. Postcolonial scholars are often interested in looking at possibilities of resistance or alternatives to these Eurocentric structures, for example, practices of hybridity which resists binary oppositions of colonizer/colonized (Bhabha 2012: 296) and thus constitute moments where the colonial discourse of *otherness* breaks down. Also, postcolonial scholars are prone to criticize the universal applicability of categories developed in theories of European history, and rather try to show the failing of such categories in encounters between colonizers and colonized (for some examples see Seth 2009). Thirdly, most postcolonial scholars were interested in the question of (global) modernity, for example by arguing that modernity emerged out of mutual influences between Europe and the colonies (Quijano 2008; Randeria 2002). Thus, most works reject the 'Eurocentric diffusionism' (Blaut 1993), which tells us that modernity was invented in Europe and then diffused over the globe. But the theoretical alternative to diffusionism is not a claim for purely endogenous change within one country such as the 'China-centered approach' (Cohen 1984). Instead, postcolonial scholars look at the way 'modernity' emerges out of global, multidirectional flows, and entanglements – albeit often colonial and thus fundamentally asymmetric entanglements (Randeria 2002).

In China Studies these concerns have led to research on a wide field of topics so heterogeneous that no specific 'postcolonial topic' can be identified. However, the heterogeneous research shows some common theoretical topics, that are tied together by their theoretical interest rather than by the specific cases they study, and which largely mirror the above mentioned three postcolonial concerns: First, the topic of modernity is looming large in postcolonial works on China. Following postcolonial concerns, the idea of modernity is tied to colonial origins and criticized for its colonial assumptions, most frequently for the idea of a 'backwardness' (落后), which needs to be erased, and the social effects this idea has. Second, knowledge production on China is debated specifically in works on orientalism. Here, China Studies have been especially productive in theory building. While there are relatively few works on orientalism in China, a large number of them provide considerable theoretical additions to Said's theory. Third, research on Chinese occidentalism shows how some orientalist ideas are embedded into a Chinese discourse on the West which rather than constituting a mirror image of Western orientalism leads to a coproduction of colonial discourse between China and the West.

In all these three topics, postcolonial perspectives lead to a fruitful approach to problems in China. However, most postcolonial scholars working on China seem to agree that postcolonial thinking must not be applied from elsewhere, but must be redeveloped for China. They prefer to develop new approaches befitting the social situations in China but based on postcolonial concerns.

This is based on the insight that, with respect to postcolonial concerns, China is quite a special case. Informal imperialism merged with fragmented, 'multiple colonialisms' (Goodman & Goodman 2012) in China constitutes a fascinating case of 'co-operative venture' (Osterhammel 1986) between multiple colonial powers, but it does not make China an exception to global colonialism. In fact, many of the works I will introduce below show that concepts developed in respect to colonialism elsewhere fit the semicolonial China pretty well, too. However, China underwent an exceptionally radical decolonization process, which did not just lead to a dissolution of most (today: all) formal colonies in China, but also included a radical economic restructuring and attempts to decolonize thought and culture.

To further complicate things, the constellation of discursive power is quite different in the context of China, because, as Chen (1995) and Zhang (1999) have pointed out, certain variations of postcolonial thought enjoy themselves a hegemonic status within China. Indeed, Marxist theories on imperialism and theories of third-worldism were important ancestors for postcolonial discourse. Until today, official discourse in China addresses in many respects the same issues that postcolonial theory is concerned with; that is the memories of having once been subjected to colonialism, the 'common fate' of the formerly colonized, cultural self-confidence, the question of modernity, a challenge to the existing development structures, and so on (thus is argued by Meinhof et al. 2017). Hence, the challenge for postcolonial critique in China is not simply to confront Eurocentric discourse – rather, one must think about a situation of a Chinese state discourse dominating within China, but being situated in a world where Eurocentric discourse still largely enjoys hegemonic status.

All of this makes China a special case, but certainly no exception to colonialism, and no exception to postcolonial concerns. On the contrary, it makes postcolonial perspectives on China especially relevant and interesting. The special situation of China is likely to irritate conventional ways of postcolonial thinking and to inspire complex theoretical work – work which has only just started to emerge from an academia that for far too long avoided an in-depth discussion of postcolonialism and China.

Modernity and modernization

Most postcolonial works on China have been concerned with ideas of modernity, modernization, and development in relation to colonial history. Common to these is that instead of focusing on differences of authoritarian/liberal or socialist/capitalist, one should perceive power relations in contemporary China as experiments with and struggles over modernity – a modernity that in turn is deeply related to historic experiences with colonialism.

The theoretically most elaborate approach to this is the debate on *colonial modernity* led by Tani Barlow. Barlow criticizes the silence of major parts of China Studies on colonialism (Barlow 1997a) and proposes the idea of colonial modernity as an approach to the discussion of colonialism in East Asia. The concept highlights that for many East Asian countries, modernity and colonialism were experienced as inseparable from each other (Barlow 1997b: 1). Barlow highlights the multiple continuities between colonialism and the times after decolonization, mainly mediated through the connection of colonialism and modernism (Barlow 1997b: 7). However, Barlow insists that theories on binary relations of colonizer-colonized are inappropriate for China because the experience of semicolonialism contains more ambivalence and multiplicity than the experience of formal colonization. Thus, colonial modernity is about 'monitoring semiosis as it flows in and around the breached boundaries of Chinese sovereignty' (Barlow 1997b: 10). Scholars working in colonial modernity in China have put spotlights on various issues related to modernity and colonialism, often but not always focusing on cultural aspects or aspects of everyday life. Hevia (1997) argues that the plundering of China by the Eight Nations Alliance after the Boxer Rebellion was structured in parts by the idea to destroy traditional cultural roots in China. Lydia Liu shows how the idea of the individual was negotiated in the debates on modernity in China in the 1910s and 1920s (Liu 1997). Wang (1997) analyzed the fascination of the Chinese with science and the introduction of the Japanese term *kexue* to signify science after the 1890s. Such works have outlined a very useful theoretical framework specifically designed for postcolonial approaches to the history of China. One could critically remark that Barlow's argument, that the specific complexity of semicolonialism cannot be understood in binary terms of China/West implies that binarization was appropriate everywhere else, and thus – once again – disconnects China Studies from other postcolonial discourse. However, colonial modernity is at the moment the closest to a postcolonial theory in China Studies and might be the best starting point for a comparative theoretical debate.

Taking a very different, openly normative position, Zhang Yiwu argues that since the era of colonialism, there is a deep, yet harmful desire in China for 'modernity'. This modernity is harmful to the Chinese, because it merges the spatial notion of China and the West and the temporal notion of backward and advanced into one, and in consequence compels Chinese to express their own experiences through the categories and concepts of the Other (the West) (Zhang 1994b). This places modernity at odds with 'Chineseness' (中华性), which Zhang et. al. define as a pluralized and eclectic discourse deconstructing differences like China/West, old/new or socialism/capitalism and instead assembling practices beneficial for China (Zhang et al. 1994). China, Zhang argues, must reach a post–new era (后新时代) where intellectuals and their discourse on modernity are replaced by a new discourse (Zhang 1994a) led by 'marginal' postintellectuals who would not prescribe how modern behavior should be conducted but rather observe and describe popular practices. Zhang was heavily criticized especially for his notion of 'Chineseness' (Sheng 2007). He was depicted to be a nativist with imperialistic attitudes (Xu 1998). However, a serious engagement with Zhang Yiwu's work as a theory on reform-era China rather than as an example for contemporary Chinese, although that has not yet happened in the English language. Although some of the critiques miss the point of his works, there are indeed inconsistencies of Zhang's thesis from a postcolonial perspective. For example, he stresses the right for people's self-determination, but does not elaborate how this applies to Chinese ethnic minorities self-determination versus Han modernity within the framework of 'Chineseness'.

Aside from these larger theoretical projects, a number of studies have been concerned with the idea of lagging behind or backwardness and attempts to overcome it. These works are theoretically very fascinating for postcolonial scholars because they imply that colonialism left its impact on China not because the fight to regain sovereignty failed in China, but because colonial stereotypes were internalized into the worldview of those who struggled for sovereignty. Duara (1995) presented a major study arguing that the regulation and prohibition of religious practices in China can be traced back to the notion of a progressing history which the Chinese developed in grappling with Japanese and Western ideas during the colonial era. Similarly, Yang (2011) has argued that colonial experiences made many Chinese believe that they need to modernize their country in order to secure its sovereignty, which in turn motivated Chinese leaders to crack down on religions they deemed superstitious and backward. She diagnoses a postcolonial complex, which influences state visions of a singular, secular modernity and thus becomes a resource of conflicts with popular religious practices (Yang 2004).

Meinhof (Meinhof 2017) introduces the theoretical term 'colonial temporality', which in contrast to above-mentioned works lays a stronger focus on population politics and governmentality. He argues that the idea of China lagging behind the West which guides many attempts to reform and modernize the population originates in a typical colonial outlook on the attributes of time which was internalized into Chinese discourse after 1895 and especially during the early republican period. Although colonial temporality helped to mobilized many Chinese to strive for self-improvement, it also compelled them to a 'constant comparisons with the West', which allowed modernity to be ultimately defined through 'external reference'. This has inspired some follow-up works which all focus on how ideas about Chinese 'backwardness' are influenced by colonial temporality, and why these ideas are reproduced in society. Yan and Meinhof (2018) argue, that Chinese returnee migrants in multinational corporations (MNC) do reproduce stereotypes of a 'backward Chinese mentality' in order to position themselves within the power field of the MNC as Chinese-yet-modern. Meinhof (2018) argues that antiregime and pro-regime comments in online discussions on China and the West do cooperate in producing the narrative of a backward China catching-up – the former counter the official discourse within China by arguing China was hopelessly lagging behind, the latter counter American discourses on a despotic China by arguing that China is doing great and has almost caught up. Zhu (2017) tries to understand the dynamics of colonial temporality by looking at the self-strengthening movement's discourse on importing Western weaponry after the opium war as an example of a discourse on colonialism, the West, and reforms in China that is *not* guided by the notion of modernization and/or colonial temporality.

Certainly, all of these works have in common not only their attempt to deconstruct classic notions of modernity but also an interest in a globally entangled coproduction of knowledge about China and the West, which, due to its historic origin in colonial relations, tends to reproduce an anachronistic symbolic superiority of the West. Thus, all three above mentioned concerns – the interest in modernity, in Eurocentric knowledge and in global entanglements – are visible in these works.

Orientalism

Largely independent from these works on modernity, a series of works have focused on Western orientalism with respect to China. Zhang Kuan argues that the West produces an orientalist image of China as exotic and backward, and that Chinese modernization discourses have accepted this image (Zhang 2009, 1993). His 1993 article is often considered to be the trigger for postcolonial debates in China, although he himself denies this (Zhang 2009). Dirlik argues famously, that orientalism should not be seen as a product of Western discourse alone. In accordance with the idea of global entanglements, he argues that Chinese Elites took part in constructing China as a Confucianist civilization (Dirlik 1996). This, he argues, contributed to produce the orientalist idea of China as an exotic other, in opposition to a Christian West. However, this self-orientalization is not always disempowering China, but rather can be used consciously to legitimate power relations in China and to immunize China against critique from abroad (Dirlik 1995).

From a historic perspective, a number of works have used the notions of orientalism to analyze colonial relations in China. Osterhammel's only recently translated work (Osterhammel 2018) shows that China was not always constructed as the negative other of Europe, but rather received great admiration before Europeans started to develop imperialist attitudes towards China. Mühlhahn (2000) shows how orientalist hierarchies structured life for both colonizers and colonized in German colonies in Jiaozhou, and argues that this created strong experiences of alterity for the Chinese living in these colonies. The focus on colonialism and postcolonial thoughts is also visible in Mühlhahn's major overview of the history of modern China (Mühlhahn 2019). Steinmetz (2007) looks at German colonies in Africa, China, and the Pacific in order to draw comparisons and highlight entanglements between these colonies. Villard (2019) shows how the Lyon Sino-French Institute was used to teach Chinese overseas students the values of the French Empire and the idea of colonialism as a civilizing mission. From a legal perspective, Ruskola has provided excellent works on the way consular courts worked in extraterritorial settlements in China. He argues that the legitimacy of the US court of China was based on a 'legal orientalism' (Ruskola 2013) constructing Chinese law as backward and barbaric, thus inapplicable to modern citizens of the United States. This led to the import of juridical practices established in US territories and colonies so that an American 'Colonialism without Colonies' (Ruskola 2008) emerged in China.

Theoretically, most influential on contemporary China Studies is probably Vukovich's work on the 'new sinological orientalism' (Vukovich 2012) of the late 1990s and the 21st century. Vukovich argues that new orientalism does not construct a discourse of 'otherness' but rather one of 'becoming-sameness': Orientalist stereotypes of a backward, despotic *Other* of the West are applied on the Mao-Era, while at the same time the Reform-Era is constructed as a grand historic movement of overcoming this *Otherness* and becoming similar to the West. Throughout this becoming-sameness, however, the West remains in positional superiority, because in the eyes of new orientalists, the West defines the endpoint of the trajectory of Chinese social change which China never entirely realizes.

Vukovich's notion of a new orientalism was picked up by a large number of works of which only a few can be mentioned here. Yan (Yan 2017) argues, that US and Chinese political sciences have constructed a social group of MNC-employees with presumed shared values based on an ideological discourse of becoming-sameness. Also referring to Vukovich, Ampuero, and Labarca (2017) present an exploratory yet promising study on Chilenian orientalist depictions of China. Vukovich himself in a new work depicts the challenge to liberal academic theory by the supposed success of Chinese illiberal practices (Vukovich 2019). He has however not yet elaborated how exactly shifts between a focus on otherness and on becoming-sameness happen, a discussion which would be relevant considering the recent return of US discourse to an emphasis on China as a threat.

New orientalism has won a new relevance in the discourse on the COVID-19 pandemic, especially in the United States, where China is increasingly constructed as negative other on which US leaders may lay blame for the outbreak of the pandemic. This othering of China seems part of a larger shift from 'becoming-sameness' back to a traditional 'otherness' of China in US discourse, which takes place in recent years. I have published a very preliminary paper on othering in the discourse on COVID-19 (Meinhof 2020), where I identify three types of othering: (1) racism, which attributes the virus to Chinese bodies; (2) Vukovich's New Orientalism, which attributes the virus to failures of authoritarianism; and (3) colonial temporality, which explains the outbreak with Chinese backwardness. Theoretically important, I argue that New Orientalism has often merged with racism and covered this racism in a disguise of an otherwise legitimate critique of the authoritarian system. Some other works on COVID-related racism, too, have highlighted the attribution of the disease to Chinese or Asian bodies (e.g., Roche 2020; Lai 2020). However, these are preliminary, non-peer-reviewed considerations, since it is far too early to present reliable research results on orientalism in the COVID-19 crisis. Some reports from Guangzhou indicate, that after the epicenter of the disease shifted to Europe, racist discrimination of the Black community in China has been on the increase, and this in turn seems to have triggered anti-Chinese racism in some African countries. This issue will require thorough research in the future. In times of COVID-19, it has become more visible than ever before, that there is not such a linear transition from otherness to becoming-sameness as Vukovich assumes. Although it has not been argued in any of the published papers so far, it seems obvious today that otherness and becoming-sameness co-exist as virtual ideas that can be actualized anytime. After COVID-19 hit the US hard, a discourse on Chinese otherness, even China as the enemy of the United States, spread through wide political circles driving calls for an exclusion of China – this was so far the peak of development away from becoming-sameness and back towards otherness.

Closely related to this debate on orientalism is the idea of Sinologism by Gu Mingdong (Gu 2013). Sinologism moves the focus away from ideology and hegemonic struggle and towards the 'cultural unconscious' disposition of Westerners towards China. However, from a postcolonial perspective, this constitutes a disadvantage of the theory, because it loses the sociological perspective on power-knowledge, while the idea of a 'cultural unconscious' shared by Westerners smacks of cultural essentialism.

Some authors have rejected the critique on orientalism for China Studies with varying arguments (Kluge 2019; e.g., Schwartz 1980; Zhang 1999). The most valid point is made by Kluge (Kluge 2019) who argues that China is not successfully objectified in China Studies. Chinese academics actively study and debate Western sinology, and the Chinese state does actively influence Western academic debates on China. Especially his second point is very valid in showing that a critique on orientalism in China Studies should also take the global agency of China into account. However, Kluge does not mention the still existing sharp asymmetries in academic knowledge production. The Chinese state does mainly 'defensively' try to influence or censor representations of China which are in most countries still dominated by Anglo-American voices, and these attempts are often rejected by Western academia as suspicious propaganda or censorship while on the other hand there is no 'western studies' or 'US studies' from China with relevant global influence. Thus, while Kluge is certainly right in rejecting the idea of China as a passive object of Western gaze, he does not sufficiently consider that academia is far away from an equal relation between Chinese and US scholarship.

If one tries to identify the common point in these works, aside from the common theoretical concept of orientalism, they all look at a kind of knowledge that creates a superior position for the West, and they look at how this knowledge is related to historic heritage of colonialism and/or the Cold War. Apart from the works on modernity, however, few of the studies of orientalism put an emphasis on the coproduction of this knowledge between China and the (former) colonial powers.

Occidentalism

In addition to works on orientalism, a number of scholars have focused on Chinese discourses constructing the West – often termed *occidentalism*. However, the exact understanding of occidentalism and the political implications vary between authors.

The majority of works perceive occidentalism as coproducing orientalism. While orientalism is a Western discourse on the 'East', which constructs the imaginary East as *inferior*, occidentalism is a corresponding Eastern discourse on the 'West', which constructs the imaginary West as *superior*. Thus, it is not simply the Chinese Sinocentric version of Western Eurocentric orientalism, but an equally Eurocentric discourse that accompanies orientalism. These works theoretically connect above-mentioned debates on 'modernity' and of orientalism, even though none of the authors explicates this connection. The deepest theoretical consideration into this connection is presented by Shih Shu-mei's (Shih 2001) work on modernism in the May Fourth movement that argues, that May Fourth scholars bifurcated the colonial empires into an imperialist and metropolitan culture, and rejected the former while they glorified the latter. Her work does not only develop arguably the most complex theory of orientalism-occidentalism in China up to date. She also contributes to the long-standing debates on 'Chinese agency' in Sinology by presenting a theory of Chinese agency embedded into a global power framework working in favor of (former) colonial powers.

In the Chinese language, too, scholars have critically debated the May Fourth movement's depiction of the West in light of postcolonial theory. For example, Feng Jicai (Feng 2000) claims that Lu Xun's idea of an inferior Chinese national character (国民性) is reproducing stereotypes of Western colonial discourse. This was in turn met by critiques who, for example, claimed that Missionaries influence on China had beneficial elements and that Lu Xun appropriated Western concepts and turned them into a Chinese progressive theory able to challenge traditional culture (e.g. Zhu 2002). Against this, again, Hu Yugao claimed that critiques on Feng Jicai and Lydia Liu relied too much on binary oppositions such as Western/Chinese and traditional/modern (He 2016). This debate may serve as an example of how postcolonial critique on May Fourth Occidentalism sparked a lively debate challenging not only classic readings like Lu Xun, but also world binary views widespread in China and elsewhere.

For some authors, this type of critique of occidentalism is accompanied by a call for a transformation of Chinese discourses on modernity. For example, Cao and Li (1996) have argued that Chinese acceptance of Western discourse has lead to a state of 'aphasia' (失语症) among Chinese intellectuals because they have problems to express Chinese problems without referring to Western examples or concepts. He Qing (2010) argues that the Chinese have internalized Western 'progress theory' (进步论) which keeps them from thinking about alternatives to progress. Zhang Yiwu, whose works have already been debated above, also argues that Chinese intellectuals apply an othering to themselves because their discourse on modernity accepts Western modernity as the norm and describes China as an exception in contrast to this normal modernity (Zhang 1994b). These works have been heavily criticized for their nationalist implications and their alleged misappropriation of postcolonial concepts (Sheng 2007; Zhang 1999).

A very different approach to occidentalism is used by Chen Xiaomei (Chen 1995). Chen distinguishes between an official occidentalism, which constructs the West as Evil and Imperialist in order to legitimize the communist party rule over China, and an antiofficial occidentalism that glorifies the West in order to challenge the legitimacy of the authoritarian regime. Differing from the above-mentioned authors, she argues that a glorification of the West should not be read as mirroring colonial orientalist stereotypes, but rather as a conscious counterdiscourse against the political regime in China. This book is one of the theoretically most inspiring works for scholars interested in postcolonial theory, even if they do not have any specific China focus. However, she has received some substantial critique. Shih has argued that Chen's idea of an equivalence between Chinese occidentalism and Western orientalism is oblivious to the global power structures which made orientalism a global hegemonic project (Shih 2001). I have criticized Chen for assuming too smoothly a binary scheme of Anti-Western State vs. Pro-Western People by arguing, that nationalist depictions of China in popular culture can also be read as a counterdiscourse against the perceived anti-Chinese discourses both in US-led mass media as well as in the antiofficial occidentalist discourses Chen describes (Meinhof 2018).

Another entirely different but highly inspiring perspective on occidentalism is taken by Wang Mingming. Wang argues in his historic account of the varying imaginations of the West, that China has a long tradition of imagining the West, in which images constantly transformed due to changing historic constellations. Current images of the West built during the 19th and 20th century should be seen as one in a long row of changing conceptions of the West as the other of China (Wang 2014).

Despite these very different understandings of occidentalism, what these works have in common is that they look at global entanglements in the sense of a historic trajectory of Western and Chinese stereotypes that mutually influence each other. Indeed, for most of them, Chinese occidentalism can be separated neither from Western orientalism nor from the history of colonialism and, for contemporary occidentalism, the history of the Cold War. Thus, again, we find the idea of asymmetric entanglements, asymmetric knowledge production, and a historic trajectory emerging from the colonial past in these debates, too.

Ethnic relations in China

While the main corpus of postcolonial works deals with Chinese uneasy relationships with 'the West' and 'modernity', Postcolonial perspectives can just as well be applied to ethnic relations within China. For example, several works have shown that concerns of postcolonial works are important to ethnic relations within China, too, and that these relations, in turn, need to be embedded into global postcolonial power relations. Wang Hui, for example, did debate how Western Orientalist images of Tibet do cover over the complex sociopolitical reasons for protests in Tibet by constructing an ahistoric ethnic antagonism between Han and Tibetians, and portraying the conflict as one between a pure, spiritual tradition and a polluted, industrial modernity (Wang 2010). Roche (2019) shows the transnational circulation of coloniality by arguing that small Tibetian languages are erased in a struggle between the Chinese government and exile Tibetian movements in the West, which both try to define the 'real' Tibet and thus homogenize the linguistic diversity into one 'Tibetian language' that needs to be preserved. Lan (2016) looks at images of black and white migrants in China, relating racial images to the history of colonialism/imperialism in China. Stressing another important element of postcolonialism, Wilcox (2016) engages in a search for alternatives to orientalism by looking at instances of ethnic relations. These works, however, need to reflect the complex global power relations at play when people from Anglo-American elite universities, often imbued in a new orientalist discourse, represent Han Chinese orientalist representations of Chinese minorities. Works like that of Schein (1997), which entirely focus on domestic power relations, don't draw the full potential of postcolonialism. Also, postcolonial works need to be careful not to inflate the concept of 'colonialism' until it signifies any given relation of domination. For example, some arguments on Manchu colonialism towards Han (Perdue 2009; Crossley et al. 2006: 1–2) seem to assume that any multiethnic state with a majority-minority relation qualifies as a colonial empire. The inflation of the concept of colonialism has been rightfully criticized by Zhu (2019) in her argument, that the Manchu approach to dominating Han does not fit the postcolonial notion of coloniality, because the Manchu were eager to prove their belonging to the Chinese dynasties rather than their separation from them. Postcolonialism could help to flesh out better what exactly makes unequal ethnic relations colonial.

Conclusion

Postcolonialism touches on a wide range of concerns that are very visible in China, such as questions of modernity and backwardness, sovereignty, China and the West, the humiliation of the colonial era. It puts them into terms that neither belong entirely to Chinese state discourse nor to American liberal discourse – and thus allows a fresh perspective in which both camps may appear ideological (I attempted such a perspective in Meinhof 2018).

However, one must not forget that in China Studies, postcolonialism is a marginal discourse, and postcolonial scholars did not yet have the chance to sufficiently debate and elaborate all their ideas in academic debates. Thus, their works only allow a glimpse at the potential this discourse could hold such as, for example, a better understanding of the idea of backwardness and the relation of China to the West, more explicit connections between research on the May Fourth era and contemporary China, deeper connections between China Studies and other Area Studies as well as sociological debates on modernity. Whether the similarities between Chinese official discourse and postcolonial thought are reason enough to abandon postcolonialism in China Studies needs to be debated in respect of the quality of actual empiric works – at least, most of the works introduced in this text clearly avoid the pitfall of merely reproducing official Chinese discourse.

Such a postcolonial perspective is urgently necessary. Many Western observers have erased memories of colonialism in China from their discourse to such a degree, that they have difficulties understanding that colonial memories are a fundamental part of Chinese discourses on modernity, Chineseness, and the West. Because of their own colonial amnesia, they tend to assume a strategic interest behind all Chinese memories of colonialism. Postcolonialism can show, that colonialism and the postcolonial asymmetric relations of knowledge production are of real importance, and memories of them can be sincere elements of Chinese identity – elements that might be used for strategic interests or for nationalist propaganda, but are not invented for the sake of these reasons.

In order to achieve this understanding, however, a more thorough discourse on theoretical concepts related to China will be necessary. Because so few scholars have used postcolonial perspectives on China, and because they positioned themselves in thematic debates without adopting an overall discussion on postcolonialism as theory, there has been very little theoretical synergy between individual works. The tendency of Anglo-American academia to reward scholars for belonging to 'new' paradigms has not helped in this respect, because it caught many young scholars in a never-ending fashion circle of ever new paradigmatic turns, which splits postcolonial thought into various seemingly different camps of postcolonialism, decolonialism, colonial modernity, and so on. But what exactly is the theoretical difference, for example, between Duara's 'History', Yang's 'self-imposed Orientalism' and Zhang's 'Modernity'; what are the consequences of selecting one or the other of these terms and which might be best suitable for China Studies; do case studies show any need to revise or elaborate these concepts? Such questions need to be raised in order to develop a postcolonial perspective on China – and this requires a theoretical discourse rather than a collection of singular great works on specific topics.

References

Ampuero, P. and Labarca, C. (2017) 'Chilean Business Orientalism: The Role of Non-State Actors in the Frame of Asymmetric Bilateral Relations', *International Journal of Social, Behavioral, Educational, Economic, Business and Industrial Engineering*, vol. 11, no. 6, pp. 1217–1244.

Barlow, T. (1997a) 'Colonialism's Career in Postwar China Studies', in Barlow, T. E. (ed) *Formations of Colonial Modernity in East Asia*, Durham, Duke University Press, pp. 373–411.

Barlow, T. (1997b) 'Introduction: On 'Colonial Modernity'', in Barlow, T. E. (ed) *Formations of Colonial Modernity in East Asia*, Durham, Duke University Press, pp. 1–20.

Bhabha, H. (2012) 'By Bread Alone: Signs of Violence in the Mid-Nineteenth Century', in Bhabha, H. (ed) *The Location of Culture*, 2nd edn, Hoboken, Taylor and Francis, pp. 282–302.

Blaut, J. (1993) *The Colonizer's Model of the World: Geographical Diffusionism and Eurocentric History*, New York, Guilford Press.

Callahan, W. (2004) 'National Insecurities: Humiliation, Salvation, and Chinese Nationalism', *Alternatives*, vol. 29, pp. 199–218.

Callahan, W. (2006) 'History, Identity, and Security: Producing and Consuming Nationalism in China', *Critical Asian Studies*, vol. 38, no. 2, pp. 179–208.

Cao, S. and Li, S. 曹顺庆，李思屈 (1996) '重建中国文论话语的基本路径及其方法' (Reconstruction of the basic ways and methods of Chinese literary theory), 文艺研究 *(Literature & Art Studies)* 2(13): 12–21.

Césaire, A. (1972) *Discourse on Colonialism*, 14th edn, New York, NY, Monthly Review Press.

Chakrabarty, D. (2000) *Provincializing Europe: Postcolonial Thought and Historical Difference*, Princeton, Princeton University Press.

Chen, X. (1995) *Occidentalism: A Theory of Counter-Discourse in Post-Mao China*, Oxford, New York, Oxford Univ. Press.

Chun, A. (2019) '(Post)Colonial Governance in Hong Kong and Macau: A Tale of Two Cities and Regimes', *Postcolonial Studies*, vol. 22, no. 4, pp. 413–427.

Cohen, P. (1984) *Discovering History in China: American Historical Writing on the Recent Chinese Past*, New York, Columbia Univ.Pr.

Crossley, P., Siu, H. and Sutton, D. (2006) 'Introduction', in Crossley, P., Siu, H. and Sutton, D. (eds) *Empire at the Margins: Culture, Ethnicity, and Frontier in Early Modern China*, Berkeley, University of California Press, pp. 1–24.

Dirlik, A. (1995) 'Confucius in the Borderlands: Global Capitalism and the Reinvention of Confucianism', *Boundary 2*, vol. 22, no. 3, pp. 229–273.

Dirlik, A. (1996) 'Chinese History and the Question of Orientalism', *History and Theory*, vol. 35, no. 4, pp. 96–118.

Duara, P. (1995) *Rescuing History from the Nation: Questioning Narratives of Modern China*, Chicago, University of Chicago Press.

Escobar, A. (1995) *Encountering Development: The Making and Unmaking of the Third World*, Princeton, NJ, Princeton University Press.

Fanon, F. (2017) *The Wretched of the Earth*, New York: Grove.

Feng Jicai 冯骥才 (2000) '鲁迅的功与过' (Luxun´s merits and faults), 收获 *(Harvest)* 1(2): 123–126.

Goodman, B. and Goodman, D., eds. (2012) *Twentieth Century Colonialism and China: Localities, the Everyday, and the World*, London: Taylor and Francis.

Gu, M. (2013) *Sinologism: An Alternative to Orientalism and Postcolonialism*, London, New York, Routledge.

He, Q. (2010) 'Progress Theory: The Constraints on China's Cultural Renaissance', in Cao, T. Y., Zhong, X. and Liao, K. (eds) *Culture and Social Transformations in Reform Era China*, Leiden, Boston, Brill, pp. 285–295.

He, Y. 贺玉高 (2016) '国民性论争与当代知识界的二元对立思维' (Debates on national character and the binary oppositional thinking in contemporay intellectual world), 文艺理论研究 *(Studies in Literature & Arts Theory)* 36(6): 37–45.

Hevia, J. (1997) 'Leaving a Brand of China: Missionary Discourse in the Wake of the Boxer Movement', in Barlow, T. E. (ed) *Formations of Colonial Modernity in East Asia*, Durham, Duke University Press, pp. 113–140.

Huang, H. (2017) 'National Humiliation Discourse, Historical Memories and Acculturation: An Autoethnographic Study', *Journal of Multicultural Discourses*, vol. 12, no. 2, pp. 120–133.

Kluge, R. (2019) 'Orientalism and Current Chinese Studies', *Mapping China Journal*, no. 3, pp. 26–38.

Lai, Aerin (2020) 'The Hypervisibility of Chinese Bodies in Times of Covid-19 and what it says about being british', *Discover Society*, at: https://discoversociety.org/2020/04/12/the-hypervisibility-of-chinese-bodies-in-times-of-covid-19-and-what-it-says-about-being-british/.

Lan, S. (2016) 'The Shifting Meanings of Race in China: A Case Study of the African Diaspora Communities in Guangzhou', *City & Society*, vol. 28, no. 3, pp. 298–318.

Liu, L. (1997) 'Translingual Practice: The Discourse of Individualism between China and the West', in Barlow, T. (ed) *Formations of colonial modernity in East Asia*, Durham, Duke University Press, pp. 83–112.

Meinhof, M. (2017) 'Colonial Temporality and Chinese National Modernization Discourses', *Interdisciplines*, vol. 8, no. 1, pp. 51–80.

Meinhof, M. (2018) 'Contesting Chinese Modernity? Postcoloniality and Discourses on Modernisation at a Chinese University Campus', *Postcolonial Studies*, vol. 21, no. 4, pp. 464–481.

Meinhof, M. (2020) 'Othering the Virus', *Discover Society*, at: https://discoversociety.org/2020/03/21/othering-the-virus/.

Meinhof, M., Yan, J. and Zhu, L. (2017) 'Postcolonialism and China—Some Introductory Remarks', *Interdisciplines*, vol. 8, no. 1, pp. 1–25.

Mühlhahn, K. (2000) *Herrschaft und Widerstand in der 'Musterkolonie' Kiautschou: Interaktionen zwischen China und Deutschland, 1897–1914*, München, De Gruyter Oldenbourg.

Mühlhahn, K. (2019) *Making China Modern: From the Great Qing to Xi Jinping*, Cambridge, Harvard University Press.

Osterhammel, J. (1986) 'Semi-Colonialism and Informal Empire in Twentieth-Century China: Towards a Framework of Analysis', in Mommsen, W. J. (ed) *Imperialism and after: Continuities and Discontinuities*, London, Allen & Unwin, pp. 290–314.

Osterhammel, J. (2018) *Unfabling the East: The Enlightenment's Encounter with Asia*, Princeton, Oxford, Princeton University Press.

Perdue, P. (2009) 'China and Other Colonial Empires', *The Journal of American-East Asian Relations*, vol. 16, no. ½, pp. 85–103.

Quijano, A. (2008) 'Coloniality of Power, Eurocentrism, and Latin America', in Moraña, M., Dussel, E. and Jáuregui, C. (eds) *Coloniality at Large: Latin America and the Postcolonial Debate*, Durham, Duke University Press, pp. 181–224.

Randeria, S. (2002) 'Entangled Histories of Uneven Modernities: Civil Society, Caste Solidarities and Legal Pluralism in Post-Colonial India', in Elkana, Y., Krastev, I., Macamo, E. and Randeria, S. (eds) *Unraveling ties: From Social Cohesion to New Practices of Connectedness*, Frankfurt am Main, Campus, pp. 284–311.

Roche, G. (2019) 'Articulating Language Oppression: Colonialism, Coloniality and the Erasure of Tibet's Minority Languages', *Patterns of Prejudice*, vol. 53, no. 5, pp. 487–514.

Roche, G. (2020) 'The Epidemiology of Sinophobia', *Made in China Journal*, at: https://madeinchinajournal.com/2020/02/17/the-epidemiology-of-sinophobia/.

Ruskola, T. (2008) 'Colonialism Without Colonies: On the Extraterritorial Jurisprudence of the US Court for China', *Law and Contemporary Problems*, vol. 71, no. 3, pp. 217–242.

Ruskola, T. (2013) *Legal Orientalism: China, the United States, and Modern Law*, Cambridge, Harvard University Press.

Said, E. (1978) *Orientalism*, New York, Pantheon.

Schein, L. (1997) 'Gender and Internal Orientalism in China', *Modern China*, vol. 23, no. 1, pp. 69–98.

Schwartz, B. (1980) 'Presidential Address: Area Studies as a Critical Discipline', *The Journal of Asian Studies*, vol. 40, no. 1, pp. 15–25.

Seth, S. (2009) 'Historical Sociology and Postcolonial Theory: Two Strategies for Challenging Eurocentrism', *International Political Sociology*, vol. 3, no. 3, pp. 334–338.

Sheng, A. (2007) 'Traveling Theory, or, Transforming Theory: Metamorphosis of Postcolonialism in China', *Neohelicon*, vol. 34, no. 2, pp. 115–136.

Shih, S. (2001) *The Lure of the Modern: Writing Modernism in Semicolonial China, 1917–1937*, Berkeley, University of California Press.

Spivak, G. (1988) 'Can The Subaltern Speak?', in Nelson, C. and Grossberg, L. (eds) *Marxism and the Interpretation of Culture*, Chicago, University of Illinois Press, pp. 66–111.

Steinmetz, G. (2007) *The Devil's Handwriting: Precoloniality and the German Colonial State in Qingdao, Samoa, and Southwest Africa*, Chicago, University of Chicago Press.

Villard, F. (2019) 'Civilising Mission, Transcultural Flows and National Subjectivity: Reading the Historical Experience of the Institut franco-chinois de Lyon (1921–1946) from a Postcolonial Perspective', *Postcolonial Studies*, vol. 22, no. 3, pp. 384–398.

Vukovich, D. (2012) *China and Orientalism: Western Knowledge Production and the P.R.C*, Milton Park Abingdon u.a, Routledge.

Vukovich, D. (2019) *Illiberal China*, Singapore, Springer Singapore.

Wang, H. (1997) 'The Fate of 'Mr. Science' in China: The Concept of Science and Its Application in Modern Chinese Thought', in Barlow, T. E. (ed) *Formations of Colonial Modernity in East Asia*, Durham, Duke University Press, pp. 21–81.

Wang, H. (2010) 'The 'Tibet Issue' Between East and West', *Chinese Sociology & Anthropology*, vol. 42, no. 4, pp. 7–30.

Wang, M. (2014) *The West as the Other: A Genealogy of Chinese Occidentalism*, Hong Kong, Chinese University Press.

Wang, Z. (2012) *Never Forget National Humiliation: Historical Memory in Chinese Politics and Foreign Relations*, New York, Columbia University Press.

Wilcox, E. (2016) 'Beyond Internal Orientalism: Dance and Nationality Discourse in the Early People's Republic of China, 1949–1954', *The Journal of Asian Studies*, vol. 75, no. 2, pp. 363–386.

Xu, B. (1998) ''From Modernity to Chineseness': The Rise of Nativist Cultural Theory in Post-1989 China', *Positions*, vol. 6, no. 1, pp. 203–237.

Yan, J. (2017) 'Construction and Politicization of Waiqi White-Collar Identity: Traveling Knowledge about Chinese Professionals in Multinational Corporations in China', *Interdisciplines*, vol. 8, no. 1, pp. 81–111.

Yan, J. and Meinhof, M. (2018) 'The Other Chinese: Identity Work and Self-Orientalization of Chinese Host Country Nationals in Multinational Corporations', *Social Identities*, vol. 24, no. 5, pp. 666–683.

Yang, M. (2004) 'Spatial Struggles: Postcolonial Complex, State Disenchantment, and Popular Reappropriation of Space in Rural Southeast China', *The Journal of Asian Studies*, vol. 63, no. 3, pp. 719–755.

Yang, M. (2011) 'Postcoloniality and Religiosity in Modern China: The Disenchantments of Sovereignty', *Theory, Culture and Society*, vol. 28, no. 2, pp. 3–45.

Zhang, F., Zhang, Y. and Wang, Y.张发, 张颐武, 王一川 (1994) '从'现代性'到'中华性'—新知识型的探寻' (From 'modernity' to 'Chineseness'—A new knowledge-based exploration), 文艺争鸣 *(Literary and artistic contention)* 9(2): 10–20.

Zhang, K. 张宽 (1993) '欧美人眼中的非我族类' (The other in the eyes of euro-americans), 读书 *(Dushu)* 21(9): 3–9.

Zhang, K. (2009) 'The Dilemma of Postcolonial Criticism in Contemporary China', *ARIEL: A Review of International Englisch Literature*, vol. 40, no. 1, pp. 143–159.

Zhang, L. (1999) 'Debating 'Chinese Postmoderism'', *Postcolonial Studies*, vol. 2, no. 2, pp. 185–198.

Zhang, Y. 张颐武 (1994a) '后新时期文化: 挑战与机遇'(Post-New Culture: challenge and opportunity), 战略与管理 *(Strategy and Management)* 2(1): 112–114.

Zhang, Y. 张颐武 (1994b) '现代性的终结: 一个无法回避的课题' (The termination of modernity: an unavoidable issue), 战略与管理 *(Strategy and Management)* 2(3): 104–109.

Zhu, L. (2017) 'From 'The Art of War' to 'The Force of War'. Colonialism and the Chinese Perception of War in Transition', *Interdisciplines*, vol. 8, no. 1, pp. 27–50.

Zhu, L. (2019) 'Manchu-Han Relations in Qing China: Reconsidering the Concept of Continental Colonialism in Chinese History', in Schorkowitz, D., Chavez, J. and Schroeder, I. (eds) *Shifting forms of Continental Colonialism: Between Empire and Nation*, Singapore, Palgrave Macmillan, pp. 175–195.

Zhu, Q. 竹潜民 (2002) '评冯骥才的鲁迅的功和'过''(Comments on Feng Jicai´s Luxun`s merits and faults), 浙江师范大学学报 *(Journal of Zhejiang Normal University)* 27(3): 11–13.

40

Science in China

Key problems, topics, and methodologies

Florin-Stefan Morar

Introduction

For much of the 20th century, science has been understood as a Western development. Historians have tried to explain the origins of such things as mathematization of nature, experimentation, and science-based technological developments by highlighting unique cultural aspects of Western civilization and history. This view has come into doubt as historians have begun to seriously investigate other areas of the world. China especially has demonstrated a long history of developments in the making of knowledge in technology and medicine that were analogous to those in the West and that can be reliably identified as scientific. The history of science in China is an attempt to interpret these developments.

Crucial in the discipline is the work of Joseph Needham (1900–1995), who was the first to discuss Chinese scientific achievements and compare them to the Western ones (Needham et al. 1954). Needham validated knowledge-making in China as scientific but did not see it as equivalent to 'modern' science as was developed in early modern Europe. He was therefore preoccupied in investigating a negative question: why was China on the cusp of the 'scientific revolution', but did not ultimately realize it? Needham's work remains valuable for its contribution in identifying what can be understood as 'scientific' in China's past. Yet newer approaches have widely rejected Needham's arguments, producing new understandings.

This chapter aims to chart the evolution of the history of science, and by extension of the history of technology and medicine in China. I first discuss the work of Joseph Needham, then explore how newer approaches have recast our understanding of knowledge-making in premodern, modern, and contemporary China.

Science and civilization in China

Joseph Needham was a biochemist trained at Cambridge University. He enjoyed all the honors that the British academic system can bestow upon one of its members: he was elected fellow of the Royal Society in 1941, fellow of the British Academy in 1971, and finally was conferred a Companionship of Honour by the Queen in 1992. Though having made contributions in the fields of embryology and morphogenesis, Needham best became

DOI: 10.4324/9780429059704-47

known for the multivolume work entitled *Science and Civilization in China* (Spence 2008; Winchester 2008). Needham first came to develop an interest in the problem of China's scientific development after meeting three Chinese scientists, Lu Guizhen Wang Yinglai, and Shen Shizhang, who had come to Cambridge for graduate studies. According to Needham, the three asked him the question, 'why had modern science originated in Europe and not in China' (Cohen 1994; Holorenshaw 1973). Needham then embarked on a long intellectual journey trying to answer this question, learning Chinese together with Lu, with whom he enjoyed a very close relationship, and visiting China between 1942 and 1946. Needham ultimately came to develop what is now called 'the Needham question' with the publication of the Grand Titration in 1969. Here, Needham wrote the following: 'why does modern science, the mathematization of hypotheses about Nature, with all its implications for advanced technology, take its meteoric rise only in the West at the time of Galileo? Why was it that between the second century BC and the sixteenth century AD East Asian culture was much more efficient than the European West in applying human knowledge to useful purposes?' (Needham 1969: 16).

How to evaluate Needham's arguments? First, it would be essential to note, that as much as 'the Needham question' has become a common expression in writing about science in China, the question was a Chinese question even before it became Needham's. The three Chinese students who provided Needham the impetus to embark on his intellectual journey were reflecting concerns about the state of Chinese science that were common among Chinese intellectuals at the end of the Qing dynasty and into the Republican period. Major thinkers such as Hu Shi, Chen Duxiu, Feng Youlan, and others had made such statements and uttered similar questions to that of Needham's. Moreover, the nature of Chinese science had been at the center of the 1923 'Debate on science and the philosophy of life' (科學與人生觀), triggered by the translation of social Darwinist Herber Spencer. Similar arguments to that of Needham's about the limitations of Chinese scientific endeavors in imperial times had been thrown around in this debate. Secondly, Needham's question and its popularity would have been impossible without the interest that the 'scientific revolution' of early modern Europe had sparked among historians of science in the middle of the 20th century. Historians and sociologists such as Alexandre Koyré, Herbert Butterfield, and Robert Merton identified the 16th and 17th centuries and such larger-than-life figures as Bacon, Galileo, Newton, and Leibniz as the starting point (Shapin 1998). Needham was very much interested in these contributions and even tried to participate by writing under the pseudonym Henry Holorenshaw a book on the Levellers (a religious and political movement during the English Civil War of 1642–1651, emphasizing equality) and their role in fostering a scientific mindset (Holorenshaw 1939: 19). Although providing an immense amount of details about Chinese scientific developments, the effect of Needham's work is to emphasize the special nature of Europe in having developed since the Renaissance the mathematized and experimental kind of knowledge-making at the root of modern science.

Regardless of its Euro-centrist implications, Needham's work did have an important impact on 20th-century Chinese intellectuals and policymakers. The theoretical physicist Qian Wenyuan who emigrated to the United States in 1984, published soon after his arrival *The Great Inertia: Scientific stagnation in traditional China* (Qian 1985). Qian both critiqued and echoed Needham's arguments, taking them even further. Using a blunt vocabulary, Qian speaks about China 'lagging behind' and remaining 'inert' in terms of scientific development in ancient and premodern times. The unity of China ensured through state control, according to Qian, fostered an intolerance of intellectual and scientific advancement. Qian's arguments were no doubt aimed as much at 20th-century China as they were at China's past. However, the idea of the negative impact of the centralized, state-driven bureaucratic system on innovation in ancient China, has continued to circulate even among Chinese thinkers who remained in China. The economist Justin Yifu Lin, who served as China's first senior vice-president of the World Bank, used similar arguments to demonstrate why the industrial revolution did not originate in China (Lin 1995). In the contemporary political discourse moreover, arguments about why China didn't develop science, technology, and medicine in the past, are used to argue for the importance of fostering them in the present. Even the Chinese leaders made such remarks in their speeches.

The Needham question, in spite of its widespread influence, has fared less well in the international community of historians of science. Nathan Sivin was the first prominent critic of Needham in this community. Sivin argued that to ask why the scientific revolution did not take place in China is 'analogous to the question of why your name did not appear on page 3 of today's newspapers' (Sivin 1985: 42). More recently, Kapil Raj has done much to demonstrate the inherent Eurocentrism of the center-periphery model underlying questions such as Needham's (Raj 2013, 2010). One could also show, in light of the more recent literature on early modern science, the problematic assumptions about the scientific revolution with which Needham worked. Alexandre Koyré has shown that modern science did not spring up during the early modern period as Athena did from the head of Zeus, fully clothed and with shield and spear at the ready (Koyré 1968). A more likely perspective is that it took time for modern science to institutionalize and by the time it did, it did so everywhere in the world not just in Europe. As Marwa Elshakry proposed recently, science *became* Western. That is, in the 19th century there were efforts to make science appear as having had unique European origins (Elshakry 2010).

Ancient and premodern knowledge-making in China

The critique of the work of Joseph Needham has been an important starting point for a number of alternative approaches to science in ancient and premodern China. The work of Benjamin Elman is the most methodologically robust and well-articulated. Elman built on both traditions in Chinese historiography and the social studies of science approach inspired by social constructivism. Building on this methodology Elman wrote two sweeping books on science in China: *On Their Own Terms: Science in China, 1550–1900* and *A Cultural History of Modern Science in China* (Elman 2005, 2006). Elman focuses here mostly on the early modern period and deploys language abilities in both Chinese and Western languages to reconstruct the history of modern science in China from the Chinese perspective.

The work of Dagmar Schaefer is equally important for the current state of the field. Schaefer applied to early modern China the methodological insights gained from work on artisans and craftsmen in early modern Europe (Zilsel 2000). Schaefer used these insights and sought to apply them to late Ming China. In *Crafting the 10000 Things*, a dense and detailed study using a rich variety of historical sources, Schaefer focuses on the figure of Song Yingxing (1587–1666) to reconstruct the dynamics between scholars and artisans at the end of the Ming dynasty (Dagmar Schäfer 2011).

Although much of the attention in recent decades have been on Late Imperial China, work on ancient China has also progressed beyond Needham's surveys in *Science and Civilization*. Important to note here is the work of Christopher Cullen, who succeeded Needham in leading the Science and Civilization project. Cullen gave an important critical edition and translation of the *Zhoubi Suan Jing* (周髀算經), the classic of the gnomon of Zhou, containing a mathematical demonstration parallel, although not similar to Pythagoras' theorem (Cullen 1996, 2017a, 2017b). Equally relevant for the understanding of the Chinese calendar before the arrival of the Jesuits is the work of Jean-Claude Martzloff, who has written extensively on the history of Chinese mathematics (Martzloff 1997, 1981).

Much new work has been done in the area of medicine in recent decades as well. Shigehisa Kuriyama has produced an innovative book on ancient Chinese medicine and the body (Kuriyama 1999). The book contains a comparison between ancient Chinese and Western medicine, pointing out the divergence of the practices and cultural experiences of what is essentially the same human body. More recently, there has been a focus on other aspects of Chinese medicine such as the *materia medica* and pharmacology. In the creatively written *The Monkey and the Inkpot,* Carla Nappi examined the *Bencaogangmu* (本草綱目) of Li Shizhen (1518–1593), the late Ming *materia medica* that systematized and classed plants and things according to their healing properties and medical value (Nappi 2009). Federico Marcon has looked at how the materia medica was translated and transculturated in Japan and its influence on the development of the Japanese science of Nature, up to the Meiji period (Marcon 2015). Marta Hanson produced a novel study of epidemic diseases in early modern China. Hanson examined an essential change in Chinese medicine in the Ming dynasty, by which the category of warm diseases *wen bing* (溫病) appeared as a way of describing contagious diseases in Southern China (Marta Hanson 2012).

Since the reform and opening era of the 1980s, Chinese scholars have been increasingly active in examining the history of science in China. So have a number of scholars in Hong Kong and Taiwan who were trained at American or European Institutions. In mainland China, much important work has been done at the Institute for the History of Natural Sciences, under the Chinese Academy of Social Sciences. Their research is disseminated primarily in the journal *Studies in the History of Natural Sciences* (自然科学史研究). The work of some of the researchers affiliated with the Institute for the History of Natural Sciences has recently also been translated into English in two volumes collecting lectures given at the Institute (Lu 2015). In Taiwan, new research on the history of science has been conducted at the Academia Sinica. Chu Ping-Yi in particular has been active in this field, writing on astronomy and medicine (Chu 1994, 1997, 1999). In Hong Kong the work of Angela Leung is particularly prominent. Leung's monograph on leprosy in China examines the complex cultural and medical dimensions of this disease from imperial times to the establishment of a regime of hygiene in the late 19th century (Bray, Nakayama, & Leung 2018; Leung 2009).

In the last three decades, scholars working on the history of science in China have explored new approaches and new topics than those present in the work of Joseph Needham. The discipline has aligned more closely with work in other areas of the history of science and reflected developments taken from the social studies of science. A more detailed and more finely grained picture of Chinese science emerged as a result.

The Jesuits and the Sino-Western knowledge exchanges in the early modern period

In the 16th century, Europeans increased their interactions with China. In 1557 the Portuguese were permitted to settle on a small strip of land on the coast of Canton province, which they called Macao. They were followed by the Spanish, who colonized the Philippines in 1565. Then, in 1624, the Dutch established themselves on the island of Taiwan. In this context, Christian missionaries approached China and repeatedly try to move inland with the goal of converting the country to Christianity. Among them, the Company of Jesus played an outsized role due to their deep connections with the Iberian empires (Brockey 2007; Standaert 2001). In 1582 the Jesuits Matteo Ricci and Michele Ruggieri arrived on Macao and after two years of language learning, managed to enter and obtain permission to settle in Guangdong province. Of these two, Matteo Ricci became the most prominent and prolific, having formed deep bonds with Chinese literati and having settled in Beijing (Ricci 1985). Science and technology were significant in Ricci's and later other Jesuits' missionary activities. (Feingold 2003) (Baldini n.d.; Baldini & Casanovas 1996).

As Ricci made inroads into China, reaching Beijing in 1601, he formulated for the mission a strategy of accommodation to Chinese culture. (Standaert 2001, 2002). Ever since the first days in the Canton province, Ricci noticed that Chinese literati were intrigued by things like European clocks and maps. Cartography especially proved to be an enduring magnet of literati attention. Pasquale D'Elia was the first to note the importance of cartography for the Jesuit mission, outlining with precision the chronology of various world maps that Ricci created and producing an important critical edition for Ricci's spectacular world map *Kunyuwanguo quantu* (坤輿萬國全圖) which he made in collaboration with the scholar Li Zhizao (D'Elia 1961; Ricci 1938). There were numerous editions of this map, all influential. Some were copied by palace artisans for the private viewing of the Wanli emperor and, as new research has shown, one version of the map with the title *Liangyi xuanlan tu* (兩儀玄覽圖) was obtained by the Manchus, was displayed in the Shenyang palace and was partially translated into Manchu, a testament of the early interest of the Qing rulers in European technology (Morar 2018). After Ricci, other Jesuits continued to produce world maps with important editions by Giulio Aleni, Ferdinand Verbiest, and Michele Benoit (Heirman, Troia, & Parmentier 2009; Luk 1977; Menegon 1994; Walravens 1991). As Mario Cams has recently shown, after the Manchu conquest of China, Jesuits embarked on a large-scale mapping of China using surveying techniques but also relying on local gazetteers and local knowledge, which resulted in the production of a map of unprecedented precision printed at the court as the *Huangyu quanlan tu* (皇輿全覽圖) (Cams 2017; Hostetler 2001).

Astronomy and mathematics also played an important role in the Sino-Western knowledge exchanges. The Chinese emperor had a duty to ensure the maintenance of an accurate calendar for which purpose he employed astronomers at court. The Jesuits arrived in China at a moment of crisis, when the errors in calculating the lunar calendar had accumulated and a readjustment of the lunar and solar years was necessary as the prediction of eclipses was of key interest for astrology and omens of imperial vigor had become inaccurate. Ricci could take advantage of this moment and started working together with his Chinese collaborators Xu Guangqi and Li Zhizao toward rectifying the calendar (Hashimoto 1988).

The transmission of European astronomy to China and the peculiar position the Jesuits found themselves in after the trial of Galileo has not been yet described in a full-length monograph. However, important studies by a number of scholars have extracted the crucial details of this episode (Chu 1994; Elman 2005; Hashimoto 1988; Jami 1999; Sivin 1981). The Jesuits translated into Chinese parts from Galileo's work, which they undoubtedly admired. An example is the *Discourse on the Telescope Yuanjing shuo* (遠鏡說) translated by Bell. But they were careful to exclude any mention of cosmology from these translations. Copernicanism was only disclosed in China when it became politically opportune to do so. Michel Benoit was the first to include a diagram of the heliocentric solar system on his world map *Kunyu quantu* (坤輿全圖) made in 1760 for the Qianlong emperor and the in *Diqiu tushuo* (地球圖說), which was published as a book to be disseminated among the literati (Hashimoto 1988: 1–4, 75–81; Sivin 1995: 14–16).

More recent scholarship has focused on other aspects of the Jesuit enterprise in China. Florence C. Hsia has described Jesuit conceptions of science and the icon of the missionary-scientist based on Jesuit hagiography and historiographical writing (Hsia 2009). Catherine Jami, in a masterful book, *The Emperor's new mathematics*, focused on the French Jesuit Mathematicians during the Qing at the Kangxi court (Jami 2012). Dominic Sachsenmeyer, in the *Global Entanglements of a Man Who Never Traveled*, examined one of the converts of the Jesuits in Zhejiang and explored the important Chinese reception of Jesuit ideas (Sachsenmaier 2018). Scholars from mainland China, Hong Kong, and Taiwan have also weighed in on the China Jesuits. The academician Han Qi has produced a number of articles on the Jesuit scientific activities in China such as the correspondences between Joachim Bouvet and Leibniz, mathematics at the Kangxi court or European astrology in late Ming China (2019).

The Jesuits were not only responsible for translating European ways of knowledge-making to China. They have also done the reverse, translating Chinese knowledge for the European public and also importing Chinese books and material artifacts. The figure of Athanasius Kircher is particularly important here and has been recently examined in the work of Paula Findlen (Findlen 2004). Kircher used many of the materials brought over or sent by China Jesuits and popularized them in his *China Illustrata* from 1667. In the European Enlightenment it would serve as one of the sources for the depiction of China as a secular monarchic state governed by reason. Translations of the Confucian classics, the Four Books also contributed toward bolstering this image as has been shown by Thierry Meynard (Meynard, Ruggieri (S.I.), & Villasante 2018). More recently, Alexander Statman has reworked some of the materials related to China's influence on the European Enlightenment (Statman 2016, 2019). We are also beginning to know more about the second half of the Jesuit mission in China, especially the Qianlong period. (Menegon 2019).

Much of the previous literature on the Jesuits in China has focused on countering Jesuit hagiographic history and to examine more skeptically their claims of success (Gernet 1985). Jesuits have had nevertheless an impact throughout their presence, leaving important hybrid Sino-Western artifacts and elements of architecture in the Forbidden City and elsewhere. Chinese scholars have taken over and discussed many of the new ideas brought over by the Jesuits, although no doubt Christianity especially has also found rejection and enmity among them. To what extent the Jesuits have influenced China is still a matter of debate. But the Jesuits constantly brought to the court new information and knowledge of the wider world. The absence of the Jesuits at the Qing court after 1773 and left an important gap in the empire's ability to learn about Europe's developments as Europeans were increasingly dominating world affairs and were experiencing the industrial revolution.

Science and modernization during the Late Qing dynasty and the Republic of China

The shocking outcome of the Opium Wars (1839–1860) was the immediate cause of the impetus for modernization in the late Qing dynasty. The scholarship has tended to look at the role played in scientific modernization by vast projects of translating science, technology and medicine, creating new institutions, sending students abroad and an effort at industrialization with the goal of producing military technologies such as battleships and cannon. While the Qing dynasty, which ended in 1912, and the succeeding Republican period are usually treated separately in the historiography, there is reason to consider them together for the purpose of the history of science as many of the late Qing developments continued in the Republican period.

Lin Zexu, who was appointed by the Daoguang emperor as imperial commissioner to resolve the opium smuggling crisis from 1839 and to fight against the British, was the first to initiate a project of translation of a variety of books produced in 'Western countries' (Chen 2017). The result of Lin's translation activities, which were initially kept secret to the court, were partly imported in the *Gazeteer of Maritime Kingdoms* by Wei Yuan (Barnett 1970; Wei 1880). This work compiled information on the West extracted from a variety of sources including, to an important degree, Jesuit translations of scientific works published earlier in the dynasty. Wei's work was crucial in having laid out a vision for the modernization of the dynasty which was influential not only in China (arguably even for today's China) but also Japan (Leonard 1984; Mosca 2013).

Translation is key to understanding science history in the late Qing. The Protestant missionaries filled the gap left by the Jesuits. Robert Morisson, associated with the London Missionary Society, was an important figure in this respect (Elman 2005). Morrison was deeply engaged in supporting a number of translation projects and had gathered an important library of Chinese works and Jesuit translations to facilitate the linguistic effort at coining new scientific terms in Chinese. Other Protestant missionaries, such as John Fryer, Benjamin Hobson, Joseph Edkins, and John Fryer were deeply involved in the project of scientific translation (Wright 1998; Zhang 2007).

A number of collaborators of the protestants became crucial for various efforts to build military technology in the newly founded government arsenals. The Jiangnan arsenal became a place of active scientific exploration and technological experimentation with the contributions of such figures as Li Shanlan, Hua Hengfeng, Zhao Yuanyi, He Liaoran, and Xu Shou. In the context of the arsenals, the development of the discipline of chemistry has received more scholarly attention with two monographs by Reardon Anderson and David Wright focusing on different aspects (Reardon-Anderson 1991; Wright 2000). Translation was equally important in the field of medicine with the pioneering translations by Benjamin Hobson of 19th-century treatises of anatomy, physiology and women's medicine. The reception of anatomy is particularly fascinating (Andrews 1994, 2014). Consequential for both science and the public intellectual sphere were the translations of Darwin and Spencer. Yan Fu is in this respect the most important figure. Before Yan Fu's translations, Darwin's theory of evolution has been excluded from translation by Protestant missionaries, a move not unlike that of the Jesuits who excluded discussions of Copernicus in Chinese. In the environment created by the defeat of in the Sino-Japanese war of 1895, the popularity of this translation soared, and its ideas were used to explain China's plight (Qi 2012; Schwartz 1983). In intellectual circles, science and technology became a solution toward restoring China's status in the world. The intellectual atmosphere before the end of the dynasty in 1912 was therefore marked by a pronounced scientism where Mr. Science (賽先生) along with Mr. Democracy (德先生) were seen as saviors (Kwok 1971; Wang 2002).

The role of science in Chinese society was debated in the so-called 'controversy about science and philosophy of life'. The debate was started with Liang Qichao's visit to Europe during the aftermath of World War II. Liang in conversation with European intellectuals and existentialist philosophers became aware of the dark side of Mr. Science in its ability to produce mass death and widespread destruction. Ultimately, the advocates of science gained the upper hand, but the debate had raised the important issues of Chinese identity in modernization, even as what was being perceived as 'Western' science was being adopted in China.

A number of other topics have been considered in the scholarship in relation to the history of science in the late Qing and the Republican period. The migration of students is one example. In the wake of the Boxer Rebellion, the Boxer indemnity funds were used to send Chinese students to US institutions. Hu Shi was among them, studying at Cornell and Columbia. (La Fargue 1987). Another such intersection is found in the establishment of foreign research institutions and hospitals in China (Fan 2014; Bullock 1980). The impact of scientific debate on Chinese popular culture in the Republican period and after has been explored in the work of Schmaltzer *The People's Peking man* (Schmalzer 2009). There was a complex picture of science in the second half of the Republican period with the Japanese occupation of Manchuria and the creation of colonial institutions there, the foreign concessions in Shanghai and on the China coast and Hong Kong (Rogaski 2014).

The late Qing and Republican periods were crucial to establishing modern science in China. Numerous scientific treatises and books were translated by Protestant missionaries in collaboration with Chinese translators and increasingly by bilingual Chinese as well. New institutions were formed and Chinese students began studying abroad and, once returned to China played an active role in scientific development. By the end of the Republican period, the groundwork has been laid for a Chinese system of science, technology, and medicine.

Science, technology, and medicine in the People's Republic

In a recently published article, the historian of science Fa-Ti Fan wrote that there are more Chinese restaurants around an average American university campus than books about the history of science in 20th-century China in its libraries (Fan 2007). This is a reality that is not likely to change soon and it is all the more true with regard to the PRC period. The study of the history of science in China in the PRS is marred by a number of problems: low availability of trained researchers, inadequate access to historical sources and materials, and political pitfalls in an increasingly combative relationship between China and the United States. Nevertheless, some critical research has been done in recent years both by Chinese and Western scholars.

The destiny of the scientific institutions in the PRC at the moment of its founding were closely tied to those of the Republican period. In a context of emergent nationalism, many scientists and engineers chose to stay behind and support the regime. Lines of continuity can also be traced at the scientific language and terminology level, which had already been established through translation. But overall the entire system underwent drastic restructuring to conform it to the Soviet model (Fan 2007).

In the decade following the establishment of the PRC, in 1949, the alliance with the Soviet Union led to the influx of Russian textbooks in science and engineering as well as Russian experts working in advisory roles (Zhang 2004). A number of Chinese engineers and scientists were also trained in Russian universities and institutes. Upon their return to China, they mingled with colleagues who had been trained at American and European institutions before the war, which gave Chinese science a strangely cosmopolitan flavor. Many Western-educated scientists such as Zhu Kezhen, Li Siguang, and Tao Menghe continued in the newly restructured Chinese Academy of Science in leadership roles (Mullaney 2010).

In the early years of the PRC, scientists, regardless of their background, enjoyed a level of political shielding and protection. This can be seen in the Chinese debate about Lysenkoism (Schneider 2003). Starting from 1957 with the Great Leap Forward, and even more so during the Cultural Revolution, many prominent scientists faced persecution, public shaming, and intense psychological pressure. Some died as a result (Chang 1969). Even under the dire conditions of the antirightist campaigns, Mao Zedong still protected those scientists crucial for national defense projects. One significant achievement was the development of the nuclear bomb (Lewis 1988). While rocketry and the nuclear weapons programs were arguably successful, other areas of science fared less well during the Maoist period. There were a number of questionable practices such as surgery with acupuncture induced anesthesia, mass ultrasound, backyard smelters, and disastrous agricultural techniques. On the other hand, scholarship has shown that some of these pushes for mass science had benefits (Wen 1975). One repercussion of the push for mass science was a suspicion of academic discourse and high-flying science. As Danian Hu has shown, this resulted in a rejection of Einstein's theory of relativity at the height of the Cultural Revolution (Hu 2005).

At the end of the Maoist period, one important and consequential topic was population control. Susan Greenhalgh has shown that this was a consequence of the increasingly transnational connection of Chinese scientists (Greenhalgh 2008). Chinese scientists took seriously the overly alarmist Club of Rome report from 1972 and, as Greenhalgh shows, a Chinese expert on missile control formulated a statistical model of population, which led to the one-child policy. An important area of research that is still poorly understood is the impact of migration and transnational networks on the development of science in the second half of the 20th century. Chinese émigré scientists played a key role in the history of both the United States and China. Nobel Prize winners D.T. Lee and C.N. Yang made an impact both in the United States and in China (Wang 1999). There are hundreds, perhaps thousands of Chinese students in the sciences and engineering that supported projects in the United States and Europe. Many of these emigrated permanently, but some returned and were incorporated in a reformed system of research and education in the PRC. It is important to reflect also in this context on the important role played by Hong Kong and Taiwan. Taiwanese scientists were some of the first to obtain access to the US educational system. The steep rise of the semiconductor industry on the island is a consequence of this development. Later on, the development of the technology sector on the mainland was caused by Taiwanese investment. Apple's supplier Foxconn is only the most successful example (Aberbach, Dollar, & Sokoloff 1994).

Deng Xiaoping's China and the period of reform and opening have seen far fewer contributions. Historians of science and anthropologists are still grappling with the question of how to write about this period. Zuoyue Wang was the first to describe the reform-minded atmosphere in places such as the Chinese Academy of Science in the Deng era (Wang 2007). Many scientists found courage in this period to ask openly for reform, including political reform. On the transformation of China by rapid technological and industrial growth in the last 30 years there are only a handful of works. Economists, political scientists, and journalists mostly wrote these. The development of the high-speed rail network and the Chinese internet are topics that have attracted considerable attention (Doig 2018; Griffiths 2019; Roberts 2020)

Science and technology in the PRC had experienced stunning growth, especially since the beginning of the reform and opening era. By all accounts, today's China is a leading player in a number of fields. Chinese scientists are, at least for the time being, plugged into international networks, and communicate in English. Technological development has spurned a radical transformation of Chinese society, changing the way Chinese shop, pay, and travel, even while introducing new limitations on expression – the Great Firewall of China is an example. In a certain sense, today's China is experiencing the rule of Mr. Science, that the reformers of the beginning of the 20th century envisioned.

Open questions in the study of science in China

The importance of science and technology in China today highlights its general importance for Chinese history. Although, as shown in this chapter, much progress has been made in the research of Chinese science, there are a number of questions that have still not been resolved in the scholarship.

The study of science in premodern China has had the lion's share of the scholars' attention. But, after the rejection of the Needham question, scholars have focused on the narrow study of contexts. There are still, however, broader questions that have not been answered. How does premodern Chinese science compare to premodern science in other cultures and regions of the world? Some work, notably by Nathan Sivin and G.E.R. Lloyd, has been done comparing science in ancient Greece to that of China with interesting results, but India, Africa, and the Americas have not been taken into account (Lloyd & Sivin 2002). Naturally, comparison has its pitfalls, as shown by the Needham question, but applying comparison within a global approach to the question of premodern science might reveal the anthropological quality of scientific inquiry and its variance across human experiences in all parts of the world. Leaving comparison aside, connection is another important area of exploration. To what extent was science as practiced in premodern China a result of cross-cultural contact with India, Inner Asia, the Middle East, or even Europe? We still know little, although work on the Yuan dynasty by Hyunhee Park has revealed some of the extant connections (Park 2012).

Another question that has not been explored is the following: to what extent is there a continuity between science in premodern China and science in modern China? Currently modern science in China is widely understood as a Western import. Is it the case that Chinese knowledge traditions were completely cast aside? An important area to look at would be translation. Translation becomes possible in contexts that contain the means of expressing the new translated ideas, in an understandable form. Research might show that it was the rich and sophisticated premodern Chinese scientific traditions that enabled the translation of Western science and that those traditions were still carried forward in several ways in contemporary Chinese scientific language, even though hybridized with new ideas.

The topic of environmental history has taken off in recent years, replacing, for better or worse, some of the more fundamental approaches in historical studies. We still do not have a complete picture of environmental history in China. While contributions such as those of Ruth Rogaski, Shellen Wu, and Victor Seow have shed some light on choice topics of environmental history, there is much ground to cover (Seow 2014; Shapiro 2001; Wu 2015).

These are only a few of the most obvious open questions and problems in the study of science in China. The study of science is an important part of Chinese studies and as the role of science, technology, and medicine grows in Chinese society and culture, so must also this area of research.

References

Aberbach, J. D., Dollar, D., & Sokoloff, K. L. (1994) *The Role of the State in Taiwan's Development*, Armonk, NY: M.E. Sharpe.

Andrews, B. (1994) *Tailoring Tradition: The Impact of Modern Medicine in Traditional Chinese Medicine, 1887–1937*, Publisher not identified.

Andrews, B. (2014) *The Making of Modern Chinese Medicine, 1850–1960*, Vancouver: UBC Press.

Baldini, Ugo (n.d.) 'Matteo Ricci nel Collegio Romano (1572–1577): Cronologia, maestri, studi', *Archivum Historicum Societatis Iesu*, LXXXII (2013)(1), 115–164.

Baldini, U., & Casanovas, J. (1996) *La sfera celeste di Cristoforo Clavio. In Osservatorio astronomico di Capodimonte*, Almanacco.

Barnett, S. W. (1970) 'Wei Yüan and Westerners: Notes on the Sources of the Hai-Kuo T'u-Chih', *Ch'ing-Shih Wen-t'i*, 2(4), 1–20.

Bray, F., Nakayama, I., & Leung, A. K. C. (2018) *Gender, Health, and History in Modern East Asia*, Baltimore, Maryland: Project MUSE.

Brockey, L. M. (2007) *Journey to the East: The Jesuit mission to China, 1579–1724*, Cambridge, MA: Belknap Press of Harvard University Press.

Bullock, M. B. (1980) *An American Transplant: The Rockefeller Foundation and Peking Union Medical College*, Berkeley: University of California Press.

Cams, M. (2017) *Companions in Geography: East-West Collaboration in the Mapping of Qing China (c.1685–1735)*, London: Brill.

Chang, P. H. (1969) 'China's Scientists in the Cultural Revolution', *Bulletin of the Atomic Scientists*, 25(5), 19–40. https://doi.org/10.1080/00963402.1969.11455213

Chen, S. (2017) 'Translation and Ideology: A Study of Lin Zexu's Translation Activities', *Meta: Journal Des Traducteurs/Meta: Translators' Journal*, 62(2), 313–332. https://doi.org/10.7202/1041026ar.

Chu, P. (1997) 'Scientific Dispute in the Imperial Court: The 1664 Calendar Case', *Chinese Science*, 14, 7–34.

Chu, P. (1999) 'Trust, Instruments, and Cross-Cultural Scientific Exchanges: Chinese Debate over the Shape of the Earth, 1600–1800', *Science in Context*, 12(3), 385–412. https://doi.org/10.1017/S0269889700003501.

Chu, P.-Yi. (1994) *Technical Knowledge, Cultural Practices and Social Boundaries: Wan-Nan Scholars and the Recasting of Jesuit Astronomy, 1600–1800*, Ph.D. Thesis, University of California Los Angeles.

Cohen, H. F. (1994) *The Scientific Revolution: A Historiographical Inquiry*, Chicago: University of Chicago Press.

Cullen, C. (1996) *Astronomy and mathematics in ancient China: the Zhou bi suan jing*, Cambridge, UK: Cambridge University Press.

Cullen, C. (2017a) *Heavenly Numbers: Astronomy and Authority in Early Imperial China* (1st ed), Oxford: Oxford University Press.

Cullen, C. (2017b) *The Foundations of Celestial Reckoning: Three Ancient Chinese Astronomical Systems*, New York: Routledge.

Dagmar Schäfer (2011) *The Crafting of the 10,000 Things: Knowledge and Technology in Seventeenth-Century China*, University of Chicago Press. http://portal.igpublish.com/iglibrary/search/UCHIB0001552.html.

D'Elia, P. M. (1961) 'Recent discoveries and new studies on the world map in Chinese of father Matteo Ricci S.J.', *Monumenta Serica*, 20, 82–164.

Doig, W. (2018) *High-Speed Empire: Chinese Expansion and the Future of Southeast Asia*, Columbia Global Reports.

Elman, B. A. (2005) *On Their Own Terms Science in China, 1550–1900*, Harvard University Press. http://site.ebrary.com/id/10314310

Elman, B. A. (2006) *A Cultural History of Modern Science in China*, Cambridge, MA: Harvard University Press.

Elshakry, M. (2010) 'When Science Became Western: Historiographical Reflections', *Isis*, 101(1), 98.

Fan, F. (2007) 'Redrawing the Map: Science in Twentieth-Century China', *Isis*, 98(3), 524–538. https://doi.org/10.1086/521156.

Fan, S. (2014) *The Harvard-Yenching Institute and Cultural Engineering: Remaking the Humanities in China, 1924–1951*, Lanham: Lexington Books.

Feingold, M. (2003) *Jesuit Science and the Republic of Letters*, Cambridge, MA: MIT Press.

Feingold, M. (ed) (2003) *The New Science and Jesuit Science: Seventeenth Century Perspectives*, Dordrecht: Kluwer; HistSciTechMed.

Findlen, P. (Ed.). (2004) *Athanasius Kircher: The Last Man Who Knew Everything* (1st ed). New York: Routledge.

Gernet, J. (1985) *China and the Christian Impact: A Conflict of Cultures*, Cambridge, UK: Cambridge University Press; Editions de la Maison des sciences de l'homme.

Greenhalgh, S. (2008) *Just One Child: Science and Policy in Deng's China*, http://hdl.handle.net/2027/heb.09193.

Griffiths, J. (2019) *The Great Firewall of China: How to Build and Control an Alternative Version of the Internet*, London: Zed Books.

Han, Qi 韩琦 (2019) '易学与科学:康熙、耶稣会士白晋与《周易折中》的编纂' (The Book of Changes and Science: the Kangxi Emperor, Joachim Bouvet, S. J., and the Compilation of Zhouyi zhezhong). 自然辩证法研究 (Research on dialectics) 35, 61–66.

Hashimoto, K. (1988) *Hsü Kuang-ch'i and Astronomical Reform: The Process of the Chinese Acceptance of Western Astronomy, 1629–1635*, Osaka, Japan: Kansai University Press.

Heirman, A., Troia, P. D., & Parmentier, J. (2009) 'Francesco Sambiasi, a Missing Link in European Map Making in China?' *Imago Mundi*, 61(1), 29–46.

Holorenshaw, H. (1939) *The Levelers and the English Revolution*, London: VGollancz.

Holorenshaw, H. (1973) *The Making of an Honorary Taoist*, London: Heinemann.

Hostetler, L. (2001) *Qing Colonial Enterprise: Ethnography and Cartography in Early Modern China*, Chicago: University of Chicago Press.

Hsia, F. C. (2009) *Sojourners in a Strange Land: Jesuits and Their Scientific Missions in Late Imperial China*, Chicago: The University of Chicago Press.

Hu, D. (2005) *China and Albert Einstein: The Reception of the Physicist and His Theory in China 1917–1979*, Cambridge, MA: Harvard University Press.

Jami, C. (1999) ''European Science in China' or 'Western Learning'? Representations of Cross-Cultural Transmission, 1600–1800', *Science in Context*, 12(3), 413–434. https://doi.org/10.1017/S0269889700003513

Jami, C. (2012) *The Emperor's New Mathematics: Western Learning and Imperial Authority during the Kangxi Reign (1662–1722)*, Oxford: Oxford University Press.

Koyré, A. (1968) *Metaphysics and Measurement; Essays in Scientific Revolution*, Cambridge, MA: Harvard University Press.

Kuriyama, S. (1999) *The Expressiveness of the Body and the Divergence of Greek and Chinese Medicine*, London: Zone Books.

Kwok, D. W. Y. (1971) *Scientism in Chinese Thought, 1900–1950*, Biblo and Tannen.

La Fargue, T. E. (1987) *China's First Hundred: Educational Mission Students in the United States, 1872–1881*, Pullman, Wash.: Washington State University Press.

Leonard, J. K. (1984) *Wei Yüan and China's Rediscovery of the Maritime World* (Vol. 111). Cambridge, MA: Harvard University Asia Center.

Leung, A. K. C. (2009) *Leprosy in China: A History*, New York: Columbia University Press.

Lewis, J. W. (1988) *China Builds the Bomb*, Stanford, CA: Stanford University Press.

Lin, J. Y. (1995) 'The Needham Puzzle: Why the Industrial Revolution Did Not Originate in China', *Economic Development and Cultural Change*, 43(2), 269–292.

Lloyd, G. E. R., & Sivin, N. (2002) *The Way and the Word: Science and Medicine in Early China and Greece*, New Haven: Yale University Press.

Lu, Y. (2015) *A History of Chinese Science and Technology* (1st ed. 2015.), Berlin: Springer.

Luk, B. H. (1977) 'A Study of Giulio Aleni's 'Chih-fang wai chi' 職方外紀' *Bulletin of the School of Oriental and African Studies, University of London*, 40(1), 58–84.

Marcon, F. (2015) *The Knowledge of Nature and the Nature of Knowledge in Early Modern Japan*, The University of Chicago Press. http://nrs.harvard.edu/urn-3:hul.ebookbatch.GEN_batch:EDZ0001038568201600624.

Marta, H. (2012) 'Speaking of Epidemics', in *Chinese Medicine: Disease and the Geographic Imagination in Late Imperial China*, London: Taylor and Francis. pp. 1–267. https://doi.org/10.4324/9780203829592.

Martzloff, J.-C. (1981) *Recherches sur l'œuvre mathématique de Méi Wéndǐng, 1633–1721*, Collège de France, Institut des hautes études chinoises.

Martzloff, J.-C. (1997) *A History of Chinese Mathematics*, Berlin: Springer-Verlag. https://doi.org/10.1007/978-3-540-33783-6.
Menegon, E. (1994) *Un solo cielo: Giulio Aleni S.J.*, Grafo.
Menegon, E. (2019) 'Quid pro quo: Leisure, Europeans, and their 'Skill Capital' in Eighteenth-Century Beijing', in *Testing the Margins of Leisure: Case Studies on China, Japan, and Indonesia*, Heidelberg: Heidelberg University Publishing. pp. 107–153.
Meynard, T., Ruggieri (S.I.), M., & Villasante, R. (2018) *La filosofía moral de Confucio, por Michele Ruggieri, SJ: La primera traducción de las obras de Confucio al español en 1590*, Mensajero.
Morar, F.-S. (2018) 'Relocating the Qing in the Global History of Science: The Manchu Translation of the 1603 World Map by Li Yingshi and Matteo Ricci', *Isis*: *Journal of the History of Science*, 109(4), 679–694.
Mosca, M. W. (2013) *From Frontier Policy to Foreign Policy: The Question of India and the Transformation of Geopolitics in Qing China*, Stanford, CA: Stanford University Press.
Mullaney, T. S. (2010) *Coming to Terms with the Nation*, Berkeley: University of California Press.
Nappi, C. S. (2009) *The Monkey and the Inkpot: Natural History and Its Transformations in Early Modern China*, Cambridge, MA: Harvard University Press.
Needham, J. (1969) *The Grand Titration: Science and Society in East and West*, Toronto, CA: University of Toronto Press.
Needham, J., Wang, Ling., Yates, R. D. S., & Tsien, T. (1954) *Science and Civilization in China*, Cambridge, UK: Cambridge University Press.
Park, H. (2012) *Mapping the Chinese and Islamic Worlds: Cross-Cultural Exchange in Pre-Modern Asia*, Cambridge, UK: Cambridge University Press.
Qi, S. (2012) *Western Literature in China and the Translation of a Nation*, Berlin: Springer.
Qian, W. (1985) *The Great Inertia: Scientific Stagnation in Traditional China*, London: Croom Helm.
Raj, K. (2010) *Relocating Modern Science: Circulation and the Construction of Knowledge in South Asia and Europe, 1650–1900*, London: Palgrave Macmillan.
Raj, K. (2013) 'Beyond Postcolonialism … and Postpositivism: Circulation and the Global History of Science', *Isis*, 104(2), 337–347.
Reardon-Anderson, J. (1991) *The Study of Change: Chemistry in China, 1840–1949*, Cambridge, UK: Cambridge University Press.
Ricci, M. (1938) *Il mappamondo cinese del p. Matteo Ricci*, S. I. (3. ed., Pechino, 1602.). Città del Vaticano, Biblioteca apostolica Vaticana.
Ricci, M. (1985) *Fonti Ricciane*, Roma: Libreria dello Stato.
Roberts, M. E. (2020) *Censored: Distraction and Diversion Inside China's Great Firewall*, Princeton, NJ: Princeton University Press.
Rogaski, R. (2014) *Hygienic Modernity: Meanings of Health and Disease in Treaty-Port China*, Berkeley: Univ of California Press.
Sachsenmaier, D. (2018) *Global Entanglements of a Man Who Never Traveled: A Seventeenth-Century Chinese Christian and His Conflicted Worlds*, Columbia University Press. https://doi.org/10.7312/sach18752
Schmalzer, S. (2009) *The People's Peking Man: Popular Science and Human Identity in Twentieth-Century China*, Chicago: University of Chicago Press.
Schneider, L. A. (2003) *Biology and Revolution in Twentieth-Century China*, Lanham, MD: Rowman & Littlefield.
Schwartz, B. (1983) *In Search of Wealth and Power*, Cambridge, MA: Harvard University Press.
Seow, V. (2014) 'Fuels and Flows', *Transfers*, 4(3), 112–116. https://doi.org/10.3167/TRANS.2014.040309
Shapin, S. (1998) *The Scientific Revolution* (2nd ed). Chicago: University of Chicago Press.
Shapiro, J. (2001) *Mao's War Against Nature: Politics and the Environment in Revolutionary China*, Cambridge, UK: Cambridge University Press.
Sivin, N. (1981) *Science, Medicine, and Technology in East Asia*. Ann Arbor: Center for Chinese Studies, the University of Michigan.

Sivin, N. (1985) 'Why the Scientific Revolution Did Not Take Place in China—Or Did It?' *Environmentalist*, 5(1), 39–50. https://doi.org/10.1007/BF02239866

Sivin, N. (1995) *Science in Ancient China: Researches and Reflections*, Brookfield, Vt., USA: Variorum.

Spence, J. D. (2008, August 14) 'The Passions of Joseph Needham', https://www.nybooks.com/articles/2008/08/14/the-passions-of-joseph-needham/.

Standaert, N. (2001) *Handbook of Christianity in China*, London: Brill.

Standaert, N. (2002) 'Methodology in View of Contact Between Cultures: The China Case in the 17th Century' Centre for the Study of Religion and Chinese Society, Chung Chi College, the Chinese University of Hong Kong.

Statman, A. (2016) 'Fusang: The Enlightenment Story of the Chinese Discovery of America', *Isis*, 107(1), 1–25. https://doi.org/10.1086/686247

Statman, A. (2019) 'The First Global Turn: Chinese Contributions to Enlightenment World History', *Journal of World History*, 30(3), 363–392. https://doi.org/10.1353/jwh.2019.0061

Walravens, H. (1991) 'Father Verbiest's Chinese World Map (1674)', *Imago Mundi*, 43, 31–47.

Wang, Z. (1999) 'US–China Scientific Exchange: A Case Study of State-Sponsored Scientific Internationalism during the Cold War and Beyond', *Historical Studies in the Physical and Biological Sciences*, 30(1), 249–277. https://doi.org/10.2307/27757826

Wang, Z. (2002) 'Saving China through Science: The Science Society of China, Scientific Nationalism, and Civil Society in Republican China', *Osiris*, 17, 291–322. JSTOR.

Wang, Z. (2007) 'Science and the State in Modern China', *Isis; An International Review Devoted to the History of Science and Its Cultural Influences*, 98(3), 558–570. https://doi.org/10.1086/521158

Wei, Y. 魏源 (1880) '海國圖志' (Gazetteer of maritime kingdoms), Yangzhou: Gu wei tang, Daoguang 27 [1847].

Wen, C. (1975) 'Barefoot Doctors in China', *Nursing Digest*, 3(1), 26–28.

Winchester, S. (2008) *The Man Who Loved China: The Fantastic Story of the Eccentric Scientist Who Unlocked the Mysteries of the Middle Kingdom* (1st ed.). New York: Harper.

Wright, D. (1998) 'The Translation of Modern Western Science in Nineteenth-Century China 1840–1895', *Isis*, 89(4), 653–673. JSTOR.

Wright, D. (2000) *Translating Science: The Transmission of Western Chemistry into Late Imperial China, 1840–1900*, Leiden, Neth.: E. J. Brill.

Wu, S. X. (2015) *Empires of Coal: Fueling China's Entry into the Modern World Order, 1860–1920*, Stanford, CA: Stanford University Press.

Zhang, B. 张柏春 (2004) '苏联技术向中国的转移: 1949–1966' (Technology transfer from the Soviet Union to the P.R. China: 1949–1966), Jinan Shi: Shandong jiao yu chu ban she.

Zhang, X. (2007) *The Origins of the Modern Chinese Press: The Influence of the Protestant Missionary Press in Late Qing China*, New York: Routledge.

Zilsel, E. (2000) *The Social Origins of Modern Science*, Dordrecht: Kluwer.

41

Transnational knowledge transfer

The adaptation of German psychiatric concepts during the academic evolution of modern psychiatry in China

Wenjing Li

Introduction

Psychiatry (*Jing Shen Bing Xue*, 精神病学), a term originated from the Greek 'psychiatria', refers to the treatment of soul diseases. Historically, Western psychiatry had not been included in the field of medical science until the 18th century, although as early as the fourth century BC, Hippocrates of Cos (c. 460–c. 370 BC) proposed that mental illnesses, like any other physical illnesses, were caused by natural factors, so that appropriate medical treatment was necessary.

The development of modern Western psychiatry has a history of more than one hundred years. However, given its complexity, restricted by the influence of historical background and the level of technological development, the development of Western psychiatry is still lagging behind the other biomedical disciplines.

Western psychiatry was first introduced to mainland China by medical missionaries in 1898, before which Traditional Chinese Medicine (TCM) had been dominant there. From the period of Fu Hsi (伏羲), the first legendary Chinese emperor (c. 2852 BC), the recognized types of illnesses related to *Feng* 疯 (refers to madness) included *Dian* 癫 (refers to paralysis), *Xian* 痫 (falling sickness, similar to epilepsy), and *Kuang* 狂 (excited insanity, similar to hysteria). About 2,000 years ago, mental illnesses began to be found being recorded in Chinese medical literature, referring to the speculated causes, pathogenesis, diagnosis as well as prevention and treatment (Tseng 1973). However, due to the restricted understanding of mental illnesses, a relevant independent branch within TCM had not been generated until the late 19th century when Western approaches for psychiatry were introduced into China (Xia & Zhang 1981; Xu 1995).

Correspondingly, in Europe, the 19th century was regarded as a golden age of German psychiatry (Shorter 1997; Li 2005). Professionalization was completed during this period, and in the 1860s, psychiatry became an academic discipline at the medical faculties of German universities (Schmiedebach & Priebe 2004). Historical explanation in terms of the changes of the research paradigm, the academic progress, the rise and critique of the asylums, and the protest movement associated with the debated reputation of psychiatrists

DOI: 10.4324/9780429059704-48

triggered a wide range of discussion, which constituted a panoramic picture ahead of the draw of the twentieth century (Lerner 2003; Schmiedebach & Priebe 2004; Wolpert 2006; Schmiedebach 2011). From the early 20th century, psychiatry in Germany took new steps to expand its influence.

Around the year 1900, both Germany and China underwent tremendous social changes. Many psychiatric concepts were proposed and revised in Germany; meanwhile, modern psychiatry was introduced from the West to the East under the international influence of knowledge transfer. Modern psychiatry was established and developed in China based on the thoughts that came from the West; however, the scholarship or research on the history of psychiatry in China is not yet adequate.

With the tendency of cultural convergence and the development of holistic medicine, China-related issues attracted more and more attention of Western scholars, especially the intensified discussions convened by sinologists and sociologists, as well as the related legal studies carried out by jurisprudents. The topic of psychiatry and mental health in China was under the spotlight, yet mainly due to the curiosity of exploring the cultural correlation that might exist between mental illnesses and the Chinese feudal autocratic society as well as the Confucian cultural inheritance.

Taking the main works during recent years into consideration, Vivien W. Ng (Ng 1990) first described the madness in China with a focus on the disposition of the mentally ill under the prevailing legal and political environment during the Qing dynasty (1616–1912). Veronica Pearson (Pearson 1995) depicted the state policies, professional services, and family responsibilities related to the topic of mental health care; however, the research aim lied in the exposure and evaluation of the Chinese social system. Angelika Messner (Messner 2000) discussed the weaknesses in Ng's research and put the emphasis on the recognition of mental illnesses that had been achieved in the system of TCM. Though the time span of her work crossed from the year 1600 to 1930, her research was in fact defined in the period of Qing dynasty, in which the research status was summarized and evaluated. In her research, the study of collection and analysis of historical documents during the Republic of China seemed relatively weak or insufficient.

There are some other summaries regarding the psychiatric services established in mainland China (Pearson 1991; Diamant 1993; Szto 2002; Grau 2014; Fan et al. 2020) and a few records of mentally ill cases in specific locations (Chu & Liu 1960), as well as some rough narrative historical descriptions by Chinese indigenous pioneers (Young & Chang 1983; Xu 1989, 1995; Chen 2010), most of which emphasized the linear time compiling of specific historical events or enumerating of the patients' conditions, while were lack of historical comparison and logic analysis from beyond the perspective of purely local medical consideration and treatment. The latest set is the *Psychiatry and Chinese History* (Chiang 2014) by Howard Chiang in 2014 with a few themes of minor relevance, such as dream explanation in ancient China, the short-lived psychotherapeutic culture, and the recent Psycho-Boom (*Xin Li Re*, 心理热) among the Chinese public. The discussion in his edited book is with more emphasis on sociological perspectives, rather than medical historical discourse.

Furthermore, the international relationship between different countries or between scientific communities is becoming one of the hotspots in the history of psychiatry, for instance, a collection of essays named *International Relations in Psychiatry: Britain, Germany, and the United States to World War II* (Roelcke et al. 2010). With an emphasis on the influence of German psychiatry, this book responded to the paucity of scholarship on psychiatric knowledge dissemination within Europe and between both sides of the North Atlantic. Another collection of essays was the *Two Millennia of Psychiatry in West and East* (Hamanaka &

Berrios 2003); however, the 'East' in their selected papers merely referred to Japan and, in the 'West' part, just a few of landmark figures, such as Aelius Galenus (c. 129–200), Philippe Pinel (1745–1826) and Emil Kraepelin (1856–1926), were highlighted. In addition to these collections mentioned above, the influence of German psychiatry, especially the system of Kraepelin has been also discussed in some professional articles within the medical historical community, for instance, *The British Reaction to Dementia Praecox, 1893–1913* (Ion & Beer 2002a; Ion & Beer 2002b).

However, there is insufficient historical research carried out by medical professionals, which should have taken a comprehensive view on the development of psychiatry in China by examining the processes in which Chinese practitioners accepted or rejected the various strains of academic thoughts coming from the West. Essentially, the present state of Chinese psychiatry cannot be separated from its adaptive historical development dating back to its nascent contact with Western psychiatry.

Till now, the understanding of the transfer process in terms of psychiatric knowledge from the West, especially from Germany, to China and the historical impact of German psychiatry on China still remains incomplete and inadequate, even though a great deal of convincing historical facts illustrated that Germany dominated the realm of psychiatry academically in the nineteenth century. This research responds to the paucity of scholarship on the issues of international relationship about psychiatric concepts transmission and of cultural adaptation between the West and the East, in this chapter specifically, between Germany and China.

Research concept, design, and methodology

The comparative study on the history of psychiatry between Germany and China is an attempt to underline the prominence of cultural adaptation[1] in transnational phenomena concerning the development of psychiatry.

The comparative study has been carried out with two main tasks: The first task is to figure out the differences of research paradigms, of disease classifications, of patient treatments and of patient accommodations, of a portrait of alienists and patients in different cultural contexts. The second task is to detect and collect comprehensive information during the transfer process of psychiatric knowledge from the West to the East.

There are two assumptions in this study: First, there must be some convincing facts addressing the modern psychiatric transmission of knowledge from Germany to China around 1900 in view of the highly developed status of German psychiatry during the 19th century. Second, there must be some similar features in the state of knowledge between German psychiatry around 1900 and the cognition of mental illnesses in TCM, which might serve as the root cause or the instinctive driver for the subsequent and spontaneous exploitation of the integrated psychiatry in China.

The aim of this research is to verify the impact of German psychiatry on China by illustrating the transfer process and investigating the conceptual variation of psychiatric knowledge. The question, of what kind of German psychiatric concepts around 1900 had been accepted and what had been rejected in China, has been narrated in the Chinese cultural context.

Accurate and abundant historical materials are essential for a comparative study. Systematic literature retrieval was first conducted in the databases of Embase and Medline. Further complementary information was collected via investigating in relevant monographs and biographies etc., as mutual confirmation of various sources would reduce the risk of distorting or enveloping, which could occur as per political interference and religious obstruction. Finally, 159 publications and historical pieces were taken as reference for this study.

Historical materials can only demonstrate the unique values through systematic analysis and summary, which meanwhile enables the essentials to emerge from the superficial or accidental phenomenon. Various methods shall be employed for different topics based on the characteristics of each.

First, some ideas and methods from comparative history[2] (Bloch 1953; Sewell 1967), including the macro and microhistorical comparison, have been used extensively to improve theoretical depth. This study is designed to be qualitative research, with necessary quantitative analyses. This research is a horizontal and longitudinal comparison abided by the principles of comparability and synchronism (Skocpol & Somers 1980). The several comparative aspects (see Figure 41.1) (Li 2016) strengthen the feasibility to confirm the differences and similarities during the historical development of psychiatry in Germany and China, and thereby to draw the conclusion of general patterns and dynamics, as well as to discover the historical origins behind the phenomenon (He 2004).

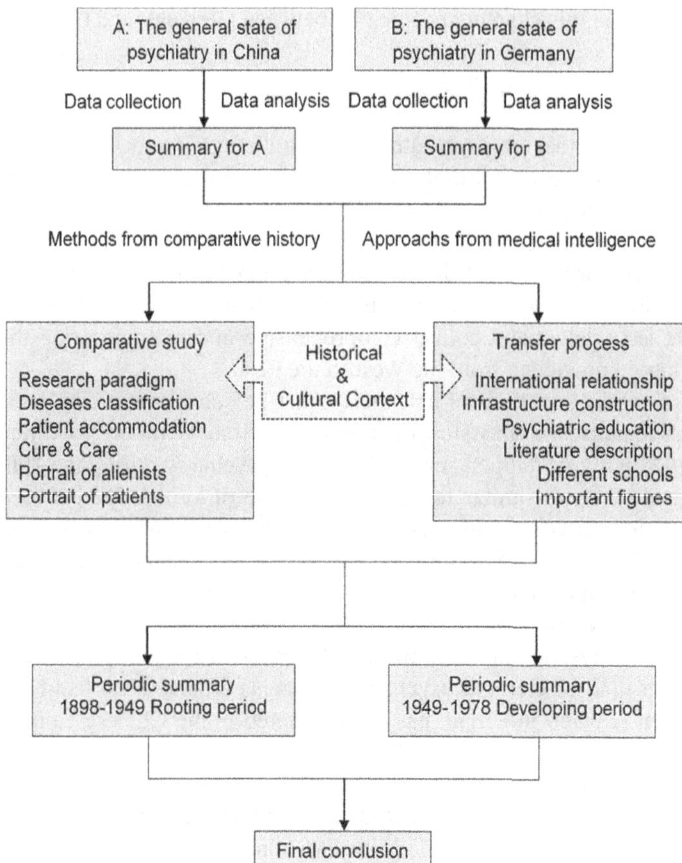

Figure 41.1 Conceptual framework for comparative research.

Second, this study drew on the way of thinking from medical intelligence science[3]. The general methods, such as literature and network resource research, the logical approaches, included comparison, analysis, and synthesis, reasoning (inductive and deductive), etc., as well as content analysis, which is dedicated to medical library and information study, all served for this study in different aspects. Conversely, classic quantitative research methods, such as principal component analysis, bibliographical analysis, regression analysis, citation analysis, cluster analysis, and so forth have been rarely employed due to the properties of the research theme.

Third, the majority of cultural or scientific exchanges in world history involved translation activities inevitably. This study is not an exception. As a large amount of translation was referred, the principle from translation research was also committed to this study. Translation implies 'negotiation' (or 'transformation'), 'which is always a shrift not between two languages, but between two cultures', as Umberto Eco (1932–2016) pointed out. From the receiver's point of view, it is a form of gain, enriching the host culture (or 'target culture') (Liu 1995) as a result of skillful adaptation; however, from the donor's point of view, on the other hand, translation is a form of loss, leading to misunderstanding and committing violence to the original. The greater the distance between the languages and cultures involved, the more clearly do the problems of translation appear (Burke & Hsia 2007). Recently, scholarship has made it clear that the imbalance of power relations[4] and 'pivot languages'[5] plays a key role in this process of relay translation.[6] Depending on which sources for written translation were selected, ignored, and compromised, relay translation could give rise to different interpretations of the original ideas (St. André & Peng 2012). Therefore, this study concentrated on such gains of China and the losses of German psychiatry during the relay of the translation process by investigating the professional individual works and the collaborative works.

Psychiatry in Germany and China before 1898

Ahead of being in contact with each other, China and Germany maintained their own beliefs in psychiatry. The term 'belief' is used not due to its original meaning from religion, but to describe the fact that, different ways of looking at and interacting with their surroundings can lead to totally different focused points in connection with ordinary issues.

As the psychiatric-related backgrounds should be compared in the context of medicine, several parallel aspects and a specific framework for contradistinction have been defined in advance. Even though different medical systems maintained remarkable autonomy respectively, common indicators could be defined as per the features that any independent medical specialty should have. In the process of brief comparison, the differences rather than similarities between countries have been emphasized (see Table 41.1) (Li 2016).

Shift of the pivotal center of modern psychiatry

In the 1950s, the sociologist John Desmond Bernal (1901–1971) gave the first description of the phenomenon of 'main area of scientific activity and its' change over time' in his famous book *Science in History* (Bernal 1954). Since then, Japanese historian of science, Mitsutomo Yuasa (湯浅光朝) (1909–2005) discovered a quantitative regularity in the shifts of the world science center. His discovery is now known as the 'Yuasa phenomenon (湯浅現象)' scientifically (Mitsutomo 1974), which reveals the great leap and imbalance of the world's scientific and technological development due to cultural upheaval, social

Table 41.1 Psychiatry in Germany and China before 1898

	Germany	*China*
Research paradigm	• From outside entering medical science • Evolution: Psychological model → Physiological model	• Described in traditional medicine but not an independent discipline • Balance of the *Yin* 阴 and *Yang* 阳[1] by holistic approach • Taoism influence
Diseases classification	• Based on syndromes and symptoms, progression and prognosis	• Based on the *Zheng Hou* 征候[2]
Accommodation	• Evolution: Asylum → Sanitarium (insanity boom) → Psychiatric hospital	• No specialized place: Buddhist temples or catholic institutions, *Yang Ji Yuan* 养济院, home (mainly), local jails, etc.
Cure & care	• Psychotherapy • Physical therapy including Spa, occupational therapy, electrotherapy, etc. • Sedative and hypnotic drugs	• Prevention is crucial: Emphasis on body-mind together,[3] adapting to the environment • No targeted herb medicine available • Acupuncture, sleep therapy
Portrait of alienists	• Observation under the microscope, therapeutic nihilism • Role of law officer rather than savior • Professionalization completed	• Absence of significant role in the discussion of criminal insanity • A Confucian bias:[4] Devaluation of the worth of specialists and professionals
Portrait of patients	• Protection of patients' rights movement • Evolution: Passive nature of human → Loss of complete freedom → Compulsory treatment	• Family-oriented stigma, family responsibility • Denial/disguise of patients' condition • Speculation of hereditary basis • Mandatory registration and confinement program

Notes: [1] In traditional Chinese philosophy, *Yin* 阴 and *Yang* 阳 describe how apparently opposite or contrary forces are complementary, interconnected, and interdependent in the natural world, and how they give rise to each other as they interrelate to one another.

[2] *Zheng Hou* 证候 was a comprehensive concept that consisted of signs that represented various life phenomena of patients' stages in the disease process. The concept of *Zheng Hou* 证候 usually included not only symptoms that could be perceived subjectively but also the signs which could be observed objectively. Moreover, *Zheng Hou* 证候 was different from the concepts of symptom and syndrome in Western medicine. The changing condition of patients in different stages was not included in the concepts of symptom or syndrome usually, but it was emphasized by the concept of *Zheng Hou* 证候.

[3] The dichotomy of body and mind did not exist in the system of Traditional Chinese Medicine (TCM). The 'somatization' here could be seen, on the one hand, it was a kind of natural expression. In TCM, each emotion was thought to be related to a specific organ in the body, which meant that any emotional disturbance was thought to originate from a corresponding organ; on the other hand, it was a result of shame avoidance as mentioned above.

[4] Compared to Western civilization, Chinese culture has been less concerned with ontological issues such as the existence of God on the fate of humans. Its two dominant philosophical traditions are Confucianism and Taoism. The specific point of view here was recorded as *Jun Zi Bu Qi* 君子不器. Not like politicians and merchants, being a doctor was not recognized by the public as a dream career in ancient China.

change, economic growth, and the rise of new disciplines as well as collective migration of scientists.

According to Yuasa, during the past 400 years, the center of world scientific activities underwent five distinct shifts. The five shifts relayed themselves as the following sequence: Italy (1540–1610), England (1660–1730), France (1770–1830), and Germany (1830–1920), as well as the United States (since the 1920s). As a part of science, the development of modern medicine followed the general regularity and the overall level of scientific and technological development.

The innovation or transformation of professional training mechanisms played a crucial role. The transfer paths and the spatial distributions of academic centers of different disciplines substantially were consistent with that of the general scientific center, only the specific time interval of which were slightly different. For example, the center of medical activity in Germany lasted from the mid-19th century to the 1930s (Zuo 2010), which was a little later than that of general science.

Before the 1890s, the United States could be considered as the medical colony of France and Germany (Stevens 1998). At the end of the 19th century, some Americans began to study medicine in Europe and were trained in German-speaking universities. Among them, the pathologist William Henry Welch (1850–1934), anatomist Franklin Paine Mall (1862–1917), and pharmacologist John Jacob Abel (1857–1938) created the Johns Hopkins Hospital, where rigorous clinical research and sophisticated experimental research was emphasized. Around 1900, the formation of the commonwealth of medicine across Europe and America was attained (Bynum 1994).

Specific to the situation in the psychiatric field, the paradigms that underpin psychiatry today are still those that were largely formulated during the 19th century and the early twentieth century. This was an era of brilliant achievements within the history of psychiatry (Beumont 1992). From the middle of the 19th century to around 1930, German psychiatry came to replace the French humanitarian genre as the dominant school of thought. With its strongly biological emphasis and a high degree of professionalization, it became the reference point for the field across the globe (Shorter 1997). From 1933 to 1938, however, German psychiatry suffered a great loss as many psychiatrists immigrated to the United States. As a result, America soon became the pivotal center of psychiatric thought (Peters 1988). Prior to World War II (1939–1945), American psychiatry was biological in its focus, but this changed shortly after the war as the emphasis shifted toward a psychoanalytic approach (Sarason 1988).

Despite these dynamics, the European school of thought continued to play a dominant role in America until the end of the 1930s. Some research departments in America strictly followed the German tradition, which meant that there was hardly any American tradition in psychiatry (Barton 1987; Shorter 1997). Before the 1940s, there were only a few significant American innovations to speak of in the field. In 1965, Benjamin Rush (1746–1813) was recognized as the founder of American psychiatry by the American Psychiatric Association (APA). However, he did little to serve as a beacon for the future, but rather agreed with his European colleagues that the brain was the origin of mental illness (Shorter 1997). The identification of a new form of neurosis, neurasthenia, by George Miller Beard (1839–1883) (Beard 1869) and the rest cure were virtually the only American contributions to the emerging discipline. As noted by Smith Ely Jelliffe (1866–1945), an American psychiatrist who had studied with Kraepelin, American psychiatry in the first quarter of the twentieth century was 'preeminently Kraepelinian psychiatry' (Brink & Jelliffe 1933). The American contribution lay rather in its expansion of psychoanalysis and a new form of biologically based psychiatry which began from the 1970s, which was featured by genetic clues and new drug therapy (Beumont 1992; Shorter 1997).

Corresponding with the view of Bynum mentioned above, between 1890 and 1914 'many of the great figures in German medicine began to explore the medical world on this side of the Atlantic', noted the historian Thomas N. Bonner (1923–2003) (Bonner 1963), and they were responsible for sparking the interest of their students about opportunities in America. Adolf Meyer (1866–1950) was among the first of a small reverse migration of physicians from German-speaking countries to America that began in 1890. As the figure with an extraordinary personal influence in America from the 1910s to the 1940s, Meyer has been referred to as the 'American Kraepelin' (Shorter 1997) because he introduced Kraepelin's system in the Worcester asylum where he was a neuropathologist in 1896 (Meyer & Winters 1951) and helped spread Kraepelin's views among the American scientific public (Peters 1990). His rejection of Kraepelin's nosology in later years led the country to the psychoanalytic direction.

Although hardly any of Meyer's work has been translated into German, he always kept up a lively intellectual exchange with his colleagues in Germany as well as August Hoch (1868–1919) in the McLean Hospital (Sutton 1986), who had been trained in Europe and also helped interpret Kraepelin's system to America academic field. Furthermore, with the continuous effort of other American practitioners, Kraepelin's system 'slipped from the interpretive grasp of Hoch and Meyer and began a new, independent journey of transformation' in America (Noll 2011).

Indirect transmission of German psychiatric concepts in China

The advances of modern medicine were closely associated with the rise of modern science in the 19th century. Most of the new doctrines, discoveries, and technologies in natural science had been applied to serve medical theory and practice, which coerced modern medicine to a status of being bundled with scientific conceptions, when modern medicine was welcomed in China.

During the introduction of modern Western medicine to China, practical effectiveness was a key factor in the acceptance of specific disciplines and methods by the Chinese medical community. Modern anatomy, physiology, pathology, and even surgery were thus recognized and accepted shortly before and after the establishment of the Republic of China. The process of 'Suspect→Try→Convince' (Xiong 2011) that Western medicine underwent in China had been completed for the most part before modern psychiatry emerged on the scene. This meant that the way had been paved for modern psychiatry to make inroads in the Chinese medical landscape as other branches of medicine had already been accepted.

Around 1900 in China, there was a lack of breakthroughs in the treatment of psychosis in contrast to the advances taking place in other branches of medicine (Pearson 1991). However, as the close relationship between mental illnesses and cerebral pathology had already been well established, psychiatry in China put down its roots in neurology. Medical academics in China were convinced that Chinese psychiatry would benefit from its close association with the rest of Western medicine.

Western psychiatry was introduced to China mainly through Anglo-American ways (Li & Schmiedebach 2015). American's contribution to modern psychiatry in China cannot be ignored. American missionaries and physicians came to China and helped establish the first mental institutions and research facilities; they also trained China's first native professionals and sent them to study abroad. They thus planted the roots of modern psychiatry in China in a very practical manner (Li 2016).

However, the process of ideas adoption was not merely one of replication, but rather a process of active selection and acceptance (Li & Schmiedebach 2015). Psychoanalysis, the representative of dynamic-psychological psychiatry, which was largely welcomed by American psychiatrists, had not been generally recognized as one of the main achievements in the psychiatric field in that era.

Most of the Westerners who helped bring psychiatry to China were either born or educated in America. All of them had a medical degree and had been trained in fields like anatomy, neurology, or neuropathology. Correspondingly, the courses they offered in mainland China related to psychiatry were almost all in neuropsychiatric orientation (Westbrook 1953). The use of foreign terms seemed to be unavoidable in neuropsychiatry, as in other branches of medicine, especially in connection with its anatomic and physiological aspects (Lyman 1937). Thus, from its inception, Chinese practitioners approached psychiatry from a biological perspective rather than a psychological one (Li 2016).

In addition to the rejection of psychoanalysis, Eugen Bleuler (1857–1939)'s psychiatry, in which Kraepelin and Sigmund Freud (1856–1939) were to be merged, was appreciated in China largely due to its contribution of rich clinical descriptions based on the tradition of German psychiatry, although the embedded philosophical explanation received little interests (see Figure 41.2) (Li 2016).

Chinese psychiatrists attributed equal importance to both physical and emotional symptoms. The belief was that the symptoms were related to each other instead of being originated from each other. They were envisaged coming from the same origin, the brain

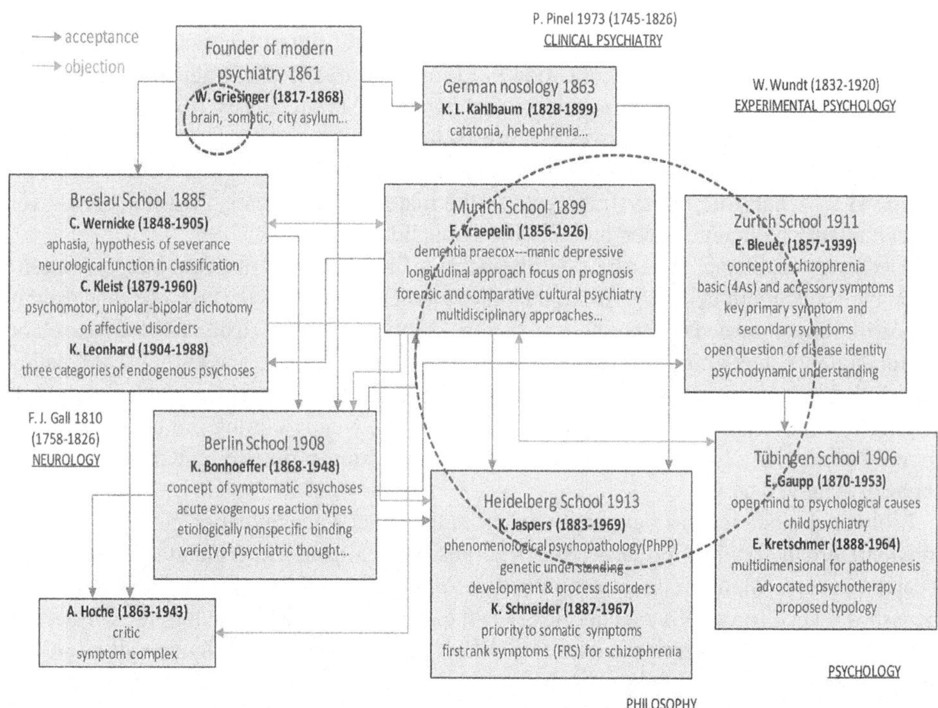

Figure 41.2 Acceptance of German psychiatric concepts around 1900 in China – concepts within the dotted circles.

dysfunction. The idea that mental illnesses are diseases of the brain, which reflected the entirely somatic-orientated psychiatry of Wilhelm Griesinger (1817–1868) and Carl Wernicke (1848–1905) in Germany, although was not exactly identical to, but was echoed with the Chinese saying *Xin Zhu Shen Ming* 心主神明[7]. In TCM, each emotion was thought to be related to a specific organ in the body, which meant that any emotional disturbance was thought to originate from a corresponding organ. Illnesses characterized by unusual or unconventional behavior were thus treated similarly to somatic manifestations. Consequently, it is not surprising that, as Lyman pointed out, 'there was no antagonism between neurology and psychiatry for a long period of time in China' (Lyman 1937). Furthermore, from the methodological point of view, TCM also relied on observations and descriptions for both diagnosis and treatment. Although it has not been discussed in depth whether clinical presentation or prognostic implication should receive more attention, the classification of mental illnesses in TCM was also based on a catalog of symptoms associated with the concept of a disease pattern. A few records of the symptoms and syndromes of mental illnesses were consistent with the descriptions of them in modern psychiatry (Tseng 1973).

Therefore, observation and description in psychiatry, as represented by Kraepelin, Bleuler, as well as Kurt Schneider (1887–1967) and the other German psychiatrists had not been difficult for Chinese scholars to understand and accept because they were still greatly influenced by traditional medicine, despite their owing modern medical training in the Western style (Li 2016).

Reevaluation of the psychiatric concepts in Germany

In China, Kraepelin was described not only as the central figure but also as the finalizer, who terminated the chaos of classification in Europe. Around 1900, Kraepelin's system did generate a high degree of attention in foreign countries, especially in America. However, around 1900 in Germany, there were various schools that represented different intentions and perspectives, and the opinions of classification far from achieving a consensus (see Figure 41.2). Therefore, many fragments in the history of psychiatry had not been given enough attention and even been ignored totally outside of Europe.

Psychiatry is distinct from the other branches of biomedicine that had become mature in the early twentieth century. Unlike the other medical branches, for instance, nephrology and cardiology, it turned out that no satisfactory solution could be easily achieved based on the fundamental recognition in terms of anatomy and physiology. The etiology and pathogenesis behind most endogenous psychoses remain unclear; current popular menu-style diagnosis is mainly based on symptoms or syndromes. Neatly cutting the cake along 'the natural boundaries existed between natural diseases entities' proposed by Kraepelin has not yet been achieved so far.

Biological medicine has benefited a lot from the exact science that originated in France and then prospered in Germany. The rigorous clinical and experimental research has received enough attention; however, biological-oriented psychiatry has not solved most of the issues related to various psychoses. Since the exact science is unequal to the correct and credible knowledge, excessive reliance on the approaches of natural science will result in a narrow horizon to contemporary psychiatry.

Exploring the suitable approach to the unknown basic mechanism of the mentally ill requires great humility, providing room for knowledge and intelligence coming from different cultures to aid in this endeavor (Shorter 2008).

In this study, it was found that ahead of Chinese elites encountering German psychiatric thoughts, the United States, as a mediator, had screened the German achievements as it prefers. However, as a beginner in this field, the United States had not adequate ability to identify the values of these concepts from Europe. Before the 1890s, the United States could be considered as a creative follower of France and Germany. Consequently, China was unaware of the whole situation of German psychiatry around 1900 and the achievements in Germany has not been tested or evaluated fully by China; the ancient country in the East experienced a longer history and owned a richer culture than most of the other countries in the world (Li 2016).

When a dying civilization was back to life through a revival movement, the existing civilization would be in touch with it. Renaissance is a quite common phenomenon in many societies. In addition to the manifestations in the Late Middle Ages and early modern Italy, renaissance could occur in other areas. German psychiatric speculations and concepts around 1900 were of great value, though seriously underestimated for sophisticated reasons. They should be reevaluated ahead of contemporary psychiatry being pushed forward hastily on the biomedical avenue without any fork.

It is imperative to convene the sincere dialogue between East and West. In the Far East, the independently generated experience and wisdom of many nations through several centuries are of great value. Being away from the 'radar' of American academic psychiatry, fortunately they have never disappeared or been strangled (Shorter 2008). East Asian psychiatry residents, who are not particularly attached to the antiquated language currently used, may be particularly equipped for the task of recreating psychiatric language together with knowledge in the twentieth century (de Leon 2013).

A broader cultural perspective for the history of psychiatry

A British historian, Arnold Joseph Toynbee (1889–1975), pointed out that the contact during the same era between different civilizations is not a prerequisite for dialogues (Toynbee 1947). Civilizations generated in the same era could meet with each other in different spaces. For example, German psychiatric concepts were transferred to the United States. Moreover, civilizations in different eras have the chance to chat with each other at an unknown future time point or time interval. German psychiatric concepts around 1900, for instance, were comprehended in Chinese circumstances.

A study with a beginning of a specific case or subject, with an emphasis on social and cultural influences, along with the complex process of interaction and construction of medical knowledge between East and West, might be one of the vibrant areas of medical history. In the process of transcultural reconstruction of civilization, exceptions, transformations, and creations in human actives are unique performances. Therefore, one of the most important duties for historians is to use their intelligence to capture such phenomena instead of just trying their best to accumulate numerous historical facts (Toynbee 1947).

So far, the historical research projects of psychiatry today had been found mainly being carried out inside single countries respectively. Although international relationships and knowledge transfer increasingly become the topic of concern, related explorations were mostly proposed among the Western world, or just between several countries in Europe, among which close contact in international relations and direct association of modern civilizations have been honored by the time.

Moreover, as one of the medical issues, psychiatry has been depicted mainly by sociologists, rather than medical professionals. Michel Foucault (1926–1984) has had a very important impact on the understanding of how modern societies and their powerful politics concerned the population, including the mentally ill. The relationship between knowledge and power did exist; however, over-interpretation of medical phenomena from the perspective of sociology is inappropriate. The inherent medical components should be supplemented and restored.

Finally, strong circumstantial evidence contributed to a better understanding of how German psychiatry has evolved in the process of transcultural knowledge construction. In order to break through the inherent mode of thinking, the issue of 'modern psychiatry in China' should be examined from the perspective of world history. In this study, the main finding is 'German wine in America bottle' (Li & Schmiedebach 2015), which means that modern psychiatry was introduced to China through a process of cultural adaptation in which the United State served as a bridge for German thought. Thus, despite the fact that there was little direct contact between Chinese and German psychiatry, a process of cultural adaptation took place: the German wine was kept, but the glittering American label on the bottle was stripped away.

Notes

1 Cultural adaptation theory was proposed by Herbert Spencer (1820–1903) originally. The concept belonged to the category of sociology. It referred to the initiative of adapting to the cultural and social environment, which was generated during the course of human interaction.

2 Comparative history is the comparison of different societies which existed during the same time period or shared similar cultural conditions. Marc Bloch (1886–1944), an early distinguished comparative historian, published a famous article named *Toward a Comparative History of European Societies* in 1928, which provided a conceptual and methodological basis for comparative history for the first time. The methods of historical comparison held by Bloch derived from 'Mill's Five Methods'. Recently, the concept of scientific history and the methods oriented by historical materialism enriched the methodology of comparative history.

3 Medical intelligence science is an emerging cross-disciplinary, which refers to the utilization of the principles, methods and techniques from intelligence science into medical field. It focuses on the medical literature and other technological information analysis, so as to provide targeted and instructive as well as comprehensive analytical conclusion. It could be seen as an important branch of intelligence science. Medical intelligence science commits to the research on the compositions and characteristics of specialized medical information, on the regularity during the whole process of medical information exchange. In other words, it is a discipline aimed to study the production, formation, collection, organization, dissemination, absorption, and utilization of all forms of medical information.

4 Translation is often embedded with asymmetrical power relations, serving as an effective means of interpretation between the colonizer and the colonized.

5 The translation of a text from language A to B, and then from language B to C, D, E, and so forth, where B is said to act as the pivot language.

6 Relay translation refers to a chain of (at least) three texts, ending with a translation made from another translation.

7 The character of '*Xin* 心' from the saying *Xin Zhu Shen Ming* 心主神明 in TCM have never referred to one precise body component, like 'the heart' or 'the brain', but have been on behalf of a broader organic and somatic-oriented conception, because each component is interdependent and interactive mutually. However, the function of brain, as a specific organ, in mental illness has never been denied.

References

Barton, W. E. (1987) *The History and Influence of the American Psychiatric Association*, Washington: American Psychiatric Publishing.

Beard, G. (1869) 'Neurasthenia, or nervous exhaustion', *The Boston Medical and Surgical Journal* 80(13): 217–221.

Bernal, J. D. (1954) *Science in History*, London: Watts & Co Ltd.

Beumont, P. (1992) 'Phenomenology and the history of psychiatry', *Australian and New Zealand Journal of Psychiatry* 26(4): 532–545.

Bloch, M. (1953) 'Toward a comparative history of European societies', *Enterprise and Secular Change Supplement*: 494–521.

Bonner, T. N. (1963) *American Doctors and German Universities: A Chapter in International Intellectual Relations, 1870–1914*, Lincoln: University of Nebraska Press.

Brink, L. and S. E. Jelliffe (1933) 'Emil Kraepelin, psychiatrist and poet', *Journal of Nervous and Mental Diseases* 77(3): 134–152.

Burke, P. and R. P.-c. Hsia (2007) *Cultural Translation in Early Modern Europe*, Cambridge: Cambridge University Press.

Bynum, W. F. (1994) *Science and the Practice of Medicine in the Nineteenth Century*, Cambridge: Cambridge University Press.

Chen, Yi Ming 陈一鸣 (2010) '北京现代精神医学早期的追索 – 先辈伍兹、雷曼、魏毓麟、许英魁的光辉历程' (Early traces of modern psychiatry in Beijing: a glorious history—Woods, Lyman, Yulin Wei, Yingkui Xu), 临床精神医学杂志 (Journal of Clinical Psychiatry) 20(2): 142–143.

Chiang, H. (2014) *Psychiatry and Chinese History (Studies for the Society for the Social History of Medicine)*, London: Pickering & Chatto.

Chu, L. and M. Liu (1960) 'Mental diseases in Peking between 1933 and 1943', *The British Journal of Psychiatry* 106(442): 274–280.

de Leon, J. (2013) 'Is psychiatry scientific? A letter to a 21st century psychiatry resident', *Psychiatry Investigation* 10(3): 205–217.

Diamant, N. (1993) 'China's great confinement? Missionaries, municipal elites, and police in the establishment of Chinese mental hospitals', *Republican China* 19(1): 3–50.

Fan, T., Q. Hu and M. Liu (2020) 'Psychiatric wards of Soochow Elizabeth Blake Hospital (1898–1937): a missing piece in the history of modern Chinese psychiatry', *History of Psychiatry* 31(2): 163–177.

Grau, C. (2014) *Die Frühphase der Psychiatrie Chinas: vergleichende Betrachtung der ersten psychiatrischen Anstalten im China der späten Kaiser-und Republikzeit (1898–1945)*, Berlin: LIT Verlag Münster.

Hamanaka, T. and G. E. Berrios (2003) *Two Millennia of Psychiatry in West and East*, Tokyo: Gakuju Shoin.

He, Ping 何平 (2004) '比较史学的理论方法和实践' (Theory and practice of comparative history), 史学理论研究 (Historiography Quarterly) 4: 137–143.

Ion, R. M. and M. Beer (2002a) 'The British reaction to dementia praecox 1893–1913. Part 1', *History of Psychiatry* 13(51): 285–304.

Ion, R. M. and M. Beer (2002b) 'The British reaction to dementia praecox 1893–1913. Part 2', *History of Psychiatry* 13(52): 419–431.

Lerner, P. F. (2003) *Hysterical Men: War, Psychiatry, and the Politics of Trauma in Germany, 1890–1930*, Ithaca: Cornell University Press.

Li, W. (2016) 'International knowledge transfer: the adaption of German Psychiatric Concepts around 1900 during the Academic Evolution of Modern Psychiatry in China', Available at: https://ediss.sub.uni-hamburg.de/volltexte/2016/8104/pdf/Dissertation.pdf (accessed 04 June 2020).

Li, W. and H.-P. Schmiedebach (2015) 'German wine in an American bottle: the spread of modern psychiatry in China, 1898–1949', *History of Psychiatry* 26(3): 348–358.

Li, Ya Ming 李亚明 (2005) '19世纪的德国精神病学' (Germany psychaitry in nineteenth century), 中华医史杂志 (Chinese Journal of Medical History) 35(2): 114–117.

Liu, L. H. (1995) *Translingual Practice: Literature, National Culture, and Translated Modernity China*; 1900–1937, Stanford: Stanford University Press.

Lyman, R. (1937) 'Psychiatry in China', *Archives of Neurology and Psychiatry* 37(4): 765–771.

Messner, A. C. (2000) *Medizinische Diskurse zu Irresein in China (1600–1930)*, Stuttgart: Steiner.

Meyer, A. and E. E. Winters (1951) *The Collected Papers of Adolf Meyer: Psychiatry*, Baltimore: Johns Hopkins University Press Vol. 3: 523.

Mitsutomo, Y. (1974) 'The shifting center of scientific activity in the West', *Science and Society in Modern Japan: Selected Historical Sources* (5): 81.

Ng, V. W. (1990) *Madness in Late Imperial China: From Illness to Deviance*, Norman: University of Oklahoma Press.

Noll, R. (2011) *American Madness: The Rise and Fall of Dementia Praecox*, Cambridge: Harvard University Press.

Pearson, V. (1991) 'The development of modern psychiatric services in China 1891–1949', *History of Psychiatry* 2(6): 133–147.

Pearson, V. (1995) *Mental Health Care in China: State Policies, Professional Services and Family Responsibilities*, London: Gaskell London.

Peters, U. H. (1988) 'Die deutsche Schizophrenielehre und die psychiatrische Emigration', *Fortschritte der Neurologie, Psychiatrie* 56(11): 347–360.

Peters, U. H. (1990) 'Adolf Meyer und die Beziehungen zwischen deutscher und amerikanischer Psychiatrie', *Fortschritte der Neurologie, Psychiatrie* 58(09): 332–338.

Roelcke, V., P. Weindling and L. Westwood (2010) *International Relations in Psychiatry: Britain, Germany, and the United States to World War II*, Rochester: University Rochester Press.

Sarason, S. B. (1988) *The Making of an American Psychologist: An Autobiography*, San Francisco: Jossey-Bass.

Schmiedebach, H.-P. (2011) 'The reputation of psychiatry in the first half of the twentieth century', *European Archives of Psychiatry and Clinical Neuroscience* 261(2) Supplement 2: 192–196.

Schmiedebach, H.-P. and S. Priebe (2004) 'Social psychiatry in Germany in the twentieth century: ideas and models', *Medical History* 48(4): 449–472.

Sewell, W. H. (1967) 'Marc Bloch and the logic of comparative history', *History and Theory* 6(2): 208–218.

Shorter, E. (1997) *A History of Psychiatry: From the Era of the Asylum to the Age of Prozac*, New York: Wiley.

Shorter, E. (2008) *A History of Psychiatry: From the Era of the Asylum to the Age of Prozac* (*in Chinese*), Shanghai: Shanghai Science and Education Press: translation by Jian Ping Han etc. of A History of Psychiatry (1997).

Skocpol, T. and M. Somers (1980) 'The uses of comparative history in macrosocial inquiry', *Comparative Studies in Society and History* 22(2): 174–197.

St. André, J. and H-y. Peng, (2012) 'Introduction: setting the terms', in St. André, James G. and Peng, Hsiao-yen (eds.), *China and Its Others: Knowledge Transfer through Translation, 1829–2010*, Amsterdam: Rodopi: 11–25.

Stevens, R. (1998) *American Medicine and the Public Interest*, Berkeley: University of California Press.

Sutton, S. B. (1986) *Crossroads in Psychiatry: A History of the McLean Hospital*, Washington: American Psychiatric Press.

Szto, P. P. (2002) 'The accommodation of insanity in Canton, China: 1857–1935', Available at: https ://search.proquest.com/docview/305507743 (accessed 04 June 2020).

Toynbee, A. J. (1947) *A Study of History*, New York: Oxford University Press.

Tseng, W.-S. (1973) 'The development of psychiatric concepts in Traditional Chinese Medicine', *Archives of General Psychiatry* 29(4): 569–575.

Westbrook, C. H. (1953) 'Psychiatry and mental hygiene in Shanghai: a historical sketch', *The American Journal of Psychiatry* 110(4): 301–306.

Wolpert, E. M. (2006) *Images in Psychiatry: German Speaking Countries; Austria, Germany, Switzerland*, Heidelberg: Universitätsverlag Winter.

Xia, Z. and M. Zhang (1981) 'History and present status of modern psychiatry in China', *Chinese Medical Journal* 94(5): 277–282.

Xiong, Yue Zhi 熊月之 (2011) 西学东渐与晚清社会 (Western Learning and the Late Qing Dynasty), Beijing: China Renmin University Press.

Xu, Tao Yuan 徐韬园 (1989) '中国精神病学四十年' (Forty years of Chinese psychiatry), 上海精神医学 (Shanghai Archives of Psychiatry) 1(1): 7–9.

Xu, Tao Yuan 徐韬园 (1995) '我国现代精神病学发展史 (History of modern psychiatry in China), 中华神经精神科杂志 (Chinese Journal of Psychiatry) 28(3): 168–176.

Young, D. and M. Chang (1983) 'Psychiatry in the People's Republic of China', *Comprehensive Psychiatry* 24(5): 431–438.

Zuo, Han Bin 左汉宾 (2010) '近代以来世界医学科学中心转移现象探析' (Analysis of the transfer of the world medical scientific center until modern times), 中华医史杂志 (Chinese Journal of Medical History) 40(2): 67–71.

42

The effects of climate change in China

Transformation of lives through cultural heritage

Elena Perez-Alvaro

Introduction

There is a general acceptance that the world's climate is changing and China, like many other countries, will be affected by these changes. Climate change includes oceans warming up, ice melting at the poles, and sea levels rising. We are also witnessing a transformation in the chemical composition of oceans, for example, in their acidity or salinity. Moreover, the pattern of currents is changing and, as a consequence, ecosystems are becoming increasingly more endangered (Perez-Alvaro 2016; Climate Central 2015). Predictions have also been made about more frequent and intense storm activity, longer and hotter drought conditions, and increased temperatures (McIntyre-Tamwoy et al. 2015). These meteorological changes will not only affect Earth's biodiversity and landscapes, but they will have a large impact on people (Gruber 2011). Climate change is not just a global process acting on the environment, but a process acting on societies that govern the environment (Morris 2011). It will have economic, political, and identity implications, and how such changes might affect lifestyles needs to be understood.

Small Island Developing States (SIDS) are a good example in understanding the reality of the situation: these states are very vulnerable to a rise in sea levels and may even become uninhabitable (UNESCO 2008). In the Pacific, Tuvalu is losing its territory as well as its heritage, and consequently, its culture as a nation is transforming (Fernandez 2013). However, it is not the only state losing its territory. Kelly (2014) explains how communities on the Torres Strait are also suffering king tides and flooding that make life nonviable. The islands will probably be completely submerged in the future, meaning that 7,000 people already have to adapt to climate change (Land and Sea Management Unit 2014). Australia has invited them to live on Australian territory, therefore, the land of such states and their culture will be lost. People may move to another country to start a new life, but their identity as citizens of their cities and countries, as members of a community with their own tangible past, complete with their cultural heritage, will disappear.

China's worries lie on the mainland as none of its islands have indigenous people and many of them are underwater at high tide or permanently submerged anyway. However, the

DOI: 10.4324/9780429059704-49

issue is that most of these islands are disputed with other sovereignties such as Vietnam (the Paracel Islands) or Taiwan (the Pratas Islands) (Perez-Alvaro & Forrest 2018). If the islands disappear, this will create disputes orientated to maritime claims on territorial waters, as this chapter later will explain.

This study explores how climate change will probably modify social and cultural behaviors, with communities changing how they live and work, migrating and abandoning their heritage, and modifying their identity. The problem is much larger than it may seem at first glance: 'identity' is a concept intrinsically linked to the concept of heritage, a process of inclusion and exclusion that defines communities (Graham & Howard 2008: 5). Heritage is necessary for an individual or a society to reinforce its socio-cultural identity. If climate change robs a culture of the land where its physical heritage is located, it would mean not only the loss of territory but also the transformation of a culture. China is a country with a variety of climates, ecosystems, cultural practices, and sites. The point of this chapter is to form a general idea of the impact that climate change may have in a country with such diversity, formulating possible solutions and concluding that, since climate change seems inevitable now and although governments and individuals need to do the impossible to minimize it, it will happen one way or another and China has to adapt and be ready for it.

Climate change in China: Floods and droughts

Some global cities have already experienced massive floods. However, it is not only coastal cities that are at risk as inland cities have suffered from overflowing riverbanks (Barthel-Boucher 2013). Some of these problems have already been experienced: for example, in 2019 a 2,000-year-old drainage system was found in East China (Xinhua 2019). The pipes were similar to those of modern underground drainage pipes, suggesting a need for draining certain flooded places.

Balica et al. (2012) studied the number of people living close to the coastline, the time needed to recover from flooding, and the measures needed to prevent floodwater and declared that Shanghai was the most vulnerable major city in the world. Coastal floods are among the most dangerous and harmful of natural disasters since urban areas adjacent to the shorelines are where major concentrations of the human population, settlements, and socio-economic activities take place. Sixty percent of China's population lives within coastal zones (Brooks et al. 2006). Due to the length of its coastline and high river discharge, Shanghai is the most exposed to coastal floods and, according to Balica et al. (2012), the most vulnerable because of its cultural heritage, shelters, flood cultural behavior, and percentage of disabled people.

Flooding may not be the only threatening issue. Some parts of the globe also suffer from increasingly dry climates due to rising temperatures, diminished rainfall, and deforestation (Barthel-Boucher 2013). According to the author, China will be particularly affected by droughts, due to its intensive development as it only has access to 10% of its water; because of over-cultivation and other pressures on water sources, more than a quarter of China will soon turn into desert. Nowadays, farming uses about 70% of the country's water, and around 21% of the country's surface water resources are unfit even for farming, due to salinity (Barthel-Boucher 2013). Furthermore, more than 80% of the glaciers in western China are in retreat so the exhaustion of the glacial water supply would have an impact on the availability of water for both agricultural and human consumption (Wheatley 2010). Carney (2018) remarked that in the past 25 years 28,000 rivers and waterways have disappeared across the country, and the iconic Yellow River often fails to reach the sea and is now a tenth of what it was in the 1940s. As a consequence, China may have a water deficit of 200 billion cubic meters in the near future.

The predicted increase of droughts on the one hand and flooding on the other are threats that are difficult to mitigate. Climate changes are accelerated by population growth and increasing urbanization (Balica et al. 2012) and human activities exert pressure on natural processes. How the different areas in China will be affected depends on many factors such as topography and elevation. What seems clear is that climate change may create environmental migration (climate refugees) due to ecological pressures, as this chapter will later explain.

Identity and heritage

Graham and Howard identify heritage as 'the way in which very selective past material artefacts, natural landscapes, mythologies, memories and traditions become cultural, political and economic resources for the present' (2008: 2). China's cultural heritage is very diverse, including indigenous sites that are ephemeral or cultural practices on more constructed sites. The loss of archaeological knowledge, the impact on indigenous identity, and community well-being due to climate change has still not been understood.

Identity and tangible cultural heritage in China

It is not the aim of this chapter to list the number of tangible cultural heritage sites in China, which would be very extensive and very difficult to categorize according to different criteria, but to link tangible heritage with the concept of identity examining the threats this heritage may suffer from climate change.

Tourism in China has emerged as a force for economic development, utilizing heritage for product development (Sofield & Li 1998). According to Hoelscher and Anheier (2011), one of the most visited World Heritage sites in 2009 was the Forbidden City (7,000,000 visitors), just short of tourist figures from the Louvre in France (8,3000,000 visitors) and the Great Smoky Mountains in the USA (9,000,000 visitors). However, tangible cultural heritage is not only located on land but also underwater: sunken cities, shipwrecks, or aircraft are a few examples of what can be found at the bottom of the sea. The South China Sea has a wealth of underwater cultural heritage as it hosted some of the busiest maritime routes of ancient times, several battlefields, and some of the oldest heritage on Earth, which represented the close interaction, activities, and accumulation of the maritime history of various civilizations over generations. The Battle of Yamen in 1279, for example, is reported to have resulted in the sinking of over 2,000 warships (Gruber 2008) which provides information on the economic and cultural link between neighboring countries. The subsequent Western age of discovery and colonization left a rich legacy of shipwrecks from Portugal, Netherlands, Spain, and England in the South China Sea over a period of more than 450 years (Adams 2013).

In general, climate changes may affect tangible cultural heritage in two substantial ways: either by exposing, damaging, or moving the current underwater cultural heritage or by transforming cultural heritage on land. Tangible cultural heritage on land can be affected by sandstorms burying both buildings and relics or by processes leading to faster decay of structures (Gruber 2011). Climate change can also transform tangible cultural heritage on land into underwater cultural heritage by flooding.

In the case of underwater cultural heritage, the most important source of information for archaeologists at underwater sites is not only ships or underwater cities but also their associated objects: context, inventory, personal belongings, and cargo, each of which has a different reaction to water and changes. Cultural heritage, once submerged, is covered by coral, mud, microorganisms, and sand. Furthermore, once they are stabilized, there is little physical disturbance by postdepositional forces (Piechota & Ciangrande 2008). Underwater cultural heritage is, as a consequence, protected by the stability that may change due to climate change in the oceans, such as currents modification or increased depth. More water means greater depth and shipwrecks lying on the seabed will be subject to greater pressure, which may be more than they can withstand. Additionally, an increase of one meter will affect the amount of time a diver can remain safely underwater and the archaeological works that a shipwreck may need for its protection would take much longer. There are already some examples of processes that underwater cultural heritage is experiencing. For instance, the raising of sea levels has disturbed the underwater graves of soldiers killed in World War II on the Marshall Islands (McGrath 2014). The tides have exposed a grave containing 26 human bodies; the coffins and human remains are being washed away, causing ethical issues due to the watery graves being disturbed (Perez-Alvaro 2019). Underwater sites that have been protected and preserved thanks to the layers of sediments may be exposed or damaged.

On the other hand, cultural heritage on land may be submerged and transformed into underwater cultural heritage sites: when there is destruction, there is also creation. If water levels rise even further, by 3, 4, or 5 meters in centuries to come, cities will have to be abandoned (Rahmstorf & Richardson 2009). These underwater cities will become future underwater cultural heritage sites. If climate change keeps progressing, by the year 2050 global temperatures will have crossed the threshold of 2°C above the preindustrial value. Sea levels will have increased another 30 cm since the year 2000 and by the year 2100, the temperature will stand at 5°C above the average (Rahmstorf & Richardson 2009). To get a clearer idea, the following images from Climate Central (2015) depict a potential scenario of a future rise in sea levels in Shanghai. The first image shows a projection of a post-2100 rise in sea level of 2°C warming from carbon pollution corresponding to the target limit by the United Nations (see Figure 42.1).

In the second image, the projection is based on 4°C (see Figure 42.2).

Buildings, cultural heritage sites, and religious erections will be covered by water. As a consequence, the question is not only how destruction can be prevented but what will destruction create. We will lose cultural heritage, but we will also gain underwater cultural heritage. However, the meaning for the society of this cultural heritage will change. The stories that society tells itself about its past are often grounded in material heritage (Viejo-Rose 2011); these objects and places nourish a sense of group identity and cohesion. Conflict, even if it is in the form of natural disasters such as climate change, changes social, urban, and power structures and, as a result, will transform the meaning of these tangible heritage places (Viejo-Rose 2011).

Identity and intangible cultural heritage in China

Cheng and Ling (2013) classified the structures of intangible cultural heritage in China into three types: traditional craft and traditional opera (the most predominant class), traditional music, customs, dancing, art, and literature and the least predominant type, traditional physical education, medicine, and drama.

Intangible heritage distribution in China has a certain correlation with big river systems (Cheng & Ling 2013). The authors state that the first factor affecting the distribution of intangible cultural heritage is the geographic environment as cultural heritage is more

Figure 42.1 Shanghai's projections image based on 2°C warming. Source: © [Climate Central]. Reproduced by permission of Climate Central. Permission to reuse must be obtained from the rights holder. Available at: http://sealevel.climatecentral.org.

Figure 42.2 Shanghai's projections image based on 4°C warming. Source: © [Climate Central]. Reproduced by permission of Climate Central. Permission to reuse must be obtained from the rights holder. Available at: http://sealevel.climatecentral.org.

evident in areas rich in products and human activities. The second factor is the existence of liveable environmental conditions because these areas are characterized by long histories and rich cultures. The last factor that the authors identify is that minority regions along border areas are subjected to less cultural invasion, therefore, more intangible cultural heritage survives over time. The main issue is that if the intangible cultural heritage of the communities in these areas is modified or disappears if the land floods or is subject to drought, these communities will need to emigrate. Because the traditions and lifestyles of those living in intangible cultural heritage areas are inherited from ancestors and passed on to descendants, the creation of intangible cultural heritage may be linked to the land, but its survival depends on descendants maintaining and transmitting it where they live.

Cultural heritage, whether tangible or intangible, as a symbolic element, is part of the national discourse of society. As Viejo-Rose (2011) argues, cultural heritage is used to evoke memories or emotions and it is highly selective depending on the nation. Cheng and Ling (2013) state that most of the cultural heritage in China is influenced by the nationality of the population. In fact, according to Hoelscher and Anheier (2011) during the period from 1999 to 2004, 55.1% of the Chinese population thought that among locality, region, country, continent, or the world, the most important for them was their country. In contrast, only 23.5 % thought so in Japan, who considered their local identity to be the most important to them. This may be the reason why cultural heritage is such a strong element in the national discourse of China: people feel they are citizens of the country as a whole. This national discourse needs to be used by Chinese policymakers to help protect cultural heritage from climate change.

Ethical issues: Land loss and change in people's lives

Climate change in China may lead to two main ethical issues: land loss and changes in people's lives.

Land loss can cause problems with shifting the delimitation of the seas. Legal disputes concerning sea boundaries are a diplomatic source of conflict nowadays; just meters of sea can be the object of dispute in international tribunals, such as the International Tribunal for the Law of the Sea (Perez-Alvaro & Forest 2018). China is already involved in a legal dispute concerning the South China Sea: A long-contested seascape manifested in disputed claims over islands, their resulting maritime zones, and maritime boundaries between a range of southeast Asian governments, including Vietnam, Malaysia, Taiwan, Brunei, and the Philippines (Perez-Alvaro & Forest 2018). The division between internal waters and territorial seas is determined by the baselines provided for in the Law of the Sea (UNCLOS 1982). The coastal state has full sovereignty in internal waters that lie landward of the baseline. The territorial sea is measured from the baseline such that its outer limit is a line 12 nm from the nearest point of the baseline. The coastal state has the sovereignty of the territorial sea subject to some limitations, mostly the concept of innocent passage of vessels through the zone. If the baseline changes due to flooding, the rights of the coastal states will also change and this may bring new disputes and international conflict. Additionally, the melting of the Arctic would open new commercial maritime routes that would most certainly bring about new economic possibilities and the claiming of new territories (Fernandez 2013).

However, it is not only complicated legal processes that climate change can affect but also changes in people's lives: coastal floods can destroy houses and cultural heritage, disrupt communication and agriculture and even cause fatalities. Many economic activities can be affected by flooding such as tourism, fisheries, industries, shipping, transportation, agriculture, navigation, availability of potable water, or sea delimitation (Balica et al. 2012). New cities might need to be constructed and old cities may be abandoned. People's lives in these areas will be modified; they may even be the new climate refugees, a term that has had growing attention in global climate governance (Bettini 2013). However, the term has been heavily criticized for being alarmist and apocalyptic for two main reasons.

First, the term 'climate refugee' has no basis in international refugee law and could undermine the international legal regime for the protection of refugees (Hartmann 2010). The use of the word refugee, according to the United Nations Convention Related to the Status of Refugees (Refugee Convention 1951) is used for those who, 'owing to a well-founded fear of being persecuted [...] is unable or [...] unwilling to avail himself of the protection of that country' (Article 1.2). As a consequence, its use as climate-related migration may vitiate the meaning to those being persecuted. Additionally, displacement due to climate change is likely to be internal, without the crossing of international borders. In the case of islands and atolls threatened by a rise in sea levels, people may need to leave their homes. In the case of China – whose total geographical area is about 10,000,000 square kilometers, being the world's third or fourth-largest country by area – these displacements will probably be internal so the loss of identity as nationals of a country is less likely. The Chinese Special Administrative Region of Macau is the world's most densely populated territory with 48,003 people per square mile.[1] Some of its population will need to migrate due to climate change. However, while the eastern half of China is highly populated (as it is where intensive agriculture is centered), the western and frontier regions are almost isolated and sparsely populated. In fact, after economic reforms in the late 1970s, there was a tidal wave of west-to-east migration, depleting the population in the western regions.[2] If the east is severely threatened by flooding in the future, the population will start a gradual reversion to the west, finding agricultural processes and settling in previously abandoned territories or creating new territories: virgin areas will be explored, new cities will be constructed and, therefore, new cultural heritage will be born.

Second, human beings have traveled for many reasons, such as an increase in population, war, famine and disease, exhaustion of habit, pressure on resources, ambition, natural acquisitiveness, and curiosity or climate change (Scarre et al. 2019) and as a consequence, the more habitable parts of the Earth have been contested sites. In addition, there have already been different periods of climate change: some glaciations with episodes of global warming with warmer temperatures than in the present. As Gruber (2011) observes, the first small human settlements were founded in approximately 12,000 BC. This period was followed by a significant rise in the sea level that led to the flooding of these coastal settlements. Furthermore, after a drop in temperature before the Little Ice Age, winegrowing was pushed to the south. These changes impacted ways of living and whether shaping the landscape or adapting buildings, human beings had to move to find better places to live or adapt to make their land more habitable. Human beings have already exhausted land and resources in the past, needing to find new land to cultivate and live on. It is logical to think that if humans have survived previous climate changes, they will survive and adapt to future ones.

Using climate change as a security threat by using the term 'climate refugees' is likely to undermine efforts that reduce poverty and promote equity (Hartmann 2010). This is not to trivialize climate change and its impact on human mobility, as people will need to move and people will need to abandon their villages. However, it is best not to draw an alarmist narrative to avoid implications such as the risk of increased xenophobia, the use of authoritarian policies, or the creation of politics of fear against those refugees (Bettini 2013).

Recommendations

There is a close interrelationship between environment, culture, and human behavior. It is a hybrid that cannot be divided. Protected areas, both terrestrial and marine, are now being regarded holistically by many states.

This chapter has directed its efforts toward triggering the debate, which needs further discussion and dissemination across academic, social, and political agendas in China. It is erroneous to assume that the most visible remains are the most threatened. Accordingly, there needs to be a practical and political response to the effects of climate change on cultural heritage, but also a priority of raising awareness of its impact. As there is a lack of creativity in managing cultural heritage, some interagency cooperation might be necessary as well as convincing climate policymakers to include climate change impact on cultural heritage in planning (Van de Noort 2013).

Cultural heritage and environment

Whereas the term 'natural environment' has traditionally been used to refer to nature and the living resources therein, it is now recognized that cultural heritage resources are part of that environment, and the inextricable link between both means that the protection and treatment of one must contemplate the consequences for the other. Maybe it is time to adopt the concept of sustainability from environmentalism as the prime motivator for cultural heritage protection (Kingsley 2011). China's biodiversity ranks eighth in the world and first in the northern hemisphere (Tisdell 1984). According to Sofield and Li (1998), the values of ecologically sustainable development have appeared in China. Tourism has been given a leading role in introducing environmentally sound development, such as new forest parks. However, these strategies seem to be separated from embracing cultural heritage. As Morris states, 'conventional divisions between nature and culture can no longer be maintained' (2011: 124). In their need to confront climate change and their desire above all to preserve, those involved with cultural heritage have to fight the same battles as those involved with natural heritage since both domains will be affected by the same changes; cultural heritage is often constructed of unique local building materials and shipwrecks are often used by fish as artificial reefs. As a consequence, the same legal and political agendas that deal with the effect of climate change on nature, such as the effects on the oceans and coral reefs, should be widened to include cultural heritage. The environment has to be included in cultural heritage's agendas and heritage protection in environmentalist agendas.

The 1972 Convention concerning the Protection of World Cultural and Natural Heritage (UNESCO 1972), ratified by China in 1985, is an instrument for the preservation of both cultural and natural heritage. The category of cultural landscape recognizes the intangible value of heritage, for instance, as 'sacred places' (Rössler 2006). Chapman (2003) established a close relationship between ecological and archaeological site management and suggests a liaison between archaeologists and other parties interested in the natural environment. Lixinski (2008: 379) claims that the 'nature and culture dichotomy' listed in the 1972 World Heritage Convention (UNESCO 1972) is simply artificial, as it is proved to be in the wording, 'the combined works of nature and man'. Maybe the artificial distinction should include all types of heritage as the common denominator to protect for the benefit of humankind. This approach should be adopted by Chinese policymakers.

The Convention does not mention climate change specifically, but Article 11.4 states:

> The Committee shall establish, […] under the title of "List of World Heritage in Danger", a list of the property appearing in the World Heritage List […] The list may include only such property forming part of the cultural and natural heritage as is threatened by serious and specific dangers, such as the threat of disappearance caused by accelerated deterioration, large-scale public or private projects or rapid urban or tourist development projects; destruction caused by changes in the use or ownership of the land; major alterations due to unknown causes; abandonment for any reason whatsoever; the outbreak or the threat of an armed conflict; calamities and cataclysms; serious fires, earthquakes, landslides; volcanic eruptions; changes in water level, floods and tidal waves. The Committee may at any time, in case of urgent need, make a new entry in the List of World Heritage in Danger and publicize such entry immediately.

As a consequence, although climate change does not receive a specific mention, the threats that cultural heritage may suffer are contemplated. China has 37 cultural properties included on the World Heritage List 14 natural properties and 4 mixed properties; none are included in the List of World Heritage in Danger. Of the 37 cultural properties, it is difficult to find a single one where the environment is not part of the property, for instance, the West Lake Cultural Landscape of Hangzhou comprises numerous temples, pagodas, pavilions, gardens, and ornamental trees, as well as causeways, artificial islands, the lake, and surrounding hills. The Great Wall, inscribed in 1987, states its historic importance is matched only by its surroundings (UNESCO 1972). However, according to Gruber (2011), the Great Wall, at 6,300 kilometers in length, is one-third intact, one-third severely damaged, and one-third has completely vanished. Some sections are built of mud and the effects of sandstorms place constant stress on the material, which has been worn out and some sections are now just dust. The question is if it should be included in the List of World Heritage in Danger. This list describes heritage that is in ascertained danger of serious deterioration of materials, structure and/or ornamental features, architecture or town-planning coherence, urban or rural space, the natural environment, a significant loss of historical authenticity, or an important loss of cultural significance. Having just one-third of the Great Wall intact seems to fit this description of danger. However, it is not listed.

Protecting those sites just by their cultural value and ignoring their natural characteristics would mean a loss of half the value of the site. Individuals and governments have the power to protect nature, for example, by restoring or creating wetlands and wildlife corridors, and by establishing protected areas. Including cultural heritage in these measures will be of benefit to preserve the identity of individuals and communities as inhabitants of a natural and cultural world.

Government strategies

Developing effective protection mechanisms against climate change is very complicated. However, public awareness of climate change has been largely pursued via the media, outreach campaigns, and education. It seems the threat has been realized by both governments and individuals and actions are now being taken. The green lobby is proving successful in ensuring that consideration is given to the environment. Wildlife biologists who make concerted efforts to promote ocean conservation with messages about saving whales and dolphins, protecting coral reefs, or promoting catch-and-release fishing have not only been well received by the public but create hordes of people defending such principles. The cultural heritage lobby has not been as successful in its strategy as the public is not as aware and/or interested in the threats to cultural heritage as it is in the threats to the environment. As Sheridan and Sheridan (2013) observe, it seems that people may need to see their cultural heritage threatened, temples washed away or cathedrals destroyed by flooding to be convinced of the effects of climate change in culture and to evaluate and propose solutions. In fact, government and individuals can already take up measures such as foregoing fossil fuels, upgrading infrastructure such as electric transport, moving closer to work, consuming less such as buying a car that will last longer, being efficient creating less waste, or unplugging electric equipment when not in use (Biello 2007).

From a policy point of view, Group I of the Intergovernmental Panel on Climate Change (IPCC 2007) already concluded that the oceans are warming, the salinification of water is changing, there is evidence for decreased oxygen concentrations and the sea level is rising. According to Climate Action Tracker[3] China is simultaneously the world's largest consumer of coal and the largest developer of renewable energy. It seems like the choice it makes will have a lasting effect on the world's ability to limit warming to 1.5°C. China has already signed the Paris Agreement (2016) with targets such as lowering the carbon intensity, increasing the share of natural gas and increasing forest stock. It is not the aim of this chapter to analyze the government strategies for flattening CO_2 emissions, but instead to propose other possible solutions to those already designed by international policymakers.

A first approach would be mitigation measures. McIntyre-Tamwoy et al. (2015: 10) identify three main measures: continual maintenance of water drainage and diversion infrastructure, maintenance and construction of flood-resistant sea walls, and mobilization and training of civil society in disaster response. However, for Gruber (2011), corrective measures against climate change should focus on adaptation rather than mitigation.

In this regard, the second approach is convincing architects and cultural heritage policymakers to include climate change impact in planning (Cassar & Pender 2005), for instance, as a combination of applying water law, land use law, and construction law, with constant monitoring or by constructing comprehensive systems of coastal and river embankments or moving heritage structures. There is a need to rank the potential impact of climate change on individual heritage sites and determine the vulnerability, sensitivity, and resilience to future changes (Howard 2012). The UNESCO Strategy for climate change does not address any solution for cultural heritage. The 1992 UN Framework Convention on Climate Change did not have any direct reference to cultural heritage and neither did the 1997 Kyoto Protocol, which agreed to reduce greenhouse gas targets. International policymakers have to understand that cultural and natural heritage has to be contemplated and taken care of because joining agendas will make the strategies stronger.

Acceptance and cultural heritage management

There will be a loss of cultural heritage sites in China and around the world. It is necessary to evaluate and specify predominant values to determine what we should preserve, why should we preserve it, and how. We need to do it as soon as possible because climate change does not wait.

However, it is essential to understand that, although climate change does destroy heritage, it also creates new heritage (for instance, flooded cities or islands will become underwater cultural heritage). Again, this is an ethical issue on heritage as a process; understanding that it is inevitable to lose some cultural heritage, but that this, in turn, leads to gains under a different label. On this premise, however, the importance of these sites must be evaluated and appropriate actions taken in line with preserving the selected ones. These future submerged sites can be as touristic as they were when not flooded: the creation of diving underwater parks and snorkeling heritage trails are a good option for accessibility. Underwater trails attract many snorkelers and divers: for instance, in the Museo Atlántico, in Lanzarote (Spain), divers can visit the only underwater museum in Europe with sculptures by artist Jason deCaires Taylor. In fact, it attracts more than 11,000 visitors a year. Other solutions will include underwater museums, such as the Baiheliang Underwater Museum in Fuling, China. Opened in 2009, this museum is an archaeological site, now submerged under the waters of the newly built Three Gorges Dam, which displays some of the world's oldest hydrological inscriptions. The museum receives around 150,000 visitors a year.

Revisionist reactions to cultural heritage are common in moments of political transition, economic crisis, and natural disasters, such as climate change. Chinese policymakers will need to decide what to protect, what to memorialize, and what to forget. Natural events can be memorialized creating a natural world with local and national identities (Morris 2011). This chapter proposes two options for future lost cultural heritage.

First, people can continue to visit future abandoned heritage left behind because of possible flooding or abandoned cities. We can call this 'absent heritage', the memorialization of places and objects whose significance relates to their destruction or absence (Harrison 2013). It was a concept applied to the destruction of the Great and Little Buddhas of the Bamiyan Valley (Afghanistan). Pieces of heritage that once contained the Buddhas have remained as a memory of their destruction. This theory, applied to destroyed tangible cultural heritage, would treat them as 'absent niches', where the heritage site is not preserved but the space is, not only for memorialization but also as a reminder of the cause of destruction (men's actions and their consequences as climate changes). We consider this an 'absent presence' (Perez-Alvaro 2019).

Another idea is treating the destroyed cultural heritage as 'invisible heritage', in that it has left its footprints behind. In this regard, when the salvage company Odyssey Marine Exploration found the wreck of Nuestra Senora de las Mercedes, it was claimed that the shipwreck was not a shipwreck, but a field of debris (Zorich 2009). Contravening this idea, the concept of 'invisible heritage' includes shipwreck fields that are known to be there but have disappeared and that have been left invisible to the rest of human existence. It is the idea of heritage as a footprint.

Conclusions

Climate change is expected to cause an accelerated rise in sea levels, increased flood frequency, accelerated erosion, increased saltwater intrusion, increased storms, and increased frequency of cyclones. China, by the year 2100, may be heavily affected by these changes, as it is a country geographically, climatically, and culturally diverse in itself.

Loss of life is the first concern in dramatic climate change situations, but a loss of heritage, buildings, and traditions need to receive urgent attention. If villages and places on the coasts are abandoned, there will be a loss of spaces with exceptional cultural significance because archaeological heritage cannot be moved. However, the issue is not only about tangible cultural heritage but also the ethical questions around the protection of cultural traditions since cultural heritage shapes identity. Fortunately, due to China's geography, changes may be less transformative than in other countries where lands may be lost, especially island states. Although China will suffer some irreparable loss of land, cultural heritage, and modification of lifestyle may experience the worst consequences of climate change, such as floods or desertification.

Old cultural heritage may be submerged but will become underwater cultural heritage and ways to memorialize these sacred places need to be found. This chapter proposes two methods – absent heritage or invisible heritage. China is a privileged country because its natural habitat allows the application of environmental measures to cultural heritage and vice versa. The distinction between cultural and natural needs to disappear and policymakers from both fields need to join forces. The Chinese government, on the other hand, needs to create mitigation and adaptation measures and foresee the future loss of land and heritage.

Inevitably, there will be a loss of heritage sites. However, dramatizing the issue might create exceptional measures that may play against the solution. Assuming the loss will allow the prioritization of what is more important, the preservation of culture and the safeguarding of identity as citizens of a country is paramount.

Notes

1 Available at: https://www.worldatlas.com/articles/most-densely-populated-countries-in-the-world.html.
2 Available at: https://www.britannica.com/place/China/Population-distribution.
3 Available at: https://www.britannica.com/place/China/Population-distribution.

References

Adams, J. (2013). The role of underwater archaeology in framing and facilitating the Chinese National Strategic Agenda. In: T. Blumenfield and H. Silverman (eds.), *Cultural Heritage Politics in China*. New York: Springer: 261–282.

Balica, S. F., Wright, N. G. and van der Meulen, F. (2012). A flood vulnerability index for coastal cities and its use in assessing climate change impacts. *Natural Hazards*, 64(1): 73–105.

Barthel-Bouchier, D. (2013). *Cultural Heritage and the Challenge of Sustainability*. London and New York: Routledge.

Bettini, G. (2013). Climate Barbarians at the Gate? A critique of apocalyptic narratives on 'climate refugees'. *Elsevier: Geoforum* 45: 63–72

Biello, D. (2007). 10 solutions for climate change. *Scientific American Online*. 26-11-2007. Available at: https://www.scientificamerican.com/article/10-solutions-for-climate-change/ Accessed 10-07-2020.

Brooks, N., Nicholls, R. and Hall, J. (2006). *Sea Level Rise: Coastal Impacts and Response*. Norwich, Berlin: WBGU.

Carney, M. (2018). Forget geopolitics, water scarcity shapes up as the biggest threat to China's rise. *ABC News*. 26-11-2018. Available at: https://www.abc.net.au/news/2018-11-23/china-water-crisis-threatens-growth/10434116 Accessed 01-04-2020.

Cassar, M. and Pender, R. (2005). The impact of climate change on cultural heritage: Evidence and response. Published in the 14th Triennial Meeting The Hague Preprints. Vol. II.

Chapman, H. P. (2003). Global warming: The implications for sustainable archaeological resource management. *Conservation and Management of Archaeological Sites* 5(4): 241–245.

Cheng, Q. and Ling, S. (2013). Geographical distribution and affecting factors of the Intangible Cultural Heritage in China. *Scientia Geographica Sinica*. Available at: http://en.cnki.com.cn/Article_en/CJFDTotal-DLKX201310002.htm.

Climate Central. (November 2015). Mapping choices: Carbon, climate and rising oceans: Our global legacy. *Abgerufen am 29*. November 2015 von Climate Central. Report: http://sealevel.climatecentral.org/research/reports/mapping-choices-carbon-climate-and-rising-seas-our-global-legacy.

Fernandez (2013). Cambio climático y derecho del mar. In: J. J. Franch (Dir.), *Derecho del mar y sostenibilidad ambiental en el Mediterráneo*. Valencia: Tirant Lo Blanch: S. 271–317.

Graham, B. and Howard, P. (2008). Introduction. In: B. Graham and P. Howard (eds.), *The Ahsgate Research Companion to Heritage and Identity*. Cornwall: Ashgate Publishing Ltd: S. 1–17.

Gruber, S. (2008). Protecting China's cultural heritage sites in times of rapid change: Current developments, practice and law. *Legal Studies Research Paper No. 08/93*. The University of Sydney. Sydney Law School.

Gruber, S. (2011). The impact of climate change on cultural heritage sites: Environmental law and adaptation. *Carbon & Climate Law Review* 5(2): 209–219.

Harrison, R. (2013). *Heritage: Critical Approaches*. New York: Routledge.

Hartmann, B. (2010). Policy Arena. Rethinking climate refugees and climate conflict: Rhetoric, reality and the politics of policy discourse. *Journal of International Development* 22: 233–246.

Hoelscher, M. and Anheier, H. (2011). Indicator suites. In: H. Anheier and Y. Raj Isar (eds.), *Heritage, Memory & Identity*. London: SAGE: The Cultures and Globalization series 4: 285–391.

Howard, A. J. (2012). Managing global heritage in the face of future climate change: The importance of understanding geological and geomorphological processes and hazards. *International Journal of Heritage Studies* 19(7): 632–658.

IPCC (2007). Intergovernmental panel on climate change fourth assessment report on climate change. Available at: https://www.ipcc-wg1.unibe.ch/.

Kelly, E. (26 November 2014). Rising seas pose a cultural threat to Australia's 'forgotten people'. Von The conversation online: http://theconversation.com/rising-seas-pose-a-cultural-threat-to-australias-forgotten-people-34359abgerufen.

Kingsley, S. (2011). Challenges of maritime archaeology: In too deep. In: T. F. King (ed.), *A Companion to Cultural Resource Management*. Wiley: Blackwell Publications: 223–244.

Land and Sea Management Unit (2014). Torres strait climate change strategy 2014–2018. Torres Strait Regional Authority. Von Available at: http://www.tsra.gov.au/__data/assets/pdf_file/0003/7419/TSRA-Climate-Change-Strategy-2014-2018-Upload4.pdfabgerufen.

Lixinski, L. (2008). World heritage and the heritage of the world: Book review. By F. Francioni and F. Lenzerini. *The 1972 World Heritage Convention: A Commentary*, Oxford: Oxford University Press: 2008. *European Journal of Legal Studies* 2(1) 2008: 371–386.

McGrath, M. (2014). Climate change helps seas disturb Japanese war dead [online]. *BBC News: Science and Environment*. 7-6-2014. Available at: http://www.bbc.com/news/science-environment-27742957.

McIntyre-Tamwoy, S., Barr, S. and Hurd, J. (2015). Ethics, conservation and climate change. In: T. Ireland and J. Schofield (eds.), *The Ethics of Cultural Heritage. Ethical Archaeologies: The Politics of Social Justice 4*. New York: Springer Science+Business Media: Chapter 5: 69–88.

Morris, B. (2011). Not just a place: Cultural heritage and the environment. In Y. R. Isar, H. K. Anheier and D. Viejo-Rose (eds.), *Heritage, Memory and Identity*. London: The Cultures and Globalization Series, vol. 4. Sage: 124–135.

Paris Agreement (2016). United Nations framework convention on climate change. Available at: https://unfccc.int/process-and-meetings/the-paris-agreement/the-paris-agreement.

Perez-Alvaro, E. (2016). Climate change and underwater cultural heritage: Impacts and challenges. *Journal of Cultural Heritage* 21: 842–848.

Perez-Alvaro, E. (2019). *Underwater Cultural Heritage: Ethical Concepts and Practical Challenges*. New York: Routledge.

Perez-Alvaro, E. and Forrest, C. (2018). Maritime archaeology and underwater cultural heritage in the disputed South China Sea. *International Journal of Cultural Property* 25(3): 375–401.

Piechota, D. and Giangrande, C. (2008). Conservation of archaeological finds from deep-water wreck sites. In R. D. Ballard (ed.), *Archaeological Oceanography*. Princeton: Princeton University Press: 65–94.

Rahmstorf, S. and Richardson, K. (2009). *Our Threatened Oceans. The Sustainability Project*. London: Haus Publishing.

Refugee Convention (1951) United Nations convention relating to the Status of Refugees (1951). Available at: http://www.unhcr.org/uk/1951-refugee-convention.html.

Rössler, M. (2006). World heritage-linking cultural and biological diversity. In: B. T. Hoffman (ed.), *Art and Cultural Heritage: Law, Policy and Practice*. Cambridge: Cambridge University Press: 201–205.

Scarre, G., Holtorf, C. and Pantazatos, A. (2019). Introduction. In: C. Holtorf, A. Pantazatos and G. Scarre (eds.), *Cultural Heritage, Ethics and Contemporary Migrations*. New York: Routledge: 1–10.

Sheridan, R. and Sheridan, J. (2013). *International Heritage Instruments and Climate Change*. Illinois: Common Ground Publishing LLC.

Sofield, T. and Li, S. (1998). Tourism Development and Cultural Policies in China. *Annals of Tourism Research* 25(2): 362–392.

Tisdell, C. (1984). Tourism, the environment, international trade and public economics (No. 6).

UNCLOS (1982) United Nations Convention on the Law of the Sea. Available at: http://www.un.org/depts/los/convention_agreements/texts/unclos/unclos_e.pdf.

UNESCO (1972). Convention concerning the protection of the world cultural and natural heritage. Paris 16 November 1972. Available at: http://whc.unesco.org/en/conventiontext/.

UNESCO (2008). Policy Document on the Impacts of Climate Change on World Heritage Properties. UNESCO World Heritage Centre publications on climate change. Vonwhc.unesco.org/document/10046abgerufen.

Van de Noort, R. (2013). Wetland archaeology in the 21st Century: Adapting to climate change. In: F. Menotti and A. O'Sullivan (eds.), *The Oxford Handbook of Wetland Archaeology*. Oxford: Oxford University Press: 719–732.

Viejo-Rose, D (2011). *Reconstructing Spain: Cultural Heritage and Memory after Civil War*. Sussex: Sussex Academic Press.

Wheatley, A. (2010). Water crisis threatens Asia's rise. *The New York Times*. 11-10-2010. Available at: https://www.nytimes.com/2010/10/12/business/global/12inside.html Accessed 01-04-2020.

Xinhua (2019). Over 2,000-year-old drainage system found in E China. *Xinhuanet News*. 22-12-2019. Available at: http://www.xinhuanet.com/english/2019-12/22/c_138649833.htm Accessed: 01-04-2020.

Zorich, Z. (2009). Television: Finding treasure and losing history [online]. *Archaeology* 62, No. 2. Available at: http://archive.archaeology.org/0903/trenches/odyssey.html.

43

Reading between the lines

How frame analysis reveals changes in policy priorities

Sabine Mokry

Introduction

Secrecy is a key feature of authoritarian rule. Since authoritarian rulers constantly operate under structural insecurity, they try to hide their internal operations and actions. With no institutional constraints forcing them to publicize their internal procedures, their capacity to do so is high (Barros 2016: 954f.). This makes the political processes of authoritarian regimes, such as the People's Republic of China (PRC), opaque. One consequence of this opacity is that the Chinese government uses vague jargon to describe its work in policy documents. As a result, researchers cannot simply read the government's statements to grasp what it intends to prioritize. This chapter shows how researchers can apply frame analysis to detect the Chinese government's policy priorities in official documents.

Frame analysis describes the systematic identification and examination of frames. A frame is a schema of interpretation that performs at least one of the following four functions: problem description, diagnosis of causes, moral interpretation, and suggestion of remedies. The chapter first reviews how others have used the PRC's policy reports, mainly the annual government work report, as primary sources. After conceptualizing frames as the result of framing, it offers a step-by-step guide for identifying and examining frames. To illustrate the technique's potential, the chapter examines how the Chinese government's policy priorities changed in education, health, and foreign policy as expressed through frames in some of the most authoritative statements in the Chinese system, the Chinese Communist Party (CCP) General Secretary's reports to party congress and the annual government work report, over the course of the past 15 years.[1] The chapter's last section summarizes the technique's benefits and discusses its limitations as well as how other sources of evidence can mitigate these limitations.

Making sense of the Chinese government's reports

Many observers of Chinese politics argue that reports issued by the party-state play an important role in how the PRC is governed and should therefore be the starting point for any analysis of Chinese politics (You et al. 2010; Miller 2017; Mattis 2019). Snape (2019), for

DOI: 10.4324/9780429059704-50

instance, argues that these documents matter because they signal what issues the Chinese leadership wants to prioritize and because they set 'vague but compelling' boundaries for the larger political discourse (Snape 2019: 685). For scholars, the documents' 'consistency and accessibility' make them one of the rare means to obtain information for gauging policy changes (Wang 2017: 202). In the Chinese-language debate, some dive deep into recent reports (Huang 2019), many trace longitudinal changes, at times going as far back as the 1950s (Zhang 2016). Most studies focus on a particular topic, for example, demographic changes (Wu & Tang 2019), the government's approach towards informatization (Wang et al. 2019), or its ocean policy (Zhang 2016).

However, there is inadequate debate on how to analyze these reports to meet research needs. A handful of studies take the critical discourse analysis or the corpus linguistics approach. For example, with corpus-linguistic techniques such as frequency lists, co-selection patterns, and concordance lines, Meng and Yu (2016) examine the underlying power distance and ideological stances conveyed in the official political discourse in mainland China and in Hong Kong. Yu and Wu (2018) focus on the linguistic choices of agency examining the official translation of the annual government reports. However, they do not engage with the substantive policy content of the reports. Only Cha (2017) and You et al. (2010) engage with the reports' policy substance examining changes in terminology and what they could imply. Cha conducts a frequency analysis of selected words which he later combines into topical areas such as political ideology, international trends, foreign policy goals, and attitudes towards foreign affairs. Similarly, You et al. identify topics and schemata through which the Chinese government constructs its foreign policy (You et al. 2010). While these analyses bring interesting results, looking only at the frequency of certain words risks overlooking qualitative changes.

Frames and framing

This chapter starts from the premise that policy priorities are conveyed in frames. Frames are understood as 'cognitive tool[s] that help actors organize information in a complex environment' (Lenz 2018: 32). The logic behind framing, the process during which frames are generated, explains why frame analysis is suitable for revealing policy priorities: Entman (2007) describes framing as the 'process of culling a few elements of a perceived reality and assembling a narrative that highlights connections among them to promote a particular interpretation' (2007: 164). In the context of this chapter, 'particular interpretation' refers to the expression of policy priorities in official documents. As the government selects and expresses what it deems important, it engages in framing. Since frames are the result of framing processes, frames from different points in time differ from each other. Hence, comparing frames across time reveals shifts in the government's policy priorities.[2]

Framing has already been applied to various aspects of Chinese politics: from assessing how environmental advocacy groups align their frames with the government's (Zeng et al. 2019) to detailing how the public participates in frame-building on the internet. The biggest contribution of this literature has been to reveal the mechanisms behind the Chinese government's framing attempts: Van Gerven (2019) showed how the government framed the aging debate and connected it to welfare reform (2019). Hu (2020) teased out how the Chinese party-state managed to refocus the discourse on democracy by applying a delicate framing strategy. Through analyzing all articles published in the People's Daily, he found that the Chinese government reframed the meaning of democracy from 'what democracy is' to 'what the government is doing for democracy' (Hu 2020). Bondes and Heep (2012) revealed how the Chinese government propagated official frames to reproduce Chinese people's belief in the leadership's qualities and their determination to serve the common interest (Bondes & Heep 2012). These studies demonstrate how the Chinese government engages in framing; however, a detailed conceptualization of frames in official documents and examinations of how frames change over time are still lacking.

The specificity of Entman's framing definition renders it useful for conceptualizing and operationalizing frames (Jecker 2017: 13). His distinction of the four functions frames can perform is a helpful starting point for identifying and analyzing the frames the Chinese government uses to convey its policy priorities. According to Entman:

> to frame is to select some aspects of a perceived reality and make them more salient in a communicating text, in such a way as to promote a particular problem definition, causal interpretation, moral evaluation, and/or treatment recommendation.
>
> *(Entman 1993: 52)*

Table 43.1 describes each function briefly by summarizing Matthes & Kohring's operationalization of Entman's definition (Matthes & Kohring 2008: 264). The table also shows how

Table 43.1 Frame functions, their operationalization, and examples for frames that perform these functions

Frame function based on Entman	*Frame variable based on Matthes & Kohring*	*What it means in the analysis of the Chinese government's policy priorities*	*Example for a frame expressing policy priorities*
Diagnosis of causes	Benefit attribution	Indicates who/what causes success of a policy	Chinese government will use IT-based approaches for oversight over childcare *(GWR 2018)*
	Risk attribution	Indicates who/what causes failure of a policy	*Does not appear in the sample*
Moral evaluation	Benefit	Describes the positive effects of a certain policy	A modern hospital management system emerges *(19th PCR)*
	Risk	Describes the negative effects of a certain policy or action	Humanity's future depends on its choices *(19th PCR)*
Suggestion of remedies	Positive judgement	Calls for adopting a certain measure	Chinese government implement pilot reforms of public hospitals *(GWR 2010, 2011)*
	Negative judgement	Calls for not adopting a certain measure	Chinese government refrain from compensation for hospital costs with overpriced drugs *(19th PCR)*
Problem definition	Actor	Describes what a causal agent is doing	Chinese government
	Topic		Underpins all the above examples

these functions manifest themselves in the analysis of the Chinese government's priorities. Entman describes the diagnosis of causes as 'identify[ing] the forces creating the problem' (Entman 1993: 52). Frames that perform the function of moral evaluation 'evaluate causal agents and their effects' (Entman 1993: 52). Entman's third frame function is the suggestion of remedies, that is to 'offer and justify treatments for the problems and predict their likely effects' (Entman 1993: 52). According to Entman, a frame can perform several of these functions simultaneously. Most frames that express policy priorities perform one of the above functions as well as the frame function problem definition. In Entman's words, this frame function allows identifying 'what a causal agent is doing with what costs and benefits (…)' (Entman 1993: 52). Following Matthes and Kohring, I operationalize this frame function as issues and actors discussing these issues whereby the issues are most often covered by another frame function (Matthes & Kohring 2008: 264).

Frame analysis technique

Frames cannot be observed directly in the material used to reveal policy priorities because policy statements, especially by authoritarian states, tend to be vague. This section describes step by step how to identify and examine frames. The basic idea is to code frame fragments in the material, retrieve them, and combine them into frames in a structured manner. For this, each retrieved frame fragment is subsumed under one of the four types of frame components: actor, frame verb, qualifier, and frame object. After identifying frames, one can describe how they evolve across the sample. Before going into the specifics of each step, we explain the technique within the spectrum of frame analysis approaches.

To contextualize, frame analysis covers a wide spectrum from fully automated coding to interpretative approaches. Automated variants of frame analysis are based on word frequencies. Examining the use and omission of certain words, they require large amounts of text. As these automated approaches cannot capture infrequent frames, they risk omitting more subtle arguments. At the other end of the spectrum, interpretive approaches are based on a high degree of subjectivity. The frame analysis technique introduced in this chapter is based on manual but highly systematic coding and is located between automated large-n and interpretive approaches. The technique's main benefit lies in teasing out changes in frames over time. It does not only reveal what issues are important, but also how attributed importance shifts. Using Entman's frame functions helps to uncover an additional layer in the Chinese government's statements. While most frames in the policy reports perform the frame function 'suggestion of remedies', other frame functions also appear revealing insights on the Chinese government's rationale and justification strategies.

I now describe each step of the frame analysis in detail. Figure 43.1 provides an overview of all the steps as they pertain to the two stages of the investigation. Since there is no similar study whose coding scheme I could use, I developed the codes for the frame fragments inductively on the material. My manual technique is supported by the MAXQDA software's dictionary function. This tool allows to automatically apply predefined codes to the entire sample. First, I automatically identified combinations of four to five words that appeared multiple times across the sample and autocoded them in all documents. Second, I went through all the documents in the sample to code frame objects manually using MAXQDA's in-vivo coding function to ensure that I did not miss frame fragments that only appeared once. I went through the material adding new codes until no more new codes appeared. The codes need to be exhaustive and mutually exclusive. Exhaustive means that there is an appropriate code for each case coded. Mutually exclusive means that there is only one

Stage I: Identifying frames

1. Develop codes for frame fragments and code all the material
2. Retrieve frame fragments and subsume fragments under frame components
3. Combine frame components into frames

Stage II: Analyzing frames

1. Discern the function a frame performs
2. Describe changes in frames and frame functions

Figure 43.1 Steps for frame analysis.

appropriate code for each case that is coded (Neuendorf 2017: 131). I performed two rounds of reliability checks to ensure that the codes were exhaustive and mutually exclusive: In the first round, I made sure that I did not miss any frame objects. In the second round, I scrutinized each code to make sure that there were no overlaps between codes. This step is completed when all the material is coded. Figure 43.2 shows examples of coded frame fragments in MAXQDA's document browser.

The coded frame fragments are the building blocks for the frame components. I first retrieve the coded fragments, then, subsume each fragment under one of the four types of frame components: actors, frame verbs, and their qualifiers and frame objects. These are the structural components frames consist of. Actors describe who is doing something. Frame verbs describe the policy action and direction. For developing the frame verbs, I clustered all frame components with similar verbs and deduced a frame verb that covers all of them. Qualifiers modify the frame verbs and describe the degree of a policy action. Frame objects describe the concrete policy dimension. To identify frame objects, I merged similar codes. Figure 43.3 illustrates this step of transforming frame fragments into frame components.

Frame components that appear within a sentence are then combined into frames. After combining the frame components into frames, one can discern which functions a frame performs. Since the frame verb describes a frame's action, it determines which frame functions the frame performs. In the last step of the frame analysis, one examines in which documents

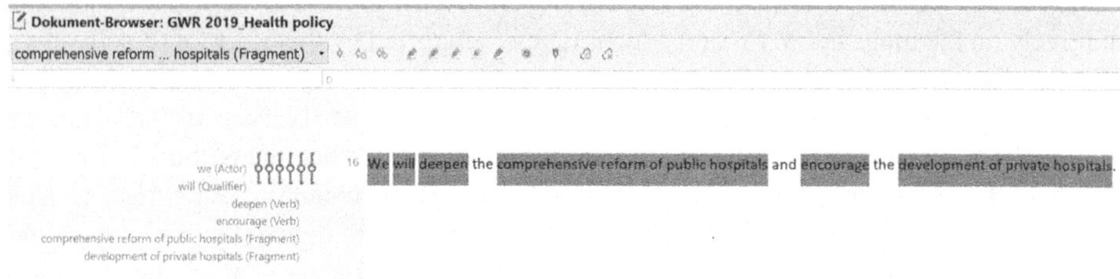

Figure 43.2 Examples of coded frame fragments.

Actor	Chinese government	Chinese government	Chinese government	Chinese government	Chinese government
Qualifier	none	none	none	none	fully
Frame verb	deepen	advocate	accelerate	extend	implement
Frame object	public hospital reform	public hospital reform	public hospital reform	public hospital reform	county-level public hospital reform
Coded frame fragment	reform of public hospitals	reform of public hospitals	reform of public hospitals	comprehensive reform of public hospitals	comprehensive reform of county-level public hospital reform

Figure 43.3 Examples of retrieved frame fragments subsumed under frame components.

and how often a particular frame appears. MAXQDA's Code Matrix Browser is a useful tool for this. It lists in which documents the identified frames appear. This graphical representation allows describing changes in frames. Figure 43.4 illustrates this.

Once the frames are identified in the material, one can analyze how they evolve. There are four ways to describe change and continuity in frames across the sample: Stable, faded, modified, and new. Stable frames appear multiple times across the documents in the same form. Faded frames disappear at some point. New frames appear only once, in the most recent edition of a document type. Modified frames change across the documents. Since each frame consists of a frame object and a frame verb, there are three possible scenarios for modification: change in frame object, change in frame verb, change in both frame object and verb. Change in frame object describes a change in issue/'what'. Change in frame verb describes a change in degree/'how'. The examples presented in Figure 43.5 are mostly changes in degree. Change in both frame object and frame verb describes changes in issue and degree. Since the frame verb determines the function a frame performs, a change in verb can be a change in frame function that would constitute a major change.

Changing priorities in the fields of health, education, and foreign policy

The following sections illustrate the research potential of the technique by examining changes in the Chinese government's policy priorities in health, education, and foreign policy through an analysis of frames in policy documents. The CCP General Secretary's report to the party congress held every five years is the most authoritative document in China's political system. It outlines the party's strategies for the coming years in all policy sectors (Jakobson 2013; Miller 2017). As a synthetic document, it reflects the consensus of the broader party leadership and provides policy guidance (Cha 2017). The annual government work report is presented by the premier to the National People's Congress usually held in March. For this chapter, all passages that deal primarily with health, education, and foreign policy were considered.[3] To increase readability, PCR stands for report to party congress, GWR stands for government work report. Figure 43.6 provides an overview of the analyzed material[4] and a first glimpse into which policy priorities appear across the documents. The darker the field, the more frequently the issue appears in the document.

Frame function	Suggestion of remedies	Suggestion of remedies	Suggestion of remedies	Suggestion of remedies	Suggestion of remedies
Variable	Positive judgement	Positive judgement	Positive judgement	Positive judgement	Positive judgement
Actor	Chinese government	Chinese government	Chinese government	Chinese government	Chinese government
Qualifier	*none*	*none*	*none*	*none*	fully
Frame verb	deepen	advocate	accelerate	extend	implement
Frame object	public hospital reform	public hospital reform	public hospital reform	comprehensive public hospital reform	county-level public hospital reform
17th PCR_Health policy	1	0	0	0	0
18th PCR_Health policy	1	0	0	0	0
19th PCR_Health policy	0	0	0	0	0
GWR 2010_Health policy	0	0	0	0	0
GWR 2011_Health policy	0	0	0	0	0
GWR 2012_Health policy	0	1	0	0	0
GWR 2013_Health policy	0	0	1	0	0
GWR 2014_Health Policy	0	0	0	0	0
GWR 2015_Health policy	0	0	0	0	1
GWR 2016_Health policy	0	0	0	0	0
GWR 2017_Health policy	0	0	0	0	0
GWR 2018_Health policy	0	0	0	0	0
GWR 2019_Health policy	0	0	0	1	0

Figure 43.4 Graphical representation of frames' appearances in the sample.

Health policy

The literature on China's health policy suggests that changes in the Chinese government's policy priorities are most likely in hospital reform, medical insurance, and the pricing of drugs (Liu et al. 2017; Cheng 2019). After discussing changed priorities as expressed through frames in these realms, the second part of the analysis will highlight changed policy priorities in areas that emerged from a close reading of the documents: doctor-patient relations, disease prevention, public health emergencies, and traditional Chinese medicine.

Regarding hospital reform, the Chinese government initially prioritized trial reforms, then ignored the issue for a couple of years. In 2019, hospital reform emerged again as a

<table>
<tr><td colspan="4">The analysed documents are available in the original Chinese version and in an official English translation. Since the two versions are directed at different audiences, they could differ significantly. This makes it necessary to consider both versions. Rather than conducting the frame analysis twice, the researcher should select the version s/he is more comfortable with and systematically compare the two version of each document before-hand. The comparison shows where and how much the two versions differ from each other. In the example below, differences are underlined. Differences can be substantive, in degree or minor. After identifying these differences, the document sections that relate to one's research interests should be analyzed in both versions of a document.</td></tr>
<tr><th>Chinese version</th><th>English version</th><th>Description of difference</th><th>Categorization of difference</th></tr>
<tr><td>中国秉持共商共建共享的全球治理观，<u>倡导国际关系民主化</u>，坚持国家不分大小、强弱、贫富一律平等，支持联合国发挥积极作用，支持扩大发展中国家在国际事务中的代表性和发言权。中国将继续发挥负责任大国作用，积极参与全球治理体系改革和建设，不断贡献中国智慧和力量。</td><td>China follows the principle of achieving shared growth through discussion and collaboration in engaging in global governance. <u>China stands for democracy in international relations</u> and the equality of all countries, big or small, strong or weak, rich or poor. China supports the United Nations in playing an active role in international affairs, and supports the efforts of other developing countries to increase their representation and strengthen their voice in international affairs. China will continue to play its part as a major and responsible country, take an active part in reforming and developing the global governance system, and keep contributing Chinese wisdom and strength to global governance.</td><td>CN: advocates democratization of international relations
EN: stands for democracy in international relations</td><td>Substantive difference</td></tr>
<tr><td><u>中华民族将以更加昂扬的姿态屹立于世界民族之林。</u></td><td><u>The Chinese nation will become a proud and active member of the community of nations.</u></td><td>EN: The Chinese nation will become a proud and active member of the community of nations
CN: The Chinese nation will stand in the forest of the nations of the world with a more magnificent attitude</td><td>Difference in degree</td></tr>
</table>

Figure 43.5 How to deal with official documents in different versions.

priority. To be more specific, between 2010 and 2016, most GWRs referred to trial reforms of public hospitals. There was a slight change in degree from implementing (抓好) (2010, 2011) to extending (扩大) (2014) such reforms. This focus on trial reforms was accompanied by frames that described the Chinese government as advocating for (推进) (2012) and accelerating (加快) (2013) the reform of public hospitals. After 2016, all these frames faded. The issue only reappeared in 2019, when a frame in the GWR put forward the call to action to 'deepen the comprehensive reform of public hospitals' (深化公立医院综合

Document type	Year	Delivered by	Hospital reform	Insurance	Drugs	Doctor-patient relations	Migrants	Disease prevention	Public health emergencies	Traditional Chinese Medicine
Report to Party Congress	2007	Hu Jintao								
	2012	Hu Jintao								
	2017	Xi Jinping								
Government Work Report	2010	Wen Jiabao								
	2011	Wen Jiabao								
	2012	Wen Jiabao								
	2013	Wen Jiabao								
	2014	Li Keqiang								
	2015	Li Keqiang								
	2016	Li Keqiang								
	2017	Li Keqiang								
	2018	Li Keqiang								
	2019	Li Keqiang								

Figure 43.6a Overview of data and policy priorities in health policy.

Document type	Year	Delivered by	Education providers	Purpose of education	Preschool education	Special needs education	Vocational education	Education inequality	Teachers	Schools' conditions
Report to Party Congress	2007	Hu Jintao								
	2012	Hu Jintao								
	2017	Xi Jinping								
Government Work Report	2010	Wen Jiabao								
	2011	Wen Jiabao								
	2012	Wen Jiabao								
	2013	Wen Jiabao								
	2014	Li Keqiang								
	2015	Li Keqiang								
	2016	Li Keqiang								
	2017	Li Keqiang								
	2018	Li Keqiang								
	2019	Li Keqiang								

Figure 43.6b Overview of data and policy priorities in education policy.

Document type	Year	Delivered by	International order	Threat perceptions	China's international role	Promotion of values	Relations to neighboring countries	Security	Interests	New initiatives
Report to Party Congress	2007	Hu Jintao								
	2012	Hu Jintao								
	2017	Xi Jinping								
Government Work Report	2010	Wen Jiabao								
	2011	Wen Jiabao								
	2012	Wen Jiabao								
	2013	Wen Jiabao								
	2014	Li Keqiang								
	2015	Li Keqiang								
	2016	Li Keqiang								
	2017	Li Keqiang								
	2018	Li Keqiang								
	2019	Li Keqiang								

Figure 43.6c Overview of data and policy priorities in foreign policy.

改革) (2019). All frames that describe the reform of public hospitals perform the frame function suggestion of remedies. Closely related to hospital reform, hospital management systems are also mentioned in the GWRs in 2011 and 2012. The reform of these systems is vaguely described as something to be explored. The fact that the management of hospitals issue appeared in the last PCR as well revealed that the government recently turned it into a priority. Another priority is the development of private hospitals. While investment into hospitals from nongovernmental actors has been welcomed frequently in the GWRs, (2012, 2013, 2015), with frames performing the frame function diagnosis of causes, recently, the priority has shifted to encouraging the development of private hospitals in the English version of the text and encouraging 'community hospitals' (促进社会办医) in the Chinese version of the text (2019).

Regarding medical insurance, extending coverage is prioritized. Recently, there was an important change from improving the medical insurance system (18th PCR) to establishing a 'distinctively Chinese system for providing basic health care and medical insurance' (全面建立中国特色基本医疗卫生制度) (19th PCR). While the reference in the

PCR signals that establishing a medical insurance system continues to be a priority, it is striking that frames that described implementing this disappeared from the GWRs after 2017. Before, there were calls to expand coverage (提高基本医疗保障水平) (2012) and to accelerate the building of a nation-wide network of basic medical insurance (加快推进基本医保全国联网和异地就医结算) (2016, 2017). In 2019, however, the government shifted its attention to financing medical insurance. From the GWRs, insurance for serious diseases emerged as another priority. Frames first appeared in 2012, with a focus on selected diseases. Since 2014, there was a stable frame that described that the government wanted to implement a major disease insurance scheme (2014, 2015, 2017). In 2017 and 2018, the idea of raising insurance benefits for such diseases was added.

The literature on China's health policy identifies drug prices as another important issue. While only a few frames describe drug pricing, a number of frames point to other priorities around drugs. Until 2014, many frames described the use of so-called basic drugs (基本药物) (2010, 2011, 2012, 2013). The 17th PCR, for example, referred to establishing a national system of basic drugs, which would ensure supply. Between 2012 and 2014, there was a frame that described the Chinese government's priority in improving this system. Another important issue around drugs calls for abolishing the practice of compensation for low income from medical services with high prices for drugs. While this frame disappeared from the GWRs in 2015, it continued to be a priority as it was mentioned in the 19th PCR.

The following highlights changed policy priorities in a number of other areas that emerged out of a close reading of the policy documents and the literature on China's health policy. Relations between doctors and patients have long been a contentious issue in China's healthcare system (Cheng 2019). In the GWRs, frames calling for harmonious relations between doctors and patients (和谐的医患关系) (2012, 2014, 2017) were first accompanied by descriptions of the benefits of a contracted family doctor system (2017) (家庭签约服务), then replaced by calls for improving such a system (2019). Migrant workers hardly appear in the Chinese government's description of its priorities. Only recently, this has begun to change: With regard to health policy, migrants appear for the first time in 2018 in the GWR. The frame performs the frame function suggestion of remedies and calls for making the interprovincial on the spot settlement of medical bills through basic insurance accounts available to migrants. A year later, the same issue is addressed. The 2019 frame performs the frame function diagnosis of causes and assesses that this system will 'make things easier for migrants'. The stable frames that call for disease prevention in all the PCRs underline that this is a priority for the Chinese government. New and faded frames in the GWR indicate shifts in priorities regarding the prevention of specific (kinds of) diseases. Cancer prevention, for example, appears for the first time in 2019. Measures to prevent influenza and HIV/AIDS appear once in 2010 and 2011, respectively. Frames that referred to public health emergencies disappeared after the 18th PCR. Before, they described the commitment to improve China's ability to handle such emergencies (17th,18th). Finally, stable frames describe the Chinese government's commitment to promoting the development of traditional Chinese medicine. In the latest PCR, there was a slight change in emphasis: the government now commits itself to ensure the preservation and development of traditional Chinese medicine (传承发展中医药事业) (19th PCR).

Education policy

The literature on education policy suggests that the Chinese government's policy priorities most likely changed in the following areas: purpose of education and education providers

(Li 2017). The analysis will further examine changes in policy priorities as they relate to vocational, preschool, and special needs education, schools' conditions, teachers as well as the links between inequality and education.

Regarding the purpose the Chinese government ascribes to education, the most significant change was that the 17th and 18th PCR frame education was described as the 'cornerstone of national rejuvenation' (教育是民族振兴的基石) and the 'bedrock of socialist modernization' (坚持教育为社会主义现代化建设服务) respectively, while such references do not appear in the 19th PCR. In fact, frames that describe how education is supposed to contribute to the country's strength disappear entirely after 2017. Before 2017, education's purpose was described as fulfilling China's strategic requirements (2012) and claimed to be important for the country's future (2012, 2016) in the GWRs. After 2017, however, the order reversed: now, the country is tasked with strengthening education (19th PCR). Some frames relate to the purpose of education on the individual level: The idea of fostering entrepreneurial abilities through (higher) education introduced in the 2010 GWR quickly disappeared. In 2017, the idea that Chinese people can realize their dreams through education was put forward for the first time (GWR 2017, 2018).

Regarding education providers, the Chinese government focuses on private actors and universities. As private/nongovernment actors appear in all PCRs, the government bestows them with an important role in the provision of education. In the 17th and 18th PCR, frames described the government's support for educational programs run by nongovernmental entities. The last PCR focused on schools run by private actors, spelling out that the government supported the well-regulated development of private schools. In the GWRs, a stable frame describes the government's support for nongovernmental actors running schools, which further illustrates that the government considers this to be a priority (2014, 2019). Another priority is the establishment of world-class universities. In addition to appearing frequently in the GWRs, the goal also appeared in the latest PCR, which shows that the government attaches even more importance to it. In the GWRs, there was a slight modification where 'world-class disciplines' was now added to the universities (2019). A new frame that appeared for the first time in 2018 was the call for establishing universities in China's Western and Central regions (2018, 2019), signaling a new priority here.

A number of frames describe specific types of education from special needs over preschool to vocational education. Special needs education (特殊教育) appears throughout the sample signaling that it is an unchanged policy priority. The establishment of a vocational education system (职业教育体系) also emerges as a policy priority because it appeared in all PCRs. In the GWRs, a change in degree is visible from developing such a system (GWR 2012) to accelerating its establishment (GWR 2013, 2014). A similar change in degree was visible in the provision of preschool education (学前教育), suggesting more emphasis on quality. Frames that describe schools' conditions do not feature in the PCRs but appear regularly in the GWRs. Between 2014 and 2017, a stable frame described the government's commitment to improving conditions in schools that are badly built and poorly operated. In 2015 and 2016, there was an additional focus on boarding schools. Recently, priorities shifted toward improving the conditions in rural schools (2019). Strengthening teachers' abilities also emerges as a policy priority from the analyzed documents, mostly expressed through a stable frame since 2010. In 2017, there was a slight shift in emphasis towards improving teachers' performance (GWR 2017) and a focus on strengthening their professional ethics (19th PCR). Several issues relate to inequality in education, for example, the government's approach towards ethnic minorities. While frames that refer to the education of ethnic minorities appear in every GWR, the precise focus is constantly changing: in

2010 it was bilingual instruction, in 2019, there was a more general reference to providing quality education for them. Another important dimension of inequality in education is access to higher education. This topic appears regularly in the GWRs with a focus on expanding the enrollment of children from poor families (2016, 2017). Granting equal access to education for migrant children is also a stable frame (2011, 2015, 2018, 2019). Generally, the aspiration to granting equal access to education seems to be a policy priority as it is reflected in the PCR (17th, 18th PCR), but with less emphasis on implementation in recent GWRs.

Foreign policy

In foreign policy, shifts in policy priorities emerge in how Chinese leaders portray the international order and China's role in it. Changes in their threat perceptions are also visible. Besides, one can gather what values China seeks to promote, how it intends to ensure security, and how it wants to pursue its interests. China's relations with neighboring states and its goals in global governance also play an important role.

Striking changes emerge in Chinese leaders' portrayal of the international order and in their perceptions of threats. In the most recent PCR, the expressed commitment to upholding the international order (国际秩序的维护者) replaced the ambition of making it fairer (朝着公正合理的方向发展) (17th, 18th PCR). These changes are also reflected in the GWRs: Until 2015, frames called for making the international order fairer. Since 2017, frames have called for upholding the international order. In the frames that describe Chinese leaders' threat perceptions, shifts in frame functions were noticeable: The frame that described traditional and nontraditional threats as intertwined in the 17th PCR highlights a risk. In the 19th PCR, it was replaced by a frame that called for combining responses to traditional and nontraditional threats, which performed the frame function suggestion of remedies. Regarding instabilities, a prominent source of threats, frames' scope expanded: In the 18th PCR, world economic growth is described as overshadowed by growing factors of instability and uncertainty. The frame in the 19th PCR does not only refer to the world economy, but to the world at large that is facing growing uncertainties and destabilizing factors.

Portrayals of China as a 'major country' appear for the first time in the 18th PCR and have been slightly modified since then: In the 18th PCR, a frame describes that China will play its due role of a major responsible country (负责任大国作用). The 19th PCR describes China as continuing to play this role. The portrayal of China's global role also includes a discussion of principles that underlie its foreign policy. In the 17th and 18th PCR, frames called for protecting the legitimate concerns and rights of others (别国合法政权), which disappeared after the 18th PCR. A slight modification can be observed in the noninterference in the internal affairs of others: In the 17th PCR, the frame described that China would never interfere in the internal affairs of others. In the 18th PCR, there was slightly less emphasis with the frame China does not interfere in the internal affairs of others. In the 19th PCR, the frame was China opposes the interference in internal affairs, suggesting that this could now also apply to other countries. Regarding the protection of China's legitimate rights, there was an increase in emphasis: In the 18th PCR, there was a frame that described that China will protect its legitimate rights and interests overseas (维护我国海外合法权益). In the 19th PCR, this changed into China will never give up its legitimate rights and interests (决不放弃自己的正当权益).

Slightly modified frames spell out goals in China's relations with its neighbors: In the 17th PCR, there was a commitment to always strengthening 'good neighborly relations', in the 18th PCR, this was replaced by a commitment to promote friendship and partnership with neighbors. In the 19th PCR, this was then replaced by deepening relations with neighbors. These shifts in emphasis were reflected in the GWRs: In 2011 and 2012, the focus was on good relations with neighbors, from 2012 to 2014, there was a focus on active participation in neighborhood diplomacy – in 2018 and 2019 there was a focus on achieving common development with neighbors as well as deepening relations with neighbors, just as in the 19th PCR.

The provision of security emerged as a key priority from the 19th PCR with many new frames describing how China's security is to be ensured. Changes were already visible since the 17th PCR: Back then, China's role in promoting international and regional security cooperation was described. In the 18th PCR, there was also a focus on others, specifically that one should share security. These frames were replaced in the 19th PCR with frames that described how exactly China's security should be sustained as well as a new focus on capacity-building for security. Related to the provision of security, the protection of interests emerges as a key goal of China's foreign policy from the analyzed policy statement. In the 17th PCR, a frame described that China will always protect its interests. There was none such mention in the following PCR. In the 19th PCR, the theme appeared again: Now China needs to put its national interests first. Other frames describe protecting Chinese and other countries' interests at the same time. There was also a slight modification here: In the 17th and 18th PCR, frames call for combining China's and other countries' interests. In the 19th PCR, China was supposed to expand the convergence with other interests. The idea of common interests faded after the 18th PCR.

Lastly, China wants to contribute new initiatives to international politics, such as the idea of establishing 'a new type of international relations' (新型国际关系). While this idea already appeared in the 18th PCR, it was much more prominently in the 19th PCR. Here, new forms of international relations and a new approach to state-to-state relations appeared prominently. This was also reflected in the GWRs since 2015. Another example is the idea of a 'community of shared future/destiny'. In the 17th PCR, there was a vague claim that China will bring about a better future. In the 18th PCR, there was a slight shift: now there was a call for raising awareness that human beings share a community of common destiny. In the 19th PCR, there was a strong shift toward building a community of shared future, now formulated as a call to action – this was also reflected in the GWRs. There were also important changes in the Chinese government's goals for global governance. There were a number of new frames in the last PCR, for example, China contributes wisdom and strength to global governance (19th PCR). There was also an important shift in the description of China's activities, there was a shift from participation in global governance (GWR 2012) to reforming it (19th PCR).

Conclusions

Applying this frame analysis technique to China's policy reports revealed a number of unexpected findings across the three policy areas. In health policy, the Chinese government's priorities include reforming the management of hospitals, extending coverage of medical insurance, and guaranteeing drug safety. For improving relations between doctors and patients, the establishment of a contracted family doctor system is prioritized. Migrant workers' healthcare only recently appeared as an issue. Disease prevention has long been a priority for the Chinese government. Frames that referred to public health emergencies disappeared after the 18th PCR. In light of the COVID-19 pandemic, the issue is likely to be prioritized again in future policy statements. Regarding education policy, frames that describe how education is supposed to strengthen the country disappeared. Regarding the

In order to successfully apply this frame analysis technique, the researcher needs:

- patience for developing frame fragments inductively on the material
- willingness to trace incremental change in professed intentions
- awareness of what official documents can tell him/her and where other sources of evidence are necessary to corroborate findings.

Figure 43.7 Special skills required for applying the frame analysis technique.

providers of education, the Chinese government bestows private actors with great importance. Besides, the development of world-class universities is prioritized. Further priorities are improving the conditions of schools and teachers' abilities. In foreign policy, leaders' expressed commitment to upholding the international order replaced the ambition of making it fairer. Regarding foreign policy goals, the provision of security recently emerged as a key priority alongside the goal of protecting China's national interests. There is also a growing ambition of China playing an increasingly important role in global governance.

This technique for applying frame analysis to Chinese policy documents has three benefits: First, it allows to trace incremental changes in policy priorities. Second, coding frame fragments in the material, retrieving them, turning them into frame components, and combining these components into frames in a structured manner makes the approach replicable. Third, the computer-assisted coding facilitates the use of relatively large amounts of texts. This allows conducting comparative analyses across time and across issue areas. Figure 43.7 summarizes the special skills required for getting the most out of applying this technique.

The careful detection of incremental changes in the Chinese government's policy priorities is well suited for generating new research questions. The high degree of detail allows researchers to ask more precise questions about the Chinese government's intentions. One could, for example, explore why comprehensive hospital reform suddenly emerged as a policy priority in 2019 after references to trial reforms disappeared in 2016. To answer such questions, findings from the frame analysis can and should be corroborated with other sources of evidence, such as interviews or statistical analyses. The technique could also be a useful starting point for assessing the implementation of various policies. Here, the results from the frame analysis provide a baseline of the government's professed intentions, for example, that it wants to provide high-quality preschool education for all children. These professed intentions can then be systematically compared to its actions.

Notes

1 The chapter covers the current and the previous administration, starting with the report to the party congress in 2007. The analysis highlights changes in frames. A comprehensive account of all frames that relate to the three policy areas is beyond the scope of this chapter.

2 I do not investigate how the Chinese government's frames come into being because it is very difficult – perhaps even impossible – to get detailed insight into how the Chinese government drafts documents and speeches. Neither do I examine how the Chinese government's frames are received by its domestic or international audience.

3 Passages that mentioned the policy areas alongside other policy areas, for example, in general rundown of goals were not considered.

4 The State Council Information Office publishes the annual government work reports on its website (http://english.www.gov.cn/). The General Secretary's report to party congress can be accessed on the Xinhua website.

References

Barros, Robert. 2016. 'On The Outside Looking In: Secrecy And The Study Of Authoritarian Regimes'. *Social Science Quarterly* 97(4), 953–73.

Bondes, Maria and Sandra Heep. 2012. 'Frames We Can Believe In: Official Framing And Ideology In The Ccp's Quest For Legitimacy'. *Giga Working Paper* 187.

Cha, Chang Hoon. 2017. 'China's Search For Ideological Values In World Politics: Chinese Adaptation To Liberal Order Drawn From Political Reports Of The Chinese Communist Party Congress Since 1977'. *Pacific Focus* 32(3), 416–44.

Cheng, Tsung-Mei. 2019. 'Between A Rock And A Hard Place: China's Health Care Reforms Over The Next Ten Years'. *Asia Dialogue*. Available at: https://theasiadialogue.com/2019/03/27/between-a-rock-and-a-hard-place-chinas-health-care-reforms-over-the-next-ten-years/ (last accessed: December 29 2020).

Entman, Robert M. 2007. 'Framing Bias: Media In The Distribution Of Power'. *Journal Of Communication* 57(1), 163–73.

Entman, Robert M. 1993. 'Framing: Towards Clarification Of A Fractured Paradigm'. *Journal Of Communication* 43(4), 51–8.

Van Gerven, Minna. 2019. 'Narrative Stories In Chinese Characters: Political Framing Of Ageing And Welfare Reform In China'. *Policy And Society* 38(3), 502–18.

Hu, Yue. 2020. 'Refocusing Democracy: The Chinese Government's Framing Strategy In Political Language'. *Democratization* 27(2), 302–20.

Huang, Shouhong 黄守宏 (2019) '着力激发市场主体活力 保持经济持续健康发展——2019年《政府工作报告》解读 (Focus on stimulating the vitality of market players to maintain sustained and healthy economic development-Interpretation of the 2019 'Government Work Report')', 行政管理改革 (*Administration Reform*) 04:4–16.

Jakobson, Linda. 2013. 'China's Foreign Policy Dilemma'. *Lowy Institute Analysis*. Available at: https://www.files.ethz.ch/isn/159724/jakobson_chinas_foreign_policy_dilemma_web_1.pdf

Jecker, Constanze. 2017. *Entmans Framing-Ansatz - Theoretische Grundlegung Und Empirische Umsetzung*. Köln: Herbert Von Halem Verlag.

Lenz, Tobias. 2018. 'Frame Diffusion And Institutional Choice In Regional Economic Cooperation'. *International Theory* 10(1), 31–70.

Li, Jun. 2017. 'Educational Policy Development In China For The 21st Century: Rationality And Challenges In A Globalizing Age'. *Chinese Education & Society* 50(3), 133–41.

Liu, Gordon G., Samantha A. Vortherms And Xuezhi Hong. 2017. 'China's Health Reform Update'. *Annual Review Of Public Health* 38(1), 431–48.

Matthes, Jörg And Mattias Kohring. 2008. 'The Content Analysis Of Media Frames: Toward Improving Reliability And Validity'. *Journal Of Communication* 58, 258–279.

Mattis, Peter. 2019. 'The Party Congress Test: A Minimum Standard For Analzying Beijing's Intentions'. *War On The Rocks* [Online]. Available at: Https://Warontherocks.Com/2019/01/The-Party-Congress-Test-A-Minimum-Standard-For-Analyzing-Beijings-Intentions/ [Accessed 10 Jun 2019].

Meng, Cheng And Yao Yu. 2016. ''We Should…' Versus 'We Will…': How Do The Governments Report Their Work In 'One Country Two Systems'? A Corpus-Driven Critical Discourse Analysis Of Government Work Reports In Greater China In: Text & Talk Band 36 Heft 2 (2016)'. *Text & Talk* 36(2), 199–219.

Miller, Alice. 2017. 'How To Read Xi Jinping's 19th Party Congress Political Report '. *China Leadership Monitor* 53, 1–7.

Neuendorf, Kimberley A. 2017. *The Content Analysis Guidebook*. 2nd Edn. Los Angeles: Sage.

Snape, Holly. 2019. 'Social Management Or Social Governance: A Review Of Party And Government Discourse And Why It Matters In Understanding Chinese Politics'. *Journal Of Chinese Political Science* 24(4), 685–99.

Wang, Luozhon Chen, Yu 王洛忠, 陈宇, Du, Mengdie 都梦蝶 (2019) '中央政府对信息化的注意力研究——基于1997—2019年国务院《政府工作报告》内容分析 (Research into the Central Government's attention towards informatization - based on the Content Analysis of the 'Government Work Report' of the State Council from 1997 to 2019)', 理论探讨 (*Theoretical Investigation*) 5: 177–182.

Wang, Zhen. 2017. 'Government Work Reports: Securing State Legitimacy Through Institutionalization'. *The China Quarterly* 229, 195–204.

Wu, Bin Tang, Wei 吴宾, 唐薇 (2019) '中国政府推进老龄事业发展的注意力配置研究——基于中央政府工作报告(1978—2018)的内容分析 (Research on the Attention Allocation of the Chinese Government to Advance the Development of Aging Causes——Based on the Content Analysis of the Work Report of the Central Government (1978–2018))', 中州学刊 (*Academic Journal of Zhongzhou*) 5: 65–71.

You, Zeshun, Jianping Chen And Hong Zhong. 2010. 'Discursive Construction Of Chinese Foreign Policy: A Diachronic Analysis Of The Chinese Government's Annual Work Report To The Npc'. *Journal Of Language And Politics* 9(4), 593–614.

Yu, Hailing And Canzhong Wu. 2018. 'Images Of The Chinese Government Projected In Its Work Reports: Transformation Through Translation'. *Lingua* 214, 74–87.

Zeng, Fanxu, Jia Dai And Jeffrey Javed. 2019. 'Frame Alignment And Environmental Advocacy: The Influence Of Ngo Strategies On Policy Outcomes In China'. *Environmental Politics* 28(4), 747–70.

Zhang, Haizhu 张海柱 (2016) '政府工作报告中的海洋政策演变——对1954–2015年国务院政府工作报告的内容分析 (The Evolution of Ocean Policy in the Government Work Report——Analysis of the Contents of the Government Work Report of the State Council from 1954 to 2015)', 上海行政学院学报 (*The Journal of Shanghai Administration Institute*) 03: 105–111.

44

Chinese media discourse analysis

A case study of the discursive strategies in the editorials in *Global Times*

Bo Wang and Yuanyi Ma

Introduction

This chapter approaches Chinese media discourse from a linguistic perspective. We will first conduct a brief survey of related studies in this area and then report on our findings of a case study on the editorials in a Chinese newspaper media. Our data are selected from *Global Times* (环球时报) – a Chinese newspaper under the auspices of *People's Daily* (人民日报), which acts as the mouthpiece of the Chinese government and reflects the ideologies of the Communist Party of China (CPC).

In the past few decades, there has been a considerable body of linguistic research investigating the various aspects of media discourse. O'Keeffe (2012) reviews the various frameworks and approaches in media discourse and points out the key characteristics of this research area, i.e., the orientations toward nonpresent readers/viewers and the absence of instantaneous responses. In practice, as media discourse is produced in contexts heavily influenced by ideology, a critical stance such as critical discourse analysis (CDA) is suitable for examining such discourse (see Wei 2019 for a comprehensive review of CDA research on Chinese discourse). For instance, in the Chinese context, Liu and Li (2017) investigate the discourses on the elderly in China's newspapers and Weibo (a social media platform, i.e. micro-blog). Their findings reveal that positive strategies are often used in newspapers to refer to the elderly while negative strategies are commonly seen in Weibo. Based on these findings, they propose two factors in relation to power and society: (i) the unequal social power between the young and the aged people and (ii) the negative stereotype created by social media.

Studies on media discourse using CDA are often assisted with corpus tools. For example, Liu (2017) illustrates the hegemony of neoliberalism in media discourse by conducting a corpus-based study. He analyzes news discourse on the Sino-US currency dispute from two newspapers: *China Daily* and the *New York Times* and finds that there are differences in the two newspapers in terms of the construction of stance toward the currency dispute. In the *New York Times*, neoliberal beliefs are evident at various levels of discourse, including thematic, lexical, and grammatical, to build a combative stance towards the policies in China. In *China Daily*, however, an ambivalent stance is constructed and a contradictory evaluation of the impact is detected.

DOI: 10.4324/9780429059704-51

Systemic Functional Linguistics (SFL) offers another linguistic approach to media discourse (see Kaltenbacher & Stöckl 2019 for recent contributions to media discourse from the SFL perspective). Some influential and comprehensive studies include Bednarek (2006) as well as Bednarek and Caple (2012), in which Martin and White's (2005) appraisal framework are applied to quantitatively evaluate newspaper articles. In another study, Huan (2018) applies the appraisal framework to the analysis of Chinese and Australian hard news in terms of journalistic stance-taking practices, using a combination of ethnographic fieldwork and corpus-based methods.

Data and methods

Our data comprise 15 editorials in *Global Times* which focus on the incident of Meng Wanzhou (孟晚舟) – the deputy chairperson of the telecom giant Huawei arrested by the Canadian authorities at the request of the United States on December 1, 2018. As previously stated, *Global Times* is an influential Chinese newspaper. With the support of the Chinese government, it aims to boost nationalism by vilifying any foreign action that seems to affect the political or economic interests of China and is widely known for its nationalist tendency (Zhang & Chen 2014). The editorials analyzed are characterized by a strong orientation to national collectivism, demonization of foreign powers, and victimization of domestic parties, thereby appealing to the emotions of Chinese audiences who are keenly aware of their national identity, highly defensive of national dignity, and easily aroused by such ideological positions. For instance, during the period of the COVID-19 pandemic, *Global Times* has published various editorials that (i) discusses the delinquency of the US government (e.g., '联邦政府严重渎职, 坑惨了美国人民' [The Misconduct of the Federal Government Seriously Entrapped the American people]), (ii) warns the Chinese people about the danger of the Sino-US conflict (e.g., '美国来势汹汹, 中国需做长期应对准备' [The US Starts a Blame Game, China Needs to Be Prepared for Long-term Confrontations]) (iii) praises the achievements of the Chinese government in dealing with the outbreak (e.g., '全球抗疫马拉松, 中国跑得好瞒不住' [Global Fight against COVID-19, Forerunner China Cannot Hide in]) and (iv) introduces the reasons for the United States to discredit China (e.g., '四大政治和心理动力推动了抹黑中国' [Four Political and Psychological Motivations for Blaming China])

In this study, to explore the discursive strategies in the editorials, we will analyze our data from lexicogrammatical and contextual perspectives. The lexicogrammatical analysis is based on the system of MODALITY, which is one of the major systems modeling on the interpersonal metafunction of language (see Figure 44.1). It includes the expressions of indeterminacy between positive and negative, constructs the semantic region of uncertainty, and helps to express the speaker's judgment or request of the judgment. There are four major types of modality: probability (the likelihood of a situation to be true), usuality (how frequently a situation is true), obligation (how confident the interactant can be to carry out the command), and readiness (how willing the interactant can be to fulfill the offer). Probability and usuality are referred to as modalization and they focus on the exchange of information; obligation and readiness are collectively known as modulation and they entail the exchange of goods and services.

Modality can be further characterized according to value and polarity. There are three values according to which modality is organized, i.e., a median value and two outer values, namely high and low. In addition, the system of POLARITY offers resources for assessing the arguability value of a clause and the two choices involved include positive and negative.

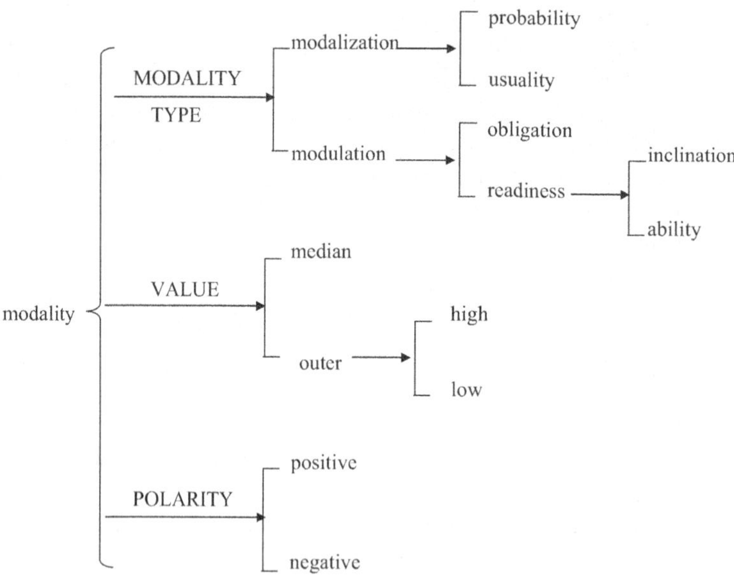

Figure 44.1 Systems of MODALITY involved in the analysis (Adapted from Halliday and Matthiessen 2014: 182).

The contextual analysis reveals the generic stages of the data. We apply Generic Structure Potential (GSP), which was first explored in SFL by Hasan (e.g., 1978, 1984, 1985), to identify the possible contextual structures that are characteristic of a situation type. In this study, the generic stages are referred to as potential because a range of structural variants that vary within the general situation type are described rather than one simple structure. In SFL, generic structures are also referred to as schematic structures and are comparable to McKeown's (1985) recursive transition networks in computational linguistics.

Analysis of modality

In total, 306 occurrences of modality were found in the data. The frequencies of modality range from 14 to 30 in one editorial. These numbers reflect the abundant use of modality in the editorials. Realizations of such choices of modality include modal auxiliaries (e.g., '能' can), modal adverbs (e.g., '一定' certainly) and projections by means of interpersonal metaphor, one of the two modes of grammatical metaphor that expand the interpersonal resources through incongruent mapping between semantics and lexicogrammar (e.g., '我们认为' we think). Table 44.1 tabulates all types of modality found in the data.

Some lexes, such as '必须' (must), '可以' (can, may), '应该' (should), '会' (can, will), '能' (can) and '要' (will, would), can be analyzed as different kinds of modality. In the analysis, they are first differentiated as modalization (modality concerning the degrees of statements and questions in the exchanges of information) and modulation (modality concerning the degrees of offer and command in the exchanges of goods and services). Furthermore, the lexical choices are categorized in accordance with the various degrees in the subtypes (e.g., the degrees of 'probability' include possibly/probably/certainly and the degrees of 'usuality' include sometimes/usually/always). In this way, one lexis will only belong to one category and will not be classified into several categories at the same time. As shown in Example 1,

Table 44.1 Examples of modality found in the data

Kind of modality				*Example*
modalization	probability		certain	必须 (must), 必然 (certainly), 想必 (surely), 应该 (should), 注定 (certainly), 一定 (certainly), 肯定 (surely), 显然 (obviously), 确实 (certainly), 无疑 (surely), 毫无疑问 (undoubtedly), 我们认为 (we think), 我们相信 (we believe)
			probable	大概 (probably), 看来 (it seems), 似乎 (it seems), 看起来 (it seems), 看上去 (it seems), 好像 (seem)
			possible	可以 (can, may), 可能 (can, may), 会 (can, will), 能 (can), 要 (will, would)
	usuality		always	一直 (always)
			usually	通常 (often), 常常 (usually)
			sometimes	——
modulation	obligation		required	须 (must), 必须 (must), 需 (need), 需要 (need), 能 (can), 要 (should), 有必要 (need)
			supposed	应 (should), 该 (should), 应该 (should), 应当 (should), 理应 (should)
			allowed	可以 (can), 会 (can, will)
	readiness	ability		能 (can), 能够 (can), 可以 (can), 有能力 (have the ability to)
		inclination	determined	要 (will, would), 会 (will)
			keen	想 (want), 欲 (want)
			willing	愿意 (wish), 希望 (wish), 可以 (can)

'应该' (should) is identified as obligation (in Example 1.1) and probability (in Example 1.2). In Example 1.1, goods and services are exchanged by way of suggesting what the United States and other countries should do. In Example 1.2, what is being assessed is the information, i.e., whether the scholars and former ambassadors understand Huawei's difficulty or not.

EXAMPLE 1

1.1 美国**应该**这样，它的小兄弟们**尤其应该**这样。 (modulation: obligation & median & positive)
(The United States *should* be like this; its little brothers *should* especially be like this.)

1.2 还是这些学者和前大使们，他们**应该**最了解华为作为中国一家民营企业，从中国市场崛起并走向全球是多么不容易...... (modalization: probability & high & positive)
(Yet, for these scholars and former ambassadors, they **should** best know that it is uneasy for Huawei, a Chinese private enterprise, to rise from the Chinese market and to reach out to the world ...)

The four basic types of modality

Among the four types of modality (see Figure 44.2), obligation is the most frequently used, which accounts for 40.8% of the total frequencies. Probability, which also has a frequency larger than 100, ranks the second, occupying 36.3% of the total occurrences. As for readiness and usuality, their frequencies are much smaller compared to the other two kinds and usuality is the least frequent.

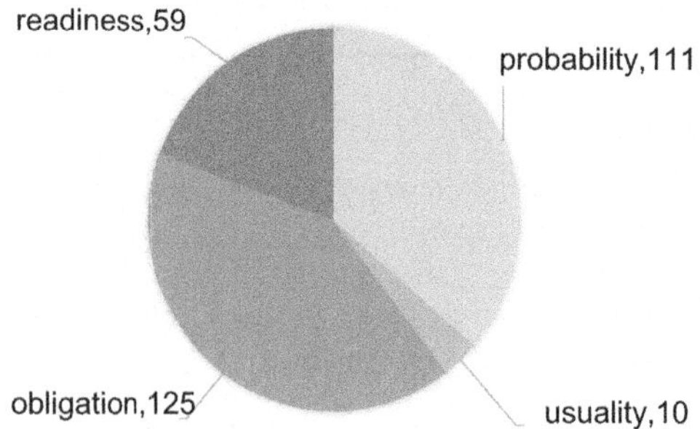

Figure 44.2 Frequencies of the four kinds of modality.

Each type of modality has three values, i.e., high, median, and low. Example 2 illustrates the three values of probability, which range from certain (high value), probable (median value) to possible (low value). From '注定' (certainly), '看起来' (it seems) to '可能' (can), the likeliness gradually weakens. In Example 2.1, probability: certain is used to attack the evidence provided by the US government, emphasizing the failure of the United States. The probability: probable in Example 2.2 evaluates the effect of the mobilization. The modality of median value suggests that the mobilization will probably but not necessarily work for the allied countries of the United States. The use of probability: possible in Example 2.3 indicates the likeliness for Huawei to encounter further trouble in the future and the low value of modality implies that the probability is not very high.

EXAMPLE 2

2.1 美方的所谓证据**注定**是漏洞百出的。 (modalization: probability & high & positive)
(The so-called evidence from the United States will *certainly* be full of loopholes.)

2.2 **看起来**美国的动员正在对它的一些盟国奏效…… (modalization: probability & median & positive)
(*It seems* that the mobilization by the United States is working in the allied countries …)

2.3 今后华为还**可能**遭遇更多麻烦。 (modalization: probability & low & positive)
(In the future, it is *possible* for Huawei to face more troubles.)

The three values of usuality include always (high value), usually (median value), and sometimes (low value). Only choices of high and median values are observed in our data, while usuality of low value, such as '有时候' (sometimes) and '偶尔' (occasionally), are not found. As shown in Example 3.1, '一直' (always) indicates the high frequency for the Chinese government to respect its Canadian counterpart, while '通常' (often) in Example 3.2 reveals how common the understanding is.

EXAMPLE 3

3.1 而在这之前中国**一直**是把加拿大真的当成独立主权国家对待并尊重的。 (modalization: usuality & high & positive)
(However, before this incident, China has *always* treated and respected Canada as a real sovereign country.)

3.2 他们在玷污人们**通常**对法律精神的认识。(modalization: usuality & median & positive)
(They smear the understanding of legal spirit that people *often* have.)

The three values of obligation are required (high value), supposed (median value) and allowed (low value). In Example 4, the lexical choices of modality from Example 4.1 to Example 4.3 include '需要' (need), '应当' (should), and '可以' (can), and the intensity of instructing the addressee to undertake a certain action gradually decreases.

EXAMPLE 4

4.1 中国**需要**用实际行动向全世界展示加拿大这样做的后果。(modulation: obligation & high & positive)
(With practical actions, China *needs* to demonstrate the consequences of Canada to the whole world.)

4.2 加拿大**应当**采取实际行动降低这种紧张和敏感。(modulation: obligation & median & positive)
(Canada *should* take some practical actions to relieve the tension and decrease the sensitivity.)

4.3 孟晚舟方面**可以**抗辩、上诉...... (modulation: obligation & low & positive)
(The Meng Wanzhou side *can* defend and appeal ...)

Readiness has two subtypes, i.e., ability and inclination. In Example 5.1, ability has no differentiation of the three values and is realized by '能够' (can), which means Huawei is capable of achieving its development. From Example 5.2 to 5.4, the value of inclination decreases from determined, i.e., '一定' (must) of high value in Example 5.2 to keen, i.e., '想' (want) of low value in Example 5.3 and then to willing, i.e., '愿意' (wish) of low value in Example 5.4.

EXAMPLE 5

5.1 华为这些年**能够**发展得这么好，很重要的一条就是它严格守法...... (modulation: readiness: ability & positive)
(One of the reasons that Huawei *can* prosper in previous years is that it strictly abides by the law ...)

5.2 中国**一定**要采取多种手段坚决将其打痛，让整个世界都了解，帮着美国伤害中国将付出沉重代价...... (modulation: readiness: inclination & high & positive)
(China *must* take various measures to attack them resolutely, so that the whole world knows that those who help the United States to hurt China will have to pay a heavy cost.)

5.3 加拿大**想**通过拉盟友对华施加压力来解决它与中国的矛盾，决不会奏效。(modulation: readiness: inclination & median & positive)
(Canada *wanted* to resolve its conflicts with China by seeking its allies to exert pressures on China, but that will definitely not work.)

5.4 然而很多人出于惧怕美国等利益关系不**愿意**去捅这层窗户纸，所以中方尤其需要坚持发声。(modulation: readiness: inclination & low & negative)
(However, due to interest relations such as fear of the United States, many people do not *wish* to talk about it, therefore the Chinese side especially needs to persist in expressing their opinions.)

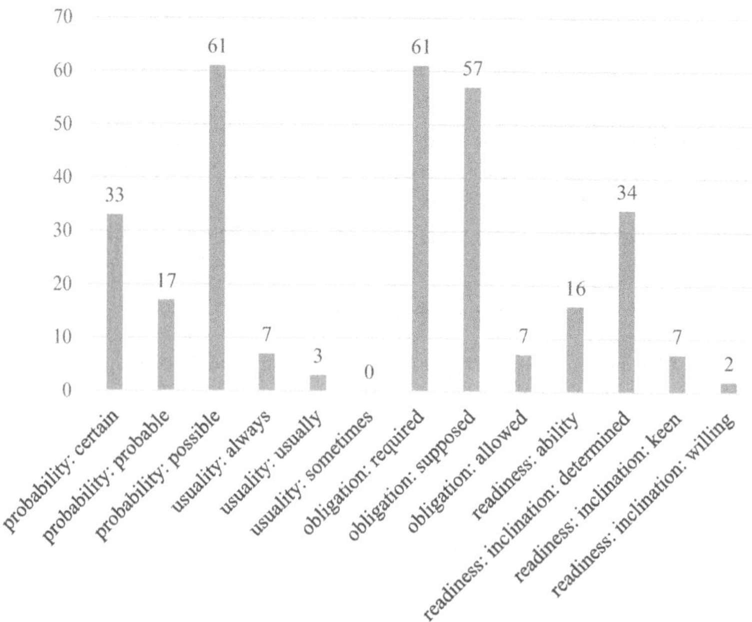

Figure 44.3 Frequencies of modality with different values.

Modality with different values

In Figure 44.3, we point out the frequencies of the modality choices and their values. It can be observed that the different kinds of modality are not evenly selected. Some choices, including probability: possible, obligation: required, and obligation: supposed are more frequently found. Among these three kinds of modality, probability: possible is used to make predictions about the future development of the Huawei incident and to denounce or ridicule the various parties involved. As shown in Example 6.1, with the help of '可以' (can), the uncertainty of the incident is portrayed (see also Example 2.3). It is also noted that the prediction can be made by the United States as shown in Example 6.2, where the use of '可能' (may) foretells the future actions of the US government. Additionally, Examples 6.3 and 6.4 illustrate how the United States and Canada criticize China and vice versa with the help of probability: possible. In Example 6.3, the choice of '会' (will) is found in the criticism against the Chinese government, underscoring the possible harmful effects of China's future actions. In Example 6.4, the use of '可能' (could) and the speech function of question suggest that it is likely that the Canadians will pay the price.

EXAMPLE 6

6.1 这一过程至少**可以**拖几个月…… (modulation: probability & low & positive)
(This process *can* be delayed for at least several months …)

6.2 美方也没有表示**可能**将抓捕中国企业高管常态化…… (modulation: probability & low & positive)
(The United States has also not declared that they *may* normalize the arrest of senior managers in Chinese enterprises …)

6.3 美加舆论鼓噪中国拘押两名加拿大人**会**破坏大的营商环境…… (modulation: probability & low & positive)
(As clamored by the public opinions in the United States and Canada, the arrest of the two Canadians in China *will* destroy the business environment …)

6.4 [加拿大]仅凭美加引渡条约就帮美迫害中国企业高管，怎么**可能**把人送走，自己欠下的账就不用还了呢？ (modulation: probability & low & positive)
(Canada helped the United States to persecute a senior manager in a Chinese enterprise by simply resorting to the extradition treaty between the United States and Canada. How *could* Canada not pay the bill it owed after sending the person away?)

The frequent use of obligation: required and obligation: supposed contribute to the high frequency of obligation among the four types of modality (see also Figure 44.2). These two subtypes of modality help to give suggestions to China, as seen in '需要' (need) from Example 7.1, which introduces a strategy at the national level. Also, they help to give warnings to the United States and Canada. The negative choice of '要' (should) in Example 7.2 warns the Canadian government not to rely on the United States, while the positive use of '应当' (should) instructs the Canadians on what to do next.

EXAMPLE 7

7.1 中国**需要**将捍卫传统国家利益与改善同西方的关系实现最大限度的协调…… (modulation: obligation & high & positive)
(China *needs* to maximize the coordination between the defense of traditional national interests and the improvement of its relationship with the West …)

7.2 加拿大不**要**指望美国帮它说话就能起什么作用…… (modulation: obligation & high & negative)
(Canada *should* not count on the vocal support from the United States …)

7.3 加拿大方面接下来**应当**做的是彻底恢复孟女士的自由…… (modulation: obligation & median & positive)
(What Canada *should* do next is to completely free Ms. Meng …)

The frequencies of some modalities are also considerable, including readiness: inclination: determined, probability: certain, probability: probable, and readiness: ability. Modalities of inclination are used to highlight the resolution of the Chinese in strategic planning and to describe the attack or charge against Huawei. Example 5.2 has previously illustrated the determination of the Chinese government to fight against Canada. In Example 8.1, four paralleled questions are addressed to query the future actions of the United States. All the questions involve the high-valued modality of '会' (will) and are of the A-not-A or unbiased type, which is characteristic of Mandarin Chinese (Shei 2014) and is absent in the grammar of English.

EXAMPLE 8

美国**会不会**扩大对中国公司的打击面？**会不会**采用抓捕中国公司高管的方式来实施这种打击？它**会不会**要求更多盟国给予引渡配合？以及美国全面打压华为的做法**会不会**今后用来对付其他国家的竞争者？ (modulation: readiness: inclination & high)

(*Will* the United States enlarge its scope of attacking the Chinese enterprises? *Will* it implement this kind of attack by arresting senior managers in Chinese enterprises? *Will* it demand more allied countries to cooperate with the extradition? And *will* the practices of the United States to completely suppress Huawei be applied to deal with competitors from other countries?)

To reinforce the actions of the Chinese, probability: certain and probability: probable help to provide further proof of such actions. However, when these two subtypes of modality are used in reference to the United States and Canada, they help to attack and discredit the actions of the United States and Canada. In Examples 9.1 and 9.2, the same lexical choices are used but are associated with the different parties of the Huawei incident.

EXAMPLE 9

9.1 中方**毫无疑问**是有权力依法抓外国人的…… (modulation: probability & high & positive)
(China *undoubtedly* has the right to arrest foreigners in accordance with its law …)

9.2 美国加拿大**毫无疑问**在滥用它们的司法体系…… (modulation: probability & high & positive)
(The United States and Canada have *undoubtedly* abused their judicial system …)

Similarly, when dealing with the Chinese government or Huawei, modalities of readiness: ability on the one hand emphasize the capability of the Chinese, as previously illustrated in Example 5.1. On the other hand, when such modalities are associated with the United States or Canada, they describe their impotence in problem-solving (see Example 10).

EXAMPLE 10

加拿大或许**能够**拉到盟友不痛不痒的几句帮腔…… (modulation: readiness: ability & positive)
(Perhaps Canada *can* find some superficial vocal support from its allies …)

Some choices of modality, such as usuality: usually (see Example 3.2), readiness: inclination: keen (see Example 5.3), and readiness: inclination: willing (see Example 5.4) are applied to a lesser extent in the editorials. For usuality: sometimes, it is not found in the data and is the choice least frequently selected.

The different generic stages

Relating the generic stages to modality choices

In total, we observe four generic stages in the editorials, including Background, Explanation, Solution, and Admonishment. The names of the generic stages have been capitalized following the convention in Halliday and Hasan (1985).

Background is found in all the editorials. It recounts the events that the rest of the discussions are based on. The date of the event is generally provided, such as '12月1日' (December 1) in Example 11. At this generic stage, the author of the editorial may also provide his evaluation of the event and criticize the United States and Canada, with lexical choices such as '卑鄙的流氓做法' (vile indecent practice) (see Example 11), '严重侵犯中国公民的合法、正当权益' (seriously invade the legitimate rights and interests of a Chinese citizen), '性质极其恶劣' (of an extremely vile nature) and '科技迫害'

(persecution in the field of science and technology) being used. The severity of the event can be stated, such as '引起轩然大波' (cause a great disturbance).

EXAMPLE 11

> 12月1日，美国与加拿大联手，以突然袭击的手段逮捕了中国华为公司的首席财务总监、华为创始人任正非之女孟晚舟女士。美方这样做，显然是在通过市场手段无法遏制华为在5G领域突出竞争力的情况下，使出了卑鄙的流氓做法。
> (On December 1, the United States cooperated with Canada to arrest Ms. Meng Wanzhou – Chief Financial Officer of Chinese Huawei Company and the daughter of Ren Zhengfei, who was the founder of Huawei, by means of a sudden onslaught. Obviously, the United States has conducted vile indecent practice under the circumstance that they are unable to suppress the outstanding competitiveness of Huawei in the 5G area.)

In terms of the modality used at the Background stage, we find the frequent use of probability. Most choices of probability are of low value, indicating the false charge of the United States to Huawei, such as '可能' (may), which is categorized as modality concerning the possible degree, in '理由是华为设备**可能**威胁这些国家的网络安全' (The reason is that Huawei's equipment *may* threaten the network security of these countries), or predicting the future development of the incident as seen in '可能' (may) from '美方是有**可能**在最后期限到来之前提出引渡要求的' (The United States *may* make their request of extradition before the deadline.).

The generic stage of *Explanation* offers an interpretation of the incident previously mentioned at the Background stage. There can be more than one stage of Explanation in one editorial. It is at this stage that the criticism of the United States and Canada is mostly found, e.g., '美国不怕露出这样的流氓相' (the United States is not afraid of appearing as a rogue), '[外国人]在华恣意妄为' (foreigners act recklessly in China), '欲加之罪何患无辞' (he who has a mind to beat his dog will easily find his stick) and '他们应该为自己的虚伪和装腔作势而感到羞耻' (They should be ashamed of their hypocrisy and grand gestures.). This generic stage is also used to defend Huawei and the Chinese government for arresting the Canadians who violated the law in mainland China as seen in '所有外国人在中国居留期间都须遵守中国法律，而不是将他们的国内法作为护身符在华恣意妄为' (All foreigners should abide by the law in China during their stay rather than regarding their domestic laws as amulets and behaving unscrupulously in China). Therefore, Explanation also abounds with sentences like '华为这些年能够发展得这么好，很重要的一条就是它严格守法' (One of the reasons for Huawei to prosper in these years is that it strictly abides by the law), and '华为一没偷，二没抢' (Huawei neither steals nor robs). Further, to prove that the arrest of Meng Wanzhou has a harmful effect on the global economy, opinions from the third party besides China and the United States are often cited at the stage of Explanation, such as '全球商界对加拿大应美国要求逮捕一名企业高管的反应都是负面的' (The business circles responded negatively to Canada's arrest of a corporate executive upon the request of the United States).

The choices of modality that are frequently used at the Explanation stage include probability and obligation. Those of probability, on the one hand, evaluate the Huawei incident by pointing out the illegitimacy of the arrest of Meng Wanzhou, as seen in '似乎' (seem) from '他们在法律程序上做得**似乎**"挺完美"' (They *seem* to have acted 'perfectly' in legal procedure.). On the other hand, these choices of probability not only help to defend

Huawei, such as '不可能' (impossible) in '华为**不可能**存在恶意违反美方规定的动机' (It is *impossible* for Huawei to intend to violate the regulations of the United States maliciously.), but also express best wishes to Huawei, such as '我们相信' (we believe) in '**我们相信**华为有能力和智慧应对当前的风险' (*We believe* Huawei has the ability and wisdom to cope with the current risk).

For choices of obligation at the Explanation stage, they are mostly of median value, with choices like '应' (should), '应该' (should), and '应当' (should) being frequently seen. They give suggestions to the Canadians and Americans with respect to what is correct and what is wrong. One example is the negative use of '应' (should) from '释不释放她就不**应**仅仅由美加引渡协议和华盛顿的态度主导' (whether to release her or not *should* not merely be dominated by the extradition agreement between the United States and Canada and the attitude from Washington), which demands the release of Meng Wanzhou from the Canadian government.

Exaggerated expressions are often found at the stage of Explanation. They are characterized by the four-character idioms in Chinese and dramatize the incident, such as '登峰造极' (reach the peak of perfection) and '载入史册' (be written into the annals of history) in '这样的登峰造极想必将被载入史册' (Such a reach of the peak of perfection will presumably be written into the annals of history). We also find the abundant use of metaphors at this stage. For instance, in '这一悍然对企业高管下手的越雷池之举，被他们披上法律的外衣' (They have garmented such an overstepped action of outrageously putting their hands to a corporate executive with law), '雷池' (Lei Chi – the name of a place in Anhui Province that is used to refer to the boundary) depicts the danger in arresting Meng Wanzhou and '外衣' (garment) is compared to the charge against Meng.

The generic stage of *Solution* informs readers about what the Chinese government, Huawei, and the Chinese citizens should do next. It is a follow-up to the Explanation stage and contains more instructions and suggestions. For instance, in Example 12, two solutions of extricating Huawei from the difficult situation are provided explicitly, with the first one concerning the development of Huawei and the other focusing on the further opening up of China to the outside world.

EXAMPLE 12

解决华为的困境，大概需要两个方向上的努力。
第一，华为唯有在技术上更加卓尔不群，更加不可替代，才能一定程度上消除来自美国的歧视。……
第二，中国需要通过扩大对外开放，缓解中美及中西的地缘政治或意识形态紧张。……

(To solve the dilemma of Huawei, we probably need to make our efforts in two directions.
First, only when Huawei is more distinguished and irreplaceable in technology can it eliminate the discrimination from the United States to some extent …
Second, China needs to relieve the tension of geopolitics or ideology between Sino-US as well as China and the West by opening up further to the outside world …)

In terms of modality, obligation is the most frequently used type at the Solution stage. Also, among all the generic stages, the frequency of obligation in Solution is the highest, as the primary purpose of Solution is to regulate the behaviors of the different parties involved and to demand further actions. Further, we observe that these choices of obligation are all of high and median values, characterized by the use of '要' (will, would) and '需要' (need), which are of high value, as well as '应当' (should) and '应该' (should), which are of median value. On the one hand, modality choices of high value are used to a large extent, such as '需要' (need) in '我们**需要**精选反制的目标' (We *need* to carefully select the target of counterattack). On the other hand, modalities of median value are all addressed to the US and Canada with the aim of regulating their behavior, as seen in '应' (should) from '加方**应**尽快彻底恢复孟晚舟女士的自由' (Canada *should* free Ms. Meng Wanzhou as soon as possible).

Admonishment, as the final generic stage in most of the editorials analyzed, serves to warn the United States and Canada about the dangers of opposing China. It often appears at the end of an editorial as a concluding remark. In some editorials, Admonishment is found in the middle and is followed by Explanation or Solution. As shown in Example 13, the likely consequences are directly stated and the possibility that China will revenge is pointed out at the Admonishment stage.

EXAMPLE 13

美国国内法不是美加可以对外作恶的挡箭牌，渥太华如果坚持不释放孟晚舟，而是将她引渡到美国，对中加关系必将造成无法挽回的沉重打击。加方不该对可能避免遭到中国的严厉报复而心存幻想。

(The domestic law of the United States is not a shield with which the United States and Canada can do evil. If Ottawa insists on not releasing Meng Wanzhou but delivering her to the United States, it will certainly be an irretrievable and heavy blow on the Sino-Canadian relationship. Canada should not fantasize that they may avoid the harsh vengeance from China.)

At the stage of Admonishment, we find the use of harsh language against the US and Canada, most of which are verbal groups (based on descriptions of group/phrase in SFL, see Halliday and Matthiessen 2014), indicating the resolution of the Chinese to fight back. Some examples include '沉重打击' (hit hard), '严厉制裁' (tough sanction), '重点反制' (counterattack the focal point), '绝不手软' (never be soft-hearted), '坚决将其打痛' (hurt it resolutely), '付出相应的代价' (pay the price accordingly), and '猛烈报复' (revenge fiercely).

The frequent-used types of modality at the Admonishment stage include obligation and probability. The use of obligation here is similar to its usage in Explanation and Solution. The value of the modality choices is often high, such as '需要' (need) in '华盛顿**需要**适可而止' (Washington *needs* to stop when it is enough), which requires Washington to stop persecuting Meng Wanzhou and Huawei. In addition, the choices of probability have predicted the negative impact of the incident, as seen in '会' (will) from '这种背离进步方向的反向干涉不仅**会**带来技术上的损失' (This kind of reverse interference that is deviated from the direction of advancement *will* not only bring about loss in technology), which suggests the possible loss to the United States in terms of scientific progress.

The Generic Structure Potential of the editorials

Based on our analysis of generic structure, we make the following observations: (i) Background and Explanation are the obligatory generic stages in all editorials; (ii) Solution and Admonishment are the optional generic stages; and (iii) Explanation and Solution can be iterated.

B^ [E ·^ (S ·) (^A)]

B = Background

E = Explanation

S = Solution

A = Admonishment

Figure 44.4 Generic Structure Potential for the editorials in *Global Times*.

In editorials where all the four generic stages are found, the actual structure is B^E^S^A, which is a structure that appeared twice in our data. (The initial letters have been used here to stand for the name of the stages. The caret sign ^ means followed by and shows the order of the stages.) Moreover, when stages of Explanation and Solution are iterated, they are numbered in sequence, such as $B^\wedge E_1{}^\wedge S_1{}^\wedge E_2{}^\wedge S_2{}^\wedge E_3{}^\wedge S_3{}^\wedge A$. We also find that Admonishment does not necessarily appear at the end of the editorial and there can be stages of Explanation and Solution following Admonishment. Thus, there are actual structures like $B^\wedge E_1{}^\wedge A^\wedge E_2{}^\wedge S$ and $B^\wedge E_1{}^\wedge A^\wedge S_1{}^\wedge E_1{}^\wedge S_2$.

Based on Hasan's (e.g., 1984; Halliday and Hasan 1985) pioneering studies on GSP, we summarize the GSP for the editorials in *Global Times* in Figure 44.4.

B is the first generic stage in all editorials and thus appears at the beginning. For the symbols used, the curved arrow ↶ marks iteration, the round brackets indicate optionality of enclosed elements, and the dot · between different elements suggests more than one option in sequence. However, such optionality of sequence does not mean complete freedom and the square bracket indicates this restraint. In this way, the GSP in the square bracket can be interpreted as follows: (i) E can occur anywhere as long as it does not precede B; (ii) E and S can be iterative; (iii) S can occur anywhere as long as it does not precede B; and (iv) S and A are optional.

The GSP presented in Figure 44.4 is a summary of the actual structures of the editorials collected. It not only points out how the contextual structure of the editorials is realized semiotically and promotes our understanding of the structure of each editorial as a separate entity, but also enhances our awareness of the editorial as a certain text type or genre. Such an approach is suitable to help us recognize the functional nature of language (Halliday and Hasan 1985).

Conclusion

In this chapter, we first discussed the different strands of linguistic research on media discourse and highlighted the contributions by SFL in this area. Drawing on SFL, we examined the discursive strategies of *Global Times* from the perspectives of lexicogrammar and context. For the lexicogrammatical analysis, we studied the interpersonal system of MODALITY, which not only deals with expressions of indeterminacy between positive and negative, but also interpersonally constructs the semantic region of uncertainty. Choices of the four types of modality, i.e. probability, usuality, obligation, and readiness were quantified, and the various delicate subtypes were examined in accordance with their values. We found that these lexical choices of modality were not randomly applied, but were selected to fulfill different purposes. For the contextual analysis, we identified four generic stages and summarized the GSP of the editorials in *Global Times*. We also identified the patterns of selecting modality choices in different generic stages.

By exploring the discursive strategies used by *Global Times* to criticize the United States and Canada, to strongly defend Huawei, and to call on the Chinese people to stand firm behind the domestic company, this chapter complements previous studies on Chinese media discourse and motivates further research in this field of inquiry. First, we point out the linguistic features of online Chinese nationalism, which is strategically manipulated by the CCP (e.g., Ma 2018). Second, the linguistic devices help to reflect the diplomatic policies of the People's Republic of China, illustrating the close link between language in the media and ideology (e.g., Fang 1994, 2001). Third, as discussed by Huan (2016), Chinese media has faced an increasingly tightening tension between the political power of the CCP and the marketing concerns of the readers. The publication of editorials that mobilize nationalist awareness and hatred in *Global Times* not only pleases the leaders who regard online nationalism as a 'safety valve' that helps relieve social tension (cf. Xiao 2011), but also pleases the readers of *Global Times* who have no access to foreign media, yearns to know about the power of the motherland and are likely to be instigated by the media.[1]

Moreover, a framework that combines lexicogrammatical and contextual analyses based on SFL was constructed. Unlike most previous SFL studies that draw on Martin and White's (2005) appraisal framework, we approached our data from the perspectives of modality and GSP. In doing so, we have demonstrated the value of SFL to the analysis of media discourse. Our study is also helpful to scholars of Chinese studies as it provides useful insights about the Chinese media, which serve as the mouthpiece of the CPC and are heavily shaped by the Chinese socialist ideology. Furthermore, the findings on the choices of modality and generic structure hold implications for news writing, especially editorial writing. An editorial with careful choices of modality will be more meaningful interpersonally and an editorial with a clear structure will be more impressive to its readers.

Acknowledgment

We thank Dr. Mark Nartey for proofreading our draft.

Acronyms in this chapter

CDA: critical discourse analysis
CPC: Communist Party of China
GSP: Generic Structure Potential
SFL: Systemic Functional Linguistics

Note

1 According to a survey conducted by *Global Times* in 2014, 82.5% of its readers have a monthly income lower than ¥5000 and 27.6% of the readers have only received a high school diploma or below (see https://wenku.baidu.com/view/7c342080f121dd36a32d8255?pcf=2).

References

Bednarek, M. (2006) *Evaluation in Media Discourse: Analysis of a Newspaper Corpus*, London and New York: Continuum.

Bednarek, M. and Caple, H. (2012) *News Discourse*, London and New York: Continuum.

Fang, Y. (1994) '"Riots" and demonstrations in the Chinese press: A case study of language and ideology', *Discourse & Society* 5(4): 463–81.

Fang, Y. (2001) 'Reporting the same events? A critical analysis of Chinese print news media texts', *Discourse & Society* 12(5): 585–613.

Halliday, M. A. K. and Hasan, R. (1985) *Language, Context, and Text: Aspects of Language in a Social-Semiotic Perspective*, Geelong, Victoria: Deakin University Press.

Halliday, M. A. K. and Matthiessen, C. M. I. M. (2014) *Halliday's Introduction to Functional Grammar*, 4th ed, London and New York: Routledge.

Hasan, R. (1978) 'Text in the systemic-functional model', in W. Dressler (ed) *Current Trends in Text Linguistics*, Berlin: de Gruyter, pp. 228–46.

Hasan, R. (1984) 'The nursery tale as a genre'. *Nottingham Linguistic Circular* 13: 71–102. Reprinted in R. Hasan (1996) *Ways of Saying: Ways of Meaning: Selected Papers of Ruqaiya* Hasan, C. Cloran, D. Butt and G. Williams (eds.), London: Cassell, pp. 51–72.

Hasan, R. (1985) *Linguistics, Language and Verbal Art*, Geelong, Victoria: Deakin University Press.

Huan, C. (2016) 'Leaders or readers, whom to please? News values in the transition of the Chinese press', *Discourse, Context and Media* 13: 114–21.

Huan, C. (2018) *Journalistic Stance in Chinese and Australian Hard News*, Singapore: Springer.

Kaltenbacher, M. and Stöckl, H. (eds.) (2019) *Analyzing the Media: A Systemic Functional Approach*, Sheffield: Equinox.

Liu, M. (2017) '"Contesting the cynicism of neoliberalism": A corpus-assisted discourse study of press representations of the Sino-US currency dispute', *Journal of Language and Politics* 16(2): 242–63.

Liu, Wenyu and Li, Ke 刘文宇, 李珂 (2017) '报刊和微博中老年人身份建构差异研究' (A study on the differences in identity construction of aged people in newspaper and Weibo), 外语与外语教学 (Foreign Languages and Their Teaching) 6: 71–80.

Ma, Y. (2018) "Online Chinese nationalism: A competing discourse? A discourse analysis of Chinese media texts relating to the Beijing Olympic torch relay in Paris", *The Journal of International Communication* 24(2): 305–25.

Martin, J. R. and White, P. R. R. (2005) *The Language of Evaluation: Appraisal in English*, Basingstoke: Palgrave Macmillan.

McKeown, K. R. (1985) *Text Generation: Using Discourse Strategies and Focus Constraints to Generate Natural Language Text*, Cambridge: Cambridge University Press.

O'Keeffe, A. (2012) 'Media and discourse analysis', in J. P. Gee and M. Handford (eds.), *The Routledge Handbook of Discourse Analysis*, London and New York: Routledge, pp. 441–54.

Shei, C. (2014) *Understanding the Chinese Language: A Comprehensive Linguistic Introduction*, London and New York: Routledge.

Wei, W. (2019) 'Critical analysis of Chinese discourse: Adaptation and transformation', in C. Shei (ed.), *The Routledge Handbook of Chinese Discourse Analysis*, Abingdon and New York: Routledge, pp. 36–50.

Xiao, Q. (2011) 'The rise of online public opinion and its political impact', in S. L. Shirk (eds.), *Changing Media, Changing China*, New York: Oxford University Press, pp. 202–24.

Zhang, Taofu and Chen, Lijuan 张涛甫, 陈丽娟 (2014) '论《环球时报》的民族主义倾向——以钓鱼岛报道为例' (On the nationalist tendency in *Global Times*: Examples from reports on Diaoyu Island), 新闻大学 (Journalism Bimonthly) 3: 66–74.

Further reading

O'Keeffe, A. (2012) 'Media and discourse analysis', in J. P. Gee and M. Handford (eds) *The Routledge Handbook of Discourse Analysis*, London and New York: Routledge, pp. 441–54.

This chapter provides an overview of media discourse analysis informed by linguistic theories, introduces the various paradigms and methodologies involved and discusses the parameters of media discourse.

Bednarek, M. and Caple, H. (2012) *News Discourse*, London and New York: Continuum.

This book presents an SFL-based approach to news discourse by applying Martin and White's (2005) appraisal framework to the quantitative analysis and assessment of newspaper articles.

Huan, C. (2018) *Journalistic Stance in Chinese and Australian Hard News*, Singapore: Springer.

This book explores the journalistic stance-taking practices in Chinese and Australian hard news by adopting an interdisciplinary approach, encompassing the appraisal framework in SFL, the concepts in journalism studies, ethnographic fieldwork and corpus-based methodology.

Index

Made in United States
North Haven, CT
29 June 2025